Greek Grammar

BEYOND *the* BASICS

With Scripture, Subject, and Greek Word Indexes

Greek Grammar

BEYOND *the* BASICS

AN EXEGETICAL SYNTAX OF THE
NEW TESTAMENT

Daniel B.
WALLACE

ZONDERVAN

Greek Grammar Beyond the Basics
Copyright © 1996 by Daniel B. Wallace

Requests for information should be addressed to:
Zondervan, 3900 *Sparks Dr. SE, Grand Rapids, Michigan 49546*

Library of Congress Cataloging-in-Publication Data

Wallace, Daniel B.
    Greek grammar beyond the basics : an exegetical syntax of the New Testament / Daniel B.
Wallace.
       p. cm.
    Includes bibliographical references and index.
    ISBN 978-0-310-21895-1
    1. Greek language, Biblical — Syntax. 2. Greek language, Biblical — Grammar. 3. Bible. N.T. — Lan-
guage, style. I. Title.
PA851.W34 1995
487' .4 — dc20   95-33112

The Greek New Testament, edited by Barbara Aland, Kurt Aland, J. Karavidopoulos, Carlo M. Martini, and
Bruce M. Metzger. Fourth Revised Edition. © 1966, 1968, 1975, 1983, 1994 by the United Bible Societies. Used
by permission.

Typeset: Teknia Software

Printed in China

16 17 18 19 20 /CTC/ 49 48 47 46 45 44 43 42 41 40 39 38 37 36 35 34 33 32 31

Two men in particular have instilled in me
a love for the Greek New Testament,
both by their scholarship and by their example of
Christian grace and humility.
To them this book is dedicated:

Dr. Buist M. Fanning

and the memory of

Dr. Harry A. Sturz

Table of Contents

Preface

I. Why This Book?

When Mounce only half-jokingly notes in his preface that "the ratio of Greek grammars to Greek professors is ten to nine,"[1] he is referring to *first*-year grammars. The situation, up until fairly recently, has been quite different for the intermediate level: such grammars could be counted on one hand. The last two decades have seen a reversal of this trend. There are now notable works by Brooks and Winbery, Vaughan and Gideon, Hoffmann and von Siebenthal (though not yet in English), Porter, and Young, to mention a few.[2] The question then arises: Why *this* book?

A. The Prehistory of This Work

Without in any way wishing to disparage the work of others (indeed, I have benefited much from them), some justification of this grammar, as well as a highlight of its distinctives, needs to be made. By way of a preliminary note, it should be pointed out that this first *published* edition is actually the *sixth* version. This book started out in 1979 as a 150-page syllabus for third semester Greek at Dallas Theological Seminary (at the time it was called *Selected Notes on the Syntax of New Testament Greek*). Within three years it went through three more versions, growing to over 300 pages. Most of the illustrations, exegetical discussions, and grammatical categories were thus present, at least in embryo form, as early as 1982. Part of the motivation for publication has been the widespread use of the various unpublished editions by former students and others. I do not say this to "toot my own horn" as much as to correct the judgments of a neophyte professor. It is my hope that the present work reflects a consistently more sober judgment about the syntax of the NT.

---

[1] W. D. Mounce, *Basics of Biblical Greek* (Grand Rapids: Zondervan, 1993) x.

[2] See abbreviations list for full bibliographic data, as these works will be mentioned at several points throughout this work. Although now slightly more than two decades old, Funk's *Beginning-Intermediate Grammar* should not be overlooked.

B. *Motivation*

My motivation from the beginning has not changed, however: to encourage students to get beyond the grammatical categories and to see the relevance of syntax for exegesis. As one who teaches both grammar and exegesis, I have felt this need acutely. Typically, by the time a student finishes intermediate Greek, disillusion and demotivation have set in via "death by categories." Greek grammars have a strong tradition of giving laundry lists of the various morpho-syntactic uses, coupled with a few illustrations. This follows the model of classical grammars, which canvass many corpora (for the idioms of any language must be based on unambiguous examples).[3] But with such an approach for the NT, the student can easily get the artificial impression that the syntactical labels will almost naturally attach themselves to the words in a given passage, thus rendering exegesis as a black-and-white *science*.

Once a little exegesis is under the student's belt, however, the opposite (and equally false) impression emerges: exegesis is the *art* of importing one's views into the text by picking a syntactical label that is in harmony with one's preunderstanding. The former attitude views syntax as a cold and rigid taskmaster of exegesis, equally indispensable *and* uninteresting; the latter assumes that the use of syntactical labels in exegesis is simply a Wittgensteinian-like game that commentators play.

Thus, too much exegesis is not properly based on syntax; too many works on syntax show little concern for exegesis. The result of this dichotomy is that intermediate students do not see the *relevance* of syntax for exegesis, and exegetes often *misuse* syntax in their exegesis. This work attempts to offer an initial corrective to this situation by properly grounding the exegesis in the idioms of the language and by orienting the syntax to its exegetical value.

C. *Distinctives*

1. Exegetically Significant Examples

After the clear illustrations of a particular category are noted, there will frequently be ambiguous and exegetically significant examples. These passages are usually discussed in some detail. Not only does this make syntax more interesting, but it also encourages the student to begin thinking exegetically (and to recognize that syntax does not solve every interpretive problem).

---

[3] This is not to say that a *reduction* of syntactical categories is to be preferred. Such a reduction, though pedagogically more manageable, is exegetically less useful for the student. The rationale for the multitude of categories in this book is discussed below.

2. **Semantics and "Semantic Situation"**

Both the semantics and the "semantic situation" of the categories are frequently developed. That is, rather than mere definitions for labels, the nuancing of the category (semantics) and the situations (e.g., contexts, lexical intrusions, etc.)[4] in which such a usage generally occurs also are analyzed. Such analyses show that syntactical description is not a Mad Hatter word-game and that the idioms of the language do offer some controls on exegesis. At times, structural clues that intermediate students might overlook are given (e.g., the historical present is always in the indicative mood and all clear examples of historical presents in the NT are in the third person). Often this discussion mulls over the semantics of a construction, thereby helping the student gain insights into the exegetical significance of various syntactical patterns.[5]

3. **Clear, User-Friendly Definitions**

This work attempts to give clear, expanded definitions, followed by a translational gloss known as the "key to identification" (e.g., for ingressive imperfect the student should translate the verb "began doing"; for customary present, he/she should try "habitually" before the verb).

4. **Plenty of Examples**

If only one or two examples were given, it would be possible for the student to focus on the atypical elements. With several examples, taken in a relatively balanced approach from the Gospels, Acts, the Pauline corpus, catholic epistles, and Revelation, the student gets exposed to the various types of literature in the NT and is able to see more clearly the essential features of a given category.[6] When the illustrations in this book are taken exclusively from one genre, this is not accidental: it indicates that the usage in view is restricted to such a genre (e.g., historical presents only occur in narrative). Almost all examples are translated with the appropriate words highlighted. Advanced students should

---

[4] "Semantic situation" is developed more fully in "The Approach of This Book."

[5] Sometimes this discussion will be nuanced and perhaps seemingly too advanced for a given intermediate Greek class. (The semantic discussion of the genitive of apposition, for example, is unusually long.) In reality, however, if a teacher wants his/her students to *think linguistically* rather than simply memorize and regurgitate grammatical categories, this section needs to be digested. Precisely because of a lack of linguistic sensitivity, many students of the NT commit exegetical blunders. Knowing how to translate and/or syntactically tag a construction is not the same as knowing how to articulate the semantics of such a construction.

[6] Some NT grammars could more appropriately be titled something like *A Syntax of Matthew and Occasionally Other New Testament Books,* for they are not consciously trying to take examples from the various genres of the NT.

appreciate the many textual variants (with their witnesses) that are mentioned.[7]

5. Grammatical Statistics

The frequencies of various morphologically tagged words and construc-tions will be listed at the beginning of major sections.[8] For a student to know that a given construction is "rare" is somewhat helpful, but when he/she finds out that the future passive participle occurs once or that the optative occurs 68 times, "rare" takes on a more precise connotation. Without this added information, a student might conclude that the first class condition is found more often than the perfect tense!

6. Charts, Tables, and Graphs

Scores of charts, graphs, and tables are included in *Exegetical Syntax*. The more pie charts, bar graphs, and Venn diagrams, the more the student understands and retains. Such visual aids represent usage, semantics, frequencies, etc. A bar graph on the frequency of various prepositions, for example, will instantly give the student a sense of the importance of ἐν.

7. Multitude of Syntactical Categories

One of the features of this work is a multitude of syntactical categories, some of which have never been in print before. A word needs to be said about this since several grammarians nowadays are retreating from a proliferation of syntactical categories. They are doing this for three inter-related reasons.

First, via the tool of modern linguistics, there is an increased apprecia-tion for and recognition of the basic meaning of various morpho-syntac-tic elements (what we are calling the *unaffected meaning*). Thus, statements such as, "at bottom, all genitives are either subjective or objective," or "the aorist is the default tense, used only when an author wishes to refrain from describing," are on the rise.

---

[7] For statistical purposes, the Nestle-Aland[26/27]/UBS[3/4] text is used. Usually, this text will also be used for the illustrations (with variants relevant to the grammatical point at hand discussed). Whenever the illustration involves a reading not found in this text, it will be noted.

A word should be said about the shape of the examples used. Occasionally, particles or other words irrelevant to the syntactical point being stressed are omitted without noti-fication (viz., ". . ."). The Greek text is thus kept as brief as possible. Usually just enough context is given to demonstrate the appropriateness of the illustration for its category.

[8] The statistics are initially taken from *acCordance*, a software program for Macintosh (marketed by the Gramcord Institute, Vancouver, WA) that performs sophisticated searches on a morphologically-tagged Greek NT (Nestle-Aland[26]), as well as the Hebrew OT (*BHS*) and LXX (Rahlfs).

Second, numerous specific categories of usage that are themselves restricted to certain *semantic situations* (such as genre, context, lexical meaning of words involved, etc.) are often interpreted as mere *applications* of the basic meaning and not legitimate semantic categories in and of themselves. Seeing analogies with lexicology, the trend now is to treat such categories as not purely grammatical and therefore not worthy of description in a book on grammar.[9]

Third, often for pedagogical reasons, the number of grammatical categories has been reduced. Several have been lumped together (e.g., in one recent grammar the dative of means, cause, agent, and manner are treated as one indistinguishable category[10]). Others, especially rare categories of usage, have been ignored.[11]

This trend is helpful to some degree, but overdrawn. The rationale for it lacks nuancing. Although our understanding of the unaffected meaning of certain morpho-syntactic categories is increasing, to *leave* the discussion of syntax at the common denominator level is neither linguistically sensitive nor pedagogically helpful. The nature of language is such that *grammar cannot be isolated from other elements* such as context, lexeme, or other grammatical features. Rather than treat these as mere applications, we prefer to see them as various uses or categories of the *affected meaning* of the basic form. Indeed, our fundamental approach to syntax is to distinguish between the unaffected meaning and the affected meaning, and to note the linguistic signs that inform such a distinction.

No one has ever seen a present tense by itself, for example. What we see is a verb that has as many as seven different morphological tags to it (one of which may be present tense), one lexical tag (the stem)–and all this in a given context (both literary and historical). Although we may be, at the time, trying to analyze the meaning of the present tense, all of these other linguistic features are crowding the picture. Indeed, one central thesis of this grammar is that *other linguistic features affect (and therefore contribute to) the meaning of the particular grammatical category under investigation.*

---

[9] For example, in many recent lexical/linguistic studies, the difference between an utterance and a sentence is pointed out. (Cf., e.g., the excellent work by Peter Cotterell and Max Turner, *Linguistics and Biblical Interpretation* [Downers Grove, IL: InterVarsity, 1989] 22-23.) An utterance is a unique, one-time statement. The same words may be repeated on a different occasion, but this would not be the same utterance. It would, however, be the same sentence. Applying this to lexical studies, a distinction must be made between meaning and instance–otherwise a dictionary would have to give all instances, labeling each of them with a distinct meaning.

[10] S. E. Porter, *Idioms of the Greek New Testament* (Sheffield: JSOT, 1992) 98-99.

[11] For an intermediate grammar (such as the present work) this *is* a legitimate reason not to list certain categories.

Grammarians' hypotheses about the unaffected meaning[12] of a particular morpho-syntactic element (such as genitive case, present tense, etc.) are supposed to be based on a decent sampling of the data and with a proper linguistic grid to run it through. Older works tended to obscure the unaffected meaning because the data on which they based their definitions were insufficient. For example, the idea that the present prohibition means, *in essence*, "stop doing" is in reality a *specific usage* that cannot be applied universally. An abstract notion of the present prohibition first needs to be found, one that is both distinctive to the present prohibition and able to explain most of the data.

But simply to rework these definitions based on a broader sampling of data does not make much of an advance. Extra-grammatical features must also be examined if meaningful categories of usage are to be articulated. Thus, the next step is to examine the present prohibition in various contexts, genres, and lexemes. As certain semantic patterns are detected, these form the backbone for the various categories. When this is done, the present prohibition used to prohibit an action in progress is found to be a legitimate category of *affected* meaning, though it does not represent the unaffected meaning.

An illustration from the classroom might help. In teaching syntax to second-year Greek students at Dallas Seminary, the NT Department has given assignments in translation and syntactical analysis. As we work through a passage, the students translate and analyze various syntactical features. On many occasions, the classroom discussion will sound something like this.

> Student: "I take this to be a genitive of possession."
>
> Teacher: "It is more probably an attributive genitive. Notice the context: in the preceding line, Paul says . . ."
>
> Student: "I thought this was a class on Greek grammar. What does the context have to do with it?"
>
> Teacher: "Everything."

From that point ensues an enlightening (I hope) discussion on how *syntax cannot be understood apart from other features of the language.* (Students typically are not prepared for this simply because they have just

---

[12] If the terminology "unaffected meaning" is difficult to grasp, you might recall a particular example of this. Verbal *aspect* (as opposed to *Aktionsart*) is the unaffected meaning of the kind of action the various tenses can have. It is not affected by lexical or contextual intrusions. *Aktionsart*, on the other hand, is the affected meaning, shaped especially by the verb's lexeme. (Of course, this illustration will not help those who have not had exposure to the term *Aktionsart*!) I am simply applying the findings and categorization of aspectual research to a larger area, viz., all of syntax. (Thus, for example, when the basic meaning of the genitive case is discussed, it is really an abstract picture, based on a multitude of concrete instances in which a common denominator, to a large degree, repeatedly occurs.)

completed a year of study in which *forms* were devoured in mass quantities. Now they are asked to think again, not simply regurgitate.) Specific syntactical categories are, in reality, almost never *merely* syntactical categories. *Syntax is, in fact, an analysis of how certain repeatable, predictable, and "organizable" features of communication (a.k.a. the semantic situation) impact discrete morpho-syntactic forms.*

It is neither helpful nor possible simply to strip syntax to the elemental thread that, to a large degree, runs through all instances of a particular form. It has been my experience that most students who learn NT Greek are not really interested in grammar or Greek or linguistics per se. But they are interested in interpretation and exegesis. Thus to refrain from discussing the various nuances of, say, the genitive case is to promote exegetical imprecision. But to compound categories without discussing the various semantic situations in which they occur promotes eisegesis. Thus, although these categories can be cumbersome at times, it is more profitable, pedagogically, to give them to the student than not, simply because the student is interested in exegesis, not just Greek.

8.   No Discussion of Discourse Analysis

Contrary to the current trend, this work has no chapter on discourse analysis (DA). The rationale for this lacuna is fourfold: (1) DA is still in its infant stages of development, in which the methods, terminology, and results tend to be unstable and overly subjective.[13] (2) DA's methods, as shifting as they are, tend not to start from the ground up (i.e., they do not begin with the word, nor even with the sentence). This by no means invalidates DA; but it does make its approach quite different from that of syntactical investigation. (3) Along these lines, since this is explicitly a work on *syntax*, DA by definition only plays at the perimeter of that topic and hence is not to be included.[14] (4) Finally, DA is too significant a topic to receive merely a token treatment, appended as it were to the end of a book on grammar. It deserves its own full-blown discussion, such as can be found in the works of Cotterell and Turner, D. A. Black, and others.[15]

---

[13] On a broader level, this is analogous to Robinson's blistering critique, now two decades old, of Noam Chomsky's transformational grammar: "Fashions in linguistics come and go with a rapidity which in itself suggests something suspect about the essential claim of linguistics, that it is a science" (Ian Robinson, *The New Grammarians' Funeral: A Critique of Noam Chomsky's Linguistics* [Cambridge: CUP, 1975] x).

[14] P. H. Matthews, in his masterful *Syntax* (Cambridge: CUP, 1981), defined syntax "as a subject distinct from stylistics and in terms of which expressions such as 'syntax beyond the sentence' are meaningless" (xvix). I would not go this far, but I am traveling in the same direction.

[15] Happily, I find Matthews in agreement with this overall assessment: "These fields [discourse analysis and sentence structure] are too important, and their methods too much of their own, for them to be handled as an appendage to a book which is basically on relations within phrases and clauses" (*Syntax*, xix).

## 9.	Structural Priority

Another trend current among grammarians (whether of Greek or other languages) is that of organizing the material by semantic priority rather than by structural priority. Thus, the focus is on *how* purpose, possession, result, condition, etc. are expressed, rather than on the *forms* used to express such notions.

Semantic priority grammars are most useful for *composition* in a living language, not analysis of a small corpus of a dead language. This is not to say that such an approach has no place in a grammar on ancient Greek, but that an intermediate and exegetical grammar is more useful if organized by morpho-syntactic features.

It is anticipated that the average user of this work will either lack the ability or the inclination to think through all the ways in which, say, purpose can be expressed in Greek. But that user should be able to recognize forms as they occur in the Greek NT. When he or she sees a ἵνα or genitive articular infinitive in the text, the first question asked will not be, "How can purpose be expressed in Greek?" but "How is this word used here?" The initial questions are thus almost always tied to *form*. The value of an exegetical grammar is related to its usability in exegesis: since exegesis begins with the forms found in the text and then moves toward its concepts, so should an exegetical grammar.

One pragmatic consequence of a structural-priority scheme is that the section on clause syntax is relatively small compared with noun and verb syntax. This does *not* mean that I view the word as the basic unit of meaning! Such an atomistic approach to language has been abandoned for decades. Rather, the decision to organize this grammar by recognizable forms is borne of pedagogical, not linguistic motives. Thus, word-grammar is preferable as a user-friendly entrance into dialogue. In other words, the *presentation* of the material is *formal*, while the *analysis* of the material is *semantic*.

## 10.	Minimal Material on Lexico-Syntactic Categories

Certain morpho-syntactic categories involve an open number of lexemes (such as nouns, adjectives, and verbs). Others involve a closed number of lexemes, such as prepositions, pronouns, and conjunctions. Those that have a closed or finite number of lexemes are lexico-syntactic categories. It is our conviction that standard lexica such as BAGD already have an admirable treatment of such categories–one that is both easy to locate (viz., alphabetical) and rich in bibliographic data, textual variants, and exegetical discussions (albeit terse).[16] Further, anyone

---

[16] One exception to this is the entry on the article. Since the article is by far the most common word in the NT (occurring about twice as often as its nearest competitor, καί), it requires a somewhat detailed treatment in a grammar.

interested in an *exegetical* syntax does not need to be encouraged to purchase a lexicon; it is (or should be!) one of the most accessible tools in the exegete's library.

In light of these considerations, it seemed superfluous to duplicate all the material already found in the lexicon.[17] Thus, for the most part, our discussions of lexico-syntactic categories will involve the following: (1) an *outline* of uses with terminology that is consistent with the rest of this book; (2) a few detailed discussions of exegetically significant passages; and (3) general principles that are useful for the larger syntactical category to which a specific lexico-syntactic category belongs (e.g., types of conjunctions, general comments on prepositions, etc.).

11. Layout

This text is designed for many users, from intermediate students still wet behind the ears to seasoned pastors who live in the Greek text. To assist you in using it to its maximum potential, we note the following:

- The **illustrations** are given both in Greek and in English, with the relevant syntactical forms highlighted.

- There are at least three **levels of discussion** in *Exegetical Syntax*:

  1) The **simplest** is the "Syntax Summaries," found near the end of this book. Almost every "Syntax Summary" includes a category title, brief definition, and a translational gloss (called "Key to Identification"). No examples or exegetical or linguistic discussions are found here. This is a bare-bones outline of the book, designed to trigger the memory of one who has worked through the categories.

  2) The **intermediate** level is found in normal-sized type in the body of the book. This includes especially the definitions and illustrations, as well as discussions of the semantics of many of the categories.

  3) The **advanced** level is found in smaller type. This includes especially footnotes. Many of these notes add extensive discussions of syntax. Exegetical discussions of select passages are also placed in smaller type, but intermediate students are encouraged to read (or at least skim) them, as they are intended to be motivational as models of syntactical exegesis.[18]

---

[17] Older grammars (such as Robertson's) spent an exorbitant amount of space on lexico-syntactic categories, but this was largely due to the non-existence of comprehensive and up-to-date lexica. Curiously, many recent grammars take the same approach but without the same necessity.

[18] Some of the exegetical discussions, however, are quite complex. Such discussions can be skimmed by the intermediate student with impunity.

- Finally, the **scripture index** is designed especially for the working pastor. Rather than merely listing the texts found in the body of this work, those that receive extended treatment (especially of an exegetical nature) are highlighted.

In the following section this layout will be discussed in greater detail, with pointers on how to use this book in a one-semester intermediate Greek course.

II. How to Use This Text in the Classroom (or, An Apology on the Length of Exegetical Syntax)

I did not write this work for linguists, though I use linguistics. I did not write it for those whose interest in the NT is mere translation, though it should help in that endeavor.[19] I wrote it for those whose concern is the interpretation of the text, exegesis, exposition. As such, it is designed for a variety of users: intermediate Greek students, advanced Greek students, expositors of scripture, and anyone whose Greek has become to him or her like a tax-collector or a Gentile! In short, this work is designed both for the classroom and for the pastor's study.

The daunting size may suggest *prima facie* that I have no classroom experience! Some teachers of intermediate Greek might have concern over such length, feeling overwhelmed at the prospect of covering all the material in the course of one semester. An explanation on its length, as well as pointers on how it can be used in the given time constraints, are thus in order.

Much of the length is due to several features, not always found in an intermediate grammar:

- an abundance of examples, laid out in an easy-to-read format
- relatively extensive footnotes
- scores of charts and tables
- discussions of exegetically significant passages
- analyses of rare categories of usage
- discussions of semantics

As you can see, not all of the extra length should cause a hardship. The charts and extra illustrations, in particular, should make your classroom efforts easier. (By analogy, Mounce's *Basics of Biblical Greek* is much longer than the average first-year grammar, but it is filled with so much pedagogically useful information that its length aids in instruction rather than detracts.) In order to cover the material in one semester, I would encourage you to follow the first two suggestions below. If the semester is crowded with many other assignments, suggestions three and four might also need to be implemented.

---

[19] Generally, seminary courses are more often taught with exegesis in mind, while college courses focus more specifically on translation skills.

1) Have the *intermediate* students ignore all *footnotes*. The footnotes are designed for teachers and advanced students.

2) Let the students skim over the *rarer* categories of usage. Some categories are so rare that it is helpful just to know of their existence and to use the grammar as a reference tool later on. Don't discuss them or quiz over them. Just have the students read the material for exposure and leave it at that. In that way, a teacher could just tell students to note the summaries and mark their texts accordingly.[20] The more common categories of usage are already noted with an *arrow* in the left margin and via bold print in the "Syntax Summaries." These, of course, should be learned.

3) Some who teach intermediate Greek might want the students to ignore or skim over the exegetical discussions (immediately below many of the examples). Personally, I think this is the very feature that will motivate students. But you may disagree so violently with my exegesis that you don't want your students to get too much exposure to it![21]

4) Some teachers (especially on the college level) may wish to have students ignore everything but the definitions, keys to identification, and clear illustrations. The rest of the material could be used for reference.[22]

A suggested approach that implements the first two suggestions above is as follows. The students should read through the day's material *three* times. The first reading (or skimming) should be for the purpose of gaining an overview and familiarity of the material; the second reading is for memorizing definitions and one or two illustrations; the third reading is for review and reflection, especially of the more recondite discussions. This should then be followed by a *weekly* refresher of the material via the "Syntax Summaries." As well, the "Syntax Summaries" can, at this stage, be utilized for any syntactical questions that are used in the analysis of the biblical text.

In sum, there are many approaches one can take to make this text manageable in a single semester. And we would hope that when the semester is concluded, though the student may not feel as if its contents were thoroughly mastered, *Exegetical Syntax* will be of some service down the road as well.[23]

---

[20] One general exception to this approach involves the rare categories that are frequently appealed to in commentaries (e.g., dative of agency, imperatival participle); these should be recognized if only to help the student become critical of their overuse in exegetical works. Most such abused categories are highlighted by a *dagger* in the left margin.

[21] College courses that focus on translation will typically skim over the exegetical discussions.

[22] By using the grammar in this way, the student actually gets *less* material than is found in some of the briefest intermediate grammars.

[23] One of the reasons for the length of this work has to do with its overall purpose. This book attempts to bridge two gaps: that between first-year textbooks such as Mounce's *Basics of Biblical Greek* and standard reference works such as BDF, and that between syntax and exegesis. All this adds to the length. Anything significantly shorter would have procrusteanized this twofold objective.

III. Acknowledgments

As this text has been used, at least in skeletal form, for over fifteen years, my debt of gratitude constitutes a long train. Unfortunately, so many have helped in bringing this work to fruition that I cannot–either because of space or memory–mention them all. The following represent the tip of the iceberg.

First, I am grateful to my students over the years who have worked through the material, taken quizzes and tests, gently corrected many of my blunders, and encouraged me to get the work published. The list includes Intermediate Greek students at Dallas Seminary (1979-81); Intermediate Greek students at Grace Seminary (1981-83); and Advanced Greek Grammar students at Dallas Seminary (1988-94).

Thanks are due as well to Pamela Bingham and Christine Wakitsch who keyed in an early draft of the work on computer for classroom use. Their painstaking accuracy freed me up to focus on content rather than on form.

Κῦδος is due to the following hand-picked "grunt workers": Mike Burer, Charlie Cummings, Ben Ellis, Joe Fantin, R. Elliott Greene, Don Hartley, Greg Herrick, Shil Kwan Jeon, "Bobs" Johnson, J. Will Johnston, Donald Leung, Brian Ortner, Richard Smith, Brad Van Eerden, and "Benwa" Wallace. These men searched for illustrations, checked the references, examined manuscript facsimiles and Greek texts for variants, gathered both primary and secondary data, prepared the indices, and offered many valuable critiques and insights. Most of these students were my interns between 1993 and 1996 at Dallas Seminary; others were simply interested friends who offered their labors out of love for the syntax and exegesis of the NT.

Also to be acknowledged are the many field testers, who examined the penultimate draft during the 1994-95 school year. Especially to be noted are Dr. Stephen M. Baugh, Dr. William H. Heth, and Dr. Dale Wheeler.

I have also been aided at every step of the process by librarians and libraries. At the top of the list are Teresa Ingalls (Interlibrary Loan Librarian) and Marvin Hunn (Assistant Librarian) of Turpin Library, Dallas Seminary. In addition, I was helped substantially by the resources at Tyndale House in Cambridge, England, Cambridge University Library, Morgan Library of Grace Seminary (particularly helpful was Jerry Lincoln, Assistant Librarian), and more than a half dozen other schools and libraries.

This grammar would not have been possible without *acCordance*, a software program for Macintosh (marketed by the Gramcord Institute, Vancouver, WA) that performs sophisticated searches on a morphologically-tagged Greek NT (Nestle-Aland[26]), as well as the Hebrew OT (*BHS*) and LXX (Rahlfs). This remarkable tool has been a *sine qua non* in the writing of this grammar. Not only has it provided many statistics, but has also proved valuable in surfacing several of the illustrations. Thanks are due especially to James Boyer, who tagged the Greek

NT; Paul Miller, the developer of the original *Gramcord* program for DOS; and Roy Brown, who developed the Macintosh version.

Appreciation is also rendered to the late Philip R. Williams, whose *Grammar Notes on the Noun and Verb* involve, *inter alia*, crystal clear definitions. Indeed, originally my literary efforts on syntax were merely classroom notes that were intended to be a supplement to Williams' notes. Dr. Williams, whose tenure at Dallas Seminary overlapped mine only briefly, has impacted my thinking on syntax substantially.

Williams' heritage was continued at Dallas Seminary where the entire NT Studies Department has been for years shaping and reshaping its own *Greek Syntax Notes* (*GSN*) for classroom use. The contributions to this work came from many minds over several years. The *GSN* have been such an intrinsic part of intermediate Greek at Dallas Seminary for the past decade that much of the organization, as well as many of the illustrations and definitions, have made their way into the warp and woof of *Exegetical Syntax*. I can only express my indebtedness to the department for its collectively clear thinking about the syntax of the NT.

To my oh-so-down-to-earth wife, Pati, I am grateful for her encouragement to get my course notes published. More than any other, she has prodded, cajoled, and insisted that this material get beyond the confines of the classroom.

To my childhood friend, Bill Mounce, I am grateful for his contagious enthusiasm and for his suggestion that this text be published in the Zondervan series on biblical Greek. Bill is also to be thanked for the final typesetting of this book.

I am thankful as well to the ever-gracious help offered by the folks at Zondervan Publishing House: to Ed Vandermaas, Stan Gundry, and Jack Kragt, for their invaluable encouragement from the beginning; and especially to Verlyn Verbrugge, the editor of the work, whose eagle eye saw the project through to its completion. Verlyn's capacity as proofreader, editor, linguist, Greek scholar, and exegete, happily wed to his kind demeanor, have rendered him the ideal editor for this sometimes curmudgeonly author.

For the financial backing to complete this project, I wish to thank especially two institutes: Dallas Seminary, for granting me both a sabbatical and a study leave (1994-95); and the Biblical Studies Foundation, for its rather generous contribution toward my trip to England in the spring of 1995. In addition, many, many friends have supported us over the years financially, in hopes that this book would finally get published. To you, I offer a special word of thanks.

Finally, I express my most profound appreciation to the two men who have most instilled in me an awareness of the rich details of the Greek NT: Dr. Buist M. Fanning III and the late Dr. Harry A. Sturz. Dr. Sturz, my first Greek teacher (Biola University), guided me through several courses in Greek grammar and textual criticism, including a year-long independent study on the solecisms of the Apocalypse. Though warm-hearted, Dr. Sturz never failed to criticize my efforts, tempering my often sophomorish exuberance. Such integrity was only matched by his own spirit of humility. And Dr. Fanning, who instructed me in Advanced

Greek Grammar in the summer of 1977 at Dallas Seminary and has continued to exercise a sobering influence on me ever since, has shaped so much of my thinking on syntax that his imprint is surely felt on virtually every page of this work. Though he would consider himself simply as my colleague, I must always regard him as my mentor in things grammatical.

One might be tempted to think that with such a great cloud of witnesses, this work would be a milestone, signaling a new era in Greek grammatical studies! A quick scan of the book will quickly dispel that notion. I have no such delusions of grandeur for this tome. Ultimately, the responsibility for the shape and content of this work belongs with me. The biggest faults surely are due to my stubborn nature and frailty of mind. Such stubbornness lays all faults at my own feet; such frailty places more there than I am aware of presently. Nevertheless, I hope that *Exegetical Syntax* does make some contribution, encouraging and motivating those who handle the sacred text to pursue truth–even at the cost of abandoning their own prejudices.

ἀγώνισαι περὶ τῆς ἀληθείας

–Sirach 4:28

List Of Illustrations

Tables

Charts[24]

---

[24]We are using the term "Chart" loosely: it includes charts, diagrams, figures, and virtually all non-tables.

Abbreviations

AB	Anchor Bible
Abel, *Grammaire*	Abel, F.-M. *Grammaire du grec biblique: Suive d'un choix de papyrus*, 2d ed. Paris: Gabalda, 1927.
acc.	accusative
acCordance	Mac software program that performs sophisticated searches on a morphologically tagged Greek NT (Nestle-Aland^{26} text) as well as a Hebrew OT (*BHS*). Marketed by the Gramcord Institute, Vancouver, WA, and programmed by Roy Brown.
AJP	*American Journal of Philology*
BAGD	*A Greek-English Lexicon of the New Testament and Other Early Christian Literature*. By W. Bauer. Trans. and rev. by W. F. Arndt, F. W. Gingrich, and F. W. Danker. Chicago: University of Chicago Press, 1979.
BDF	Blass, F., and A. Debrunner. *A Greek Grammar of the New Testament and Other Early Christian Literature*. Trans. and rev. by R. W. Funk. Chicago: University of Chicago Press, 1961.
Bib	*Biblica*
BNTC	Black's New Testament Commentaries
Brooks-Winbery	Brooks, J. A., and C. L. Winbery. *Syntax of New Testament Greek*. Washington, D.C.: University Press of America, 1979.
BSac	*Bibliotheca Sacra*
BT	*Bible Translator*
Byz	Majority of the Byzantine minuscules
CBC	Cambridge Bible Commentary
CBQ	*Catholic Biblical Quarterly*

Chamberlain, *Exegetical Grammar*	Chamberlain, W. D. *An Exegetical Grammar of the Greek New Testament.* New York: Macmillan, 1941.
CTR	*Criswell Theological Review*
Dana-Mantey	Dana, H. E., and J. R. Mantey. *A Manual Grammar of the Greek New Testament.* Toronto: Macmillan, 1927.
dat.	dative
EKKNT	Evangelisch-katholischer Kommentar zum Neuen Testament
ExpTim	*Expository Times*
Fanning, *Verbal Aspect*	Fanning, B. M. *Verbal Aspect in New Testament Greek.* Oxford: Clarendon, 1990.
FilolNT	*Filología Neotestamentaria*
Funk, *Intermediate Grammar*	Funk., R. W. *A Beginning-Intermediate Grammar of Hellenistic Greek.* 3 vols. 2d, corrected ed. Missoula, Mont.: Scholars, 1973.
gen.	genitive
GKC	Kautzsch, E., and A. E. Cowley, editors. *Gesenius' Hebrew Grammar.* 2d English ed. Oxford: Clarendon, 1910.
Gildersleeve, *Classical Greek*	Gildersleeve, B. L. *Syntax of Classical Greek from Homer to Demosthenes.* 2 vols. New York: American Book Company, 1900-11.
Givón, *Syntax*	Givón, T. *Syntax: A Functional-Typological Introduction.* Amsterdam: Benjamins, 1984.
Goetchius, *Language*	Goetchius, E. V. N. *The Language of the New Testament.* New York: Scribner's, 1965.
Gramcord	DOS software program that performs sophisticated searches on a morphologically tagged Greek NT (Nestle-Aland[26] text) as well as a Hebrew OT (*BHS*). Marketed by the Gramcord Institute, Vancouver, WA, and programmed by Paul Miller.
GTJ	*Grace Theological Journal*

Hoffmann-von Siebenthal, *Grammatik*	Hoffmann, E. G., und H. von Siebenthal. *Griechische Grammatik zum Neuen Testament*. Riehen, 1985.
HTKNT	Herders theologischer Kommentar zum Neuen Testament
ICC	International Critical Commentary
Jannaris, *Historical Greek Grammar*	Jannaris, A. N. *An Historical Greek Grammar Chiefly of the Attic Dialect.* Hildesheim: Georg Olms, 1968 (reprint ed.).
JB	Jerusalem Bible
JBL	*Journal of Biblical Literature*
JBR	*Journal of Bible and Religion*
JETS	*Journal of the Evangelical Theological Society*
JT	*Journal of Theology*
KJV	King James Version
KNT	Kommentar zum Neuen Testament
LSJ	Liddell, H. G., and R. Scott. *A Greek-English Lexicon*. 9th ed. with supplement. Rev. by H. S. Jones. Oxford: Oxford University Press, 1968.
LXX	Septuagint
𝔐	Majority of Greek witnesses, most of which are of the Byzantine texttype
Matthews, *Syntax*	Matthews, P. H. *Syntax*. Cambridge: Cambridge University Press, 1981.
Metzger, *Textual Commentary*	Metzger, B. M. *A Textual Commentary on the Greek New Testament*. 2d ed. Stuttgart: Deutsche Bibelgesellschaft, 1994.
MM	Moulton, J. H., and G. Milligan. *The Vocabulary of the Greek Testament: Illustrated from the Papyri and Other Non-Literary Sources*. Grand Rapids: Eerdmans, 1930.

Moule, *Idiom Book*

Moule, C. F. D. *An Idiom Book of New Testament Greek*. 2d ed. Cambridge: Cambridge University Press, 1959.

Moulton, *Prolegomena*

Moulton, J. H. *A Grammar of New Testament Greek*. 4 vols. Edinburgh: T. & T. Clark, 1908-76. Vol. 1 (1908): *Prolegomena*, by J. H. Moulton. 1st ed. (1906); 3d ed. (1908).

Moulton-Howard, *Accidence*

Moulton, J. H. *A Grammar of New Testament Greek*. 4 vols. Edinburgh: T. & T. Clark, 1908-76. Vol. 2 (1929): *Accidence and Word Formation*, by W. F. Howard.

Mounce, *Basics of Biblical Greek*

Mounce, W. D. *Basics of Biblical Greek*. Grand Rapids: Zondervan, 1993.

MS(S)

manuscript(s)

NAC

The New American Commentary

NASB

New American Standard Bible

NCBC

New Century Bible Commentary

NEB

New English Bible

Neot

Neotestamentaria

Nestle-Aland[26]

Novum Testamentum Graece. Ed. by K. Aland. M. Black, C. M. Martini, B. M. Metzger, A. Wikgren. 26th ed. Stuttgart: Deutsche Bibelgesellschaft, 1979.

Nestle-Aland[27]

Novum Testamentum Graece. Ed. by B. Aland, K. Aland, J. Karavidopoulos, C. M. Martini, B. M. Metzger. 27th ed. Stuttgart: Deutsche Bibelgesellschaft, 1993.

NIBC

New International Biblical Commentary

NICNT

New International Commentary on the New Testament

NIGTC

New International Greek Testament Commentary

NKJV

New King James Version

NIV

New International Version

nom.

nominative

NovT

Novum Testamentum

NRSV	New Revised Standard Version
NT	New Testament
NTC	New Testament Commentary
NTD	Das Neue Testament Deutsch
NTS	*New Testament Studies*
OT	Old Testament
Porter, *Idioms*	Porter, S. E. *Idioms of the Greek New Testament.* Sheffield: JSOT, 1992.
Porter, *Verbal Aspect*	Porter, S. E. *Verbal Aspect in the Greek of the New Testament, with Reference to Tense and Mood.* Bern/New York: Peter Lang, 1989.
Radermacher, *Grammatik*	Radermacher, L. *Neutestamentliche Grammatik.* 2d ed. Tübingen: J. C. B. Mohr, 1925.
Robertson, *Grammar*	Robertson, A. T. *A Grammar of the Greek New Testament in the Light of Historical Research.* 4th ed. New York: Hodder & Stoughton, 1923.
Robertson, *Short Grammar*	Robertson, A. T., and W. H. Davis. *A New Short Grammar of the Greek Testament, for Students Familiar with the Elements of Greek.* 10th ed. New York: Harper & Brothers, 1958.
Rosenthal	Rosenthal, F. *A Grammar of Biblical Aramaic.* Wiesbaden: Otto Harrassowitz, 1963.
RSV	Revised Standard Version
Schmidt, *Hellenistic*	Schmidt, D. D. *Hellenistic Greek Grammar and Noam Chomsky: Nominalizing Transformations.* Chico, CA: Scholars Press, 1981.
Smyth, *Greek Grammar*	Smyth, H. W. *Greek Grammar.* Rev. by G. M. Messing. Cambridge, MA: Harvard University Press, 1956.
TAPA	*Transactions of the American Philological Association*
TDNT	*Theological Dictionary of the New Testament.* Ed. by G. Kittel and G. Friedrich. 10 vols. Grand Rapids: Eerdmans, 1964-76.

TG	transformational grammar
THNT	Theologischer Handkommentar zum Neuen Testament
Tischendorf	Tischendorf, C. *Novum Testamentum Graece*, 8th ed., 2 vols. Lipsiae: Giesecke & Devrient, 1869-72.
TNTC	Tyndale New Testament Commentaries
TS	*Theological Studies*
Turner, *Insights*	Turner, N. *Grammatical Insights into the New Testament*. Edinburgh: T. & T. Clark, 1965.
Turner, *Syntax*	Moulton, J. H. *A Grammar of New Testament Greek*. 4 vols. Edinburgh: T. & T. Clark, 1908-76. Vol. 3 (1963): *Syntax*, by N. Turner.
Turner, *Style*	Moulton, J. H. *A Grammar of New Testament Greek*. 4 vols. Edinburgh: T. & T. Clark, 1908-76. Vol. 4 (1976): *Style*, by N. Turner.
TynBul	*Tyndale Bulletin*
UBS³	*The Greek New Testament*. Ed. by K. Aland. M. Black, C. M. Martini, B. M. Metzger, A. Wikgren. 3d ed., corrected. Stuttgart: United Bible Societies, 1983.
UBS⁴	*The Greek New Testament*. Ed. by B. Aland, K. Aland, J. Karavidopoulos, C. M. Martini, B. M. Metzger. 4th ed., corrected. Stuttgart: United Bible Societies, 1994.
Vaughan-Gideon	Vaughan, C., and V. E. Gideon. *A Greek Grammar of the New Testament*. Nashville: Broadman, 1979.
VE	*Vox Evangelica*
v.l.(l)	textual variant(s)
voc.	vocative
WBC	Word Biblical Commentary
Williams, *Grammar Notes*	Williams, P. R. *Grammar Notes on the Noun and the Verb and Certain Other Items*, rev. ed. Tacoma, WA: Northwest Baptist Seminary, 1988.

Winer-Moulton

Winer, G. B. *A Treatise on the Grammar of New Testament Greek*. Trans. and rev. by W. F. Moulton. 3d ed., rev. Edinburgh: T. & T. Clark, 1882.

Young, *Intermediate Greek*

Young, R. A. *Intermediate New Testament Greek: A Linguistic and Exegetical Approach*. Nashville: Broadman, 1994.

Zerwick, *Biblical Greek*

Zerwick, M. *Biblical Greek Illustrated by Examples*. Rome: Pontificii Instituti Biblici, 1963.

ZNW

Zeitschrift für Neutestamentliche Wissenschaft

✚

Abused categories that students should be aware of

➡

Common categories that students should know.

The Approach of This Book

In light of the inroads that modern linguistics has been making into biblical studies for over three decades and in light of the substantial disagreement among various schools of linguistics regarding terminology, methodology, and objectives, it is important to state at the outset of this book my approach to syntax. The syntax of the Greek NT will be examined with eight methodological considerations in mind. Most of these will seem self-evident, yet surprisingly most have been violated by grammatical and exegetical studies in this century (some of which were highly touted).[1] Overall, it must be kept in mind that this is an *exegetical* syntax; hence, our goal at all times is to see the value of grammar for the interpretation of the text of scripture.[2]

1. Sufficient Data Base

Any *significant* statements as to the semantics of a given construction must be based on a large number of examples. Statements such as "every clear instance of this construction in the NT means X" are worthless in and of themselves. To argue, for example, that "there is apparently no instance in the New Testament of the Aorist Infinitive in indirect discourse representing the Aorist Indicative of the direct form"[3] or "γευσαμ[ένους] here [in Heb 6:4] as elsewhere, [means] to know experientially [as opposed to a mere taste]" is meaningless if there are only two instances of the word or construction in question.[4] This is not too far removed from saying something like, "All Indians walk single-file. At least the one I saw did."[5] In the least, such statements can be misleading because they are often assumed to be intrinsic to the construction at hand.

---

[1] The criteria adopted here are, for the most part, self-evident from a linguistic, logical, or empirical viewpoint. Cf. D. A. Carson, *Exegetical Fallacies* (Grand Rapids: Baker, 1984) for numerous illustrations on the broader scale of methodological considerations one must take into account when doing exegesis.

[2] This chapter is intended primarily for teachers and advanced students. Intermediate students should normally begin with the following chapter.

The bulk of this chapter is adapted from D. B. Wallace, "The Article with Multiple Substantives Connected by Καί in the New Testament: Semantics and Significance" (Ph.D. dissertation, Dallas Theological Seminary, 1995) 8-23.

[3] E. D. W. Burton, *Syntax of the Moods and Tenses in New Testament Greek*, 3d ed. (Chicago: University of Chicago, 1900) 53, §114. Burton provides none of the data. Yet this view of the aorist infinitive is often assumed in exegeses of Eph 4:22, as if the matter of the ἀποθέσθαι were thereby settled.

[4] M. Dods, "The Epistle to the Hebrews," vol. 4 in *The Expositor's Greek Testament* (ed. W. R. Nicoll; New York: Dodd, Mead & Co., 1897) 296. Cf. P. E. Hughes, *A Commentary on the Epistle to the Hebrews* (Grand Rapids: Eerdmans, 1977) 209, for a similar comment.

[5] An illustration oft-repeated by A. Duane Litfin, a former professor of mine, in his homiletics courses at Dallas Theological Seminary.

2. *Semantic Situation of Undisputed Examples a Prerequisite*

Any semantic patterns (i.e., what is called the "semantic situation" in this book[6]) of the undisputed examples need to be analyzed before the disputed passages are considered. Only from the starting point of clearly established meaning can a proper analysis be conducted. Responsible exegesis has always recognized this principle in broad strokes, but has not always attended to its details. To argue, for instance, that the first person present tense verbs in Rom 7:14-25 are historical presents ignores the semantic pattern of this category of usage: of the hundreds of undisputed historical presents in the NT, all are in the *third* person. Or to pigeonhole, without comment, ὀργίζεσθε in Eph 4:26 as a conditional imperative[7] is a tacit assumption that such imperatives can be joined by καί to another imperative with a different semantic force; but there are no undisputed instances of this in the NT. Any judgment as to the semantics of the disputed passages must be based on clear examples that parallel, in all the essentials, the semantic situation of the target construction.

3. *Unaffected Vs. Affected Meaning*

Along the same lines, a careful distinction needs to be made between the unaffected or ontological meaning of the construction and the affected or phenomenological meaning. By "unaffected" is meant the meaning of the construction in a vacuum–apart from contextual, lexical, or other grammatical intrusions. By "affected" is meant the meaning of the construction in its environment–i.e., "real life" instances. (This distinction is similar to that between aspect and *Aktionsart* for the verb as perceived by many grammarians: the former refers to the kind of action a verb tense would have stripped of its lexeme and context, while the latter is the kind of action a verb displays in combination with lexemic and contextual considerations.) Since the unaffected or ontological meaning[8] is an abstraction that can only be derived from observed phenomena, it is imperative that any deduction about ontology be made on the basis of carefully scrutinized and representative phenomena.

---

[6]This is essentially the same as what some linguists call the "environmental conditions under which a particular rule applied" (P. H. Matthews, "Formalization," in *Linguistic Controversies: Essays in Linguistic Theory and Practice in Honour of F. R. Palmer*, ed. D. Crystal [London: Edward Arnold, 1982] 7). Considerations of morpho-syntactic features, other lexico-grammatical features, context, genre (including discourse analysis), and figures of speech all contribute to the semantic situation.

[7]So *BDF*, 195 (§387). Cf. also H. Schlier, *Der Brief an die Epheser* (Düsseldorf: Patmos, 1963) 224, n. 3.

[8] With the term "ontological" we do not mean that this meaning is always present in full force. It can be overridden to some degree by the lexical, contextual, or grammatical intrusions. It is not, therefore, the lowest common denominator. An author chooses his particular tense for a reason, just as he chooses his mood, lexical root, etc. All of these contribute to the meaning he wishes to express. They are all, as it were, vying for control. To call any one of these nonviolable is to undervalue the interplay of the semantic forces at work.

Illustrations abound in grammatical studies where this distinction has not been observed. Instances of semantic myopia are legion, but perhaps the most infamous example in NT studies is the "barking dog" illustration. For over eighty years, students of the NT assumed a certain view about the semantics of commands and prohibitions. This view is often traced to a brief essay written in 1904 by Henry Jackson.[9] He tells of a friend, Thomas Davidson, who had been struggling with commands and prohibitions in modern Greek:

> Davidson told me that, when he was learning modern Greek, he had been puzzled about the distinction, until he heard a Greek friend use the present imperative to a dog which was barking. This gave him the clue. He turned to Plato's *Apology*, and immediately stumbled upon the excellent instances 20 E μὴ θορυβήσητε, before clamour begins, and 21 A μὴ θορυβεῖτε, when it has begun.[10]

This view was promoted two years later in J. H. Moulton's *Prolegomena*,[11] in which he speaks of the aorist as prohibiting an action not yet begun and the present as prohibiting an action that is in progress. From there this "already/not yet" view of the present and aorist prohibitions made its way into many of the textbook grammars of the NT for the next several decades.[12]

The fundamental problem with this approach was that it took a legitimate phenomenological usage and assumed that such affected meanings expressed the unaffected or basic idea. But the sampling was not large enough to make meaningful conclusions about the *essential* differences between aorist and present. A hunch was promoted. When certain passages did not fit the view, they were ignored, abused, or conveniently called exceptions.[13]

---

[9] "Prohibitions in Greek," *Classical Review* 18 (1904) 262-63.

[10] Jackson, "Prohibitions in Greek," 263.

[11] J. H. Moulton, *Prolegomena*, vol. 1 of *A Grammar of New Testament Greek* (Edinburgh: T. & T. Clark, 1906) 122.

[12] Dana-Mantey are representative. They give as their basic definition of each tense usage the following: "(1) Thus a prohibition expressed with the *present tense* demands the cessation of some act that is already in progress" (301-2); "(2) A prohibition expressed in the *aorist tense* is a warning or exhortation against doing a thing not yet begun" (302). Similar are the remarks of Brooks-Winbery, 116.

[13] In 1985 K. L. McKay challenged this view in his important essay "Aspect in Imperatival Constructions in New Testament Greek," *NovT* 27 (1985) 201-226. Among other things, he produced numerous examples from which he extrapolated that "in the imperative the *essential* difference between the aorist and the imperfective is that the former urges an activity *as whole action* and the latter urges it as *ongoing process*" (206-7). Whether or not the action had already begun is not a part of the ontology of either tense of the imperative (cf. Eph 5:18 for present; John 3:7 for aorist).

We will later argue that the significance of this distinction was also not made sufficiently by S. E. Porter in his view of verbal aspect. That is to say, he does not carefully distinguish between unaffected meaning and affected meaning, but instead attempts to extract the unaffected idea from selected affected instances.

4. *Synchronic Priority*

Since the genesis of modern linguistics with Ferdinand de Saussure's *Cours de linguistique générale*,[14] most lexicologists and many lexicographers have recognized the priority of synchrony over diachrony.[15] (*Synchrony* has to do with the language as used at a given time; *diachrony* looks at a language throughout its history or, at least, over a much longer period of time.) Grammarians (notoriously those of ancient Greek), however, have been much slower to change from long-standing practices.[16] In this work synchrony also takes priority over diachrony. Specifically, it is assumed that light shed on the NT will come mostly from Greek writings that fall within the Hellenistic period (roughly from 330 BCE to 330 CE). This is not at all to say that diachronic study is without value, just that synchronic texts will be judged more relevant to the syntactical phenomena embedded in the NT.

Sometimes, however, linguists overstate the case for synchronic priority. The analogy of a chess game in progress (made famous by Saussure)[17] has sometimes been pressed into the service of synchrony: one does not need to know all of the prior moves to understand the status of the game at present. A better analogy might be a football game: although the most important thing is what is on the scoreboard, how the scoring was done, how much time is left, which team has the momentum (and the ball!), whether any injuries have recently occurred, etc., are all important factors for understanding the present status and predicting the final outcome of the game. Applied to lexical and syntactical studies–especially in the biblical field–an understanding of the past and how it relates to the present is sometimes critical for gaining a proper picture of the present. It must be stressed that *the value of diachronics is for the modern researcher, not the ancient Hellenistic reader.*[18] Because of the frequent paucity and historical accident of the extant synchronic materials, because all native speakers of Koine Greek are dead, and

---

[14] F. de Saussure, *Cours de linguistique générale* (Paris: Payot, 1916). The work has been translated by W. Baskin into English as *Course in General Linguistics* (New York: Philosophical Library, 1959). All citations will be from the English translation unless otherwise noted.

[15] Saussure, *General Linguistics*, 101-90. Saussure's insights (among others') were applied to biblical criticism in the landmark tome by James Barr, *Semantics of Biblical Language*, in which a rather lengthy and pungent critique was leveled at the numerous linguistic fallacies found in *TDNT*.

[16] See J. P. Louw, "New Testament Greek–The Present State of the Art," *Neot* 24.2 (1990), for a brief history of the situation. Among other things, he points out that the etymological approach–"that there must be one basic meaning of each word or grammatical construction that will highlight and explain all of the various usages" (161)–is still largely to be found in NT grammars, though it has been abandoned by NT lexica.

[17] Saussure, *General Linguistics*, 22-23, 110, and especially 88-89.

[18] Linguistic works routinely disparage diachronic analysis from the ancient reader's perspective. But to ignore diachronics from the modern reader's perspective almost tacitly assumes that the linguist at least has an easy passageway into the synchronic scenario and, at most, is omniscient.

because there often exist deeply ingressed preunderstandings of the nature of NT Greek on the part of researchers, diachronic analysis also needs to be judiciously employed.[19]

5. *Structural Priority*

The starting point of our investigations will be the given structures, from which we hope to make semantic conclusions. The movement, then, is from structure (or more specifically, morpho-syntactic structure) to semantics.[20] To begin with semantics and impose a supposed meaning on the structure under investigation involves, to some degree, the prescriptive fallacy.

One of the most well-known rules of NT grammar articulated in this century encompassed just such an approach. What has become known as "Colwell's rule" was first published in 1933, in E. C. Colwell's "A Definite Rule for the Use of the Article in the Greek New Testament."[21] The rule is simply that "Definite predicate nouns which precede the verb usually lack the article ... a predicate nominative which precedes the verb cannot be translated as an indefinite or a 'qualitative' noun solely because of the absence of the article; if the context suggests that the predicate is definite, it should be translated as a definite noun . . . ."[22] The rule is valid as far as it goes, though it is relatively worthless for *syntactical* purposes since it presupposes a

---

[19] The need for diachronic analysis in syntax can be illustrated by the subjunctive mood. Discussions in many NT grammars of the third class condition assume that Hellenistic authors had at their disposal the optative mood just as readily as they had the subjunctive mood: that is, they treat the third class condition as the probable condition, while the fourth class condition is considered potential or possible. Cf., e.g., *BDF*, 188-89 (§371.2, 4); Robertson, *Grammar*, 1016-1022; Radermacher, *Neutestamentliche Grammatik*, 160, 174-76. Yet there are no complete fourth class conditions in the NT and only 68 optatives (according to the Nestle-Aland[26/27] text). The model that NT grammars follow is, in reality, a classical Greek model, even though in Hellenistic Greek the subjunctive has largely encroached on the domain of the optative. This portrait is therefore not completely valid, but because of the preunderstanding of grammarians the alleged synchronous description is too often a subconscious adoption of an obsolete model.

[20] L. C. McGaughy's insightful *Toward a Descriptive Analysis of Εἶναι as a Linking Verb in New Testament Greek* (Missoula, Mont.: Society of Biblical Literature, 1972) is based on this principle. Along the same lines, Haiim B. Rosén (*Early Greek Grammar and Thought in Heraclitus: The Emergence of the Article* [Jerusalem: Israel Academy of Sciences and Humanities, 1988]) has observed: "While grammatical analysis is strictly empirical and objective the next step, that of determination . . . of the conceptual or notional content of meaningful elements, or rather of formal elements in the environments where they are meaningful, is not . . ." (30). My method has greater kinship to his than to that of most linguists.

[21] E. C. Colwell, "A Definite Rule for the Use of the Article in the Greek New Testament," *JBL* 52 (1933) 12-21.

[22] Ibid., 20.

certain semantic force for the predicate nominatives in question.[23] Colwell
did not begin with structure (anarthrous precopulative predicate nominatives) but with semantics (definite predicate nominatives). Although it has
been largely assumed (even by Colwell himself) that his "study may be said
to have increased the definiteness of a predicate noun before the verb without the article . . . ,"[24] even to the point that precopulative predicate nominatives are often viewed as *normally* definite,[25] such a conclusion presupposes
that the converse of the rule is as valid as the rule itself. This would be like
saying, "Whenever it rains there are clouds in the sky; therefore, whenever
there are clouds in the sky it is raining."[26] A proper syntactical approach
investigates all of the relevant morpho-syntactic structures and then draws
conclusions about the semantics, rather than foisting a semantic meaning on
such structures when only a small sampling has been examined.

Surprisingly, as much as the prescriptive fallacy is an anathema to modern
linguists, much of linguistics is generated by a rather sophisticated form of
prescription.[27] This is an occupational hazard of linguists (especially of

---

[23] Colwell's legacy was to be in the field of textual criticism far more than in grammar.
His rule is valuable, as he noted (ibid., 20), for textual criticism (for once it is determined
that a precopulative predicate nominative is definite, a reading that lacks the article is to
be preferred over one that has it), yet Colwell believed that it was even more valuable as
a syntactical rule (ibid.).

[24] Ibid., 21.

[25] Cf., e.g., Turner, *Grammatical Insights*, 17; Zerwick, *Biblical Greek*, 56; L. Cignelli and
G. C. Bottini, "L'Articolo nel Greco Biblico," *Studium Biblicum Franciscanum Liber Annuus*
41 (1991) 187.

[26] Theological conservatives have especially applied the converse of the rule to John
1:1 (cf., e.g., B. M. Metzger, "On the Translation of John i.1," *ExpTim* 63 [1951-52] 125-26;
among Roman Catholics, cf. Zerwick), not realizing that Colwell *assumed* the definiteness
of θεός (Colwell, "Definite Rule," 20). His rule did nothing to demonstrate it. For a helpful
critique of "Colwell's rule" see P. B. Harner, "Qualitative Anarthrous Predicate Nouns:
Mark 15:39 and John 1:1," *JBL* 92 (1973) 75-87.

[27] Linguists are usually careful to avoid expressions such as "correct grammar" and
"bad grammar." By such a restraint they are able to avoid (in their minds) any notions of
prescriptive grammar. But to speak of a particular construction as "ungrammatical" or
"non-English" or "non-Greek" because it does not conform to the linguist's perception of
what can occur in the language under consideration is very much a prescriptive view of
language.

On the other hand, although it would be errant to speak of language in terms of
"good" and "bad" on an absolute and diachronic level, there is a sense in which the time-
bound and space-bound conventions of communication do indeed dictate what is good
and bad in language. On a graded scale, issues of good and bad grammar are linked to
the level of language (whether vulgar, conversational, or literary), the competence of the
speaker and audience, discourse setting, and the like. (Thus a lecturer at the Society of
Biblical Literature would surely be scorned for using "ain't" and "we goes," while in
some pockets of rural and inner-city America, the *avoidance* of such slang would be
frowned upon.) Seen in this light, even though some of the solecisms of the Apocalypse
may occasionally find parallels in other Greek literature, it is an entirely different matter
to call such peculiarities *normal* Greek (*contra* S. E. Porter, "The Language of the Apocalypse in Recent Discussion," *NTS* 35 [1989] 582-603; Young, *Intermediate Greek*, 13).

semanticists), since meaning and predictability are their stock-in-trade. David Crystal complains, in the preface to the *Festschrift* he edited, *Linguistic Controversies*, that "the process of theory construction and model-building has left empirical research too far behind: the need for better data-bases is a major conclusion of over half the chapters in the book . . . . "[28] And Ian Robinson, in his blistering critique of Noam Chomsky's linguistics,[29] notes that

> He [Chomsky] *always* writes as if all rules are mathematically precise. And the obvious danger is that grammar then becomes logically *analytic*, rather than a way of referring to language. If the language happens not to fit the well-defined systems of rules it is declared ungrammatical: rules take precedence over language and grammar returns to prescriptivism.[30]

The structure-semantics grid, in reality, involves something of a hermeneutical spiral. Whereas "traditional grammar is largely descriptive and often provides little more than names assigned to constructions"[31] and sometimes ample illustrations, modern semantic approaches are often prescriptive, doctrinaire, and lacking in substance. Though the goal of syntax should be to ascertain the meaning of given structures, it must be based on at least representative phenomena. In sum, traditional (and formal) syntax often falls short in that it does not pursue meaning; modern semantics often falls short in that it does not have an adequate empirical base.[32]

6. The Cryptic Nature of Language

Language, by its nature, is compressed, cryptic, symbolic. We can see this on many levels. *Words* in isolation mean next to nothing–simply because they

---

[28] *Linguistic Controversies*, xi. See also S. C. Dik, *Coordination: Its Implication for the Theory of General Linguistics* (Amsterdam: North-Holland, 1968) 5.

[29] Ian Robinson, *The New Grammarians' Funeral: A Critique of Noam Chomsky's Linguistics* (Cambridge: CUP, 1975). Though two decades old, this slender tome is still valuable reading, injecting as it does much common sense into the linguistic scene.

[30] Ibid., 21.

[31] Louw, "Present State," 165.

[32] Sometimes older methods have been abandoned not because of principle but because of expedience. Ironically, the occasions when traditional grammar often went awry were when it turned *linguistic* hunches into dogma without a sufficient empirical base. (To be sure those hunches were, linguistically speaking, woefully naïve, but they erred also in being a hasty product of the philologist's calling.) What is *not* needed is entirely to abandon the old approaches for the new, but to cull out the best things of the old and the new, forming a new alloy serviceable to grammarian and linguist alike. Louw comes *close* to this when he writes, "One should not assume that all of the philological ... approaches to New Testament Greek are to be discarded" (Louw, "Present State," 161). But he errs in thinking that these traditional approaches have run their course. Where the traditional approach is especially valuable is in the painstaking collection of data; with the advent of the electronic age it is evident that even this task is far from complete.

are capable of so many meanings. Given no context, it would be impossible to define, for example, "bank," or "fine," or "trust."[33] In the NT, ἀφίημι can have a variety of meanings such as "forgive," "abandon," divorce," "leave," "permit," etc. Without a context, we are at a loss to decide.

Even whole *sentences*, without a context, are filled with ambiguities. Thus pronouns are used precisely because there is a shared meaning that precedes the sentence. "He went to the bank and sat down" has many ambiguities: who is "he"? What exactly is meant by "bank"? Which bank (for the presence of the article implies a well-known one)? In John 1:21 we read, "He answered, 'no.'" Without a context, this means nothing.[34]

Further, on a *paragraph* level, though ambiguities lessen, there is still room for interpretation. Thus a broader context than merely the immediate literary context is needed for understanding. The famous Abbott and Costello baseball shtick ("Who's on First?") is a well-known instance of massive misunderstanding. Many TV sit-coms are based on the tried-and-true plot of sustained misunderstanding of one's meaning. And biblically, examples abound. Jesus tells a simple parable and no one understands. Who the branches are in John 15, the "I" in Rom 7, or those addressed in Heb 6 are topics of great debate.

On an even larger scale misunderstanding takes place–once again, because language is by its nature compressed, cryptic, and symbolic. Whole epistles are interpreted in widely divergent ways. In part, this is due to the distance between the original author-reader matrix and the modern interpreter. It is as if we were listening in on half of a phone conversation. Yet, even the original readers did not necessarily fully grasp an author's meaning (cf. 1 Cor 5:9-13; 2 Pet 3:15-16). That is, not everything in language is fully explained. Indeed, few things are.[35]

---

[33] Yet even the collocation of these words in a sentence would not necessarily indicate just one meaning. "I trust this fine bank," could refer to more than one thing: a financial institute or a river bank.

[34] But even with the preceding question ("Are you the prophet?") there can be little understanding without getting into Jewish history, Jewish expectations, and the OT (particularly Deut 18:15). In a Muslim context, this question would mean something quite different!

[35] R. M. Krauss and S. Glucksberg, "Social and Nonsocial Speech," *Scientific American* 236 (February 1977) 100-105, describe an experiment in communication that illustrates how language compresses the more shared preunderstanding there is between speaker and listener. A researcher goes to Harvard Square in Cambridge and inquires from passers-by how to get to Central Square. In his dress, mannerisms, and inquiry he gives the appearance of being a native Bostonian. The respondents, assuming him to be a local, give a correspondingly brief answer: "First stop on the subway." The following day the same researcher goes to the same spot, but this time presents himself as a tourist. The respondents, noting this, give a detailed and elaborate response.

When we read the NT letters, it is as if we are tourists eavesdropping on a conversation between two locals. We are at a communications disadvantage that can only be overcome as we immerse ourselves in the customs, culture, history, and language of the first century, not to mention the specific interaction between, say, Paul and his churches.

How does all this relate to a book on *syntax*? In three ways:

1)　Any examination of the syntax of the NT will be filled with miscues if it fails to recognize the compressed nature of language. When the doctor says to the nurse, "Scalpel!" this is a noun, but the utterance is taken as a command. We err if we cannot see that. One of our objectives is to "unpack" such compressed language. This will especially be necessary in the chapters on the genitive case and the participle (hence, these chapters are among the longest in the book).

2)　Humility needs to be exercised where the data are insufficient *or* where the language is capable of many interpretations. For example, although we would reject the probability that the present tenses in Rom 7 are historical presents (since all undisputed historical presents in the NT are in the third person), we cannot, on syntactical grounds, reject the notion that the "I" refers to Paul's presaved state. Other issues besides syntax (notably the strong possibility of figurative language) are at work here. This brings us to the third point.

3)　Much in language that is easily misunderstood is outside the scope of syntax, even broadly defined. Although a decent grasp on syntax is a *sine qua non* for sound exegesis, it is not a panacea for all of one's exegetical woes. Only rarely does the grammar hand the exegete his or her interpretation on a silver platter. In most cases, the better we understand the syntax of the NT, the shorter is our list of viable interpretive options.

7. *Probability Vs. Possibility*

In a historical-literary investigation we are dealing with probability vs. possibility. We are attempting to recover meaning without all the data. This is not a hard science. None of the examples culled from the literature are repeatable in a pristine laboratory. Unlike the hard sciences, a falsifiable hypothesis in the humanities is difficult to demonstrate because of the vacillations in the levels of ambiguity in the data examined (in our case, the ambiguities in texts whose authors cannot be consulted).[36] In particular, many of the so-called undisputed examples may well be disputed by some; conversely, some of what we consider disputed examples may be patently undisputed to others. But in literature and linguistics statistical probabilities

---

[36] Karl Popper, the noted scientific philosopher, argued with reference to the hard sciences that a good hypothesis must involve statements that can, *in principle*, be proved false by empirical observation (*The Logic of Scientific Discovery* [New York: Basic, 1959] 40-42). Since in most cases a complete induction is an impossibility, a hypothesis cannot be conclusively verifiable. But a good hypothesis can be falsifiable. This principle is no less important in the humanities (so N. Chomsky, *Syntactic Structures* [The Hague: Mouton, 1957] 5), though it is more difficult to practice because observations are both nonrepeatable and more subjective. That is why the database must be large enough and the semantics clear enough for any significant syntactical conclusions to be drawn.

are not ultimately to be measured in decimal points, but in patterns and composite pictures. Rather than creating reproducible results in a test tube, our objective is, first, to detect any linguistic patterns in the surviving literature and, second, to apply such patterns to exegetically problematic texts.

To *require* that a particular morpho-syntactic construction always fit the straitjacket of a particular semantic force before any exegetical conclusions can be drawn is to treat the vagaries of human behavior as though they followed the laws of physics. That some have taken just such a tack in biblical and/or linguistic studies does not thereby validate the approach.

Conversely, it must be admitted that most heterodox (whether theological or exegetical) positions are built upon what is *possible*; but whether they are probable is a different matter. Just because a view is *possible* does not make it likely in a given text.

8. *Portrayal Vs. Reality*

One of the fundamental keys to understanding language is the recognition that *there is not necessarily any correspondence between language and reality.* If such were the case, neither irony nor novels could be penned.[37] Unfortunately, students of scripture (both exegetes and grammarians) too often assume such a correspondence. For example, not infrequently the indicative mood is erroneously considered to be the mood of *fact*. On this point, A. T. Robertson astutely pointed out:

> The indicative does *state* a thing as true, but does not guarantee the *reality* of the thing. In the nature of the case only the *statement* is under discussion. A clear grip on this point will help one all along. The indicative has nothing to do with reality ('an sich'). The speaker *presents* something as true. . . . Whether it is true or no is another matter. Most untruths are told in the indicative mode.[38]

---

[37] Robinson gives the following illustration to this effect (*New Grammarians' Funeral*, 48): "One attraction of the kernel sentences, as we shall see, is that they make propositions, and 'she was wearing her old blue coat' appears to be making a factual, verifiable statement. But what if it is the opening sentence of a novel? It is not then verifiable, but does that make it extraordinary? On the contrary it would be extraordinary for a story to begin with something verifiable. 'Once upon a time there was a very wicked old witch who lived in the dismal depths of a dank dark forest–' If you interrupt and say, 'But that can't be so! for there are no such people as witches' you are falling in 'aspect-blindness', for nobody has asserted that there *are* witches." A similar point could be made about many of the characters in Jesus' parables.

On the following page Robinson adds: "TG grammar has no way of showing (although it is implied by common parlance) that saying something ironically is less basic to language than saying something straight. One linguistic universal I do believe in: I cannot imagine a language in which it would be impossible to say something ironically."

[38] Robertson, *Grammar*, 915.

The aorist tense has often been the target of such abuse, due largely to the exegete's misunderstanding of the grammarians' terms such as "punctiliar" or "point action." What is meant by such verbiage is not that the aorist describes the action as occurring at a point (a notion that gave rise to the "once and for all" aorist), but that the aorist's mode of presentation is punctiliar. In other words, the aorist takes something of a snapshot of the action.[39] The action itself may be iterative, durative, progressive, etc., but the aorist refrains from describing such intricacies.

These are well-known gaffes. But such are only the tip of the iceberg. On a broader scale, grammarians are still fond of speaking of particular morpho-syntactic categories–such as the subjunctive mood or μή in questions or first-class conditions–as somehow intrinsically tied to the speaker's *viewpoint* of reality. The notion that verbal aspect is subjective while *Aktionsart* is objective is another instance, for it is often supposed that *Aktionsart* more closely corresponds to reality. In truth, language *qua* language does not tell us anything about either reality or even a speaker's viewpoint about reality. It only records the speaker's/writer's *presentation*. Thus, for Robertson to argue that the devil used the first class condition in his temptation of Jesus (εἰ υἱὸς εἶ τοῦ θεοῦ in Luke 4:3) because "the devil knew it to be true"[40] is to make several faulty assumptions about the nature of language and its correspondence to reality.

Whether there is, in a given instance, any correspondence between language and reality is not up to the grammarian to decide. The atheist would deny that any "God-talk" in scripture has such correspondence. As a believer, my own convictions are decidedly different. Yet, even for one who has embraced the cardinal doctrines of the Christian faith, there must be room for irony, perspective, rhetoric, and hyperbole in the canon.

---

[39] Recent studies have refined this view further, but suffice it to say for now that this was the idea that grammarians had in mind.

[40] Robertson, *Grammar*, 1009.

The Language of the
New Testament

Overview of Chapter

In this chapter our goal is twofold: (1) to see where NT Greek fits in the history of the Greek language (this is known as a diachronic and external study) and (2) to look at certain issues related to NT Greek per se (this is a synchronic and internal study). The material is not all equally important; some of it may be glossed over quickly and merely used for reference. The chapter can be outlined as follows (with the more immediately relevant sections for intermediate students highlighted in bold letters):

Select Bibliography

A. W. Argyle, "Greek Among the Jews of Palestine in New Testament Times," *NTS* 20 (1973) 87-89; **M. Black**, *An Aramaic Approach to the Gospels and Acts*, 3d ed. (Oxford, 1967); *BDF*, 1-6 (§1-7); **C. D. Buck**, *Introduction to the Study of the Greek Dialects*, 2d ed. (1928) 3-16, 136-40; **C. F. Burney**, *The Aramaic Origin of the Fourth Gospel* (Oxford, 1922); **E. C. Colwell**, "The Character of the Greek of the Fourth Gospel . . . Parallels from Epictetus" (Ph.D. dissertation, University of Chicago, 1930); **G. A. Deissmann**, *Bibelstudien* (1895); **idem**, *Light from the Ancient East* (1923); **J. A. Fitzmyer**, "The Languages of Palestine in the First Century A.D.," *CBQ* 32 (1970) 501-31; **R. G. Hoerber**, "The Greek of the New Testament: Some Theological Implications," *Concordia Journal* 2 (1976) 251-56; **Hoffmann—von Siebenthal**, *Grammatik*, 2-5; **G. Horsley**, "Divergent Views on the Nature of the Greek of the Bible," *Bib* 65 (1984) 393-403; **P. E. Hughes**, "The Languages Spoken by Jesus," *New Dimensions in New Testament Study* (ed. R. N. Longenecker and M. C. Tenney; Grand Rapids: Zondervan, 1974) 127-43; **A. N. Jannaris**, *Historical Greek Grammar*; **E. V. McKnight**, "Is the New Testament Written in 'Holy Ghost' Greek?", *BT* 16 (1965) 87-93; **idem**, "The New Testament and 'Biblical Greek'," *JBR* 34 (1966) 36-42; **B. M. Metzger**, "The Language of the New Testament," *The Interpreter's Bible* (New York: Abingdon, 1951) 7.43-59; **E. M. Meyers and J. F. Strange**, *Archaeology, the Rabbis, and Early Christianity* (Nashville: Abingdon, 1981) 62-91, 92-124, 166-73; **Moule**, *Idiom Book*, 1-4; **Moulton**, *Prolegomena*, 1-41; **Moulton-Howard**, *Accidence*, 412-85 (on Semitisms in the NT); **G. Mussies**, *The Morphology of Koine Greek* (Leiden: Brill, 1971); **E. Oikonomos**, "The New Testament in Modern Greek," *BT* 21 (1970) 114-25; **L. R. Palmer**, *The Greek Language* (London: Faber & Faber, 1980); **S. E. Porter**, *Verbal Aspect in the Greek of the New Testament* (Bern: Peter Lang, 1989) 111-56; **idem**, "Did Jesus Ever Teach in Greek?" *TynBul* 44 (1993) 195-235; **L. Radermacher**, "Besonderheiten der Koine-Syntax," *Wiener Studien (Zeitschrift für Klassische Philologie)* 31 (1909) 1-12; **Robertson**, *Grammar*, 31-75; **L. Rydbeck**, "What Happened to Greek Grammar after Albert Debrunner?" *NTS* 21 (1975) 424-27; **E. Schürer**, *The History of the Jewish People in the Age of Jesus Christ* (rev. and ed. by G. Vermes, F. Millar, M. Black; Edinburgh: T. & T. Clark, 1979) 2.29-80, esp. 74-80; **J. N. Sevenster**, *Do You Know Greek? How Much Greek Could the First Jewish Christians have Known?* (Leiden: E. J. Brill, 1968); **M. Silva**, "Bilingualism and the Character of New Testament Greek," *Bib* 69 (1980) 198-219; **Smyth**, *Greek Grammar*, 1-4b; **Turner**, *Insights*, 174-88; **idem**, "The Literary Character of New Testament Greek," *NTS* 20 (1973) 107-114; **idem**, *Syntax*, 1-9; **idem**, "The Unique Character of Biblical Greek," *Vetus Testamentum* 5 (1955) 208-213; **Zerwick**, *Biblical Greek*, 161-64.[1]

---

[1] This bibliography and the others in this book are not meant to be exhaustive, but suggestive. (The bibliography listed here is more comprehensive than the others, however, due to the nature of the topic.) The more commonly cited sources are here given in abbreviated form (e.g., an author's last name, or initials for journals); for such sources, consult the abbreviations list.

I. The Roots of the Greek Language

What is the relationship of Greek to other languages? By tracing certain linguistic features of various languages (especially stable lexical terms–e.g., parts of the body), linguists are able to determine how languages relate to each other genealogically (e.g., *tres* [Latin], τρεῖς [Greek], and *tryas* [Sanskrit]). It is often argued that although Sanskrit is not the mother of Greek and Latin, it is their older sister. All of these go back to a now lost Indo-European language.

The Mother Tongue of all languages apparently had as many as ten children, each of whom were in turn parents of rather large families. One of these ten children was "Proto-Indo-European," from which we get Greek, Latin, Romance languages, Germanic languages, etc.

II. Stages of the Greek Language (Diachronic)

There are five great stages of the Greek language.[2]

A. Pre-Homeric (up to 1000 BCE)

As early as the third millennium BCE, tribes of Indo-European peoples wandered into Greece. The natural barriers there eventually created several dialects. That is, as they settled they were cut off from one another–consequently, a different dialect emerged for each local group. Unfortunately, because we lack literary remains, we know very little from this period about the Greek language.[3]

B. The Age of the Dialects, or the Classical Era (1000 BCE-330 BCE)

Geography and politics (e.g., independent city-states) caused Greek to fracture into several dialects, four of which were predominant.[4] There exist today few literary remains of the other dialects.[5]

The main dialects[6] were *Aeolic* (whose extant remains are only poetic, e.g., Sappho), *Doric* (also with only poetic remains, most notably of Pindar and

---

[2] For numerous sub-divisions, see Jannaris, 1-20.

[3] For a discussion of the history of proto-Greek (esp. Linear B which was identified as proto-Greek in 1952), see Palmer, *The Greek Language*, 27-56. The inscriptionary evidence does not reveal different dialects until after the 12th century BCE.

[4] Buck, *The Greek Dialects*, lists 18-20 dialects altogether.

Theocritus), *Ionic* (found in Homer, Hesiod, Herodotus, and Hippocrates), and by far the most influential, *Attic*.

An offspring of Ionic, Attic was the dialect of Athens, during the "golden age" of classical Greek (4th-5th centuries BCE). In this golden age, Athens was both the political and literary center of Greece. "Classical Greek," though technically referring to all four dialects, is normally equated with Attic Greek, because of the proliferation of literary works that come from this dialect. Attic was thus a vehicle of refinement, precision, and beauty[7] through which some of the world's great literature was conveyed: "In it were composed the tragedies of Aeschylus, Sophocles, and Euripides, the comedies of Aristophanies, the histories of Thucydides and Xenophon, the orations of Demosthenes, and the philosophical treatises of Plato."[8]

C. Κοινή *Greek (330 BCE–330 CE)*

When primitive tribes of Indo-Europeans moved into Greece, presumably they spoke a single language. Geography and politics caused it to fracture into a score of dialects, only to be united once again on the battlefield. Thus, ironically, the first military campaign in the third millennium BCE brought confusion of tongues, while the last campaign not only restored linguistic unity, but forged a new language which was destined to become a *Weltsprache* (world language).

The Koine was born out of the conquests of Alexander the Great. First, his troops, which came from Athens as well as other Greek cities and regions, had to speak to one another. This close contact produced a melting-pot Greek that inevitably softened the rough edges of some dialects and abandoned the subtleties of others. Second, the conquered cities and colonies learned Greek as a second language. By the first century CE, Greek was the *lingua franca* of the whole Mediterranean region and beyond. Since the majority of Greek-speakers learned it as a second language, this further increased its loss of subtleties and moved it toward greater explicitness (e.g., the repetition of a preposition with a second noun where Attic Greek was usually comfortable with a single preposition).

---

[5] The inscriptional remains reveal a somewhat different picture. Indeed, we could examine the dialects geographically or literarily. Geographically, there were four main dialects (Arcado-Cypriot, West Greek [including Doric and Northwest Greek], Attic-Ionic [including both Ionic and Attic], and Aeolic [including Lesbian (named after the island Lesbos) and Boeotian]). See Palmer, *The Greek Language*, 57-58, for a brief description. Our approach above is literary, dealing with the major dialects in terms of their literary remains.

[6] See Smyth, *Greek Grammar*, 3-4, and Palmer, *The Greek Language*, 57-58, for a discussion.

[7] Smyth, 4.

[8] Metzger, 44.

D. Byzantine (or Medieval) Greek (330 CE-1453 CE)

1. Koine Greek was transformed into Byzantine Greek when Constantine was converted. By reversing the edicts of Diocletian's persecution (303-311), Constantine gave the language a largely religious hue. Ecclesiastical Greek was born.

2. When the Empire split between East and West, Greek lost its *Weltsprache* status. Latin was used in the West (Rome), Greek in the East (Constantinople).

E. Modern Greek (1453 CE to present)

In 1453 the Turks invaded Byzantium. Greek was no longer isolated from the rest of the world. The Renaissance was born in the West as scholars fled with copies of Greek classics under their arms; the Reformation was born in northern Europe as Christian scholars (such as Erasmus and Luther) were made aware of NT Greek manuscripts.

Nevertheless, although Greek got out of the East, Europe did not get in. That is to say, copies of ancient Greek literature finally brought Europe out of the dark ages, but Europe had no impact on the living language. The Turks largely cut the East off from the rest of Europe, retarding the growth of the language (that is, until 1820, when the Greeks rebelled against the Turks and regained their freedom). The net effect is that "the modern Greek popular speech does not differ materially from the vernacular Byzantine, and thus connects directly with the vernacular κοινή."[9] By way of analogy, Hoerber points out that "the Greek language has fewer changes over three thousand years than English has since Chaucer (?1340-1400) or *Beowulf* (8th century) …"[10]

Today, there are two levels of Greek:

1. Katharevousa (καθαρεύουσα = "literary language")

This is not really a historical development of the language, but is "book Greek" or an artificial attempt at resurrecting the Attic dialect in modern times. Moulton sarcastically suggests that "it is just as valuable as Volapük to the student of linguistic evolution" and that "it is a medley far more mixed than we should get by compounding together Cynewulf and Kipling."[11]

---

[9] Robertson, 44.
[10] Hoerber, 253.
[11] Moulton, *Prolegomena*, 26.

2. *Demotic* (δημοτική)

This is the spoken language of Greece today, the "direct descendant of the Koine."[12]

III. Κοινή *Greek (Synchronic)*

A. Terminology

Κοινή is the feminine adjective of κοινός ("common"). The feminine is used because it (implicitly) modifies διάλεκτος, a (second declension) feminine noun. Synonyms of Koine are "common" Greek, or, more frequently, Hellenistic Greek (which normally implies that Greek is a second language–i.e., the speakers have become Hellenized [cf. Acts 6:1]).

Both New Testament Greek and Septuagintal Greek are considered substrata of the Koine. (The LXX, however, is so heavily Semitized–precisely because it is entirely translation Greek–that it is normally treated as in a class by itself.)

B. Historical Development

The following are eight interesting historical facts about the Hellenistic Greek:

1. The golden age of Greek literature effectively died with Aristotle (322 BCE).

2. The Koine was born with Alexander the Great's conquests.

3. Hellenistic Greek began with Alexander's troops who came from all the regions of Greece. The troops, then, produced a *leveling* influence.

4. It developed further as a second language of conquered peoples, when new Greek colonies sprang up due to Alexander's victories. The conquests, then, gave Greek its *universal* nature.

5. Koine Greek grew largely from Attic Greek (which, if you recall, was the dialect of the "golden age" of Greece), as this was Alexander's dialect, but was also influenced by the other dialects of Alexander's soldiers. "Hellenistic Greek is a compromise between the rights of the stronger minority (i.e., Attic) and the weaker majority (other dialects)."[13]

---

[12] *BDF,* 2, n. 1 (§ 3).
[13] Moule, 1.

6. This new dialect, however, should not be perceived to be inferior to Attic. It was not a contamination of the pure gold of classical Greek, but a more serviceable alloy for the masses.[14]

7. It became the *lingua franca* of the whole Roman Empire by the first century CE.[15]

8. When is Koine Koine?

   Though Koine Greek had its birth in c. 330 BCE, this was its physical birth, not its linguistic. One should not suppose that all of a sudden, with the conclusion of Alexander's final battle, everyone began speaking Koine Greek! (Remember that Greece still retained its dialects while Alexander was conquering the world.) Just as a newborn baby does not immediately speak, it took some time before Koine really took shape.

C. *Scope of Κοινή Greek*

1. Time

Roughly, 330 BCE to 330 CE. Or, from Alexander's conquests to the removal of the Roman Empire's capital from Rome to Constantinople. With the death of Aristotle in 322 BCE, classical Greek as a living language was phasing out. Koine was at its peak in the first century BCE and first century CE.

2. Place

For the first time, Greek was universalized. As colonies were established well past Alexander's day, and as the Greeks continued to rule, the Greek language kept on thriving in foreign lands. Even after Rome became the world power in the first century BCE, Greek continued to penetrate distant lands. (This was due largely to Rome's policy of assimilation of cultures already in place, rather than destruction and replacement.) Consequently, even when Rome was in absolute control, Latin was not the *lingua franca*. Greek continued to be a *universal* language until at least the end of the first century. From about the second century on, Latin began to win out in Italy (among the populace), then the West in general, once Constantinople became the capital of the Roman empire. For only a brief period, then, was Greek the universal language.

---

[14] Ibid.

[15] Cf. esp. Porter, "Did Jesus Ever Teach in Greek?" 205-23 (205-9 addresses Greek as the *lingua franca* of the Roman Empire; 209-23 deals with Greek in Palestine per se).

D. *Changes from Classical Greek*

In a word, Greek became *simpler*. In terms of morphology, the language lost certain aspects, decreased its use of others, and assimilated difficult forms into more frequently seen patterns. The language tended toward shorter, simpler sentences. Some of the syntactical subtleties were lost or at least declined. The language replaced the precision and refinement of classical Greek with greater explicitness.[16]

1. Morphology

Since Hellenistic Greek is an amalgam of other dialects, we should be wary of inventing prescriptive rules for morphology, only to call most verb forms "exceptions" to the rules. Many of the so-called exceptions are traceable to an unsystematic borrowing from the various dialects (e.g., the Aeolic third singular first aorist optative ending -αι for the Attic ending -ειε[ν]); still others are due to the Koine shaping itself into familiar or analogous patterns (such as putting first aorist endings on second aorist verbs–εἶπαν for εἶπον). The sometimes multiple forms of a particular principal part (e.g., fourth and fifth principal parts of ἀνοίγω) that occur in the NT are to be explained along these same lines.

In sum, not all irregular forms in the NT have pat linguistic solutions, as if the mere memorizing of rules is all that is needed to recognize them. Many of these irregularities are simply due to historical accident, not linguistic principle.[17]

2. Sentence Structure

a. Shorter, simpler sentences replaced the often complex sentences of classical Greek.

b. Fewer particles and conjunctions were used, several of which were pressed into service to accomplish many different tasks.

c. Parataxis (coordinated clauses) increased; hypotaxis (complex sentences in which a subordinate clause is used) decreased.

d. Direct discourse was favored over indirect discourse.

---

[16] This is essentially the argument of Zerwick, who sustains it with many examples throughout his *Biblical Greek*.

[17] Some examples of morphological changes are as follows: (1) σσ for ττ (e.g., θάλασσα for θάλαττα); (2) decline in the use of -μι verbs, optatives, superlatives; (3) loss of the dual (a form on nouns, verbs, adjectives used to indicate two persons); (4) assimilation of forms to more familiar patterns, e.g., first aorist endings on second aorist verbs (e.g., ἦλθαν for ἦλθον, εἶπαν for εἶπον, etc.), first declension endings on third declension nouns (e.g., θυγατέραν for θυγατέρα [though only the true third declension form occurs in the NT]); and (5) more frequent use of diminutive, though the meaning is often unaltered from the normal form.

3. Style/Syntax of the Noun and Verb

Since Hellenistic Greek is both a melting pot of previous dialects and a second language to conquered peoples, three predictable features occur: (1) subtleties drop out; (2) refinements blur; (3) the language tends toward greater explicitness.[18] Some examples:

a. **Prepositions:**

    1) repeated before nouns where Attic Greek would have used one preposition.

    2) preference for compound verbs with prepositions where either the compound or the preposition is all that is necessary.

    3) the use of prepositions where Attic Greek often used a mere noun in the proper case.

    4) confusion/overlapping of prepositions (e.g., εἰς/ἐν, ὑπέρ/περί).

b. **Pronouns:** more frequently used (more explicit).

c. **Personal Pronouns:** used as subjects of verbs where Attic usually left them out.

d. **Number:** dual drops out.

e. **Tenses:** use of present tense for future (vivid futuristic present).

f. **Voices:** Direct middle declining; active voice with reflexive pronoun normally used.

g. **Moods:** optative dying out.

h. **ἵνα replaces infinitive; uses of ἵνα are broadening.**

i. **Participles:** greater frequency of periphrastic constructions.

E. *Types of Κοινή Greek*

Many scholars admit of only two real levels: vulgar and literary.[19] This is a wrong-headed approach for the following reasons: (1) This view is not

---

[18] Metzger, 45; Zerwick, 161.

[19] *BDF* pose the question this way: "Where between the two extremes do the NT documents belong, to the everyday idiom reflected in the papyrus letters, or to the Atticized literary monuments? By and large it may be said that *the language of the NT authors is nearer to the simple popular language* . . ." (2 [§ 3]).

sensitive to the differences between a truly literary Koine and an artificial Atticistic Greek; (2) the issue is presented as black-or-white: the "two extremes" are seen as the only grids through which the rest of Koine material must be seen; (3) most of the books of the NT were never intended to be literary works–thus, it is not an apt analogy to compare them to works intended to be literary. On the other hand, they do not fully parallel receipts, wills, laundry lists, business documents, memos, legal documents, even personal letters written by soldiers from the field; for they were written, for the most part, for an audience, not just a private individual–and they were usually intended to be read aloud. Further, their subject matter and their frequent apologetic tone dictate that parallels cannot easily be found in the papyri.

It is for these reasons that a few scholars have suggested that there may be at least one intermediate level of Koine Greek between the extremes of vulgar and literary. That assessment seems to be correct; the following breakdown reflects this.

1. **Vernacular** or **Vulgar** (e.g., papyri, ostraca)

    This is the language of the streets–colloquial, popular speech. It is found principally in the papyri excavated from Egypt, truly the *lingua franca* of the day.

    > The papyri remains are similar to a hypothetical situation in which Americans of the twentieth century would empty their waste-baskets in rubbish heaps in a location sufficiently dry to preserve them for two thousand years; then scholars would discover them and study such material, noticing particularly the type of English employed in the twentieth century. We dare surmise that the deductions of those scholars would give a narrow and warped picture of the linguistic ability and practice of twentieth-century Americans.[20]

2. **Literary** (e.g., Polybius, Josephus, Philo, Diodorus, Strabo, Epictetus, Plutarch)

    A more polished Koine, this is the language of scholars and littérateurs, of academics and historians. The difference between literary Koine and vulgar Koine is the difference between English spoken on the streets and English spoken in places of higher education. Epictetus would probably represent the lowest form of literary Koine–in fact, E. C. Colwell went so far as to say that the Greek of the Fourth Gospel was quite similar to that of Epictetus. Josephus' Greek, though at times heavily Semitized, is often quite good.

---

[20] Hoerber, 252.

3. **Conversational** (New Testament, some papyri)

Conversational Koine is typically the *spoken* language of educated people. It is grammatically correct for the most part, but not on the same literary level (lacks subtleties, is more explicit, shorter sentences, more
parataxis) as literary Koine. By its very nature, one would not expect to
find many parallels to this—either in the papyri (usually the language of
uneducated people) or among literary authors (for their language is a
written language). Evidence/analogies for this level of language can be
found plentifully, however, in western civilization.

a. This analogy can be seen further in *sermons*. A sermon is typically
above the level of vulgar, below the level of literary. In fact, many
homileticians today argue that an ideal sermon should be put on a
"lively conversational level" (so, e.g., Haddon Robinson). Here is a
decent analogy to the NT: much of the NT was originally sermonic
in nature, now transcribed for posterity. Some of the letters were
intended to be sermons; most were intended at least to be read aloud
in the churches. Perhaps we can never recover the living language
of spoken Koine, but the NT seems to come very close to it.

b. "Practically every age of Western civilization, particularly after the
composing and recording of the Homeric epics, exhibits three basic
levels of language: literary, conversational, and 'vulgar'. . . The
extant compositions of ancient Greece and Rome are almost entirely
on the literary level."[21] Cicero's speeches are a good example of conversational Latin.

c. Finally, there are at least three levels of Greek for all its periods, as
Jannaris notes:

> The literary masterpieces of this period [Classical era] then do not rep-
> resent the language as actually spoken at the time…. For in ordinary
> intercourse both the educated classes and uneducated multitudes
> could not rise above the simple colloquial or popular speech, in many
> cases degenerating into a vernacular or even rustic idiom. The co-exist-
> ence at all times of an artistic or literary style, and a colloquial or pop-
> ular speech…with an intermediate conventional language, is a fact
> indisputably established by the force of logic, by historical investiga-
> tion, and by modern analogies, as well as by daily experience.[22]

Jannaris further articulates the difference between the spoken and
written language:

> …no writer whatever uses the same diction both in writing and speak-
> ing. On the contrary, every penman makes it a special point to clothe
> his thoughts in a more or less elegant expression…. The whole [classi-
> cal] Greek literature, the glory of ancient Greece, is composed almost

---

[21] Hoerber, 252.
[22] Jannaris, 4.

exclusively in the literary diction. With regard to the colloquial or popular speech, it is hardly represented in the written monuments extant.[23]

Finally, for the Koine period, Jannaris argues that there are four different levels of Greek: (1) Atticistic, (2) conventional [=literary], (3) Levantine [=conversational; specifically the Greek of Hellenized foreigners, including the NT], and (4) colloquial or popular speech (=vulgar).[24]

   d. In conclusion, it seems that the initial excitement over the papyri parallels to the NT was perhaps overstated. That is to say, as helpful as the papyri have been for our understanding of NT vocabulary stock, we have not found perfect *syntactical* parallels in the papyri. Most of the papyri are beneath most of the NT syntactically, while the NT is not on the same literary level as such authors as Josephus or Polybius. It largely holds a middle ground between vulgar and literary, known as conversational.[25]

4.   **Atticistic** (e.g., Lucian, Dionysius of Halicarnasus, Dio Chrysostom, Aristides, Phrynichus, Moeris)

This is an artificial language revived by littérateurs who did not care for what had become of the language (much like many advocates of the KJV today argue for that version's renderings because it represents English at the height of its glory, during the Shakespearean era).

As the language developed under such conditions and influences [of Roman rule, where culture and intellectual life were brought to a low ebb] compared unfavourably with the Attic of the glorious olden times of Athenian hegemony, many scholars now, and after them the great majority of their successors, acting in a tacit conspiracy, endeavored to check the further progress of this "Common" (i.e., unclassical Attic) Greek and revive the ancient pure Attic, a circumstance which gave them the nickname of *Atticists*, i.e., "purists." Not originality, but *imitation* and *form* …[26]

IV. New Testament Greek

There are two separate though related questions that need to be answered regarding the nature of NT Greek: (1) What were the current languages of first-century Palestine? and (2) Where does NT Greek fit into Koine?

---

[23] Ibid., 5.

[24] Ibid., 8.

[25] Hoffmann-von Siebenthal have arrived at similar conclusions (2-3).

[26] Jannaris, 7.

A. *The Language Milieu of Palestine*

It is being increasingly recognized that Aramaic, Hebrew, and Greek were in use in Palestine in the first century CE.[27] How commonplace each of these languages was is debated. Related to this issue is the language(s) Jesus spoke. Since this latter issue is separate from the issue of NT Greek (though related to it), we will only treat it briefly.

1. Aramaic

By the first century CE, it is probable that Aramaic was the primary tongue of at least several Jewish regions. It is doubtful, however, that it was the primary language for all Jews in Palestine, particularly those from Galilee. Most scholars today say that this was the primary (if not exclusive) language in which Jesus taught, though he probably knew Hebrew (cf. Luke 4), and probably spoke Greek as well.

2. Hebrew

Some scholars argue that (Mishnaic) Hebrew was actually the primary language of first-century Palestine. Yet Hebrew was apparently not widely used by the masses, as is evident by the lack of evidence: there is almost no trace of Hebrew inscriptions in Palestine at this time.

3. Greek

An increasing number of scholars are arguing that Greek was the primary language spoken in Palestine in the time of, and perhaps even in the ministry of Jesus. "The arguments for this position rest firmly on the role of Greek as the *lingua franca* of the Roman Empire, the linguistic and cultural character of lower Galilee during the first century, the linguistic fact that the New Testament has been transmitted in Greek from its earliest documents, and diversity of epigraphic evidence, significant literary evidence, and several significant contexts in the Gospels ...."[28]

B. *Place of the Language of the New Testament in Hellenistic Greek*

1. The Issue

How much Semitic influence is there on the Greek of the NT? How much is the Greek of the NT affected by other influences?

---

[27] For a summary, see Porter, *Verbal Aspect*, 111-56.

[28] Porter, "Did Jesus Ever Teach in Greek?" 204. For a detailed presentation of the arguments and an excellent bibliography, see idem, 195-235.

2. The Proposals

In 1863, J. B. Lightfoot anticipated the great discoveries of papyri parallels when he said, "If we could only recover letters that ordinary people wrote to each other without any thought of being literary, we should have the greatest possible help for the understanding of the language of the NT generally."[29]

Thirty-two years later, in 1895, Adolf Deissmann published his *Bibelstudien*–an innocently titled work that was to revolutionize the study of the NT. In this work (later translated into English under the title *Bible Studies*) Deissmann showed that the Greek of the NT was not a language invented by the Holy Spirit (Hermann Cremer had called it "Holy Ghost Greek," largely because 10 percent of its vocabulary had no secular parallels).

Deissmann demonstrated that the vast bulk of NT vocabulary was to be found in the papyri. The pragmatic effect of Deissmann's work was to render obsolete virtually all lexica and lexical commentaries written before the turn of the century. (Thayer's lexicon, published in 1886, was consequently outdated shortly after it came off the press–yet, ironically, it is still relied on today by many NT students).

James Hope Moulton took up Deissmann's mantle and demonstrated parallels in syntax and morphology between the NT and the papyri. In essence, *what Deissmann did for lexicography, Moulton did for grammar.* He noted that some previously unparalleled NT constructions were found in the papyri (e.g., instrumental ἐv). However, his case has not proved as convincing. For this reason, the debate still rages as to how much Semitic influence there is on NT Greek.

Today, there are generally three broad views of NT Greek, ranging from vernacular Koine to heavily Semitized Greek.

a. NT Greek = Vernacular Greek

This was the view of Deissmann and Moulton, and it has been promoted (with some modification) by Robertson, Radermacher, Colwell, Silva, and Rydbeck. All these scholars allow for Semitisms when it comes to quotations from the OT and some sayings of Jesus.

The problems with this view are: (1) It does not allow for the rich variety of authors of the NT–some may fit this mold, others may fit one of the following two categories; (2) much of the papyri are found in Jewish settlements–thus, these too may be Semitized; and, most seriously, (3) the syntactical parallels are not nearly as convincing as the lexical parallels: the NT seems, for the most part, to be on a higher plane than the papyri.

---

[29] Cited in Moulton, *Prolegomena*, 242.

b. **NT Greek = Vernacular Greek with Some Portions Heavily Semitized**

Some scholars (e.g., Dalman, Torrey, Burney, Black, R. H. Charles, M. Wilcox) view the Gospels, the first fifteen chapters of Acts, and the Apocalypse as virtual translation Greek. That is, the original was in Aramaic, and what we have in our extant copies is a Greek translation.

The problems with this view are: (1) There is absolutely no early textual evidence for this theory (i.e., no early Aramaic MS has been produced that could purport to be behind the Greek text of the Gospels, Acts, or Revelation); (2) most of the alleged Semitisms (e.g., word-plays lost in the Greek translation, mistranslations, etc.), though ingenious, are subject to serious objections.

c. **NT Greek = A Distinct Dialect**

This view, which looks very much like a throw-back to the days of "Holy Ghost Greek," has been strongly promoted by Nigel Turner. Turner goes so far as to say, when pondering the question of Holy Ghost Greek, "We now have to concede that not only is the subject-matter of the Scriptures unique but so also is the language in which they came to be written or translated."[30] Elsewhere he bluntly states, "Bibl[ical] Greek is a unique language with a unity and character of its own."[31] It is essential to understand that by "biblical Greek" Turner includes the LXX. Indeed, the LXX is the mother of the NT, linguistically speaking.

The problems with this view–in addition to the problems with the second view–are: (1) A number of studies have shown that the syntax of the NT is hardly identical with the LXX, and the two are not really of the same genre;[32] (2) the parallels are drawn selectively;[33] (3) this view confuses style with syntax (more on this point later).

---

[30] Turner, *Syntax*, 9.

[31] Ibid., 4.

[32] For example, the genitive absolute is used frequently in the NT, infrequently in the LXX–and it is a distinctively Greek idiom; several features of NT Greek verbal aspect have no parallels in the Semitic tongues; the article-noun-καί-noun construction is frequent in the NT, infrequent (and not carrying the same semantic force) in the LXX; the relation of adjective to noun in anarthrous constructions in the NT is more similar to Attic and the papyri than to the LXX.

[33] This is especially the case in the recent article by L. Cignelli and G. C. Bottini, "L'Articolo nel Greco Biblico," *Studium Biblicum Franciscanum Liber Annuus* 41 (1991) 159-99. They argue that the use of the article in the NT stands in opposition to that of the Attic (159). Their approach, however, is to take examples from the LXX (which is translation Greek) and assume that such are equally valid in the NT. But to lump the NT in with the LXX as though all were the same genre is an overstatement.

In sum, most scholars today would hold to a view somewhere between the first and second one. But there are increasing studies that promote the first view, viz., that the Greek of the NT was good, common Greek that could be understood on the streets of Athens as easily as in the suburbs of Jerusalem. Nevertheless, there are problems with all these views, especially in terms of how the issue is stated.

3. Restating the Issue

Perhaps there are other ways of looking at the nature of NT Greek. The following considerations offer a complex grid of considerations that need to be addressed.

a. Distinction between Style and Syntax[34]

Those who hold that the Greek of the NT is conventional Koine make an important distinction between syntax and style (e.g., Deissmann, Moulton, Radermacher, Debrunner), while the "distinct dialect" view does not. Semitisms affect the *style* of the NT, while the *syntax* is still Hellenistic Greek. Syntax is something external to an author–the basic linguistic features of a community without which communication would be impossible. Style, on the other hand, is something internal to each writer. For example, the frequency of the use of the preposition or of the coordinating conjunctions (such as καί) is a stylistic matter: the fact that Attic writers used prepositions and coordinating conjunctions less often than Koine writers does not mean the syntax changed. Many of the arguments for a distinct dialect are based on these quantitative differences between Attic and NT Greek; only if such a view could prove *qualitative* changes (and on a large scale)–and not only between Attic and NT Greek, but also between NT Greek and other Koine–would the case for a unique language be feasible.

b. Levels of Koine Greek

As we argued earlier, the Greek of the NT is neither on the level of the papyri, nor on the level of literary Koine, but is conversational Greek. That many scholars seem to be unaware of this intermediate level is part of the reason there is confusion over the nature of NT Greek.

c. Multi-Faceted, not Linear

Grammar and style are not the only issues that need to be addressed. Vocabulary is also a crucial matrix. Deissmann has well shown that the lexical stock of NT Greek is largely the lexical stock

---

[34] See Rydbeck, 424-27, for discussion.

of vernacular Koine. It is our conviction that *the language of the NT needs to be seen in light of three poles*, not one: style, grammar, vocabulary. To a large degree, the *style* is Semitic, the *syntax* is conversational/literary Koine (the descendant of Attic), and the *vocabulary* is vernacular Koine. These cannot be tidily separated at all times, of course.[35] The relationship can be illustrated as follows.

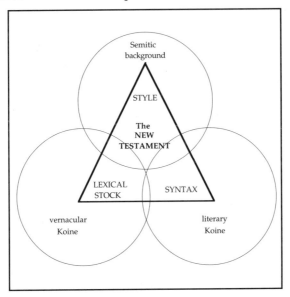

Chart 1
The Multi-Faceted Nature of NT Greek

d. Multiple authorship

One other factor needs to be addressed: the NT was written by several authors. Some (e.g., author of Hebrews, Luke, sometimes Paul) aspire to literary Koine in their sentence structure; others are on a much lower plane (e.g., Mark, John, Revelation, 2 Peter). *It is consequently impossible to speak of NT Greek in monotone terms.* This, it seems, is decisively an argument against Turner, for the language of the NT is not a "unique language" (a cursory comparison of Hebrews and Revelation will reveal this); but it also argues against Deissmann and Moulton to some degree, for the Greek of the NT is not altogether to be put on the same level as the papyri. For some of the NT authors, it does seem that Greek was their native tongue; others grew up with it in a bilingual environment, though probably learned Greek after Aramaic; still others may have learned it as adults.

---

[35] That is to say, the Semitic background of the authors can, at times, affect their syntax and their vocabulary (especially due to the LXX's influence); the vernacular Koine can impact their syntax, as well as their style, etc.

4. Some Conclusions

The issues relating to the Greek of the NT are somewhat complex. We can summarize our view as follows:

a. For the most part, the Greek of the NT is *conversational Greek* in its *syntax*–somewhat below the refinement and sentence structure of literary Koine, but above the level found in most papyri (though, to be sure, there are Semitic intrusions into the syntax on occasion).

b. Its *style*, on the other hand, is largely *Semitic*–that is, since almost all of the writers of the NT books are Jews, their style of writing is shaped both by their religious heritage and by their linguistic background. Furthermore, the style of the NT is also due to the fact that these writers all share one thing in common, faith in Jesus Christ. (This is analogous to conversations between two Christians at church and the same two at work: the linguistic style and vocabulary to some extent are different in both places.)

c. The NT *vocabulary* stock, however, is largely shared with the ordinary *papyrus* documents of the day, though heavily influenced at times by the LXX and the Christian experience.

There are exceptions to each of these areas, as they are not neatly compartmentalized. Not only this, but since the NT was written by authors with various linguistic backgrounds and abilities, it is quite impossible to view their Greek as merely one kind. Nevertheless, it is possible to gain an overall impression of NT Greek, and Moule has summarized this nicely:

> The pendulum has swung rather too far in the direction of equating Biblical with "secular" Greek; and we must not allow these fascinating discoveries to blind us to the fact that Biblical Greek still does retain certain peculiarities, due in part to Semitic influence (which must be far stronger in the New Testament than in an equivalent bulk of colloquial or literary "secular" Greek, even allowing for the permeation of society by Jewish settlements), and in part to the moulding influence of the Christian experience, which did in some measure create an idiom [=style] and vocabulary of its own.[36]

---

[36] Moule, 3-4.

5. **Individual NT Authors**

Generally speaking, the range of literary levels of the NT authors can be displayed as follows:[37]

Semitic/Vulgar	Conversational	Literary Koine
Revelation Mark John, 1-3 John 2 Peter	most of Paul Matthew	Hebrews Luke-Acts James Pastorals 1 Peter Jude

Table 1
Literary Levels of NT Authors

N.B. In the above table, the books are listed in descending order of purity. Thus, Hebrews is more literary than 1 Peter, Revelation is more Semitic than Mark, etc.[38]

---

[37] For detailed discussion, see Metzger, 46-52 and standard critical commentaries.

[38] One deficiency in this table is that one cannot tell whether Matthew is closer to vulgar or literary Koine; another is that we are mixing style, syntax, and vocabulary (although this illustration is primarily of the syntax of various books) and then treating them all on a linear level.

The Cases:
An Introduction

In determining the relation of words to each other, case plays a large role. Although there are only five distinct case forms (nominative, vocative, genitive, dative, accusative), they have scores of functions. Further, of the almost 140,000 words[1] in the Greek NT, about three-fifths are forms that have cases[2] (including nouns, adjectives, participles, pronouns, and the article). Such a massive quantity, coupled with the rich variety of uses that each case can have, warrants a careful investigation of the Greek cases.[3] The breakdown can be visualized in the chart below.

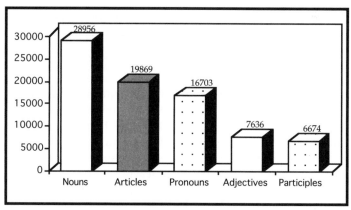

Chart 2
Frequency of Case-Forms in the New Testament (According to Word Class)

---

[1] The Nestle-Aland[27]/UBS[4] has 138,162.

[2] Included in the list are indeclinable nouns (such as Semitic names), even though technically they do not have case endings. The specific number, according to the current version of *acCordance*, is 79,838 (out of 138,162 words).

[3] Pragmatically, the study of the cases is restricted to substantives—i.e., words that function as nouns. Although participles, adjectives, and even the article can stand in the place of a noun, the most common substantives are nouns and pronouns. Altogether, close to 50,000 words in the NT are substantival.

Case Systems:
The Five- Vs. Eight-Case Debate

Introduction: The Significance of the Issue

The question of how many cases there are in Greek may seem as relevant as how many angels can dance on the head of a pin. However, the question of case does have *some* significance.

First of all, grammarians are not united on this issue (although most today hold to the five-case system). This by itself is not necessarily significant. But the fact that grammars and commentaries assume two different views of case could be confusing if this issue were not brought to a conscious level.[4] (See table 2 below for a comparison of the case names in the two systems.)

Second, the basic difference between the two systems is a question of *definition*. The eight-case system defines case in terms of *function*, while the five-case system defines case in terms of *form*.

Third, such a difference in definition can affect, to some degree, one's hermeneutics. In both systems, with reference to a given noun in a given passage of scripture, only one case will be seen. In the eight-case system, since case is defined as much by function as by form, seeing only *one case* for a noun usually means seeing only one function. But in the five-case system, since case is defined more by form than by function, the case of a particular word *may*, on occasion, have more than one function. (A good example of the hermeneutical difference between these two can be seen in Mark 1:8—ἐγὼ ἐβάπτισα ὑμᾶς **ὕδατι,** αὐτὸς δὲ βαπτίσει ὑμᾶς ἐν πνεύματι ἁγίῳ ["I baptized you in water, but he will baptize you in the Holy Spirit"].[5] Following the eight-case system, one must see ὕδατι as either instrumental or locative, but not both. In the five-case system, it is possible to see ὕδατι as *both* the means and the sphere in which John carried out his baptism. [Thus, his baptism would have been done both by means of water and in the sphere of water.] The same principle applies to Christ's baptism ἐν πνεύματι, which addresses some of the theological issues in 1 Cor 12:13).[6]

In summary, the real *significance*[7] in this issue over case systems is a hermeneutical one. In the eight-case system there is a tendency for precision of function

---

[4] On the side of the eight-case system are the grammars by Robertson, Dana-Mantey, Summers, Brooks-Winbery, Vaughan-Gideon, and a few others. Almost all the rest (whether grammars of the NT or of classical Greek) embrace the five-case system. Interestingly, the common thread that runs through the eight-case supporters is that they are typically Southern Baptists (A. T. Robertson's influence is most likely the major reason for the popularity of the eight-case system in that denomination).

[5] Although most MSS have ἐν before ὕδατι (e.g., A [D] E F G L P W Σ *f*[1, 13] 28 565 579 700 1241 1424 *Byz*), this seems to be a later addition. Our point is not affected either way.

[6] We will discuss this text in the chapter on prepositions.

while in the five-case system there is more room to see an author using a particular form to convey a fuller meaning than that of one function.

I. *The Eight-Case System*

A. Support

Two arguments are used in support of the eight-case system—one historical, the other linguistic. First, through comparative philology (i.e.,
the comparing of linguistic phenomena in one language with those of
another), since Sanskrit is an older sister to Greek and since Sanskrit has
eight cases, Greek must also have eight cases. Second, "this conclusion
is also based upon the very obvious fact that case is a matter of function
rather than form."[8]

B. Critique

First, the historical argument is *diachronic* in nature rather than synchronic. That is to say, it is an appeal to an earlier usage (in this case, to
another language!), which may have little or no relevance to the present
situation. But how a people understood their own language is determined much more by current usage than by history.[9] Further, the appeal
to such older languages as Sanskrit is on the basis of *forms*, while the
application to Greek is in terms of function.[10] A better parallel would be
that both in Sanskrit and in Greek, case is a matter of form rather than
function. We have few, if any, proto-Greek or early Greek remains that
would suggest more than five forms.[11]

---

[7] That is not to say that the issue is solved by hermeneutics, although this certainly
has a place in the decision. Current biblical research recognizes that a given author may,
at times, be *intentionally* ambiguous. The instances of double entendre, *sensus plenior* (conservatively defined), puns, and word-plays in the NT all contribute to this fact. A full
treatment of this is still to be done. But cf. Saeed Hamidkhani's doctoral thesis, "Revelation and Concealment: The Nature and Function of Ambiguity in the Fourth Gospel"
(Cambridge University, 1996).

[8] Dana-Mantey, 65.

[9] Giving priority to synchronics over diachronics is one of the great achievements of
modern linguistics (cf. F. de Saussure, *Cours de linguistique générale* [Paris: Payot, 1916]).
The work has been translated into English as *Course in General Linguistics* (New York:
Philosophical Library, 1959). The discussion of synchronics is on 101-90.

[10] Cf. W. D. Whitney, *A Sanskrit Grammar, Including Both the Classical Language, and the
Older Dialects, of Veda and Brahmana*, 3d ed. (Leipzig: Breitkopf & Härtel, 1896) 89 (§266),
103-5 (§307) on the eight case forms of Sanskrit.

[11] In his section on "The Greekness of Greek," Palmer notes that, even from the earliest inscriptional evidence, one of the distinguishing features of Greek was its five case
forms: "In the morphology of the noun the most striking innovation of Greek was the
reduction of the eight cases of IE [Indo-European] to five . . ." (L. R. Palmer, *The Greek Language* [London: Faber & Faber, 1980] 5).

Second, the "very obvious fact" that case is a matter of function rather than form is not as obvious to others as it is to eight-case proponents. And it is not carried out far enough. If case is truly a matter of function only, then there should be over *one hundred* cases in Greek. The genitive alone has *dozens* of functions.[12]

C. Pedagogical Value

The one positive thing for the eight-case system is that with eight cases one can see somewhat clearly a *root idea* for each case[13] (although there are many exceptions to this), while in the five-case system this is more difficult to detect. The eight-case system is especially helpful in remembering the distinction between genitive, dative, and accusative of time.

II. *Definition of Case Under the Five-Case System*

Case is the inflectional variation in a noun[14] that encompasses various syntactical functions or relationships to other words.

Or, put more simply, case is a matter of *form* rather than *function*. Each case has one form but many functions.

Five-Case System	Eight-Case System
Nominative	Nominative
Genitive	Genitive Ablative
Dative	Dative Locative Instrumental
Accusative	Accusative
Vocative	Vocative

Table 2
Five-Case System Vs. Eight-Case System

---

[12] We might add that to begin with semantic categories is to put the cart before the horse. Syntax must first of all be based on an examination and interpretation of the structures. To start with semantics skews the data. (See "Introduction: Approach of This Book" for discussion.)

[13] Indeed, much of our organization of the case uses will be built on this root idea. Thus, e.g., the genitive will have a broad section called "Adjectival Uses" and one called "Ablatival Uses."

[14] Technically, of course, case is not restricted to nouns. Pragmatically, however, the discussion of cases focuses on nouns and other substantives because adjectives and other modifiers "piggy back" on the case of the substantive and do not bear an independent meaning.

On the assumption that the five-case system is legitimate, we can now determine how many of the various cases there are in the NT on the basis of formal features alone. According to the five-case system, the breakdown is as follows:

Nominatives:[15]	24,618
Genitives:[16]	19,633
Datives:[17]	12,173
Accusatives:[18]	23,105
Vocatives:[19]	317
Total:	**79,846**[20]

---

[15] Nominatives: 7794 nouns, 3145 pronouns, 6009 articles, 4621 participles, 3049 adjectives.

[16] Genitives: 7681 nouns, 4986 pronouns, 5028 articles, 743 participles, 1195 adjectives.

[17] Datives: 4375 nouns, 3565 pronouns, 2944 articles, 353 participles, 936 adjectives.

[18] Accusatives: 8815 nouns, 5009 pronouns, 5889 articles, 957 participles, 2435 adjectives.

[19] Vocatives: 292 nouns, 0 pronouns, 0 articles, 1 participle, 24 adjectives. Although these data were based initially on the current release of *acCordance,* this software database was flawed in its treatment of the vocative, for all nominatives *used* as vocatives were declined as vocatives. In addition, since there is no distinction in form between a plural nominative and a plural vocative, a syntactical decision needed to be made (which is, of course, wholly arbitrary). All plurals in such cases were considered to be vocatives by *acCordance*, nominatives by us. (As well, we considered all indeclinable nouns to be nominatives for vocatives.)

[20] A discrepancy of 8 cases exists between the two *acCordance* searches done in this chapter: 79,838 vs. 79,846. As we pointed out earlier, *acCordance* is not a perfect tool, but its accuracy is still extremely high (in this instance, 99.99%).

The Nominative Case

Overview of Nominative Uses

Select Bibliography

Abel, *Grammaire*, 165-67; *BDF*, 79-82 (§143-45, 147); **Brooks-Winbery**, 4-7, 59; **Dana-Mantey**, 68-71 (§83); **Goetchius**, *Language*, 45-46; **Funk**, *Intermediate Greek*, 395-404 (§530-37), 709-10 (§885-86); **Hoffmann-von Siebenthal**, *Grammatik*, 214-16; **L. C. McGaughy**, *Toward a Descriptive Analysis of Εἶναι as a Linking Verb in New Testament Greek* (Missoula, Mont.: Society of Biblical Literature, 1972); **Matthews**, *Syntax*, 96-120; **Moule**, *Idiom Book*, 30-31; **Moulton**, *Prolegomena*, 69-71; **Porter**, *Idioms*, 83-87; **Radermacher**, *Grammatik*, 118-19; **Robertson**, *Grammar*, 456-61; **Smyth**, *Greek Grammar*, 256-57 (§906-18); **Turner**, *Syntax*, 34, 230-31; **Young**, *Intermediate Greek*, 9-15; **Zerwick**, *Biblical Greek*, 9-11 (§25-34).

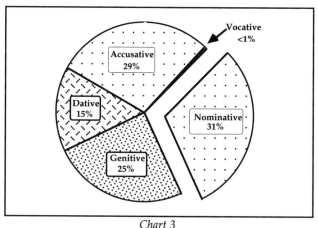

Chart 3
Frequency of Cases in the New Testament

Introduction: Unaffected Features

The nominative is the case of specific designation. The Greeks referred to it as the "naming case" for it often names the main topic of the sentence. The main topic in a sentence *semantically* is, of course, very similar to the *syntactical* subject, but the two are not always identical.[1] Hence, the most common use of the nominative case is as subject.[2] The nominative[3] occurs more than any other case form in the NT, though the accusative and genitive are not far behind.[4]

---

[1] Technically, the topic in a sentence is broader than a single word. However, even in English usage we use the term "subject" to refer both to the topic and grammatical subject. E.g., in the sentence "The boy hit the ball," the grammatical subject is "boy," but the topic (or semantic/logical subject) has to do both with an actor (a boy) *and* an action (hitting the ball).

[2] Gildersleeve adds an interesting note as to why the neuter has no distinct forms between nom. and acc.: "The nominative implies person or personification . . . . That is the reason why the neuter has no nominative [form] and the free personification of abstract nouns would be foreign to a simple, practical prose style, would be native to poetry, to philosophy" (B. L. Gildersleeve, "I. — Problems in Greek Syntax," *AJP* 23 [1902] 17-18). That is to say, the subject of a sentence is frequently if not normally the agent and hence usually personal (since things do not normally perform volitional acts). There are many exceptions, of course, but Gildersleeve's point is related to the historical roots of the language rather than its usage.

[3] The breakdown is as follows. Of the 24,618 nominatives in the NT, 32% are nouns (7794), 24% are articles (6009), 19% are participles (4621), 13% are pronouns (3145), and 12% are adjectives (3049).

[4] The term "unaffected" will be used throughout this book to refer to the characteristics or features of a particular morphological tag (such as nom. case, present tense, indicative mood, etc.) which can be seen only as an ideal composite. In other words, the unaffected features are those that, say, the present tense has when there are no intrusions on this basic meaning (such as context, lexical meaning of the verb, or other grammatical features like indicative mood, etc.). For a detailed discussion of unaffected features and specific uses, see "The Approach of This Book."

Specific Uses

Primary Uses of the Nominative

➡ I. Subject

    A. **Definition**

        The substantive[5] in the nominative case is frequently the subject of a finite verb.[6] The verb may be explicitly stated or implied.[7] Conversely, the subject may be implied, "embedded" as it were, in the verb (e.g., ἔρχεται means "*he* comes"). This usage is the most common of the nominative case uses.

    B. **Amplification**

        1. **Relation to Verb Voice**

            The relation of the subject to the action or state of the verb is largely determined by the voice of the verb. If the voice is *active*, the subject does the acting (e.g., ἦλθεν ὁ Ἰησοῦς εἰς τὴν Ἰουδαίαν γῆν ["Jesus came into the Judean region"] in John 3:22); if *passive*, the subject is acted upon (e.g., ὁ νόμος ἐδόθη ["the law was given"] in John 1:17); if *middle*, the subject acts on itself or in its own behalf, or the stress is placed on the subject (e.g., ὁ θεὸς ἐξελέξατο ["God chose (for himself)"] in Eph 1:3-4).

            Of course, there are exceptions to this: e.g., the deponent middle and passive have active meanings, and the equative verb does not imply action, but a state.

---

    [5] "Substantive" is any word functioning as a noun. As we pointed out in the introduction to the cases, nouns will fill this role more than other words. But pronouns, adjectives, participles, and even other parts of speech can function like a noun. For sake of completeness, the following forms should be noted as being capable of filling the *subject* slot: (1) noun; (2) pronoun; (3) participle (esp. articular); (4) adjective (also usually articular); (5) numeral; (6) article with: (a) μέν or δέ, (b) prepositional phrase, (c) a gen. phrase, (d) adverb, or (e) virtually any other part of speech, even a finite verb (see discussion in chapter on the article); (7) an infinitive, whether anarthrous or articular; (8) preposition + numeral; (9) an entire clause that gives no morphological indication that it is the subject (such as a ἵνα or ὅτι clause). Cf. Smyth, *Greek Grammar*, 256 (§908); Young, *Intermediate Greek*, 11.

    [6] By *finite* verb we mean any verb which when parsed includes *person*. Thus indicative, subjunctive, optative, and imperative verbs will take a nom. subject, while infinitives and participles technically take no subject.

    [7] The most frequent implied verb is the equative verb, usually εἰμί, and usually in the third person. Other verbs can also be implied, though almost always only if the preceding context has such a verb.

2. Relation to Verb Type

In addition to analyzing verbs by their voice, it is profitable to analyze them as to whether they are transitive, intransitive, or equative. Briefly, *transitive* verbs take a direct object and can typically be transformed into a passive construction ("the boy hit the ball" can become "the ball was hit by the boy"). *Intransitive* verbs do not take a direct object and cannot be transformed into a passive ("she came to the church" *cannot* be changed to "the church was come to by her"). *Equative* verbs are somewhat in between: they function like transitive verbs in that there are typically two substantives joined by a verb. But they also function like intransitives in that they cannot be transformed. They are unlike either in that the second substantive will be in the same case as the first substantive ("John was a man").

Although our analysis at this point is minimal, it is important to keep these verb types in mind as you think about syntax in general. For example, it becomes self-evident that subjects will be far more common than predicate nominatives simply because a predicate nominative can occur only with an *equative* verb, while a subject can occur with all three types of verbs.[8]

3. Types of Subjects Semantically

Subjects can be analyzed morpho-syntactically (i.e., by formal features such as number and gender), in relation to the form of the verb voice, or lexico-semantically. On a lexico-semantic level, not all subjects of active verbs function in the same way. For example, statements such as "I heard the speech," "I received the gift," or "I have a dog" do not necessarily imply an active role on the part of the subject, even though the verb is active (and transitive).[9] Thus one cannot say that the subject of an active verb is necessarily the *doer* of the action. There is much profit in analyzing subjects in relation to the kinds of lexical nuances seen in the verbs. This topic will be taken up in our chapter, "The Tenses: An Introduction."[10]

4. Missing Elements

The verb (especially the equative verb) may be absent from the clause, though implied (e.g., ἐγὼ φωνή ["I am a voice"] in John 1:23). Also, the subject may be absent, though implied in the verb (e.g., προσέφερον αὐτῷ παιδία ["they were bringing children to him"] in Mark 10:13).

---

[8] In our analysis of the oblique cases (i.e., gen., dat., acc.) we will note these verb types as well. For example, subjective genitives will be more common than objective genitives because they can occur with verbal nouns whose implied verbal idea is transitive or intransitive, while objective genitives can occur only with implied transitive verbal ideas.

[9] Matthews, *Syntax*, 99.

[10] For a helpful discussion, see especially Fanning, *Verbal Aspect*, 126–96; cf. also Givón, *Syntax*, 139–45 (§5.3).

C. Illustrations

John 3:16   ἠγάπησεν ὁ θεός τὸν κόσμον
God loved the world

Heb 11:8   πίστει ᾿Αβραάμ ὑπήκουσεν
by faith **Abraham** obeyed

Rom 6:4   ἠγέρθη **Χριστὸς** ἐκ νεκρῶν
Christ was raised from the dead

Acts 1:7   ὁ **πατὴρ** ἔθετο ἐν τῇ ἰδίᾳ ἐξουσίᾳ
the **Father** established by his own authority

Eph 5:23   ὁ **Χριστὸς** κεφαλὴ τῆς ἐκκλησίας
Christ [is] the head of the church

➡ II. *Predicate Nominative*

A. Definition

The predicate nominative (PN) is *approximately* the same as the subject (S) and is joined to it by an equative verb, whether stated or implied. The usage is very common. The equation of S and PN does not necessarily or even normally imply complete correspondence (e.g., as in the interchangeability of A=B, B=A in a mathematical formula). Rather, the PN normally describes a larger category (or *state*) to which the S belongs. It is important to keep in mind, however, that there are two distinct types of S-PN constructions; these will be discussed below.

B. Amplification

1. The Kinds of Verbs Used

The verbs used for this "equation" are, most frequently, εἰμί, γίνομαι, and ὑπάρχω. In addition, the passives of some transitive verbs can also be used: e.g., καλέω (φίλος θεοῦ ἐκλήθη ["he was called the friend of God"] in Jas 2:23), εὑρίσκω (εὑρέθημεν καὶ αὐτοὶ ἁμαρτωλοί ["we ourselves were even found to be sinners"] Gal 2:17), etc.[11]

2. Translation of Subject-Predicate Nominative Clauses

English translation requires that the S be translated first.[12] Such is

---

[11] Occasionally even μένω can be used as an equative verb. When it does so, it does not bear its normal intransitive force (cf. Acts 27:41; 1 Cor 7:11; 2 Tim 2:13; Heb 7:3).

[12] This is true for virtually all sentences except interrogatives where the order is reversed (e.g., τίς ἐστιν ἡ μήτηρ μου ["who is my mother?"] in Matt 12:48; the subject is "my mother" and the predicate nom. is "who"). Interrogatives, by their nature, indicate the unknown component and hence cannot be the subject (see McGaughy, *Descriptive Analysis of Εἶναι,* 46, 68-72). (Another class of exceptions, though much rarer, is demonstrative pronouns followed by appositional or epexegetical statements, for the pronoun's contents are *revealed* in the following statement [cf., e.g., Jas 1:27].)

not the case in Greek. In John 1:1, for example, θεὸς ἦν ὁ λόγος should be translated "the Word was God" rather than "God was the Word." But since Greek word order is far more flexible than English, this creates a problem: How do we distinguish S from PN if word order is not a clear guide? The following section will offer a detailed solution.

3. The Semantics and Exegetical Significance of the Subject-Predicate Nominative Construction

a. Two Kinds of Semantic Relationships

The significance of the S-PN construction affects more than mere translation precisely because S and PN do not normally involve total interchangeability. The usual relationship between the two is that *the predicate nominative describes the class to which the subject belongs.*[13] This is known as a **subset proposition** (where S is a subset of PN). Thus the meaning of "the Word was flesh" is not the same as "flesh was the Word," because flesh is broader than "the Word." "The word of the cross is foolishness" (1 Cor 1:18) does not mean "foolishness is the word of the cross," for there are other kinds of foolishness. "God is love" is not the same as "love is God." It can thus be seen from these examples that *"is" does not necessarily mean "equals."*[14]

But there is another, less frequent semantic relationship between S and PN. Sometimes called a **convertible proposition**, this construction indicates an identical exchange. That is to say, both nouns have an identical referent. The mathematical formulas of A=B, B=A are applicable in such instances. A statement such as "Michael Jordan is the greatest basketball player in NBA history" means the same thing as "the greatest player in NBA history is Michael Jordan." There is complete interchange between the two.[15]

---

[13] In linguistic terms, the narrower category (subject) is the hyponym and the broader category (predicate nom.) is the superordinate. For example, football player is a hyponym of athlete; athlete is a superordinate of football player. In such relationships, mutual interchangeability will not take place.

[14] The assumption that the grammatical equative verb bears the same force as the mathematical equal sign is one of the fundamental flaws in the thinking of Jehovah's Witnesses regarding the deity of Christ. On John 1:1, cf. their booklet, *Should You Believe in the Trinity?* (New York: Watchtower Bible and Tract Society, 1989), where it is argued that since John 1:1b states that "the Word was *with* God," John 1:1c cannot mean "The Word was God": "Someone who is 'with' another person cannot be the same as that other person" (27). This argument seems to assume that all S-PN constructions are of the convertible proposition type.

[15] However, this does not mean that it is not important to distinguish which one is the subject: the first sentence answers the question, "Who is Michael Jordan?" while the second answers "Who is the greatest player in NBA history?" Cf. McGaughy, *Descriptive Analysis of Εἶναι*, 68-72.

These two kinds of relationships are graphically represented in the chart below.

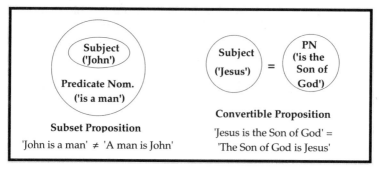

Chart 4

Semantic Relation of Subject and Predicate Nominative

Thus in examining S-PN clauses, two fundamental questions need to be answered: (1) How can we distinguish between S and PN since word order is not an infallible guide? and (2) what is the semantic relationship between the two: Is the S a particular within the larger class of the PN, or is it interchangeable with the PN?

b. How to Distinguish Subject from Predicate Nominative[16]

The general principle for distinguishing S from PN is that the S is the *known* entity.[17] This principle is valid for both kinds of S-PN constructions. In Greek equative clauses, the known entity

---

[16] The seminal work in this area was done by Goetchius, *Language*, 45-46. He articulates five distinguishing features of the S: (a) proper name, (b) articular noun, (c) if both are equally definite, the one with the narrower reference is S; (d) S is mentioned in immediately preceding context, and (e) pronoun. Goetchius' rules were examined and found wanting by McGaughy, *Descriptive Analysis of Εἶναι*, 29-33. McGaughy finds two general flaws in Goetchius' method (32): "(1) Goetchius has a mixture of categories: (a), (b), and (e) are grammatical (morphological and syntactical); (d) is contextual and (c) is meaning-based (semantic). (2) Goetchius has not ordered his rules." As well, he notes that "while Goetchius' analysis represents progress in the identification of subjects in S-II, the fact that he begins with a semantic principle [definite vs. indefinite] defeats his ultimate purpose" (33).

McGaughy follows the principle of structural linguistics (which is also largely adopted in this grammar) that proper grammatical analysis must begin with structure and end with semantics (ibid., 10-16). Otherwise hopeless confusion arises and built-in biases do not get properly challenged. The grammatical features of the language will be a surer guide than the lexical or semantic features that change from author to author and from time to time (and from interpreter to interpreter!). See our "Approach of This Book."

Finally, I wish to express my thanks to Steve Casselli and Gennadi Sergienko, whose work in the course Advanced Greek Grammar at Dallas Theological Seminary (1992 and 1993 respectively) helped to substantiate and clarify the argument of this section.

[17] McGaughy, *Descriptive Analysis of Εἶναι*, 68-72.

(S) will be distinguished from the PN in one of three ways (discussed below).[18]

The significance of the following three rules is that *when only one nominative substantive has such a grammatical "tag," the semantic relationship will be that of particular (subject) to class (predicate nominative).*[19] That is, the construction will be a subset proposition.

1) The subject will be a pronoun, whether stated or implied in the verb.[20]

Matt 3:17 **οὗτός** ἐστιν ὁ υἱός μου ὁ ἀγαπητός
this is my beloved Son

Luke 1:18 εἶπεν Ζαχαρίας πρὸς τὸν ἄγγελον, **ἐγὼ** εἰμι πρεσβύτης
Zachariah said to the angel, "**I** am an old man."

Acts 2:15 ἔστιν ὥρα τρίτη τῆς ἡμέρας
(**it**) is the third hour of the day

Cf. also Matt 27:54; John 9:8; Rom 5:14; Jude 12; Rev 13:18; 21:7.

2) The subject will be articular.

John 4:24 πνεῦμα **ὁ θεός**
God is spirit

Heb 1:10 ἔργα τῶν χειρῶν σού εἰσιν **οἱ οὐρανοί**
the heavens are the works of your hands

Mark 2:28 κύριός ἐστιν **ὁ υἱὸς** τοῦ ἀνθρώπου καὶ τοῦ σαββάτου.
The Son of man is Lord even of the Sabbath.

3) The subject will be a proper name.[21]

Luke 11:30 ἐγένετο **Ἰωνᾶς** τοῖς Νινευίταις σημεῖον[22]
Jonah became a sign to the Ninevites

1 Cor 3:5 τί οὖν ἐστιν **Ἀπολλῶς**;
What then is **Apollos**?
Interrogative pronouns are translated first even though the other nom.

---

[18] This is by and large McGaughy's approach, with some modification.

[19] The apparent exceptions to this have to do with instances in which a PN may be definite without being a pronoun, proper name, etc. See the chapter on the article for discussion.

[20] This is true except for the interrogative pronoun which is the PN.

[21] This does not always hold true when the other nom. is ὄνομα. The reason that ὄνομα is an exception is due to its lexical force: The very nature of the word connotes a known quantity. E.g., in Luke 1:63 (Ἰωάννης ἐστὶν ὄνομα αὐτοῦ) the text could be translated "his name is John" or "John is his name." But the fact that the child must have a name is the known quantity; what it is exactly is not yet known. Hence, the semantically correct translation is "His name is John." Cf. also Matt 13:55 (discussed below).

[22] B Λ *et pauci* insert ὁ before Ἰωνᾶς.

is the S. Following our general principle that the S is *known* this can easily be seen here. The semantic force of this sentence can be restated: "Apollos belongs to what larger category?"

Jas 5:17   Ἡλίας ἄνθρωπος ἦν
            Elijah was a man

c. The "Pecking" Order[23]

What if *both* S and PN have one of these three tags? Which is the S? And what is the semantic relationship? First, when both substantives bear such grammatical tags, the "pecking" order is as follows:

1) **The pronoun has greatest priority:** It will be the S regardless of what grammatical tag the other substantive has.[24]

Matt 11:14   καὶ εἰ θέλετε δέξασθαι, **αὐτός** ἐστιν Ἡλίας
             and if you will receive it, **he** is Elijah

Acts 9:20   **οὗτός** ἐστιν ὁ υἱὸς τοῦ θεοῦ
             he is the Son of God

1 John 5:9   ἡ μαρτυρία τοῦ θεοῦ μείζων ἐστίν, ὅτι **αὕτη** ἐστὶν ἡ μαρτυρία τοῦ θεοῦ
             the testimony of God is greater: **this** is the testimony of God

2) **Articular nouns and proper names seem to have equal priority.** In instances where one substantive is articular and the other is a proper name (or where both are articular), word order may be the determining factor.[25]

John 8:39   **ὁ πατὴρ** ἡμῶν Ἀβραάμ ἐστιν
             our **father** is Abraham[26]

John 15:1   **ὁ πατήρ** μου ὁ γεωργός ἐστιν
             my **Father** is the vinedresser

---

[23] We are not interacting here with Goetchius' rule that S will have been referred to in the immediately preceding context for two reasons. First, as McGaughy noted, it is context-based rather than morphologically-based. Second, pragmatically, there are few places in the NT in which one of the other rules cannot also be invoked. That is, the term in the preceding context is almost always specified with an anaphoric article or as a pronoun (both of which are better guides for distinguishing S from PN). The context rule is apparently valid when neither substantive in a given S-PN construction is a pronoun, articular, or a proper name (cf. Heb 11:1, where both substantives are anarthrous, but πίστις is the S being mentioned in 10:38-39 [similar is Eph 5:23]). But in such instances no ordering is necessary because the context rule is not in conflict with any other rule.

[24] Again, this is true except for interrogative pronouns. The reason that personal, demonstrative, and relative pronouns function differently than interrogative pronouns is this: the former are a substitute for something already revealed in the context (a known quantity), while the latter are anticipatory of a substantive not yet revealed (an unknown quantity). One refers back to an antecedent; the other looks forward to a postcedent.

Matt 13:55   οὐχ **ἡ μήτηρ** αὐτοῦ λέγεται Μαριὰμ καὶ **οἱ ἀδελφοὶ** αὐτοῦ Ἰάκωβος καὶ
Ἰωσὴφ καὶ Σίμων καὶ Ἰούδας;
Is not his **mother** named Mary and his **brothers** James and Joseph
and Simon and Judas?[27]

Cf. also Matt 6:22; 1 John 2:7.

d. The Semantic Relationship: Convertible Proposition

Second, the semantic relationship in such instances is that of a
convertible proposition. That is to say, when both substantives
meet one of the three qualifications for S, then they become
interchangeable. (See examples in the preceding section.)

e. Exegetically Significant Passages

There are scores of passages impacted by the semantics of the S-
PN construction. Just a few will be noted below.

1) Subset Propositions

1 John 4:8   **ὁ θεὸς** ἀγάπη ἐστίν
God is love

A subset proposition is clearly seen in this passage. God has the *quality*
of love, but is not identical with it. If this were a convertible proposition, it would affirm pantheism, or, in the least, panentheism.

John 1:1   ὁ λόγος ἦν πρὸς τὸν θεόν, καὶ θεὸς ἦν **ὁ λόγος**.
The Word was with God, and **the Word** was God.

Again, a subset proposition is envisioned here. The λόγος belongs to the
larger category known as θεός. The force of this construction is most

---

[25] McGaughy, *Descriptive Analysis of Εἶναι*, 51-52, argues that the arthrous noun will
be the subject. His exceptions, though, seem to disprove this. Indeed, it is possible to
argue just the opposite, viz., that the proper name will be the S. There are few passages
that fit this paradigm, so judgments must be somewhat tentative. But in most clear passages, the proper name is the S, regardless of word order (cf. the formulaic construction
in 1 John 2:22; 4:15; 5:1; 5:5). Cf. also John 8:39 (mentioned below).

The complexity of the problem can be illustrated in 1 Cor 11:3 [anarthrous Χριστός in
B* D* F G *et pauci*] (παντὸς ἀνδρὸς ἡ κεφαλὴ **Χριστός** ἐστιν ["**Christ** is the head of every
man" or "the head of every man is Christ"]). Although κεφαλή is normally treated as the
S in most translations, the parallel structure with the rest of the clause, where κεφαλή is
anarthrous each time, may indicate that κεφαλή is the PN: κεφαλὴ δὲ γυναικὸς ὁ ἀνήρ,
κεφαλὴ δὲ τοῦ Χριστοῦ ὁ θεός ("and the husband is the head of the wife, and God is the
head of Christ"). On the other hand, since κεφαλή is followed by a gen. in each instance,
and since it seems to be the known (the implied question being, "Who is the head of the
husband?" rather than "What is Christ in relation to the husband?"), κεφαλή could be
taken as the S. The paucity of data in the NT certainly makes for tentative conclusions
until more work in a broader range of Hellenistic Greek is done.

[26] It is possible that this should be translated "Abraham is our father" (so RSV; but cf.
McGaughy, *Descriptive Analysis of Εἶναι*, 50).

[27]Cf. note above on Luke 1:63 for a possible explanation.

likely to emphasize the *nature* of the Word, not his identity.[28] That is to say, the Word is true deity but he is not the same *person* as the θεός mentioned earlier in the verse.

Phil 2:13   θεὸς γάρ ἐστιν **ὁ ἐνεργῶν** ἐν ὑμῖν
for **the one working** in you is God

Although most English translations render θεός as S,[29] the substantival participle is the S since it is articular.[30] The reason θεός stands first in the sentence, then, is for emphasis. Further, there is a subtle difference between ὁ θεός and θεός: The anarthrous θεός seems to be viewed somewhat qualitatively. Paul is stressing God's power more than his person, for the issue raised by v 12 has to do with the *how* of sanctification, not the who.

2) Convertible Propositions

John 20:31   ταῦτα γέγραπται ἵνα πιστεύσητε ὅτι **Ἰησοῦς** ἐστιν ὁ χριστὸς
These things have been written that you might believe that **Jesus** is the Christ.[31]

D. A. Carson has an interesting hypothesis on John 20:31. His view is that the question John is answering is not "Who is Jesus?" (one that Christians would ask), but "Who is the Messiah?" (one that Jews would ask). Thus the text should be translated "that you might believe that the Messiah is Jesus." Hence, the Fourth Gospel was written essentially for a Jewish audience. One fundamental argument Carson uses is grammatical, viz., that an articular noun takes priority over a proper name.[32] He considers the NT to contain "firm syntactical evidence"[33] to this effect. But, as we have seen, the evidence is ambiguous and, if anything, moves in the opposite direction: Either the first noun is S or the proper name is S. Thus the grammatical leg of this argument is invalid. In addition, in 1 John, this same construction occurs four times (specifically, either Ἰησοῦς ἐστιν ὁ υἱός τοῦ θεοῦ [1 John 4:15; 5:5] or Ἰησοῦς ἐστιν ὁ Χριστός [1 John 2:22; 5:1]), yet the audience seems clearly to be of a Gentile nature (cf. 5:21). In short, there is no *grammatical* argument that John is written to Jews. Such a view must be based on other than grammar where, in fact, the case seems less well founded.[34]

---

[28] See later discussion in "The Article: Part II."

[29] It could in fact be argued that θεός, by its position and nature, almost begs to be the subject. This is probably why the majority of MSS, from the ninth century on, add ὁ before θεός (besides 𝔐, note D¹ L Ψ 075 0278 1739ᶜ *et alii*).

[30] θεός is not a proper name in Greek. One rule of thumb for detecting proper names in Greek is simply to ask the question, Can the noun in question be pluralized? Since θεοί is possible (cf. John 10:34), θεός is not a proper name. For a detailed discussion on the grammatical use of θεός in the NT, cf. B. Weiss, "Der Gebrauch des Artikels bei den Gottesnamen," *TSK* 84 (1911) 319-92, 503-38. Note also the recent theological use made of θεός as a common noun in N. T. Wright, *The New Testament and the People of God* (Minneapolis: Fortress, 1992) xiv-xv and *passim*.

[31] The variants found in D (Ἰησοῦς Χριστὸς υἱός ἐστιν τοῦ θεοῦ) and W (Ἰησοῦς ὁ χριστὸς ἐστιν ὁ υἱός τοῦ θεοῦ) are obvious corruptions.

[32] D. A. Carson, "The Purpose of the Fourth Gospel: John 20:31 Reconsidered," *JBL* 106 (1987) 639-51; cf. especially 642-44. Carson depends on E. V. N. Goetchius' critique of McGaughy's dissertation in *JBL* 95 (1976) 147-49 for his grammatical evidence.

[33] D. A. Carson, *The Gospel According to John* (Grand Rapids: Eerdmans, 1991) 90.

C. Substitution for Predicate Nominative (εἰς + accusative)

Εἰς + the accusative is occasionally found replacing the predicate nominative in the NT. Although this construction is found in the papyri,[35] it is usually due to a Semitic influence (Hebrew לְ). This idiom is frequent in OT quotations (as can be seen in the references below). That the construction is equivalent to the S-PN construction can be seen in Matt 19:5-6. In v 5 the entrance into the new state is mentioned with this construction (ἔσονται οἱ δύο εἰς σάρκα μίαν ["the two shall become one flesh"]), followed in the next verse by a declaration of the resultant state with a normal PN (ὥστε οὐκέτι εἰσὶν δύο ἀλλὰ σὰρξ μία).

This construction occurs with (1) **γίνομαι**; (2) **εἰμί**, typically in the future tense; and, less frequently, (3) **λογίζομαι**.[36]

1. With Γίνομαι[37]

Acts 4:11 ὁ λίθος . . . ὁ *γενόμενος* **εἰς κεφαλὴν** *γωνίας*
the stone . . . that *has become* **the chief** cornerstone
> Alluding to Ps 118:22, a text frequently applied to Christ in the NT.

Rom 11:9 *γενηθήτω* ἡ τράπεζα αὐτῶν **εἰς παγίδα** καὶ **εἰς θήραν**
Let their table *become* **a snare** and **a trap** (=Ps 68:23)

2. With Εἰμί[38]

Mark 10:8 ἔσονται οἱ δύο **εἰς σάρκα μίαν**
the two shall *become* **one flesh**

---

[34] Yet Carson's *main* argument is grammatical (*John*, 662): "Above all, it can be shown that, with very high probability, the *hina*-clause must on syntactical grounds be rendered 'that you may believe that the Christ, the Son of God, is Jesus.'" Significantly, in the object-complement construction, which is semantically parallel to the S-PN construction, either word order is the determining factor or the *proper name* takes priority over the arthrous noun. Cf., e.g., Acts 18:28: "[Paul] was refuting the Jews publicly, demonstrating that {Jesus was the Christ/the Christ was Jesus}" (τοῖς Ἰουδαίοις διακατηλέγχετο δημοσίᾳ ἐπιδεικνὺς . . . εἶναι τὸν Χριστὸν Ἰησοῦν). This is the kind of situation (an address to the Jews) that Carson envisions in John 20:31. But unlike John 20:31, Ἰησοῦς follows the arthrous noun. Goetchius (on whose arguments Carson bases his case) cites Acts 18:5, 28; 5:42 to prove that the arthrous noun takes priority. But in each instance, the arthrous noun stands first in order. (Overlooked by Goetchius is Acts 11:20, where the proper name, though in second place, takes priority.)

[35] See Moulton, *Prolegomena*, 71-72; BAGD, s.v. εἰς, 8.a.

[36] Cf. Zerwick, *Biblical Greek*, 10-11 (§32); BDF, 80 (§145); BAGD, s.v. εἰς, 8.a.

[37] Besides the texts listed above, note Matt 21:42=Mark 12:10=Luke 20:17 (Ps 118:22); Luke 13:19; John 16:20; Acts 5:36; 1 Pet 2:7 (Ps 118:22); Rev 8:11; 16:19.

[38] Besides the texts listed above, cf. Matt 19:5=Mark 10:8 (Gen 2:24); Luke 3:5 (Isa 40:4); John 17:23 (present subjunctive here); 2 Cor 6:18 (2 Sam 7:14); Eph 5:31 (Gen 2:24); Heb 8:10 (2 Kgs 6:16); 1 John 5:8. This last text is somewhat unusual (for εἰμί constructions) in two senses: the form of εἰμί is present indicative rather than future (or present subjunctive), and it does not allude to any OT text. The closest parallels to this construction are in John 17:23 (with εἰς + acc.) and John 10:30 (ἕν + εἰμί).

Heb 1:5   ἐγὼ ἔσομαι αὐτῷ **εἰς πατέρα**, καὶ αὐτὸς ἔσται μοι **εἰς υἱόν**
I shall *become* **a father** to him, and he *shall be* **a son** to me
> Quoting 2 Sam 7:14, a passage often cited in the NT as having Messianic significance.

3. With Λογίζομαι[39]

Acts 19:27   τὸ τῆς μεγάλης θεᾶς ᾿Αρτέμιδος ἱερὸν **εἰς οὐθὲν** *λογισθῆναι*
the temple of the great goddess Artemis *might be regarded* **as nothing**

Rom 4:3   ἐπίστευσεν ᾿Αβραὰμ τῷ θεῷ, καὶ *ἐλογίσθη* αὐτῷ **εἰς δικαιοσύνην**
Abraham believed God, and it *was reckoned* to him as righteousness

➡ III. Nominative in Simple Apposition

The nominative case (as well as the other cases) can be an appositive to another substantive in the *same* case. The usage is quite common. There are four features of simple apposition to be noted (the first two are structural clues; the last two features are semantic): *An appositional construction involves (1) two adjacent substantives (2) in the same case,*[40] *(3) which refer to the same person or thing, (4) and have the same syntactical relation to the rest of the clause.*

The first substantive can belong to *any* category (e.g., subject, predicate nom., etc.) and the second is merely a clarification, description, or identification of who or what is mentioned.[41] Thus, the appositive "piggy-backs" on the first nominative's use, as it were. For this reason simple apposition is not an *independent* syntactical category.

The appositive functions very much like a PN in a convertible proposition—that is, it refers to the same thing as the first noun.[42] The difference, however, is that a PN makes an *assertion* about the S (an equative verb is either stated or implied); with appositives there is assumption, not assertion (no verb is in mind). In the sentence "Paul is an apostle," *apostle* is a PN; in the sentence, "Paul the apostle is in prison," *apostle* is in apposition to *Paul*.

---

[39] Cf. also Rom 2:26; 4: 5, 22 (like Rom 4:3, quoting Gen 15:6); 9:8; Gal 3:6 (Gen 15:6); Jas 2:23 (Gen 15:6).

[40] The nom. occasionally is in apposition to an oblique case, but the semantics are the same. See discussion below.

[41] An appositive, strictly speaking, is *substantival*, not adjectival. Thus, adjectives or participles in second attributive position are not generally appositives, but usually have an adjectival force.

[42] The significance of this will be seen in our discussion of the gen. case, for the gen. can *also* involve a syntactical category, viz., the gen. of apposition. The semantics involved in such a category are quite different from those involved in simple apposition.

With proper names typically the first noun is anarthrous and the apposi-tional noun is articular.[43]

Matt 3:1   παραγίνεται Ἰωάννης **ὁ βαπτιστὴς** κηρύσσων
          John **the Baptist** came preaching

Mark 15:40   ἐν αἷς καὶ Μαρία **ἡ Μαγδαληνή** . . .
          among them also were Mary **the Magdalene** . . .

Luke 1:24   συνέλαβεν Ἐλισάβετ **ἡ γυνὴ** αὐτοῦ
          Elizabeth his **wife** conceived

Rev 1:5   ὁ μάρτυς ὁ πιστός, **ὁ πρωτότοκος** τῶν νεκρῶν
          the faithful witness, **the firstborn** from the dead

Grammatically Independent Uses of the Nominative

Some grammars include nominative absolute, independent nominative, paren-thetic nominative, *nominativus pendens* (pendent nom.), and nominative in pro-verbial expressions under this broad category without making any further refinement. However, not only should some distinction be made among these subgroups, but other uses of the nominative are also, technically, independent.

All independent nominatives follow this general rule: *The substantive in the nom-inative case is grammatically unrelated to the rest of the sentence.*

➡ **I. Nominative Absolute**

     A. Definition

         The nominative absolute and the *nominativus pendens* are the two inde-pendent nominatives that are especially lumped together in most treat-ments.[44] But there are distinctions in the semantic situations in which they occur.[45] *The nominative absolute is the use of the nominative case in introductory material (such as titles, headings, salutations, and addresses), which are not to be construed as sentences.*[46]

---

[43] Though structurally similar, semantically different is the phenomenon of two jux-taposed substantives in which the first functions adjectivally (e.g., ἄνδρες ἀδελφοί in Acts 1:16) and is usually left untranslated. This idiom occurs with ἀνήρ as in classical Greek (cf. *BDF*, 126 [§242]).

[44] This is due to the fact that nom. absolute is normally construed to mean any nom. used without grammatical connection. We are adopting a more specific usage for this title, since the semantic situations of the various independent nominatives are varied.

[45] In Attic Greek this nom. was used "in the citation of names, in enumerations, and in indefinite predications" (Gildersleeve, *Syntax of Classical Greek*, 1.2).

[46] Funk, *Intermediate Grammar*, 2.710 (§886.4).

B. Simplification

The easiest way to remember the difference between a pendent nominative and a nominative absolute is that a *nominative absolute does not occur in a sentence,* but only in titles, salutations, and other introductory phrases.

C. Exception

The only exception to this definition is that when a *participle* in the nominative case is grammatically unrelated to the rest of the sentence, it is traditionally *called* a nominative absolute participle (because it shares similarities with the gen. absolute participle). This area is where confusion between nominative absolute and *nominativus pendens* has arisen, for the nominative absolute participle belongs to the pendent nominative category, though it is called nominative absolute. Only when the *participle* is used, then, is there overlap between these two categories. (However, the nom. absolute participle will be dealt with under the *nominativus pendens* category because it shares *features* with that category, while it shares only its *designation* with the category of nom. absolute.)

D. Illustrations

1. Titles

Matt 1:1   **Βίβλος** γενέσεως Ἰησοῦ Χριστοῦ
              The book of the genealogy of Jesus Christ

Mark 1:1   **Ἀρχὴ** τοῦ εὐαγγελίου Ἰησοῦ Χριστοῦ
              The beginning of the gospel of Jesus Christ

Rev 1:1   **Ἀποκάλυψις** Ἰησοῦ Χριστοῦ
              The revelation of Jesus Christ

2. Addresses[47]

Rom 1:1   **Παῦλος** δοῦλος Χριστοῦ Ἰησοῦ
              Paul, a bond-servant of Christ Jesus

1 Cor 1:1   **Παῦλος** . . . καὶ **Σωσθένης**
              Paul . . . and **Sosthenes**

---

[47] Some grammarians regard such introductory formulae to have an implied verb such as γράφει (thus, "Paul *writes* . . ."). But, as Young points out, "inserting a verb, such as 'writes' or 'sends' is just as unnecessary as inserting a verb on the mailing label of a package" (*Intermediate Greek,* 14).

3. Salutations

Rom 1:7 **χάρις** ὑμῖν καὶ **εἰρήνη** ἀπὸ θεοῦ πατρὸς ἡμῶν καὶ κυρίου Ἰησοῦ Χριστοῦ
grace to you and **peace** from God our Father and the Lord Jesus
Christ

> Salutations need to be treated somewhat differently from addresses, for
> occasionally a verb does show up, in which cases the nom. is not abso-
> lute but functions as the S of a finite verb (cf. 1 Pet 1:2; 2 Pet 1:2; Jude 2;
> 2 John 3). The verb never appears in the *corpus Paulinum*, however. This
> may be significant, especially if the suggestion that Paul invented (or at
> least popularized) the "grace and peace" salutation is taken seriously,
> for what would be a "signature" item for him (and hence so under-
> stood by his churches) may have needed expansion via an explicit verb
> in other writers.

Cf. also 1 Cor 1:3; 2 Cor 1:2; Gal 1:3; Eph 1:2; Phil 1:2; Col 1:2; 1 Thess 1:1; 2 Thess 1:2; 1
Tim 1:2; 2 Tim 1:2; Titus 1:4; Phlm 3.[48]

➡ II. Nominativus Pendens *(Pendent Nominative)*

A. Definition

The pendent nominative is similar to the nominative absolute in that it
is grammatically independent. However, while the nominative absolute
is not used in a sentence, the pendent nominative is. This nominative
substantive is *the logical rather than syntactical subject* at the beginning of
a sentence, followed by a sentence in which this subject is now replaced
by a pronoun in the case required by the syntax.[49]

B. Clarification

The "subject" (logical, not grammatical) may be a noun or a participle,[50]
which is grammatically unrelated to the rest of the sentence. The pronoun (in a different case) is used later on simply because it would be too
redundant to name the noun again. The pendent nominative illustrates

---

[48] All the letters in the Pauline corpus have χάρις and εἰρήνη, but the Pastorals
exchange a singular personal noun in the dat. for ὑμῖν and 1-2 Timothy add ἔλεος to the
formula. Nevertheless, even these epistles do not have a verb in the salutation, whereas
all similar salutations in the Catholic epistles do.

[49] Zerwick, *Biblical Greek*, 9 (§25), gives an excellent definition, though he does not
distinguish *nominativus pendens* from nom. absolute.

[50] When the participle is the pendent nom., it is traditionally called a nom. absolute
participle (see discussion above, under "nominative absolute").

the genius of the nominative case: It is used to focus on the main *topic* of the sentence, whether or not it is the grammatical subject.[51]

The pendent nominative carries one of two semantic forces: *emotion* or *emphasis*. The second usage, which is far more common, could be labeled *nominative of reference*. (In fact, a helpful key to testing whether a certain nom. is pendent is the question, Can I translate the nom. at the beginning of the clause, "With reference to . . ."?)

C. Illustrations

1. Emphasis

Rev 3:12   ὁ **νικῶν** ποιήσω *αὐτὸν* στῦλον[52]

         the one who overcomes: I will make *him* a pillar

> This is a nom. absolute participle followed by a pronoun in the acc. case as required by the syntax of the sentence. This could be read, "With reference to the one who overcomes, I will make him . . ."

John 1:12   **ὅσοι** δὲ ἔλαβον αὐτόν, ἔδωκεν *αὐτοῖς* ἐξουσίαν

         but **as many as** received him, *to them* he gave authority

Acts 7:40   ὁ γὰρ **Μωϋσῆς οὗτος** . . . οὐκ οἴδαμεν τί ἐγένετο *αὐτῷ*

         for **this Moses** . . . we do not know what has happened *to him*

Cf. also Luke 21:6; John 7:38; Rev 2:26; 3:21.

2. Emotion

The following two examples are doubtful. In both, the pendent nominative may be suggesting emphasis rather than emotion (or possibly both). It should be kept in mind, however, that these sentences are placed in highly charged emotional settings.

Luke 12:10   **πᾶς ὃς** ἐρεῖ λόγον εἰς τὸν υἱὸν τοῦ ἀνθρώπου, ἀφεθήσεται *αὐτῷ*

         everyone who shall speak a word against the Son of Man, it shall be forgiven *him*[53]

> The topic of the sentence (those who speak against the Son of Man) is thrown forward, followed by a pronoun in the dative. This has much

---

[51] This construction constitutes a part of primitive speech. When a child learns to speak, frequently complete sentences will be uttered with one word and an index finger. "Toy!" is a pedocrypt for "That toy over there—that's what I want!" At a later stage of speech development, the *logical* subject is thrown to the front of the sentence, followed by a sentence in which this "subject" now takes its rightful syntactical place. E.g., "Ice cream! I want ice cream!" In these examples it is easy to see that *emotion* at the time of an utterance is what sometimes produces a pendent nom.

In more sophisticated speech, the pendent nom. may function more as a heading to a sentence in which its introduction at the proper syntactical location might be somewhat awkward to communicate. E.g., "John—didn't I see him at the game last night?" or, "The drug problem: I don't think it will go away."

[52] A few MSS have αὐτῷ for αὐτόν (ℵ* 241 1611 1854 2027 2351 *et pauci*).

greater emotional force than "It shall be forgiven everyone who shall speak a word against the Son of Man."

John 18:11   τὸ ποτήριον ὃ δέδωκέν μοι ὁ πατὴρ οὐ μὴ πίω αὐτό;
  The cup that my Father gave me to drink, shall I not drink *it*?

➡ III. Parenthetic Nominative

A. Definition

A parenthetic nominative is actually the subject in a clause inside a sentence that may or may not have a different subject.

B. Clarification

Although this is similar to the nominative absolute and the *nominativus pendens*, it is distinct from these two nominatives in the following ways: (1) Unlike the nominative absolute, the parenthetic nominative occurs in sentences; (2) unlike both the nominative absolute and pendent nominative, the parenthetic nominative is not usually found at the head of its construction (especially not at the head of a sentence); (3) unlike the pendent nominative, the parenthetic nominative is not used to indicate the author's emotion at the time of writing, nor is it primarily emphatic in nature. Its use is primarily *explanatory* and is frequently an editorial aside, especially in the Fourth Gospel.

C. Simplification

*A parenthetic nominative is the subject of an explanatory clause **within** another clause.* Although editions of the Greek NT are not consistent about putting such clauses in parentheses, if such a clause seems so unnatural in translation that mere commas do not seem to set it enough apart, then it is probably a parenthesis and its *subject* is a parenthetic nominative.

D. Amplification

Labeling an explanatory clause a parenthesis (and consequently, its subject as a parenthetic nom.[54]), is not a cut-and-dried matter. Robertson

---

[53] In *The Five Gospels: The Search for the Authentic Words of Jesus,* edd. R. W. Funk, R. W. Hoover, and the Jesus Seminar (New York: Macmillan, 1993), this text is not considered to go back to the historical Jesus in any sense (the words are printed in black, which means "Jesus did not say this; it represents the perspective or content of a later or different tradition" [p. 36]). Yet, the syntax is uncharacteristic of Luke, except when it is an ostensible statement from Jesus (cf., e.g., Luke 21:6). Perhaps syntax ought to have been one of the criteria of authenticity employed by the Jesus Seminar.

[54] It is possible, of course, to treat parenthesis exclusively in the section on clause, rather than isolate the nom. case here. But for pedagogical reasons we include the discussion here as well.

gives many examples in which the editors of different Greek New Testaments are far from unanimous.[55] In general, the parentheses found in the Gospels will be milder and are merely editorial asides, while those in the epistles border on anacoluthon, disrupting the flow of thought much more dramatically.[56]

E. Illustrations

John 1:6   ἐγένετο ἄνθρωπος ἀπεσταλμένος παρὰ θεοῦ, **ὄνομα** αὐτῷ Ἰωάννης.
There came a man sent from God (his **name** was John).

Matt 24:15   ὅταν οὖν ἴδητε τὸ βδέλυγμα τῆς ἐρημώσεως τὸ ῥηθὲν διὰ Δανιὴλ τοῦ προφήτου ἑστὸς ἐν τόπῳ ἁγίῳ, **ὁ ἀναγινώσκων** νοείτω, τότε
Whenever you see the abomination of desolation, spoken of by Daniel the prophet, standing in the holy place (let the **reader** understand), then ...

Gal 2:6   ἀπὸ δὲ τῶν δοκούντων εἶναί τι – ὁποῖοί ποτε ἦσαν οὐδέν μοι διαφέρει· πρόσωπον **ὁ θεὸς** ἀνθρώπου οὐ λαμβάνει – ἐμοὶ γὰρ οἱ δοκοῦντες οὐδὲν προσανέθεντο.
And from those who were supposed to be something (what they were makes no difference to me; **God** shows no partiality) for those who had a reputation added nothing to me.[57]

> There is a double parenthesis here: "God shows no partiality" is within a larger parenthesis with its subject embedded in the verb "they were" (ἦσαν).

Rev 2:9   οἶδα σου τὴν θλῖψιν καὶ τὴν πτωχείαν, ἀλλὰ πλούσιος **εἶ**
I know your trial and your poverty (yet **you** are [in reality] rich)

> Here the nom. is embedded in the verb.

Cf. also Mark 2:10 (nom. embedded in verb, as in Rev 2:9); John 1:15; 3:1; 4:1-3; Gal 2:5; Rev 3:9.

IV. Nominative in Proverbial Expressions[58]

A. Definition

A substantive in the nominative is used in proverbial expressions that have no *finite* verb.[59] Generally speaking, the syntax is either compressed and elliptical (as in "once a thief, always a thief") or else fragmentary and foreign to its new context (such as when an author quotes just a subordinate clause). The reason for the unusual syntax is that the

---

[55] Robertson, *Grammar*, 433-35.

[56] Ibid. Many grammarians (Robertson, Moulton, Williams, *et al.*) consider the nom. for time as a parenthetic nom.

[57] B C D F G K L 1739 1881 𝔐 *et alii* lack the article before θεός. Though a significant reading, the syntactical category is the same either way.

[58] See Brooks-Winbery, 7, for a seminal discussion.

proverbial saying, even if fragmentary, has become a fixed part of the literary heritage. Since it is well known in that particularly pithy form, to round out the syntax would be to spoil the effect.[60]

B. Illustrations

2 Pet 2:22   **κύων** ἐπιστρέψας ἐπὶ τὸ ἴδιον ἐξέραμα,
               καί **ὗς** λουσαμένη εἰς κυλισμὸν βορβόρου
               a dog returns to its own vomit,
               and **a sow** washes herself by wallowing in the mire[61]

> Both clauses need to be translated into English as though the participles were finite verbs (*contra* ASV). It is likely that the verbal forms are dependent participles because the lines were lifted from their original contexts.[62] The first line is from Prov 26:11 (though not quoted exactly as in the LXX, in both the NT and LXX it is in a subordinate clause); the source of the second is disputed.[63]

1 Cor 3:19   **ὁ δρασσόμενος** τοὺς σοφοὺς ἐν τῇ πανουργίᾳ αὐτῶν
               He catches the wise in their craftiness

> The substantival participle needs to be translated like a finite verb. It is not that there are any syntactical reasons for this, but since the quotation is fragmentary the syntax is elliptical. The original statement in Job 5:12 is an appositional participial clause, referring back to "God" in v 8 (vv 9-11 function similarly). Thus, "I make my appeal to God . . . who catches . . ."[64]

---

[59] This is not to say that proverbial expressions never have a finite verb, of course (cf. Luke 4:23; Acts 20:35; 1 Cor 15:33), just that those that do fall under the normal rules of syntax and do not need to be treated here.

The verbless proverb in Titus 1:12, perhaps from Epimenides (whose extant remains do not include it), is typically translated as a sentence "(Cretans *are* always liars, evil beasts, lazy gluttons")" but without access to the source, this is not certain. J. D. Quinn, *The Letter to Titus* (AB; New York: Doubleday, 1990) 107, translates it in the spirit of the Greek hexameter as:

> Liars ever, men of Crete,
> Nasty brutes that live to eat.

[60] There is no necessity, of course, in the substantive being nom. (cf., e.g., Matt 5:38).

[61] For other translation possibilities of this line, see BAGD, s.v. βόρβορος.

[62] In the least, due to genre considerations, it is difficult to argue that the participles are true independent participles.

[63] Heraclitus has often been mentioned, but this is doubtful. See R. J. Bauckham, *Jude, 2 Peter* (WBC; Waco: Word, 1983) 279-80.

[64] There are some notable differences between this form and the LXX: The latter employs an acc. case (in keeping with the syntax of v 8), a different verb, and no article.

➡ *V. Nominative for Vocative (Nominative of Address)*[65]

A. Definition

A substantive in the nominative is used in the place of the vocative case. It is used (as is the voc.) in direct address to designate the addressee.

B. Amplification: A Legitimate Category?

The reason the nominative came to be used for the vocative was due to formal overlap. There is no distinction in form in the plural or neuter singular, as well as in some forms of the masculine and feminine singular. "Hence the tendency to eliminate the distinction even where the vocative has a form of its own. . . ."[66]

Grammarians who hold to the eight-case system typically object to the category nominative for vocative, since their definition of case is functional rather than morphological.[67] Part of the reason for this objection, too, is that eight-case proponents tend to view language more diachronically than synchronically and more in terms of etymology than usage. But the nominative for vocative is a natural development of the nominative as the naming case, especially among peoples whose native tongue did not include a distinct vocative form.[68]

C. Structure and Semantics[69]

The nominative for vocative can be broken down into two structural categories: anarthrous and articular. The *anarthrous* use has two further structures: with ὦ and without ὦ. Each anarthrous use parallels the similar vocative construction (viz., with the particle ὦ, the address is much more emphatic or emotional; without it, less so).[70]

---

[65] Thanks are due J. Will Johnston, whose work on this area in the course Advanced Greek Grammar (Dallas Seminary, Spring 1993) helped to substantiate and clarify the argument of this section.

[66] Zerwick, 11 (§33). Cf. also *BDF*, 81 (§147).

[67] The *Gramcord/acCordance* data base also implicitly objects to it, labeling *every* nom. for voc. as a voc.

[68] Besides the question of form and legitimacy of this category, note the rather succinct and helpful discussion on semantic situation in *BDF*, 81 (§147).

[69] Gildersleeve, in commenting on this phenomenon in *classical* Greek, points out: "In the absence of a vocative form, the nominative is used as a vocative. When the vocative exists, the use of the nominative as a vocative has often a perceptible difference of tone. It is graver and more respectful, because it appeals to character, though sometimes metrical considerations come into play" (*Syntax of Classical Greek*, 1.4). NT Greek has a different force. First, with reference to the *articular* nom.: "There is a very marked increase in the use of the articular nominative in address. Nearly sixty examples of it are found in the NT. . . we may still recognize a survival [from classical Greek] of the *decisiveness* of the older use. *Descriptiveness*, however, is rather the note of the articular nom. of address in the NT. . . . The *anarthrous* nom. should probably be regarded as a mere substitute for the vocative . . ." (Moulton, *Prolegomena*, 70).

The *articular* use also involves two nuances: address to an inferior and simple substitute for a Semitic noun of address, regardless of whether the addressee is inferior or superior.[71] The key for determining which use is being followed has to do with whether the text in question can be attributed to a Semitic source (such as quotation from the LXX).

There is a further use that is technically not syntactical but merely functional: a nominative in apposition to a vocative.

D. Illustrations[72]

1. Anarthrous

a. Without ὦ[73]

John 17:25   **πατὴρ** δίκαιε,[74] καὶ ὁ κόσμος σε οὐκ ἔγνω
righteous **Father**, even the world has not known you
> The nom. for voc. is different from the subject of the main sentence ("the world"). Note that the adjective that modifies the nom. is voc.

Matt 16:17   μακάριος εἶ, **Σίμων** Βαριωνᾶ
blessed are you, **Simon** son of John

Rom 1:13   οὐ θέλω δὲ ὑμᾶς ἀγνοεῖν, **ἀδελφοί**
I do not want you to be ignorant, **brothers**

b. With ὦ

Mark 9:19   Ὦ **γενεὰ** ἄπιστος, ἕως πότε πρὸς ὑμᾶς ἔσομαι;
O unfaithful **generation**![75] How long will I be with you?
> Cf. parallels in Matt 17:17 and Luke 9:41.

---

[70] For a more detailed discussion of direct address with this particle, see the chapter on the vocative.

[71] In Hebrew typically the noun of address will have the article; cf. 2 Sam 14:4 (a superior can even be addressed in this way [GKC, 405 (§126f)]). In the LXX, God (*Elohim*) is customarily addressed with an articular nom. (θεέ occurs only seven times, five of which are in the Apocrypha). Porter has a different view of the nom. for voc., following Louw ("Linguistic Theory," 80), viz., the nom. is less direct, more formal and reserved than the voc. (Porter, *Idioms*, 87). Though probably true in Hellenistic Greek as a whole, the NT usage frequently has a more Semitic coloring. Jesus' tender "Child, rise" (Luke 8:54) is hardly formal, reserved, less direct.

[72] There are almost 600 instances of nom. for voc. in the NT—about twice as many as there are true vocatives. Only about 60 nominatives for vocatives are articular (Moulton, *Prolegomena*, 70).

[73] On the significance of the voc. with and without ὦ, see the chapter on the vocative case.

[74] πάτερ in UBS[3,4], with 𝔓[59vid] ℵ C D L W Θ Ψ 𝔐 *et al.* in support; πατήρ in Nestle-Aland[25] supported by A B N *pauci*.

[75] D W Θ 565 have the voc. adjective ἄπιστε.

Gal 3:1   ὦ ἀνόητοι **Γαλάται**, τίς ὑμᾶς ἐβάσκανεν;
O foolish **Galatians**! Who has bewitched you?

> The pathos of Paul is seen clearly in this text. He is deeply disturbed (or better, outraged) at the Galatians' immediate defection from the gospel.

Cf. also Matt 17:17=Mark 9:19=Luke 9:41; 24:25; Acts 13:10 (with adjective here); 18:14; 27:21; Rom 11:33 (βάθος could also be labeled a nom. of exclamation; see later discussion).[76]

2. Articular

Mark 5:8   ἔξελθε **τὸ πνεῦμα** τὸ ἀκάθαρτον ἐκ τοῦ ἀνθρώπου.
Come out of that man, [you] unclean **spirit**!

Luke 8:54 **ἡ παῖς**, ἔγειρε.
Child, rise.

> This address to an inferior could either be due to Luke's Greek (which could be styled literary Koine) or simply the Greek equivalent of a Semitic utterance (cf. the parallel in Mark 5:41).

John 19:3 χαῖρε, **ὁ Βασιλεὺς** τῶν Ἰουδαίων
Hail, **King** of the Jews![77]

> It is probable that the evangelist is representing the soldiers as using the articular nom. in what *BDF* consider to be the classical usage: "Attic used the nominative (with article) with simple substantives only in addressing inferiors. . ." (*BDF*, 81, [§147]). Thus, although they call him "King," the *form* in which they make this proclamation denies the address. Cf. Acts 26:7. Note also that in Mark 15:18 the voc. is used (a parallel passage, where most later MSS change the voc. to an articular nom). Moulton, who agrees textually with the voc., declares that it "is merely a note of the writer's imperfect sensibility to the more delicate shades of Greek idiom" (*Prolegomena*, 71).

Eph 5:22   **αἱ γυναῖκες** τοῖς ἰδίοις ἀνδράσιν
Wives, [be submissive] to your own husbands

> It would not be correct to argue that the articular nom. indicates an inferior in this instance, for it is also used in 5:25 when addressing the husbands.

John 20:28 Θωμᾶς εἶπεν αὐτῷ, **ὁ κύριός** μου καὶ **ὁ θεός** μου.
Thomas said to him, "My **Lord** and my **God**!"

> In all but two instances in the NT (both in the same verse, Matt 27:46), God is addressed with the nom., most likely due to Semitic influence.

3. In apposition to vocative (always articular)

Rev 15:3   μεγάλα καὶ θαυμαστὰ τὰ ἔργα σου, κύριε **ὁ θεὸς** ὁ παντοκράτωρ
Great and wonderful are your works, Lord **God Almighty**

---

[76] ὦ with nom. actually occurs more often than with the voc. in the NT: 9 instances (listed above) to 8 (Matt 15:28; Acts 1:1; Rom 2:1, 3; 9:20; 1 Tim 6:11, 20; Jas 2:20).

[77] Instead of the articular nom., the voc. βασιλεῦ is found in 𝔓[66] ℵ.

E. A Theologically Significant Passage

Heb 1:8   πρὸς δὲ τὸν υἱόν, ὁ θρόνος σου, **ὁ θεός**, εἰς τὸν αἰῶνα τοῦ αἰῶνος
But to the Son [he declares], "Your throne, **O God**, is forever and
ever"

> There are three syntactical possibilities for θεός here: as a subject ("God
> is your throne"),[78] predicate nom. ("your throne is God"),[79] and nom.
> for voc. (as in the translation above).[80] The S and PN translations can be
> lumped together[81] and set off against the nom. for voc. approach. It is
> our view that the nom. for voc. view is to be preferred for the following
> reasons: (1) It is an overstatement to argue that if a writer wanted to
> address God he could have used the vocative θεέ, because no where in
> the NT is this done except in Matt 27:46. The articular nom. for voc. is
> the almost universal choice. (2) This is especially the case in quoting
> from the LXX (as in Heb 1:8; cf. Heb 10:7), for the LXX is equally reticent
> to use the voc. form, most likely since Hebrew lacked such a form. (3)
> The accentuation in the Hebrew of Ps 45:7 suggests that there should be
> a pause between "throne" and "God" (indicating that tradition took
> "God" as direct address).[82] (4) This view takes seriously the μέν . . . δέ
> construction in vv 7-8, while the S-PN view does not adequately handle
> these conjunctions. Specifically, if we read v 8 as "your throne is God"[83]
> the δέ loses its adversative force, for such a statement could also be
> made of the angels, viz., that God reigns over them.[84]

VI. *Nominative of Exclamation*

A. Definition

The nominative substantive is used in an exclamation without any
grammatical connection to the rest of the sentence.

---

[78] So Westcott, Moffatt, RSV margin, NRSV margin, NEB margin.

[79] In his excellent study of Heb 1:8, Harris could only find Hort and Nairne among
the commentators to hold this view (M. J. Harris, *Jesus as God: The New Testament Use of
Theos in Reference to Jesus* [Grand Rapids: Baker, 1992] 212).

[80] The majority of translations, commentators, grammarians, *et al.* hold this view.

[81] As to which of these two options is better, we have already argued that with two
articular nouns, the first in order is the subject (see section on predicate nom.). Hence, ὁ
θρόνος σου would be the subject rather than ὁ θεός (*contra* most NT scholars who opt for
either of these views). Harris' argument that θεός as a PN should be anarthrous (ibid., 215)
is linguistically faulty, for it fails to recognize convertible proposition as a live option for
S-PN constructions.

[82] Harris argues cogently that in both the LXX and Hebrew of Ps 45:7 "God" is
directly addressed (ibid., 215).

[83] Turner's objection to this translation that it is a "grotesque interpretation" is curiously oblique; it seems almost as if he envisions Christ sitting on God by such a gloss
(*Insights*, 15)! But the biblical language is patently metaphorical.

[84] For other arguments, see Harris, *Jesus as God*, 212-18.

B. Clarification and Significance

This use of the nominative is actually a subcategory of the nominative for vocative. However, we will treat it separately and make this (somewhat) arbitrary distinction: Nominative of exclamation will not be used in direct address. It is a primitive use of the language where emotion overrides syntax: The emotional topic is exclaimed without any verb stated.[85]

Robertson points out that this is "a sort of interjectional nominative,"[86] something of an emotional outburst. The keys to identifying a nominative of exclamation are: (1) the lack of a verb (though one may be implied), (2) the obvious emotion of the author, and (3) the necessity of an exclamation point in translation. Sometimes ὦ is used with the nominative

C. Illustrations

Rom 7:24   ταλαίπωρος ἐγὼ **ἄνθρωπος**

[O] wretched **man** [that] I am!

Rom 11:33   ῝Ω **βάθος** πλούτου καὶ σοφίας καὶ γνώσεως θεοῦ

Oh the **depth** both of the riches and wisdom and knowledge of God![87]

Notice that in these examples the nominative of exclamation is *not used in a sentence*. Even in Rom 7:24 the implied "that" removes this from being a complete thought. It is a good rule of thumb that if the construction in which a supposed nom. of exclamation appears can be construed as a sentence, then the nom. should be simply considered as the subject. Thus, 1 Cor 15:57, which implies the optative of the copula, should probably not be considered as containing a nominative of exclamation.

Mark 3:34   ἴδε **ἡ μήτηρ** μου καὶ **οἱ ἀδελφοί** μου

Behold, my **mother** and my **brothers**!

> In NT usage, ἴδε and ἰδού are customarily followed by a nom.[88] These were originally verb forms (the active and middle aorist imperatives of ὁράω respectively) and should, according to classical usage, take an accusative. But in Koine Greek, and especially the NT, they normally function like mere interjections.

---

[85] Smyth, *Greek Grammar*, 607 (§2684).

[86] Robertson, *Grammar*, 461.

[87] Although some editions have ῎Ω instead of ῝Ω here, the Ω with the acute is used with a nom. while the Ω with the circumflex is usually found with the voc. (so BAGD).

[88] Though other constructions also follow (esp. whole clauses); the acc. follows as direct object of ἴδε or ἰδού twice (John 20:27; Rom 11:22), *contra* Porter, *Idioms*, 87. With nom. following: Mark 13:1 (though ἴδε is omitted in W); 16:6 (though D has εἴδετε . . . τὸν τόπον for ἴδε ὁ τόπος); John 1:29, 36; 19:14, 26, 27.

Nominatives in Place of Oblique Cases [89]

I. Nominative of Appellation [90]

A. Definition

A title appears in the nominative and functions as though it were a proper name. Another case would normally be more appropriate, but the nominative is used because of the special character of the individual described.

B. Clarification and Semantics

The key is that the nominative is *treated* as a proper name, which is expected to be in another case. It is as if a common noun is dignified when it is attached to a particular individual. Although ancient Greek did not have the convention of quotation marks, it could express essentially the same idea with a nominative of appellation. There are only a few examples of this use of the nominative in the NT.

This is a *par excellence* use of a given noun. The key to identification is one of two things: either capitalize the noun or put it in quotation marks.

C. Illustrations

John 13:13   ὑμεῖς φωνεῖτέ με **ὁ διδάσκαλος** καὶ **ὁ κύριος**
              you call me **Teacher** and **Lord**

Rev 9:11   ἐν τῇ Ἑλληνικῇ ὄνομα ἔχει **Ἀπολλύων**
            In Greek he has the name **Appollyon**

Cf. also Rev 2:13 for another example. In Luke 19:29 and 21:37 if the reading Ἐλαιών rather than Ἐλαιῶν is accepted [so BAGD], then we have two more instances of this use of the nom. In Rev 1:4 if we treat ὁ ὤν as a name, then this would be another instance (the unchangeable nature of God is accented in this verse).

---

[89] Such uses of the nominative are rare, occurring mostly in Revelation. The cause of such unusual grammar in the Apocalypse is highly debated. It may be due to Semitic influence, or could be in keeping with the vulgar Greek of the day. It is also possible that the author alludes to the LXX, retaining the same case-form (even though it now lacks concord in its new context), to signal his audience that he is quoting from the OT. In any event, *some* of the following syntactical categories should be regarded as somewhat unusual (in some cases, bizarre), even by Koine standards.

[90] The independent uses of the nom. can be laid out in concentric circles. There is much overlap among them. However, the one key element is that they pick up the ontological nuances of the nom.—viz., to render the topic of the sentence prominent whether or not it is the grammatical subject.

II. *Nominative in Apposition to Oblique Cases*

A. Definition

An appositional construction involves two adjacent substantives that refer to the same person or thing and have the same syntactical relation to the rest of the clause. The second substantive is said to be in apposition to the first. Normally, both substantives will be in the same case (whether it is nom., voc., gen., dat., or acc.).[91] The semantics of all but the genitive of apposition are the same—i.e., both substantives have an identical referent.[92]

A rarely seen phenomenon in the NT (but particularly in the Apocalypse) is a nominative in apposition to an oblique case.

B. Significance

The Seer of Revelation, seems, for the most part, either to have considered the substantive in the nominative case as an indeclinable title (2:13), a quotation (1:5; 17:5),[93] or simply as imitating the LXX usage (1:5; 17:4). It seems that he used this *to emphasize* the word in the nominative, for his audience would certainly take note of such a construction.

C. Illustrations

Rev 1:5   ἀπὸ Ἰησοῦ Χριστοῦ, **ὁ μάρτυς** ὁ πιστός
              from Jesus Christ, the faithful **witness** (or perhaps, "the witness, the faithful one")

> The quotation from Ps 89:38 preserves the case of the original (LXX); the Seer juxtaposes this nom. to the gen. so as to identify the faithful witness with Jesus Christ.

Rev 9:14   λέγοντα τῷ ἕκτῳ ἀγγέλῳ, **ὁ ἔχων** τὴν σάλπιγγα
              saying to the seventh angel, **the one who has** the trumpet

Cf. also Rev 3:12; 7:9; 14:12; 16:13.

III. *Nominative After a Preposition*

There is apparently only one example of this in the NT.[94]

Rev 1:4   ἀπὸ **ὁ ὢν**[95] καὶ **ὁ ἦν** καὶ **ὁ ἐρχόμενος**
              from "**he who is**" and "**the he was**" and "**he who is coming**"

---

[91] The only exceptions to this are nom. in apposition to voc., nom. in apposition to an oblique case (i.e., gen., dat., acc.), or the gen. of apposition.

[92] The gen. of apposition would approximate the subset proposition rather than the convertible proposition of S-PN constructions. See section under genitive.

[93] In this instance such a nom. also fits under the category of appellation.

[94] Unless the reading found in ℵ* B D* 131 1319 (εἰς . . . Βηθανία) in Luke 19:29 is accepted. (εἰς) Βηθφαγή also in Luke 19:29, is most likely an indeclinable noun (BAGD, 140), though a few late MSS have Βηθφαγήν (063 1 179 713) or a similar form (Γ Θ 22 118 205 209 230 472 *pauci*).

This is the first and worst grammatical solecism in Revelation, but many more are to follow. There are two broad options for how to deal with it: Either the author unintentionally erred or he intentionally violated standard syntax.[96] If unintentional, it could be due to a heavily Semitized Greek, or merely represent the level of linguistic skill that a minimally educated man might achieve (as in the vulgar papyri).[97] Either of these is doubtful here because (1) such a flagrant misunderstanding of the rudiments of Greek would almost surely mean that the author simply could not compose in Greek, yet the Apocalypse itself argues against this; (2) nowhere else does the Seer use a nom. immediately after a preposition (in fact, he uses ἀπό 32 times with a gen. immediately following).

If intentional, the question of what the author intends. Few scholars would disagree with Charles' assessment: "The Seer has deliberately violated the rules of grammar in order to preserve the divine name inviolate from the change which it would necessarily have undergone if declined. Hence the divine name is here in the nominative."[98] It would be like one American saying to another, "Do you believe in 'We the People'?" If the question had been, "Do you believe in us the people?" the allusion to the Preamble to the Constitution would have been lost.

The Seer is no doubt alluding to Exod 3:14 in the LXX (ἐγώ εἰμι ὁ ὤν – "I am who I am"), a text well familiar to early Gentile Christians. Although there are other views on the grammar of Revelation as a

---

[95] It is not surprising to find the majority of MSS inserting τοῦ θεοῦ before ὁ ὤν, in light of the nature and severity of this grammatical anomaly.

[96] Many linguistically-oriented works do not like either of these options. For example, Young (*Intermediate Greek*, 13) has argued that the grammar of Rev 1:4 "can only be a violation if grammar is viewed prescriptively. With a descriptive view of grammar, it merely illustrates the range of expression that Koine Greek tolerates." This seems to be a case of circular reasoning: Because this occurs in the language, it must be tolerable. We have argued in "The Approach of This Book" that the present-day thinking about prescriptive vs. descriptive grammar lacks sufficient nuancing.

[97] Many linguists nowadays prefer not to speak of "good grammar" and "bad grammar," because such language sounds prescriptive (so Young, *Intermediate Greek*, 13, commenting on Rev 1:4). Prescriptivism needs to be more carefully defined, however. To be sure, it is inappropriate to judge the Greek of the NT by Attic standards (a diachronic approach), just as it would be inappropriate to judge modern English by Elizabethan standards (or vice versa). But if a syntactical structure is highly unusual in a given place and time, the community may well judge it to be bad grammar. (See our "Approach of This Book" for discussion on prescription vs. description.)

This would most likely have been the case with Rev 1:4, at least initially. In the least, it is rather doubtful that any audience would accept the syntax here as merely illustrating "the range of expression that koine Greek tolerates" (Young, *Intermediate Greek*, 13). (It is as if Young is saying that there can be no mistakes in grammar—ever! I bet his high school English teacher did not take the same position!) Prescriptivism has to do with applying standards of one place and time to another, or applying universals where none exist (as is so often done in modern linguistic circles—cf. Ian Robinson, *A New Grammarians' Funeral* [CUP, 1975], esp. ch. 2). But it seems self-evident that all peoples of all cultures of all times have had certain standards of communication by which they judged whether communication took place.

[98] R. H. Charles, *A Critical and Exegetical Commentary on the Revelation of St. John* (ICC; Edinburgh: T. & T. Clark, 1920) 1.10.

whole,[99] it seems that 1:4 may function somewhat paradigmatically for many of the solecisms. The Seer had just instructed the readers to pay careful attention to his words (1:3)—something he ostensibly fails to do in the next verse! But, in reality, he is driving his audience back into the OT by preserving the very forms found in the LXX, even when they lack concord in the new context. (E.g., he continues to do this in 1:5, where a nom. is in apposition to a gen.: the nom. is a quotation from Ps 89). Without even once saying, "It is written," the author is thus able to signal the readers that he is using the OT.[100]

IV. Nominative for Time

A. Definition

Very rarely in the NT the nominative case is used rather than another case to indicate a measurement of time. The data are insufficient to tell which oblique case the nominative normally is substituting for (though most have argued that it is the rough equivalent of an acc. of time). Each instance needs to be determined by its own context.[101]

B. Illustration

Mark 8:2   ἤδη **ἡμέραι τρεῖς** προσμένουσίν μοι
already [for the extent of?] **three days** they have been with me

Cf. also Matt 15:32; Luke 9:28.

V. Nominative ad Nauseum

Also known as the *aporetic* nominative (from the Greek word ἀπορέω, "I am at a loss"), this is the category one should appeal to when another slot cannot be found. The title is descriptive not of the nominative but of the feeling one has in the pit of his/her stomach for having spent so much time on this case and coming up with nothing.

---

[99] Among the more notable treatments are the following: T. C. Laughlin, *The Solecisms of the Apocalypse* (Princeton: University Publishers, 1902 [originally a doctor's dissertation at Princeton Seminary]); Charles, *Revelation*, 1.cxvii-clix; D. R. Younce, "The Grammar of the Apocalypse" (unpublished doctoral dissertation, Dallas Theological Seminary, 1968); G. Mussies, *The Morphology of Koine Greek as Used in the Apocalypse of St. John* (Leiden: E. J. Brill, 1971); S. Thompson, *The Apocalypse and Semitic Syntax* (Cambridge: Cambridge University Press, 1985); S. E. Porter, "The Language of the Apocalypse in Recent Discussion," *NTS* 35 (1989) 582-603; D. D. Schmidt, "Semitisms and Septuagintalisms in the Book of Revelation," *NTS* 37 (1991) 592-603.

[100] This approach does not address all of the solecisms in the Apocalypse of course. Some of them are due to the apocalyptic genre or the emotional state at the time of composition. The issue of whether the syntax is Semitically-colored or is typical Koine, though an important one, does not seem to resolve some of the most fundamental problems (such as 1:4).

[101] That the scribes were uncomfortable with this usage is evident by the textual variants in each of these verses. But which oblique case they substituted for the nom. differed, even in parallel passages: Mark 8:2 (for the nom. ἡμέραι τρεῖς, ἡμέραις τρίσιν is found in B pc); but the parallel passage in Matt 15:32 has ἡμέρας in ℵ Θ Ω fam[13] et al.); in Luke 9:28, for the nom. ἡμέραι ὀκτώ, ἡμέρας ὀκτώ is found in 1313 and 1338.

The Vocative Case

Overview of Vocative Uses

Select Bibliography

Abel, *Grammaire*, 67; **K. Barnwell**, "Vocative Phrases," *Notes on Translation* 53 (1974) 9-17; *BDF*, 81 (§146); **Brooks-Winbery**, 59; **Dana-Mantey**, 71-72 (§84); **Funk**, *Intermediate Greek*, 710-11 (§886); **Hoffmann-von Siebenthal**, 215-16 (§148); **Moule**, *Idiom Book*, 31-32; **Moulton**, *Prolegomena*, 60, 71-72; **Porter**, *Idioms*, 87-88; **Robertson**, *Grammar*, 461-66; **Smyth**, *Greek Grammar*, 312-13 (§1283-88); **Turner**, *Syntax*, 34, 230-31; **Young**, *Intermediate Greek*, 15-16; **Zerwick**, *Biblical Greek*, 11-12 (§35).[1]

I. Definition

The vocative is the case used for addressing someone or, on occasion, for uttering exclamations. It technically has no syntactical relation to the main clause. In this respect it is much like the nominative absolute.

As in English, the connotations of direct address vary on the circumstances, ranging from delight to astonishment to anger.[2] Although the context plays a

---

[1] Thanks are due especially to Buist M. Fanning, Kevin Warstler, and J. Will Johnston for their input on this chapter.

major role in determining the force of the vocative, the absence or presence of ὦ is also significant (see below).

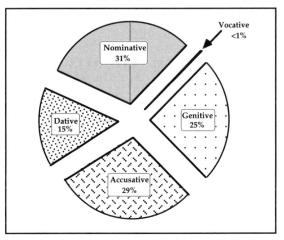

Chart 5
Frequency of Cases in the New Testament[3]

II. Is It a Legitimate Case?

Whether the vocative is a legitimate case is debated on two grounds: (1) *form*: it is not a completely distinct case-form. It does not occur at all in the plural, and not even in every gender-declension combination in the singular (e.g., the feminine first declension);[4] (2) *function*: the vocative is syntactically independent from the rest of the sentence. Hence, if we define case essentially as having to do with syntactical function on a sentence level, then the vocative would not qualify.

These two objections are not as strong as they appear. First, although not fully developed, the vocative can, at times, be distinguished formally. If the vocative is not a true case in some gender-declension combinations, then neither is the accusative for the neuter-second/third declension (since it is not distinct from the neuter nom.). The fact that there is *some* formal (and accentual[5]) difference is sufficient to regard it as a separate case, at least in the singular. Second, although on a *sentence* level the vocative is grammatically absolute, on a *discourse* level it

---

[2] See Smyth, *Greek Grammar*, 312 (§1284); Turner, *Syntax*, 33; Barnwell, "Vocative Phrases," 9-17.

[3] The breakdown of vocatives is as follows: 292 nouns, 0 pronouns, 0 articles, 1 participle (Acts 23:3), 24 adjectives.

[4] For a discussion of forms, see Mounce, *Basics of Biblical Greek*, 105 (§13.10); Moulton-Howard, *Accidence*, 54-55, 59, 118-20, 129, 134-37, 142; and W. D. Mounce, *The Morphology of Biblical Greek* (Grand Rapids: Zondervan, 1994) 167.

does bear semantic weight. That is, even though the vocative shows up within a sentence, it really is an audience indicator and thus is "supra-sentential," helping the reader understand who is being addressed as well as how.[6]

III. Uses of the Vocative Case

There are three basic uses of the vocative: direct address, exclamation, and apposition. The third category, as in all simple appositions, is not really a separate syntactical category (for the case merely "piggy-backs" on the substantive to which it is in apposition). The first category, direct address, is by far the most frequent use.

A. Direct Address

A substantive in the vocative is used in direct address to designate the addressee. Except for two texts in the NT, the addressee is always personal.[7] This category may be divided into two subgroups. The first category is used quite frequently; the second, only nine times.[8]

➡ ## 1. Simple Address

a. Definition

This is the use of the vocative *without* ὦ preceding it. For the most part, no special significance is to be attached to the use of the vocative in such

---

[5] The accent of the voc. in Greek is frequently thrown forward, toward the first syllable of the word (thus γυνή becomes γύναι, πατήρ becomes πάτερ, θυγάτηρ becomes θύγατερ, etc. Note, too, that the inflection also frequently becomes shortened). This was possibly due to pitch in oral language, as can be seen even in English (in the following sentences, the word "father" is pronounced slightly differently each time, with greater pitch placed on the first syllable in the direct address: "My father works at a bank"; "Father, may I borrow some money?").

[6] The nom. for voc. is encroaching on the voc. so much that there are twice as many of these as there are vocs. in the NT. (Since the voc. and nom. are identical in the plural, we are counting all such forms as nominatives. This must of course be the case in the several instances that are articular, for the voc. does not take an article.) See discussion of direct address in the previous chapter, under "Nominative for Vocative."

[7] In 1 Cor 15:55 θάνατε ("death") is twice addressed; in Rev 18:20 οὐρανέ ("heaven") is addressed.

[8] That is, ὦ with the voc. is used only nine times in the NT. Not all of these are emphatic (the usage in Acts is an exceptional case, following classical idiom for the most part). Not counted are ὦ with plurals (for the plurals are identical in form to nominatives).

instances. (In many instances, however, there will obviously be great emotion in the utterance. In such cases, the context will be determinative.)[9]

b. Illustrations

Matt 9:22   ὁ Ἰησοῦς . . . εἶπεν, Θάρσει, **θύγατερ**· ἡ πίστις σου σέσωκέν σε.[10]
Jesus said, "Take heart, **daughter**! Your faith has saved you."

Luke 4:23   πάντως ἐρεῖτέ μοι τὴν παραβολὴν ταύτην· **Ἰατρέ**, θεράπευσον σεαυτόν·
No doubt you will quote to me this proverb: "**Physician**, heal yourself."

1 Cor 7:16   τί γὰρ οἶδας, **γύναι**, εἰ τὸν ἄνδρα σώσεις;
How do you know, **woman**, whether you will save your husband?

Heb 1:10   Σὺ κατ᾽ ἀρχάς, **κύριε**, τὴν γῆν ἐθεμελίωσας
You, **Lord**, established the earth in the beginning.
> In this example we see the most common word placed in the voc. case in the NT, κύριος (which accounts for 119 of the 317 vocatives, though found in only 8 books).

Cf. also Matt 7:21; 20:13; Mark 8:33; Luke 7:14; John 2:4; Rom 11:3; Phil 4:3; Rev 7:14; 22:20.

2. *Emphatic (or, Emotional) Address*

a. Definition

This is the use of the vocative *with* ὦ preceding it. Here the presence of the particle ὦ is used in contexts where deep emotion is to be found. As can be seen from the following examples, "This is but a little particle, but it casts such a light on the state of mind of our Lord and of His apostles, that no one, surely, in reading the Scriptures, would wish to neglect its indications."[11]

b. Illustrations

Matt 15:28   ὁ Ἰησοῦς εἶπεν αὐτῇ, **Ὦ γύναι**, μεγάλη σου ἡ πίστις
Jesus said to her, "**O woman**, great is your faith!"
> Jesus' surprise at the Canaanite woman's humble and insightful response ("even the puppies eat the scraps that fall from their masters' table" [v 27]) elicited this remark.

---

[9] The voc. on the lips of Jesus (and others at times) seems to be occasionally emotional even without this particle. Cf. Matt 4:10; 7:5; 8:29; 11:21; 18:32; 23:26; 25:26; 27:46; Mark 1:24; 8:33; 10:47; Luke 4:34; 19:22; Acts 5:3; 1 Cor 15:55. It may be that the "naked vocative" is really a catch-all, encompassing both simple address and emphatic/emotional address. That is to say, it is unmarked, but the context may of course inform its flavor.

[10] The nom. θυγάτηρ is found in D G L N W Θ *et pauci*.

[11] Zerwick, *Biblical Greek*, 12 (§35).

Jas 2:20   θέλεις δὲ γνῶναι, **ὦ ἄνθρωπε κενέ**, ὅτι ἡ πίστις χωρὶς τῶν ἔργων ἀργή ἐστιν;

Do you want to learn, **O empty man**, that faith without works is worthless?

Cf. also Rom 2:1, 3; 9:20; 1 Tim 6:11, 20.[12]

3. *The Exceptional Usage in Acts*

Classical Greek was different from Hellenistic Greek in the use of the vocative in two ways[13]: (1) The vocative with ὦ was unmarked—that is, it was the normal usage, employed in polite or simple address; (2) the vocative, whether with or without ὦ, was usually located deep in the sentence rather than at the front. Hellenistic usage has reversed especially the first trend, but also, to some degree, the second. Thus, generally speaking, ὦ with the vocative, is marked or used for emphasis, emotion, etc., and the vocative is usually near the front of the sentence.

The usage in Acts is more like the classical norm than typical Koine. One cannot say, however, that this is due to Luke's more literary Koine, precisely because *the idiom occurs only in Acts, not in Luke*.[14] Descriptively we could say that (1) ὦ with the vocative (or nom.) in mid-sentence in Acts is unemphatic (Acts 1:1 [in addressing Theophilus in the preface to his work—ὦ Θεόφιλε]; 18:14; 27:21), while (2) ὦ at the front of the sentence is emphatic/emotional (Acts 13:10 [where Paul rails against Elymas the magician; see discussion below]). Whether this leads to any satisfactory explanation as to *why* Acts is different is difficult to assess. One attractive hypothesis is that when Luke is his *own source* (as in the prologue and in chs. 16-28 [the "we"-sections of Acts]), his style is more literary; but when he uses other sources, it follows the Hellenistic idiom. This would account for the differences between Luke and Acts, but is not without difficulties.[15]

---

[12] There are only 8 instances of ὦ with the voc. in the NT (Matt 15:28; Acts 1:1; Rom 2:1, 3; 9:20; 1 Tim 6:11, 20; Jas 2:20), as well as 9 with the nom. (Matt 17:17=Mark 9:19=Luke 9:41; 24:25; Acts 13:10; 18:14; 27:21; Rom 11:33; Gal 3:1). For discussion of Acts 1:1, see below ("Exceptional Usage in Acts").

[13] For a succinct discussion, see Smyth, *Greek Grammar*, 312-13 (§1283-88).

[14] ὦ with the nom. in Acts follows the same pattern.

[15] It is not really an argument against this hypothesis to say that it assumes the "we"-sections to be eye-witness accounts, for that debate is hardly settled. Rather, if this hypothesis could be reasonably demonstrated, it may well contribute to the other concern (as well as indicate, to some degree, how the author used his sources). The problems are rather that certain texts do not comfortably fit in with this approach (note, e.g., Luke 1:3, where the greeting to Theophilus is made without ὦ).

4. Simplification/Keys to Identification

The keys to remembering the use and significance of the vocative are:

1) *without* ὦ preceding it (except in Acts): simple address

2) *with* ὦ preceding it (except in Acts): emphatic address or vocative of exclamation

B. Exclamation

The vocative substantive is only rarely used in an exclamation without any grammatical connection to the rest of the sentence. The vocative in such instances, though used to address someone, is something of a sustained emotional outburst. All of the instances are disputed and may well belong under vocative of emphatic address. Cf. Rom 2:1, 3; Acts 13:10 (also discussed below).

C. Apposition

1. Definition

The substantive in the vocative case can stand in apposition to another vocative. In such instances the first vocative will bear one of the above-mentioned forces (i.e., direct address or exclamation). The presence of an appositional vocative almost always indicates that the whole vocative construction is emphatic/emotional address or exclamation (as opposed to simple address), for the piling on of vocatives, once the addressee has already been established with the first one, is linguistically unnecessary, but rhetorically effective.[16]

2. Illustrations

Mark 5:7   Τί ἐμοὶ καὶ σοί, Ἰησοῦ **υἱὲ** τοῦ θεοῦ τοῦ ὑψίστου
            Leave me alone, Jesus, **Son** of the most high God!
               The demonic response is filled with emotion and terror, as can be seen
               both by the compounding of vocatives and the idiomatic expression Τί
               ἐμοὶ καὶ σοί.[17]

---

[16] An exception to this would be expressions of *tight* apposition such as "King Agrippa" (Acts 25:26; 26:19). That is, such expressions are not for rhetorical effect.

[17] For a decent discussion on this expression, see BAGD, s.v. ἐγώ, 217.

Acts 1:24   Σὺ κύριε, **καρδιογνῶστα** πάντων, ἀνάδειξον ὃν ἐξελέξω ἐκ τούτων τῶν δύο ἕνα

You, Lord, **Knower of the hearts** of all men, show us which of these two you have chosen.

> This prayer, uttered on the occasion of the apostles' selection of one to replace Judas, revealed the somber tone with which they approached their task.

Acts 13:10   Ὦ πλήρης παντὸς δόλου καὶ πάσης ῥᾳδιουργίας, υἱὲ διαβόλου, **ἐχθρὲ** πάσης δικαιοσύνης . . .

O you son of the devil, full of every kind of guile and wickedness, **enemy** of all righteousness . . .

> Obviously Paul's reaction to Elymas the magician's attempt to subvert the gospel was hardly a hand-slapping! According to Luke's record, Paul subsequently brought down the curse of darkness on the magician. (One might suspect that if the ACLU had been around in Paul's day, they'd be pretty silent on this occasion!)

Rev 22:20   Ναί, ἔρχομαι ταχύ. Ἀμήν, ἔρχου, κύριε Ἰησοῦ.

Yes, come quickly. Amen, come Lord **Jesus**!

Cf. also Mark 10:47; Luke 4:34; 8:28; 10:21; 17:13; 18:38.

The Genitive Case

Overview of Genitive Uses

Select Bibliography

Abel, *Grammaire*, 175-92 (§44); *BDF*, 89-100 (§162-86); **Brooks-Winbery**, 7-29; **Funk**, *Intermediate Grammar*, 711-17 (§888-90); **Hoffmann-von Siebenthal**, *Grammatik*, 227-45 (§158-72); **E. Mayser**, *Grammatik der griechischen Papyri aus der Ptolemäerzeit* (Berlin/Leipzig: Walter de Gruyter, 1933) 2.2.185-240; **Moule**, *Idiom Book*, 36-43; **Moulton**, *Prolegomena*, 72-74; **Porter**, *Idioms*, 92-97; **Radermacher**, *Grammatik*, 123-26; **Robertson**, *Grammar*, 491-520; **Smyth**, *Greek Grammar*, 313-37 (§1290-1449); **Turner**, *Syntax*, 231-36; **G. H. Waterman**, "The Greek 'Verbal Genitive',", *Current Issues in Biblical and Patristic Interpretation: Studies in Honor of Merrill C. Tenney Presented by his Former Students*, ed. G. F. Hawthorne (Grand Rapids: Eerdmans, 1975) 289-93; **Young**, *Intermediate Greek*, 23-41; **Zerwick**, *Biblical Greek*, 12-19 (§36-50).

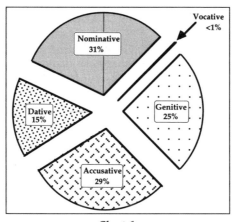

Chart 6
Frequency of Cases in the New Testament[1]

I. Introduction

A. Preliminary Remarks

1. Relation to the English Preposition "Of"

The genitive case is one of the most crucial elements of Greek syntax to master. Fortunately, for English speakers, many of the uses of the Greek genitive

---

[1] The genitive breakdown is as follows: 7681 nouns, 4986 pronouns, 5028 articles, 743 participles, 1195 adjectives.

are similar to our preposition "of." This not only makes learning the genitive easier, but it also makes it easier to explain to a lay audience the meaning of a passage that might hinge, in part, on the use of a genitive. For example, in Rom 8:35, when Paul wrote, "What shall separate us from the love of Christ?" it is clear in both English and Greek that he meant "the love Christ has for us" rather than "the love we have for Christ."

At the same time, we should be cautioned that the Greek genitive has some different uses than the English "of" (e.g., comparison, purpose, etc.). Explaining such to a lay audience needs to be handled carefully, especially when your interpretation differs from the "of" translation the audience is using. Further, only with diligence and a desire to look at the text from the Greek viewpoint will you be able to see for yourself such interpretive possibilities.

2. *Semantics and Exegetical Significance of the Genitive Case*

Learning the genitive uses well pays big dividends. It has a great deal of exegetical significance, far more so than any of the other cases, because it is capable of a wide variety of interpretations.[2] This, in turn, is due to three things:[3] elasticity in its uses, embedded kernels, and antithetical possibilities.

a. Elasticity

The genitive is more elastic than any other case, able to stretch over much of the syntactical terrain. In part this is due to this one form encompassing what are frequently two case-forms in other Indo-European languages (viz., gen. and ablative–the "of" and "from" ideas).

b. Embedded Kernels

Language, by its nature, is compressed, cryptic, symbolic.[4] One of the areas of great ambiguity in language involves the genitive case. Genitives are routinely used in compressed situations which need to be unpacked. The genitive is typically related to another substantive. But what that relation involves can be quite varied. "The revelation of Jesus Christ," "the love of God," "children of wrath," "mystery of godliness" are all capable of more than one interpretation precisely because

---

[2] Moule calls the gen. an "immensely versatile" and "hard-worked" case (*Idiom Book,* 37).

[3] These are not technically three separate notions; there is much overlap between them (particularly elasticity and embeds). To *some* degree, they are three ways of saying the same thing.

[4] See "Introduction: Approach of This Book" for discussion.

"of" covers a multitude of semantic relationships. In essence, the Noun–Noun–$_{\text{gen.}}$[5] construction is used to compress a number of different sentence types (such as subject-predicate nominative, transitive verb-direct object, subject-transitive verb, etc.).[6] A large part of our task in this chapter is to *unpack* the N-N$_g$ construction,[7] attempting to show for the most part the semantic situation[8] in which the various usages occur.

c. Antithetical Possibilities

Unlike the nominative and vocative cases (whose structural clues are generally sufficient to show which usage is involved), the genitive case typically requires a rather nuanced examination of context, lexical meanings of the words involved (i.e., in the N-N$_g$ construction), and other grammatical features (such as articularity or number).[9] Furthermore, in certain constructions (such as those which involve a "verbal" noun) the meaning possibilities can be somewhat antithetical. Thus, "revelation of Christ" can be unpacked to mean "the revelation *about* Christ" or "the revelation *from* Christ." Because of such widely divergent nuances, the genitive case requires careful examination.

3. *Genitive Chains*

Genitive chains (also known as concatenative genitives) can be somewhat complicated. In general, each succeeding genitive depends on the one that preceded it, though this is not always the case. (See discussion under Rom 8:21 in "Attributive Genitive" for more help.)

---

[5] Traditionally called *nomen regens-nomen rectum* or head noun-gen. noun. We will use compressed and symbolic terminology: from here on called N-N$_g$.

[6] For a seminal and stimulating study, in which the author applied transformational grammar to the N-N$_g$ construction, see Waterman, "The Greek 'Verbal Genitive'," 289-93. This approach is applied, using the language of Chomskyan linguistics, in Young, *Intermediate Greek*, 29. (Although we have benefited much from Chomsky, the labels used in this chapter are more traditional and descriptive.)

Note also Kiki Nikiforidou, "The Meanings of the Genitive: A Case Study in Semantic Structure and Semantic Change," *Cognitive Linguistics* 2.2 (1991) 149-205, who argues that all genitives came from the possessive idea. Nevertheless, through a diachronic analysis the author points out how the various uses evolved into notions that ultimately were far removed from the thought of possession.

[7] The gen. is used, of course, with other than a noun (such as verb, adverb, adjective, etc.). But most of its uses occur in N-N$_g$ constructions, and most of the exegetically problematic uses are also so used.

[8] See "Approach of This Book" for a discussion of this expression. For a summary, see below.

[9] As you will recall, these three elements (context [in its broadest sense, including literary and historical], lexeme, and other grammatical features) are the basic ingredients of the "semantic situation."

B. Definition of the Genitive Case: The Unaffected Meaning[10]

1. A Note About Oblique Cases in General

a. Genitive Distinct from Accusative

The genitive and the accusative are similar in that both are cases expressing some kind of *limitation*. The limiting function of the genitive can be seen in "the kingdom **of God**," specifying whose kingdom it is; "Simon **of Cyrene**," indicating which Simon is in view; "the flesh **of birds**," where the kind of flesh is marked out. The accusative also limits, as in "I heard **a voice**," indicating what it is that was heard; "they worshipped **the Lord**," specifying the object of the worship.

As can be seen from the examples above, the difference between these two is generally twofold: (1) The "genitive limits as to kind, while the accusative limits as to extent."[11] Another way to put this is that the genitive limits as to *quality* while the accusative limits as to *quantity*. (2) The genitive is usually related to a noun while the accusative is usually related to a verb.

b. Genitive Distinct from Dative

While the force of the genitive is generally adjectival, the force of the dative is basically adverbial. There is some overlap between the uses of these cases, but these distinctions should help you to see more clearly the significance of each case. Also, the genitive is usually related to a noun, while the dative (as the acc.) is usually related to a verb.[12]

2. Within the Eight-Case System

In the eight-case system, the genitive defines, describes, qualifies, restricts, limits.[13] In this respect it is similar to an adjective, but is more emphatic.[14] One should be cautioned that several grammars and commentaries assume

---

[10] That is, unaffected by context, genre, lexical intrusions, etc. This is the meaning the gen. would have if it were seen in isolation. See "Approach of This Book" for discussion of terms.

[11] Dana-Mantey, 73.

[12] There are of course gen. direct objects (thus, related to a verb). Such instances do not mitigate the *qualifying* force of the gen. The significance of the gen. direct object will be seen in relation to the acc. direct object (thus, kind vs. extent is often the difference), for many verbs take both acc. and gen., but there is, to my knowledge, no verb in the Greek NT which takes both a gen. *and dat.* direct object.

the eight-case system; when they speak of the genitive, this is all they mean (i.e., the ablatival notion of separation is not included). But for those who embrace the five-case system, a more encompassing definition is needed.

3. *Within the Five-Case System*

Since the genitive and ablative have the same form, we shall consider them both as *one* case ("case" being defined as a matter of form rather than function). In some respects, the definition of the genitive case in the five-case system simply combines genitive and *ablative* from the eight-case system. The ablative notion is fundamentally that of *separation*. This is the *from* idea. Such separation may be viewed statically (i.e., in a separated state), or progressively (movement away from, so as to become separated). Further, the emphasis may be on either the result or the cause (in the latter, origin or source is emphasized).

Another way to view the genitive case is to see all uses, both adjectival and ablatival, generating from one idea. Whether such a root idea was that of possession,[15] or restriction,[16] or some other notion, is of greater interest to the philologist (and the field of diachronics) than the exegete. In Hellenistic Greek, the *of* idea and the *from* idea are usually distinct–so much so that the ablatival concept is increasingly expressed with ἀπό or ἐκ rather than with the "naked" genitive form. (In the least, this suggests a growing uneasiness on the part of Koine speakers to use the gen. case to express the idea of separation.[17])

Therefore, under the five-case system, the genitive case may be defined as *the case of qualification (or limitation as to kind) and (occasionally) separation.*

II. Specific Uses

Our approach to the genitive is to break its uses down into a few major categories with many subgroups under each of these. This approach (followed by many

---

[13] We are not by any means arguing on behalf of the eight-case system here, just recognizing a reality as to how case has been treated in the literature. Remarkably, more than one grammar has defined the gen. case simply as qualification (or the like), in spite of adopting the *five*-case system!

[14] Dana-Mantey, 72-74.

[15] So Nikiforidou, "The Meanings of the Genitive," who presents a plausible argument.

[16] So Louw, 83-85, followed by Porter, *Idioms*, 92.

[17] Some grammars mix the naked case uses with those of preposition + case (e.g., Brooks-Winbery, 7-64). This only confuses the issue and promotes a great deal of exegetical misunderstanding. For a more detailed discussion, see the chapter on prepositions.

grammarians) is helpful in showing the similarities that different types of genitives have toward one another.

N. B. The layout in this chapter may seem a bit industrious. The immediate reaction of looking at the following categories might be to rush through the material before the categories, like rabbits, multiply any further! What appears at first glance to be microscopic hair-splitting is governed by the principles of *semantic reality* and *exegetical significance*. That is, in light of the great diversity of established uses of the genitive, as well as of the often profound exegetical significance that this case can play in given texts, an acquaintance with these categories is justified.[18]

A. Adjectival Genitive

This broad category really touches the heart of the genitive. If the genitive is primarily descriptive, then it is largely similar to the adjective in functions. "The chief thing to remember is that the Genitive often practically does the duty of an adjective, distinguishing two otherwise similar things. . . ."[19] However, although the genitive is primarily adjectival in force, it is more emphatic than a simple adjective would be.[20]

---

[18] It is important to keep in mind this tension between established semantic categories and the exegetical mileage we can get out of them. On the one hand, any *clear* examples establish a semantic category. If we were to rigorously break down the descriptive gen., for example, we may well end up with more than 100 categories of genitives! (It will not do to object that such usages are contextually based, because *context* is just as much a part of syntax as morphology or lexeme [*contra* Porter, *Idioms*, 82, who makes a hard-and-fast distinction between syntax and context]. Thus, it is conceivable that *some* gen. uses in the NT will not be found in certain other corpora of Hellenistic Greek.) On the other hand, such a multiplication of categories, as useful as it might be on a linguistic level, is reigned in by our governing principle of exegetical value. Thus, although there are more categories of the gen. in this chapter than are found in most grammars, we believe that the additional categories are both valid and useful for exegesis.

[19] Moule, *Idiom Book*, 38.

[20] Another difference between an adjectival gen. and an adjective is that a gen. does not lose its nominal force in that it can take adnominal modifiers, while an adjective usually takes only adverbial modifiers. The one gen. that does not apparently not take adnominals is the attributive gen., but even here its connotation is decidedly more pronounced than a mere adjective would be.

✝ **1. Descriptive Genitive ("Aporetic" Genitive[21]) [characterized by, described by]**

a. Definition

The genitive substantive describes the head noun in a loose manner. The nature of the collocation of the two nouns in this construction is usually quite ambiguous.

b. Amplification

This is the "catch-all" genitive, the "drip pan" genitive, the "black hole" of genitive categories that tries to suck many a genitive into its grasp! In some respects, *all adjectival genitives are descriptive, yet no adjectival genitive is descriptive.* That is to say, although all adjectival genitives are, by their nature, descriptive, very few, if any, belong only to this specific category of usage. This use truly embodies the root idea of the (adjectival) genitive. It is often the usage of the genitive when it has not been affected by other linguistic considerations–that is, when there are *no* contextual, lexemic, or other grammatical features that suggest a more specific nuance.[22]

Frequently, however, it is close to the attributive genitive, being either *other than or broader than* the attributive use.[23] (See chart 7 below.) Hence, this use of the genitive should be a *last resort.* If one cannot find a *narrower* category to which a genitive belongs, this is where he or she should look for solace.[24]

---

[21] That is, the "I am at a loss" gen. (from the Greek word, ἀπορέω, "I am at a loss," a tongue-in-cheek title suggested to me by J. Will Johnston). This is the category one should appeal to when another slot cannot be found. The title is descriptive not of the gen., but of the feeling one has in the pit of his/her stomach for having spent so much time on this case and coming up with nothing.

[22] Actually, this could be called the "gen. of limited application." The context does suggest this usage sometimes (in that the gen. is generally descriptive), but more frequently the gen. use has simply not been "unpacked." The advanced student can experiment with such unpacking along the lines of TG.

[23] Williams, *Grammar Notes*, 5.

[24] Since there is already a plethora of gen. categories, we had to stop somewhere. The descriptive gen. covers a multitude of syntactical categories which have, as yet, to receive published sanction (though this would be a worthy project). It seems that one of the chief situations in which descriptive genitives occur is when either the head noun or the gen. noun is highly idiomatic, figurative, or informed by Semitic usage. Thus, υἱός + noun$_{gen}$ is perhaps frequently descriptive (e.g., "son of disobedience"). To call this merely attributive ("disobedient son") is not adequate, for "son" then does not get interpreted. (υἱός with gen. is notoriously complex; see Zerwick, *Biblical Greek*, 15-16 [§42-43] for summary of uses.) Also, when the head noun is figurative, such as in "root of bitterness" ῥίζα πικρίας, Heb 12:15), the gen. can frequently be described as descriptive.

At the same time, our approach in this chapter overall is different from grammars that refuse to analyze the descriptive gen. (e.g., Young, *Intermediate Greek*, 23; Moule, *Idiom Book*, 37), because we believe that such analysis is not intuitive with most students of Greek and, further, that the additional categories have exegetical value.

c. **Key to Identification**

For the word *of* insert the paraphrase *characterized by* or *described by*. If
this fits, and if *none* of the other uses of the genitive fits, then the genitive
is probably a genitive of description.[25]

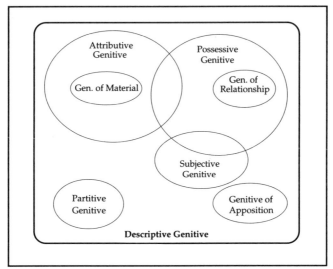

Chart 7
The Relation of Descriptive Genitive to Various Other Genitive Uses

d. **Illustrations**

Mark 1:4   Ἰωάννης . . . κηρύσσων βάπτισμα **μετανοίας**
           John . . . [was] preaching a baptism **of repentance**
           > There are various *possible* interpretations of this phrase: "baptism that
           > is based on repentance" (causal), "baptism that points toward/pro-
           > duces repentance" (purpose or production), "baptism that symbolizes
           > repentance." In light of such ambiguity, it may well be best to be non-
           > committal: "baptism that is somehow related to repentance."

John 2:16 μὴ ποιεῖτε τὸν οἶκον τοῦ πατρός μου οἶκον **ἐμπορίου**
           do not make my Father's house into a house **of merchandise**
           > The idea is "a house in which merchandise is sold."

Rom 13:12 ἐνδυσώμεθα τὰ ὅπλα **τοῦ φωτός**
           let us put on the full armor **of light**

2 Cor 6:2 ἐν ἡμέρᾳ **σωτηρίας**
           in [the] day **of salvation**
           > This cannot be an attributive gen., for then the idea would be "a *saved*
           > day"! A day which is "characterized by" salvation is acceptably clear.

---

[25] Commentators are often fond of merely labeling a gen. as "descriptive" without
giving any more precision to the nuance involved. We suggest that an attempt at least
ought to be made to see if a given gen. plugs into another category.

We could unpack this further, however: "the day in which salvation is revealed," or "the day in which salvation comes."[26]

1 Thess 5:5 πάντες γὰρ ὑμεῖς υἱοὶ **φωτός** ἐστε

for you all are sons **of light**

This does not mean "lightful sons" but "enlightened sons" comes closer. The figurative and compressed language involves a connotation which has more emotive force than merely "sons who dwell in the light," though that is surely close to the denotative meaning.[27]

Rev 9:1 ἐδόθη αὐτῷ ἡ κλεὶς **τοῦ φρέατος** τῆς ἀβύσσου

the key **to the shaft** of the abyss was given to him

This is not a possessive gen., even though our idiom "belongs to" fits (for the shaft does not possess the key). The idea is "the key *which opens* the shaft of the abyss."[28]

Cf. also Matt 24:37; 2 Cor 11:14; Eph 2:2; perhaps Heb 1:9; Heb 12:15.

➡ 2. *Possessive Genitive [belonging to, possessed by]*

a. Definition

The substantive in the genitive possesses the thing to which it stands related. That is, in some sense the head noun is owned by the genitive noun. Such ownership at times can be broadly defined and need not imply the literal (and sometimes harsh) idea of possession of physical property. This usage is quite common.

b. Key to Identification

Instead of the word *of* replace it with *belonging to* or *possessed by*. If this paraphrase fits, then the genitive is probably a genitive of possession.

c. Amplification

Although this category can be broadly defined, it really ought to be used only when a genitive cannot fit more neatly under some other category (it will still be of very common occurrence). A genitive should not be

---

[26] This text illustrates a certain pattern, viz., the head noun establishes a framework (such as time or space) in which an *implied* event takes place whose subject is embedded in the gen. This is especially frequent with ἡμέρα. E.g., in Matt 11:12 "the days of John the Baptist" means "the days when [temporal framework] John the Baptist [subject embedded in gen.] lived [implied verb]"; in Matt 10:15/11:22 "the day of judgment" means "the day when judgment occurs." (Cf. also Luke 21:22; Acts 7:45; Eph 4:30; Phil 2:16. Slightly different is the idiom in Luke 1:80; 1 Pet 2:12.) As suggested earlier, much profit could be gained by analyzing this rather broad and amorphous category.

[27] As there is no gen. category such as gen. of domicile (which would have probably rather limited instances in the NT), descriptive gen. will have to do: "sons characterized by light."

[28] See discussion above under 2 Cor 6:2; the embedded clause is apparently similar.

labeled possessive unless this is the *narrowest* sense it can have. If it is related to a verbal noun, then, it is probably objective or subjective.[29]

Further, possessive *pronouns* will be the primary words used for the genitive of possession. In fact, when one sees a possessive pronoun he/she can *usually* assume that its primary nuance is that of possession.

Finally, the head noun and the genitive noun will routinely have *lexical* nuances that naturally fit in with the idea of possession. E.g., John's book, the name of the woman, the dog's tail, etc. In these instances, it is observed that *the genitive noun is animate and is usually personal*; the head noun, normally the kind of thing that *can* be possessed (e.g., entities, not abstract ideas).

d. Illustrations[30]

Matt 26:51   τὸν δοῦλον **τοῦ ἀρχιερέως**
the slave **of the high priest**

Matt 26:51   **αὐτοῦ** τὸ ὠτίον
his ear

> The difference between this and a partitive gen. is typically that with a partitive gen. the head noun is impersonal or conceived of as wielding power/authority over the gen. Thus, "the car's bumper" is not the same as "the man's foot." This illustrates the fact that the specific uses cannot be understood apart from the phenomenological instances in which they occur–e.g., lexical intrusions.[31]

John 20:28   Θωμᾶς εἶπεν αὐτῷ, ὁ κύριός **μου** καὶ ὁ θεός **μου**
Thomas said to him, "**My** Lord and **my** God"

> The idea of possession in such expressions is not to be pressed in the sense that the Lord is owned fully by Thomas. But in a broad sense, the Lord belongs to Thomas–now, on this occasion, in a way not true before.

1 Cor 1:12   ἕκαστος ὑμῶν λέγει, ἐγὼ μέν εἰμι **Παύλου**, ἐγὼ δὲ **Ἀπολλῶ**
each of you says, "I am **of Paul**"; "I am **of Apollos**"

---

[29] My colleague, Prof. John Grassmick, has suggested the following scheme: The subjective gen., possessive gen. and the gen. of source are closely related. Other things being equal, and if the context allows, *possession* takes precedent over source, and the *subjective* gen. takes precedent over possession *when* a verbal noun is involved.

[30] Several grammars suggest that references such as "children of God" (John 1:12), "apostle of Christ Jesus" (2 Cor 1:1); "their brothers" (Heb 7:5), "prisoner of Christ Jesus" (Eph 3:1) embody possessive genitives. All of these are indeed genitives of possession, but their nuances also go *beyond* mere possession. E.g., "children of God" would be a gen. of relationship; "apostle of Christ Jesus" is also subjective gen. (indicating that Christ Jesus sent out Paul). Hence, although in a broad sense the gen. of possession is quite common, in a narrow sense (which is adopted in this grammar) the instances are more restricted.

[31] At the same time, such lexical intrusions are not automatic guides as to the use of the gen. For example, in 1 Cor 15:39, although "flesh of men, flesh of beasts, flesh of birds, flesh of fish" meets the body parts criterion, the overall context indicates that attributive genitives (i.e., manly flesh, beastly flesh, birdly flesh, fishy flesh") is the idea in view.

> The proper name in each of these instances does not refer to the person, but to the sect that follows him. If it were otherwise, a possessive gen. might imply personal ownership. Once the figurative language is analyzed, however, the meaning is clear: "I belong to the Pauline sect," etc.[32]

Heb 11:25   τῷ λαῷ **τοῦ θεοῦ**
             the people **of God**

Cf. also Mark 12:17; John 18:15; Acts 17:5; 21:8; Jas 3:3; Rev 13:17.

3. Genitive of Relationship

a. Definition

The substantive in the genitive indicates a *familial* relationship, typically the progenitor of the person named by the head noun. This category is relatively rare.

b. Key to Identification/Amplification

This is a subset of the possessive genitive (See chart 7 above for a visual representation.) The key to determining whether or not a possessive genitive is a genitive of relationship is (1) if the noun to which the genitive is related is a *family* relation noun (e.g., son, mother, etc.) or (2) if the noun to which the genitive is related is *understood* (i.e., must be supplied from the context) and what one supplies is a family relation noun, then the possessive genitive is a genitive of relationship.[33] As well, the genitive noun is routinely a proper name.

c. Clarification

Often, especially in the Gospels, the noun related to the genitive is to be supplied. If this is the case, the genitive alone *usually* suggests the idea of "who comes from" or "who is a descendant of." Thus, when the noun to which the genitive is related is *not* named, it can usually be assumed that the genitive alone speaks of the ancestor (but cf. Mark 16:1 for an exception; here the genitive speaks of the descendant rather than of the ancestor).

d. Illustrations

Matt 20:20   ἡ μήτηρ **τῶν υἱῶν Ζεβεδαίου**
            the mother **of the sons of Zebedee**
               This is a *double* example in which the first gen. ("sons") indicates

---

[32] Not altogether common in this example is the possessive gen. in the predicate, making an assertion about the subject. Cf. also Matt 5:10.

[33] Differently, Young (*Intermediate Greek*, 25-26), who includes "social" relationships in this category.

descendant of the first noun ("mother"), followed by a gen. indicating progenitor ("Zebedee").

John 21:15   Σίμων Ἰωάννου
             Simon, [son] **of John**

Luke 24:10   Μαρία ἡ Ἰακώβου
             Mary, the [mother] **of James**

Matt 4:21   Ἰάκωβον τὸν **τοῦ Ζεβεδαίου**
             James, the [son] **of Zebedee**

➡ 4. *Partitive Genitive ("Wholative") [which is a part of]*[34]

a. Definition

The substantive in the genitive denotes *the whole of which* the head noun is a part. This usage is relatively common in the NT.

b. Key to Identification

Instead of the word *of* substitute *which is a part of.*

c. Amplification and Semantics[35]

1) This is a phenomenological use of the genitive that requires the head noun to have a lexical nuance indicating *portion*. For example, "some of the Pharisees," "one of you," "a tenth of the city," "the branch of the tree," "a piece of pie."

2) This use of the genitive is similar to *one* kind of possessive genitive (e.g., the possessive gen. with anatomy) with one significant difference. "The tail of the dog" is possessive, while "the bumper of the car" is partitive. As can be seen, the difference between these two has to do with animateness. One *crude* way to test whether a genitive is partitive or possessive is to ask whether the genitive substantive would object to the head noun's departure. A dog would (possession); a car would not (partitive).[36]

3) The partitive genitive is *semantically the opposite of the genitive of apposition.* While the partitive designates the whole of which the head noun is a part, the genitive of apposition designates a particular within the class described by the head noun. The important thing to

---

[34] The term "partitive" is confusing, for it suggests that the gen. itself will designate the part of which the head noun is the whole. Hence, it has been suggested that "wholative" is a better designation. Some call it the gen. of the divided whole, but this is hardly better than partitive.

[35] Our discussion here could easily be protracted beyond what it is presently. For further analysis, cf. *BDF,* 90-91 (§164).

keep in mind here is that, though semantically opposite, sometimes they are structurally identical. (See under "Genitive of Apposition" for discussion and diagram.)

4) Occasionally, the noun to which the genitive is related is absent, understood from the context. (One will also see this frequently with ἐκ + the gen. [e.g., Matt 27:48; John 11:49; 16:17], which often has a partitive force to it.[37]) Therefore, sometimes it is necessary to *supply* the "part" in order to determine whether or not the genitive is partitive.

5) An almost invariable formula that the partitive genitive follows includes such head substantives as: τις,[38] ἕκαστος,[39] and especially εἷς.[40] That is to say, in such constructions, the genitive will routinely be partitive.[41]

d. Illustrations

1) Clear Examples

Luke 19:8 τὰ ἡμίσιά μου **τῶν ὑπαρχόντων**
half **of** my **possessions**

Rom 11:17 τινες **τῶν κλάδων**
some **of the branches**

Rom 15:26 τοὺς πτωχοὺς **τῶν ἁγίων**
the poor **of the saints**

Rev 11:13 τὸ δέκατον **τῆς πόλεως**
[one] tenth **of the city**

---

[36] This test has many exceptions however. For example, in "a tenth of the city" the nine-tenths would probably object if the one tenth were no longer! But in certain contexts (such as Rev 11:13, where this expression occurs) animation is not in view as much as place. In the expression "some of the women" it is hardly possible that the gen. noun possesses the head noun (so also "one third of the people" in Rev 9:18). Consequently, partitive is the only option. Perhaps part of the solution has to do with individual vs. group distinctions (a point hinted at by Winer long ago [Winer-Moulton, 244]): this rule of thumb does not work on semantically plural partitives (like "city," "women," etc.), only on singulars.

[37] The partitive gen. is in fact being squeezed out in Koine Greek by ἐκ + gen. (*BDF*, 90 [§164]).

[38] E.g., Mark 14:47; Luke 9:8; Jas 1:18 (modifying ἀπαρχήν).

[39] E.g., Heb 11:21; Rev 21:21.

[40] E.g., Matt 5:19; Mark 5:22; Luke 5:3, 12, 17.

[41] However, πάντες ὑμῶν never occurs in the NT. The two instances where we see the partitive idea for πᾶς + personal pronoun both have the prep. ἐκ (Luke 14:33; 1 John 2:19). It is thus likely that in, say, Phil 1:4, 7 πάντων ὑμῶν is not partitive, but simple apposition ("you all"); cf. v 7 (πάντας ὑμᾶς), v 8 (πάντας ὑμᾶς), which seem to confirm this.

Jas 1:18   εἰς τὸ εἶναι ἡμᾶς ἀπαρχήν τινα **τῶν** αὐτοῦ **κτισμάτων**
              that we should be a kind of first fruit **of** his **creatures**

Cf. also Matt 21:11; Mark 2:16; Luke 4:29; 8:44; 16:24; 18:11; John 2:1; Jude 13.

2) Debated Example

Eph 4:9   τὸ δὲ ᾽Ανέβη τί ἐστιν εἰ μὴ ὅτι καὶ κατέβη εἰς τὰ κατώτερα μέρη **τῆς γῆς**
              Now the statement "he ascended"–what does it mean except that he
              also descended into the lower parts **of the earth**?

> Although popularly taken to be a partitive gen. (thus referring to the
> Lord's descent into hell), this is not the only possibility here. It is more
> likely a gen. of apposition. (See discussion and defense under "Geni-
> tive of Apposition.")

➡ ## 5. *Attributive Genitive (Hebrew Genitive, Genitive of Quality)*[42]

a. Definition

The genitive substantive specifies an *attribute* or innate quality of the
head substantive. It is similar to a simple adjective in its semantic force,
though more emphatic: it "expresses quality like an adjective indeed,
but with more sharpness and distinctness."[43] The category is very
common in the NT, largely due to the Semitic mindset of most of its
authors.[44]

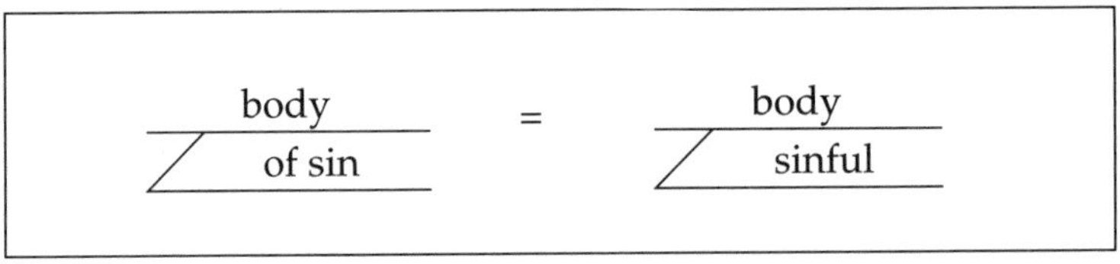

Chart 8
The Semantics of the Attributive Genitive

---

[42] Cf. especially the helpful studies in Robertson, *Grammar*, 496, Moule, *Idiom Book*, 37-38, Zerwick, *Biblical Greek*, 14-15, BDF, 91-92 (§165).

[43] Robertson, *Grammar*, 496.

[44] "Hebrew usage is . . . reflected, in that this construction compensates for the nearly nonexistent adjective. Classical Greek exhibits very sparse parallels in poetry only" (*BDF*, 91 [§165]). (For classical examples, see A. C. Moorhouse, *The Syntax of Sophocles* [Leiden: Brill, 1982] 54; Smyth, *Greek Grammar*, 317 [§1320].) This is not to say that the attributive gen. was nonexistent in classical or Hellenistic Greek. Rather, the frequency of it (as well as certain peculiar collocations) is due largely to the linguistic and religious (esp. LXX influence) background of the NT authors.

Further, that this usage is found just as much in Luke or Paul as it is in John or Mark puts it on the plane of Semitic *style* rather than *syntax per se* and hence contributes nothing to the notion that NT Greek is a unique language. Cf. Lars Rydbeck, "What Happened to Greek Grammar after Albert Debrunner?", *NTS* 21 (1974-75) 424-27.

b. **Key to Identification**

If the noun in the genitive can be converted into an attributive adjective, modifying the noun to which the genitive stands related, then the genitive is very likely an attributive genitive.

c. **Semantics and Significance**

1) This genitive is more emphatic than an adjective would have been. Thus, although the denotation is the same, the connotation is not. "Body of sin" has a stronger force than "sinful body."

2) The genitive of *material* is technically a subset of the attributive genitive, but it involves other nuances as well. If a genitive could be classified as either attributive or material, it should classified as the latter.[45]

3) Certain words are frequently found in this construction, such as σῶμα as a head noun (cf. Rom 6:6; 7:24; Phil 3:21; Col 2:11)[46] or δόξης as the genitive term (cf. Matt 19:28; 25:31; Acts 7:2; Rom 8:21; 1 Cor 2:8).

4) The *specific* relation of the two substantives, though frequently obvious, is not always so. For example, once the genitive is converted into an adjective, should it have an active or passive force? Would, for example, "man of peace" mean "peaceful man" or "peacemaking man"? Or take "body of death"–does it mean "deadly body" or "dying body"? Each one needs to be examined in its context.

d. **Illustrations**

Luke 18:6 ὁ κριτὴς **τῆς ἀδικίας**
judge **of unrighteousness** (= "**unrighteous** judge")

Rom 6:6 τὸ σῶμα **τῆς ἁμαρτίας**
body **of sin** (= "**sinful** body")

> By using the attributive gen. rather than a mere adjective, Paul laid more emphasis on the sinfulness of humanity's condition.

Rom 8:21 τὴν ἐλευθερίαν **τῆς δόξης** τῶν τέκνων τοῦ θεοῦ
the freedom **of the glory** of the children of God (= "the **glorious** freedom of the children of God")

> Normally in gen. chains (a.k.a. concatenative genitives) each successive gen. modifies the one that precedes it.[47] But when an attributive gen. is in the mix, matters are a bit more complicated. Since an attributive gen.

---

[45] See later discussion on gen. of material. With anatomical descriptions, either category seems acceptable.

[46] *BDF*, 91 (§165) suggest that ἡμέρα occurs as head noun in this construction frequently. We would treat all such examples differently (see footnote at 2 Cor 6:2, under "Descriptive Genitive," for discussion.)

[47] *BDF*, 93 (§168) says "always."

is by its nature strongly adjectival, it is best to convert it into an adjective and take it "out of the loop" of the gen. chain. Doing this in Rom 8:21 produces a dependency hierarchy of:

freedom
of children
of God.

Factoring in δόξης and putting the whole construction in a diagram, the relationships are clearly seen:

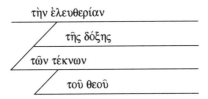

It is evident in the above diagram that although δόξης depends on ἐλευθερίαν, τῶν τέκνων does not depend on δόξης. As we suggested earlier, an attributive gen. does not normally, if ever, take a modifier.

Col 1:22   ἐν τῷ σώματι **τῆς σαρκὸς** αὐτοῦ
in the body **of his flesh** (= "in his **fleshly** body")
> This could equally be labeled gen. of material (see below).

1 Tim 1:17   τῷ δὲ βασιλεῖ **τῶν αἰώνων**
now to the king **of the ages** (="**eternal**" king)
> The problem with taking this as attributive is that the gen. is plural. However, if it were put in the singular, the meaning would not be "eternal king" ("king of the age" would be a temporal king). RSV, NRSV take it as "king of the ages";[48] ASV *et al.* take it as "eternal king."

Jas 2:4   ἐγένεσθε κριταὶ **διαλογισμῶν** πονηρῶν
you have become judges **with** evil **motives**
> The idea here is not "you have become judges **of** evil motives" (which would be an objective gen.). But the translation "evil-motived judges" is cumbersome. This illustrates the fact that one should think about the *sense* of the passage more than merely do a translational gloss.

Cf. also Luke 16:9; Acts 9:15; Rom 11:8; 2 Cor 1:12 (possible)[49]; Gal 6:1; Phil 2:1 (possible); 3:21; Col 1:25 (possible); Heb 1:3; 7:2.

---

[48] "King of the ages" would be a gen. of subordination–i.e., the "one who rules over the ages." See below.

[49] The instances with θεοῦ or πνεύματος are not frequent, but they are nevertheless intriguing. Too often exegetes assume a member of the Godhead when a qualitative force to the gen. gives a quite satisfactory interpretation.

6. The Attributed Genitive

a. Definition

This is just the opposite, semantically, of the attributive genitive. The head noun, rather than the genitive, is functioning (in sense) as an attributive adjective. Although rarer than the attributive genitive, this is not altogether uncommon.[50]

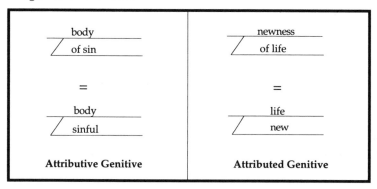

Chart 9
A Semantic Diagram of the Attributive Genitive and Attributed Genitive

As can be seen in the chart above, with the attributed genitive, the diagram "flip-flops" (thus illustrating, *inter alia*, the limited value of diagrams[51]). Some grammarians thus refer to this as a "reverse genitive."[52]

b. Key to Identification

If it is possible to convert the noun to which the genitive stands related into a mere adjective, then the genitive is a good candidate for this category.

One simple way to do this conversion is to omit the *of* in translation between the head noun and genitive, and change the head noun into its corresponding adjective. Thus "newness *of* life" becomes "new life."

c. Semantics

If the whole N-N$_g$ construction is envisioned, the semantics of both the attributive and attributed genitive are similar. For the most part, one could profitably consult our discussion of the semantics of the

---

[50] Since this category gets minimal or no attention in most grammars, most commentators do not wrestle with this usage as a possibility. Here is another area of syntax that could profitably be exploited, for there are surely scores of texts in which this idiom is both a viable and unrecognized option.

[51] Diagramming in Greek is very helpful for seeing the surface structure more clearly. However, it is limited in that it normally is unable to reflect a different "deep structure."

[52] *BDF*, 91 (§165); Zerwick, *Biblical Greek*, 15 (n. 6); BAGD, s.v. ἀλήθεια, for Rom 1:25.

attributive genitive and simply replace "genitive" with "head noun." Thus, (1) the head noun is more emphatic than an adjective would have been: "newness of life" has a stronger force than "new life." (2) The *specific* relation of the two substantives, though usually intuitively obvious, needs to be brought to the conscious level. For example, once the head noun is converted into an adjective, it will sometimes have an active or passive force.

d. Illustrations

1) Clear Examples

Rom 6:4   οὕτως καὶ ἡμεῖς ἐν καινότητι **ζωῆς** περιπατήσωμεν
> Thus also we should walk in newness **of life.**
>> Here "newness of life" = "new life." An attribu*tive* gen. would be nonsensical: "living/lively newness"![53]

Eph 1:19   καὶ τί τὸ ὑπερβάλλον μέγεθος **τῆς δυνάμεως** αὐτοῦ
> and what is the surpassing greatness **of** his **power**
>> Here "surpassing greatness of his power" might = "surpassingly great power."

Phil 1:22   τοῦτό μοι καρπὸς **ἔργου**
> this [will mean] [the] fruit **of labor** to me
>> Here "the fruit of labor" = "fruitful labor." An attributive gen. would mean "laboring fruit"!

1 Pet 1:7   τὸ δοκίμιον ὑμῶν **τῆς πίστεως** πολυτιμότερον χρυσίου
> the genuineness **of** your **faith** which is much more precious than gold
>> The idea is that their genuine faith is more precious than gold.

Cf. also Phil 3:8; Jas 3:9.

2) Possible (and Exegetically Significant) Examples

Eph 1:18   τίς ὁ πλοῦτος **τῆς δόξης** τῆς κληρονομίας αὐτοῦ
> what are the riches **of the glory** of his inheritance
>> Possibly "riches of the glory" = "rich glory," though attribu*tive* gen. is more likely ("glorious riches").

Rom 1:25   οἵτινες μετήλλαξαν τὴν ἀλήθειαν **τοῦ θεοῦ**
> they exchanged the truth **of God**
>> It is likely that "truth of God" = "true God."

Eph 1:17   πνεῦμα **σοφίας** καὶ **ἀποκαλύψεως**
> spiritual **wisdom** and **revelation**
>> In this text we have three possibilities: (1) "a spirit" of wisdom and revelation, (2) "the Spirit" of wisdom and revelation, or (3) "spiritual" wisdom and revelation. This last option would treat "wisdom" and "revelation" as attributed genitives. It has much in its favor, both

---

[53] Remarkably, Robertson calls this attributive (*Grammar*, 496)!

grammatically and exegetically. Exegetically, to say that the author is praying that God might give the readers the Holy Spirit seems to contradict what he stated just three verses earlier, in vv 13-14 (though this could easily be a metonymy of cause for effect). On the other side, the meaning of "a spirit of wisdom, etc." is vague. Grammatically, when an anarthrous gen. is related to an anarthrous head noun both nouns will usually be equally definite, indefinite, or qualitative.[54] Here, since "wisdom" and "revelation" are *qualitative* words, it is most natural to also consider "spirit" as qualitative. To translate πνεῦμα as "spiritual" brings out this qualitative force.[55]

Cf. also Eph 4:18; 2 Thess 2:11 (NRSV).

7. Genitive of Material [made out of, consisting of]

a. Definition

The genitive substantive specifies the material out of which the head noun is made. This usage is quite rare in the NT (the notion of material is somewhat more frequently stated with ἐκ + gen.).

b. Key to Identification

Replace the word *of* with the paraphrase *made out of* or *consisting of*. If this paraphrase fits, the genitive is probably a genitive of material.

c. Semantics

The genitive of material is technically a subset of the attributive genitive, but it involves other nuances as well. If a genitive is equally attributive and material, it should be classified as the latter. It relates specifically to physical properties and is therefore a lexico-syntactic category. That is to say, both substantives in the N-N$_g$ construction must express something concrete if a genitive of material is to be seen. As well, this genitive is a more nuanced qualifier than attributive. Whereas the scope of qualification is quite broad for attributive genitive, it is *focused* with material.[56] (See chart 7 above for further help.)

d. Illustrations

Mark 2:21   ἐπίβλημα **ῥάκους** ἀγνάφου
            a patch [made out] **of** unshrunk **cloth**

---

[54] See chapter on the article where "Apollonius' Corollary" is discussed.

[55] Eph 1:17 is a notorious problem, but discussions are almost always shut up to the options of "a spirit" and "the Spirit." Cf., e.g., A. T. Lincoln, *Ephesians* (WBC; Dallas: Word, 1990) 57-58; M. Barth, *Ephesians* (AB; Garden City, New York: Doubleday, 1974) 1.148; T. K. Abbott, *A Critical and Exegetical Commentary On the Epistles to the Ephesians and to the Colossians* (ICC; Edinburgh, T. & T. Clark, 1897).

[56] Even though the gen. of material is a subset of the attributive gen., it is typically awkward to translate it as an adjective.

Rev 18:12   γόμον **χρυσοῦ** καὶ **ἀργύρου** καὶ **λίθου** τιμίου[57]
             cargo **of gold** and **silver** and precious **stone** (= cargo *consisting of*
             gold and silver and precious stone)

Cf. also John 19:39; perhaps Col 1:22 and 2:11 (but see "Attributive Genitive").

8. Genitive of Content [full of, containing]

a. Definition

The genitive substantive specifies the contents of the word to which it is
related. This word may be either a noun, adjective or verb. This is fairly
common in the NT, though only with certain kinds of words.

b. Key to Identification

If the word to which this genitive is related is a noun, replace the word
of with the paraphrase *full of* or *containing*.[58] If the word is a verb, the typical translational force of the genitive is *with*. (This key is not as helpful
as the others, for there are many exceptions. For this category, the real
key is to notice the lexical nuance of the word to which the gen. is
related.)

c. Amplification

(1) There are *two* kinds of genitive of content: one related to a noun or
adjective (*nominal* gen. of content), the other to a verb (*verbal* gen. of content).[59] A genitive of content is a lexico-syntactic category in that the
verb or head noun will be a term indicating *quantity*[60] (e.g., for verbs:
γέμω, πίμπλημι, πληρόω; for nouns/adjectives: βάθος, μέστος, πλήρης, πλήρωμα, πλοῦτος, etc.). (2) The nominal genitive of content is distinct from
the genitive of material in that content indicates the item contained
while material indicates the material made out of. The figure below
illustrates this difference.

---

[57] The adjectives χρύσουν, ἀργύρουν, and λίθουν τιμίουν are found, respectively, for
χρυσοῦ, ἀργύρου, λίθου, τιμίου in C P *et pauci*.

[58] In reality, most of the time the head noun/adjective will already indicate this lexical meaning.

[59] Most grammars treat the verbal type under gen. direct object (with verbs of filling).
Though that is an equally valid location, to list it only there would not be as helpful (since
it is an important category, in its own right, exegetically as well as syntactically).

[60] For the nominal usage, "the word to which the genitive is related implies a quantity
or amount of the thing in the genitive, rather than being a container which is actually containing something" (Williams, *Grammar Notes*, 6).

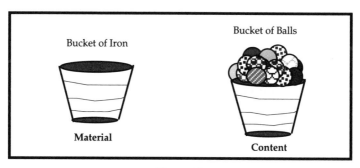

Figure 10
Genitive of Content Vs. Genitive of Material

d. Semantics

For the *nominal* use, the genitive term bears the brunt of the semantic weight. It is the important word rather than the head noun. Typically this construction is used in figurative language as a rhetorical device.[61]

The important thing to remember for the *verbal* use is that *in Greek the genitive, rather than the dative, is the case used to indicate the content of a verb.* Thus although the dative can frequently be translated "with," when a verb of filling is used, it is vital to examine the Greek text to see whether a genitive or dative substantive follows. If it is genitive, the translation "with" is appropriate; if a dative, some other translation (such as "by, in, because of") better reflects the Greek idiom–because *the dative case does not, as a rule, indicate the content of the verb.*[62]

e. Illustrations

1) Nominal Genitive of Content

John 21:8   τὸ δίκτυον **τῶν ἰχθύων**
the net [**full**] **of fish**

Acts 6:3   ἄνδρας . . . ἑπτὰ πλήρεις **πνεύματος** καὶ **σοφίας**
seven men full **of** [the] **Spirit** and **wisdom**
     Here the genitives of content are related to an adjective.

Col 2:3   πάντες οἱ θησαυροὶ **τῆς σοφίας** καὶ **γνώσεως**
all the treasures **of wisdom** and **knowledge**

---

[61] Williams, *Grammar Notes*, 6.

[62] There are only three or four places in the NT in which a *naked* dat. is used for content (one of which has the gen. for a variant [cf. Luke 2:40, discussed below]). There are apparently no instances of ἐν + dat. for content in biblical Greek after πληρόω. One of the most misunderstood passages in the NT is Eph 5:18, where πληρόω is followed by (ἐν) πνεύματι. A typical translation is "be filled with the Spirit" which implies that the Spirit is the content of the filling. But this is highly suspect from the Greek point of view. See later discussion under the preposition ἐν.

Col 2:9   ἐν αὐτῷ κατοικεῖ πᾶν τὸ πλήρωμα **τῆς θεότητος** σωματικῶς

             in him dwells all the fulness **of deity** bodily

Cf. also Rom 11:33; 2 Cor 8:2.

2) Verbal Genitive of Content

Luke 2:40   τὸ δὲ παιδίον ηὔξανεν καὶ ἐκραταιοῦτο πληρούμενον **σοφίας**[63]

             now the child continued to grow and become strong, (being)
             filled **with wisdom** (or full **of wisdom**)

Luke 4:28   ἐπλήσθησαν πάντες **θυμοῦ** ἐν τῇ συναγωγῇ

             all in the synagogue were filled **with anger**

John 6:13   ἐγέμισαν δώδεκα κοφίνους **κλασμάτων**

             they filled twelve baskets **with fragments**

Acts 2:4   ἐπλήσθησαν πάντες **πνεύματος** ἁγίου, καὶ ἤρξαντο λαλεῖν ἑτέραις
             γλώσσαις

             all were filled **with the** Holy **Spirit** and they began to speak in other
             tongues

> It is to be noted that neither the verb nor the case following the verb are
> the same as in Eph 5:18 (here, πίμπλημι; there, πληρόω; here, gen.; there,
> [ἐν +] dat.). The command there to be filled by the Spirit has nothing to
> do with tongues-speaking. The Spirit-filling (with πίμπλημι) in Acts is
> never commanded, nor is it related particularly to sanctification.
> Rather, it is a special imbueing of the Spirit for a particular task (similar
> to the Spirit's ministry in the OT). Furthermore, every time the case
> used to indicate the content of filling is the gen., never the dat. Cf. Acts
> 4:8, 31; 9:17; 13:9 (cf. also Luke 1:15, 41).

Cf. also Luke 6:11; Acts 3:10; 5:17; 13:45; 19:29.

➡ ## 9. *Genitive in Simple Apposition*

See following section for a discussion of this genitive use and genitive of
apposition. The two need to be distinguished carefully. (It should be noted
the gen. in simple apposition is a legitimate category, but because of confusion over its semantics we are treating it in the next section.) Simple apposition requires that both nouns be in the same case (whether nom., gen., dat.,
acc., voc.), while the genitive of apposition requires only the second noun to
be in the genitive case. If the syntax of the sentence requires the head noun
to be in the genitive, a possibility of confusion between these two appositional uses results.

---

[63] σοφίας is the reading found in ℵ* A D Θ X Γ Δ Λ Π *f*[1, 13] *Byz*; σοφίᾳ is found in ℵ[c] B
L W Ψ 33 *et pauci*.

→ **10. *Genitive of Apposition (Epexegetical Genitive, Genitive of Definition)***

This use of the genitive is fairly common, though largely misunderstood. It is sometimes lumped in together with the genitive of content or the genitive of material, though there are legitimate semantic differences among all three categories. It is also often confused with the genitive in simple apposition.

a. **Definition**

The substantive in the genitive case refers to the same thing as the substantive to which it is related. The equation, however, is not exact. The genitive of apposition typically states a specific example that is a part of the larger category named by the head noun. It is frequently used when the head noun is ambiguous or metaphorical (hence the name "epexegetical genitive" is quite appropriate).

b. **Key to Identification (*which is, who is*)**

Every genitive of apposition, like most genitive uses, can be translated with *of* + the genitive noun. To test whether the genitive in question is a genitive of apposition, replace the word *of* with the paraphrase *which is* or *that is, namely*, or, if a personal noun, *who is*. If it does not make the same sense, a genitive of apposition is unlikely; if it does make the same sense, a genitive of apposition is likely.[64]

c. **Semantics: Genitive of Apposition Distinct from Simple Apposition**

1) **Expanded Definitions**

These two uses of the genitive can easily get confused: whenever the head noun to which the genitive is related is also in the genitive case, and apposition is suspected, which *kind* of appositional genitive is it? This is not merely an academic question. There is a significant semantic difference between a genitive of apposition and a genitive in simple apposition—hence it is important to decipher such genitive constructions and try to determine which use is involved.

a) As we have said, in a *genitive of apposition* construction, the head noun: (1) will state a large category, (2) will be ambiguous, or (3) will be metaphorical in its meaning, while the genitive names a concrete or specific example that either falls *within* that category, clarifies its ambiguity, or brings the metaphor down to earth:

1) "the land of Egypt" (category-example)

2) "the sign of circumcision" (ambiguity-clarification)

3) "the breastplate of righteousness" (metaphor-meaning)

---

[64] The next step, of course, is to analyze this and other possibilities by way of sound exegesis.

Indeed, one of the chief reasons to identify a particular genitive as a genitive of apposition is that it is related to a noun which begs to be defined. The ambiguity of the head noun is forcefully dissipated with the genitive. But the reason for an author using the head noun in the first place becomes clear: the collocation of the two nouns often suggests provocative imagery ("the breastplate of righteousness," "the down payment of the Spirit," "the temple of his body") which would be the poorer if the genitive simply replaced the head noun. Thus, the two nouns stand in symbiotic relation: they need each other if both clarification and connotation are to take place!

b) In *simple apposition*, however, both nouns are in the same case and the appositive does *not* name a specific example that falls within the category named by the noun to which it is related. Rather, it simply gives a different designation that either clarifies who is the one named or shows a different relation to the rest of the clause than what the first noun by itself could display. Both words thus have the same referent, though they describe it in different terms.

For example, in "Paul the apostle," "the apostle" is in simple apposition to "Paul." The appositive clarifies who is the one named. In "God, our Father," "Father" is in simple apposition to "God" and shows a different relation to the rest of the clause than the first noun by itself could display.

2) Embedded Equative Clauses

As we saw in the introduction to the genitive case, there is value in unpacking the $N\text{-}N_g$ construction, so as to see the larger phrase or clause that this embedded construction represents. With the appositional genitives (both kinds), generally speaking, the two kinds of *subject-predicate nominative* constructions are represented.[65]

In a *genitive of apposition* construction, the genitive is semantically equivalent to a subject that designates a particular belonging to a larger group (predicate nominative). Thus, "the sign of circumcision" can be unpacked as "circumcision is a sign" (but not "a sign is circumcision"). In this example, the lexical field of "sign" is much larger than that for "circumcision."[66]

For a *genitive in simple apposition* the two nouns are equivalent to a convertible proposition. Thus, "Paul the apostle" could be unpacked as "Paul is the apostle" or "the apostle is Paul."

---

[65] See chapter on the nominative case under "Predicate Nominative" for discussion.

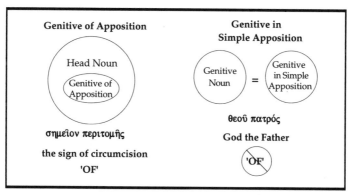

Chart 11
Genitive of Apposition Vs. Genitive in Simple Apposition

In light of these genuine semantic differences, it becomes evident that a genitive of apposition will not occur when both nouns are personal. "The apostle of Paul" does not mean the same thing as "the apostle is Paul." We will see the value of this distinction when we explore exegetically significant texts.

d. Simplification

Our discussion of the genitive of apposition has been unusually lengthy. It may be helpful, therefore, to simplify this discussion by giving a two-step procedure by which to determine whether a particular genitive fits this category.

1) Appositional Genitive vs. another Genitive Use

By "appositional genitive" we mean *both* kinds of apposition (simple and gen. of apposition). The first thing to determine, of course,

---

[66] Further analysis along the lines of an embedded sentence suggest two kinds of gen. of apposition. One kind is related to a "nominal" noun and the other to a "verbal" noun. For example, "the city of Jerusalem" (nominal) can only represent one kind of sentence, viz., one involving a subject and predicate nom. ("Jerusalem is a city"). But "the sign of circumcision" (verbal) can represent either an equative sentence ("circumcision is a sign") or a transitive sentence ("circumcision signifies"). The nominal use seems to be rarer than the verbal use.

The nominal construction differs very little (in terms of its semantic force) from the gen. in simple apposition: "the city of Jerusalem" can be converted to "Jerusalem, the city" with relative ease, while "the down payment of the Spirit" does not as naturally become "the Spirit, the down payment." (*BDF* §167 suggest that "The gen. [of apposition] of the names of cities is seldom found in class., and then nearly always in poetry...." They cite 2 Pet 2:6 as the only legitimate instance of this in the NT [which text even some grammarians dispute].) In such examples, the issue is related to the ambiguity/figurative language of the head noun: the referent of "city" in a given context would be quite clear, while "down payment," "gift," "sign," etc. would need to be explained by the following gen. In general, such vague head nouns will be verbal, but occasionally a nominal head noun will also be vague (cf., e.g., John 2:21).

is whether one of the appositional uses is applicable. To do this, insert "which is," "namely," or "who is" between the head noun and the genitive noun. If this makes sense, an appositional genitive is likely.

2) Genitive of Apposition vs. Simple Apposition

Both will fit the "which is" formula so another test needs to be used to distinguish the two. If the word "of" can be used before the genitive in question, then it is a genitive of apposition. If it cannot, then it is simple apposition related to another genitive. (Keep in mind that the only time there could be any confusion is when both head noun and genitive noun are in the same case, but this does occur frequently.)

e. Illustrations

1) Clear Examples

a) Of a Genitive of Apposition

Luke 22:1   ἡ ἑορτὴ **τῶν ἀζύμων**
the feast **of unleavened bread**
(="the feast, **namely** [the festival] **of unleavened bread**"[67])

John 2:21   ἔλεγεν περὶ τοῦ ναοῦ **τοῦ σώματος** αὐτοῦ
he was speaking concerning the temple **of** his **body** (= "the temple, **which is** his **body**")

> Here the gen. of apposition is related to another gen. Thus there is the *structural* possibility of it being simple apposition. However, it fits the translation "of. . .", rendering simple apposition out of the question.
>
> Exegetically, John 2:19-21, culminating in this verse, is triply significant. First, it clearly indicates that the NT viewed the resurrection of Christ as a *bodily* resurrection.[68] Second, Jesus is here represented as an *agent* of his own resurrection. The NT thus speaks of the entire Trinity as participants in Christ's resurrection (cf. Eph 1:20; 1 Pet 3:18). Third, the reason for the collocation of "temple" with "body" thus becomes clear: the Shekinah glory, which had long ago departed from the temple, now resides in Jesus bodily.[69]

---

[67] Cf. *BDF* §141.3; BAGD, s.v. ἄζυμος 1.b.

[68] Occasionally the view is suggested that the gen. is possessive rather than appositional. If so, the temple would belong to the Lord's body. The resultant meaning could be other than a bodily resurrection. But such a view not only ignores the semantic situation of the gen. of apposition (viz., related to a metaphorical or vague head noun), but also wreaks havoc with the imagery: a temple is not itself *housed*–it is the house that contains the Shekinah glory.

[69] Significantly, this theme of God's glory in the "body" is developed by more than one author in the NT–and in two directions: first, with reference to Christ (cf., e.g., John 1:14; Col 2:9); second, with reference to those who are "in Christ" (cf. 1 Cor 6:19; Eph 2:20-22).

Rom 4:11   καὶ σημεῖον ἔλαβεν **περιτομῆς**[70]
            and he received [the] sign **of circumcision** (= "the sign, **which is
            circumcision**")

2 Pet 2:6   πόλεις **Σοδόμων** καὶ **Γομόρρας**
            the cities **of Sodom** and **Gomorrah**

Rev 1:3   τοὺς λόγους **τῆς προφητείας**
            the words **of the prophecy**

Cf. also Luke 2:41; John 11:13; 13:1; Acts 2:33; 2 Cor 1:22; 5:5; Eph 1:14; Rev 14:10.

b) Of Simple Apposition

Matt 2:11   εἶδον τὸ παιδίον μετὰ Μαρίας **τῆς μητρὸς** αὐτοῦ
            they saw the child with Mary, his **mother**

Eph 1:2   χάρις ὑμῖν καὶ εἰρήνη ἀπὸ θεοῦ **πατρὸς** ἡμῶν
            grace to you and peace from God our **Father**
            > If "of" were placed before "Father" the idea would be "from the God **of**
            > our Father"! It is obviously simple apposition here.

Col 1:18   αὐτός ἐστιν ἡ κεφαλὴ τοῦ σώματος, **τῆς ἐκκλησίας**
            he is the head of the body, **the church**

Titus 2:13 σωτῆρος ἡμῶν **Ἰησοῦ Χριστοῦ**
            our Savior, **Jesus Christ**
            > This is, again, obviously not a gen. of apposition, for the translation
            > "our Savior of Jesus Christ"/"the Savior of our Jesus Christ" is quite
            > different from that given above (and, of course, foreign to the NT)!

Cf. also Matt 2:1; Mark 6:17; Luke 3:4; John 7:42; Acts 22:20; Rom 5:17.[71]

2) Debatable (and Exegetically Significant) Examples

Eph 4:9   τὸ δὲ Ἀνέβη τί ἐστιν εἰ μὴ ὅτι καὶ κατέβη εἰς τὰ κατώτερα μέρη **τῆς γῆς**
            now the statement "he ascended"–what does it mean except that he
            also descended into the lower parts **of the earth**?
            > "Of the earth" is popularly taken to be a partitive gen. However, it may
            > well be a gen. of apposition, thus, "he descended into the lower parts
            > [of the universe], that is, the earth." At first glance this second option
            > seems awkward because the noun to which the singular gen. is related
            > is *plural*. However, it is a common idiom for a singular gen. of apposi-
            > tion to be related to μέρη (plural)–cf. Isa 9:1 (LXX); Matt 2:22. In such
            > constructions it seems that there is a *partitive* gen. that needs to be sup-
            > plied from the context (as seems to be the case in Eph 4:9). For example,
            > in Matt 2:22 we read ἀνεχώρησεν εἰς τὰ μέρη τῆς Γαλιλαίας. The transla-
            > tion might either be "he departed for the regions [of Israel], namely,

---

[70] The acc. περιτομήν is found in a few MSS (A C* 1506 1739 1881 *pc*), turning the construction into an object-complement ("he received circumcision as a sign").

[71] A common instance of simple apposition (in any case) is that of an anarthrous
proper name followed by an arthrous descriptive noun. Many of our examples are of this
sort.

Galilee" or, "he departed for the regions that constitute Galilee." Thus since the gen. of apposition occurs in the singular related to the plural μέρη as a *geographical* term, there is sufficient grammatical evidence to see it used in Eph 4:9. (For other examples of this phenomenon, cf. Matt 15:21; 16:13; Mark 8:10; Acts 2:10.)

The difference between the partitive gen. and the gen. of apposition in this text is no less than the difference between a descent at the Lord's *death* into hell and a descent at his *incarnation* to the earth.[72] Grammar certainly will not solve this problem, but it at least opens up the interpretive possibilities.[73]

Cf. also Eph 2:2 (in which the πνεύματος is sometimes incorrectly taken as a gen. of apposition to ἄρχοντα).[74] Eph 2:20 also has a possible gen. of apposition (τῷ θεμελίῳ τῶν ἀποστόλων καὶ προφητῶν), though the gen. construction may be subjective.[75] Cf. also Col 1:5, 13.

11. *Genitive of Destination (a. k. a. Direction) or Purpose [destined for, toward]*

a. Definition

The genitive substantive indicates where the head noun is going (or the direction it is "moving" in) or the purpose of its existence.[76] This is a somewhat rare category.

b. Key to Identification

For the word *of* supply the paraphrase *for the purpose of, destined for, toward,* or *into.*

c. Amplification

Technically, there are really two subgroups that share the idea of movement toward an end. The direction of a particular person or thing is not necessarily purposed, such as in "The car's brakes accidentally released

---

[72] Another interpretation (which has much to commend it) based on a gen. of apposition is that the descent occurs *after* the ascent and, hence, is the descent of the Spirit on the day of Pentecost. Cf. W. Hall Harris III, "The Ascent and Descent of Christ in Ephesians 4:9-10,"*BSac* 151 (1994) 198-214.

[73] It could also be noted that the gen. of apposition is a mark of the author's style in Ephesians, occurring over a dozen times (cf. Harris, "Ephesians 4:9-10,"204, for a complete list).

[74] Recall that a gen. of apposition never involves two personal nouns. "The ruler of the spirit" does not mean "the ruler who is the spirit." Most likely, the gen. use is that of subordination ("the ruler **over** the spirit"). See later discussion of this category.

[75] The fact that the gen. nouns and not the head noun are personal does not deny the possibility of an appositional gen. here.

[76] *BDF,* 92 (§166) list John 10:7 (ἡ θύρα τῶν προβάτων) as an example, but since doors don't move off their hinges this is doubtful. The idea is "the door that opens for the sheep," where the collocation of head noun and gen. noun implies a certain verbal notion (see discussion under 2 Cor 6:2 in "Descriptive Genitive," above).

and it rolled off the cliff *toward* the sea." This sentence does not mean "it rolled off the cliff *for the purpose of going into* the sea," but the gloss *"destined for, in the direction of"* would fit nicely.

Thus, one kind involves intention, the other mere direction (or sometimes even tendency).

d. Illustrations

1) Clear Examples

Rom 8:36 ἐλογίσθημεν ὡς πρόβατα **σφαγῆς**
we were regarded as sheep **destined for slaughter**

Gal 2:7 πεπίστευμαι τὸ εὐαγγέλιον **τῆς ἀκροβυστίας** καθὼς Πέτρος **τῆς περιτομῆς**
I have been entrusted with the gospel **for the uncircimcision,** just as Peter [has been entrusted with the gospel] **for the circumcision**

Cf. also Matt 10:5; Heb 9:8.

2) Debatable Examples

John 5:29 ἀνάστασιν **ζωῆς**. . . ἀνάστασιν **κρίσεως**
resurrection **of life**. . . resurrection **of judgment**
> Here the genitives seem to express both purpose and *result*–thus, "the resurrection for the purpose of and which results in life/judgment." The gloss that seems to encompass both ideas is "the resurrection *that leads to* life/judgment."[77]

Acts 16:17 οὗτοι οἱ ἄνθρωποι . . . καταγγέλλουσιν ὑμῖν ὁδὸν **σωτηρίας**
these men . . . are proclaiming to you the way **that leads to salvation**

Rom 9:22 σκεύη **ὀργῆς** κατηρτισμένα εἰς ἀπώλειαν
vessels **of wrath**, prepared for destruction (= "vessels **destined for wrath**")
> Some view the gen. as merely descriptive or attributive, but the parallel with "prepared for destruction" seems to indicate in the least that these vessels were destined for destruction.[78] More may be implied, depending on whether the participle κατηρτισμένα is middle or passive.

Eph 2:3 καὶ ἤμεθα τέκνα φύσει **ὀργῆς** ὡς καὶ οἱ λοιποί·
and we were children **of wrath** (= "children **destined for wrath**"), even as the rest
> The point of the text, in light of 2:1-10, is not to describe humanity in terms of attributes (such as wrathful children), but to speak of the hopeless situation of those who were without Christ.

---

[77] Cf. *BDF*, 92 (§166).

[78] Further, the evidence within the Pauline corpus is that ὀργή frequently has a particularly eschatological tinge to it, especially in Romans (cf. Rom 2:5, 8; 3:5; 5:9; Eph 5:6; Col 3:6; 1 Thess 1:10; 5:9).

12. Predicate Genitive

a. Definition

The genitive substantive makes an assertion about another genitive substantive, much like a predicate nominative does. The difference, however, is that with the predicate genitive the equative verb is a participle (in the gen. case) rather than a finite verb. This category is relatively uncommon.

b. Key to Identification: see definition

c. Clarification and Significance

This kind of genitive is in reality an *emphatic kind of simple apposition* in the genitive (emphatic due to the presence of the participial form of the equative verb).[79] Both adjectival participles and the genitive absolute participle (which is always circumstantial) can be used in this way.

d. Illustrations

Acts 1:12   ὄρους τοῦ καλουμένου **Ἐλαιῶνος**
             [the] mountain which is called "**Olivet**"

Acts 7:58   νεανίου καλουμένου **Σαύλου**
             a young man called **Saul**

Rom 5:8   ἔτι **ἁμαρτωλῶν** ὄντων ἡμῶν Χριστὸς ὑπὲρ ἡμῶν ἀπέθανεν
             while we were yet **sinners** Christ died for us
                 This is an instance of a gen. absolute construction that involves an
                 equative verb as participle.[80]

Eph 2:20   ὄντος **ἀκρογωνιαίου** αὐτοῦ Χριστοῦ Ἰησοῦ
             Christ Jesus himself being **the chief cornerstone**
                 This is another gen. absolute construction.

Cf. also John 4:9; Acts 18:12;[81] Acts 21:8.[82]

---

[79] Note from some of the examples that follow that this equative verb will not necessarily be a form of εἰμί (just as is true with predicate nominatives).

[80] It should also be noted that the same rules for distinguishing S from PN seem to apply to this construction. The apparent exceptions in Acts 1:12 and 7:58 fall under our general rule that when something is *named*, the proper name is the predicate noun.

[81] This also is a gen. absolute construction.

[82] In this instance the predicate gen. (ἑνός) needs to be supplied.

13. Genitive of Subordination [over]

a. Definition

The genitive substantive specifies that which is subordinated to or under the dominion of the head noun.

b. Key to Identification

Instead of *of* supply the gloss *over* or something like it that suggests dominion or priority.

c. Amplification/Semantics

This kind of genitive is a lexico-semantic category. That is, it is related only to certain kinds of head substantives–nouns (or participles) that lexically imply some kind of rule or authority. Words such as βασιλεύς and ἄρχων routinely belong here. For the most part, this genitive is a subset of the objective genitive,[83] but not always.[84]

d. Illustrations

1) Clear Examples

Matt 9:34   τῷ ἄρχοντι **τῶν δαιμονίων**
            the ruler **over the demons**

Mark 15:32   ὁ βασιλεὺς **Ἰσραήλ**
            the king **over Israel**

2 Cor 4:4   ὁ θεὸς **τοῦ αἰῶνος τούτου**
            the god **of this world**

Cf. also John 12:31; Acts 4:26; Rev 1:5; 15:3.

2) Disputed Examples

1 Tim 1:17   τῷ δὲ βασιλεῖ **τῶν αἰώνων**
            now to the king **of the ages** (=the one who rules **over the ages**)
              The problem with taking this as attributive (as ASV *et al.* do) is that the

---

[83] For this reason, most likely, such a category is not to be found in standard grammars.

[84] When the head noun does not imply a verbal idea, the gen. of subordination parts company from the objective gen.

A further subset of the gen. of subordination category might be "the genitive in relation to a *par excellence* noun" (though, at times, the nuances depart some from the subordination notion). That is, rarely a gen. indicates the class of which the head noun is the supreme member. When this occurs, both head noun and gen. noun have the *same lexeme*. For example, note βασιλεὺς βασιλέων in Rev 19:16; ἅγια ἁγίων in Heb 9:3 (where the meaning is *not* strictly speaking that of subordination, just *par excellence*); cf. also Rev 17:14. Acts 23:6 is similar ("a Pharisee, son of a Pharisee"), as is Phil 3:5 ("a Hebrew of Hebrews," though the usage here is with ἐκ).

gen. is plural. However, if it were put in the singular, the meaning would not be "eternal king" ("king of the age" would be a temporal king). RSV, NRSV treat it as a gen. of subordination–"king of the ages."[85]

Eph 2:2   ποτε περιεπατήσατε . . . κατὰ τὸν ἄρχοντα **τῆς ἐξουσίας** τοῦ ἀέρος, **τοῦ πνεύματος** τοῦ νῦν ἐνεργοῦντος ἐν τοῖς υἱοῖς τῆς ἀπειθείας

you formerly walked according to the ruler **of the domain** of the air, [the ruler] **of the spirit** which now works in the sons of disobedience

> The semantic force of subordination here would be "the one who rules **over the domain** of the air, **over the spirit** . . ." Although some take πνεύματος as a gen. of apposition to ἄρχοντα, this is semantically impossible because such cannot occur when both nouns are personal.[86] (See discussion under gen. of apposition, mentioned above.) The idea of this text, then, is that the devil controls non-believers both externally (the environment or domain of the air) and internally (attitudes or spirit).

Col 1:15   ὅς ἐστιν εἰκὼν τοῦ θεοῦ τοῦ ἀοράτου, πρωτότοκος πάσης **κτίσεως**

who is the image of the invisible God, the firstborn **over** all **creation**

> Though some regard this gen. to be partitive (thus, firstborn who is a part of creation), both due to the lexical field of "firstborn" including "preeminent over"[87] (and not just a literal chronological birth order) and the following causal clause ("for [ὅτι] in him all things were created")–which makes little sense if mere chronological order is in view, it is far more likely that this expresses subordination. Further, although most examples of subordination involve a verbal head noun, not all do (notice 2 Cor 4:4 above, as well as Acts 13:17). The resultant meaning seems to be an early confession of Christ's lordship and hence, implicitly, his deity.

14. *Genitive of Production/Producer [produced by]*[88]

a.   Definition

The genitive substantive *produces* the noun to which it stands related. This usage of the genitive is not common.

---

[85] See earlier discussion under attributive gen. (thus "eternal king"). The question is whether innate character or actual domain is emphasized. The gen. is elastic enough to include both; perhaps the expression was left in the gen. for this very reason, as a sort of pregnant gen.

[86] It is true that in our view both nouns are not personal (since we are treating "spirit" as an internal attitude), but the appositional view does treat both as personal, for it equates "ruler" with "spirit."

[87] Cf. the theological statements to this effect in 1 Chron 5:1; Ps 89:27; Rom 8:29; Rev 1:5.

[88] Thanks are due to Jo Ann Pulliam for her work in Advanced Greek Grammar at Dallas Seminary in 1994 on the genitives of production and product.

b. **Key to Identification**

For the word *of* supply *produced by.*

c. **Amplification**

This usage is similar to a subjective genitive, but the genitive of production is either not related to a verbal noun or expresses a relation to a verbal noun that is better translated as "produced by" than by converting the genitive into the subject and converting the noun to which it stands related into a verbal form.[89]

It is also similar to a genitive of source, but tends to involve a more active role on the part of the genitive. Thus, "angel from heaven" (source) simply indicates the source or origin from which the angel came. But "peace of God" suggests both source and involvement on the part of God.

d. **Illustrations (possible)**

Eph 4:3   τὴν ἑνότητα **τοῦ πνεύματος**
the unity **of the Spirit**
> Here, "the unity of the Spirit" probably = "the unity produced by the Spirit." Although the gen. is related to a verbal noun, it would lose some of its force to say, "[by being diligent to maintain] what the Spirit unites." Thus, to call τοῦ πνεύματος a subjective gen. does not seem to do full justice to the author's thought here.

Phil 2:8   θανάτου δὲ **σταυροῦ**
even death **of a cross**
> σταυροῦ may be a gen. of means; thus, "death by means of a cross." Or it may possibly be a gen. of place; thus, "death on a cross." However, to take it as a gen. of production brings out the force of the author's thought a little better: "death produced by, brought about by a cross." The δέ makes the statement emphatic ("even"),[90] which fits well with a gen. of production.

Eph 5:9   ὁ γὰρ καρπὸς **τοῦ φωτὸς** ἐν πάσῃ ἀγαθωσύνῃ . . .
for the fruit **of the light**[91] consists in all goodness . . .
> Fruit produced by the light seems to fit well in this context where the light imagery seems to involve the status of salvation.

---

[89] Most scholars treat what we are calling a gen. of producer as a subjective gen., but the semantics are not quite the same. With a subjective gen., the head noun is transformed into a verb; with a gen. of producer, the head noun is transformed into the direct object of the verb "who produces." Thus, if "unity of the Spirit" becomes "the Spirit produces unity," the gen. is producer rather than subjective. Other scholars would not differentiate this category from source or origin. (The discussion of this category is admittedly in seminal form.)

[90] In fact so emphatic that some felt that this one phrase ruined the meter of this hymn (cf. J. Jeremias, "Zur Gedankenführung in den paulinischen Briefen,"*Studia Paulina in Honorem J. de Zwaan,* ed. J. N. Sevenster and W. C. van Unnik [Haarlem, 1953] 146-54)! If so, it is most likely a point added by Paul to the original hymn, adapting it for the sake of his present audience.

[91] Several MSS have "fruit of the Spirit" (καρπὸς τοῦ πνεύματος) here (e.g., 𝔓⁴⁶ Dᶜ Ψ *Byz et alii*).

Phil 4:7   καὶ ἡ εἰρήνη **τοῦ θεοῦ** ἡ ὑπερέχουσα πάντα νοῦν φρουρήσει τὰς καρδίας
            ὑμῶν[92]

and the peace **of God** which surpasses all understanding will guard
your hearts

> Although this could be an attributed gen. (thus, "peacemaking God"),
> in this context it is doubtful, for it is obvious that God surpasses all
> understanding (further, that point is later made in v 9 [ὁ θεὸς τῆς
> εἰρήνης]). Subjective will not do for it is the entity, peace, not the act of
> making it, which is in view. And a gen. of source, though certainly pos-
> sible, typically does not imply the element of volition which is seen
> here. The thought of production is: "the peace produced by God."

Cf. also Rom 1:5 (perhaps); 4:11; Gal 3:13 (perhaps); 5:22; 1 Thess 1:3.

15. Genitive of Product [which produces]

a. Definition

The genitive substantive is the *product* of the noun to which it stands
related. Frequently θεός will be the head noun and the genitive an
abstract term. This category is similar to an objective genitive, but
whereas with the objective genitive the head noun is to be converted into
a *verb*, the head noun in this construction remains a noun. The verbal
idea is implied from the *of*. This usage of the genitive is not common.

b. Key to Identification

For the word *of* supply the words *which produces*.

c. Illustrations

1) Clear Examples

Rom 15:13   ὁ θεὸς **τῆς ἐλπίδος**

the God **of hope**

> Obviously, attributive gen. will not do ("the hopeful God"?), nor will
> objective gen., for that would turn the head noun into a verb. "The God
> *who produces* hope [in us]" makes excellent sense.

Rom 15:33   ὁ δὲ θεὸς **τῆς εἰρήνης** μετὰ πάντων ὑμῶν

now may the God **of peace** be with you all

> =Now may the God who produces peace [in you] be with you all.

Cf. also Rom 16:20.

---

[92] Χριστοῦ is found for θεοῦ in A *pc*. The grammatical point is not affected by this,
however.

2) Possible Examples

Rom 15:5 ὁ θεὸς τῆς ὑπομονῆς καὶ τῆς παρακλήσεως
the God **of steadfastness** and **of encouragement**

> Although this text might involve two attributive genitives, such would have to be carefully nuanced: the steadfast and encouraging God (as opposed to encouraged God).[93] Further, if God is encouraging, this implies a verbal idea: he is the God who *produces* encouragement in us. The syntactic parallels between the two genitives thus suggests that τῆς ὑπομονῆς means "[the God who] *produces perseverance* in us." (What may be significant is the fact that θεός is used thrice in Romans 15 with a gen. modifier, each time in what appears to be a gen. of product construction.)

Heb 1:9 ἔλαιον **ἀγαλλιάσεως**
oil **of gladness**

> It *may* be possible that the author is conceiving of the oil as that which produces gladness (or, perhaps, the oil produced by gladness–a gen. of production). When half of the expression under study is metaphorical, grammatical decisions are notoriously difficult. Hence, many simply park this in the black hole of the descriptive gen.

Cf. also 1 Cor 14:33; 2 Cor 13:11; Phil 4:9.[94]

B. Ablatival Genitive

The ablatival genitive basically involves the notion of separation. (Though frequently translated *from*, such a gloss will not work for the genitive of comparison, which requires *than* as its gloss). This idea can be static (i.e., in a separated state) or progressive (movement away from, so as to become separated). The emphasis may be on either the state resulting from the separation or the cause of separation (in the latter, origin or source is emphasized). For the most part, the ablatival genitive is being replaced in Koine Greek by ἐκ or ἀπό with the genitive.[95]

1. Genitive of Separation [out of, away from, from]

a. Definition

> The genitive substantive is that from which the *verb* or sometimes head noun is separated. Thus the genitive is used to indicate the point of departure. This usage is rare in the NT.

---

[93] See previous discussion about active and passive ideas for attributive genitives.

[94] Cf. also ὕδατος² in John 4:14 as another possible example (though here the gen. may be material or content, depending on the lexical force of πηγή in this context).

[95] For more detailed treatment, see the introduction to this chapter.

b. Key to Identification

For the word *of* supply the words *out of, away from,* or *from.* Another key is to note that *usually* this genitive will be dependent on a verb (or verbal form) rather than a noun.

c. Amplification/Semantics

1) In classical Greek, the idea of separation was found frequently enough with the simple genitive. In Koine Greek, however, the idea of separation was increasingly made more explicit by the presence of the preposition ἀπό or sometimes ἐκ.[96] Hence, a genitive of separation will be rare in the NT, while the preposition ἀπό (or ἐκ) + genitive will be somewhat commonly used for separation.[97]

2) This is a lexico-syntactic category: it is determined by the lexical meaning of the word to which the genitive is related. Only if that word, usually a verb, connotes motion away from, distance, or separation can the genitive be one of separation.[98]

3) The notion of separation may be physical (spatial) or metaphorical. The first example below is spatial, the second is metaphorical.

d. Illustrations

Matt 10:14   ἐκτινάξατε τὸν κονιορτὸν **τῶν ποδῶν** ὑμῶν[99]
shake the dust **from** your **feet**

Acts 15:29   ἀπέχεσθαι **εἰδωλοθύτων** καὶ **αἵματος** καὶ **πνικτῶν** καὶ **πορνείας**
[that you should] abstain **from things offered to idols** and **from blood** and **from things strangled** and **from fornication**

Eph 2:12   ἀπηλλοτριωμένοι **τῆς πολιτείας** τοῦ Ἰσραήλ
having been alienated **from the commonwealth** of Israel

1 Pet 3:21   καὶ ὑμᾶς . . . νῦν σῴζει βάπτισμα, οὐ **σαρκὸς** ἀπόθεσις ῥύπου
and baptism . . . now saves you–not as a removal of dirt **from the body**

> Here is an example in which the gen. separates from a head noun, though it has a verbal notion.

---

[96] This, of course, was in keeping with the tendency of the Koine toward greater explicitness and simplicity. Cf. the excellent and succinct treatment by Zerwick, *Biblical Greek,* 161-64 (§480-94).

[97] Cf. Heb 7:26, where even in the most literary Koine of the NT, ἀπό is used explicitly to indicate separation.

[98] See *BDF,* 97 (§180) for a list of frequently used verbs.

[99] ἐκ is found before τῶν ποδῶν in ℵ C 33 0281 892 *et pauci.* This is hardly surprising in light of the Koine tendency toward greater explicitness and away from the simple gen. to express an ablatival notion.

1 Pet 4:1 πέπαυται **ἁμαρτίας**[100]
he has ceased **from** [doing] **sin**

Cf. also Luke 2:37; Rom 1:4; 1 Cor 9:21; 15:41; Gal 5:7; Rev 8:5. Rom 1:17 might also fit, though this is debatable.

2. Genitive of Source (or Origin) [out of, derived from, dependent on]

a. Definition

The genitive substantive is the source from which the head noun derives or depends. This is a rare category in Koine Greek.

b. Key to Identification

For the word *of* supply the paraphrase *out of, derived from, dependent on,* or *"sourced in."*

c. Amplification

Again, as with the genitive of separation, the simple genitive is being replaced in Koine Greek by a prepositional phrase (in this instance, ἐκ + gen.) to indicate source. This corresponds to the fact that *source* is an emphatic idea: emphasis and explicitness often go hand in hand.

Since this usage is not common, it is not advisable to seek it as the most likely one for a particular genitive that may fit under another label. In some ways, the possessive, subjective, and source genitives are similar. In any given instance, if they all make good sense, subjective should be given priority. In cases where there is no verbal head noun, possessive still takes priority over source as an apt label. The distinction between source and separation, however, is more difficult to call. Frequently, it is a matter merely of emphasis: separation stresses result while source stresses cause.[101] (Some of the illustrations below could belong under either source or separation.)[102]

---

[100] ἁμαρτίας is found in 𝔓[72] ℵ* A C K L P 1739 *Byz;* ἁμαρτίαις is found in ℵ² B Ψ *et pauci;* ἀπὸ ἁμαρτίας is found in 1881 *pauci.*

[101] In this respect the two categories are analogous to the extensive perfect and the intensive perfect tenses.

[102] At the same time, the gen. of separation seems to be more common than the gen. of source. (This is also true in the prepositional constructions, for separation can be represented either by ἐκ or ἀπό, while source is usually restricted to ἐκ.)

d. Illustrations

Rom 9:16   οὐ **τοῦ θέλοντος** οὐδὲ **τοῦ τρέχοντος**, ἀλλὰ **τοῦ** ἐλεῶντος **θεοῦ**
             It is not **dependent on the one who wills** nor **on the one who runs**,
             but **on the God** who shows mercy

Rom 10:3   ἀγνοοῦντες τὴν **τοῦ θεοῦ** δικαιοσύνην
             being ignorant of the righteousness **that comes from God**

2 Cor 3:3   ἐστὲ ἐπιστολὴ **Χριστοῦ**
             you are a letter **from Christ**

Rev 9:11   ἔχουσιν ἐπ᾽ αὐτῶν βασιλέα τὸν ἄγγελον **τῆς ἀβύσσου**
             they have over them as king the angel **from the Abyss**

> It is possible that this is an attributive or descriptive gen., but gen. of
> source indicates origin more than character and hence seems more
> appropriate in this context.

Cf. also Rom 15:18, 22 (here, with an infinitive as the word in the gen.); 2 Cor 4:7; 11:26;
Col 2:19 (possible).

→ 3. *Genitive of Comparison [than]*

a. Definition

The genitive substantive, almost always after a comparative *adjective*, is
used to indicate comparison. The genitive, then, is the standard against
which the comparison is made (i.e., in "X is greater than Y," the gen. is
the Y). This usage is relatively common.

b. Key to Identification

The definition gives the key: a genitive after a *comparative* adjective,
which requires the word *than* before the genitive (instead of the usual *of*).

c. Amplification and Semantics

First, it should be noted that the comparative adjective will not be an
attributive adjective. That is, it will not be found in the construction article-adjective-noun.[103] Second, the comparison is *usually* made between
the known and the unknown, with the genitive substantive being the
known item. Sometimes, however, both quantities will be known, but an
explicit comparison between them involves a certain emphasis (whether
it be rhetorical, surprise, or an unusual collocation). Third, not every
instance of a comparative adjective (in predicate position) followed by a

---

[103] Although I have not done anything like an exhaustive study of this phenomenon
in extra-NT Greek, this is true in the NT. That it, *there are no clear cases of a genitive of comparison after an attributive adjective.* Semantically as well, such seems unlikely: in order for
the comparative adjective to make a comparison explicitly, it needs to assert something
about the noun it is related to–and thus it needs to be predicate, not attributive.

genitive will necessarily involve a comparative genitive,[104] in part because not every comparative adjective is functioning according to form: a comparative adjective may act like a superlative or an elative.[105] Finally, very rarely the genitive of comparison follows other than a comparative adjective (viz., a verb that lexically suggests comparison or a comparative *adverb*).

d. Illustrations

1) Clear Examples

Matt 6:25   οὐχὶ ἡ ψυχὴ πλεῖόν ἐστιν **τῆς τροφῆς;**
Is not your life worth more **than food**?

> Here the collocation of "life" with "food" has a powerful emotive effect: the response intended on the part of the hearer is something like, "Well, yes–my life is worth more than food! You mean that God knows this and wants to take care of me?"

Matt 10:31 **πολλῶν στρουθίων** διαφέρετε ὑμεῖς
you are worth more **than many sparrows**

> Here is an example with a verb rather than a comparative adjective. διαφέρω is perhaps the most commonly used verb with a gen. of comparison, though even it is rarely used.[106]

John 14:28 ὁ πατὴρ μείζων **μού** ἐστιν
the Father is greater **than I [am]**

> In this context, it is obvious that Jesus is speaking with reference to his office, not his person. That is, the Father has a greater rank, but the Son is no less deity than is the Father (cf. John 14:8). This is in line with one of the chief themes of the Fourth Gospel–to point out emphatically the deity of the Word.

John 20:4   ὁ ἄλλος μαθητὴς προέδραμεν τάχιον **τοῦ Πέτρου**
the other disciple ran more quickly **than Peter**

> This is a rare example of a gen. of comparison after a comparative *adverb*.

1 Cor 1:25 τὸ μωρὸν τοῦ θεοῦ σοφώτερον **τῶν ἀνθρώπων** ἐστίν
the foolishness of God is wiser **than men**

Heb 1:4   κρείττων γενόμενος **τῶν ἀγγέλων**
[the Son] having become better **than the angels**

Heb 7:26   ἀρχιερεύς . . . ὑψηλότερος **τῶν οὐρανῶν**
a high priest . . . higher **than the heavens**

---

[104] Cf., e.g., 1 Cor 12:23; 1 Cor 15:19 (partitive gen.); Phil 1:14 (partitive); Heb 3:3 (the comparative adjective *modifies* the gen. noun [there is a legitimate comparative gen. in this verse, too]; similarly, Heb 7:19, 22).

[105] See chapter on adjectives for discussion.

[106] Cf. Luke 12:7 (though v 24 adds the comparative adj.); perhaps 1 Cor 15:41 (but this is probably a gen. of separation); Gal 4:1.

1 Pet 1:7   τὸ δοκίμιον ὑμῶν τῆς πίστεως πολυτιμότερον **χρυσίου**
the genuineness of your faith which is much more precious **than gold**

> The comparative adjective relates back to "genuineness" (not faith *per se*)[107] and is thus a predicate adjective. The known quantity in this statement is the preciousness of gold–and a genuine faith is much more precious than that!
>
> Cf. also Heb 3:3; 11:26 (it is to be noticed that the comparative adjective plays a large role in Hebrews, for the theme is built around the idea that Christ is *better than* prophets, angels, the old covenant, Moses, etc.).

2) Disputed Examples

Mark 4:31   (=Matt 13:32)–cf. discussion under adjective.

Eph 4:9   τὸ δὲ Ἀνέβη τί ἐστιν εἰ μὴ ὅτι καὶ κατέβη εἰς τὰ κατώτερα μέρη **τῆς γῆς**
Now the statement "he ascended"–what does it mean except that he also descended into the lower parts **of the earth**?

> See our earlier discussion of this text under "Genitive of Apposition." Here we simply wish to point out that some scholars take the gen. as comparative–"he also descended into the parts lower *than the earth*."[108] Although a partitive gen. is possible and a gen. of apposition is likely, a comparative gen. is syntactically improbable, if not impossible: the comparative adjective is in *attributive* position to μέρη. If one were to ignore such a syntactical feature in, say, Matt 23:23, the meaning there would be "you have neglected the matters which are weightier *than the law*" (instead of "you have neglected the weightier matters *of the law*").[109]

C. Verbal Genitive
(i.e., Genitive Related to a Verbal Noun)

Although the subgroups under this category actually belong under "Adjectival Genitive," there are some advantages to placing these uses under a separate umbrella, the "Verbal Genitive." This is partially due to the fact that the objective and the subjective genitives are both crucial and confusing, but also due to the fact that included here is a category not normally listed in NT grammars.

The subjective, objective, and plenary genitives are used with head nouns that involve a verbal idea. That is, the head noun has a verb as a cognate (e.g., βασιλεῦς has βασιλεύω as cognate). The verbal genitive construction, then, is a sentence embed involving, typically, a transitive verbal idea in the head noun. The order below (subjective, objective, plenary) displays the descending order of frequency.

---

[107] At least not grammatically. But "genuineness of faith" = "genuine faith"–thus, an attributed gen. See earlier discussion.

[108] Cf., e.g., Meyer, *Ephesians* (MeyerK) 213; F. Büchsel, "κατώτερος,"*TDNT* 3.641-43. Turner, *Syntax*, 215, also entertains the possibility.

[109] ἀφήκατε τὰ βαρύτερα τοῦ νόμου. Cf. also Heb 6:9.

➡ 1. *Subjective Genitive*

a. Definition

The genitive substantive functions semantically as the subject of the verbal idea implicit in the head noun. This is common in the NT.

b. Key to Identification

If a subjective genitive is suspected, attempt to convert the verbal noun to which the genitive is related into a verbal form and turn the genitive into its subject. Thus, for example, "the revelation of Jesus Christ ..." in Gal 1:12 becomes "[What/the fact that] Jesus Christ reveals ..."

c. Semantics/Amplification

1) This category is lexico-syntactic–i.e., it is related to a *specific lexical meaning* for one of the words involved (in this case, the head noun). The head noun, which is here called a "verbal noun,"[110] must have an implicit verbal idea. Words such as "love," "hope," "revelation," "witness," and "word," can imply, in a given situation, a verbal idea. The perspective must, of course, be from Greek rather than English: "king," for example, has no verbal cognate in English (there is no verb "to king") but it does in Greek (βασιλεὺς has βασιλεύω).

2) The subjective genitive, by its very nature, can occur in more types of constructions than the objective genitive can. This is due to the semantic force of both: a subject can take a transitive or intransitive verb,[111] while an object can only be object of a transitive verb. Thus, in ἡ παρουσία τοῦ Χριστοῦ ("the coming of Christ") the genitive *cannot* be objective because the verbal idea is not transitive, but it can be subjective ("[when] Christ comes").[112]

3) Where objective and subjective genitives occur in the same constructions–therefore allowing for semantically opposite interpretations–the head noun implies a *transitive* verb. This is by far the more frequent type of verbal noun, however. In a given context, "love of God" could mean "[my/your/their] love for God" (objective) or "God's love for me [you/them]." Since the lexico-syntactic features in such instances are identical, appeal must be made to context, authorial usage, and broader exegetical issues.

See Chart 12 below for a diagram of both subjective and objective genitives.

---

[110] Not to be confused with an infinitive, which is *syntactically* a verbal noun. The expression as used here is a *lexical* title.

[111] It also can take an equative verb, but the subjective gen. will not be used in such constructions. Greek expresses such ideas with predicate genitives and with appositional genitives. (However, in Luke 9:43, for example, "the majesty of God" can be read as "how majestic God is.")

[112] For an exceptional usage, see discussion below under "Objective Genitive."

d. Illustrations

1) Clear Examples

Matt 24:27 οὕτως ἔσται ἡ παρουσία **τοῦ υἱοῦ** τοῦ ἀνθρώπου

so shall the coming **of the Son** of Man be (="so shall it be when the Son of Man comes").

Mark 14:59 οὐδὲ οὕτως ἴση ἦν ἡ μαρτυρία **αὐτῶν**

nor was **their** testimony thus the same (="nor did they testify the same thing")

Acts 12:11 ἐξείλατό με ἐκ χειρὸς Ἡρῴδου καὶ πάσης τῆς προσδοκίας **τοῦ λαοῦ** τῶν Ἰουδαίων

[the angel of the Lord] has delivered me from Herod's hand and from all the expectation **of the** Jewish **people** (="all that the Jewish people expected")

Rom 8:35 τίς ἡμᾶς χωρίσει ἀπὸ τῆς ἀγάπης **τοῦ Χριστοῦ;**[113]

who shall separate us from the love **of Christ** (= Who shall separate us from the Christ's love for us?)

> The context is very clear that a subjective gen. is in view. The stress is not on what we do to maintain the ties to heaven, but on what God has done in Christ to bring our election to glory. Cf. vv 30-39, in which the emphasis is on God's past, present, and future activity. Verse 39, which caps the chapter, especially brings this out: "[not one thing] will be able to separate us from *the love of God* (τῆς ἀγάπης τοῦ θεοῦ) which is in Christ Jesus our Lord."

2 Cor 7:15 τὴν **πάντων ὑμῶν** ὑπακοήν

the obedience **of you all** (= "the fact that you obeyed")

Cf. also Luke 7:30; Rom 9:11; 13:2; 1 Cor 16:17; 2 Cor 7:6; 8:24; 1 John 5:9; Rev 3:14.

2) Possible (and Exegetically Significant) Examples involving Πίστις Χριστοῦ

Arguably the most debated group of texts involves the expression, πίστις Χριστοῦ: should it be translated "faith *in* Christ" (objective gen.) or "the faith/faithfulness *of* Christ" (subjective gen.)?

Rom 3:22 δικαιοσύνη δὲ θεοῦ διὰ πίστεως Ἰησοῦ Χριστοῦ

even the righteousness of God, through the faithfulness **of Jesus Christ**

Phil 3:9 μὴ ἔχων ἐμὴν δικαιοσύνην τὴν ἐκ νόμου ἀλλὰ τὴν διὰ πίστεως **Χριστοῦ**

not by having a righteousness of my own which is based on the law, but [one] which is through the faithfulness **of Christ**

---

[113] Although a few MSS have θεοῦ for Χριστοῦ (e.g., ℵ [B] 365 *et pauci*), the syntax is not affected.

Eph 3:12   ἔχομεν τὴν παρρησίαν καὶ προσαγωγὴν . . . διὰ τῆς πίστεως **αὐτοῦ**
we have boldness and access through **his** faithfulness

Cf. also Rom 3:26; Gal 2:16 (twice), 20; 3:22, for similar wording.

Older commentaries (probably as a Lutheran reflex) see Χριστοῦ as an objective gen., thus, "faith *in* Christ." However, more and more scholars are embracing these texts as involving a subjective gen. (thus, either "Christ's faith"[114] or "Christ's faithfulness"). Without attempting to decide the issue, we simply wish to interact with a couple of grammatical arguments, one used for each position.

1)   On behalf of the objective gen. view, it is argued that πίστις in the NT takes an objective gen. when both nouns are anarthrous; it takes a subjective gen. when both are articular.[115] In response, the data need to be skewed in order for this to have any weight: most of the examples have a possessive pronoun for the gen., which almost always requires the head noun to have an article.[116] Further, *all* of the πίστις Χριστοῦ texts are in prepositional phrases (where the object of the preposition, in this case πίστις, is typically anarthrous).[117] Prepositional phrases tend to omit the article, even when the object of the preposition is definite.[118]

---

[114] Cranfield, whose first volume on Romans appeared in 1975, calls the subjective gen. view (in Rom 3:22) "altogether unconvincing," without giving much support for this conclusion (*Romans* [ICC], 1.203). He only cites an early articulation of the subjective view, J. Haussleiter, "Der Glaube Jesu Christi und der christliche Glaube: ein Beitrag zur Erklärung des Römerbriefes," *NKZ* 2 (1891) 109-45. In the last two or three decades, however, the defense of the subjective gen. view has found several advocates, though it has not gone without opposition. Note, e.g., for the *subjective* view: R. N. Longenecker, *Paul, Apostle of Liberty* (New York: Harper & Row, 1964) 149-52; G. Howard, "The 'Faith of Christ'," *ExpTim* 85 (1974) 212-15; S. K. Williams, "The 'Righteousness of God' in Romans," *JBL* 99 (1980) 272-78; idem, "Again *Pistis Christou*," *CBQ* 49 (1987) 431-47; R. B. Hays, *The Faith of Jesus Christ: An Investigation of the Narrative Substructure of Galatians 3:1-4:11* (SBLDS 56; Chico: Scholars, 1983); M. D. Hooker, "Πίστις Χριστοῦ," *NTS* 35 (1989) 321-42; R. B. Hays, "ΠΙΣΤΙΣ and Pauline Christology: What Is at Stake?", *SBL 1991 Seminar Papers*, 714-29; B. W. Longenecker, "Defining the Faithful Character of the Covenant Community: Galatians 2.15-21 and Beyond," preliminary draft of a paper presented in Durham, England, 1995. For the *objective* view, note, e.g., A. Hultgren, "The *Pistis Christou* Formulations in Paul," *NovT* 22 (1980) 248-63; J. D. G. Dunn, "Once More, ΠΙΣΤΙΣ ΧΡΙΣΤΟΥ," *SBL 1991 Seminar Papers*, 730-44; as well as virtually all older commentaries on Romans and Galatians.

[115] See Dunn, "Once More," 732-34. Dunn regards this as one of his three main arguments (ibid., 744).

[116] Cf. *BDF*, 148-49 (§284). Dunn recognizes the weakness of this argument with ὑμῶν, but not with μου (Dunn, "Once More," 732), as if to say that one pronoun will act differently than another (true lexically of course, but the issue here is syntactical).

[117] Here it could be pointed out that in the Pauline corpus, there are almost twice as many preposition + anarthrous noun constructions as there are preposition + article + noun constructions (1107 to 599). When πίστις is the object, the difference is even greater (40 to 17).

[118] See later discussion in the chapter on the article.

The grammatical argument for the objective gen., then, has little to commend it.[119]

2) On behalf of the subjective gen. view, it is argued that "*Pistis* followed by the personal genitive is quite rare; but when it does appear it is almost always followed by the non-objective genitive. . . ."[120] This has much more going for it, but still involves some weaknesses. There are two or three clear instances of πίστις + *objective personal* gen. in the NT (Mark 11:22; Jas 2:1; Rev 2:13), as well as two clear instances involving an impersonal gen. noun (Col 2:12; 2 Thess 2:13). Nevertheless, the predominant usage in the NT is with a subjective gen.[121] Practically speaking, if the subjective gen. view is correct, these texts (whether πίστις is translated "faith" or "faithfulness")[122] argue against "an implicitly docetic Christology."[123] Further, the faith/faithfulness of Christ is not a denial of faith *in* Christ as a Pauline concept (for the idea is expressed in many of the same contexts, only with the verb πιστεύω rather than the noun), but implies that the object of faith is a worthy object, for he himself is faithful. Although the issue is not to be solved via grammar, on balance grammatical considerations seem to be in favor of the subjective gen. view.

➡ *2. Objective Genitive*

a. **Definition**

The genitive substantive functions semantically as the *direct object* of the verbal idea implicit in the head noun. This is common in the NT.

---

[119] Dunn ("Once More," 732-33) offers four passages in which he sees the subjective gen., pointing out that, unlike Rom 3:22, *et al.*, these involve an articular πίστις (Rom 3:3; Jas 2:1; Rev 2:13; 14:12). What he does not mention, however, is that not only are most of these texts highly disputed–or rather, almost certainly instances of the *objective* gen. (Jas 2:1; Rev 2:13; 14:12)–but in each one of them πίστις is the direct object and is therefore usually articular. In the least, we would expect an article with πίστις when a particular faith is in view.

[120] Howard, "The 'Faith of Christ'," 213.

[121] Cf. Matt 9:2, 22, 29; Mark 2:5; 5:34; 10:52; Luke 5:20; 7:50; 8:25, 48; 17:19; 18:42; 22:32; Rom 1:8, 12; 3:3 (here "the faithfulness of God"); 4:5, 12, 16; 1 Cor 2:5; 15:14, 17; 2 Cor 10:15; Phil 2:17; Col 1:4; 2:5; 1 Thess 1:8; 3:2, 5, 10; 2 Thess 1:3; Titus 1:1; Phlm 6; 1 Pet 1:9, 21; 2 Pet 1:5. Besides the πίστις Χριστοῦ formula in Paul, Acts 3:16 and Rev 14:12 are now also debatable. Phil 1:27 ("faith of the gospel") is likewise ambiguous.

[122] Longenecker suggests that "faithfulness" is a better translation, since it embraces both concepts and fits in better with Paul's theology ("Galatians 2.15-21 and Beyond," 4, n. 14).

[123] Hays, "ΠΙΣΤΙΣ and Pauline Christology," 728.

b. Key to Identification

When an objective genitive is suspected, attempt to convert the verbal noun to which the genitive is related into a verbal form and turn the genitive into its direct object. Thus, for example, "a demonstration of his righteousness" in Rom 3:25 becomes "demonstrating his righteousness."

A simpler and less fool-proof method is to supply for the word *of* the words *for, about, concerning, toward,* or sometimes *against.*

c. Semantics/Amplification

1) This category is lexico-syntactic—i.e., it is related to a *specific lexical meaning* for one of the words involved (in this case, the head noun). The head noun, which is here called a "verbal noun,"[124] must have an implicit verbal idea. Words such as "love," "hope," "revelation," "witness," and "word," can imply, in a given situation, a verbal idea. The perspective must, of course, be from Greek rather than English: "king," for example, has no verbal cognate in English (there is no verb "to king") but it does in Greek (βασιλεύς has βασιλεύω).

2) The objective genitive, by its very nature, can occur in less types of constructions than the subjective genitive can. This is due to the semantic force of both: a subject can take a transitive or intransitive verb,[125] while an object can only be object of a transitive verb. It follows, then, that *an objective genitive can only occur with verbal nouns which imply a transitive verb.*[126]

3) Where objective and subjective genitives occur in the same constructions—and therefore allows for semantically opposite interpretations—the head noun implies a *transitive* verb. This is by far the more frequent type of verbal noun, however. In a given context, "love of God" could mean "[my/your/their] love for God" (objective) or "God's love for me [you/them]." Since the lexico-syntactic features in such instances are identical, appeal must be made to context, authorial usage, and broader exegetical issues.

---

[124] Not to be confused with an infinitive which is *syntactically* a verbal noun. The expression as used here is a *lexical* title.

[125] It also can take an equative verb, but the subjective gen. will not be used in such constructions. Greek expresses such ideas with predicate genitives and with appositional genitives.

[126] Thus, in ἡ παρουσία τοῦ Χριστοῦ ("the coming of Christ") the gen. *cannot* be objective because the verbal idea is not intransitive. But it could be subjective ("[when] Christ comes"). Luke 6:12 presents an interesting exception to this: τῇ προσευχῇ τοῦ θεοῦ means "prayer to God" (the gen. is thus objective, but after an intransitive verbal noun). Even here, some scribes were not comfortable with the construction (D, it[d] omit τοῦ θεοῦ). Cf. also Acts 4:9; perhaps Matt 1:12 (though Βαβυλῶνος could be a gen. of destination).

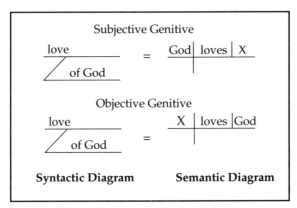

Chart 12
Diagrams of Subjective and Objective Genitive[127]

d. Illustrations[128]

1) Clear Examples

Matt 12:31   ἡ δὲ **τοῦ πνεύματος** βλασφημία οὐκ ἀφεθήσεται
but the blasphemy **of the Spirit** shall not be forgiven (= "blasphemy **against the Spirit**" or "blaspheming the Spirit")

Luke 11:42   οὐαὶ ὑμῖν τοῖς Φαρισαίοις, ὅτι . . . παρέρχεσθε τὴν κρίσιν καὶ τὴν ἀγάπην **τοῦ θεοῦ**
Woe to you Pharisees! For you have neglected justice and love **for God!**

Rom 3:25   ὃν προέθετο ὁ θεὸς . . . εἰς ἔνδειξιν **τῆς δικαιοσύνης** αὐτοῦ
whom God publicly displayed as a demonstration **of his righteousness**

> The idea is "God publicly displayed Jesus Christ in order to demonstrate his righteousness."[129]

---

[127] It should be noted that this semantic equivalence is not exact. An N-N$_g$ construction cannot simply be converted into an S-V-O construction because one is a noun phrase and the other is a full-blown sentence. Thus, "the love of Christ constrains me" cannot simply be converted into either "Christ loves me constrains me" or "I love Christ constrains me," because it would not make good sense. The "I love Christ/Christ loves me" still needs to be retained as a noun phrase. In this instance, "the fact that Christ loves me constrains me" would make good sense as well as "the fact that I love Christ constrains me" (though some of the connotative force is lost by such a gloss). Each situation is different, however. The main thing to remember is that a noun phrase cannot simply be converted into a sentence. Some adjustments need to be made.

[128] Slightly different is the expression in Rom 1:19 (τὸ γνωστὸν τοῦ θεοῦ), where "that which is known about God" is not the same as "the fact of knowing God" directly. The passive ending on the adjective removes this phrase from being considered an objective gen.

[129] This verse can be unpacked even further: "God publicly displayed Jesus Christ in order to demonstrate that he is righteousness."

Rom 11:34 τίς γὰρ ἔγνω νοῦν κυρίου; ἢ τίς σύμβουλος **αὐτοῦ** ἐγένετο;

For who has known the mind of God, or who has become **his** counselor?

The force of this expression is "who has counseled God?"[130]

1 Pet 3:21 καὶ ὑμᾶς . . . νῦν σῴζει βάπτισμα, οὐ σαρκὸς ἀπόθεσις **ῥύπου**

and baptism . . . now saves you–not as a removal **of dirt** from the body

The semantic force of this sentence is: "And baptism now saves you. I'm not talking about the kind which removes dirt from the body. . . ." That is to say, there is no salvific value to the water *per se*.

There are two genitives related to ἀπόθεσις (removal)–ῥύπου (dirt) and σαρκός (flesh, or here, body). One is objective, the other is a gen. of separation.

Cf. also Mark 11:22; Luke 22:25;[131] Acts 2:42; Rom 2:23; 13:4; 1 Cor 15:34; 2 Cor 9:13; Eph 4:13; Col 1:10; Heb 4:2; 1 Pet 2:19; 2 Pet 1:2.

2) Disputed Examples

Rom 8:17 (see later discussion); John 5:42; 1 Pet 3:21 ("the resurrection of Christ").[132] In addition, see discussion under "Subjective Genitive" of the πίστις Χριστοῦ formula and the various passages involved.

3. Plenary Genitive

a. Definition

The noun in the genitive is *both* subjective and objective. In most cases, the subjective produces the objective notion.

Though most grammarians would not like to see a case functioning in a double-duty sense, Zerwick astutely points out that "in interpreting the sacred text, however, we must beware lest we sacrifice to clarity of meaning part of the fulness of the meaning."[133] Only if we treat the language of the Bible as in a class by itself (in that it cannot employ puns, double entendres, and the like) can we deny the possibility of a category such as this. It may

---

[130] See discussion of this text under "Genitive of Association," where the idea of association is rejected on lexical grounds.

[131] This could equally be classified as a gen. of subordination ("kings of the Gentiles").

[132] The issue here and in similar expressions is whether we should see this as "Christ rising [from the dead]" or as "[God] raising Christ [from the dead]." Both are taught in the NT–even to the extent that Christ is considered an active participant in his own resurrection (cf. John 2:21 and our discussion of that text under "Genitive of Apposition").

[133] Zerwick, *Biblical Greek*, 13 (§39).

be that the examples below do not fit the plenary gen., but this is not to deny the inherent plausibility of this usage.[134]

The larger issue at stake here is not the exegesis of a particular passage, but how we approach exegesis as a whole, as well as how we approach the Bible. Almost universally, when a particular gen. is in question, commentators begin their investigation with the underlying assumption that a decision needs to be made. But such an approach presupposes that there can be no intentional ambiguity or pregnant meaning on the part of the speaker. Yet if this occurs elsewhere in human language (universally, I believe, even if somewhat rare in every culture), why is it that we tend to deny such an option to biblical writers?

b. Key to Identification

Simply apply the "Keys" used for the subjective and objective genitives. If *both* ideas seem to fit in a given passage, *and do not contradict but rather complement one another*, then there is a good possibility that the genitive in question is a plenary (or full) genitive.

c. (Possible) Illustrations

2 Cor 5:14   ἡ γὰρ ἀγάπη **τοῦ Χριστοῦ** συνέχει ἡμᾶς
              for the love **of Christ** constrains us

> Here most Protestants take the gen. to be subjective, while others typically consider it to be objective. However, it is possible that both ideas were intended by Paul.[135] Thus, "The love that comes from Christ produces our love for Christ–and this [the whole package] constrains us." In this example, then, the subjective *produces* the objective: "Christ's love for us, which in turn motivates and enables our love for him, constrains us."[136]

Rev 1:1   ἀποκάλυψις **Ἰησοῦ Χριστοῦ**, ἣν ἔδωκεν αὐτῷ ὁ θεός, δεῖξαι τοῖς δούλοις αὐτοῦ
              the revelation **of Jesus Christ**, which God gave to him to show to his servants

> This is the title John gave to his work. Is the revelation that which

---

[134] One of the reasons that most NT grammarians have been reticent to accept this category is simply that most NT grammarians are Protestants. And the Protestant tradition of a singular meaning for a text (which, historically, was a reaction to the fourfold meaning employed in the Middle Ages) has been fundamental in their thinking. However, current biblical research recognizes that a given author may, at times, be *intentionally* ambiguous. The instances of double entendre, *sensus plenior* (conservatively defined), puns, and word-plays in the NT all contribute to this view. Significantly, two of the finest commentaries on the Gospel of John are by Roman Catholic scholars (Raymond Brown and Rudolf Schnackenburg): John's Gospel, more than any other book in the NT, involves double entendre. Tradition has to some degree prevented Protestants from seeing this. But see now, from a Protestant perspective, the work by Saeed Hamidkhani, "Revelation and Concealment: The Nature, Significance and Function of Ambiguity in the Fourth Gospel" (Ph.D. thesis, Cambridge University, to be completed in c. 1996).

[135] So Spicq, "L'étreinte de la charité," *Studia Theologica* 8 (1954) 124; cf. also the commentaries by Lietzmann, Allo, *loc. cit.*

comes *from* Christ or is it *about* Christ? In 22:16 Jesus tells John that *his* angel was the one proclaiming the message of the book to John. Thus, the book is certainly a revelation *from* Christ (hence, we may have a subjective gen. in 1:1). But the revelation is supremely and ultimately *about* Christ. Thus, the gen. in 1:1 may also be an objective gen. The question is whether the author intended both in 1:1. Since this is the *title* of his book–intended to describe the whole of the work–it may well be a plenary gen.

Rom 5:5   ἡ ἀγάπη **τοῦ θεοῦ** ἐκκέχυται ἐν ταῖς καρδίαις ἡμῶν διὰ πνεύματος ἁγίου τοῦ δοθέντος ἡμῖν

the love **of God** has been poured out within our hearts through the Holy Spirit who was given to us

Many older commentators interpret this as objective (e.g., Augustine, Luther), while the majority of modern commentators see it as subjective (so Dunn, Fitzmyer, Moo, Käsemann, Lagrange). It is true that the context is clearly about what God has done for us, rather than about what we have done for God. Thus, contextual considerations seem to indicate that the gen. is subjective: "the love which comes from God has been poured out within our hearts." However, the fact that this love has been poured out *within* us (as opposed to simply upon or toward us) suggests that such love is the source for a reciprocated love. Thus, the gen. may *also* be objective. The idea, then, would be: "The love that comes *from* God and that produces our love *for* God has been poured out within our hearts through the Holy Spirit who was given to us."

Cf. for other possible examples, John 5:42; 2 Thess 3:5; and many instances of εὐαγγέλιον θεοῦ (Mark 1:1, 14; Rom 1:1; 15:16; 1 Thess 2:2, 8, 9).

D. Adverbial Genitive

This is the use of the genitive that is similar in force to an adverb. As well, often this use of the genitive has the force of a prepositional phrase (which, of course, is similar in force to an adverb). Thus the genitive will normally be related to a verb or adjective rather than a noun. (Even in instances where it is dependent on a noun, there is usually an implicit verbal idea in the noun.)

---

[136] ἀγάπη θεοῦ/Χριστοῦ is used in the NT in an objective sense (cf. Luke 11:42; 1 John 2:5, 15; 5:3), as well as a subjective sense (cf. Rom 8:35, 39; 2 Cor 13:13; Eph 3:19; 1 John 4:9). But some texts are difficult to decide (e.g., Rom 5:5; 2 Cor 5:14; 2 Thess 3:5 [where the preceding context suggests objective gen., but the following parallel seems to argue for subjective; Jude 21 is similar]; 1 John 3:17; even John 5:42 [so Robertson, *Grammar*, 499]). It will not do to argue, as several commentators have (e.g., Meyer, Plummer, Furnish, Thrall), that this expression is apparently never objective in the *corpus Paulinum,* since it only occurs seven times in the entire Pauline corpus, three of which texts are debatable! Further, such a view is disputed even here.

1. Genitive of Price or Value or Quantity [for]

a. Definition

The genitive substantive specifies the price paid for or value assessed for the word to which it is related. This is relatively rare in the NT.

b. Key to Identification

For the word *of* supply the word *for* (in answer to the question, "How much?"). Also, remember that the noun in the genitive is a monetary/material word, and is related to a verb (once or twice with a noun) which is lexically colored (i.e., usually involving the notion of buying, selling, worth, etc., such as ἀγοράζω, πιπράσκω, πωλέω).

c. Illustrations

Matt 20:13 οὐχὶ **δηναρίου** συνεφώνησάς μοι;
Did you not agree with me [to work] **for a denarius**?
The lexical notion of worth is sometimes only implicit, as here.

John 6:7 **διακοσίων δηναρίων** ἄρτοι οὐκ ἀρκοῦσιν αὐτοῖς
bread **worth two hundred denarii** is not sufficient for them
English idiom would render this "two hundred denarii worth of bread." This is an unusual instance of the gen. of price related to a noun (cf. also Rev 6:6).

Acts 7:16 τῷ μνήματι ᾧ ὠνήσατο Ἀβραὰμ **τιμῆς** ἀργυρίου
the tomb that Abraham had purchased **for a [certain] amount** of silver

1 Cor 6:20 ἠγοράσθητε γὰρ **τιμῆς**
for you were bought **for a price**

The following are most of the remaining references: Matt 10:29; 16:26; 20:2; 26:9; Mark 6:37; 14:5; Luke 12:6; John 12:5; Acts 5:8; 22:28; 1 Cor 7:23; Heb 12:16; Jude 11.[137]

→ 2. Genitive of Time (within which or during which)

a. Definition

The genitive substantive indicates the *kind* of time, or time *within which* the word to which it stands related takes place.

The easiest way to remember the genitive of time (as opposed to the dat. and acc. of time) is to relate the genitive back to its basal significance. The genitive is the case of quality, attribute, description, or *kind*.[138] Thus, the genitive of time indicates the *kind* of time. (This usage is not very

---

[137] Rom 3:1 ("value of circumcision") does not fit this category because the *gen.* noun does not indicate price or value.

common, but can frequently be expected with words that lexically involve a temporal element.[139])

b. Key to Identification

Just remember that the noun in the genitive expresses an indication of time. The *of* typically becomes *during* or *at* or *within*.

c. Amplification/Semantics

When the simple genitive (i.e., without a preposition) is used for time, it expresses the *kind* of time. However, with ἐκ or ἀπό the meaning is quite different–with emphasis placed on the beginning (cf., e.g., Mark 9:21– ἐκ παιδιόθεν ["from childhood"]).[140] This is *not* a confusion of case uses–one indicating time within which and the other indicating extent of time. The classification of a genitive indicating a time element that follows ἐκ or ἀπό is properly "object of the preposition." The preposition then needs to be classified.

The genitive of time, as we said, puts a stress on the *kind* of time in view. An author has the choice of three cases to indicate time: genitive, dative, accusative. *Generally* speaking, their semantic forces are, respectively: kind of time (or time during which), point in time (answering the question, "When?"), and extent of time (answering the question, "How long?"). Such cases ought to be carefully observed to see what point an author is trying to make–a point not always easily translated into English.

d. Illustrations

Luke 18:12 νηστεύω δὶς **τοῦ σαββάτου**
I fast twice **a week**
> The idea is that the Pharisee fasted twice *during* the week.

John 3:2 ἦλθεν πρὸς αὐτὸν **νυκτός**
he came to him **during the night**
> Had the evangelist used the *dative*, the point would have been that Nicodemus came at a particular point in the night. With the gen., however, the emphasis is on the *kind* of time in which Nicodemus came to

---

[138] Of course, we are speaking about the eight-case system. This is the one area in which this system seems to be helpful, viz., it is pedagogically of some use, even though linguistically (from a synchronic perspective at least) it is faulty.

[139] Although ὥρας is never so used in the NT.

[140]This shows the fallacy of lumping preposition + case uses with simple case uses (a practice followed in more than one intermediate grammar). The preposition does not simply make explicit what the simple case means; in this instance, ἐκ + gen. indicates *source* or separation, while the simple gen. indicates *kind*. But there is no simple gen. use for *time* which indicates source. This notion requires a preposition. Cf. Phil 1:5, for example, ἀπὸ τῆς πρώτης ἡμέρας ἄχρι τοῦ νῦν ("from the first day until now"): this is *not* kind of time, but span of time.

see the Lord. The gospel writer puts a great deal of emphasis on dark vs. light; the gen. for time highlights it here. In the least we can say that Nicodemus is not cast in a good light (contrast John 19:39)!

1 Thess 2:9   **νυκτὸς** καὶ **ἡμέρας** ἐργαζόμενοι
　　　　　　working **night** and **day**

> Paul is not suggesting here that he and his colleagues were working 24-hour shifts among the Thessalonians, but that they labored both in day-time and nighttime. The stress is not on the duration, but on the kind of time in which they worked.[141]

Rev 21:25   καὶ οἱ πυλῶνες αὐτῆς οὐ μὴ κλεισθῶσιν **ἡμέρας**
　　　　　　and its gates will never be shut **during the day**

Cf. also Matt 2:14; 14:25; 24:20; 28:13; Mark 6:48; Luke 2:8; 18:7; John 11:9, 49; Acts 9:25; 1 Thess 3:10; 1 Tim 5:5; Rev 7:15.

3. *Genitive of Place /Space (where or within which)*

a. Definition

The genitive substantive indicates the place *within which* the *verb* to which it is related occurs. This usage is rather rare in the NT and ought to be suggested only if no other category fits.

b. Key to Identification

For the word *of* supply *in, at,* or sometimes *through.*

c. Semantics

Like the genitive of time, this use focuses on *kind* or *quality* (as opposed to the dat., which focuses on a point or specific location).

d. Illustrations

Luke 16:24   πέμψον Λάζαρον ἵνα βάψῃ τὸ ἄκρον τοῦ δακτύλου αὐτοῦ **ὕδατος**
　　　　　　send Lazarus in order that he might dip the tip of his finger **in water**

Luke 19:4   **ἐκείνης** ἤμελλεν διέρχεσθαι
　　　　　　he was about to pass **through that way**

> Here "through" is the translation both of the prepositional prefix on the verb and the nuance of the gen.

Phil 2:8   γενόμενος ὑπήκοος μέχρι θανάτου, θανάτου δὲ **σταυροῦ**
　　　　　　becoming obedient unto death, even death **on a cross**

> This is a possible example: it could equally fit under gen. of means ("by

---

[141] The same stress seems to be found in Rev 4:8, even though it is added that the worship of the four living creatures continued without ceasing. It is, of course, possible that this expression "day and night" is merely a stereotyped phrase that has lost its original grammatical nuances. Similarly, Rev 20:10.

means of a cross") or, better, production ("produced by a cross"). See discussion above and below.

Cf. also 1 Cor 4:5; 1 Pet 3:4 (both metaphorical) for other possible instances.[142]

4. Genitive of Means [by]

a. Definition

The genitive substantive indicates the means or instrumentality by which the verbal action (implicit in the head noun [or adjective] or explicit in the verb) is accomplished. It answers the question, "How?" This usage is quite rare. (With the preposition ἐκ it is much more frequent, though that technically is not a gen. of means because of the presence of the preposition.)

b. Key to Identification

For *of* supply *by*. This will be followed by a noun in the genitive case that is impersonal, or at least conceived of as such.

c. Semantics/Amplification

The genitive of means seems to be, *at times*, slightly closer to a causal idea than a dative of means is (the dat. is the normal case used to indicate means).[143] The construction ἐκ + genitive is used more frequently for means than the simple genitive is.

d. Illustrations

Rom 4:11   τῆς δικαιοσύνης **τῆς πίστεως**
the righteousness **by** [means of] **faith**

1 Cor 2:13   ἃ καὶ λαλοῦμεν οὐκ ἐν διδακτοῖς ἀνθρωπίνης **σοφίας** λόγοις
which things we speak–not in words taught **by** human **wisdom**

Jas 1:13   ὁ γὰρ θεὸς ἀπείραστός ἐστιν **κακῶν**
for God is not tempted **by evil**

Phil 2:8   θανάτου δὲ **σταυροῦ**
death **by** [means of] **a cross**
     This is a doubtful example. The gen. here might rather be place, or even better, production.

---

[142] Phil 2:10 also may belong here (πᾶν γόνυ κάμψῃ **ἐπουρανίων** καὶ **ἐπιγείων** καὶ **καταχθονίων**)–thus, "every knee should bow, **in the heavenly** and **earthly** and **subterranean** places." But it is more likely that the genitives are possessive, referring to those whose knees are bent ("the knees of those in heaven, etc.").

[143] Note, e.g., Acts 1:18 (ἐκτήσατο χωρίον ἐκ μισθοῦ **τῆς ἀδικίας**) in which the gen. connotes "the wages **that he earned from his wickedness**." It is difficult to distinguish means from cause/production here.

5. Genitive of Agency [by]

a. Definition

The genitive substantive indicates the *personal* agent by whom the action in view is accomplished. It is almost always related to a verbal adjective that is typically used as a substantive and has the characteristically passive ending -τος. The usage is fairly rare.

b. Key to Identification

The red flag of this usage is an adjective, usually ending in -τος, followed by a personal noun in the genitive. For *of* supply *by*. Thus, e.g., διδακτὸς θεοῦ, "taught of God," becomes "taught by God." Look for combinations such as ἀγαπητός + genitive, διδακτός + genitive, ἐκλεκτός + genitive.

c. Structure and Semantics

The genitive will normally be related to an adjective that (a) is substantival (i.e., in the place of a noun), (b) ends in -τος, and (c) implies a passive idea.[144]

The genitive of agency is closer in force to ὑπό + the genitive (expressing ultimate agent) than to διά + the genitive (expressing intermediate agent).

d. Illustrations

1) Clear Examples

John 18:16   ὁ μαθητὴς ὁ ἄλλος ὁ γνωστὸς **τοῦ ἀρχιερέως**[145]
             the other disciple, who was known **by the high priest**

John 6:45   ἔσονται πάντες διδακτοὶ **θεοῦ**
             they shall all be taught **by God**

Rom 1:7   πᾶσιν τοῖς οὖσιν ἐν Ῥώμῃ ἀγαπητοῖς **θεοῦ**[146]
             to all who are in Rome, beloved **by God**

Rom 8:33   τίς ἐγκαλέσει κατὰ ἐκλεκτῶν **θεοῦ**;
             Who will bring a charge against those chosen **by God**?

---

[144] See *BDF*, 98 (§ 183) for a succinct and helpful discussion. *BDF* point out but two exceptions to this threefold rule: (1) in 1 Cor 2:13 the adjective modifies a noun; (2) in Matt 25:34 a perfect passive participle (instead of an adjective) is used with the gen. But John 6:45 is also an exception, involving a predicate adjective. So too is John 18:16, which has an attributive adjective.

[145] This reading is found in B C*[vid] L *et pauci*; ὁ ἄλλος ὃς ἦν γνωστὸς τῷ ἀρχιερεῖ is found in ℵ A C² Dˢ W Υ Γ Δ Θ Λ Π Ψ f¹, ¹³ 33 *Byz*.

[146] ἐν ἀγάπῃ θεοῦ is found in G *et pauci*.

1 Cor 2:13   ἐν διδακτοῖς **πνεύματος**
               in [words] taught **by [the] Spirit**

2) Disputed Example

Rom 1:6   ἐν οἷς ἐστε καὶ ὑμεῖς κλητοὶ **Ἰησοῦ Χριστοῦ**
            among whom you also are called **by Jesus Christ**

> In light of the structural parallel with v 7 (ἀγαπητοὶ θεοῦ), it is possible that this expression indicates agency. Another possibility is that this is a possessive gen.: thus, "called *to belong to* Jesus Christ."[147] First, only rarely in the NT is it said that Christ does the *calling* of the saints.[148] Second, ultimate agency is normally in view for the gen. of agency, while only rarely is Christ considered to be the ultimate agent.[149] Third, it is not infrequent to find a possessive gen. after an adjective ending in -τος, especially in Romans.[150] Syntax does not solve this problem by any means, but it at least helps to lay out on the table some of the evidence for each view.

➡ ## 6. *Genitive Absolute*

See under "Adverbial Participles."

7. *Genitive of Reference [with reference to]*

a. Definition

The genitive substantive indicates that in reference to which the noun or adjective to which it stands related is true. This usage is not common.

b. Key to Identification

For the word *of* supply *with reference to, with respect to.*

c. Amplification

This genitive usually modifies an adjective (although rarely it will be connected to a noun), and as such its adverbial force is self-evident. The genitive limits the frame of reference of the adjective.

---

[147] So *BDF*, 98 (§183); NRSV. Against this, see Cranfield, *Romans* (ICC) 1.68, who calls the possessive view "doctrinaire."

[148] The calling of the apostles (e.g., in Matt 4:21) is different. But cf. Matt 9:13.

[149] This argument is not as strong as it could be, however, in light of 1 Cor 2:13 (where πνεῦμα is the agent).

[150] Cf., e.g., Rom 1:20, 21; 2:4, 6:12; 8:11; 9:22; for less clear examples, cf. Matt 24:31; Luke 18:7; Rom 2:16; 16:5, 8, 9. Some of these examples may also belong to another category, but it is hardly disputable that they are at least possessive and not at all indicating agency. On the other hand, all of the *clear* examples involve the possessive pronoun, unlike Rom 1:6.

All oblique cases, as well as the nominative (known as pendent nom.), can be used to indicate reference. By far the most common is the dative of reference. The genitive of reference is the least common.

d. Illustrations

1) With an Adjective

Heb 3:12   καρδία πονηρὰ **ἀπιστίας**
            a heart evil **with reference to unbelief**

Heb 5:13   πᾶς γὰρ ὁ μετέχων γάλακτος ἄπειρος **λόγου** δικαιοσύνης
            for everyone who lives on milk is unskilled **with reference to the word** of righteousness

2) With a Noun (or Substantive)

Matt 21:21 οὐ μόνον τὸ **τῆς συκῆς** ποιήσετε
            you shall do not only what [was done] **with reference to the fig tree**

Col 1:15   ὅς ἐστιν. . . πρωτότοκος **πάσης κτίσεως**
            who is. . . the first-born **with reference to all creation**

> The other possibilities are partitive and subordination. If this were partitive, the idea would be that Christ was *part* of creation, i.e., a created being. But Paul makes it clear throughout this epistle that Jesus Christ is the supreme Creator, God in the flesh–e.g., cf. 1:15a, 2:9. In the section in which this verse is found, 1:9-20, he could hardly be more emphatic about the deity of his Lord.[151] However, a gen. of subordination is, in all probability, the best option (see discussion of this text earlier).

8. Genitive of Association [in association with]

a. Definition

The genitive substantive indicates the one with whom the noun to which it stands related is associated. This usage is somewhat common, but only in certain collocations (see below).

b. Key to Identification

For *of* supply *with*, or *in association with*.

c. Amplification and Significance

The head noun to which this kind of genitival use is connected is normally prefixed with συν-. Such compound nouns naturally lend

---

[151] One of the arguments for Christ's deity being affirmed here is that this is a *hymn* (1:15-20). Hymns were sung to deities, not mere mortals. Cf., e.g., R. T. France, "The Worship of Jesus–A Neglected Factor in Christological Debate?" *VE* 12 (1981) 19-33.

themselves to the associative idea. As well, some nouns and adjectives already embrace lexically the idea of "in association with" and hence can take a genitive of association without συν- prefixed to them.

This usage has particular exegetical weight in the Pauline letters, for it typically makes explicit some ramification of the ἐν Χριστῷ formula (since believers are said to be in Christ, because of their organic connection to him,[152] they now associate with him in many and profound ways).[153]

d. Illustrations

1) Clear Examples

Matt 23:30 οὐκ ἂν ἤμεθα **αὐτῶν** κοινωνοὶ ἐν τῷ αἵματι τῶν προφητῶν[154]
> we would not have shared **with them** in the blood of the prophets
>> This is one of the less frequent examples involving a head noun/adjective not prefixed by συν-.

Rom 8:17 εἰ δὲ τέκνα, καὶ κληρονόμοι· κληρονόμοι μὲν θεοῦ, συγκληρονόμοι δὲ **Χριστοῦ**
> now if we are children, [we are] also heirs: on the one hand, heirs of God, on the other hand, fellow heirs **with Christ**
>> The first gen. (θεοῦ) may be either possessive (God would then possess the believer) or objective (the believer inherits God). The second gen., however, follows a συν- noun, and the inheritance that Christ himself enjoys also belongs to believers because of their association with him.

Eph 2:19 ἐστὲ συμπολῖται **τῶν ἁγίων**
> you are fellow-citizens **with the saints**

Eph 5:7 μὴ οὖν γίνεσθε συμμέτοχοι **αὐτῶν**
> therefore, do not become fellow-sharers **with them**

Col 4:10 Ἀρίσταρχος ὁ συναιχμάλωτός **μου**
> Aristarchus, **my** fellow-prisoner (="fellow-prisoner **with me**")
>> In English usage "my" is more natural than "with me," though the force is obviously not that Paul *possesses* Aristarchus.

Rev 19:10 καὶ ἔπεσα ἔμπροσθεν τῶν ποδῶν αὐτοῦ προσκυνῆσαι αὐτῷ. καὶ λέγει μοι, Ὅρα μή· σύνδουλός **σού** εἰμι
> and I fell before [the angel's] feet to worship him. And he said to me, "See that you do not do that! I am a fellow-servant **with you**"
>> The reaction of the angel to the prophet's veneration of him was quite different from Jesus' reaction to Thomas' exclamation, "My Lord and

---

[152] And not *just* their legal or forensic connection: cf. especially Rom 5, where both the forensic and organic connections are made.

[153] Cf. also the more common idiom of συν- verbs followed by a dative in the *corpus Paulinum*.

[154] αὐτῶν is omitted in Θ Σ *et pauci*.

my God!" (John 20:28). Whereas the angel rejected it because he and John were equals in the service of God, Jesus accepted it from Thomas.

Cf. also Matt 18:29, 31, 33; Acts 19:29; Rom 16:3; Phlm 24.

2) Disputed Examples

Phil 3:17   συμμιμηταί **μου** γίνεσθε, ἀδελφοί

become fellow-imitators **with me**, brothers

> The NRSV has "join in imitating me" (taking the gen. as objective and the head noun as implying association—i.e., "join one another"). It is also possible (but not as likely) to regard the gen. as associative, in which case the one who is to be imitated is only implied. The following context, however, seems to make clear that Paul is the one to be imitated. The NRSV translation is thus to be preferred.

Rom 11:34   Τίς γὰρ ἔγνω νοῦν κυρίου; ἢ τίς σύμβουλος **αὐτοῦ** ἐγένετο;

For who has known the mind of God, or who has become a counselor **with him**?

> Although etymologically possible, the usage of σύμβουλος in both classical and Koine Greek meant simply "advisor," not "fellow advisor."[155] The gen. must be taken then as objective ("who has counseled God"), the thought being all the more pernicious, for the hypothetical counselor would not be in league with God, but above him.

1 Cor 3:9   **θεοῦ** γὰρ ἐσμεν συνεργοί

for we are **God's** fellow-workers

> Here, Paul *may* be saying that he and Apollos *and* God are in association with one another in the work of the ministry.[156] However, it is better to see an ellipsis of "with one another" and to see θεοῦ as a possessive gen. (thus, "we are fellow-workers [with each other], belonging to God"). Contextually, the argument in this section is very explicit: Paul and Apollos are nothing, but God is the one who brought about both salvation and sanctification (vv 5-7). Syntactically, there are other examples of συν- prefixed nouns taking an *implied* gen. of association while the gen. mentioned in the text functions in another capacity[157]—cf., e.g., Rom 11:17 (fellow-sharers [with the Jewish believers] *of the root*); 1 Cor 1:20; 9:23; Eph 3:6; 1 Pet 3:7.[158] Thus it is likely that the apostle is not claiming that he and Apollos are God's partners, but his servants.

---

[155] Most commentators simply assume this, however, without any discussion (e.g., Cranfield, *Romans* [ICC] 2.590-91). On the other hand, *BDF* seem to assume the opposite without any proof (104, [§194.2]). For ancient parallels, cf. Herodotus 5.24; Aristophanes, *Thesmophoriazusae* 9.21; P Petr II. 13. 6. 11.

[156] So Robertson-Plummer, *I Corinthians* (ICC) 58-59. The view is often assumed in exegetical literature on this passage.

[157] Cf. also Acts 21:30 for something similar, viz., a subjective gen. after a συν- noun.

[158] In 1 Thess 3:2 both genitives are used: one association, one possessive ("our brother and co-worker *for God*"). This text also closely parallels 1 Cor 3:9 in thought and word. Cf. also Phil 1:7.

E. After Certain Words

There are some uses of the genitive that do not neatly fit into any of the above categories. Or, if they do fit into one of the above categories, they are related to a word other than a noun. These constitute the large and amorphous group known as the use of the genitive after certain words.

➡ ## 1. *Genitive After Certain Verbs (as a Direct Object)*

a. Definition

Certain verbs take a genitive substantive as direct object.

b. Key to Identification

A number of verbs characteristically take a genitive direct object. These verbs commonly correspond in meaning to some other function of the genitive, e.g., separation, partitive, source, etc. The predominant uses can be grouped into four types of verbs: *sensation, emotion/volition, sharing, ruling.*

If all the verb groups are included, they can fit into nine categories. *BDF* breaks these verbs down into ten categories (one of which, the gen. after verbs meaning "to fill, to be full of," we have labeled a [verbal] gen. of content): 1) Verbs of sharing or partaking and verbs with a partitive genitive idea; 2) Verbs meaning "to touch, take hold of"; 3) Verbs meaning "to strive after, desire" and "to reach, obtain"; 4) Verbs meaning "to fill, be full of" [which I have listed elsewhere]; 5) Verbs of perception; 6) Verbs meaning smell; 7) Verbs meaning "to remember, forget"; 8) Verbs of emotion; 9) Verbs meaning "to rule, govern, surpass"; 10) Verbs of accusing. [159]

c. Clarification and Semantic Significance

It has already been pointed out that such genitive direct objects usually imply one of the genitive functions. This, in part, is the semantic significance of genitive direct objects. As well, several of the verbs which take genitive direct objects also take accusative direct objects. Thus, when an author has a choice for the case of his direct object, the case he chooses in which to express his idea may be significant.

---

[159] See *BDF*, 93-96 (§§169-78) for a list of such verbs. Rather than duplicate the list in these notes, since such genitives can easily be noted via the lexicon, the student is advised to consult BAGD under the verb in question if in doubt.

d. Illustrations

Because this is such a broad category, and because the liberal use of a good lexicon easily reveals this usage, only a few examples will be given.

1) Sensation

Mark 5:41   κρατήσας **τῆς χειρὸς** τοῦ παιδίου λέγει αὐτῇ, Ταλιθα κουμ

touching **the hand** of the little girl, he said to her, "Talitha cum"

> There is a note of tenderness seen in the gen., contrasted with the acc.: κρατέω + acc. normally indicates grasping the whole of or completely embracing (cf. Matt 12:11; 28:9; Mark 7:3; Acts 3:11), with frequent negative connotations such as seizing or arresting (cf. Matt 14:3; 18:28; Mark 3:21). By contrast, κρατέω + gen. is partitive, with the usual implication of a gentle touch (cf. Matt 9:25; Mark 1:31).[160]

Mark 7:33   πτύσας ἥψατο **τῆς γλώσσης** αὐτοῦ

after spitting, he touched his **tongue**

> ἅπτομαι naturally takes a gen. direct object (exclusively so in the NT when the meaning is "to touch"[161]). The partitive notion is embedded in the lexical force of the verb.

2) Emotion/Volition

Luke 10:35   ἐπιμελήθητι **αὐτοῦ**

take care **of him**

1 Tim 3:1   εἴ τις ἐπισκοπῆς ὀρέγεται, **καλοῦ ἔργου** ἐπιθυμεῖ.

If anyone aspires to the office of bishop, he desires **a noble work**.

> Nothing can be made of the gen. with ἐπιθυμέω, for it always takes a gen. direct object in the NT, except when it is followed by a complementary infinitive. (It finds a counterpart in the English expression, "he is desirous of a noble work.")

3) Sharing

Heb 12:10   ὁ δὲ ἐπὶ τὸ συμφέρον εἰς τὸ μεταλαβεῖν **τῆς ἁγιότητος** αὐτοῦ

but he [disciplines us] for our benefit, that we might share **in** his **holiness**

> This is an instance of the *partitive* direct object. (Generally speaking, if a verb can take either a gen. or acc. direct object, the *accusative* will be used when the object is apprehended *as a whole*; the *genitive*[162] will be

---

[160] This may be due more to set idiom, for χείρ is frequently the gen. noun. As well, Heb 4:14 does not fit this picture: the gen. is used, even though the grasping of the confession is presumably to be a total embrace (as in Mark 7:3, 8; Col 2:19; 2 Thess 2:15; Rev 2:13, 14–all of which have the acc.).

[161] The verb can also mean "to light, kindle," in which case it always takes an acc. (cf. Luke 8:16; 11:33; 15:8; Acts 28:2).

[162] Or, much more frequently in the NT, ἐκ + gen.

used when the object is apprehended *in part*.[163]) The participation that believers can have in God's holiness is not complete, but derived and partial. The gen. seems to be used to reflect this.[164]

Acts 9:7   οἱ δὲ ἄνδρες οἱ συνοδεύοντες αὐτῷ εἱστήκεισαν ἐνεοί, ἀκούοντες μὲν **τῆς φωνῆς** μηδένα δὲ θεωροῦντες.

The men who traveled with him stood speechless, hearing **the voice** but seeing no one.

> There seems to be a contradiction between this account of Paul's conversion and his account of it in Acts 22, for there he says, "those who were with me. . . did *not* hear the voice. . ." However, in Acts 22:9 the verb ἀκούω takes an *accusative* direct object. On these two passages, Robertson states: ". . . it is perfectly proper to appeal to the distinction in the cases in the apparent contradiction between ἀκούοντες μὲν τῆς φωνῆς (Ac. 9:7) and τὴν δὲ φωνὴν οὐκ ἤκουσαν (22:9). The accusative case (case of extent) accents the intellectual apprehension of the sound, while the genitive (specifying case) calls attention to the sound of the voice without accenting the sense. The word ἀκούω itself has two senses which fall in well with this case-distinction, one 'to hear,' the other 'to understand'."[165]

> The NIV seems to follow this line of reasoning: Acts 9:7 reads "they heard the *sound* but did not see anyone"; 22:9 has "my companions saw the light, but did not understand the voice." The field of meaning for both ἀκούω (hear, understand) and φωνή (sound, voice), coupled with the change in cases (gen., acc.), can be appealed to to harmonize these two accounts.

> On the other hand, it is doubtful that this is where the difference lay between the two cases used with ἀκούω in Hellenistic Greek: the NT (including the more literary writers) is filled with examples of ἀκούω + *genitive indicating understanding* (Matt 2:9; John 5:25; 18:37; Acts 3:23; 11:7; Rev 3:20; 6:3, 5;[166] 8:13; 11:12; 14:13; 16:1, 5, 7; 21:3) as well as instances of ἀκούω + *accusative where little or no comprehension takes place*[167] (explicitly so in Matt 13:19; Mark 13:7/Matt 24:6/Luke 21:9; Acts 5:24; 1 Cor 11:18; Eph 3:2; Col 1:4; Phlm 5; Jas 5:11; Rev 14:2). The exceptions, in fact, are seemingly more numerous than the rule!

---

[163] Cf. *BDF*, 93 (§169.2).

[164] There is but one instance of μεταλαμβάνω taking an acc. direct object in the NT (2 Tim 2:6), although this was a standard idiom outside the NT (cf. LSJ, s.v. μεταλαμβάνω).

[165] Robertson, *Grammar*, 506.

[166] Rev 6:7 finds a parallel with the acc.!

[167] In some of these examples, the hearing is indirect (e.g., hearing *about* wars [Mark 13:7 and parallels]; *of* divisions [1 Cor 11:18]) where, on Robertson's scheme, a gen. would be expected. Other examples showing the fallacy of this approach: in Jesus' urging his audience to listen to his words and obey them, cf. the parallels in Matt 7:24 (acc.) and Luke 6:47 (gen.); the parallels of the angels' articulate cry of "Come!" when they dispense with the seal judgments (Rev 6:3, 5 have the gen.; 6:7 has the acc.).

Thus, regardless of how one works through the accounts of Paul's conversion, an appeal to different cases probably ought *not* form any part of the solution.[168]

4) Ruling

Luke 22:25 οἱ βασιλεῖς τῶν ἐθνῶν κυριεύουσιν **αὐτῶν**
the kings of the Gentiles lord it **over them**

Rom 15:12 ἔσται ἡ ῥίζα τοῦ Ἰεσσαί, καὶ ὁ ἀνιστάμενος ἄρχειν **ἐθνῶν**
The root of Jesse will come, even he who will rise to rule **over the Gentiles**

2. *Genitive After Certain Adjectives (and Adverbs)*

a. Definition

Certain adjectives (such as ἄξιος, "worthy [of]") and adverbs normally take a genitive "object." In many instances the adjective/adverb is an embedded transitive verb, thus taking an objective genitive (e.g., "he is deserving of X" means "he deserves X") or involving a partitive idea.

b. Key to Identification/Amplification

As with the genitive direct object, you should check BAGD under various adjectives and adverbs or *BDF* (98, [§182]) for a list. In reality, most of these examples also fit under some other genitive use equally well–such as partitive, objective, content, reference, etc. However, the fact that certain adjectives, by their very nature, take genitives after them, renders this a predictable and stable category (since a fixed group of lexemes is involved).[169]

c. Illustrations

Only a few illustrations will be given as this is a usage easily discovered through a judicious use of the lexicon.

---

[168] It is still most reasonable to conclude that these accounts are not presenting contradictory views about what Paul's companions heard. The most probable solution sees the various traditions that Luke gathered (including Acts 26:14) as from different sources. Luke then compiled the information in a conservative manner, even to the point of preserving much of the wording of his sources (where both ἀκούω and φωνή carried different nuances in each source). Hence, what looks like a contradiction is in reality evidence of Luke's reticence to drastically alter the traditions as handed down to him.

[169] Nevertheless, the NT is not nearly as rich as classical Greek in this usage.

Matt 26:66   ἔνοχος **θανάτου** ἐστίν
     he is deserving **of death**
      This is the equivalent of "he deserves **death**," an objective gen.

Luke 12:48   ποιήσας ἄξια **πληγῶν**
     having done things worthy **of blows**

Luke 23:15   οὐδὲν ἄξιον **θανάτου** ἐστὶν πεπραγμένον αὐτῷ
     nothing worthy **of death** has been done by him
      The phrase ἄξιος θανάτου also occurs in Acts 23:29; 25:11; Rom 1:32.

Phil 1:27   ἀξίως **τοῦ εὐαγγελίου** τοῦ Χριστοῦ πολιτεύεσθε
     conduct yourselves worthily **of the gospel** of Christ

Cf. also Luke 7:6; 1 Cor 6:2; Heb 9:7; 2 Pet 2:14.

3. *Genitive After Certain Nouns*[170]

a. Definition

A genitive substantive may *rarely* occur after certain nouns whose lexical nature requires a genitive. The genitive in such instances will not fit into one of the "standard" genitive categories. The most common instances involve two genitives joined by καί, with the meaning "between." This category is quite rare.

b. Key to Identification

The student should check BAGD if in doubt.

c. Illustrations

Acts 23:7   ἐγένετο στάσις **τῶν Φαρισαίων** καὶ **Σαδδουκαίων**
     a dissension arose **between the Pharisees** and **Sadducees**

Rev 5:6   ἐν μέσῳ **τοῦ θρόνου** καὶ **τῶν τεσσάρων ζῴων**
     between **the throne** and **the four living creatures**

Cf. also Rom 10:12; 1 Tim 2:5.

---

[170] The idea of "between" is normally found with the "improper" preposition μεταξύ or, on at least one occasion, ἐκ (Phil 1:23).

→ **4. *Genitive After Certain Prepositions***

    a. **Definition and Key to Identification**

Certain prepositions take the genitive after them. See the chapter on prepositions for discussion. For review of which prepositions take which cases, cf., e.g., Mounce, *Basics of Biblical Greek*, 55-62.[171]

    b. **Significance**

When a genitive follows a preposition, you should *not* attempt to identify the genitive's function by case usage *alone*. Rather, consult either BAGD or the chapter on prepositions for the specific usage of that case with that preposition. Many of the simple genitive uses overlap those of the preposition + the genitive (especially with ἐκ + the gen.). But the parallels are not exact: there are some simple genitive uses that cannot be duplicated with prepositions and some preposition + genitive uses that find no parallel with the simple genitive. Furthermore, where there is overlap of usage, there is usually *not* overlap of frequency of occurrence.

---

[171] In addition, forty of the forty-two "improper prepositions" take the gen. case (e.g., ἄχρι(ς), ἔμπροσθεν, ἕνεκα, ἕως, ὀψέ, πλησίον, ὑπεράνω, ὑποκάτω, χωρίς). One should consult the lexicon if in doubt.

The Dative Case

Overview of Dative Uses

Select Bibliography

BDF, 100-109 (§187-202); **Moule**, *Idiom Book*, 43-47; **Moulton**, *Prolegomena*, 62-64; **Porter**, *Idioms*, 97-102; **Robertson**, *Grammar*, 520-44; **Smyth**, *Greek Grammar*, 337-53 (§1450-1550); **Turner**, *Syntax*, 236-44; **Winer-Moulton**, 260-77; **Young**, *Intermediate Greek*, 43-54; **Zerwick**, *Biblical Greek*, 19-23 (§51-65).

Introduction

The dative case is not as exegetically significant as the genitive. This is not to say that the dative does not play a vital role in exegetical decisions. Rather, a particular instance of the dative is usually easier to classify than a given genitive. This is due to two things: (1) the broad classes of dative uses are generally more easily distinguishable; and (2) the embedded clause needs less "unpacking" since the dative is already related to a verb, while the genitive is more cryptic and elliptical since it is usually related to a noun.[1]

At the same time, there are some instances in which a given dative may function in more than one capacity (e.g., both instrumental and local), and not a few in which a decision is still hard to come by. In such places, the dative takes on greater significance.

Finally, the simple dative is phasing out in Koine Greek, being replaced largely by prepositions, especially ἐν + the dative.[2] This is not to say that the simple dative and ἐν + dative mirror each other completely, as will become abundantly clear in our examination of various uses of the dative case.

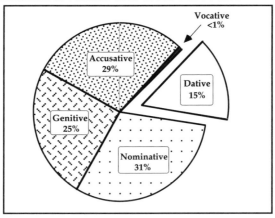

Chart 13
Frequency of Cases in the New Testament[3]

---

[1] On more distinctions between the oblique cases, see the introduction to the gen. case.

[2] Cf. BAGD, 258-61, esp. 261, §IV.4.a.

Definition of the Dative Case

1. *Within the Eight-Case System*

"The dative, locative, and instrumental cases are all represented by the same inflectional form, but the distinction in function is very clear—much more so than the distinction between the ablative and genitive."[4] However, this does *not* mean that, within the eight-case system, it is always easy to tell to which case this particular inflectional form belongs. Furthermore, there will be a few occasions in which the same case form will have a double-duty function. The eight-case system cannot handle such a double function because such would involve two different cases. Thus, the definition of case as a matter of function rather than form can sometimes be so rigid that it excludes part of the meaning intended by the author.[5]

The true dative is used to designate the person more remotely concerned.[6] It is the case of *personal interest*, pointing out the person *to* or *for* whom something is done.[7]

This is not to say that the dative cannot relate to things, for there are numerous examples of this. When it does so, it has a referring force. In general, when the dative is used of persons, it speaks about the one(s) concerned about (or affected by) the action; when it is used of things, it addresses the *framework* in which an act occurs.

2. *Within the Five-Case System*

However, since the dative, instrumental, and locative share the same form, we will consider them as *one* case ("case" being defined as a matter of form rather than function within the five-case system).[8] The *instrumental* idea involves means and generally answers the question, "How?" The *locative* notion involves place and answers the question, "Where?" Thus, a broad view of the dative case (including pure dative, locative, and instrumental uses) suggests that it answers one of three questions: To/for whom? How? or Where?

---

[3] The dative breakdown is 4375 nouns, 3565 pronouns, 2944 articles, 936 adjectives, 353 participles.

[4] Dana-Mantey, 83.

[5] Cf. "The Cases: An Introduction" for a more extended discussion of this point.

[6] *BDF*, 100.

[7] So Funk, *Intermediate Grammar*, 2.718.

[8] It is not insignificant that even Dana-Mantey vacillate slightly here in saying that "we cannot ignore form entirely while we are in the realm of syntax, for it often happens that we would be utterly unable to determine what the intended function is except for the form" (Dana-Mantey, 86).

In connection with this, Chamberlain (although he holds to the eight-case system) gives a very helpful exegetical tip:

> When the interpreter is confronted with a "dative" form, he should remember that any one of three basic ideas may be expressed by this case-form:
>
> 1. The idea of place
> 2. The idea of the instrument
> 3. The true dative
>
> A good passage upon which to test this is: τῇ γὰρ ἐλπίδι ἐσώθημεν (Rom 8:24). Does Paul mean to say "We are saved by hope" (instrumental), "in hope" (locative), or "to" (or "for") "hope" (dative)? If the case is [pure] dative, hope is, in a sense, personified and becomes the end of salvation rather than a means to that end. If the case is locative, hope is regarded as the sphere in which salvation occurs. If the case is instrumental, hope is considered as a means used in saving men. The only scientific way in which to decide this sort of question is to appeal to the Pauline viewpoint as reflected in the New Testament.[9]

Therefore, within the five-case system, the dative case may be defined as the case of *personal interest, reference/respect* (pure dative), *position* (locative), and *means* (instrumental).

Specific Uses

Pure Dative Uses

The subgroups here are specific uses built on the root idea of *personal interest* and *reference/respect*.

➡ ## 1. *Dative Indirect Object*

a. Definition

The dative substantive is that to or for which the action of a verb is performed. The indirect object will *only occur with a transitive verb*. When the transitive verb is in the *active* voice,[10] the indirect object receives the direct object ("the boy hit the ball *to me*"); when the verb is in the *passive* voice, the indirect object receives the subject of the verb ("the ball was

---

[9] Chamberlain, *Exegetical Grammar*, 34-35.

[10] Sometimes in the middle (deponent middles are treated as though they are actives).

hit *to me*"). The indirect object is the receiver of the direct object of an active[11] verb, or of the subject of a passive verb.

Stated more succinctly: "The noun or pronoun in the dative is the person or thing to which is given (or which receives) the direct object (of a transitive verb) (or [receives the] subject of a passive verb)."[12] This category is far and away the *most common* of the dative uses.

b. Key to Identification

The key is: (1) the verb must be transitive;[13] and (2) if the dative can be translated with *to* or *for* it is most likely indirect object.

c. Semantics and Clarification

1) To translate a dative as *to* or *for* with a transitive verb is easily the most common translation (like *of* for the genitive). There are many uses of the dative which actually fall under the larger umbrella of the indirect object (e.g., interest, ethical). The indirect object, therefore, is normally recognized as the most common dative. Just as the *of* idea for the genitive, the *to* idea for the dative is the most common. However, the *to* idea for the dative is more "unpacked" than the genitive, since the dative is already related to an explicit verb (as distinguished from an implicit verb with the genitive). Consequently, dative uses are more easily detected than the genitive, and therefore their exegetical significance is easier to determine, since there is less ambiguity (the presence of the verb reduces the ambiguity).

2) In the sentence "He gave the book to the boy," "to the boy" is the indirect object. It receives the direct object, "the book," of the transitive (and active) verb, "gave." Such a sentence can be put into a *passive transform*: "The book was given to the boy by him." Here, "The book" has become the subject (formerly the direct object), but "to the boy" is still the indirect object. The subject of the active voice verb "gave" has become the agent of the passive voice verb "was given." In both sentences the indirect object remains the same and it receives the same thing semantically, though not grammatically (i.e., it receives the *book* each time, but does not receive the same part of the sentence each time).

---

[11] Active from an English perspective.

[12] Williams, *Grammar Notes*, 15.

[13] "Transitive" should probably be defined in two ways, one grammatical and the other lexical. Grammatically, a transitive verb is one that takes a direct object and can be put into the passive voice. Lexically, the kinds of transitive verbs that take dative indirect objects are generally those that, in the strict sense, move the direct object from one place to another. Thus, "give," "repay," "send," "bring," "speak," etc. naturally occur with indirect objects, while verbs such as "have" or "live" do not.

d. Illustrations

John 4:10   καὶ ἔδωκεν ἄν **σοι** ὕδωρ ζῶν
and he would have given **to you** living water

Luke 1:13   ἡ γυνή σου Ἐλισάβετ γεννήσει υἱόν **σοι**, καὶ καλέσεις τὸ ὄνομα αὐτοῦ
Ἰωάννην.[14]
Your wife Elizabeth will bear a son **to you**, and you will call his
name John.

Jas 2:16   εἴπῃ δέ τις **αὐτοῖς** ἐξ ὑμῶν, Ὑπάγετε ἐν εἰρήνῃ, θερμαίνεσθε καὶ
χορτάζεσθε, μὴ δῶτε δὲ **αὐτοῖς** τὰ ἐπιτήδεια τοῦ σώματος, τί τὸ ὄφελος;
But one of you says to them, "Go in peace, be warmed and be filled,"
but you do not give **them** the things necessary for the body, what is
the benefit?

> In this example, the *statement* that follows is the direct object, or that
> which is received by the dat. indirect object.

2 Cor 5:11   **θεῷ** πεφανερώμεθα
we are manifested **to God**

2 Cor 12:7   ἐδόθη **μοι** σκόλοψ τῇ σαρκί
a thorn in the flesh was given **to me**

> This is a passive transform of the clause, ἔδωκεν **μοι** σκόλοπα τῇ σαρκί,
> "He gave **me** a thorn in the flesh." For other examples of passive trans-
> forms, cf. Matt 14:11; 21:43; Acts 7:13; 14:26, Eph 3:8; Rev 6:2, etc.

Cf. also Matt 7:6; Mark 14:44; John 10:28; Acts 13:22; 1 Pet 4:19; Rev 16:6.

➡ ### 2. *Dative of Interest (including Advantage* [commodi] *and Disadvantage* [incommodi])

a. Definition

The dative substantive indicates the person (or, rarely, thing) interested
in the verbal action. The dative of advantage has a *to* or *for* idea, while
the dative of disadvantage has an *against* idea. The dative of advantage
occurs more frequently than disadvantage, though both are common
enough.

Even though both fall under the umbrella of dative of interest, it is
important to distinguish between dative of advantage and disadvantage
(since the resultant meanings are opposite).

b. Key to Identification

Instead of the words *to* or *for*, supply *for the benefit of* or *in the interest of*
for the dative of *advantage*, and *for/unto the detriment of*, *to the disadvantage
of* or *against* for the dative of *disadvantage*. The translation *for the benefit of*

---

[14] σοι is missing in D Δ 1 579 *et pauci*.

etc. is helpful for getting the sense of the dative, not as a final translation, since it is too awkward.

c. Semantics/Significance

- Dative of interest typically (but not always) belongs to the larger category of indirect object. The difference in the two is that, in the former, interest is stressed, while in the latter it is not.

- The connotation of the *verb* used is frequently a major clue as to whether a particular dative is merely indirect object or a dative of interest. For example, "If I say ἔδωκεν τὸ βιβλίον μοι ['He gave the book to me'], it is clear that the giving of the book was in my interest, and the sense is not materially changed if it be said that τὸ βιβλίον μοι ἠγοράσθη, *the book was bought for me*, only making the idea of personal interest more emphatic."[15]

- Since the root idea of the pure dative is personal interest (i.e., with reference to person), one should not think in such clear-cut categories as to divorce this idea from other uses of the pure dative. That is, *every pure dative use is a dative of interest in a general sense.* However, the category *dative of interest* really involves a more specific use of the dative, which emphasizes either advantage or disadvantage. Thus, for example, "This is food to me" would be a dative of interest in a general sense. However, a lousy meal would mean a dative of disadvantage, while *my* wife's culinary fare would mean a dative of advantage! A dative of disadvantage/advantage will usually belong to some other category as well; but when the idea of advantage/disadvantage is prominent, it is to be classified as such.

d. Illustrations

1) Disadvantage (*Incommodi*)

Matt 23:31   μαρτυρεῖτε **ἑαυτοῖς**
You testify **against yourselves**

1 Cor 11:29   ὁ γὰρ ἐσθίων καὶ πίνων κρίμα **ἑαυτῷ** ἐσθίει καὶ πίνει
For the one who eats and drinks eats and drinks judgment **upon himself**

Phil 1:28   ἥτις ἐστὶν **αὐτοῖς** ἔνδειξις ἀπωλείας
which is a sign of destruction **to them**

> Here the dat. indicates both ref. ("which is a sign of destruction with reference to them") *and* disadvantage. The *emphasis*, however, is that of disadvantage ("which is a sign of destruction unto their detriment"). In such cases where both are true, treat the term as belonging to the more particular category, in this case *disadvantage*. The apostle's point is

---

[15] Dana-Mantey, 84-85.

heightened by the following *genitive*: ὑμῶν δὲ σωτηρίας.[16] That is, the enemies of the gospel do not possess their destruction, but are the unfortunate recipients of it; but believers do possess their salvation. The contrast in the two cases here is not merely stylistic, but involves rich subtleties that are often not brought out in translation.

Heb 6:6   ἀνασταυροῦντας **ἑαυτοῖς** τὸν υἱὸν τοῦ θεοῦ
             again crucifying **to themselves** the Son of God

Cf. also 1 Cor 4:4; Jas 5:3; perhaps also Mark 13:9.

2)   Advantage (*Commodi*)

1 Cor 6:13   τὰ βρώματα **τῇ κοιλίᾳ**
             food is **for** [the benefit of] **the stomach**

2 Cor 5:13   εἴτε γὰρ ἐξέστημεν, **θεῷ·** εἴτε σωφρονοῦμεν, **ὑμῖν.**
             For if we are beside ourselves, it is **for God**; if we are in our right minds, it is **for you.**

Matt 5:39   ὅστις σε ῥαπίζει εἰς τὴν δεξιὰν σιαγόνα σου, στρέψον **αὐτῷ** καὶ τὴν ἄλλην
             whoever strikes you on the right cheek, turn **to him** also the other

Eph 5:19   λαλοῦντες **ἑαυτοῖς** ἐν ψαλμοῖς καὶ ὕμνοις καὶ ᾠδαῖς πνευματικαῖς, ᾄδοντες καὶ ψάλλοντες τῇ καρδίᾳ ὑμῶν τῷ κυρίῳ
             speaking **to one another** in psalms and hymns and spiritual songs, singing and making melody in your heart to the Lord
             > This is indirect object, but it is for the advantage of the recipients, as the context makes clear.

Jude 1   τοῖς ἐν θεῷ πατρὶ ἠγαπημένοις καὶ **Ἰησοῦ Χριστῷ** τετηρημένοις κλητοῖς[17]
             to those who are called, beloved in God the Father and kept **for Jesus Christ**
             > Though some would treat the dat. as agency ("kept **by** Jesus Christ") it is probably better to take it as advantage. See discussion of agency below.

Rev 21:2   Ἰερουσαλὴμ καινὴν εἶδον . . . ὡς νύμφην κεκοσμημένην **τῷ ἀνδρὶ** αὐτῆς.
             I saw the new Jerusalem . . . adorned as a bride **for her husband.**

→ ## 3. *Dative of Reference/Respect [with reference to]*

a.   Definition

The dative substantive is that in reference to which something is presented as true. An author will use this dative to qualify a statement that

---

[16] This point was lost on many scribes as can be seen in the plethora of variants for ὑμῶν, such as ὑμῖν in D¹ K L P 075 *et pauci*, ἡμῖν in C* D* F G *et pauci*.

[17] Ἰησοῦ Χριστῷ τετηρημένοις is omitted in a few late MSS (e.g., 1505 1611 1898 2138).

would otherwise typically not be true.[18] This dative can thus be called a frame of reference dative, limiting dative, qualifying dative, or contextualizing dative. This is a common use of the dative case; further, the dative is the most common case used for reference/respect.[19]

b. Key to Identification

Instead of the word *to*, supply the phrase *with reference to* before the dative. (Other glosses are *concerning*, *about*, *in regard to*, etc.) When the noun in the dative is a *thing*, the sentence typically makes no sense if the dative is removed, as, e.g., in Rom 6:2—"How shall we who died [to sin] still live in it?"

c. Amplification

The pure dative, when referring especially to things, reduces the element of interest and relation to that of reference or framework. It is frequently found with adjectives. But the dative of reference can also occasionally be used of persons (see examples below).[20]

d. Caution

Sometimes it is easy to confuse a dative of reference/respect with a dative of sphere. However, the resulting ideas frequently have the opposite meaning. In Eph 2:1, whether ὑμᾶς ὄντας νεκροὺς. . .ταῖς ἁμαρτίαις ὑμῶν means "although you were dead *in the realm of your sins*" or "although you were dead *with reference to your sins*" makes a great deal of difference (so also Rom 6:2). (On other occasions, sphere and reference shade off into one another [as in Matt 5:8, discussed below]). One ought to be careful, then, in the syntactical choices he or she makes and not be guided merely by what seems to fit *grammatically*, but also by the context and the author's intent.

e. Illustrations

Rom 6:2   οἵτινες ἀπεθάνομεν **τῇ ἁμαρτίᾳ,** πῶς ἔτι ζήσομεν ἐν αὐτῇ;
           How shall we who died [with reference] **to sin** still live in it?

---

[18] Some grammarians distinguish ethical dat. from the dat. of reference. They would say, for example, that "beautiful to God" means "beautiful as far as God is concerned" (Acts 7:20). Another way to look at this is to regard it as a dat. of reference with a personal noun in the dat. case. We will treat the two as separate categories, recognizing that most ethical datives constitute a subset of the dat. of reference.

[19] The acc. is the next most common, but it is a distant second (acc. stands first in classical Greek). There is also a gen. of reference, and, in fact, a nom. of reference (i.e., *nominativus pendens*).

[20] For distinction between dat. of ref. and ethical dat. with personal nouns, see "Ethical Dative" below.

Rom 6:11   λογίζεσθε ἑαυτοὺς εἶναι νεκροὺς μὲν **τῇ ἁμαρτίᾳ**, ζῶντας δὲ **τῷ θεῷ**
            Consider yourselves to be dead **to sin**, but alive **to God**
> The parallel between τῇ ἁμαρτίᾳ and τῷ θεῷ suggests that both function
> in the same way. The first is a dat. of reference ("dead with reference to
> sin") and, although the second is a personal noun, it also fits this cate-
> gory ("but alive with reference to God").

Luke 18:31 πάντα τὰ γεγραμμένα διὰ τῶν προφητῶν **τῷ υἱῷ** τοῦ ἀνθρώπου[21]
            all the things written by the prophets **concerning the Son** of Man
> Here is another example of dat. of ref. with a personal noun. Although
> **τῷ υἱῷ** is not the grammatical object, it is the semantic object—i.e., that
> which is talked about in the text.

Acts 16:5   αἱ ... ἐκκλησίαι ἐστερεοῦντο **τῇ πίστει**[22]
            the churches grew **in faith/with reference to faith**

Matt 5:8   μακάριοι οἱ καθαροὶ **τῇ καρδίᾳ**
            blessed are the pure **with reference to the heart**
> This could equally be considered a dat. of sphere ("pure in heart").
> Both nuances are equally applicable in this context.

Cf. also Acts 14:22; Rom 4:19; 1 Cor 14:20; Phil 2:7; Titus 2:2; Jas 2:5; 1 Pet 4:6.

4. *Ethical Dative*[23] *(Dative of Feeling) [as far as I am concerned]*

a. Definition

The dative substantive indicates the person whose feelings or viewpoint
are intimately tied to the action (or state) of the verb. This usage is quite
rare.

b. Key to Identification

Instead of *to*, paraphrase the *personal* noun in the dative with *as far as I
am concerned* (or you, he, she, etc.), *as I look at it*, or *in my opinion*.[24]

c. Semantics and Clarification

1) One might call this the *existential dative* or *dative of opinion*, in that it
    speaks of something that is true (or ought to be true) only with ref-
    erence to the one whose identity (either via noun or pronoun) is put
    in the dative. Thus, it does not speak of absolutes but of a particular
    point of view.

---

[21] περὶ τοῦ θεοῦ replaces τῷ υἱῷ in D (Θ) f^{13} 1216 1579 *et pauci*.

[22] The dat. τῇ πίστει is lacking in D.

[23] See previous section. It is possible to treat this as merely a subset of the dat. of reference.

[24] So Robertson, *Short Grammar*, 243.

2) This usage shares some kinship with the dative of reference. The differences are as follows: (1) reference normally involves a thing, while the ethical dative is always personal; (2) whereas the personal dative of reference indicates the framework (and therefore tends to be objective), the ethical dative indicates the person whose attitude is involved (and hence this usage tends to be subjective).

3) This category also shares kinship with the dative of interest (esp. dat. of advantage). The difference is one of perspective. In the sentence, τοῦτο τὸ βρῶμα μοι, if the dative is ethical, the translation would be "This is food as far as I am concerned"; if a dative of advantage, the idea would be "This is food for me."

d. Illustrations

Acts 7:20   ἀστεῖος **τῷ θεῷ**
          beautiful **to God** (= "beautiful as far as God is concerned")

Phil 1:21   **ἐμοὶ** γὰρ τὸ ζῆν Χριστός
          For **to me** to live is Christ (= "As I look at it, to live is Christ," or "As far as I am concerned, to live is Christ")

Cf. also 2 Pet 3:14 (possibly).

5. *Dative of Destination*

a. Definition

This is a dative that is similar to an indirect object, except that it appears with *intransitive* verbs (esp. ἔρχομαι). It is the "to" idea when a non-transitive verb is used. There is typically a transfer of something from one place to another. It indicates the final point of the verb, where the verb is going. This usage is relatively infrequent, being replaced in Koine Greek with explicit prepositions (such as ἐν, ἐπί, εἰς).

b. Key to Identification (and Clarification)

Basically, remember that this broad "to" idea is in relation to *intransitive* verbs (i.e., verbs that do *not* take a direct object). The dative with ἔρχομαι accounts for most examples.

c. Illustrations

Matt 21:5   ὁ βασιλεύς σου ἔρχεταί **σοι**
          your king is coming **to you**

Luke 15:25   ὡς ἐρχόμενος ἤγγισεν **τῇ οἰκίᾳ**
          when he came, he approached **the house**

Heb 12:22   προσεληλύθατε Σιὼν **ὄρει** καὶ **πόλει** θεοῦ ζῶντος. . .καὶ **μυριάσιν**
             ἀγγέλων[25]

             you have come **to Mount** Zion and **to the city** of the living God . . .
             and **to myriads** of angels

> Not every dat. of destination is impersonal, as can be seen by the last
> dat. used here, μυριάσιν (ἀγγέλων). Cf. also Matt 21:5 above.

Cf. also Luke 7:12; 23:52; John 12:21; Acts 9:1; 21:31; Heb 11:6; Rev 2:5.

6. Dative of Recipient

a. Definition

This is a dative that would ordinarily be an indirect object, except that it
appears in *verbless constructions* (such as in titles and salutations).[26] It is
used to indicate the person(s) who receives the object stated or implied.
This usage is not common.

b. Key to Identification/Semantics[27]

Basically, remember that this is a *personal* noun in the dative case occurring *in verbless constructions*. This dative occurs in two types of constructions: (1) titles and salutations in which no verb is implied;
(2) constructions within a sentence in which the dative is related to a *verbal noun* that implies a transitive verb.

c. Illustrations

Acts 23:26   Κλαύδιος Λυσίας **τῷ κρατίστῳ ἡγεμόνι Φήλικι** χαίρειν.
              Claudius Lysius, **to his Excellency, the governor Felix**, greetings.

1 Cor 1:2   **τῇ ἐκκλησίᾳ** τοῦ θεοῦ τῇ οὔσῃ ἐν Κορίνθῳ
              to the church of God which is in Corinth

Phil 1:1   **πᾶσιν τοῖς ἁγίοις**
              to all the saints

---

[25] Instead of the dat. μυριάσιν D* has μυρίων ἅγιων (corrected to μυριάσιν ἅγιων in D²),
making the καί join θεοῦ with ἀγγέλων, and both subordinate to πόλει (you have come to
Mount Zion and to the city of the living God and of the myriads of holy angels).

[26] Some prefer to take the dat. in salutations as an indirect object with an implied verb
such as γράφω (as in "Paul writes to the Corinthians . . ."). An implied verb, however, is
no more necessary in NT salutations than it is on addresses of envelopes today.

[27] The dat. of destination and the dat. of recipient are similar, though differing in two
respects: (1) destination is typically impersonal while recipient is personal; and (2) destination occurs with intransitive verbs, while recipient occurs in verbless constructions.

1 Pet 3:15   κύριον δὲ τὸν Χριστὸν ἁγιάσατε ἐν ταῖς καρδίαις ὑμῶν, ἕτοιμοι ἀεὶ πρὸς ἀπολογίαν **παντὶ τῷ αἰτοῦντι** ὑμᾶς λόγον περὶ τῆς ἐν ὑμῖν ἐλπίδος

But sanctify Christ as Lord in your hearts, be ready always with a defense **to everyone who asks** you for a word about the hope that is in you.[28]

Cf. also Rom 1:7; 2 Cor 1:1; Gal 1:2; Jude 11.

7. Dative of Possession [belonging to]

a. Definition

The dative of possession functions like a genitive of possession under certain conditions; see semantic discussion below.

The dative substantive possesses the noun to which it is related. In other words, the dative of possession is that to which the subject of an equative verb belongs. This occurs with equative verbs such as εἰμί, γίνομαι, and ὑπάρχω. It possesses the subject of such verbs. The usage is not especially common.

b. Key to Identification

Instead of the word *to*, supply *possessed by* or *belonging to*.

On occasion (especially if the dative is in predicate position after an equative verb), it may be more helpful to regard the dative as the semantic equivalent of a nominative subject and put the actual subject in the predicate (e.g., treat as direct object). For example:

Acts 8:21   οὐκ ἔστιν **σοι** μερὶς οὐδὲ κλῆρος ἐν τῷ λόγῳ τούτῳ

neither a share nor a lot in this matter **belong to you**

> This could be converted to "you have neither a share nor a lot in this matter." (The dat. becomes the subject and the subject is placed in the predicate—here, as direct object.)

Acts 2:43   Ἐγίνετο δὲ **πάσῃ ψυχῇ** φόβος, πολλά τε τέρατα καὶ σημεῖα διὰ τῶν ἀποστόλων ἐγίνετο.

And fear came **upon every soul**, and many signs and wonders were taking place through the apostles.

> The first clause could be converted to "every soul became afraid." Once again, the dat. becomes the subject, and the subject is placed in the predicate (in this instance, it becomes a predicate adjective).

---

[28] Perhaps = "defend yourselves to anyone." The construction with πρὸς ἀπολογίαν seems to be the semantic equivalent of a transitive verb and thus embeds an indirect object. For a similar example, cf. 1 Cor 9:3.

c.   **Semantics**

1)   In general, the difference between an indirect object and a possessive dative has to do with *act* (as seen in the transitive verb) and
resultant *state* (as seen in the equative verb). For example, ἔδωκεν τὸ
βιβλίον μοι ("he gave me the book") becomes τὸ βιβλίον ἐστί μοι ("the
book is mine").[29]

2)   In this connection, the distinction in *force* between a genitive of possession and a dative of possession can be analyzed: "the genitive is
used when the acquisition is recent or the emphasis is on the pos-
sessor . . . and the dative [is used] when the object possessed is to be
stressed."[30] The reason for this distinction seems to be more related
to the verb than the case: the dative of possession is used almost
exclusively with the equative verb, and the object to be possessed is
typically the *subject* of the verb. Hence, since a state rather than an
act is in view, the emphasis naturally falls on the object, and any
notion of recent acquisition is absent.

d.   **Illustrations**

Matt 18:12   Τί ὑμῖν δοκεῖ; ἐὰν γένηταί **τινι ἀνθρώπῳ** ἑκατὸν πρόβατα
What do you think? If a hundred sheep **[belong] to a certain man**

Luke 1:14   καὶ ἔσται χαρὰ **σοι** καὶ ἀγαλλίασις
and joy and gladness shall be **to you** (="joy and gladness shall be
yours")

John 1:6   ὄνομα **αὐτῷ** Ἰωάννης
The name [belonging] **to him** was John (= "His name was John")

Rom 7:3   ἐὰν γένηται **ἀνδρὶ ἑτέρῳ**
if she becomes **to another man** (= "if she becomes another man's" or,
"if she becomes possessed by another man")[31]

John 2:4   λέγει αὐτῇ ὁ Ἰησοῦς, Τί **ἐμοὶ** καὶ **σοί**, γύναι;
Jesus said to her, "What **to me** and **to you**, woman?"
> This text is problematic for more reasons than the classification of the
> dat. The entire expression is idiomatic and has been variously rendered
> as "What do I have to do with you?"; "What do we have in common?
> Leave me alone!"[32] If this construction is a legitimate dat. of possession,

---

[29] Cf. Dana-Mantey, 85.

[30] *BDF*, 102 (§189).

[31] *BDF* label this text as an "exception" to the rule that the possessive dat. is not used
for recent acquisition (ibid.). But this is not an exception to the structural pattern of *equative* verb + possessive dat. Further, as we argued above, the reason that the dat. does not
usually emphasize recent acquisition is because it is used with equative verbs (most of
which speak of state, not act). That the dat. in Rom 7:3 is used of recent acquisition is due
to the lexical force of γίνομαι, not to any confusion of the cases. Winer (264) has it right
when he suggests that with εἰμί the idea is "belonging to," and with γίνομαι "becoming
the property of."

the idea is "What do we have in common?"[33] Besides this text, it occurs in Mark 5:7; Luke 8:28; and with ἡμῖν for ἐμοί, in Matt 8:29; Mark 1:24; Luke 4:34.

Cf. also Acts 8:21; 2 Pet 1:8.

8. Dative of Thing Possessed (a debatable category) [who possesses]

a. Definition

The dative substantive denotes that which is possessed by someone (the noun to which the dative is related). This usage is exceedingly rare and, in fact, is debatable for the simple dative.

b. Key to Identification

First, remember that this use of the dative is semantically the *opposite* of the dative of *possession*. Second, remember that *with* + the dative often expresses possession in English. Third, convert the *with* to *who possesses* before the noun in the dative.

c. Is It a Legitimate Category?

There are *no clear instances* in the NT with the *simple* dative, although ἐν + the dative sometimes occurs in this sense (cf. Mark 1:23; Eph 6:2). In the least, this illustrates the difference in nuances between the simple dative and the dative after a preposition.

d. Illustrations

2 Cor 1:15 Καὶ **ταύτῃ τῇ πεποιθήσει** ἐβουλόμην πρότερον πρὸς ὑμᾶς ἐλθεῖν
And **with this confidence** I planned to come to you earlier.
> Other possibilities present themselves here: sphere, means, adverbial (manner).

Similarly, Acts 28:11.[34]

---

[32] Cf. BAGD, s.v. ἐγώ; *BDF*, 156-57 (§299.3). Though typically considered a Semitism, it did occur in wholly secular Greek (so BAGD, ibid.; Smyth, *Greek Grammar*, 341 [§1479]).

[33] So Smyth, *Greek Grammar*, 341-42 (§1479-80).

[34] Sometimes 1 Cor 4:21; 15:35; Phil 2:6 are offered as examples, but all can be otherwise explained.

9. Predicate Dative

a. Definition

The dative substantive makes an assertion about another dative substantive, much like a predicate nominative does.[35] The difference, however, is that with the predicate dative, the equative verb is a participle (in the dative case) rather than a finite verb. This category is quite rare.

b. Key to Identification: see definition

c. Clarification and Significance

This kind of dative is in reality an *emphatic kind of simple apposition* in the dative (emphatic due to the presence of the participial form of the equative verb).

d. Illustrations

Acts 16:21   ἡμῖν . . . ᾿ **Ρωμαίοις** οὖσιν
               for us . . . being **Romans**

Acts 24:24   Δρουσίλλῃ τῇ ἰδίᾳ γυναικὶ οὔσῃ ᾿Ιουδαίᾳ
               to Drusilla, his wife, who was **a Jewess**

Gal 4:8   ἐδουλεύσατε τοῖς φύσει μὴ οὖσιν **θεοῖς**
               you were enslaved to beings that were not **gods**

⮕ ## 10. Dative in Simple Apposition

a. Definition

Though not technically a syntactical category,[36] the dative case (as well as the other cases) can be an appositive to another substantive in the *same* case. An appositional construction involves two adjacent substantives that refer to the same person or thing and have the same syntactical relation to the rest of the clause. The first dative substantive can belong to *any* dative category and the second is merely a clarification of who or what is mentioned. Thus, the appositive "piggy-backs" on the first dative's use, as it were.[37] This usage is common.

---

[35] The predicate dat. follows the same rules as does the predicate nom. in terms of distinguishing between subject and predicate term (e.g., the "subject" has the article or is a pronoun). See "Nominative: Predicate Nominative" for discussion, and note the illustrations below.

[36] Hence, this category could belong in the dat., locative, or instrumental groups. It is listed here for convenience' sake.

[37] For more information on simple apposition, cf. the sections on the nominative and genitive.

b. Illustrations

Matt 27:2　παρέδωκαν Πιλάτῳ **τῷ ἡγεμόνι**
they handed [him] over to Pilate, **the governor**

Luke 1:47　ἠγαλλίασεν τὸ πνεῦμά μου ἐπὶ τῷ θεῷ **τῷ σωτῆρί** μου
my spirit rejoices in God my **Savior**

Acts 24:24　Δρουσίλλῃ **τῇ ἰδίᾳ γυναικί**
to Drusilla, **his wife**

Rom 6:23　ἐν Χριστῷ Ἰησοῦ **τῷ κυρίῳ** ἡμῶν
in Christ Jesus, our **Lord**

Heb 12:22　προσεληλύθατε Σιὼν ὄρει καὶ πόλει θεοῦ ζῶντος, **Ἰερουσαλὴμ ἐπουρανίῳ**, καὶ μυριάσιν ἀγγέλων
you have come to Mount Zion and to the city of the living God, **the heavenly Jerusalem**, and to myriads of angels

> This text also involves parallel datives not in apposition. There are no absolute structural clues for determining whether a case is appositional or parallel; a determination needs to be made on grounds other than syntactical.

Cf. also Mark 1:2; Luke 11:15; John 4:5; Acts 5:1; Rev 11:18.

Local Dative Uses

The subgroups here are specific uses built on the root idea of *position*, whether spatial, nonphysical, or temporal.

1. Dative of Place

See dative of sphere.[38]

➡ 2. Dative of Sphere [in the sphere of]

a. Definition

The dative substantive indicates the sphere or realm in which the word to which it is related takes place or exists. Normally this word is a verb, but not always.[39] This is a common use of the dative.

---

[38] I do not at the present regard this as a valid category, distinct from sphere. I am including its title because some users might question the oversight otherwise. My sense is that sphere and place are simply different applications of the same category—one figurative, the other literal. The only difference is lexical, not semantic.

[39] In our view, sphere and place are really the same thing. The distinction is lexical, not grammatical—and on such a subtle level that it is not worth mentioning since exegesis is not materially affected by such a distinction.

b. Key to Identification

Before the noun in the dative supply the words *in the sphere of* or *in the realm of.*

c. Caution/Clarification

As was pointed out earlier, it is easy to confuse a dative of reference/ respect with a dative of sphere, even though the resulting ideas *frequently* have the opposite meaning. In Eph 2:1, whether ὑμᾶς ὄντας νεκροὺς ... ταῖς ἁμαρτίαις ὑμῶν means "although you were dead *in the realm of your sins*" or "although you were dead *with reference to your sins*" makes a great deal of difference (so also Rom 6:2). (On other occasions, sphere and reference shade off into one another, as in Matt 5:8, discussed below). One ought to be careful, then, in the syntactical choices he or she makes and not be guided merely by what seems to fit *grammatically*, but also by the context and the author's intent.

In general, it is safe to say that the dative of *reference* views the word to which the dative stands related as detached or *separated* somehow from the dative, while the dative of *sphere* views the word to which the dative stands related as *incorporated* within the realm of the dative. For example, in Rom 6:2 Paul uses the dative of reference: "How shall we who died [with reference] to sin still live in it?" Here, "we who died" is detached or separated from "sin." In Eph 2:1 we see the dative of sphere: "Though you were dead in [the sphere of] your sins." Here, "you were dead" is incorporated within the realm of sin. There are exceptions to this rule of thumb, but in those passages that seem to violate this "rule," the distinction between reference and sphere also seems to be more blurred.[40]

d. Illustrations

Acts 16:5   αἱ ... ἐκκλησίαι ἐστερεοῦντο **τῇ πίστει**[41]
the churches grew **in faith**
> This could equally be considered a dat. of reference ("grew with reference to faith"). Both nuances are equally applicable.

Matt 5:8   μακάριοι οἱ καθαροὶ **τῇ καρδίᾳ**
blessed are the pure **in heart**
> This could equally be considered a dat. of reference ("pure with reference to the heart").

---

[40] The reason for the occasional blurring is that reference/respect emphasizes that *concerning which* some act is accomplished. Sphere, on the other hand, emphasizes the realm *within which* something is done. In a given instance, these two realms can blend imperceptibly into one another.

[41] D omits τῇ πίστει.

1 Pet 3:18   Χριστὸς ἅπαξ περὶ ἁμαρτιῶν ἔπαθεν, δίκαιος ὑπὲρ ἀδίκων, ... θανατωθεὶς μὲν **σαρκί**

Christ suffered once for all for sins, the just for the unjust, having been put to death **in the flesh**

Matt 5:3   οἱ πτωχοὶ **τῷ πνεύματι**

the poor **in spirit**

> Here the dat. is practically equivalent to an adverb, thus, "the spiritually poor."

John 21:8   **τῷ πλοιαρίῳ** ἦλθον

they came **in a small boat**

Luke 3:16   ἐγὼ μὲν **ὕδατι** βαπτίζω ὑμᾶς

I baptize you **in water**

> Here ὕδατι, as occasionally happens with the dat. of sphere, seems to function in a double-duty capacity—specifying both the *place* of baptism and the *means* of baptism.

Cf. also Rom 4:19; Eph 2:1 (discussed above); 1 Pet 4:1; Jude 11.

➡ 3. *Dative of Time (when)*

a. Definition

The noun in the dative indicates the *time when* the action of the main verb is accomplished. The dative routinely denotes *point of time*, answering the question, "When?" In the eight-case system, this would be the locative of time.[42] Though common enough, this usage is being increasingly replaced in Koine Greek with ἐν + the dative.[43]

b. Key to Identification

Remember that the noun in the dative expresses an indication of time.

---

[42] Though the time may be specific from the perspective of the speaker, this does not imply that the audience was privy to it. Cf., e.g., Luke 12:20 (discussed below); 17:29-30. At other times the dat. may be used simply to ask the general question, "When?" in an undefined sense. That is, though the answer may be general ("on that day," "in that hour"), the emphasis is not on the *kind* of time as it would be with the gen., but simply on the time when. Thus the dat. of time may *seem* to behave like a gen. of time, when actual cases of such are extremely rare.

The difference, as I see it, is that the gen. focuses on kind of time and/or time during which an *extended* event takes place; the dat., on the other hand, focuses on a point of time in which a usually *instantaneous* event takes place. Whether this event is known, or anticipated as such, the dat. still focuses on this feature. It is as if the dat. is equal to an aorist (in the sense of summary action) and the gen. is equal to a present tense (in that the event is looked at internally).

[43] This was not a new feature of the Koine, for ἐν + dat. for time "was already widespread in the classical language" (*BDF*, 107 [§200]).

c. Significance/Semantics

The dative of time is distinct from the genitive of time as well the accusative of time. The easiest way to remember the distinction between these cases for time is to remember the root idea of each case. The root idea of the (pure) genitive is quality, attribute, or kind. Thus, the genitive of time expresses *kind* of time (or time during which). The root idea of the accusative is limitation as to extent. Thus, the accusative of time expresses *extent* of time. The root idea of the *local* dative is position. Thus, the dative of time expresses a *point* in time. (Just remember that the local dative is "a case in point.")

d. Clarification

Although the dative largely has the force of *point*, it occasionally overlaps with the accusative of time,[44] and rarely with the genitive of time.[45]

e. Illustrations

Matt 17:23   τῇ τρίτῃ ἡμέρᾳ ἐγερθήσεται[46]

[at a point in time] **on the third day** he will be raised

Every occurrence of "the third day" with reference to Jesus' resurrection in the Gospels is put in the dat. without an accompanying preposition. Cf. Matt 16:21; 20:19; Luke 9:22; 18:33; 24:7, 46.[47]

---

[44] *BDF* suggest that the only certain examples of the dat. for acc. of time occur with transitive verbs, either active or passive (108 [§201]), citing only Luke 8:29 (which can be explained as a true dat. in a distributive sense: "on many occasions"); Rom 16:25. But cf. also Luke 1:75; 8:27; John 14:9; Acts 8:11; 13:20; and possibly John 2:20 (though the use of the case here is complicated by several factors; see discussion of this in the chapter on the aorist tense). (Most of these examples use either "time" [χρόνος] or "year" [ἔτος] as the dat. term.) It is possible to take μιᾷ ὥρᾳ in Rev 18:10 as indicating extent, as is evident by the acc. in codex A and a dozen other MSS, but the context suggests more a "time within which" notion (thus = gen. of time).

Various reasons for the dative's behavior have been suggested: attraction to Latin ablative (*BDF*, 108 [§201]) and an instrumental (as opposed to locative) use of the dat. (so Robertson, *Grammar*, 527) are among the leading contenders. Robertson is surely closer to the truth; cf. his critique of Blass on 528.

[45] *BDF* argue that the simple dat. is never used for a "period within which" (=gen. of time) in the NT, calling such "impossible," though they admit that ἐν + dat. is sometimes so used (*BDF*, 107 [§200]). Yet, though quite rare, even the simple dat. can be used like a gen. of time (cf. Rev 18:10, 17, 19 [with *v.ll.* for each text]).

[46] μετὰ τρεῖς ἡμέρας is found in D.

[47] It might not be insignificant that this expression only occurs in Matthew and Luke, Mark exclusively having the more primitive expression "after three days" (cf. Mark 9:31; 10:34).

Matt 24:20   προσεύχεσθε δὲ ἵνα μὴ γένηται ἡ φυγὴ ὑμῶν χειμῶνος μηδὲ **σαββάτῳ**[48]
             But pray that your flight will not be during the winter nor **on the
             sabbath**

> A nice contrast is seen here between the genitive of time (χειμῶνος),
> indicating time during which, and the dative of time, indicating a
> point.

Mark 6:21   Ἡρῴδης **τοῖς γενεσίοις** αὐτοῦ δεῖπνον ἐποίησεν
             Herod **on** his **birthday** prepared a feast

Luke 12:20   **ταύτῃ τῇ νυκτὶ** τὴν ψυχήν σου ἀπαιτοῦσιν ἀπὸ σοῦ
             [at a point in time] **in this night** your soul shall be required of you[49]

Gal 6:9   τὸ δὲ καλὸν ποιοῦντες μὴ ἐγκακῶμεν, **καιρῷ** γὰρ **ἰδίῳ** θερίσομεν μὴ
             ἐκλυόμενοι
             let us not cease from doing good, for we shall reap **at the proper
             moment** if we do not give up

> Though frequently translated "in due season" (so KJV, ASV, RSV), the
> dat. construction more probably implies something like "at just the
> right moment."[50]

Cf. also Matt 24:42; Mark 12:2; 14:12, 30; Luke 9:37; 13:14, 16; 20:10; Acts 12:6; 23:11;
2 Cor 6:2.

4. Dative of Rule [in conformity with]

a.   Definition

The dative substantive specifies the rule or code a person follows or the
standard of conduct to which he or she conforms. This usage is rare.

b.   Key to Identification

Before the dative supply the words *according to*, or *in conformity with*.

c.   Clarification/Semantics

(1) This category seems to fit under the broader umbrella of local dative
in a loose way. It seems close to sphere as well as means in its nuance. In
fact, there are occasions when a dative of rule apparently functions in a
double-duty capacity with one or the other of these nuances. However,

---

[48] σαββάτου is found in D L M Φ 047 *et pauci*; σαββάτων in 094 (both gen. readings are
motivated by the parallel with χειμῶνος); ἐν σαββάτῳ is found in E F G H 28 565 1424 *et
alii*. But the naked dat. reading has the earliest and most widespread support (א B K S U
V W Y Z Γ Δ Θ Π Σ Ω *f*[1,13] *et alii*).

[49] See the category "Indefinite Plural" in the chapter on "Person and Number," for
rationale on the translation above (as opposed to "in this night they will require your
soul").

[50] This is the only occurrence of the singular καιρῷ ἰδίῳ in the NT, though the plural
always has this force (cf. 1 Tim 2:6; 6:15; Titus 1:3, and cf. the RSV in these places).

we have placed it under the group of local dative because it suggests boundary—that is, a "standard" is a measure within which one remains.

(2) The dative term is lexically nuanced: it is a word that implies some sort of standard, rule, code of conduct, etc. (such as ἔθος, ἴχνος, κανών, and the like). As well, most examples occur with certain kinds of verbs that also imply a code of conduct (such as περιπατέω and στοιχέω).

d. Illustrations

1) Clear Examples

Acts 14:16 εἴασεν πάντα τὰ ἔθνη πορεύεσθαι **ταῖς ὁδοῖς** αὐτῶν
He allowed all the nations to walk **in** their own **ways** (= "according to their own ways")

Gal 6:16 ὅσοι **τῷ κανόνι τούτῳ** στοιχήσουσιν, εἰρήνη ἐπ᾽ αὐτοὺς
as many as will live **according to this standard**, peace upon them

1 Pet 2:21 Χριστὸς ἔπαθεν ὑπὲρ ὑμῶν, ὑμῖν ὑπολιμπάνων ὑπογραμμὸν ἵνα ἐπακολουθήσητε **τοῖς ἴχνεσιν** αὐτοῦ
Christ suffered for you, leaving you an example, that you should follow **in** his **steps**

Cf. also Luke 6:38; Acts 15:1; 21:21; Rom 4:12; 2 Cor 10:12; 12:18; Phil 3:16.

2) An Improbable Example

Gal 5:16 **πνεύματι** περιπατεῖτε καὶ ἐπιθυμίαν σαρκὸς οὐ μὴ τελέσητε
walk **by the Spirit** and you will not fulfill the lust of the flesh

> The dat. πνεύματι could be variously interpreted. It is possible to see it as sphere or means. Although there is a collocation of the dat. with στοιχέω in v 25, it is unnecessary to postulate, as some have done, this as a dat. of rule. Such is unlikely on two grounds: (1) πνεῦμα does not inherently imply a rule or standard; (2) the force of the immediate context and the whole of Galatians is against this: it is not the *standard* of the Spirit that enables one to resist the flesh, but the *empowering* of the Spirit. Paul is clear that the law, any law, cannot do anything to counter the fleshly forces within.

Instrumental Dative Uses

The subgroups here are specific uses built on the root idea of *means*, although some loosely fit under this umbrella.

➡ **1. Dative of Association (Accompaniment, Comitative) [in association with]**

a. Definition

The dative substantive indicates the person or thing one associates with or accompanies. This usage is relatively common.

b. Key to Identification

Before the noun in the dative supply the phrase *in association with*.

c. Clarification

- This usage of the dative only loosely belongs under the broad category of instrumental datives. Nevertheless, it belongs here more naturally than elsewhere.[51]

- Frequently, though not always, the dative word will be related to a compound verb involving σύν. This is especially so in Acts, less frequently in the Pauline letters. On the other hand, not every dative following a σύν- prefixed verb is a dative of association (see discussion of the debatable example below).[52]

- The difference between genitive of association and dative of association is simply this: the genitive is used with *nouns* (which begin with σύν-) while the dative is used with *verbs* (which are frequently prefixed with σύν-).

d. Caution

Although there is a close relation between means and association, one should be careful to distinguish them. In the sentence, "He walked with his friend with a cane," "with his friend" expresses association and "with a cane" expresses means. The difference, of course, is that for the purposes of walking the cane is necessary, while the friend is expendable!

e. Illustrations

1) Clear Examples

Acts 9:7   οἱ δὲ ἄνδρες οἱ συνοδεύοντες **αὐτῷ**
the men who were traveling **with him**
> A typical example in which the verbal prefix is σύν.

---

[51] Dana-Mantey (88) suggest an ingenious though improbable relationship between association and instrumentality: "the second person supplies the means of fellowship."

[52] Cf. *BDF*, 103-4 (§193) for discussion of the kinds of verbs used. Besides σύν- verbs, *BDF* mention verbs prefixed with παρά, ἐπί, πρός, διά, κτλ., as well as verbs whose lexemes carry an associative idea (such as κοινωνέω, ἑτεροζυγέω, κολλάω).

2 Cor 6:14   μὴ γίνεσθε ἑτεροζυγοῦντες **ἀπίστοις**
              do not become unequally yoked [in association] **with unbelievers**
              This is an example in which the verb *root* carries an associative idea.

Eph 2:5   συνεζωοποίησεν **τῷ Χριστῷ**[53]
              he made us alive together **with Christ**

Heb 11:31   Πίστει Ῥαὰβ ἡ πόρνη οὐ συναπώλετο **τοῖς ἀπειθήσασιν**
              By faith Rahab the harlot did not perish **along with those who were disobedient**

Jas 2:22   ἡ πίστις συνήργει **τοῖς ἔργοις** αὐτοῦ
              faith cooperated **with** his **works**
              Here is an unusual instance of a dat. of association with an *impersonal* noun. Yet even here πίστις and ἔργοις are personified by the author.

Cf. also Mark 2:15; 9:4; John 4:9; 6:22; Acts 9:39; 10:45; 11:3; 13:31; 1 Cor 5:9; 6:16, 17; Col 3:1; 2 Thess 3:14; Heb 11:25; 3 John 8; Rev 8:4.

2) A Debatable Example

Rom 8:16   αὐτὸ τὸ πνεῦμα συμμαρτυρεῖ **τῷ πνεύματι** ἡμῶν ὅτι ἐσμὲν τέκνα θεοῦ
              the Spirit himself bears witness **along with** our **spirit** that we are God's children
              At issue, grammatically, is whether the Spirit testifies *alongside of* our spirit (dat. of association), or whether he testifies *to our spirit* (indirect object) that we are God's children. If the former, the one receiving this testimony is unstated (is it God? or believers?). If the latter, the believer receives the testimony and hence is assured of salvation via the inner witness of the Spirit. The first view has the advantage of a σύν- prefixed verb, which might be expected to take an accompanying dat. of association (and is supported by NEB, JB, etc.).

              But there are three reasons why πνεύματι should *not* be taken as association: (1) Grammatically, a dat. with a σύν- prefixed verb does not necessarily indicate association.[54] This, of course, does not preclude such here, but this fact at least opens up the alternatives in this text. (2) Lexically, though συμμαρτυρέω originally bore an associative idea, it developed in the direction of merely intensifying μαρτυρέω. This is surely the case in the only other NT text with a dat. (Rom 9:1).[55] (3) Contextually, a dat. of association does not seem to support Paul's argument: "What standing has our spirit in *this* matter? Of itself it surely has no right at all to testify to our being sons of God."[56]

---

[53] ἐν is read before τῷ Χριστῷ in 𝔓[46] B 33 *et pauci.*

[54] Although most nonassociative datives following σύν- verbs are impersonal (e.g., Luke 11:48; Acts 8:1; 18:7; Rom 7:22; 8:26; 12:2; Eph 5:11; Phil 1:27; 2 Tim 1:8; Rev 18:4), personal datives are not without representation (in 1 Cor 4:4 ἐμαυτῷ is a dat. *incommodi* after σύνοιδα; in Acts 6:9 τῷ Στεφάνῳ is indirect object after συζητέω [a construction in which the direct object is only implied, but cf. Mark 9:10, 16; Luke 22:23]).

[55] BAGD note that as early as the sixth century BCE "the prefix συν- has in the highest degree the effect of strengthening" (s.v. συμμαρτυρέω, 778).

[56] Cranfield, *Romans* (ICC) 1.403 (italics original).

In sum, Rom 8:16 seems to be secure as a text in which the believer's assurance of salvation is based on the inner witness of the Spirit. The implications of this for one's soteriology are profound: The objective data, as helpful as they are, cannot by themselves provide *assurance* of salvation; the believer also needs (and receives!) an existential, ongoing encounter with God's Spirit in order to gain that familial comfort.[57]

2. Dative of Manner (or Adverbial Dative)[58] [with, in (answering "How?")]

a. Definition

The dative substantive denotes the manner in which the action of the verb is accomplished. Like many adverbs, this use of the dative answers the question "How?" (and typically with a "with" or "in" phrase). The manner can be an accompanying action, attitude, emotion, or circumstance. Hence, such a dative noun routinely has an abstract quality. This usage is relatively common,[59] being supplanted by ἐν + dative (or μετά + gen.) in Koine Greek.

b. Key to Identification

Supply *with* or *in* before the dative noun. Also, if the dative can be converted into an adverb (e.g., "with thanksgiving" becomes "thankfully"), it is most likely a dative of manner. (It should be noted, however, that not always can one easily convert this dative into an adverb.)

c. Clarification

The real key is to ask first whether the dative noun answers the question "How?" and then ask if the dative *defines* the action of the verb (dative of means) or adds color to the verb (manner). In the sentence, "She walked with a cane with a flare," "with a cane" expresses means, while "with a flare" expresses manner. Thus, *one* of the ways in which you can distinguish between means and manner is that a dative of manner typically employs an abstract noun while a dative of means typically employs a more concrete noun.

---

[57] Perhaps the most neglected factor in modern American evangelical debates over soteriology is the role of the Spirit in the process.

[58] A subcategory of dat. of manner is the cognate dat. (discussed below).

[59] If the cognate dat. is included. Many a Koine adverb may have started out as a dat. of manner: e.g., εἰκῇ, κρυφῇ, λάθρᾳ, κτλ., but to regard these as true datives would be anachronistic. However, some words, such as δημοσίᾳ, continue to vacillate between adnominal (Acts 5:18) and adverbial functions (cf. Acts 16:37).

d. Illustrations

John 7:26   **παρρησίᾳ** λαλεῖ
he speaks **with boldness** (= **boldly**)

1 Cor 10:30   εἰ ἐγὼ **χάριτι** μετέχω
if I partake [of the food] **with thanksgiving** (= **thankfully**)

Phil 1:18   εἴτε **προφάσει** εἴτε **ἀληθείᾳ**, Χριστὸς καταγγέλλεται
whether **in pretext** or **in truth**, Christ is being proclaimed

Mark 14:65   οἱ ὑπηρέται **ῥαπίσμασιν** αὐτὸν ἔλαβον
the guards received him **with blows**

> In this instance a concrete noun is used, but the force is still manner. The violence was not a necessary means of "welcoming" Jesus, but it depicts the attitude and actions that accompanied this reception.

2 Cor 7:4   ὑπερπερισσεύομαι **τῇ χαρᾷ** ἐπὶ πάσῃ τῇ θλίψει ἡμῶν[60]
I overflow **with joy** in all our affliction

Cf. also John 7:13; Acts 11:23; 16:37; 1 Cor 11:5; Rev 5:12; 18:21.

➡ 3. *Dative of Means/Instrument [by, by means of, with]*

a. Definition

The dative substantive is used to indicate the means or instrument by which the verbal action is accomplished. This is a very common use of the dative, embracing as it does one of the root ideas of the dative case (viz., instrumentality).

b. Key to Identification

Before the noun in the dative, supply the words *by means of*, or simply *with*.

c. Amplification

The dative noun is typically concrete, as opposed to manner, where the noun is typically abstract. The noun in the dative is *conceived of as impersonal*. It is not necessarily so, however. But it is distinguished from personal agency in two ways: (1) personality is not in view, and (2) means involves an agent who uses it (whether that agent is stated or implied).

d. Illustrations

Matt 8:16   ἐξέβαλεν τὰ πνεύματα **λόγῳ**
he cast out the spirits **by** [means of] **a word**

---

[60] Codex B has ἐν before τῇ χαρᾷ.

John 11:2   ἐκμάξασα τοὺς πόδας αὐτοῦ **ταῖς θριξὶν** αὐτῆς
she wiped his feet **with** her **hair**

Acts 12:2   ἀνεῖλεν δὲ Ἰάκωβον τὸν ἀδελφὸν Ἰωάννου **μαχαίρῃ**
now he put to death James, John's brother, **with a sword**

Rom 3:28   λογιζόμεθα δικαιοῦσθαι **πίστει** ἄνθρωπον[61]
we maintain that a person is justified **by faith**

Gal 2:8   ὁ γὰρ ἐνεργήσας **Πέτρῳ** εἰς ἀποστολὴν τῆς περιτομῆς ἐνήργησεν καὶ **ἐμοὶ** εἰς τὰ ἔθνη
For the one who worked **through Peter** for the apostleship of circumcision also worked **through me** for the Gentiles

> Although Peter and Paul are persons, their personality is not in view here: rather, they are presented as instruments in the hands of God.

Phil 4:6   ἐν παντὶ **τῇ προσευχῇ καὶ τῇ δεήσει** μετὰ εὐχαριστίας τὰ αἰτήματα ὑμῶν γνωριζέσθω πρὸς τὸν θεόν
in everything, **by prayer and petition** with thanksgiving, let your requests be made known to God

Cf. also Acts 12:6; 26:18; 2 Cor 1:11; 8:9 (unless this is cause); Heb 11:17; 2 Pet 3:5; Rev 22:14.[62]

† 4. Dative of Agency [by, through]

a. Definition

The dative substantive is used to indicate the *personal* agent by whom the action of the verb is accomplished. This is an *extremely rare* category in the NT, as well as in ancient Greek in general.

b. Keys to Identification, Structure and Semantics

(1) According to the above definition, if the dative is used to express agency, the noun in the dative must not only be personal, but must also be the agent who performs the action. Much confusion exists among students of the NT over this category. In general, it is invoked *far* more often than is legitimate.[63]

---

[61] For πίστει F G read διὰ πίστεως, a *v.l.* which, in the least, confirms the notion of means.

[62] John 8:6 (**τῷ δακτύλῳ** κατέγραφεν) affords a concrete example of means, though the *pericope adulterae* is almost surely not a part of the original text.

[63] Even by grammarians on occasion. Cf., e.g., Young, *Intermediate Greek*, 50 (his examples from Rom 8:14 and 1 Tim 3:16 are doubtful; see discussion of these texts below); Brooks-Winbery, 45.

There are *four keys* to identification for the dative of agency: (a) *Lexical*: the dative must be personal. (b) *Contextual*: the person specified by the dative noun is portrayed as exercising volition.[64] (c) *Grammatical*: the only clear texts involve a perfect passive verb,[65] as in the classical idiom.[66] (d) *Linguistic*: a good *rule of thumb* for distinguishing between agent and means is simply this: the agent of a passive verb can become the subject of an active verb, while the means normally cannot.[67]

(2) When the dative expresses the idea of *means*, the instrument is used *by an agent*. When agent is indicated, the agent so named is *not used* by another, but is the one who either performs an act directly or uses an instrument. Thus, a dative of means *can* be (and often is) used of *persons*, though they are conceived of as impersonal (i.e., used as an instrument by someone else). For example, in the sentence, "God disciplined me by means of my parents," "God" is the agent who uses the "parents" as the *means* by which he accomplished something. The parents are, of course, persons! But they are conceived of as impersonal in that the focus is not on their personality, but on their instrumentality as used by an agent.

c. **How Agency is Expressed in the NT**

Apart from naming the agent as the subject, there are two common ways to express agency in the NT: ὑπό + the genitive is used for *ultimate* agent; διά + the genitive is used for *intermediate* agent. For example, in Matt 1:22 we read that "all this happened in order that what was spoken **by the Lord** (ὑπὸ κυρίου) **through the prophet** (διὰ τοῦ προφήτου) might be ful-filled." The Lord is the ultimate agent, though he communicates his mes-sage through the prophet.[68]

In summary, this clarification is important because when one sees a dative used with a person and some sort of instrumentality is implied, he/she should seek to discover the *agent* who uses the (personal) instru-ment.

---

[64] Recall that in Gal 2:8 (noted above under "Dative of Means") Peter and Paul are treated as instruments in God's hands; their volition is not in view.

[65] *BDF* (102 [§191]) may be too pessimistic in seeing Luke 23:15 as the lone "genuine example" in the NT.

[66] See Smyth, *Greek Grammar*, 343-44 (§1488-94), for an extended discussion. Smyth offers the insight that "the usual restriction of the dative to tenses of completed action seems to be due to the fact that the agent is represented as placed in the position of view-ing an already completed action in the light of its relation to himself . . ." (ibid., 343-44 [§1489]).

[67] See T. Givón, *Syntax*, 139, n. 7 (§ 5.3): "To my knowledge, no clear cases exist of the *instrument* or *manner* ever becoming subjects of simple/active clauses." Cf. also § 5.3.4 (142) and § 5.3.5 (143). But Givón gives examples that seem to contradict this, such as: "the hammer broke the window" transforms "the window was broken by the hammer" (143).

[68] The issue of agency with prepositions will be developed more fully in the chapters on prepositions and verb voice.

d. Illustrations

1) Clear Examples

Luke 23:15 οὐδὲν ἄξιον θανάτου ἐστὶν πεπραγμένον **αὐτῷ** [69]
nothing worthy of death had been done **by him**

> As is apparently always the case in the NT, the only clear examples involve a perfect passive verb form.

Jas 3:7 πᾶσα γὰρ φύσις θηρίων . . . δεδάμασται **τῇ φύσει τῇ ἀνθρωπίνῃ**
for every kind of beast . . . has been tamed **by humankind**

Cf. also John 18:15; Rom 14:18;[70] 2 Pet 2:19 (if ᾧ is personal) for other possible texts.

2) Debatable Examples

Jude 1 τοῖς ἐν θεῷ πατρὶ ἠγαπημένοις καὶ **Ἰησοῦ Χριστῷ** τετηρημένοις κλητοῖς[71]
to those who are called, beloved by God, and kept **by Jesus Christ**

> It is probably better to take Ἰησοῦ Χριστῷ as a dat. of advantage ("kept *for* Jesus Christ"). But if this is agency, it fits the pattern of dat. after a perfect passive verb.

1 Tim 3:16 ὤφθη **ἀγγέλοις**
he was seen **by angels**

> This text (as well as others with ὤφθη and similar verbs) can be variously interpreted: either "he *appeared* **to angels**" or "he *was seen* **by angels**." If the former, the dat. would be recipient (and the passive verb could be perceived as merely intransitive).[72] If the latter, the dat. would still not fit the contours of clearly definable datives of agency, either contextually (no volition is required in the act of seeing) or grammatically (the verb is aorist, not perfect).

Gal 5:16 **πνεύματι** περιπατεῖτε καὶ ἐπιθυμίαν σαρκὸς οὐ μὴ τελέσητε
walk **by the Spirit** and you will not fulfill the lust of the flesh

> Taking πνεύματι as a dat. of agency is a popular view among commentators,[73] but there are two basic problems with this interpretation: (1) This usage is quite rare in the NT (unless, of course, we assume that πνεύματι on many occasions belongs here!); (2) πνεύματι does not occur with a passive verb, let alone a perfect passive; yet every clear example

---

[69] The addition of ἐν before αὐτῷ in D N X Γ 0211 *f*[13] *et pauci* is a later emendation.

[70] These texts employ an adjective ending in -τος , as was also done in classical Greek (Smyth, *Greek Grammar*, 343 [§1488]). However, they are capable of other interpretations.

[71] Ἰησοῦ Χριστῷ τετηρημένοις is omitted in a few late MSS (e.g., 1505 1611 1898 2138).

[72] It is not insignificant that virtually every time ὤφθη is used in the NT with a simple dat., the subject of the verb consciously *initiates* the visible manifestation; in no instance can it be said that the person(s) in the dat. case initiate(s) the act. In other words, volition rests wholly with the subject, while the dat. noun is merely recipient. Cf. Luke 1:11; 22:43; 24:34; Acts 7:2, 26, 30; 13:31; 16:9; 1 Cor 15:5, 6, 7, 8. (The only problematic texts are Mark 9:4 and its parallel, Matt 17:3; but even here the appearance of Elijah and Moses was clearly not anticipated by the disciples.)

[73] Cf., e.g., E. D. W. Burton, *Galatians* (ICC) 303; Hendriksen, *Galatians* (NTC) 216-17; Bruce, *Galatians* (NIGTC) 245-46; Guthrie, *Galatians* (NCBC) 136.

of dat. of agency in the NT occurs with a perfect passive verb. The implication of these considerations is this: It unmasks an *assumption* by many commentators that the Spirit's distinct personality was fully recognized in the early apostolic period. It appeals to a possible category in light of later theological articulations. But such an assumption is clearly question-begging if the grammatical data are hardly on its side.[74]

This certainly raises some questions that can be addressed only in part here: We are not arguing that the distinct personality and deity of the Spirit are foreign to the NT, but just that there is progressive revelation *within* the NT, just as there is *between* the Testaments. Thus in the earlier books (such as Galatians) we might see the Spirit's personality only "through a glass darkly," as it were.[75] As much as theologians can glean from the text, it must be admitted that the Bible is not a systematic theology. The books of the Bible must be examined in their historical setting.

What then is the use of the dat.? Most likely, means.[76] This label does *not* deny the personality of the Holy Spirit. It should be noted that, in all probability, *none* of the examples involving πνεύματι in the NT should be classified as agency.[77]

5. *Dative of Measure/Degree of Difference [by]*

a. Definition

The dative substantive, when following or preceding a comparative adjective or adverb, may be used to indicate the extent to which the comparison is true or the degree of difference that exists in the comparison. This usage is fairly rare.

b. Key to Identification

Rather than supply *than* as with the genitive of comparison (the two ideas are similar, but not identical),[78] supply *by* before a quantitative

---

[74] It is interesting that all of the NT examples of ὑπό + πνεύματος, indicating as they apparently do the personality of the Spirit, occur in later books (cf. Matt 4:1; Luke 2:26; Acts 13:4; 16:6; 2 Pet 1:21).

[75] This finds a parallel with articulation about Christ's deity: Only in the later books is he explicitly called θεός. The reasons for this are surely related to the strict monotheistic soil out of which the NT grew. As R. T. France has articulated, "It was such shocking language that, even when the beliefs underlying it were firmly established, it was easier, and perhaps more politic, to express these beliefs in less direct terms. The wonder is not that the NT so seldom describes Jesus as God, but that in such a milieu it does so at all" ("The Worship of Jesus—A Neglected Factor in Christological Debate?" *VE* 12 [1981] 25).

[76] As we will demonstrate in the discussion of ἐν πνεύματι in 1 Cor 12:13 (in the chapter on prepositions), to treat (ἐν) πνεύματι as agent causes other theological and exegetical difficulties.

[77] Cf. Rom 8:13, 14; 1 Cor 14:2; Gal 3:3; 5:5, 18, 25; Eph 1:13; 1 Pet 3:18, all of which are probably datives of means.

[78] Both may even occur in the same clause; cf. Heb 1:4 below.

word in the dative. Typically the formula in Greek will be πολλῷ (the dative word) + μᾶλλον.

c. Illustrations

Rom 5:8-9   ἔτι ἁμαρτωλῶν ὄντων ἡμῶν Χριστὸς ὑπὲρ ἡμῶν ἀπέθανεν. (9) **πολλῷ** οὖν μᾶλλον δικαιωθέντες νῦν ἐν τῷ αἵματι αὐτοῦ σωθησόμεθα δι᾽ αὐτοῦ ἀπὸ τῆς ὀργῆς.

While we were yet sinners, Christ died for us. **Much** more [literally, "more **by much**"], then, since we have now been justified by his blood, we shall be saved from the [coming] wrath through him.

Phil 2:12   ὑπηκούσατε . . . **πολλῷ** μᾶλλον ἐν τῇ ἀπουσίᾳ μου

you obeyed . . . **much** more in my absence

Heb 1:4   **τοσούτῳ** κρείττων γενόμενος τῶν ἀγγέλων

having become **by so much** better than the angels

> A key theme in Hebrews is the superiority of the Son. In 1:4-14 the Son is contrasted to angels, with the clear implication (made explicit in v 8) that he is God incarnate.

Cf. also Matt 6:30; Mark 10:48; Luke 18:39; Rom 5:10, 15, 17; 2 Cor 3:9, 11; Phil 1:23; Heb 10:25.

➡ 6. Dative of Cause [because of]

a. Definition

The dative substantive indicates the cause or basis of the action of the verb. This usage is fairly common.

b. Key to Identification

Before the dative insert the phrase *because of* or *on the basis of.*

c. Clarification

This use of the dative is similar to but not the same as the dative of means. (At times, however, it is impossible to distinguish the two.)[79] The dative of *means* indicates the *how*; the dative of *cause* indicates the *why*; the dative of *means* indicates the *method*; the dative of *cause* indicates the *basis*. Also, it is not always best to translate the dative of cause as "because of." This is due to the fact that in English, "because" may express cause *or* motive. The two ideas are similar, but not identical. Thus, occasionally it is best to translate the dative of cause with "by " or "on the basis of." In Eph 2:8, for example (τῇ γὰρ χάριτί ἐστε σεσῳσμένοι διὰ πίστεως), τῇ χάριτι is the cause of our salvation (and διὰ πίστεως

---

[79] This is due to the fact that the ultimate cause may also, at times, be the accomplishing means of an action.

expresses the means). However, it would be better to translate it as "by grace" or "on the basis of grace" instead of "because of grace," since this last phrase might be construed as indicating only God's motive, but not the basis of our salvation.

d. Illustrations

Luke 15:17   Πόσοι μίσθιοι τοῦ πατρός μου περισσεύονται ἄρτων, ἐγὼ δὲ **λιμῷ** ὧδε ἀπόλλυμαι;
How many of my father's hirelings are overflowing in bread, but I am perishing here **because of a famine?**

Rom 4:20   οὐ διεκρίθη **τῇ ἀπιστίᾳ**
he did not waver **because of unbelief**

Gal 6:12   μόνον ἵνα **τῷ σταυρῷ** τοῦ Χριστοῦ μὴ διώκωνται
only that they might not be persecuted **because of the cross** of Christ

Phil 1:14   . . . τοὺς πλείονας τῶν ἀδελφῶν ἐν κυρίῳ πεποιθότας **τοῖς δεσμοῖς** μου
. . . most of the brothers having become confident in the Lord **because of** my **bonds**

Cf. also Rom 11:30-32; 2 Cor 2:7; Eph 2:8 (discussed above); 1 Pet 4:12.

7. *Cognate Dative*[80]

a. Definition

The dative noun[81] is cognate to the verb either formally (where both noun and verb have the same root) or conceptually (where the roots are different). This is not common.

b. Key to Identification

The key, of course, will be the cognate *force* of the dative. However, another clue will be that the dative can usually be translated as an adverb modifying the verb.[82]

c. Significance and Clarification

The force of the cognate dative will be primarily to *emphasize the action of the verb*. However, this use of the dative will usually fit under another

---

[80] See dat. of manner for the larger category to which this dat. belongs.

[81] This use of the dat., by definition, cannot be used with pronouns, since the *lexical* meaning of the dat. word is related to that of the verb.

[82] Some of the examples below do not fit this adverbial notion, but are cognate datives in a broader sense.

category of the dative as well (in particular, manner). But when an author chooses his words so that the noun in the dative is cognate to the verb, this is a clue that the cognate idea (i.e., that of emphasizing the action of the verb) is the main thrust of the dative.

d. Illustrations

1) Cognate in Form

Luke 22:15 **ἐπιθυμίᾳ** ἐπεθύμησα
I desired **with desire**
(= "I earnestly desired")

Acts 2:17 οἱ πρεσβύτεροι ὑμῶν **ἐνυπνίοις** ἐνυπνιασθήσονται
your old men will dream **dreams**
The dat. here seems also to function as the direct object.

Jas 5:17 Ἠλίας . . . **προσευχῇ** προσηύξατο
Elijah . . . prayed **earnestly**

Rev 14:2 κιθαρῳδῶν κιθαριζόντων **ταῖς κιθάραις** (*v.l.*)
harpists harping **on their harps**
Not only is the dat. cognate to the verb (participle), but so is the gen. noun! Cf. also Heb 8:10 and 10:16 for a similar phenomenon (in these instances, of cognate nom.).[83]

Cf. also Mark 1:26; John 3:29; Col 2:11; Rev 14:18.

2) Cognate in Meaning

1 Pet 1:8 ἀγαλλιᾶσθε **χαρᾷ**
you rejoice **with joy**

Rev 5:11-12 ἤκουσα φωνὴν. . . λέγοντες **φωνῇ μεγάλῃ**
I heard a voice. . . saying **with a loud voice**

Cf. also Rev 5:2; 7:10; 8:13; 10:3; 14:7, 9.[84]

8. *Dative of Material*

a. Definition

The dative substantive denotes the material that is used to accomplish the action of the verb. This use is fairly rare.

---

[83] The dat. ταῖς κιθάραις is preceded by ἐν in almost all Greek witnesses. Thus, though the above is an illuminating example, it is hardly original.

[84] Its frequency in Revelation is due largely to the Semitic mindset of the author. Whether he was thinking in Hebrew and writing in Greek, however, is a separate issue.

b. Key to Identification and Clarification

The noun in the dative will usually be a *quantitative* word (although an occasional metaphorical application will be seen). The difference between this usage and that of means has to do with whether or not the item used is a *tool*. If it is a tool, the dative indicates means; if it is not, the dative indicates material. (For example, one writes with ink and with a pen. The ink is the material, the pen is the means.) The difference between this and the *genitive* of material is that the genitive of material is related to a *noun* while the dative of material is related to a *verb*.

c. Illustrations

John 11:2   Μαριὰμ . . . ἀλείψασα τὸν κύριον **μύρῳ**
             Mary . . . anointed the Lord **with ointment**
             > The verbal notion of anointing suggests the application of some sub-
             > stance to an object. Thus, even in Acts 10:38 ("God anointed [ἔχρισεν]
             > him *with the Holy Spirit* and *with power*"), the datives are presented as
             > material.

2 Cor 3:3   ἐγγραμμένη οὐ **μέλανι**
             written not **with ink**

Heb 2:7   **δόξῃ** καὶ **τιμῇ** ἐστεφάνωσας αὐτόν
             he has crowned him **with glory** and **honor**

Cf. also Mark 6:13; Luke 7:38, 46; Gal 6:11; Heb 2:9; Jas 5:14.

† 9. *Dative of Content*

a. Definition

The noun in the dative denotes the content that is used by a verb of *filling*. This usage is debatable in the NT (in part because it is difficult to distinguish it from material; in part because even in its own right, it is extremely rare).

b. Key to Identification

The dative is a quantitative word related to a verb of *filling*. Indeed, the key differences between content and material are that (1) material will involve a quantitative word, while content may be qualititative (or even abstract); (2) content is specifically related to a verb of filling.

c. Clarification

Normally, a verb of filling takes a *genitive* of content. However, there are possibly three instances in the NT when πληρόω takes a *dative* of content. It must be noted, however, that there are no clear examples in biblical Greek in which ἐν + the dative indicates content.[85] (Thus the popular interpretation of πληροῦσθε ἐν πνεύματι in Eph 5:18 as "be filled with the Spirit" in the sense that the Spirit is the content with which one is filled is most likely incorrect.)[86]

d. Illustrations

Rom 1:29   πεπληρωμένους **πάσῃ ἀδικίᾳ** κτλ.
            being filled **with all wickedness**, etc.

2 Cor 7:4   πεπλήρωμαι **τῇ παρακλήσει**
            I am filled **with comfort**

Luke 2:40   πληρούμενον **σοφίᾳ**[87]
            being filled **with wisdom**

The Uses of the Dative After Certain Words

There are some uses of the dative that do not *neatly* fit into any of the above categories. These constitute the large and amorphous group known as *the use of the dative after certain words*.

➡ ## 1. Dative Direct Object

a. Definition

A number of verbs take the dative as their direct object. Also, it should be noted that such datives are usually related to verbs implying personal relation. Thus the meanings of the verbs correspond in meaning to the basic idea of the pure dative. This category yields many illustrations.

b. Key to Identification and Clarification

See BAGD, a good concordance, or *BDF* for a list of such verbs.[88] Usually it will be obvious when the dative is the direct object. But since the dative is normally related to a *verb* rather than to a noun, there may be times of confusion.

---

[85] Abbott notes that "the use of ἐν with πληρόω to express the content with which a thing is filled would be quite unexampled" (*Ephesians* [ICC] 161). See his discussion on 161-62 of ἐν πνεύματι in Eph 5:18.

[86] This text will be discussed at some length in the chapter on prepositions.

[87] σοφίας is the reading found in ℵ* A D Θ X Γ Δ Λ Π *f*[1, 13] *Byz*; σοφίᾳ is found in ℵ[c] B L W Ψ 33 *et pauci*.

[88] Although many intermediate grammars list all such verbs, it is our conviction that grammars do much unnecessary duplication with lexica. Our approach is to try to refrain from trespassing into the domain of the lexicon as much as possible.

A good rule of thumb is that verbs taking a dative direct object can usually be translated with *to* or *in*. Thus ὑπακούω can be translated, "I am obedient to," διακονῶ can be rendered "I minister to," εὐχαριστῶ can be translated as "I am thankful to," πιστεύω can be rendered "I trust in." (One has to use a little imagination with these verbs because they are normally rendered "I obey," "I serve," "I thank," and "I believe.")

Another way to look at the verbs taking dative direct objects is that the majority of them can be placed in one of the following groups (all of which, quite incidentally, are terms used for discipleship): *trusting* (e.g., πιστεύω), *obeying* (e.g., ὑπακούω), *serving* (e.g., διακονέω), *worshiping* (e.g., λατρεύω), *thanksgiving* (e.g., εὐχαριστέω), *following* (e.g., ἀκολουθέω).

c. **Significance**

It has already been pointed out that such dative direct objects are usually related to verbs implying personal relation. This, in part, is the significance of dative direct objects. As well, some of the verbs that take dative direct objects also take accusative direct objects. Thus, when an author has a choice for the case of his direct object, the case he chooses in which to express his idea may be significant.

d. **Illustrations**

Obviously, because this is such a broad category, the examples selected cannot possibly reflect the usage adequately. I have chosen one of the more significant verbs that takes a dative direct object as well as an accusative direct object (προσκυνέω).

1) **Introductory Remarks about Προσκυνέω + Dative Direct Object**

Since the dative is the case of personal interest, it is easy to see the root idea coming through when an author chooses to use the dative direct object of προσκυνέω. The idea of personal interest lends itself to personal relation, so it *may* be significant that usually in the NT, the dative direct object is used with προσκυνέω when true Deity is the object of worship (cf. Matt 14:33; 28:9; John 4:21; 1 Cor 14:25; Heb 1:6; Rev 4:10; 7:11; 11:16; 19:10; 22:9). The implication, in part, may be that God is a true God—one with whom human beings can have a personal relation. And usually, when false deity is worshiped, the accusative direct object is used (cf. Rev 9:20; 13:8, 12; 14:9, 11; 20:4).

It seems, too, that when the dative direct object is used with προσκυνέω for the worship of *false* deity, the stress is on the personal relation involved (cf. Rev 13:4) because the object of worship is a real *person*,[89] though not true Deity. Occasionally, the accusative direct object is used with προσκυνέω when true Deity is worshiped. Such instances may imply either a misconception of God on the part of the worshiper (cf. John 4:22) or worship that is at a distance (cf. discussion on Matt 4:10 below).[90]

2) Examples of Προσκυνέω + the Dative

Heb 1:6 ὅταν δὲ πάλιν εἰσαγάγῃ τὸν πρωτότοκον εἰς τὴν οἰκουμένην, λέγει καὶ προσκυνησάτωσαν **αὐτῷ** πάντες ἄγγελοι θεοῦ.

And when he again brings the firstborn into the [inhabited] world, he says, "And let all the angels of God worship **him**."

> It is only fitting that in Heb 1, the chapter in which the author establishes the superiority of Christ over the angels—a superiority belonging to God alone—the *dative* direct object should be used of Christ.

Matt 4:9 ταῦτά σοι πάντα δώσω, ἐὰν πεσὼν προσκυνήσῃς **μοι**.

I will give you all these things if you fall down and worship **me**.

> Here, the tempter attempts to tempt Jesus to worship him. But by the evangelist's use of the dat. direct object, the devil is not asking for mere homage, but for a confession that he is God.

Cf. also Matt 2:11; 8:2; 14:33; 28:9; John 4:21; Rev 4:10; 19:4.

3) Examples of Προσκυνέω + the Accusative

Matt 4:10 **κύριον τὸν θεόν** σου προσκυνήσεις

you shall worship **the Lord** your **God**

> Jesus is refuting the tempter with scripture. He quotes Deut 6:13, which has φοβηθήσῃ for προσκυνήσεις. Thus the use of the acc. with προσκυνέω is not due to the LXX. Rather, it seems that a personal application of this text to the tempter is being made. Although only the Lord God is the true God, the devil will have no chance for a *personal* relation with him, though he does have an obligation (cf. Phil 2:10 for a similar theme).

Cf. also Rev 9:20; 13:8; 14:9, 11.

2. *Dative After Certain Nouns*

a. Definition

A few nouns take datives after them. Again, the notion of personal interest is almost always seen. This category is not particularly common.

---

[89] Even "the image of the beast" is put in the dat. in Rev 13:15; 16:2; 19:20. But in its first occurrence, it is "made to speak" (13:15) and thus appears to be personal.

[90] Admittedly, more work needs to be done on the cases with προσκυνέω. The explanation given above is only suggestive and cannot handle all of the data. Further, it does not wield Occam's razor well. Some of the most problematic texts are Luke 24:52 (acc.); John 4:23-24 (interchange between dat. and acc.); and the seemingly capricious shifts in the Apocalypse. (One approach to resolve the use in Revelation is to take note of compound objects: they are always put in the acc. [such as "the beast and its image"] even when separately the dat. is used.) But whatever final solution is to be offered for this syntactical conundrum, the difference between the cases in terms of personal relation (dat.) and extent (acc.) needs to be taken into account.

b.   Key to Identification

These nouns are *verbal* nouns (i.e., they are cognate to a verb, such as ὀφειλέτης [ὀφείλω], ὑπάντησις [ὑπαντάω]). Furthermore, frequently that noun finds its counterpart in one of the verbs taking a dative direct object: διακονία-διακονέω, εὐχαριστία-εὐχαριστέω, etc.

c.   Illustrations

Matt 8:34   πᾶσα ἡ πόλις ἐξῆλθεν εἰς ὑπάντησιν **τῷ Ἰησοῦ**
all the city came out for a meeting **with Jesus**
> The verbal cognate, ὑπαντάω, takes what could be called a dat. of association or dat. direct object (cf. Mark 5:2; John 4:51).

1 Cor 16:15 διακονίαν **τοῖς ἁγίοις**
service **to the saints**

Cf. also Rom 8:12 (ὀφειλέτης); 2 Cor 9:11 (εὐχαριστία).

3. *Dative After Certain Adjectives*

a.   Definition

A few adjectives are followed by the dative case. Once again, when the idea of personal interest appears, the dative is naturally used. This broad category is fairly common.

b.   Key to Identification

There really is no one key to identification since this is a rather amorphous group: the most common group is adjectives of "likeness" (i.e., correspondence) such as ὅμοιος, ἴσος.[91] As well, many of the adjectives belong to the larger category of dative of *reference*.

c.   Illustrations

Matt 13:31 ὁμοία ἐστὶν ἡ βασιλεία τῶν οὐρανῶν **κόκκῳ** σινάπεως
the kingdom of heaven is like a mustard **seed**

Rom 1:30   **γονεῦσιν** ἀπειθεῖς
disobedient **to parents**

Phil 2:6   οὐχ ἁρπαγμὸν ἡγήσατο τὸ εἶναι ἴσα **θεῷ**
he did not regard being equal **with God** as something to be grasped

1 Tim 4:15 ἵνα σου ἡ προκοπὴ φανερὰ ᾖ **πᾶσιν**
that your progress might be manifest **to all**

---

[91] Cf. Robertson's *Short Grammar*, 240.

Rev 2:18   ὁ υἱὸς τοῦ θεοῦ . . . οἱ πόδες αὐτοῦ ὅμοιοι **χαλκολιβάνῳ**
             the Son of God . . . his feet are like **burnished bronze**

Cf. also Matt 20:12; John 18:15; Acts 7:13; 26:19; Titus 2:11.

→ 4. *Dative After Certain Prepositions*

a. Definition and Key to Identification

Certain prepositions take the dative after them. See the chapter on prepositions for discussion. For review of which prepositions take which cases, cf., e.g., Mounce, *Basics of Biblical Greek*, 55-62.

b. Significance

When a dative follows a preposition, you should *not* attempt to identify the dative's function by case usage *alone*. Rather, consult BAGD for the specific usage of that case with that preposition. Although many of the case uses overlap with the uses of the preposition + the dative (especially with ἐν + the dative), the parallels are not exact. Furthermore, where there is overlap of usage, there is usually not overlap of frequency of occurrence (e.g., although the naked dative as well as ἐν + the dative can express sphere, the frequency of such usage is much higher with ἐν + the dative).[92]

---

[92] For a more detailed discussion of the differences between simple case uses and preposition + case uses, see the chapter on prepositions.

The Accusative Case

Overview of Accusative Uses

Select Bibliography

BDF, 82-89 (§148-61); **Brooks-Winbery**, 45-59; **E. Crespo**, "The Semantic and Syntactic Functions of the Accusative," *In the Footsteps of Raphael Kühner*, ed. A. Rijksbaron, H. A. Mulder, G. C. Wakker (Amsterdam: J. C. Gieben, 1986) 99-120; **Dana-Mantey**, 91-95 (§96); **A. C. Moorhouse**, "The Role of the Accusative Case," *In the Footsteps of Raphael Kühner*, 209-18; **Moule**, *Idiom Book*, 32-37; **Porter**, *Idioms*, 88-92; **Robertson**, *Grammar*, 466-91; **Smyth**, *Greek Grammar*, 353-64 (§1551-1633); **Turner**, *Syntax*, 220-21, 244-48; **Young**, *Intermediate Greek*, 16-22; **Zerwick**, *Biblical Greek*, 23-26 (§66-74).

Introduction

1. *The Accusative in Classical Greek*

The accusative case was employed "as the oblique case *par excellence*"[1] in classical Greek. This was so for two reasons: (1) It was by far the most frequent of the oblique cases (gen., dat., acc.);[2] and (2) it was the least specific of the oblique cases, allowing it to be used in a greater number of circumstances. It could thus be said that the accusative case was "unmarked" or the default case among the oblique cases. It was the routine case used, unless there was some reason for using the genitive or dative.

2. *The Accusative in the NT*

Although NT grammarians have generally assumed the same situation for that corpus,[3] the statistics tell a somewhat different story. Unlike classical Greek, the NT has more nominatives (31% of all case-forms) than accusatives (29%). Further, typically in classical Greek the accusative outnumbers genitives and datives together. But in the NT, although there are more accusatives than either genitives (25%) or datives (15%), the combination of the two cases (40%) has a significantly higher yield than accusatives.

What is to account for these differences? Several factors seem to be involved. First, many of the subtleties of the language naturally began to drop out as Greek passed from classical to Koine and became the language of commerce to many nonnatives. Thus, for example, the accusative of address, pendent accusative, accusative of exclamation, accusative as a heading in introductions, accusative in apposition to a sentence, and accusative absolute, though frequent enough in classical Greek,[4] are rare or nonexistent in the NT.[5] Second, in keeping with the Hellenistic spirit toward greater explicitness, prepositions take a decidedly more prominent role in the NT in places where a simple case (in particular the acc.) would have been used in earlier times. Many such prepositions take other than the accusative case. Third, the high proportion of genitive uses is apparently due, in part, to the Semitic influence (e.g., the "Hebrew" or attributive gen.).

---

[1] Moorhouse, "The Role of the Accusative Case," 209.

[2] Moorhouse (ibid., 211) notes that "in samples taken from eight authors, ranging in time from Homer to Demosthenes, the number of accusatives exceeds even that of nominatives without exception, and for oblique case usage considered by itself, the accusatives outnumber genitives and datives taken together with only one exception (in Thucydides)." Our comparisons in the following paragraph are based on this representative sampling.

[3] Cf., e.g., Robertson, *Grammar*, 466-67; Porter, *Idioms*, 88.

[4] See Moorhouse, "The Role of the Accusative Case," 212-17, for examples.

[5] These uses, known collectively as independent accusatives, are the primary roles that prompted classical grammarians to regard the acc. as the unmarked case.

3. *General Definition*

In sum, although the accusative could justifiably be considered the default case in classical Greek, more nuancing is required to understand its role in the NT. Yes, the accusative was certainly the unmarked case as far as direct objects were concerned. But for most other categories, it carried some semantic force. It is for this reason that we cannot simply call it the undefined case in the NT.

Instead, the least objectionable umbrella for the accusative uses is to describe it as the case of *extent*, or *limitation*. "The accusative measures an idea as to its content, scope, direction."[6] *It is primarily used to **limit** the action of a verb as to **extent**, **direction**, or **goal**.* Thus it most frequently answers the question, "How far?"[7] In many respects, this will be a fluid, undefined idea.[8] The precise force of the accusative is determined by its lexeme and that of the verb.[9]

4. *Relation to the Other Oblique Cases*

The accusative is similar to the genitive in that both cases have as part of their root idea limitation. But the *genitive* limits as to *quality* while the *accusative* limits as to *quantity*. Also, the accusative and the dative are similar in that both cases are primarily related to the verb. However, the dative is concerned about that to which the action of the verb is related, located, or by which it is accomplished, while the accusative is concerned about the extent and the scope of the verb's action.

---

[6] Robertson, *Grammar*, 468. This still does not cover every usage. Robertson reminds us that Brugmann and Delbrück long ago "despair[ed] of finding a single unifying idea" (*Grammar*, 467). In some respects, largely because of the historical antecedents that gave shape to the Koine in general and the NT in particular, we can only describe the various uses of the acc. without attempting to lump them under a conceptual unity. Thus the notion of *extent* works well with most acc. uses, but certainly not all. In particular, the *adverbial* uses of the acc. involve many exceptions to the notion of extent.

[7] So Robertson, *Grammar*, 215-16.

[8] This may be said to be closest to the unaffected meaning, yet even here there are many exceptions.

[9] Crespo, "The Semantic and Syntactic Functions of the Accusative," 100-101, takes some exception to this, noting that, depending on the kind of verb used, the acc. could be defined pretty much like the gen. or dat. He seems to suggest that the nuance of syntactical object is the unaffected meaning for the acc. case (115). But since his study was restricted to Homeric Greek, the synchronic realities of the first century CE prevent us from taking the same route.

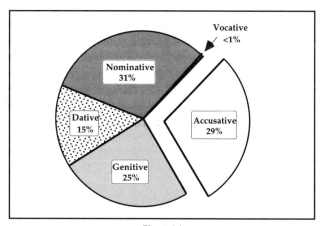

Chart 14
Frequency of Cases in the New Testament[10]

Specific Uses

The accusative categories can be generally grouped under one of three rubrics: substantival, adverbial, and after certain prepositions. These groupings are not entirely discrete, but may be viewed as helpful guides.

Substantival Uses of the Accusative

➡ ### 1. *Accusative Direct Object*

   a. Definition

      The accusative substantive indicates the immediate object of the action of a transitive verb. It receives the action of the verb. In this way it limits the verbal action. This usage is so common as to be routine: when one sees an accusative substantive, he/she normally should think of it as the direct object; conversely, when one anticipates the direct object, the case expected is usually the accusative.

   b. Key to Identification: see definition

   c. Clarification and Significance

      First, the accusative will be related to a transitive verb.[11] The verb is

---

[10] The breakdown of acc. forms is as follows: 8815 nouns, 5009 pronouns, 5889 articles, 957 participles, 2435 adjectives (for a total of 23,105).

[11] Not all verbs are consistently transitive or intransitive, nor do transitive verbs always have an explicit direct object. Some of the issues related to verb types will be taken up in the chapter on voice.

typically in the active voice, but some verbs in the middle or even the passive (deponents) take a direct object. Second, the accusative case is not the only case for the direct object; the genitive and dative also can, with certain kinds of verbs, function as the direct object. The exegetical significance of the direct object will normally be when a case *other than* the accusative is used (thus the acc. is the unmarked case as far as direct object is concerned).

d. Illustrations

Matt 5:46 ἐὰν ἀγαπήσητε τοὺς ἀγαπῶντας **ὑμᾶς**
if you love *those who love* **you**
> Just as ὑμᾶς is the direct object of the participle ἀγαπῶντας, so ἀγαπῶντας is the direct object of the finite verb, ἀγαπήσητε.

Mark 2:17 οὐκ ἦλθον καλέσαι **δικαίους** ἀλλὰ **ἁμαρτωλούς**
I did not come to call **the righteous** but **sinners**

John 3:16 ἠγάπησεν ὁ θεὸς **τὸν κόσμον**
God loved **the world**

Acts 10:14 οὐδέποτε ἔφαγον **πᾶν κοινὸν** καὶ **ἀκάθαρτον**
I have never eaten **anything that is common** or **unclean**

Acts 14:24 διελθόντες **τὴν Πισιδίαν**
passing through **Pisidia**
> Occasionally an intransitive verb (such as ἔρχομαι) can be transformed into a transitive verb by way of prepositional prefix (such as διά, to become διέρχομαι).[12]

Eph 2:7 ἵνα ἐνδείξηται. . . **τὸ ὑπερβάλλον πλοῦτος** τῆς χάριτος αὐτοῦ[13]
in order that he might display **the surpassing riches** of his grace

Jas 2:6 ὑμεῖς δὲ ἠτιμάσατε **τὸν πτωχόν**
but you have dishonored **the poor man**

Rom 8:28 τοῖς ἀγαπῶσιν τὸν θεὸν **πάντα** συνεργεῖ [ὁ θεὸς] εἰς ἀγαθόν[14]
God causes **all things** to work together for good to those who love God
> Sometimes it is difficult to tell whether a particular sentence even has a direct object. In this instance, such doubt is due to textual uncertainty and the syntactical range of the verb. συνεργέω is one of the verbs that can be either transitive or intransitive. If ὁ θεός is original, the verb is transitive here (and πάντα is the acc. direct object). But since ὁ θεός is textually suspect,[15] it is better to read the text without it. This leaves

---

[12] See BDF, 83-84 (§150). BAGD calls this an acc. of place (s.v. διέρχομαι).

[13] τὸν ὑπερβάλλοντα πλοῦτον is found in D¹ E K L P Ψ *Byz.*

[14] 𝔓⁴⁶ has the singular πᾶν for πάντα.

[15] ὁ θεός is found in 𝔓⁴⁶ A B 81 *et pauci* which, though certainly formidable MSS, are opposed by ℵ C D F G 33 1739 and a host of other witnesses over a widespread region. Further, the longer reading could easily be motivated by the scribal tendency toward explicitness.

two probable options: either *"he* works all things together for good" or "all things work together for good." In the first instance the subject is embedded in the verb and "God" is clearly implied (as in v 29). In the second instance, πάντα becomes the subject of an intransitive verb.[16] In either case, "What is expressed is a truly biblical confidence in the sovereignty of God."[17]

It is difficult to pass over a verse such as this without noting two additional items: (1) the good that is accomplished is specifically *for believers*; and (2) that good is in connection with conformity to Christ through suffering (so vv 17-30). Thus to say (as is frequently done nowadays, even in non-Christian circles), "Everything will work together for the good," as if things work out by themselves and the good is human comfort, is hardly Pauline and hardly biblical. Such a worldview C. H. Dodd rightly derided as "evolutionary optimism."

➡ 2. *Double Accusatives*

There are two types of double accusative constructions—i.e., constructions in which a verb takes two accusatives. Because the semantics are different, it is important to distinguish them.

➡ ### a. Double Accusative of the Person and Thing

1) Definition

Certain verbs take two direct objects, one a person and the other a thing. The thing is the nearer object; the person is the more remote object.[18] Another way to put this is that the person is the object *affected*, while the thing is the object *effected*. This is a fairly common category.

2) Amplification and Illustrations

Typically we would expect the accusative of person to be in the dative rather than the accusative case. Thus "I teach you Greek," means the same thing as "I teach Greek to you."[19] But in Greek certain verbs take two accusatives rather than a dative of person and accusative of thing. In most instances the person *receives* the thing, just as a dative indirect object receives a direct object (hence, the person is considered the more remote object). The verbs used with

---

[16] This is possible, of course, because neuter plural subjects regularly take singular verbs. For a discussion of the problem, as well as presentation of other options, cf. BAGD, s.v. συνεργέω; Cranfield, *Romans* (ICC) 1.425-29.

[17] Cranfield, *Romans* (ICC) 1.427.

[18] Cf. Moule, *Idiom Book*, 33; Winer-Moulton, 284-85.

[19] At the same time, there may be a real semantic difference between these two. Smyth suggests that "When the dative of the person is used, something is done *for . . .* , not *to* him . . ." (*Greek Grammar*, 363 [§1624]).

person-thing double accusatives can be grouped into at least four basic lexical categories.

a) Teaching, Reminding

John 14:26   ἐκεῖνος **ὑμᾶς** διδάξει **πάντα**
             he will teach **you**[p] **all things**[th]

1 Cor 4:17   ὅς **ὑμᾶς** ἀναμνήσει **τὰς ὁδούς** μου
             who will remind **you**[p] **of** my **ways**[th]

b) Clothing, Anointing

Matt 27:31   ἐξέδυσαν **αὐτὸν τὴν χλαμύδα** καὶ ἐνέδυσαν **αὐτὸν τὰ ἱμάτια** αὐτοῦ
             They stripped **him**[p] **of** [his] **robe**[th] and put his own **garments**[th] **on him**[p]

Heb 1:9   ἔχρισέν **σε**. . . **ἔλαιον**
             he anointed **you**[p] **with oil**[th]

c) Inquiring, Asking

Matt 21:24   ἐρωτήσω **ὑμᾶς** κἀγὼ **λόγον ἕνα**
             I shall ask **you**[p] **one thing**[th]

Mark 6:22   αἴτησόν **με ὅ** ἐὰν θέλῃς
             ask **me**[p] [for] **whatever**[th] you wish

d) Other Types of *Causative* Ideas

1 Cor 3:2   **γάλα ὑμᾶς** ἐπότισα
             I gave **you**[p] **milk**[th] to drink

Luke 11:46   φορτίζετε **τοὺς ἀνθρώπους φορτία**
             you burden **men**[p] **with burdens**[th]

➡ ## b. Double Accusative of Object-Complement[20]

1) Definition

An object-complement double accusative is a construction in which one accusative substantive is the direct object of the verb and the other accusative (either noun, adjective, participle, or infinitive) complements the object in that it predicates something about it. The complement may be substantival or adjectival.[21] This usage occurs

---

[20] For a more comprehensive treatment, see D. B. Wallace, "The Semantics and Exegetical Significance of the Object-Complement Construction in the New Testament," *GTJ* 6 (1985) 91-112. This section summarizes the salient points of that article.

[21] The substantive used as an object can be a noun, pronoun, participle, adjective, or infinitive.

only with certain kinds of verbs. It is a common usage of the accusative.

The proper label for the direct object in such a construction is "object in object-complement construction"; for the complement, "complement in object-complement construction," or simply "the object complement."[22]

2)   Structural and Semantic Clues

This usage of the accusative is exegetically strategic in many texts. It is therefore important to understand how to identify it as well as how to interpret it. There is no one key to identification, but several features of this construction should be noted:

a)   The direct object usually combines with the verb to form a new verbal idea that has another accusative (the complement) as its object.[23]

b)   Like the person-thing double accusative, this usage is lexically nuanced. That is to say, it is related to a particular kind of verb, lexically speaking.[24] But every verb that *can* take such a construction is not *required* to do so.[25] This creates special problems in exegesis: not infrequently a crucial issue in the text is decided on the basis of whether the two accusatives are appositional or object-complement.[26]

---

[22] Note that the lack of hyphen indicates this acc. term; the hyphen (object-complement) refers to the whole construction. The reason for these distinctions is due to the semantics involved in this construction. Thus, direct object and predicate acc., respectively, are not specific enough since these labels could apply to other acc. categories. For terminology used by other grammars, see Wallace, "Object-Complement Construction," 93.

[23] So W. W. Goodwin, *Greek Grammar*, rev. by C. B. Gulick (Boston: Ginn & Co., 1930) 227.

[24] Among the verbs in the NT that can take object-complements are the following: ἁγιάζω, ἄγω, αἰτέω, ἀνατρέφω, ἀποδείκνυμι, ἀπολύω, ἀποστέλλω, γεύομαι, γινώσκω, δέχομαι, δίδωμι, δοκέω, ἐγείρω, ἐκβάλλω, ἐκλέγω, ἐνδείκνυμι, ἐπιδείκνυμι, ἐπικαλέω, εὑρίσκω, ἔχω, ἡγέομαι, θέλω, θεωρέω, ἱκανόω, ἵστημι, καθίστημι, καλέω, κηρύσσω, κρίνω, λαμβάνω, λέγω, λογίζομαι, νομίζω (*contra BDF*, 86 [§157] and Robertson, *Grammar*, 480; cf. 1 Cor 7:26; 1 Tim 6:5), οἶδα, ὁμολογέω, ὀνομάζω, ὁράω, παραλαμβάνω, παρέχω, παρίστημι, πείθω, περιάγω, πιστεύω, ποιέω, προορίζω, προσφέρω, προτίθημι, προχειρίζω, συνίημι, συνίστημι (συνιστάνω), τίθημι, ὑποκρίνομαι, ὑπονοέω, ὑψόω, φάσκω, χρηματίζω. For a more complete list, see Wallace, "Object-Complement Construction," 96, n. 23.

[25] See E. V. N. Goetchius, *The Language of the New Testament* (New York: Charles Scribner's Sons, 1965) 141. Some verbs in the NT, however, regularly or almost exclusively take object-complements (e.g., ἡγέομαι, ὀνομάζω, φάσκω).

[26] For debatable texts, cf. Matt 27:32; Acts 11:20; 13:6, 23; Rom 10:9; 13:14; Phil 3:18; Col 2:6; 1 Pet 3:15; Rev 13:17.

c) Occasionally, the construction is marked by the presence of εἰς or ὡς before the complement, or εἶναι[27] between the two accusatives. Thus, in 1 Cor 4:1 Paul says, "let a person regard us *as* servants of Christ" (ἡμᾶς λογιζέσθω ἄνθρωπος ὡς ὑπηρέτας Χριστοῦ).[28]

Although such elements are usually lacking, one should normally translate the construction with "as," "to be," or "namely" between the two accusatives.

d) Frequently, the complement is an adjective. When this is the case, it is always a *predicate* adjective. The object is, in such cases, usually articular.

3) Identification and Semantics of the Components

a) Identification of the Components

Identification of the components in the construction is also not a given. Although normally the object comes first, about twenty percent of the examples reverse this order. (For example, in Phil 3:17 Paul says, "you have us as a pattern" [ἔχετε τύπον ἡμᾶς].) However, it is easy to determine which is which because *the object-complement construction is semantically equivalent to the subject-predicate nominative construction.*[29] This is because such a construction is an embedded subject-predicate nominative clause.[30] Thus, the principles used to sort out subject from predicate nominative can equally be used here.[31] Specifically:

- If one of the two is a *pronoun*, it will be the object;
- If one of the two is a *proper name*, it will be the object;
- If one of the two is *articular*, it will be the object.[32]

---

[27] When the infinitive is present, it is equally possible to call one acc. the subject of the infinitive and the other, a predicate acc. For a discussion of the semantics of such constructions, see discussions under "Subject of Infinitive" and "Predicate Accusative."

[28] It should be noted, however, that not every instance of ὡς or εἰς with a second acc. indicates an object-complement construction (cf., e.g., Matt 9:38; Rom 6:22; 2 John 10).

[29] For proof, see Wallace, "Object-Complement Construction," 101-3.

[30] There is one significant difference between S-PN constructions and object-complement. While in the former, the equation usually indicates a state or class, in the latter the relationship is frequently one of *progress* toward a state. This is not due to any innate differences in the respective constructions, but rather to the controlling verb. Thus, with verbs of making, sending, presenting, etc., the object *becomes* the complement (e.g., ἐποίησεν τὸ ὕδωρ οἶνον in John 4:46).

[31] See chapter on nom. case, under predicate nom., for a detailed discussion.

[32] The "pecking order" between these elements seems to be the same as for the S-PN construction: pronouns take priority, followed by (apparently) proper names, then articular nouns. Cf. Acts 5:42 for an example in which the proper name is second, but the articular noun is the complement.

b) Semantics of the Components

In general, the *semantics* (not the identification) of the components is guided by word order. On a continuum from definite to qualitative to indefinite, the object will normally fall in the definite range, while the complement will tend toward the qualitative-indefinite range.[33] Thus, for example, in Mark 10:45 we are told that the Son of Man came "to give his life as *a ransom* for many" (δοῦναι τὴν ψυχὴν αὐτοῦ *λύτρον* ἀντὶ πολλῶν); in Acts 28:6 Paul is claimed to be "*a god*" (ἔλεγον αὐτὸν εἶναι θεόν).

But when the order of the elements is *reversed*, the complement *tends* toward the definite-qualitative range.[34] This is no doubt due to the prominence of its location in the clause: the more it is thrust forward, the more specific it becomes.

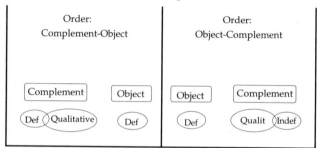

Chart 15
The Semantics of the Object-Complement Construction

4) Illustrations

The principal verbs that can take an object-complement construction are grouped below.

a) Calling, Designating, Confessing

Matt 22:43   Δαυὶδ ἐν πνεύματι καλεῖ **αὐτὸν κύριον**[35]
             David in the Spirit calls **him**[obj] **Lord**[comp]

John 5:18   **πατέρα** ἴδιον ἔλεγεν **τὸν θεόν**
             he was calling **God**[obj] his own **Father**[comp]
                 This text illustrates a couple of semantic issues. The complement comes

---

[33] Many complements are actually predicate adjectives (cf. Acts 5:10; 16:15; Jas 2:5), but even the nouns tend toward qualitative-indefinite. Cf. John 4:46; Acts 24:5; Rom 6:13, 19; Phil 3:7; Heb 1:7; 1 John 4:10, 14.

[34] This has analogies with the S-PN construction as well, but there are many exceptions for the acc. construction. For discussion, see Wallace, "Object-Complement Construction," 106-8.

[35] The object-complement construction has a number of variants such as the following: καλεῖ κύριον αὐτόν in ℵ L Z 892; κύριον αὐτὸν καλεῖ in W E F G H K Γ Δ 0102 (0161) *f*[1, 13] *Byz*.

first and is anarthrous; the object comes second and is articular. The same rules for distinguishing subject from predicate nom. apply here. If one simply followed word order, the meaning would be "he was calling his own father God"! Further, the complement is thrown forward for emphasis and to render it definite. If it were placed second in order, the meaning would tend toward qualitative-indefinite ("calling God a father of his"?). To clear up this confusion, the evangelist could have used the article, but this would have created a problem for distinguishing the object from the complement. The wording here is a concise theological statement.

John 15:15   οὐκέτι λέγω **ὑμᾶς δούλους**
              no longer do I call **you**[obj] **servants**[comp]

b) Making, Appointing

Matt 4:19   ποιήσω **ὑμᾶς ἁλιεῖς** ἀνθρώπων[36]
              I will make **you**[obj] **fishers**[comp] of men

John 4:46   ἐποίησεν **τὸ ὕδωρ οἶνον**
              he turned **the water**[obj] [into] **wine**[comp]

John 5:11   ὁ ποιήσας **με ὑγιῆ**
              the one who made **me**[obj] **well**[comp]

c) Sending, Expelling

1 John 4:14   πατὴρ ἀπέσταλκεν **τὸν υἱὸν σωτῆρα**
              the Father sent **the Son**[obj] [as] **Savior**[comp]

Luke 6:22   ὅταν . . . ἐκβάλωσιν **τὸ ὄνομα** ὑμῶν ὡς **πονηρόν**
              whenever . . . they cast out your **name**[obj] as **evil**[comp]

d) Considering, Regarding

Phil 3:7   **ταῦτα** ἥγημαι. . . **ζημίαν**
              I regard **these things**[obj] [to be] **loss**[comp]

Rom 6:11   λογίζεσθε **ἑαυτοὺς** εἶναι **νεκροὺς** τῇ ἁμαρτίᾳ
              consider **yourselves**[obj] to be **dead**[comp] to sin

Phil 2:6   ὃς ἐν μορφῇ θεοῦ ὑπάρχων οὐχ **ἁρπαγμὸν** ἡγήσατο τὸ **εἶναι** ἴσα θεῷ
              who, although he existed in the form of God, did not regard **the [state of] being**[obj] equal to God [as] **something to be grasped**[comp]
              > In this text the infinitive is the object and the anarthrous term, ἁρπαγμόν, is the complement.[37] The most natural reason for the article with the infinitive is simply to mark it out as the object.[38]

---

[36] ℵ[c] D 33 *et alii* add γενέσθαι before ἁλιεῖς.

[37] This follows a Greek idiom, ἁρπαγμὸν τι ἡγεῖσθαι.

e) Having, Taking

Mark 12:23   οἱ γὰρ ἑπτὰ ἔσχον **αὐτὴν γυναῖκα**
for the seven [brothers] had **her**[obj] [as] **a wife**[comp]

Jas 5:10   **ὑπόδειγμα** λάβετε . . . **τοὺς προφήτας**
[as] **an example**[comp] take . . . **the prophets**[obj]

f) Declaring, Presenting

Rom 3:25   ὃν προέθετο ὁ θεὸς **ἱλαστήριον**
whom[obj] God put forth [as] **a propitiation**[comp]

Col 1:28   ἵνα παραστήσωμεν **πάντα ἄνθρωπον τέλειον** ἐν Χριστῷ
in order that we might present **every person**[obj] [as] **perfect**[comp] in Christ

> Avoid the temptation of seeing τέλειον as an attributive adjective. (Remember that an adjectival complement is *always* a predicate adjective.) If you were to do so, the ensuing translation would be radically different: "in order that we might present every perfect person. . ." The point, then, would *not* be that in Christ or because of Christ every believer shall be presented as perfect before God, but rather that *only* those believers who are perfect in Christ shall be presented! Obviously, how one takes τέλειον has profound theological implications.

Cf. also Mark 1:3; Luke 6:22; John 7:23; 10:35; 14:18; Acts 10:28; 26:29; 1 Cor 4:9; 7:26; Eph 5:2; Phil 2:20; 1 Tim 2:6; 6:14; 1 John 4:10.

5) Debatable Passages

John 4:54   **τοῦτο δεύτερον σημεῖον** ἐποίησεν ὁ Ἰησοῦς
Jesus made **this**[obj] [to be] **the second sign**[comp]

> Most translations treat τοῦτο as though it were the subject rather than object (cf. ASV, RSV, NASB, NIV, etc.): "This was the second sign which Jesus did . . ." A more accurate rendering sees the construction as object-complement.[39] The issue is not merely pedantic: as an object-complement, the evangelist's emphasis becomes clearer: Jesus was both powerful *and* sovereign. John 2:11 has a similar construction (ταύτην ἐποίησεν ἀρχὴν τῶν σημείων ὁ Ἰησοῦς ["Jesus made this (to be) the beginning of (his) signs"]).[40]

Rom 10:9   ἐὰν ὁμολογήσῃς ἐν τῇ στόματί σου **κύριον Ἰησοῦν** . . . σωθήσῃ
if you confess with your mouth **Jesus** [as] **Lord** . . . you shall be saved (or, "if you confess with your mouth [that] **Jesus** is **Lord** . . . ")

---

[38] *Contra* N. T. Wright, "ἁρπαγμός and the Meaning of Philippians 2:5-11," *JTS*, NS 37 (1986) 344, who sees the article as anaphoric to μορφῇ θεοῦ. As attractive as this view is theologically, it has a weak basis grammatically.

[39] Although τοῦτο could be nom., in this context it is the object of ἐποίησεν.

[40] The NASB has "This beginning of [his] signs Jesus did . . ." The problem with this translation is that it takes the demonstrative as a modifying adjective rather than an independent pronoun. But such could not be the case without an article before ἀρχήν.

Two issues are at stake here.[41] First, which is the object and which is the complement? Since the object-complement construction is an embedded subject-predicate nom. clause, the same rules apply here. Thus, since Ἰησοῦν is a proper name, it is the object (and κύριον is the complement).

Second, what are the semantics of the components? That is, what does Paul mean here by "Lord"? Since the complement κύριον *precedes* the object, it is possible that it is definite though anarthrous. Thus, the confession would be that Jesus is *the* Lord, that is, *Yahweh*.[42] This is substantiated by the context: Since Paul is alluding to and even directly quoting the OT here, his thought is colored by it. In vv 11 and 12, Christ is still clearly in view. And in v 13 he again mentions κύριος without indicating that a different Lord is in view. Thus to confess that Jesus is *the* Lord is to confess that he is the Lord mentioned in v 13. This verse is a quotation of Joel 3:5 (Hebrew; 2:32 in LXX), in which "Lord" is in reference to Yahweh. Such an allusion is hardly accidental, but part of the Pauline soteriological confession.[43] For Paul, to confess that Jesus is Lord is to confess that he is Yahweh.

Titus 2:10   **πᾶσαν πίστιν** ἐνδεικνυμένους **ἀγαθήν**[44]

showing **all faith** [to be] **good**

This text is universally regarded to mean "showing forth all good faith." That is, ἀγαθήν is taken as an *attributive* adjective rather than as the complement to πίστιν. But there is grammatical and exegetical evidence on the side of a predicate ἀγαθήν and thus an object-complement construction: (1) ἐνδείκνυμι does take an object-complement elsewhere in the NT (cf. Rom 2:15).[45] (2) In answer to the objection that πίστιν

---

[41] Although almost all English translations understand the construction to be object-complement (*contra* Douay, KJV, and NKJV), a preliminary issue is whether this is so or whether it is merely simple apposition (viz. "the Lord Jesus"). We should most likely take it as an object-complement construction because of the following: (a) the verb used (ὁμολογέω) can take an object-complement (cf. John 9:22; 1 John 4:2 ; 2 John 7); (b) with a verb of confessing, all anarthrous constructions of κύριος Ἰησοῦς are other than a tight apposition (cf. 1 Cor 8:6; 12:3; Phil 2:11). It is significant that in each of these texts a confession is also made); and (c) some MSS (most notably, Vaticanus) converted the acc. construction into a subject-predicate nom. construction.

[42] That Yahweh is meant by "the Lord" is argued on the basis of its *par excellence* nuance (in the sense that Yahweh deserves this title more than anyone else, especially since in the LXX κύριος regularly translates YHWH).

[43] In two other texts involving a confession of Jesus as Lord, there is an allusion to the OT and specifically to Yahweh himself (Isa 45:23 in Phil 2:11; Isa 8:13 in 1 Pet 3:15). In these two parallel texts where the κύριος clearly refers to Yahweh, even though this predicate noun is anarthrous, the biblical author places it before the object/subject to indicate that it is definite. Apparently, not only was the article unnecessary, but the reversed order seems to be the "normal" way to express the idea that κύριος is definite. For more discussion of Rom 10:9, cf. Wallace, "Object-Complement Construction," 108-11.

[44] The syntax of this text is complicated by a rich variety of textual variants, though none has a compelling pedigree. Further, the most plausible *v.ll.* merely involve a transposition of the elements (33 has πᾶσαν ἐνδεικνυμένους ἀγάπην). Some MSS link πίστιν and ἀγαθήν more closely (e.g., πᾶσαν ἐνδεικνυμένους πίστιν ἀγαθήν in F^gr G), though others flip just the first two words (πίστιν πᾶσαν ἐνδεικνυμένους ἀγαθήν in K L Ψ *Byz*). The first hand of ℵ has πᾶσαν ἐνδεικνυμένους ἀγαθήν, a nonsensical reading.

[45] As well, the stem -δείκνυμι frequently takes an object-complement.

cannot be an object in a double acc. construction because it is anarthrous, there are several parallels that exhibit an anarthrous object and a predicate adjective.[46] (3) It is highly unusual for an attributive adjective to be separated from the anarthrous noun it modifies by an intervening word—esp. a *verb*,[47] but this is normal for predicate adjectives.[48] (4) A rendering of the text along these lines unveils a synthetic (or even a synonymous) parallel between the two halves of v 10: "Slaves should be wholly subject to their masters . . . demonstrating that all [genuine][49] faith is productive, with the result [ecbatic ἵνα] that they will completely adorn the doctrine of God." If taken this way, the text seems to support the idea that saving faith does not fail, but even results in good works.

For other debatable (and exegetically significant) texts, cf. Phil 3:18; 1 Pet 3:15.

3. Cognate Accusative (or Accusative of the Inner Object)

a. Definition

The accusative noun is cognate either in lexical root or meaning to the verb. It functions as the direct object of the verb.[50] Both uses are rare.

b. Semantics and Significance

This is different from the cognate dative in that the cognate dative is more adverbial,[51] making emphatic the action implied in the verb (or, sometimes the cognate picks up on some other nuance), while the cognate accusative is simply a direct object. If the accusative has a modifier (either adjective or genitive), the overall construction is more emphatic.[52]

---

[46] Cf., e.g., Luke 3:8; John 9:1; Acts 10:28; Col 1:28.

[47] Though John 10:32 may afford an example. It is of course impossible for an attributive adjective to be separated from an *articular* noun by a verb.

[48] Cf. Mark 7:2; 8:19; Acts 4:16; Rev 15:1.

[49] "Genuine" may either be implied from the flow of argument or may be considered a part of the field of meaning for πᾶς when it is used with abstract nouns (cf. BAGD, s.v. πᾶς, 1.a.δ.).

[50] On a rare occasion, the cognate acc. will be the thing in a person-thing double acc. (e.g., ἐνέδυσαν αὐτὸν τὰ ἱμάτια αὐτοῦ in Matt 27:31, cited under "direct object"; δοξάσατε αὐτὸν δόξαν in 𝔓[47] in Rev 14:7), or a complement in an object-complement construction (e.g., κατακλίνατε αὐτοὺς κλισίας in Luke 9:14). BDF call the first an acc. of object and cognate acc. (86 [§156]), and the second an acc. of object and of result (87 [§158]), as though they are distinguishable from person-thing and object-complement respectively. But these are merely lexically-colored instances of the broader categories. The notion of result is frequently embedded in an object-complement construction (see previous discussion under "Object-Complement").

[51] Although the cognate acc. is also known as acc. of the inner object, this description presupposes a strongly adverbial force. But only rarely is the cognate acc. functioning adverbially (e.g., Luke 2:9; perhaps Matt 6:19) rather than as direct object.

[52] So BDF, 84-85 (§153). Cf. also Smyth, *Greek Grammar*, 355-56 (§1563-77) for a helpful discussion.

c.   Illustrations

1)   Lexical Cognate

Matt 2:10   ἐχάρησαν **χαρὰν** μεγάλην σφόδρα
they rejoiced exceedingly **with** great **joy**

Matt 6:19   μὴ θησαυρίζετε ὑμῖν **θησαυρούς**
do not treasure up **treasures** for yourself

Eph 4:8   ἀναβὰς εἰς ὕψος ᾐχμαλώτευσεν **αἰχμαλωσίαν**
when he ascended on high, he led captive **captivity**

1 Tim 6:12   ἀγωνίζου τὸν καλὸν **ἀγῶνα** . . . ὡμολόγησας τὴν καλὴν **ὁμολογίαν**
Fight the good **fight** . . . when you confessed the good **confession**

Cf. also Matt 22:3; Mark 4:41; Luke 2:8-9; John 7:24; Acts 2:17; Col 2:19; 2 Tim 4:7; 1 Pet 5:2; 1 John 5:16.

2)   Conceptual Cognate

1 Pet 3:6   μὴ φοβούμεναι μηδεμίαν **πτόησιν**
without being frightened **by** any **fear**

Luke 1:73   **ὅρκον** ὃν ὤμοσεν πρὸς Ἀβραὰμ τὸν πατέρα ἡμῶν
[the] **oath** which he swore to Abraham our father
This is similar to an acc. in oaths, but the latter is an adverbial use of the acc., not direct object.

John 21:16   ποίμαινε τὰ **πρόβατά** μου
shepherd my **sheep**

4.   *Predicate Accusative*

a.   Definition

The accusative substantive (or adjective) stands in predicate relation to another accusative substantive. The two will be joined by an equative verb, either an infinitive or participle. Neither type is especially frequent outside of Luke or Paul.

b.   Clarification (and Significance)

There are two types of predicate accusatives. First is the one that is similar to the predicate genitive and the predicate dative. That is, it is (normally) simple apposition made emphatic by a copula in *participial* form.

Second, there is the predicate accusative in which one accusative is the subject of the *infinitive* and the second makes an assertion about the first. Thus, it is similar to the nominative subject and predicate nominative construction,[53] following the same principles for distinguishing them.[54] Frequently the infinitive will be in indirect discourse.[55]

c. Illustrations

1) Examples with the Participle

John 2:9   ἐγεύσατο ὁ ἀρχιτρίκλινος τὸ ὕδωρ **οἶνον** γεγενημένον

the head waiter tasted the water which had become **wine**

> The construction here is *semantically* different from most predicate accusatives with the participle in that the predication is more emphatic than mere apposition would be. As well, the construction is *structurally* different from most in that the participle is anarthrous even though the first acc. is articular.[56] The construction could also be treated as an object-complement.

Acts 9:11   τὴν ῥύμην τὴν καλουμένην **Εὐθεῖαν**

the street which is called **Straight**

Eph 2:1   ὑμᾶς ὄντας **νεκροὺς** τοῖς παραπτώμασιν

although you were **dead** in [your] trespasses

> This text is similar to John 2:9 in its semantics and structure. The participle is circumstantial, most likely with a concessive force.

1 Tim 1:12-13   πιστόν με ἡγήσατο. . . (13) τὸ πρότερον ὄντα **βλάσφημον**

he considered me faithful . . . who formerly was **a blasphemer**

Cf. also Matt 4:18; 9:9; Luke 21:37; 23:33; Acts 3:2; 15:37; 17:16; 27:8, 16; Rom 16:1; Col 1:21; 2:13; Rev 16:16.

2) Examples with the Infinitive

Matt 16:13   **τίνα** λέγουσιν οἱ ἄνθρωποι εἶναι τὸν υἱὸν τοῦ ἀνθρώπου;

Who do people say that the Son of Man is?[57]

Luke 4:41   ἤδεισαν **τὸν Χριστὸν** αὐτὸν εἶναι

they knew that he was **the Christ**

Rom 4:18   εἰς τὸ γενέσθαι αὐτὸν **πατέρα** πολλῶν ἐθνῶν

with the result that he became **[the] father** of many nations

---

[53] It is of course possible to have predication in the acc. without an equative verb. All object-complement constructions, for example, involve predication, though most do not have an explicit infinitive.

[54] I.e., the "subject" will be a pronoun, proper name, or articular noun. See examples below.

[55] The examples in this second category also usually belong to the object-complement category, though several are in result or purpose clauses introduced by εἰς.

[56] It is possible to take the participle circumstantially ("the water when it had become wine"), although this is not necessary since its relation to the predicate acc. can be conceived of as adjectival.

[57] It should be remembered that, just as in S-PN constructions, *interrogative* pronouns are the predicate term rather than the "subject."

Eph 3:5-6   νῦν ἀπεκαλύφθη . . . εἶναι τὰ ἔθνη **συγκληρονόμα** καὶ **σύσσωμα** καὶ **συμμέτοχα**
it has now been revealed . . . that the Gentiles are **fellow-heirs** and **fellow body-members** and **fellow-sharers**

Jas 1:18   εἰς τὸ εἶναι ἡμᾶς **ἀπαρχήν τινα** τῶν αὐτοῦ κτισμάτων
that we might be **a kind of firstfruits** of his creation

Cf. also Luke 11:8; 20:6, 41; 23:2; Acts 17:7; 18:5, 28; 27:4; Rom 2:19; 3:26; 4:11, 16; 7:3; 15:16; 2 Cor 9:5; Phil 1:13; 1 Tim 3:2; Titus 2:2; 1 Pet 5:12.[58]

➡ 5. *Accusative Subject of the Infinitive*

a. Definition

The accusative substantive frequently functions semantically as the subject of the infinitive. Though older grammars insist that technically this is an accusative of respect, from a descriptive and functional perspective, it is better to treat it as subject. This is a common use of the accusative, especially with personal pronouns.

b. Clarification

Normally the subject of the infinitive is the same as the subject of the main verb and thus is in the nominative case. For example, in Luke 19:47 we read οἱ γραμματεῖς ἐζήτουν αὐτὸν ἀπολέσαι ("the scribes were seeking to kill him").[59] But when the infinitive requires a different agent, it is almost always put in the accusative case.[60]

1) English Analogies

Though this usage of the accusative is difficult to grasp, it is not without some parallels in English. In the sentence "She wanted me to learn something," "me" is both the direct object of "wanted" and the subject of "to learn." Greek usage is similar, though more varied (that is to say, the subject of an infinitive is not always going to do double-duty as a direct object, too). Note, for example, Phil 1:12-13: γινώσκειν δὲ **ὑμᾶς** βούλομαι . . . ὥστε **τοὺς δεσμούς** μου φανεροὺς . . . γενέσθαι ("now I want **you** to know. . . so that my **bonds** have become manifest"). In v 12 the accusative is both object of the verb

---

[58] A debatable passage is 1 Pet 1:21.

[59] Cf. also Matt 16:25; Mark 8:11; 13:5; 15:8; Luke 9:12; John 11:8; Acts 13:44. The complementary infinitive is especially used with a nom. subject. On a rare occasion, the subject and object involve a reciprocal relationship, with the result that the infinitive takes an acc. subject that is the same individual as the nom. subject (e.g., Heb 5:5).

[60] Occasionally even another oblique case can *function* as the subject of the infinitive. In such instances it functions almost as a relative pronoun. Cf., e.g., John 4:7; Phil 1:7, 29; Jude 24.

βούλομαι and subject of the infinitive γινώσκειν;[61] while in v 13 the accusative is functioning as the subject of γενέσθαι in a result clause after ὥστε.

2) When an Infinitive has two Accusatives

Often in the NT a construction will have an accusative subject as well as an accusative predicate or an accusative direct object. In such cases, how can one tell which is which? For example, in Phil 1:7 does διὰ τὸ ἔχειν **με** ἐν τῇ καρδίᾳ **ὑμᾶς** mean "because **I** have you in my heart" or "because **you** have me in your heart"? Early analyses suggested that word order or proximity to the infinitive were the determining factors. But word order has since been shown to be at best a *secondary* consideration, and only with certain kinds of constructions.[62]

---

[61] Technically, the embedded *clause* γινώσκειν ὑμᾶς κτλ. is the direct object of βούλομαι, but the "you" as its leading agent is naturally put in the acc. case (cf. also Luke 11:1). See the chapter on the infinitive for more discussion on complementary infinitives with the acc.

[62]The issue was raised more than three decades ago by Henry R. Moeller and Arnold Kramer, "An Overlooked Structural Pattern in New Testament Greek," *NovT* 5 (1963) 25-35. To be sure, it had been discussed albeit briefly in older works, most notably by Clyde Votaw's *The Use of the Infinitive in Biblical Greek* (Chicago: by the author, 1896). Moeller and Kramer concluded that "of two consecutive accusative case substantives constructed with an infinitive, the first in order functions as the subject term, the second as the predicate term . . ." (27).

The issue was again raised almost thirty years later by Jeffrey T. Reed, "The Infinitive with Two Substantival Accusatives: An Ambiguous Construction?", *NovT* 33 (1991) 1-27. His conclusions were essentially the same ("Of two accusative case nominal, pronominal or adjectival substantives with an infinitive, the first in order functions as the subject, the second as the object/predicate" [ibid., 8]), though he found fault with Moeller and Kramer for overlooking several constructions (they listed 77 relevant texts; Reed found 95).

Neither of these approaches adequately dealt with the differences between subject-predicate acc. constructions (S-P) and subject-direct object constructions (S-O)—that is, between constructions involving an equative verb infinitive and one involving a transitive verb infinitive. They both assumed that a principle of word order was valid for all constructions.

A year after Reed's article appeared, another study treated this very issue in depth. Though unpublished, the essay by Matthew A. Cripe ("An Analysis of Infinitive Clauses Containing Both Subject and Object in the Accusative Case in the Greek New Testament" [Th.M. thesis, Dallas Seminary, 1992]) has taken issue with Reed's approach on several fronts and has elevated the discussion to a new height. Among other things, he criticizes the former studies for (1) forcing a principle of word order on the construction when 26% of the equative clauses involve a P-S order (18 out of 68 such constructions [ibid., 57]) and 17% of the transitive constructions involve an O-S order (14 out of 81 constructions [ibid., 67]); (2) not distinguishing between S-P and S-O constructions; and (3) overlooking many of the relevant constructions (Cripe found 149). (Cripe's third criticism of Reed, however, was unjustified in that Reed explicitly limited his study to two acc. *substantives*, while Cripe also included non-substantival adjectives and participles as predicate accusatives.)

In the most recent analysis, M. A. Cripe[63] notes that:

- **subject accusative-predicate accusative** (S-P) constructions need to be *treated just like their **nominative** counterparts*. Neither word order nor proximity to the infinitive are helpful guides for determining the subject.[64] What matters is whether one of the accusatives is a pronoun or articular or a proper name (in which case, it is the subject term).[65]

- **subject accusative-direct object** (S-O) constructions need to be analyzed differently since there is no semantic correlation between this construction and the S-P construction.[66] Cripe notes that for the S-O construction, there are only four potentially ambiguous passages[67] and the rest, regardless of word order, can be deciphered by applying common sense (e.g., noticing the context).

Although it is hoped that further analysis outside the NT will shed light on the S-O construction, the notion that either word order or proximity[68] to the infinitive solves the problem is both simplistic and misleading. To be sure, word order can be used as a *secondary* guide, but it is not even on the level of a rule of thumb.

c. **Illustrations**

1) **Unambiguous Constructions (with one Accusative Substantive)**

Matt 22:3   ἀπέστειλεν **τοὺς δούλους** αὐτοῦ καλέσαι τοὺς κεκλημένους
he sent his **servants** to call those who had been invited

Luke 18:16 ἄφετε **τὰ παιδία** ἔρχεσθαι πρός με
let **the children** come to me

Acts 11:15 ἐν δὲ τῷ ἄρξασθαί **με** λαλεῖν ἐπέπεσεν τὸ πνεῦμα τὸ ἅγιον ἐπ᾽ αὐτούς
as **I** began to speak, the Holy Spirit fell on them

---

[63] See bibliographic data in previous note.

[64] Cf., e.g., Luke 20:20, 23:2; Acts 17:7; Rom 2:19, 4:16; 1 Cor 10:20; 1 Tim 6:5; 2 Pet 3:11; Rev 2:9. He sums up his critique of Reed at this point: "74% is much too low a number to base a word order rule on as Reed attempts to do" (ibid., 58).

[65] See our section on the predicate nom. for more information.

[66] For example, "It is possible to have an indefinite subject with a definite object as in 'someone hit the ball'" (ibid., 59). Cripe gives the biblical example of Heb 5:12 to this effect.

[67] Luke 18:5; 2 Cor 2:13; 8:6; Phil 1:7 (all discussed on 83-87).

[68] The rule of proximity was Votaw's, taken up again by M. Silva in application to Phil 1:7 (*Philippians*, Wycliffe Exegetical Commentary [Chicago: Moody, 1988] 56, n. 21). Cripe remarks: "This idea of proximity has been shown to be in error by this study since it ignores constructions in which the infinitive splits the accusatives" (Cripe, 86).

1 Cor 10:13 πιστὸς ὁ θεός, ὃς οὐκ ἐάσει **ὑμᾶς** πειρασθῆναι ὑπὲρ ὃ δύνασθε

God is faithful, who will not allow **you** to be tempted beyond what you are able

Rev 10:11 δεῖ **σε** πάλιν προφητεῦσαι

it is necessary **for you** to prophesy again

Cf. also Matt 5:32; John 6:10; Acts 7:19; 8:31; Rom 1:13; Gal 2:14; 1 Thess 5:27; 2 Tim 2:18; Heb 9:26; Rev 19:19; 22:16.

2) Potentially Ambiguous Constructions (with two Accusatives)

a) Subject and Predicate Accusative (with Equative Verb Infinitives)

Mark 14:64 κατέκριναν **αὐτὸν** ἔνοχον εἶναι θανάτου[69]

they judged **him** to be guilty of death

> Frequently one of the accusatives is a predicate adjective (as here) or predicate participle.[70] Unless the adjective is functioning substantivally (which is rare), it must be considered the predicate term.

Acts 28:6 ἔλεγον **αὐτὸν** εἶναι θεόν

they were saying that **he** was a god

> Just as with subject-predicate nom. constructions (S-PN), if one of the two is a pronoun, it is the subject.[71]

1 Tim 6:5 νομιζόντων πορισμὸν εἶναι **τὴν εὐσέβειαν**

supposing that **godliness** is a means of gain

> Just as with S-PN, if one of the two is articular, it is the subject.[72] In this instance, the subject term follows the predicate term, illustrating that word order is not a valid guide.

Luke 20:6 πεπεισμένος ἐστιν **Ἰωάννην** προφήτην εἶναι

they are convinced that **John** was a prophet

> Just as with S-PN, if one of the two is a proper name, it is the subject.[73]

---

[69] D* has αὐτῷ for αὐτόν.

[70] Cf. also Acts 19:36; Rom 14:14; 2 Cor 7:11; 11:16; Eph 1:4.

[71] For other examples of acc. pronoun as subject of an equative verb infinitive, cf. Mark 1:17; Luke 23:2; Rom 2:19; 4:11, 18; 7:3; 8:29; 1 Cor 10:6, 20; 1 Thess 1:7; Jas 1:18; 1 Pet 5:12; Rev 2:9; 3:9. In Luke 9:18 (and parallels) two pronouns are connected (τίνα με λέγουσιν οἱ ὄχλοι εἶναι). The *interrogative* pronoun is the predicate term, since *lexically* it fills the slot of the unknown (who?). Thus, although as a pronoun it would grammatically be expected to fill the slot of subject, as an *interrogative* pronoun it *lexically* fills the slot of predicate. (This well illustrates the interplay that lexeme and syntax have on one another; they cannot be treated in isolation.) Cf. also Matt 16:15; Mark 8:27, 29; Luke 9:20; and Acts 2:12; 17:20 for similar constructions with interrogative pronouns, and Acts 5:36; 8:9 for constructions with an indefinite pronoun as the predicate term.

[72] For other examples of articular acc. as subject of an equative verb infinitive, cf. Luke 20:41; Acts 26:29 (here with qualitative pronoun as predicate term); Eph 3:6. Although Cripe lists several examples, most have an adjective for the predicate term.

[73] Cripe found only three examples: Luke 20:6; Acts 17:7; Rom 15:8.

Luke 4:41   ἤδεισαν τὸν χριστὸν **αὐτὸν** εἶναι
             they knew that **he** was the Christ

> Just as with S-PN, if one of the two substantives is a pronoun and the other is articular (or a proper name), the pronoun is the subject term (again, regardless of word order).[74]

b) Subject and Direct Object (with Transitive Verb Infinitives)

Luke 2:27   ἐν τῷ εἰσαγαγεῖν **τοὺς γονεῖς** τὸ παιδίον Ἰησοῦν[75]
             when **the parents** brought in the child Jesus

> Obviously, common sense is helpful in determining which acc. is the subject and which is the object!

John 1:48   πρὸ τοῦ σε **Φίλιππον** φωνῆσαι ὄντα ὑπὸ τὴν συκῆν εἶδόν σε
             before **Philip** called you, while you were under the fig tree, I saw you

Heb 5:12   χρείαν ἔχετε τοῦ διδάσκειν ὑμᾶς **τινά**
             you need **someone** to teach you

> In this text the order is O-S with an indefinite acc. subject. Neither proximity to the infinitive nor word order indicates which acc. is the subject; but the context does.[76]

Cf. also Mark 8:31; Acts 16:30; Rom 12:2; 1 Cor 7:11; Phil 1:10; 2 Tim 3:15.

3) Problematic Texts

Phil 1:7   διὰ τὸ ἔχειν **με** ἐν τῇ καρδίᾳ ὑμᾶς
             because **I** have you in [my] heart *or*
             because **you** have me in [your] heart

> This is the one passage that Cripe felt was highly ambiguous. It is possible to translate, "because *you* have *me* in your heart . . ." or "because *I* have *you* in my heart . . ." Either is possible because: (a) both subject and direct object are in the acc.; (b) the article τῇ (καρδίᾳ) implies possession (which could be either "my" or "your"); and (c) in Pauline literature "heart" is often used as a collective singular (i.e., referring to plural possession). The context must be determinative. But this has been argued both ways. In cases such as this, the best approach *is* to bring in word order—not as though nothing else mattered, but as the factor that tips the scales.[77]

2 Cor 2:13   οὐκ ἔσχηκα ἄνεσιν τῷ πνεύματί μου τῷ μὴ εὑρεῖν **με Τίτον**
             I had no rest in my soul when **I** did not find Titus *or*
             I had no rest in my soul when **Titus** did not find me

> Although this text could, in a given context, be read either way, it

---

[74] Cf. also Rom 4:13.

[75] τοὺς γονεῖς is omitted in a few late MSS (245 1347 1510 2643).

[76] For similar constructions, cf. Acts 3:21; 1 Cor 5:1; Heb 8:3.

[77] This is due to the fact that although *normal* word order in Greek is difficult to determine, almost all studies conclude that the subject term usually precedes the object term. Thus, in an otherwise ambiguous text, an author might be expected to give us some clue on what he means.

probably means "I did not find Titus." The connection between the ἔσχηκα ἄνεσιν and the infinitive clause suggests this: if Paul is looking for Titus, he is not resting.

Cf. also 2 Cor 8:6 (S-O); Acts 18:5, 28 (S-P). Both Acts passages read, εἶναι τὸν χριστὸν Ἰησοῦν. Note the differences in translation: "Jesus was the Christ" (AV, NASB, NIV) vs. "the Christ was Jesus" (RSV, NEB).[78]

6. Accusative of Retained Object

a. Definition

The *accusative of thing* in a double accusative person-thing construction with an active verb *retains its case* when the verb is put in the *passive*. The accusative of person, in such instances, becomes the subject.[79] This use of the accusative occurs most frequently with causative verbs, though it is rare in the NT.

"I taught you *the lesson*" becomes, with the verb converted to a passive, "You were taught *the lesson* by me." When the verb is transformed into a passive, the accusative of person becomes the subject (nom.), the accusative of thing is retained.

b. Illustrations

1 Cor 12:13   πάντες **ἓν πνεῦμα** ἐποτίσθημεν[80]
           all were made to drink [of] **one Spirit**
              "All" is the person, put in the nom. with passive verbs. The acc. of thing, "one Spirit," is retained. If the verb had been in the active voice, the text would be read: "he made all to drink of one Spirit" (ἐπότισε πάντα ἓν πνεῦμα).

Luke 7:29   οἱ τελῶναι ἐδικαίωσαν τὸν θεὸν βαπτισθέντες **τὸ βάπτισμα** Ἰωάννου
           the tax-collectors, having been baptized with **the baptism** of John, recognized that God was right

2 Th 2:15   κρατεῖτε τὰς παραδόσεις **ἃς** ἐδιδάχθητε
           hold fast to the traditions **that** you were taught

Rev 16:9   ἐκαυματίσθησαν οἱ ἄνθρωποι **καῦμα μέγα**
           people were scorched [with] **a scorching heat**
              This is also an example of cognate acc.

Cf. also Gal 2:7; Phil 1:11; Heb 6:9.

---

[78] Most likely τὸν χριστόν should be regarded as the subject. This is not, however, due to its articularity, but word order. See discussion of this kind of problem in the section on predicate nom.

[79] It is not always explicit, however. Cf. 2 Thess 2:15, mentioned below.

[80] Some witnesses have πόμα for πνεῦμα (177 630 920 1505 1738 1881): "all were made to drink one *drink*," turning the expression into an allusion to the Lord's Supper (so BAGD, s.v. πόμα).

7. Pendent Accusative (Accusativum Pendens)

a. Definition

The pendent accusative is a grammatically independent use of the accusative. The accusative is *pendent* or "hanging" in that it is introduced into the sentence as though it were going to be the direct object, but the sentence is completed in a syntactically awkward manner, leaving the accusative dangling. Like the pendent nominative, this accusative is thrown forward to the beginning of the clause, followed by a sentence in which it is now replaced by a pronoun in the case required by the syntax. This category has very few examples.

b. Clarification/Key to Identification

In some ways it may be helpful to think of the *accusativum pendens* as a subset of the accusative of reference. A helpful key to testing whether a certain accusative is pendent in fact is the question, Can I translate the accusative at the beginning of the clause, "With reference to . . ."? On the other hand, it is different from the standard accusative of reference in that this usage really belongs to *anacoluthon*—i.e., it is a poorly constructed sentence, syntactically speaking.

c. Illustrations

Matt 21:42 **λίθον** ὃν ἀπεδοκίμασαν οἱ οἰκοδομοῦντες, οὗτος ἐγενήθη εἰς κεφαλὴν γωνίας
the stone that the builders rejected—this has become the cornerstone

> This could be read: "With reference to the stone that the builders rejected: this has become the cornerstone." As is often true of such constructions in the NT, this is a quotation from the OT (Ps 118:22 here).

Mark 6:16 ὃν ἐγὼ ἀπεκεφάλισα **Ἰωάννην**, οὗτος ἠγέρθη[81]
John, whom I beheaded—this one has been raised!

Cf. also John 15:2; Gal 5:17; 6:7.

→ 8. Accusative in Simple Apposition

a. Definition

Though not technically a syntactical category, the accusative case (as well as the other cases) can be an appositive to another substantive in the *same* case. An appositional construction involves two adjacent substantives that refer to the same person or thing and have the same syntactical

---

[81] A few scribes apparently felt uncomfortable with the acc. Ἰωάννην, replacing it with Ἰωάννης (ℵ* has οὗτος Ἰωάννης; οὗτος ἐστιν Ἰωάννης is read in Θ 565 700 *et pauci*).

relation to the rest of the clause. The first accusative substantive can belong to *any* accusative category, and the second is merely a clarification of who or what is mentioned. Thus, the appositive "piggy-backs" on the first accusative's use, as it were.[82] It is a common use of the accusative, though occasionally the function of the trailing accusative substantive may be difficult to determine (i.e., apposition or parallel are options [cf. Eph 2:2 below]).

b. Illustrations

Mark 1:16   Ἀνδρέαν **τὸν ἀδελφὸν** Σίμωνος
            Andrew **the brother** of Simon

Acts 16:31 πίστευσον ἐπὶ τὸν κύριον **Ἰησοῦν** καὶ σωθήσῃ σύ
            believe in the Lord **Jesus** and you shall be saved

Eph 1:7   ἐν ᾧ ἔχομεν τὴν ἀπολύτρωσιν διὰ τοῦ αἵματος αὐτοῦ, **τὴν ἄφεσιν** τῶν παραπτωμάτων
            in whom we have the redemption through his blood, **the forgiveness** of [our] trespasses

Eph 2:2   ἐν αἷς ποτε περιεπατήσατε κατὰ τὸν αἰῶνα τοῦ κόσμου τούτου, κατὰ **τὸν ἄρχοντα** τῆς ἐξουσίας τοῦ ἀέρος
            in which you formerly walked according to the Aeon of this world, according to **the ruler** of the domain of the air

> This text is debatable. If τὸν αἰῶνα refers to a supernatural being,[83] then it may well be in apposition to τὸν ἄρχοντα.[84] But if it refers to "the age of this world," then the constructions are parallel rather than appositional. For similarly ambiguous texts, cf. Luke 3:8; Acts 11:20; 13:23; Rom 13:14; Col 2:6; 1 Pet 3:15; Rev 13:17.

Cf. also Matt 2:6; Acts 1:23; 2:22; 3:13; Phil 2:25; Col 1:14; 1 Thess 3:2; Heb 13:23; Rev 2:20.

Adverbial Uses of the Accusative

The difficulty with most adverbial accusatives is that they do not find ready analogies with English. The accusative in classical Greek was the workhorse of the oblique cases, functioning in many different capacities. But when the Koine language was born and nonnatives began to speak Greek, the adverbial accusatives took on a more restricted role. Many were replaced by datives or prepositional phrases. Hence, the modern student can take some measure of comfort in knowing that the unnatural feel of many adverbial accusatives was shared by other peoples learning this language as well.

---

[82] For more information on simple apposition, cf. the sections on the nom. and gen. in simple apposition.

[83] See BAGD, s.v. αἰών, 4 (28).

[84] Technically, the two prepositional phrases would be in apposition to one another.

1. Adverbial Accusative (Accusative of Manner)

a. Definition

The accusative substantive functions semantically like an adverb in that it *qualifies* the action of the verb rather than indicating *quantity* or extent of the verbal action. It frequently acts like an adverb of manner, though not always (hence, the alternative category title is really a *sub*category, although the most frequently used one). Apart from the occurrence with certain words, this usage is not common.[85]

b. Amplification and Caution

This usage has structural similarities to a cognate accusative, but there the similarity ends. It is restricted to a certain group of words that, historically, were used adverbially. That is to say, many adverbs developed from the accusative form of the noun or (especially) adjective.

There are two distinct kinds of adverbial accusatives: nominal and adjectival. The noun δωρεάν is frequently used for an adverbial accusative.[86] But few other nouns are so used. There is a much larger number of adjectives that are used adverbially.[87]

c. Illustrations

1) Nominal Examples

Matt 10:8   **δωρεὰν** ἐλάβετε, **δωρεὰν** δότε
              you received **freely, freely** give
> If δωρεάν were a cognate acc., the translation would be: "You received a gift, [so] give a gift." As an adverbial acc. the typical acc. idea of "extent" has disappeared.

Gal 2:21   εἰ γὰρ διὰ νόμου δικαιοσύνη, ἄρα Χριστὸς **δωρεὰν** ἀπέθανεν
              for if justification comes by law, then Christ died **for nothing**

---

[85] Many grammarians lump adverbial acc. and acc. of respect together. This is certainly legitimate, but our treatment of the adverbial acc. is more restrictive. Generally speaking, we consider an adverbial acc. *noun* to be one that can be translated like an adverb, while an acc. of respect should receive the gloss "with respect to . . . ."

[86] Every anarthrous instance of δωρεάν in fact is best treated as an adverbial accusative (each time indicating manner). Cf. John 15:25; Rom 3:24; 2 Cor 11:7; Gal 2:21; 2 Thess 3:8; Rev 21:6; 22:17. Curiously, the NRSV treats many of these substantivally (typically in an object-complement construction), though they do not fit the normal contours of such a construction (e.g., often both substantives are anarthrous).

[87] Technically, adjectives do not normally belong under any case category because they are normally dependent on substantives and hence "piggy-back" on whatever case (and case usage) the substantive has. But the acc. adjective, when it is not dependent on a noun, almost defies classification. To discuss it under "Adjectives" is somewhat misleading, as is a discussion of it under "Accusative."

2) Adjectival Examples

Matt 6:33 ζητεῖτε δὲ **πρῶτον** τὴν βασιλείαν τοῦ θεοῦ
but seek **first** the kingdom of God

John 10:10 ἐγὼ ἦλθον ἵνα ζωὴν ἔχωσιν καὶ **περισσὸν** ἔχωσιν.[88]
I have come that they might have life and that they might have it **abundantly.**

Phil 3:1 **τὸ λοιπόν**, ἀδελφοί μου, χαίρετε ἐν κυρίῳ
finally, my brothers, rejoice in the Lord

Cf. also Matt 8:30 (μακράν)[89]; 9:14 (πολλά); 15:16 (ἀκμήν); Luke 17:25 (πρῶτον); John 1:41 (πρῶτον); Acts 27:20 (λοιπόν); 2 Cor 13:11 (λοιπόν).

➡ 2. *Accusative of Measure (or Extent of Time or Space)*

a. Definition

The accusative substantive indicates the extent of the verbal action. This can either be how far (extent of space) or for how long (extent of time). The usage is quite rare with space, though somewhat common with time.

b. Key to Identification

Supply before the accusative *for the extent of* or (with reference to time) *for the duration of.*

c. Significance and Clarification

This use of the accusative has in view the basic idea of this case: limitation as to extent. The accusative of space answers the question, "How far?" while the accusative of time answers the question "How long?" It is important to specify to which subgroup a particular accusative belongs (i.e., whether it is the acc. of time or the acc. of space).

With ὥρα the accusative functions like a *dative* of time in that it answers the question "When?" In such instances, the accusative should simply be labeled an accusative of *time* (rather than acc. of *extent* of time).[90]

---

[88] καὶ περισσὸν ἔχωσιν is omitted in 𝔓[66*] D *et pauci*; the adjective is comparative (περισσότερον) in 𝔓[44] 𝔓[75] Χ Γ Ψ 69 1010 *et pauci*.

[89] Instances of μακράν could be classified either as adverbial acc. or acc. of extent of space, with ὁδόν implied (so BAGD). Cf. also Mark 12:34; Luke 15:20; John 21:8; Acts 22:21; Eph 2:13, 17.

[90] See *BDF*, 88 (§161) for discussion. Perhaps this is due more to the growing lexical latitude of ὥρα, for it came to be used both for "hour" and "moment" (BAGD, s.v. ὥρα, 2.b: "as a moment of time that takes its name fr. the hour that has just passed").

d. Illustrations

1) Accusative for Extent of Space

Luke 2:44   νομίσαντες δὲ αὐτὸν εἶναι ἐν τῇ συνοδίᾳ ἦλθον ἡμέρας **ὁδόν**
            but assuming that he was in the group, they went a day's **journey**

John 6:19   ἐληλακότες οὖν ὡς **σταδίους** εἴκοσι πέντε ἢ τριάκοντα
            therefore, when they had rowed about twenty-five or thirty **stades**

Cf. also Matt 4:15; Mark 12:34; Luke 22:41.

2) Accusative for Extent of Time

Matt 20:6   τί ὧδε ἑστήκατε **ὅλην τὴν ἡμέραν** ἀργοί;
            Why have you been standing here idle **the whole day**?

Matt 4:2   νηστεύσας **ἡμέρας** τεσσεράκοντα καὶ **νύκτας** τεσσεράκοντα
            fasting forty **days** and forty **nights**
            > Had the evangelist said that Jesus was fasting forty days and forty
            > nights with the *genitive* of time, it would have meant that he was fasting
            > *during* that time period, but not necessarily for the whole of it. Indeed,
            > the meaning might have been that he had fasted during the daytime,
            > but ate at night.[91] Cf. also Mark 1:13.

Acts 7:20   ἀνετράφη **μῆνας τρεῖς** ἐν τῷ οἴκῳ τοῦ πατρός
            [Moses] was raised **for three months** in his father's house

Matt 28:20 μεθ᾽ ὑμῶν εἰμι **πάσας τὰς ἡμέρας** ἕως τῆς συντελείας τοῦ αἰῶνος
            I shall be with you **all the days** until the end of the age
            > Jesus' promise to his disciples is not just that he would be with them
            > *during* the present dispensation [which would have been expressed by
            > the genitive], but for the *extent* of it.

Luke 2:37   ἀφίστατο τοῦ ἱεροῦ . . . λατρεύουσα **νύκτα καὶ ἡμέραν**
            [Anna] did not leave the temple, worshiping . . . **night and day**
            > The expression "night and day" means "throughout the night and
            > day." It could be translated "all the time," but in a distributive or itera-
            > tive sense. Cf. also Mark 4:27; Acts 26:7; 2 Thess 3:8 (*v.l.*).

Cf. also Mark 2:19; Acts 9:9; 10:30; 21:7; Rev 9:10.

e. Summary of Genitive, Dative, and Accusative of Time

One way to remember the distinctions between the cases used for time
is to remember the root idea of each case. However, under the five-case

---

[91] Cf. Luke 18:12, though not much can be made of the gen. there ("on two occasions
during the week"). But the Pharisees often fasted during the daytime only (cf. E. Schürer,
The History of the Jewish People in the Age of Jesus Christ, rev. and ed. by G. Vermes, F. Millar,
M. Black [Edinburgh: T. & T. Clark, 1979] 2.484). Further, the Didache seems to suggest a
qualitative distinction between the two. In *Didache* 8.1 the author exhorts the readers not
to fast like the Jews do, on Mondays and Thursdays (using the dat. case [δευτέρᾳ σαββάτων
καὶ πέμπῃ]), but on Wednesdays and Fridays (acc. case [τετράδα καὶ παρασκευήν]).

system this may prove a bit confusing. Therefore, for the cases used for time, it may be helpful to think in terms of the *eight*-case system. The root idea of the *genitive* is *kind*. Thus the genitive of time expresses the *kind* of time or time within which. The root idea of the *locative* (not dat.) is *position*, expressing *point* in time. The root idea for the *accusative* is *extent*. Thus the accusative of time expresses the *extent* of time.

One illustration may help. If I were to say, "I worked last night" it could mean (1) during the night, (2) all night, or (3) at a point of time in the night. But in Greek, the case of *night* would indicate what I meant. If I had said νυκτός (gen.), I would mean "during the night." If I had said νυκτί (dat.) I would mean "at a point of time in the night (e.g., 1 a.m.)." If I had said νυκτά (acc.) I would mean "for the length of the night." This can be illustrated graphically as well (see chart 16 below).

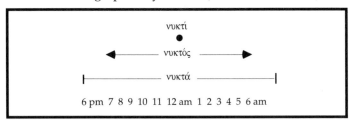

Chart 16
The Cases for Time

3. Accusative of Respect or (General) Reference

a. Definition

The accusative substantive restricts the reference of the verbal action. It indicates *with reference to what* the verbal action is represented as true.

An author will use this accusative to qualify a statement that would otherwise typically not be true. This accusative could thus be called a frame of reference accusative or limiting accusative. This is not very common in Koine Greek.[92]

b. Key to Identification

Before the accusative substantive you can usually supply the words *with reference to*, or *concerning*. The usage is rare enough in the NT that this should be employed as a last resort—that is, only after other categories are exhausted.

---

[92] In classical Greek the acc. was the most common case used for reference. In Koine, it is a distant second to the dat. of reference, being supplanted by the dat., no doubt, because the dat. more naturally connotes reference to nonnative speakers. There is also a gen. of reference, and a nom. of reference (i. e., *nominativus pendens*).

c. Illustrations

Matt 27:57 ἄνθρωπος πλούσιος ἀπὸ Ἀριμαθαίας, **τοὔνομα** Ἰωσήφ
a rich man from Arimathea, Joseph **by name**

John 6:10 ἀνέπεσαν οὖν οἱ ἄνδρες **τὸν ἀριθμὸν** ὡς πεντακισχίλιοι
then the men sat down—**with reference to number** about 5000

Rom 10:5 Μωϋσῆς γὰρ γράφει **τὴν δικαιοσύνην** τὴν ἐκ τοῦ νόμου
for Moses writes that, **with reference to the righteousness** which
comes from the law . . .

Rev 1:20 **τὸ μυστήριον** τῶν ἑπτὰ ἀστέρων οὓς εἶδες ἐπὶ τῆς δεξιᾶς μου, . . . · οἱ
ἑπτὰ ἀστέρες ἄγγελοι εἰσιν . . .
as for the mystery of the seven stars which you saw in my right
hand: . . . the seven stars are angels . . .

Cf. also Acts 2:37; Rom 8:28 (possible);[93] 1 Cor 9:25; 2 Cor 12:13.; Eph 4:15; Phil 1:27 (possible); Heb 2:17.

4. *Accusative in Oaths*

a. Definition

The accusative substantive indicates the person or thing by whom or by which one swears an oath. This usage is not common in the NT.

b. Key to Identification

Before the noun in the accusative supply the word *by*. Note also that it will *only* be used with verbs of *swearing* (such as ὁρκίζω, ὀμνύω), followed typically (though not always) by a divine title.

c. Amplification

Although structurally it often looks like one of the double accusatives (person-thing or object-complement), semantically it is different. (1) The accusative in oaths can be a person even when the direct object is a person. Hence, it is not a person-thing double accusative. (2) The two accusatives do not refer to the same thing. Hence, it is not an object-complement construction.[94] In reality, this is one kind of adverbial accusative, though it would be inappropriate to translate the accusative as an adverb.[95]

---

[93] See Cranfield, *Romans* (ICC) 1.425-29, who discusses and dismisses the likelihood of πάντα as acc. of reference (assuming the longer reading). He is surely correct. In our view, if an acc. could just as naturally fit some other category (such as direct object), calling it reference is *petitio principii.*

[94] It is not even necessary for the acc. in oaths to be found with another acc., illustrating another difference from double accusatives.

A preposition sometimes replaces the simple accusative for the person or thing by whom or which one swears,[96] as does the simple dative.[97]

d. Illustrations

Mark 5:7　Ἰησοῦ υἱὲ τοῦ θεοῦ τοῦ ὑψίστου; ὁρκίζω σε **τὸν θεόν**, μή με βασανίσῃς
Jesus, Son of the Most High God, I adjure you **by God**, do not torment me!

1 Th 5:27　ἐνορκίζω ὑμᾶς **τὸν κύριον**
I adjure you **by the Lord**

Jas 5:12　μὴ ὀμνύετε, μήτε **τὸν οὐρανὸν** μήτε **τὴν γῆν** μήτε ἄλλον τινὰ ὅρκον
do not swear—either **by heaven** or **by earth** or with any other oath
> The last expression, "with any other oath" (μήτε ἄλλον τινὰ ὅρκον) seems to involve a cognate acc., though the parallel with the two previous μήτε phrases might suggest an implicit acc. in oaths (something like "nor by the person or thing in any other oath").

Cf. also Acts 19:13; 2 Tim 4:1.

Accusative After Certain Prepositions

1. Definition

Certain prepositions take the accusative after them. See the chapter on prepositions for discussion. For review of which prepositions take which cases, cf. Mounce, *Basics of Biblical Greek*, 55-62.

2. Significance

When an accusative follows a preposition, you should *not* attempt to identify the accusative's function by case usage *alone*. Rather, consult BAGD for the specific usage of that case with that preposition.

Conclusion on the Cases

The section on the cases has been unusually long for two reasons: (1) the frequency of the cases warrants a lengthy treatment (about 60% of all words in the NT are case-forms), and (2) the cases are extremely elastic in their uses and thus play a key role in exegesis. As Robertson so aptly puts it, "The cases have kept us for a good while, but the subject is second to none in importance in Greek syntax."[98]

---

[95] In classical usage this category belongs under the larger umbrella of acc. in invocations. See Moorhouse, "The Role of the Accusative Case," 212-13.

[96] E.g., ἐν in Matt 5:34, 36; 23:16; Rev 10:6; κατά + gen. in Matt 26:63; Heb 6:13.

[97] Cf. Acts 2:30.

[98] Robertson, *Grammar*, 543.

The Article, Part I

Origin, Function, Regular Uses, and Absence of the Article

Select Bibliography

BAGD, 549-52; *BDF*, 131-45 (§249-76); **Brooks-Winbery**, 67-74; **L. Cignelli, and G. C. Bottini**, "L'Articolo nel Greco Biblico," *Studium Biblicum Franciscanum Liber Annuus* 41 (1991) 159-199; **Dana-Mantey**, 135-53 (§144-50); **F. Eakin**, "The Greek Article in First and Second Century Papyri," *AJP* 37 (1916) 333-40; **R. W. Funk**, *Intermediate Grammar*, 2.555-60 (§710-16); **idem**, "The Syntax of the Greek Article: Its Importance for Critical Pauline Problems" (Ph.D. dissertation, Vanderbilt University, 1953); **Gildersleeve**, *Classical Greek*, 2.514-608; **T. F. Middleton**, *The Doctrine of the Greek Article Applied to the Criticism and Illustration of the New Testament*, new [3d] ed., rev. by H. J. Rose (London: J. G. F. & J. Rivington, 1841); **Moule**, *Idiom Book*, 106-17; **Porter**, *Idioms*, 103-14; **Robertson**, *Grammar*, 754-96; **H. B. Rosén**, *Early Greek Grammar and Thought in Heraclitus: The Emergence of the Article* (Jerusalem: Israel Academy of Sciences and Humanities, 1988); **D. Sansone**, "Towards a New Doctrine of the Article in Greek: Some Observations on the Definite Article in Plato," *Classical Philology* 88.3 (1993) 191-205; **Turner**, *Syntax*, 13-18, 36-37, 165-88; **Völker**, *Syntax der griechischen Papyri*, vol. 1: *Der Artikel* (Münster: Westfälischen Vereinsdruckerei, 1903); **Young**, *Intermediate Greek*, 55-69; **Zerwick**, *Biblical Greek*, 53-62 (§165-92).

A. Introduction

One of the greatest gifts bequeathed by the Greeks to Western civilization was the article. European intellectual life was profoundly impacted by this gift of clarity.[1] By the first century CE, it had become refined and subtle. Consequently, the article is one of the most fascinating areas of study in NT Greek grammar. It is also one of the most neglected and abused. In spite of the fact that the article is used far more frequently than any other word in the Greek NT (almost 20,000 times, or one out of seven words),[2] there is still much mystery about its usage.[3] The most comprehensive treatment, *The Doctrine of the Greek Article* by

---

[1] See P. Chantraine, "Le grec et la structure les langues modernes de l'occident," *Travaux du cercle linguistique de Copenhague* 11 (1957) 20-21.

[2] In light of its frequency and finesse, we cannot hope to classify all uses of the article. This chapter will focus on the main categories. One should consult the bibliography for some of the more comprehensive treatments.

[3] Sansone remarks, "Even to examine exhaustively the use of the article in a single author requires a study the length of a dissertation and, until several such studies have been adequately and accurately carried out, there can be no hope of giving a full account of the use of the definite [*sic*] article in ancient, or even classical, Greek" ("New Doctrine of the Article," 195).

Middleton, is over one hundred and fifty years old.[4] Nevertheless, although there is much that we do not understand about the Greek article, there is much that we do understand. As Robertson pointed out, "The article is never meaningless in Greek, though it often fails to correspond with the English idiom . . . . Its free use leads to exactness and finesse."[5] In the least, we cannot treat it lightly, for its presence or absence is the crucial element to unlocking the meaning of scores of passages in the NT.

In short, there is no more important aspect of Greek grammar than the article to help shape our understanding of the thought and theology of the NT writers.

> As a side note, it should be mentioned that the KJV translators often erred in their treatment of the article. They were more comfortable with the Latin than with the Greek. Since there is no article in Latin, the KJV translators frequently missed the nuances of the Greek article. Robertson points out:
>
>> The translators of the King James Version, under the influence of the Vulgate, handle the Greek article loosely and inaccurately. A goodly list of such sins is given in "The Revision of the New Testament," such as "a pinnacle" for τὸ πτερύγιον (Mt. 4:5). Here the whole point lies in the article, the wing of the Temple overlooking the abyss. So in Mt. 5:1 τὸ ὄρος was the mountain right at hand, not "a mountain." On the other hand, the King James translators missed the point of μετὰ γυναικός (Jo. 4:27) when they said "the woman." It was "a woman," any woman, not the particular woman in question. But the Canterbury Revisers cannot be absolved from all blame, for they ignore the article in Lk. 18:13, τῷ ἁμαρτωλῷ. The vital thing is to see the matter from the Greek point of view and find the reason for the use of the article.[6]

B. Origin

The article was originally derived from the demonstrative pronoun. That is, its original force was to *point out* something. It has largely kept the force of drawing attention to something.

---

[4] The two-volume work by Adrian Kluit, *Vindiciae Articuli Ὁ, Ἡ, Τό in Novo Testamento* (Paddenburg: Traiecti ad Rhenum, 1768) is arguably more comprehensive, though it is largely preoccupied with the interface of syntax and lexical issues, viz., how the article is used with various terms, rather than with a systematic presentation. Middleton's work, by contrast, includes one hundred and fifty pages on the syntax of the article in classical Greek, followed by something of a syntactical exegesis of the article in the NT (over 500 pages marching *seriatim* from Matthew through Revelation).

[5] Robertson, *Grammar*, 756.

[6] Ibid., 756-57.

C. Function

1. What it is NOT

The function of the article is *not* primarily to make something definite that would otherwise be indefinite. It does *not* primarily "definitize."[7] There are at least ten ways in which a noun in Greek can be definite without the article. For example, proper names are definite even without the article (Παῦλος means "Paul," not "*a* Paul"). Yet, proper names sometimes take the article. Hence, when the article is used with them it must be for some other purpose. Further, its use with other than nouns is not to make something definite that would otherwise be indefinite, but to *nominalize* something that would otherwise not be considered as a concept.

To argue that the article functions primarily to make something definite is to commit the "phenomenological fallacy"–viz., that of making ontological statements based on truncated evidence. No one questions that the article is used frequently to definitize, but whether this captures the essential idea is another matter.

One further note: There is no need to speak of the article in Greek as the *definite* article because there is no corresponding indefinite article.[8]

2. What it IS

a. At bottom, the article intrinsically has the ability to *conceptualize*. Or, as Rosén has put it, the article "has the power of according nominal status to any expression to which it is appended, and, by this token, of conveying the status of a concept to whatever 'thing' is denoted by that expression, for the reason that whatever is conceived by the mind–so it would appear–becomes a concept as a result of one's faculty to call it by a name."[9] In other words, the article is able to turn just about any part of speech into a noun and, therefore, a concept. For example, "poor" expresses a quality, but the addition of an article turns it into an entity, "the poor." It is this ability to conceptualize that seems to be the basic force of the article.

b. Does it ever do more than conceptualize? Of course. A distinction needs to be made between the essential force of the article and what it is most frequently used for. In terms of basic force, the article conceptualizes. In terms of predominant *function*, it *identifies*.[10] That is to say, it is used pre-

---

[7] *Contra* Brooks-Winbery, 67; Young, *Intermediate Greek*, 55.

[8] Rosén (*Heraclitus*, 25) observes, "this term is justified only when a language has at least two of these elements, one of which is a determinator. I know of no language which, having only one 'article,' assigns to it an 'undetermining' function."

[9] Ibid., 27.

[10] That this is its normal use does not mean that its conceptual powers disappear, but rather that the identifying force of the article is a subset of the conceptual. Further, if we said that its essential value was to identify, we would be hard-pressed to explain its use with non-nouns.

dominantly to stress the identity of an individual or class or quality. There are a variety of ways in which the article stresses identity. For example, it may distinguish one entity (or class) from another, identify something as known or unique, point to something physically present, or simply point out. The identifying function of the article covers a multitude of uses.

c.   The Greek article also serves a determining function at times–i.e., it *definitizes*. On the one hand, although it would be incorrect to say that the article's basic function is to make something definite, on the other hand, whenever it is used, the term it modifies must of necessity be definite. These three relationships (conceptualize, identify, definitize) can be envisioned as concentric circles: all articles that make definite also identify; all articles that identify also conceptualize.

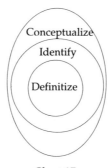

Chart 17
The Basic Forces of the Article

D. Regular Uses of the Article

The major categories of this section (e.g., as a pronoun, with substantives, etc.) look at the article in certain constructions. But one caveat is in order: to label the use of the article in one *structural* category is not necessary to bar it from membership in one of the *semantic* categories. As Sansone remarks, "The reason it is so difficult to account for its use is that the article, small word though it is, attempts to do too much."[11]

The major semantic categories normally occur with nouns, but such semantics are not infrequently found in other constructions. Thus, for example, the articles in Acts 14:4 belong to the category "Alternative Pronouns," in which they are used in the place of nouns: ἐσχίσθη δὲ τὸ πλῆθος τῆς πόλεως, καὶ **οἱ** μὲν ἦσαν σὺν τοῖς Ἰουδαίοις **οἱ** δὲ σὺν τοῖς ἀποστόλοις ("but the people of the city were divided; **some** sided with the Jews, but **others** sided with the apostles"). Yet they are also anaphoric, referring back to "the people/multitude" (τὸ πλῆθος). It would be

----

[11] Sansone, "New Doctrine of the Article," 205.

erroneous to say that the articles cannot be anaphoric because they are pronominal. A good rule of thumb to follow is this: Plug the article into its appropriate structural category, then examine it to see whether it also follows one of the semantic categories as well.

1. As a Pronoun ([partially] Independent Use)

The article is not a true pronoun in Koine Greek, even though it derived from the demonstrative. But in many instances it can function semantically in the place of a pronoun. Each category needs to be analyzed on its own.

- The use of the article for the *personal* and *alternating* pronouns comes the closest to an actual independent use in which the article no longer functions in its normal capacity. There is no noun that it modifies; normally, such an article involves no other force.

- What we call the use of the article for the *relative* pronoun is, in reality, an English way of looking at the matter. In such cases, the article has lost none of its articular nuances. That is to say, it is still dependent on a noun or other substantive.

- The article used for the *possessive* pronoun is also dependent. The possessive idea can be inferred from the presence of the article alone in certain contexts. In such instances, the article still retains the full range of semantic options it has when used with substantives.

a. Personal Pronoun *[he, she, it]*

1) Definition

The article is often used in the place of a *third* person personal pronoun in the nominative case. It is only used this way with the μὲν. . . δέ construction or with δέ alone. (Thus, ὁ μὲν. . . ὁ δέ or simply ὁ δέ) These constructions occur frequently in the Gospels and Acts, almost never elsewhere.

2) Amplification

a) The δέ is used to indicate that the subject has changed; the article is used to refer back to someone prior to the last-named subject. Most frequently, the subjects are speakers and the interchange is one of words, not action.

b) Typically, the ὁ δέ (or ὁ μέν) construction is immediately followed by a finite verb or circumstantial participle.[12] By

---

[12] Matthew uses the participle far more frequently than any author. Luke and John employ the article almost exclusively with the verb following. On a few occasions no verbal form follows, but a finite verb is to be supplied (cf. Luke 7:40; Acts 17:18; 19:2).

definition, a circumstantial participle is *never* articular, but in
such constructions the beginning student might see the article
and assume that the following participle is substantival. However, if you remember that the article as a pronoun is independent and therefore *not* modifying the participle, you can see that
the force of the participle is circumstantial. There will almost
never be any confusion about this, as the context will make clear
whether the participle is circumstantial or substantival.[13]

3) Illustrations

Mt 15:26-27 ὁ δὲ ἀποκριθεὶς εἶπεν, Οὐκ ἔστιν καλὸν λαβεῖν τὸν ἄρτον τῶν
τέκνων . . . (27) ἡ δὲ εἶπεν . . .
But **he**, answering, said, "It is not good to take the bread from the
children . . ." (27) but **she** said . . .

Luke 5:33 οἱ δὲ εἶπαν πρὸς αὐτόν· οἱ μαθηταὶ Ἰωάννου νηστεύουσιν. . . , οἱ δὲ σοὶ
ἐσθίουσιν καὶ πίνουσιν
But **they** said to him, "John's disciples fast . . . , but your [**disciples**]
eat and drink

John 4:32 ὁ δὲ εἶπεν αὐτοῖς
but **he** said to them

Acts 15:3 οἱ μὲν οὖν προπεμφθέντες ὑπὸ τῆς ἐκκλησίας
when **they** had been sent on their way by the church

Heb 7:24 ὁ δὲ . . . εἰς τὸν αἰῶνα . . . ἔχει τὴν ἱερωσύνην
but **he** . . . holds his priesthood . . . forever

Cf. also Matt 13:28, 29; 14:8; 17:11; 27:23 (twice); Mark 6:24; Luke 8:21; 9:45; John 2:8; 7:41;
20:25; Acts 3:5; 4:21; 5:8; 16:31.

b. Alternative Personal Pronoun *[the one . . . the other]*

1) Definition

Like the use of the article as a personal pronoun, the alternative use
is also found with μέν and δέ (and, as with the personal pronoun use,
the article is only found in the nom. case). This usage is distinct from
that of the personal pronoun use in that (1) structurally, both μέν and
δέ are almost always present,[14] and (2) semantically, a mild contrast
is implied. (It is probably best to consider this a subset of the

---

[13] Young, *Intermediate Greek*, lists Matt 4:20; 8:32; 26:57 as potentially ambiguous texts,
though all of them involve circumstantial participles. At first glance Matt 14:21, 33 might
also seem ambiguous, but these texts involve substantival participles.

[14] In Acts 17:18 we have τινες . . . οἱ δέ.

personal pronoun use.) The singular is typically translated "the one . . . the other"; the plural is rendered "some . . . others." This usage is quite rare in the NT.[15]

2) Illustrations

Acts 17:32 ἀκούσαντες δὲ ἀνάστασιν νεκρῶν **οἱ** μὲν ἐχλεύαζον, **οἱ** δὲ εἶπαν, Ἀκουσόμεθά σου περὶ τούτου καὶ πάλιν

Now when they heard of the resurrection of the dead, **some** began scoffing, but **others** said, "We will hear you again on this matter."

1 Cor 7:7 ἕκαστος ἴδιον ἔχει χάρισμα ἐκ θεοῦ, **ὁ** μὲν οὕτως, **ὁ** δὲ οὕτως[16]

each one has his own gift from God, **one** has this kind, **another** has that kind

> The articles here also function anaphorically, referring back to ἕκαστος.

Heb 7:5-6 **οἱ** μὲν ἐκ τῶν υἱῶν Λευὶ τὴν ἱερατείαν λαμβάνοντες ἐντολὴν ἔχουσιν ἀποδεκατοῦν . . . τοὺς ἀδελφοὺς αὐτῶν, καίπερ ἐξεληλυθότας ἐκ τῆς ὀσφύος Ἀβραάμ· (6) **ὁ** δὲ μὴ γενεαλογούμενος ἐξ αὐτῶν δεδεκάτωκεν Ἀβραάμ . . .

The descendants of the sons of Levi who receive the priestly office have a commandment to take tithes from . . . their brothers, even though they also are descended from Abraham. (6) But **this man**, not having their genealogy, received tithes from Abraham . . .

> It is possible that this twofold example belongs in different categories: the first article οἱ could be considered a substantiving article (with a prepositional phrase); the second might be considered a substantiver with a participle (in which case the translation would be: "this man, who does not have their genealogy").

Cf. also John 7:12; Acts 14:4; 17:18; 28:24; Gal 4:23; Eph 4:11; Phil 1:16-17; Heb 7:20-21; 12:10.

➡ ### c. Relative Pronoun *[who, which]*

1) Definition

Sometimes the article is equivalent to a relative pronoun in *force*. This is especially true when it is repeated after a noun before a phrase (e.g., a gen. phrase). For example, in 1 Cor 1:18 ὁ λόγος **ὁ** τοῦ σταυροῦ means "the word **which is** of the cross."

---

[15] Sometimes the article is also anaphoric, referring back to an already specified noun (e.g., Acts 14:4); other times, the nominal content is to be supplied from the context (e.g., Gal 4:23). On one occasion the article apparently functions as the object in an object-complement construction (Eph 4:11). The example in Acts 14:4 is instructive on another front: since the article functions in more than one capacity here, it illustrates the multi-functional character of the article overall.

[16] Most MSS read ὅς instead of ὁ ($\mathfrak{P}^{46}$ ℵ^C K L Ψ *Byz*).

2) Amplification and Semantics

a) Specifically, this is the use of the article with second and third attributive positions in which the modifier is *not* an adjective. (The second attributive position is article-noun-article-modifier; the third attributive position is noun-article-modifier.) Thus when the modifier is (a) a *genitive phrase* (as above), (b) a *prepositional phrase* (as in Matt 6:9–"our Father **who** is in heaven" [Πάτερ ἡμῶν ὁ ἐν τοῖς οὐρανοῖς]), or (c) a *participle* (e.g., Mark 4:15–"the word **which was** sown" [τὸν λόγον **τὸν** ἐσπαρμένον]), the article is translated as a relative.

b) To say that the article is functioning like a relative pronoun is only an *English* way of looking at the matter. Thus it is not truly the semantic force of the article. The article is still dependent on a noun or other substantive. It typically bears an anaphoric force, pointing back to the substantive with which it has concord. We translate it as a relative pronoun because this is less cumbersome than something like "our Father, the [one] in heaven."

c) When a genitive or prepositional phrase follows the substantive, the article could be omitted without altering the basic sense.[17] Returning to 1 Cor 1:18, we note that some important MSS omit the article before the genitive phrase (ὁ λόγος τοῦ σταυρου).[18] The notion conveyed is less emphatic ("the word of the cross"), but it is not essentially different. Why then is the article sometimes added before genitives and prepositional phrases? It is used primarily for emphasis and secondarily for clarification.[19]

3) Illustrations

Luke 7:32   ὅμοιοί εἰσιν παιδίοις **τοῖς** ἐν ἀγορᾷ καθημένοις
they are like children **who** [are] sitting in the marketplace

Acts 15:1   ἐὰν μὴ περιτμηθῆτε τῷ ἔθει **τῷ** Μωϋσέως[20]
unless you are circumcised according to the custom **which** [is] of Moses

> A less cumbersome translation would simply be, "the custom of Moses." The use of the article, however, emphasises the link with the old covenant.

---

[17] This is not true with participles; an anarthrous participle following an articular noun will be other than an attributive participle (either adverbial or predicate). However, when an anarthrous participle follows an anarthrous noun, it could be attributive.

[18] E.g., 𝔓46 B 1739 *pauci*.

[19] The clarifying value of the article is especially seen before prepositional phrases, since such phrases could otherwise be construed as subordinate to more than one substantive in the sentence.

[20] A few MSS omit the second article (Cᶜ D E H L P *alii*).

Phil 3:9   εὑρεθῶ ἐν αὐτῷ, μὴ ἔχων ἐμὴν δικαιοσύνην **τὴν** ἐκ νόμου ἀλλὰ **τὴν** διὰ πίστεως Χριστοῦ
[that] I might be found in him, not by having a righteousness of my own **which** [is] from the law, but **which** [is] through the faithfulness of Christ[21]

> This text involves the third attributive position as well as two prepositional phrases. The second article resumes the argument; it is as if the apostle said, "a 'not-of-my-own-righteousness, but one that comes by way of Christ's faithfulness.'"

Jas 2:7   τὸ καλὸν ὄνομα **τὸ** ἐπικληθὲν ἐφ' ὑμᾶς
the good name **that** [was] invoked over you

Cf. also Matt 2:16 ; 21:25; Mark 3:22; 11:30; Luke 10:23; John 5:44; Acts 3:16; Rom 4:11; 1 Cor 15:54; 1 Thess 2:4; Titus 2:10; Heb 9:3; Rev 5:12; 20:8.

d. Possessive Pronoun *[his, her]*

1) Definition

The article is sometimes used in contexts in which possession is implied. The article itself does not involve possession, but this notion can be inferred from the presence of the article alone in certain contexts.

2) Amplification

a) The article is used this way in contexts in which the idea of possession is obvious, especially when human anatomy is involved. Thus, in Matt 8:3, there is no need for the evangelist to add αὐτοῦ to what is patently evident: "stretching out **his** hand" (ἐκτείνας **τὴν** χεῖρα).

b) Conversely, it is important to note that unless a noun is modified by a possessive pronoun or at least an article, possession is almost surely not implied. Thus, in Eph 5:18, πληροῦσθε ἐν πνεύματι most probably does not mean "be filled in *your own* spirit" but "be filled in/with/by the Spirit."[22] And in 1 Tim 2:12 the instruction for a woman not to teach or exercise authority over ἀνδρός most likely is not related to her husband, but to men in a more general way.

3) Illustrations

Matt 4:20   οἱ δὲ εὐθέως ἀφέντες **τὰ** δίκτυα ἠκολούθησαν αὐτῷ
and immediately they left **their** nets and followed him

> The article is also anaphoric, pointing back to v 18.

---

[21] For discussion on the use of the gen. Χριστοῦ, see the chapter on the gen. case under "Subjective Genitive."

[22] Some appeal to the parallel in 1 Cor 14:15, but there the article is used.

Rom 7:25   ἐγὼ **τῷ** μὲν νοΐ δουλεύω νόμῳ θεοῦ, **τῇ** δὲ σαρκὶ νόμῳ ἁμαρτίας.
           I serve the law of God with **my** mind, but with **my** flesh, the law of
           sin.

Eph 5:25   οἱ ἄνδρες, ἀγαπᾶτε **τὰς** γυναῖκας
           husbands, love **your** wives

> The article is also generic in a distributive sense: each husband is to
> love his own wife.

Matt 13:36 ἀφεὶς τοὺς ὄχλους ἦλθεν εἰς **τὴν** οἰκίαν[23]
           leaving the crowd, he came into **his** house

> It is possible that the article is merely anaphoric, pointing back to the
> previous reference in v 1. But that is thirty-five verses away. It is equally
> possible that Jesus is here returning to his own home.

Cf. also Matt 27:24; Mark 1:41; 7:32; Phil 1:7.

2. With Substantives (Dependent or Modifying Use)

The article with substantives is the most fruitful area, exegetically speaking,
to study within the realm of the article. The two broadest categories are (1)
individualizing and (2) generic. The individualizing article particularizes,
distinguishing otherwise similar objects; the generic (or categorical) article is
used to distinguish one category of individuals from another.

➡   ### a. Individualizing Article

"Nearest to the real genius of [the article's] function is the use of the article to *point out* a particular object [italics mine]."[24] But this category is not
specific enough and can be broken down into at least eight subgroups.

➡   #### 1) Simple Identification

a) Definition

The article is frequently used to distinguish one individual from
another.

b) Clarification

This is our "drip-pan" category and should be used only as a
last resort. In reality, not many examples of the article fit under
this category *only*. Yet the article is still a largely unmined
territory by grammarians. Hence, pragmatically, unless
the article fits under one of the other seven categories of
the individualizing article or under the generic use (or one of

---

[23] A number of late MSS add αὐτοῦ (*f*[1] 118 1424 *et alii*).

[24] Dana-Mantey, 141.

the special uses), it is acceptable to list it as "the article of simple identification."

c) Illustrations

Matt 5:15 οὐδὲ καίουσιν λύχνον καὶ τιθέασιν αὐτὸν ὑπὸ **τὸν** μόδιον ἀλλ᾽ ἐπὶ **τὴν** λυχνίαν

nor do people light a lamp and place it under **the** bowl, but they [place it] on **the** lampstand

> This is a good twofold example of simple identification: both the bowl and the lampstand are in the room and are pointed out as such with the article.

Luke 4:20 πτύξας τὸ βιβλίον ἀποδοὺς **τῷ** ὑπηρέτῃ ἐκάθισεν

he closed the book and gave it back to **the** attendant and sat down

> The book was the book of Isaiah, referred to previously in v 17 (thus, anaphoric). But the attendant has not been mentioned. He is not apparently a well-known attendant, but simply a typical attendant at the synagogue. The article identifies him as such.

Acts 10:9 ἀνέβη Πέτρος ἐπὶ **τὸ** δῶμα προσεύξασθαι

Peter went up to **the** housetop to pray

> There is no previous reference to any house, but in the background is the custom of praying on a housetop. Luke is simply specifying this location as opposed to some other.

1 Cor 4:5 τότε **ὁ** ἔπαινος γενήσεται ἑκάστῳ ἀπὸ τοῦ θεοῦ

then **the** praise will come to each one from God

> A smoother translation would be, "then praise will come to each one from God," but this would miss the point of the article: each individual believer is to receive specific praise. The idea is "each one will receive his or her praise from God."

1 Cor 5:9 ἔγραψα ὑμῖν ἐν **τῇ** ἐπιστολῇ . . .

I wrote to you in **the** letter . . .

> Paul had previously written to the Corinthians and is here reminding them of that letter. Simple identification is an acceptable label for the article, though other possibilities present themselves. In a general sense, the article is anaphoric, referring back to this letter. It could also loosely be taken as possessive ("my letter"), but the force would be "the letter from me." As well, the letter could be treated as well-known or even monadic (assuming it is the only letter the Corinthians had received from Paul to date).

Cf. also John 13:5; Rom 4:4; Rev 1:7.

2) Anaphoric (Previous Reference)

a) Definition

The anaphoric article is the article denoting previous reference. (It derives its name from the Greek verb ἀναφέρειν, "to bring back, to bring up.") The first mention of the substantive is usually anarthrous because it is merely being introduced. But subsequent mentions of it use the article, for the article is now pointing back to *the* substantive previously mentioned. The anaphoric article has, by nature, then, a pointing force to it, reminding the reader of who or what was mentioned previously. It is the most common use of the article and the easiest usage to identify.

For example, in John 4:10 Jesus introduces to the woman at the well the concept of living water (ὕδωρ ζῶν). In v 11 the woman refers to the water, saying, "Where, then, do you keep *the* living water?" (πόθεν οὖν ἔχεις **τὸ** ὕδωρ **τὸ** ζῶν). The force of the article here could be translated, "Where do you keep **this** living water **of which** you just spoke?"

b) Amplification

1] Most individualizing articles will be anaphoric *in a very broad sense*. That is, they will be used to point out something that had been introduced earlier–perhaps even much earlier. For example, in John 1:21 the Jews ask John the Baptist, "Are you **the** prophet?" (ὁ προφήτης εἶ σύ;). They are thinking of the prophet mentioned in Deut 18:15 ("a prophet like me"). Technically, this instance belongs under the *par excellence* article (best/extreme of a class), but again, broadly, it is anaphoric. Thus to call an article anaphoric is not enough: one has to probe to see if it belongs more specifically to some other category as well.

Practically speaking, labeling an article as anaphoric requires that it have been introduced at most in the same book, preferably in a context not too far removed.

2] In terms of exposition, the anaphoric article is crucial, but primarily in a negative way. When you come across a word with the article, you might be tempted to make more out of it than the author intended. For example, in John 4:9 we read ἡ γυνὴ ἡ Σαμαρῖτις ("the Samaritan woman"). This is clearly anaphoric, going back to the anarthrous γυνή in v 7 (where the woman is introduced). However, if you did not know that it was anaphoric, you might wonder why the evangelist calls attention to her by the article, "the Samaritan woman." Your conclusion might be (1) she is well known as the embodiment of all Samaritan women, or (2) she is the Samaritan woman *par excellence*–no one else has the right to the title "*the* Samaritan woman." But when you realize that the article is anaphoric, merely pointing out the fact that the woman mentioned earlier is still under discussion, you will be accurate in your exposition and not say something that the author never intended.

3] Finally, the anaphoric article may be used with a noun whose *synonym* was mentioned previously. That is to say, although the terms used to describe may differ, the article is anaphoric if the reference is the same.

c) Illustrations

Jn 4:40, 43 ἔμεινεν ἐκεῖ δύο ἡμέρας . . . μετὰ δὲ **τὰς** δύο ἡμέρας...

he stayed there two days . . . after **the** two days. . .

John 4:50 λέγει αὐτῷ ὁ Ἰησοῦς· πορεύου, ὁ υἱός σου ζῇ. ἐπίστευσεν **ὁ** ἄνθρωπος τῷ λόγῳ ὃν εἶπεν αὐτῷ ὁ Ἰησοῦς καὶ ἐπορεύετο

Jesus said to him, "Go, your son lives." **The** man believed the word that Jesus spoke to him and went on his way.

> In v 46 this man is introduced as τις βασιλικός (a certain royal official). This subsequent mention uses a rather plain synonym, ὁ ἄνθρωπος, with the article reminding us which man is in view.

Acts 19:15 **τὸν** Παῦλον ἐπίσταμαι

this Paul I recognize

> The antecedent in v 13 (Παῦλος) is anarthrous.

Rom 6:4 συνετάφημεν αὐτῷ διὰ **τοῦ** βαπτίσματος

we were buried with him through **the** baptism

> The previous reference to baptism, in v 3, is the verb ἐβαπτίσθημεν. The anaphoric article thus can refer back not only to a synonym, but even to a word that is not substantival.

Jas 2:14 Τί τὸ ὄφελος, ἀδελφοί μου, ἐὰν πίστιν λέγῃ τις ἔχειν, ἔργα δὲ μὴ ἔχῃ; μὴ δύναται **ἡ** πίστις σῶσαι αὐτόν;

What is the benefit, my brothers, if someone says he has faith, but does not have works? **This** [kind of] faith is not able to save him, is it?

> The author introduces his topic: faith without works. He then follows it with a question, asking whether this kind of faith is able to save. The use of the article both points back to a certain kind of faith as defined by the author and is used to particularize an abstract noun.

> Against the vast bulk of commentators, Hodges argues that the article is not anaphoric, since otherwise the articular πίστις in the following verses would also have to refer back to such a workless faith.[25] He translates the text simply as "Faith cannot save him, can it?"[26] Although it may be true that the article with πίστις in vv 17, 18, 20, 22, and 26 is anaphoric, the antecedent needs to be examined in its own immediate context. In particular, the author examines two kinds of faith in 2:14-26, defining a non-working faith as a non-saving faith and a productive faith as one that saves. Both James and Paul would agree, I believe, with the statement: "Faith alone saves, but the faith that saves is not alone."

---

[25] Z. C. Hodges, *The Gospel Under Siege* (Dallas: Redención Viva, 1981) 23.
[26] Ibid., 21.

2 Tim 4:2   κήρυξον **τὸν** λόγον
             preach **the** word

> Here τὸν λόγον most likely goes back to 3:16, in which it is stated that
> πᾶσα γραφὴ θεόπνευστος καὶ ὠφέλιμος–"Every scripture [is] inspired
> and profitable." Identifying the article with λόγον as anaphoric here is
> both natural (since the anaphoric article frequently refers back to a syn-
> onym) and suggestive that 3:16 should *not* be translated "Every
> inspired scripture is also profitable. . ." as the ASV and NEB have done.
> If 3:16 were to be translated "every inspired scripture is also profit-
> able," we might expect a qualifier in 4:2, such as "preach the *inspired*
> word."[27]

Phil 2:6   ὃς ἐν μορφῇ θεοῦ ὑπάρχων οὐχ ἁρπαγμὸν ἡγήσατο **τὸ** εἶναι ἴσα θεῷ
             who, although he existed in the form of God, did not regard **the**
             [state of] being equal to God [as] something to be grasped

> This is a debatable example. Wright argues that the article is anaphoric,
> referring back to μορφῇ θεοῦ.[28] As attractive as this view may be theo-
> logically, it has a weak basis grammatically. The infinitive is the object
> and the anarthrous term, ἁρπαγμός, is the complement. The most natu-
> ral reason for the article with the infinitive is simply to mark it out as
> the object (see "Article as Function Marker" for discussion of this
> usage). Further, there is the possibility that μορφῇ θεοῦ refers to essence
> (thus, Christ's deity), while τὸ εἶναι ἴσα θεῷ refers to function. If this is
> the meaning of the text, then the two are not synonymous: although
> Christ was true deity, he did not usurp the role of the Father.

Cf. also Matt 2:1, 7; John 1:4; 2:1, 2; Acts 9:4, 7; 2 Cor 5:1, 4; Rev 15:1, 6.

3) Kataphoric (Following Reference)

a) Definition

A rare use of the article is to point to something in the text that
immediately follows. (It derives its name from the Greek verb
καταφέρειν, "to bring down.") The first mention, with the article,
is anticipatory, followed by a phrase or statement that defines or
qualifies the thing mentioned.

b) Illustrations

2 Cor 8:18   **τὸν** ἀδελφὸν οὗ ὁ ἔπαινος ἐν τῷ εὐαγγελίῳ
             the brother whose praise [is] in the gospel

1 Tim 1:15   πιστὸς **ὁ** λόγος . . . ὅτι Χριστὸς Ἰησοῦς ἦλθεν εἰς τὸν κόσμον ἁμαρτωλοὺς
             σῶσαι
             faithful is **the** saying . . . that Christ Jesus came into the world to save
             sinners

> Cf. also 1 Tim 3:1; 4:9; 2 Tim 2:11; Titus 3:8 for other "faithful sayings."
> The articles in 1 Tim 3:1 and 2 Tim 2:11 could possibly be anaphoric, but

[27] For a greater defense of this translation, see the chapter on adjectives.
[28] N. T. Wright, "ἁρπαγμός and the Meaning of Philippians 2:5-11," *JTS*, NS 37 (1986) 344.

are most likely kataphoric.[29] In 1 Tim 4:9, however, the article is most likely anaphoric, referring back to the second half of v 8.[30] This is also the case in Titus 3:8.[31]

Cf. also John 17:26; Phil 1:29.

4) Deictic ("Pointing" Article)

a) Definition

The article is occasionally used to point out an object or person which/who is *present* at the moment of speaking. It typically has a demonstrative force. This usage comes very near to the original idea of the article,[32] though it is largely replaced (or strengthened) in Koine Greek with the demonstrative pronoun.

b) Illustrations

Matt 14:15 προσῆλθον αὐτῷ οἱ μαθηταὶ λέγοντες· ἔρημός ἐστιν **ὁ** τόπος
the disciples came to him, saying, "**This** place is deserted"

Luke 17:6 εἶπεν ὁ κύριος· εἰ ἔχετε πίστιν ὡς κόκκον σινάπεως, ἐλέγετε ἂν **τῇ** συκαμίνῳ[33]
The Lord said, "If you had faith like a mustard seed, you could say to **this** mulberry tree. . . ."

John 19:5 ἰδοὺ **ὁ** ἄνθρωπος[34]
Behold, **the** man!
Here we can envision Pilate putting Jesus on display and gesturing toward him to show the crowd precisely *which* man is on trial.

1 Th 5:27 ἀναγνωσθῆναι **τὴν** ἐπιστολήν.
have **the** letter read.
The force of the article is: "Have the letter–the one in your hands–read."

Rev 1:3 μακάριος ὁ ἀναγινώσκων καὶ οἱ ἀκούοντες τοὺς λόγους **τῆς** προφητείας καὶ τηροῦντες τὰ ἐν αὐτῇ γεγραμμένα
blessed is the one who reads and those who hear the words of **this** prophecy and keep the things written in it
The Seer is referring to the prophetic book that the readers now have in their possession.

Cf. also Mark 6:35; Luke 1:66 (*v.l.* in MS 1443); Rom 16:22; 1 Cor 16:21; Col 4:16; Rev 22:7 (*v.l.*).

---

[29] G. D. Fee, *1 and 2 Timothy, Titus* (NIBC) 79, 248-49.

[30] Ibid., 104-5.

[31] Ibid., 206-7.

[32] Some grammarians label the individualizing article deictic. We prefer to reserve the term for this specific category.

[33] This is the reading of 𝔓75 ℵ D L X 213 579 *pauci*; the Nestle-Aland[27] adds ταύτῃ following A B W Θ 𝔐 *et alii*.

[34] Codex Vaticanus omits the article; the first hand of 𝔓66 omits the entire phrase.

➡   **5) *Par Excellence***

         a) Definition

              The article is frequently used to point out a substantive that is,
              in a sense, "in a class by itself." It is the only one deserving of the
              name. For example, if in late January someone were to say to
              you, "Did you see the game?" you might reply, "Which game?"
              They might then reply, "*The* game! The only game worth watch-
              ing! The *BIG* game! You know, the Super Bowl!" This is the arti-
              cle used in a *par excellence* way.

              It is used by the speaker to point out an object as the only one
              worthy of the name, even though there are many other such
              objects by the same name.

         b) Amplification

              The *par excellence* article is not necessarily used just for the *best*
              of a class. It could be used for the *worst* of a class–if the lexical
              nuance (or contextual connotation) of that particular class sug-
              gests it. In essence, *par excellence* indicates the *extreme* of a partic-
              ular class. "I am **the** chief of sinners" does not mean the best of
              sinners, but the worst of sinners. If I make a "pig" of myself
              while eating ice cream and then get labeled "**the** pig," it cer-
              tainly would not be a valued appellation.

              The article *par excellence* and the well-known article are often
              difficult to distinguish. Technically, this is due to the fact that the
              article *par excellence* is a subset of the well-known article. A rule
              of thumb here is that if the article points out an object that is not
              conceived as the *best* (or worst) of its category, but is neverthe-
              less well known, it is a well-known article. The question one
              must always ask is, *Why* is it well known?

         c) Illustrations

John 1:21   ὁ προφήτης εἶ σύ;
              Are you **the** prophet?
                   Here the interrogators are asking John if he is *the* prophet mentioned in
                   Deut 18:15. Of course, there were many prophets, but only one who
                   deserved to be singled out in this way.

Mark 1:10   εἶδεν . . . **τὸ** πνεῦμα ὡς περιστερὰν καταβαῖνον εἰς αὐτόν
              He saw **the** Spirit descending on him like a dove

Acts 1:7   οὐχ ὑμῶν ἐστιν γνῶναι χρόνους . . . οὓς **ὁ** πατὴρ ἔθετο ἐν τῇ ἰδίᾳ ἐξουσίᾳ
              It is not for you to know the times . . . which **the** Father has
              appointed by his own authority

1 Cor 3:13   ἡ ἡμέρα δηλώσει
              the day will reveal it
                   That is, the day of judgment–the *great* day.

Jas 5:9   ἰδοὺ **ὁ** κριτὴς πρὸ τῶν θυρῶν ἔστηκεν.
Behold, **the** judge is standing at the doors.

Rev 1:5   **ὁ** μάρτυς, **ὁ** πιστός
the witness, **the** faithful one
> In this allusion to Ps 89, Christ is described as the preeminent one who deserves such accolades.

Luke 18:13   **ὁ** θεός, ἱλάσθητί μοι **τῷ** ἁμαρτωλῷ
O God, be merciful to me, **the** sinner
> Here the article is either *par excellence* or simple identification [or, *possibly* well-known]. If it is simple identification, this tax-collector is recognizing the presence of the Pharisee and is distinguishing himself from him by implying that, as far as he knew, the Pharisee was *the* righteous one (between the two of them) and he was *the* sinner. But if the article is *par excellence*, then the man is declaring that he is the worst of all sinners (from his perspective). This seems to fit well with the spirit of his prayer, for only the Pharisee explicitly makes a comparison with the other person present.

John 3:10   **ὁ** διδάσκαλος τοῦ Ἰσραήλ
the teacher of Israel
> There were many teachers of Israel, but Nicodemus was either well known or, if the article is *par excellence*, the number one professor on the Gallup poll!

Often "**the** gospel" (τὸ εὐαγγέλιον) and "**the** Lord" (ὁ κύριος) employ articles *par excellence*. In other words, there was only *one* gospel and *one* Lord worth mentioning as far as the early Christians were concerned.[35]

Cf. also Matt 4:3; John 1:32, 45; Rom 1:16; Jas 4:12; 1 Pet 2:3, 8; 2 Pet 3:18; 1 John 2:1, 22.

➡   **6) Monadic ("One of a Kind" or "Unique" Article)**

     a) Definition

> The article is frequently used to identify monadic or one-of-a-kind nouns, such as "*the* devil," "*the* sun," "*the* Christ."

     b) Amplification and Clarification

> 1] The difference between the monadic article and the article *par excellence* is that the monadic article points out a *unique* object, while the article *par excellence* points out the *extreme* of a certain category, thus, the one deserving the name more than any other. The article *par excellence*, therefore, has a superlative idea. For example, "the sun" is monadic because there is only one sun. It is not the best of many suns,

---

[35] ὁ θεός also may be regarded as *par excellence* rather than monadic in many contexts. This is not to say that to the NT writers there were many gods, but that there were many entities and beings *called* θεός. Only one truly deserved the name.

but is the only one.[36] In *reality,* it is in a class by itself. But "the Lord" is *par excellence* because there are many lords. However, the article is used with the word to convey the idea that, according to the speaker's presented viewpoint, there is only one Lord.

2] When the articular substantive has an adjunct (such as an adjective or gen. phrase), the entire expression often suggests a monadic notion. If no modifier is used, the article is typically *par excellence.* Thus, "**the** kingdom of God" (ἡ βασιλεία τοῦ θεοῦ) in Mark 9:47 is monadic, while "**the** kingdom" (ἡ βασιλεία) in Matt 9:35 is *par excellence;* "**the** way of God" (ἡ ὁδὸς τοῦ θεοῦ) in Acts 18:26 is monadic,[37] while "**the** Way" (ἡ ὁδός) in Acts 9:2 is *par excellence.*

c) Illustrations

Matt 4:1 ὁ Ἰησοῦς ἀνήχθη εἰς τὴν ἔρημον ὑπὸ τοῦ πνεύματος πειρασθῆναι ὑπὸ **τοῦ** διαβόλου

Jesus was led into the wilderness by the Spirit to be tempted by **the** devil

> The KJV translators translate both διάβολος and δαιμόνιον as "devil,"[38] as if "*the* devil" were *par excellence.* But in the Greek text, διάβολος only occurs in the plural thrice, all three instances functioning adjectivally and in reference to humans (1 Tim 3:11; 2 Tim 3:3; Titus 2:3). διάβολος used substantivally can properly be regarded as monadic.

Mark 13:24 ὁ ἥλιος σκοτισθήσεται, καὶ ἡ σελήνη οὐ δώσει τὸ φέγγος αὐτῆς

the sun will be darkened and the moon will not shed its light

John 1:29 ἴδε ὁ ἀμνὸς τοῦ θεοῦ ὁ αἴρων τὴν ἁμαρτίαν τοῦ κόσμου.

Behold **the** lamb of God who takes away the sin of the world!

> John's description of Jesus may be regarded as monadic as long as the gen. "of God" is considered part of the formula, for it is used of Jesus alone in the Bible.

Jas 5:8 ἡ παρουσία τοῦ κυρίου ἤγγικεν

the coming of the Lord is near

Cf. also Matt 4:5, 8, 11; Rom 14:10; Eph 4:26; Jas 1:12; 2 Pet 2:1; Rev 6:12.

---

[36] One must at all times keep in mind the universe of discourse of the original readership. Thus, although there truly is more than one sun, the first-century reader would not have thought so.

[37] In Cantabrigiensis the reading is *par excellence:* ἡ ὁδός.

[38] The KJV never uses the word "demon." Sixty-two of the 63 NT instances of δαιμόνιον are translated "devil" (in Acts 17:18 the plural is translated "gods"). This can get confusing in places where the singular "devil" is used: Is Satan or one of the demons in view (cf. Matt 9:33 [demon]; 13:39 [devil]; 17:18 [demon]; Mark 7:26 [demon]; Luke 4:2 [devil]; etc.)?

➡ 7) **Well-Known ("Celebrity" or "Familiar" Article)**

a) **Definition**

The article points out an object that is well known, but for reasons *other* than the above categories (i.e., not anaphoric, deictic, *par excellence*, or monadic). Thus it refers to a well-known object that has not been mentioned in the preceding context (anaphoric), nor is considered to be the best of its class (*par excellence*), nor is one of a kind (monadic).

b) **Illustrations**

Matt 13:55   οὐχ οὗτός ἐστιν **ὁ** τοῦ τέκτονος υἱός;
Is this not **the** carpenter's son?

> Although the Christian reader would see the article as *par excellence*, the evangelist portrays the villagers of Capernaum as simply recognizing him as an offspring of Joseph.

Gal 4:22   **τῆς** παιδίσκης . . . **τῆς** ἐλευθέρας
the bond-woman . . . **the** free woman

> These women were not the best of their respective categories, but were well known because of the biblical account.

Jas 1:1   ταῖς δώδεκα φυλαῖς ταῖς ἐν **τῇ** διασπορᾷ
to the twelve tribes that are in **the** dispersion

2 John 1   ʽΟ πρεσβύτερος ἐκλεκτῇ κυρίᾳ καὶ τοῖς τέκνοις αὐτῆς
The elder to the elect lady and her children

> Whether translated "the elder," "the presbyter," or "the old man," the article almost certainly is used to indicate someone well-known to the readers.

3 John 15   ἀσπάζονταί σε **οἱ** φίλοι. ἀσπάζου **τοὺς** φίλους κατ᾽ ὄνομα.
The friends greet you. Greet **the** friends by name.

> The elder had his associates (οἱ φίλοι) and Gaius had his (τοὺς φίλους). Obviously, neither group is singled out as more prominent than the other, though both are well known to the correspondents of this letter.

Acts 2:42   **τῇ** διδαχῇ. . . **τῇ** κοινωνίᾳ, **τῇ** κλάσει
the teaching. . . **the** fellowship, **the** breaking [of the bread]

> Either this pattern of worship was well known in the early church because it was the *common* manner in which it was done, or Luke was attempting to convey that each element of the worship was the only one deserving of the name (*par excellence*).

Cf. also Mark 1:3; 2 Pet 2:1 (τῷ λαῷ); 3 John 1; possibly Matt 5:1.

➡   **8)   Abstract (i.e., the Article with Abstract Nouns)**

     a) Definition

Abstract nouns by their very nature focus on a quality.[39] However, when such a noun is articular, that quality is "tightened up," as it were, defined more closely, distinguished from other notions. This usage is quite frequent (articular abstract nouns are far more frequent than anarthrous abstracts).

     b) Amplification

In translating such nouns, the article should rarely be used (typically, only when the article also fits under some other individualizing category, such as anaphoric). But in exposition, the force of the article should be brought out. Usually, the article with an abstract noun fits under the *par excellence* and well-known categories but in even a more technical way. As well, frequently it particularizes a general quality.

The article with abstract nouns often has a certain affinity with articular *generic* nouns in that both focus on traits and qualities. But there are differences: one focuses on a quality via its lexeme (abstract), while the other focuses on a category grammatically (generic).

     c) Illustrations

Matt 7:23   οἱ ἐργαζόμενοι **τὴν** ἀνομίαν
               the workers of lawlessness

John 4:22   ἡ σωτηρία ἐκ τῶν Ἰουδαίων ἐστίν
               salvation is from the Jews

                     Although the article should not be translated here, the force of it is that this is the only salvation worth considering and the one that needs no clarification because it is well known.

Acts 6:10   οὐκ ἴσχυον ἀντιστῆναι **τῇ** σοφίᾳ καὶ τῷ πνεύματι ᾧ ἐλάλει
               they were not able to withstand **the** wisdom and the spirit with which he spoke

                     This may also be regarded as a kataphoric article, for the kind of wisdom mentioned is described further by the relative clause.

---

[39] We are restricting our definition of abstract nouns, for the most part, to what Lyons calls "third-order entities" (J. Lyons, *Semantics* [Cambridge: CUP, 1977] 2.442-46). First-order entities are physical objects; second-order entities are "events, processes, states-of-affairs, etc., which are located in time and which, in English, are said to occur or take place, rather than to exist" (ibid., 444); third-order entities are "unobservable and cannot be said to occur or to be located either in space or in time . . . . 'true,' rather than 'real,' is more naturally predicated of them; they can be asserted or denied, remembered or forgotten; they can be reasons, but not causes. . . . In short, they are entities of the kind that may function as the objects of such so-called propositional attitudes as belief, expectation and judgement: they are what logicians often call intensional objects" (ibid., 443-45).

Rom 12:9 ἡ ἀγάπη ἀνυπόκριτος. ἀποστυγοῦντες **τὸ** πονηρόν, κολλώμενοι **τῷ**
ἀγαθῷ

Let love be without hypocrisy. Hate **the** evil; hold fast to **the** good.

> English more naturally translates the article with the last two terms
> because they are adjectives and, with the article, they are somewhat
> "concretized." Thus, τὸ πονηρόν means "that which is evil."

Cf. also Luke 22:45; John 1:17; Acts 4:12; 1 Cor 13:4-13; Gal 5:13; 1 Thess 1:3; Phlm 9; Heb
3:6; 2 Pet 1:7.

➡ **b. Generic Article (Categorical Article) [*as a class*]**

1) Definition

While the *individualizing* article distinguishes or identifies a particular object belonging to a larger class, the *generic* article distinguishes
one class from another. This is somewhat less frequent than the individualizing article (though it still occurs hundreds of times in the
NT). It categorizes rather than particularizes.

2) Key to Identification

The key to determining whether or not the article might be generic
is the insertion of the phrase "as a class" after the noun that the article is modifying.

3) Amplification

a) If ὁ ἄνθρωπος is understood as a generic article, the sense would
be: "humankind" (i.e., human beings as a class). The use of the
article here distinguishes this *class* from among other classes
(such as "the animal kingdom" or "the realm of angels").

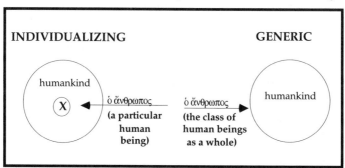

Chart 18
Individualizing Vs. Generic Article

b) Most grammarians agree with Gildersleeve that "the principle
of the generic article is the selection of a *representative* or normal
individual [italics mine]."[40] However, this could only be true if

---

[40] Gildersleeve, *Classical Greek*, 2.255.

the generic article were used exclusively with *singular* nouns, never with plurals. But even the example Dana-Mantey give is plural (αἱ ἀλώπεκες φωλεοὺς ἔχουσιν–"Foxes have dens"). This dominical saying is not referring to any *particular* foxes that the Lord knows have dens. Rather, he is saying, "Foxes, *as a class*, have dens."

Therefore, it is better to see the generic article as simply distinguishing one class from among others, rather than as pointing out a representative of the class. Such a view is more in accord with the facts, for all grammarians agree that the plural article can be used in a generic sense.[41]

c) At times, the most natural translation is to replace the article with an indefinite article. This is because both indefinite nouns and generic nouns share certain properties: while one categorizes or stresses the characteristics of a given class (generic), the other points to an individual within a class, without addressing any traits that would distinguish it from other members (indefinite).

4) Illustrations

Matt 18:17 ἔστω σοι ὥσπερ ὁ ἐθνικὸς καὶ ὁ τελώνης
he shall be [with reference] to you as **the** Gentile [as a class] and **the** tax-collector [as a class]

> In translation we would probably say, "**a** Gentile and **a** tax-collector." However, this is due to the fact that the *force* of the generic article is qualitative, since it indicates the class to which one belongs (thus, *kind*), rather than identifying him as a particular individual. Sometimes the English indefinite article brings out this force better. Note also that if the articles in this text were *not* taken as generic, then Jesus would be identifying the sinning brother with a *particular* Gentile or a *particular* tax-collector he had in mind, though giving no clue as to which one it was.

Luke 10:7 ἄξιος ὁ ἐργάτης τοῦ μισθοῦ αὐτοῦ
the laborer is worthy of his wages

John 2:25 καὶ ὅτι οὐ χρείαν εἶχεν ἵνα τις μαρτυρήσῃ περὶ **τοῦ** ἀνθρώπου αὐτὸς γὰρ ἐγίνωσκεν τί ἦν ἐν **τῷ** ἀνθρώπῳ.
And because he did not need anyone to testify concerning man [as a class–mankind], for he himself knew what was in man [as a class].

> Although generally today the use of the masculine "man" as a generic for humanity is unacceptable, not to translate ἄνθρωπος as "man" here is to miss the author's point. Immediately after this pronouncement about Jesus' insight into *man*, the evangelist introduces the readers to a

---

[41] The frequent refrain of "everyone who," "husbands, love your wives," "my little children," etc. are generic expressions.

particular *man* who fits this description of depravity (3:1–"there came a *man*")–a man named Nicodemus.[42]

Rom 13:4   οὐ εἰκῇ **τὴν** μάχαιραν φορεῖ

he does not bear **the** sword without reason

Eph 5:25   **οἱ** ἄνδρες, ἀγαπᾶτε τὰς γυναῖκας

Husbands [as a class], love your wives

> The command is not meant to distinguish some of the Ephesian/Asia Minor husbands as opposed to others, but to distinguish the husbands in the church as opposed to the wives or children. They are viewed collectively, as a whole.

1 Tim 3:2   δεῖ **τὸν** ἐπίσκοπον ἀνεπίλημπτον εἶναι

the overseer must be above reproach

> Grammatically speaking, the article could either be monadic (indicating that for each church there is *one* overseer,) or it could be generic (indicating that overseers as a class are in view). When other considerations are brought to bear, however, it is unlikely that only one overseer is in view: (1) The monadic view cannot easily handle 1 Tim 5:17 ("let the elders who rule well be considered worthy of double honor") or Titus 1:5 ("appoint elders in every town"); and (2) the context of 1 Tim 2:8-3:16 involves an interchange of singular and plural generic nouns, suggesting strongly that the singular is used as a generic noun.[43]

Heb 7:7   **τὸ** ἔλαττον ὑπὸ **τοῦ** κρείττονος εὐλογεῖται

the inferior is blessed by **the** superior

> The author is indicating a principle here, which he applies to the blessing of Abraham by Melchizedek. Note that the terms are adjectives and as such do not have a fixed gender. The author could have put them in the masculine, as if to point back specifically to Abraham and Melchizedek. By using the neuter form, he is indicating a generic principle: whatever is inferior is blessed by whatever is superior.

---

[42] The NRSV has "[Jesus] needed no one to testify about *anyone* [ὁ ἄνθρωπος]; for he himself knew what was in *everyone* [ὁ ἄνθρωπος]. (3:1) Now there was a Pharisee named Nicodemus, a leader of the Jews." ἄνθρωπος in 3:1 is not even translated and the connection is thereby lost.

[43] Note the following generic terms: τοὺς ἄνδρας (2:8), γυναῖκας (2:9), γυναιξίν (2:10), γυνή (2:11), γυναικί, ἀνδρός (2:12). This is followed by the singular reference to Eve/woman in 2:15, embedded in the verb σωθήσεται, then the plural generic reference to women embedded in μείνωσιν. In such a context it is difficult to assert that ἐπίσκοπον in 3:2 is monadic.

Part of the issue here revolves around the date and authorship of the Pastoral Letters. The later they are, the more likely is the monarchical episcopate view. Certain parallels are usually drawn between the Pastorals and Ignatius (d. 117 CE). But if the Pastoral Letters were written by Paul (and, hence, well within the first century), they are more likely to comport with the ecclesiology seen everywhere else in the NT, viz., that there are to be multiple elders in the church. Cf. G. W. Knight, *Commentary on the Pastoral Epistles* (NIGNTC; Grand Rapids: Eerdmans, 1992) 175-77. Sometimes, in fact, part of the argument against Pauline authorship involves the assumption that 1 Tim 3:2 avers the monarchical episcopate, rendering the ecclesiology of the Pastorals different from the rest of Paul's letters. Such an argument is at best circular.

1 John 2:23   πᾶς ὁ ἀρνούμενος τὸν υἱὸν οὐδὲ τὸν πατέρα ἔχει, ὁ ὁμολογῶν τὸν υἱὸν
καὶ τὸν πατέρα ἔχει.[44]

Everyone who denies the Son does not have the Father; **the** one who
confesses the Son also has the Father.

> This is a double example, with the first instance involving the fre-
> quently used πᾶς ὁ formula (cf. also Matt 5:22, 28, 32; Luke 6:47; 14:11;
> 20:18; John 3:16; 4:13; Acts 13:39; Rom 10:11; Gal 3:13; 2 Tim 2:19; 1 John
> 3:6).

Rev 2:11   ὁ νικῶν οὐ μὴ ἀδικηθῇ ἐκ τοῦ θανάτου τοῦ δευτέρου

the one who conquers will not at all be hurt by the second death

Cf. also Matt 12:35; 15:11, 18; Luke 4:4; John 8:34; Rom 13:4; Gal 2:10; Jas 2:26; 3:5; 5:6 (possible), 7; 1 Pet 1:24; 2 John 9; Rev 13:18; 16:15.

The following chart depicts the semantic relationships of the individualizing
article. The chart is designed to show the student in pictorial form that the seven
categories of the individualizing article are not entirely distinct. Rather, they are
related, for the most part, in a general-to-specific manner. That is, every monadic
article is, in a sense, a specific kind of *par excellence* article (in the sense that the
only one of a class is, *ipso facto*, the best of a class). And every *par excellence* article
is well known (but it is more specific, for it is well known *because* it is the best of
a class). And every well-known article is anaphoric (in the broadest sense possible). But it is more specific than a simple anaphoric article would be.

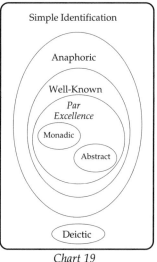

Chart 19
The Semantic Relations Of The Individualizing Article

The flow chart below presupposes that the student understands the chart on this
page. In order to use the flow chart, you should attempt to find the *narrowest*

---

[44] The Byzantine MSS have an uncharacteristic omission of an entire clause (ὁ
ὁμολογῶν τὸν υἱὸν καὶ τὸν πατέρα ἔχει), due no doubt to homoioteleuton in which the eye
skipped over the ἔχει just preceding and wrote the ἔχει that ended the sentence. Among
other things, such a reading offers a clue about the roots of the Byzantine text, at least in
the Johannine letters (viz., that it seems to have originated in a single archetype).

category to which a particular article can belong. As long as you can say "yes" to a particular semantic force, you should continue on until you get to the narrowest category for a particular article.

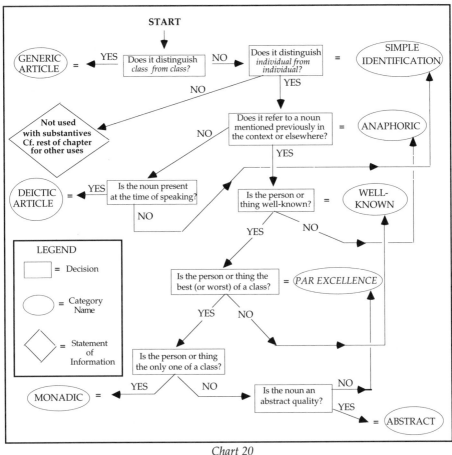

Chart 20
Flow Chart on the Article with Substantives

→ 3. As a Substantiver (With Certain Parts of Speech)

a. Definition

The article can turn almost any part of speech into a noun: adverbs, adjectives, prepositional phrases, particles, infinitives, participles, and even finite verbs. As well, the article can turn a phrase into a nominal entity. This incredible flexibility is part of the genius of the Greek article. Such usage is quite frequent overall, more so with the adjective and participle than with other parts of speech.[45]

---

[45] Although articular infinitives are commonplace, they are not all substantival. See the chapter on the infinitive for a discussion.

b. **Amplification**

The substantiving use of the article can only minimally be considered a *semantic* category, in the sense that its essential semantic role is to conceptualize. Beyond this, the article also functions in one of the above-mentioned semantic roles; that is, it either individualizes or categorizes, just as it does with nouns. The usage with participles and adjectives is routine and unremarkable, so much so that many of these examples were discussed in the preceding sections.

c. **Illustrations**

1) **With Adverbs**

The usage with adverbs occurs frequently. Some of the more commonly used adverbs include αὔριον, ἐπαύριον, νῦν, πέραν, and πλησίον.

Matt 8:28   ἐλθόντος αὐτοῦ εἰς **τὸ** πέραν
             when he came to **the** other side

Matt 24:21   ἔσται τότε θλῖψις μεγάλη οἵα οὐ γέγονεν ἀπ᾽ ἀρχῆς κόσμου ἕως **τοῦ** νῦν
             then there will be a great tribulation [the likes of] which have not happened from the beginning of the world until **the** present

Mark 11:12   **τῇ** ἐπαύριον ἐξελθόντων αὐτῶν ἀπὸ Βηθανίας ἐπείνασεν
             on **the** next [day], when they came from Bethany, he was hungry

             Every instance of the adverb ἐπαύριον in the NT occurs with a feminine dat. article (cf., e.g., Matt 27:62; John 1:29; Acts 21:8). Although the adverb itself simply means "following, next," the usage in the NT each time implies the noun ἡμέρα (hence, the article is feminine) and suggests that the event took place at a point in time (hence, the article is dat.).[46]

John 4:31   ἐν **τῷ** μεταξὺ ἠρώτων αὐτὸν οἱ μαθηταὶ λέγοντες· ῥαββί, φάγε.
             in **the** meantime, the disciples were asking him, saying, "Rabbi, eat."

John 8:23   ὑμεῖς ἐκ **τῶν** κάτω ἐστέ, ἐγὼ ἐκ **τῶν** ἄνω εἰμί
             you are from **the** [places] below; I am from **the** [places] above

             The articles indicate more than a mere general sentiment as to origins; heaven and hell are implied.

Acts 18:6   ἀπὸ **τοῦ** νῦν εἰς τὰ ἔθνη πορεύσομαι[47]
             from now [this point] on, I will go to the Gentiles

---

[46] αὔριον is different in two respects: (1) it is not always articular (cf. Luke 12:28; 13:32, 33; Acts 23:20; 25:22; 1 Cor 15:32); and (2) the articular form never occurs in the dat., though it does appear in the nom. (Matt 6:34), gen. (Jas 4:14), and acc. (Luke 10:35; Acts 4:3, 5).

[47] D* has ἀφ᾽ ὑμῶν for ἀπὸ τοῦ.

Col 3:2 τὰ ἄνω φρονεῖτε, μὴ τὰ ἐπὶ τῆς γῆς

Set [your] mind on **the** [things] above, not on the [things] on earth

Cf. also Matt 5:43; 23:26; Mark 12:31; Luke 11:40; Acts 5:38; Rom 8:22; 1 Cor 5:12; 1 Tim 3:7; Heb 3:13.

2) With Adjectives

Adjectives often stand in the place of nouns, especially when the qualities of a particular group are stressed. Instances in the plural are especially frequently generic, though in both singular and plural the individualizing article occurs often enough.

Matt 5:5 μακάριοι **οἱ** πραεῖς, ὅτι αὐτοὶ κληρονομήσουσιν τὴν γῆν

blessed are **the** meek, for they shall inherit the earth

Matt 6:13 μὴ εἰσενέγκῃς ἡμᾶς εἰς πειρασμόν, ἀλλὰ ῥῦσαι ἡμᾶς ἀπὸ **τοῦ** πονηροῦ

do not lead us into temptation, but deliver us from **the** evil [one]

> Although the KJV renders this "deliver us from evil," the presence of the article indicates not evil in general, but the evil one himself. In the context of Matthew's Gospel, such deliverance from the devil seems to be linked to Jesus' temptation in 4:1-10: Because the Spirit led him into temptation by the evil one, believers now participate in his victory.

Mark 6:7 προσκαλεῖται **τοὺς** δώδεκα

he summoned **the** twelve

> "The twelve" takes on a technical nuance in the Gospels by virtue of how well known the disciples were. The article thus belongs to the "well-known" category as well. Cf. also Matt 26:14, 20; Mark 9:35; 10:32; 14:10; Luke 9:1; 18:31.

Luke 23:49 εἱστήκεισαν πάντες **οἱ** γνωστοὶ αὐτῷ ἀπὸ μακρόθεν

all **those** who knew him stood off at a distance

Rom 5:7 ὑπὲρ **τοῦ** ἀγαθοῦ τάχα τις καὶ τολμᾷ ἀποθανεῖν

for **the** good [person] perhaps someone would dare even to die

Heb 1:6 ὅταν εἰσαγάγῃ **τὸν** πρωτότοκον εἰς τὴν οἰκουμένην

when he brings **the** firstborn into the world

2 Pet 3:16 ἃ **οἱ** ἀμαθεῖς καὶ ἀστήρικτοι στρεβλοῦσιν . . . πρὸς τὴν ἰδίαν αὐτῶν ἀπώλειαν

which things **the** ignorant and unstable twist . . . to their own destruction

Cf. also Mark 1:24; 3:27; Luke 6:35; 16:25; John 2:10; 3:12; Acts 3:14; 7:14; Gal 6:10; Titus 2:4; Jas 2:6; 5:6; 3 John 11; Jude 15; Rev 13:16.

3) With Participles

The usage with participles is commonplace. As with adjectives, the article with participles can be individualizing or generic.

Matt 2:23　　ὅπως πληρωθῇ **τὸ** ῥηθὲν διὰ τῶν προφητῶν
　　　　　　　in order that **that** which was spoken by the prophets might be ful-
　　　　　　　filled

Luke 7:19　　σὺ εἶ **ὁ** ἐρχόμενος;
　　　　　　　Are you **the** one who is to come?

2 Cor 2:15　　Χριστοῦ εὐωδία ἐσμὲν τῷ θεῷ ἐν **τοῖς** σῳζομένοις
　　　　　　　we are a fragrance of Christ to God among **the** ones who are being
　　　　　　　saved

Eph 4:28　　ὁ κλέπτων μηκέτι κλεπτέτω
　　　　　　　let **the** one who steals no longer steal

1 John 3:6　　πᾶς **ὁ** ἁμαρτάνων οὐχ ἑώρακεν αὐτόν
　　　　　　　everyone who sins has not seen him

Rev 1:3　　μακάριος **ὁ** ἀναγινώσκων καὶ **οἱ** ἀκούοντες τοὺς λόγους τῆς προφητείας
　　　　　　　καὶ τηροῦντες **τὰ** ἐν αὐτῇ γεγραμμένα[48]
　　　　　　　blessed is **the** one who reads and **those** who hear the words of this
　　　　　　　prophecy and keep **the** things written in it

Cf. also Matt 4:3; Luke 6:21; John 3:6; Acts 5:5; Rom 2:18; 1 Cor 1:28; Gal 5:12; Eph 1:6;
1Thess 2:10; Phlm 8; Jas 2:5; 1 Pet 1:15; 2 John 9; Rev 20:11.

4) With Infinitives

Although infinitives frequently take an article, the article is usually
not used to nominalize the infinitive. This usage is relatively rare,
though more common in the epistles than in narrative literature.
(The infinitive can also function substantivally without the article.)
The article is always neuter singular.

Mark 10:40　**τὸ** δὲ καθίσαι ἐκ δεξιῶν μου ἢ ἐξ εὐωνύμων οὐκ ἔστιν ἐμὸν δοῦναι
　　　　　　　but to sit at my right hand or my left hand is not mine to give
　　　　　　　　　The articular infinitive is the subject of the verb ἔστιν.

Acts 27:20　περιῃρεῖτο ἐλπὶς πᾶσα **τοῦ** σῴζεσθαι ἡμᾶς
　　　　　　　all hope **of** our being saved was abandoned
　　　　　　　　　The gen. articular infinitive is an objective gen. with an acc. subject of
　　　　　　　　　the infinitive. A woodenly literal rendering would be "all hope of the
　　　　　　　　　being saved with reference to us."

Rom 7:18　**τὸ** θέλειν παράκειταί μοι, **τὸ** δὲ κατεργάζεσθαι τὸ καλὸν οὔ.
　　　　　　　the willing is present with me, but **the** doing [of] the good is not.

1 Cor 14:39　ζηλοῦτε **τὸ** προφητεύειν καὶ **τὸ** λαλεῖν μὴ κωλύετε γλώσσαις[49]
　　　　　　　seek **the** prophesying and do not forbid **the** speaking in tongues

---

[48] 2053 and 2062 read ἀκούων for οἱ ἀκούοντες, making the reader the same as the
hearer in a construction that follows Granville Sharp's rule.

[49] The article is omitted before λαλεῖν in B 0243 630 1739 1881 *pauci.*

Phil 1:21-22 **τὸ** ζῆν Χριστὸς καὶ **τὸ** ἀποθανεῖν κέρδος. (22) εἰ δὲ **τὸ** ζῆν ἐν σαρκί . . .
to live is Christ and to die is gain. (22) Now if **the** living [on] in the
flesh . . .

> The articular infinitives in v 21 are subjects of their respective clauses.
> τὸ ζῆν is repeated in v 22, with the article functioning both as a substan-
> tiver of the infinitive and anaphorically. Verse 22 is more smoothly
> translated as "now if I am to live on in the flesh," but the more literal
> rendering makes a stronger connection to v 21.

The following references include most of the other instances of articular substantival infinitives in the NT: Matt 20:23; Mark 12:33; Luke 10:19; Rom 13:8; 14:21;
1 Cor 9:10; 2 Cor 1:8; 8:10-11; 9:1; Phil 1:24; 2:6; 2:13 (possible);[50] 3:21; Heb 2:15;
10:31; 1 Pet 3:10.

5) With a Genitive Word or Phrase

A non-genitive article is often followed by a genitive word or
phrase. Although there is no concord, the article may be viewed as
"bracketing" the word or phrase that follows. Two of the more frequent idioms are (1) the masculine singular article followed by a
proper name in the genitive, where the article implies "son" (and the
gen. that follows is a gen. of relationship), and (2) the neuter plural
article with a genitive, where the neuter article implies "things."

Matt 10:3 Ἰάκωβος **ὁ** τοῦ Ἀλφαίου
James, **the** [son] of Alphaeus[51]

Matt 16:23 οὐ φρονεῖς **τὰ** τοῦ θεοῦ ἀλλὰ **τὰ** τῶν ἀνθρώπων[52]
you are not thinking **the** [things] of God, but **the** [things] of men

Luke 5:33 **οἱ** τῶν Φαρισαίων
the [disciples] of the Pharisees

Rom 14:19 **τὰ** τῆς εἰρήνης διώκωμεν καὶ **τὰ** τῆς οἰκοδομῆς
let us pursue **the** [things] of peace and **the** [things] of edification

1 Cor 15:23 **οἱ** τοῦ Χριστου. . .
[those who are] Christ's. . .

---

[50] If ἐνεργῶν is transitive, then the articular infinitives τὸ θέλειν and τὸ ἐνεργεῖν should
be taken as a compound direct object: "For the one causing both the desiring and the
working in you is God."

[51] This could equally be regarded as an article used for a relative pronoun (in the
third attributive position). Occasionally the construction has no proper name preceding
the article, as in John 21:2: "**the** [sons] of Zebedee" (**οἱ** τοῦ Ζεβεδαίου).

[52] D has τοῦ ἀνθρώπου for τὰ τῶν ἀνθρώπων.

Jas 4:14   οὐκ ἐπίστασθε **τὸ** τῆς αὔριον[53]
            you do not know **that** [which is] of tomorrow

> The idea is "the stuff of tomorrow" or "whatever tomorrow brings." The readers may know something about tomorrow, but they do not know the details.

Cf. also Matt 22:21; Mark 8:33; 15:40; Luke 2:49; Acts 19:26; Rom 2:14; 1 Cor 2:14; 2 Cor 11:30; 1 John 4:3.

6) With a Prepositional Phrase

Similar to the use with genitive words and phrases is the use of the article to nominalize a prepositional phrase. This is a fairly common use of the article.

Acts 11:2   **οἱ** ἐκ περιτομῆς
             those of the circumcision [party]

1 Cor 13:9-10   ἐκ μέρους γινώσκομεν καὶ ἐκ μέρους προφητεύομεν· (10) ὅταν δὲ ἔλθῃ τὸ τέλειον, **τὸ** ἐκ μέρους καταργηθήσεται
             [now] we know in part and we prophesy in part; (10) but when the perfect comes, **the** partial will be done away

> The article in v 10 is anaphoric, referring back to the twofold ἐκ μέρους of v 9. It is as if Paul said, "when the perfect comes, the 'in part' will be done away." The point is that with the coming of the perfect (most likely, the return of Christ), both the gift of prophecy and the gift of knowledge will vanish.

Phil 1:27   **τὰ** περὶ ὑμῶν
             the things concerning you [= your circumstances]

Phil 1:29   ὑμῖν ἐχαρίσθη **τὸ** ὑπὲρ Χριστοῦ, οὐ μόνον τὸ εἰς αὐτὸν πιστεύειν ἀλλὰ καὶ τὸ ὑπὲρ αὐτοῦ πάσχειν
             to you it has been granted, for Christ's sake, not only to believe in him, but also to suffer for him

> The first article in this text turns the prepositional phrase ὑπὲρ Χριστοῦ into the subject of the sentence. But English cannot express the idea adequately, in part because the article is also kataphoric–that is, it refers to a twofold concept that is to follow. An overly literal translation, which at least brings out the force of the article (as well as the following two articles), is as follows: "**the** on-behalf-of-Christ thing has been given to you, namely, not only **the** believing in his name, but also **the** suffering for him." The Greek is far more concrete than the English in this instance.

Col 3:2   **τὰ** ἄνω φρονεῖτε, μὴ **τὰ** ἐπὶ τῆς γῆς
           Set [your] mind on the [things] above, not on **the** [things] on earth

1 John 2:13   ἐγνώκατε **τὸν** ἀπ᾽ ἀρχῆς
               you knew **the** [one who was] from the beginning

Cf. also Luke 11:3; 24:19; Acts 13:13; Rom 3:26; Gal 2:12; 3:7; Heb 13:24.

---

[53] B omits the article; a number of other MSS have the neuter plural.

7) With Particles

Included in the list of particles are interjections, negatives, emphatic particles, etc. This usage is rare.

1 Cor 14:16   πῶς ἐρεῖ **τὸ** ἀμὴν;
How will he say **the** "Amen"?

2 Cor 1:17   ἢ παρ᾿ ἐμοὶ **τὸ** ναὶ ναὶ καὶ **τὸ** οὒ οὔ
the "yes" should be "yes" and **the** "no" [should be] "no" with me

Jas 5:12   ἤτω δὲ ὑμῶν **τὸ** ναὶ ναὶ καὶ **τὸ** οὒ οὔ
let your "yes" be "yes" and your "no" be "no"[54]

Rev 3:14   τάδε λέγει **ὁ** ἀμήν . . .
these things says **the** Amen . . .

Rev 11:14   **ἡ** οὐαὶ ἡ δευτέρα ἀπῆλθεν· ἰδοὺ **ἡ** οὐαὶ ἡ τρίτη ἔρχεται ταχύ[55]
The second woe has passed; behold, **the** third woe is coming quickly.

Cf. also 2 Cor 1:20; Rev 9:12.

8) With Finite Verbs

This usage occurs only in one set phrase found in the Apocalypse alone.

Rev 1:4   χάρις ὑμῖν καὶ εἰρήνη ἀπὸ ὁ ὢν καὶ **ὁ** ἦν καὶ ὁ ἐρχόμενος
grace to you and peace from the one who is and **the** [one who] was and the one who is coming

> The syntax here is doubly bizarre: Not only does the preposition ἀπό govern a nom. form,[56] but the Seer has turned a finite verb into a substantive. The imperfect verb is possibly used since no imperfect participle was available and the Seer did not wish to use the aorist of γίνομαι. If the author of this book is the same as the evangelist who wrote the Gospel of John, the parallel between the ἦν in the Johannine prologue and here may be more than coincidental: Both would affirm something about the eternality of the Lord.

Cf. also Rev 1:8; 4:8; 11:17; 16:5.

9) With Clauses, Statements, and Quotations

The neuter singular article is sometimes used before a statement, quotation, or clause. For some clauses, the article needs to be translated in various ways; only the context will help. For direct

---

[54] The dominical saying from which this is apparently derived does not use the article (ἔστω δὲ ὁ λόγος ὑμῶν ναὶ ναί, οὒ οὔ in Matt 5:37 [though Θ 213 *lectionary* 184 *et pauci* include an article before the first ναί and first οὔ]).

[55] A few late MSS omit the article before τρίτη (1006 1424 1854 2050 2053 2329 2351).

[56] See discussion of this text in the chapter on the "Nominative Case."

statements and quotations, it is usually best to supply the phrase "statement" after the article followed by quotation marks.

Mark 9:23 Ἰησοῦς εἶπεν αὐτῷ· **τὸ** εἰ δύνῃ, πάντα δυνατὰ τῷ πιστεύοντι.[57]
Jesus said to him, "[Concerning your request,] 'If you can . . .' all things are possible to the one who believes.

> In v 22 a man whose son was demon-possessed pleaded with Jesus, "If you can do anything, help us!" (εἴ τι δύνῃ, βοήθησον ἡμῖν). Jesus' response picks up the very wording of the man's request. The article functions anaphorically. A paraphrase would be "You said 'if you can.' Let me tell you, all things are possible to the one who believes."

Luke 9:46 εἰσῆλθεν διαλογισμὸς ἐν αὐτοῖς, **τὸ** τίς ἂν εἴη μείζων αὐτῶν.
An argument arose among them, **namely**, who was greatest among them.

> The neuter article refers back to the masculine διαλογισμός only in a loose way. Although it is anaphoric, its force could be brought out with "to the effect that," "with reference to," "the point of which concerned," etc.

Rom 13:9 **τὸ** οὐ μοιχεύσεις, οὐ φονεύσεις, οὐ κλέψεις, οὐκ ἐπιθυμήσεις, καὶ εἴ τις ἑτέρα ἐντολή, ἐν τῷ λόγῳ τούτῳ ἀνακεφαλαιοῦται ἐν τῷ· ἀγαπήσεις τὸν πλησίον σου ὡς σεαυτόν.[58]
The [list of commandments], "You shall not commit adultery, you shall not murder, you shall not steal, you shall not covet"–and if there is any other commandment–is summed up in this word, namely, "You shall love your neighbor as yourself."

> The neuter article at the beginning of the verse introduces the second table of the Ten Commandments; ἐν τῷ toward the end of the verse is most likely resumptive, referring back to the masculine λόγῳ. Similarly, Gal 5:14.

Eph 4:9 **τὸ** δὲ ἀνέβη τί ἐστιν . . . ;
Now **the** [statement], "he ascended. . . ," what does it mean . . . ?

> Although only one word from the preceding quotation of Ps 68:18 is repeated, the idiom suggests that the whole verse is under examination. In other words, the author is not asking "What does 'he ascended' mean?" but "What does the quotation from Ps 68:18 mean?"

Cf. also Matt 19:18; Rom 8:26; Heb 12:27.

➡ **4. *As a Function Marker***

When the article is used as a grammatical function marker, it may or may not also bear a semantic force. But even when it does bear such a force, the grammatical (structural) use is usually prominent.

---

[57] A number of important witnesses omit the article (D K Θ f^{13} 28 131 565 700ᶜ) while others have τοῦτο instead ($\mathfrak{P}^{45}$ W). The more difficult reading (and therefore most likely original) is that which is printed as our text.

[58] For the article a couple of Western MSS (F G) have γέγραπται.

a. To Denote Adjectival Positions

Especially when the article is used to denote the second attributive position would we say that it has almost no semantic meaning.[59]

Mark 8:38 ὅταν ἔλθῃ ἐν τῇ δόξῃ τοῦ πατρὸς αὐτοῦ μετὰ **τῶν** ἀγγέλων **τῶν** ἁγίων
whenever he comes in his Father's glory with **the** holy angels

Luke 15:22 ταχὺ ἐξενέγκατε στολὴν **τὴν** πρώτην καὶ ἐνδύσατε αὐτόν
quickly bring a robe–**the** best [one]–and put it on him

> The article is in the rarely used third attributive position here (an anarthrous noun followed by an article and modifier). A smoother translation (though one that misses the connotation) is, "quickly bring the best robe . . ."

Cf. also Mark 14:10; Luke 11:44; John 3:16; Acts 19:6; 1 Cor 7:14.

b. With Possessive Pronouns

Almost invariably the article is used when a possessive pronoun is attached to the noun. (On the other hand, the article alone can be used, in certain contexts, to imply possession [see "The Article as a Possessive Pronoun" above].)

Mark 1:41 ἐκτείνας **τὴν** χεῖρα αὐτοῦ
stretching out his hand

Rom 5:9 δικαιωθέντες νῦν ἐν **τῷ** αἵματι αὐτοῦ
having been justified by his blood

Cf. also Heb 3:5; 1 Pet 2:22; Rev 1:14.

c. In Genitive Phrases

In genitive phrases both the head noun and the genitive noun normally have or lack the article.

This construction is known as Apollonius' Canon, named after Apollonius Dyscolus, the second-century Greek grammarian. Apollonius observed that both the head noun and genitive noun mimicked each other with regard to articularity. Rarely did they go their own separate ways. Thus, we would expect either ὁ λόγος τοῦ θεοῦ or λόγος θεοῦ, but not λόγος τοῦ θεοῦ or ὁ λόγος θεοῦ. The canon, however, has many exceptions in classical Greek as well as the NT.[60] Nevertheless, for the most

---

[59] The attributive and predicate positions of adjective to noun are discussed in the chapter on the adjective. Although grammars routinely address such under the rubric of the article, with over 2,000 wholly anarthrous noun-adjective constructions in the NT, a large proportion of the examples are categorically overlooked.

[60] See S. D. Hull, "Exceptions to Apollonius' Canon in the New Testament: A Grammatical Study," *TrinJ* NS (1986) 3-16, for a detailed discussion. Hull notes seven conditions under which the exceptions can be accounted for; only 32 of the 461 exceptions do not fit one of these conditions (5).

part, when the article is present in the construction, it is expected with both head noun and genitive noun. In such cases, the article often carries little semantic weight.[61] This is due to the fact that even when both nouns lack the article, they are normally definite.[62]

Matt 3:16   εἶδεν **τὸ** πνεῦμα **τοῦ** θεοῦ καταβαῖνον ὡσεὶ περιστερὰν
              he saw **the** Spirit of God coming down like a dove

> The MSS vacillate over the presence of the articles before πνεῦμα and θεοῦ. ℵ B cop[bo] lack the articles; most other witnesses have them. What is important to note is that the MSS *uniformly* either have both articles or lack both articles. With or without the articles, the translation and sense are the same.

Mark 1:15   ἤγγικεν **ἡ** βασιλεία **τοῦ** θεοῦ
              the kingdom of God is near

Acts 26:13   **τὴν** λαμπρότητα **τοῦ** ἡλίου
              the brightness of **the** sun

1 Cor 13:1   **ταῖς** γλώσσαις **τῶν** ἀνθρώπων
              the tongues of men

Cf. also Luke 4:9; John 3:14; Acts 27:19; 1 Cor 10:16; Eph 1:7; Heb 10:23.

d.   With Indeclinable Nouns

The article is used with indeclinable nouns to show the case of the noun.

---

[61] One exception to this is ὁ υἱὸς τοῦ ἀνθρώπου. As Moule has recently pointed out, this phrase is not, as some have supposed, "linguistically odd" (C. F. D. Moule, "The 'Son of Man': Some of the Facts," *NTS* 41 [1995] 277). What is unusual about the phrase is that both in nascent Christian literature and Judaica, almost all instances occur in dominical material. Moule draws the conclusion that "the simplest explanation of the almost entire consistency with which the definite singular is confined to Christian sayings is to postulate that Jesus did refer to Dan 7, speaking of '*the* Son of man [whom you know from that vision]' . . . . To attribute the phrase to Jesus himself is not to deny that some of the Son of Man sayings in the Gospels may well be an addition modelled on the original sayings; but I can think of no reason why there should not be a dominical origin for each of the main types of sayings" (ibid., 278). In the least, Moule is arguing from the criterion of dissimilarity for the authenticity of such "Son of Man" sayings in the Gospels. Grammatically, he treats (correctly I think) the articular construction as well-known, in that it refers back to Dan 7:13.

As a sidenote, it is curious that even though the scholars who produced *The Five Gospels: The Search for the Authentic Words of Jesus* (viz., R. W. Funk, R. W. Hoover, and the Jesus Seminar; New York: Macmillan, 1993) embrace the criterion of dissimilarity in theory (23-24), in practice they categorically deny the authenticity of the vast bulk of "Son of Man" sayings. For example, the following passages are treated as "black"–i.e., "Jesus did not say this; it represents the perspective or content of a later or different tradition" (ibid., 36): Matt 9:6; 10:23; 12:32, 40; 13:37, 41; 16:13, 27-28; 17:9, 12, 22; 19:28; 20:18; 23:30, 37, 39, 44; 25:31; 26:2, 24, 45, 64; Mark 2:10; 8:31, 38; 9:12, 31; 10:33; 13:26; 14:21, 41, 62; Luke 5:24; 9:22, 26, 44; 11:30; 12:8, 10, 40; 17:26, 30; 18:8, 31; 19:10; 21:27, 36; 22:22, 48, 69; 24:7; John 1:51; 3:13; 5:27; 6:27, 53, 62; 8:28; 9:35; 12:23; 13:31.

[62] See below under the section "Absence of the Article."

Luke 1:68   εὐλογητὸς κύριος ὁ θεὸς **τοῦ** Ἰσραήλ
            blessed is the Lord God of Israel

John 4:5   πλησίον τοῦ χωρίου ὃ ἔδωκεν Ἰακὼβ **τῷ** Ἰωσὴφ
            near the place which Jacob gave to Joseph

> Without the dat. article, it would be possible to misconstrue Ἰωσήφ as the subject of ἔδωκεν. The article serves no other purpose than clarifying the roles of Joseph and Jacob.[63]

Gal 3:29   **τοῦ** Ἀβραὰμ σπέρμα ἐστέ
            you are the seed of Abraham

Cf. also Matt 3:9; 8:10; Luke 1:55; John 1:45, 49; 4:6; 8:39; Acts 7:40; 1 Pet 3:6.

e. With Participles

The article before participles functions both as a substantiver and as a function marker. The presence of the article indicates a substantival (or adjectival) function for the participle. Of course, the participle can also often be substantival or adjectival without the article, though there is the greater possibility of ambiguity in such instances.

Luke 6:21   μακάριοι **οἱ** κλαίοντες νῦν
            blessed are **those** who weep now

Rom 1:16   δύναμις γὰρ θεοῦ ἐστιν εἰς σωτηρίαν παντὶ **τῷ** πιστεύοντι
            for it is the power of God unto salvation to everyone who believes

John 4:11   πόθεν οὖν ἔχεις τὸ ὕδωρ **τὸ** ζῶν
            Where then do you keep **this** living water?

Cf. also Acts 1:19; Rom 7:2; 2 Cor 4:3.[64]

f. With Demonstratives

The article is used with the demonstratives in predicate position to indicate attributive function. Demonstratives cannot stand in attributive position (e.g., between the article and noun). If they are related to an anarthrous noun, they function independently, as pronouns. Only when they are in predicate position to an *articular* noun can demonstratives be considered dependent and attributive.[65]

---

[63] Even so, it is likely to be a later addition, intended to clarify the relationship to the reader. Most MSS omit the article (A C D L W^S Γ Δ Θ Π Ψ 086 $f^{1, 13}$ 33 *Byz*). The sense was evidently assumed to be clear enough to these scribes.

[64] Some translations (e.g., KJV, ASV) mistakenly take the participle in John 4:39 as adjectival ("the woman who testified"). But since the noun is articular and the participle is not (τῆς γυναικὸς μαρτυρούσης), it must be treated adverbially ("the woman when she testified").

[65] A demonstrative may, of course, function as a pronoun even when adjacent to an articular noun, as in Luke 8:11 ("Now this is the parable" [Ἔστιν δὲ αὕτη ἡ παραβολή]). But it almost never functions adjectivally if the noun is anarthrous.

Occasionally translations miss this basic rule of Greek grammar. For example, in John 2:11 (ταύτην ἐποίησεν ἀρχὴν τῶν σημείων ὁ Ἰησοῦς) the ASV has "This beginning of his signs Jesus did"–an invalid translation since ἀρχήν is anarthrous.[66]

Matt 16:18   ἐπὶ ταύτῃ **τῇ** πέτρᾳ οἰκοδομήσω μου τὴν ἐκκλησίαν
             on this rock I will build my church

Mark 15:39   ἀληθῶς οὗτος **ὁ** ἄνθρωπος υἱὸς θεοῦ ἦν.
             Truly this man was God's Son.

Luke 7:44   βλέπεις ταύτην **τὴν** γυναῖκα;
             Do you see this woman?

Cf. also Mark 1:9; John 4:15; Acts 1:11; 1 Cor 11:25; Titus 1:13; 2 Pet 1:18; Jude 4; Rev 11:10.

g. With Nominative Nouns (to denote subject)

Normally a subject will have the article (unless it is a pronoun or proper name).[67]

Luke 11:7   **ἡ** θύρα κέκλεισται
             the door is shut

John 13:31   **ὁ** θεὸς ἐδοξάσθη ἐν αὐτῷ
             God has been glorified in him

Cf. also Mark 13:28; John 4:11; Acts 10:38; Col 3:1; Titus 2:11.

h. To Distinguish Subject from Predicate Nominative and Object from Complement

Generally speaking, the subject will be distinguished from the predicate nominative by having the article. This rule of thumb also applies to objects in the object-complement double accusative construction.[68]

---

[66] This is most curious since in John 4:54, where the same idiom occurs (τοῦτο δὲ πάλιν δεύτερον σημεῖον ἐποίησεν ὁ Ἰησοῦς), most modern translations (including the ASV) recognize the anarthrous noun. However, they miss some of the other syntactical features of the language, resulting in a less than satisfactory translation. The NRSV is typical: "Now this was the second sign that Jesus did." This errs as follows: (a) it treats τοῦτο as though it were the nom. subject rather than direct object of ἐποίησεν; (b) consequently, it relegates the main verb to a relative clause, as though the Greek read τοῦτο δὲ πάλιν ἦν δεύτερον σημεῖον ὃ ἐποίησεν ὁ Ἰησοῦς. This may seem a petty issue, but the translation masks the intention of the author–both here and in 2:11. In both places the demonstrative is the object of an object-complement construction, with the trailing noun functioning as the complement. The idea is, in 2:11, "Jesus made this [to be] the beginning of his signs" and 4:54, "Jesus again made this [to be] the second of his signs." The evangelist is not simply emphasizing Jesus' power, but his sovereignty as well.

[67] Even with non-proper nouns, however, there are plenty of examples where the subject is anarthrous. Cf. Rom 1:16, 17, 18; John 1:18.

[68] Cf. detailed discussions in the chapters on "The Nominative Case" (under predicate nominative) and "The Accusative Case" (under both object-complement and subject of infinitive).

Matt 12:8 κύριος ἐστιν τοῦ σαββάτου **ὁ** υἱὸς τοῦ ἀνθρώπου
the Son of Man is lord of the Sabbath

John 5:18 πατέρα ἴδιον ἔλεγεν **τὸν** θεὸν
he was claiming God [to be] his own Father

Phil 1:8 μάρτυς μου **ὁ** θεός
God is my witness

1 Tim 6:5 νομιζόντων πορισμὸν εἶναι **τὴν** εὐσέβειαν
thinking that godliness is a means of gain

Cf. also John 1:1; Phil 2:6; Jas 5:10; 1 John 4:14.

i.   With the Infinitive to Denote Various Functions[69]

E. Absence of the Article

1. Clarification

It is not necessary for a noun to have the article in order for it to be definite. But conversely, a noun *cannot* be *in*definite when it has the article. Thus it *may* be definite without the article, and it *must* be definite with the article.

2. Significance

When a substantive is anarthrous, it may have one of three forces: indefinite, qualitative, or definite. There are not clear-cut distinctions between these three forces, however. If we were to place them on a continuum graph, we would see that the *qualitative* aspect is sometimes close to being definite, sometimes close to being indefinite:

Chart 21
The Semantics of Anarthrous Nouns

---

[69] See chapter on infinitives for discussion.

➡ **a.   Indefinite**

An indefinite noun refers to one member of a class, without specifying which member. For example, in John 4:7 we have "**A** woman from Samaria. . ." The anarthrous γυνή is indefinite, telling us nothing about this particular woman. Thus an indefinite noun is unmarked in that (next to) nothing is revealed about it apart from its membership in a class of others that share the same designation. It lacks, as Givón says, "unique referential identity."[70]

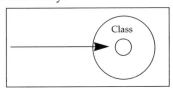

Chart 22
The Semantics of Indefinite Nouns

➡ **b.   Qualitative**

A qualitative noun places the stress on quality, nature, or essence. It does not merely indicate membership in a class of which there are other members (such as an indefinite noun), nor does it stress individual identity (such as a definite noun).

It is akin to a generic noun in that it focuses on the *kind*. Further, like a generic, *it emphasizes class traits*. Yet, unlike generic nouns, a qualitative noun often has in view one individual rather than the class as a whole.

Abstract nouns deserve special treatment. For the most part, they are not normally conceived of in terms of membership in a class. For example, ὁ θεὸς ἀγάπη ἐστιν cannot naturally be translated, "God is **a** love" or "God is **the** love." The lexical nature of the word ἀγάπη is abstract rather than particular. Hence, on the one hand, most abstract nouns will be qualitative; on the other hand, abstract nouns will *not* normally be generic because no *class* is in view, just a certain quality.

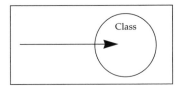   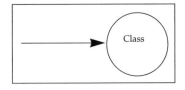

Chart 23   *Chart 24*
The Semantics of Qualitative Nouns   *The Semantics of Generic Nouns*

---

[70] Givón defines indefinite as follows: "Speakers code a referential nominal as indefinite if they think that they are *not* entitled to assume that the hearer can–by whatever means–assign it unique referential identity" (*Syntax*, 399).

1 John 4:8 ὁ θεὸς **ἀγάπη** ἐστίν
God is **love**

John 1:4 ἐν αὐτῷ **ζωὴ** ἦν
in him was **life**

> ζωή is a typically abstract term in the NT. It would be difficult to read this as an indefinite, "in him was **a** life."

Heb 1:2 ἐπ᾽ ἐσχάτου τῶν ἡμερῶν τούτων ἐλάλησεν ἡμῖν ἐν **υἱῷ**
In these last days, [God] has spoken to us in **Son**

> Although this should probably be translated "a Son" (there is no decent way to express this compactly in English), the force is clearly qualitative (though, of course, on the continuum it would be closer to the indefinite than the definite category).[71] The point is that God, in his final revelation, has spoken to us in one who has the characteristics of a son. His credentials are vastly different from the credentials of the prophets (or from the angels, as the following context indicates).

c. Definite

A definite noun lays the stress on individual identity. It has in view membership in a class, but this particular member is already marked out by the author. Definite nouns have unique referential identity.[72]

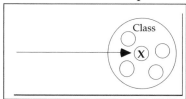

Chart 25
The Semantics of Definite Nouns

Though by definition an articular noun is definite, an anarthrous noun may also be definite under certain conditions. As was mentioned earlier, there are at least ten constructions in which a noun may be definite though anarthrous. The following is a brief look at these constructions.

1) Proper Names

By the nature of the case, a proper name is definite without the article. If we read Παῦλος we do not think of translating it "a Paul." Further, "the use of the art. w. personal names is varied; as a general rule the presence of the art. w. a personal name indicates that the pers. is known; the absence of the art. simply names him. . . . This rule,

---

[71] Some translations render this "his Son," though this is probably too definite and introduces the idea of possession without either the article or a possessive pronoun.

[72] Givón, *Syntax*, 399. He defines definite as follows: "Speakers code a referential nominal as definite if they think that they are entitled to assume that the hearer can–by whatever means–assign it unique reference."

however, is subject to considerable modification . . . ."[73] Robertson adds to this:

> This seems rather odd to us in English, since the proper name itself is supposed to be definite enough. . . . But, just because proper names are so obviously definite, the article was frequently used where we in English cannot handle it. But this is very far from saying that the article meant nothing to the Greek.[74]

The difficulty with the article with proper names is twofold: (1) English usage does not correspond to it, and (2) we still cannot achieve "explanatory adequacy"[75] with reference to the use of the article with proper names–that is, we are unable to articulate clear and consistent principles as to why the article is used in a given instance. (For example, although sometimes it is due to anaphora, there are too many exceptions to make this a major principle.)[76] What we can say, however, is that a proper name, with or without the article, is definite.[77]

Luke 5:8   Σίμων Πέτρος προσέπεσεν τοῖς γόνασιν Ἰησοῦ[78]
            Simon Peter fell at the feet **of Jesus**

---

[73] BAGD, s.v. ὁ, ἡ, τό, II. 1. b.

[74] Robertson, *Grammar*, 759.

[75] To borrow a phrase from Chomsky, by which he has articulated one of the main goals of modern linguistics.

[76] Few detailed studies have been done on the article with proper names in the NT (for classical Greek, see B. L. Gildersleeve, "On the Article with Proper Names," *AJP* 11 [1890] 483-87). In G. D. Fee's stimulating study, "The Use of the Definite Article with Personal Names in the Gospel of John," *NTS* 17 (1970-71) 168-83, the author argues against anaphora as a major guiding principle. The Fourth Gospel is not the only NT book in this camp. In Matthew's genealogy, for example, the article is only used with the direct object (e.g., Ἀβραὰμ ἐγέννησεν τὸν Ἰσαάκ, Ἰσαὰκ δὲ ἐγέννησεν τὸν Ἰακώβ, Ἰακὼβ δὲ ἐγέννησεν τὸν Ἰούδαν καὶ τοὺς ἀδελφοὺς αὐτοῦ in 1:2), never for previous reference. It is understandable that the article would be used with the acc. nouns: With indeclinable nouns, the article is typically found with oblique case nouns to distinguish them from the subject. But this usage does not preclude a nom. article used for previous reference.

More recently, J. Heimerdinger and S. Levinsohn, "The Use of the Definite Article before Names of People in the Greek Text of Acts with Particular Reference to Codex Bezae," *FilolNT* 5.9 (1992) 15-44, argue that the first mention of names is almost always anarthrous and that later references are also anarthrous when the author wishes to draw attention to them for a particular reason (a feature the authors describe as "salience"). This approach has real merit, but needs to be more broadly based before any conclusions can be made for the NT as a whole.

[77] One of the difficulties in determining any principles relates to the definition of a proper name. A good rule of thumb to follow is that a proper name is one that cannot be pluralized. Thus, Χριστός, θεός, and κύριος are not proper names; Παῦλος, Πέτρος, and Ἰησοῦς are. See later discussion of this point in "The Article: Part II."

[78] D W 13 69 828 892 983 1005 1241 add an article before Σίμων; others add one before Ἰησοῦ (A C F L M X Θ Λ Ψ f[1, 13] 33 579 1241 1424).

John 1:45   εὑρίσκει **Φίλιππος** τὸν Ναθαναήλ
Philip found Nathanael
> The article is used with Ναθαναήλ, an indeclinable name, to identify him as the direct object.

Acts 19:13   ὁρκίζω ὑμᾶς τὸν Ἰησοῦν ὃν **Παῦλος** κηρύσσει
I adjure by the Jesus whom **Paul** preaches
> In this instance the article with Ἰησοῦν is kataphoric.

1 Cor 1:13   μὴ **Παῦλος** ἐσταυρώθη ὑπὲρ ὑμῶν, ἢ εἰς τὸ ὄνομα **Παύλου** ἐβαπτίσθητε;
Paul was not crucified for you, was he? or, you were not baptized into **Paul's** name, were you?

Cf. also Luke 3:21; Acts 26:24; Gal 2:1, 11.

➡ ### 2)   Object of a Preposition

There is no need for the article to be used to make the object of a preposition definite.[79] However, this is not to say that all prepositional objects are definite. An anarthrous noun as object of a preposition is not *necessarily* definite. It is often qualitative (e.g., υἱῷ in Heb 1:2, mentioned above),[80] or even occasionally indefinite (cf. μετὰ γυναικὸς ἐλάλει–"he was speaking with **a** woman" [John 4:27]).[81] Thus, when a noun is the object of a preposition, it does not *require* the article to be definite: if it has the article, it *must* be definite; if it *lacks* the article, it *may* be definite. The reason for the article, then, is usually for other purposes (such as anaphora or as a function marker).

Luke 5:12   πεσὼν ἐπὶ **πρόσωπον**
falling on [his] **face**

John 1:1   Ἐν **ἀρχῇ** ἦν ὁ λόγος
In **the beginning** was the Word
> Here the noun is also monadic, giving it additional reason to be definite.

Rom 1:4   τοῦ ὁρισθέντος υἱοῦ θεοῦ ἐν δυνάμει κατὰ **πνεῦμα** ἁγιωσύνης ἐξ **ἀναστάσεως** νεκρῶν
who was designated the Son of God in power according to **the Spirit** of holiness by **the resurrection** from the dead
> Two of the three prepositional phrases include definite objects; ἐν δυνάμει is qualitative.

Cf. also Matt 10:22; Mark 2:1; Luke 2:14; John 1:13; 6:64; 2 Cor 10:3; Heb 4:3; 9:12; 1 Pet 1:12; Rev 7:5.

---

[79] This is recognized by most grammarians. Cf. Robertson, *Grammar*, 791; *BDF*, 133; Zerwick, *Biblical Greek*, 58-59.

[80] Cf. also Luke 1:39; Acts 4:27; 1 Cor 3:13; Jas 1:6. It is our impression that most anarthrous nouns after prepositions seem to be qualitative unless they are monadic, proper names, in a gen. construction, or have a qualifying adjective.

[81] Cf. also Mark 4:1; 5:2; Luke 4:11; 5:18; 1 Pet 3:15; Rev 1:11.

➡   **3)   With Ordinal Numbers**

The number identifies the "amount" of the substantive, making it definite.

Matt 14:25   τετάρτη **φυλακῇ** τῆς νυκτὸς
in **the** fourth **watch** of the night

Mark 15:25   ἦν **ὥρα** τρίτη καὶ ἐσταύρωσαν αὐτόν
it was [about] **the** third **hour** when they crucified him

John 4:6   **ὥρα** ἦν ὡς ἕκτη
it was about **the** sixth **hour**

Cf. also Mark 12:20; John 4:52; Acts 2:15; 2 Cor 12:2.

➡   **4)   Predicate Nominative**

If the predicate nominative *precedes* the copula, it *may* be definite though anarthrous. For more information, see "Colwell's rule" under "Special Uses (and Non-Uses) of the Article."

➡   **5)   Complement in Object-Complement Construction**

If the complement precedes the object, it may be definite though anarthrous. For more information, see "Object Complement" in the chapter on the "Accusative Case."

John 5:18   **πατέρα** ἴδιον ἔλεγεν τὸν θεόν
he was calling God his own **father**

Rom 10:9   ἐὰν ὁμολογήσῃς ἐν τῇ στόματί σου **κύριον Ἰησοῦν** . . . σωθήσῃ
if you confess with your mouth **Jesus** [as] **Lord** . . . you shall be saved

➡   **6)   Monadic Nouns**

A one-of-a-kind noun does not, of course, require the article to be definite (e.g., "sun," "earth," "devil," etc.). One might consider πνεῦμα as monadic when it is modified by the adjective ἅγιον. If so, then the expression πνεῦμα ἅγιον is monadic and refers only to *the* Holy Spirit.[82] In the least this illustrates the fact that we need to think of the entire *noun phrase*, not just a single word, when identifying it as monadic. The expression "Son of God," for example, is monadic, while "son" is not. "Heavenly Father" is monadic; "father" is not.

---

[82] Cf. Robertson, *Grammar*, 795; Moule, *Idiom Book*, 112-113 ("it seems to me rather forced to interpret the anarthrous uses . . . as uniformly meaning something less than *God's Holy Spirit*").

Luke 21:25 ἔσονται σημεῖα ἐν **ἡλίῳ** καὶ **σελήνῃ**

there will be signs in **the sun** and **moon**

John 19:13 ὁ οὖν Πιλᾶτος ἀκούσας τῶν λόγων τούτων ἤγαγεν ἔξω τὸν Ἰησοῦν καὶ ἐκάθισεν ἐπὶ βήματος εἰς τόπον λεγόμενον **λιθόστρωτον** . . .

when Pilate heard these words, he brought out Jesus and sat on the judgment seat in a place called **the Pavement** . . .

Luke 1:35 κληθήσεται **υἱὸς** θεοῦ

he shall be called **the Son** of God

John 6:70 ἀπεκρίθη αὐτοῖς ὁ Ἰησοῦς· οὐκ ἐγὼ ὑμᾶς τοὺς δώδεκα ἐξελεξάμην; καὶ ἐξ ὑμῶν εἷς **διάβολός** ἐστιν.

Jesus answered them, "Have I not chosen you, the twelve? Yet one of you is **the devil**."

> A curious phenomenon has occurred in the English Bible with reference to one particular monadic noun, διάβολος.[83] The KJV translates both διάβολος and δαιμόνιον as "devil." Thus in the AV translators' minds, "devil" was not a monadic noun. Modern translations have correctly rendered δαιμόνιον as "demon" and have, for the most part, recognized that διάβολος is monadic (cf., e.g., 1 Pet 5:8; Rev 20:2).[84] But in John 6:70 modern translations have fallen into the error of the King James translators. The KJV has "one of you is **a** devil." So does the RSV, NRSV, ASV, NIV, NKJV, and JB. Yet there is only one devil.[85] A typical objection to the rendering "one of you is **the** devil" is that this would identify Judas with the devil. Yes, that is true–on the surface. Obviously that is not what is *literally* meant–any more than it is literally true that Peter is Satan (Mark 8:33 and parallels). The legacy of the KJV still lives on, then, even in places where it ought not.

Cf. also Luke 1:15; Acts 13:10; 1 Cor 15:41.

➡ 7) **Abstract Nouns**

Words such as love, joy, peace, faith, etc. are commonly anarthrous though they are not *in*definite. They could be classified as qualitative-definite, however, and consequently occur with and without the article. Nevertheless, for the most part, "no vital difference was felt between articular and anarthrous abstract nouns."[86] Occasionally, however, the article is used for anaphora or some other reason where at least a recognition of its presence (whether translated or not) is beneficial to an understanding of the passage.

---

[83] Technically, an adjective. But it functions substantivally in the singular consistently in the NT.

[84] These are two of the occurrences where the word is anarthrous. Usually it is articular. On occasion, the word is in the plural and adjectival.

[85] Another reason why "devil" here should not be taken as an indefinite noun is that it precedes the equative verb. See below on "Colwell's rule."

[86] Robertson, *Grammar*, 794.

Luke 19:9   σήμερον **σωτηρία** τῷ οἴκῳ τούτῳ ἐγένετο
today **salvation** has come to this house

John 1:16   ἐκ τοῦ πληρώματος αὐτοῦ ἡμεῖς πάντες ἐλάβομεν καὶ **χάριν** ἀντὶ **χάριτος**
out of his fullness we all have received, even **grace** upon **grace**

John 17:17   ὁ λόγος ὁ σὸς **ἀλήθειά** ἐστιν
your word is **truth**

Gal 5:22-23   ὁ καρπὸς τοῦ πνεύματός ἐστιν **ἀγάπη χαρὰ εἰρήνη, μακροθυμία χρηστότης ἀγαθωσύνη, πίστις πραΰτης ἐγκράτεια**
The fruit of the Spirit is **love, joy, peace, patience, kindness, goodness, faithfulness, gentleness, self-control**

Eph 2:5, 8   **χάριτί** ἐστε σεσῳσμένοι . . . τῇ **χάριτί** ἐστε σεσῳσμένοι
by **grace** you are saved . . . by grace you are saved

> The first reference to χάρις is anarthrous (v 5), followed by a resumption of the point in v 8 with the anaphoric article. Although the force of the article is not naturally brought out in translation, its presence should not go unobserved in exegesis.

Cf. also Luke 21:15; John 1:4, 12; Acts 7:10; Rom 1:29; 11:33; 2 Cor 11:10; Gal 5:19-21; 2 Tim 2:10; Phlm 3; Heb 1:14; Rev 1:4; 17:9.

➡   ### 8)   A Genitive Construction (Apollonius' Corollary)

The general rule (discussed earlier in this chapter) is that *both* the head noun and the genitive noun either have the article or lack the article (known as Apollonius' Canon). It makes little semantic difference whether the construction is articular or anarthrous. Thus ὁ λόγος τοῦ θεοῦ=λόγος θεοῦ.

The corollary to this rule (Apollonius' Corollary), developed by David Hedges,[87] is that *when both nouns are anarthrous, both will usually have the same semantic force.* That is, both will be, for example, definite (D-D), the most commonly shared semantic force. Somewhat less common is qualitative-qualitative (Q-Q). The least likely semantic force is indefinite-indefinite (I-I). Further, although not infrequently was there a one-step difference between the two substantives (e.g., D-Q), only rarely did the two nouns differ by two steps (either I-D or D-I). Hedges worked only in the Pauline letters, but his conclusions are similar to other work done in the rest of the NT.[88]

---

[87] David W. Hedges, "Apollonius' Canon and Anarthrous Constructions in Pauline Literature: An Hypothesis" (M.Div. thesis, Grace Theological Seminary, 1983).

[88] Though Hedges worked only on the *corpus Paulinum*, his work has been supplemented by Charles Cummings in a paper done in Advanced Greek Grammar at Dallas Seminary in 1992. Cummings worked on the Petrine epistles. My preliminary work in narrative literature also confirms the findings of Hedges and Cummings.

The investigation consisted of an inductive examination of 289 Pauline anarthrous constructions selected using GRAMCORD. These constructions were classified as N (containing a proper noun or κύριος), T (containing θεός), P (object of a preposition), E (subject or predicate of an equative verb), combinations of the above (e.g., NP), or Z (none of the above), and the definiteness of each noun was determined. The results indicated that the hypothesis, though not an absolute rule, had general validity. On the average, absolute agreement was observed in 74% of the cases, while 20% of the pairs differed by only one semantic step [e.g., Q-D] and only 6% differed by two steps. It was further determined that in general if the construction involved θεός, the nouns were probably both definite (68%), if the construction involved only a preposition, they were probably both qualitative (52%), and if the construction involved neither proper nouns, θεός, prepositions, nor equative verbs, then the nouns, though agreeing, had about an equal chance of being any of the three definiteness classes.[89]

What is noteworthy here is that at most only 6% of the constructions involve an indefinite noun and a definite noun.[90] Yet in many exegetical discussions, it is presupposed that I-D is a normal, even probable force for the construction. In addition, it should be noted that (1) just as rare as I-D is I-I; (2) only rarely is the genitive noun less definite than the head noun;[91] hence, (3) the genitive noun is the "driving force" behind the construction: It tends to be definite and to make the head noun definite as well.[92]

a) Clear Examples (Definite-Definite)

Matt 3:16   πνεῦμα θεοῦ[93]

the Spirit of God

> A nonsensical translation would be "**a** spirit of **a** god." The point of Apollonius' Corollary is that when both nouns are anarthrous and it can be determined that one is definite, then the other is also definite. Thus in the above example, if θεοῦ is definite, so is πνεῦμα. If one wants to claim that the text should be translated, "a spirit of God," the burden of proof is on him or her and he/she would have to establish such a translation on a basis other than normal grammatical usage. Recall that I-D is the *least* likely possibility for this construction.

---

[89] Hedges, "Apollonius' Canon," 66-67.

[90] Although almost all of these were I-D rather than D-I, this two-step variation was still considered to be rare.

[91] Hedges, "Apollonius' Canon," 43, n. 1. He gives as his best example 1 Cor 12:10, where ἑρμηνεία γλωσσῶν means "**the** interpretation of tongues," "where it is clear that the single correct interpretation (definite) is in view for each of the various tongues (indefinite)." Cf. also Acts 6:15 (πρόσωπον ἀγγέλου ["**the** face of **an** angel"]).

[92] Part of the reason for this is that once an adjunct is added to a noun, that noun moves toward greater specificity.

[93] This is the reading of ℵ B; most other MSS have τὸ πνεῦμα τοῦ θεοῦ. Cf. also Heb 9:3 for a similar *v.l.*

John 5:29   οἱ τὰ ἀγαθὰ ποιήσαντες εἰς **ἀνάστασιν ζωῆς**, οἱ δὲ τὰ φαῦλα πράξαντες
             εἰς **ἀνάστασιν κρίσεως**

             those who have done good, to **the resurrection of life**; but those
             who have done evil, to **the resurrection of judgment**

Acts 7:8   ἔδωκεν αὐτῷ **διαθήκην περιτομῆς**

             he gave to him **the covenant of circumcision**

Rom 1:18   ἀποκαλύπτεται **ὀργὴ θεοῦ**

             the wrath of God is revealed

Cf. also Acts 1:19; 2:36; Rom 8:9; 1 Cor 10:21; 1 Thess 2:13.

b) Ambiguous Examples

1] Texts Involving ἄγγελος κυρίου

One of the many theologically significant constructions is
ἄγγελος κυρίου (cf. Matt 1:20; 28:2; Luke 2:9; Acts 12:7; Gal
4:14 [ἄγγελος θεοῦ]). In the LXX this is the normal phrase
used to translate מלאך יהוה ("**the** angel of **the** Lord").[94]
The NT exhibits the same phenomenon, prompting Nigel
Turner to suggest that "ἄγγελος κυρίου is not *an angel* but *the
angel* [of the Lord]."[95] Indeed, although most scholars treat
ἄγγελος κυρίου in the NT as "an angel of the Lord,"[96] there
is no *linguistic* basis for doing so. Apart from theological argument, it is most probable that ἄγγελος κυρίου is *the* angel
of the Lord in the NT and is to be identified with the *the* angel of the Lord of the OT.[97]

2] Other Theologically Significant Texts

Other theologically significant texts include Mark 15:39;
1 Cor 15:10; 1 Thess 4:15-16; 5:2.

---

[94] Neither in the Hebrew nor the LXX is the expression articular, except when the reference is anaphoric. The same is true for the NT (compare Matt 1:20 with v 24).

[95] *Syntax*, 180.

[96] Cf. NRSV, NASB, NIV, most commentaries and theologians.

[97] W. G. MacDonald ("Christology and 'The Angel of the Lord'," *Current Issues in Biblical and Patristic Studies*, 324-35) feels the weight of the linguistic argument, in that he recognizes no difference between the OT and NT usage of the phrase. But his conclusion is
that it should be translated "*an* angel of the Lord" in *both* Testaments. I agree that the
phrase in both Testaments must almost surely be translated the same, but considerations
both from Apollonius' Canon and Corollary and the identification of the angel of the Lord
with YHWH himself (which strikes me as more than mere representation or functional
deity [see L. W. Hurtado, *One God, One Lord: Early Christian Devotion and Ancient Jewish
Monotheism* (Philadelphia: Fortress, 1988)]) lead me to think that a particular "angel" is in
view.

→   **9) With a Pronominal Adjective**

Nouns with πᾶς, ὅλος,[98] etc. do not need the article to be definite, for either the class as a whole ("all") or distributively ("every") is being specified.[99] Either way, a generic force is given to such constructions.

Matt 3:15   πρέπον ἐστὶν ἡμῖν πληρῶσαι πᾶσαν **δικαιοσύνην**
it is fitting for us to fulfill all **righteousness**

Luke 3:5   πᾶν **ὄρος** καὶ **βουνὸς** ταπεινωθήσεται
every **mountain** and **hill** will be brought low

Luke 5:5   ἐπιστάτα, δι᾽ ὅλης **νυκτὸς** κοπιάσαντες[100]
Master, we labored all **night**

Rom 11:26   πᾶς **Ἰσραὴλ** σωθήσεται
all **Israel** will be saved

Rev 21:4   ἐξαλείψει πᾶν **δάκρυον** ἐκ τῶν ὀφθαλμῶν αὐτῶν
he will wipe away every **tear** from their eyes

Cf. Matt 23:35; Mark 13:20; John 1:9; Acts 1:21; 24:3; 2 Cor 1:3; Eph 3:15; Titus 2:11; 1 Pet 1:24; 2 Pet 1:20; Jude 15.

→   **10) Generic Nouns**

The generic article is not always necessary in order for a noun to have a generic idea.[101] There is little semantic difference between articular generics and anarthrous generics, though it is true that some nouns usually take the article and others do not. Just as with articular generics, sometimes it is more appropriate to translate the anarthrous generic noun with an indefinite article (with the understanding that the whole class is still in view).

a) Clear Examples

Luke 18:2   κριτής τις ἦν . . . **ἄνθρωπον** μὴ ἐντρεπόμενος
there was a certain judge. . . who did not respect **people**

1 Cor 1:20   ποῦ **σόφος**; ποῦ **γραμματεῦς**;
Where is **the wise man**? Where is **the scribe**?

---

[98] An exception with ὅλος is found in John 7:23 (ὅλον **ἄνθρωπον** ὑγιῆ ἐποίησα), where the translation is indefinite: "I made **a** whole **man** well."

[99] The issue of the translation of πᾶς + noun as "every [noun]" or "all/the whole [noun]" will not be taken up here in any detail. Suffice it to say that "all/the whole [noun]" is exampled in biblical literature for the anarthrous construction (cf., e.g., 1 Chron 28:8; Amos 3:1; Matt 3:15; Acts 1:21), thus permitting such a translation in Eph 2:21; 3:15; and 2 Tim 3:16. Cf. Moule, *Idiom Book*, 94-95.

[100] The majority of MSS (in particular, late ones) add τῆς before νυκτός (C D X Γ Δ Θ Λ *f*[1, 13] Byz).

[101] Cf. Robertson, *Grammar*, 757.

1 Cor 11:7   ἡ γυνὴ δόξα **ἀνδρός** ἐστιν
               the wife is the glory of **the husband**

> Here the article is used with γυνή, but it is not used with ἀνδρός. Yet both terms are generic.

1 Tim 2:11   **γυνὴ** ἐν ἡσυχίᾳ μανθανέτω
               let **a woman** learn in silence

Cf. also Matt 10:35; John 2:10; 1 Cor 11:8, 9; 12:13; 1 Tim 2:12; 1 Pet 3:18.

b) Possible Example

Rev 13:18   ἀριθμὸς **ἀνθρώπου** ἐστιν
              it is the number of **humankind**

> If ἀνθρώπου is generic, then the sense is, "It is [the] number of **humankind**." It is significant that this construction fits Apollonius' Canon (i.e., both the head noun and the genitive are anarthrous), suggesting that if one of these nouns is definite, then the other is, too. Grammatically, those who contend that the sense is "it is [the] number of **a man**" have the burden of proof on them (for they treat the head noun, ἀριθμός, as definite and the genitive, ἀνθρώπου, as indefinite–the rarest of all possibilities[102]). In light of Johannine usage, we might also add Rev 16:18, where the Seer *clearly* uses the anarthrous ἄνθρωπος in a generic sense, meaning "humankind." The implications of this grammatical possibility, exegetically speaking, are simply that the number "666" is the number that represents humankind. Of course, an individual is in view, but his number may be the number representing all of humankind. Thus the Seer might be suggesting here that the antichrist, who is the *best* representative of humanity without Christ (and the best counterfeit of a perfect man that his master, that old serpent, could muster), is still less than perfection (which would have been represented by the number seven).

---

[102] Cf. our discussion of Apollonius' Corollary above.

The Article, Part II

Special Uses and Non-Uses of the Article

Introduction

Here we will consider two constructions. One of these involves the non-use of the article and the other involves the use of the article: anarthrous pre-verbal predicate nominatives and the article-noun-καί-noun construction. They deserve their own extended treatment both because of rich theological implications (especially related to explicit NT affirmations of the deity of Christ) and because of common abuse in NT circles. The material is not all equally important; some of it may be glossed over quickly and merely used for reference. The chapter can be outlined as above (with the more immediately relevant sections for intermediate students highlighted in bold letters).

A. *Anarthrous Pre-Verbal Predicate Nominatives (Involving Colwell's Rule)*

Introduction

1) Definition of Terms

First, it would be helpful to review some basic terminology.

- anarthrous = without the article
- pre-verbal = *before* the equative verb
- predicate nominative (PN) = the noun in the nominative case which is the same as the subject (more or less)

Therefore, an anarthrous pre-verbal predicate nominative is a predicate nominative that does not have the article and occurs before the equative verb. This is the kind of construction Ernest Cadman Colwell investigated when he wrote his now well-known article in 1933. To economize on our verbiage, therefore, we will consider every anarthrous pre-verbal predicate nominative construction as a "Colwell's *construction*" (though not necessarily fitting Colwell's *rule*).

2) Predicate Nominatives in General

In general, a predicate nominative is anarthrous and it *follows* the copula. It is usually qualitative or indefinite.

1. Discovery of "Colwell's Rule"

E. C. Colwell completed his doctor's dissertation on "The Character of the Greek of John's Gospel" in 1931. His intensive research into the grammar of John's Gospel led to the discovery of his rule.

In 1933 he published an article entitled, "A Definite Rule for the Use of the Article in the Greek New Testament," in *JBL* 52 (1933) 12-21. Ever since, his rule has been known simply as "Colwell's rule."

➡ ## 2. Statement of the Rule

Colwell's rule is as follows: "Definite predicate nouns which precede the verb usually lack the article . . . a predicate nominative which precedes the verb cannot be translated as an indefinite or a 'qualitative' noun solely because of the absence of the article; if the context suggests that the predicate is definite, it should be translated as a definite noun. . . ."[1]

Colwell illustrated this principle with John 1:49: ἀπεκρίθη αὐτῷ Ναθαναήλ· ῥαββί, σὺ εἶ ὁ υἱὸς τοῦ θεοῦ, σὺ βασιλεὺς εἶ τοῦ Ἰσραήλ (Nathanael answered him, "Rabbi, you are the Son of God, you are the king of Israel"). Colwell observed that the structural parallels between the two statements differed at two points: (a) in the second statement, the PN is anarthrous while in the first it is articular; (b) in the second statement, the PN is before the verb, while in the first it is after the verb. Yet the grammatical sense was the same for both statements: the PN in each should be regarded as definite. From this, Colwell assumed that definiteness of the PN could be achieved either by the article or by a shift in word order. His essay dealt with the latter.

In other words, a PN that precedes the copula, and which is apparently definite *from the context*, usually lacks the article.

3. Misunderstanding of the Rule

a. By Scholars Since Colwell

Almost immediately many scholars (especially of a more conservative stripe) misunderstood Colwell's rule. They saw the benefit of the rule for affirming the deity of Christ in John 1:1. But what they thought Colwell was articulating was actually the *converse* of the rule, not the rule itself. That is, they thought that the rule was: An anarthrous predicate nominative that precedes the verb is usually definite. This is not the rule, nor can it be implied from the rule.

For the most part, they either quote Colwell without much interaction or they read *into* the rule what is not there. For example, Nigel Turner argued: "[In John 1:1] there need be no doctrinal significance in the dropping of the article, for it is simply a matter of word-order."[2] This means that θεὸς ἦν ὁ λόγος meant the same thing as ὁ λόγος ἦν ὁ θεός.[3] Bruce Metzger summarizes: "As regards Jn 1¹,

---

[1] Colwell, "A Definite Rule," 20.

[2] Turner, *Grammatical Insights into the New Testament*, 17.

[3] Cf. also Zerwick, *Biblical Greek*, 56; L. Cignelli, and G. C. Bottini, "L'Articolo nel Greco Biblico," *Studium Biblicum Franciscanum Liber Annuus* 41 (1991) 187.

Colwell's research casts the most serious doubts on the correctness of such translations as 'and the Logos was divine' (Moffatt, Strachan), 'and the Word was divine' (Goodspeed), and (worst of all) 'and the Word was a god' (. . . *New World Translation*)."[4] Actually, Colwell's rule does not address this issue at all.[5] Walter Martin goes so far as to say: "Colwell's rule clearly states that a definite predicate nominative . . . *never* takes an article when it precedes the verb . . . as in John 1:1."[6] Although Martin states the rule rather than the converse (though too dogmatically, for Colwell did not say "never"), he assumes the converse of the rule in the very next breath!

Our point is that Colwell's rule has been misunderstood and abused by scholars. By applying Colwell's rule to John 1:1 they have jumped out of the frying pan of Arianism and into the fire of Sabellianism.

b. By Colwell Himself

In his article Colwell overstates his case: "Loosely speaking, this study may be said to have increased the definiteness of a predicate noun before the verb without the article. . . ."[7] Shortly, I will explain how this is not a very accurate statement.[8]

Further, he was inconsistent elsewhere when he said: "[The data presented here] show that a predicate nominative which precedes the verb cannot be translated as an indefinite or a 'qualitative' noun solely because of the absence of the article; *if the context suggests* that the predicate is definite, it should be translated as a definite noun in spite of the absence of the article."[9] This is an accurate statement in that he recognizes that contextual factors need to be brought in to argue for a definite PN. But this is followed on the next page with: "The absence of the article does *not* make the predicate [nominative] indefinite or qualitative when it precedes the verb; it is indefinite in

---

[4] B. M. Metzger, "On the Translation of John i. 1," *ExpTim* 63 (1951-52) 125-26.

[5] We will contend later that, in fact, Moffatt's, Strachan's, and Goodspeed's translations are (1) not at all to be lumped in with the *New World Translation*, and (2) this is probably the most satisfactory translation of the passage.

[6] Walter Martin, *The Kingdom of the Cults: An Analysis of the Major Cult Systems in the Present Christian Era*, rev. ed. (Minneapolis: Bethany Fellowship, 1968) 75, n. 31. For others who have misunderstood the rule, note, e.g., Moule, *Idiom Book*, 116; C. Kuehne, "The Greek Article and the Doctrine of Christ's Deity: II. Colwell's Rule and John 1:1," *Journal of Theology* 15.1 (1975) 12-14; L. Morris, *The Gospel According to John* (NICNT) 77, n. 15.

[7] Colwell, "A Definite Rule," 21.

[8] Nevertheless, from one perspective it is quite acceptable. Colwell brought to NT students' attention that anarthrous pre-verbal PNs were frequently definite. He provided many undisputed examples of this and thus established a clear category of usage. This allowed NT students to see definiteness in many such constructions where they might not have otherwise.

[9] Colwell, "A Definite Rule," 20 (italics mine).

this position *only* when the context *demands* it."[10] In the first statement Colwell pointed out that the burden of proof rests with the definite PN view, but in the second statement he assumes the opposite: now the burden of proof rests with any view other than the definite PN! To make either statement, in reality, was to embrace a methodological error, for Colwell had stated at the outset of his study that he only examined definite predicate nominatives.

Even after his rule had become well-known and even abused by others, Colwell affirmed that the converse of the rule seemed to be as valid as the rule itself.[11] He stated that he felt his rule suggested that an anarthrous pre-verbal PN would *normally* be definite.

➡ ### 4. Clarification of Colwell's Rule

a. By Harner

Forty years after Colwell's article appeared in *JBL*, Philip B. Harner's essay was published in the same journal. Harner pointed out that "Colwell was almost entirely concerned with the question whether anarthrous predicate nouns were definite or indefinite, and he did not discuss at any length the problem of their qualitative significance."[12] This was probably due to the fact that many older grammarians saw *no* distinction between qualitative nouns and indefinite nouns.[13]

Second, Harner produced evidence that an anarthrous pre-verbal PN is usually *qualitative*–not definite nor indefinite. His findings, in general, were that 80% of Colwell's constructions involved qualitative nouns and only 20% involved definite nouns.

b. By Dixon

Paul Stephen Dixon[14] begins the third chapter of his thesis by quoting Colwell's crucial statement of his rule: "A definite predicate nominative . . . does not have the article when it precedes the verb." Dixon goes on, however, to point out an invalid inference which has been made from this rule:

---

[10] Ibid., 21 (italics mine).

[11] This was learned second-hand from my first Greek professor, Dr. Harry A. Sturz. He was a student of Colwell's at Claremont and pointedly asked him, toward the end of Colwell's life, whether the converse of the rule was as valid as the rule itself.

[12] Philip B. Harner, "Qualitative Anarthrous Predicate Nouns: Mark 15:39 and John 1:1," *JBL* 92 (1973) 76. The entire essay is on 75-87.

[13] Even Kuehne, who is more recent, thinks qualitative = indefinite (C. Kuehne, "A Postscript to Colwell's Rule and John 1:1," *Journal of Theology* 15 [1975] 22).

[14] Paul Stephen Dixon, "The Significance of the Anarthrous Predicate Nominative in John" (Th.M. thesis, Dallas Theological Seminary, 1975).

The rule does not say: an anarthrous predicate nominative which precedes the verb is definite. This is the converse of Colwell's rule and as such is not a valid inference. (From the statement "A implies B," it is not valid to infer "B implies A."' From the statement "Articular nouns are definite," it is not valid to infer "Definite nouns are articular." Likewise, from the statement "Definite predicate nominatives preceding the verb are anarthrous," it is not valid to infer "Anarthrous predicate nominatives preceding the verb are definite.")[15]

Dixon, too, suggests that the anarthrous pre-verbal predicate nominative (in John's Gospel at least) is primarily qualitative in force.[16]

➡   c. **Summary**

1) Colwell stated that a definite PN that precedes the verb is usually anarthrous. He did *not* say the *converse*, namely, an anarthrous PN that precedes the verb is usually definite. However, this is how the rule has been misunderstood by most scholars (including Colwell) since the article in *JBL* was written.

2) Colwell restricted his study to anarthrous pre-verbal predicate nominatives which were, as far as he could tell, determined as definite *by the context*. He did not deal with *any* other anarthrous pre-verbal predicate nominatives. However, the misunderstanding has arisen because scholars have not recognized that Colwell only tested these constructions. In other words, Colwell started off with a *semantic* category rather than a *structural* category. He did *not* begin by asking the question, What does the anarthrous pre-verbal PN construction mean? Rather, he began by asking, Will a definite PN be articular or anarthrous? And will it follow or precede the verb? In his initial question, he *assumed* a particular meaning (i.e., definiteness) and sought the particular constructions involved.[17]

Colwell, therefore, did not do an exhaustive research on the construction under consideration. He assumed what many since have thought that he proved![18]

---

[15] Dixon, "Anarthrous Predicate Nominative," 11-12.

[16] He concluded that 94% of these predicate nominatives in John were qualitative, while only 6% were definite.

[17] "It is obvious that the significance of these figures rests upon the accuracy with which definite predicate nouns without the article have been identified" (Colwell, "A Definite Rule," 17).

[18] This is not to say that his rule is invalid. Rather, it is to say that its validity is for *textual criticism* rather than for grammar. Textual criticism was Colwell's real love anyway (he is frequently regarded as the father of modern American NT textual criticism). The rule's validity for textual criticism is as follows: If it is obvious that a pre-verbal PN is definite, the MSS that lack the article are more likely to support the original reading. The issue of *meaning* is not in view; rather, the presence or absence of the article is.

3) Colwell had a simplistic understanding of qualitative and indefinite nouns. He believed that the way we can tell whether a noun is indefinite or "qualitative" or definite is by its *translation*. But as was pointed out in Part I of this chapter, translation does not always bring out whether a word is qualitative or indefinite or definite. Apparently, if it seemed unnatural to put in the article "a/an" before the noun, Colwell assumed that the noun was *definite*. Greek and English are dissimilar enough, however, that we must argue from *sense*, not translation.

4) We can illustrate the faulty assumptions in two ways. (a) Suppose a study were made of the divorce rate of people married by a justice of the peace. And suppose that the findings were that 90% of the people married by a justice of the peace got divorced within five years. The findings then might support a "rule": If you were married by a justice of the peace, you will probably (9 out of 10 chances) get divorced within five years. The *converse* of this rule, however, would *not* be true: If you are divorced, you probably got married by a justice of the peace. The reason the converse would not necessarily follow is that the study was made *only* of people who were married by a justice of the peace, *not* of all divorced people. Only when all divorcees are considered, can *any* statement be made about their probability of being married by a justice of the peace.

(b) A simpler illustration: Suppose a little boy were to examine as best he could the relationship of rain to clouds. Every time it rains, he runs outside and notices that there are clouds in the sky. He will conclude the following principle: *If it is raining, there must be clouds in the sky.* In such a statement the *only* time the sky is examined is when it is raining. The study is not exhaustive to include all occasions in which the sky is cloudy. If this boy were to formulate the *converse* of his rule, we could all see its logical fallacy: *If there are clouds in the sky, it must be raining.*

With reference to Colwell's rule, only anarthrous pre-verbal predicate nominatives were studied which were previously determined by their contexts to be most probably definite. Not *all* anarthrous pre-verbal predicate nominatives were studied. But the *converse* of the rule, commonly embraced in NT scholarship, assumes that all such constructions have been examined. In Harner's study, the net was cast wider. He examined all pre-verbal predicate nominatives. And his conclusion was that 80% were qualitative. Therefore, when one sees an anarthrous pre-verbal PN, he should consider its force to be *most likely* qualitative, and only to be definite if the context or other factors strongly suggest otherwise.

In sum, Colwell's rule proves nothing about definiteness. Its value is not for grammar per se, but for textual criticism: It proves something about articularity and word order.

The following chart displays the different databases that were examined by Colwell ("Colwell's rule") and Harner ("Colwell's construction").

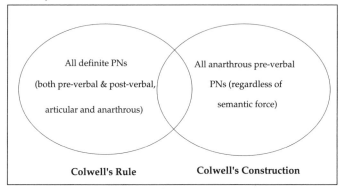

Chart 26
The Different Databases for Colwell's Rule Vs. Colwell's Construction

As can be seen from the chart, the databases were not the same. The fact of some overlap is what has given rise to the confusion over the rule.

5. Significance of Colwell's Construction for Exegesis

The studies by Dixon and especially Harner demonstrate that the anarthrous pre-verbal PN is still *closer* to definiteness than is the anarthrous *post*-copulative predicate nominative,[19] and that an anarthrous predicate nominative that *follows* the verb will usually be either qualitative or *in*definite.[20]

A general rule about the construction can now be stated: *An anarthrous pre-verbal PN is normally qualitative, sometimes definite, and only rarely indefinite.* In neither of the two studies were any indefinite PNs found. We believe there may be some in the NT, but this is nevertheless the most poorly attested semantic force for such a construction.

---

[19] Dixon himself denies its significance for exegesis, stating, "Obviously, this rule has very little exegetical value" (14). This is true for the rule, but not for the construction. Specifically, of the 53 Colwell's constructions Dixon found in John, not one was considered *indefinite*.

[20] That is, of course, unless there is some other ground for considering it to be definite (such as a monadic noun).

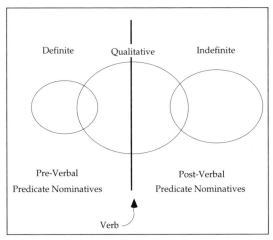

Chart 27
The Semantic Range of Anarthrous Predicate Nominatives

The chart illustrates the fact that anarthrous *pre-verbal* predicate nomina-tives usually fall within the qualitative-*definite* range, while anarthrous *post*-verbal predicate nominatives usually fall within the qualitative-*indefinite* range. The presumption, therefore, when one faces an anar-throus pre-verbal PN is that it will be qualitative unless there are contex-tual or other considerations suggesting that it is definite or, less likely, indefinite.

a. Definite Predicate Nominatives

Matt 27:42 ἄλλους ἔσωσεν, ἑαυτὸν οὐ δύναται σῶσαι· **βασιλεὺς** Ἰσραήλ ἐστιν, καταβάτω νῦν ἀπὸ τοῦ σταυροῦ

He saved others, [but] he cannot save himself. He is **the king** of Israel; let him come down now from the cross . . .

> It is plain that the PN cannot be anything but definite here, for there is only one king of Israel at a time.[21]

John 1:49 σὺ εἶ ὁ υἱὸς τοῦ θεοῦ, σὺ **βασιλεὺς** εἶ τοῦ Ἰσραήλ[22]

you are the Son of God, you are **the king** of Israel

> Nathanael's response to Jesus is a twofold identification. In the first construction the PN follows the verb and has the article. In the second

---

[21] Still, it is to be observed that the PN has a genitive adjunct. What is most interesting about many of Colwell's constructions is that those very PNs that are to be considered to be definite frequently have some other feature (e.g., monadic noun, genitive modifier, proper name) that suggests definiteness independently of Colwell's construction.

[22] Several MSS place the βασιλεύς after the verb and add an article before it (e.g., $\mathfrak{P}^{66}$ א X Γ Δ Θ 063 1241 f^{13} *Byz*). Colwell noted such variants as evidence for the validity of his rule: either a definite PN preceded the verb and was without the article or followed the verb with the article.

construction the PN precedes the verb and lacks the article. This text was Colwell's main illustration of his principle.[23]

1 Cor 1:18   ὁ λόγος τοῦ σταυροῦ τοῖς δὲ σῳζομένοις ἡμῖν **δύναμις** θεοῦ ἐστιν
              the word of the cross to us who are being saved is **the power** of God

Heb 1:10   **ἔργα** τῶν χειρῶν σού εἰσιν οἱ οὐρανοί·
              the heavens are **the works** of your hands

Cf. also Matt 4:3, 6; 5:34, 35; 13:39; 14:33; John 3:29; 10:2; 11:51; Acts 13:33; Rom 1:16; 10:4; 1 Cor 4:4; 11:3; 2 Cor 6:16; Gal 3:25; Jas 2:23; 1 John 2:2.

b. Qualitative Predicate Nominatives[24]

John 1:14   ὁ λόγος **σὰρξ** ἐγένετο
              the Word became **flesh**

> The idea is not that the Word became "the flesh," nor "a flesh," but simply "flesh." That is, the Word partook of humanity. Many pre-1933 exegetes (i.e., before Colwell's rule was published) saw a parallel between this verse and John 1:1, noting that both PNs were qualitative.

John 5:10   ἔλεγον οὖν οἱ Ἰουδαῖοι τῷ τεθεραπευμένῳ, **σάββατόν** ἐστιν
              Then the Jews said to the man who had been healed, "It is **Sabbath**"

> Although this could be translated "it is **the Sabbath**" or, a bit less naturally, "**a Sabbath**," one must remember to argue from *sense* rather than from translation. The point the Pharisees were making had to with the *kind* of day on which this man was working–hence, a qualitative noun.

1 John 4:8   ὁ θεὸς **ἀγάπη** ἐστίν
              God is **love**

> The meaning is certainly not convertible: "love is God." The idea of a qualitative ἀγάπη is that God's essence or nature is love, or that he has the quality of love. Thus love is an attribute, not an identification, of God.

Phil 2:13   **θεὸς** ἐστιν ὁ ἐνεργῶν
              the one working in you is **God**

> Although it is certainly possible that θεός is definite,[25] the force in this context seems to be a bit more on what God does in the believer rather than who it is that does it. In the previous verse, the apostle exhorts his audience to work out their own salvation. Lest they think they are alone in this endeavor, he hastens to remind them that the one working in them has the ability to bring about their complete sanctification.

---

[23] "It was a study of these passages, especially John 1[:]49, that suggested the rule which is advocated in this study. . . . When the passage is scrutinized, it appears at once that the variable quantum is not definiteness but word-order" (Colwell, "A Definite Rule," 13).

[24] One of the ways to test whether a PN is qualitative or definite is to swap the S with the PN. If the sentence makes the same sense, then the PN is definite since the construction involves a convertible proposition. For a more detailed discussion, see the chapter on the "Nominative Case" under "Predicate Nominative."

[25] To clarify this, the majority of MSS added an article before θεός (so D^C E L Ψ 1 69 104 326 1739^C *Byz et alii*).

Cf. also Mark 14:70; Luke 22:59; 23:6; John 3:6; 9:27, 28; 10:33; 12:36, 50; 13:35; 18:35; Acts 7:26, 33; 16:21; Rom 14:23; 1 Cor 2:14; 3:19; 2 Cor 11:22, 23; 1 John 1:5.

c. Indefinite Predicate Nominatives

The following examples comprise potential indefinite predicate nominatives in Colwell's construction. None in the NT have been positively classified as belonging here either by Harner or Dixon (though a few predicate nouns almost certainly belong here). However, in other Hellenistic literature, this usage is established. An example outside the NT is given below.

1 Tim 6:10 ῥίζα πάντων τῶν κακῶν ἐστιν ἡ φιλαργυρία

> This is a difficult text to translate, having the following possibilities: (1) "the love of money is **a** root of all evils," (2) "the love of money is **the** root of all evils," (3) "the love of money motivates all evils," (4) "the love of money is **a** root of all kinds of evils," (5) "the love of money is **the** root of all kinds of evils," (6) "the love of money motivates all kinds of evils." The reason for these six possibilities is that first, it is difficult to tell whether ῥίζα is indefinite (options 1 & 4), definite (2 & 5), or qualitative (3 & 6), and secondly, πάντων may mean "all without exclusion" (1, 2, & 3) or "all without distinction" (4, 5, & 6).
>
> Logically, it would be difficult to say that ῥίζα is definite, for then the text would be saying either (1) the *only* root of all evils is the love of money or that (2) the *greatest* root (*par excellence*) of all evils is the love of money. These are the options *if* πάντων means "all without exclusion." However, the definite idea would fit if πάντων means "all without distinction."
>
> Grammatically, it would be difficult to take ῥίζα as indefinite, since this is the least attested meaning for the anarthrous pre-verbal PN in the NT. However, grammatically the most probable option is to see ῥίζα as qualitative. The idea would be either that all evils *can be* motivated or initiated by the love for money or that all kinds of evils *can be* motivated by the love for money. The qualitative idea makes no comment about anything else that might motivate or produce evil. It simply states that loving money does motivate/produce all (kinds of) evils.

John 6:70 ἐξ ὑμῶν εἷς **διάβολός** ἐστιν
one of you is **a/the devil**

> This text has been discussed above (in greater detail) under "Monadic Nouns." In sum, although the majority of translations treat διάβολος as indefinite (because of the English tradition of the KJV), there is only one devil. Hence, since it is a monadic noun, the meaning is "one of you is **the** devil."

John 4:19 λέγει αὐτῷ ἡ γυνή, Κύριε, θεωρῶ ὅτι **προφήτης** εἶ σύ
The woman said to him, "Sir/Lord, I perceive that you are **a/the prophet**"

> This is the most likely candidate of an indefinite pre-verbal PN in the NT. Yet there is some doubt about it. First, it is slightly possible that the evangelist is representing the Samaritan woman as thinking about the great prophet of Deut 18. This, however, is doubtful because of the verb θεωρῶ. Her *perception* would be that he was *a* prophet, but Jesus' statement to her in v 18 is too insufficient a base to make her think of *the*

prophet. Further, it is quite unnatural to "perceive" the identity of someone; perception belongs to class characteristics, not exact identity. In other words, we would expect her to say, "You're the prophet!" or, perhaps, "Are you the prophet?" if indeed she was thinking of Deut 18. However, this is not to say that the PN must be indefinite. The woman seems to be focusing on the attributes of a prophet, rather than merely listing Jesus as a member of that class. Again, θεωρῶ contributes to this. Although the translation is most naturally "Sir, I perceive that you are a prophet," the sense may be better characterized as indefinite-qualitative. It could almost be translated, "I perceive that you are prophetic," or "I perceive that you have the prophetic gift." The focus of an indefinite noun is on a *member* of class, while the focus of a qualitative noun is on the *attributes* that the class members share.

Didache 11.8 οὐ πᾶς ὁ λαλῶν ἐν πνεύματι **προφήτης** ἐστίν

Not everyone who speaks in/by the Spirit is **a prophet**.

In Didache 11.3-12 προφήτης or ψευδοπροφήτης is an anarthrous PN five times. The focus on the passage is on anyone who claims to have membership in that elite group known as prophets. If a particular individual acts unbecoming of that group, he is called a false prophet (ψευδοπροφήτης). The focus of the pericope, then, is on any individual member without specifying which member is in view (apart from his own actions pointing him out). This is an indefinite PN.[26]

For other potential indefinite predicate nominatives (many of which might better be classified as indefinite-qualitative or qualitative-indefinite), cf. Matt 14:26; Luke 5:8; John 8:34; Acts 28:4; Rom 13:6; 1 Cor 6:19.

6. Application of Colwell's Construction to John 1:1[27]

John 1:1 states: Ἐν ἀρχῇ ἦν ὁ λόγος, καὶ ὁ λόγος ἦν πρὸς τὸν θεόν, καὶ θεὸς ἦν ὁ λόγος. In the last part of the verse, the clause καὶ θεὸς ἦν ὁ λόγος (John 1:1c), θεός is the PN. It is anarthrous and comes before the verb. Therefore, it fits Colwell's *construction*, though it might not fit the rule (for the rule states that definiteness is determined or indicated by the context, not by the grammar). Whether it is indefinite, qualitative, or definite is the issue at hand.

a. Is Θεός in John 1:1c Indefinite?

If θεός were indefinite, we would translate it "*a god*" (as is done in the *New World Translation* [NWT]). If so, the theological implication would be some form of polytheism, perhaps suggesting that the Word was merely a secondary god in a pantheon of deities.

The grammatical argument that the PN here is indefinite is weak. Often, those who argue for such a view (in particular, the translators

---

[26] It is nevertheless difficult to distinguish indefinite from qualitative nouns at times (just as at other times it is difficult to distinguish qualitative from definite nouns). The very fact that any member of a class is mentioned highlights to some degree that particular class–hence, making some kind of qualitative statement.

[27] Cf. also Mark 15:39 (and Harner's article) for a similar theologically significant text.

of the NWT) do so on the sole basis that the term is anarthrous. Yet they are inconsistent, as R. H. Countess pointed out:

> In the New Testament there are 282 occurrences of the anarthrous θεός. At sixteen places NWT has either a god, god, gods, or godly. Sixteen out of 282 means that the translators were faithful to *their* translation principle only six percent of the time. . . .
>
> The first section of John–1:1-18–furnishes a lucid example of NWT arbitrary dogmatism. Θεός occurs eight times–verses 1, 2, 6, 12, 13, 18–and has the article only twice–verses 1, 2. Yet NWT six times translated "God," once "a god," and once "the god."[28]

If we expand the discussion to other anarthrous terms in the Johannine Prologue, we notice other inconsistencies in the NWT: It is interesting that the *New World Translation* renders θεός as "a god" on the simplistic grounds that it lacks the article. This is surely an insufficient basis. Following the "anarthrous = indefinite" principle would mean that ἀρχῇ should be "a beginning" (1:1, 2), ζωή should be "a life" (1:4), παρὰ θεοῦ should be "from a god" (1:6), Ἰωάννης should be "a John" (1:6), θεόν should be "a god" (1:18), etc. Yet none of these other anarthrous nouns is rendered with an indefinite article. One can only suspect strong theological bias in such a translation.

According to Dixon's study, if θεός were *indefinite* in John 1:1, it would be the only anarthrous pre-verbal PN in John's Gospel to be so. Although we have argued that this is somewhat overstated, the general point is valid: The indefinite notion is the most poorly attested for anarthrous pre-verbal predicate nominatives. Thus, grammatically such a meaning is improbable. Also, the context suggests that such is not likely, for the Word already existed in the beginning. Thus, contextually and grammatically, it is highly improbable that the Logos could be "a god" according to John. Finally, the evangelist's own theology militates against this view, for there is an exalted Christology in the Fourth Gospel, to the point that Jesus Christ is identified as God (cf. 5:23; 8:58; 10:30; 20:28, etc.).

b. Is Θεός in John 1:1c Definite?

Grammarians and exegetes since Colwell have taken θεός as definite in John 1:1c. However, their basis has *usually* been a misunderstanding of Colwell's rule. They have understood the rule to say that an anarthrous pre-verbal PN will usually be definite (rather than the converse). But Colwell's rule states that a PN which is probably definite as determined from the *context* which precedes a verb will

---

[28] R. H. Countess, *The Jehovah's Witnesses' New Testament: A Critical Analysis of the* New World Translation of the Christian Greek Scriptures (Philipsburg, N. J.: Presbyterian and Reformed, 1982) 54-55.

usually be anarthrous. If we check the rule to see if it applies here, we would say that the previous mention of θεός (in 1:1b) is articular. Therefore, if the same person being referred to there is called θεός in 1:1c, then in both places it is definite. Although certainly possible grammatically (though not nearly as likely as qualitative), the evidence is not very compelling. The vast majority of *definite* anarthrous pre-verbal predicate nominatives are monadic, in genitive constructions, or are proper names, none of which is true here, diminishing the likelihood of a definite θεός in John 1:1c.

Further, calling θεός in 1:1c definite is the same as saying that if it had followed the verb it would have had the article. Thus it would be a convertible proposition with λόγος (i.e., "the Word" = "God" *and* "God" = "the Word"). The problem of this argument is that the θεός in 1:1b is the Father. Thus to say that the θεός in 1:1c is the same person is to say that "the Word was the *Father*."[29] This, as the older grammarians and exegetes pointed out, is embryonic Sabellianism or modalism.[30] The Fourth Gospel is about the least likely place to find modalism in the NT.

---

[29] This is not to say that in a given context Jesus could not be identified with ὁ θεός. In John 20:28, for example, where the crescendo of the Gospel comes in Thomas' confession, Jesus is called ὁ θεός. But there is nothing in that context that would identify him with the Father.

[30] Before 1933 NT commentators saw θεός as qualitative. For example, in Westcott's commentary on John: "It is necessarily without the article (θεός not ὁ θεός) inasmuch as it describes the nature of the Word and does not identify His Person. It would be pure Sabellianism to say 'the Word was ὁ θεός.'"

Robertson, *Grammar*, 767-68: "ὁ θεὸς ἦν ὁ λόγος (convertible terms) would have been pure Sabellianism . . . . The absence of the article here is on purpose and essential to the true idea."

Lange's commentary on John: "Θεός without the article signifies divine essence, or the generic idea of God in distinction from man and angel; as σάρξ, ver. 14, signifies the human essence or nature of the Logos. The article before θεός would here destroy the distinction of pesonality and confound the Son with the Father."

Chemnitz says: "θεός sine artic. essentialiter, cum artic. personaliter."

Alford points out: "The omission of the article before θεός is not *mere usage*; it could not have been here expressed, whatever place the words might hold in the sentence. ὁ λόγος ἦν ὁ θεός would destroy the idea of the λόγος altogether. θεός must then be taken as implying **God**, *in substance and essence*, –not ὁ θεός , 'the Father,' *in Person* . . . . as in σὰρξ ἐγένετο [John 1:14], σάρξ expresses that *state* into which the Divine Word entered by a definite act, so in θεὸς ἦν, θεός expresses that *essence* which was His ἐν ἀρχῇ: –that He was *very* God. So that this first verse might be connected thus: the Logos was from eternity, –was with God (the Father), –and was Himself God."

Luther states it succinctly: "'the Word was God' is against Arius; 'the Word was with God' against Sabellius."

c. Is Θεός in John 1:1c Qualitative?

The most likely candidate for θεός is qualitative. This is true both grammatically (for the largest proportion of pre-verbal anarthrous predicate nominatives fall into this category) and theologically (both the theology of the Fourth Gospel and of the NT as a whole). There is a balance between the Word's deity, which was already present in the beginning (ἐν ἀρχῇ . . . θεὸς ἦν [1:1], and his humanity, which was added later (σὰρξ ἐγένετο [1:14]). The grammatical structure of these two statements mirrors each other; both emphasize the nature of the Word, rather than his identity. But θεός was his nature from eternity (hence, εἰμί is used), while σάρξ was added at the incarnation (hence, γίνομαι is used).

Such an option does not at all impugn the deity of Christ. Rather, it stresses that, although the person of Christ is not the person of the Father, their *essence* is identical. Possible translations are as follows: "What God was, the Word was" (NEB), or "the Word was divine" (a modified Moffatt). In this second translation, "divine" is acceptable only if it is a term that can be applied *only* to true deity. However, in modern English, we use it with reference to angels, theologians, even a meal! Thus "divine" could be misleading in an English translation. The *idea* of a qualitative θεός here is that the Word had all the attributes and qualities that "the God" (of 1:1b) had. In other words, he shared the *essence* of the Father, though they differed in person. *The construction the evangelist chose to express this idea was the most concise way he could have stated that the Word was God and yet was distinct from the Father.*[31]

7. Appendix to Colwell's "Construction": When the Verb is Absent

When there is no verb, a PN, of course, cannot properly be called *pre*-verbal. However, there is one construction in which an *a*-copulative (that is, no verb) PN will have the same semantic value as the pre-verbal PN, viz., when the PN precedes the *subject*. Thus, although there are several passages in which the copula is lacking, the force of such texts can be determined by the word order of the PN and the subject.[32]

When the anarthrous PN stands before the subject, it will either be qualitative or definite. This is due to the fact that (1) had the verb been present, it more than likely would have come after the PN, and (2) by

---

[31] Although I believe that θεός in 1:1c is qualitative, I think the simplest and most straightforward translation is, "and the Word was God." It may be better to clearly affirm the NT teaching of the deity of Christ and then explain that he is *not* the Father, than to *sound* ambiguous on his deity and explain that he is God but is not the Father.

[32] The reason this is so is that whenever a word is thrown forward in the sentence it tends to be emphasized. Thus an anarthrous pre-verbal PN, by this word order shift, tends toward definiteness. So also an anarthrous a-verbal pre-subject PN.

placing the PN before the subject, an author is making the PN emphatic and if emphatic, then either qualitative or definite (since it is not normal to conceive of an *in*definite PN being emphasized, though not entirely impossible).

In John 4:24 Jesus says to the woman at the well, πνεῦμα ὁ θεός. The anarthrous PN comes before the subject and there is no verb. Here, πνεῦμα is qualitative–stressing the nature or essence of God (the KJV incorrectly renders this, "God is *a* spirit").

In Phil 2:11 Paul proclaims that κύριος Ἰησοῦς Χριστός ("Jesus Christ is Lord"). Here, as in John 4:24, there is no copula and the anarthrous PN comes before the subject. The PN in this instance is apparently definite; Jesus Christ is *the* Lord. Cf. also Phil 1:8 (with Rom 1:9).

In summary, when an anarthrous PN precedes a verbless subject, it will either be qualitative or definite just as would a pre-verbal anarthrous PN.

B. *The Article with Multiple Substantives Connected by Καί (Granville Sharp Rule and Related Constructions)*[33]

Introduction

In Greek, when two nouns are connected by καί and the article precedes only the first noun, there is a close connection between the two. That connection always indicates at least some sort of *unity.* At a higher level, it may connote *equality.* At the highest level it may indicate *identity.* When the construction meets three specific demands, then the two nouns *always* refer to the same person. When the construction does not meet these requirements, the nouns may or may not refer to the same person(s)/object(s).

1. Discovery of "Granville Sharp's Rule"

Granville Sharp, son of an archdeacon and grandson of an archbishop, was an English philanthropist and abolitionist (1735-1813). He is known to students of history as "the Abraham Lincoln of England" for his key role in the abolition of slavery there. Though untrained theologically, he was a student of the scriptures. His strong belief in Christ's deity led him to study the Bible in the original in order to defend more ably that belief. Through such motivation he became a relatively good linguist, able to handle both the Greek and Hebrew texts.[34] As he studied the scriptures in the original, he noticed a certain pattern, viz., when the construction article-substantive-καί-substantive (TSKS) involved personal nouns

---

[33] For a comprehensive treatment of this subject, see D. B. Wallace, "The Article with Multiple Substantives Connected by Καί in the New Testament: Semantics and Significance" (Ph.D. dissertation, Dallas Theological Seminary, 1995), to be published by Peter Lang Publishers, c. 1997.

which were singular and not proper names, they always referred to the same person. He noticed further that such a rule applied, in several texts[35] to the deity of Jesus Christ. So in 1798 he published a short volume entitled, *Remarks on the Definitive Article in the Greek Text of the New Testament, Containing Many New Proofs of the Divinity of Christ, from Passages Which Are Wrongly Translated in the Common English Version* [KJV].[36] The volume went through four editions (three English and one American).[37]

➡ ### 2. Statement of the Rule

Sharp actually penned six rules on the use of the article, but the first of these is what has become known as Sharp's rule because of its import for texts dealing with the deity of Christ. Hence, "it is of much more consequence than the rest. . . ."[38] The rule is as follows:

> When the copulative καὶ connects two nouns of the same case, [viz. nouns (either substantive or adjective, or participles) of personal description, respecting office, dignity, affinity, or connexion, and attributes, properties, or qualities, good or ill], if the article ὁ, or any of its cases, precedes the first of the said nouns or participles, and is not repeated before the second noun or participle, the latter always relates to the same person that is expressed or described by the first noun or participle: i.e. it denotes a farther description of the first-named person . . . .[39]

Although Sharp discusses here only personal substantives in the singular, it is not clear from this statement whether he intended to restrict his rule to such. However, a perusal of his monograph reveals that he felt the rule could be applied absolutely only to personal, singular, non-proper nouns.[40]

In other words, in the TSKS construction, the second noun[41] refers to the *same* person mentioned with the first noun when:

---

[34] Among the nearly 70 volumes that Sharp wrote (most of which had to do with social issues, especially slavery) were 16 works in biblical studies. One of his first books, in fact, dealt with the textual criticism of the OT and was a critique of the work of the great Oxford Hebrew scholar, Benjamin Kennicott. Sharp also penned a volume on Hebrew pronunciation as well as one on Hebrew syntax in which he formulated rules about the *waw*-consecutive still considered valid today.

[35] He had more than the two we here consider to be legitimate. His other texts involved either textual variants which we do not regard as original or items which do not meet Sharp's basic criteria as he has laid them down.

[36] Published in Durham by L. Pennington.

[37] For a more detailed life of Granville Sharp, see Wallace, "The Article with Multiple Substantives," 30-42. All citations of Sharp's monograph are from the latest edition, the first American edition (Philadelphia: B. B. Hopkins, 1807).

[38] Sharp, *Remarks on the Uses of the Definitive Article*, 2.

[39] Ibid., 3 (italics in the original).

[40] See Wallace, "The Article with Multiple Substantives," 47-48, for documentation.

[41] By "noun" we mean what Sharp meant: substantival adjective, substantival participle, or noun.

(1) neither is *im*personal;

(2) neither is *plural*;

(3) neither is a *proper* name.[42]

Therefore, according to Sharp, the rule applied absolutely *only* with personal, singular, and non-proper nouns. The significance of these requirements can hardly be overestimated, for those who have misunderstood Sharp's principle have done so almost without exception because they were unaware of the restrictions that Sharp set forth.

3.   The Neglect and Abuse of Sharp's Rule

One of the interesting ironies in the history of biblical studies is that Sharp's rule, which early on found massive and well-documented support among classical grammarians and patristic scholars, was almost felled by one unsubstantiated footnote. G. B. Winer, the great NT grammarian of the nineteenth century, wrote:

> In Tit. ii. 13. . . considerations derived from Paul's system of doctrine lead me to believe that σωτῆρος is not a second predicate, co-ordinate with θεοῦ.
>
> . . . .
>
> [In n 2 at the bottom of the same page] In the above remarks it was not my intention to deny that, in point of *grammar*, σωτῆρος ἡμῶν may be regarded as a second predicate, jointly depending on the article τοῦ; but the dogmatic conviction derived from Paul's writings that this apostle cannot have called Christ *the great God* induced me to show that there is no grammatical obstacle to our taking the clause καὶ σωτ. . . . Χριστοῦ by itself, as referring to a second subject.[43]

Although he advances no real grammatical arguments, because he was a highly regarded grammarian Winer was able to cancel out, by the intimidation of his own opinion, the use of Sharp's rule in passages such as Titus 2:13 and 2 Pet 1:1. This statement virtually sounded the death knell to Sharp's rule.[44] From this point on, scholars were either tentative about the validity of Sharp's rule or else were unsure about its requirements.[45] For example, Moulton flatly states: "We cannot discuss here the problem of Tit 2[13], for we must, *as grammarians*, leave the matter open:

---

[42] A *proper* noun is defined as a noun which *cannot* be "pluralized"–thus it does *not* include titles. A person's name, therefore, is proper and consequently does not fit the rule. But θεός is not proper because it can be pluralized–thus, when θεός is in a TSKS construction in which both nouns are singular and personal, it fits Sharp's rule. Since θεοί is possible (cf. John 10:34), θεός is not a proper name. For a detailed discussion on the grammatical use of θεός in the NT, cf. B. Weiss, "Der Gebrauch des Artikels bei den Gottesnamen," *TSK* 84 (1911) 319-92, 503-38; R. W. Funk, "The Syntax of the Greek Article: Its Importance for Critical Pauline Problems" (Ph.D. dissertation, Vanderbilt University, 1953) 46, 154-67; Wallace, "The Article with Multiple Substantives," 260-63.

[43] Winer-Moulton, 162.

[44] Today, scholars tend either to reject Pauline authorship of the pastorals or an affirmation of Christ's deity in them. One cannot have both Paul and Christ, it seems.

[45] For documentation, see Wallace, "The Article with Multiple Substantives," 53-80, esp. 66-80.

see WM [Winer-Moulton] 162, 156n."[46] And Dana and Mantey–on whose grammar many American students have been weaned–actually reproduce (almost) verbatim Sharp's rule, but neglect to specify more clearly the limitations.[47]

The upshot of the imprecise knowledge of Sharp's limitations is that those who invoke his canon on behalf of the argument for Christ's deity in Titus 2:13, etc., since they place plurals and impersonals under the rubric of the rule, are unable to regard the rule as absolute. In other words, the exceptions they find to the rule are actually outside the scope of the rule and are thus not exceptions at all.[48]

➡ **4.   Validity of the Rule Within the New Testament**

We have not established the validity of Sharp's canon thus far, but we have argued that it has been widely misunderstood. In this section our goal is to demonstrate its validity within the pages of the NT.

➡   **a.   In General**

Not counting the christologically significant passages, there are 80 constructions in the NT which fit the *requirements* for Sharp's rule.[49] But do they all fit the *semantics* of the rule–that is, do the substantives always refer to one and the same person? In a word, yes. Even Sharp's opponents could not find any exceptions; all had to admit that the rule was valid in the NT.[50]

---

[46] Moulton, *Prolegomena*, 84 (italics added).

[47] Dana-Mantey, 147.

[48] The list of those who have misunderstood the rule include such notable scholars as J. H. Moulton, A. T. Robertson, Dana-Mantey, M. J. Harris, F. F. Bruce, C. F. D. Moule, et al.

[49] This number is disputed by some, either due to textual variants, inclusion of impersonal nouns and/or plural nouns, or a different interpretation on certain participles (viz., those which I consider to be adjectival are sometimes regarded as substantival by others and hence included in the count by them).

[50] The most formidable foe to Sharp's rule was Calvin Winstanley (*A Vindication of Certain Passages in the Common English Version of the New Testament: Addressed to Granville Sharp, Esq.*, 2d ed. [Cambridge: University Press–Hilliard and Metcalf, 1819]). Yet even he agreed that Sharp's principle was generally valid, going so far as to say, "your first rule has a real foundation in the idiom of the language . . ." (36). And further, within the pages of the NT, Winstanley conceded "There are, you say, no exceptions, in the New Testament, to your rule; that is, I suppose, unless these particular texts [i.e., the ones Sharp used to adduce Christ's deity] be such. . . . it is nothing surprising to find all these particular texts in question appearing as exceptions to your rule, and the sole exceptions . . . in the New Testament . . ." (39-40)–an obvious concession that he could find no exceptions save for the ones he supposed to exist in the christologically pregnant texts.

On the other side of the ledger, in C. Kuehne's lengthy study, "The Greek Article and the Doctrine of Christ's Deity," *Journal of Theology* 13 (September 1973) 12-28; 13 (December 1973) 14-30; 14 (March 1974) 11-20; 14 (June 1974) 16-25; 14 (September 1974) 21-33; 14 (December 1974) 8-19, the Lutheran scholar summarizes his findings: ". . . we have seen that in the New Testament there are no exceptions at all to the rule!" (*Journal of Theology* 14.4 [1974] 10).

Below are listed several representative passages of Sharp's rule, including nouns, participles, adjectives, and mixed constructions.

1) Nouns in the TSKS Personal Construction

Mark 6:3   οὗτός ἐστιν ὁ τέκτων, **ὁ υἱὸς** τῆς Μαρίας **καὶ ἀδελφὸς** Ἰακώβου[51]
             this is the carpenter, **the son** of Mary **and brother** of James

John 20:17   **τὸν πατέρα** μου **καὶ πατέρα** ὑμῶν **καὶ θεόν** μου **καὶ θεὸν** ὑμῶν
             my **Father and** your **Father and** my **God and** your **God**

> The construction here is unusual in that it involves four nouns. The possessive pronouns are used to show the differences in how Jesus and his disciples relate to God, but they do not imply that a different person is in view: the first person of the Trinity is the referent for all four nouns. It is also significant that one of the substantives is θεός. This is a good illustration of the fact that θεός is not a proper noun (from the Greek perspective), for whenever a proper name occurs in Sharp's construction two persons are in view. Yet, whenever θεός is in this construction, one person is in view.

Eph 6:21   Τυχικὸς ὁ ἀγαπητὸς **ἀδελφὸς καὶ** πιστὸς **διάκονος**
             Tychicus, **the** beloved **brother and** faithful **servant**

Heb 3:1   **τὸν ἀπόστολον καὶ ἀρχιερέα** τῆς ὁμολογίας ἡμῶν Ἰησοῦν
             Jesus, **the apostle and high priest** of our confession

1 Pet 1:3   **ὁ θεὸς καὶ πατὴρ** τοῦ κυρίου ἡμῶν Ἰησοῦ Χριστοῦ
             the God and Father of our Lord Jesus Christ

Rev 1:9   ἐγὼ Ἰωάννης, **ὁ ἀδελφὸς** ὑμῶν **καὶ συγκοινωνός** ἐν τῇ θλίψει καὶ βασιλείᾳ
             I, John, your **brother and fellow-partaker** in the tribulation and kingdom

> This text involves two TSKS constructions, one personal and one impersonal. It is obvious that the personal construction fits the rule (John is both brother of and fellow-participant with his readers), while the impersonal construction just as obviously does not (the tribulation is not identical with the kingdom).

Cf. also Luke 20:37; Rom 15:6; 2 Cor 1:3; 11:31; Gal 1:4; Eph 1:3; 5:20; Phil 4:20; Col 4:7; 1 Thess 1:3; 3:11, 13; 1 Tim 6:15; Heb 12:2; Jas 1:27; 3:9; 1 Pet 2:25; 5:1; 2 Pet 1:11; 2:20; 3:2, 18; Rev 1:6.

2) Participles in the TSKS Personal Construction

Matt 27:40   **ὁ καταλύων** τὸν ναὸν **καὶ** ἐν τρισὶν ἡμέραις **οἰκοδομῶν**, σῶσον σεαυτόν
             [you,] **the one who would destroy** the temple **and** in three days **build** [it up], save yourself

John 6:33   **ὁ καταβαίνων** ἐκ τοῦ οὐρανοῦ **καὶ** ζωὴν **διδούς**
             the one who comes down from heaven **and who gives life**

---

[51] ℵ D L 892* add ὁ before ἀδελφός; (Θ) 565 700 892ᶜ omit the καί, thus retaining the apposition.

Acts 15:38 τὸν **ἀποστάντα** ἀπ᾽ αὐτῶν ἀπὸ Παμφυλίας **καὶ** μὴ **συνελθόντα** αὐτοῖς
the one who had withdrawn from them in Pamphilia **and had** not
gone on with them

Eph 2:14 ὁ **ποιήσας** τὰ ἀμφότερα ἓν **καὶ** τὸ μεσότοιχον τοῦ φραγμοῦ **λύσας**
the one who made both into one **and who destroyed** the middle
wall of partition

> This text well illustrates that even when there are several intervening
> words, the construction is not thereby invalidated.

Jas 1:25 ὁ δὲ **παρακύψας** εἰς νόμον τέλειον τὸν τῆς ἐλευθερίας **καὶ παραμείνας**
. . . οὗτος μακάριος ἐν τῇ ποιήσει αὐτοῦ ἔσται
but **the one who looks** into [the] perfect law, the law of liberty, **and**
perseveres . . . he shall be blessed in what he does

Rev 22:8 κἀγὼ Ἰωάννης ὁ **ἀκούων καὶ βλέπων** ταῦτα
And I, John, **the one who hears and sees** these things

Cf. also Matt 7:26; 13:20; Mark 15:29; Luke 6:47; 16:18; John 5:24; 6:54; 9:8; Acts 10:35; 1 Cor
11:29; 2 Cor 1:21, 22; Gal 1:15; 2 Thess 2:4; Heb 7:1; 1 John 2:4, 9; 2 John 9; Rev 1:5; 16:15.

3) Adjectives in the TSKS Personal Construction

Acts 3:14 ὑμεῖς δὲ **τὸν ἅγιον καὶ δίκαιον** ἠρνήσασθε
you have denied **the holy and righteous one**

Rev 3:17 σὺ εἶ ὁ **ταλαίπωρος καὶ ἐλεεινὸς καὶ πτωχὸς καὶ τυφλὸς καὶ γυμνός**[52]
you are the **wretched and pitiable and poor and blind and naked**
one!

Cf. also Phlm 1.

4) Mixed Elements in the TSKS Personal Construction

Phil 2:25 Ἐπαφρόδιτον **τὸν ἀδελφὸν καὶ συνεργὸν καὶ συστρατιώτην** μου
Epaphroditus, my **brother and fellow-worker and fellow-soldier**

> This passage illustrates the fact that a possessive pronoun added to one
> of the nouns does not invalidate the rule.

1 Tim 5:5 ἡ ὄντως **χήρα καὶ μεμονωμένη**
the one who is really **a widow and left alone**[53]

Cf. also 1 Thess 3:2.

The monotonous pattern of personal singular substantives in the
TSKS construction indicating an identical referent immediately
places such substantives in a different category from proper names,
impersonal nouns, or plural nouns. The statistics accentuate this difference: In the TSKS construction there are about a dozen personal
proper names in the NT (none having an identical referent); close to

---

[52] An article before ἐλεεινός is added by A 1006 1611 1841 2329 2351 *et alii*.

[53] Although it is possible that μεμονωμένη is a predicate participle, its linkage to χήρα
by καί suggests that it, too, is substantival.

fifty impersonal nouns (only one unambiguously having the same referent); more than seventy plural substantives (little more than a third having an identical referent); and *eighty* TSKS constructions fitting the structural requirements of the rule (the christologically significant texts excepted), *all* of which apparently having an identical referent. It is evident that Sharp's limitation to personal singular substantives does indeed have substance.

➡ **b. For Christologically Significant Texts**

Granville Sharp believed that several christologically significant texts involved the TSKS construction.[54] However, several of these involved dubious textual variants (e.g., Acts 20:28; Jude 4), and others had proper names (Eph 5:5; 2 Thess 1:12; 1 Tim 5:21; 2 Tim 4:1).[55]

This leaves two passages, Titus 2:13 and 2 Pet 1:1.

Titus 2:13   τοῦ μεγάλου **θεοῦ καὶ σωτῆρος** ἡμῶν Ἰησοῦ Χριστοῦ
our great **God and Savior**, Jesus Christ

> It has frequently been alleged that θεός is a proper name and, hence, that Sharp's rule cannot apply to constructions in which it is employed. We have already argued that θεός is not a proper name in Greek.[56] We simply wish to point out here that in the TSKS construction θεός is used over a dozen times in the NT (e.g., Luke 20:37; John 20:27; Rom 15:6; 2 Cor 1:3; Gal 1:4; Jas 1:27) and always (if we exclude the christologically significant texts) in reference to one person. This phenomenon is not true of any other proper name in said construction (every instance involving true proper names always points to two individuals). Since that argument carries no weight, there is no good reason to reject Titus 2:13 as an explicit affirmation of the deity of Christ.

2 Pet 1:1   τοῦ **θεοῦ** ἡμῶν **καὶ σωτῆρος**, Ἰησοῦ Χριστοῦ[57]
our God and Savior, Jesus Christ

> Some grammarians have objected that since ἡμῶν is connected with θεοῦ, two persons are in view.[58] The pronoun seems to "bracket" the

---

[54] One text that Sharp did not deal with is 1 John 5:20. Whether this even fits Sharp's rule is debatable. For a discussion, see Wallace, "The Article with Multiple Substantives," 271-77.

[55] It is somewhat surprising that many scholars (most notably, R. Bultmann) have embraced 2 Thess 1:12 as an explicit affirmation of Christ's deity. Only by detaching κυρίου from Ἰησοῦ Χριστοῦ could one apply Sharp's rule to this construction. But significantly, Middleton, whose *Doctrine of the Greek Article* was the first major work to support Sharp's rule, rejects 2 Thess 1:12, arguing that (1) κυρίου should not be detached from Ἰησοῦ Χριστοῦ, since the whole forms a common title in the epistles, thus partaking of the properties of a proper name; and (2) although Greek patristic writers employed the wording of Titus 2:13 and 2 Pet 1:1 on numerous occasions to affirm the deity of Christ, they have hardly noticed this passage (*Doctrine of the Greek Article*, 379-82). Cf. also Matthews, *Syntax*, 228-29, for modern linguistic arguments related to gradations of apposition (in 2 Thess 1:12 most exegetes would see "Lord Jesus Christ" as constituting a "close apposition").

[56] See earlier discussion under "Statement of the Rule."

[57] ℵ Ψ *et pauci* have κυρίου instead of θεοῦ.

noun, effectively isolating the trailing noun. However in v 11 of this same chapter (as well as in 2:20 and 3:18), the author writes τοῦ κυρίου ἡμῶν καὶ σωτῆρος, Ἰησοῦ Χριστοῦ, an expression which refers to one person, Jesus Christ: "Why refuse to apply the same rule to 2 Peter i. 1, that all admit . . . to be true of 2 Peter i. 11 [not to mention 2:20 and 3:18]?"[59] Further, more than half of the NT texts that fit Sharp's rule involve some intervening word between the two substantives. Several of them have an intervening possessive pronoun or other gen. modifier.[60] Yet, in all of these constructions only one person is clearly in view.[61] In all such instances the intervening term had no effect on breaking the construction. This being the case, there is no good reason for rejecting 2 Pet 1:1 as an explicit affirmation of the deity of Christ.[62]

➡ 5. Constructions Involving Impersonal, Plural, and Proper Nouns

a. Proper Names

Always in the NT, whenever proper names are in the equation, distinct individuals are in view. For example, we read of "Peter and James and John" (τὸν Πέτρον καὶ Ἰάκωβον καὶ Ἰωάννην) in Matt 17:1; "Mary Magdalene and Mary . . ." (ἡ δὲ Μαρία ἡ Μαγδαληνὴ καὶ Μαρία) in Mark 15:47; "Martha and Mary" (τὴν Μάρθαν καὶ Μαριάμ) in John 11:19; "Barnabas and Saul" (τὸν Βαρναβᾶν καὶ Σαῦλον) in Acts 13:2. Yet at the same time they are united under one article for the purposes at hand. Peter and James and John were the inner circle of disciples (Matt 17:1), Martha and Mary were sisters (John 11:19),

---

[58] E.g., E. Stauffer, θεός, *TDNT* 3.106.

[59] A. T. Robertson, "The Greek Article and the Deity of Christ," *The Expositor*, 8th Series, vol 21 (1921) 185.

[60] Cf. John 20:17; 2 Cor 1:3; 1 Thess 3:2; 1 Tim 6:15; Heb 12:2; Rev 1:9.

[61] In a sampling of the non-literary papyri, I have found the same phenomenon, and, once again, the genitive attached to the first noun *never* broke the force of Sharp's principle. For example, P. Lond. 417.1 reads "to my master and beloved brother" (τῷ δεσπότῃ μου καὶ ἀγαπητῷ ἀδελφῷ); P. Oxy. 2106. 24-25 addresses "my lord and brother" (τῷ κυρίῳ μου καὶ ἀδελφῷ).

[62] There is some interesting confirmation of Sharp's rule, as applied to the christologically pregnant texts, in patristic literature. In 1802 a fellow (and later, master) of Trinity College in Cambridge, Christopher Wordsworth, published his *Six Letters to Granville Sharp, Esq. Respecting his Remarks on the Uses of the Definitive Article, in the Greek Text of the New Testament* (London: F. and C. Rivington, 1802). Wordsworth tested Sharp's principle in the patristic literature. He felt that if the principle was valid, then the Greek fathers would certainly have understood the christologically significant texts in the same way that Sharp had. At one point he gushed, "I fully believe, that there is no one exception to your first rule in the whole New Testament: and the assertion might be extended infinitely further" (ibid., 103). After an exhaustive investigation, from Greek Christian literature covering a span of over 1000 years, Wordsworth was able to make the astounding comment, "I have observed . . . some hundreds of instances of the ὁ μέγας θεὸς καὶ σωτήρ (Tit. ii. 13); and not fewer than several thousands of the form ὁ θεὸς καὶ σωτήρ (2 Pet. i. 1.)[,] while in no single case, have I seen (where the sense could be determined) any of them used, but only of *one* person" (ibid., 132). Therefore, as far as Wordsworth was concerned, the TSKS constructions which involve the deity of Christ, both in the NT and in the Greek church fathers, were never ambiguous, but fully supported Sharp's proposition.

Barnabas and Saul had been set apart for a particular task (Acts 13:2). There is a reason for the lone article in every instance, viz., to conceptualize a contextually-defined coherent group. But because the nouns are proper, the article does not identify one with the other.

➡   **b.   Plural Personal Constructions**[63]

1)   Semantics and the NT Data

Several NT scholars who embraced Sharp's rule have assumed without warrant that it applied to plural substantives. Others who have understood Sharp's requirement of singular substantives have nevertheless assumed that plural substantives either must have the same referent or entirely discrete referents. Their semantic approach is inadequate in that the only question they raise is: Are the two groups identical or distinct? Such a question for the singular, personal construction is of course adequate; either the first-named person is identical with the second-named person or he is distinct. But the very nature of a *plural* construction demands that several other questions be asked if we are to see its full semantic range. That is, since the plural construction deals with *groups*, there may be other possibilities besides absolute distinction and absolute identity.

Theoretically, in fact, there are five semantic possibilities for the plural TSKS construction: (1) distinct groups, though united; (2) overlapping groups; (3) first group subset of second; (4) second group subset of first; and (5) both groups identical. In the NT all groups are represented, though they are not evenly distributed. We will discuss the statistics after a brief look at some examples.

2)   Unambiguous Illustrations

a)   Distinct Groups, though United

At all times the lone article in the TSKS construction suggests some sort of unity. A large number of instances in the NT imply nothing more. We can readily see this in English. In the sentence "the Democrats and Republicans approved the bill unanimously," the two political parties, though distinct, are united on a particular issue.[64]

---

[63] For a detailed discussion, see Wallace, "The Article with Multiple Substantives," 136-63, 219-44. In more embryonic form, though with largely the same conclusions, see D. B. Wallace, "The Semantic Range of the Article-Noun-Καί-Noun Plural Construction in the New Testament," *GTJ* 4 (1983) 59-84.

[64] Perhaps this illustration is not as true to life as intended!

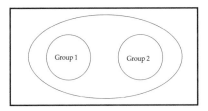

Chart 28
Distinct Groups, though United[65]

Matt 3:7   τῶν Φαρισαίων καὶ Σαδδουκαίων
the Pharisees and Sadducees

> Although these two parties were distinct, the article unites them for the purposes at hand. This is the first mention of either Pharisees or Sadducees in Matthew's Gospel, and it may be significant that the evangelist presents these two parties which were historically opposed to one another as united in their opposition to the Messiah's forerunner. The Pharisees and the Sadducees are listed together only four other times in Matthew; in each instance the structure is TSKS and the two groups are set in opposition to Jesus.[66]

Matt 16:21   τῶν πρεσβυτέρων καὶ ἀρχιερέων καὶ γραμματέων
the elders and chief priests and scribes

> These were the three distinct parties which comprised the Sanhedrin. (Some have erroneously insisted that this construction fits Sharp's rule because these three groups all refer to the Sanhedrin. However, to say that A + B + C = D is not the same as saying A = B = C, the latter equation being what Sharp's rule asserts.[67])

Acts 17:12   τῶν . . . γυναικῶν . . . καὶ ἀνδρῶν
the . . . women . . . and men

Cf. also Matt 2:4; Mark 15:1; Luke 9:22.

b)   Overlapping Groups

> English illustrations suggesting overlapping groups are easily produced: "the poor and sick," "the blind and elderly," etc. In the NT, however, this is a scantily attested category, with only three examples.

---

[65] In this and the following figures, the article before the first substantive and the καί between the substantives are omitted because the figures are intended to depict the *semantics*, not the structure, of the TSKS construction.

[66] See Matt 16:1, 6, 11, 12. See also Acts 23:7 for the only other instance of those two groups in this construction.

[67] The difference between the two formulae is the difference between equality of status and identity of referent. Only if the scribes referred to the same group as the elders could Sharp's principle be invoked.

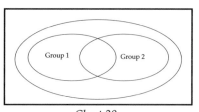

Chart 29
Overlapping Groups

Rev 21:8   τοῖς δὲ **δειλοῖς καὶ ἀπίστοις καὶ ἐβδελυγμένοις καὶ φονεῦσιν καὶ πόρνοις καὶ φαρμάκοις καὶ εἰδωλολάτραις** . . . τὸ μέρος αὐτῶν ἐν τῇ λίμνῃ τῇ καιομένῃ πυρὶ καὶ θείῳ

now as for **the cowardly and unfaithful and abominable and murderers and fornicators and sorcerers and idolaters** . . . their portion shall be in the lake that burns with fire and sulfur

> It is obvious here that the Lake of Fire is not reserved *only* for those who meet *all* of the "qualifications," nor for those meeting only one requirement. Overlapping groups is the intended meaning.

Cf. also Matt 4:24; Luke 14:21.

c)   First Group Subset of Second

When we say that the first group is a subset of the second, we mean that it is entirely subsumed within the second-named group. The idea would be "the X and [other] Y." For example, "the deaf and handicapped," the angels and created beings," "the citizens and residents."

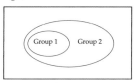

Chart 30
First Group Subset of Second

Matt 9:11   **τῶν τελωνῶν καὶ ἁμαρτωλῶν**
          the tax-collectors and [other] sinners

Luke 14:3   ὁ Ἰησοῦς εἶπεν πρὸς **τοὺς νομικοὺς καὶ Φαρισαίους**
          Jesus spoke to **the lawyers and [other] Pharisees**

Cf. also Matt 5:20; 12:38; Mark 2:16; Luke 5:30; 6:35.

d)   Second Group Subset of First

Sometimes the order between the elements is reversed from "first subset of second." The terms in the illustrations above can be flip-flopped: "the created beings and angels," "the handicapped and deaf," etc. The idea is "the X and [in particular] Y."

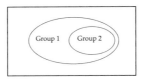

Chart 31
Second Group Subset of First

Mark 2:16 ἰδόντες ὅτι ἐσθίει μετὰ **τῶν ἁμαρτωλῶν καὶ τελωνῶν** ἔλεγον τοῖς μαθηταῖς αὐτοῦ· ὅτι μετὰ τῶν τελωνῶν καὶ ἁμαρτωλῶν ἐσθίει;[68]

when they saw that he was eating with **the sinners and tax-collectors** they said to his disciples, "Why does he eat with the tax-collectors and sinners?"

> There are two plural TSKS constructions in this verse, both using the same wording but in different order. The first instance is that of second group subset of first; the second instance is first subset of second.

1 Cor 5:10 τοῖς πλεονέκταις καὶ ἅρπαξιν[69]

the greedy and swindlers

> Although one could be greedy without being branded a swindler, it is doubtful that the reverse could be true. The idea, then, is "the greedy and [especially] swindlers."

Cf. also 1 Tim 5:8; 3 John 5.

e) Both Groups Identical

The idea of identical groups is "the X who are Y." The second substantive functions either in a descriptive or restrictive manner. For example, "the San Francisco Forty-Niners and world champions of football," "those eating well and exercising will get strong." This category has greater attestation than any of the others in the NT, though it is not

---

[68] ℵ A C *f*[1, 13] *Byz et alii* have τῶν τελωνῶν καὶ ἁμαρτωλῶν for τῶν ἁμαρτωλῶν καὶ τελωνῶν.

[69] ἤ is read for καί in 𝔓[46] ℵ[2] D[2] Ψ *Byz*, nullifying the construction in a large (though admittedly inferior) portion of the Greek witnesses to this text. The Chester Beatty papyrus, though early, is hardly a carefully copied MS. Unless it is found in company with other early and reliable witnesses, its voice needs to be somewhat discounted. See the magisterial study by Günther Zuntz on this codex (*The Text of the Epistles: A Disquisition on the Corpus Paulinum* [London: Oxford University Press, 1953]). From my preliminary research, I have noticed that the second corrector of codex Claromontanus almost always assimilates to the Byzantine text. Thus, this reading is not as formidable as it at first appears.

at all found among noun+noun TSKS plural constructions.[70]

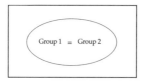

Chart 32
Both Groups Identical

John 20:29   μακάριοι **οἱ μὴ ἰδόντες καὶ πιστεύσαντες**
             blessed are **those who have** not **seen and** [yet] **believe**

> The negative stipulation of not seeing the risen Lord is inadequate to
> procure a blessing. And, in this context, the Lord is pronouncing a
> blessing on those who believe apart from seeing him, in contrast to
> Thomas.

Eph 1:1   **τοῖς ἁγίοις** τοῖς οὖσιν [ἐν Ἐφέσῳ] **καὶ πιστοῖς** ἐν Χριστῷ Ἰησοῦ
             to the saints who are [in Ephesus] **and who are faithful** in Christ
             Jesus

> A. T. Lincoln, who regards Ephesians as a pseudonymous work, still
> can argue that in light of the detectable fingerprints of Pauline theology,
> it is doubtful that the author would be specifying two groups which
> could be distinguished in any way.[71] And M. Barth, who embraces
> Pauline authorship of Ephesians, makes a good case that
>
> > It is unlikely that Paul wanted to distinguish two classes
> > among the Christians, i.e. a "faithful" group from another
> > larger or smaller group that is "holy." Such a distinction
> > would be unparalleled in the Pauline letters. Even the wild
> > Corinthians are called "sanctified" and "perfect" (1 Cor 1:2;
> > 2:6). While occasionally Paul presupposes a sharp division
> > between "those outside" and "those inside," between "the
> > unbelieving" and "the faithful," he has no room for half- or
> > three-quarter Christians. It is probable that here the Greek
> > conjunction "and" has the meaning of "namely." It serves the
> > purpose of explication and may therefore occasionally be
> > omitted in translation if its intent is preserved.[72]

---

[70] That is, of those texts that are unambiguous. A basic reason that participles (and
occasionally adjectives) fit this "identical" category, but not nouns, is that nouns tend to
focus on innate, stable, or permanent qualities, while participles tend to focus on activities
within an (often unstated) time-frame which may or may not be characteristic. Thus one
who is presently telling the truth is not necessarily an honest person, one playing baseball
is not necessarily a baseball player, those who study are not necessarily students. However, when an activity marks a person in such a way that it becomes characteristic, the
descriptions of such a person sometimes metamorphose from participles into nouns.

[71] Lincoln, *Ephesians* (WBC) 3-7.

[72] Barth, *Ephesians* (AB) 1.68.

Rev 1:3   μακάριος ὁ ἀναγινώσκων καὶ **οἱ ἀκούοντες** τοὺς λόγους τῆς προφητείας **καὶ τηροῦντες** τὰ ἐν αὐτῇ γεγραμμένα[73]

blessed is the one who reads and **those who hear** the words of this prophecy **and keep** the things written in it

> It is evident that the one who only hears the prophecy and does not obey it falls short of the blessing. The twofold response of hearing and keeping is necessary if one is to be counted among the μακάριοι.

Cf. also Matt 5:6; Mark 12:40; Luke 7:32; John 1:20; 2 Cor 12:21; Phil 3:3; 1 Thess 5:12; 2 Pet 2:10; 2 John 9; Rev 18:9.

f) Summary

There are 62 unambiguous passages out of 73; the breakdown is as follows:

Distinct	26% of total; 31% of clearly marked constructions
Overlap	4% and 5%
First subset	10% and 11%
Second subset	5.5% and 6.5%
Identical	40% and 47%

Table 3
Semantics of Plural Personal TSKS Constructions

With reference to the types of substantives used (counting only the unambiguous passages), the following table reveals some interesting patterns:

	Distinct	*Overlap*	*1st Subset of 2nd*	*2nd Subset of 1st*	*Identical*	**Totals**
Noun + Noun	11		2			13
Adjective + Adjective		1	1	1	2	5
Participle + Participle					24	24
Mixed: Non-Participial	8		4	3	2	17
Mixed: With Participle		2			1	3
Totals	19	3	7	4	29	62

Table 4
Types of Substantives Used in the Plural Personal Construction

---

[73] 2053 2062 *et pauci* read ἀκούων instead of οἱ ἀκούοντες.

3) Exegetically and Theologically Significant Texts

There are several ambiguous plural TSKS constructions, two of which have particular exegetical value.[74]

Eph 4:11   αὐτὸς ἔδωκεν τοὺς μὲν ἀποστόλους, τοὺς δὲ προφήτας, τοὺς δὲ εὐαγγελιστάς, **τοὺς δὲ ποιμένας καὶ διδασκάλους**

he gave some as apostles, some as prophets, some as evangelists, **some [as] pastors and teachers**

> This text discusses the gifted leaders whom Christ has given to the Church for her maturity. The debate over this text has focused on the issue of whether one gift or two are mentioned. Most commentators have seen only one gift here, but primarily because they erroneously thought that the Granville Sharp rule absolutely applied to plural constructions. Also, against the "one gift" view, there are no clear examples of *nouns* being used in a plural TSKS construction to specify one group. However, we are not shut up to the "entirely distinct groups" option only.

> The uniting of these two groups by one article sets them apart from the other gifted leaders. Absolute distinction, then, is probably not in view. In light of the fact that elders and pastors had similar functions in the NT,[75] since elders were to be teachers,[76] the pastors were also to be teachers.[77] Further, presumably not all teachers were elders or pastors.[78] This evidence seems to suggest that the ποιμένας were a part of the διδασκάλους in Eph 4:11. This likelihood is in keeping with the semantics of the plural noun construction, for the first-subset-of-second category is well-attested in both the clear and ambiguous texts in the NT. Thus, Eph 4:11 seems to affirm that all pastors were to be teachers, though not all teachers were to be pastors.[79]

Eph 2:20   ἐποικοδομηθέντες ἐπὶ τῷ θεμελίῳ **τῶν ἀποστόλων καὶ προφητῶν**

having been built upon the foundation **of the apostles and prophets**

> This text has become something of a theological lightning rod in conservative circles in America in the past several years, largely due to the work of Wayne Grudem.[80] Grudem argues that the apostles and prophets are identical here. This is important to his view of NT prophecy: on the one hand, he holds to a high view of scripture, viz., that the autographs are inerrant; on the other hand, he believes that *non*-apostolic

---

[74] For a detailed discussion of these texts, as well as the other ambiguous passages (e.g., Matt 21:12; Acts 15:2; Eph 3:5; Heb 5:2), see Wallace, "The Article with Multiple Substantives," 219-44.

[75] See A. M. Malphurs, "The Relationship of Pastors and Teachers in Ephesians 4:11" (Th.M. thesis, Dallas Theological Seminary, 1978) 46-53.

[76] Ibid., 52-53.

[77] Ibid., 41-46.

[78] This is difficult to assess since only in Eph 4:11 are pastors and teachers mentioned together. But a few texts mention teachers without any hint that they must also be pastors. Cf. Rom 12:7; 1 Cor 12:28-29; Heb 5:12; Jas 3:1; perhaps also 2 Tim 2:2.

[79] Cf. also F. Rienecker, *Der Brief des Paulus an die Epheser* (Wuppertal: R. Brockhaus, 1961) 146; [J.] Calvin, *The Epistles of Paul to the Galatians, Ephesians, Philippians and Colossians* (Grand Rapids: Eerdmans, 1965) 179, for a similar conclusion (though neither one bases his views on syntactical considerations).

prophets both in the early church and today mixed error with truth. If in Eph 2:20 the Church is built on the foundation of apostles and *other* prophets, then it would seem that Grudem either has to deny inerrancy or affirm that non-apostolic prophets only spoke truth (and were thus on par with OT prophets). Hence, he spends much ink arguing that *in this text* the prophets are identical with the apostles, while elsewhere in the NT the prophets are a separate class of individuals. This distinction allows him the luxury of embracing an inerrant NT while admitting that today's prophets (as well as first century non-apostolic prophets) can commit error in their predictions.

We must refrain from entering into the larger issues of charismata and fallible prophecy in our treatment of this text.[81] Our point is simply that the syntactical evidence is very much against the "identical" view, even though syntax has been the primary grounds used in behalf of it. As we have seen, there are no clear examples of plural *nouns* in TSKS fitting the "identical" group in the NT, rendering such a possibility here less likely on grammatical grounds.[82]

The strongest possibilities are either that two distinct groups are in view or the apostles are seen as a subset of the prophets. If the OT prophets are in view, then obviously two distinct groups are meant. But if NT prophets are in view, this would favor the apostles as being a subset of the prophets. In favor of this second view: (1) If OT prophets were

---

[80] Grudem has written a number of books and articles on the subject of NT prophecy, growing out of his doctoral dissertation, "The Gift of Prophecy in 1 Corinthians 12-14," Ph.D. dissertation, Cambridge University, 1978). Cf. also his *The Gift of Prophecy in 1 Corinthians* (Washington, D.C.: University Press of America, 1982) where he devotes 24 pages (82-105) to a discussion of Eph 2:20.

[81] Others have argued against Grudem's thesis on this point. Note the following: D. G. McCartney, review of Wayne A. Grudem, *The Gift of Prophecy in 1 Corinthians*, in *WTJ* 45 (1983) 191-97; R. A. Pyne, "The Cessation of Special Revelation as Related to the Pentecostal Movement" (Th.M. thesis, Dallas Theological Seminary, 1985) 36-39; M. Turner, "Spiritual Gifts Then and Now," *VE* 15 (1985) 15-17; K. L. Gentry, *The Charismatic Gift of Prophecy: A Reformed Response to Wayne Grudem* (Memphis: Footstool, 1986); F. D. Farnell, "The New Testament Prophetic Gift: Its Nature and Duration" (Ph.D. dissertation, Dallas Theological Seminary, 1990) 7-8, 102-111, 189-309 (especially 243-53), 382-85, and *passim*; idem, "Fallible New Testament Prophecy/Prophets? A Critique of Wayne Grudem's Hypothesis," *Master's Seminary Journal* 2.2 (1991) 157-79; idem, "Is the Gift of Prophecy for Today? The Current Debate about New Testament Prophecy," *BSac* 149 (1992) 277-303; idem, "Is the Gift of Prophecy for Today? The Gift of Prophecy in the Old and New Testaments," *BSac* 149 (1992) 387-410; idem, "Does the New Testament Teach Two Prophetic Gifts?" *BSac* 150 (1993) 62-88; idem, "When Will the Gift of Prophecy Cease?" *BSac* 150 (1993) 171-202; R. F. White, "Gaffin and Grudem on Eph 2:20: In Defense of Gaffin's Cessationist Exegesis," *WTJ* 54 (1992) 303-20; R. L. Thomas, "Prophecy Rediscovered? A Review of *The Gift of Prophecy in the New Testament and Today*," *BSac* 149 (1992) 83-96; D. B. McWilliams, "Something New Under the Sun?" [review of Wayne A. Grudem, *The Gift of Prophecy in the New Testament and Today*], *WTJ* 54 (1992) 321-330.

[82] In Grudem's study he mixed singular TSKS constructions and plural *participial* TSKS constructions in with Eph 2:20. But the semantic patterns of each of these constructions do not match noun+noun plural TSKS constructions:There are no clear examples of plural nouns displaying identity, while all singular and virtually all plural participles fit this category.

For a more detailed discussion, see Wallace, "The Article with Multiple Substantives," 223-40.

in view, it seems unnatural that they would be mentioned second. (2) Whenever apostles are in a TSKS plural construction they always come first and the semantic value of the construction involves the first group as a subset of the second. (3) Since the picture of a building which apparently consists of the true Church is what is being described here, and since the apostles and prophets are viewed as foundational to this building, it seems hardly conceivable that OT prophets would be in the author's mind here. (4) The same construction occurs in 3:5 in which it is declared that the mystery has *now* been revealed "to his holy apostles and prophets"; thus, the NT prophets are clearly in view there. Since the context is still about the foundation and beginning of the Church, it would be consistent for the reference to be about the same group of prophets in both 2:20 and 3:5. Our conclusion, then, is that Eph 2:20 speaks of "the apostles and [other] prophets."

➡   c.   **Impersonal Constructions**

There are about 50 impersonal TSKS constructions in the NT.[83] Theoretically, such constructions can have the same semantic range as plural personal constructions (i.e., distinct, overlapping, first subset of second, second subset of first, and identical [see figures above]). However, the "identical" category is quite rare, with only one clear example. Far more common is the distinct category and the overlapping groups (especially first subset of second).

1)   Unambiguous Examples

a)   Distinct Entities, though United

Luke 21:12   διώξουσιν, παραδιδόντες εἰς **τὰς συναγωγὰς καὶ φυλακάς**[84]

they will persecute [you], handing [you] over to **the synagogues and prisons**

> The reason for the single article is that both groups are hostile to the disciples.

Eph 3:12   ἐν ᾧ ἔχομεν **τὴν παρρησίαν καὶ προσαγωγήν**

in whom we have **the boldness and access**

> There is a very close relationship between boldness and access, one being the internal attitude which corresponds to the external reality.

Eph 3:18   **τὸ πλάτος καὶ μῆκος καὶ ὕψος καὶ βάθος**

the breadth and length and height and depth

> The author is speaking about God's love in figurative language, as if he were using a spiritual plumb-line. Although each term refers to God's love, each refers to a different aspect of it and thus the terms are *not* identical.[85]

---

[83] Impersonal substantives present special problems that are beyond the scope of a non-specialized study. For discussion, see Wallace, "The Article with Multiple Substantives," 167-84.

[84] A L W X Γ Δ Θ Λ Ψ 0102 33 $f^{1, 13}$ *Byz* omit τάς.

Rev 1:9 ἐγὼ Ἰωάννης, ὁ ἀδελφὸς ὑμῶν καὶ συγκοινωνὸς ἐν **τῇ θλίψει καὶ βασιλείᾳ**

I John, your brother and fellow-partaker in **the tribulation and kingdom**

> There are two TSKS constructions in this, one personal and one impersonal. The personal construction involves an identical referent; the impersonal referent obviously does not (the tribulation and kingdom are not the same). The article shows that John and his readers are *united* in both suffering and glory.

Cf. also Luke 24:44; Acts 10:12; 21:25; 2 Cor 6:7; Col 2:19; Rev 20:10.

b) Overlapping Entities

2 Cor 12:21 τῶν προημαρτηκότων καὶ μὴ μετανοησάντων ἐπὶ **τῇ ἀκαθαρσίᾳ καὶ πορνείᾳ καὶ ἀσελγείᾳ**

those who have previously sinned and not repented over **the impurity and immorality and licentiousness**

> This is the only clear instance in the NT,[86] and even here the overlap is partial: immorality and licentiousness are kinds of impurity.

c) First Entity Subset of Second

Col 2:22 **τὰ ἐντάλματα καὶ διδασκαλίας** τῶν ἀνθρώπων
the commandments and teachings of men

> Not all teachings are commandments, but all commandments would seem to be teachings.

Rev 9:15 ἐλύθησαν οἱ τέσσαρες ἄγγελοι οἱ ἡτοιμασμένοι εἰς **τὴν ὥραν καὶ ἡμέραν καὶ μῆνα καὶ ἐνιαυτόν**

the four angels who had been prepared for **the hour and day and month and year** were released

Cf. also Mark 12:33; Luke 1:6; 9:12; Rom 1:20; 16:18; Phil 1:7.

d) Second Group Subset of First

Matt 24:36 Περὶ δὲ **τῆς ἡμέρας** ἐκείνης **καὶ ὥρας** οὐδεὶς οἶδεν
Now concerning that **day and hour**, no one knows

Luke 6:17 **πάσης τῆς Ἰουδαίας καὶ Ἰερουσαλήμ**
all Judea and Jerusalem

Cf. also Mark 6:36; Luke 5:17; Heb 13:16; Rev 14:7.

---

[85] Some have been confused over this text, assuming that it fits Sharp's rule. Generally this confusion is exacerbated because (1) all of the terms do apparently refer to God's love, yet even here it would not be appropriate to say that the length is identical with the height; (2) the figurative language compounds the problem because the imagery and its referent are both somewhat elusive; and (3) there is a widespread confusion about what Sharp's rule actually addresses: it is not mere equality, but identity that is in view.

[86] Other potential candidates include 1 Cor 7:35; 2 Cor 10:1; Heb 7:18; Rev 17:13.

e) Both Entities Identical

There is only one clear example of this in the NT.

Acts 1:25   ἀνάδειξον ὃν ἐξελέξω . . . (25) λαβεῖν τὸν τόπον **τῆς διακονίας** ταύτης **καὶ ἀποστολῆς**

Show [us] which one you have chosen . . . (25) to take the place of this **ministry and apostleship**

> The presence of the demonstrative ταύτης seems to restrict διακονία in the context so that the noun phrase "*this* ministry" becomes, in the discourse, the exact equivalent of ἀποστολή.

2) Exegetically and Theologically Significant Texts

There are several ambiguous impersonal TSKS constructions, some of which are exegetically significant.[87] Three of them will be taken up here.

Acts 2:23   τοῦτον **τῇ** ὡρισμένη **βουλῇ καὶ προγνώσει** τοῦ θεοῦ

this [Jesus, having been delivered up] by **the** predetermined **plan and foreknowledge** of God

> If "foreknowledge" defines "predetermination," this opens the door that (according to one definition of πρόγνωσις) God's decree is dependent on his omniscience. But if the terms are distinguishable, the relationship may be reversed, viz., omniscience is dependent on the eternal decree. Without attempting to resolve this theological issue entirely, it can nevertheless be argued that the "identical" view is unlikely: the least attested meaning of impersonal constructions is referential identity.[88] The relationship between the two terms here may be one of distinctness or the subsumption of one under the other. In the context of Acts 2 and in light of Luke's christological argument "from prophecy and pattern,"[89] the most likely option is that the πρόγνωσις is grounded in the ὡρισμένη βουλή (thus "foreknowledge" is a part of the "predetermined plan"), for one of the foci of the chapter is on the divine *plan* in relation to the Messiah's death and resurrection.[90] Thus, God's decrees are not based on him simply foreknowing what human beings will do; rather, humanity's actions are based on God's foreknowledge and predetermined plan.

---

[87] Cf. Matt 24:3; Acts 2:23; 20:21; 2 Thess 2:1; Titus 2:13; 1 Pet 1:21; 2 Pet 1:10. For a discussion, see Wallace, "The Article with Multiple Substantives," 188-219.

[88] If referential identity were implied, the second term would define and clarify the first. Yet ὡρισμένη βουλή, *prima facie*, is less ambiguous than πρόγνωσις due to (1) the clarifying participle and (2) the lack of exegetical debate over ὁρίζω in comparison with πρόγνωσις (cf. R. Bultmann on πρόγνωσις in *TDNT* 1.715-16, and K. L. Schmidt on ὁρίζω in *TDNT* 5.452-53).

[89] To borrow the phrase and theme of D. L. Bock, *Proclamation from Prophecy and Pattern: Lucan Old Testament Christology* (Sheffield: JSOT, 1987).

[90] See Bock, ibid., 155-87, for a discussion of the use of the OT in Acts 2 in support of this theme.

Acts 20:21   διαμαρτυρόμενος Ἰουδαίοις τε καὶ Ἕλλησιν **τὴν** εἰς θεὸν **μετάνοιαν καὶ πίστιν** εἰς τὸν κύριον ἡμῶν Ἰησοῦν
testifying to both Jews and Greeks of **the repentance** toward God **and faith** in our Lord Jesus Christ

> One major exegetical problem of the text relates to the Pauline kerygma and the use of μετάνοια here. Two of the most commonly-held views are at odds with each other. On the one hand, some scholars regard the construction as a chiasmus: Jews were to have faith and Greeks were to repent.[91] Although it is true that turning toward God is a typical component in Paul's gospel presentation to Gentiles (cf. Gal 4:8; 1 Thess 1:9),[92] it is hardly atypical of the message he addressed to the Jews.[93] Nor is it atypical of Luke's theology.[94] Further, the TSKS construction in the least implies some sort of unity between μετάνοια and πίστις. Those who embrace the chiastic view do not address this problem. On the other hand, several scholars argue that the two terms have an identical, or nearly identical referent, being persuaded apparently by the supposed force of the TSKS construction.[95] Although this second view takes into account the structure in Greek, it does not reckon with the impersonal nature of this construction.

> The evidence suggests that, in Luke's usage, saving faith *includes* repentance. In those texts which speak simply of faith, a "theological shorthand" seems to be employed: Luke envisions repentance as the inceptive act of which the entirety may be called πίστις.[96] Thus, for Luke, conversion is not a two-step process, but one step, faith–but the kind of faith that *includes* repentance. This, of course, fits well with the frequent idiom of first subset of second for impersonal TSKS constructions.

---

[91] Cf. J. Roloff, *Die Apostelgeschichte: Übersetzt und Erklärt* (NTD; Göttingen: Vandenhoeck & Ruprecht, 1981) 303; R. Pesch, *Die Apostelgeschichte* (EKKNT; Zürich: Benziger, 1986) 2.202.

[92] It is equally true that μετάνοια is hardly a characteristic word used in the *corpus Paulinum* to describe this gospel. (The μετανο- word-group is used only five times in the letters attributed to Paul, principally in 2 Corinthians and mostly with reference to believers [Rom 2:4; 2 Cor 7:9, 10; 12:21; 2 Tim 2:25].) While one must not make the linguistic mistake of verbal-conceptual equations, it is nevertheless the case that Luke's representation of Paul's speech in Acts 20 has many parallels with the verbiage found in Paul's letters.

[93] Repeatedly in the Pauline letters the apostle addresses the Jews' unrepentant attitude not only toward Christ, but also toward God and their own sin (cf. Rom 2:17-29; 3:1-8; 9:1-3; 10:1-3, 18-21; 11:11-32; 1 Thess 2:13-16). Luke's portrayal of Paul's kerygma also includes the need for Jews to repent (Acts 13:44-47; 18:5-6; 19:8-9; 26:20; 28:24-28).

[94] The programmatic statement is found in the dominical saying in Luke 24:47, where repentance is to be preached to all people, starting with the Jews. Cf. also Acts 2:38; 3:19; 5:31.

[95] Cf., e.g., F. F. Bruce, *The Acts of the Apostles: The Greek Text with Introduction and Commentary,* 3d ed. rev. (Grand Rapids: Eerdmans, 1990) 431; S. D. Toussaint, "Acts," *The Bible Knowledge Commentary: An Exposition of the Scriptures by Dallas Seminary Faculty. New Testament Edition* (J. F. Walvoord and R. B. Zuck, editors; Wheaton: Victor, 1983) 413.

[96] See Wallace, "The Article with Multiple Substantives," 210-13, for a discussion.

2 Thess 2:1 Ἐρωτῶμεν δὲ ὑμᾶς, ἀδελφοί, ὑπὲρ **τῆς παρουσίας** τοῦ κυρίου ἡμῶν Ἰησοῦ Χριστοῦ **καὶ** ἡμῶν **ἐπισυναγωγῆς** ἐπ᾽ αὐτόν

Now we ask you, brothers, concerning **the coming** of our Lord Jesus Christ **and** our **gathering together** with him

> This text impacts the discussion in some American evangelical circles over the time of the rapture. Many posttribulationists/non-dispensationalists have considered the two to have the same referent precisely because of their misunderstanding of Sharp's rule and its specific requirements.[97]

> Since the TSKS construction involves impersonal substantives, the highest degree of doubt is cast upon the probability of the terms referring to the same event. This is especially the case since the terms look to concrete temporal referents (the parousia and the gathering of the saints), for the identical category is unattested for *concrete* impersonals in the NT.

> This is not to say that one could not see a posttribulational rapture in the text, for even if the words do not have an identical referent, they could have simultaneous ones. Our only point is that because of the misuse of syntax by some scholars, certain approaches to the theology of the NT have often been jettisoned without a fair hearing.

7. Conclusion

As has been demonstrated, the TSKS construction is used in several texts which have to do with some rich theological issues (e.g., our Lord's deity, ecclesiology, the biblical concepts of election and foreknowledge, eschatology, etc.). Although this section has been disproportionately long, since Greek grammar has been improperly invoked in support of various positions, a detailed corrective was in order.

C. *Conclusion of The Article, Part II*

The history of NT studies involves many ironies. One has to do with the syntax of the article: On the one hand, Colwell's rule, as applied to John 1:1, has been played as a trump card by Trinitarians in many christological debates, even though the rule really says nothing about the definiteness of θεός. Indeed, an examination both of pre-verbal anarthrous predicate nominatives and of the Christology of the Fourth Gospel strongly suggests a *qualitative* force to θεός (a view which affirms the deity of Christ just as strongly but for different reasons).

On the other hand, Sharp's rule has also been misunderstood, the net effect being to lessen certainty as to its value in christologically pregnant texts. It has been applied only with great hesitation to Titus 2:13 and 2 Pet 1:1 by Trinitarians in the past two centuries. However, a proper understanding of the rule shows it to have the highest degree of validity within the NT. Consequently, these two passages are as secure as any in the canon when it comes to identifying Christ as θεός.

---

[97] Cf., e.g., F. F. Bruce, *1 & 2 Thessalonians* (WBC; Waco, TX: Word, 1982) 163; L. Morris, *The First and Second Epistles to the Thessalonians* (NICNT; Grand Rapids: Eerdmans, 1959) 214.

Adjectives

Overview

Select Bibliography

Abel, *Grammaire*, 127-30 (§32), 149-53 (§37); *BDF*, 125-29 (§241-46); **Brooks-Winbery**, 65-67; **Dana-Mantey**, 115-22 (§127-32); **Moule**, *Idiom Book*, 93-98; **Porter**, *Idioms*, 115-24; **Robertson**, *Grammar*, 401, 413, 650-75; **Turner**, *Syntax*, 29-32, 185-87, 225-26; **D. B. Wallace**, "The Relation of Adjective to Noun in Anarthrous Constructions in the New Testament," *NovT* 26 (1984) 128-67; **Young**, *Intermediate Greek*, 80-84; **Zerwick**, *Biblical Greek*, 47-51 (§140-53).

Introduction

Basically, only three questions need to be asked of the adjective: (1) What is its relationship to a noun (or other substantive) and how can one tell? (2) Are the positive, comparative, and superlative forms of the adjective ever used for other than positive, comparative, and superlative ideas respectively? (3) Can the adjective function other than in dependence on a noun?

These questions will be dealt with in reverse order (or chiastically), beginning with the least significant question (exegetically) to the most significant question.

I. "Non-Adjectival" Uses of the Adjective

Introduction

The basic role of the adjective is as a modifier of a noun or other substantive. As such, it can be modified by an adverb. Not infrequently, however, it deviates from this role by one step in either direction. That is, it can either stand in the place of a noun or in the place of an adverb. Its nominal role is a natural extension of the adjective in which the noun is elided; its adverbial role is more idiomatic, usually reserved for special terms.

Substantival	Adjectival	Adverbial
Independent	Dependent on Noun	Dependent on Adjective or Verb

Table 5
The Functions of the Adjective

A. The Adverbial Use of the Adjective

1. Definition

The adjective is sometimes used in the place of an adverb. Some of the uses are analogous to colloquial English, such as "I am doing good," or "Come here quick!" Other, more frequent, instances involve idiomatic uses of the adjective, such as the accusative adjective in the neuter used adverbially. (Surprising as it may seem, this idiomatic adverbial use is frequently, if not normally, articular.) These include a large group of stereotyped terms, such as βραχύ, λοιπόν, μίκρον, μόνον, πολύ, πρῶτον, ὕστερον, κτλ.

2. Illustrations

Matt 6:33   ζητεῖτε δὲ **πρῶτον** τὴν βασιλείαν τοῦ θεοῦ
but seek **first** the kingdom of God

John 1:41   εὑρίσκει οὗτος **πρῶτον** τὸν ἀδελφὸν τὸν ἴδιον Σίμωνα
he **first** found his own brother, Simon
> If the variant πρῶτος (found in ℵ* L W^supp Γ Δ Λ *Byz et alii*) were original, the idea would be that "Andrew was the first follower of Jesus who made a convert. The reading πρῶτον . . . means that the first thing that Andrew did after having been called was to find his brother . . . ."[1]

John 4:18   πέντε ἄνδρας ἔσχες καὶ νῦν ὃν ἔχεις οὐκ ἔστιν σου ἀνήρ· τοῦτο **ἀληθὲς** εἴρηκας.[2]
You have had five husbands and the one whom you now have is not your husband; this you have spoken **truly**.

John 10:10   ἐγὼ ἦλθον ἵνα ζωὴν ἔχωσιν καὶ **περισσὸν** ἔχωσιν
I have come that they might have life and that they might have it **abundantly**

Phil 3:1   **τὸ λοιπόν**, ἀδελφοί μου, χαίρετε ἐν κυρίῳ
finally, my brothers, rejoice in the Lord

Cf. also Matt 9:14 (πολλά); Matt 15:16 (ἀκμήν); Mark 12:27 (πολύ); Luke 17:25 (πρῶτον); Acts 27:20 (λοιπόν); 2 Cor 13:11 (λοιπόν); 1 Pet 1:6 (ὀλίγον).

---

[1] B. M. Metzger, *A Textual Commentary on the Greek New Testament* (New York: United Bible Societies, 1971) 200.

[2] The adj. is harsh even in Greek. Predictably, some scribes changed it to the adverb ἀληθῶς (so ℵ E *pauci*). Note also the *v.l.* in Acts 14:19 (ἀληθὲς λέγουσιν) found in 81 1739 *et alii*.

➡

B. The Independent or Substantival
Use of the Adjective

1. Definition

The adjective is frequently used independently of a noun. That is, it can function as a substantive (in which case it either implies a noun or takes on the lexical nuance of a noun).

2. Clarification

Usually, though not always, such a substantival adjective will have the article with it to point out that its use is indeed substantival. Some words, such as κύριος ("lord"),[3] ἔρημος ("desert"), διάβολος ("slanderous," or, as a noun, "the devil"), and ἅγιος ("holy," or, as a noun, "saint"), often function as substantives without the article since they are either often or usually independent of nouns in the NT. Other adjectives, however, usually require the article to make clear that they are being used substantivally.

Furthermore, when the adjective is substantival, its gender is generally fixed by sense rather than by grammatical concord.[4] That is to say, if it refers to a male, it will usually be masculine; if it refers to a female, it will usually be feminine; if it refers to an entity or concept, it will be neuter.

3. Illustrations

Matt 6:13   ῥῦσαι ἡμᾶς ἀπὸ τοῦ **πονηροῦ**
deliver us from the **evil** [one]
> The devil is in view here, not evil in general. (However, in 5:39 just the evil man is in view.) This is one of the many passages mistranslated in the KJV: "deliver us from evil." The prayer is not a request for deliverance from evil in general, but from the grasp of the evil one himself.

Matt 13:17   πολλοὶ προφῆται καὶ **δίκαιοι**
many prophets and **righteous** [men]
> In this text there is no article, but δίκαιοι clearly should be taken substantivally. This is probably due to the fact that since πολλοί is a pronominal adj. the article is not required. This being the case, the

---

[3] Although κύριος was originally an adj., it always functions as a noun in the NT (BAGD, s.v. κύριος, I).

[4] An exception to this is when a particular noun is consistently elided, such as ἡμέρα (cf. ἡ ἑβδόμη in Heb 4:4) or χείρ (cf. ἡ δεξιά in Matt 6:3). The term κοινή with reference to Greek modifies an understood διαλέκτος (a second declension feminine noun). In such instances, the gender of the adj. is fixed by its concord with the elided noun. As well, a number of terms are consistently used in the neuter, even though they refer to people (see Robertson, *Grammar*, 653-54).

construction then approximates a *plural* Granville Sharp construction (see last chapter, Part II, for a discussion of this phenomenon).

Luke 6:45 ὁ ἀγαθὸς ἄνθρωπος ἐκ τοῦ ἀγαθοῦ θησαυροῦ τῆς καρδίας προφέρει **τὸ ἀγαθόν**, καὶ ὁ πονηρὸς ἐκ τοῦ πονηροῦ προφέρει **τὸ πονηρόν**[5]
the good man out of the good treasure of his heart brings forth **the good**, and **the evil** [man] out of **the evil** [treasure of his heart] brings forth **the evil**

Acts 2:33 τῇ **δεξιᾷ** τοῦ θεοῦ ὑψωθεὶς
having been exalted at the **right** [hand] of God

Rom 1:17 ὁ δὲ **δίκαιος** ἐκ πίστεως ζήσεται
but the **righteous** [person] shall live by faith

2 Cor 6:15 τίς μερὶς **πιστῷ** μετὰ **ἀπίστου**;
What portion does **a believer** have with **an unbeliever**?

1 Cor 13:10 ὅταν δὲ ἔλθῃ τὸ **τέλειον**, τὸ ἐκ μέρους καταργηθήσεται
whenever the **perfect** comes, the partial will be done away

Although there can be no objection to the τέλειον referring to the completion of the canon *grammatically* (for the adj. would naturally be neuter if it referred to a thing, even if the inferred noun were feminine, such as γραφή), it is difficult to see such a notion in this passage, for this view presupposes that (1) both Paul and the Corinthians knew that he was writing scripture, and (2) the apostle foresaw the completion of the NT before the Lord's return.[6] A more likely view is that "the perfect" refers to the coming of Christ[7] (note the terminus given in v 12 [τότε] as "face to face," a personal reference that does not easily comport with the canon view).[8]

Cf. also Matt 19:17; 27:29; Mark 1:4; Acts 5:31; Rom 8:34; 12:9, 21; 1 Cor 1:20, 25-28; Gal 4:27; Eph 1:20; 2:14, 16; 1 Tim 5:16; Heb 1:3; 1 Pet 4:18; 1 John 2:20; Rev 3:7.

---

[5] The article is omitted before ἀγαθόν in D W *et pauci*.

[6] G. D. Fee, *The First Epistle to the Corinthians* (NICNT) 645, n. 23, remarks that this "is an impossible view, of course, since Paul himself could not have articulated it."

[7] One cannot object that the reference is not to the coming of Christ because the adj. is neuter, since the neuter adj. is sometimes used for persons for reasons of rhetoric, aphoristic principle, suspense, etc. Cf. Matt 12:6, 41; 1 Cor 1:27-28; Heb 7:7.

[8] This is not necessarily to say that the sign gifts would continue until the Second Coming, for in Paul's mind he would be alive when Christ returned (cf. 1 Thess 4:15). Such an anticipation summarily removes this text from supporting either the charismatic or cessationist position on sign gifts.

II. The Use of the Positive, Comparative, and Superlative Forms of the Adjective

Introduction

The terms "positive," "comparative," and "superlative" refer to different forms of the same adjective that have to do with degree. Thus in English we have "nice" (positive form), "nicer" (comparative), and "nicest" (superlative).[9]

The *positive* adjective focuses on the properties of a noun in terms of *kind*, not degree. In a sense, it infers an absolute notion. Thus, "the green house" does not compare the "greenness" of one house to another; rather, it simply identifies a particular house as green. But in "the tall woman," although an absolute notion is inferred (in that regardless of how many other tall women there might be, this one still belongs to that class), an *implicit* comparison is often seen. In such instances, we might say that the comparison is *inter*-categorical, that is, between two different categories (such as "tall" and "short"). With the positive adjective, contrast and comparison are not explicit; the focus is on quality, not degree.

The *comparative* adjective and the *superlative* adjective focus on the properties of a noun in terms of *degree*, not kind. They infer a relative rather than an absolute notion. Thus, "the taller woman" only speaks of the height of one woman in comparison with another. It may be that both are short. The issue is thus degree, since height is a quality that both share. Thus, comparative and superlative adjectives may be said to be *intra*-categorical in focus.

The difference between the comparative adjective and the superlative is not that of kind, or degree, but of *number*. Comparative adjectives basically compare only *two* entities (or persons, ideas, etc.). Superlative adjectives basically compare *three* or more. In the NT, however (and Koine Greek in general), there is much overlap in usage among these categories.

Finally, *elative* is a term used of either the comparative or superlative adjective to describe an *intensification* of the positive notion (with the translation *very* before the positive form). That is, like a positive adjective, an elative adjective focuses on kind rather than degree. Although the *form* of such an adjective is either comparative or superlative, in meaning it does not make an explicit comparison. For example, μείζων (comparative in form, "greater") may on occasion have an elative force, "*very* great."

---

[9] Thanks are due to Roberts ("Bobs") Johnson for his superlative work on the comparative and superlative adjectives in the NT, done in the course Advanced Greek Grammar at Dallas Seminary, Spring 1993.

A. The Use of the Positive Adjective

➡ ## 1. Normal Usage

Normally, the positive adjective makes no comment about any other object than the one that it modifies (or, if a predicate adjective, the object it makes an assertion about). It simply qualifies the noun to which it stands related (e.g., "a good man" does not indicate that this particular man is *better* [the comparative idea] than other men). This usage is routine.

Acts 27:14   ἄνεμος **τυφωνικός**
             a **violent** wind

Rom 7:12   ἡ ἐντολὴ **ἁγία** καὶ **δικαία** καὶ **ἀγαθή**
             the commandment is **holy** and **righteous** and **good**

Rev 20:2   ὁ ὄφις ὁ **ἀρχαῖος**
             the **old** serpent

2. Positive for Comparative

On a rare occasion, the positive adjective can be used for the comparative.

Matt 18:8   **καλόν** σοί ἐστιν εἰσελθεῖν εἰς τὴν ζωὴν κυλλόν
             it is **better** to enter life crippled
             > Here, ἤ is used later in the sentence to indicate comparison. Obviously, the idea of the positive adj. is insufficient, i.e., it is *not* good in and of itself to enter life *crippled*!

Luke 18:14   κατέβη οὗτος **δεδικαιωμένος** εἰς τὸν οἶκον αὐτοῦ παρ᾿ ἐκεῖνον
             this man went down to his house **more justified** than the other
             > In this text the adjectival participle functions as an adj. Zerwick notes that the true force of Jesus' words here is that the tax-collector was "justified whereas the other was not." A better gloss would thus be *justified rather than the other.*[10]

1 Cor 10:33 μὴ ζητῶν τὸ ἐμαυτοῦ σύμφορον ἀλλὰ τὸ **τῶν πολλῶν**
             not seeking my own advantage, but that **of the majority**
             > Certain substantival adjectives which have the notion of comparison embedded lexically (esp. πολύς) are used for an implicit comparison. Such examples do not follow the structural pattern of comparative adjectives (e.g., they are not followed by a gen. or ἤ).

Cf. also Matt 24:12; Luke 16:10; John 2:10.

---

[10] Zerwick, *Biblical Greek*, 48. What renders the adjectival participle function comparatively is its collocation with παρ᾿ ἐκεῖνον. παρά + acc. is regularly used in comparisons (cf. Luke 3:13; Heb 1:4; 3:3; 9:23; 11:4; 12:24). However, in such a comparison "one member [of the comparison] may receive so little attention as to pass fr. consideration entirely, so that 'more than' becomes *instead of, rather than, to the exclusion of*" (BAGD, s.v. παρά, III. 3 [p. 611]).

3. Positive for Superlative

Occasionally, the positive adjective is used in the place of a superlative adjective. When the positive adjective is in the attributive position and is used with the *par excellence* article, it has the force of the superlative adjective. Rarely, a predicate adjective also functions as a superlative.

Matt 22:38   αὕτη ἐστὶν ἡ **μεγάλη** καὶ πρώτη ἐντολή
              this is the **great** [=greatest] and first commandment

Luke 9:48   ὁ μικρότερος ἐν πᾶσιν ὑμῖν . . . ἐστιν **μέγας**
              the least among you all . . . is **greatest**

Luke 10:42   Μαριὰμ τὴν **ἀγαθὴν** μερίδα ἐξελέξατο
              Mary has chosen the **good** [=best] part

> It is of course possible that the adj. is here functioning for a comparative ("Mary has chosen the **better** part").

Heb 9:3   **ἅγια** ἁγίων[11]
              the **Holy** of Holies

> The idea is "the holiest of all holy places." Since Hebrew lacked the comparative and superlative forms, some sort of circumlocution was necessary to suggest this notion. Often a gen. having the same lexeme as the head noun (or adj.) was so used, as here. Such expressions were rare in Greek; most in the NT are due to Semitic influence and many are stock phrases from the OT. Cf. also βασιλεὺς βασιλέων and κύριος κυρίων in Rev 17:14 and 19:16; Ἑβραῖος ἐξ Ἑβραίων in Phil 3:5.[12]

Cf. also Luke 1:42 (adjectival participle); Rev 22:13.

B. The Use of the Comparative Adjective

Much less frequent than the positive form of the adjective are the comparative and superlative. There are *approximately* 7399 positive adjectives, 198 comparatives, and 191 superlatives in the NT.[13]

---

[11] The double articular construction (τὰ ἅγια τῶν ἁγίων) is found in several witnesses (e.g., ℵ^C B D^C K L 1241 *et pauci*).

[12] Unless κύριος is counted as an adj., Heb 9:3 is the only place in the NT of this construction with two adjectives.

[13] The numbers, based initially on a search in *acCordance*, are not exact. According to *acCordance*, there are only 39 superlatives in the NT. This number needs to be modified, however, since the current version of *acCordance* has mistagged a number of terms, treating them functionally rather than morphologically. For example, neither πρῶτος (100 instances) nor ἔσχατος (52 instances), both superlative adjectives in form, are *ever* tagged as such in *acCordance/Gramcord*. Yet, these comprise 152 of the 191 superlatives in the NT. As well, not infrequently, *acCordance* labels an adj. functioning adverbially as an adverb. It is not known how many adjectives are so tagged.

➡ ## 1. Normal Usage

The comparative adjective normally makes a comparison (as its name suggests). The largest group of instances involves an explicit comparison in which the adjective is followed by a genitive of comparison or the particle ἤ or, less frequently, by παρά or ὑπέρ. But the comparative adjective not infrequently is used substantivally, often leaving the comparison implicit.

Matt 12:6   λέγω ὑμῖν ὅτι τοῦ ἱεροῦ **μεῖζόν** ἐστιν ὧδε
I tell you, [something] **greater** than the temple is here

Mark 10:25 **εὐκοπώτερον** ἐστιν κάμηλον διὰ τῆς τρυμαλιᾶς τῆς ῥαφίδος διελθεῖν ἢ πλούσιον εἰς τὴν βασιλείαν τοῦ θεοῦ εἰσελθεῖν
it is **easier** for a camel to enter the eye of a needle than for a rich man to enter the kingdom of God

Phil 1:14   τοὺς **πλείονας** τῶν ἀδελφῶν ἐν κυρίῳ πεποιθότας τοῖς δεσμοῖς μου περισσοτέρως τολμᾶν . . .
[with the result that] **most** of the brothers, since they are confident in the Lord because of my bonds, dare all the more . . .

Heb 4:12   ζῶν ὁ λόγος τοῦ θεοῦ καὶ ἐνεργὴς καὶ **τομώτερος** ὑπὲρ πᾶσαν μάχαιραν δίστομον
the word of God is living and active and **sharper** than any two-edged sword

Cf. also John 4:41; Rom 9:12; Heb 1:4; 1 Pet 3:7.

2. Comparative for Superlative

Although relatively rare, the comparative adjective can be used with a superlative sense. As Turner points out, significant for exegesis "is the infiltration of the comparative into the old preserves of the superlative, so that the alert translator will not lose the opportunity of translating the one as the other, if necessary. . . ."[14]

Luke 9:48 ὁ **μικρότερος** ἐν πᾶσιν ὑμῖν . . . ἐστιν μέγας
the **least** among you all . . . is greatest
Notice too that the *positive* form μέγας is used in a superlative sense.

1 Tim 4:1 ἐν **ὑστέροις** καιροῖς ἀποστήσονταί τινες τῆς πίστεως
in the **last** times some will depart from the faith

1 Cor 13:13 νυνὶ δὲ μένει πίστις, ἐλπίς, ἀγάπη, τὰ τρία ταῦτα· **μείζων** δὲ τούτων ἡ ἀγάπη
But now remain faith, hope, love, these three. And the **greatest** of these is love
It is sometimes disputed that μείζων is functioning in a superlative

---

[14] Turner, *Syntax*, 2-3.

manner here. On behalf of the "true comparative" view is the fact that although there is a good deal of elasticity in the functions of the comparative and superlative adjectives in Hellenistic Greek, it is nevertheless true that the comparative for superlative is relatively rare in the NT. Winer-Moulton argue, for example, that faith and hope are a unity and hence love is compared only to one entity, "faith-hope."[15] One problem with this view is its subtlety and lack of grammatical basis: faith and hope are not set off against love; rather, all are grouped together.[16]

More recently, Martin has taken μείζων as a true comparative, arguing that the sense of the passage is "but greater than these [three] is the love [of God]."[17] This, too, suffers from being overly subtle: Why should we supply "of God"? Not only are there no contextual clues that this should be the case, but the article with ἀγάπη in the last clause of the verse is almost certainly anaphoric, and if so, then the same love is in view throughout the verse.[18]

Cf. also Matt 18:1; Mark 9:34.

3. *Comparative for Elative*

Sometimes the comparative adjective is used with an elative sense. That is, the quality expressed by the adjective is intensified, but is not making a comparison (e.g., ὁ ἰσχυρότερος ἀνήρ might mean "the *very* strong man" rather than "the stronger man"). The elative sense in classical Greek was normally reserved for the superlative form, but in Koine the comparative has encroached on the superlative's domain.

a.   Clear Examples

Acts 13:31   ὃς ὤφθη ἐπὶ ἡμέρας **πλείους**
             who appeared for **very many** days

Acts 17:22   κατὰ πάντα ὡς **δεισιδαιμονεστέρους** ὑμᾶς θεωρῶ
             I perceive how **very religious** you are in every way

> The KJV has "I perceive that in all things ye are too superstitious." But such a translation is unnecessary linguistically, since the comparative has a well-established usage as an elative in Koine Greek. Furthermore, this particular term, δεισιδαίμων, is used in other literature in a neutral

---

[15] "We must render, *greater of* (among) *these is love*; the comparative being chosen because love is contrasted with faith and hope as *one* category" (Winer-Moulton, 303 [italics original]).

[16] Further, this view virtually demands a different sense for οὗτος in the two halves of the verse ("these three," "greater than these [two]"), an approach that is unnatural at best. Yet Winer-Moulton attempt to skirt this problem by the translation "greater among these is love," which, on its face, is really a superlative notion!

[17] Cf. R. P. Martin, "A Suggested Exegesis of 1 Corinthians 13:13," *ExpTi* 82 (1970-71) 119-20.

[18] For other arguments against Martin's view, see D. A. Carson, *Showing the Spirit: A Theological Exposition of 1 Corinthians 12-14* (Grand Rapids: Baker, 1987) 72-74.

> sense often enough;[19] and "in the laudatory introduction of Paul's speech before the Areopagus . . . it must mean *religious*. . . ."[20]

Cf. also Acts 21:10; 24:17; 2 Cor 8:17.

b. A Possible and Exegetically Significant Example

Matt 13:32 ὃ **μικρότερον** μέν ἐστιν πάντων τῶν σπερμάτων
[the mustard seed. . .] which is **smaller** than all the seeds
or perhaps which is **very small** among all the seeds

> The first translation given for this text treats the adj. in its comparative sense, while the second translation treats it in an elative sense. This text has created a theological difficulty for some American evangelicals: Jesus seems to be declaring the mustard seed to be smaller than all other seeds when, in fact, it is *not* the smallest (the wild orchid is smaller). A typical resolution is that the adj. is elative. The justification for taking it so is twofold: (1) As has already been established, the comparative adj. occasionally had the elative sense in the NT, and (2) the gen. πάντων τῶν σπερμάτων, rather than being a gen. of comparison, might mean "among . . . ," as it does in Matt 23:11, John 8:7, Acts 19:35, 1 Cor 2:11, Gal 2:15, etc.
>
> Nevertheless, it seems on the surface that though it is *possible* to take μικρότερον as an elative, it is not likely. Apart from our modern-day scientific knowledge, few would understand μικρότερον as an elative. Like 1 Cor 13:13, a comparative adj. followed by a gen. should be taken in a comparative way; in both cases the comparison is between more than two items and hence functions as a superlative. Other approaches (all of which take μικρότερον in a superlative sense) are as follows: (1) σπέρμα is used, indicating a sown seed; the mustard seed is the smallest of all sown seeds;[21] (2) within the world view of Palestinian farmers, the mustard seed was the smallest seed; (3) the statement is proverbial (hence, Jesus is alluding to the proverb for rhetorical effect). Grammar does not solve this problem, of course, but it does lean in one direction (viz., comparative for superlative). It seems that many have made a mountain out of a mole hill with this text (or, a shade tree out of a mustard seed, as the case may be)!

C. The Use of the Superlative Adjective

➡ 1. "Normal" Usage

In Hellenistic Greek, the true superlative sense for the superlative adjective is on its way out. Thus the superlative sense for the superlative adjective is "normal" more in name than in reality. Although it is more frequent than other uses, the margin is negligible.

---

[19] See BAGD, s.v. δεισιδαίμων; Moulton-Milligan, s.v. δεισιδαιμονία, δεισιδαίμων.

[20] BAGD, ibid. Cf. F. J. F. Jackson and K. Lake, *The Beginnings of Christianity, Part I: The Acts of the Apostles* (Grand Rapids: Baker, 1979 [reprint ed.]), vol. 4 (by K. Lake and H. J. Cadbury), 214, for other arguments.

[21] Mark 4:31 adds the qualifier "when it is sown, it is smaller" (ὅταν σπαρῇ ἐπὶ τῆς γῆς, μικρότερον). However, σπέρμα is also the typical word for seed, whether sown or not.

This "normal" usage is due largely to the instances of πρῶτος and ἔσχατος, which together account for most of the superlative forms in the NT. These two need to be treated separately, since they skew the data. Apart from these two terms, approximately half of the superlative forms in the NT function as superlatives.[22]

John 11:24   ἀναστήσεται ἐν τῇ ἀναστάσει ἐν τῇ **ἐσχάτῃ** ἡμέρᾳ
              he will rise again in the resurrection on the **last** day

Acts 16:17   οὗτοι οἱ ἄνθρωποι δοῦλοι τοῦ θεοῦ τοῦ **ὑψίστου** εἰσίν
              these men are servants of the **most high** God

1 Cor 15:9   ἐγώ εἰμι ὁ **ἐλάχιστος** τῶν ἀποστόλων
              I am the **least** of the apostles

Eph 3:8   ἐμοὶ τῷ **ἐλαχιστοτέρῳ** πάντων ἁγίων
              to me, **less than the least** of all the saints

> This is the comparative of the superlative, perhaps coined for the occasion![23] A more literal translation would be something like "leaster."[24] An interesting argument for the authenticity of Ephesians is this autobiographical note in comparison with 1 Cor 15:9. First Corinthians, on any reckoning, was written earlier than Ephesians. There, Paul viewed himself as the least of the apostles; here, the circle has widened. Several scholars (e.g., Barth, Beare, Bruce, Wood) see in this statement the stamp of apostolic authenticity, for a forger would be unlikely to make Paul lower than he himself had done.
>
> Lincoln argues against this: "but this intensification also fits the tendency of the post-apostolic churches to accentuate the unworthiness of the apostles in order to highlight the greatness of Christ's grace in their lives (cf. 1 Tim 1:15, where Paul now becomes not just the least worthy Christian, but the foremost of sinners). . . ."[25] But Lincoln's approach equally assumes that the pastorals are inauthentic (a view increasingly abandoned nowadays), rendering his argument circular. When one actually compares the apostolic autobiographical notes found in the NT with those in the postapostolic pseudepigrapha, he notices a marked difference in tone. In the pseudepigrapha, the apostles are typically put on a pedestal; in the NT letters, they marvel at the grace of God in their lives.[26]

Cf. also Matt 2:6; 20:8; 21:9; 22:25; Mark 5:7; 9:35; 10:31; Luke 2:14; 16:5; 20:29; Acts 26:5; 1 Tim 1:15; Jude 20; Rev 1:17; 4:7; 21:19; 22:13.

---

[22] Most of the "true" superlative instances (not including πρῶτος and ἔσχατος) are found with ὕψιστος, frequently as a title for God (Luke 1:35, 76; 6:35; Acts 7:48; Heb 7:1).

[23] There is no other superlative-comparative form in the NT, though a double comparative occurs in 3 John 4 (μειζοτέραν).

[24] Though Robertson suspects that it has the elative sense (*Grammar*, 670).

[25] Lincoln, *Ephesians* (WBC) 183.

[26] Lincoln cites *Barnabas* 5.9 as an illustration of the postapostolic denigration of the apostles. But this statement is not autobiographical, nor is it even typical of most postapostolic writings (cf., e.g., Ignatius, *Ephesians* 12.1-2).

➡ ## 2. Superlative for Elative

Apart from πρῶτος and ἔσχατος, the superlative is used about as frequently for the elative as it is for the superlative.[27] When πρῶτος and ἔσχατος are factored in, however, this category gets a smaller piece of the pie.[28]

Mark 4:1   συνάγεται πρὸς αὐτὸν ὄχλος **πλεῖστος**
           a **very great** crowd gathered before him

Luke 1:3   **κράτιστε** Θεόφιλε
           most excellent Theophilus

> κράτιστος was used often in Hellenistic literature as a technical term in reference to a government official.[29] Cf. also Acts 23:26; 24:3; 26:25.

1 Cor 4:3 ἐμοὶ εἰς **ἐλάχιστόν** ἐστιν, ἵνα ὑφ' ὑμῶν ἀνακριθῶ
           to me, it is a **very small thing** that I should be judged by you

Cf. also Matt 21:8; Luke 12:26 (probable); 16:10 (probable); 19:17; 2 Cor 12:9, 15; Jas 3:4; 2 Pet 1:4; Rev 18:12 (probable); 21:11.

➡ ## 3. Superlative for Comparative

Not infrequently, the superlative has the same sense as the comparative in that it compares only *two* things rather than three or more. This is frequent with πρῶτος (although it normally has a superlative force), rare with ἔσχατος, and nonexistent with other superlative forms.

a. Clear Examples

Matt 21:28 ἄνθρωπος εἶχεν τέκνα δύο. καὶ προσελθὼν τῷ **πρώτῳ** εἶπεν . . .
            a man had two sons. He came to the **first** and said . . .

John 20:4   ὁ ἄλλος μαθητὴς . . . ἦλθεν **πρῶτος** εἰς τὸ μνημεῖον
            the other disciple came **first** to the tomb

> In classical Greek, the use of πρῶτος would usually indicate that at least *three* things were being compared. If this were the case here, then three disciples would be in view (*contra* οἱ δύο earlier in the verse). But the NT usage, like modern colloquial English, relaxed some of the grammatical standards of a former generation.

Cf. also John 1:15, 30; 20:8; 1 Tim 2:13; Heb 8:7; 9:1; 10:9; 2 Pet 2:20; Rev 20:5.[30]

---

[27] Robertson inexplicably says that this usage "comprises the great majority of the superlative forms that survive in the N.T." (*Grammar*, 670). *BDF* make a similar comment: "In the NT the remnants of the superlative forms are used mostly with 'elative' force as in the papyri" (32-33 [§60]).

[28] Very few examples with these two adjectives could be regarded as elative. The most likely instances are in Luke 14:9, 10 and Acts 2:17.

[29] BAGD, s.v. κράτιστος, 1.

[30] With the exception of 2 Pet 2:20 (ἔσχατος), all of these texts employ πρῶτος.

b. Debatable and Exegetically Significant Examples

Acts 1:1   Τὸν μὲν **πρῶτον** λόγον ἐποιησάμην
              The **first** account which I composed

> On this text Zerwick writes: "The use of πρῶτος in the sense of 'former, prior' is of a certain exegetical importance, for if this use were not taken into account, and the canons of classical usage were applied, it would follow from the prologue to the Acts that Luke wrote, or at least intended to write, not merely the gospel and the Acts but at least one other book of the same series; for. . . πρῶτος would in classical usage suppose plurality and not duality, for which πρότερος would have to be used."[31] The opposite view was taken by Theodor Zahn who argued that Luke intended to write three volumes. Zahn's view has largely been abandoned today.

Luke 2:2   αὕτη ἀπογραφὴ **πρώτη** ἐγένετο ἡγεμονεύοντος τῆς Συρίας Κυρηνίου[32]
             this was the **first** census [taken] when Quirinius was governor of Syria

> This text casts serious doubts on Luke's accuracy for two reasons: (1) The earliest known Roman census in Palestine was taken in 6-7 CE, and (2) there is little, if any, evidence that Quirinius was governor of Syria before Herod's death in 4 BCE. In light of this, many scholars believe that Luke was thinking about the census in 6-7 CE, when Quirinius was governor of Syria. At the same time, Luke demonstrates remarkable historical accuracy overall and even shows both an awareness of this later census (cf. Acts 5:37) and an understanding that Jesus was not born this late (cf. Luke 1:5).
>
> This issue cannot be resolved with certainty, though a couple of views are unlikely. First, it is doubtful that πρώτη here is used superlatively: "first of at least three." Not only is the usage of πρῶτος for a comparative well established in the NT, but it is unnecessary to compound the historical difficulty this text presents.[33]
>
> Second, it has sometimes been suggested that the text should be translated, "this census was *before the census* which Quirinius, governor of Syria, made."[34] It is argued that other comparative expressions sometimes have elided words (as in John 5:36 and 1 Cor 1:25) and, therefore, such is possible here. But this basis is insufficient, for the following reasons: (a) In both John 5:36 and 1 Cor 1:25, the gen. immediately follows the comparative adj., making the comparison explicit, while in this text Κυρηνίου is far removed from πρώτη and, in fact, is gen. because it is part of a gen. absolute construction.[35] Thus, what must necessarily be supplied in those texts is neither necessary nor natural in this one.[36] (b) This view presupposes that αὕτη *modifies* ἀπογραφή. But since the construction is anarthrous, such a view is almost impossible (because when a demonstrative functions attributively to a noun, the noun is

---

[31] Zerwick, *Biblical Greek*, 50.

[32] The addition of ἡ after αὕτη is found in several MSS, though predominantly late (e.g., ℵ^C A C L W *f*^1, 13 33 *Byz*).

[33] Inexplicably, Robertson suggests that the census is the "first in a series of enrollments as we now know" (669)!

[34] See Turner, *Insights*, 23-24, for a defense of this view. The view was articulated as early as the seventeenth century by Herwartus and maintained by Huschke, Tholuck, Lagrange, Heichelheim, Bruce, Turner, et al.

almost always articular);[37] a far more natural translation would be "This is the first census . . ." rather than "this census is . . ."

Third, πρώτη is sometimes regarded as adverbial: "this census took place *before* Quirinius was governor of Syria."[38] The advantage of this approach is that it eludes the historical problem of Quirinius' governorship overlapping the reign of Herod. However, like the previous view, it erroneously presupposes that αὕτη modifies ἀπογραφή. Further, it ignores the concord between πρώτη and ἀπογραφή, making the adj. most likely to function adjectivally, rather than adverbially.

In conclusion, facile solutions do not come naturally to Luke 2:2. This does not, of course, mean that Luke erred. In agreement with Schürmann, Marshall "warns against too easy acceptance of the conclusion that Luke has gone astray here; only the discovery of new historical evidence can lead to a solution of the problem."[39] This is where we must leave the matter.

The various forces of the three forms of the adjective are conveniently summarized below.

Form	*Positive*	*Comparative*	*Superlative*
Function			
Positive	X	0	0
Comparative	X	X	X
Elative	0	X	X
Superlative	X	X	X

Chart 33
The Semantic Range of the Forms of the Adjective

---

[35] H. Hoehner, *Chronological Aspects of the Life of Christ* (Grand Rapids: Zondervan, 1977) 21, argues similarly: "one notable difference between Luke 2:2 and the other passages cited is that Luke 2:2 has the participial phrase, 'when Quirinius was governor of Syria,' which is cumbersome, namely, 'This census was earlier than [the census] when Quirinius was governor of Syria.'"

[36] Winer-Moulton, 306, rightly calls this view "awkward, if not ungrammatical."

[37] BAGD point out that "when the art. is lacking there is no real connection betw. the demonstrative and the noun, but the one or the other belongs to the predicate . . ." (οὗτος, 2.c. [597]). They list but two exceptions, calling them "more difficult" (Acts 1:5) and "most difficult of all" (Acts 24:21).

[38] Cf. A. J. B. Higgins, "Sidelights on Christian Beginnings in the Graeco-Roman World," *EvanQ* 41 (1969) 200-1.

[39] I. H. Marshall, *Luke: Historian and Theologian* (Grand Rapids: Zondervan, 1971) 69, n. 5, enlisting H. Schürmann, *Das Lukasevangelium* (Freiburg, 1969) 1.98-101, on his side.

For an excellent treatment of the problem overall, especially from a historical perspective, see Hoehner, *Chronological Aspects*, 13-23.

III. The Relation of Adjective to Noun

The adjective may be either attributive or predicate in relation to the noun. That is, it may either modify the noun or assert something about it. Except for the use of pronominal adjectives with nouns (e.g., πᾶς, ὅλος, εἷς), when the article is present, it is usually easy to discern the relationship.

A. When the Article Is Present

1. The Attributive Positions

a. First Attributive Position

The first attributive position is article-adjective-noun (e.g., ὁ ἀγαθὸς βασιλεύς = the good king). In this construction "the adjective receives greater emphasis than the substantive."[40] This usage is quite common.

Matt 4:5   τὴν **ἁγίαν** πόλιν
             the **holy** city

Luke 6:45   ὁ **ἀγαθὸς** ἄνθρωπος
             the **good** man

Phil 3:2   βλέπετε τοὺς **κακοὺς** ἐργάτας
             watch out for the **evil** workers

1 John 4:18 ἡ **τελεία** ἀγάπη ἔξω βάλλει τὸν φόβον
             perfect love casts out fear

Cf. also Matt 5:26; John 2:10; Acts 9:31; Rom 7:2; Eph 3:5; Jas 1:21; Jude 3.

b. Second Attributive Position

The second attributive position is article-noun-article-adjective (e.g., ὁ βασιλεὺς ὁ ἀγαθός = the good king). This difference in the placement of the adjective is not one of relation, but of position and emphasis. In the second attributive position "both substantive and adjective receive emphasis and the adjective is added as a sort of climax in apposition with a separate article."[41] A literal, though awkward, gloss, bringing out the force of such a construction of ὁ βασιλεὺς ὁ ἀγαθός, is "the king, the good one." This construction occurs frequently.

Matt 5:29   εἰ ὁ ὀφθαλμός σου ὁ **δεξιὸς** σκανδαλίζει σε
             if your **right** eye causes you to stumble

---

[40] Robertson, *Grammar*, 776.
[41] Ibid., 777.

Acts 11:15   ἐπέπεσεν τὸ πνεῦμα τὸ **ἅγιον** ἐπ᾽ αὐτούς
              the **Holy** Spirit fell on them

Heb 6:4   γευσαμένους τῆς δωρεᾶς τῆς **ἐπουρανίου**
              having tasted the **heavenly** gift

Rev 19:2   ἔκρινεν τὴν πόρνην τὴν **μεγάλην**
              he has judged the **great** harlot

Cf. also Mark 3:29; Luke 1:59; 1 Cor 7:14; 1 Tim 5:25; Heb 4:4; Jas 3:7.

c.   Third Attributive Position

The third attributive position is noun-article-adjective (e.g., βασιλεὺς ὁ ἀγαθός = the good king). "Here the substantive is [often] indefinite and general, while the attribute [adjective] makes a particular application."[42] To bring out the *force* of such a construction one might translate βασιλεὺς ὁ ἀγαθός as "a king, the good one." This is the least frequent of the attributive positions, occurring only a few times with adjectives.[43]

Luke 15:22   ταχὺ ἐξενέγκατε στολὴν τὴν **πρώτην**[44]
             quickly bring out the **best** robe
             > The idea is "bring out a robe–the **best** one."

John 1:18   μονογενὴς θεὸς ὁ **ὢν** εἰς τὸν κόλπον τοῦ πατρός
             the unique God **who was** near the heart of the Father
             > More frequent than the adj. in third attributive positions is the partici-
             > ple. When a participle is used, the article should normally be translated
             > like a relative pronoun.

Cf. also Matt 4:13; Luke 23:49 (adjectival participle); Acts 2:20; Rom 16:10; Gal 1:1 (adjectival participle); Rev 14:8.

2. *The Predicate Positions*

➡   ### a.   First Predicate Position

The first predicate position is adjective-article-noun (e.g., ἀγαθὸς ὁ βασιλεύς = the king is good). Here, the adjective seems to be slightly more emphatic than the noun. Thus, to bring out the *force* of such a construction, one might translate ἀγαθὸς ὁ βασιλεύς as "good is the king." This usage is relatively common.

---

[42] Ibid.

[43] There are only a couple dozen such examples in the NT (apart from instances with proper names). However, the third attributive position is frequent when the modifier is other than an adj. (such as a participle, prepositional phrase, or gen. adjunct). In such instances the article is translated as though it were a relative pronoun. See "Article, Part I: The Article as Relative Pronoun," for discussion.

[44] Several MSS add τήν before στολήν (so 𝔓⁷⁵ D² *f*[1, 13] *Byz et alii*).

Matt 5:9   μακάριοι οἱ εἰρηνοποιοί
                blessed are the peacemakers

Mark 9:50   **καλὸν** τὸ ἅλας
                salt is **good**

2 Cor 1:18   **πιστὸς** ὁ θεός
                God is **faithful**

1 John 3:10   ἐν τούτῳ **φανερά** ἐστιν τὰ τέκνα τοῦ θεοῦ
                in this the children of God are **manifest**

Cf. also Matt 7:13; Mark 6:35; Luke 10:7; John 3:19; Acts 7:39; Rom 7:13; Titus 3:8; Heb 6:10; 1 Pet 2:3; Rev 5:12.

➡   **b.   Second Predicate Position**

     The second predicate position is article-noun-adjective (e.g., ὁ βασιλεὺς ἀγαθός = the king is good). Here, the emphasis seems to be either equally placed on both noun and adjective or is slightly heavier on the noun. This usage is relatively common.

John 3:33   ὁ θεὸς **ἀληθής** ἐστιν
                God is **true**

Rom 12:9   ἡ ἀγάπη **ἀνυπόκριτος**
                [Let] love be **without hypocrisy**

Jas 2:26   ἡ πίστις χωρὶς ἔργων **νεκρά** ἐστιν
                faith without works is **dead**

1 Pet 2:12   τὴν ἀναστροφὴν ὑμῶν ἐν τοῖς ἔθνεσιν ἔχοντες **καλήν**
                keep your conduct among the Gentiles **good**
                    The predicate adj. in this instance is also the complement of an object-complement construction.

Cf. also Matt 5:12; Mark 9:3; Luke 11:34; Acts 8:21; 1 Cor 14:14; Gal 4:1; Heb 4:12; 3 John 12.

3. *Summary*

When the article is present, the relation of adjective to noun is easy to determine. When the adjective is *within* the article-noun group (i.e., when it has an article immediately before it), it is attributive to the noun and hence modifies or qualifies the noun in some way. When the adjective is *outside* the article-noun group, it is predicate to the noun and hence makes an assertion about it.

The only exception to these rules when the article is present is with pronominal adjectives (i.e., words that function sometimes as adjectives and sometimes as pronouns, such as πᾶς, ὅλος). These may stand in a predicate *position* but have an attributive *relation* to the noun. Other than with pronominal adjectives, then, when the article is present, the adjective's (structural) position to the noun will determine and be the same as its (semantic) relation to the noun.

	1st	*2nd*	*3rd*
Attributive	Art-Adj-Noun (ὁ ἀγαθὸς ἄνθρωπος= the good man)	Art-Noun-Art-Adj (ὁ ἄνθρωπος ὁ ἀγαθός= the good man)	Noun-Art-Adj (ἄνθρωπος ὁ ἀγαθός= the good man)
Predicate	Adj-Art-Noun (ἀγαθὸς ὁ ἄνθρωπος= the man is good)	Art-Noun-Adj (ὁ ἄνθρωπος ἀγαθός= the man is good)	None

Table 6
Attributive and Predicate Positions of the Adjective

B. When the Article Is Absent

When no article is present, the relation of adjective to noun is more difficult to ascertain. This type of construction occurs almost 2400 times in the NT, over one fourth of all adjective-noun constructions. Conceivably, the anarthrous adjective-noun construction could express either an attributive or predicate relation.[45] For example, βασιλεὺς ἀγαθός could mean either "a good king" or "a king is good." However, there are some rules of thumb to follow here that will be discussed toward the end of this section.

➡ ## 1. The Anarthrous Adjective-Noun Construction

Rather than treat attributive and predicate positions separately, both will be dealt with under the same structural heading. The reason for this is that only when the article is present will the structure dictate the semantics. In the anarthrous construction, since the article is absent, the position of the adjective does not determine its relation to the noun.

a. (Anarthrous) First Attributive Position

Thus when it has been determined *from the context* that an adjective in an adjective-noun construction (note the order: adj., then noun) expresses an attributive relation to the noun, it is in the *first* (anarthrous) *attributive* position (e.g., ἀγαθὸς βασιλεύς = a good king). This is common enough, occurring hundreds of times in the NT.

---

[45] However, of the 30+ NT grammatical works I examined, only seven allowed the possibility of an adj. in such a construction expressing a predicate relation to the noun, while none gave any true examples of this phenomenon (cf. Wallace, "Anarthrous Constructions," 129-30, n. 3).

b. Illustrations

Luke 19:17 εὖγε, **ἀγαθὲ** δοῦλε
well done, **good** servant

1 Cor 3:10 ὡς **σοφὸς** ἀρχιτέκτων θεμέλιον ἔθηκα
as a **wise** master builder, I laid a foundation

2 Pet 1:19 ὡς λύχνῳ φαίνοντι ἐν **αὐχμηρῷ** τόπῳ
like a lamp shining in a **dark** place

Cf. Matt 15:14; 2 John 1; Jude 6; Rev 3:8.

c. (Anarthrous) First Predicate Position

When, however, the same construction has been determined *from the context* to express a predicate relation, the adjective is in the *first* (anarthrous) *predicate* position to the noun (e.g., ἀγαθὸς βασιλεύς = a king is good). Though much less common than the attributive relation, in equative clauses (viz., a clause in which an equative verb is stated or implied), this is not too uncommon.

Mark 12:31 **μείζων** τούτων ἄλλη ἐντολὴ οὐκ ἔστιν
no other command is **greater** than these

1 Cor 12:17 εἰ **ὅλον** ἀκοή, ποῦ ἡ ὄσφρησις;
If the **whole** [body] were an ear [lit. hearing], where would the sense of smell be?

Jas 1:12 **μακάριος** ἀνὴρ ὃς ὑπομένει πειρασμόν
blessed is the man who endures a trial

Cf. Rom 9:2 (possible);[46] Heb 6:5 (possible);[47] 10:4; Jude 14.

→ 2. *The Anarthrous Noun-Adjective Construction*

a. Fourth Attributive Position

When it has been determined *from the context* that an adjective in a noun-adjective construction expresses an attributive relation to the noun, such a construction is in the *fourth* attributive position. The reason for this is that *both* the second and third attributive positions involve an adjective following a noun.[48] Thus to say that an adjective is in the *fourth*

---

[46] λύπη μοί ἐστιν μεγάλη καὶ ἀδιάλειπτος ὀδύνη τῇ καρδίᾳ μου could either mean "there is great grief and unceasing anguish in my heart" or "my grief is great and the anguish in my heart is unceasing" (*contra* Wallace, "Anarthrous Constructions," 157, where this construction is considered with certainty to be predicate).

[47] καλὸν γευσαμένους θεοῦ ῥῆμα could either be translated "having tasted the good word of God" or "having tasted that the word of God is good."

[48] See Wallace, "Anarthrous Constructions," 133-35, for a discussion of the problem of terminology.

attributive position is to say that the article does *not* occur in the construction at all (e.g., βασιλεὺς ἀγαθός = a good king). This usage is quite common.

b. Illustrations

Mark 1:8   αὐτὸς βαπτίσει ὑμᾶς ἐν πνεύματι **ἁγίῳ**
               he will baptize you in the **Holy** Spirit

John 3:16   μὴ ἀπόληται ἀλλ᾽ ἔχῃ ζωὴν **αἰώνιον**
               he should not perish but have **eternal** life

Phil 1:6   ὁ ἐναρξάμενος ἐν ὑμῖν ἔργον **ἀγαθὸν** ἐπιτελέσει
               the one who began a **good** work in you will complete it

Cf. also Matt 7:19; Acts 7:60; Rom 5:21; Rev 1:15; 19:17.

c. (Anarthrous) Second Predicate Position

When the same construction has been determined *from the context* to express a predicate relation, the adjective is in the *second* (anarthrous) *predicate* position to the noun (e.g., βασιλεὺς ἀγαθός = a king is good). This usage is relatively common, especially in equative clauses.

Matt 13:57   οὐκ ἔστιν προφήτης **ἄτιμος** εἰ μὴ ἐν τῇ πατρίδι
               a prophet is not **without honor** except in his homeland

Rom 7:8   χωρὶς νόμου ἁμαρτία **νεκρά**
               apart from the law, sin is **dead**

Heb 9:17   διαθήκη ἐπὶ νεκροῖς **βεβαία**
               a covenant is **confirmed** at death

Cf. Matt 12:10; Mark 6:4; John 9:1; 1 Tim 3:8; Heb 4:13; 1 John 3:3.

3. Determining the Relation of Adjective to Noun in Anarthrous Constructions: Some Guidelines

The general rule is that in *nonequative* clauses (i.e., a clause that does not primarily make an assertion about the subject; thus its main verb is other than the copula), an anarthrous adjective related to an anarthrous noun is normally attributive (cf., e.g., 1 Cor 3:10; 2 John 1; Jude 6; Rev 3:3). There are some exceptions, however (cf. e.g., Heb 6:18; 10:4; Jude 14).

In *equative* clauses (i.e., a clause that primarily makes an assertion about the subject; thus its main verb [whether expressed or implied] is the copula), the general rule is that an anarthrous adjective related to an anarthrous noun is normally predicate. This is especially true when the order is noun-adjective.[49] For the predicate relations, cf., e.g., 1 Cor 12:17; Rom 7:8;

---

[49] In this construction in equative clauses I have discovered 127 definite predicate relations and only 40 attributive relations.

Heb 9:17; Jas 1:12. The example in Rom 7:8 is most illustrative: ἀμαρτία νεκρά ("sin is dead"). But the attributive relation also occurs, though not as frequently (cf., e.g., Matt 7:15; Luke 5:8; Eph 6:2; Heb 12:11; 1 John 2:18).

4. Some Exegetically and Theologically Significant Passages

In anarthrous constructions there are a few passages that deserve some discussion due to their exegetical and/or theological significance. In all of these texts, NT scholars have seen the adjectives in question as ambiguous or definitely attributive. But a case can be made that the adjective in question is predicate.

Acts 19:2   οὐδ᾽ εἰ πνεῦμα **ἅγιον** ἔστιν ἠκούσαμεν[50]

There are three translation possibilities for this text: (1) "we have not heard whether there is a **Holy** Spirit"; (2) "we have not heard whether the **Holy** Spirit was [given]" (cf. John 7:39); or (3) "we have not heard whether a spirit can be **holy**."

The first two options are typically addressed in the literature. A defense of the third translation is taken up here. It is at least possible for the following reasons: (1) There is no article to define the relation of adj. to noun, thus it might be predicate (indeed, in equative clauses the anarthrous second predicate adj. outnumbers the fourth attributive adj. three to one). (2) The flurry of activity of evil spirits in Jesus' day and the early apostolic period makes it feasible. (3) The fact that these disciples were from Ephesus, a known hotbed for cults, renders this a possible translation. Still, this is only a possibility that simply needs to be put on the exegetical table for further discussion.

Titus 2:10   πᾶσαν πίστιν ἐνδεικνυμένους **ἀγαθήν**[51]

There are two possibilities here: (1) "showing forth all **good** faith" and (2) "showing forth all faith [to be] **good**."

Again, the first gloss is all that is found in the literature. But the case for the second translation is by no means weak: (1) In nonequative clauses in the NT, there are apparently *no* instances in which the adj. following the noun is attributive when (a) there is an adj. before the noun and (b) there is an intervening word between the noun and second adj. (2) On the other hand, there are four other instances (besides this one) that involve the construction adj.-noun-adj. in a nonequative clause in which the second adj. has a word between it and the noun: the second adj. each time is predicate (cf. Mark 7:2; 8:19; Acts 4:16; Rev 15:1). (3) Lexically, the use of πίστις in the Pastorals (if the faith has been clarified as genuine) is a faith that produces good works (cf., e.g., 2 Tim 3:15-17; Titus 1:13-16). (4) The verb ἐνδείκνυμι is one of the verbs that takes an object-complement double acc. Thus, when such a verb has a noun and adj. in the acc., the burden of proof seems to be on those who would see the adj. as attributive rather than as predicate (and thus acting as the complement to the noun in the acc.). (5) Contextually, a rendering of the text along these lines unveils a synthetic (or even a synonymous)

---

[50] A few MSS, particularly of the Western text, have λαμβάνουσιν τινες for ἔστιν (𝔓[38,41] D*): "We have not heard if some have received the Holy Spirit."

[51] A number of MSS shuffle the word order and/or substitute terms in this text.

parallel between the two halves of v 10: "Slaves should be wholly subject to their masters . . . demonstrating that all [genuine][52] faith is productive, with the result [ecbatic ἵνα] that they will completely adorn the doctrine of God." The point of the text, then, if this understanding is correct, is an exhortation to slaves to demonstrate that their faith is sincere and results in holy behavior. If taken this way, the text seems to support the idea that saving faith does not fail, but even results in good works.

2 Tim 3:16 πᾶσα γραφὴ **θεόπνευστος** καὶ ὠφέλιμος

every[53] scripture is **inspired** and profitable

Many scholars feel that the translation should be: "Every **inspired** scripture is also profitable." This is probably not the best translation, however, for the following reasons: (1) Contextually: (a) Among those who see the Pastorals as authentic, the argument has been that Paul would not need to assert the inspiration of scripture to Timothy. Indeed, that the author might be doing so here has been used as an argument against authenticity. But it is possible for the Pastorals to be both authentic and for the apostle to be making an assertion:[54] He has a habit of reminding Timothy of truths he already knows, such as that Jesus Christ was raised from the dead and that Paul himself was a minister of the gospel to the Gentiles. Thus, as Fairbairn points out, "it could not be superfluous to impress upon him a sense of the divine character of Old Testament Scripture."[55] (b) If the author were merely asserting the profitableness of scripture, then what would be the basis for his very forceful command in 4:1-2? Could he "solemnly charge [Timothy] in the presence of God and of Christ Jesus, [to] preach the word" if he had simply asserted that scripture is profitable?

(2) Grammatically: (a) The fact that v 16 is asyndetic (i.e., begins without a conjunction) cannot be due to new subject matter, but to the solemnity of the statement because the author had been discussing the holy writings in v 15. Thus seeing θεόπνευστος as predicate fits in better with the solemn tone established at the beginning of the verse. (b) Since the copula is lacking, it needs to be supplied in English. And the most natural place to supply the equative verb is between the subject and the *first* word that follows it. It is in fact significant that an author typically leaves out the copula when he assumes the audience knows where it naturally should go. (c) The fact that καί means "and" twelve times as often as it means "also," as well as the fact that it is unnatural to translate it adverbially as "also" between two adjectives in the same case,

---

[52] "Genuine" may either be implied from the flow of argument or may be considered a part of the field of meaning for πᾶς when it is used with abstract nouns (cf. BAGD, s.v. πᾶς, 1.a.δ.).

[53] It is of course possible to translate πᾶσα as "all," but normal usage would require the noun (γραφή) to be articular.

[54] Although the view that the Pastorals are not authentic has held sway for most NT scholars in this century, a number of scholars are now arguing for Pauline authorship. Cf. the commentaries by Guthrie, Fee, Knight, Mounce, etc.

[55] P. Fairbairn, *Commentary on the Pastoral Epistles* (Grand Rapids: Zondervan, 1956) 380.

argues for a predicate θεόπνευστος.[56] (d) Since the article may be ana-phoric when referring back to a synonym, and since the author has been discussing the scriptures with three different synonyms in this context (vv 15, 16, and 4:2), it seems likely that the article is anaphoric in 4:2 when he declares, "Preach *the* word!" (κήρυξον **τὸν** λόγον). If the writer had said that only inspired scripture was profitable in 3:16 and then tells his reader(s) to preach *all* scripture (= "the word"), it might be a misleading statement, for [Timothy] might inadvertently preach some scripture that was not inspired. But since the writer leaves λόγον unqualified apart from the fact that it referred back to γραφή of v 16, it is perhaps likely that he meant to make an assertion about all scripture in v 16, viz., that it is inspired.[57] (e) Finally, what bears on the relation of adj. to noun most directly: In the NT, LXX, in classical and Koine Greek, the overwhelming semantic force of an adj.-noun-adj. construc-tion in an equative clause is that the first adj. will be attributive and the second will be predicate.[58] There are almost 50 instances in the NT and LXX in which the second adj. in such a construction is predicate and the first is attributive (39 of which involve πᾶς before the noun; most in the LXX) and none on the other side. The evidence is so overwhelming that we may suggest a "rule": *In πᾶς + noun + adjective constructions in equa-tive clauses the πᾶς, being by nature as definite as the article, implies the arti-cle, thus making the adjective(s) following the noun outside the implied article-noun group and, therefore, predicate.*[59] In the least, the evidence ren-ders translations of this verse such as the NEB's ("every inspired scrip-ture has its use") highly suspect.

---

[56] There is a textual variant which omits the καί. If original, then almost surely θεόπνευστος is attributive. However, support for it is weak (neither Nestle[27] nor Tischen-dorf list any Greek MSS omitting the καί; they give only versions and patristic writers).

[57] This argument, however, may be less weighty than presented. Even an attributive θεόπνευστος would not necessarily imply that not all scripture was inspired, for this adj. could be descriptive (of all scripture) rather than restrictive.

[58] There is possibly one exception to this in the NT and none in the LXX. I have found perhaps one or two exceptions in Hellenistic Greek (one in Josephus, one in the Didache), though none so far in Attic Greek. The research has not been exhaustive, but the odds are against taking θεόπνευστος as attributive.

[59] For a lengthier discussion of this text, cf. D. B. Wallace, "The Relation of Adjective to Noun in Anarthrous Constructions in the New Testament" (Th.M. thesis, Dallas Theo-logical Seminary, 1979) 51-61. The article in *NovT* with the same title is virtually identical with the thesis except that it lacks two parts: (a) an appendix listing all definite and ques-tionable predicate adjectives in anarthrous constructions (73-102), and (b) a detailed dis-cussion of some of the exegetically significant texts (46-61).

The Pronouns

Overview

I. Select Bibliography

BAGD, s.v. various lexical entries; *BDF*, 145-61 (§277-306); **H. J. Cadbury**, "The Relative Pronouns in Acts and Elsewhere," *JBL* 42 (1923) 150-57; **Dana-Mantey**, 122-35 (§133-43); **Hoffmann-von Siebenthal**, *Grammatik*, 194-211 (§139-44); **W. Michaelis**, "Das unbetonte καὶ αὐτός bei Lukas," *Studia Theologica* 4 (1950) 86-93; **Moule**, *Idiom Book*, 118-25; **Moulton**, *Prolegomena*, 84-98; **Porter**, *Idioms*, 128-38; **H. K. Moulton**, "Pronouns in the New Testament," *BT* 27.2 (1976) 237-40; **Robertson**, *Grammar*, 676-753; **Smyth**, *Greek Grammar*, 298-311 (§1190-1278); **V. Spottorno**, "The Relative Pronoun in the New Testament," *NTS* 28 (1982) 132-41; **Turner**, *Syntax*, 37-50; **Young**, *Intermediate Greek*, 71-80; **Zerwick**, *Biblical Greek*, 7-8, 63-71 (§16-21, 195-223).

II. General Remarks

A. Definition

A pronoun is a word used "to designate an object without naming it, when that which is referred to is known from context or usage, has been already mentioned or indicated, or, being unknown, is the subject or object of inquiry."[1] Since pronouns are grammatical proxies, they must indicate in some manner that to which they are referring. The basic rule for the Greek pronoun is that it agrees with its antecedent in gender and number, but its case is determined by the pronoun's function in its own clause. This concord principle, however, has many exceptions.

B. A Linguistic Luxury

In many respects, pronouns are a linguistic luxury. They are unnecessary because, for the most part, they stand in the place of a noun, other substantive, or noun phrase. This antecedent could just as easily be repeated. In Greek, there is a second reason why at least some of the pronouns are often unnecessary, viz., the pronoun's force is either already embedded in the structure of the sentence (e.g., verbal endings) or could be inferred by some other means (e.g., possessive adjective).

---

[1] *Oxford English Dictionary,* s.v. "pronoun."

C. Reduction of Redundancy

One might think that with so much going against them, pronouns would be scarcely employed. This is hardly the case. The NT has about 16,500 pronouns![2] They show up in four-fifths of the verses. Why are pronouns used so frequently, when they are a luxury of the language? The reasons are stylistic as much as syntactical. That is to say, as terms that most frequently replace nouns, pronouns are able to sidestep monotonous redundancy and keep the discourse moving.

D. Clarification and Misunderstanding

On the one hand, this extended use of pronouns also makes them susceptible to misinterpretation. For example, in Eph 2:8 we read τῇ γὰρ χάριτί ἐστε σεσῳσμένοι διὰ πίστεως· καὶ **τοῦτο** οὐκ ἐξ ὑμῶν ("for by grace you are saved through faith; and **this** is not of yourselves"). To what does τοῦτο refer? Is it "grace," "faith," or something altogether different? The antecedent is anything but clear.

On the other hand, pronouns are often used to *clarify.* In the dialogue between Jesus and the Samaritan woman, for example, the personal pronoun is used to distinguish speaker from hearer (John 4:15-16): λέγει πρὸς αὐτὸν ἡ γυνή· κύριε, δός μοι τοῦτο τὸ ὕδωρ, ἵνα μὴ διψῶ μηδὲ διέρχωμαι ἐνθάδε ἀντλεῖν. λέγει **αὐτῇ** ... ("the woman said to him, 'Sir, give me this water, in order that I might not thirst nor come here to draw.' He said **to her** ...").

Sometimes this penchant for clarity results in a redundant (or pleonastic) pronoun, as in John 5:11: ὁ ποιήσας με ὑγιῆ **ἐκεῖνός** μοι εἶπεν ("the one who made me well–**that one** [*or* he] said to me"). To a lesser degree, pronouns are often used in Hellenistic Greek simply for the sake of explicitness. To an Attic writer, such explicitness would seem redundant, since the pronominal notion is already carried in the verbal inflection or by some other means. But as the language expanded beyond the borders of Greece and Macedonia, the subtleties of the Attic dialect were often replaced by express terms. The frequent use of pronouns was part of this tendency.[3]

---

[2] A search in *acCordance* yielded 16,703 pronouns. But when the *acCordance* search was broken down by categories, only 16,298 pronouns were found (408 instances of τις were not included in the indefinite pronoun category; three instances of pronouns are unaccounted for). But the larger number is still too big by our reckoning. The difference is definitional: What *acCordance/Gramcord* regards as a pronoun, we take to be an adjective (e.g., *acCordance* regards ἐμός, σός, ἡμέτερος, and ὑμέτερος as possessive pronouns; we view them as possessive adjectives).

[3] Zerwick, *Biblical Greek,* 63 (§196): "The great frequency with which pronouns are used is due to what may be called the 'analytic' tendency of any living spontaneous popular speech, a tendency that is to express explicitly what is already contained implicitly in the expression used or in the nature of the subject matter ...."

E. Connotative Value

Pronouns are also used, at times, exclusively with *connotative* value. What they denote may be obvious from the text; but they can be used for emphasis, contrast, etc. This is especially the case with personal pronouns. But all is not cut and dried. As we have said, one of the marks of Koine Greek was its movement away from the subtleties of Attic. Thus, even when αὐτός is used with a third person verb, it may be for emphasis *or* for clarity. Not a few exegetical debates hinge on which force it has in a given text.

F. Relaxing of Classical Distinctions Between Pronouns

Furthermore, there is overlap in the use of the pronouns; again, the classical distinctions are not always maintained. The NT authors, for example, do not always maintain the near-far distinction with the demonstrative pronouns οὗτος and ἐκεῖνος.[4] In John especially, the demonstratives are used interchangeably with the personal pronoun and often simply mean "he."

G. Antecedents and Postcedents

Finally, we should mention a word about terminology. When the noun (or other nominal) that the pronoun refers to *precedes* the pronoun, it is called the pronoun's *antecedent* (as in "**Bob** read the book. Then *he* gave it to Jane"). This is the most frequent usage. When the noun comes after the pronoun, it is the pronoun's *postcedent* (as in "After *he* read the book, **Bob** gave it to Jane"). In the latter case, the pronoun may be said to be "proleptic."

---

[4] Dana-Mantey suggest, for example, that ἐκεῖνος is used "for that which is relatively distant in actuality or thought" (128), while οὗτος is used "for that which is relatively near in actuality or thought" (127). This is a good description of their usage in Attic Greek, but there are many exceptions in the NT.

III. Semantic Categories: Major Classes

The number of pronoun classes in Greek is difficult to assess, though most grammars have between eight and twelve.[5] A major part of the difficulty in determining the number of classes has to do with whether a particular term is an adjective or a pronoun.[6] Nevertheless, certain classes are not disputed as pronominal: personal, demonstrative, relative, interrogative, indefinite, intensive, reflexive, and reciprocal. These constitute the core of our discussion. In addition, the possessive pronoun will receive treatment below, but it is not a true *Greek* category.

The relative frequency of the eight main categories can be seen in the following chart.[7]

---

[5] *BDF* list at least 10; Robertson has 11; Dana-Mantey have 9; Smyth mentions 10; Porter and Hoffman-von Siebenthal each have 8; Young and *acCordance* each give 9. None of these lists is identical, however. Correlative, possessive, and identical are the most debatable categories, all of which are considered to be adjectives in this grammar (though the possessive class requires some explanation [see discussion below]).

[6] Grammarians are not agreed as to what distinguishes a pronoun from an adjective. Indeed, many terms are given double labels (adjective and pronoun [i.e., substantive]) in BAGD. Young (*Intermediate Greek*, 71) notes that "the distinctions between different kinds of pronouns and even between pronouns and adjectives are often blurred.... Pronouns that function as pronouns agree with their antecedent in gender and number. Those that function as adjectives agree with the noun they modify in gender, number, and case." The problem with this distinction is that it gives no criteria for telling whether a word is a pronoun acting like an adjective, or an adjective acting like a pronoun. Are the terms ἐμός, σός, ἡμέτερος, and ὑμέτερος adjectives or pronouns? They predominantly function in a dependent role, modifying a noun. In all syntactical respects they behave just like adjectives, yet many grammarians consider them to be pronouns.

The problems of definition are real. To some extent, then, the determination of what constitutes a pronoun is an arbitrary choice. Some words are clearly pronouns (e.g., ἐγώ), others are clearly adjectives (e.g., ἀγαθός), while several words may be classed somewhere in between, either as pronominal adjectives or adjectival pronouns. For the most part, *we are regarding those words as pronouns which, when functioning substantively, do not take the article.* Adjectives, on the other hand, regularly take the article when substituting for a noun.

[7] The statistics are those of *acCordance* with some modification.

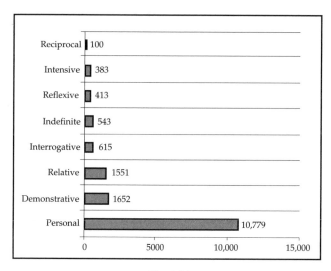

Chart 34
Frequency of Pronoun Classes in the New Testament

A. Personal Pronouns

1. Definition and Terms Used

The personal pronouns are ἐγώ (ἡμεῖς) for the first person, and σύ (ὑμεῖς) for the second person. In Hellenistic Greek, αὐτός is used for the third person pronoun (and sometimes for the first or second person).[8]

Personal pronouns are far and away the most frequently used pronouns in the NT. Two out of three pronouns belong to this classification. About half of the instances in this class involve αὐτός. The uses of personal pronouns can be broken down by cases, viz., nominative and non-nominative (= oblique).[9]

Other pronouns that fill the slot of personal pronouns are ἐκεῖνος and οὗτος. Though technically demonstrative pronouns, not infrequently their demonstrative force is diminished (see "Demonstrative Pronouns" for discussion).

---

[8] It is sometimes alleged that the Attic third person pronouns, οὗ (gen. singular, there being no nom.) and σφεῖς (nom. plural), have been replaced in the NT by αὐτός. Although true, even in Attic these pronouns were rarely used: "Of the forms of the third personal pronoun only the datives οἷ and σφίσι(ν) are commonly used in Attic prose, and then only as indirect reflexives. . . ." (Smyth, *Greek Grammar*, 92 [§326.d]).

[9] The gen. is the most common case, accounting for about 40% of all personal pronouns. Most of these *function* semantically as possessive pronouns. As well, the gen. is the most frequent with every form of the personal pronoun except the second person plural (dat. has 608 to 561 for the gen.), while the nom. is the least frequent for every form except the first person singular.

2. Functions

a. Nominative Uses[10]

1) Emphasis

The nominative personal pronoun is most commonly used for emphasis. The emphasis may involve some sort of *contrast*. In such instances, two subjects are normally in view, though one might be only implied. This contrast is either of kind (antithetical) or degree (comparison). For example, in "He washed and she dried," the contrast is comparative (both people doing the dishes). In the sentence "He slept and she worked," the contrast is antithetical.

Emphasis may also focus on the *subject* more than the verb. The reasons for such focus may be to identify, give prominence to, clarify, etc.[11] In such instances, contrast with other subjects is not necessarily absent, but neither is it prominent.

a) Contrast

Matt 2:6   καὶ **σὺ** Βηθλέεμ, γῆ Ἰούδα, οὐδαμῶς ἐλαχίστη εἶ ἐν τοῖς ἡγεμόσιν Ἰούδα
and **you**, Bethlehem, in the land of Judah, are by no means least among the leaders of Judah

Mark 8:29   **σὺ** εἶ ὁ χριστός
you are the Christ

> Jesus is not Elijah, one of the prophets, or John raised from the dead. He is in a league by himself. Peter's declaration as to Jesus' identity, on a discourse level, may be viewed as the pivotal point in the Gospel of Mark. Up until this point, Jesus is progressively revealed as the Servant

---

[10] In addition to the two uses below, many grammars list the "epistolary plural" (a. k. a. "editorial 'we'"), as well as the use of the first or second person for third. Since almost all such examples occur in the nom. case as subject of the verb, thereby making an explicit pronoun dispensable (because it is embedded in the verbal inflection), we felt it best to locate this category in the chapter "Person and Number" in the section on "Verbs and Verbals." In other words, these categories do not have to do with the pronoun per se, but with the person.

[11] Classifying emphasis is notoriously difficult. Some helpful approaches are as follows. Dana-Mantey speak of two kinds of emphasis as "antithetical" and "prominence" (123 [§134]). Porter lists three kinds of emphasis: antithetical, selective, and descriptive (*Idioms*, 129). The descriptive use might be better labeled "anaphoric" because it points back to a *previous* description. Young takes a discourse approach in which emphasis is broken down into "importance, gravity, surprise, anger, contrast, comparison, or identity" (*Intermediate Greek*, 72). These uses are helpful handles, but are, for the most part, applicational instances of emphasis rather than intrinsic or syntactical labels. Other discourse categories could be added to the list, such as joy (1 John 1:4), insignificance (1 Cor 15:9), servility (Eph 4:1), personal responsibility (Acts 16:31), etc. One only needs to use his or her imagination to look at the *reason* for the emphasis in the discourse. Furthermore, such uses are not restricted to the nom. case. Nevertheless, Young's point is well taken: One must not stop at syntactical labels when doing exegesis.

of Yahweh. After this, he is seen to be the *suffering* Servant of Yahweh. The pronoun, of course, says none of this. But the reasons for its presence in a given passage need to be ascertained.

Mark 10:28 Ἤρξατο λέγειν ὁ Πέτρος αὐτῷ· ἰδοὺ **ἡμεῖς** ἀφήκαμεν πάντα καὶ ἠκολουθήκαμέν σοι[12]

Peter began to say to him, "Behold, **we** have left everything and have followed you."

> Peter's comment stands in bold relief with the statement in v 22 of the failure of the rich young ruler to abandon his wealth to follow Jesus.

Luke 11:48 μάρτυρές ἐστε καὶ συνευδοκεῖτε τοῖς ἔργοις τῶν πατέρων ὑμῶν, ὅτι **αὐτοὶ** μὲν ἀπέκτειναν αὐτούς, **ὑμεῖς** δὲ οἰκοδομεῖτε.

You are witnesses and consent to the deeds of your fathers, for **they** killed [the prophets] and **you** build [their tombs].

> Although their relation to the prophets is different, both the Pharisees and their ancestors are cut from the same cloth (thus, a comparison is made).

Luke 24:18 **σὺ** μόνος παροικεῖς Ἰερουσαλὴμ καὶ οὐκ ἔγνως τὰ γενόμενα ἐν αὐτῇ;

Are **you** the only one visiting Jerusalem and yet you do not know the things that have happened in it?

John 15:16 οὐχ **ὑμεῖς** με ἐξελέξασθε, ἀλλ᾽ **ἐγὼ** ἐξελεξάμην ὑμᾶς

you did not choose me, but **I** chose you

> The contrast between Jesus and the disciples is categorical: Election was accomplished by him, a point strengthened by the ἀλλά. A comparative contrast would mean, "You did not choose me as much as I chose you," but that is foreign to the context.

1 Th 2:18 ἠθελήσαμεν ἐλθεῖν πρὸς ὑμᾶς, **ἐγὼ** μὲν Παῦλος καὶ ἅπαξ καὶ δίς, καὶ ἐνέκοψεν ἡμᾶς ὁ σατανᾶς

We wanted to come to you, [especially] **I**, Paul, more than once, yet Satan hindered us.

> Whether the contrast here is one of kind or degree is difficult to assess: Does this text "mean *we [all]* wanted . . . *[at least,]* I did? or does it mean simply I *wanted [though others did not]*?"[13] Since the plural is repeated (ἡμᾶς) after Paul singles himself out, the force of ἐγώ is most likely comparative (Satan hindered all of us, but I especially tried to come).

Cf. also Matt 5:28; Mark 1:8; 5:40; John 2:10; 4:22; Acts 27:31; Rom 8:23; 2 Cor 11:29; Heb 1:11; 5:2; 1 John 4:19; Rev 3:10.

b) Subject Focus

John 1:23 **ἐγὼ** φωνὴ βοῶντος ἐν τῇ ἐρήμῳ

I am a voice of one crying in the wilderness

> This is John's answer in response to the question, "Who are you?" (v 22). There is of course a contrast implied as well: John is not Elijah (v 21), but the focus seems more to be on his positive identity.

---

[12] ἡμεῖς is omitted in W.

[13] Moule, *Idiom Book*, 119.

Jas 1:13   πειράζει δὲ **αὐτὸς** οὐδένα
          but **he** tempts no one

2 Pet 1:17   ὁ υἱός μου ὁ ἀγαπητός μου οὗτός ἐστιν εἰς ὃν **ἐγὼ** εὐδόκησα[14]
          this is my beloved Son, in whom **I** am well pleased

Rev 3:9   **ἐγὼ** ἠγάπησά σε[15]
          I have loved you

> The risen Christ says to the church at Philadelphia that he will make the members of the synagogue of Satan learn "that I have loved you." The implication (both from the context and the personal pronoun) seems to be that the Lord's love for his church was disputed by this group.

Cf. also Matt 22:32; Rom 10:19; Heb 12:1; 1 Pet 1:16; 1 John 2:25; 3 John 1; Jude 17.

2) Redundancy

The presence of the personal pronoun in the nominative is not always for emphasis. Occasionally, it is a mere redundancy of the pronominal notion embedded in the verb.[16] Only the context can help determine whether a personal pronoun is emphatic or not. Many of these instances could be functioning in the narrative as a "switch-reference device, signifying a change in subject to someone or something that had been mentioned previously."[17]

Luke 5:1   Ἐγένετο δὲ ἐν τῷ τὸν ὄχλον ἐπικεῖσθαι αὐτῷ καὶ ἀκούειν τὸν λόγον τοῦ θεοῦ καὶ **αὐτὸς** ἦν ἑστὼς παρὰ τὴν λίμνην Γεννησαρέτ[18]
          When the crowd began to press upon him and to hear the word of God, **he** was standing by the lake of Gennesaret.

John 6:24   ὅτε οὖν εἶδεν ὁ ὄχλος ὅτι Ἰησοῦς οὐκ ἔστιν ἐκεῖ οὐδὲ οἱ μαθηταὶ αὐτοῦ, ἐνέβησαν **αὐτοὶ** εἰς τὰ πλοιάρια καὶ ἦλθον εἰς Καφαρναοὺμ ζητοῦντες τὸν Ἰησοῦν.[19]
          Then when the crowd saw that Jesus was not there, nor were his disciples, **they** got into the boats and came to Capernaum, seeking Jesus.

Cf. also Matt 14:2; Luke 2:28; 3:23; 4:15; 9:44; Acts 22:19.

---

[14] ἐν ᾧ is read in Ψ 0209 33 1241 *et pauci* for εἰς ὅν.

[15] The majority of MSS, though all of them late, omit ἐγώ (cf. 1006 1841 2351 & 𝔐^k), while the earliest and best witnesses (e.g., ℵ A C P *alii*) have it.

[16] Luke especially uses καὶ αὐτός this way. See Michaelis, "Das unbetonte," for a detailed discussion. He has largely been followed by BAGD, *BDF*, 146 (§277), Zerwick, *Biblical Greek*, 64 (§199), et al.

[17] Young, *Intermediate Greek*, 75.

[18] For καὶ αὐτὸς ἦν ἑστώς codex D has the gen. absolute ἑστῶτος αὐτοῦ.

[19] A number of witnesses alter the construction αὐτοὶ εἰς τὰ πλοιάρια, although only the Western text (D it) changes the personal pronoun to a reflexive pronoun (ἑαυτοῖς πλοιάρια). D also has ἔλαβον for ἐνέβησαν (thus, "they took for themselves boats").

b. Oblique Cases

The almost exclusive use of the personal pronouns in the oblique cases (i.e., gen., dat., acc.) is simply to stand in the place of a noun or other nominal. This use of the pronoun can be called *anaphoric* in that it refers back to its antecedent. Two other uses deserve special mention.

1) Normal Use: Anaphoric

John 4:7   ἔρχεται γυνή . . . λέγει **αὐτῇ** ὁ Ἰησοῦς
           a woman came . . . Jesus said **to her**
> This is followed by "the woman said **to him**" (λέγει **αὐτῷ** ἡ γυνή) in v 9, "Jesus said **to her**" (Ἰησοῦς εἶπεν **αὐτῇ**) in v 10, "the woman said **to him**" (λέγει **αὐτῷ** ἡ γυνή) in v 11, and so on in vv 13, 15, 16, 17, 19, etc.

Acts 27:32   ἀπέκοψαν οἱ στρατιῶται τὰ σχοινία τῆς σκάφης καὶ εἴασαν **αὐτὴν** ἐκπεσεῖν
           the soldiers cut the ropes of the skiff and let **it** fall

Rom 6:8   εἰ ἀπεθάνομεν σὺν Χριστῷ, πιστεύομεν ὅτι καὶ συζήσομεν **αὐτῷ**[20]
           if we have died with Christ, we believe that we will also live **with him**

Rev 17:16   μισήσουσιν τὴν πόρνην καὶ ἠρημωμένην ποιήσουσιν **αὐτὴν** καὶ γυμνὴν καὶ τὰς σάρκας **αὐτῆς** φάγονται καὶ **αὐτὴν** κατακαύσουσιν ἐν πυρί[21]
           they will hate the harlot and make **her** desolate and naked and they will eat **her** flesh and burn **her** up with fire

Cf. also Matt 19:7-8; Phlm 10; Jas 2:16; 2 John 5.

2) Possessive

The genitive of the personal pronoun frequently, if not usually, indicates possession. As such it could be treated in one of three ways: (1) as a subclass of the normal use of the personal pronoun because it, too, refers back to the antecedent (see Rev 17:16 above); (2) as a possessive genitive, since the notion of possession is not a part of the stem, but of the case ending; (3) as a possessive pronoun (see discussion there). It is so routine that no examples need be given here. (See the chapter on the genitive case for examples and discussion.)

3) Reflexive

The personal pronoun is rarely used for the reflexive pronoun in the NT. In such instances it has the force of *himself, herself, itself.*[22]

---

[20] αὐτῷ is replaced with τῷ Χριστῷ in D* F G. The pronoun has a superior pedigree: ℵ A B C Dᶜ E K L P *alii.*

[21] A few late MSS have some interesting though implausible readings in this text. For αὐτῆς: 1597 reads αὐτῶν; 2025 2037 omit the pronoun. For αὐτήν²: 203 452 506 read αὐτοί.

Matt 6:19 μὴ θησαυρίζετε **ὑμῖν** θησαυροὺς ἐπὶ τῆς γῆς
do not store up **for yourselves** treasures on the earth

> This and the following verse are perhaps the only two places in the NT where a *second* person personal pronoun is used in a reflexive sense.[23] All others are third person (αὐτός).

John 2:24 Ἰησοῦς οὐκ ἐπίστευεν **αὐτὸν** αὐτοῖς[24]
Jesus was not entrusting **himself** to them

Eph 2:15 ἵνα τοὺς δύο κτίσῃ ἐν **αὐτῷ** εἰς ἕνα καινὸν ἄνθρωπον[25]
that he might create in **himself** one new man

Cf. also Mark 9:16; John 20:10; Acts 14:17; Phil 3:21; Heb 5:3; 1 John 5:10 (*v.l.*); Rev 8:6; 18:7.

B. Demonstrative Pronouns

1. Definition and Terms Used

A demonstrative pronoun is a pointer, singling out an object in a special way. The three demonstrative pronouns used in the NT are οὗτος, ἐκεῖνος, and ὅδε. (This last one is rare, occurring only ten times.) οὗτος regularly refers to the *near* object ("this"), while ἐκεῖνος regularly refers to the *far* object ("that"). There are exceptions to this rule in that both demonstratives sometimes function like personal pronouns. As well, they sometimes "violate" the general rules of concord that pronouns normally follow. Such exceptions are often freighted with exegetical significance.

2. Functions

a. Regular Use (As Demonstratives)

The near-far distinctions of οὗτος and ἐκεῖνος can refer either to that which is near/far in the (1) context, (2) in the writer's mind, or (3) in space or time of the writer or audience.[26] Sometimes these realms are in

---

[22] Due to the more broadly based usage in Hellenistic Greek of the gen. personal pronoun for ἑαυτοῦ, the most recent editions of the Greek NT have replaced the contracted reflexive αὐτοῦ/αὐτῶν with the personal pronouns αὐτοῦ/αὐτῶν. See BAGD, s.v. ἑαυτοῦ, *BDF,* 35 (§64), Robertson, *Grammar,* 226; Turner, *Syntax,* 190; Metzger, *Textual Commentary,* 616 (on Phil 3:21), 718 (on 1 John 5:10).

[23] So Dana-Mantey, 124.

[24] The tension as to whether a personal pronoun was appropriate here is felt in the MSS. 𝔓[66] ℵ[2] A[C] W[C] Θ Ψ 050 083 *f*[1, 13] 33 *Byz* replace it with the reflexive ἑαυτόν, while 𝔓[75] 579 *et pauci* omit the pronoun altogether. The personal pronoun is found in ℵ* A* B L 700 *et alii*. Although the witnesses are fractured, the personal pronoun is found in decent texts and is the most difficult reading.

[25] A number of witnesses, principally Western and Byzantine, alter the personal pronoun to the more natural ἑαυτῷ (ℵ[2] D G Ψ *Byz*).

[26] So Winer-Moulton, 195-96; Dana-Mantey, 127-28 (§136); Young, *Intermediate Greek,* 78. Zerwick, *Biblical Greek,* 68 (§214), summarizes the issue nicely: "the proximity or remoteness may be not grammatical . . . but psychological."

conflict: What might be the nearest antecedent contextually might not be the nearest antecedent in the author's mind, etc. A little imagination is sometimes needed to see the reason for the pronoun.

1) οὗτος (Proximity)

Matt 8:27 ποταπός ἐστιν **οὗτος** ὅτι καὶ οἱ ἄνεμοι καὶ ἡ θάλασσα αὐτῷ ὑπακούουσιν;[27]
What sort of man is **this**, that even the winds and the sea obey him?

John 9:2 τίς ἥμαρτεν, **οὗτος** ἢ οἱ γονεῖς αὐτοῦ;
Who sinned–**this** [man] or his parents?

Acts 4:11 **οὗτός** ἐστιν ὁ λίθος, ὁ ἐξουθενηθεὶς ὑφ' ὑμῶν τῶν οἰκοδόμων
this is the stone, which was rejected by you builders
> The reference is to Christ, mentioned in v 10. But Ἰησοῦ Χριστοῦ is not the nearest antecedent in the context. Verse 10 reads: ἐν τῷ ὀνόματι Ἰησοῦ Χριστοῦ τοῦ Ναζωραίου ὃν ὑμεῖς ἐσταυρώσατε, ὃν ὁ θεὸς ἤγειρεν ἐκ νεκρῶν, ἐν τούτῳ οὗτος παρέστηκεν ἐνώπιον ὑμῶν ὑγιής ("by the name of Jesus Christ of Nazareth, whom you crucified, whom God raised from the dead, by him this man is standing before you well"). θεός is the nearest noun and οὗτος (referring to the healed man) is the nearest substantive. But since Ἰησοῦ Χριστοῦ is the "nearest *psychologically*, –was more vividly present to [the writer's] mind than any other,"[28] it is the antecedent.

Gal 4:24 **αὗται** εἰσιν δύο διαθῆκαι
these [women] are the two covenants

Phlm 18 εἰ δέ τι ἠδίκησέν σε ἢ ὀφείλει, **τοῦτο** ἐμοὶ ἐλλόγα
if he has done anything wrong to you, or owes you anything, charge **this** to me

1 Pet 1:25 τὸ ῥῆμα κυρίου μένει εἰς τὸν αἰῶνα. **τοῦτο** δέ ἐστιν τὸ ῥῆμα τὸ εὐαγγελισθὲν εἰς ὑμᾶς.
The word of the Lord abides forever. And **this** is the word that was proclaimed to you.

1 John 5:20 **οὗτός** ἐστιν ὁ ἀληθινὸς θεὸς καὶ ζωὴ αἰώνιος
this is the true God and eternal life
> This text is exegetically problematic for a variety of reasons. What concerns us here is what the antecedent is. Many scholars see ὁ θεός rather than Χριστός as the antecedent, even though Χριστός is closer. Winer argues, for example, that "in the first place, ἀληθινὸς θεός is a constant and exclusive epithet of the Father; and, secondly, there follows a warning against idolatry, and ἀληθινὸς θεός is always contrasted with εἴδωλα."[29]
> On behalf of seeing Χριστός as the antecedent are the following arguments: (1) Although it is true that ἀληθινὸς θεός is not elsewhere

---

[27] Codex W adds ὁ ἄνθρωπος after οὗτος.
[28] Winer-Moulton, 195.
[29] Winer-Moulton, 195.

referred to Christ, ἀλήθεία is, and is so in Johannine literature (John 14:6). Further, ἀληθινὸς θεός is not a "constant . . epithet" as Winer supposes, being found only in John 17:3 and 1 John 5:20! (2) Christ is also said to be ζωή in John's writings (John 11:25; 14:6; 1 John 1:1-2), an epithet nowhere else used of the Father. (3) The demonstrative pronoun, οὗτος, in the Gospel and Epistles of John seems to be used in a theologically rich manner.[30] Specifically, of the approximately seventy instances in which οὗτος has a personal referent, as many as forty-four of them (almost two-thirds of the instances) refer to the Son. Of the remainder, most imply some sort of positive connection with the Son.[31] What is most significant is that *never* is the Father the referent. For what it is worth, this datum increases the probability that Ἰησοῦ Χριστῷ is the antecedent in 1 John 5:20.[32]

The issue cannot be decided on grammar alone. But suffice it to say here that there are no grammatical reasons for denying that ἀληθινὸς θεός is descriptive of Jesus Christ.[33]

Cf. also Matt 9:3; Mark 1:38; 8:4; 9:7; Luke 1:29; Acts 1:18; 6:13; 1 Cor 6:13; 13:13; 16:3; Phil 1:6; 4:8; 2 Tim 3:8; Rev 1:19.

2) ἐκεῖνος (Remoteness)

Matt 13:11   ὑμῖν δέδοται γνῶναι τὰ μυστήρια τῆς βασιλείας τῶν οὐρανῶν, **ἐκείνοις** δὲ οὐ δέδοται

To you it has been given to know the mysteries of the kingdom of heaven, but **to those** [people] it has not been given.

John 7:45   ἦλθον οὖν οἱ ὑπηρέται πρὸς τοὺς ἀρχιερεῖς καὶ Φαρισαίους, καὶ εἶπον αὐτοῖς **ἐκεῖνοι**· διὰ τί οὐκ ἠγάγετε αὐτόν;

Then the officers came back to the chief priests and Pharisees, and **the latter** said to them, "Why have you not brought him?"

Although ἐκεῖνοι is used, the antecedent is the nearest in the context ("the chief priests and Pharisees"), as can be seen from the following verse (ἀπεκρίθησαν οἱ ὑπηρέται . . .). ἐκεῖνος is used, most likely, because the officers had been dispatched to find Jesus in v 32 and were nearer in the writer's mind than was the Sanhedrin. The narrative progresses from the dispatch, to Jesus' discourse in the temple (vv 33-43), to the anticipation of arrest by the officers (v 44), to the return of the officers back to the Sanhedrin (v 45). ἐκεῖνος is thus used, it seems, because the chief priests and Pharisees are "behind the scenes" in this discourse.

---

[30] Thanks are due to Dr. W. Hall Harris for alerting me to the possible significance of the demonstrative pronoun in Johannine literature.

[31] If this usage does indicate a theological motif, the author is not altogether consistent, for there are a few places that do not at all fit this model (e.g., John 6:71; 1 John 2:22). The same could be said for the use of ἐγώ εἰμί, too, though (cf. John 9:9), yet all agree that ἐγὼ εἰμί is a theological motif in John.

[32] For other arguments on behalf of Ἰησοῦ Χριστῷ as the antecedent, see especially Marshall, *The Epistles of John*, 254, n. 47; Brown, *The Epistles of John*, 625-626.

[33] The grammatical issues are rather complex. For a discussion, see D. B. Wallace, "The Article with Multiple Substantives Connected by Καί in the New Testament: Semantics and Significance" (Ph.D. dissertation, Dallas Theological Seminary, 1995) 271-77.

Rom 6:21   τίνα καρπὸν εἴχετε τότε ἐφ᾿ οἷς νῦν ἐπαισχύνεσθε; τὸ γὰρ τέλος **ἐκείνων** θάνατος.
What benefit did you get then from the things of which you are now ashamed? For the end **of those things** is death.
> Although another pronoun would in this context fit just as nicely, evidently ἐκεῖνος is used because of the *temporal* distance between the readers and their former lifestyle (notice the "then" and "now").

Jas 4:15   ἐὰν ὁ κύριος θελήσῃ καὶ ζήσομεν καὶ ποιήσομεν τοῦτο ἢ **ἐκεῖνο**
If the Lord wills, then we will live and do this or **that.**
> The activity options, though unspecified, are listed in order of priority. The idea is, "If we can't do this, then we'll do that."

Cf. also Mark 12:4; Luke 11:42; Acts 15:11; 1 Cor 9:25; 2 Tim 3:9; Heb 11:15.

3) ὅδε

This pronoun is used only ten times in the NT, eight of which are in the expression τάδε λέγει. The force of this expression is always proleptic or anticipatory: "He says the following [things]." Seven of the eight are used in the Apocalypse,[34] all of which are in the messages to the churches. The pronoun is used to add solemnity to the prophetic utterance that follows.[35]

Acts 21:11   **τάδε** λέγει τὸ πνεῦμα τὸ ἅγιον . . .
the Holy Spirit says **these things** . . .

Rev 2:18   **τάδε** λέγει ὁ υἱὸς τοῦ θεοῦ . . .
the Son of God says **these things** . . .

Cf. also Luke 10:39; Rev 2:1, 8, 12; 3:1, 7, 14.

b. For Personal Pronouns

Although technically οὗτος and ἐκεῖνος are demonstrative pronouns, sometimes their demonstrative force is diminished.[36] In such cases, they act as third person personal pronouns with a simple anaphoric force. This usage is especially frequent in John, occurring more with ἐκεῖνος than with οὗτος.

John 5:6   **τοῦτον** ἰδὼν ὁ Ἰησοῦς
when Jesus saw **him**

John 8:44   **ἐκεῖνος** ἀνθρωποκτόνος ἦν ἀπ᾿ ἀρχῆς
he was a murderer from the beginning

---

[34] Of the other two instances, one is retrospective (Luke 10:39) and the other is adjectival (Jas 4:13).

[35] In classical drama, it was used to introduce a new actor to the scene (Smyth, *Greek Grammar*, 307 [§1241]). But the τάδε λέγει formula in the NT derives from the OT, where it was used to introduce a prophetic utterance (BAGD, s.v. ὅδε, 1). The use of ὅδε is even more emphatic than that of οὗτος (Smyth, *Greek Grammar*, 307 [§1241]).

[36] This was also true in Attic Greek (Smyth, *Greek Grammar*, 92 [§326.d]).

John 11:29 **ἐκείνη** ὡς ἤκουσεν ἠγέρθη ταχὺ καὶ ἤρχετο πρὸς αὐτόν
when **she** heard [that Jesus had arrived], she rose quickly and came
to him

2 Tim 2:26 ἀνανήψωσιν ἐκ τῆς τοῦ διαβόλου παγίδος, ἐζωγρημένοι ὑπ᾽ αὐτοῦ εἰς τὸ
ἐκείνου θέλημα
they might return to their senses [and escape] from the snare of the
devil, after having been captured by him to [do] **his** will

> The antecedents of αὐτοῦ and ἐκείνου are not certain. Older commen-
> taries, in which it was assumed that classical standards obtained in the
> NT, felt that two antecedents had to be in view. With two pronouns so
> close together, the force in Attic Greek would be "he (αὐτός) . . . the
> other one (ἐκεῖνος)." This yielded one of two interpretations: (1) αὐτοῦ
> refers back to the Lord's servant (v 24) and ἐκείνου refers to God (v 25):
> "they might return to their senses [and escape] from the snare of the
> devil, after having been captured by *the Lord's servant* to [do] *the Lord's*
> will. (2) αὐτοῦ refers to the devil and ἐκείνου refers to God: "they might
> return to their senses [and escape] from the snare of the devil, after hav-
> ing been captured by *the devil*, [but after escaping,] to [do] *God's* will.
> The first interpretation is implausible because of the distance of the
> antecedents; the second is implausible because of what must be
> inferred for it to work.[37]
>
> Most modern commentators see διαβόλου as the antecedent for both
> pronouns. This is in keeping with Koine usage, in which the demon-
> strative pronouns, especially ἐκεῖνος, are sometimes used for αὐτός. But
> why the change of pronouns? Could not αὐτός be used each time? Han-
> son makes the intriguing suggestion that ἐκεῖνος is used for its occa-
> sional connotative value of "'we-know-who,' 'the dreaded one.'"[38] If
> so, the force of the passage would be "they might return to their senses
> [and escape] from the snare of the devil, after having been captured by
> him to [do] the will **of that [dreaded] one**."

Cf. also John 1:7, 8; 3:2; 10:6.

c. **Unusual Uses (from an English perspective)**

The following categories of usage are unusual in that the pronoun seems
to be unnecessary (redundant), or is lacking in concord with its antecedent, or is used for some other reason. Most of the uses, however, are normal in terms of the pronoun having its full demonstrative force.

1) **Pleonastic (Redundant)**

Occasionally a demonstrative is used when no ambiguity would
result if it had been deleted. This especially occurs in the nominative
case: The demonstrative repeats a subject just mentioned (usually a

---

[37] For other arguments against these views, see M. Dibelius-H. Conzelmann, *The Pastoral Epistles* (Hermeneia) 114; J. N. D. Kelly, *A Commentary on the Pastoral Epistles*, 191-92;
A. T. Hanson, *The Pastoral Epistles* (NCB) 142-43.

[38] Hanson, *Pastoral Epistles*, 143. Although he bases this nuance on the usages listed
in LSJ, BAGD also mentions that ἐκεῖνος is sometimes used "w. ref. to well-known or notorious personalities . . . . W. an unfavorable connotation" (s.v. ἐκεῖνος, 1.c.).

substantival participle), even though the verb is not introduced until *after* the pronoun. In effect, the pronoun resumes the subject that is now separated from the verb by the participial construction. The pronoun is called pleonastic, redundant, or resumptive. In such cases, the pronoun is usually best left untranslated. However, at times, it has great rhetorical power and the English should reflect this.

John 5:11   ὁ ποιήσας με ὑγιῆ **ἐκεῖνός** μοι εἶπεν· ἆρον τὸν κράβαττόν σου καὶ περιπάτει
              The one who made me well said to me, "Take up your mattress and walk!"

Rom 8:30   οὓς δὲ προώρισεν, **τούτους** καὶ ἐκάλεσεν· καὶ οὓς ἐκάλεσεν, **τούτους** καὶ ἐδικαίωσεν· οὓς δὲ ἐδικαίωσεν, **τούτους** καὶ ἐδόξασεν
              and the ones whom he predestined, **these** he also called; and the ones whom he called, **these** he also justified; and the ones whom he justified, **these** he also glorified

> The usage here seems to be emphatic and not merely resumptive. The idea is that the very ones whom God predestined, called, and justified are also glorified. The compounding of pronouns thus has a dramatic effect: No one is lost between the eternal decree and the eternal state.

Jas 1:25   ὁ παρακύψας εἰς νόμον τέλειον τὸν τῆς ἐλευθερίας καὶ παραμείνας, οὐκ ἀκροατὴς ἐπιλησμονῆς γενόμενος ἀλλὰ ποιητὴς ἔργου, **οὗτος** μακάριος ἐν τῇ ποιήσει αὐτοῦ ἔσται.[39]
              The one who looks into the perfect law, the [law] of liberty, and perseveres–not becoming a forgetful hearer but an effectual doer–**this one** shall be blessed in what he does.

> Even in English usage the resumptive pronoun needs to be translated because the subject is removed from the verb by a score of words!

2 John 9   ὁ μένων ἐν τῇ διδαχῇ, **οὗτος** καὶ τὸν πατέρα καὶ τὸν υἱὸν ἔχει
              the one who abides in this teaching has both the Father and the Son

Cf. John 5:37; 12:48; 14:21; Acts 7:35; Rom 8:14; Phil 3:7; Jas 3:2.

2) *Constructio ad Sensum*

A small group of demonstrative pronouns involve a *natural* agreement with their antecedents that overrides strict grammatical concord. As such, they are illustrations of constructions according to sense (*constructio ad sensum*). This natural agreement may involve gender or, much more rarely, number. Frequently, the agreement is conceptual only, since the pronoun refers to a phrase or clause rather than a noun or other substantive. As might be expected, not a few of these instances are debatable and exegetically significant.

---

[39] 𝔓[74] *et pauci* omit the pronoun here.

a) Gender

1] Clear Illustrations

Acts 8:10   **οὗτός** ἐστιν ἡ δύναμις τοῦ θεοῦ
this [man] is the power of God

Rom 2:14   ὅταν ἔθνη τὰ μὴ νόμον ἔχοντα φύσει τὰ τοῦ νόμου ποιῶσιν, **οὗτοι** νόμον
μὴ ἔχοντες ἑαυτοῖς εἰσιν νόμος[40]
whenever Gentiles who do not have the law naturally practice the
things of the law, **these**, not having law, are a law unto themselves

> The pronoun's antecedent is ἔθνη which, though neuter, refers to
> human beings.

1 Cor 6: 10-11 οὔτε κλέπται οὔτε πλεονέκται, οὐ μέθυσοι, οὐ λοίδοροι, οὐχ ἅρπαγες
βασιλείαν θεοῦ κληρονομήσουσιν. (11) καὶ **ταῦτά** τινες ἦτε
nor thieves, nor the greedy, nor drunkards, nor abusive people, nor
robbers will inherit the kingdom of God. (11) And **these things** were
some [of you].

> Although all the antecedent nouns are masculine, the demonstrative
> used is neuter. Robertson notes that "here ταῦτα is much like τοιοῦτοι,
> but more definite and emphatic."[41] The neuter is used to express the
> horror of depravity, as if they had been subhuman before conversion.

Cf. also Acts 9:15; Phil 3:7; 1 Pet 2:19; Jude 12.

2] Debatable Examples

John 15:26   ὅταν ἔλθῃ ὁ παράκλητος ὃν ἐγὼ πέμψω ὑμῖν παρὰ τοῦ πατρός, τὸ
πνεῦμα τῆς ἀληθείας ὃ παρὰ τοῦ πατρὸς ἐκπορεύεται, **ἐκεῖνος**
μαρτυρήσει περὶ ἐμοῦ
whenever the Comforter comes, whom I am sending to you from the
Father–the Spirit of truth which/who proceeds from the Father–**that
one** will testify concerning me

> The use of ἐκεῖνος here is frequently regarded by students of the NT to
> be an affirmation of the personality of the Spirit. Such an approach is
> based on the assumption that the antecedent of ἐκεῖνος is πνεῦμα: "the
> masculine pronoun ἐκεῖνος is used in John 14:26 and 16:13-14 to refer to
> the neuter noun πνεῦμα to emphasize the personality of the Holy
> Spirit."[42]
>
> But this is erroneous. In all these Johannine passages, πνεῦμα is apposi-
> tional to a masculine noun. The gender of ἐκεῖνος thus has nothing to

---

[40] Codex G has οἱ τοιοῦτοι for οὗτοι.

[41] Robertson, *Grammar*, 704.

[42] Young, *Intermediate Greek*, 78. Similarly, G. B. Stevens, *The Johannine Theology* (New
York: Scribner's, 1899) 196; L. Morris, *The Gospel According to John* (NICNT) 656. The view
is especially popular among theologians, not infrequently becoming the mainstay in their
argument for the personality of the Spirit (cf., e.g., J. I. Packer, *Keep In Step With the Spirit*
[Old Tappan, NJ: Fleming H. Revell, 1984] 61; C. C. Ryrie, *The Holy Spirit* [Chicago:
Moody, 1965] 14; R. C. Sproul, *The Mystery of the Holy Spirit* [Wheaton, Ill.: Tyndale, 1990]
17-18).

do with the natural gender of πνεῦμα. The antecedent of ἐκεῖνος, in each case, is παράκλητος, not πνεῦμα. John 14:26 reads ὁ παράκλητος, τὸ πνεῦμα τὸ ἅγιον, ὃ πέμψει ὁ πατὴρ ἐν τῷ ὀνόματί μου, **ἐκεῖνος** ὑμᾶς διδάξει πάντα ("the Comforter, the Holy Spirit whom the Father sends in my name, **that one** will teach you all things"). πνεῦμα not only is appositional to παράκλητος, but the relative pronoun that follows it is neuter! This hardly assists the grammatical argument for the Spirit's personality. In John 16:13-14 the immediate context is deceptive: ὅταν δὲ ἔλθῃ **ἐκεῖνος**, τὸ πνεῦμα τῆς ἀληθείας, ὁδηγήσει ὑμᾶς ἐν τῇ ἀληθείᾳ πάσῃ· **ἐκεῖνος** ἐμὲ δοξάσει ("whenever **that one** comes–the Spirit of truth–he will guide you in all truth . . . . **he** will glorify me"). The ἐκεῖνος reaches back to v 7, where παράκλητος is mentioned.[43] Thus, since παράκλητος is masculine, so is the pronoun. Although one might argue that the Spirit's personality is in view in these passages, the view must be based on the nature of a παράκλητος and the things said about the Comforter, not on any supposed grammatical subtleties. Indeed, it is difficult to find *any* text in which πνεῦμα is grammatically referred to with the masculine gender.[44]

b) Number

2 John 7   πολλοὶ πλάνοι ἐξῆλθον εἰς τὸν κόσμον, οἱ μὴ ὁμολογοῦντες Ἰησοῦν Χριστὸν ἐρχόμενον ἐν σαρκί· **οὗτός** ἐστιν ὁ πλάνος καὶ ὁ ἀντίχριστος.

Many deceivers have gone out into the world, the ones who do not confess that Jesus Christ has come in the flesh. **This** is the deceiver and the antichrist.

> The demonstrative has virtually a generic force here: "Such a person is the deceiver and the antichrist."

3 John 4   μειζοτέραν **τούτων** οὐκ ἔχω χαράν, ἵνα ἀκούω τὰ ἐμὰ τέκνα ἐν τῇ ἀληθείᾳ περιπατοῦντα

I have no greater joy than **this**, to hear that my children are walking in the truth.

---

[43] Although translations of v 13 such as that of the NRSV may be misleading as to what the subject of the sentence is ("When the Spirit of truth comes, he will guide you. . . "), their objective is not to be a handbook for Greek students.

[44] Besides the Johannine texts, three other passages are occasionally used for this: Eph 1:14; 2 Thess 2:6-7; and 1 John 5:7. All of these have problems. In Eph 1:14 ὅς ἐστιν ἀρραβών refers back to τῷ πνεύματι (v 13), but the masculine relative pronoun (*v.l.*) is easily explained without resorting to seeing theological motifs. (See discussion below, under "Relative Pronouns.") In 2 Thess 2:6-7 πνεῦμα is nowhere mentioned; τὸ κατέχον/ὁ κατέχων are often assumed to both refer to the Holy Spirit. But in spite of the fact that there is much to commend this view, it certainly cannot use clear natural-gender passages in support, nor can such a known *crux interpretum* become the basis for such a syntactical point. First John 5:7 is perhaps the most plausible of the passages enlisted. The masculine participle in τρεῖς εἰσιν οἱ μαρτυροῦντες refers to τὸ πνεῦμα καὶ τὸ ὕδωρ καὶ τὸ αἷμα (v 8), all neuter nouns. Some see this as an oblique reference to the Spirit's personality (so I. H. Marshall, *The Epistles of John* [NICNT] 237, n. 20), but the fact that the author has personified water and blood, turning them into witnesses along with the Spirit, may be enough to account for the masculine gender. This interpretation also has in its behalf the allusion to Deut 19:15 (the necessity of "two or three witnesses"), for in the OT the testimony only of males was acceptable. Thus, the elder may be subtly indicating (via the masculine participle) that the Spirit, water, and blood are all valid witnesses.

Although the postcedent to which τούτων refers is the content of the ἵνα clause, the pronoun would normally be expected to be in the singular.

Cf. also 1 Cor 6:8 (*v.l.*); Heb 11:12.

c) Conceptual Antecedent/Postcedent

The neuter of οὗτος is routinely used to refer to a phrase or clause. In such cases, the thing referred to is not a specific noun or substantive. The singular is used to refer both to an antecedent and a postcedent on a regular basis, while the plural is almost exclusively shut up to retrospective uses.[45] Certain formulaic phrases are often employed, such as διὰ τοῦτο, referring back to the previous argument (cf. Matt 6:25; 12:27; Mark 6:14; Luke 11:19; Rom 1:26; Heb 1:9),[46] or μετὰ ταῦτα, referring to the previous events (Luke 17:8; John 5:1; 21:1; Acts 13:20; 1 Pet 1:11; Rev 4:1).

1] Clear Illustrations

Luke 4:28   ἐπλήσθησαν πάντες θυμοῦ ἐν τῇ συναγωγῇ ἀκούοντες **ταῦτα**[47]
when they heard **these things**, all in the synagogue were filled with rage

> What the people heard was the words of Jesus. Even though λόγος ("message") or λόγοι ("words") could naturally be supplied, the *neuter* pronoun is the normal means of referring to an unspecified concept in Greek.[48]

Luke 14:20   γυναῖκα ἔγημα καὶ διὰ **τοῦτο** οὐ δύναμαι ἐλθεῖν[49]
I have [just] married a woman and for **this reason** I cannot come

> Obviously, the pronoun must refer to the marriage event, not the woman![50]

Rom 6:6   **τοῦτο** γινώσκοντες ὅτι ὁ παλαιὸς ἡμῶν ἄνθρωπος συνεσταυρώθη
since we know **this**, that our old man has been cocrucified [with him]

---

[45] So Young, *Intermediate Greek*, 78. He says that "ταῦτα seems only to point to what precedes," but see 3 John 4 (mentioned above).

[46] Not every instance is retrospective (cf. Matt 13:13; Mark 12:24; John 1:31; 1 Thess 2:13; Phlm 15).

[47] Instead of ταῦτα, codex 579 reads αὐτά and 827 reads αὐτοῦ.

[48] By extension, this may have implications for τὸ τέλειον in 1 Cor 13:10 (see the chapter on adjectives for a discussion).

[49] For καὶ διὰ τοῦτο D has διό; 157 omits διὰ τοῦτο.

[50] Of course, if the neuter term γύναιον ("little woman" [infrequently a term of endearment, though normally one of derision]) had been used, this might give the interpreter pause!

1 Cor 11:24   τοῦτό μού ἐστιν τὸ σῶμα τὸ ὑπὲρ ὑμῶν· **τοῦτο** ποιεῖτε εἰς τὴν ἐμὴν
ἀνάμνησιν.

This is my body which is [given] for you. Do **this** in remembrance of
me.

> The second τοῦτο refers to the act of eating the bread, even though in
> the preceding context a neuter noun (σῶμα), along with its pronoun
> (τοῦτο), is seen.

Heb 9:27   καθ᾽ ὅσον ἀπόκειται τοῖς ἀνθρώποις ἅπαξ ἀποθανεῖν, μετὰ δὲ **τοῦτο**
κρίσις

just as it is appointed for humans to die once, and after **this** the judgment

Cf. also Luke 1:18; 4:18; 6:6; 7:32; 8:30; Acts 1:9; 4:7; Rom 5:12; 8:31; 14:9; 1 Cor 4:6; 11:22;
Gal 3:2; Col 3:20; 1 Thess 4:15; Heb 4:5.

2] Debatable Example

Eph 2:8   τῇ γὰρ χάριτί ἐστε σεσῳσμένοι διὰ πίστεως· καὶ **τοῦτο** οὐκ ἐξ ὑμῶν, θεοῦ
τὸ δῶρον

for by grace you are saved through faith; and **this** is not of yourselves, it is the gift of God

> This is the most debated text in terms of the antecedent of the demon-
> strative pronoun, τοῦτο. The standard interpretations include: (1)
> "grace" as antecedent, (2) "faith" as antecedent, (3) the concept of a
> grace-by-faith salvation as antecedent, and (4) καὶ τοῦτο having an
> adverbial force with no antecedent ("and especially").
>
> The first and second options suffer from the fact that τοῦτο is neuter
> while χάριτι and πίστεως are feminine. Some have argued that the gen-
> der shift causes no problem because (a) there are other examples in
> Greek literature in which a neuter demonstrative refers back to a noun
> of a different gender,[51] and (b) the τοῦτο has been attracted to the gen-
> der of δῶρον, the predicate nominative. These two arguments need to
> be examined together.
>
> While it is true that on rare occasions there is a gender shift between
> antecedent and pronoun, the pronoun is almost always caught
> between two nouns of different gender. One is the antecedent; the other
> is the predicate nom. In Acts 8:10, for example (**οὗτός** ἐστιν ἡ δύναμις τοῦ
> θεοῦ), the pronoun is masculine because its antecedent is masculine,
> even though the predicate nom. is feminine. In Matt 13:38 inverse
> attraction takes place (the pronominal subject is attracted to the gender
> of the predicate nom.): τὸ δὲ καλὸν σπέρμα, **οὗτοί** εἰσιν οἱ υἱοὶ τῆς
> βασιλείας ("the good seed, **these** are the sons of the kingdom").[52] The
> construction in Eph 2:8, however, is not parallel because δῶρον is not
> the predicate nom. of τοῦτο, but of the implied "it" in the following

---

[51] In particular, note R. H. Countess, "Thank God for the Genitive!" *JETS* 12 (1969)
117-22. He lists three examples from Attic Greek, arguing that such a phenomenon occurs
frequently in Greek literature (120). His approach has weaknesses, however, for not only
does he cite no NT examples, but two of his classical illustrations are better seen as referring to a concept than to a noun. Further, the usage is not at all frequent and in every
instance requires explanation.

[52] Cf. also Matt 7:12; Luke 2:12; 8:11; John 1:19; Rom 11:27; Gal 4:24.

clause. On a grammatical level, then, it is doubtful that either "faith" or "grace" is the antecedent of τοῦτο.

More plausible is the third view, viz., that τοῦτο refers to the concept of a grace-by-faith salvation. As we have seen, τοῦτο regularly takes a conceptual antecedent. Whether faith is seen as a gift here or anywhere else in the NT is not addressed by this.[53]

A fourth view is that καὶ τοῦτο is adverbial, though this view has surprisingly made little impact on the exegetical literature.[54] If adverbial, καὶ τοῦτο is intensive, meaning "and at that, and especially," without having any antecedent. It focuses on the *verb* rather than on any noun. In 3 John 5 we see this usage: πιστὸν ποιεῖς ὃ ἐὰν ἐργάσῃ εἰς τοὺς ἀδελφοὺς **καὶ τοῦτο** ξένους[55] ("you do a faithful [deed] whenever you render service for the brothers, **and especially** [when you do it] for strangers"). If this is the force in Eph 2:8, the text means "for by grace you are saved through faith, **and** [you are saved] **especially** not by your own doing; it is the gift of God."

The issues here are complex and cannot be solved by grammar alone. Nevertheless, syntactical considerations do tend toward one of the latter two views.[56]

C. Relative Pronouns

1. Definition and Terms Used

Relative pronouns (ὅς and ὅστις) are so called because they *relate* to more than one clause. Typically, they are "hinge" words in that they both refer back to an antecedent in the previous clause and also function in some capacity in their own clause. For example, in the sentence "The house *that* Jack built fell down," *that* refers to its antecedent ("house") and heads up its own clause as well.

---

[53] On an exegetical level, I am inclined to agree with Lincoln that "in Paul's thinking faith can never be viewed as a meritorious work because in connection with justification he always contrasts faith with works of the law (cf. Gal 2:16; 3:2-5, 9, 10; Rom 3:27, 28)" (A. T. Lincoln, *Ephesians* [WBC] 111). If faith is not meritorious, but is instead the *reception* of the gift of salvation, then it is not a gift per se. Such a view does not preclude the notion that for faith to save, the Spirit of God must initiate the conversion process.

[54] But cf. *BDF*, 151 (§290.5), BAGD, s.v. οὗτος 1.b.γ. Both authorities assume this force for καὶ τοῦτο in Eph 2:8 without discussion.

[55] τοῦτο is replaced by εἰς τούς in P *Byz* and by τούς in 81 *et pauci*. The pronoun is solidly established in early and widespread witnesses, however (e.g., א A B C Ψ 048 33[vid] 323 1241[vid] 1739).

[56] For what it is worth, an examination of all 22 instances of καὶ τοῦτο in the NT (not including Eph 2:8) yielded the following results: 14 or 15 had a conceptual referent (e.g., Luke 3:20; 5:6; John 11:28; 18:38; John 20:20; Acts 7:60; 1 Cor 7:37; Phil 1:9; Heb 6:3 [Phil 1:28 was probable]); four were adverbial (Rom 13:11; 1 Cor 6:6, 8; 3 John 5 [Heb 11:12 is listed by BAGD as adverbial, but the plural is used (καὶ ταῦτα), following more closely the Attic idiom]); three involved the same gender (Luke 2:12; 13:8; 1 John 4:3); no clear examples involved different genders (though Phil 1:28 was possible).

Converting this sentence into Greek, we see some basic principles of relative pronouns at work: ὁ οἶκος **ὃν** Ἰάκωβος ᾠκοδόμησεν ἔπεσε. The relative pronoun is singular and masculine because οἶκος is singular and masculine. But ὅν is accusative, rather than nominative, because it is the direct object of ᾠκοδόμησεν. In other words, *the relative pronoun (RP) agrees with its antecedent in gender and number, but its case is determined by the function it has in its own clause.*

2. Functions

The definite RP is ὅς; the indefinite RP is ὅστις. These two need to be treated separately as the major exegetical issues are different for each.

a. ὅς

1) Regular Use

ὅς is routinely used to link a noun or other substantive to the relative clause, which either describes, clarifies, or restricts the meaning of the noun.

John 1:26   μέσος ὑμῶν ἔστηκεν **ὃν** ὑμεῖς οὐκ οἴδατε
            in your midst stands [one] **whom** you do not know

Acts 4:10   Ἰησοῦ Χριστοῦ . . . **ὃν** ὑμεῖς ἐσταυρώσατε, **ὃν** ὁ θεὸς ἤγειρεν ἐκ νεκρῶν
            Jesus Christ . . . **whom** you have crucified, **whom** God has raised from the dead

Eph 2:2-3   τοῖς υἱοῖς τῆς ἀπειθείας, (3) ἐν **οἷς** καὶ ἡμεῖς πάντες ἀνεστράφημέν ποτε
            . . . in the sons of disobedience, among **whom** we also all formerly lived

> The relative clauses in vv 2-3 provide a balanced structure: ἐν αἷς, ἐν οἷς: we walked in sin, we lived among sinners. The case for the depravity of humanity and its need for salvation in the opening verses of Eph 2 is masterfully and concisely stated.

Rev 1:1   Ἀποκάλυψις Ἰησοῦ Χριστοῦ **ἣν** ἔδωκεν αὐτῷ ὁ θεός
            The revelation of Jesus Christ, **which** God gave to him

Matt 1:16   Ἰακὼβ ἐγέννησεν τὸν Ἰωσὴφ τὸν ἄνδρα Μαρίας, ἐξ **ἧς** ἐγεννήθη Ἰησοῦς[57]
            Jacob became the father of Joseph, the husband of Mary, by **whom** was born Jesus

> The English translation does not bring out the gender in Greek: "by

---

[57] The reading of the Sinaitic Syriac MS, in which Joseph's paternity of Jesus is suggested ("Joseph, to whom was betrothed Mary the virgin, begot Jesus who is called the Christ"), has little to commend it, not being found in any Greek witnesses and, most likely, without support anywhere else (for discussion, see Metzger, *Textual Commentary,* 2-7).

whom" (ἐξ ἧς) is feminine, referring to Mary. To list women indirectly in a Jewish genealogy was unusual (as was done with Tamar, Rahab, Ruth, and "the wife of Uriah"), but to list a woman by directly linking her to the offspring was startling. The discourse follows with an explanation: Jesus was miraculously conceived (vv 18-25).

Cf. also Mark 14:71; Luke 2:11; John 1:13; Acts 17:3; Rom 1:2; 2 Cor 7:7; Eph 1:6; Phil 3:8; 1 Pet 2:22.

2) "Unusual" Uses

Not infrequently relative pronouns do not follow the basic rules of agreement. Sometimes the gender of the RP does not match that of the antecedent, usually because of sense agreement superseding syntactical agreement (*constructio ad sensum*). As you recall, the rules of agreement do not normally involve *case* for the RP. Yet sometimes the case of the relative is attracted to that of the antecedent (known as attraction or direct attraction); at other times, though much less often, the antecedent is drawn to the case of the RP (known as inverse or indirect attraction).

To make matters more difficult, the relation of the RP to its antecedent is sometimes complicated: the antecedent may be lacking, or the relative phrase may be adverbial and thus not refer to a noun or other substantive. As with the demonstratives, the discovery of these syntactical "glitches" occasionally yields a point of exegetical value as well.

a) Gender

1] Clear Illustrations

John 4:22   ὑμεῖς προσκυνεῖτε ὃ οὐκ οἴδατε· ἡμεῖς προσκυνοῦμεν ὃ οἴδαμεν
you [Samaritans] worship **what** you do not know; we [Jews] worship **what** we know

> In Jesus' response to the Samaritan woman about worship, he noted in v 21 that true worshipers will worship the Father (ὁ πατήρ). He continues with the principle articulated in v 22, but this time uses the neuter pronoun to describe the object of worship. The implication seems to be that, since he is aligning himself with his people (not with true worshipers per se), he grants them doctrinal fidelity but not spiritual relationship.[58]

Phlm 10   παρακαλῶ σε περὶ τοῦ ἐμοῦ τέκνου, ὃν ἐγέννησα ἐν τοῖς δεσμοῖς
I urge you concerning my child, **of whom** I have become a father in my bonds

> Although τέκνον is neuter, the RP is masculine due to natural gender.

---

[58] This text also could belong under "Omission of the Antecedent," since the antecedent is embedded in the RP. Nevertheless, the RP refers back–contextually, not syntactically–to "the Father" in the previous verse.

1 Cor 15:10 χάριτι θεοῦ εἰμι **ὅ** εἰμι

> by the grace of God I am **what** I am

>> The antecedent is implicit, but it is naturally masculine. By using the neuter, Paul is not affirming his person as much as his office of apostleship.

Cf. also Acts 26:17; 1 Cor 4:17; Col 2:19; Gal 4:19; 2 Pet 2:17; 2 John 1; Rev 13:14.

2] Debatable Example

Eph 1:13-14 ἐσφραγίσθητε τῷ πνεύματι τῆς ἐπαγγελίας τῷ ἁγίῳ, (14) **ὅς** ἐστιν ἀρραβὼν τῆς κληρονομίας ἡμῶν

> you were sealed with the Holy Spirit of promise, (14) **who** is the down payment of our inheritance

>> The reading ὅς, which is doubtful on text-critical grounds,[59] is sometimes invoked as grammatical proof of the Spirit's personality.[60] But the masculine RP is to be explained simply as attraction to the gender of the predicate nom. ἀρραβών. Such gender attraction is common enough in the NT (cf. Mark 15:16; Gal 3:16; Eph 6:17; 1 Tim 3:15). It occurs when the focus of the discourse is on the predicate nom.: the dominant gender reveals the dominant idea of the passage.

>> Neither in Eph 1:14 nor in any other text is there clear *syntactical* evidence for the personality of the Spirit.[61] There are, of course, many lines of evidence that demonstrate this, but the attempt to use Greek grammar in such a manner is facile and often creates theological problems that are greater than the cure.[62]

b) Case

1] Attraction (a.k.a. Direct Attraction)

> The case of the RP, unlike its gender and number, usually has no relation to that of the antecedent, since it is normally determined by the function it has in its own clause.

---

[59] UBS[4] reads ὅ instead of ὅς. Several issues make the decision difficult. Not only are there weighty MSS on both sides (though antiquity and geographical distribution favor the neuter), but the potential for an accidental alteration is great. As a side note, the evidence from the Itala as listed in UBS[4] may be misleading due to the inner grammar of each language: in Greek the antecedent, πνεῦμα, is neuter, while the predicate nom., ἀρραβών, is masculine; in Latin the antecedent is masculine (*spiritus*), while the predicate nom. (in most MSS) is neuter (*pignus*). Thus it may be that the neuter RP in some Latin MSS reflects a *masculine* RP in the Greek Vorlage and the masculine RP in other Latin witnesses reflects a *neuter* RP in their Greek Vorlage!

[60] Older commentaries especially argued this point, and even Barth (*Ephesians* [AB] 1.96) sees this theological motif as a possible reason for the use of the masculine ὅς by the author.

[61] See earlier discussion of John 15:26 in the section on demonstrative pronouns.

[62] For example, the use of Colwell's rule to affirm the deity of Christ in John 1:1 is an inadvertent support for modalism. See discussion of this text in "The Article, Part II." Similarly, note the discussion of Gal 5:16 in "The Dative Case: Dative of Agency," and the argument on 1 Cor 12:13 in "Prepositions: ἐν" (both of which have to do with the personality of the Spirit).

Sometimes, however, it is attracted to the case of the antecedent. This is especially common with the attraction of the *accusative* of the RP to either the *genitive* or *dative* of the antecedent. (That is to say, in places where we expect to see an acc. RP, sometimes we see a gen. or dat. because of attraction.)

Matt 24:50 ἐν ὥρᾳ **ᾗ** οὐ γινώσκει
in an hour **which** he does not know

John 4:14 ὃς δ᾽ ἂν πίῃ ἐκ τοῦ ὕδατος **οὗ** ἐγὼ δώσω αὐτῷ
whoever drinks of the water **which** I will give him

Heb 6:10 τῆς ἀγάπης **ἧς** ἐνεδείξασθε εἰς τὸ ὄνομα αὐτοῦ[63]
the love **which** you showed for his name

1 John 3:24 ἐκ τοῦ πνεύματος **οὗ** ἡμῖν ἔδωκεν
by the Spirit **which** he has given us

Cf. also Mark 7:13; Luke 5:9; 12:46; John 15:20; 17:5; Acts 2:22; 1 Cor 6:19; Col 1:23; Rev 18:6.

2] Inverse Attraction (a.k.a. Indirect Attraction)

Inverse attraction takes place when the antecedent is attracted to the case of the RP.

Mark 12:10 λίθον **ὃν** ἀπεδοκίμασαν οἱ οἰκοδομοῦντες, οὗτος ἐγενήθη . . .
the stone **which** the builders rejected, this has become . . .

1 Cor 10:16 τὸν ἄρτον **ὃν** κλῶμεν, οὐχὶ κοινωνία τοῦ σώματος τοῦ Χριστοῦ ἐστιν;
the bread, **which** we break, is it not communion in the body of Christ?

> The previous line reads τὸ ποτήριον τῆς εὐλογίας **ὃ** εὐλογοῦμεν, οὐχὶ κοινωνία ἐστὶν τοῦ αἵματος τοῦ Χριστοῦ; ("the cup of blessing, **which** we bless, is it not communion in the blood of Christ?") Although τὸ ποτήριον could conceivably be nom., in light of the parallel with τὸν ἄρτον, it is most likely acc.

Cf. also Matt 21:42; Mark 6:16; Luke 1:73; Acts 21:16; Rom 6:17.

c) Antecedent Complexities

1] Omission of Antecedent

The antecedent may be omitted for a variety of reasons in Greek. For example, the RP may incorporate a *demonstrative* pronoun, in which case the object is clear enough from the context. Less frequent, but no less significant exegetically,

---

[63] A wide variety of witnesses have the acc. ἥν, reflecting a tension over the direct attraction (cf. 𝔓[46] B[2] 1505 1739 1881 *et pauci*). The gen., however, is both the harder reading and has a better pedigree (cf. ℵ A B* C D 0278 33 𝔐).

are instances of *poetic* material woven into the fabric of a discourse (see discussion of 1 Tim 3:16 below).

a] Embedded Demonstrative

John 4:18   πέντε ἄνδρας ἔσχες καὶ νῦν **ὃν** ἔχεις οὐκ ἔστιν σου ἀνήρ
you have had five husbands and **[the one] whom** you now have is not your husband

Heb 5:8   καίπερ ὢν υἱός, ἔμαθεν ἀφ᾽ **ὧν** ἔπαθεν τὴν ὑπακοήν
although he was a son, he learned obedience from **[those things] which** he suffered

Other clear examples include Luke 9:36; John 7:31.

1 Pet 1:6   ἐν **ᾧ** ἀγαλλιᾶσθε[64]
in **this** [*or* **which**?] you rejoice

> The previous context reads: εἰς σωτηρίαν ἑτοίμην ἀποκαλυφθῆναι ἐν καιρῷ ἐσχάτῳ ("for a salvation prepared to be revealed in the last time"). The Nestle-Aland[27] text ends v 5 with a period, making the relative pronoun in v 6 embed a demonstrative. But such an embed is rare and should not be invoked when the sentence structure makes good sense, complex though it may be. Furthermore, this is unnatural: The Nestle-Aland[27] text's punctuation suggests that the RP is used exclusively for a demonstrative, rather than in a double-duty capacity as both RP and demonstrative.
>
> This outlook seems to have impacted English translations as well (especially the NIV). The sentences are getting shorter. On a larger scale, this impacts several other grammatical issues, such as the frequency of imperatival participles or whether clauses exist in a hierchical relationship (i.e., one subordinate to the other) or are coordinate.[65]
>
> These issues are more than grammatical: If, for example, 1 Pet 5:7 (πᾶσαν τὴν μέριμναν ὑμῶν ἐπιρίψαντες ἐπ᾽ αὐτόν, ὅτι αὐτῷ μέλει περὶ ὑμῶν) is read as an independent clause, the idea would be, "Cast all your cares on him because he cares for you." But if the participle is dependent on the preceding verse ("humble yourselves under the mighty hand of God . . ."), the idea is that the path of humility is found in casting one's cares on God ("humble yourselves . . . [by] casting"). Putting a period between the two verses obscures this connection.

b] Poetry

> Most scholars now see hymn fragments here and there in the NT, such as Phil 2:6-11; Col 1:15-20; 1 Tim 3:16; Heb 1:3-4; etc. Frequently, such texts begin with a relative clause that has been woven into the syntax of the

---

[64] For ἐν ᾧ ἀγαλλιᾶσθε 𝔓[72] has the participle ἀγαλλιάσαντες; the second corrector of C drops the ἐν ᾧ but keeps the imperative.

[65] Other sentences that are shortened in the Nestle-Aland[27] text without sufficient warrant include the following: 1 Pet 1:9-10, 11-12 (1 Pet 1:3-12 is actually one long sentence in Greek); Eph 1:3-14 (also one sentence in Greek) is broken down into vv 3-6, 7-10, 11-12, 13-14 (each new section beginning with ἐν ᾧ); Eph 5:18-21 (unwarranted hard break at v 21).

surrounding prose discourse. Indeed, one of the standard features of Greek poetry is the introductory use of the relative pronoun.[66] Sometimes, however, the RP has no antecedent because the hymnic fragment is introduced without syntactic connection.

1 Tim 3:16   καὶ ὁμολογουμένως μέγα ἐστὶν τὸ τῆς εὐσεβείας μυστήριον·

δς ἐφανερώθη ἐν σαρκί,

ἐδικαιώθη ἐν πνεύματι,

ὤφθη ἀγγέλοις,

ἐκηρύχθη ἐν ἔθνεσιν,

ἐπιστεύθη ἐν κόσμῳ,

ἀνελήμφθη ἐν δόξῃ.

and confessedly great is the mystery of godliness:

who was manifested in the flesh,

vindicated in the spirit,

appeared to angels,

proclaimed among Gentiles,

believed on in the world,

taken up to glory.

> The rhythmic patterns of this text are obvious: six lines of parallel passive verbs, followed by parallel (ἐν +) dat. constructions. These features, coupled with an introductory ὅς, are signatures of poetry.[67] Among other things, the implications of such an identification are the following: (1) To seek outside the hymn for an antecedent to ὅς, as some have done, is an unnecessary expedient, which, in fact, misreads the genre and misunderstand the force of τὸ τῆς εὐσεβείας μυστήριον.[68] (2) The textual variant θεός in the place of ὅς, has been adamantly defended by some scholars, particulary those of the "majority text" school. Not only is such a reading poorly attested,[69] but the syntactical

---

[66] See especially R. P. Martin, "Aspects of Worship in the New Testament Church," *VE* 2 (1963) 16-18, for the lingustic criteria used to detect poetry.

[67] P. T. O'Brien nicely summarizes the criteria for detecting hymnic material in the NT: "(a) *stylistic:* a certain rhythmical lilt when the passages are read aloud, the presence of *parallelismus membrorum* (i.e., an arrangement into couplets), the semblance of some metre, and the presence of rhetorical devices such as alliteration, *chiasmus*, and antithesis; and (b) *linguistic:* an unusual vocabulary, particularly the presence of theological terms, which is different from the surrounding context" (*Commentary on Philippians* [NIGTC] 188-89). On the structure of 1 Tim 3:16, see Fee, *1 and 2 Timothy, Titus* (NIBC) 92-93.

[68] Young, *Intermediate Greek*, 76, enlists this text as an example of a gender shift, arguing that "the mystery of godliness" refers to Christ since it is followed by ὅς. Most commentators prefer to see "the mystery of godliness" as referring to the Christian faith. So Conzelmann-Dibelius, Fee, Guthrie, Hanson, et al.

[69] In particular, it is impossible to explain the Latin reading of a neuter RP as deriving from θεός, showing that ὅς was quite early. Not one firsthand of any Greek witnesses prior to the 8th century read θεός. Since θεός was a *nomen sacrum,* it was contracted as $\overline{\Theta C}$ in the MSS. The possibility thus exists that OC was misread as $\overline{\Theta C}$ in about the fourth century and, owing to its richer theological content, thereby ended up in the vast majority of MSS. (See the discussion in Metzger, *Textual Commentary,* 641.)

argument that "'*mystery*' (μυστήριον) being a neuter noun, *cannot* be followed by the masculine pronoun (ὅς)"[70] is entirely without weight. As attractive theologically as the reading θεός may be, it is spurious. To reject it is not to deny the deity of Christ, of course; it is just to deny any *explicit* reference in *this* text.[71]

2] Adverbial/Conjunctive Uses

The RP is often used after a preposition. Frequently, such prepositional phrases have an adverbial or conjunctive force. In such instances, the RP either has no antecedent, or else its antecedent is conceptual, not grammatical.[72]

Luke 12:3 **ἀνθ᾽ ὧν** ὅσα ἐν τῇ σκοτίᾳ εἴπατε ἐν τῷ φωτὶ ἀκουσθήσεται
therefore, whatever you said in the dark will be heard in the light

Acts 26:12 **ἐν οἷς** πορευόμενος εἰς τὴν Δαμασκὸν
meanwhile/therefore, when I traveled to Damascus
The prepositional expression could either point back to the preceding clause in a general way (="therefore," "because of these things"), or it could be temporal ("meanwhile," "in the meantime"). Cf. also Luke 12:1 (where ἐν οἷς is clearly temporal).

Rom 5:12 εἰς πάντας ἀνθρώπους ὁ θάνατος διῆλθεν, **ἐφ᾽ ᾧ** πάντες ἥμαρτον
death passed to all people, **because** all sinned
The prepositional phrase here is often debated. It is possible that ᾧ refers back to "one man" (ἑνὸς ἀνθρώπου) mentioned earlier in the verse. If so, the idea is either "all sinned in one man," or "all sinned because of one man." But the distance to ἑνὸς ἀνθρώπου is too great for this to be a natural reading. But if ἐφ᾽ ᾧ functions as a conjunction, it does not look back at any antecedent, but explains how death passed to all: "Death is universal for the precise reason that sin is universal."[73] This usage finds parallels in the papyri and in the rest of the Pauline corpus (cf. 2 Cor 5:4; Phil 3:12). The theological issues at stake are profound and complex (e.g., whether humanity's sinning is personal or participatory in Adam's sin), but such things are only partially resolved by the grammar of the RP.[74] Nevertheless, without compelling

---

[70] J. W. Burgon, *The Revision Revised* (London: John Murray, 1883) 426 (cf. also 497-501). Burgon adds: "Such an expression is abhorrent alike to Grammar and to Logic, –is intolerable, in Greek as in English." Though eloquent in rhetoric, Burgon's argument is lacking in substance.

[71] For a comprehensive treatment on explicit references to Jesus as θεός in the NT, see M. J. Harris, *Jesus as God: The New Testament Use of Theos in Reference to Jesus* (Grand Rapids: Baker, 1992). The discussion of 1 Tim 3:16 is found on 267-68.

[72] See BAGD, s.v. ὅς, I.11. (585).

[73] S. L. Johnson, Jr., "Romans 5:12–An Exercise in Exegesis and Theology" *New Dimensions in New Testament Study,* edd. R. N. Longenecker and M. C. Tenney (Grand Rapids: Zondervan, 1974) 305. The entire essay (298-316) is a penetrating treatment of the exegetical and theological issues involved in the verse.

[74] For a convenient discussion of the interpretive options, see Cranfield, *Romans* (ICC) 1.274-79. On the basis of the context he rejects the independent personal sin view (that of Pelagius), because "it reduces the scope of the analogy between Christ and Adam to such an extent as virtually to empty it of real significance" (277).

evidence on the other side, the force of ἐφ᾽ ᾧ ought to be taken as conjunctive since it is both well established in Greek literature and makes excellent sense here.[75]

2 Pet 3:4   ἀφ᾽ ἧς οἱ πατέρες ἐκοιμήθησαν, πάντα οὕτως διαμένει ἀπ᾽ ἀρχῆς κτίσεως
ever since the fathers fell asleep, all things have continued in the same manner from the beginning of creation

1 Pet 3:19   ἐν ᾧ καὶ τοῖς ἐν φυλακῇ πνεύμασιν πορευθεὶς ἐκήρυξεν
in which he also went and preached to the spirits in prison

> The antecedent of the RP is by no means certain. Some take it to refer to πνεύματι immediately preceding, the meaning of which might be either the Holy Spirit or the spiritual state.[76] Others see the phrase as causal ("for which reason," "because of this"), referring back to the entire clause, while still other scholars read the phrase as temporal (if so, it could be with or without an antecedent: "on which occasion" or "meanwhile"). None of these options is excluded by syntax.[77] It may be significant, however, that every other time ἐν ᾧ is used in 1 Peter it bears an adverbial/conjunctive force (cf. 1:6; 2:12; 3:16 [here, temporal]; 4:4).[78]

Cf. also Luke 1:20; 7:45; 19:44; Acts 24:11; Rom 11:25; 2 Thess 1:11; 2:10.

b. ὅστις

1) General Use

In general, ὅστις is indefinite while ὅς is definite (though ὅς used with ἄν also has an indefinite force). All but half a dozen instances are in the nominative case.[79]

---

[75] For a discussion of the force of ἐφ᾽ ᾧ, see D. L. Turner, "Adam, Christ, and Us: The Pauline Teaching of Solidarity in Romans 5:12-21" (Th.D. dissertation, Grace Theological Seminary, Winona Lake, Ind., 1982) 129-49, who opts, however, for a normal prepositional use, without committing to any particular antecedent.

[76] It is often objected that the Holy Spirit cannot be in view because the two datives of v 18 (σαρκί, πνεύματι) would then have a different syntactical force (sphere, means). But if 1 Pet 3:18 is a hymnic or liturgical fragment, this can be no objection because of "poetic license": Poetry is replete with examples of grammatical and lexical license, not the least of which is the use of the same morpho-syntactic categories, in parallel lines, with different senses (note, e.g., the dat. expressions in 1 Tim 3:16). For a general introduction to the syntax of poetry, see V. Bers, *Greek Poetic Syntax in the Classical Age* (New Haven: Yale University Press, 1984).

[77] This is so, despite Selwyn's objection that nowhere does πνεύματι as a dat. of reference function antecedently to an RP (E. G. Selwyn, *The First Epistle of Peter*, 2d ed. [London: Macmillan, 1947] 197), because, as W. A. Grudem (*The First Epistle of Peter: An Introduction and Commentary* [TNTC] 228) points out, "it is exegetically illegitimate to demand parallel examples which are so narrowly specified that one would not expect to find many, if any, examples. Thus, Selwyn has based his exegetical judgment on an artificial distinction. . . ."

[78] This is not a syntactical issue per se, but it is a stylistic one–and one that is distinctly Petrine (BAGD lists only these texts as examples of a conjunctive ἐν ᾧ in the NT).

[79] According to *acCordance*, there are five instances of the gen. in the fixed expression ἕως ὅτου, one instance of the acc. ὅτι (1 John 3:20), and 139 of the nom. BAGD also lists ἀφ᾽ ὅτου occurring in D at Luke 13:25.

2) Clarification and Subcategories

Although traditionally used, "indefinite" is not the best choice of terms for this pronoun. The notion needs to be defined broadly: It is typically either *generic* in that the RP focuses on the whole class (thus, "whoever" = "everyone who") or *qualitative* in that the RP focuses on the nature or essence of the person or thing in view. In this second sense, it can usually be translated intensively ("the very one who," "who certainly," "who indeed").[80] Distinguishing between these two is not always an easy matter, however.

a) Illustrations of the Generic RP

Matt 5:39 ὅστις σε ῥαπίζει εἰς τὴν δεξιὰν σιαγόνα σου, στρέψον αὐτῷ καὶ τὴν ἄλλην
whoever strikes you on your right cheek, turn to him also the other cheek

Luke 14:27 ὅστις οὐ βαστάζει τὸν σταυρὸν ἑαυτοῦ καὶ ἔρχεται ὀπίσω μου, οὐ δύναται εἶναί μου μαθητής
whoever does not bear his own cross and come after me cannot be my disciple

Gal 5:4 κατηργήθητε ἀπὸ Χριστοῦ, **οἵτινες** ἐν νόμῳ δικαιοῦσθε
you have become separated from Christ, [all] **who** would be justified by the law

b) Illustrations of the Qualitative RP

Matt 7:15 προσέχετε ἀπὸ τῶν ψευδοπροφητῶν, **οἵτινες** ἔρχονται πρὸς ὑμᾶς ἐν ἐνδύμασιν προβάτων, ἔσωθεν δέ εἰσιν λύκοι ἅρπαγες
beware of false prophets, **the very ones who** come to you in sheep's clothing, but inside are ravenous wolves

Rom 1:25 **οἵτινες** μετήλλαξαν τὴν ἀλήθειαν τοῦ θεοῦ ἐν τῷ ψεύδει
these indeed exchanged the truth of God for a lie

1 Pet 2:11 παρακαλῶ . . . ἀπέχεσθαι τῶν σαρκικῶν ἐπιθυμιῶν **αἵτινες** στρατεύονται κατὰ τῆς ψυχῆς
I urge [you] . . . to abstain from fleshly lusts, **the very things that** wage war against the soul

3) Confusion with ὅς

Not infrequently, ὅστις seems to function just like ὅς in the NT in that it has a definite referent in view. In such places there is little or no discernible difference in the force of the two pronouns. This is especially common in Luke-Acts.[81]

---

[80] For more nuancing of the categories, cf. BAGD.
[81] See H. J. Cadbury, "The Relative Pronouns in Acts and Elsewhere," *JBL* 42 (1923) 150-57, for the seminal study.

Luke 9:30 ἄνδρες δύο συνελάλουν αὐτῷ, **οἵτινες** ἦσαν Μωϋσῆς καὶ Ἠλίας[82]
two men were conversing with him, **who** were Moses and Elijah

Acts 16:12 κἀκεῖθεν εἰς Φιλίππους, **ἥτις** ἐστὶν πρώτης μερίδος τῆς Μακεδονίας πόλις
and from there to Philippi, **which is** the leading city of the district of Macedonia

2 Tim 2:18 Ὑμέναιος καὶ Φίλητος, (18) **οἵτινες** περὶ τὴν ἀλήθειαν ἠστόχησαν
Hymenaeus and Philetus, **who** have deviated from the truth

D. Interrogative Pronouns

1. Definition and Terms Used

An interrogative pronoun asks a question. The most common interrogative pronoun is τίς, τί (occurring over 500 times), typically asking an *identifying* question ("Who?" or "What?"). ποῖος, used far more sparingly in the NT (only 33 times), normally asks a *qualitative* question ("What sort?"), while πόσος (27 times) asks a *quantitative* question ("How much?").

2. Functions of τίς

Τίς is used to introduce both direct and indirect questions. As such, it is used both substantivally (as a true pronoun) and adjectivally. The neuter is also used adverbially ("Why?").[83] For the most part, τίς asks an identifying question, especially when a person is in view. But it is also used to ask a categorical or qualitative question ("What sort?"), thus encroaching on the domain normally reserved for ποῖος.

Mark 8:27 **τίνα** με λέγουσιν οἱ ἄνθρωποι εἶναι;
Who do people say that I am?
The substantival use is the most common use of the interrogative pronoun. Cf. also Matt 6:3; Mark 2:7; 5:9; Luke 4:34; Rev 5:2.

Mark 9:34 πρὸς ἀλλήλους διελέχθησαν . . . **τίς** μείζων
they were discussing with each other . . . **who** was the greatest
This is an example of the interrogative pronoun used in an indirect question. Cf. also Luke 1:62; John 4:10; Acts 10:17.

Matt 5:46 **τίνα** μισθὸν ἔχετε;
What reward do you have?

---

[82] For οἵτινες, ἦν δέ is read in D, οἵ in C.

[83] See BAGD for examples of other uses such as (a) which of two (=πότερος), (b) as a substitute for the RP, and (c) as an exclamation (τί = "How!").

This is an illustration of the adjectival use of the interrogative pronoun. Cf. also Matt 7:9; John 2:18; Rom 6:21; 1 Thess 3:9; Heb 12:7.

Mark 1:27 ἐθαμβήθησαν ἅπαντες ὥστε συζητεῖν πρὸς ἑαυτοὺς λέγοντας· **τί** ἐστιν τοῦτο; διδαχὴ καινή[84]

they were all amazed so that they queried among themselves, saying, "**What** is this? A new teaching!"

> This is an example of a categorical question (= "What sort of thing is this?"). Cf. also Luke 1:66; Eph 1:19; Col 1:27; Heb 2:6.

Acts 1:11 **τί** ἑστήκατε ἐμβλέποντες εἰς τὸν οὐρανόν;

Why do you stand, gazing into heaven?

> For other examples of the adverbial use of τί, cf. Matt 6:28; Mark 8:12; Luke 2:48; Acts 3:12; Rom 9:19; 1 Cor 10:30; Col 2:20.

3. *Functions of* ποῖος *and* πόσος

Ποῖος and πόσος are normally qualitative and quantitative interrogative pronouns respectively: ποῖος asks "What sort?" and πόσος asks "How much?" Such a distinction for ποῖος is not always maintained, however; rarely it functions like τίς (cf. John 10:32)[85] in that it asks an identifying question.

Mark 11:28 ἐν **ποίᾳ** ἐξουσίᾳ ταῦτα ποιεῖς;

By **what kind of** authority do you do these things?

John 12:33 τοῦτο ἔλεγεν σημαίνων **ποίῳ** θανάτῳ ἤμελλεν ἀποθνῄσκειν

he was saying this, signifying **by what sort of** death he was about to die

1 Pet 1:11 ἐραυνῶντες εἰς τίνα ἢ **ποῖον** καιρὸν ἐδήλου τὸ ἐν αὐτοῖς πνεῦμα Χριστοῦ προμαρτυρόμενον τὰ εἰς Χριστὸν παθήματα

inquiring as to what or **what kind of time** the Spirit of Christ within them was indicating by testifying ahead of time about the sufferings of Christ

> It is also possible to take τίνα as substantival in the sense of "who" (so RSV, NASB, NRSV ["inquiring about the person or time"]).[86]

Matt 15:34 **πόσους** ἄρτους ἔχετε;

How many loaves do you have?

Luke 16:7 σὺ **πόσον** ὀφείλεις;

How much do you owe?

---

[84] τί ἐστιν τοῦτο is omitted in D W.

[85] BAGD also list Matt 22:36, but the translation of ποία ἐντολὴ μεγάλη as "Which is the great commandment?" is not at all demanded; an equally plausible rendering is, "What sort of commandment is great?" Even John 10:32 might not fit; διὰ ποῖον αὐτῶν ἔργον ἐμὲ λιθάζετε; could mean, "Which category of works of these are you about to stone me for?"

[86] For a discussion of the options, see the tidy summary in Porter, *Idioms*, 137.

E. Indefinite Pronoun

1. Definition and Terms Used

The indefinite pronoun (τις, τι) is used to introduce a member of a class without further identification. It is used both substantivally (as a true pronoun) and adjectivally. It can be translated *anyone, someone, a certain,* or simply *a(n)*.[87]

2. Functions

a. Substantival Uses

Matt 16:24   εἴ **τις** θέλει ὀπίσω μου ἐλθεῖν, ἀπαρνησάσθω ἑαυτὸν
            if **anyone** wants to come after me, let him deny himself

John 6:51   ἐάν **τις** φάγῃ ἐκ τούτου τοῦ ἄρτου ζήσει εἰς τὸν αἰῶνα
            if **anyone** eats from this bread, he will live forever

Heb 3:4   πᾶς οἶκος κατασκευάζεται ὑπό **τινος**
            every house is built by **someone**

Cf. also John 3:3; Acts 4:35; Rom 5:7; Phlm 18; Heb 2:9; Jas 1:5; 1 Pet 4:11; 2 John 10; Rev 3:20.

b. Adjectival Uses

Luke 10:25   νομικός **τις** ἀνέστη ἐκπειράζων αὐτόν[88]
            a lawyer stood up, testing him

Rom 8:39   οὔτε ὕψωμα οὔτε βάθος οὔτε **τις** κτίσις ἑτέρα δυνήσεται ἡμᾶς χωρίσαι ἀπὸ τῆς ἀγάπης τοῦ θεοῦ[89]
            neither height nor depth nor **any** other created thing will be able to separate us from the love of God

Phil 2:1   εἴ **τις** παράκλησις ἐν Χριστῷ
            if there is **any** encouragement in Christ

Jas 1:18   εἰς τὸ εἶναι ἡμᾶς ἀπαρχήν **τινα**
            that we might be **a kind** of firstfruits

Cf. also Matt 18:12; Luke 8:27; 9:8; John 4:46; Acts 3:2; 27:8; Gal 6:1; Heb 10:27; Jude 4.

---

[87] Cf. BAGD for a detailed treatment of τις, including its various permutations.

[88] τις is omitted in 0211.

[89] τις is omitted in 𝔓[46] D F G 1505, perhaps due to homoiomeson with the following word (κτίσις).

F. Possessive "Pronouns" (= Adjectives)

1. Definition and Terms Used

Greek does not have a distinct possessive pronoun. Instead, it usually employs either the possessive adjective (ἐμός, σός, ἡμέτερος, ὑμέτερος)[90] or the genitive of the personal pronoun.[91] The one *lexicalizes* possession (i.e., the notion of possession is part of the lexical root); the other *grammaticalizes* possession (i.e., the notion of possession is part of the inflection). No detailed treatment needs to be given since (a) possessive pronoun is not a bona fide Greek category, and (b) the notion of possession can be examined either via the lexicon or other sections of this grammar.

2. How Possession is Expressed

Possession can be expressed in four ways in the New Testament:

1) by the possessive adjectives
2) by the genitive of the personal pronoun
3) by the article
4) by ἴδιος.

G. Intensive Pronoun

1. Definition and Term Used

The intensive pronoun, αὐτός, is far and away the most common pronoun used in the NT. Technically, however, as an intensive (with the sense of –*self*) it is relatively infrequent. The predominant function of αὐτός is as a stand-in for the third person personal pronoun in oblique cases. What will be illustrated below are the two main categories of usage *other* than as a personal pronoun.[92]

---

[90] Are the terms ἐμός, σός, ἡμέτερος, and ὑμέτερος adjectives or pronouns? They predominantly function in a dependent role, modifying a noun. In all syntactical respects they behave just like adjectives. Yet many grammarians consider them to be pronouns.

In the NT they almost always stand in attributive position, usually dependent on a noun, agreeing with it in gender, number, and case. Furthermore, these terms, even when not modifying a noun, consistently have the article (a structural clue for adjectives, not pronouns).

[91] The inclusion, then, of the possessive adjective in the semantic category of possession is really an English way of looking at things.

[92] See BAGD, 122-24, for a detailed description of the various uses of αὐτός.

2. Functions

a. As an Intensive Pronoun

When αὐτός is in *predicate* position to an articular noun (or to an anarthrous proper name), it has the force of *himself, herself, itself,* etc. αὐτός can also bear this force when it stands alone, either as the subject of the verb or in any of the oblique cases. In general, the intensive use of αὐτός is intended "to emphasize identity. It is the demonstrative force intensified."[93]

Mark 12:36   **αὐτὸς** Δαυὶδ εἶπεν ἐν τῷ πνεύματι
David **himself** spoke in the Spirit

John 2:24   **αὐτὸς** Ἰησοῦς οὐκ ἐπίστευεν **αὐτὸν** αὐτοῖς διὰ τὸ **αὐτὸν** γινώσκειν πάντας[94]
Jesus **himself** was not entrusting **himself** to them, because **he himself** knew all men

> This text affords an interesting and insightful example. It is first used as an intensifier to the subject, then as direct object (with an intensive-reflexive force). On the surface, the pronoun looks redundant, but its very repetition contrasts Jesus with the rest of humanity, setting him apart in his sinlessness.

1 Th 4:16   **αὐτὸς** ὁ κύριος ἐν κελεύσματι . . . καταβήσεται ἀπ᾿ οὐρανοῦ
the Lord **himself** will descend from heaven with a shout

Jas 2:7   οὐκ **αὐτοὶ** βλασφημοῦσιν;
do not **they themselves** blaspheme?

Cf. also Mark 16:8; Acts 18:15; 1 Cor 15:28; Rev 21:3.

b. As an Identifying Adjective

When modifying an articular substantive in the *attributive* position, αὐτός is used as an identifying adjective. As such, it is translated *same.*

Luke 23:40   τῷ **αὐτῷ** κρίματι
in the **same** judgment

1 Cor 12:5   ὁ **αὐτὸς** κύριος
the **same** Lord

> The unity-in-diversity refrain is repeated in this chapter, as witnessed by the identifying adjective use of αὐτός. Cf. also vv 8, 9, 11 (each time with τὸ αὐτὸ πνεῦμα).

---

[93] Dana-Mantey, 129.

[94] The second αὐτόν is replaced by the more natural reflexive pronoun, ἑαυτόν, in 𝔓[66] ℵ[2] A[c] W[c] Θ Ψ 050 083 *f*[1, 13] 33 *Byz.* 𝔓[75] 579 *et pauci* omit the pronoun altogether. The personal pronoun is found in ℵ* A B L 700 *et alii*. Although the witnesses are fractured, the personal pronoun is found in decent texts and is the most difficult reading grammatically. It adds a touch of rhetorical power to the statement.

Phil 2:2   τὴν **αὐτὴν** ἀγάπην ἔχοντες
            having the **same** love

Jas 3:10   ἐκ τοῦ **αὐτοῦ** στόματος ἐξέρχεται εὐλογία καὶ κατάρα
            from the **same** mouth come forth blessing and cursing

Cf. also Matt 26:44; Mark 14:39; Rom 9:21; 2 Cor 3:14; Heb 10:1; 2 Pet 3:7.

H. Reflexive Pronouns

1. Definition and Terms Used

The reflexive pronouns are ἐμαυτοῦ (*of myself*), σεαυτοῦ (*of yourself*), ἑαυτοῦ (*of himself*), ἑαυτῶν (*of themselves*). The force of the reflexive is *frequently* to indicate that the subject is also the object of the action of the verb. The pronoun thus "reflects back" on the subject. But since the reflexive pronoun also occurs as *other than* the direct object, this description is incomplete.[95]

On a broader scale, the reflexive pronoun is used to *highlight the participation of the subject* in the verbal action, as direct object, indirect object, intensifier, etc. Although predominantly the reflexive pronoun is used as direct object, this is by no means its only function. Especially common is the pronoun as object of a preposition. As might be expected, then, the reflexive pronoun only occurs in the oblique cases. In this respect, it overlaps to some degree with the intensive pronoun in oblique cases.

2. Illustrations

Matt 4:6   εἰ υἱὸς εἶ τοῦ θεοῦ, βάλε **σεαυτὸν** κάτω
            if you are the Son of God, throw **yourself** down

Mark 5:30   ὁ Ἰησοῦς ἐπιγνοὺς ἐν **ἑαυτῷ**[96]
            Jesus knowing within **himself**

Luke 1:24   περιέκρυβεν **ἑαυτήν**[97]
            she hid **herself**

Luke 2:39   ἐπέστρεψαν . . . εἰς πόλιν **ἑαυτῶν** Ναζαρέθ[98]
            they returned . . . to **their own** city, Nazareth

---

[95] Several standard grammars describe the reflexive pronoun as though it only occurred as direct object (cf. Dana-Mantey, 131; Porter, *Idioms*, 79).

[96] The prepositional phrase ἐν ἑαυτῷ is omitted in codex D.

[97] αὐτήν is read for ἑαυτήν in L 118 205 209 579 700 716 1247 1579 2643 2766 *et pauci.* ἑαυτήν is found in early and widespread witnesses, however.

[98] αὐτῶν is found in the *TR* and is supported by D² H Λ *et alii.*

Rom 5:8   συνίστησιν τὴν **ἑαυτοῦ** ἀγάπην εἰς ἡμᾶς ὁ θεός
           God demonstrated **his own** love for us

Eph 5:19   λαλοῦντες **ἑαυτοῖς** ἐν ψαλμοῖς καὶ ὕμνοις
           speaking **to one another** in psalms and hymns
           > Here is a rare instance of the reflexive pronoun used like a reciprocal
           > pronoun. Cf. also 1 Pet 4:10.

Phil 2:7   **ἑαυτὸν** ἐκένωσεν μορφὴν δούλου λαβών
           he emptied **himself** by taking on the form of a servant

Heb 5:5   ὁ Χριστὸς οὐχ **ἑαυτὸν** ἐδόξασεν
           Christ did not glorify **himself**

Jas 2:17   ἡ πίστις, ἐὰν μὴ ἔχῃ ἔργα, νεκρά ἐστιν καθ᾽ **ἑαυτήν**
           faith, if it does not have works, is dead [being] by **itself**

Cf. also Matt 8:4; 14:15; 16:24; Mark 5:5; 9:10; Luke 2:3; John 5:18; Acts 1:3; 12:11; Rom 2:14;
Gal 1:4; 1 Tim 2:6; Heb 6:6; Jas 1:22; 1 Pet 3:5; 1 John 1:8; Rev 19:7.

I. Reciprocal Pronouns

1. Definition and Terms Used

The reciprocal pronoun, ἀλλήλων (*of one another*), is used to indicate an interchange between two or more groups. It is thus always *plural* and, like the
reflexive pronoun, occurs only in the oblique cases. One frequently finds this
pronoun in paraenetic contexts, basing the exhortation on the organic connection that believers have with the risen Christ.

2. Illustrations

Matt 24:10   τότε σκανδαλισθήσονται πολλοὶ καὶ **ἀλλήλους** παραδώσουσιν
             then many will fall away and betray **one another**

Mark 9:50   εἰρηνεύετε ἐν **ἀλλήλοις**
             be at peace with **one another**

John 13:34   ἀγαπᾶτε **ἀλλήλους**
             love **one another**

Eph 4:25   ἐσμὲν **ἀλλήλων** μέλη
             we are members **of one another**

Jas 5:16   εὔχεσθε ὑπὲρ **ἀλλήλων**
             pray for **one another**

Cf. also Matt 25:32; Luke 12:1; John 5:44; Acts 15:39; Rom 12:5; 2 Cor 13:12; Gal 6:2; Heb
10:24; 1 Pet 4:9; 2 John 5; Rev 6:4.

IV. Lexico-Syntactic Categories: Major Terms

The previous section approached the pronouns from a *semantic priority* grid. This section begins with a *formal priority*. The rationale for this is that it is more user-friendly to the student who can recognize certain words in the text as being pronouns, but may not be able to articulate to which semantic category they belong. This section, however, is little more than an outline of uses: When the student notices the various semantic options for a particular form, he or she should turn to the relevant discussions in the previous section. The semantic uses are listed in order of frequency for each word.

A. Ἀλλήλων
  1. Instances: 100
  2. Use: Reciprocal pronoun

B. Αὐτός
  1. Instances: 5596
  2. Uses
    • Personal pronoun (usually third person)
    • Possessive pronoun (gen. case)
    • Intensive pronoun (including identifying adjective)

C. Ἑαυτοῦ
  1. Instances: 319
  2. Use: Reflexive pronoun

D. Ἐγώ
  1. Instances: 1804
  2. Uses
    • Personal pronoun
    • Possessive pronoun (gen. case)

E. Ἐκεῖνος
  1. Instances: 265
  2. Uses
    • Demonstrative pronoun
    • Personal pronoun

F. Ἐμαυτοῦ
  1. Instances: 37
  2. Use: Reflexive pronoun

G. Ἡμεῖς
1. Instances: 864
2. Uses
- Personal pronoun
- Possessive pronoun (gen. case)

H. Ὅδε
1. Instances: 10
2. Use: Demonstrative pronoun

I. Ὅς
1. Instances: 1406
2. Use: Relative pronoun (definite)

J. Ὅστις
1. Instances: 145
2. Use: Relative pronoun (indefinite)

K. Οὗτος
1. Instances: 1387
2. Uses

- Demonstrative pronoun
- Personal pronoun

L. Ποῖος
1. Instances: 33
2. Use: Interrogative pronoun (qualitative)

M. Πόσος
1. Instances: 27
2. Use: Interrogative pronoun (quantitative)

N. Σεαυτοῦ
1. Instances: 43
2. Use: Reflexive pronoun

O. Σύ
1. Instances: 1067
2. Uses
- Personal pronoun
- Possessive pronoun (gen. case)

P. Τίς
1. Instances: 546
2. Use: Interrogative pronoun

Q. Τις
  1. Instances: 543
  2. Use: Indefinite pronoun

R. Ὑμεῖς
  1. Instances: 1840
  2. Use
    • Personal pronoun
    • Possessive pronoun (gen. case)

The relative frequencies of these pronouns are visually displayed in the chart below.

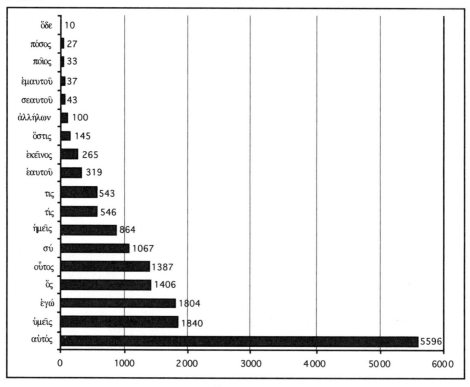

Chart 35
Frequency of Pronoun Terms in the New Testament

The Prepositions

Overview of the Chapter

Select Bibliography

BDF, 110-25 (§203-40); **M. J. Harris**, "Prepositions and Theology in the Greek New Testament," *New International Dictionary of New Testament Theology*, ed. Colin Brown (Grand Rapids: Zondervan, 1978) 3.1171-1215; **Howard**, *Accidence* 292-332; **E. Mayser**, *Grammatik der griechischen Papyri aus der Ptolemäerzeit* (Berlin/Leipzig: Walter de Gruyter, 1933) II. 2.152-68, 337-543; **Moule**, *Idiom Book*, 48-92; **Moulton**, *Prolegomena*, 98-107; **Porter**, *Idioms*, 139-80; **Radermacher**, *Grammatik* 137-46; **Robertson**, *Grammar*, 553-649; **Young**, *Intermediate Greek*, 85-104; **Zerwick**, *Biblical Greek*, 27-46 (§78-135).[1]

Preface

This chapter has three modest objectives: to give a general overview of prepositions, to *outline* the basic uses of the various prepositions, and to discuss a few exegetically significant texts impacted by the use of a preposition. The student should always consult BAGD when attempting to determine the special nuances of the prepositions, as the discussion in BAGD is more complete than what is found here.[2]

I. General Considerations

A. *The Nature of Prepositions*

Prepositions are, in some respects, extended adverbs. That is, they frequently modify verbs and tell how, when, where, etc. But, unlike adverbs, they govern a noun and hence can give more information than a mere adverb can. "Christ dwells in you" is more specific than "Christ dwells inside." Prepositions show how the verb connects to various objects. The realities expressed by such connections are, at times, breathtaking.

---

[1] See also works listed in BAGD, s.v. ἀνά, 49; and the select bibliography in Harris, "Prepositions and Theology," 3.1214-15. For literature dealing with each of the various prepositions, consult the respective entries in BAGD.

[2] Although several intermediate grammars have a detailed chapter on the prepositions, our conviction is that grammars do much unnecessary duplication with lexica. Since anyone using this text should no doubt own a copy of BAGD, we felt that the best approach in this work would be to provide things not normally accessible in a lexicon: general principles, the *basic* uses with labels consistent with our case categories, and exegetical discussions. We have given a highly selective treatment of lexico-syntactic categories to urge students to use BAGD and other tools.

There are exceptions to the adverbial force of prepositions. Some function at times adjectivally. In general, the prepositions that take accusative and dative case objects function adverbially, while those that take a genitive case object often function adjectivally.[3] All of this is in keeping with the simple case uses: The accusative and dative are usually connected to a verb and the genitive is usually connected to a noun.

A proper understanding of prepositions is vital to exegesis. Many an exegetical debate has turned on the use of a particular preposition.[4] One can gain some sense of the value of learning the nuances of the prepositions by noting their sheer number (over 10,000 of them in the NT).[5] Prepositions are so common that four out of five verses have at least one.[6] In general, the more common a preposition is, the more varied are its uses.

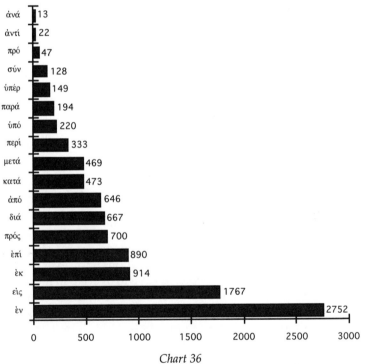

Chart 36
Frequencies of Prepositions in the New Testament[7]

---

[3] Nevertheless, the prepositions that take a gen. are normally adverbial. E.g., ἐκ and ἀπό usually have an ablatival force and hence are usually related to a verb.

[4] The most accessible sustained discussion of the exegetical and theological value of prepositions is that of Harris, "Prepositions and Theology."

[5] 10,384 to be exact (not including improper prepositions).

[6] They occur in 5728 verses.

[7] This list does not include improper prepositions, so-called because they cannot be prefixed to a verb.

B. *Spatial Functions of Prepositions*

1.   In General

The following diagram may prove helpful in understanding the local or spatial functions that prepositions have at times. The circle represents the object of the preposition.

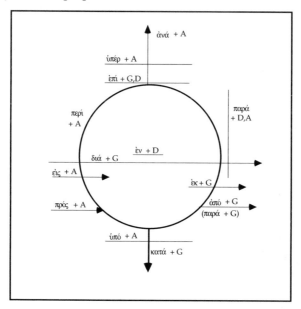

Chart 37
The Spatial Functions of Prepositions

This diagram is designed to be a "rough and ready" chart to help you see the spatial differences in the prepositions. However, there are many exceptions to the nuances depicted (due to overlap in meaning between prepositions, the influence of verbs, etc.). The chart, therefore, has its primary value in showing the *normal* distinctions between the nuances of the prepositions, but it does not make any absolute statements that the relations will always be as they are pictured.

In order to determine the potential uses of a given preposition, one should consult BAGD to see the shades of meaning each preposition can have spatially.

2.   Motion, State, Prepositions, and Verbs

One observation to be made about prepositions is whether they are stative or transitive. That is, does a given preposition suggest merely a *state* or does it imply *motion*? The chart above indicates transitive prepositions by the use of arrows, while stative prepositions are displayed with simple lines having no arrows.

All is not as it seems, however. A stative preposition can occur with a verb of motion, just like a transitive preposition can occur with a stative verb. In such instances, how are we to interpret the data? For example, πρός + accusative indicates *movement toward* the object as in Luke 6:47: πᾶς ὁ ἐρχόμενος **πρός** με ("everyone who comes **to** *me*"). The verb and preposition match each other: they both imply motion. But in John 1:1 πρός is translated *with*: ὁ λόγος ἦν **πρὸς** τὸν θεόν ("the Word was **with** God"). In this instance the verb and preposition do not match: The verb is stative and the preposition is transitive.[8]

Πρός is not the only preposition whose force is overridden by a verb. Virtually all instances of stative verbs with prepositions of motion go in this direction.[9] Note, for example, the uses of εἰς with a stative verb. εἰς generally has the meaning of movement *into from without*. However, when it is used with a stative verb, such as τηρέω, κάθημαι, εἰμί, etc., the idea of *motion* is negated by the stative nature of the verb (cf., e.g., τηρέω εἰς in Acts 25:4; κάθημαι εἰς in Mark 13:3).

These texts illustrate a general principle: *Stative verbs* **override** *the transitive force of prepositions.* Almost always, when a stative verb is used with a transitive preposition, the preposition's natural force is neutralized; all that remains is a stative idea.

When a verb of motion is used with a stative preposition, again the verb is usually dominant: The entire construction indicates motion. For example, πιστεύω + ἐν is the equivalent of πιστεύω + εἰς (cf. Mark 1:15; John 3:15).[10] The idea is "put one's faith *into*" even though ἐν is used.[11]

What is the value of this discussion for exegesis? It is simply that too often prepositions are analyzed simplistically, etymologically, and without due consideration for the verb to which they are connected. Prepositions are often treated in isolation, as though their ontological meaning were still completely intact. Note, for example, the following illustration.

---

[8] For other examples of stative verbs (especially εἰμί) with πρός indicating state, cf. Matt 13:56; 26:18, 55 (*v.l.*); Mark 6:3; 9:19; 14:49; Luke 9:41; Acts 10:48; 12:20; 18:3 (*v.l.*); 1 Cor 16:6-7; 2 Cor 5:8; 11:9; Gal 1:18; 2:5; 4:18, 20; 1 Thess 3:4; 2 Thess 2:5; 3:10; Phlm 13; Heb 4:13; 1 John 1:2.

[9] The most common exception to this rule is the use of εἰμί with ἐκ. In this instance, the preposition still retains its transitive force. E.g., **ἐκ** Ναζαρὲτ δύναταί τι ἀγαθὸν εἶναι; ("Can any good thing *be* **from** Nazareth?") in John 1:46. In this expression the combination of preposition and verb is virtually equivalent to "Can any good thing *come* **from** Nazareth?" Cf. also John 3:31.

[10] However, in some texts ἐν with πιστεύω indicates the location where belief takes place rather than the object of belief (e.g., Rom 10:9; 1 Thess 1:7; 1 Tim 3:16).

[11] For instances of πιστεύω εἰς (a construction far more common in the NT [esp. in John] than πιστεύω ἐν), cf. Matt 18:6; Mark 9:42; John 1:12; 2:11, 23; 3:16; 4:39; 8:30; 9:35; 11:25; 12:44; Acts 10:43; 1 John 5:10, 13.

John 1:18   μονογενὴς θεὸς ὁ ὢν **εἰς** τὸν κόλπον τοῦ πατρός

the unique One, God, who *was* **in** the bosom of the Father

> One cannot press the idea of motion here, as though the meaning is "who was **into** the bosom of the Father." Although a few scholars try to see a theologically rich concept here (either a dynamic and energetic relationship between Son and Father, or the eternal generation of the Son), in Koine Greek, the interchange of εἰς with ἐν, coupled with the overwhelming force of stative verb + transitive preposition, suggests otherwise. This is not to say that the relationship of Son to Father was not dynamic or energetic, just that this text affirms only their intimate relationship.

For other texts impacted by this discussion, cf. John 1:1;[12] Rev 3:10.

C. Prepositions and Simple Case Constructions

1. Do Prepositions Govern or Merely Clarify?

Older NT grammars generally denied that prepositions govern their cases. For example, Dana and Mantey argue,

> It is incorrect . . . to say that prepositions *govern* cases [italics mine]. But it is true that as cases limit and define the relations of verbs to substantives, so also prepositions help to express more exactly and effectively the very distinctions for which cases were created. . . .[13]

This statement is generally accurate for *classical* Greek, but not Koine. Some of the case uses in the classical period were quite subtle. As the language progressed in the Koine period, such subtleties were replaced with more explicit statements. For example, the genitive of separation, a common idiom in the Attic dialect, is rare in Koine. It has been replaced, by and large, by ἀπό + genitive. Likewise, ἐκ + genitive has replaced for the most part the genitive of source. Hence, the prepositional phrase does not always communicate more *explicitly* what a naked case could communicate; sometimes it communicates something *other* than what a simple case would normally communicate. In this respect it is legitimate to speak of prepositions as *governing* nouns.[14]

2. Prepositions Vs. Simple Case Constructions

In light of the preceding discussion, a proper grammatical method separates prepositional phrases from simple case uses. Whenever any of the oblique cases follows a preposition, you should examine the use of the *preposition*, rather than the case usage, to determine the possible nuances involved.

---

[12] Discussed briefly above.

[13] Dana-Mantey, 97-98 (§101). Robertson says, "The notion, therefore, that prepositions 'govern' cases must be discarded definitely" (*Grammar*, 554). Cf. also Moule, *Idiom Book*, 48. More recently, Porter, *Idioms*, argues this same point (140).

The beginning exegete often has a tendency to treat the use of a case after a preposition as though there were no preposition present. That is, he or she attempts to determine the nuance of the case according to the categories for that case rather than according to the categories for the preposition. This is imprecise exegesis for it assumes that the preposition does not alter how the case can be used. But in Hellenistic Greek, because of the tendency toward explicitness, the preposition increasingly gained independent value. Thus, the preposition does not just clarify the case's usage; often, it *alters* it.

It is true that there are many *overlaps* in case usage and preposition + case usage. In such instances, you may check the case usage (as described in the grammars) for a better understanding of the *nuance* involved, but you would err if you shut yourself up to the categorical *possibilities* of the naked case. For example, if you came across ἐν + the dative, you would first want to consult the lexicon for the nuances of ἐν. Once you have determined, via the *lexicon*, that the idea of sphere is a likely candidate in this instance, you may want to look at the dative of sphere in the grammars. The grammars will clarify and expand what the lexica state in cursory form. But it is not the place of the grammar to dictate that the idea of sphere is used in this instance. It would be a wrong procedure, therefore, for a student to turn to the discussion of the dative case in a grammar in order to determine the categorical *possibilities* of ἐν + the dative case.

To restate and summarize: Prepositions are used with cases either to *clarify, strengthen,* or *alter* the basic case usage. For example, ἐν + the dative is very frequently, if not most frequently, used to strengthen the idea of sphere. ἐκ + the genitive often clarifies that source is the idea meant (but in Koine Greek a gen. of source is scarce). When ἀπό is used to indicate a temporal nuance, the idea is radically altered from the use of the naked genitive for time (the former speaking of the *extent* of time, stressing the beginning; the latter, speaking of the *kind* of time).[15] Therefore, *the use of a particular preposition with a particular case **never** exactly parallels–either in*

---

[14] Young offers the helpful insight that there are two schools of thought about prepositions: One school views them as simply clarifying the meaning of the cases, often with the result that the prepositions are not treated separately from case uses; the other school sees the preposition as the dominant element, with the result that prepositions deserve their own special treatment (Young, *Intermediate Greek*, 85). Young correctly takes the latter approach, recognizing that "in koine Greek the preposition gained more independent force, while the case lost some of its significance" (ibid.). An example of the former view is to be found in Brooks-Winbery, 2-59, where they entirely subsume the discussion of prepositions under case uses (although an appendix isolating prepositional uses is added [60-64]). See also Vaughan-Gideon, 30-77, who have no separate treatment of prepositions. Note our discussion in the following section.

[15] Remarkably, more than one recent grammar mixes the case uses in with the preposition uses in such a way that the particular case uses are *systematically* described with and without the preposition. For example, Brooks and Winbery, 9-10, list under "Adverbial Genitive of Time" (1) the Substantive without a Preposition, (2) The Substantive with

category possibilities or in relative frequency of nuances—the use of a case without a preposition.

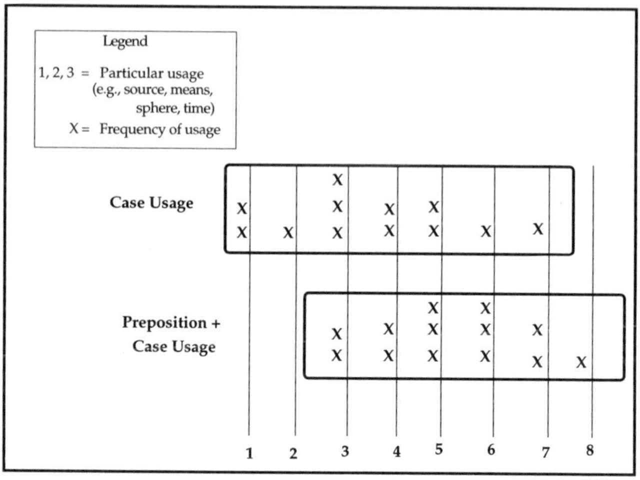

Chart 38
Semantic Overlap Between Simple Case and Preposition + Case

D. Influence of Koine Greek

In addition to the points mentioned above about preposition + case uses vs. simple case uses, Hellenistic Greek impacts prepositional uses in two other ways.

1. Overlapping Usage

Besides the tendency toward explicitness (in which prepositions are used increasingly in Koine rather than naked cases), there is also a tendency toward *laxity* in meaning. That is, many prepositions in Hellenistic Greek have overlapping semantic domains.[16] This finds an analogy with modern English. "This morning, I jumped **in** a pool," for most English-speakers, indicates entrance into the pool, rather than an

the Preposition διά, (3) the Substantive with the Preposition ἐπί, and (4) the Substantive with Adverbial Prepositions. Although they state that such a genitive usage "usually indicates kind of time" (9), the examples with ἕως, ἄχρι, and μέχρι do not at all fit this. Nor would any uses with ἀπό. This approach can only lead to massive confusion for the student.

[16] See Zerwick, *Biblical Greek*, 28-35 (§87-106) for an extended treatment of several overlapping pairs (including ἀπο = ἐκ, ἀπό = ὑπό and παρά, ὑπέρ = ἀντί, ὑπέρ = περί, εἰς = πρός, εἰς = ἐν). Note also Harris, "Prepositions and Theology," 3.1198, for a discussion of the overlap between ὑπό and διά, ὑπό and ἀπό, ὑπό and παρά.

activity already within it ("I jumped **into** a pool" rather than "I jumped **within** a pool").

One caveat is in order, however: The overlap does not flow equally in both directions. In some instances, one preposition encroaches on the meaning of another without a reciprocal laxity (such as with ὑπέρ in the place of ἀντί). In other instances, the overlap goes in both directions (e.g., εἰς and ἐν), but even here there is no equilibrium. (The significance of this point will be developed under ὑπέρ.)

The most frequent examples include the following:

- ἐκ and ἀπό (cf. ἐκ τῶν οὐρανῶν in 1 Thess 1:10 with ἀπ᾽ οὐρανοῦ in 2 Thess 1:7; note ἀπό/ἐκ interchange in 1 Thess 2:6).[17]
- εἰς and ἐν (cf. Luke 9:62; 11:7; John 1:18; 3:15).[18]
- ὑπέρ and περί (cf. Matt 26:28; John 1:30; 17:9; Rom 8:3; Eph 6:18).[19]

2. Root Fallacy

As lexicographers have long noted, the root meaning of a word is not necessarily an accurate guide to the meaning of the word in later literature. The same is true of morpho-syntactic categories: One ought not look for some kind of invariant meaning that is always present with the preposition. The meaning of words changes in time. Further, a word has a *field* of meaning rather than a *point*. Such is no less true for prepositions than for other words.[20]

---

[17] This overlap is clearly seen in statements about Christ's resurrection. If the classical Greek distinctions still obtained, ἀπὸ τῶν νεκρῶν might imply something less than a genuine resurrection (*away from* the dead), while ἐκ (τῶν) νεκρῶν would refer to the real thing (*out from among* the dead). Not all NT writers make such a distinction, however. Matthew 28:6 has ἀπὸ τῶν νεκρῶν (cf. also 27:64) while Luke 24:46 has ἐκ νεκρῶν, both referring to Christ's resurrection. Elsewhere Matthew uses ἐκ (τῶν) νεκρῶν (Matt 17:9). Paul, on the other hand, never uses ἀπὸ (τῶν) νεκρῶν to refer to Christ's resurrection.

[18] In the least, such overlap in meaning would render ἐβαπτίσθη **εἰς** τὸν Ἰορδάνην in Mark 1:9 as less than an iron-clad argument for baptismal immersion, even though εἰς is used (Young, *Intermediate Greek*, 86). It should be noted further that although ἐν is the most frequent preposition in the NT, εἰς is encroaching on its domain more than vice versa. In modern Greek εἰς has almost entirely replaced ἐν.

[19] As with εἰς and ἐν, the overlap is generally in one direction: ὑπέρ increasingly is broadening its horizons, both toward περί and, more significantly, toward ἀντί.

[20] Some grammars still seem to embrace a root meaning for each preposition. E.g., Porter, *Idioms*, 142, argues that "most prepositions have a fundamental sense related to being situated in, moving toward[,] or moving away from a location." This leads him to the conclusion that μονογενὴς θεὸς ὁ ὢν εἰς τὸν κόλπον τοῦ πατρός in John 1:18 means "[the] only begotten [*sic*] God who is directed toward the bosom of the father" (ibid., 153).

II. Specific Prepositions

This section *outlines* the prepositions according to their basic uses and discusses a few exegetically significant texts. For a more detailed treatment of the various uses of the prepositions, consult especially BAGD. The prepositions to be discussed in any detail will only be those that occur independently (i.e., not prefixed to a verb) and are considered by BAGD as "proper" prepositions.

'Aνά

A. Basic Uses (with Accusative only)

1. Distributive: *in the midst of* (ἀνὰ μέσον + G); *each, apiece* (with numbers)
2. Spatial (in composition with verbs): *up, motion upwards.*

B. Significant Passage Involving 'Aνά

There are a few interesting passages in which this preposition occurs in composition (i.e., prefixed to a verb). E.g., Mark 16:4; Acts 17:6; 2 Cor 1:13; 3:2, 2 Tim 1:6.

'Aντί

A. Basic Uses (with Genitive only)

1. Substitution: *instead of, in place of*
2. Exchange/Equivalence: *for, as, in the place of*

   The notions of exchange and substitution are quite similar, often blending into each other.
3. Cause (debatable): *because of*[21]

---

[21] Even granting ἀντί a causal force is not to deny the notion of substitution/exchange. See discussion below.

B. Significant Passages Involving Ἀντί

1. Concerning the Nature of the Atonement

The two passages related to the atonement that involve ἀντί are Matt 20:28 and Mark 10:45. Except for the introductory conjunctions, they are identical (καὶ γὰρ ὁ υἱὸς τοῦ ἀνθρώπου οὐκ ἦλθεν διακονηθῆναι ἀλλὰ διακονῆσαι καὶ δοῦναι τὴν ψυχὴν αὐτοῦ λύτρον **ἀντὶ** πολλῶν), and so will be treated as one text. Some scholars reject the meaning of *in place of* for ἀντί here, accepting instead the vaguer meaning of *on behalf of*, thus effectively denying substitutionary atonement in this passage. Such a usage for ἀντί (i.e., *on behalf of*) is based on two passages—Gen 44:33 (LXX) and Matt 17:27. Arndt, Gingrich, and Danker, following Bauer's lead, hold to this view for this *crux interpretum*.[22] Büchsel also thinks that ἀντί=ὑπέρ in Matt 17:27,[23] but he does not apply this meaning to Matt 20:28.[24]

The argument that ἀντί ever bore the mere sense of *representation* (i.e., = ὑπέρ) has a surprisingly slim basis. In support of the substitutionary atonement view of this text, note the comments of the following scholars.[25]

Nigel Turner on the use of ἀντί in Matt 17:27:[26]

> From Exodus 30[11] it is clear that originally the half-shekel tax was a redemption tax, for at a public census Moses was commanded to exact this amount, so that each man could give a ransom for himself, and this was understood to be the purchase money required to buy the subject from a hypothetical servitude. So "yourself and me" can be conceived as the objects desired to purchase, preceded as they are by *anti*, and the half-shekel paid by Simon was the price of purchase.

He concludes: "In consequence, we may safely rule out (4) ["on behalf of"] as a separate category of meaning for *anti*; the sole significance of the preposition in each New Testament context is that of substitution and exchange."[27]

R. E. Davies comments on the use of ἀντί in Gen 44:33 (LXX):

> Walter Bauer thinks that Genesis 44:33 shows how the meaning "in place of" can develop into "in behalf of" someone, so that ἀντί becomes equivalent to ὑπέρ. However, the meaning is clearly "in place of" as is evident from a most cursory reading of the verse: "Now therefore, let your servant, I pray you, remain *instead of the lad* as a slave to my lord; and let the lad go back with his brothers."[28]

---

[22] See BAGD, s.v. ἀντί, 3 (p. 73).

[23] *TDNT*, 1.372.

[24] Ibid., 373.

[25] We are here giving extensive quotations because of the significance of the issue.

[26] *Insights*, 173.

[27] ibid.

[28] "Christ in Our Place—The Contribution of the Prepositions," *TynBul* 21 (1970) 76.

Davies concludes on the use of ἀντί in extra-NT literature (including the LXX):

> This brief survey of the background literature to the New Testament should suffice to show that the meaning of ἀντί is basically that of *substitution* or *exchange*. No instances have been found where the "broader" meaning appears.[29]

As for the NT, and Matt 20:28 in particular, Davies concludes that ἀντί must mean *in place of*: "What we would add to this is that the preposition ἀντί *demands* this sort of interpretation. It *cannot* be understood otherwise."[30]

Harris [31] writes:

> As in 1 Tim. 2:6 (*antilytron hyper pantōn*), the notions of exchange and substitution are both present. It is hardly a sound hermeneutical procedure to appeal to a contestable "wider" sense of *anti* (viz. "on behalf of") in Matt. 17:27 (or Gen. 44:33) as the key to the proper understanding of *anti* in this passage. . . .

Waltke, after an exhaustive discussion of ἀντί in extra-NT literature, writes:

> It should also be observed that there is very little development in the usage of the preposition from the time of Homer to modern times; that is to say, that the word is quite static for it did not expand or become eclectic to assume other significations. In this respect ἀντί is unlike ὑπέρ.
>
> Also important is the conclusion that ἀντί always maintains its individual notion of substitution whether in the meaning *in exchange for* with its concrete meanings or its more logical or mental inferences, or in the meaning *instead of* for in the thought of exchange is the basic thought of something taking the place of another in order to transact the exchange, and in the signification of *instead of* the substitutionary aspect is plain.
>
> . . . ἀντί always has either the local meanings of *opposite, over against* or the metaphorical meaning of substituting one thing for another which may result in either the meaning *in exchange for* or *instead of*.
>
> This fact has been confirmed in two ways: 1) by refutation; and 2) by exhaustive investigations of the different periods of Greek literature. The examples of both Liddell and Scott and Bauer which might disprove that ἀντί always has a substitutionary sense outside of its local signification have been examined and found wanting in that in every example cited the individual notion of counter-balancing and substituting has been found in a very prominent way. In no instance was the meaning *on behalf of, for the sake of* necessary to the understanding of the preposition in any particular context. . . . the writer agrees with Moulton that even as the individual notion

---

[29] Ibid.

[30] Ibid., 80-81.

[31] "Prepositions and Theology," 3.1180.

is always to be found in the New Testament so also it is always to be found in literature outside of the New Testament.[32]

With reference to the NT, Waltke summarizes: "It is concluded that the usage of ἀντί in New Testament passages not considered by the writer to be theologically important is consistent with its usage in Greek literature outside the New Testament."[33]

Finally, with reference to Matt 20:28/Mark 10:45, Waltke writes:

> It appears to the writer, therefore, that it is best to accept and recognize both theological significations of ἀντί in this passage. The life of Christ not only is the price paid for the redemption of the many, stressing the redemptive work on the cross, but also He did this by "... nothing less than to step into their places...," enduring the divine wrath to make propitiation. The meaning *in exchange for* points to the results of His vicarious suffering; and the meaning *in the place of* points to the method in which this redemptive work is accomplished. The blending of two concepts into the one preposition is not unusual.[34]

In summary, the evidence appears to be overwhelmingly in favor of viewing ἀντί in Matt 20:28/Mark 10:45 as meaning *in the place of* and very possibly with the secondary meaning *in exchange for*, while the evidence for it meaning simply the vague idea of *on behalf of* is suspect at best. However, it is important to note that the theory of substitutionary atonement is usually based on passages involving ὑπέρ. As Davies points out:

> However, although it may be admitted that Mark 10:45 does teach substitution, it is often argued that our understanding of the work of Christ must not rest on a single passage which, according to some, is of doubtful authenticity anyway. It is said that we must take account of the fact that the preposition most frequently used in statements about the death of Christ is ὑπέρ with the genitive, which [allegedly] means "on behalf of" and cannot mean "in the place of."[35]

Consequently, the issue of whether the NT writers perceived Christ's death as substitutionary must be fought on ὑπέρ's turf as well.

2. Other Significant Passages

a) Hebrews 12:2

The text reads: ὃς **ἀντί** τῆς προκειμένης αὐτῷ χαρᾶς ὑπέμεινεν σταυρόν ("who [i.e., Jesus] **because of/instead of** the joy that lay before him endured the cross"). If ἀντί means *because of*, then Jesus endured the

---

[32] B. K. Waltke, "The Theological Significations of Ἀντί and Ὑπέρ in the New Testament," Th.D. dissertation (Dallas Theological Seminary, 1958), 1.127-28.

[33] ibid., 152.

[34] Ibid, 166.

[35] Davies, "Christ in Our Place," 81.

cross in anticipation of the joy (i.e., glory, inheritance?) that would be his afterwards. If it means *instead of*, then Jesus forsook the joy that was his (cf. Phil. 2:6-7) that he might bring others into the kingdom of God.[36]

b) John 1:16

For a discussion of this passage and its possible interpretations, cf. Waltke, "Theological Significations of Ἀντί and Ὑπέρ," 1.166-76; Harris, "Prepositions and Theology," 3.1179-80.

Ἀπό

A. Basic Uses (with Genitive only)

The basic force of ἀπό in classical Greek was *separation from*. "In the NT it has encroached on the domain of Att. ἐκ, ὑπό, παρά, and the gen. of separation . . . ."[37]

1. Separation (from place or person): *away from*
2. Source: *from, out of*
3. Cause: *because of*
4. Partitive (i.e., substituting for a partitive gen.): *of*
5. Agency (rare): *by, from*

B. Significant Passages Involving Ἀπό

Just a few of the more significant passages are Rom 5:9; Rev 1:4; 12:6.

Διά

A. Basic Uses (with Genitive and Accusative)

1. With Genitive

   a.   Agency: *by, through*

---

[36] Note the following: (1) *because of*: P. E. Hughes, *A Commentary on the Epistle to the Hebrews*, 523-24; Waltke, "Theological Significations of Ἀντί and Ὑπέρ," 1.176-80. (2) *instead of*: BAGD, s.v. ἀντί, 1 (p. 73); Dana-Mantey, 100; Harris, "Prepositions and Theology," 3.1180; Turner, *Insights*, 172.

[37] BAGD, s.v. ἀπό, 86.

      b.   Means: *through*

      c.   Spatial: *through*

      d.   Temporal: *through(out), during*

2. With Accusative

      a.   Cause: *because of, on account of, for the sake of*

      b.   Spatial (rare): *through*

B. Significant Passages Involving Διά

Some of the more significant texts involving διά, to which the aspiring exegete can practice some of his/her analytical skill, are Matt 1:22; John 1:3; Rom 3:25; 4:25; Eph 2:8; 1 Tim 2:15; Heb 2:10; 1 John 5:6.[38]

Εἰς

A. Basic Uses (with Accusative only)

1.   Spatial: *into, toward, in*

2.   Temporal: *for, throughout*

3.   Purpose: *for, in order to, to*

4.   Result: *so that, with the result that*

5.   Reference/Respect: *with respect to, with reference to*

6.   Advantage: *for*

7.   Disadvantage: *against*

8.   In the place of ἐν (with its various nuances)

B. Significant Passages Involving Εἰς

1. Causal Εἰς in Acts 2:38?

An interesting discussion over the force of εἰς took place several years ago, especially in relation to Acts 2:38. The text reads as follows: Πέτρος δὲ πρὸς αὐτούς· μετανοήσατε, φησίν, καὶ βαπτισθήτω ἕκαστος ὑμῶν ἐπὶ τῷ ὀνόματι Ἰησοῦ Χριστοῦ **εἰς** ἄφεσιν τῶν ἁμαρτιῶν ὑμῶν. . . ("And Peter said to them, "Repent, and be baptized—each one of you—at the name of Jesus Christ **because of/for/unto** the forgiveness of your sins. . ."").

---

[38] For a discussion of some of these texts, see "Voice: Passive Constructions (with Agency Expressed)."

On the one hand, J. R. Mantey argued that εἰς could be used causally in various passages in the NT, among them Matt 3:11 and Acts 2:38. It seems that Mantey believed that a salvation by grace would be violated if a causal εἰς was not evident in such passages as Acts 2:38.[39]

On the other hand, Ralph Marcus questioned Mantey's nonbiblical examples of a causal εἰς so that in his second of two rejoinders he concluded (after a blow-by-blow refutation):

> It is quite possible that εἰς is used causally in these NT passages but the examples of causal εἰς cited from non-biblical Greek contribute absolutely nothing to making this possibility a probability. If, therefore, Professor Mantey is right in his interpretation of various NT passages on baptism and repentance and the remission of sins, he is right for reasons that are non-linguistic.[40]

Marcus ably demonstrated that the linguistic evidence for a causal εἰς fell short of proof.

If a causal εἰς is not in view, what are we to make of Acts 2:38? There are at least four other interpretations of Acts 2:38.

1) *The baptism referred to here is **physical** only,* and εἰς has the meaning of *for* or *unto.* Such a view, if this is all there is to it, suggests that salvation is based on works. The basic problem of this view is that it runs squarely in the face of the theology of Acts, namely: (a) repentance precedes baptism (cf. Acts 3:19; 26:20), and (b) salvation is entirely a gift of God, not procured via water baptism (Acts 10:43 [cf. v 47]; 13:38-39, 48; 15:11; 16:30-31; 20:21; 26:18).

2) *The baptism referred to here is **spiritual** only.* Although such a view fits well with the theology of Acts, it does not fit well with the obvious meaning of "baptism" in Acts—especially in this text (cf. 2:41).

3) *The text should be repunctuated* in light of the shift from second person plural to third person singular back to second person plural again. If so, it would read as follows: "Repent, and let each one of you be baptized at the name of Jesus Christ, for the forgiveness of your sins. . . ." If this is the correct understanding, then εἰς is subordinate to μετανοήσατε alone, rather than to βαπτισθήτω. The idea then would be, "Repent *for/with reference to* your sins, and let each one of you be baptized. . . ." Such a view is an acceptable way of handling εἰς, but its subtlety and awkwardness are against it.

4) Finally, it is possible that to a first-century Jewish audience (as well as to Peter), *the idea of baptism might incorporate both the spiritual reality*

---

[39] See J. R. Mantey, "The Causal Use of *Eis* in the New Testament," *JBL* 70 (1952) 45-58 and "On Causal *Eis* Again," *JBL* 70 (1952) 309-311.

[40] Ralph Marcus, "The Elusive Causal *Eis*," *JBL* 71 (1953) 44. Cf. also Marcus' first article, "On Causal *Eis,*" *JBL* 70 (1952) 129-130.

and the physical symbol. In other words, when one spoke of baptism, he usually meant *both* ideas—the reality and the ritual. Peter is shown to make the strong connection between these two in chapters 10 and 11. In 11:15-16 he recounts the conversion of Cornelius and friends, pointing out that at the point of their conversion they were *baptized* by the Holy Spirit. After he had seen this, he declared, "Surely no one can refuse the water for these to be baptized who have received the Holy Spirit. . ." (10:47). The point seems to be that if they have had the internal testimony of the Holy Spirit via spiritual baptism, there ought to be a public testimony/acknowledgment via water baptism as well. This may not only explain Acts 2:38 (viz., that Peter spoke of both reality and picture, though only the reality removes sins), but also why the NT speaks of only baptized believers (as far as we can tell): Water baptism is not a cause of salvation, but a *picture*; and as such it serves both as a public acknowledgment (by those present) and a public confession (by the convert) that one has been Spirit-baptized.

In sum, although Mantey's instincts were surely correct that in Luke's theology baptism was not the cause of salvation, his ingenious solution of a causal εἰς lacks conviction. There are other ways for us to satisfy the tension, but adjusting the grammar to answer a backward-looking "Why?" has no more basis than the notion that ἀντί ever meant mere representation (see prior discussion).

2. Other Significant Passages

For some other significant uses of εἰς, see John 1:18 (=ἐν); Eph 4:12-13 (5 instances; the problem here is not so much meaning as it is the question of subordination and coordination); Phil 1:10; 1 Pet 1:11.

Ἐκ

A. Basic Uses (with Genitive only)

In general, ἐκ has the force of *from, out of, away from, of.*

1. Source: *out of, from*
2. Separation: *away from, from*
3. Temporal: *from, from* [this point] . . . *on*
4. Cause: *because of*[41]
5. Partitive (i.e., substituting for a partitive gen.): *of*
6. Means: *by, from*

---

[41] BAGD call this "the 'perfectivizing' force of ἐκ . . . in compounds. . . ."

B. Significant Passages Involving Ἐκ

Matt 26:27   πίετε ἐξ **αὐτοῦ** πάντες
            drink **from it**, all [of you]

> The unfortunate translation found in the King James Version ("Drink ye all of it") has caused a great deal of confusion. S. Lewis Johnson, Jr. has often told the story of the country preacher who, having no knowledge of Greek, assumed that "all" referred to the wine and "of it" modified the "all" (in which case it would have to be put in the acc. case as the direct object of πίετε). Having a rather small congregation, coupled with a liturgical tradition that required a pitcher of wine to be filled for the weekly Communion, the pastor found himself in a moral quandary. Every Sunday, after the tiny flock departed, the good reverend would down the pitcher and become drunk—all because he misunderstood this verse![42]

Some of the other significant passages involving ἐκ are Rom 1:17; Eph 3:15; Rev 3:10.

Ἐν

A. Basic Uses (with Dative only)

Ἐν is the workhorse of prepositions in the NT, occurring more frequently and in more varied situations than any other. It overlaps with the simple dative uses to a great extent, but not entirely. The following categories are for the most part painted with broad strokes.[43]

1. Spatial/Sphere: *in* (and various other translations)

2. Temporal: *in, within, when, while, during*[44]

3. Association (often close personal relationship): *with*

4. Cause: *because of*

5. Instrumental: *by, with*

6. Reference/Respect: *with respect to/with reference to*

7. Manner: *with*

8. Thing Possessed: *with* (in the sense of *which possesses*)[45]

9. Standard (=Dative of Rule): *according to the standard of*

10. As an equivalent for εἰς (with verbs of motion)

---

[42] This text is not really significant exegetically, except perhaps by way of comic relief.

[43] Even BAGD (s.v. ἐν, 258) recognizes the difficulty of cataloging every usage: "The uses of this prep. are so many-sided, and oft. so easily confused, that a strictly systematic treatment is impossible. It must suffice to list the main categories, which will help in establishing the usage in individual cases." BAGD's treatment is nevertheless extensive (258-61).

[44] This "time within which" notion is almost never found with the simple dat. (*BDF*, 107 [§200] deny it altogether, but see chapter on "Dative Case" for examples).

[45] Cf. Mark 1:23 (cf. Luke 4:33); Eph 6:2.

B. *Significant Passages Involving* Ἐv

As varied as the uses of ἐv are, sometimes it is considered even more elastic than it really is. The following discussion focuses on a few passages in which the preposition has been viewed as expressing *agency* or *content*.

1. ᾽Ev + Dative for Personal Agency?

Some have suggested that either the naked dative or ἐv + the dative can express personal agency in the NT.[46] However, once a clear definition is given for personal agency, this will be seen to be a rare or nonexistent category. Williams defines the dative of agency as denoting "the agent (personal) by whom something is done. The only difference between means and agency is that means is impersonal, agency is personal."[47]

This definition is a little too general. It would be better to say that when ἐv + the dative expresses the idea of means (a *different* category), the instrument is used *by an agent*. When agency is indicated, the agent so named is not used by another, but is the one who uses an instrument. (It may be noted here that an intermediate agent, usually expressed by διά + the genitive, is an agent who acts *on behalf of* another or in the place of another. This agent is not, strictly speaking, *used* by another as an instrument would be.) Thus, ἐv + dative to express *means* can be (and often is) used of *persons*, though they are conceived of as impersonal (i.e, used as an instrument by someone else). For example, in the sentence "God disciplined me by means of my parents," "God" is the agent who used the "parents" as the *means* by which he accomplished something. The parents are, of course, persons. But they are conceived of as impersonal in that they are the instruments used by another.

According to our definition, if ἐv + dative is used to express agency, the noun in the dative must not only be personal, but must also be the agent who performs the action.[48] BDF accurately assess the NT situation of the naked dative used for personal agency: "Dative of agency is perhaps represented by only one genuine example in the NT and this with the perfect: Luke 23:15."[49] In summary, we can say that there are very few clear examples of the dative of agency in the NT, and all of them involve a perfect passive verb.

---

[46] See "Dative of Agency" in the chapter on the dative case for a discussion of other passages, especially those involving πνεύματι.

[47] Williams, *Grammar Notes*, 18.

[48] Andrews sought to demonstrate agency with ἐv + the dative in the NT, but his whole thesis breaks down at the very beginning—at the definition: "Agency is a term used to attribute a thing done *to* [*sic*] a personal *instrument* [italics mine]" (James Warren Andrews, "The Use of ᾽Ev with the Passive Voice to Denote Personal Agency," [Th.M. thesis, Dallas Theological Seminary, 1963], 8).

[49] BDF, 102 (§191).

The slightly different phenomenon of ἐν + the dative is also considered by many to express agency on a rare occasion. Yet no unambiguous examples are forthcoming. Thus what can be said about the dative of agency can also be said of ἐν + the dative to express agent: it is *rare*, at best.[50]

Mark 1:8   αὐτὸς δὲ βαπτίσει ὑμᾶς **ἐν** πνεύματι ἀγίῳ[51]
            but he shall baptize you **with** the Holy Spirit
> Here it is obvious that Christ is the agent (since αὐτός is the subject), and the Holy Spirit is the means (and perhaps sphere) that the Lord uses to baptize.

1 Cor 12:13   γὰρ **ἐν** ἐνὶ πνεύματι ἡμεῖς πάντες εἰς ἓν σῶμα ἐβαπτίσθημεν
            for **by** one Spirit we all were baptized into one body
> Our contention is that this is an illustration of ἐν used for *means*. By calling "Spirit" means here does *not* deny the personality of the Holy Spirit.[52] Rather, the Holy Spirit is the instrument that Christ uses to baptize, even though he is a person. Since πνεύματι ἀγίῳ clearly indicated means in Mark 1:8 (as in several other passages dealing with Spirit-baptism), it is surely not unreasonable to see "Spirit" as the means here.
>
> Furthermore, if the Holy Spirit is the agent in this text, there is a theological problem: When is the prophecy of Mark 1:8 fulfilled? When would *Christ* baptize with the Holy Spirit? Because of the grammatical improbability of πνεύματι expressing agent in 1 Cor 12:13, it is better to see it as means *and* as the fulfillment of Mark 1:8. Thus, Christ is the unnamed agent. This also renders highly improbable one popular interpretation, viz., that there are *two* Spirit baptisms in the NT, one at salvation and one later.[53]

2.   'Eν + Dative for Content?

Rare is the usage of the simple dative to denote the content that is used by a verb of *filling*.[54] For ἐν + the dative, this usage is debatable.

Normally, a verb of filling takes a *genitive* of content; rarely, a simple dative of content.[55] However, we know of no clear examples in biblical

---

[50] The best example is found in 1 Cor 6:2: **ἐν** ὑμῖν κρίνεται ὁ κόσμος ("the world is to be judged **by** you"). But this is by no means certain. Robertson-Plummer suggest that it speaks of sphere/locality: "in your court," "in your jurisdiction" (*First Corinthians* [ICC] 112). So also BDF, 118 (§219.1), noting parallels in profane literature.

[51] The preposition is omitted in B L 2427 *et pauci*.

[52] At this point in salvation history, however, there is some question as to the apostolic recognition of the personality of the Spirit. Further, because ἐν was the preposition of choice with the Spirit up until this time (i.e., when agency/means was in view), the tradition of continuing this practice, even once the Spirit's personality had been recognized, is likely.

[53] Typically associated with Pentecostal theology.

[54] See "Dative of Content" in the chapter on the dative case for discussion.

[55] There are three clear examples in the NT of this phenomenon (Luke 2:40; Rom 1:29; 2 Cor 7:4), though the Lukan text is textually suspect.

Greek in which ἐν + the dative indicates content.[56] We should, therefore, seek some other nuance in such instances, as in Eph 5:18 (discussed below).

Eph 5:18 πληροῦσθε **ἐν** πνεύματι
be filled [**with, by, in**] [the] Spirit

> To see ἐν πνεύματι here as indicating content is grammatically suspect (even though it is, in many circles, the predominant view). Only if the flow of argument and/or the lack of other good possibilities strongly point in the direction of content would we be compelled to take it as such. There are no other examples in biblical Greek in which ἐν + the dative after πληρόω indicates content.[57] Further, the parallel with οἴνῳ as well as the common grammatical category of *means* suggest that the idea intended is that believers are to be filled *by means of* the [Holy] Spirit. If so, there seems to be an unnamed agent.
>
> The meaning of this text can only be fully appreciated in light of the πληρόω language in Ephesians. Always the term is used in connection with a member of theTrinity. Three considerations seem to be key: (1) In Eph 3:19 the "hinge" prayer introducing the last half of the letter makes a request that the believers "be filled with all the fullness of God" (πληρωθῆτε εἰς πᾶν τὸ πλήρωμα τοῦ θεοῦ). The explicit *content* of πληρόω is thus God's fullness (probably a reference to his moral attributes). (2) In 4:10 Christ is said to be the agent of filling (with v 11 adding the specifics of his giving spiritual gifts). (3) The author then brings his argument to a crescendo in 5:18: Believers are to be filled *by* Christ *by means of* the Spirit *with* the content of the fullness of God.

3. Other Significant Passages

One group of significant passages involves the phrase ἐν Χριστῷ, an expression found almost solely in the Pauline corpus. The student is encouraged to consult standard lexical and biblico-theological sources for a treatment of this phrase.[58]

Other significant passages include: John 14:17; 1 Cor 7:15; Gal 1:16; 1 Pet 2:12.

---

[56] This illustrates, in a minute way, that the naked dative does *not* exactly parallel the usage of ἐν + the dative.

[57] Abbott notes that "the use of ἐν with πληρόω to express the content with which a thing is filled would be quite unexampled" (*Ephesians* [ICC] 161). See his discussion on 161-62 of ἐν πνεύματι in Eph 5:18.

[58] *BDF,*118 (§219) despair of a treatment of the phrase because it "is copiously appended by Paul to the most varied concepts" and hence "utterly defies definite interpretation...." Cf. BAGD, s.v. ἐν, I.5.d. (259-60) (and the bibliography listed there). See also Oepke's essay in *TDNT* 2.541-2; C. F. D. Moule, *Origin of Christology* (Cambridge: Cambridge University Press, 1977) 54-69 (esp. 54-62); Harris, "Prepositions and Theology," 3.1192-93 (for a succinct summary).

Ἐπί

A. Basic Uses (with Genitive, Dative, and Accusative)

1. With Genitive

    a. Spatial: *on, upon, at, near*

    b. Temporal: *in the time of, during*

    c. Cause: *on the basis of*

2. With Dative

    a. Spatial: *on, upon, against, at, near*

    b. Temporal: *at, at the time of, during*

    c. Cause: *on the basis of*

3. With Accusative

    a. Spatial: *on, upon, to, up to, against*

    b. Temporal: *for, over a period of*

B. Significant Passages Involving Ἐπί

Some of the more significant texts involving ἐπί are: Matt 19:9; Mark 10:11; Rom 5:12;[59] Eph 2:10; 2 Cor 5:4; 1 Pet 2:24.

Κατά

A. Basic Uses (with Genitive and Accusative)

1. With Genitive

    a. Spatial: *down from, throughout*

    b. Opposition: *against*

    c. Source: *from*

---

[59] For discussion of the text, cf. Cranfield, *The Epistle to the Romans* (ICC) 1.274-81; F. Danker, "Romans V. 12 Sin Under Law," *NTS* 14 (1968) 424-39; S. Lyonnet, "Le sens de ἐφ' ᾧ en Rom 5, 12 et l'exégèse des Pères grecs," *Bib* 36 (1955) 436-56; S. L. Johnson, Jr., "Romans 5:12—An Exercise in Exegesis and Theology," in *New Dimensions in New Testament Study,* ed. R. N. Longenecker and M. C. Tenney (Grand Rapids: Zondervan, 1974) 298-316; D. L. Turner, "Adam, Christ, and Us: The Pauline Teaching of Solidarity in Romans 5:12-21" (Th.D. dissertation, Grace Theological Seminary, Winona Lake, Ind., 1982) 129-49. Note our treatment of this text in the chapter on pronouns, under the relative pronoun ὅς.

2. With Accusative

   a.   Standard: *in accordance with, corresponding to*

   b.   Spatial: *along, through* (extension); *toward, up to* (direction)

   c.   Temporal: *at, during*

   d.   Distributive: "indicating the division of a greater whole into individual parts"[60]

   e.   Purpose: *for the purpose of*

   f.   Reference/Respect: *with respect to, with reference to*

B. *Significant Passages Involving Κατά*

Some of the more significant passages involving κατά are: Acts 14:23 (if taken distributively here, it argues for plurality of elders); Rom 8:5; 1 Cor 15:3-4; 1 Pet 3:7.

Μετά

A. *Basic Uses (with Genitive and Accusative)*[61]

1. With Genitive

   a.   Association/Accompaniment: *with, in company with*

   b.   Spatial: *with, among*

   c.   Manner (Attendant Circumstance): *with*

2. With Accusative

   a.   Temporal: *after, behind*

   b.   Spatial (rare): *after, behind*

B. *Significant Passages Involving Μετά*

1. The Relation of Μετά to Σύν

Though not all would agree with Harris that "in Hel. Greek they are virtually synonymous,"[62] even he would concede that

> it is significant that Paul regularly ends his letters with the prayer that grace

---

[60] BAGD, s.v. κατά II.3 (406).

[61] In other literature this preposition also occurred with the dat. case, but not in the NT.

[62] Harris, "Prepositions and Theology," 3.1206.

be with (*meta*, never *syn*) his addressees, whereas he depicts the Christian life as one of identification with Christ and the Christian's destiny as "being with Christ" (*syn*, not *meta*, in both cases). This would suggest that, of the two preps., *syn* was the more suited to express intimate personal union (e.g., Col. 3:4), and *meta* the more suited to denote close association or attendant circumstances (e.g., 1 Thess. 3:13).[63]

2. Other Significant Passages

Cf. Matt 27:66; Rev 2:16; 12:7; 13:4; 17:14.

Παρά

A. Basic Uses (with Genitive, Dative, and Accusative)

1. With Genitive

Generally, the idea is *from (the side of)* (almost always with a personal object).

a.   Source/Spatial: *from*

b.   Agency: *from, by*

2. With Dative

In general, the dative uses suggest *proximity* or nearness.

a.   Spatial: *near, beside*

b.   Sphere: *in the sight of, before* (someone)

c.   Association: *with* (someone/something)

d.   Virtually equivalent to simple dative

3. With Accusative

a.   Spatial: *by, alongside of, near, on*

b.   Comparison: *in comparison to, more than*

c.   Opposition: *against, contrary to*

B. Significant Passages Involving Παρά

Some of the more significant passages are: John 1:6; 6:46; 1:14; 15:26[64]; Rom 1:25; 1 Cor 7:24; 12:15.

---

[63] Ibid., 3.1206-1207.

[64] For an excellent, though brief, discussion of these verses and how they relate to the alleged eternal generation of the Son and eternal procession of the Spirit, cf. Harris, "Prepositions and Theology," 3.1202-3.

Περί

A. Basic Uses (with Genitive and Accusative)[65]

1. With Genitive

   a. Reference: *concerning*

   b. Advantage/Representation: *on behalf of, for* (= ὑπέρ)

2. With Accusative

   a. Spatial: *around, near*

   b. Temporal: *about, near*

   c. Reference/Respect: *with regard/reference to*

B. Significant Passages Involving Περί

Some of the more significant passages are: Acts 25:18; 3 John 2; John 11:19 (*v.l.*); 1 Thess 5:1.[66]

Πρό

A. Basic Uses (with Genitive only)

1. Spatial: *before, in front of, at*
2. Temporal: *before*
3. Rank/Priority: *before*

B. Significant Passages Involving Πρό

Not a whole lot can be said about significant passages involving πρό, for its usage in almost every instance neatly falls into one of the three definitions given in BAGD. However, the following texts are either important theologically or slightly ambiguous: Luke 21:12; John 1:48; 12:1; 13:19; 17:5, 24; 1 Cor 2:7; Gal 3:23; Eph 1:4; Col 1:17; 2 Tim 1:9; Titus 1:2; 1 Pet 1:20; Jude 25.[67]

---

[65] In other literature this preposition also occurred with the dat. case, but not in the NT.

[66] For the construction περὶ ἁμαρτίας cf. Harris, "Prepositions and Theology," 3.1203.

[67] Most of these texts are unambiguous, though helpful in affirming various aspects of God's sovereignty in that he did or knew something before time/eternity. In two passages there may be some ambiguity: Luke 21:12 (time vs. rank, though time is far more probable) and Col 1:17 (again, times vs. rank; here, it is possible that a double nuance is intended—thus, Jesus Christ takes priority over and is before all things).

Πρός

A. Basic Uses (with Accusative almost exclusively)

This preposition occurs only once with the genitive and only six times with the dative case, but almost 700 times with the accusative. Our treatment will be restricted thus to the accusative case (for the other cases used, see BAGD's treatment).

1. Purpose: *for, for the purpose of*
2. Spatial: *toward*
3. Temporal: *toward, for* (duration)
4. Result: *so that, with the result that*
5. Opposition: *against*
6. Association: *with, in company with* (with stative verbs)

B. Significant Passages Involving Πρός

1. Revelation 3:20

One of the more significant and, at the same time, most misunderstood passages (at least in popular circles) involving πρός, is Rev 3:20. The text reads: Ἰδοὺ ἕστηκα ἐπὶ τὴν θύραν καὶ κρούω· ἐάν τις ἀκούσῃ τῆς φωνῆς μου καὶ ἀνοίξῃ τὴν θύραν, καὶ εἰσελεύσομαι **πρὸς** αὐτὸν καὶ δειπνήσω μετ᾽ αὐτοῦ καὶ αὐτὸς μετ᾽ ἐμοῦ ("Behold, I stand at the door and knock. If anyone hears my voice and opens the door, I will come in **to** him and will dine with him and he [will dine] with me"). The crucial phrase for our purposes is "I will come *in to* him." This text has often been taken as a text offering salvation to a lost sinner. Such a view is based on two assumptions: (1) that the Laodiceans, or at least some of them, were indeed lost, and (2) that εἰσελεύσομαι πρός means "come *into*."

Both of these assumptions, however, are based on little evidence. With reference to the first assumption, that those in the Laodicean church were not believers, it is important to note that in the preceding verse, the resurrected Lord declares, "Those whom I love, I reprove and discipline." Here φιλέω is used for "love"—a term that is never used of God/Jesus loving unbelievers in the NT. (Indeed, it would be impossible for God to have this kind of love for an unbeliever, for it routinely speaks of enjoyment and fellowship. ἀγαπάω, rather, is the verb used of God's love for unbelievers [cf. John 3:16], for it frequently, if not normally, speaks of commitment and, when used with God/Jesus as the subject, the idea is often of an unconditional love.[68]) This φιλέω must be applied to the Laodiceans here, for the verse concludes, "Be zealous, *therefore*, and repent." The inferential οὖν connects the two parts of the verse, indicating that the *Laodiceans* are to repent because Christ *loves* (φιλέω) *them!*[69]

The second assumption is that εἰσελεύσομαι πρός means "come into." Such an assumption is based on a less than careful reading of the *English* text! The ASV, NASB, RSV, NRSV, for example, all correctly render it "come in to." (Note the space between the prepositions.) The idea of "come into" would be expressed with εἰς as the independent preposition and would suggest a penetration into the person (thus, spawning the idea of entering into one's heart). However, spatially πρός means *toward*, not *into*. In all eight instances of εἰσέρχομαι πρός in the NT, the meaning is "come in toward/before a person" (i.e., enter a building, house, etc., so as to be in the presence of someone), *never penetration* into the person himself/herself. In some instances, such a view would not only be absurd, but inappropriate (cf. Mark 6:25; 15:43; Luke 1:28; Acts 10:3; 11:3; 16:40; 17:2; 28:8).[70]

What, then, can we say that this verse is affirming? First, we should answer in the negative: it is *not* an offering of salvation. The implications of this are manifold. Among other things, to use this text as a salvation verse is a perversion of the simplicity of the gospel. Many people have allegedly "received Christ into their hearts" without understanding what that means or what the gospel means. Although this verse is picturesque, it actually muddies the waters of the truth of salvation.

---

[68] This is not to deny that there is some overlap between these two verbs, of course (such as seems to be the case in John 21). But when φιλέω, the rarer word, is used, and when it is used apart from ἀγαπάω, we would expect it to bear its normal nuance.

[69] This, by the way, may have some implications for the perseverance of the saints, for it is impossible that God could have this kind of love for a person unless, in some sense, God could *enjoy* him. The implication, then, may be that the Laodiceans, even in their backslidden state, were still growing in some way.

[70] In the LXX this expression is used frequently, especially for sexual intercourse (cf., e.g., Gen 16:2, 4; 19:31; 29:21, 23, 30; 30:3, 4, 10; 38:2, 8, 16; Deut 21:13; 25:5; Judg 15:1; 16:1; Ruth 4:13; 2 Sam 3:7; 16:21; Ps 50:2; Prov 6:29). However, in each of such instances it seems to suggest "enter into [the tent/house] *toward* her." This conclusion is based on the probability of euphemistic (and therefore subtle) language; the obvious meaning when sexual intercourse is not intended, even in instances where it could be (cf. Gen 6:20; 7:9, 15; 19:5; 20:3; 40:6; Exod 1:19; 5:1; 8:1; 9:1; 10:1; Josh 2:4; Judg 3:20; 4:21, 22; 18:10; Ruth 3:16, 17; 1 Sam 10:14; 16:21; 28:21; 2 Sam 1:2; 3:24; 6:9; 11:7; 12:1; 14:33; 1 Kings 1:15; Esth 4:11, 16; Ps 42:4; Hos 9:10; Jer 43:20; 48:6; Dan 2:12, 24); and the fact that sometimes the act of sexual intercourse needs to be explicitly stated (cf. Gen 39:14; 2 Sam 11:4; 12:24). Further, apart from the sexually-colored texts, there are no instances in which entrance *into* the object of πρός can be said to occur. All of this suggests that εἰσέρχομαι πρός almost always functions idiomatically with an *implied* object of εἰσέρχομαι and a *stated* object of πρός. But the two objects are *never* identical. Judges 4:21 is instructive: "Jael, the wife of Heber, took a tent peg, and took a hammer in her hand, and went quietly in to (εἰσῆλθεν **πρός**) him and drove the peg into his temple." Obviously, Jael went into the tent (cf. v 20) *toward* Sisera. Hence, the notion of entrance into the heart in Rev 3:20 lacks a sufficient parallel in biblical Greek and must be judged a misunderstanding of this text.

Reception of Christ is a *consequence*, not a condition, of salvation.[71] As far as the *positive* meaning of this verse, it may refer to Christ having supremacy in the assembly or even to an invitation (and, consequently, a reminder) to believers to share with him in the coming kingdom. But to determine which of these is correct is beyond the scope of grammar. All grammar can tell us here is which view is almost certainly *not* correct—namely, that which sees this as an offering of salvation.

2.   Other Significant Passages

Some other significant passages involving πρός include: John 1:1;[72] 2 Cor 5:8; 2 Tim 3:16; 1 John 5:16.[73]

Σύν

A. *Basic Uses (with Dative only)*

The predominant usage of this preposition is to indicate accompaniment/association: *with, in association (company) with.*

B. *Significant Passages Involving Σύν*

1.   The Relation of Σύν to Μετά

See discussion above, under μετά.

2.   Significant Passages Involving Σύν as an Independent Preposition

These include, *inter alia*, Phil 1:23 and 1 Thess 4:17. For a concise discussion of these texts (both of which have to do with believers' fellowship with Christ) see Harris, "Prepositions and Theology," 3.1207.[74]

3.   Significant Passages Involving Σύν- Prefixed to Verbs

For a discussion of some of the more important of these texts, the student should consult B. McGrath, "'Syn'- Words in Paul," *CBQ* 14 (1952) 219-26; G. W. Linhart, "Paul's Doctrinal Use of Verbs Compounded with *Sun*" (Th.M., Dallas Theological Seminary, 1949).

---

[71] The idea that one is to receive Christ into one's heart is based on essentially two texts, Rev 3:20 and John 1:12. But neither passage addresses this. In John 1:12 those who *received* the word were Jews in Palestine who received Jesus into their homes and treated him as a true prophet. It is a historical statement, not a soteriological one.

[72] See our discussion in the introduction to this chapter.

[73] For a discussion of John 1:1; 2 Cor 5:8 and 1 John 5:16, see Harris, "Prepositions and Theology," 3.1204-6.

[74] Harris also lists 2 Cor 5:8, but the preposition used there is πρός.

Ὑπέρ

A. Basic Uses (with Genitive and Accusative)

1. With Genitive

a. Representation/Advantage: *on behalf of, for the sake of*

b. Reference/Respect: *concerning, with reference to* (= περί)

c. Substitution: *in place of, instead of* (= ἀντί)
   (such instances also involve representation)

2. With Accusative

a. Spatial: *over, above*

b. Comparison: *more than, beyond*

B. Significant Passages Involving Ὑπέρ

1. Concerning the Substitutionary Atonement (Ὑπέρ + Genitive)

As was pointed out in the discussion on ἀντί, the normal preposition used in texts that purportedly deal with Christ's substitutionary atonement is ὑπέρ. Further, it was pointed out that although the case against a substitutionary sense for ἀντί is weak, the case for a substitutionary sense for ὑπέρ is faced with the difficulty that the preposition can bear several other nuances that, on a lexical level, at least, are equally plausible in the theologically significant passages. It is to be noted, however, that BAGD do consider ὑπέρ to have a substitutionary sense on occasion (though they list only one text that bears on the atonement—2 Cor 5:14).

This issue is important enough that an extended discussion is warranted. Although the following treatment may be a bit heady in places, it should become evident that grammar is relevant for exegesis and theology.

It is our conviction that ὑπέρ is naturally suited to the meaning of substitution and is in fact used in several passages dealing with the nature of Christ's atonement. On behalf of the view that ὑπέρ has at least a substitutionary sense to it in passages dealing with the atonement are the following arguments:

a. The substitutionary sense is found in extra-NT Greek literature.

1) In Classical Greek

Admittedly, this usage is rare in the classical period, but cf. Plato, *Republic* 590a; Xenophon, *Anabasis* 7.4.9-10, etc.[75]

---

[75] For a discussion, cf. Davies, "Christ in Our Place," 82-83; Waltke, "Theological Significations of Ἀντί and Ὑπέρ," 2.199-210, 214-15.

2) In the LXX

Cf. Deut 24:16; Isa 43:3-4; Judith 8:12; etc.[76]

3) In the Papyri

Cf. Oxyrhynchus Papyrus 1281.11, 12; Tebtunis Papyrus 380:43, 44, etc.[77] In Robertson's study of this phenomenon he noted the following:

> But the papyri, particularly the business documents, show that Paul is following current usage when he prefers ὑπέρ [over ἀντί] for the idea of substitution. . . . Certainly in all these instances the writing is done on behalf of one, but one cannot stop there. Winer (Winer-Thayer, p. 382) rightly says: "In most cases one who acts in behalf of another takes his place." This is absolutely true in the case of this recurrent idiom so common in the papyri, where a scribe writes a document in behalf of and instead of one who does not know letters. The scribe writes "for" one who is not able to write. . . .ἔγραψα ὑπὲρ αὐτοῦ μὴ ἰδότος γράμματα. This solemn asseveration makes the loan binding on the illiterate party to the contract. There is not the slightest doubt about the meaning of ὑπέρ in this sentence. The phraseology becomes almost a set formula in such documents.
>
> . . . .
>
> One cannot break the force of these examples by saying that they all reflect the same set idiom. The point is rather strengthened than otherwise. The set idiom for substitution employs ὑπέρ rather than ἀντί.
>
> . . . .
>
> It is needless to add more. They tell the same almost monotonous story of the substitionary use of ὑπέρ.[78]

As helpful as Robertson's study was, it has had little impact on lexica and grammars.[79] Perhaps part of the reason was that he produced less than ten examples, all following the same set idiom. Further, some of these were somewhat later than the NT, while others had gaps in them at the very point where

---

[76] For discussion, cf. Davies, "Christ in Our Place," 83; Waltke, "Theological Significations of Ἀντί and Ὑπέρ," 2.227, 238-39.

[77] For a discussion, cf. Mayser, *Grammatik der griechischen Papyri* II.2.460; A. T. Robertson, "The Use of Ὑπέρ in Business Documents in the Papyri," *The Expositor* 8.19 (1920) 321-27, reprinted in Robertson, *The Minister and His Greek New Testament* (Nashville: Broadman, 1977) 35-42 (all of our citations are from *Minister*).

[78] Robertson, *Minister*, 36-38.

[79] Although *BDF* cite Robertson's article, they list it under ὑπέρ + the accusative (*BDF*, 121 [§230])! Further, in the next paragraph (§231, dealing with ὑπέρ + genitive), they do not allow for a substitutionary meaning.

Robertson reconstructed ὑπέρ.[80] Thus, even though it could be argued that this particular idiom was in use, unless this preposition was used in other idioms, was found amply, and was in papyri that were at least roughly coeval with the NT, the force of Robertson's point is diminished. His study clearly needs to be supplemented.

I have examined some representative papyri for the purpose of supplementing Robertson's study.[81] It is our purpose in this section to supplement Robertson's list in three ways: (1) multiplicity of examples; (2) a few *early* examples; and (3) a few examples that do not fall into the above-mentioned idiom. A few select illustrations are noted here; the rest are in a footnote. Altogether, to Robertson's nine illustrations we can add another 78 instances.[82]

---

[80] Robertson produces nine examples of this phenomenon in the papyri. However, in his two earliest examples (both of which are from the same document, dated 30-29 BCE) the word in question is in brackets—i.e., not recoverable from the extant papyrus due to a lacuna (gap) or smudge, etc. Besides this twofold example, he has only *one* more that is BCE (Tebt. P. 386, 25-28 [12 BCE]). All the rest are first or second century.

[81] The two volumes on non-literary prose papyri in the Loeb Classical Library were examined. One of my former students, Charles Powell, also did work in the Oxyrhynchus papyri, supplementing my study, though the results of his work are not included here.

[82] For those texts that are either *very early* (150 CE or before) or which use *a different idiom* from the one identified by Robertson, an asterisk (*) is placed at the front of the entry. If a reference is double asterisked (**), this indicates that it is both early and non-idiomatic. The arrangement is the same as is found in *Select Papyri*, volume 1, and *Select Papyri*, volume 2 (*SP* 1, *SP* 2)—that is, I am simply numbering and listing the uses as they appear on the pages of these two edited volumes.

1. P. Oxy. 1631.39 (280 CE/*SP* 1.58);
2. Stud. Pal. xiii. p. 6 (line 25) (322 CE/*SP* 1.66);
3. P. Grenf. ii.87.40 (602 CE/*SP* 1.68);
4. P. Oxy. 138.46 (610-611 CE/*SP* 1.74);
5. P. Oxy. 139.32 (612 CE/*SP* 1.76);
6. P. Lond. 1722.46 (573 CE/*SP* 1.94);
7. P. Lond. 1722.51 (573 CE/*SP* 1.94);
8. P. Lond. 1164.30 (212 CE/*SP* 1.116);
9. P.S.I. 961,11.38 (176 CE/*SP* 1.138);
10. P. Oxy. 1129.18 (449 CE/*SP* 1.138);
11. P. Oxy. 1038.36 (568 CE/*SP* 1.142);
12. P. Oxy. 1890.21 (508 CE/*SP* 1.146);
13. P. Oxy. 1636.45 (249 CE/*SP* 1.150);
14. P. Grenf. ii.68.18-19 (247 CE/*SP* 1.150);
15. BGU 405.24 (348 CE/*SP* 1.170);

*16. P. Tebt. 392.37 (134-35 CE/*SP* 1.176);
17. P. Lond. 992.24 (507 CE/*SP* 1.184);
18. P. Ryl. 177.17 (246 CE/*SP* 1.190);
19. P. Oxy. 1892.44 (581 CE/*SP* 1.192);
*20. P. Oxy. 269.17-18 (57 CE/*SP* 1.204);
*21. P. Amh. 104.15-17 (125 CE/*SP* 1.212);
*22. P. Ryl. 174.35-36 (112 CE/*SP* 1.216);
23. P. Ryl. 174.37 (112 CE/*SP* 1.216);
24. P. Lond. 334.36 (166 CE/*SP* 1.222);
25. P. Oxy. 91.39-40 (187 CE/*SP* 1.230);
26. P. Oxy. 1900.33 (528 CE/*SP* 1.232);
27. PSI 786.23 (581 CE/*SP* 1.234);
28. P. Oxy. 494.18 (156-165 CE/*SP* 1.246): ;
29. P. Lond. 1727.7 (CE 583-4/*SP* 1.254)//(ὑπέρ is in brackets);

(*)30. P. Oxy. 1295.8 (2nd or 3rd cent. CE/*SP* 1.332) (?): Perhaps here only "on behalf of" is meant;
*31. P. Grenf. ii.77.20 (3rd-4th cent. CE/*SP* 1.372) ;
*32. P. Fay. 100.21 (99 CE/*SP* 1.406);
*33. P. Fay. 100.28 (99 CE/*SP* 1.406);
The idea in the following examples from P. Oxy. 2144 is *exchange* (all found in *SP* 1.430):
*34. P. Oxy. 2144.5 (late 3rd cent. CE/*SP* 1.430);
*35. P. Oxy. 2144.7;
*36. P. Oxy. 2144.9;
*37. P. Oxy. 2144.11;
*38. P. Oxy. 2144.13;
*39. P. Oxy. 2144.18;
*40. P. Oxy. 2144.21;
*41. P. Hamb. i.4.14 (87 CE/*SP* 2.176);

In P. Oxy. 494, line 18 (156-165 CE) we see the notion of *exchange*: "And my wife will supply 200 drachma *in exchange for* garments each year." So also in P. Grenf. ii. 77, line 20 (3rd-4th century CE): "[in exchange for] expenditures on loaves and relishes, 16 drachma." In P. Bour. 20, line 2 (350+ CE) is an example of ὑπέρ as a "proxy" (*in the place of*). In P. Lond. 23, lines 28-29 (158 BCE), ὑπέρ is used for representation and substitution: "I may be able to perform the sacrifices *on behalf of/in place of* you and your children."

Although our list is not exhaustive (as I gave only a cursory glance at the evidence), 78 examples nicely supplement Robertson's initial study, confirming his understanding.[83] This evidence is overwhelming in favor of treating ὑπέρ as bearing a substitutionary force in the NT era.

One reason for previous resistance to this idea is due to the fact that in classical times ὑπέρ only rarely transgressed into the boundary of ἀντί. As one carefully looks at the examples that have been provided here, he/she will no doubt detect that the

---

42. P. Oxy. 1881.23 (427 CE/*SP* 2.184);
*43. P. Ryl. 94.15 (14-37 CE/*SP* 2.188);
*44. P. Bour. 20.2 (350+ CE/*SP* 2.210);
*45. P. Bour. 20.3 (350+ CE/*SP* 2.212);
**46. P. Lond. 23.28-29 (158 BCE/*SP* 2.244): ;
47. BGU 648.23-24 (164 or 196 CE/*SP* 2.272);
48. BGU 1022.30 (196 CE/*SP* 2.280);
49. P. Ryl. 114.28 (c.280 CE/*SP* 2.294): "in exchange for";
50. P. Thead. 17.21 (332 CE/*SP* 2.302);
51. PSI 1067.26 (235-37 CE/*SP* 2.320);
*52. P. Fay. 28.15 (150-51 CE/*SP* 2.332);
53. P. Oxy. 1464.16 (250 CE/*SP* 2.352);
54. P. Ryl. 12.10 (250 CE/*SP* 2.354);
*55. P. Oxy. 1453.39 (30-29 BCE/*SP* 2.370): N.B. ὑπέρ is in brackets;
*56. Raccolta Lumbroso, p. 46.22 (25 CE/*SP* 2.372);
57. P. Oxy. 83.27 (327 CE/*SP* 2.378);
58. P. Oxy. 2124.22 (316 CE/*SP* 2.404);
59. P. Oxy. 1425.15 (318 CE/*SP* 2.404): N.B. Cf. line 8 which uses ἀντί in the strict sense of "in place of";
60. P. Oxy. 2109.63-64 (261 CE/*SP* 2.432);
61. P. Oxy. 896.21 (316 CE/*SP* 2.440);
*62. P. Oxy. 1626.12 (325 CE/*SP* 2.442): "exchange";
63. P. Oxy. 1626.26 (325 CE/*SP* 2.442);
64. P. Oxy. 1627.27 (342 CE/*SP* 2.44?): N.B. Cf. ἀντί in line 19 in the sense of "instead of";
*65. P. Cairo Masp. 67032.48 (551 CE/*SP* 2.448): "in exchange for";
*66. P. Cairo Masp. 67032.50 (551 CE/*SP* 2.450): "in exchange for";
67. P. Strassb. 46.27 (566 CE/*SP* 2.456);
68. P. Hamb. 39 (33).19 (179 CE/*SP* 2.468);
*69. P. Thead. 35.7 (325 CE/*SP* 2.494): exchange;
**70. P. Lond. 1177.39 (113 CE/*SP* 2.536): exchange;
**71. P. Lond. 1177.55 (113 CE/*SP* 2.538): exchange;
*72-76. P. Oxy. 1920.5,7,10,12,14 (late 6th cent. CE/*SP* 2.544): exchange;
*77. P. Oxy. 1920.15 (late 6th cent. CE/*SP* 2.546): exchange;
*78. P.Oxy. 106.24 (135 CE/*SP* 2.578).

[83] Powell also discovered a couple hundred instances in the Oxyrhynchus Papyri. The substitutionary use of ὑπέρ is well known to papyrologists, of course, but our data are given here for the sake of NT students who are not always aware of extra-NT research.

vast majority of them are quite late, suggesting that the broad use of ὑπέρ was a development of the language in the Koine period, becoming more and more fixed as time progressed. Our hypothesis is simply this: *Throughout the Koine period ὑπέρ began to encroach more and more on the meanings of ἀντί, though never fully phasing it out.*[84] It was a relatively common phenomenon for one grammatical or lexical form to swallow up the uses of another in the Hellenistic period.

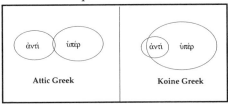

Chart 39
Overlap in Uses of Ἀντί and Ὑπέρ

b. **The substitutionary sense is found in soteriologically insignificant texts in the NT.**

Ὑπέρ is used in a substitutionary sense in soteriologically insignificant passages, thus establishing such a nuance in the NT. Cf. Rom 9:3; Phlm 13.[85]

c. **The substitutionary sense occurs in *at least* one soteriologically significant text.**

Ὑπέρ is used with a substitutionary force in at least one soteriologically significant passage, admitted even by BAGD: 2 Cor 5:14.[86] As well, there are other soteriologically significant texts in which it is difficult to deny a substitutionary sense to ὑπέρ: Gal 3:13;[87] John 11:50.[88]

---

[84] One means of comparison is simply quantitative: ἀντί occurs 22 times in the NT; ὑπέρ occurs 149. If the evidence from biblical Greek is at all indicative, a diachronic trend can be seen toward the encroachment of ὑπέρ on ἀντί's domain, for in the LXX ἀντί is used 390 times, while ὑπέρ is found 430 times. Both prepositions are still in use in modern Greek.

[85] See discussion in Waltke, "Theological Significations of Ἀντί and Ὑπέρ," 2.295-305.

[86] For a discussion see Davies, "Christ in Our Place," 87-88; Waltke, "Theological Significations of Ἀντί and Ὑπέρ," 2.370-78.

[87] Cf. Leon Morris, *The Apostolic Preaching of the Cross,* 59; Davies, "Christ in Our Place," 89; Robertson, *Minister,* 39-40; Waltke, "Theological Significations of Ἀντί and Ὑπέρ," 2.379-81.

[88] Cf. Davies, "Christ in Our Place," 85; Robertson, *Minister,* 39; Waltke, "Theological Significations of Ἀντί and Ὑπέρ," 2.358-61.

d. ˊΥπέρ also occurs with λύτρον on one occasion.

Once ὑπέρ is even used with a form of λύτρον that has been strengthened by prefixing ἀντί to it: 1 Tim 2:6. On this text, Davies points out that

> clearly the reference in I Timothy 2:6 which speaks of "the man Christ Jesus, who gave himself as a ransom for all," (ἀντίλυτρον ὑπὲρ πάντων) has a substitutionary meaning. The prefixed ἀντι- reinforces the idea of substitution already present in the λύτρον concept, and so even if the ὑπέρ were taken with the meaning "for the benefit of," the concept of substitution would be present in the text.[89]

e. ˊΥπέρ is a richer term than ἀντί

Finally, the question might be asked: If the Pauline doctrine of the atonement is at least a substitutionary one, why does he *never* choose the less ambiguous preposition ἀντί to express such an idea? In answer to this question, consider the following:

1) "In the New Testament period ἀντί suffered a great reduction in use."[90]

2) As Robertson has demonstrated, in Koine Greek, "The set idiom for substitution employs ὑπέρ rather than ἀντί."[91]

3) As Trench long ago noted:

> We obtain a perfect right to claim such declarations of Christ's death *for us* as also declarations of his death *in our stead*. And in them beyond doubt the preposition ὑπέρ is the rather employed, that it may embrace both these meanings, and express how Christ died at once *for our sakes* . . . and *in our stead*; while ἀντί would only have expressed the last of these.[92]

In sum, although it is possible that substitution is not the sense of ὑπέρ in some of the soteriologically significant texts, because this must be the sense in many such texts, the burden of proof falls on those who would deny such a sense in the others. In the least, in light of the well-established usage of substitution in Hellenistic Greek, there seems to be

---

[89] Davies, "Christ in Our Place," 89-90. Of course, this last sentence tells us nothing about the force of ὑπέρ. For more discussion of this passage, cf. Morris, *Apostolic Preaching*, 48, 59.

[90] Davies, "Christ in Our Place," 90. See our chart above and note the statistics: ὑπέρ is almost seven times as frequent as ἀντί.

[91] Robertson, *Minister*, 38.

[92] R. C. Trench, *Synonyms of the New Testament*, 291. My quoting of Trench is not to be taken as a wholesale endorsement of his now rather outdated work. I just think that on this point he was particularly insightful. Along the same lines, cf. Waltke, "Theological Significations of ˊΑντί and ˊΥπέρ," 2.403; Harris, "Prepositions and Theology," 3.1177-78, 1197.

no reason not to adopt this nuance as part of the Pauline doctrine of the atonement. In the final analysis, what we can say about the atonement can be summarized as follows:

> ... no one of the theories of the atonement states all the truth nor, indeed, do all of them together. The bottom of this ocean of truth has never been sounded by any man's plumb-line. There is more in the death of Christ for all of us than any of us has been able to fathom. . . . However, one must say that substitution is an essential element in any real atonement.[93]

2. Ὑπέρ with the Accusative

Here the most significant text is 1 Cor 4:6.[94]

Ὑπό

A. *Basic Uses (with Genitive and Accusative)*[95]

1. With Genitive

a. (Ultimate) Agency: *by*[96]

b. Intermediate Agency (with active verbs): *through*

c. Means: *by* (rare)

2. With Accusative

a. Spatial: *under, below*

b. Subordination: *under* (the rule of)

B. *Significant Passages Involving* Ὑπό

Some of the more important/interesting texts include: Matt 1:22; 2:15, etc.; Rom 3:9; 6:14, 15.[97]

---

[93] Robertson, *Minister*, 40-41.

[94] Cf. A. Legault, "Beyond the Things Which Are Written," *NTS* 18 (1972) 227-31.

[95] In the NT and other early Christian literature, the dat. case is not used with ὑπό, although this was the case in other ancient Greek writings.

[96] For details, see the discussion on the passive voice with agency expressed in the chapter on voice.

[97] For a discussion of the overlap between ὑπό and διά, ὑπό and ἀπό, ὑπό and παρά, see Harris, "Prepositions and Theology," 3.1198.

Person and Number

Overview

Select Bibliography

E. H. Askwith, "'I' and 'We' in the Thessalonian Epistles," *Expositor*, 8th Series, 1 (1911) 149-59; *BDF*, 72-79, 146-47 (§129-37, 139-42, 280-82); **J. Beekman and J. Callow**, *Translating the Word of God* (Grand Rapids: Zondervan, 1974) 107-16; **M. Carrez**, "Le Nous en 2 Corinthiens," *NTS* 26 (1980) 474-86; **Dana-Mantey**, 164-65 (§159); **K. Dick**, *Der Schriftstellerische Plural bei Paulus* (Halle: Max Niemeyer, 1900); **J. H. Greenlee**, "II Corinthians (The Editorial 'We')," *Notes on Translation* 60 (1976) 31-32; **U. Holzmeister**, "De 'Plurali Categoriae' in Novo Testamento et a Patribus Adhibito," *Bib* 14 (1933) 68-95; **W. R. Hutton**, "Who Are We?" *BT* 4 (1953) 86-90; **M. P. John**, "When Does 'We' Include 'You'?" *BT* 27 (1976) 237-40; **J. J. Kijne**, "We, Us, and Our in I and II Corinthians," *NovT* 8 (1966) 171-79; **W. F. Lofthouse**, "'I' and 'We' in the Pauline Letters," *ExpTi* 64 (1952) 241-45; **Moule**, *Idiom Book*, 118-19, 180-81; **V. A. Pickett**, "Those Problem Pronouns, *We*, *Us*, and *Our* in the New Testament," *BT* 15.2 (1964) 88-92; **Robertson**, *Grammar*, 402-09, 1028-29; **Turner**, *Syntax*, 311-17; **T. K. Weis**, "'We' Means Who? An Investigation of the Literary Plural," Th.M. thesis, Dallas Theological Seminary, 1995; **Young**, *Intermediate Greek*, 73-74; **Zerwick**, *Biblical Greek*, 1-4 (§1-8).

Preface

In general, it can be said that a verb usually agrees with the subject in both person and number (known as *concord*). Such routine usage is already part of the intermediate student's preunderstanding and need not be discussed here.[1] There are also exceptional uses. Specifically, with regard to *person*, the lack of agreement is not between subject and verb, but between the linguistic person and the real person. With regard to *number*, there are several instances of discord between the verb number and the subject number. A few of the more interesting and/or exegetically significant phenomena with regard to person and number will be noted in this chapter.[2]

I. Person

A. First Person for Third Person ("I" = "Someone")

On a rare occasion, the first person singular may be used for the sake of vividness when a more universal application is in view.[3] Normally such a usage is inclusive of the first person (thus, "I" would mean something like "all of us"), but apparently it can also be used in an exclusive way ("I" would mean "others, but not myself").

1 Cor 10:30   εἰ **ἐγὼ** χάριτι μετέχω, τί **βλασφημοῦμαι** ὑπὲρ οὗ **ἐγὼ** εὐχαριστῶ;

If **I** partake with thanksgiving, why am **I** denounced for that for which **I** give thanks?

> In the preceding context, Paul addressed the Corinthians in the second person (note the hypothetical situation described in vv 27-29). He switches to the first person singular in vv 29-30, then back to the second person plural again in v 31. He seems to be sympathizing with the stronger brother by the use of the first person.

Gal 2:18   εἰ γὰρ ἃ **κατέλυσα** ταῦτα πάλιν **οἰκοδομῶ**, παραβάτην **ἐμαυτὸν συνιστάνω**.

For if **I** build up again those things that **I** have destroyed, **I** prove **myself** [to be] a transgressor.

> In this context Paul seems to associate with the situation that the Galatians were facing, not in terms of sympathy, but judgment. The first

---

[1] For a discussion, see Mounce, *Biblical Greek*, 116-18 (§15.3-15.5).

[2] Some grammars address one or more of these uses in other sections, such as the epistolary plural in the chapter on pronouns. Since almost all such examples occur in the nom. case as subject of the verb, thereby making an explicit pronoun dispensable (because it is embedded in the verbal inflection), it seemed more logical to discuss such in the unit on "Verbs and Verbals."

[3] This usage is both rarer in Greek than in other languages and appears relatively late, just prior to the Koine period (*BDF*, 147 [§281]).

person thus functions as a sort of polite way of condemning the actions of the readers.

The use of the first person singular in Rom 7:7-25 may well fit this category as well. The issues here are quite complex and cannot be resolved at the grammatical level. But suffice to say that (1) Rom 7:7-25 is an extraordinarily difficult passage exegetically; none of the standard views can claim at all points normal or routine syntax for itself; (2) if the "I" of vv 7-13 is the same as the "I" of vv 14-25, then it is almost certainly used in a universal sense, for v 9 ("I was once alive apart from sin") can hardly refer to Paul in his pre-conversion state, while v 14 ("I am carnal, sold under sin") does not seem able to describe him after his conversion. A universal notion would focus on humanity's (whether believers or unbelievers) inability to please God by subjecting oneself to law. Thus, even though the use of the first person in a universal sense is quite rare, it is the only one that consistently interprets "I."

† B. *Second Person for Third Person ("You" = "Someone") ?*

In the Greek NT there is, most likely, *no indefinite second person* as there is in modern colloquial English.[4] (By "indefinite" I mean the use of the second person for either the first or the third person.) Webster's defines the indefinite second person of modern English as referring to "a person or people generally: equivalent in sense to indefinite *one*, as, *you* can never tell!" (*New World Dictionary*).

By way of illustration, suppose the son of a University of Texas alumnus asked him, "How do you become an Aggie?" the father might respond, "You first must train yourself in exercising bad judgment." In such an interchange, neither father nor son would be referring to each other directly!

The Greeks, however, would use the appropriate person to express what we colloquially say with the second person. Older English and literary English are quite similar.[5] The point, however, is that when you (I mean *you*, the reader) come across a second person in the Greek NT, you must think in terms other than colloquial English. If you can think on a literary level, very good! If you can capture the *Greek* point of view, this is even better! But you must remember that the NT apparently does *not* employ the second person in an indefinite sense.

---

[4] *BDF*, 147 (§281) suggest that such a phenomenon occurs in the NT, but none of the examples is convincing. In particular, they cite Rom 8:2 (ὁ γὰρ νόμος τοῦ πνεύματος τῆς ζωῆς ἐν Χριστῷ Ἰησοῦ ἠλευθέρωσέν **σε** ἀπὸ τοῦ νόμου τῆς ἁμαρτίας καὶ τοῦ θανάτου) as a clear example. However, this is the use of the singular for the plural (not the second person for the third), for the apostle is not making a universal statement, true of believers and unbelievers alike. In any event, *BDF* admit that this usage of the second person is quite rare.

[5] It is rare in both classical Greek (*BDF*, 147 [§281]) and literary English (*Oxford English Dictionary*, s.v. "you," III. 6., gives as its earliest example an illustration from 1577; interestingly, no instances are cited for "thou").

John 4:11   πόθεν οὖν **ἔχεις** τὸ ὕδωρ τὸ ζῶν

Where then do **you** keep this living water?

> The woman is *not* asking, "Where do you **get** this living water?" as if to refer to herself (i.e., "Where does one get this living water?"). She is asking where Jesus *keeps* it or, more colloquially, "Where have you got this living water?"

Rom 8:13   εἰ γὰρ κατὰ σάρκα **ζῆτε**, **μέλλετε** ἀποθνήσκειν . . .

For if **you** live by the flesh, **you** are about to die . . .

> Paul is not referring to an indefinite third person here, but to his *Christian* audience in Rome. In 1:7 he identifies them as "saints." It is very possible that here he is referring to physical death, i.e., that a Christian who conducts his or her life according to the flesh has no guarantee that he or she will live out the lifespan God originally intended (desired will, *not* decreed will) that believer to have. This interpretation has good support in the rest of the verse which declares, "but if by the Spirit you are putting to death the deeds of the flesh, you will live." This is certainly not the way to gain *spiritual* life–by works! But if one sees *spiritual* death in the first part (either in reference to believers who were in danger of losing their salvation, or in reference to unbelievers), then to be consistent he/she should see *spiritual* life in the latter part of the verse. Such an interpretation, however, seems to fly in the face of Pauline theology, especially as seen in this very chapter.

The basic exegetical point here is that the NT authors' distinctions between second and third person are not to be overlooked (because they will not be blurred in Greek as they are in English). Theologically, this is significant for it seems that in many of the texts which *on the surface* seem to suggest that a believer can lose his/her salvation, the "insecure" part of the text is in the third person (cf. John 15:1-11 [note especially the change of persons between vv 5 and 6]; Heb 6:4-6, 9).

➡ ## C. *First Person Plural Constructions: The Scope of "We"*

In many situations in the NT, especially in the epistles, the use of *we* is not always clear.[6] Does the author mean to include his associates (or co-authors), or his audience, or is this simply an *editorial* way of referring to himself? The use of the first person plural to refer only to the author is known as the *editorial "we"* (or *epistolary plural*); the use of the first person plural to refer to the author and his associates as distinct from the audience is called *exclusive "we"*; and the use of the first person plural to refer to both author(s) and his reader(s) is called the *inclusive "we."* The potential referents can be diagrammed as follows.

---

[6] Thanks are due to Ted Weis for clarifying many issues of "we" in his research of first person plural pronouns in Paul for the course Advanced Greek Grammar at Dallas Seminary in the spring semester, 1994. See now his thesis, "'We' Means Who?"

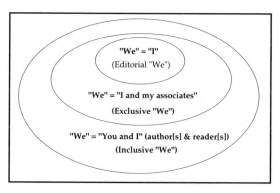

Chart 40
The Scope of "We" in the NT

1. **Editorial "We" (Epistolary Plural)**

   a. **Definition**

   The *editorial "we"* (also known as the *epistolary plural*) is the use of the first person plural by an author when he is in reality referring only to himself.[7] The use of the epistolary plural, though established in the papyri letters, is neither common in the papyri nor in the NT letters.[8] Many texts are debatable; the ambiguity in such instances usually has to do with whether the author includes his associates in the first person plural or is referring only to himself; not infrequently, such passages are triply ambiguous: Does the author refer to himself alone, himself and his associates, or does he include the *audience* in the *we*?

   b. **Keys to Identification**

   The normal presupposition is that a given first person plural is not editorial. But when an author shifts unexpectedly from the singular to the plural, there is grounds for suspecting an epistolary plural. The *context* is thus the primary factor involved in determining whether or not *we* is editorial. There is, however, a morphological clue as well: *The epistolary plural normally occurs in the nominative case.*[9] Even in contexts where the oblique cases are used, the nominative usually leads off the discourse.

   ---

   [7] Some grammarians lump the epistolary plural in with the literary plural. In our terminology, the latter refers to the inclusive *we* (i.e., the use of the first person plural to include the audience).

   [8] Moule, *Idiom Book*, 118; Zerwick, *Biblical Greek*, 4.

   [9] Moulton cites a couple of exceptions to this "rule" from the papyri (*Prolegomena*, 86). There are also exceptions in the NT, especially the gen. of the personal pronoun (though this is usually attached to the subject): It is a natural shift to say, for example, "We ask" to "Our request."

c. Illustrations

1) (Relatively) Clear Examples

All of the examples of the editorial *we* in the NT are debatable,[10] though some are excellent candidates for this category with few detractors among the commentators.

2 Cor 10:11 οἷοί **ἐσμεν** τῷ λόγῳ δι' ἐπιστολῶν ἀπόντες, τοιοῦτοι καὶ παρόντες

what **we** are when absent in word through [our] letters, these things also [we are] in deed when present

The preceding context speaks of Paul alone as the author of his letters (vv 9-10). The sudden change to the plural is thus best explained as an editorial *we*.

2 Cor 10:13 **ἡμεῖς** οὐκ εἰς τὰ ἄμετρα καυχησόμεθα

we will not boast beyond the limit

Again, the preceding context speaks only of Paul boasting, though he does seem to include reference to his companions in other things (vv 1-2, 8 mention Paul's boasting/boldness; vv 5, 7 seem to refer to Paul and his associates). Second Corinthians 10-13 includes several instances of what many regard as epistolary plurals, especially since they are sprinkled among the more frequent first person singulars. These two texts (10:11 and 10:13) are but two of them. For other possible epistolary plurals in this section, note 10:12, 14, 15; 13:4, 6-9 (bracketed by singulars in vv 1-3 and v 10); more doubtful are 11:6, 12, 21. In 2 Cor 12:18-19, the plural is now used after an explicit mention of Titus (v 17) and is thus to be explained as an exclusive *we*.

One possible reason for the use of the epistolary plural throughout these chapters is that Paul, being obviously self-conscious about displaying the credentials of his apostleship under the present circumstances, occasionally reverts to the plural out of modesty. Significantly, he does not use the plural when he makes an autobiographical note (which, if the plural had been used, could be construed by his opponents as false testimony since only Paul received the thirty-nine lashes five times, only Paul was stoned, etc.).

Rom 1:5 **ἐλάβομεν** χάριν καὶ ἀποστολήν

we have received grace and an apostleship

Paul mentions only himself as author (v 1), rendering the plural here as most likely epistolary. Further, it is unlikely that he has in mind other apostles because of the prepositional phrase, detailing the purpose of the apostleship, that immediately follows: εἰς ὑπακοὴν πίστεως ἐν πᾶσιν τοῖς ἔθνεσιν (for the obedience of the faith among all the Gentiles). Since Paul alone was the apostle to the Gentiles, the *we* is evidently editorial.

---

[10] *Contra* Lofthouse, "'I' and 'We' in the Pauline Letters," who argues that in every instance of *we* in Paul "he was thinking of himself as one of a number, either the little band of his companions, or his readers, or the whole company of believers always in the background of his mind. The circle expands or contracts; but it is always there when the plural is used; never when it is not" (241). Some exegetical gymnastics need to be performed to arrive at this conclusion, however. (Similar is Askwith's statement that "I can see no reason for thinking that he [Paul] ever says 'we' when he means 'I'" ["'I' and 'We' in the Thessalonian Epistles," 159].)

Gal 1:8-9   ἀλλὰ καὶ ἐὰν **ἡμεῖς** ἢ ἄγγελος ἐξ οὐρανοῦ εὐαγγελίζηται ὑμῖν παρ᾽ ὃ
            εὐηγγελισάμεθα ὑμῖν, ἀνάθεμα ἔστω. (9) ὡς **προειρήκαμεν** καὶ ἄρτι
            πάλιν λέγω· εἴ τις ὑμᾶς εὐαγγελίζεται παρ᾽ ὃ παρελάβετε, ἀνάθεμα
            ἔστω. . . .

            But even if **we**, or an angel from heaven, should preach to you a gos-
            pel other than the one **we** preached to you, let him be accursed. (9)
            As **we** just stated, I now also say it again: if any one preaches to you
            a gospel other than that which you received, let him be accursed.

> Although the letter to the Galatians opens with "Paul . . . and all the
> brothers who are with me," the body of the letter begins with the sin-
> gular verb θαυμάζω (v 6) and vv 8-9 are surrounded by first person sin-
> gulars (vv 10-24). Further, the interchange between *we* and *I* in vv 8-9 is
> more easily explained if only Paul is in view. The brothers in v 2, then,
> seem to function in a supporting role, as witnesses to the truth of Paul's
> gospel.

Cf. also 2 Cor 3:1-6, 12; 7:12-16; 8:1-8; 9:1-5.

2) Debatable Illustrations

1 Th 2:18   **ἠθελήσαμεν** ἐλθεῖν πρὸς ὑμᾶς, ἐγὼ μὲν Παῦλος καὶ ἅπαξ καὶ δίς, καὶ
            ἐνέκοψεν **ἡμᾶς** ὁ σατανᾶς
            we wanted to come to you–I Paul more than once–yet Satan
            hindered **us**

> Is the plural referring to Paul alone, or to Paul and Silvanus, or to Paul
> and Silvanus and Timothy? Cf. also 3:1, 2, 5 where the plural continues
> to be used, though punctuated by the first person singular.

1 John 1:4 ταῦτα γράφομεν **ἡμεῖς,** ἵνα ἡ χαρὰ ἡμῶν ᾖ πεπληρωμένη
            we write these things that our joy might be made complete

> Is the Elder writing alone or in association with others? Complicating
> the issue is the fact in vv 5 and 6 the plural continues, but each time
> with a different force: In v 5 it seems to refer to the author and other
> ministers; in v 6, it is an inclusive *we* (the author and audience
> together). The author uses γράφω another dozen times in this letter, but
> each time in the singular.

Heb 6:9   **πεπείσμεθα** περὶ ὑμῶν, ἀγαπητοί, τὰ κρείσσονα
            we are convinced of better things concerning you, beloved

> The letter to the Hebrews is typically regarded as employing only two
> types of first person plurals: epistolary and inclusive. (For potential
> epistolary plurals, note, e.g., 2:5; 5:11; 6:9, 11; 8:1; 9:5; 13:18, 23; for inclu-
> sive *we*, cf. 2:1, 3; 3:6; 4:2, 11, 13, 14; 7:26; 10:10, 19; 12:1.) The second cat-
> egory is without dispute: The author clearly and often associates
> himself with the audience. But whether the epistolary plural is used is
> more difficult to assess. For one thing, this letter is unlike other NT let-
> ters: In every other letter the author uses "I" before getting half way
> through. But the situation is different in Hebrews: The first person sin-
> gular does not appear until chapter 11 (v 32), and then in only three
> more verses (13:19, 22, 23). This is very unusual and suggests the pos-
> sibility that Hebrews was actually written by at least *two* persons with
> one being the better known to the audience.[11]

Cf. also Rom 3:28; 2 Cor 4:1-6; 5:11-16; 11:6, 12, 21.

➡️ **2. Inclusive "We" (Literary Plural) Vs. Exclusive "We"**

    a. Definition

        The inclusive *we* is the use of the first person plural to include both author(s) and audience. This contrasts with the exclusive *we* in which the first person plural restricts the group to the author and his associates (whether co-authors, those physically present, even those who, distinct from the audience, have participated in some of the author's experiences, etc.).

    b. Significance

        The issue of whether *we* is inclusive or exclusive is both difficult to resolve in many texts and of more than academic interest to many Bible translators. Although the first person plural–whether inclusive or exclusive–is the same form in most Indo-European languages, two distinct forms are used in many Asian, Pacific Island, Indian, African, and Latin American cultures. Thus, to the field translator there is no luxury of referential ambiguity; a decision needs to be made in each instance.[12]

        Resolving the issue must be done on a case-by-case basis. The context and overall thrust of the book are the best clues.[13] In particular, the presence of the second person plural in the same context often signals an exclusive *we* (but there are many exceptions). Below are offered only a handful of texts impacted by this issue. Those interested in seeing more comprehensive treatments are urged to examine the works cited in the bibliography.

---

[11] This possibility is strengthened by the author(s)'s appeal to the audience in 13:18 to "pray for *us*." ἡμῶν here would be an unusual epistolary plural, without parallel in the NT, partially because the epistolary plural does not naturally occur in the oblique cases, and partially because none of the reasons for the use of an epistolary plural (e.g., modesty, politeness in asserting authority, etc.) would easily fit a personal request for prayer.

[12] One will observe in the bibliography for this chapter the disproportionate number of articles in *Bible Translator* and *Notes on Translation,* as opposed to the standard NT journals that deal with exegesis (even Kijne's essay in *NovT* has to do with issues of translation more than exegesis).

[13] Pickett, "Those Problem Pronouns," suggests five analytical questions to ask to resolve the issues. She offers a stimulating discussion of several thorny passages. Although discussed in the essay, she does not list as a separate question the text-critical problems surrounding the ἡμεῖς/ὑμεῖς interchange. Usually the textual issue (which is quite frequent) needs to be resolved first, however, because one cannot tell what the text means unless he or she first knows what the text *says*.

c.   Illustrations

1)   Clear Examples

a)   Of Inclusive *We*

Rom 5:1   δικαιωθέντες οὖν ἐκ πίστεως εἰρήνην **ἔχομεν** πρὸς τὸν θεόν

therefore, since we have been justified by faith, **we** have peace with God

Eph 2:18   δι᾽ αὐτοῦ **ἔχομεν** τὴν προσαγωγὴν οἱ ἀμφότεροι ἐν ἑνὶ πνεύματι πρὸς τὸν πατέρα

through him **we** both have access in one Spirit to the Father

> The presence of ἀμφότεροι and the entire section (2:11-22) addresses issues of reconciliation between Jew and Gentile in the body of Christ.

Jas 3:2   πολλὰ **πταίομεν** ἅπαντες

we all stumble in many ways

Cf. also Rom 1:12; Gal 2:4; Eph 3:20; Titus 3:3, 5; Heb 12:1; 1 Pet 2:24; 2 Pet 3:13; 3 John 8.

b)   Of Exclusive *We*

1 Cor 4:10   **ἡμεῖς** μωροὶ διὰ Χριστόν, ὑμεῖς δὲ φρόνιμοι ἐν Χριστῷ· **ἡμεῖς** ἀσθενεῖς, ὑμεῖς δὲ ἰσχυροί

we are fools for Christ, but you are wise in Christ; **we** are weak, but you are strong

2 Thess 2:1   **ἐρωτῶμεν** δὲ ὑμᾶς, ἀδελφοί, ὑπὲρ τῆς παρουσίας τοῦ κυρίου ἡμῶν Ἰησοῦ Χριστοῦ καὶ ἡμῶν ἐπισυναγωγῆς ἐπ᾽ αὐτόν

now **we** ask you, brothers, concerning the coming of our Lord Jesus Christ and our gathering together with him

> The first person plural passes almost imperceptibly from exclusive to inclusive in this verse: *"we* ask you" is clearly exclusive, while *"our* Lord" and *"our* gathering" are clearly inclusive. This illustrates that even in the same text one cannot assume that the presence of the second person pronoun ("we ask **you**") renders all first person pronouns exclusive.

Cf. also John 4:12; 1 Cor 3:9; 15:15; Gal 2:9; Col 1:3; 2 Pet 1:16-19.

2)   Debatable Examples

John 8:53   μὴ σὺ μείζων εἶ τοῦ πατρὸς **ἡμῶν** Ἀβραάμ;

You are not greater than **our** father Abraham, are you?

> Although it could be argued that the pronoun is inclusive (viewing the Jews as regarding Abraham as Jesus' ancestor, too), in light of their allegation of his illegitimate birth (v 41), and the issue of paternity as the key to authority in this pericope, it is more likely that the *we* is exclusive. Perhaps an underlying assumption on their part is that not only was Jesus illegitimate, but that he was half-Gentile.

2 Cor 5:18 τὰ δὲ πάντα ἐκ τοῦ θεοῦ τοῦ καταλλάξαντος **ἡμᾶς** ἑαυτῷ διὰ Χριστοῦ
     καὶ δόντος **ἡμῖν** τὴν διακονίαν τῆς καταλλαγῆς

     and all these things [come] from God who reconciled **us** to himself
     through Christ and who gave **to us** the ministry of reconciliation

> Although there is no linguistic basis for seeing a shift in referent, from
> the content side of things and the context (cf. v 20) the first pronoun
> seems to be inclusive (God reconciled all believers) and the second pro-
> noun seems to be exclusive (Paul and his companions are ministers of
> such reconciliation). It can be no argument that Paul should have
> warned the reader of his change in meaning, because in the rapid-fire,
> emotion-laden literary efforts of the apostle to the Gentiles–especially
> in this letter–reflective precision sometimes gives way to passionate
> involvement with his flock.

1 John 1:4 ταῦτα γράφομεν ἡμεῖς, ἵνα ἡ χαρὰ **ἡμῶν** ᾖ πεπληρωμένη

     we write these things that **our** joy might be made complete

> Is the purpose of writing that the author might have joy or that both
> author and audience might experience joy? Complicating the issue is
> the MS testimony: Some witnesses have ἡμῶν (e.g., ℵ B L Ψ 1241) while
> others read ὑμῶν (e.g., A C K P 33 1739). The issue is quite difficult to
> decide, but in the least the second person pronoun implicitly suggests
> that the scribes saw the audience as participating in the joyous purpose
> of the epistle.

Cf. also Mark 4:38; 6:37; Luke 24:20 (probably inclusive[14]); John 21:24; Acts 6:3; Rom 10:16;
1 Cor 9:10; 2 Cor 1:20-21; Gal 5:5; Eph 1:12; 2:3; 1 Thess 3:4; 4:15; Rev 5:10.

II. Number

→ ## A. *Neuter Plural Subject with Singular Verb*

Although there is a lack of concord in such constructions, they are not infrequent. Indeed, a neuter plural subject *normally* takes a singular verb. It is an
example of *constructio ad sensum* (construction according to sense, rather
than according to strict grammatical concord). Since the neuter usually
refers to impersonal things (including animals), the singular verb regards
the plural subject as a *collective* whole. It is appropriate to translate the subject as a plural as well as the verb, rather than translate both as singulars.

Mark 4:4 ἦλθεν **τὰ πετεινὰ** καὶ κατέφαγεν αὐτό
    the birds came and devoured it

John 9:3 φανερωθῇ **τὰ ἔργα** τοῦ θεοῦ ἐν αὐτῷ
    [in order that] **the works** of God might be manifest in him

> The "works of God" are viewed as a collective singular–a united group.

---

[14] Pickett notes that in the conversation between the disciples on the road to Emmaus
and Jesus, "*our* chief priests and rulers" is probably inclusive since they invited this
stranger to eat with them (vv 29-30).

Acts 2:43   **πολλὰ τέρατα** καὶ **σημεῖα** διὰ τῶν ἀποστόλων ἐγίνετο
             many wonders and **signs** happened through the apostles
             > In this text not only is the subject neuter plural, but it is compound: *two* neuter plural nouns constitute the subject.

1 Cor 10:7   **τὰ τέλη** τῶν αἰώνων κατήντηκεν
             the ends of the age have come

2 Cor 5:17   εἴ τις ἐν Χριστῷ, καινὴ κτίσις· **τὰ ἀρχαῖα** παρῆλθεν, ἰδοὺ γέγονεν **καινά**
             If anyone is in Christ, he is a new creation; **the old things** have passed away—behold, **new things** have come!
             > Here the state of a believer is viewed positionally and in its entirety.

Rev 20:7   ὅταν τελεσθῇ **τὰ χίλια ἔτη**
             whenever **the thousand years** are completed

Cf. also Matt 13:4; 15:27; Luke 4:41; 8:2; 10:20; John 7:7; 10:4, 21; 19:31; Acts 18:15; 26:24; Eph 4:17; Heb 3:17; Jas 5:2; 1 John 3:12; Rev 11:18.

However, when the author wants to *stress* the individuality of each subject involved in a neuter plural subject, the plural verb is used. "Usually a neuter plural in the N.T. that has a personal or collective meaning has a plural verb."[15] The following are examples of the *neuter plural subject with a plural verb*.

Matt 13:38   **τὰ ζιζάνιά** εἰσιν οἱ υἱοὶ τοῦ πονηροῦ
             the weeds are the sons of the evil one

John 10:27   **τὰ πρόβατα** τὰ ἐμὰ τῆς φωνῆς μου ἀκούουσιν, καγὼ γινώσκω αὐτὰ καὶ ἀκολουθοῦσίν μοι
             my **sheep** hear my voice, and I know them and they follow me
             > The "sheep" represent people and Jesus is emphasizing their individuality, even though "sheep" is neuter. Each sheep hears Jesus' voice for himself. The plural verb is no accident: v 27 contrasts with v 3 where real sheep hear the shepherd's voice as a group (**τὰ πρόβατα** τῆς φωνῆς αὐτοῦ ἀκούει), and v 4 where the sheep follow the shepherd collectively (τὰ πρόβατα αὐτῷ ἀκολουθεῖ).

Jas 2:19   **τὰ δαιμόνια** πιστεύουσιν καὶ φρίσσουσιν
             the demons believe and shudder

Cf. also Matt 6:32; 10:21; 25:32; Mark 5:13; Luke 12:30; Acts 13:48; Rom 15:12; Rev 5:14; 17:9.

B. *Collective Singular Subject with Plural Verb*

Normally collective singular subjects take a singular verb. In such constructions the group is viewed as a whole (cf. Mark 3:7; Luke 21:38; 23:35).

---

[15] Robertson, *Grammar*, 403. This is not always the case, however; sometimes even a personal plural subject in the neuter takes a singular verb (cf. 1 Cor 7:14; Eph 4:17; Heb 2:14; Rev 11:18). As well, occasionally an impersonal subject takes a plural verb (cf. Matt 13:16; Heb 1:12; 11:30; Rev 16:20).

However, on a rare occasion such a collective subject takes a plural verb (another instance of *constructio ad sensum*), in which case the individuals in the group receive greater stress.[16]

Mark 3:32 ὄχλος . . . λέγουσιν

a crowd was saying

Luke 6:19 πᾶς ὁ **ὄχλος** ἐζήτουν ἅπτεσθαι αὐτοῦ

all **the crowd** was seeking to touch him

Cf. also Matt 21:8; John 7:49; Acts 6:7.

➡ ## C. *Compound Subject with Singular Verb*

When two subjects, each in the singular, are joined by a conjunction, the verb is usually in the plural (e.g., in Acts 15:35 we read: Παῦλος καὶ **Βαρναβᾶς** διέτριβον ἐν Ἀντιοχείᾳ [Paul and Barnabas were staying in Antioch]). However, when an author wants to *highlight* one of the subjects, the verb is put in the singular.[17] (This even occurs when one of the subjects is in the plural.) The *first*-named subject is the one being stressed in such instances.[18]

This kind of construction occurs frequently enough, as we might have expected, when "Jesus and his disciples" is the compound subject. It is almost as if the disciples are merely tagging along while all of the action centers on Jesus.

Matt 13:55 οὐχ ἡ **μήτηρ** αὐτοῦ λέγεται Μαριὰμ καὶ οἱ **ἀδελφοὶ** αὐτοῦ Ἰάκωβος καὶ Ἰωσὴφ καὶ Σίμων καὶ Ἰούδας;

Is not his **mother** called Mary and his **brothers** [called] James and Joseph and Simon and Judas?

> The use of the singular verb, λέγεται, singles out Mary above Jesus' brothers.

John 2:2 ἐκλήθη ὁ **Ἰησοῦς** καὶ οἱ **μαθηταὶ** αὐτοῦ εἰς τὸν γάμον

Jesus was invited to the wedding and [so were] his disciples

> The connotation seems to be "Jesus was invited to the wedding and his disciples tagged along."

---

[16] This is frequent when the verb follows at some distance, especially in the next clause (cf., e.g., Luke 8:40; John 6:2; 7:49; 12:18). Sometimes, however, the verbs used with collective singulars change from singular to plural (cf., e.g., Mark 5:24; John 7:49). Should we say that the one verb viewed the group collectively and the other viewed it individually? More likely, the author subconsciously shifts from one to the other due to natural number.

[17] *BDF*, 75 (§135) argue that this also occurs when both subjects are viewed equally, but their *personal* examples are unconvincing (John 18:15; 20:3). However, non-personal subjects can behave this way (e.g., παρέλθῃ ὁ οὐρανὸς καὶ ἡ γῆ [Matt 5:18]).

[18] *BDF* suggest only that the verb precedes both subjects (74 [§135]), but sometimes the verb stands between both (cf., e.g., Matt 13:55).

John 4:36   ἵνα **ὁ σπείρων** ὁμοῦ χαίρῃ καὶ **ὁ θερίζων**
in order that **the sower** and **the reaper** might rejoice together

> It is significant that in this dominical saying, prominence is given to the sower: This is the one who really rejoices! How different this attitude is from many modern-day evangelists whose criterion for successful ministry is in the number of the scalps, not the depths of the plowing.

Acts 16:31   πίστευσον ἐπὶ τὸν κύριον Ἰησοῦν καὶ σωθήσῃ **σὺ** καὶ **ὁ οἶκός** σου
believe in the Lord Jesus and **you** shall be saved–and your **house**

> It is sometimes argued that only the Philippian jailer needed to exercise faith in order for his household to be saved. This view is based on the use of the singular verbs πίστευσον and σωθήσῃ. Such a notion is foreign to the Greek, for in the other instances of a compound subject with a singular verb the second nom. was still subject of the verb. Applied here, since the two verbs are linked by καί, there is no reason to treat them differently: πίστις is required of the jailer's family if they are to receive σωτηρία. The reason for the singular each time is evidently that the jailer is present while his family is not (Paul could not very easily have said, "All of you believe . . ." when speaking to one man). An expanded translation brings this out: "Believe in the Lord Jesus and you shall be saved–and if members of your house believe they too will be saved." The condition is the same for both and the offer is the same for both.

Cf. also Mark 8:27; 14:1; John 3:22; 4:53; Acts 5:29; 1 Tim 6:4.

D. *The Indefinite Plural ("They" = "Someone")*

1.   Definition

The indefinite plural is the use of the third person plural to indicate no one in particular, but rather "someone." This has parallels with modern colloquial English. For example, "I understand that *they* have discovered a cure for cancer." In this sentence, "they" = "someone." Frequently it is better to convert an indefinite plural into a *passive* in which the object becomes the subject (e.g., in the sentence above, this would = "I understand that a cure for cancer has been discovered").

Sometimes the indefinite plural is a circumlocution for naming God as subject.[19]

2.   Illustrations

a.   Clear Instances

Matt 7:16   μήτι **συλλέγουσιν** ἀπὸ ἀκανθῶν σταφυλάς;
they do not **gather** grapes from thornbushes, do they?

> Jesus had just declared that false prophets would be known by their fruits. Since the verb συλλέγουσιν is in concord with "false prophets" *grammatically* it is possible to see it referring back to them. But

---

[19] So Zerwick, *Biblical Greek*, 1.

semantically this is absurd: "[False prophets] do not gather grapes from thornbushes, do they?"! A principle is being suggested, requiring a generic subject. The point here is that "grapes are not gathered from thornbushes." One should translate the verb, then, as a passive so as not to construe the wrong impression that false prophets are the subject.

Luke 12:20 ταύτῃ τῇ νυκτὶ τὴν ψυχήν σου **ἀπαιτοῦσιν** ἀπὸ σοῦ

in this night, **they** will require your soul from you

> Here, "they" seems to refer to God. It is not legitimate, however, to infer from this that the Trinity is in view (as some have done), for this same usage was found in classical Greek with reference to one person.

Cf. also Matt 5:15; 9:2; Luke 6:38; 12:48; 23:31; John 15:6.

b. A Debatable Passage

Mark 3:21 ἀκούσαντες οἱ παρ᾽ αὐτοῦ ἐξῆλθον κρατῆσαι αὐτόν· **ἔλεγον** γὰρ ὅτι ἐξέστη.

When his family heard it, they went out to seize him, for **they** were saying, "He has lost his senses."

> Zerwick comments: "These παρ᾽ αὐτοῦ are later (v. 31) said to be 'His mother and his brethren'. Were they necessarily the ones who thought Jesus was deranged? Not at all."[20] His motivation for seeing an indefinite plural here is admitted earlier in the same paragraph: "[This] text seems offensive to the honour of the Mother of God . . ."[21] Suffice it to say here that since there is a perfectly natural antecedent, both grammatically and semantically, the burden of proof would seem to rest with the one who sees an indefinite plural in this text.[22] Further, Jesus' implicit rebuke of his family (including his mother) in vv 31-34 seems to make better sense if ἔλεγον found its antecedent in οἱ παρ᾽ αὐτοῦ.

E. *The Categorical Plural (a.k.a. Generalizing Plural)*

1. Definition

This is very similar to the indefinite plural. The differences are three: (1) the categorical plural construction cannot easily be converted into a passive; (2) the categorical plural can be a *noun* while the indefinite plural is only a pronoun (whether stated or implied);[23] and (3) rather than *they*

---

[20] Zerwick, *Biblical Greek*, 2.

[21] Turner (a Protestant) also sees an indefinite plural in Mark 3:21 (*Syntax*, 292; he translates ἔλεγον as "rumour had it"). A number of Protestant or ecumenical translations also so regard the plural (e.g., RSV, NRSV).

[22] On Zerwick's side is evidence of sudden shifts in person in gospel narrative literature, such as in Matt 7:16 (discussed above).

[23] This is due to the fact that the categorical plural refers to a generic subject, while the indefinite plural refers to an indefinite subject. Thus, although particular subjects might be mentioned ("the disciples," "the prophets") with the categorical plural, a particular class is still in view; with the indefinite plural, no particular class of people is in view, just "someone."

meaning *someone*, *they* means *he* (or *she*). "What is called the generalizing or categorical plural has a certain affinity with the indefinite plural. It ... consists in a plural referring in reality to a singular subject (class for individual)."[24] This category is not very common, but several potential texts come to mind.

2. Semantics and Significance

- The reason that the plural is used is that it more easily yields itself to a *generic* notion: The force of this usage, it seems, is to focus more on the *action* than on the actor. This is not to say that the actor is unimportant; rather, the actor is important only in a generic sense: "This is the kind of person who does this." Thus, one way to test this in a given passage is to convert the plural into a generic singular.

- The categorical plural is also used when a single grammatical *object* (not subject) is in view.

- Recognition of this category opens up the possibility that several texts say something other than what is normally construed. In particular, seeing the categorical plural in certain places seems to harmonize two texts that stand in tension. This does not, of course, mean that such an expedient should be employed at one's whim; but neither should one assume contradictions in the biblical record when the basis for doing so is the *English* way of looking at things.

3. Illustrations

a. Clear Examples

Matt 2:20   **τεθνήκασιν οἱ ζητοῦντες** τὴν ψυχὴν τοῦ παιδίου
                    those who sought the child's life are **dead**

> The previous verse states that Herod had died. As well, v 15 signals that Jesus would stay in Egypt until the death of Herod. In 2:20, then, the idea is that "the **one** who sought. . . " But the point, semantically, is that the child's life is no longer in danger and therefore he can safely return to Israel. The plural, then, is used to draw the focus away from the particular actor and onto the action.

Heb 11:37   **ἐπρίσθησαν**
                    they were sawn in two

> In this chapter, specifically in vv 32-38, the author speaks generally about the accomplishments of men of faith. He begins by saying, "For time will fail me if I tell of Gideon, Barak, Samson, Jephthah, of David and Samuel and the prophets, who by faith conquered kingdoms . . . shut the mouths of lions . . ." Obviously not *all* of the above-mentioned saints of old conquered kingdoms and shut the mouths of lions! It is

---

[24] Zerwick, *Biblical Greek*, 3. Robertson puts this plural under the broader umbrella of the literary plural which, in his terminology, also includes the epistolary plural (*Grammar*, 406). We prefer to distinguish these several categories.

likely, too, then that in verse 37 the author is using the categorical plural, thinking only of one man, Isaiah the prophet.

Cf. also Matt 2:23; 14:9; John 6:26 (cf. v 14).

b. Possible (and Exegetically Significant) Examples

Mark 15:32 **οἱ συνεσταυρωμένοι** σὺν αὐτῷ ὠνείδιζον αὐτόν

those who were crucified with him reviled him

> The parallel in Luke 23:39 explicitly says that only one of the thieves railed against Jesus. One explanation for the differences might be that Mark emphasized the generic while Luke focused on the particular. It is as if Mark had said, "It was not even beneath the kind of person crucified with Jesus to revile him."

Matt 26:8 ἰδόντες **οἱ μαθηταὶ** ἠγανάκτησαν

the disciples were indignant when they saw [this]

> The disciples had just witnessed a woman pour costly perfumes on Jesus' head. However, another evangelist records that Judas was the one indignant at this act (John 12:4-6). It may be that other disciples too were indignant, but the categorical plural allows for the possibility that Matthew only meant *one* disciple, though his interests were on the class of individuals who were indignant rather than the particular person.

Mk 16:17-18 δαιμόνια **ἐκβαλοῦσιν**, γλώσσαις **λαλήσουσιν** καιναῖς, (18) . . . ὄφεις **ἀροῦσιν**, κτλ.

they will cast out demons, **they** will speak in new tongues . . . **they** will pick up serpents, etc.

> If the longer ending of Mark is original,[25] then these verses need to be wrestled with. Many religious groups assume two things about Jesus' words at the beginning of verse 17 ("And these signs will accompany those who have believed"): (1) The future tense (παρακολουθήσει) is a *promise* rather than a prediction; and (2) it is a promise to *all* believers. However, not only might this statement be a prediction rather than a promise, but the plurals might also be categorical plurals, indicating that the statement need have only *one* person in view for each prediction. The main problem with this view is that in v 18 we are told, according to the NASB, "and if they drink any deadly [poison], it shall not hurt them" (the RSV is similar). The phrase in Greek is κἂν θανάσιμόν τι πίωσιν οὐ μὴ αὐτοὺς βλάψῃ. There is certainly an element of contingency here, which the NASB has forcefully brought out by translating this as a conditional clause. However, because κἂν is used with the indefinite pronoun τι, the element of contingency is probably the *type* of poison that will be drunk, rather than the *fact* of it being drunk. Thus, a better translation might be, "and whatever deadly [poison] they should drink, it shall not hurt them." In this case, then both the protasis and the apodosis are predictive and the whole statement may be seen as other than a promise.

---

[25] There is a general scholarly consensus that these last twelve verses are not original. I am not here arguing for authenticity (for, in fact, I think that the Gospel was intentionally concluded at v 8), just that since this is part of the text that many pulpiteers will need to wrestle with in their preaching ministries (due to their own bias or that of their audience), it ought to be addressed.

This lengthy discussion is *not* intended to *prove* either that (1) the longer ending in Mark is original (for it most likely is not), or (2) the plurals are categorical. Rather, it is intended to demonstrate that even *assuming* the longer ending to be original, vv 17-18 do not necessarily need to be construed as promises to all believers. On this assumption, the point of this discussion is to show that more than one grammatical option is open to us. This being the case, the way in which a choice is made is by the flow of the argument of the text. The question to be asked to determine that is, Is the *stress* in this passage on promises given to believers (which would apparently strengthen their faith), or is it on the authentication of Christianity (which would apparently establish its validity as from God before an unbelieving world)? But such a question is outside the realm grammar. Without an adequate understanding of grammar (with references to the uses of the plural), though, we could not even have posed such a question.

Voice

Overview of Chapter

Select Bibliography

BDF, 161-66 (§307-17); **Brooks-Winbery**, 99-103; **G. T. Christopher**, "Determining the Voice of New Testament Verbs Whose Middle and Passive Forms are Identical: A Consideration of the Perfect Middle/Passive" (Th.M thesis, Grace Theological Seminary, 1985); **Dana-Mantey**, 154-64 (§151-58); **Hoffmann-von Siebenthal**, *Grammatik*, 292-303 (§188-91); **S. E. Kemmer**, "The Middle Voice: A Typological and Diachronic Study" (Ph.D. dissertation, Stanford University, 1988); **Moule**, *Idiom Book*, 24-26; **Moulton**, *Prolegomena*, 152-64; **Porter**, *Idioms*, 62-73; **Robertson**, *Grammar*, 330-41, 797-820; **G. L. Ryle**, "The Significance of the Middle Voice in the Greek New Testament" (Th.M. thesis, Dallas Theological Seminary, 1962); **Smyth**, *Greek Grammar*, 389-98 (§1703-60); **Turner**, *Syntax*, 51-58; **Young**, *Intermediate Greek*, 133-36; **Zerwick**, *Biblical Greek*, 72-76 (§225-36).

Introduction: Definition of Terms

A. *Voice*

Voice is that property of the verb that indicates how the subject is related to the action (or state) expressed by the verb.[1] In general, the voice of the verb may indicate that the subject is *doing* the action (active), *receiving* the action (passive), or both doing and receiving (at least the results of) the action (middle).

> The English term "voice," first used in the grammatical sense above in the prolegomena to Wycliffe's translation of the Bible (1382), has never been a happy term in English.[2] The Greek term is διάθεσις, which bears a variety of meanings such as "arrangement, condition, state, force, function." This is better, but it is not English. Perhaps something like "turn" (suggested by Jesperson) or "direction" (viz., the direction the action takes with reference to the subject) would be more descriptive. But since *voice* has such a long history, it is probably too entrenched in grammar books to be replaced in the near future.[3]

The three voices in Greek may be graphically (and simplistically) illustrated as follows:[4]

---

[1] Dr. W. Hall Harris is to be thanked for his input into this chapter.

[2] Hardly better is the German *Genus*, which is also used for gender. Hoffmann-von Siebenthal, *Grammatik*, have simply transliterated the Greek διάθεσις, which, though more accurate, still does not communicate the meaning to the uninitiated.

[3] Indeed, Kemmer even assumes the terminology of *middle* voice in her excellent cross-linguistic study, even for languages that do not have such a formal category ("Middle Voice," 1-6).

[4] The chart is simplistic in that it has in view only transitive verbs and depicts for the middle voice only the direct (reflexive) use. However, it may be useful for students to get a handle on the general distinctions.

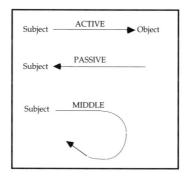

Chart 41
The Direction of the Action in Greek Voices

B. Distinct From Transitiveness

Voice is easy to confuse with transitiveness. However, the two should be distinguished.

Transitiveness relates the action of a verb to an *object*, while *voice* relates the action of a verb to its *subject*.

> If a verb is transitive, it requires a direct object (whether stated or implied[5]). If it is intransitive, it does not take a direct object. Further distinctions: A transitive verb has both an active (or middle) and passive form, while an intransitive verb does not have a passive.[6] The equative verb (copula) is like an intransitive verb in that it does not have a passive, but like a transitive verb in that it has a *complement* (i.e., a predicate nominative/adjective). It is different from both, however, in that its primary function is to assert a quality about the subject.

> Occasionally it is difficult to tell whether a verb is transitive or intransitive (indeed, some verbs can function both ways, depending on contextual and other factors). An easy way to check for transitiveness is the "passive transform" test: Transitive verbs can be converted to the passive; when this happens, the object becomes the subject and the subject becomes the agent (after "by"). The sentence, "The boy hit the ball" can be converted to "the ball was hit by the boy." But the sentence, "the girl came home," in which the verb may look transitive, cannot be converted to "the home was come by the girl."

---

[5] In keeping with its economical nature, Greek regularly implies an object that was already mentioned in the preceding context, rather than restating it. Cf., e.g., Mark 14:16–ἐξῆλθον οἱ μαθηταὶ καὶ ἦλθον εἰς τὴν πόλιν καὶ εὗρον καθὼς εἶπεν αὐτοῖς (his disciples when out and came to the city and found [*it*] just as he had told them). Cf. also John 19:1; Phil 3:12.

[6] These are, of course, distinctions in English that do not always apply in Greek (especially with deponent verbs).

C. *Distinguishing Middle From Passive*

Only in the future and aorist tenses are there distinct forms for the passive and middle voice. In the present, imperfect, perfect, and pluperfect tenses, the middle and passive forms are identical. Although for purposes of parsing, many teachers of Greek allow students to list these as simply "middle/passive," for syntactical purposes a choice needs to be made. This is not always easy and needs to be done on a case-by-case basis.[7] A few of the exegetically significant passages discussed below are connected to this problem. As well, tagging such double-terminal voices for statistical and computer-search purposes is sometimes difficult and open to interpretation. Nevertheless, the vast majority of middle-passive forms pose no problem.[8]

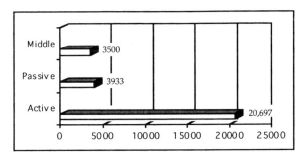

Chart 42
Voice Statistics in the NT

I. Active Voice

Definition

In general it can be said that in the active voice the subject *performs, produces,* or *experiences the action* or *exists* in the *state* expressed by the verb.

---

[7] See Christopher, "Determining the Voice of New Testament Verbs Whose Middle and Passive Forms are Identical," for some help along these lines.

[8] The data in the following chart are supplied by *AcCordance*. This program regards all 2,462 instances of εἰμί in terms of form, in spite of the vacillations it undergoes throughout its paradigm. Thus, the first person singular imperfect indicative (ἤμην) is considered middle, while the third singular form (ἦν) is considered active. All sixty-six instances of φημί are considered active (and, incidentally, all of the forty-three augmented forms are considered either imperfect or aorist). Not all grammarians would agree with this assessment, many preferring to assign no voice at all either to εἰμί or φημί.

Curiously, the problematic καταρτισμένα in Rom 9:22 is assigned no morphological value of any sort (no tense, voice, mood, number, etc.).

➡ A. Simple Active

The subject *performs* or *experiences* the action. The verb may be transitive or intransitive. This is the normal or routine use, by far the most common.

Mark 4:2 **ἐδίδασκεν** αὐτοὺς ἐν παραβολαῖς πολλά
    he **was teaching** them many things in parables

John 1:7 οὗτος **ἦλθεν** εἰς μαρτυρίαν
    he **came** for a testimony

Acts 27:32 **ἀπέκοψαν** οἱ στρατιῶται τὰ σχοινία
    the soldiers **cut off** the ropes

Titus 3:5 κατὰ τὸ αὐτοῦ ἔλεος **ἔσωσεν** ἡμᾶς
    according to his mercy he **saved** us

Jude 23 **μισοῦντες** καὶ τὸν ἀπὸ τῆς σαρκὸς ἐσπιλωμένον χιτῶνα
    hating even the clothing soiled by the flesh

Rev 20:4 **ἐβασίλευσαν** μετὰ τοῦ Χριστοῦ χίλια ἔτη
    they reigned with Christ for a thousand years

➡ B. Causative Active (a.k.a. Ergative Active)

1. Definition

The subject is not directly involved in the action, but may be said to be the ultimate source or cause of it. That cause may be volitional, but is not necessarily so. As might be expected, often the causative idea is part of the lexeme (especially with -όω and -ίζω verbs), though other verbs can also be ergative without any help from the verbal stem (as in most examples listed below). This usage is fairly common if such lexically-colored verbs are taken into account.

2. Key to Identification

For the simple verb, sometimes the gloss *cause to* can be used before the verb and its object; in such cases it is usually best to convert the verb to a passive (e.g., *he causes him to be baptized*). However, this is not always appropriate. The best key is to understand the semantics involved: The subject is not the direct agent of the act, but the source behind it.

3. Illustrations

Matt 5:45 τὸν ἥλιον αὐτοῦ **ἀνατέλλει** ἐπὶ πονηροὺς καὶ ἀγαθοὺς καὶ **βρέχει** ἐπὶ δικαίους καὶ ἀδίκους
    he **causes** his sun **to rise** on [both] evil and good [people], and he **causes it to rain** on [both] the righteous and unrighteous

John 3:22   ἦλθεν ὁ Ἰησοῦς καὶ οἱ μαθηταὶ αὐτοῦ εἰς τὴν Ἰουδαίαν γῆν καὶ ἐκεῖ διέτριβεν μετʼ αὐτῶν καὶ **ἐβάπτιζεν**

Jesus and his disciples came into the land of Judea and he remained there with them and **was baptizing**

> The immediate context gives no clue that this is causative, but in 4:1-2 the evangelist mentions that the Pharisees had misunderstood Jesus to be directly involved in the baptisms, for "Jesus was not baptizing but his disciples were" (v 2).

John 19:1   **ἐμαστίγωσεν**
he scourged [him]

> Pilate **caused** Jesus to be scourged, but did not perform the act himself.

Acts 21:11   Τάδε λέγει τὸ πνεῦμα τὸ ἅγιον, Τὸν ἄνδρα οὗ ἐστιν ἡ ζώνη αὕτη οὕτως **δήσουσιν** ἐν Ἰερουσαλὴμ οἱ Ἰουδαῖοι καὶ **παραδώσουσιν** εἰς χεῖρας ἐθνῶν.

The Holy Spirit says this: "Thus the Jews in Jerusalem **will bind** the man who owns this belt and **will hand** [him] **over** to the hands of the Gentiles."

> The prophecy by Agabus (already identified as a true prophet in Acts 11:28) was fulfilled in Acts 21:33 (where a Roman tribune arrested Paul and ordered him to be bound) and in the remainder of the book (where Paul is successively brought, as a prisoner, up the chain of command until he got to Rome). Paul was not, strictly speaking, *bound* by the Jews, but by the Romans because a riot was breaking out in the temple over Paul. And he was not, strictly speaking, *handed over* by the Jews to the Romans, but was in fact arrested and later protected by the Romans because of a Jewish plot to kill him. What are we to say of this prophecy? Only that because of the Jews' *actions* Paul was bound and handed over to the Gentiles. They were the unwitting cause, but the cause nevertheless.[9]

1 Cor 3:6   ἐγὼ ἐφύτευσα, Ἀπολλῶς **ἐπότισεν**, ἀλλὰ ὁ θεὸς **ηὔξανεν**
I planted, Apollos **watered**, but God **caused** [it] **to grow**

> The verb ποτίζω, like many verbs, is causative lexically (note the -ίζω ending).

Cf. also Acts 16:3; Gal 2:4; Eph 4:16; 1 Pet 1:22; Jude 13; Rev 7:15; 8:6.

→ ## C. *Stative Active*

1. Definition

The subject exists in the state indicated by the verb. This kind of active includes both equative verbs (copulas) and verbs that are *translated* with

---

[9] Recently some scholars have argued that Agabus' prophecy was not "right on target" and that one could not appeal to the causative verb to support its accuracy. The argument is that causative verbs imply volition on the part of the ultimate agent. This is not necessarily so. Luke's usage, in particular, involves unwitting causative agents. See discussion of Acts 1:18 below. Note also 1 John 1:10 ("If we say that we have not sinned, we cause him to be a/the liar").

an adjective in the predicate (e.g., πλουτέω–"I am rich"). This usage is quite common, even routine.

2. **Key to Identification** (*I am* "*X*")

The key is simple: The stative active occurs either with the equative verb or one that in translation uses *am* + a predicate adjective.

3. **Illustrations**

Luke 16:23   **ὑπάρχων** ἐν βασάνοις
            [the rich man] **existing** in a state of torment

John 1:1   Ἐν ἀρχῇ **ἦν** ὁ λόγος
            In the beginning **was** the Word

Acts 17:5   **ζηλώσαντες** οἱ Ἰουδαῖοι
            the Jews **were jealous**

1 Cor 13:4   ἡ ἀγάπη **μακροθυμεῖ, χρηστεύεται** ἡ ἀγάπη
            love **is patient**, love **is kind**

2 Cor 8:9   **ἐπτώχευσεν** πλούσιος **ὤν**
            although he was rich, **he became poor**

2 John 7   οὗτός **ἐστιν** ὁ πλάνος καὶ ὁ ἀντίχριστος
            this **is** the deceiver and the antichrist

Cf. also Matt 2:16; Luke 1:53; 15:28; Phil 2:6; 1 Thess 5:14; Heb 6:15; 2 Pet 3:9; Jude 16; Rev 12:17.

→ **D. Reflexive Active**

1. **Definition**

The subject acts upon himself or herself. In such cases naturally the *reflexive pronoun* is employed as the direct object (e.g., ἑαυτόν), while the corresponding reflexive middle omits the pronoun. This usage is relatively common.

In classical Greek, this idea would have often been expressed by the middle voice.[10] However, due to the Koine tendency toward greater explictness and the concomitant erosion of subtleties, the active voice with a reflexive pronoun has increasingly replaced the (direct) reflexive

---

[10] Some NT grammarians suggest that the direct middle was the norm in classical Greek. But even here, the reflexive active was predominant (Smyth, *Greek Grammar,* 391 [§1723]: "Instead of the direct middle the active voice with the reflexive is usually employed").

middle.[11] The reason is that the subtleties of a language that could easily be mastered by native speakers tend to fall away when that language is learned by nonnatives. The direct middle is one of the subtleties in Greek that is not shared by many other languages.[12]

2. Illustrations

Mark 15:30 **σῶσον** σεαυτόν
            save yourself

John 13:4   λαβὼν λέντιον **διέζωσεν** ἑαυτόν
            taking a towel, **he girded** himself[13]

1 Cor 11:28 **δοκιμαζέτω** ἄνθρωπος ἑαυτόν
            let a person **examine** himself

Gal 6:3   εἰ δοκεῖ τις εἶναί τι μηδὲν ὤν, **φρεναπατᾷ** ἑαυτόν
            if a person thinks he is something, being nothing, **he deceives** himself

1 Tim 4:7   **γύμναζε** σεαυτὸν πρὸς εὐσέβειαν
            train yourself toward godliness

1 Pet 3:5   αἱ ἅγιαι γυναῖκες αἱ ἐλπίζουσαι εἰς θεὸν **ἐκόσμουν** ἑαυτάς
            the holy women who hoped in God would **adorn** themselves

Rev 19:7   ἡ γυνὴ αὐτοῦ **ἡτοίμασεν** ἑαυτήν
            his bride **has prepared** herself

Cf. also Matt 4:6; 19:12; Luke 1:24; John 5:18; Acts 13:46; 2 Cor 4:2; Phil 2:8; Heb 9:25; 2 Pet 2:1; 1 John 5:21; Rev 8:6 (*v.l.*).

II. Middle Voice

Definition

Defining the function of the middle voice is not an easy task because it encompasses a large and amorphous group of nuances. But in general, in the middle voice the subject *performs* or *experiences the action* expressed by the verb in such a way that *emphasizes the subject's participation*. It may be said

---

[11] In fact, the reflexive active has even encroached on the domain of the indirect middle. However, in such instances the reflexive pronoun is in the dative case, indicating benefaction (cf. ἀγοράσωσιν ἑαυτοῖς in Matt 14:15; cf. also Matt 25:9; Acts 5:35; Rom 2:5, 14; 11:4; 1 Tim 3:13; Heb 6:6). The indirect middle still predominates in the NT over the reflexive active.

[12] For more information on the shift from classical to Koine, see the chapter on "The Language of the New Testament."

[13] Luke, as a more literary author, occasionally uses the direct middle with –ζώννυμι verbs (cf. Luke 12:37; 17:8).

that the subject acts "with a vested interest." "The middle voice shows that the action is performed with special reference to the subject."[14] Perhaps the best definition is this: "The middle calls special attention to the subject . . . the subject is acting in relation to himself somehow."[15]

The difference between the active and middle is one of emphasis. The active voice emphasizes the *action* of the verb; the middle emphasizes the *actor* [subject] of the verb. "It, in some way, relates the action more intimately to the subject."[16] This difference can be expressed, to some degree, in English translation. For many middle voices (especially the indirect middle), putting the subject in *italics* would communicate this emphasis.

Clarification

A few points of clarification are in order before we proceed:

- For Koine Greek, the term *middle* has become a misnomer, because it inherently describes that voice that stands halfway between the active and the passive. Only the direct middle truly does this (in that the subject is both the agent and receiver of the action). Since the direct middle is phasing out in Hellenistic Greek, the term is hardly descriptive of the voice as a whole.

- Not infrequently the difference between the active and middle of the same verb is more lexical than grammatical. Sometimes the shift is between transitive and intransitive, between causative and non-causative, or some other similar alteration. Though not always predictable, such changes in meaning from active to middle usually make good sense and are true to the genius of the voices.[17] For example:

---

[14] Smyth, *Greek Grammar*, 390.

[15] Robertson, *Grammar*, 804. Another helpful definition, though somewhat more restricted in its application, is that the "subject intimately participates in the results of the action" (Young, *Intermediate Greek*,134).

[16] Dana-Mantey, 157.

[17] Some verbs have followed separate paths for active and middle, in which, by the Koine period, there is virtually no overlap in the field of meaning. E.g., ἅπτω (I light, kindle)–ἅπτομαι (I touch, take hold of); ἄρχω (I begin)–ἄρχομαι (I rule).

For other verbs, the distinctions in classical Greek virtually disappeared in the Hellenistic era. E.g., in the classical period γαμέω meant *I marry* (used of the man), while γαμέομαι meant *I marry, am given in marriage* (used of the woman). But in the Koine period this distinction is often blurred (cf. P. Eleph. 2.8; BGU 717.16; Mark 10:12; 1 Cor 7:9-10; 1 Tim 4:3). Cf. also τίθημι–τίθεμαι (BAGD, 816: "II. middle, basically not different in mng. fr. the act."). γράφω–γράφομαι is not to be listed as a blurred distinction in the NT, since the middle form does not occur. In any event, the technical force of γράφομαι as *bring a lawsuit* would not find too many occasions for usage in the NT, and even where it would be appropriate (e.g., 1 Cor 6) the verb γράφω–in any voice–is not used at all.

Active	Middle
αἱρέω–*I take*	αἱρέομαι–*I choose, prefer*
ἀναμιμνῄσκω–*I remind*	ἀναμιμνῄσκομαι–*I remember*
ἀποδίδωμι–*I give away*	ἀποδίδομαι–*I sell*
ἀπόλλυμι–*I destroy*	ἀπόλλυμαι–*I perish*[18]
δανείζω–*I lend*	δανείζομαι–*I borrow*
ἐνεργέω–*I work*	ἐνεργέομαι–*I work* (only impersonal)[19]
ἐπικαλέω–*I call upon, name*	ἐπικαλέομαι–*I appeal*
ἔχω–*I have, hold*	ἔχομαι–*I cling to*
κληρόω–*I appoint, choose*	κληρόομαι–*I obtain, possess, receive*
κομίζω–*I bring*	κομίζομαι–*I get, receive*
κρίνω–*I judge*	κρίνομαι–*I bring a lawsuit*
παύω–*I stop* (transitive)	παύομαι–*I cease* (intransitive)
πείθω–*I persuade, convince*	πείθομαι–*I obey, trust*[20]
φυλάσσω–*I guard*	φυλάσσομαι–*I am on my guard*

† A. Direct Middle (a.k.a. Reflexive or Direct Reflexive)

1. Definition

With the direct middle, the subject acts *on* himself or herself. The genius of the middle can most clearly be seen by this use. But because of its very subtlety, nonnative speakers tended to replace this with more familiar forms.[21] Thus although the direct middle was frequently used in classical Greek, because of the Hellenistic tendency toward explicitness, this usage has increasingly been replaced by the reflexive active. In the NT, the direct middle is quite rare, used almost exclusively with certain verbs whose lexical nuance included a reflexive notion (such as putting on clothes), or in a set idiom that had become fixed in the language.[22]

---

[18] With ἀπόλλυμι the change from active to middle is more pronounced: the middle now has the force of a passive (which form does not occur in the NT).

[19] In the NT and early patristic literature, the difference in meaning between the two voices is not lexical, but syntactical. Although an impersonal subject occurs with the active frequently enough (cf. Matt 14:2; 1 Cor 12:11; Eph 2:2 [probable]), the middle occurs only with impersonal subjects. Thus, in 1 Thess 2:13 the subject of ἐνεργεῖται is apparently λόγος rather than θεός.

[20] This distinction is sometimes blurred in the NT, especially with the perfect and pluperfect forms (in which the active voice is used for *I trust, am persuaded*). But cf. Rom 2:8; Gal 5:7.

[21] Indeed, the direct middle was not even the most common way to express the reflexive idea in the classical period; the reflexive active was more common even at that time (Smyth, *Greek Grammar*, 391 [§1723]).

[22] As well, such direct middles are usually restricted to "external and natural acts" (ibid., 390 [§1717]).

Some grammarians dispute whether the direct middle even occurs in the NT,[23] but such a position is overstated. Even though it is rare and not all the proposed examples are clear, there is a sufficient number to establish its usage.

2. **Key to Identification** (verb + *self* [as direct object])

This is semantically equivalent to an active verb with a reflexive pronoun as object: simply add *himself, herself,* etc. as direct object to the verb.

3. **Illustrations**

   a. **Clear Examples**

Matt 27:5 &ἀπήγξατο
he hanged himself

> Moulton considers this to be the best example in the NT, but still disputes it, arguing that the meaning is "he choked."[24] But ἀπάγχομαι regularly bore the force of hanging oneself in the classical period[25] and this apparently became something of a stereotyped idiom by the Koine era.

Mark 14:54 ἦν . . . **θερμαινόμενος** πρὸς τὸ φῶς
[Peter] was **warming himself** by the fire

Luke 12:37 **περιζώσεται**
he will gird himself

Acts 12:21 ὁ Ἡρῴδης **ἐνδυσάμενος** ἐσθῆτα βασιλικὴν
Herod **clothed himself** with royal clothing

> Since the aorist has distinct forms for the middle and passive, this can hardly mean "Herod was clothed."[26]

Rev 3:18 ἀγοράσαι παρ᾽ ἐμοῦ . . . ἱμάτια λευκὰ ἵνα **περιβάλῃ**
buy from me . . . white garments that **you might clothe yourself**

Cf. also Matt 6:29; 27:24; Mark 14:67; Luke 7:6 (possible); 12:15 (possible); John 18:18; 1 Cor 14:8 (possible); 2 Cor 11:14 (possible); 2 Thess 2:4 (possible).

   b. **Debatable and Exegetically Significant Passage**

Rom 9:22 σκεύη ὀργῆς **κατηρτισμένα** εἰς ἀπώλειαν
vessels of wrath, **prepared/having prepared themselves** for destruction

> The view that the perfect participle is middle, and therefore a direct middle, finds its roots in Chrysostom, and is later echoed by Pelagius.

---

[23] See especially Moulton, *Prolegomena*, 155–57.

[24] Moulton, *Prolegomena*, 155; Moule, *Idiom Book*, 24.

[25] See LSJ, 174; Smyth, *Greek Grammar*, 391 (§1723).

[26] This text is an instance of a direct middle with the implied reflexive pronoun in an implied double accusative construction. Occasionally, the reflexive pronoun also occurs with reflexive actives and redundant middles in double accusatives constructions.

The idea would be that these vessels of wrath "had prepared themselves for destruction." Along these lines, it is also sometimes argued that such vessels can change their course: Although they were preparing themselves for destruction, they have the ability to avert disaster.[27] To take the verb as a passive would mean that they "had been prepared for destruction," without a specific mention of the agent.

The middle view has little to commend it. First, grammatically, the direct middle is quite rare and is used almost exclusively in certain idiomatic expressions, especially where the verb is used consistently with such a notion (as in the verbs for putting on clothes). This is decidedly not the case with καταρτίζω: nowhere else in the NT does it occur as a direct middle.[28] Second, in the perfect tense, the middle-passive form is always to be taken as a passive in the NT (Luke 6:40; 1 Cor 1:10; Heb 11:3)–a fact that, in the least, argues against an idiomatic use of this verb as a direct middle. Third, the lexical nuance of καταρτίζω, coupled with the perfect tense, suggests something of a "done deal." Although some commentators suggest that the verb means that the vessels are *ready* for destruction,[29] both the lexical nuance of complete preparation and the grammatical nuance of the perfect tense are against this. Fourth, the context argues strongly for a passive and completed notion. In v 20 the vessel is shaped by God's will, not its own ("Will that which is molded say to its maker, 'Why have you made me this way?'"). In v 21, Paul asks a question with οὐκ (thus expecting a positive answer): Is not the destiny of the vessels (one for honor, one for dishonor) entirely predetermined by their Creator? Verse 22 is the answer to that question. To argue, then, that κατηρτισμένα is a direct middle seems to fly in the face of grammar (the normal use of the voice and tense), lexeme, and context.[30]

B. Redundant Middle

1. Definition

The redundant middle is the use of the middle voice in a reflexive manner with a reflexive pronoun.[31] In terms of overall force, this use of the voice could be regarded as a subcategory of the direct middle; however,

---

[27] For the argument, see Cranfield, *Romans* (ICC) 2.495-96.

[28] The verb occurs 13 times in the NT, seven as a middle or passive form. Of those seven, two are definitely middle, being aorist (Matt 21:16; Heb 10:5), and both are obviously indirect middles. The other four (Rom 9:22 being excluded from the count) are all almost surely passive (Luke 6:40; 1 Cor 1:10; 2 Cor 13:11; Heb 11:3).

[29] So B. Weiss in MeyerK and Cranfield (ICC), *loc. cit.* Against this, G. Delling notes that the lexical notion of ripeness for destruction has "no philological justification" (*TDNT* 1.476, n. 2).

[30] Cranfield argues against this view by pointing out that in v 23 Paul used an active verb with a προ- prefix for the divine preparations of the vessels of mercy. Although true, the reason for the switch in verbs seems to be that the focus of the passage is on the benefit that accrues to the elect (note the ἵνα-clause at the beginning of v 23 ["in order to make known the riches of his glory on the vessels of mercy"], indicating the purpose of God's dealing with the vessels of wrath in v 22). Further, this view ignores the context in which God's predetermining will for both kinds of vessels is asserted (vv 20-23).

whereas the direct middle is inherently reflexive, the redundant middle requires an explicit pronoun to convey the reflexive notion.[32] Like its more subtle counterpart, the redundant middle is not common in the NT, being replaced by the reflexive active.

2. Key to Identification

The presence of a reflexive pronoun as the direct object of the middle voice verb is the key.

3. Illustrations

Luke 20:20   ἀπέστειλαν ἐγκαθέτους **ὑποκρινομένους** ἑαυτοὺς δικαίους εἶναι
they sent spies **who made** themselves out to be righteous

Rom 6:11   **λογίζεσθε** ἑαυτοὺς εἶναι νεκροὺς τῇ ἁμαρτίᾳ
consider yourselves to be dead to sin

2 Tim 2:13   **ἀρνήσασθαι** ἑαυτὸν οὐ δύναται
he is unable **to deny** himself

> The idiom of "denying oneself" is also found in the dominical calls to discipleship, with the same voice–pronoun combination (cf. Matt 16:24; Mark 8:34; Luke 9:23).

Jas 1:22   **παραλογιζόμενοι** ἑαυτούς
deceiving yourselves

➡ ## C. Indirect Middle (a.k.a. Indirect Reflexive, Benefactive, Intensive, Dynamic Middle[33])

1. Definition

The subject acts *for* (or sometimes *by*) himself or herself, or in his or her *own interest*. The subject thus shows a special interest in the action of the verb. This is a common use of the middle in the NT; apart from the deponent middle, it is the most common. This usage is closest to the general definition of the middle suggested by many grammarians. For example, Robertson says that "the middle calls special attention to the subject . . .

---

[31] Some examples of middle verb plus reflexive pronoun function reciprocally and do not fit this category, though they usually have the pronoun in a prepositional phrase (cf. Mark 11:31; Luke 20:5).

[32] Another distinction is that the redundant middle is normally used with verbs that have no active forms (e.g., ἀρνέομαι). Some of these could arguably be labelled as deponents, though the personal involvement of the subject (a litmus test for middles) usually seems to be inherent in the lexeme.

[33] Some grammars treat the dynamic middle and the deponent middle as synonymous terms.

the subject is acting in relation to himself somehow."[34] This is an apt description of the indirect middle.

2. Clarification and Semantics

The indirect middle is regarded as a broad, amorphous category in our treatment. Some grammars, however, distinguish the *intensive* middle from the *indirect* middle, arguing that the intensive middle focuses attention on the subject, as if the intensive pronoun (αὐτός) had been used with the subject,[35] while with the indirect middle it is as if the reflexive pronoun in the dative case had been used. This is a helpful distinction. We have lumped them together because, pragmatically, they are too similar to distinguish in most situations.

3. The Middle Voice and the Nature of NT Greek

One's view of the nature of NT Greek has strong implications for this use of the middle voice. If one thinks that NT Greek has abandoned the rules of classical Greek, then he/she would not put much emphasis on the force of the middle voice in a given passage. Moule, for example, argues that "as a rule, it is far from easy to come down from the fence with much decisiveness on either side in an exegetical problem if it depends on the voice."[36]

However, if one thinks that the NT Greek has, for the most part, retained the rules of classical Greek, then he/she will see more significance in the use of the middle voice. On this side of the fence, Zerwick writes: "The 'indirect' use of the middle voice ... especially shows the writers to have retained a feeling for even the finer distinctions between the sense of active and middle forms."[37]

It is our contention that a careful examination of the usage of a particular middle voice verb in Hellenistic Greek will shed light on how much can be made of the voice. What is frequently at stake, grammatically speaking, is whether the middle is to be considered indirect or deponent.[38] The student is urged to examine both this section on the indirect middle and the section on the deponent middle for guidelines in making a decision.

---

[34] Robertson, *Grammar*, 804.

[35] There are actually a few instances in which an "intensive" middle occurs with an intensive αὐτός: Should such examples collectively be labeled *indirect redundant middle*? Cf. Acts 27:36; 28:28; Heb 5:2.

[36] Moule, *Idiom Book*, 24.

[37] Zerwick, *Biblical Greek*, 75.

[38] Other factors that affect one's view of a particular middle verb are set idiom, lexically-colored verb stems, and a given author's literary background and finesse. Winer-Moulton notes that "even in classical Greek the use of this voice seems to have often depended on the culture and tact of the individual writer" (322). In this respect, I can agree with Moule's assessment, for the difficulty lay not with the power of the middle voice per se, but with the interpreter's apprehension of its force.

4. Illustrations

a. Clear Examples

Matt 27:12 ἐν τῷ κατηγορεῖσθαι αὐτὸν ὑπὸ τῶν ἀρχιερέων καὶ πρεσβυτέρων οὐδὲν **ἀπεκρίνατο**

When he was accused by the chief priests and elders, **he answered** nothing **[in his own defense]**.

> ἀποκρίνομαι is almost always put in the aorist passive in the NT and in that form has a deponent force. In the middle (seven instances in the aorist[39]) the verb connotes a solemn or legal utterance.[40] This is in keeping with the genius of the middle voice, for a legal defense is more than a mere response–it involves a vested interest on the part of the speaker. Cf. also Mark 14:61; Luke 3:16; 23:9; John 5:17, 19; Acts 3:12.

Matt 27:24 ὁ Πιλᾶτος . . . **ἀπενίψατο** τὰς χεῖρας . . . λέγων· ἀθῷός εἰμι ἀπὸ τοῦ αἵματος τούτου

Pilate **washed his hands** saying, "I am innocent of this man's blood"

> The force of the middle of ἀπονίπτω puts a special focus on Pilate, as though this act could absolve him.

Luke 10:42 Μαριὰμ τὴν ἀγαθὴν μερίδα **ἐξελέξατο**

Mary **has chosen [for herself]** the good part

> The idea is that Mary chose *for herself* the good part. Although ἐκλέγω does not occur as an active verb in the NT, it does in Hellenistic Greek in general and hence ought not to be taken as a deponent.

Acts 5:2 καὶ **ἐνοσφίσατο** ἀπὸ τῆς τιμῆς

and he **kept back** [some] of the price **[for himself]**

Eph 1:4 **ἐξελέξατο** ἡμᾶς

he chose us **[for himself]**

> God chose us *for* himself, *by* himself, or for his own interests. This does not, of course, imply that God needed believers. Rather, just as the chief end of human beings is to glorify God and enjoy him forever, so too God is in the business of glorifying himself. And as is mentioned three times in Eph 1, the elect belong to God "for the praise of his glory." On ἐκλέγω in general, see discussion above under Luke 10:42.

Eph 5:16 **ἐξαγοραζόμενοι** τὸν καιρόν

redeeming the time **[for yourself]**

Jas 1:21 **δέξασθε** τὸν ἔμφυτον λόγον

receive [for yourselves] the implanted word

> Although δέχομαι never occurs as an active, it should not be treated as a deponent verb. The lexical notion of receiving, welcoming connotes a special interest on the part of the subject.

Cf. also Matt 10:1; 20:22; Acts 10:23; 25:11; 27:38; Rom 15:7; 2 Cor 3:18; Gal 4:10; Phil 1:22; Col 4:5; Heb 9:12.

---

[39] The present also occurs, but since there is no distinction in form between the middle and passive in the present, it is not easy to tell which voice is meant.

[40] So BAGD.

b. A Debatable and Exegetically Significant Text

1 Cor 13:8   εἴτε προφητεῖαι, καταργηθήσονται· εἴτε γλῶσσαι, **παύσονται**· εἴτε γνῶσις, καταργηθήσεται

If there are prophecies, they will be done away; if there are tongues, **they will cease [on their own]**; if there is knowledge, it will be done away.

> If the voice of the verb here is significant, then Paul is saying either that tongues will cut themselves off (direct middle) or, more likely, cease of their own accord, i.e., "die out" without an intervening agent (indirect middle). It may be significant that with reference to prophecy and knowledge, Paul used a different verb (καταργέω) and put it in the *passive* voice. In vv 9–10, the argument continues: "for we *know* in part and we *prophesy* in part; but when the perfect comes, the partial shall be done away [καταργηθήσονται]." Here again, Paul uses the same passive verb he had used with prophecy and knowledge and he speaks of the verbal counterpart to the nominal "prophecy" and "knowledge." Yet he does *not* speak about *tongues* being done away "when the perfect comes." The implication *may* be that tongues were to have "died out" of their own *before* the perfect comes. The middle voice in this text, then, must be wrestled with if one is to come to any conclusions about when tongues would cease.
>
> The dominant opinion among NT scholars today, however, is that παύσονται is not an indirect middle. The argument is that παύω in the future is deponent, and that the change in verbs is merely stylistic. If so, then this text makes no comment about tongues ceasing on their own, apart from the intervention of "the perfect." There are three arguments against the deponent view, however. First, if παύσονται is deponent, then the second principal part (future form) should not occur in the *active* voice in Hellenistic Greek. But it does, and it does so frequently.[41] Hence, the verb *cannot* be considered deponent. Second, sometimes Luke 8:24 is brought into the discussion: Jesus rebuked the wind and sea and they *ceased* (ἐπαύσαντο, aorist middle) from their turbulence.[42] The argument is that inanimate objects cannot cease of their own accord; therefore, the middle of παύω is equivalent to a passive. But this is a misunderstanding of the literary features of the passage: If the wind and sea cannot cease voluntarily, why does Jesus *rebuke* them? And why do the disciples speak of the wind and sea as having *obeyed* Jesus? The elements are personified in Luke 8 and their ceasing from turbulence is therefore presented as volitional obedience to Jesus. If anything, Luke 8:24 supports the indirect middle view. Third, the idea of a

---

[41] A search of the *TLG* database revealed *hundreds* of such instances, normally bearing the meaning "stop something." Further, the future middle of παύω was consistently used in the same period with the meaning of "stop" or "cease." (Thanks are due to Ronnie Black for his research on this topic done for the course Advanced Greek Grammar at Dallas Seminary, Spring 1992.)

It is somewhat surprising that the "deponent view" is so often assumed without a prior investigation into extra-NT Greek. Since the second principal part occurs in the active voice in Hellenistic Greek, to maintain that παύσονται is deponent is to imply that the language of the NT is a unique dialect. The very scholars who call it deponent, however, are equally adamant that NT Greek was a part of the Hellenistic language.

[42] Again, the *TLG* database revealed that the third principal part, like the second principal part, was an active form in Koine Greek.

deponent verb is that it is middle in form, but *active* in meaning. But παύσονται is surrounded by *passives* in 1 Cor 13:8, not actives.[43] The real force of παύω in the middle is *intransitive*, while in the active it is transitive. In the active it has the force of stopping some other object; in the middle, it ceases from its own activity.

In sum, the deponent view is based on some faulty assumptions as to the labeling of παύσονται as deponent, the parallel in Luke 8:24, and even the meaning of deponency. Paul seems to be making a point that is more than stylistic in his shift in verbs. But this is not to say that the middle voice in 1 Cor 13:8 *proves* that tongues already ceased! This verse does not specifically address *when* tongues would cease, although it is giving a *terminus ad quem*: when the perfect comes.[44]

D. *Causative Middle*

1. Definition

The subject *has* something done *for* or *to* himself or herself. As well, the subject may be the *source* behind an action done in his/her behalf. This usage, though rare, involves some exegetically important texts.

2. Key to Identification

See definition.

3. Semantics

The semantics of the causative middle need to be seen in light of three poles: volition vs. involuntary cause, causative active vs. causative middle, and causative middle vs. permissive middle.

- The cause may be *volitional*, but is not necessarily so. Volition is sometimes incorrectly assumed to be an essential part of a causative verb. Certainly it is one kind of source behind an action, but both personal and impersonal subjects act involuntarily at times and in such a way that they become unwitting sources of another action.

- The difference between the causative *active* and causative *middle* is that the causative active simply implies the source behind an action, while the causative middle implies both source and results: The action was caused by someone who also was the recipient of its

---

[43] Although it is true that the future middle is occasionally used in a passive sense (Smyth, *Greek Grammar*, 390 [§1715]; Winer-Moulton, 319), it is apparently so with certain verbs because of a set idiom. Such is not the case with παύω.

[44] As we discussed in the chapter on adjectives, there is no good reason for taking τὸ τέλειον as the close of the canon. Unfortunately, the view presented above about παύσονται is typically associated with the canon-view of the "perfect." Perhaps this is why it has gotten little respect.

outcome in some sense. The causative middle is thus an indirect middle or occasionally a direct middle as well.

- The *causative* middle is very close to the *permissive* middle. The former implies ultimate source and often volition; the latter suggests that the prompting lay elsewhere and only that consent or permission or toleration was wrung from the subject. Some of the illustrations below could conceivably belong in either category, depending on extra-grammatical features (such as context, historical background, etc.).

4. Illustrations

Luke 11:38 ὁ Φαρισαῖος ἰδὼν ἐθαύμασεν ὅτι οὐ πρῶτον **ἐβαπτίσατο** πρὸ τοῦ ἀρίστου[45]

When the Pharisee saw this, he was amazed because [Jesus] did not first **have himself washed** before the meal

> This is an example of a *direct* middle (not uncommon with verbs for bathing), and is probably causative: Jesus as a guest in the Pharisee's house would be washed by another.

Acts 21:24 τούτους παραλαβὼν . . . καὶ δαπάνησον ἐπ᾽ αὐτοῖς ἵνα **ξυρήσονται** τὴν κεφαλήν

take these men . . . and pay their expenses that **they might have** their head **shaved**

Gal 5:12 ὄφελον καὶ **ἀποκόψονται** οἱ ἀναστατοῦντες ὑμᾶς[46]

Would that those who are troubling you **have themselves castrated!**

> This is an example of a causative *direct* middle.

Rev 3:5 ὁ νικῶν **περιβαλεῖται** ἐν ἱματίοις λευκοῖς

the one who conquers **will cause himself to be clothed** in white clothing

> Like Gal 5:12, this is an example of a causative *direct* middle. Direct middles are not uncommon with verbs meaning "to put on clothes."

Acts 1:18 **ἐκτήσατο** χωρίον

he purchased a field [**for himself**]

> The text seems to suggest that Judas himself purchased the field in which he was later buried. However, Matt 27:7 specifically states that the *chief priests* purchased the field after Judas had died. It would be difficult to reconcile these two texts from the English point of view. But from the Greek, it is easy to see ἐκτήσατο as a *causative* middle, indicating that ultimately Judas purchased the field, in that it was purchased with his "blood money." Another possibility here is that since this verb never had an active form, it might be deponent, having the force of a

---

[45] The reading ἐβαπτίσατο is found in 𝔓[45] 700, while almost all other witnesses read ἐβαπτίσθη. Most likely the passive is original, being better attested externally and even more difficult (since the Pharisee's amazement would presumably be due to Jesus intentionally not washing his hands).

[46] ἀποκόψωνται is found in 𝔓[46] D E F G *et alii.*

causative *active*.[47] However, it seems that it retains a middle *force* from classical to Koine Greek, and thus should be considered a true middle. In classical Greek (especially in Sophocles, Euripides, and Thucidydes) κτάομαι often had the causative nuance of "bring misfortune upon oneself" (cf. LSJ, BAGD). Such a nuance may even be appropriate in a secondary role to "acquire" in Acts 1:18.

Cf. also Matt 5:42; 20:1.

E. Permissive Middle

1. Definition

The subject *allows* something to be done *for* or *to* himself or herself. This usage, though rare, involves some exegetically important texts.

Not infrequently a particular verb will be used almost in a set idiom, giving rise to the notion that the permissive (or causative) middle is due to the lexical force of the verb stem.[48] βαπτίζω is often cited as such a verb. But since the same verb is often used without any hint of permission, it is better to regard this as an occasional idiom that is not intrinsically related to the lexeme. Nevertheless, if a particular verb has established instances of permissive middle, this strengthens the case in the debatable passages.

2. Key to Identification

See definition. As well, a good "rough and ready" test is to translate the verb as a *passive*. If this makes sense–and if the notion of permission or allowance seems also to be implied–the verb is a good candidate for permissive middle. (It should be noted that most permissive middles are usually best translated as passives; the glosses provided below are intended only to illustrate the usage.)

3. Semantics

The semantics of the permissive middle can be seen in the light of three other grammatical categories:[49]

- The *permissive* middle is very close to the *causative* middle. The latter implies ultimate source and often volition; the former suggests that the prompting lay elsewhere and only that consent or permission or toleration was wrung from the subject. Some of the illustrations below could conceivably belong in either category, depending on extra-grammatical features (such as context, historical background, etc.).

---

[47] If so, then it forms an even greater parallel to the involuntary causative active in Acts 21:11, mentioned above.

[48] So Robertson, *Grammar*, 808.

[49] See the semantics of the causative middle above for comparison.

- The *permissive* middle has a certain affinity with the *direct* middle in that with both the subject is the receiver of the action. But whereas with the direct middle the subject is also the actor, with the permissive middle the subject does not perform the action.

- The *permissive* middle is also like a *passive* in that the subject is the receiver of the action, but it is unlike the passive in that the middle always implies acknowledgment, consent, toleration, or permission of the action of the verb. The passive normally implies no such cognition.[50]

> An exception to this principle is the permissive passive. It is important to note that although both categories are rare (some grammarians even dispute the legitimacy of the permissive passive), the volitional element is almost always a part of the middle voice while it is almost always lacking in the passive.[50]

4. Illustrations

Luke 2:5   ἀνέβη Ἰωσὴφ ἀπὸ τῆς Γαλιλαίας . . . (5) **ἀπογράψασθαι** σὺν Μαριὰμ

Joseph went up from Galilee . . . (5) **to be enrolled** with Mary

> The idea seems to be that Joseph "allowed himself to be enrolled." That this is permissive is evident by vv 1, 3, in which the passive is apparently used (ἀπογράφεσθαι). The permissive middle makes explicit the notion of volition that is not naturally borne by the passive.

Acts 22:16   ἀναστὰς **βάπτισαι** καὶ **ἀπόλουσαι** τὰς ἁμαρτίας σου

Rise, **have yourself baptized** and **allow** your sins **to be washed away**

> If βάπτισαι were a direct middle, the idea would be "baptize yourself"–a thoroughly unbiblical concept.[51] If ἀπόλουσαι were an indirect middle, the idea would be "wash away your sins by yourself"–also thoroughly unbiblical. This particular verb occurs as a causative or permissive middle in 1 Cor 6:11 (see below), its only other NT occurrence. The force of the voices here seems to be causative or permissive direct middle for βάπτισαι and permissive indirect middle for ἀπόλουσαι.[52]

---

[50] This is not to say that the subject of a passive verb is *not* cognizant of the action, but rather that the passive makes *no comment* about the subject's recognition of it. A mistake often made by students is the assumption that grammatical forms regularly make negative statements. Thus, the pluperfect is popularly conceived to mean that something accomplished in the past had results that continued in the past, but stopped before the present began; or the aorist is typically assumed not to be able to describe an action that, in reality, was progressive, or iterative, etc. Such a "negative assessment" is the argument from silence run amock.

[51] Though this was the method that Judaism practiced in the first century. βαπτίζω occurs 77 times in the NT: 45 passives, 30 actives, only two in the middle voice (Acts 22:16 and Mark 7:4 [referring to ritual cleansing]), unless the *v.ll.* in Luke 11:38 (see above, under causative middle) and in 1 Cor 10:2 (see below) are accepted. In all this there is no evidence that believers baptized themselves. In particular, in the earlier version of Paul's conversion (Acts 9:1-19), the passive is used (ἀναστὰς **ἐβαπτίσθη** in v 18).

[52] So Robertson, *Grammar*, 808.

1 Cor 6:11   ταῦτά τινες ἦτε· ἀλλὰ **ἀπελούσασθε**, ἀλλὰ ἡγιάσθητε, ἀλλὰ ἐδικαιώθητε

Such things were some [of you]. But **you allowed yourselves to be washed**, you were sanctified, you were justified

1 Cor 10:2   πάντες εἰς τὸν Μωϋσῆν **ἐβαπτίσαντο**

all **were baptized** into Moses

> The force of the middle here is close to a passive, but it adds the element of cognition of the action and permission or voluntary cause (this example might even fit better under causative middle). It is significant that many manuscripts have the passive ἐβαπτίσθησαν instead of the middle here (indeed, the passive is most likely original).[53] A translation that might bring out the force of the middle would be, "and all allowed themselves to be baptized into Moses" (permissive) or "and all had themselves baptized into Moses" (causative).

Cf. also John 13:10;[54] Acts 15:22 (possible);[55] 1 Cor 6:7 (forms could be passive or middle); 11:6; Gal 5:12*(or, more likely, causative).

F. Reciprocal Middle

1. Definition

The middle voice may be used with a *plural subject* to represent interaction among themselves. There is an interchange of effort among the subjects. This idiom is being replaced in Koine by an active with the reciprocal pronoun ἀλλήλων.[56] It is quite rare in the NT, most of the examples being disputed.

2. Illustrations

Matt 26:4   **συνεβουλεύσαντο** ἵνα τὸν Ἰησοῦν . . . κρατήσωσιν

they resolved together that they should arrest Jesus

John 9:22   ἤδη **συνετέθειντο** οἱ Ἰουδαῖοι

the Jews **had already agreed with one another**

Cf. also John 12:10; 1 Cor 5:9 (possible).[57]

---

[53] The middle is the reading found in 𝔓⁴⁶ᶜ B K L P *et plu* (𝔓⁴⁶* has ἐβαπτίζοντο), though not supported by NA²⁷. Although it may have a superior pedigree internally, the early and widespread nature of the passive ἐβαπτίσθησαν argues strongly for its originality.

[54] That νίψασθαι is most likely a permissive middle rather than a direct middle is due to the context: This pronouncement is made while Jesus is washing Peter's feet. Thus the idea of v 10 is "the one who has been bathed does not need *to allow himself to be washed,* except for his feet."

[55] ἐκλεξαμένους–if the subject is the men (ἄνδρας), the idea would be that Silas and Barsabbas *allowed themselves to be chosen* for the mission. It is more probable, however, that ἄνδρας is the object and "the apostles and elders" is the implied subject. See Winer-Moulton, 320.

[56] In 1 Cor 16:20 a middle verb takes the reciprocal pronoun as its object: ἀσπάσασθε ἀλλήλους. This could be regarded as a *redundant reciprocal middle*, in spite of the fact that ἀσπάζομαι, on the surface, appears to be deponent.

[57] Robertson, *Grammar*, also lists John 6:52; Acts 19:8; and 1 Cor 6:1 among his examples, but these are doubtful for various reasons.

➡ G. Deponent Middle

1. Definition

A deponent middle is a middle voice verb that has no active *form* but is active in *meaning*.[58] This is the most common middle in the NT, due to the heavy use of certain verbs. English (as well as other modern Indo-European languages) has few analogies, making analysis of this phenomenon particularly difficult.[59] But in the *AV*, we read on occasion "he is come" in the sense of "he comes" (cf. Matt 12:44; John 4:25). Older English thus employed something akin to a deponent passive.[60]

The term deponent, from the Latin *deponere*, has to do with something *laid aside*. The rarely used English verb *depone* means *lay aside*. Thus, it is easy to see that a deponent verb is one that has *laid aside* its original force (whether it be middle or passive deponent) and has replaced it with an active meaning.[61]

2. Clarification

These two elements (no active form, but active force) are at the root of the definition. However, just because a verb has no active form in the *New Testament* is not reason enough to label it deponent. For example, although ἐκλέγω does not occur as an active in the NT, the middle retains its true force (cf. Luke 10:42; Eph 1:4, discussed above under "Indirect Middle"). The following are tips for wrestling with the issue of deponency (whether for middle or passive verbs):

a. The basic principle is this: *A deponent middle verb is one that has no active form for a particular **principal part** in **Hellenistic** Greek, **and** one whose force in that principal part is evidently active.* Thus, for example, ἔρχομαι has no active form for the first principal part, but it is obviously active in force. Likewise, λήμψομαι, the second principal part

---

[58] Robertson, et al., speak of the deponent middle as the *dynamic* middle (Robertson, *Grammar*, 811-12). Other grammars treat the dynamic as a synonym for the indirect middle, as we have done.

[59] "Like the rest of us, Stahl has to go into bankruptcy," admits Gildersleeve on Stahl's explanation of the deponent middle (in B. L. Gildersleeve's review of Stahl's *Syntax* in *AJP* 29 [1908] 278).

[60] This analogy is only intended to be of pedagogical, not historical value. The roots of the English "is come" and the like are not the same as the Greek deponent verb.

[61] Although Robertson objects to the term as "very unsatisfactory" since many deponents never had an active form and hence could not have laid it aside (*Grammar*, 811). But other grammarians, seeing that the thing laid aside is the middle (or passive) *force*, not the active form, are content with this term as truly descriptive of this category. Besides, the term was used originally to describe *Latin* verbs, where many of the deponents originally had an active form (so B. L. Gildersleeve and G. Lodge, *Latin Grammar*, 3rd ed., rev. and enlarged [New York: Macmillan, 1895] 110-14 [§163-66]). Further, the earliest (and consistent) usage in English of *deponent* involved the laying aside of meaning, not form (*Oxford English Dictionary*, s.v., "deponent").

of λαμβάνω, is a deponent middle. Verbs such as these that have active forms for one or more of the principal parts are called *partially deponent*. Other verbs (such as δύναμαι) that have no active form in any principal part are *completely* deponent. Many deponent verbs never had an active form; the restriction to Hellenistic Greek is thus meant to be a bare minimum requirement.[62]

b. There are some verbs that never had an active form, but the true middle force is clearly seen. For example, δέχομαι means *I receive, I welcome*–an idea that is inherently reflexive.[63] It is not enough, then, to note merely that a verb lacks an active form throughout its history; it must also be demonstrated that the middle *force* is absent.

c. Pragmatically, how should one decide whether a verb is deponent? There is no easy solution.[64] Below are listed two different approaches, the *ideal* and the *rough and ready* approach.

1) *Rough and Ready Rule*

The simplest procedure is to consider a middle (or passive) to be deponent if the lexical form of the word in BAGD is middle (or passive), not active.

The problem with this approach is that BAGD frequently lists as the lexical form of a word the only form that occurs in biblical and early patristic literature, even though in a wider context the active is used. Thus, for example, ἐκλέγομαι is the lexical form for a verb that appears as an active in Hellenistic literature. BAGD's note here, as often, should tip the student off that all is not as it appears: "the act. does not occur in our lit."

2) *The Ideal Approach*

When an exegetical decision depends in part on the voice of the verb, a more rigorous approach is required. In such cases, you should investigate the form of the word in Koine (conveniently, via Moulton–Milligan) and classical Greek

---

[62] At the same time it must be admitted that the scarcity of some active forms in the Koine period might suggest that, for one author, the middle form is deponent while for another it is a true middle. As with lexical stock, the morphological stock of various writers at a given period cannot be presumed to be identical. Much work needs to be done in this area. For the most part, NT exegetes have been content to cite lexical entries as though the NT usage *in toto* fairly represented the pool of idioms available to its authors. Such an approach, though convenient, is hardly adequate.

[63] Robertson lists this verb as a deponent, but states that "it is not hard to see the reflexive idea in δέχομαι" (*Grammar*, 813).

[64] Indeed, no two grammars agree on this issue, especially when lexical middles that seem to have a reflexive flavor are involved.

(Liddell–Scott–Jones) before you declare a verb deponent. Even then, you should not be able to see a middle *force* to the verb.[65]

d. Some *true* deponents are:
- ἅλλομαι
- ἀποκρίνομαι (deponent in sixth principal part, but not in third)
- βούλομαι
- γίνομαι (but active in the fourth principal part [γέγονα])
- δύναμαι
- ἐργάζομαι
- ἔρχομαι (but active in the third and fourth principal parts [ἦλθον, ἐλήλυθα])
- λήμψομαι (the second principal part of λαμβάνω)
- πορεύομαι
- προσεύχομαι (?)[66]
- χαρίζομαι

e. Some verbs that look deponent but most likely are not:
- ἀπεκρινάμην (only the third principal part is a true middle)[67]
- ἀρνέομαι
- ἀσπάζομαι
- βουλεύομαι
- δέχομαι
- ἐκλέγομαι
- καυχάομαι
- λογίζομαι[68]
- μιμνήσκομαι
- παύσομαι (second principal part of παύω)[69]
- προσκαλέομαι[70]

---

[65] Robertson correctly notes that verbs of mental action often have an intensive flavor (*Grammar*, 812), but he still regards them as true deponents. The issue is compounded with many middles that have a lexeme that is intrinsically reflexive: Are these true middles in which the inflection emulates what is already resident in the stem, or are they deponent (in which case the stem needs to be examined apart from the inflection)? The criteria for determining deponency still await a definitive treatment.

[66] So BAGD. It takes little imagination to see a true (indirect) middle force to this verb, however.

[67] The fact that the aorist passive as a deponent verb is most often used suggests that when the aorist middle is used it bears some force. See previous discussion under "Indirect Middle."

[68] The "thought" that is attached to this verb is usually one of a vested interest. BAGD offers among its definitions *take into account, evaluate, think (about), consider, ponder, let one's mind dwell on, be of the opinion.*

[69] See previous discussion of παύσονται in 1 Cor 13:8 under "Indirect Middle."

[70] BAGD, 715: "in secular Gk. predom., in LXX and our lit. exclusively mid."

III. Passive Voice

Definition

In general it can be said that in the passive voice the subject *is acted upon* or *receives the action* expressed by the verb. No volition–nor even necessarily awareness of the action–is implied on the part of the subject. That is, the subject may or may not be aware, its volition may or may not be involved. But these things are not stressed when the passive is used.

The passive can be treated either structurally or semantically. Older grammars tend to take just the former approach.[71] Both ways of viewing the passive are important because they ask different questions and impact exegesis in different ways.

A. Passive Constructions

1. The Passive With and Without Expressed Agency

The passive voice occurs sometimes with an agent (or means) expressed, sometimes without an agent (or means) expressed. All uses of the passive (except the deponent) naturally occur both with and without an agent. Hence, the presence or absence of an agent is not an intrinsic part of the passive's meaning, but belongs to the force of the clausal construction in which the passive is used. Nevertheless, the issue of agency does shed much light on an author's overall meaning and ought to be included in a discussion of the passive voice.

a. With Agency Expressed

Three types of agency can be expressed in Greek: ultimate agency, intermediate agency, and impersonal means. The *ultimate* agent indicates the person who is ultimately responsible for the action.[72] Sometimes the ultimate agent uses an *intermediate* agent who carries out the act for the ultimate agent. The *impersonal means* is that which an agent uses to perform an act. (Technically, means does not indicate agency, except in a broad sense.)

Three further points:

- English does not formally distinguish these categories easily, but relies largely on context. "By" covers a multitude of

---

[71] E.g., Dana-Mantey, 161-63 (§157); Robertson, *Grammar*, 814-20. But cf. also Porter, *Idioms*, 64-66.

[72] Many grammars refer to this as the *direct* agent, but this is not always an appropriate term; in fact, it could better describe the intermediate agent, because the ultimate agent's actions are mediated through an intermediate agent.

agencies. For example, when the President of the United States wants to make a statement, sometimes he does so through his press secretary. It would be appropriate to say that "a statement was made *by the president*," just as it would be appropriate to say that "a statement was made *by the press secretary*." The first sentence indicates the ultimate agent; the second the intermediate agent. Or when a baseball player steps up to the plate and, at the direction of his manager, bunts the ball, we could say that "the ball was hit *by the bat*" (impersonal means). But we could also say that "the ball was hit *by the baseball player*" (intermediate agent, acting at the manager's direction). There is no formal grammatical distinction between the two sentences.

But in Greek, a different prepositional phrase is used to indicate each kind of agency. For means a simple dative without preposition is also frequently used.[73]

- The third category is not meant to imply that the instrument used is necessarily inanimate or impersonal. Indeed, on occasion a person might be the means used by another. Impersonal means simply means that the instrument is portrayed as that which is used by another. In the sentence "God disciplined me by means of my parents," the parents are portrayed as an instrument in God's hands. Although their personalities are not in view in this sentence, it would not be legitimate to say that the speaker felt they were inanimate objects.

- Agency can be expressed with active and middle verbs, just as it can with passive verbs, although it is more common with passives. (Some of our examples below include actives and middles.)

The following table summarizes the major ways agency is expressed in the NT.[74]

Agency	Preposition (Case)	Translation
Ultimate Agent	ὑπό (gen) ἀπό (gen) παρά (gen)	by by, of from, by
Intermediate Agent	διά (gen)	through, by
Impersonal Means	ἐν (dat) dative (no prep) ἐκ (gen)	by, with by, with by, of

Table 7
How Agency is Expressed in the New Testament

---

[73] See "Dative of Means" for detailed discussion.

[74] The table is a general guideline, not an absolute rule. Not all writers are consistent. Rarely, for example, ὑπό is used with an intermediate agent (Rev 6:8) or an impersonal means (Matt 8:24). διά is rarely used for ultimate agent (see next note).

1) Ultimate Agent

The subject of a passive verb receives the action that is usually expressed by ὑπό + genitive. Sometimes ἀπό + genitive is used, rarely παρά + genitive. The ultimate agent indicates the person who is ultimately responsible for the action, who may or may not be directly involved (though he or she usually is).

Luke 1:26   **ἀπεστάλη** ὁ ἄγγελος Γαβριὴλ *ἀπὸ* τοῦ θεοῦ[75]
the angel Gabriel **was sent** *from* God

John 1:6   ἐγένετο ἄνθρωπος, **ἀπεσταλμένος** *παρὰ* θεοῦ
there came a man, **who was sent** *from* God

Acts 10:38   πάντας τοὺς **καταδυναστευομένους** *ὑπὸ* τοῦ διαβόλου
all **who were oppressed** *by* the devil

Rom 13:1   οὐ γὰρ ἔστιν ἐξουσία εἰ μὴ *ὑπὸ* θεοῦ[76]
there is no authority except *by* God

2 Cor 1:4   **παρακαλούμεθα** αὐτοὶ *ὑπὸ* τοῦ θεοῦ
we ourselves **are comforted** *by* God

Heb 11:23   Μωϋσῆς γεννηθεὶς **ἐκρύβη** τρίμηνον *ὑπὸ* τῶν πατέρων αὐτοῦ
After Moses was born, **he was hid** for three months *by* his parents.

> The preposition indicates that the parents were ultimately responsible for the hiding of the baby, but does not exclude the possibility that others (such as Moses' sister) also carried out the clandestine activity.

Jas 1:13   μηδεὶς πειραζόμενος λεγέτω ὅτι *ἀπὸ* θεοῦ **πειράζομαι**[77]
let no one say when he is tempted, "**I am tempted** *by* God"

Rev 12:6   τόπον **ἡτοιμασμένον** *ἀπὸ* τοῦ θεοῦ[78]
a place **prepared** *by* God

For ὑπό, cf. also Matt 2:15; 11:27; 14:8; Luke 4:2; 7:30; 8:29; 17:20; 21:16; John 14:21; Acts 10:33, 41, 42; 22:30; 27:11; Rom 15:15; 1 Cor 11:32; 2 Cor 2:11; Gal 3:17; 4:9; Phil 3:12; 1 Thess 2:4; Heb 5:4; 2 Pet 1:17; 3 John 12.

For ἀπό, cf. also Matt 10:28; 12:38; 20:23; 27:9; Mark 1:13; 15:45; Luke 7:35; Acts 2:22; 1 Cor 1:30; 4:5; Gal 1:1; 1 Tim 3:7; Phlm 3; Heb 6:7; 2 Pet 1:21.

For παρά, cf. Matt 21:42; Mark 12:11; Luke 1:37, 45; John 1:6.

2) Intermediate Agent

The subject of a passive verb receives the action that is expressed by διά + genitive. Here, the agent named is intermediate, not

---

[75] ὑπό is found for ἀπό in A C D X Γ Λ Π 33 *Byz.*

[76] ἀπό is found for ὑπό in D* E* F G 629 *et pauci.*

[77] ὑπό is found for ἀπό in ℵ 429 630 1505 1611 *et alii.*

[78] ὑπό is found for ἀπό in 1611 2351 *et plu.*

ultimate.[79] Though common, this usage is not as frequent as ὑπό + genitive for ultimate agency.

Matt 1:22   τὸ **ῥηθὲν** ὑπὸ κυρίου *διὰ* τοῦ προφήτου
             what **was spoken** by the Lord *through* the prophet

> In this text we see both the ultimate and intermediate agent with the passive verb. The emphasis seems to be that the prophecy is ultimately from God, but the prophet's personality was involved in the shaping of its wording. The evangelist consistently uses ὑπό for God's agency, διά for the prophet's. On διὰ προφήτου cf. Matt 2:5, 15, 17, 23; 3:3; 4:14; 8:17; 12:17; 13:35; 21:4; 24:15; 27:9. On ὑπὸ θεοῦ cf. Matt 2:15; 22:31.[80]

John 1:3   πάντα *δι'* αὐτοῦ ἐγένετο
             all things came into existence *through* him

> The Logos is represented as the Creator in a "hands-on" sort of way, with the implication that God is the ultimate agent. This is the typical (though not exclusive) pattern seen in the NT: Ultimate agency is ascribed to God the Father (with ὑπό), intermediate agency is ascribed to Christ (with διά), and "impersonal" means is ascribed to the Holy Spirit (with ἐν or the simple dative).[81]

John 3:17   **σωθῇ** ὁ κόσμος *δι'* αὐτοῦ
             the world **might be saved** *through* him

Gal 3:19   ὁ νόμος . . . **διαταγεὶς** *δι'* ἀγγέλων
             the law . . . **was ordained** *through* angels

Eph 3:10   ἵνα **γνωρισθῇ** . . . *διὰ* τῆς ἐκκλησίας ἡ πολυποίκιλος σοφία τοῦ θεοῦ
             in order that the manifold wisdom of God **might be made known** . . . *through* the church

> The implication seems to be that God's wisdom should be displayed by what the church collectively does, rather than via its mere existence (which would be expressed by ἐν ἐκκλησίᾳ).

1 Pet 4:11   **δοξάζηται** ὁ θεὸς *διὰ* Ἰησοῦ Χριστοῦ
             God **might be glorified** *through* Jesus Christ

Cf. also Luke 18:31; John 1:2, 17; Acts 2:16; Rom 5:9; 2 Cor 1:19; Eph 3:16; Phil 1:11; Col 1:16; 1 Thess 4:14; Phlm 7; Heb 2:3; 7:25.

3) Impersonal Means

The impersonal means by which the verbal action is carried out is expressed by ἐν + dative, the dative case alone (the most common construction), or rarely, ἐκ + genitive. The noun in the

---

[79] Only once is διὰ θεοῦ used in the NT (Gal 4:7 [the *v.l.* διὰ Χριστοῦ, found in numerous late MSS, indicates a scribal tension over the expression; see discussion in J. Eadie, *Galatians*, 305-06]; Gal 1:1 comes close with διὰ Ἰησοῦ Χριστοῦ καὶ θεοῦ πατρός; cf. also 1 Cor 1:9), although διὰ θελήματος θεοῦ occurs 8 times, exclusively in the *corpus Paulinum* (Rom 15:32; 1 Cor 1:1; 2 Cor 1:1; 8:5; Eph 1:1; Col 1:1; 2 Tim 1:1).

[80] Not all NT writers make this tidy of a distinction (cf. 2 Pet 3:2; Jude 17).

[81] See discussion of the NT authors' treatment of the agency of the Spirit under "Dative of Agency," in particular on Gal 5:16.

dative is not necessarily impersonal, but is conceived of as such (i.e., usually there is an implied agent who *uses* the noun in the dative as his or her instrument).[82]

Luke 14:34 ἐὰν τὸ ἅλας μωρανθῇ, ἐν τίνι **ἀρτυθήσεται**;
if the salt has lost its flavor, *by* what **will [it] be salted?**

Rom 3:28 λογιζόμεθα **δικαιοῦσθαι** πίστει ἄνθρωπον[83]
we maintain that a person **is justified** *by faith*

Heb 9:22 ἐν αἵματι πάντα **καθαρίζεται**
all things **are cleansed** *by* blood

Jas 2:22 ἐκ τῶν ἔργων ἡ πίστις **ἐτελειώθη**
faith **was perfected** *by* works

1 Cor 12:13 ἐν ἑνὶ πνεύματι ἡμεῖς πάντες εἰς ἓν σῶμα **ἐβαπτίσθημεν**
by one Spirit **we were** all **baptized** into one body

> By calling "Spirit" means here does not deny the personality of the Holy Spirit. Rather, the Holy Spirit is the instrument that Christ uses to baptize, even though he is a person. Just as John baptized ἐν ὕδατι, so Christ baptized ἐν πνέματι.[84]

For ἐν, cf. also Matt 26:52; Acts 11:16; Rom 5:9 (probable); 2 Thess 2:13; Rev 2:27; 6:8; 12:5; 17:16.

For simple dative, cf. also Matt 8:16; John 11:2; Acts 12:2; Gal 2:8; Phil 4:6; Heb 11:17; 2 Pet 3:5; Rev 22:14.

For ἐκ, cf. also John 4:6; Rev 3:18; 9:2; 18:1.

b. Without Agency Expressed

There are a number of reasons why an agent is not always expressed with a passive verb.[85] A few of the more common ones are as follows.[86]

1) The suppressed agent is often *obvious from the context* or the audience's preunderstanding. In Matt 5:25 the sequence of the legal action is that one **is thrown** into prison (εἰς φυλακὴν **βληθήσῃ**) after being handed over by his accuser to the judge, and from the judge to the bailiff. It is obvious that the bailiff does

---

[82] Cf. "Dative of Agency" for examples and a more complete discussion.

[83] For πίστει F G read διὰ πίστεως, a *v.l.* which, in the least, confirms the notion of means.

[84] See the detailed discussion of this text in the chapter on prepositions, under ἐν.

[85] See J. Callow, "Some Initial Thoughts on the Passive in New Testament Greek," *Selected Technical Articles Related to Translation* 15 (1986) 32-37, for a seminal discussion, followed by Young, *Intermediate Greek*, 135-36. Note also the more general treatment by Givón, *Syntax*, 153-65. Since the research on this topic is still in its infant stages, our presentation will only be suggestive and not follow our normal layout.

[86] Many of the "suppressed agent" passive uses overlap. Further, some of these categories are on a discourse level, others are more syntactical.

the "throwing." In Jude 3 both author and audience know who delivered "the faith that **has been delivered** once for all to the saints" (τῇ ἅπαξ **παραδοθείσῃ** τοῖς ἁγίοις πίστει). In John 3:23 there is no need for the evangelist to repeat that "John was baptizing" (from the first part of the verse) when he writes that "they were coming and **were getting baptized**" (παρεγίνοντο καὶ **ἐβαπτίζοντο**).[87]

2) *The focus of the passage is on the subject*; an explicit agent might detract from this focus.[88] In Matt 2:12, for example, the magi "**were warned** in a dream" (**χρηματισθέντες** κατ᾽ ὄναρ), evidently by the angel of the Lord, though this is not mentioned here. In the explanation of the parable of the soils, the sower is mentioned once (Mark 4:14), followed by a discourse in which the passive of σπείρω is stated five times (4:15 [twice], 16, 17, 18, 20). In none of the Synoptic accounts is the sower identified: The focus of the parable is on the seed and the soils.[89]

3) The nature of some passive verbs is such that *no agency is to be implied* (e.g., **συντελεσθεισῶν** αὐτῶν [**when** (those days) **were completed**] in Luke 4:2).[90]

4) The verb in question is functioning as an *equative verb* (e.g., πόλιν **λεγομένην** Ναζαρέτ . . . Ναζωραῖος **κληθήσεται** [a city **called** Nazareth . . . he **shall be called** a Nazarene] in Matt 2:23).[91]

5) Similar to this usage is an *implicit generic agent*. Greek frequently uses the simple passive without an expressed agent where colloquial English might use "they say": "They say a cure for cancer has been discovered" would often be expressed in Greek as "it is said that a cure for cancer has been found." Thus, in Matt 5:21 Jesus declares, "You have heard that **it was said**" (ἠκούσατε ὅτι **ἐρρέθη**). John 10:35 has "scripture cannot **be broken**" (οὐ δύναται **λυθῆναι** ἡ γραφή), the implied agent being "by anyone."[92]

6) An *explicit agent would sometimes be obtrusive* or would render the sentence too complex, perhaps reducing the literary effect. In 1 Cor 1:13 three passives are used without an agent mentioned.

---

[87] Cf. also Matt 3:16; Mark 4:6; 5:4; Luke 4:16; 5:6; 10:9; John 2:10; Rom 3:19; 1 Cor 3:10; Gal 2:7; Rev 7:4.

[88] Young points out that this is the fundamental reason for the use of the passive even when an agent is present: "The most common function of the passive voice is to keep the topic of the passage or the previous subject as the subject of the sentence" (*Intermediate Greek*, 135). That focus is heightened even further when no agent is expressed.

[89] Cf. also Matt 2:2-3, 12, 18; 4:12; 5:10; John 5:10, 13; 7:47; Rom 1:18; 1 Cor 4:11. Some of these examples may have suppressed agents for rhetorical effect (see below).

[90] Cf. also John 7:8; Acts 2:1; Heb 1:11.

[91] Cf. also Matt 4:18; John 4:5; 5:2; Acts 1:23.

[92] Cf. also Acts 2:25; Gal 3:15; 2 Pet 2:2.

μεμέρισται ὁ Χριστός; μὴ Παῦλος **ἐσταυρώθη** ὑπὲρ ὑμῶν, ἢ εἰς τὸ ὄνομα Παύλου **ἐβαπτίσθητε**; (Is Christ **divided**? **Was** Paul **crucified** for you, or **were you baptized** into the name of Paul?).[93] In 1 Cor 12:13 to mention Christ as the agent who baptizes with the Spirit would be cumbersome and a mixture of metaphors, since believers are baptized into *Christ's* body (ἐν ἑνὶ πνεύματι ἡμεῖς πάντες εἰς ἓν σῶμα **ἐβαπτίσθημεν** [by one Spirit **we** all **were baptized** into one body]).[94]

7) Similar to the above is *the suppression of the agent for rhetorical effect*, especially for the purpose of drawing the reader into the story. Note, for example, Jesus' pronouncement to the paralytic (Mark 2:5): τέκνον, **ἀφίενταί** σου αἱ ἁμαρτίαι (child, your sins **are forgiven**).[95] In Rom 1:13 Paul declares his desire to have visited the Romans, adding that he was prevented thus far (ἐκωλύθην). In Jas 2:16, the suppression of the agent serves as an indictment: εἴπῃ τις αὐτοῖς ἐξ ὑμῶν· ὑπάγετε ἐν εἰρήνῃ, **θερμαίνεσθε** καὶ **χορτάζεσθε**, μὴ δῶτε δὲ αὐτοῖς τὰ ἐπιτήδεια τοῦ σώματος, τί τὸ ὄφελος; ([if] one of you says to them [the destitute brother or sister], "Go in peace; **be warmed** and **be filled**," but you do not give them the things necessary for the body, what is the benefit?).[96]

8) The passive is also used when *God is the obvious agent*. Many grammars call this a *divine passive* (or *theological passive*), assuming that its use was due to the Jewish aversion to using the divine name.[97] For example, in the Beatitudes, the passive is used: "they shall be comforted" (παρακληθήσονται [Matt 5:4]), "they shall be filled" (χορτασθήσονται [v 6]), "they shall receive mercy" (ἐλεηθήσονται [v 7]). Young argues that "this circumlocution occurs most often in the Gospels."[98] And Jeremias especially finds it on the lips of Jesus, seeing in such examples the *ipsissima verba* (very words) of the Lord.[99]

---

[93] The passives in 1 Cor 1:13 also belong to other categories: μεμέρισται involves no agent; the other two passives could perhaps belong to the generic category as well.

[94] Cf. also Acts 1:5; Rom 3:2; Rev 5:6 (ἐσφαγμένον). The suppression of the agent because of *negative* connotations, if it were made explicit, also fits here (cf. John 2:20–"this temple **was built**..." [οἰκοδομήθη ὁ ναὸς οὗτος]).

[95] ἀφέωνται is found in several MSS, including 𝔓[88] ℵ A C D L W Γ Π Σ 579 700 892 *f*[1] *Byz*; ἀφέονται is in G Φ 0130 828 1010 1424 *f*[13] *et pauci*; ἀφίονται is read in Δ; ἀφίωνται is the reading of Θ.

[96] Cf. also Matt 5:29; Mark 2:20; Luke 4:6, 43; John 3:14; 9:10; Rom 1:1, 21; 3:19; 2 Thess 2:2-3, 8; Titus 1:15; Rev 2:13; 6:2. In some of these texts there is overlap with the so-called "divine passive," while others leave the agent tantalizingly vague.

[97] So *BDF*, 72 (§130.1); Zerwick, *Biblical Greek*, 76 (§236); Young, *Intermediate Greek*, 135-36. Cf. also J. Jeremias, *New Testament Theology* (New York: Scribner's, 1971) 9-14.

[98] Young, *Intermediate Greek*, 135.

[99] Jeremias, *New Testament Theology*, 9-14. Cf. also Zerwick, *Biblical Greek*, 76 (§236).

Although there are certainly several divine passives in the NT, perhaps the explanation given above is overstated.[100] For not only is "God" frequently the subject, even in sayings of Jesus,[101] but θεός as nominative subject occurs *more frequently* when Jesus is the speaker than otherwise.[102] Further, the divine passive seems to occur frequently enough throughout the whole NT. Statements such as the following could be multiplied many times over; all of them seem to imply God as the unstated agent: "a man **is justified**" (**δικαιοῦσθαι** . . . ἄνθρωπον [Rom 3:28]); "the grace of God [was] **given** to me" (τὴν χάριν τοῦ θεοῦ τὴν **δοθεῖσάν** μοι [1 Cor 3:10]); "you **were bought** with a price" (τιμῆς **ἠγοράσθητε** [1 Cor 7:23]); "you **were called** to freedom" (ὑμεῖς ἐπ᾽ ἐλευθερίᾳ **ἐκλήθητε** [Gal 5:13]); "by grace **you have been saved**" (χάριτί **ἐστε σεσῳσμένοι** [Eph 2:5]); "**you were ransomed** from your futile life" (**ἐλυτρώθητε** ἐκ τῆς ματαίας ὑμῶν ἀναστροφῆς [1 Pet 1:18]).

Such expressions are obviously not due to any reticence on the part of the author to utter the name of God. It might be better to say that this phenomenon is due to certain collocations that would render the repetition of the divine name superfluous, even obtrusive. In other words, *the divine passive is simply a specific type of one of the previous categories* listed above (e.g., obvious from the passage, due to focus on the subject, otherwise obtrusive, or for rhetorical effect). That God is behind the scenes is self-evidently part of the worldview of the NT writers.[103] The nature of this book demands that we see him even when he is not mentioned.

2.   Passive With an Accusative Object

a.   Definition

Although it seems a bit odd to native English speakers, Greek sometimes uses an accusative with a true passive verb. The major usage for such a structure involves the accusative of retained object.[104] In this instance, the *accusative of thing* in a double accusative

---

[100] So Porter, *Idioms*, 65-66.

[101] Cf., e.g., Matt 3:9; 6:30; 15:4; 19:6; 22:32; Mark 10:18; 12:27; Mark 13:19; Luke 1:32; 8:39; 12:20, 24, 28; 16:15; 18:7; 20:38; John 3:16; 4:24. θεός as subject in dominical sayings even occurs in places where it is self-evident and therefore somewhat gratuitous (from the perspective of Jewish reticence). For example, in Mark 13:19 Jesus speaks of the tribulation that is greater than any "from the beginning of creation which **God** created until now" (ἀπ᾽ ἀρχῆς κτίσεως ἣν ἔκτισεν ὁ **θεὸς** ἕως τοῦ νῦν).

[102] For example, 7 out of 9 instances of θεός in Matthew are in dominical sayings.

[103] Cf. also Matt 3:10, 16; 5:4-9; Rom 1:18; 2:13; 3:2; 4:7; 9:22; 1 Cor 15:4; Heb 3:3; Jas 2:12; 1 John 4:12. Perhaps also the well-worn γέγραπται should be read as a divine passive.

[104] Other, less frequent uses also occur. See *BDF*, 87 (§159).

person-thing construction with an active verb *retains its case* when the verb is put in the *passive*. The accusative of person, in such instances, becomes the subject.[105] This use of the accusative occurs most frequently with causative verbs, though it is rare in the NT.

"I taught you *the lesson*" becomes, with the verb converted to a passive, "You were taught *the lesson* by me." When the verb is transformed into a passive, the accusative of person becomes the subject (nom.), the accusative of thing is retained.

b. Illustrations

1 Cor 12:13 πάντες **ἓν πνεῦμα** ἐποτίσθημεν[106]
> all were made to drink [of] **one Spirit**
>> "All" is the person, put in the nom. with passive verbs. The acc. of thing, "one Spirit," is retained. If the verb had been in the active voice, the text would be read: "he made all to drink of one Spirit" (ἐπότισε πάντα ἓν πνεῦμα).

Luke 7:29 οἱ τελῶναι . . . βαπτισθέντες **τὸ βάπτισμα** Ἰωάννου
> the tax-collectors, having been baptized with **the baptism** of John

2 Th 2:15 κρατεῖτε τὰς παραδόσεις **ἃς** ἐδιδάχθητε
> hold fast to the traditions **that** you were taught

Rev 16:9 ἐκαυματίσθησαν οἱ ἄνθρωποι **καῦμα μέγα**
> people were scorched [with] **a scorching heat**

Cf. also Gal 2:7; Phil 1:11; Col 1:9; Heb 6:9.

B. Passive Uses

➡ ### 1. Simple Passive

a. Definition

The most common use of the passive voice is to indicate that the subject receives the action. No implication is made about cognition, volition, or cause on the part of the subject. This usage occurs both with and without an expressed agent.

b. Illustrations

Mark 4:6 ὅτε ἀνέτειλεν ὁ ἥλιος **ἐκαυματίσθη**
> when the sun rose, **it was scorched**

---

[105] It is not always explicit, however. Cf. 2 Thess 2:15, mentioned below.

[106] Some witnesses have πόμα for πνεῦμα (177 630 920 1505 1738 1881): "all were made to drink one *drink*," turning the expression into an allusion to the Lord's Supper (so BAGD, s.v. πόμα).

Luke 6:10   ἀπεκατεστάθη ἡ χεὶρ αὐτοῦ
            his hand **was restored**

Acts 1:5   ὑμεῖς ἐν πνεύματι **βαπτισθήσεσθε** ἁγίῳ
            you **will be baptized** with the Holy Spirit

Rom 5:1   **δικαιωθέντες** οὖν ἐκ πίστεως εἰρήνην ἔχομεν πρὸς τὸν θεόν
            Therefore, **having been justified** by faith, we have peace with God.

1 Cor 12:13 ἐν ἑνὶ πνεύματι ἡμεῖς πάντες εἰς ἓν σῶμα **ἐβαπτίσθημεν** . . . καὶ πάντες
            ἓν πνεῦμα **ἐποτίσθημεν**[107]
            we all **were baptized** by one Spirit into one body . . . and **we** all **were**
            made to drink [of] one Spirit

> Some suggest that Spirit-baptism is normally a post-conversion event
> (as on the day of Pentecost), but the double emphasis on "all," coupled
> with the passive verbs, suggests that this took place at the point of con-
> version. The analogy with Pentecost fails, too, because the disciples did
> not fully realize nor apprehend the spiritual events of that day at the
> moment they occurred (note the passive verbs in Acts 2:3, 4).

Heb 3:4   πᾶς οἶκος **κατασκευάζεται** ὑπό τινος
            every house **is built** by someone

Cf. also Luke 1:4; John 12:5; Acts 1:2; 2:3; 4:9; Rom 1:13; 2:13; 7:2; 1 Cor 5:5; 2 Cor 1:6; Gal
1:12; 3:1, 16; Phil 1:29; 2:17; Col 2:7; Phlm 15; Jas 2:7; 1 Pet 2:4; 3 John 12; Jude 13; Rev 7:5.

2.   Causative/Permissive Passive

a.   Definition

The causative/permissive passive, like its middle counterpart,
implies consent, permission, or cause of the action of the verb on the
part of the subject. This usage is rare,[108] usually shut up to imperatives (as would be expected, since imperatives intrinsically involve
volition).[109] It is difficult to decide whether a given passive is causative or permissive;[110] hence, the two categories are combined for
pragmatic reasons.

---

[107] Codex A has σῶμα ἔστιν for πνεῦμα ἐποτίσθημεν.

[108] Not all grammarians view this as a legitimate category (e.g., Robertson, *Grammar*,
808).

[109] Not all passive imperatives could be labeled as causative/permissive, however.
For example, in Mark 1:41 Jesus' command to the leper "be clean!" (καθαρίσθητι) could
hardly be rendered "allow yourself to be clean." Rather, it is a pronouncement (performative statement) couched in imperatival terms. Cf. also Matt 21:21; Mark 7:34; 11:23; Rom
11:10. Of the 155 passive imperatives listed in *acCordance*, the majority are deponent passives (e.g., πορεύθητι in Matt 8:9; δεήθητε in Matt 9:38; ἀποκρίθητε in Mark 11:30) or performative statements given as imperatives for rhetorical effect. Further, the causative/
permissive passive imperatives are often either prohibitions (e.g., μὴ φοβοῦ in Luke 1:13)
or commands addressing emotional states, to the effect of "be in control of yourself" (e.g.,
πεφίμωσο in Mark 4:39; cf. also John 14:1; Rom 11:20).

b. Illustrations

Luke 7:7   ἰαθήτω ὁ παῖς μου[111]
            let my servant **be healed**

Luke 11:38 ὁ Φαρισαῖος ἰδὼν ἐθαύμασεν ὅτι οὐ πρῶτον **ἐβαπτίσθη** πρὸ τοῦ
            ἀρίστου[112]
            When the Pharisee saw this, he was amazed because [Jesus] did not
            first **allow himself to be washed** before the meal.
               Jesus as a guest in the Pharisee's house would be washed by another.

1 Cor 6:7   διὰ τί οὐχὶ μᾶλλον **ἀδικεῖσθε**; διὰ τί οὐχὶ μᾶλλον **ἀποστερεῖσθε**;
            Why not **allow yourselves to be wronged**? Why not **allow your-
            selves to be defrauded**?

Eph 5:18   μὴ **μεθύσκεσθε** οἴνῳ . . . ἀλλὰ **πληροῦσθε** ἐν πνεύματι
            Do not be drunk with wine . . . but **be filled** with the Spirit.

1 Pet 5:6   **ταπεινώθητε** ὑπὸ τὴν κραταιὰν χεῖρα τοῦ θεοῦ
            Allow yourselves to be humbled under the mighty hand of God.

Cf. also Mark 10:45; 16:6; Luke 15:15; 18:13; Acts 2:38; 21:24, 26; Rom 12:2; 14:16; Col 2:20; Heb 13:9; Jas 4:7, 10.

→   ### 3. Deponent Passive

A verb that has no active *form* may be active in meaning though passive in form. Two of the most common deponent passives are ἐγενήθην and ἀπεκρίθην. See the discussion of the deponent middle for material that is equally relevant for the deponent passive.

---

[110] Most of these texts can be translated with "allow," but this does not solve the problem. Is mere toleration in view, or is a request on the part of the subject implied? E.g., in Acts 2:38 does βαπτισθήτω ἕκαστος ὑμῶν mean "each one of you, permit yourselves to be baptized" or "each one of you, ask to be baptized"?

[111] ἰαθήσεται is found in a majority of MSS, including ℵ A C D W Δ Θ Ψ *f*[1, 13] 28 33 565 579 700 892 1292 1424 *Byz.* The passive imperative is found in 𝔓[75vid] B L 1241 *et pauci.*

[112] The reading ἐβαπτίσατο is found in 𝔓[45] 700, while almost all other witnesses read ἐβαπτίσθη. Most likely the passive is original, being better attested externally and even more difficult (since the Pharisee's amazement would presumably be due to Jesus intentionally not washing his hands).

Moods

Overview of Moods and their Uses

Select Bibliography

BDF, 181-96 (§357-87); **J. L. Boyer**, "The Classification of Imperatives: A Statistical Study," *GTJ* 8 (1987) 35-54; **idem**, "The Classification of Optatives: A Statistical Study," *GTJ* 9 (1988) 129-40; **Burton**, *Moods and Tenses*, 73-143 (§157-360); **Chamberlain**, *Exegetical Grammar*, 82-87; **Dana-Mantey**, 165-76 (§160-65); **Moule**, *Idiom Book*, 20-23, 142-47; **Moulton**, *Prolegomena*, 164-201; **Porter**, *Idioms*, 50-61; **Robertson**, *Grammar*, 911-1049; **Smyth**, *Greek Grammar*, 398-412 (§1759-1849); **Young**, *Intermediate Greek*, 136-46; **Zerwick**, *Biblical Greek*, 100-24 (§295-358).

Introduction

A. The Matter of Definition

1. General Definition

Just as with tense and voice, mood is a morphological feature of the verb. *Voice* indicates *how* the subject *relates* to the *action* or state of the verb; *tense* is used primarily to portray the *kind* of action. In general, *mood* is the feature of the verb that presents the verbal action or state with reference to its *actuality* or *potentiality*. Older grammars referred to this as "mode";[1] others call it

---

[1] E.g., Robertson, *Grammar*, 911; Chamberlain, *Exegetical Grammar*, 82.

"attitude."[2] There are four moods in Greek: indicative, subjunctive, optative, and imperative.[3]

2. *Critique of Shorthand Definitions of Mood*

Grammars tend to describe mood in somewhat of a shorthand manner (even as we have done above).[4] Such truncated language, however, can be misleading. Two kinds of definitions need to be critiqued. First, some grammars speak of mood as having an *objective correspondence to reality*. This is particularly so in their definition of the *indicative* mood. Some say, for example, that the indicative mood signifies a "simple fact."[5] But this is manifestly not true: lies are usually stated in the indicative; false perceptions are in the indicative; exaggerations and fictional accounts are in the indicative. "Little green men *live* in shoe boxes on my front lawn" involves an indicative, as does "I no longer *sin*," or "Forrest Gump *is* the greatest basketball player alive." In none of these sentences is there an objective or one-to-one correspondence to reality.[6]

The second kind of definition is an improvement, yet still misleading. Many grammars speak of mood as indicating a speaker's *perception* of reality. But to say that mood "indicates how the speaker *regards* what he or she is saying with respect to its factuality"[7] seems to suggest that the speaker is attempting to draw an accurate portrayal of the verbal action.[8] He may have failed in this attempt, but accuracy was his goal. Again, this is not the case.

---

[2] E.g., Moulton, *Prolegomena*, 164: "The moods in question are characterized by a common subjective element, representing an *attitude* of mind on the part of the speaker" (italics mine). Porter, *Idioms*, titles his second chapter "Mood and Attitude" and defines mood as "the mood forms indicate the speaker's 'attitude' toward the event" (50).

[3] Most grammars do not include the infinitive or participle under the rubric of mood, and for good reason. As dependent verbals, their attitude toward certainty is dependent on some finite verb. Hence, since such an affirmation is derivative, they cannot be said to have mood per se. Nevertheless, for parsing purposes, these two verbals are usually labeled as infinitive and participle in the "mood slot."

[4] In our simple definition we have avoided linking mood to the speaker's viewpoint, however. The basic fault with the simple definition is that it does not indicate *why* a speaker uses the grammatical form he does.

[5] Dana-Mantey, 168 (§162). Though they add a qualification, the impression is that the indicative is somehow objectively connected to reality. See also Burton, *Moods and Tenses*, 73 (§157). We are not arguing that these grammarians misunderstand the force of mood, just that they have not articulated it as clearly as they might have.

[6] In fact, as has been pointed out throughout this grammar, there is not necessarily any one-to-one correspondence between *language* and reality. The two, of course, intersect, but not at every point. To claim such a correspondence would mean that, for example, the gospel writers always quoted Jesus verbatim, the parables are true stories (not just true to life), there is virtually no overlap in lexical or grammatical fields (because only one description of an event would be possible), and figurative language does not exist! Obviously, such a view of language is absurd. In short, *all of language is an interpretive activity*.

[7] Young, *Intermediate Greek*, 136 (italics mine).

Otherwise, misinformation, sarcasm, hyperbole, fiction, dualistic world-view, etc., could never be communicated. Regarding the subjunctive, for example, is it not possible to say, "I think the Rams *might win* the Super Bowl this year," when they have already been eliminated from the competition? I could say this for the sake of sarcasm; it would not necessarily have to indicate my perception. The imperative could be used for rhetorical effect, such as when expressing an impossible demand: "*Give* a detailed description of the universe in three sentences or less"; "Vote for the candidate who agrees with you, point for point."

Occasionally, these two statements (viz., that the moods either correspond to reality or to one's perception of reality) coexist in the same grammar. Thus, the indicative mood is stated to be objective, while the other moods are subjective.[9]

It is no wonder that one grammarian said that mood was "far and away the most difficult theme in Greek syntax"![10]

3. Detailed Definition

A more accurate definition, in light of the discussion above, is as follows: *Mood is the morphological feature of a verb that a speaker uses to **portray** his or her affirmation as to the certainty of the verbal action or state (whether an actuality or potentiality).* The key elements in this definition are that mood (a) does not necessarily correspond to reality, (b) does not indicate even a speaker's *perception* of reality, but (c) does indicate a speaker's *portrayal* or *representation*.[11]

B. Semantics of the Moods

Five additional points need to be considered to understand the force of the moods.

- First, the general semantics of the moods can be compared as follows:

---

[8] Young affirms this when he says that the moods "express the speaker's *perception* of the action or state in relation to reality . . ." (ibid.). See also Moulton, *Prolegomena*, 164; Robertson, *Grammar*, 911-12; Zerwick, *Biblical Greek*, 100 (§296).

[9] E.g., Dana-Mantey (166, [§161]) speak of mood as embracing two viewpoints, "that which is actual and that which is possible."

[10] Robertson, *Grammar*, 912.

[11] In fairness to others, *all* grammarians have to resort to shorthand definitions from time to time in order to avoid cumbersome definitions. The trade-off, then, is between pedantic accuracy and pedagogical simplicity. No doubt this work will be perceived as typically erring on the side of the former, although it is not immune from the error of the latter.

Moods	Indicative	Subjunctive	Optative	Imperative
Greek example	λύεις	λύῃς	λύοις	λῦε
Portrayal	certain/ asserted	probable/ desirable	possible	intended
Translation	you are loosing/ you loose	you might be loosing/ you should be loosing	you may be loosing	loose!

Table 8
The Semantics of the Moods Compared

It must be kept in mind that this table is very much of an oversimplification, intended only to give the student a handle on the basic forces of the various moods. There are many exceptions to the general semantics, as a result of other factors (see discussion below).

• Second, the moods need to be seen in light of two poles. (1) The moods affirm various *degrees* of certainty; they are on a "continuum of certainty in the speaker's presentation,"[12] from *actuality* to *potentiality*. In general, the indicative mood is set apart from the others in that it is the mood normally used to address actuality, while the others–collectively known as the *oblique* moods–normally address potentiality.[13] Hence, since the oblique moods do not address actuality, they do not involve a time element. (2) The imperative mood is normally used to address the *volition*, while the optative, subjunctive, and especially indicative address *cognition*. In other words, the imperative appeals to the will, while the other moods appeal more frequently to the mind.

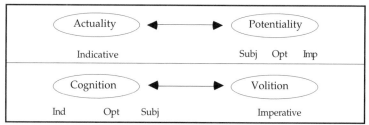

Chart 43
The Moods Viewed In Two Continua

• Third, the significance of this dual matrix is that *an author often does not have a choice* in the mood used.[14] Narrative, for example, almost always requires the indicative. Elsewhere, when a potential action is in view, certain moods (indicative and to a large degree, optative) are weeded

---

[12] Credit is due Dr. Hall Harris for this nice turn of expression.

[13] There are, of course, exceptions to this generalization. First class conditions address an *argument* from certainty (viz., "if X" means "assuming for the sake of argument the truth of X"). But the particle εἰ has influenced the mood in such instances: It is this combination that gives the clause its flavor.

out if it is addressed to one's will. But when a potential action is addressed to one's cognition, the imperative is no longer (normally) a viable option.

- Fourth, the indicative is by far the most frequently used mood, though it would perhaps be an overstatement to say that it is the "unmarked mood."[15] Other factors are involved that severely limit the choice of mood in a given instance (see previous discussion). The statistics of mood frequencies in the NT are as follows:

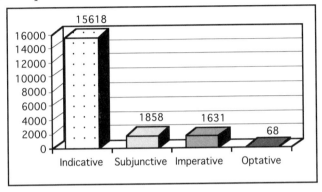

Chart 44
Mood Frequencies in the NT[16]

- Fifth, even when there is a choice, *the mood used is not always in line with its general force*. For example, in the language of prayer, when pronouncing a blessing (such as "May God grant you . . ."), the optative is virtually required. Yet this does not mean that the speaker thinks of such a blessing as less likely to occur than if he had used the subjunctive. Prohibitions are often given in the subjunctive rather than the imperative. But this does not mean that the speaker thought that they would be heeded any more than if he had used the imperative. As well, the imperative is sometimes used in the protasis of a conditional clause (e.g., in

---

[14] *Contra* Porter, *Idioms*, 50: "The choice of attitude [mood] is probably the second most important semantic choice by a language user in selection of a verbal element in Greek, second only to verbal aspect." Although there is certainly some overlap in the use of the moods (e.g., the first and third class conditions [indicative and subjunctive], volitional clauses [imperative, subjunctive, future indicative]), in most instances the choice is already largely predetermined by other factors (such as tense in volitional clauses, a purpose statement in a ἵνα clause). (Further, even in volitional clauses, the choice of subjunctive over imperative seems to be arbitrary or merely stylistic, for no modal difference is detectable.) It seems that a speaker has more freedom, generally speaking, in the *voice* he or she chooses than in the mood.

[15] *Contra* Robertson, *Grammar*, 915; Porter, *Idioms*, 51.

[16] The count is based on the text of UBSGNT³ as tagged in *acCordance*. There is some doubt about the parsing of some of the forms (e.g., whether certain second person plural forms are indicative or subjunctive, whether some forms such as δώη should be considered optative [δῴη] or subjunctive [δώῃ]); further, the text is not certain in every place. But the overall proportions and general contours are not affected by such matters.

John 2:19 Jesus says, "*Destroy* this temple and in three days I will raise it up"); but this does not mean that the speaker perceives the fulfillment of such to be a remote possibility. Along these lines, since in the Hellenistic era the optative was dying, the subjunctive encroached on its domain (see discussion below). Therefore, even in places where the optative would have been well suited, the subjunctive is frequently found simply because the author was more comfortable using this form. The use of the subjunctive, then, does not necessarily indicate that a speaker saw the event as more likely to occur than if he had used the optative. On the other hand, the subjunctive is (virtually) required after ἵνα, but this does not always indicate that the speaker viewed the event as merely probable.

The exegetical import of this final point is that the moods especially need to be examined in light of other intrusions, whether lexical, contextual, or other grammatical features. It is a dangerous thing simply to argue that a given mood is unaffected by other features of the language. Fortunately, the various semantic situations of most uses of the moods are usually distinctive. This means that the proportion of debatable passages for moods is less than it is for many other morpho-syntactical categories.

C. Categories of Moods

This chapter will deal only with the major categories of usage. For detailed study, see especially the relevant materials in Burton, *Moods and Tenses*; Robertson, *Grammar*; and Moulton, *Prolegomena*.

I. The Indicative Mood

A. Definition

The indicative mood is, in general, the mood of assertion, or *presentation of certainty*. It is not correct to say that it is the mood of certainty or reality. This belongs to the presentation (i.e., the indicative may *present* something as being certain or real, though the speaker might not believe it). To call the indicative mood the mood of certainty or fact would imply (1) that one cannot lie in the indicative (but cf. Acts 6:13), and (2) that one cannot be mistaken in the indicative (but cf. Luke 7:39). Thus it is more accurate to state that the indicative mood is the mood of assertion, or *presentation* of certainty.

B. Specific Uses

➡ 1. Declarative Indicative

a. Definition

The indicative is routinely used to *present* an assertion as a non-contingent (or unqualified) statement. This is by far its most common use.

b. Illustrations

Mark 4:3   **ἐξῆλθεν** ὁ σπείρων σπεῖραι
the sower **went out** to sow

John 1:1   Ἐν ἀρχῇ **ἦν** ὁ λόγος
In the beginning **was** the Word

Acts 6:8   Στέφανος. . . **ἐποίει** τέρατα καὶ σημεῖα μεγάλα ἐν τῷ λαῷ
Stephen. . . **was performing** signs and great wonders among the people

Rom 3:21   χωρὶς νόμου δικαιοσύνη θεοῦ **πεφανέρωται**
Apart from the law the righteousness of God **has been manifested**.

Phil 4:19   ὁ θεός μου **πληρώσει** πᾶσαν χρείαν ὑμῶν[17]
my God **will fulfill** your every need

1 Pet 4:7   πάντων δὲ τὸ τέλος **ἤγγικεν**
the end of all things **is near**

Cf. also Acts 27:4; Phil 3:20; Heb 1:2; Jas 2:18; 2 Pet 1:21; 1 John 3:6; Rev 1:6.

➡ 2. Interrogative Indicative

a. Definition

The indicative can be used in a question. The question *expects an assertion* to be made; it expects a declarative indicative in the answer. (This contrasts with the subjunctive, which asks a question of moral "oughtness" or obligation, or asks whether something is possible.) The interrogative indicative typically probes for information. In other words, it does not ask the *how* or the *why*, but the *what*.[18]

---

[17] The optative πληρώσαι is found in several MSS, including D* F G Ψ 075 33 69 81 1739 1881 1962 *et alii*.

[18] This is not to exclude the rhetorical use of this question. Not infrequently, no answer is anticipated (cf., e.g., Jas 2:4; Rev 7:13-14).

Frequently an interrogative particle is used with the indicative, especially to distinguish this usage from the declarative indicative.[19] The interrogative indicative is a common usage, though the *future* indicative is not normally used in this way (cf. deliberative subjunctive below).[20]

b. Illustrations

Matt 27:11   σὺ **εἶ** ὁ βασιλεὺς τῶν Ἰουδαίων;
             Are you the king of the Jews?

John 1:38   λέγει αὐτοῖς, Τί **ζητεῖτε**; οἱ δὲ εἶπαν αὐτῷ, Ῥαββί, . . . ποῦ **μένεις**;
             He said to them, "What **do you seek**?" And they said to him, "Rabbi,
             . . . where **are you staying**?"

John 11:26   πᾶς ὁ ζῶν καὶ πιστεύων εἰς ἐμὲ οὐ μὴ ἀποθάνῃ εἰς τὸν αἰῶνα. **πιστεύεις**
             τοῦτο;
             Everyone who lives and believes in me shall never die. **Do you
             believe** this?

Rom 11:2   οὐκ οἴδατε . . . τί **λέγει** ἡ γραφή;
             Do you not **know** what the scripture **says**?

> Here is a question within a question. It thus anticipates an assertion
> within an assertion: "You do know that the scripture says . . ."

Jas 2:5   οὐχ ὁ θεὸς **ἐξελέξατο** τοὺς πτωχοὺς τῷ κόσμῳ πλουσίους ἐν πίστει;
             Did God not **choose** the poor in the world [to become] rich in faith?

Cf. also Matt 16:13; 21:25; 27:23; Mark 8:23; 15:2; Acts 12:18 (indirect question); John 9:17; Rom 2:21-23; 1 Cor 1:13; Jas 2:7; Rev 7:13.

➡ 3. *Conditional Indicative*

a. **Definition**

This is the use of the indicative in the protasis of conditional sentences. The conditional element is made explicit with the particle εἰ. This is a relatively common usage of the indicative, though much more so with the first class condition (over 300 instances) than with the second (less than 50 examples).

The first class condition indicates *the assumption of truth for the sake of argument*, while the second class condition indicates *the assumption of an untruth for the sake of argument*.[21]

---

[19] Robertson, *Grammar*, 915-16. He lists 1 Cor 1:13 and Rom 8:33-34 as potentially ambiguous texts.

[20] But cf. Mark 13:4.

[21] For a detailed treatment, see the chapter on conditional clauses.

b. **Illustrations**

The first two examples are second class conditions; the last three are first class conditions.

John 5:46 εἰ **ἐπιστεύετε** Μωϋσεῖ, ἐπιστεύετε ἂν ἐμοί
If **you believed** Moses, you would believe me
> The second class condition assumes the untruth of the assertion. The idea is "If you believed Moses–but you did not . . ."

1 Cor 2:8 εἰ **ἔγνωσαν**, οὐκ ἂν τὸν κύριον τῆς δόξης ἐσταύρωσαν
If **they had known**, they would not have crucified the Lord of glory.

Matt 12:27 εἰ ἐγὼ ἐν Βεελζεβοὺλ **ἐκβάλλω** τὰ δαιμόνια, οἱ υἱοὶ ὑμῶν ἐν τίνι ἐκβάλλουσιν;
If I **cast out** demons by Beelzebul, by whom do your sons cast them out?
> The first class condition assumes the truth of the assertion for the sake of argument; it does *not* mean that the speaker necessarily believes it to be true. The force in this verse is "If I cast out demons by Beelzebul–and let us assume that this is true for argument's sake–then by whom do your sons cast them out?"

1 Cor 15:44 εἰ **ἔστιν** σῶμα ψυχικόν, ἔστιν καὶ πνευματικόν
If **there is** a physical body, [then] there is also a spiritual [body].

Rev 20:15 εἴ τις οὐχ **εὑρέθη** ἐν τῇ βίβλῳ τῆς ζωῆς γεγραμμένος, ἐβλήθη εἰς τὴν λίμνην τοῦ πυρός
If [the name of] someone **was** not **found** written in the book of life, he was cast into the lake of fire.

Cf. also Matt 23:30 (second class); Luke 4:9 (first class); 6:32 (first); Acts 16:15 (first); Rom 2:17 (first); 9:29 (second); Gal 2:18 (first); 1 Thess 4:14 (first); Heb 4:8 (second); Jas 2:11; 2 John 10 (first); Rev 13:9 (first).

➡ *4. Potential Indicative*

a. **Definition**

The indicative is used with verbs of obligation, wish, or desire, followed by an infinitive. The nature of the verb root, rather than the indicative, is what makes it look like a potential mood in its semantic force. This usage is fairly common.

Specifically, verbs indicating obligation (such as ὀφείλω, δεῖ), wish (e.g., βούλομαι), or desire (e.g., θέλω) are used with an infinitive. They *lexically* limit the overall assertion, turning it into a potential action. It is important to understand that the normal force of the indicative mood is not thereby denied; rather, the assertion is simply in the desire, not the doing. Thus, this usage is really a subcategory of the declarative indicative.[22]

---

[22] With the imperfect, however, the desire itself is often tendential; cf., e.g., Rom 9:3.

b. Illustrations

Luke 11:42   ταῦτα **ἔδει** ποιῆσαι
It was necessary [for you] to have done these things.

Acts 4:12   οὐδὲ ὄνομά ἐστιν ἕτερον ὑπὸ τὸν οὐρανὸν τὸ δεδομένον ἐν ἀνθρώποις ἐν
ᾧ **δεῖ** σωθῆναι ἡμᾶς
There is no other name under heaven given among men by which
we **must** [lit., **it is necessary** for us] be saved.

1 Cor 11:7   ἀνὴρ οὐκ **ὀφείλει** κατακαλύπτεσθαι τὴν κεφαλὴν
a man **should** not cover his head

1 Tim 2:8   **βούλομαι** προσεύχεσθαι τοὺς ἄνδρας
I want the men to pray

Rev 2:21   ἔδωκα αὐτῇ χρόνον ἵνα μετανοήσῃ, καὶ οὐ **θέλει** μετανοῆσαι[23]
I have given her time to repent, yet **she does** not **want** to repent.

Cf. also Matt 2:18 (θέλω); Acts 5:28 (βούλομαι); Rom 15:1 (ὀφείλω); 1 Cor 11:10 (ὀφείλω); Jude
5 (βούλομαι); Rev 11:5 (θέλω; here, in a first class conditional clause).

5. *Cohortative (Command, Volitive) Indicative*

The *future* indicative is sometimes used for a command, almost always in OT
quotations (due to a literal translation of the Hebrew).[24] However, it was
used infrequently even in classical Greek. Outside of Matthew, this usage is
not common.[25] Its force is quite emphatic, in keeping with the combined
nature of the indicative mood and future tense. "It is not a milder or gentler
imperative. A prediction may imply resistless power or cold indifference,
compulsion or concession."[26]

Matt 19:18   οὐ **φονεύσεις**, οὐ **μοιχεύσεις**, οὐ **κλέψεις**, οὐ **ψευδομαρτυρήσεις**
You shall not **murder, you shall** not **commit adultery, you shall** not
steal, you shall not **bear false witness**.
> The parallels in Mark 10:19 and Luke 18:20 have the aorist subjunctive
> after μή, a prohibitive subjunctive.

Matt 6:5   οὐκ **ἔσεσθε** ὡς οἱ ὑποκριταί[27]
you shall not **be** like the hypocrites
> This is an example of the cohortative indicative that is not from an OT
> quotation.

---

[23] Instead of οὐ θέλει, some MSS (viz., A 1626 2070) read οὐκ ἠθέλησεν.

[24] See also the chapter on the future tense for a discussion.

[25] For a succinct discussion, see *BDF*, 183 (§362).

[26] Gildersleeve, *Classical Greek*, 1.116 (§269).

[27] Numerous MSS read ἔσῃ here, a *v.l.* that nevertheless does not disturb the grammatical point at issue.

1 Pet 1:16   ἅγιοι **ἔσεσθε**, ὅτι ἐγὼ ἅγιός εἰμι[28]
              you shall be holy, because I am holy

Cf. also Matt 4:7, 10; 5:21, 27, 33, 43, 48; 21:3; 22:37, 39; Mark 9:35; Rom 7:7; 13:9; Gal 5:14.

→ ### 6. *The Indicative with* Ὅτι

The indicative mood occurs both in independent clauses and dependent clauses. One of the most frequent and complex dependent clauses in which the indicative mood occurs is the ὅτι clause.

Technically, the subcategories included here are not restricted to the syntax of the indicative mood, but involve the function of the ὅτι (+ indicative) clause. But the indicative occurs so frequently after ὅτι that a description of this construction is called for here. There are three broad groups: substantival, epexegetical, and causal.[29]

a. Substantival Ὅτι Clauses

A ὅτι (+ indicative) frequently functions substantivally. It is known as a noun (or nominal) clause, content clause, or sometimes a declarative clause (though we prefer to use this last term for indirect discourse clauses). In such instances the translation of the ὅτι is usually "that." Like a noun, the ὅτι clause can function as subject, direct object, or in apposition to another noun.

In order to see the substantival function of the clause better, brackets are put around it in the illustrations below. If you suspect that a particular ὅτι clause is substantival, replace the entire clause with a pronoun. If it makes sense, the ὅτι clause is most likely substantival. How would such a pronoun function in the sentence? Your answer will tell you which substantive the ὅτι clause is replacing.

1) Subject Clause

On a rare occasion the ὅτι clause functions as the subject of a verb.

Mark 4:38   οὐ μέλει σοι [*ὅτι* **ἀπολλύμεθα**;]
             Does not [the fact] [*that* **we are perishing**] concern you?

John 9:32   ἐκ τοῦ αἰῶνος οὐκ ἠκούσθη [*ὅτι* **ἠνέῳξέν** τις ὀφθαλμοὺς τυφλοῦ γεγεννημένου]
             [*That* anyone **has opened** the eyes of a person who was born blind] has not been heard from eternity.[30]

---

[28] Several MSS have γένεσθε for ἔσεσθε (such as K P 049 1 323 1241 1739), while the majority of MSS read γίνεσθε.

[29] The uses discussed here are the major uses of the ὅτι clause with an indicative. For others, consult BAGD, 588-89.

[30] It is possible to treat this construction as an accusative of retained object after a passive verb.

Acts 4:16		[ὅτι γνωστὸν σημεῖον **γέγονεν** δι᾽ αὐτῶν] πᾶσιν τοῖς κατοικοῦσιν
			Ἰερουσαλὴμ φανερόν
			[*That* a remarkable sign **has taken place** through them] is manifest
			to all the inhabitants of Jerusalem.

Cf. also John 8:17 (possible).

2) Direct Object Clause

The direct object clause involves three subgroups, the latter two
being common in the NT: direct object proper, direct discourse, and
indirect discourse. It is not always easy to distinguish these three. In
the Greek mind there was surely much overlap. In the Koine period,
however, with its tendency toward explicitness, direct discourse
was on the rise, although indirect discourse was still the most frequent.

a) Direct Object Clause Proper

The ὅτι clause occasionally functions as the direct object of a
transitive verb that is *not* a verb of perception (such as saying,
hearing, seeing). Some of the instances are debatable.

Luke 20:37	[ὅτι **ἐγείρονται** οἱ νεκροί], καὶ Μωϋσῆς ἐμήνυσεν
		even Moses demonstrated [*that* the dead **are raised**]
			This may well be a declarative ὅτι clause.

John 3:33	ὁ λαβὼν αὐτοῦ τὴν μαρτυρίαν ἐσφράγισεν [ὅτι ὁ θεὸς ἀληθής **ἐστιν**]
		The one who receives his testimony has sealed [*that* God **is** true].

Rev 2:4		ἔχω κατὰ σοῦ [ὅτι τὴν ἀγάπην σου τὴν πρώτην **ἀφῆκες**]
		I have against you [*that* **you have forsaken** your first love].

Cf. also Luke 10:20b; Rev 2:20.

b) Direct Discourse (a.k.a. Recitative Ὅτι Clause, Ὅτι *Recitativum*)

1] Definition

This is a specialized use of the direct object clause after a
verb of perception. It is a very common use of the ὅτι clause
in the Hellenistic era. In direct discourse, the ὅτι is not to be
translated; in its place you should put quotation marks.

2] Clarification

One must keep in mind that the use of quotation marks for
ὅτι is a modern way of thinking about such constructions.
You should not assume by such a device that such a quotation is verbatim. Several such clauses could be taken as
declarative [indirect discourse] clauses as well, but only
when the *person* of the embedded verb matches the person
of direct discourse; see discussion below.

3] Illustrations

Luke 15:2   διεγόγγυζον οἵ τε Φαρισαῖοι καὶ οἱ γραμματεῖς λέγοντες [ὅτι οὗτος ἁμαρτωλοὺς **προσδέχεται** καὶ **συνεσθίει** αὐτοῖς.]
Both the Pharisees and the scribes were grumbling, saying, ["This man **welcomes** sinners and **eats** with them."]

John 6:42   πῶς νῦν λέγει [ὅτι ἐκ τοῦ οὐρανοῦ **καταβέβηκα**;]
How does he now say, ["**I have come down** from heaven"]?

John 4:17   ἀπεκρίθη ἡ γυνὴ καὶ εἶπεν αὐτῷ· οὐκ ἔχω ἄνδρα. λέγει αὐτῇ ὁ Ἰησοῦς· καλῶς εἶπας [ὅτι ἄνδρα οὐκ **ἔχω**]
The woman answered and said to him, "I do not have a husband." Jesus said to her, "Correctly you have said, ['**I do** not **have** a husband.'"]

> In this text Jesus quotes the woman's words, but the word order has now been reversed. Such a change in word order does not turn this into indirect discourse; that would require, in this case, person-concord between the controlling verb (εἶπας) and the embedded verb (ἔχεις would have to be used instead of ἔχω); thus, "correctly you have said *that* **you do** not **have** a husband."
>
> There is great rhetorical power in the altered word order, for by placing ἄνδρα first the emphasis is on what the woman does not have ("*A husband* I don't have"). It is as if Jesus had said, "Lady, you are quite correct: you've got *somebody* at home, but he's not your husband!" The following verse indicates that this is exactly why the word order was altered ("for you have had five husbands, and the one whom you now have is not your husband. What you said was true.")
>
> Occasionally intermediate students feel uncomfortable calling this a recitative ὅτι clause, precisely because they have a mistaken notion of what direct discourse involves. Ancient writers and speakers, by and large, were not concerned about getting the words exact. They were not writing master's theses; verbal accuracy was not always high on their agenda (though they were usually concerned to reflect accurately the concepts). This can easily be seen in the NT as well: note, for example, how various writers quote the OT, or how the synoptists record the sayings of Jesus, or even how John the Baptist is recorded as quoting himself (John 1:15, 30).
>
> The discomfort that many intermediate students feel over a text such as this was shared by earlier saints. The scribes of two of the earliest uncial MSS, א and D, apparently felt that something was awry, so they altered the word order. But they did not change Jesus' word order–they changed the woman's. It was as if they were saying, "Jesus didn't quote her incorrectly; she said it wrong in the first place!"[31]

Cf. also Matt 2:23 (perhaps); 4:6; 16:7; 19:8; Mark 1:15, 37; 3:28; 5:23; John 1:20; 8:33; Rom 3:10; 2 Cor 6:16; Heb 11:18; Jude 18; Rev 18:7 (second ὅτι).

---

[31] Several MSS also change the ἔχω in Jesus' statement to ἔχεις (א C* D L *pauci*); most Itala MSS retain the first person verb both times, changing the word order of the woman's speech. Among other things, this illustrates that early scribes–even non-Byzantine scribes–performed their duties out of pious motives. Dean Burgon's charge that the five great uncials (א A B C D) were byproducts of heresy flies in the face of the evidence.

c) Indirect Discourse (a.k.a. Declarative ῞Οτι Clause)

1] Definition

This is a specialized use of the direct object clause after a verb of perception. The ὅτι clause contains *reported speech* or *thought*. This contrasts with ὅτι *recitativum*, which involves direct speech. It is a very common use of the ὅτι clause. When the ὅτι introduces indirect discourse, it should be translated *that*.

2] Clarification/Semantics

Like its recitative counterpart, the declarative ὅτι comes after a verb of perception (e.g., verbs of saying, thinking, believing, knowing, seeing, hearing). One could think of it as a recasting of an original saying or thought into a reported form. But two caveats are in order.

First, *in many instances there is no original statement that needs to be recast*. For example, "when the apostles heard *that* Samaria had received the word of God" (ἀκούσαντες οἱ . . . ἀπόστολοι ὅτι δέδεκται ἡ Σαμάρεια τὸν λόγον τοῦ θεοῦ [Acts 8:14]), it is unnecessary to formulate a direct statement "The Samaritans have heard the word of God." Luke is *summarizing* what they heard. And when the Samaritan woman tells Jesus, "I perceive *that* you are a prophet" (θεωρῶ ὅτι προφήτης εἶ σύ [John 4:19]), there is no need to formulate an original statement ("You are a prophet") that *precedes* the reported speech. In Matt 2:16 ("when Herod saw *that* he had been tricked by the magi" [Ἡρῴδης ἰδὼν ὅτι ἐνεπαίχθη ὑπὸ τῶν μάγων]) we must not suppose that there was an original statement, "I have been tricked by the magi." Indirect discourse, then, should not be taken to mean that there is always an underlying direct discourse.[32]

Second, on the other hand, there are several clauses that could be taken either as declarative or recitative. The ambiguity comes when the person of the embedded verb matches the person of direct discourse. Thus, for example, in John 4:35 we read οὐχ ὑμεῖς λέγετε ὅτι ἔτι τετράμηνός ἐστιν καὶ ὁ θερισμὸς ἔρχεται; ("Do you not say, 'There are still four months and then the harvest comes'?" *or* "Do you not say *that* there are still four months and then the harvest comes?"). In most instances, of course, it matters very little.

---

[32] Indeed, indirect discourse is something of a misnomer. Perhaps it should be called something like "perceived formulation," "summary assessment object clause," or the like. Indirect discourse (proper) would then become a subgroup of this larger category.

And again, we must keep in mind that ancient writers did not think in terms of precise quotation.

3] Translation Differences Between Greek and English

One last point needs to be mentioned. Generally speaking, *the tense* of the Greek verb in indirect discourse is *retained* from the direct discourse.[33] This is unlike English: in indirect discourse we usually push the *tense* back "one slot" from what it would have been in the direct discourse (especially if the introductory verb is past tense)–that is, we render a simple past as a past perfect, a present as a past tense, etc. Note the English usage in the table below.[34]

Direct Discourse	Indirect Discourse
He said, "I **see** the dog"	He said that he **saw** the dog
He said, "I **saw** the dog"	He said that he **had seen** the dog
"I **am doing** my chores"	I told you that I **was doing** my chores
"I **have done** my chores"	I told you that I **had done** my chores

Table 9
English Tenses in Direct and Indirect Discourse

In Greek, however, the tenses of the original utterance are usually retained in the indirect discourse. Note the illustrations below.

4] Illustrations

Matt 2:23   πληρωθῇ τὸ ῥηθὲν διὰ τῶν προφητῶν [ὅτι Ναζωραῖος **κληθήσεται**]
what was spoken through the prophet might be fulfilled [*that* **he should be called** a Nazarene]

> Although normally taken as a ὅτι *recitativum*, this could just as easily be considered a declarative ὅτι. Seeing it as such circumvents the problem of the OT citation (viz., what passage is the evangelist thinking of?). Cf. also Acts 6:14 for a declarative ὅτι clause with a future indicative.

Matt 5:17   μὴ νομίσητε [ὅτι **ἦλθον** καταλῦσαι τὸν νόμον ἢ τοὺς προφήτας]
Do not think [*that* **I have come** to destroy the law or the prophets].

> This summarizes the views of Jesus' opponents. The supposed direct discourse would have been, "He has come to destroy the law."

Mark 2:1   ἠκούσθη [ὅτι ἐν οἴκῳ **ἐστίν**]
It was heard [*that* **he was** at home].

> Note that although the equative verb ἐστίν is here translated as a past

---

[33] There are exceptions to this general rule, especially with the imperfect standing in the place of the present. See Burton, *Moods and Tenses*, 130-42 (§334-56).

[34] See also Burton, *Moods and Tenses*, 136-37 (§351-2), for more examples.

tense, it is *not* a historical present. The semantics of historical presents are quite different from the present tense retained in indirect discourse. In particular, the verb εἰμί does not occur as a historical present in the NT or, arguably, anywhere else in Greek literature.

John 4:1   ὡς ἔγνω ὁ Ἰησοῦς [ὅτι **ἤκουσαν** οἱ Φαρισαῖοι [ὅτι Ἰησοῦς πλείονας μαθητὰς **ποιεῖ** καὶ **βαπτίζει** ἢ Ἰωάννης]]

when Jesus knew [*that* the Pharisees **had heard** [*that* Jesus **was making** and **baptizing** more disciples than John]]

> This text involves indirect discourse embedded within *another* indirect discourse. It affords a good illustration of the differences between English and Greek. The Greek retains the tenses from the direct discourse, while English moves them back one slot. Thus, ἤκουσαν is translated *had heard* even though it is aorist (the original statement also would have been aorist: "the Pharisees have heard . . ."). And both ποιεῖ and βαπτίζει, although present tenses, are translated as though they were imperfects (the original statement would have been "Jesus *is making* and *baptizing* more disciples than John").

> Once again, it is important to distinguish the historical present from the present tense retained in indirect discourse. For one thing, historical presents are aspectually "flat"–that is, they are translated just like an aorist, as a simple past tense. But ποιεῖ and βαπτίζει are naturally translated as though they were imperfects.

John 5:15   ὁ ἄνθρωπος ἀνήγγειλεν τοῖς Ἰουδαίοις [ὅτι Ἰησοῦς **ἐστιν** ὁ ποιήσας αὐτὸν ὑγιῆ]

The man announced to the Jews [*that* Jesus **was** the one who made him well].

Acts 4:13   θεωροῦντες τὴν τοῦ Πέτρου παρρησίαν καὶ Ἰωάννου καὶ καταλαβόμενοι [ὅτι ἄνθρωποι ἀγράμματοί **εἰσιν** καὶ ἰδιῶται], ἐθαύμαζον ἐπεγίνωσκόν τε αὐτοὺς [ὅτι σὺν τῷ Ἰησοῦ **ἦσαν**]

When they saw the boldness of Peter and John, and when they discerned [*that* **they were** unlearned and ignorant men], they marveled; and they recognized [*that* **they had been** with Jesus].

> This is an excellent illustration of the differences between Greek and English. Both ὅτι clauses are declarative. In each instance the tense is retained in Greek, but in English translation the tense must be moved back one slot. Thus, εἰσιν is translated *they were* and ἦσαν is translated *they had been*. The purported direct statements would have been "They *are* unlearned and ignorant men" and "They *were* with Jesus."

Cf. also Matt 2:16; 5:17, 21, 33; Luke 8:47; 17:15; John 6:22; 11:27; Acts 8:14; Phlm 21; 1 John 2:18; Rev 12:13.

3) Apposition [*namely, that*]

a) Definition and Key to Identification

> Not infrequently a ὅτι clause stands in apposition to a noun, pronoun, or other substantive. When it does so the translation of the ὅτι as *namely, that* should make good sense (although *that* will also work). Another way to test whether a ὅτι clause is

appositional is to try to *substitute* the clause for its antecedent (in which case you translate the ὅτι simply as *that*). This contrasts with the epexegetical ὅτι clause, which cannot be substituted for its antecedent.

This usage is normally in apposition to the demonstrative τοῦτο in such expressions as "I say *this* to you, *namely, that . . .*" and the like. As such, the pronoun is kataphoric or proleptic, in that its content is revealed by what follows rather than by what precedes.

b) Illustrations

Luke 10:20   ἐν τούτῳ μὴ χαίρετε [ὅτι τὰ πνεύματα ὑμῖν **ὑποτάσσεται**]
Do not rejoice in this, [*namely, that* the spirits **are subject** to you].
The ὅτι clause stands in apposition to ἐν τούτῳ. It could replace it entirely ("Do not rejoice *that* the spirits are subject to you"), as is done in the second half of the verse.

John 3:19   αὕτη ἐστιν ἡ κρίσις [ὅτι τὸ φῶς **ἐλήλυθεν** εἰς τὸν κόσμον καὶ **ἠγάπησαν** οἱ ἄνθρωποι μᾶλλον τὸ σκότος ἢ τὸ φῶς]
This is the judgment, [*namely, that* the light **has come** into the world and [that] people **loved** the darkness rather than the light.
The antecedent is αὕτη; the ὅτι clause could substitute for it: "The judgment is *that* the light has come . . ."

Rom 6:6   τοῦτο γινώσκοντες [ὅτι ὁ παλαιὸς ἡμῶν ἄνθρωπος **συνεσταυρώθη**]
knowing this, [*namely, that* our old man **was co-crucified**]

Phil 1:6   πεποιθὼς αὐτὸ τοῦτο, [ὅτι ὁ ἐναρξάμενος ἐν ὑμῖν ἔργον ἀγαθὸν **ἐπιτελέσει** ἄχρι ἡμέρας Χριστοῦ Ἰησοῦ]
being convinced of this very thing, [*namely, that* the one who began a good work in you **will perfect** it until the day of Christ Jesus]

Rev 2:14   ἔχω κατὰ σοῦ ὀλίγα [ὅτι **ἔχεις** ἐκεῖ κρατοῦντας τὴν διδαχὴν Βαλαάμ]
I have against you a few things, [*namely, that* **you have** (some there) who hold the teaching of Balaam].
This is an unusual instance of the antecedent being a substantival *adjective*.

Cf. also John 5:28; 9:30; 21:23; Acts 20:38; 24:14; 1 Cor 1:12; 15:50; 2 Cor 5:14; 10:11; Eph 5:5; 2 Thess 3:10; 1 Tim 1:9; 2 Tim 3:1; 2 Pet 1:20; 1 John 1:5; Rev 2:6, 14.

b. Epexegetical

The ὅτι clause is sometimes used epexegetically. That is, it *explains* or *clarifies* or *completes* a previous word or phrase. This is similar to the appositional ὅτι clause except that epexegetical ὅτι clause (1) does not identify or name, but instead explains its antecedent; and (2) *cannot be substituted for its antecedent*; and (3) can explain (or complement) something other than a substantive. In some instances (especially after a substantive) the gloss *to the effect that* brings out the explanatory force of the ὅτι clause. Many examples, however, could be treated either as appositional or epexegetical (although the appositional use is more common than the epexegetical).

Luke 2:49   εἶπεν πρὸς αὐτούς· τί [ὅτι **ἐζητεῖτέ** με;][35]
            He said to them, "How is it [*that* **you were seeking** me?]"

Luke 8:25   τίς οὗτός ἐστιν [ὅτι καὶ τοῖς ἀνέμοις **ἐπιτάσσει** καὶ τῷ ὕδατι, καὶ **ὑπακούουσιν** αὐτῷ;]
            Who is this man [*that* **he commands** the winds and the sea, and **they obey** him?]

Rom 5:8   συνίστησιν τὴν ἑαυτοῦ ἀγάπην εἰς ἡμᾶς ὁ θεός, [ὅτι ἔτι ἁμαρτωλῶν ὄντων ἡμῶν Χριστὸς ὑπὲρ ἡμῶν **ἀπέθανεν**]
            God demonstrated his own love toward us [*to the effect that* while we were yet sinners, Christ **died** for us].

Cf. also Matt 8:27; Luke 12:24; John 2:18; 14:22; 1 Cor 1:4-5.

c. Causal (Adverbial) [*because*]

1) Definition

Quite frequently ὅτι introduces a dependent causal clause. In such instances it should be translated *because* or *for*. It is important to distinguish this usage from the declarative ὅτι, even though in many contexts there may be some ambiguity. There are two questions to ask of a particular ὅτι clause[36]: (1) Does it give the *content* (declarative) or the *reason* (causal) for what precedes? (2) Are the verb tenses in the ὅτι clause translated normally (causal), or should they be moved back one "slot" (declarative[37])?

2) Illustrations

Matt 5:3   μακάριοι οἱ πτωχοὶ τῷ πνεύματι, ὅτι αὐτῶν **ἐστιν** ἡ βασιλεία τῶν οὐρανῶν
            Blessed are the poor in spirit, *because* the kingdom of heaven **is** theirs.

Acts 10:38 ὃς διῆλθεν εὐεργετῶν καὶ ἰώμενος πάντας τοὺς καταδυναστευομένους ὑπὸ τοῦ διαβόλου, ὅτι ὁ θεὸς **ἦν** μετ᾽ αὐτοῦ
            who went about doing good and healing all those who were oppressed by the devil, *because* God **was** with him

---

[35] ℵ* W Δ 161 346 828 *et pauci* have ζητεῖτε.

[36] The only instances in which there could be confusion are when the verb in the main clause is a *transitive* verb of perception (because declarative ὅτι clauses are a subgroup of direct object after verbs of perception).

[37] It should be kept in mind, however, that not all tenses in declarative ὅτι clauses are to be moved back. See previous discussion.

Eph 4:25   λαλεῖτε ἀλήθειαν ἕκαστος μετὰ τοῦ πλησίον αὐτοῦ, *ὅτι* **ἐσμὲν** ἀλλήλων
             μέλη
             Speak the truth, each one [of you], with his neighbor, *because* **we are**
             members of one another.

Rev 3:10   *ὅτι* **ἐτήρησας** τὸν λόγον τῆς ὑπομονῆς μου, καγώ σε τηρήσω ἐκ τῆς ὥρας
             τοῦ πειρασμοῦ
             Because **you have kept** the word of my perseverance, even I will
             keep you from the hour of trial.

John 4:27   ἐπὶ τούτῳ ἦλθαν οἱ μαθηταὶ αὐτοῦ καὶ ἐθαύμαζον *ὅτι* μετὰ γυναικὸς
             ἐλάλει
             At this [moment] his disciples came and began marveling *because* **he
             was speaking** with a woman.

> Most English translations render this as a declarative ὅτι clause; thus,
> "at this moment his disciples came and began marveling *that* **he was
> speaking** with a woman." Either translation is possible,[38] but what
> may tip the scales in favor of a causal ὅτι is the fact that the imperfect
> ἐλάλει is not to be translated as a past perfect ("he had been speaking"),
> since the dialogue between Jesus and the woman was still in progress
> when the disciples returned. Consequently, because the rendering of
> ἐλάλει as a past perfect can only occur after a declarative ὅτι and, in fact,
> is to be expected,[39] it is probably best to translate ὅτι as *because*.

Cf. also Matt 5:7, 8, 9; Mark 4:29; 5:9; Luke 2:30; 6:20; John 1:17; Acts 1:5; 4:21; 1 Cor 3:13;
Gal 4:6; 1 Pet 2:15; Rev 17:14; 22:5.

II. The Subjunctive Mood

A. Definition

1. General Definition

The subjunctive is the most common of the oblique moods in the NT. In general, the subjunctive can be said to *represent the verbal action (or state) as uncertain but probable*. It is *not* correct to call this the mood of uncertainty because
the optative also presents the verb as uncertain. Rather, it is better to call it
the mood of *probability* so as to distinguish it from the optative. Still, this is
an overly simplistic definition in light of its usage in the NT.

---

[38] If declarative, ἐθαύμαζον is transitive; if causal, it is intransitive.

[39] Cf., e.g., John 9:18. The imperfect, however, admits of many exceptions in declarative ὅτι clauses.

2. Detailed Description

The subjunctive mood encompasses a multitude of nuances. An adequate description of it requires more nuancing than the mere notion of probability, especially in the Hellenistic era. The best way to describe it is in relation to the other potential moods, the optative and the imperative.

a. In Relation to the Optative

Descriptions of the subjunctive and optative moods in standard grammars sometimes tacitly assume that the optative was still in full flower in the Koine period. But it was in fact dying out. The reason is that it was too subtle for people acquiring Greek as a second language to grasp fully.[40] You can see why: English-speaking students also have a great difficulty grasping the difference between these two moods. In the table given at the beginning of this chapter, for example, we described the subjunctive with "might" and the optative with "may." We would be hard-pressed to state the difference between those two helper verbs, however. In the NT there are 1858 subjunctives and less than 70 optatives–a ratio of 27:1! This simple statistic reflects the fact that in the Hellenistic era *the subjunctive is encroaching on the uses of the optative*. The subjunctive thus, at times, is used for mere *possibility* or even *hypothetical* possibility (as well as, at other times, probability). This is especially true in conditional sentences (there are about 300 third class conditional sentences in the NT [this class involves the subjunctive], and not one complete fourth class condition [this class involves the optative]).

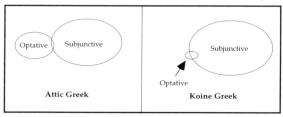

Chart 45
Semantic Overlap of Subjunctive and Optative

On the other hand, sometimes the subjunctive acts like a future indicative. The two morpho-syntactic categories are really quite similar (and perhaps derive from the same root).[41] In dependent clauses, for example, often it functions more like an indicative than an optative. When used in result clauses, for example, the subjunctive cannot be said to express "probability." In any event, the one-word descriptions for the moods are meant to be mere handles, not final statements. Only careful nuancing of the moods' uses will yield helpful insights exegetically.

---

[40] Moulton, *Prolegomena*, 165, notes: "No language but Greek has preserved both Subjunctive and Optative as separate and living elements in speech, and Hellenistic Greek took care to abolish this singularity in a fairly drastic way."

b. In Relation to the Imperative

As we noted at the beginning of this chapter, the moods can be seen against the poles of actuality vs. potentiality and cognition vs. volition. The indicative is primarily used for actuality, while the oblique moods usually remain in the realm of potentiality. Further, the imperative is the primary volitional mood. However, *the subjunctive is also used for volitional notions* quite frequently, in particular as a hortatory subjunctive and prohibitive subjunctive. Even in dependent clauses (such as after ἵνα), the subjunctive commonly has a volitional flavor to it. An acceptable gloss is often *should*, since this is equally ambiguous (it can be used for *probability, obligation,* or *contingency*).

c. Summary

In sum, the subjunctive is used to grammaticalize *potentiality*. It normally does so in the realm of *cognitive probability*, but may also be used for *cognitive possibility* (overlapping with the optative) or *volitional intentionality* (overlapping with the imperative).[42]

It should be added here that the tenses in the subjunctive, as with the other potential moods, involve only *aspect* (kind of action), not time. Only in the indicative mood is time a part of the tense.

B. Specific Uses

1. In Independent Clauses

There are four primary uses of the subjunctive in independent clauses: hortatory, deliberative, emphatic negation, and prohibition. The first two are usually found without negatives, while the latter two, by definition, are preceded by negative particles. Hortatory and prohibitive subjunctive appeal to the volition; deliberative may be volitional or cognitive; emphatic negation is cognitive.

---

[41] Moule, *Idiom Book,* 21-22, reminds us that there is no future subjunctive, and that the future indicative and aorist subjunctive were "mutually exclusive" forms. The *v.l.* at 1 Cor 13:3, καυθήσωμαι is a future subjunctive, but it is, of course, an impossible form. Had it been found in one witness, we could perhaps treat it as a mere itacism. But as the reading of the *majority* of Byzantine minuscules, its roots are clearly post-Koine and as such is a "grammatical monstrosity that cannot be attributed to Paul" (Metzger, *Textual Commentary* , 498). Cf. also the notes in *BDF,*15 (§28); Howard, *Accidence,* 219.

[42] Robertson, *Grammar,* 928-35, has a somewhat similar breakdown. He sees the subjunctive as falling into three general uses: futuristic (cognitive eventuality), volitional, and deliberative. What is missing in his analysis is the overlap between the subjunctive and optative.

➡️ a. **Hortatory Subjunctive (a.k.a. Volitive)** *[let us]*

   1) **Definition**

   The subjunctive is commonly used to exhort or command oneself and one's associates. This use of the subjunctive is used "to urge some one to unite with the speaker in a course of action upon which he has already decided."[43] Since there is no first person imperative, the hortatory subjunctive is used to do roughly the same task. Thus this use of the subjunctive is an exhortation in the *first person plural*. The typical translation, rather than *we should . . .* is *let us . . . .*

   On five occasions, the first person *singular* is also used in a hortatory way. The force is akin to asking *permission* for the verbal action. *Let me* or *permit me* brings out its meaning. The key to the singular hortatory usage is the presence of ἄφες ("permit" [aorist imperative of ἀφίημι]) or the adverb δεῦρο ("come") *preceding*[44] the subjunctive.[45]

   2) **Illustrations**

Mark 4:35   καὶ λέγει αὐτοῖς, . . . **Διέλθωμεν** εἰς τὸ πέραν
   And he said to them, . . . "**Let us go** to the other side."

Luke 6:42   ἄφες **ἐκβάλω** τὸ κάρφος τὸ ἐν τῷ ὀφθαλμῷ σου
   Let me take out the beam that is in your eye.

Acts 4:17   **ἀπειλησώμεθα** αὐτοῖς μηκέτι λαλεῖν ἐπὶ τῷ ὀνόματι τούτῳ
   Let us warn them not to speak in this name.

Acts 7:34   δεῦρο **ἀποστείλω** σε εἰς Αἴγυπτον[46]
   Come, **let me send** you to Egypt.

Rom 5:1   δικαιωθέντες οὖν ἐκ πίστεως εἰρήνην **ἔχωμεν** πρὸς τὸν θεόν[47]
   Therefore, since we have been justified by faith, **let us** have peace with God.

   This textual variant has often been translated something like, "Let us *enjoy* the peace that we already have." Only rarely in the NT does the verb mean *enjoy* (cf. Heb 11:25), and it probably never has this as a primary force in the subjunctive.[48] Thus, if the subjunctive is original, it probably means "let us come to have peace with God," but this notion is entirely foreign to the context, particularly to the fact that justification has already been applied.

---

[43] Chamberlain, *Exegetical Grammar*, 83.

[44] The subjunctive must be preceded, not followed, by one of these terms. The subjunctive in Luke 17:3, which precedes ἄφες, is a conditional subjunctive.

[45] Robertson, *Grammar*, 931, notes that all singular hortatory subjunctives in the NT are so prefaced

[46] ἀποστελῶ is found in H P Ψ 33 *Byz et plu*. The reading of the text above is a solid Alexandrian and Western reading (though ℵ and E have the itacistic ἀποστίλω).

[47] The subjunctive here is a well-known textual variant to the indicative ἔχομεν found in the Nestle-Aland[27]/UBS[4]. Although ἔχωμεν has the better external pedigree, the intrinsic evidence is sufficiently compelling to cause the UBS[4] editors to give the indicative an "A" rating (two letters higher than the UBS[3]!).

1 Cor 15:32 εἰ νεκροὶ οὐκ ἐγείρονται, **φάγωμεν** καὶ **πίωμεν**, αὔριον γὰρ ἀποθνῄσκομεν
If the dead are not raised, **let us eat** and **drink**, for tomorrow we die.

Gal 6:9 τὸ καλὸν ποιοῦντες μὴ **ἐγκακῶμεν**
Let us not grow weary in doing good.

Heb 4:14 **κρατῶμεν** τῆς ὁμολογίας
Let us hold on to the confession.

Rev 21:9 δεῦρο, **δείξω** σοι τὴν νύμφην τὴν γυναῖκα τοῦ ἀρνίου
Come, **let me** show you the bride, the wife of the Lamb.

> It is possible that δείξω is future indicative (as the RSV, NRSV, NIV take it), in which case the translation would be "Come, I will show you . . ." Similarly, Rev 17:1.

Cf. also (singular) Matt 7:4 (parallels Luke 6:42); Rev 17:1.[49]

Cf. also (plural) Matt 27:49 (here with ἄφες); Rom 13:12; 1 Cor 5:8; 2 Cor 7:1; Gal 5:25, 26; Eph 4:15; Phil 3:15; 1 Thess 5:6; Heb 4:1; 12:1; 1 John 3:18; 1 John 4:19 (possible);[50] Rev 19:7.

➡ ### b. Deliberative Subjunctive (a.k.a. Dubitative)

Definition

The deliberative subjunctive asks either a *real* or *rhetorical* question. In general, it can be said that the deliberative subjunctive is "merely the hortatory turned into a question," though the semantics of the two kinds of questions are often quite different. Both imply some *doubt* about the response, but the *real* question is usually in the *cognitive* area (such as "How can we . . . ?" in which the inquiry is about the means), while the *rhetorical* question is *volitive* (e.g., "Should we . . . ?" in which the question has to do with moral obligation). Both are fairly common with *first person* verbs, though second and third person verbs can be found. The *future indicative* is also used in deliberative questions, though the subjunctive is more common.[51]

---

[48] The subjunctive of ἔχω occurs 44 times. John 10:10 comes close, but the connotation of enjoyment is not in the verb but in περισσόν. Note also John 16:33 (εἰρήνην ἔχητε), but the parallel in the second part of the verse does not help (ἐν τῷ κόσμῳ θλῖψιν ἔχετε). Likewise, John 17:13; 2 Cor 1:15; 1 John 1:3 have similar glitches. Elsewhere the subjunctive (even present subjunctive) *nowhere* seems to suggest the enjoyment of something *already* possessed. For example, in John 5:40, Jesus in speaking to unbelievers (note v 38) says, "You do not want to come to me that you might have (ἔχητε) life." This cannot mean "that you might enjoy the life you already have"! If enjoyment is part of the connotation, so is acquiring it. Cf., e.g., Matt 17:20; 19:16; 21:38; John 3:16; 6:40; 13:35; Rom 1:13; 15:4; 1 Cor 13:1-3; 2 Cor 8:12; Eph 4:28; Heb 6:18; Jas 2:14; 1 John 2:28.

[49] All singular hortatory subjunctives are accounted for.

[50] The form ἀγαπῶμεν is probably an indicative.

[51] Cf. Matt 12:11; 16:26; 17:17; 18:12, 21; Mark 6:37; 8:4; Luke 6:39; Acts 13:10; Rom 2:26; 3:3; 8:32.

Because of the differences in the semantics it is best to distinguish the two kinds of questions. The table below illustrates the *usual* differences.[52]

Name	*Type of Question*	*Expected Response*	*Area of Doubt*
Real	Is it possible?	resolution of problem	cognitive
Rhetorical	Is it right?	volitional/ behavioral	conduct

Table 10
The Semantics of Deliberative Questions

1) Deliberative *Real* Subjunctive

a) Definition

As the name implies, the *real* question expects some kind of answer and is a genuine question. In the speaker's presentation, there is uncertainty about the answer. Unlike the interrogative indicative, it does not ask a question of fact, but of *possibility, means, location,* etc. In other words, it does typically not ask *What?* or *Who?*, but *How? Whether?* and *Where?* Occasionally it can ask a question of moral obligation, like the rhetorical question, but when it does, the expected answer is in doubt.

b) Illustrations

Matt 6:31   μὴ μεριμνήσητε λέγοντες· τί **φάγωμεν**; ἤ· τί **πίωμεν**; ἤ· τί **περιβαλώμεθα**;
Do not be anxious, saying, "What **should we eat**?" or "What **should we drink**?" or "What **should we wear**?"

> Although the question appears to be asking for a specific content, as indicated by the τί (thus, a question of fact), the subjunctive tells a different story. The subjunctive indicates some doubt as to *whether* food or drink or clothing will be available.

Mark 6:37   λέγουσιν αὐτῷ· ἀπελθόντες **ἀγοράσωμεν** δηναρίων διακοσίων ἄρτους καὶ δώσομεν αὐτοῖς φαγεῖν;
They said to him, "**Should we** go and **buy** two hundred denarii worth of bread and give it to them to eat?"

> The question here is one of possibility. The disciples are essentially asking, *How* do you expect us to feed these people? To be noted is the future indicative, δώσομεν, that is joined to the aorist subjunctive. It, too, is deliberative.

---

[52] Not all deliberative questions can be easily distinguished. The basic reason is that we cannot penetrate the mind of the author to see the reasons for his use of the subjunctive.

Mark 12:14 ἔξεστιν δοῦναι κῆνσον Καίσαρι ἢ οὔ; **δῶμεν** ἢ μὴ **δῶμεν**;[53]

> Is it lawful to pay the tax to Caesar or not? **Should we give** or **should we** not **give**?

>> This question from the Pharisees and Herodians would have gotten a different response from each group. Asked of Jesus, it was a genuine question, the answer to which was uncertain.

Cf. also Matt 26:17, 54 (third person); Mark 11:32; Luke 3:12; 23:31 (third person); John 18:39; 1 Cor 14:7 (*v.l.*); Heb 11:32.

2) Deliberative *Rhetorical* Subjunctive

a) Definition

> As the name implies, the *rhetorical* question expects no *verbal* response, but is in fact a thinly disguised statement, though couched in such a way as to draw the listener into the text. In the speaker's presentation, there is uncertainty about whether the listener will heed the implicit command. Unlike the interrogative indicative, it does not ask a question of fact, but of *obligation*. It is supremely a question of "oughtness."

b) Illustrations

Mark 8:37 τί **δοῖ** ἄνθρωπος ἀντάλλαγμα τῆς ψυχῆς αὐτοῦ;

> What **can** a person **give** in exchange for his life?[54]

>> The implication is that "there is nothing that would compensate for such a loss."[55] Although the question appears to be asking whether such an exchange is possible, it is really an indictment against gaining the world and losing one's life in the process.

Rom 6:1 **ἐπιμένωμεν** τῇ ἁμαρτίᾳ, ἵνα ἡ χάρις πλεονάσῃ;[56]

> **Should we continue** in sin that grace might increase?

>> The question is not whether one will continue to sin, but whether it is morally acceptable to continue in sin. Paul's answer quickly follows: μὴ γένοιτο!

Rom 10:14 πῶς **ἀκούσωσιν** χωρὶς κηρύσσοντος;[57]

> How **can they hear** without a preacher?

>> The implication is that there is no way that they will hear without a

---

[53] D 346 (1424) omit the clause δῶμεν ἢ μὴ δῶμεν;

[54] The Attic subjunctive δῷ is found in ℵ[C] L; the future indicative δώσει is the reading of 𝔓[45] A C D W X Γ Θ Π Σ Φ 33 *f*[1, 13] *Byz*.

[55] BAGD, s.v. ἀντάλλαγμα.

[56] The subjunctive ἐπιμένωμεν has two indicative rivals and one subjunctive rival: ἐπιμενοῦμεν in 614 945 1505 *alii*; ἐπιμένομεν in ℵ K P 1175 1881 2464 *et pauci*; ἐπιμείνωμεν in L 88 1928.

[57] For ἀκούσωσιν 𝔓[46] reads ἀκούσωνται; ℵ* D F G K P 104 309 365 436 1505 1739 1881 *et alii* read ἀκούσονται; the Byzantine cursives have ἀκούσουσιν. In the least, this shows the semantic overlap between aorist subjunctive and future indicative.

➡   preacher. But it is framed as a question to get the audience to ponder on
                     the point, reflecting on their own response.

Cf. also Matt 23:33(second person); Luke 14:34; John 6:68 (*v.l.*); Rom 6:15; Rev 15:4.

➡   c. **Emphatic Negation Subjunctive**

           1) **Definition**

                     Emphatic negation is indicated by *οὐ μή* plus the *aorist subjunctive* or,
                     less frequently, οὐ μή plus the *future indicative* (e.g., Matt 26:35;
                     Mark 13:31; John 4:14; 6:35). This is the strongest way to negate
                     something in Greek.

                     One might think that the negative with the subjunctive could not be
                     as strong as the negative with the indicative. However, while οὐ +
                     the indicative denies a *certainty*, οὐ μή + the subjunctive denies a
                     potentiality. The negative is not weaker; rather, the affirmation that is
                     being negatived is less firm with the subjunctive. οὐ μή rules out
                     even the idea as being a possibility: "ου μή is the most decisive way
                     of negativing someth. in the future."[58]

                     Emphatic negation is found primarily in the reported sayings of
                     Jesus (both in the Gospels and in the Apocalypse); secondarily, in
                     quotations from the LXX. Outside of these two sources it occurs only
                     rarely. As well, a *soteriological* theme is frequently found in such
                     statements, especially in John: what is negatived is the possibility of
                     the loss of salvation.

           2) **Illustrations**

Matt 24:35 οἱ λόγοι μου *οὐ μὴ* **παρέλθωσιν**[59]
            My words **will** *not at all* **pass away.**

John 10:28 δίδωμι αὐτοῖς ζωὴν αἰώνιον καὶ *οὐ μὴ* **ἀπόλωνται** εἰς τὸν αἰῶνα
            I give them eternal life, and **they will** *not at all* **perish.**

John 11:26 πᾶς ὁ ζῶν καὶ πιστεύων εἰς ἐμὲ *οὐ μὴ* **ἀποθάνῃ**
            Everyone who lives and believes in me **will** *never* **die.**

Rom 4:8   μακάριος ἀνὴρ οὗ *οὐ μὴ* **λογίσηται** κύριος ἁμαρτίαν
            Blessed is the man whose sin the Lord **will** *not at all* **count.**

Heb 13:5   *οὐ μή* σε **ἀνῶ** οὐδ᾽ *οὐ μή* σε **ἐγκαταλίπω**[60]
            I will *not at all* **fail** you nor **will I** *ever* **leave** you.

---

[58] Cf. BAGD, s.v. μή, 515-17, esp. III. D. on 517.

[59] The future indicative παρελεύσονται is found in ℵ² W X Γ Δ Θ Π *f*[1, 13] *Byz.*

[60] On external grounds, ἐγκαταλείπω is a superior reading, found in 𝔓[46] ℵ A C D² K
L M P Ψ 0243 33 1739 1881 *Byz et plu.* The aorist subjunctive (the reading of NA[27]), given
above, has a poorer pedigree, led by D* 81 326 365 1175 1505 *et alii.* However, the present
subjunctive (Ellingworth calls it an itacism [*Commentary on Hebrews*, NIGNTC, *loc. cit.*]) is
impossible.

Cf. also Matt 5:18, 20; 13:14; Mark 9:1, 41; 13:2; Luke 6:37; 18:7; 21:18; John 6:37; 8:12, 51; 20:25; Acts 13:41; Gal 5:16; 1 Thess 5:3; Heb 8:12; 1 Pet 2:6; Rev 2:11; 3:5, 12; 21:27.

➡ **d. Prohibitive Subjunctive**

1) Definition

This is the use of the subjunctive in a prohibition–that is, a negative command. It is used to forbid the occurrence of an action. The structure is usually μή + *aorist subjunctive,* typically in the *second* person.[61] Its force is equivalent to an imperative after μή; hence, it should be translated *Do not* rather than *You should not.*[62] The prohibitive subjunctive is frequently used in the NT.

2) Illustrations

Matt 1:20   μὴ **φοβηθῇς** παραλαβεῖν Μαρίαν τὴν γυναῖκά σου
Do *not* **be afraid** to take Mary as your wife

John 3:7   μὴ **θαυμάσῃς** ὅτι εἶπόν σοι· δεῖ ὑμᾶς γεννηθῆναι ἄνωθεν.
Do *not* **be amazed** that I said to you, "You must be born again."

Rom 10:6   μὴ **εἴπῃς** ἐν τῇ καρδίᾳ σου· τίς ἀναβήσεται εἰς τὸν οὐρανόν;
Do *not* **say** in your heart, "Who will ascend into heaven?"

Rev 22:10   μὴ **σφραγίσῃς** τοὺς λόγους τῆς προφητείας τοῦ βιβλίου τούτου
Do *not* **seal up** the words of the prophecy of this book.

Cf. also Matt 3:9; 5:17; Mark 10:19; Luke 3:8; 21:9; Acts 7:60; Col 2:21; Heb 3:8; Jas 2:11; 1 Pet 3:14; Rev 6:6.

2. In Dependent (Subordinate) Clauses

The following categories of the subjunctive are the primary uses when the subjunctive is in a dependent or subordinate clause. By far the most common category is the use of the subjunctive after ἵνα.

➡ **a. Subjunctive in Conditional Sentences**

1) Definition

This is the use of the subjunctive in the protasis of conditional sentences. The conditional element is made explicit by the particle ἐάν. Both the particle (a combination of εἰ and the contingent particle ἄν) and the subjunctive give the condition a sense of contingency. This

---

[61] In fact, nowhere in the NT is the *second person aorist imperative* used after μή. If one wanted to express prohibition in the second person, the subjunctive was always the mood of choice.

[62] See chapter on volitional clauses for discussion.

is a relatively common usage of the subjunctive, occurring nearly 300 times in the NT.

2) Clarification and Semantics

The subjunctive is used in the *third class condition* as well as the *fifth class condition*. Structurally, these two are virtually identical: The *fifth* class condition requires a present indicative in the apodosis, while the *third* class can take virtually any mood-tense combination, including the present indicative.

Semantically, their meaning is a bit different. The *third* class condition encompasses a broad range of potentialities in Koine Greek. It depicts what is *likely to occur* in the *future*, what could *possibly occur*, or even what is only *hypothetical* and will not occur. In classical Greek the third class condition was usually restricted to the first usage (known as *more probable future*), but with the subjunctive's encroaching on the domain of the optative in the Hellenistic era, this structural category has expanded accordingly. The context will always be of the greatest help in determining an author's use of the third class condition.

The *fifth* class offers a condition the fulfillment of which is realized in the *present time*. This condition is known as the *present general condition*. For the most part this condition is a *simple* condition;[63] that is, the speaker gives no indication about the likelihood of its fulfillment. His presentation is neutral: "If A, then B."

Because of the broad range of the third class condition and the undefined nature of the fifth class, many conditional clauses are open to interpretation. If in doubt, it is perhaps best to label them as *third* class, since the fifth class is truly a subcategory of the third.[64]

3) Illustrations

Matt 4:9   ταῦτά σοι πάντα δώσω, ἐὰν πεσὼν **προσκυνήσῃς** μοι
I will give you all these things, *if* **you will** fall down and **worship** me.
>This is a true third class since the apodosis involves a future indicative.

Mark 5:28   ἔλεγεν ὅτι ἐὰν **ἅψωμαι** κἂν τῶν ἱματίων αὐτοῦ σωθήσομαι
She was saying [to herself], "*If* only **I touch** his garments, I shall be healed."

---

[63] Although many grammarians, especially those of the Goodwin school, treat the first class condition as the "simple" condition, I think it more appropriately belongs to the fifth class. See the chapter on conditional clauses for discussion.

[64] For a detailed treatment on the subjunctive in conditions, see the chapter on conditional clauses.

> This woman, who had been hemorrhaging for a dozen years, was desperate. She had gotten worse by doctors' hands. The imperfect ἔλεγεν is perhaps iterative: "she was saying over and over again," as if to muster up enough courage and enough faith. Thus, in Mark's portrayal, there seems to be a great deal of doubt in this woman's mind that such an act would even heal her.

John 3:12   εἰ τὰ ἐπίγεια εἶπον ὑμῖν καὶ οὐ πιστεύετε, πῶς ἐὰν **εἴπω** ὑμῖν τὰ ἐπουράνια πιστεύσετε;

If I have told you earthly things and yet you do not believe, how will you believe *if* **I should tell** you heavenly things?

> This is a third class condition, embedded within a deliberative question. It follows a first class condition in which the apodosis is a denial of belief. In light of this parallel, as well as the context, we should read the third class condition as follows: "If I should tell you heavenly things–and it is likely that I will–how is it possible for you to believe?"

John 5:31   ἐὰν ἐγὼ **μαρτυρῶ** περὶ ἐμαυτοῦ, ἡ μαρτυρία μου οὐκ ἔστιν ἀληθής

If **I bear testimony** about myself, my testimony is not true.

> The present tense in the apodosis (ἔστιν) permits this to be taken as a fifth class condition. In the context, it seems to be the best option: Jesus is not saying that it is probable that he will bear testimony about himself. Rather, he is simply stating a supposition ("If A, then B").

1 Cor 13:2   ἐὰν **ἔχω** προφητείαν καὶ **εἰδῶ** τὰ μυστήρια πάντα καὶ πᾶσαν τὴν γνῶσιν καὶ ἐὰν **ἔχω** πᾶσαν τὴν πίστιν ὥστε ὄρη μεθιστάναι, ἀγάπην δὲ μὴ **ἔχω**, οὐθέν εἰμι.

If **I have a** prophetic gift and **I understand** all mysteries and all knowledge, and *if* **I have** all faith so as to remove mountains, but **do** not **have** love, I am nothing.

> The fourfold condition is used in a broad way. Paul builds his argument from the actual (he does have prophetic powers) to the hypothetical (he does not understand all mysteries or have all knowledge [otherwise, he would be omniscient!]). This is his pattern in the first three verses of 1 Cor 13: to argue from the actual to the hypothetical. It is therefore probable that Paul could speak in the tongues of human beings, but *not* in the tongues of *angels* (v 1). 1 Cor 13:1, then, offers no comfort for those who view tongues as a heavenly language.

Cf. also Luke 5:12; Acts 9:2; 15:1 (present general); Rom 2:25 (present general); 10:9; 1 Cor 11:15; Col 4:10; 1 Tim 3:15; Heb 10:38; Jas 2:17; 1 John 1:8, 9, 10; Rev 3:20.

➡ b. Ἵνα + the Subjunctive

The single most common category of the subjunctive in the NT is after ἵνα, comprising about *one third* of all subjunctive instances. There are seven basic uses included in this construction: purpose, result, purpose-result, substantival, epexegetical, complementary, and command. Its usage in the Koine period has increased from the classical as this construction came to be used as a periphrasis for the simple infinitive.

### 1)	Purpose Ἵνα Clause (a.k.a. Final or Telic Ἵνα)

The most frequent use of ἵνα clauses is to express purpose. In classical Greek, this idea would have been expressed more often by the infinitive. The focus is on the *intention* of the action of the main verb, whether accomplished or not. In keeping with the genius of the subjunctive, this subordinate clause answers the question *Why?* rather than *What?* An appropriate translation would be *in order that*, or, where fitting, as a simple infinitive (*to . . .*).

We must not suppose that this use of the subjunctive necessarily implies any doubt about the fulfillment of the verbal action on the part of the speaker. This may or may not be so; each case must be judged on its own merits. The subjunctive is used, however, because it answers the implicit deliberative question. Further, many instances of purpose clauses shade off into result as well, especially when the divine will is in view. (See purpose-result category below.)

Matt 12:10	ἐπηρώτησαν αὐτὸν λέγοντες· εἰ ἔξεστιν τοῖς σάββασιν θεραπεῦσαι; *ἵνα* **κατηγορήσωσιν** αὐτοῦ
They questioned him, saying, "Is it lawful to heal on the Sabbath?" *in order that* **they might accuse** him.

Matt 19:13	προσηνέχθησαν αὐτῷ παιδία *ἵνα* τὰς χεῖρας **ἐπιθῇ** αὐτοῖς καὶ **προσεύξηται**
Children were brought to him *in order that* **he might lay** his hands on them and **pray** [for them].
> The next line indicates that only purpose is in view: "but the disciples rebuked [the people who brought the children]."

Mark 6:8	παρήγγειλεν αὐτοῖς *ἵνα* μηδὲν **αἴρωσιν** εἰς ὁδόν[65]
He ordered them *to* **take** nothing for the journey.

John 1:7	οὗτος ἦλθεν εἰς μαρτυρίαν *ἵνα* **μαρτυρήσῃ** περὶ τοῦ φωτός, *ἵνα* πάντες **πιστεύσωσιν** δι᾽ αὐτοῦ
He came for a testimony, *to* **testify** concerning the light, *that* all **might believe** through him.

Acts 16:30	τί με δεῖ ποιεῖν *ἵνα* **σωθῶ**;
What must I do *to* **be saved**?

1 John 2:1	ταῦτα γράφω ὑμῖν *ἵνα* μὴ **ἁμάρτητε**[66]
I am writing these things to you *in order that* **you might** not **sin**.

Cf. also Mark 1:38; Luke 9:12; John 20:31; Acts 4:17; Rom 1:11; 1 Cor 4:6; Eph 2:9; Jas 1:4; 1 John 3:8; Rev 2:21; 8:6.

---

[65] ἄρωσιν is found in ℵ C L W Δ Θ Π Φ 565 579 *f*[13].

[66] ἁμαρτάνητε is the reading of of few late minuscules (e.g., 35 429 614 630 1505).

2) **Result Ἵνα Clause (a.k.a. Consecutive or Ecbatic Ἵνα)**

This use of ἵνα + subjunctive expresses the result of the action of the main verb. It indicates a consequence of the verbal action that is *not intended*. The ἵνα is normally translated *so that, with the result that*.

In classical Greek ἵνα was not used to indicate result. However, in the NT ἵνα is also used to express result, though only on a rare occasion.

John 9:2   ῥαββί, τίς ἥμαρτεν, οὗτος ἢ οἱ γονεῖς αὐτοῦ, ἵνα τυφλὸς **γεννηθῇ**;

Rabbi, who sinned, this man or his parents, *with the result that* **he should be born** blind?

Rom 11:11   μὴ ἔπταισαν ἵνα **πέσωσιν**;

They did not stumble *so as to* **fall**, did they?

Cf. also Mark 4:12 (par. Luke 8:10);[67] Luke 9:45 (possible); 1 Cor 5:2 (possible); Gal 5:17; 1 Thess 5:4; 1 John 1:9 (possible); 2:27.

3) **Purpose-Result Ἵνα Clause**

Not only is ἵνα used for result in the NT, but also for purpose-result. That is, it indicates *both the intention and its sure accomplishment*. BAGD point out in this connection: "In many cases purpose and result cannot be clearly differentiated, and hence ἵνα is used for the result which follows according to the purpose of the subj[ect] or of God. As in Jewish and pagan thought, purpose and result are identical in declarations of the divine will."[68] Likewise, Moule points out that "the Semitic mind was notoriously unwilling to draw a sharp dividing-line between purpose and consequence."[69] In other words, the NT writers employ the language to reflect their theology: what God purposes is what happens and, consequently, ἵνα is used to express both the divine purpose and the result.

This probably does not represent a change in syntax from classical to Koine, but a change in subject matter. It is, of course, possible to treat each of these examples as simply purpose ἵνα clauses in which there is evidently no doubt about the accomplishment from the speaker's viewpoint. Hence, *in order that* is an acceptable gloss.[70]

---

[67] This text is a theological conundrum: it could be treated as purpose, result, or purpose-result.

[68] BAGD, s.v., ἵνα, II. 2. (p. 378).

[69] Moule, *Idiom Book*, 142.

[70] BAGD state that the meaning is both *in order that* and *so that*, although they give no such double glosses.

John 3:16   τὸν υἱὸν τὸν μονογενῆ ἔδωκεν, *ἵνα* πᾶς ὁ πιστεύων εἰς αὐτὸν μὴ **ἀπόληται** ἀλλ᾽ **ἔχη** ζωὴν αἰώνιον

He gave his only Son, *in order that* everyone who believes in him **should** not **perish** but **should have** eternal life.

> The fact that the subjunctive is all but required after ἵνα[71] does not, of course, argue for uncertainty as to the fate of the believer. This fact is obvious, not from this text, but from the use of of οὐ μή in John 10:28 and 11:26, as well as the general theological contours of the gospel of John.

Phil 2:9-11   ὁ θεὸς αὐτὸν ὑπερύψωσεν . . . *ἵνα* ἐν τῷ ὀνόματι Ἰησοῦ πᾶν γόνυ **κάμψῃ**. . .καὶ πᾶσα γλῶσσα **ἐξομολογήσηται** ὅτι κύριος Ἰησοῦς Χριστός[72]

God highly exalted him . . . *in order that* at the name of Jesus every knee **should bow**. . . and every tongue **should confess** that Jesus Christ is Lord.

> Paul here is not declaring *only* God's *intention* in exalting Christ. Much more than that. The apostle is indicating that what God intends he will carry out. The evidence for this is that he is quoting Isa 45:23 here, though weaving it into his text in such a way that he alters it by turning it into a purpose clause (in the LXX it is a declarative statement using future indicatives after ὅτι). Paul quotes this text in Rom 14:11, though there he introduces it with an introductory formula (γέγραπται γάρ) and, consequently, leaves the moods and tenses as they were in the LXX. The point is simply that since Paul is not directly or formally quoting the OT here, but has worked that quotation into his text by making it the purpose of the exaltation, the subjunctive is required after ἵνα. If both in Isa 45:23 and in Rom 14:11 the future indicative is a predictive future, then Paul seems to be using the Isaiah passage to declare that Jesus Christ is the one who will fulfill the prophecy made about Yahweh. If this is an accurate assessment of the future indicative, then Paul in Phil 2:10-11 is either misunderstanding the OT or he is declaring that Jesus Christ is true deity. This text is one of scores of incidental or almost casual uses of the OT by NT writers in which the OT spoke of YHWH while the NT writer applies the statement to Christ.

Cf. also Matt 1:22; 4:14; Luke 11:50; John 4:36; 12:40; 19:28; Rom 3:19; 5:20; 7:13; 8:17.

For other possible instances, cf. Mark 4:12 (par. Luke 8:10);[73] Rom 7:4; Eph 2:7; 2 Pet 1:4; 1 John 1:9.[74]

4)   Substantival Ἵνα Clause (a.k.a. Sub-Final Clause)

As with ὅτι plus the indicative, ἵνα plus the subjunctive can be used substantivally. There are four basic uses: subject, predicate nominative, direct object, and apposition. As with substantival ὅτι clauses,

---

[71] There are over a dozen future indicatives after ἵνα in the NT, with another dozen or so among the variants.

[72] The future indicative ἐξομολογήσεται is found in A C D F G 33 1739 *et plu.*

[73] This could also be taken as epexegetical or result.

[74] This text is a theological conundrum: It could be treated as purpose, result, or purpose-result.

the ἵνα clause will be bracketed so as to highlight its substantival force. None is especially frequent.

a) Subject Clause

Matt 18:6   συμφέρει αὐτῷ [ἵνα **κρεμασθῇ** μύλος ὀνικὸς περὶ τὸν τράχηλον αὐτοῦ]
[*that* a millstone **should be tied** around his neck] is better for him . . .

1 Cor 4:2   ζητεῖται ἐν τοῖς οἰκονόμοις, [ἵνα πιστός τις **εὑρεθῇ**]
[*That* a man **should be found** faithful] is sought in stewards.

Cf. also Matt 5:29; 10:25 (possible); 18:14; John 16:7; 1 Cor 4:3.

b) Predicate Nominative Clause

John 4:34   ἐμὸν βρῶμά ἐστιν [ἵνα **ποιήσω** τὸ θέλημα τοῦ πέμψαντός με καὶ **τελειώσω** αὐτοῦ τὸ ἔργον]
My food is [*that* **I should do** the will of the one who sent me and **complete** his work].

c) Direct Object Clause (a.k.a. Content Ἵνα Clause)

In this usage the direct object often follows a verb of commanding, urging, praying. The ἵνα clause thus gives the content to the main verb and in this respect answers the question *What?* rather than *Why?*[75]

Matt 12:16   ἐπετίμησεν αὐτοῖς [ἵνα μὴ φανερὸν αὐτὸν **ποιήσωσιν**]
He ordered them [*that* **they should** not **make** him known].

Luke 4:3   εἰ υἱὸς εἶ τοῦ θεοῦ, εἰπὲ τῷ λίθῳ τούτῳ [ἵνα **γένηται** ἄρτος]
If you are God's Son, say to this stone [*that* **it should become** bread].

Cf. also Matt 4:3; 16:20; Rom 16:1-2 (possible); 1 Cor 1:10; Eph 1:17; 3:16;[76] 1 Tim 5:21; 2 Pet 1:4 (possible); 1 John 5:16.

d) Apposition Clause

The force of the appositional ἵνα is *namely, that*. Although not frequent, it is almost idiomatic of Johannine literature.

John 17:3   αὕτη ἐστιν ἡ αἰώνιος ζωὴ [ἵνα **γινώσκωσιν** σὲ τὸν μόνον ἀληθινὸν θεόν][77]
This is eternal life, [*namely, that* **they might know** you, the only true God].

---

[75] The direct object ὅτι clause also answers *What?* but it fills in a *statement*, not a command. Each type of clause is thus well-suited to the verb it depends on.

[76] This clause expresses the content of the *implied* verb of prayer in v 14 (in the phrase "I bow my knees before the Father").

[77] γινώσκουσιν is read instead of γινώσκωσιν in A D G L N W Y Δ Λ 0109 0301 33 579 1241 *et alii*.

1 John 3:11   αὕτη ἐστὶν ἡ ἀγγελία ἣν ἠκούσατε ἀπ᾽ ἀρχῆς, [ἵνα **ἀγαπῶμεν** ἀλλήλους]
               This is the message that you have heard from the beginning, [*namely,
               that* **we should love** one another].

Cf. also Luke 1:43 (possible); John 15:8, 12; Acts 17:15; 1 Cor 4:6 (second ἵνα);[78] 1 John 3:23;
4:21; 5:3; 2 John 6; 3 John 4.

5)   Epexegetical Ἵνα Clause

The epexegetical ἵνα is the use of ἵνα after a *noun* or *adjective* to
explain or clarify that noun or adjective. In classical Greek this
would have more often been expressed by an epexegetical infinitive.

Luke 7:6   οὐ ἱκανός εἰμι [ἵνα ὑπὸ τὴν στέγην μου **εἰσέλθῃς**]
              I am not worthy [*that* **you should enter** under my roof].

John 2:25   οὐ χρείαν εἶχεν [ἵνα τις **μαρτυρήσῃ**]
              he did not have a need [*that* anyone **should testify**]

Cf. also Matt 8:8; 10:25 (possible); 1 Cor 9:18; Phil 2:2 (possible);[79] 1 John 1:9.[80]

6)   Complementary Ἵνα

The complementary ἵνα *completes* the meaning of a helping verb
such as θέλω, δύναμαι, and the like. In classical Greek this would
have been expressed by a complementary infinitive. Although complementary, the force of the entire construction (verb + ἵνα clause) is
usually that of *purpose* (in keeping with the lexeme of the main verb).

Matt 26:4   συνεβουλεύσαντο [ἵνα τὸν Ἰησοῦν . . . **κρατήσωσιν** καὶ **ἀποκτείνωσιν**]
              They counseled together [*to* **arrest** Jesus . . . and *to* **kill** (him)].

Luke 6:31   καθὼς θέλετε [ἵνα **ποιῶσιν** ὑμῖν οἱ ἄνθρωποι] ποιεῖτε αὐτοῖς ὁμοίως
              Just as you wish [*that* people **should do** to you], do likewise to them.

1 Cor 14:5   θέλω πάντας ὑμᾶς λαλεῖν γλώσσαις, μᾶλλον δὲ [ἵνα **προφητεύητε**]
              I want you all to speak in tongues, but even more [*to* **prophesy**].
                   Note the parallel between the first half of the verse, which uses a com-
                   plementary infinitive, and the second half, which uses a complemen-
                   tary ἵνα clause.

Cf. also Mark 9:30; 10:35; John 9:22; 17:24.

7)   Imperatival Ἵνα

The subjunctive is rarely used after ἵνα with the force of a *command*.
Although *structurally* this looks to be a subordinate use of the subjunctive, it occurs in clauses where the subjunctive is the main verb.

---

[78] This could also be taken as result.

[79] *Contra* Moule, *Idiom Book*, 145 (he considers it a direct object/content ἵνα clause).

[80] This could also be taken as purpose-result or simply result.

Thus, this usage could just as easily be treated under independent use of the subjunctive.[81]

Mark 5:23   τὸ θυγάτριόν μου ἐσχάτως ἔχει, ἵνα ἐλθὼν **ἐπιθῇς** τὰς χεῖρας αὐτῇ ἵνα σωθῇ καὶ ζήσῃ

My little girl is near death. Come and **place** your hands on her that she may be healed and live.

> It is evident that the ἵνα clause does not logically follow what is previously said and, therefore, is not subordinate to it.

Eph 5:33   ἕκαστος τὴν ἑαυτοῦ γυναῖκα οὕτως ἀγαπάτω ὡς ἑαυτόν, ἡ δὲ γυνὴ ἵνα **φοβῆται** τὸν ἄνδρα

Let each one [of you] love his own wife as himself, and **let** the wife **respect** [her own] husband.

> The parallel with the imperative ἀγαπάτω in the first half of the verse shows the independent force of the ἵνα clause.

Cf. also Matt 20:33; Mark 10:51; 1 Cor 7:29; 2 Cor 8:7;[82] Gal 2:10; Rev 14:13.

Cf. for other *possible* references: Mark 14:49; John 1:8; 14:31; 15:25; 1 Cor 16:16; 1 John 2:19.

c. Subjunctive with Verbs of Fearing, Etc.

1) Definition

Μή plus the subjunctive can be used after verbs of *fearing, warning, watching out for*, etc. Not unusual in the better writers (Paul, Luke, Hebrews), this construction serves as a warning or suggests caution or anxiety.

2) Illustrations

Luke 21:8   βλέπετε μὴ **πλανηθῆτε**
Watch out that **you are** *not* **deceived.**

1 Cor 8:9   βλέπετε μή πως ἡ ἐξουσία ὑμῶν αὕτη πρόσκομμα **γένηται** τοῖς ἀσθενέσιν
Take care *lest* somehow this liberty of yours **should become** a stumbling block to the weak.

Heb 4:1   φοβηθῶμεν . . . *μήποτε* . . . **δοκῇ** τις ἐξ ὑμῶν ὑστερηκέναι
Let us fear . . . *lest* . . . anyone of you **should appear** to have failed.

Cf. also Mark 13:5; Acts 13:40; 23:10; 27:17, 29; 2 Cor 11:3; 12:20.

---

[81] We have dealt with it here in keeping with our organizational principle of structural priority.

[82] A different view is taken by V. Verbrugge, "The Collection and Paul's Leadership of the Church in Corinth" (Ph.D. dissertation, University of Notre Dame, 1988) 195-204. He argues that the ἵνα clause of 2 Cor 8:7 is "more of a wish" than a command (204). To do this, θέλομεν must be understood, as Verbrugge admits.

d. **Subjunctive in Indirect Questions**

1) **Definition**

The subjunctive is sometimes used in indirect questions. In such a usage, it follows the main verb, but appears awkward, even unconnected, in the sentence structure. Because of this the subjunctive (and its accompanying interrogative particle) needs to be smoothed out in translation. The subjunctive in indirect questions reflects a subjunctive from the direct question–hence, this may be considered an indirect *deliberative* question.[83]

2) **Illustrations**

Matt 15:32   ἤδη ἡμέραι τρεῖς προσμένουσίν μοι καὶ οὐκ ἔχουσιν τί **φάγωσιν**

They have already been with me [for] three days and they do not have anything **to eat**.

> Literally, "they do not have *what* **they might eat**." The direct question would have been, τί φάγωμεν ("What are we to eat?").

Luke 9:58   ὁ υἱὸς τοῦ ἀνθρώπου οὐκ ἔχει ποῦ τὴν κεφαλὴν **κλίνῃ**

The Son of Man has no place where **he could lay** his head.

Cf. also Matt 6:25; 8:20; Mark 6:36; 8:1-2; Luke 12:17.

➡   e. **Subjunctive in Indefinite Relative Clause**

1) **Definition**

The subjunctive is frequently used after ὅστις (ἄν/ἐάν) or ὅς (δ᾽) ἄν. The construction normally indicates a generic (or sometimes an uncertain) subject (but cf. Luke 9:4; John 1:33; Rom 9:15; 2 Cor 11:21); hence, the particle of contingency and the need for a subjunctive. The construction is roughly the *equivalent of a third class or fifth class condition*. (The difference is that in indefinite relative clauses the element of contingency is not that of time but of person.) Hence, the subjunctive is often translated like an indicative, since the potential element belongs to the subject rather than the verb.

2) **Illustrations**

Mark 3:29   ὃς δ᾽ ἂν **βλασφημήσῃ** εἰς τὸ πνεῦμα τὸ ἅγιον, οὐκ ἔχει ἄφεσιν εἰς τὸν αἰῶνα

Whoever **blasphemes** against the Holy Spirit never has forgiveness.

---

[83] What marks it as a bit unusual, however, is that it characteristically follows ἔχω–a verb not comfortable asking direct questions.

John 4:14 ὃς δ᾽ ἂν **πίῃ** ἐκ τοῦ ὕδατος οὗ ἐγὼ δώσω αὐτῷ, οὐ μὴ διψήσει εἰς τὸν αἰῶνα[84]

Whoever **drinks** of the water that I will give him will never thirst again.

Gal 5:10 ὁ ταράσσων ὑμᾶς βαστάσει τὸ κρίμα, ὅστις ἐὰν **ᾖ**

The one who is troubling you will bear [his] judgment, *whoever* **he is.**

Jas 2:10 ὅστις ὅλον τὸν νόμον **τηρήσῃ πταίσῃ** δὲ ἐν ἑνί, γέγονεν πάντων ἔνοχος[85]

Whoever **keeps** the whole law, yet **stumbles** in one point, has become guilty of all.

Cf. also Matt 5:19, 21; 10:33; 12:50; Luke 8:18; Acts 2:21; 3:23; Rom 9:15; 10:13; 1 Cor 11:27; 2 Cor 11:21; 1 John 3:17.

➡   **f.   Subjunctive in Indefinite Temporal Clause**

1) **Definition**

The subjunctive is frequently used after a *temporal adverb* (or *improper preposition*) meaning *until* (e.g., ἕως, ἄχρι, μέχρι), or after the temporal conjunction ὅταν with the meaning, *whenever*. It indicates a future contingency from the perspective of the time of the main verb.

2) **Illustrations**

Matt 5:11 μακάριοί ἐστε ὅταν **ὀνειδίσωσιν** ὑμᾶς

Blessed are you *whenever* **they revile** you

Matt 5:26 οὐ μὴ ἐξέλθῃς ἐκεῖθεν, ἕως ἂν **ἀποδῷς** τὸν ἔσχατον κοδράντην

You will not at all leave from there *until* **you have paid back** the last cent.

John 13:38 οὐ μὴ ἀλέκτωρ φωνήσῃ ἕως οὗ **ἀρνήσῃ** με τρίς

The cock will not at all crow *until* **you have denied** me three times.

Rom 11:25 πώρωσις ἀπὸ μέρους τῷ Ἰσραὴλ γέγονεν ἄχρι οὗ τὸ πλήρωμα τῶν ἐθνῶν **εἰσέλθῃ**

A partial hardening to Israel has happened *until* the fulness of the Gentiles **should come.**

1 Cor 11:26 τὸν θάνατον τοῦ κυρίου καταγγέλλετε ἄχρι οὗ **ἔλθῃ**

you do proclaim the Lord's death *until* **he comes**

---

[84] The Western reading of ὁ δὲ πίνων is found in ℵ* D, in obvious assimilation with the preceding line.

[85] One would expect a contingent particle used with ὅστις (either ἄν or ἐάν) and subjunctive verbs. The scribes apparently succumbed to the temptation and altered the text: The readings τηρήσῃ and πταίσῃ are supported only by ℵ B C and a few other MSS. The more grammatically correct reading of indicative verbs is found in the majority of MSS, but the verbs employed vary: τηρήσει πταίσει is the reading found in K L P 𝔐; πληρώσει πταίσῃ is found in A; Ψ 81 1241 *et alii* have τελέσει πταίσει; πληρώσας τηρήσει πταίσει is the reading of 33.

2 Cor 12:10 ὅταν **ἀσθενῶ**, τότε δυνατός εἰμι.

>					*Whenever* **I am weak**, then I am strong.

Cf. also Matt 2:13; 5:18; 6:5; Mark 13:30; Luke 8:13; 12:11; 22:16; John 2:10; 15:26; Acts 2:35; 23:12; Rom 11:27; 1 Cor 4:5; Gal 3:19; Eph 4:13; 1 Thess 5:3; Heb 1:13; Jas 1:2; 2 Pet 1:19; Rev 6:11; 20:7.

III. The Optative Mood

A. Description

There are less than 70 optatives in the entire NT. In general, it can be said that the optative is the mood used when a speaker wishes to portray an action as *possible*. It usually addresses cognition, but may be used to appeal to the volition. Along with the subjunctive and imperative, the optative is one of the potential or oblique moods.

As we pointed out above (in the section on the subjunctive mood), the optative is becoming absorbed by the subjunctive in the Koine period. This is quite different from the classical period. Once Greek became a second language and expanded well beyond the borders of its native homeland, the subtleties of the language tended to drop out. And about one fourth of the optatives used in the NT occur in a set formula (μὴ γένοιτο). As well, other optatives occur in similar formulas. Such optatives most likely should not be given their full Attic value. Still, it would be an overstatement to say that the NT writers did not generally grasp the force of the optative. The very paucity of the optative in the NT illustrates a principle of syntactical shifts between Attic and Koine: *When one morphosyntactic feature is becoming absorbed by another in Hellenistic Greek and when a Hellenistic author uses the **rarer** form, he normally does so consciously and with understanding.* What this means is that the absorption moves in one direction only: A Hellenistic author may use a subjunctive while in classical Greek an optative would have been used. But a Hellenistic author will not use an optative in a situation which, in the classical era, required a subjunctive.[86]

---

[86] This is an important concept for students to grasp. Two analogous examples illustrate this point: (1) ἀντί is not used in the sense of *on behalf of* (substitution) in Koine Greek, but ὑπέρ is used in the sense of *in the place of* (representation). The overlap of usage moves in one direction only. Thus, when an author uses ἀντί, there is an antecedent presumption of its proper use, and when he uses ὑπέρ we should have no hesitation accepting this as indicating substitution at times. (2) ὥστε + the indicative (used but twice in the NT in subordinate clauses [John 3:16 and Gal 2:13]) still bears the force of "actual result," while ὥστε + the infinitive can be used to mean "natural result" *or* "actual result." The rarer category, when used, is still used correctly. (On the use of ὥστε + the indicative, note *BDF* for some ingenious but bizarre conclusions: Because they assume that such a subtlety cannot occur in the NT–it is "not genuine NT idiom" [197, §391.2]–they emend the text of John 3:16 based on incredibly scanty evidence that would make even a rigorous eclectic blush [198, §391.2]!)

B. Specific Uses

→ 1. ***Voluntative Optative (a.k.a Optative of Obtainable Wish, Volitive Optative)***

a. Definition

This is the use of the optative in an independent clause to express an *obtainable wish* or a *prayer*. It is frequently an appeal to the *will*, in particular when used in prayers.

b. Semantics

The use of the volitive optative in the NT seems to fit into one of three nuances:

- *mere possibility* that something will take place; a great deal of doubt in the presentation. This is more in keeping with the classical idiom. It is quite rare in the NT.

- *stereotyped formula* that has lost its optative "flavor": μὴ γένοιτο usually has the force of abhorrence,[87] and may in some contexts be the equivalent of οὐ μή + aorist subjunctive (a very strong negative).

- *polite request* without necessarily a hint of doubting what the response will be. We have a similar usage of polite speech ourselves. I might, for example, ask my wife, "Do you think you might be able to help me with the dishes tonight?" This is much less blunt than "Please, help me with the dishes!" But the response expected from either request would be the same.

  The voluntative optative seems to be used this way in the language of *prayer*. Again, as with μὴ γένοιτο, it is largely a carry-over from Attic even though its meaning has changed. This is not due to any substantive change in syntax, but is rather due to a *change in theological perspective*. Prayers offered to the semi-gods of ancient Athens could expect to be haggled over, rebuffed, and left unanswered. But the God of the NT was bigger than that. The prayers offered to him depend on his sovereignty and goodness. Thus, although the *form* of much prayer language in the NT has the tinge of remote possibility, when it is offered to the God who raised Jesus Christ from the dead, its *meaning* often moves into the realm of expectation. If uncertainty is part of the package, it is not due to questions of God's ability, but simply to the petitioner's humility before the transcendent one.

---

[87] In 12 of Paul's 14 uses "it expresses the apostle's abhorrence of an inference which he fears may be (falsely) drawn from his argument" (Burton, *Moods and Tenses*, 79 [§177]).

The voluntative optative is the most common optative category (at least 35 of the 68-69 uses belong here).[88] One set idiom makes up almost half of all the voluntative optatives: μὴ γένοιτο, an expression that occurs 15 times (14 of which occur in Paul).

c. Illustrations

Luke 20:16 ἐλεύσεται καὶ ἀπολέσει τοὺς γεωργοὺς τούτους, καὶ δώσει τὸν ἀμπελῶνα ἄλλοις. ἀκούσαντες δὲ εἶπαν, Μὴ **γένοιτο.**

"He will come and destroy those tenants, and will give the vineyard to others." Now when they heard this, they said, "**May it** never **be!**"

This seems to fit the first category: "We would hope that he would never do this," a request in vain.

Rom 3:3-4 εἰ ἠπίστησάν τινες, μὴ ἡ ἀπιστία αὐτῶν τὴν πίστιν τοῦ θεοῦ καταργήσει; (4) μὴ **γένοιτο·** γινέσθω δὲ ὁ θεὸς ἀληθής, πᾶς δὲ ἄνθρωπος ψεύστης

If some did not believe, their unbelief will not nullify the faithfulness of God, will it? (4) **May it** never **be!** But let God be [found] true, and every man [be found] a liar!

Obviously Paul's usage of μὴ γένοιτο is not the same as Luke's. Here it indicates, as it usually does, his repulsion at the thought that someone might infer an erroneous conclusion from the previous argument. The apostle could have expressed his sentiment with οὐ μὴ γένηται, except that the optative seems to appeal to the volition: *You should never conclude such a thing! God forbid that you should think this! No way!* and the like. Cf. also Rom 3:6, 31; 6:2, 15; 7:7, 13; 9:14; 11:1, 11; 1 Cor 6:15; Gal 2:17; 3:21; 6:14.

1 Th 3:11 Αὐτὸς δὲ ὁ θεὸς καὶ πατὴρ ἡμῶν καὶ ὁ κύριος ἡμῶν Ἰησοῦς **κατευθύναι** τὴν ὁδὸν ἡμῶν πρὸς ὑμᾶς

Now **may** our God and Father himself, and our Lord Jesus, **direct** our path to you

There may be some significance in the use of a singular verb with this compound subject. Some possibilities are: (1) At this early stage of the new faith (1 Thessalonians being the second earliest Pauline letter), a clear distinction between the Father and Son was not yet hammered out (but the distinction in persons is made by the distinct articles before each name); (2) the optative is uniting the Father and Son in terms of purpose and, to some degree therefore, placing Jesus Christ on the same level as God; (3) as is common in the NT, when a compound subject is used with a singular verb, the first-named subject is the more important of the two[89] (though this normally or exclusively occurs in narrative literature, and typically with the indicative mood).[90]

---

[88] All except the first verb in Phlm 20 are third singular; all except the one in Acts 8:20 are aorists. Mark 11:14, Acts 8:20, and probably Jude 9 are the only imprecatory prayers in the NT.

[89] Cf., e.g., Mark 8:27; 14:1; John 2:2; 3:22; 4:53; Acts 5:29.

[90] See the discussion of "Compound Subject with Singular Verb" in the chapter on person and number.

2 Tim 1:16 **δῴη** ἔλεος ὁ κύριος τῷ Ὀνησιφόρου οἴκῳ
May the Lord **grant** mercy on the house of Onesiphorus!
> This is an instance of polite request. There is an evident expectation of fulfillment in the request.

2 Pet 1:2 χάρις ὑμῖν καὶ εἰρήνη **πληθυνθείη** ἐν ἐπιγνώσει τοῦ θεοῦ καὶ Ἰησοῦ τοῦ κυρίου ἡμῶν
May grace to you and peace **be multiplied** in the knowledge of God and of Jesus our Lord
> There is every likelihood that the author expected such blessings for his audience. The language, borrowed no doubt from the Pauline corpus, adds the optative explicitly.

Cf. also Mark 11:14; Luke 1:38; Acts 8:20; Rom 15:5, 13; 1 Thess 5:23; 2 Thess 2:17; 3:5, 16; 2 Tim 1:18; Phlm 20; Heb 13:21; 1 Pet 1:2; Jude 2, 9 (probable).

➡ *2. Oblique Optative*

a. Definition

The optative may be used in *indirect questions after a secondary tense* (i.e., one that takes the augment–aorist, imperfect, pluperfect). The *optative substitutes for an indicative or subjunctive* of the direct question. This occurs about a dozen times, depending on textual variants,[91] but only in Luke's writings.

b. Illustrations

Luke 1:29 διελογίζετο ποταπὸς **εἴη** ὁ ἀσπασμὸς οὗτος
She was pondering what sort of greeting this **might be**.
> The direct question would have been, "She wondered, 'What sort of greeting **is** [ἐστίν] this?'"

Luke 8:9 ἐπηρώτων αὐτὸν οἱ μαθηταὶ αὐτοῦ τίς αὕτη **εἴη** ἡ παραβολή
His disciples began asking him what this parable **might mean**.
> The direct question would be, "What *does* this parable *mean*?"

Acts 21:33 ἐπυνθάνετο τίς **εἴη**
He inquired who **he might be**.

Cf. also Luke 18:36; 22:23; Acts 17:11; 25:20.

3. Potential Optative

This use of the optative occurs with the particle ἄν in the *apodosis* of an *incomplete* fourth class condition.[92] It is used to indicate a consequence in the

---

[91] Specifically, whether ἄν is used or not. The presence of ἄν most likely removes this from consideration as an oblique optative.

[92] See the chapter on conditional sentences for a fuller discussion.

future of an unlikely condition. There are no complete fourth class conditions in the NT. The protasis (which also uses the optative) needs to be supplied. The idea is, *If he* ***could do*** *something, he* ***would*** *do this.* Only a handful of examples occur in the NT, all in Luke's writings.

Luke 1:62   ἐνένευον τῷ πατρὶ αὐτοῦ τὸ τί ἂν **θέλοι** καλεῖσθαι αὐτό
            They were making signs to his father as to what **he would want** to call him.

> The implicit protasis is, "If he had his voice back so that he could give him some name."

Acts 17:18 τινὲς ἔλεγον· τί ἂν **θέλοι** ὁ σπερμολόγος οὗτος λέγειν;
            Some [of the philosphers] were saying, "What **would** this babbler **say**?"

> The implicit protasis is, "If he could say anything that made sense!"

Cf. also Acts 5:24; 8:31.

4. *Conditional Optative*

This is the use of the optative in the *protasis* of a *fourth class* condition (the conditional particle used is εἰ). It is used to indicate a *possible* condition in the future, usually a remote possibility (such as, *if he could do something, if perhaps this should occur*). There are no complete fourth class conditions in the NT. Sometimes the conditional clause is mixed, with a non-optative in the apodosis (e.g., Acts 24:19). On other occasions, no apodosis is to be supplied, the protasis functioning as a sort of stereotyped parenthesis (e.g., 1 Cor 15:37).[93] This usage, like the potential optative, is quite rare.[94]

Acts 20:16 ἔσπευδεν εἰ δυνατὸν **εἴη** αὐτῷ τὴν ἡμέραν τῆς πεντηκοστῆς γενέσθαι εἰς Ἱεροσόλυμα
            He was making haste to be in Jerusalem, *if* **it might be** possible, on the day of Pentecost.

1 Pet 3:14 εἰ καὶ **πάσχοιτε** διὰ δικαιοσύνην, μακάριοι
            Even *if* **you should suffer** for righteousness, [you would be] blessed.

> This text comes as close as any to a complete fourth class condition in the NT. *Prima facie*, the readership of this letter has not yet suffered for righteousness, and the possibility of such happening soon seems remote. The author reinforces this point in v 17, again with a conditional optative: "It is better to suffer for doing good than for doing evil, *if* the will of God **should** *so* **will** it (εἰ **θέλοι** τὸ θέλημα τοῦ θεοῦ). Although the occasion of 1 Peter is frequently assumed to involve suffering on the part of the readership, this text seems to argue against that. It is probably better to see the author in the midst of suffering, out of which experience he offers his counsel to believers who may have been insulated from it thus far.

Cf. also Acts 17:27; 20:16; 24:19; 27:12, 39; 1 Cor 14:10; 15:37; 1 Pet 3:17.

---

[93] Boyer, "Optatives," 135.

[94] See the chapter on conditional sentences for a fuller discussion.

IV. The Imperative Mood

A. Description

The imperative mood is the mood of *intention*. It is the mood furthest removed from certainty. (Those who have strong-willed children understand this!) Ontologically, as one of the potential or oblique moods, the imperative moves in the realm of *volition* (involving the imposition of one's will upon another) and *possibility*.

There are many exceptions to this twofold "flavor" of the imperative in actual usage, although in almost every instance the *rhetorical* power of the imperative is still felt. Thus, when Paul says, "If the unbeliever departs, **let him depart** (χωριζέσθω)**"** (1 Cor 7:15), the permissive imperative is more strongly addressed to the heart than if he had said, "If the unbeliever departs, that is OK!" In Jas 4:7 the conditional imperative has not lost its injunctive flavor: "**If you resist** (ἀν-τίστητε) the devil–and you should!–he will flee from you." Technically, then, it is *not* best to call this the mood of *command* because it may be used for *other than* a command. But that volitional force is nevertheless still lurking beneath the surface, even when the speaker is not barking orders.

B. Specific Uses

➡ ### 1. Command

a. Definition

The imperative is most commonly used for commands,[95] outnumbering prohibitive imperatives about five to one. As a command, the imperative is usually from a superior to an inferior in rank. It occurs frequently with the aorist and present (only rarely with the perfect tense[96]).

The basic force of the imperative of command involves somewhat different nuances with each tense. With the *aorist*, the force generally is to *command the action as a whole*, without focusing on duration, repetition, etc. In keeping with its aspectual force, the aorist puts forth a *summary command*. With the *present*, the force generally is to *command the action as an ongoing process*. This is in keeping with the present's aspect, which portrays an *internal* perspective. Much more can be said about the interplay between the tenses and the imperative mood (see chapter on volitional

---

[95] See the chapter on volitional clauses for a more detailed discussion.

[96] Cf. Mark 4:39 (πεφίμωσο); Acts 15:29 (ἔρρωσθε); 23:30 (ἔρρωσθε [*v.l.*, found in P 1241], ἔρρωσο [*v.l.*, found in ℵ *Byz et plu*]); Eph 5:5; Heb 12:17; Jas 1:19. In these last three texts, ἴστε could be either perfect active imperative or indicative.

clauses for detailed discussion). For now, the important thing to get is that the imperative is most often used to make a *command*.

One final note: the *third person* imperative is normally translated *Let him do*, etc. This is easily confused in English with a permissive idea. Its force is more akin to *he must*, however, or periphrastically, *I command him to* . . .[97] Regardless of how it is translated, the expositor is responsible to observe and explain the underlying Greek form.

b. Illustrations

Mark 2:14   **ἀκολούθει** μοι
            Follow me!

Mark 6:37   **δότε** αὐτοῖς ὑμεῖς φαγεῖν
            Give them [something] to eat.

John 5:11   **ἆρον** τὸν κράβαττόν σου καὶ **περιπάτει**
            Take up your mattress and **walk.**

1 Cor 1:31 ὁ καυχώμενος ἐν κυρίῳ **καυχάσθω**
            Let the one who boasts **boast** in the Lord.

> The force of this is not an option; the one who boasts *must* boast in the Lord.

2 Cor 13:5 ἑαυτοὺς **πειράζετε** εἰ ἐστὲ ἐν τῇ πίστει
            Test yourselves [to see] if you are in the faith.

Heb 13:17   **πείθεσθε** τοῖς ἡγουμένοις ὑμῶν
            Obey those who lead you.

Jas 1:5   εἰ τις ὑμῶν λείπεται σοφίας, **αἰτείτω** παρὰ τοῦ . . . θεοῦ
            If anyone of you lacks wisdom, **let him ask** of God.

> The force of the imperative is probably not a mere urging or permission, but a command, in spite of the typical English rendering. An expanded gloss is, "If anyone of you lacks wisdom, *he must ask* of God." In other words, lacking wisdom (in the midst of trials [vv 2-4]) does not give one the option of seeking God, but the obligation.

Cf. also Mark 6:10; Luke 12:19; John 2:5, 16; Acts 5:8; Rom 6:13; 2 Cor 10:7; Gal 6:1; 2 Tim 1:14; Heb 12:14; Jude 21; Rev 1:19; 19:10.

---

[97] A number of passages could be easily misunderstood as mere permission in most English translations. (Some of these examples involve the ambiguity of who is being addressed, even though their imperatival flavor is still evident. For example, in 1 Tim 4:12 ["Let no one despise your youth"], does this mean "Don't *you* let anyone despise your youth" or "I command *others* not to despise your youth"? The first translation would have a second person verb; the second would have a third person, as it does in the Greek [κατα-φρονείτω]). The Greek is stronger than a mere option, engaging the volition and placing a requirement on the individual: Matt 5:31, 37; 11:15; 13:9, 43; 16:24; 18:17; 19:12; Mark 4:9; 8:34; Luke 16:29; Acts 1:20; 2:14; Rom 14:5; 15:11; 1 Cor 1:31; 3:18; 4:1; 7:3, 9 (probable); 11:6; 2 Cor 10:17; Gal 6:4; Eph 5:33; Phil 4:5, 6; Col 2:16; 1 Tim 2:11; 3:10; 4:12; 5:16, 17; Heb 1:6; 13:1; Jas 1:4-6, 9; 5:14, 20; Rev 2:7; 3:22; 13:18.

➡ ## 2. *Prohibition*

a. Definition

The imperative is commonly used to forbid an action.[98] It is simply a negative command (see discussion above). μή (or a cognate) is used before the imperative to turn the command into a prohibition. Almost all instances in the NT involve the present tense. The aorist is customarily found as a prohibitive *subjunctive*.[99]

b. Illustrations

Matt 6:3   μὴ **γνώτω** ἡ ἀριστερά σου τί ποιεῖ ἡ δεξιά σου
    Do *not* let your left hand **know** what your right hand is doing.

Mark 5:36   μὴ **φοβοῦ**, μόνον πίστευε.
    Do *not* **be afraid**; only believe.

Acts 10:15   ἃ ὁ θεὸς ἐκαθάρισεν, σὺ μὴ **κοίνου**
    What God has made clean, **do** *not* **make unclean.**
        The force of this prohibition is strengthened by the pronoun σύ. The idea is "Don't you defile what God has made clean!"

Rom 6:12   μὴ **βασιλευέτω** ἡ ἁμαρτία ἐν τῷ θνητῷ ὑμῶν σώματι
    Do *not* let sin **reign** in your mortal body.

Eph 5:18   μὴ **μεθύσκεσθε** οἴνῳ
    Do *not* **get drunk** with wine.

1 Tim 5:16   μὴ **βαρείσθω** ἡ ἐκκλησία
    Do *not* let the church **be burdened.**
        In English this looks as if the author is saying, "I don't permit the church to be burdened." But the Greek is stronger; it is as if he is saying, "I order the church not be burdened." There is a permissive imperative (see below), but its semantics are quite different from this.

Cf. Luke 10:4; John 2:16; 5:14 (with μηκέτι); 20:17; Acts 1:20; 27:24; 1 Cor 3:18; Gal 6:17; Col 2:16; 1 Thess 5:19-20; Heb 12:5; 1 John 2:15; Rev 5:5.

➡ ## 3. *Request (a.k.a. Entreaty, Polite Command)*

a. Definition

The imperative is often used to express a request. This is normally seen when the speaker is addressing a superior. Imperatives (almost always

---

[98] See the chapter on volitional clauses for a more detailed discussion, particularly of the use of tenses in prohibitions.

[99] There are, by my count, only 8 instances of the aorist imperative in prohibitions, all with Jesus as the speaker (Matt 6:3; 24:17, 18; Mark 13:15 [*bis*], 16; Luke 17:31 [*bis*]). Such multiple attestation, coupled with the criterion of dissimilarity (in that no one else uses this morpho-syntactical convention) suggests that such sayings are authentic.

in the *aorist* tense) directed toward God in prayers fit this category. The request can be a positive one or a *negative* one (*please, do not . . .*); in such cases the particle μή precedes the verb.

On occasion, the request imperative will be used by a superior when addressing an inferior, especially when one in authority is pleading. The difficulty in determining when this is the case is the fact that we are dealing with a *written* language. Thus we cannot hear the *tone* of the speaker.

b. Illustrations

Mt 6:10-11   **ἐλθέτω** ἡ βασιλεία σου· **γενηθήτω** τὸ θέλημά σου . . . τὸν ἄρτον ἡμῶν τὸν ἐπιούσιον **δὸς** ἡμῖν σήμερον

Let your kingdom **come, let** your will **be done** . . . **give** us today our daily bread

Luke 11:1   κύριε, **δίδαξον** ἡμᾶς προσεύχεσθαι

Lord, **teach** us [how] to pray

Luke 15:6   συγκαλεῖ τοὺς φίλους καὶ τοὺς γείτονας λέγων αὐτοῖς· **συγχάρητέ** μοι

He assembles his friends and neighbors, saying to them, "**Rejoice** with me!"

John 4:7   λέγει αὐτῇ ὁ Ἰησοῦς, **Δός** μοι πεῖν

Jesus said to her, "**Give** me [water] to drink"

John 4:31   ἠρώτων αὐτὸν οἱ μαθηταὶ λέγοντες, Ῥαββί, **φάγε**.

His disciples began asking him, saying, "Rabbi, **eat**."

> The introductory verb ("asking" [ἠρώτων]) indicates that a request is being made rather than a command.

2 Cor 5:20   δεόμεθα ὑπὲρ Χριστοῦ, **καταλλάγητε** τῷ θεῷ

We ask you for the sake of Christ, **be reconciled** to God.

Cf. also Matt 6:9; 26:39, 42; Mark 9:22; Luke 7:6 (with μή), 7; 17:5; John 17:11; John 19:21 (with μή); Acts 1:24; 2 Cor 12:13; Phlm 18; Rev 22:20.

4. *Permissive Imperative (Imperative of Toleration)*

a. Definition

The imperative is rarely used to connote permission or, better, *toleration*. This usage does *not* normally imply that some deed is optional or approved. It often views the act as a *fait accompli*. In such instances, the mood could almost be called "an imperative of resignation." Overall, it is best to treat this as a statement of *permission, allowance,* or *toleration.* The connotations of "permission" are usually too positive to convey adequately the nuances involved in this type of imperative.

b. Illustrations

Mt 8:31-32   εἰ ἐκβάλλεις ἡμᾶς, ἀπόστειλον ἡμᾶς εἰς τὴν ἀγέλην τῶν χοίρων. (32) καὶ εἶπεν αὐτοῖς· **ὑπάγετε**.

"If you cast us out, send us into the herd of swine." (32) And he said to them, "**Go!**"

> In this instance the imperative carries a double nuance: the Lord is casting them out (thus, a command) and granting their request to enter the swine (permission).

1 Cor 7:15   εἰ ὁ ἄπιστος χωρίζεται, **χωριζέσθω**
If the unbeliever departs, **let him depart**.

1 Cor 7:36   ἐὰν ᾖ ὑπέρακμος καὶ οὕτως ὀφείλει γίνεσθαι, ὃ θέλει **ποιείτω**, οὐχ ἁμαρτάνει, **γαμείτωσαν**
If he has strong passions and it has to happen, **let him do** what he desires, he does not sin; **let them marry**.

Cf. also Matt 23:32; 26:45 (possible);[100] 2 Cor 12:16 (possible).[101]

5. *Conditional Imperative*

a. Definition

The imperative may at times be used to state a condition (protasis) on which the fulfillment (apodosis) of another verb depends. There are at least twenty such imperatives in the NT.[102]

b. Structure and Semantics

This use of the imperative is always or almost always found in the construction *imperative + καί + future indicative*.[103] The idea is "If X, then Y will happen." As well, there are a few constructions in which the verb in the apodosis is either another imperative[104] or οὐ μή + subjunctive,[105] though all of these are disputed.

---

[100] See Robertson, *Grammar*, 948.

[101] This could also be taken as a conditional imperative.

[102] Boyer, "Imperatives," 39.

[103] All of the undisputed texts discovered by Boyer involved this construction ("Imperatives," 39).

[104] Cf. John 1:46; 7:52; etc. For other references and discussion, see D. B. Wallace, "'Op-γίζεσθε in Ephesians 4:26: Command or Condition?" *CTR* 3 (1989) 352-72, specifically 367-71. (This essay was reprinted in *The Best in Theology*, vol 4, ed. J. I. Packer [Carol Stream, Ill.: Christianity Today, 1990] 57-74. All page references will be to the original *CTR* article.)

[105] E.g., Luke 6:37. Burton, *Moods and Tenses*, 81 (§183) argues that in this text the "imperative [is] suggesting a hypothesis...." In my previous study on conditional imperatives, I inadvertently overlooked the possibility of the subjunctive in the apodosis (Wallace, "Ephesians 4:26").

Even if these disputed constructions are valid, it is significant that in each one of them *the trailing verb is semantically equivalent to a future indicative.* Take John 1:46, for example:

εἶπεν αὐτῷ Ναθαναήλ· ἐκ Ναζαρὲτ δύναταί τι ἀγαθὸν εἶναι; λέγει αὐτῷ ὁ Φίλιππος· **ἔρχου** καὶ **ἴδε**

Nathanael said to him, "What good thing can come out of Nazareth?" Philip said to him, "**Come** and **see!**"

If ἔρχου is conditional, then the trailing imperative bears the force of a future indicative: "If you come, you will see." All of the disputed examples display these same semantics, viz., that the trailing verb functions as though it were a future indicative.[106]

Thus, we can argue that all of the undisputed conditional imperatives in the NT have a future indicative in the apodosis; and all of the possible conditional imperatives make the second verb (either imperative or subjunctive) act as if it were a future indicative. As we will see, this point becomes significant in our discussion of a debatable passage.

Further, *none of the undisputed conditional imperatives seems to have lost its injunctive force.* That is to say, even though the imperative is translated by *if you do* and the like, the imperative was used precisely because it communicated something that another mood could not.[107] Thus, in John 1:39 ἔρχεσθε καὶ ὄψεσθε ("come and you will see") means *if you come–and I want you to–you will see.*

c. **Illustrations**

1) **Clear Examples**

Matt 7:7 **αἰτεῖτε** καὶ δοθήσεται ὑμῖν
Ask and it will be given to you.
　　The idea is "If you ask (and you should), it will be given to you."

Matt 8:8 μόνον **εἰπὲ** λόγῳ, καὶ ἰαθήσεται ὁ παῖς μου
Just **say** the word, and my servant will be healed.

John 2:19 **λύσατε** τὸν ναὸν τοῦτον καὶ ἐν τρισὶν ἡμέραις ἐγερῶ αὐτόν
Destroy this temple and in three days I will raise it up.
　　The sense of the imperative here is, minimally, "If you destroy...." But if λύσατε follows the normal semantic pattern of conditional imperatives, the force is even stronger: "If you destroy this temple–and I *command* you to–in three days I will raise it up." Though this may seem farfetched at first glance, it is in fact likely. Such a prophetic statement is reminiscent of the "ironic commands" of the Jewish prophets (cf.

[106] Wallace, "Ephesians 4:26," 367-71.

[107] One or two of the imperative + καί + future indicative clauses are arguable (in particular John 2:19, but see discussion below). However, what is significant is that "All of the 21 *potentially* conditional imperatives in imperative + καί + imperative constructions retained their injunctive force" (Wallace, "Ephesians 4:26," 371).

Isa 8:9; Amos 4:4). It thus functions as a taunt or a dare, akin to "Go ahead! Destroy this temple, if you dare! I will still raise it up!"[108] Such a view is very much in keeping with the Johannine portrait of Jesus.[109]

Jas 4:7   ἀντίστητε τῷ διαβόλῳ, καὶ φεύξεται ἀφ᾽ ὑμῶν·
Resist the devil and he will flee from you.

The idea is "if you resist the devil–and you should–then he will flee from you."

Cf. also John 1:39; Eph 5:14; Jas 4:10.

2) A Debatable and Exegetically Significant Text

Eph 4:26   ὀργίζεσθε καὶ μὴ ἁμαρτάνετε
Be angry and do not sin.

Some grammarians think that a conditional imperative may have an *imperative* in the apodosis. However, this is usually assumed for the very passage that is highly debatable, Eph 4:26.[110] The gloss suggested is *if you are angry, do not sin.*

Grammatically, there are three fundamental problems with taking ὀργίζεσθε as a conditional imperative.[111] First, there are no other undisputed examples of conditional imperatives in the construction imperative + καί + imperative in the NT.[112] Unlike Eph 4:26, all clear texts have a future indicative in the apodosis. But there are, admittedly, a few good candidates, even if not undisputed. This brings us to our second point.

Second, all of the possible conditional imperatives in the construction imperative + καί + imperative require the trailing imperative to function semantically like a *future indicative*. In John 1:46, the translation would then be, instead of "Come and see", "If you come, you *will* see." (Cf. also John 7:52). If applied to Eph 4:26, this would mean, "If you are angry, you will *not sin*"–an obviously ludicrous meaning.

Third, all of the conditional imperatives in the NT (both undisputed and potential) retained their *imperatival force*. This is semantically dissimilar to an alleged conditional imperative in Eph 4:26. Those who espouse a conditional view here would not translate the passage "If you are angry–and I want you to be. . . ." When combined with the semantics noted above for all other conditional imperatives, the conditional view is *prima facie* self-defeating: "If you are angry (and I want you to be), then you will not sin"! This, of course, is not what the text means. But to argue for a conditional ὀργίζεσθε virtually requires this meaning, since all the parallels point in this direction.

---

[108] Credit is due to Dr. Hall Harris for suggesting the rhetorical force of the imperative here, as well as the parallels with the prophets.

[109] The ironic command also occurs in the Apocalypse (22:11 says, "Let the evildoer still do evil and let the filthy still be filthy!" [ὁ ἀδικῶν ἀδικησάτω ἔτι καὶ ὁ ῥυπαρὸς ῥυπανθήτω ἔτι]).

[110] Cf. *BDF*, 195; Robertson, *Grammar*, 949; Boyer, "Imperatives," 39. *BDF* use this text as their *only* proof-text of the conditional imperative with an imperative in the apodosis. Boyer likewise provides no other examples.

[111] There are also contextual and other exegetical arguments against a conditional ὀργίζεσθε here. See Wallace, "Ephesians 4:26," for discussion.

[112] See discussion in Wallace, "Ephesians 4:26," 367-71.

If ὀργίζεσθε is not conditional, what then is the meaning of Eph 4:26? Both imperatives should be taken at face value (command and prohibition, respectively): "Be angry and do not sin." What supports this interpretation, among other things, is the rest of the verse: "Do not let the sun go down on *the cause of* your *anger* (παροργισμῷ)."[113] Verse 27, in this reconstruction, would thus mean that one should not give a place to the devil *by doing nothing about the sin in the midst of the believing community.* Entirely opposite of the "introspective conscience" view, this text seems to be a shorthand expression for church discipline, suggesting that there is biblical warrant for δικαία ὀργή (as the Greeks put it)–righteous indignation.

† 6. *Potential Imperative* (debatable category)

The use of the imperative might, perhaps, be used in the apodosis of an implied condition. This occurs when another imperative occurs in the implied protasis (the conditional imperative). But the potential imperative is quite disputed. All of the possible instances (apart from ἁμαρτάνετε in Eph 4:26) are semantically equivalent to a future indicative. For discussion, see conditional imperative above.

7. *Pronouncement Imperative*

Occasionally an imperative in the *passive voice* is the equivalent of a statement that is fulfilled at the moment of speaking. Such usage is reserved for passives that cannot be fulfilled by the recipient of the imperative. On the surface, it looks like a command, but its nature is such that it cannot be obeyed by the recipient and yet it comes true at the moment it is uttered. The pronouncement (or, performative statement) is couched in imperatival terms for rhetorical effect.

Mk 1:40-41   ἐὰν θέλῃς δύνασαί με καθαρίσαι. (41) καὶ σπλαγχνισθεὶς ἐκτείνας τὴν χεῖρα αὐτοῦ ἥψατο καὶ λέγει αὐτῷ· θέλω, **καθαρίσθητι**
"If you want to, you can cleanse me." (41) And having compassion, [Jesus] stretched out his hand and touched him and said to him, "I want to: **Be cleansed!**"
> Jesus' command to the leper could hardly be rendered, "Allow yourself to be cleansed."

---

[113] The term παροργισμός is used almost exclusively of the source of anger, not the result. That is, it refers to an external cause or provocation, not an internal reaction. Cf., e.g., 1 Kings 15:30; 2 Kings 23:26; Neh 9:18; Ps Sol 8:8-9 (a text that bears more than a passing resemblance to Eph 4:26, both probably referring back to a common Jewish source). The only text not to have this force is Jer 21:5 (*v.l.*).

Matt 21:21   κἂν τῷ ὄρει τούτῳ εἴπητε· **ἄρθητι** καὶ **βλήθητι** εἰς τὴν θάλασσαν,
γενήσεται·
Even if you tell this mountain, "**Be uprooted** and **be thrown** into the
sea," it will happen.

Cf. also Mark 7:34; 11:23; Rom 11:10.

8. As a Stereotyped Greeting

Sometimes the imperative is used in a stereotyped manner in which it has
suppressed its original injunctive force. The imperative is reduced to an
exclamation. This occurs especially in greetings.

Luke 1:28   **χαῖρε**, κεχαριτωμένη, ὁ κύριος μετὰ σοῦ
Greetings, favored [lady]! The Lord is with you.

John 19:3   **χαῖρε** ὁ βασιλεὺς τῶν Ἰουδαίων
Hail, king of the Jews!

Acts 15:29 **ἔρρωσθε**
Farewell!
> The Jerusalem decree to the Gentile churches ends with a stereotyped
> perfect imperative. Cf. also Acts 23:30 (*v.l.*).

2 Cor 13:11 λοιπόν, ἀδελφοί, **χαίρετε**
Finally, brothers, farewell.
> This, of course, could be taken as a command: "Rejoice!" But in light of
> the well-worn usage in Hellenistic literature of this term as a greeting,
> it may be better to translate it as we have above in this context.

Cf. also Matt 26:49; 27:29; Mark 15:18; Phil 3:1 (possible).[114]

---

[114] The possibility of taking χαίρετε as a final greeting is seen by its collocation with
τὸ λοιπόν ("finally"), just as in 2 Cor 13:11. It is more likely, however, that it is a simple
command or request, since (1) it has an adjunct (ἐν κυρίῳ); (2) it is immediately followed
by a sentence that makes good sense if χαίρετε is taken as a command, since the clause has
an anaphoric reference ("to write the *same* things" [cf. 2:18, 28]); (3) the letter goes on for
two more chapters (could this be a *final* greeting, then?); and (4) the thought of rejoicing
is thematic throughout Philippians, even following this verse (cf. 1:18; 2:17, 18, 28; 4:4, 10).

The Tenses: An Introduction

Overview of Chapter

Select Bibliography

BDF, 166-67 (§318); **Burton**, *Moods and Tenses*, 6-7, 46 (§5-7, 95); **D. A. Carson**, "An Introduction to the Porter/Fanning Debate," *Biblical Greek Language and Linguistics: Open Questions in Current Research*, Journal for the Study of the New Testament, Supplement Series 80; ed. by S. E. Porter and D. A Carson (Sheffield: Sheffield Academic Press, 1993) 18-25; **B. M. Fanning**, "Approaches to Verbal Aspect in New Testament Greek: Issues in Definition and Method," *Biblical Greek Language and Linguistics*, 46-62; **idem**, *Verbal Aspect*, 1-196; **K. L. McKay**, *A New Syntax of the Verb in New Testament Greek: An Aspectual Approach* (New York: Peter Lang, 1994); **idem**, "Time and Aspect in New Testament Greek," *NovT* 34 (1992) 209-28; **Moule**, *Idiom Book*, 5-6; **Moulton**, *Prolegomena*, 108-19; **Porter**, *Verbal Aspect*, 75-109; **idem**, *Idioms*, 20-28; **idem**, "In Defence of Verbal Aspect," *Biblical Greek Language and Linguistics*, 26-45; **Robertson**, *Grammar*, 821-30; **D. D. Schmidt**, "Verbal Aspect in Greek: Two Approaches," *Biblical Greek Language and Linguistics*, 63-73; **Moisés Silva**, "A Response to Fanning and Porter on Verbal Aspect," *Biblical Greek Language and Linguistics*, 74-83; **Turner**, *Syntax*, 59-60; **Young**, *Intermediate Greek*, 105-07; **Zerwick**, *Biblical Greek*, 77-78 (§240-41).

Preface

In Douglas Adams' delightfully insane *The Restaurant at the End of the Universe*[1] is a brief chapter describing the major problem in time travel:

> The major problem is quite simply one of grammar, and the main work to consult in this matter is Dr. Dan Streetmentioner's *Time Traveler's Handbook of 1001 Tense Formations*. It will tell you, for instance, how to describe something that was about to happen to you in the past before you avoided it by time-jumping forward two days in order to avoid it. The event will be described differently according to whether you are talking about it from the standpoint of your own natural time, from a time in the further future, or a time in the further past and is further complicated by the possibility of conducting conversations while you are actually traveling from one time to another with the intention of becoming your own mother or father.

> Most readers get as far as the Future Semiconditionally Modified Subinverted Plagal Past Subjunctive Intentional before giving up; and in fact in later editions of the book all the pages beyond this point have been left blank to save on printing costs.[2]

Judging by the complexities of the Greek verb and the recent plethora of treatments on the same, students of the NT can certainly empathize with the time

---

[1] The edition cited here is incorporated as the third section in Adams' *The More than Complete Hitchhiker's Guide*, complete and unabridged (New York: Wings Books, 1989).

[2] Ibid., 213.

traveler's plight![3] Our approach will attempt to simplify things as much as possible, but since a large part of the genius of the Greek verb is the tense, we would do well to view its complexities as riches to be mined. "Though it is an intricate and difficult subject, no phase of Greek grammar offers a fuller reward."[4]

I. Definition of Tense

In general, *tense* in Greek involves two elements: *aspect* (kind of action, [sometimes called *Aktionsart*, though a difference does need to be made between the two]) and *time*. Aspect is the primary value of tense in Greek and time is secondary, if involved at all. In other words, *tense is that feature of the verb that indicates the speaker's presentation of the verbal action (or state) with reference to its aspect and, under certain conditions, its time.*

The tenses in Greek are the present, future, perfect, imperfect, aorist, pluperfect.[5]

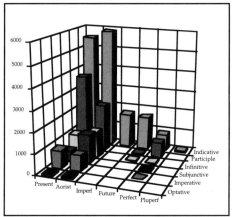

Chart 46
Relative Frequency of Tenses in the NT

---

[3] Our treatment on tenses is intentionally simpler than other elements of the verb, largely because there are at the moment so many unresolved issues in the Greek tense. (Note that the first half of *Biblical Greek Language and Linguistics: Open Questions in Current Research* is dedicated to this issue.) The modest proposals suggested in this and the following chapters on the tenses should be seen as a working hypothesis subject to revision. The major bone of contention has to do with whether tenses in the indicative grammaticalize time (see appendix to this chapter); even here there is usually little difference in the *resultant* (pragmatic) views of the two sides (cf. Fanning, *Verbal Aspect*; McKay, "Time and Aspect"). There are other issues, however, leading one scholar to sigh, "This difference of opinion gives the strongest support to the view that exegetes and pastors are well advised to say as little as possible about aspect" (Silva, "A Response to Fanning and Porter," 81-82).

[4] Dana-Mantey, 177 (§166).

[5] The future perfect also occurs, but in the NT only in periphrasis.

The specific breakdown of each tense is as follows: Present–11,583; Aorist–11,606; Imperfect–1682; Future–1623; Perfect–1571; Pluperfect–86.[6]

II. The Element of Time

A. *Three Kinds of Time*

Three kinds of time may be portrayed by tense: past, present, future. These are natural to English, but some languages employ other ideas–e.g., past, non-past; near, far; completed, uncompleted; etc.

B. *Mood Dictates the Time Element*

For the most part, the *mood* of the verb dictates whether or not time will be an element of the tense.[7]

1. Indicative

Time is clearly involved. We could in a sense speak of time as *absolute* (or *independent*) in the indicative in that it is dependent directly on the speaker's time frame, not on something within the utterance itself. There are occasions, of course, when time is not involved in the indicative. This is due to other phenomena such as genre, lexeme, the nature of the subject or object (e.g., whether general or specific), etc. But in their unaffected meaning (i.e., in their essence, undisturbed by other considerations), the tenses in the indicative mood include a temporal marker.

2. Participle[8]

Time is very often involved, although here it is *relative* (or *dependent*). Time with participles (especially adverbial participles) depends on the time of the main verb. The participle is not directly connected to the time

---

[6] This number does not take into account periphrastics. That is, a pluperfect periphrastic will be counted as an imperfect indicative and a perfect participle. The totals were determined using *acCordance*. However, the breakdown by moods did not add up to exactly the same total for the present and aorist tenses. Still, the figures are within about one-tenth of one percentage point of each other.

[7] This is the traditional view of tense. Several recent grammarians (principally Porter and McKay for the Greek NT) have disputed this view. See discussion of the nontemporal vs. temporal view of tense in the appendix to this chapter.

[8] Participles and infinitives are technically not moods, but since they take the place of a mood it is both convenient and semantically suitable to discuss them with reference to time.

frame of the speaker and hence cannot be said to be absolute. Still, the three kinds of time are the same: past, present, future. But with the participle "past" means past with reference to the verb, not the speaker (it is called *antecedent*), present is present in relation to the verb (*contemporaneous*), and future is future only with reference to the verb (*subsequent*). The times are for the most part the same; the frame of reference is all that has changed.

3. **Subjunctive, Optative, Imperative, Infinitive**

Except in indirect discourse, time is not seen with these moods. Thus an aorist subjunctive would have a futuristic (or potential) flavor, while in the indicative it would have a past idea. We can say, then, that for the most part time is irrelevant or nonexistent in the oblique (nonindicative) moods.

To sum up: In general, *time is absolute in the indicative, relative in the participle, and nonexistent in the other moods.*

C. *Portrayal Vs. Reality of Time*

Although an author may use a tense in the indicative, the time indicated by that tense *may* be other than or broader than the *real* time of the event. All such examples belong to phenomenological categories. As such, there will normally be sufficient clues (context, genre, lexeme, other grammatical features) to signal the temporal suppression.

1. **Other Than**

Examples of time *other than* what the tense (in the indicative) signifies include the historical present, futuristic present, proleptic aorist, epistolary aorist.

2. **Broader Than**

Examples of time *broader than* what the tense (in the indicative) signifies include gnomic present, extension-from-past present, gnomic aorist, gnomic future.

III. The Element of Aspect (Kind of Action)

A. *Definition of Aspect*

1. Basic Definition

Verbal aspect is, in general, the portrayal of the action (or state) as to its *progress*, *results*, or *simple occurrence*.

2. Aspect Vs. *Aktionsart*

It is important to distinguish *aspect* from *Aktionsart*. In general, we can say that **aspect** *is the unaffected meaning* while **Aktionsart** *is aspect in combination with lexical, grammatical, or contextual features*. Thus, the present tense views the action from within, without respect to beginning or end (aspect), while some uses of the present tense can be iterative, historical, futuristic, etc. (all of these belong to *Aktionsart* and are meanings of the verb affected by other features of the language). This is the same kind of distinction we have earlier called ontological vs. phenomenological (terms that can be applied to *any* morpho-syntactic category, not just the verb tense).

It is not technically correct to say that aspect is subjective while *Aktionsart* is objective (although some grammars suggest this kind of distinction). Such a statement tacitly assumes that there is a one-to-one correspondence between language and reality. *Aktionsart* is not actually objective, although it may be *presented* as more in tune with the actual event.[9]

Pragmatically, this distinction between aspect and *Aktionsart* is helpful in three ways:

1) The basic definition of a given tense deals with aspect, while the various categories of usage deal with *Aktionsart*. Thus, although the basic definition is the "purest," least-affected meaning, it is also the most artificial. This is because no one has ever seen, for instance, a present tense by itself. What we see is a verb that has as many as seven different morphological tags to it (one of which may be present tense), one lexical tag (the stem)–and all this in a given context (both literary and historical). Although we may be, at the time, trying to analyze the meaning of the present tense, all of these other linguistic features are crowding the picture.

---

[9] To argue that *Aktionsart* is objective is akin to saying that the indicative mood is the mood of fact. There is no necessary reality that corresponds to either the indicative or a particular *Aktionsart*, otherwise parables, fiction, hyperbole, deliberate misrepresentation, or faulty perception could not be communicated.

2) One error in this regard is to see a particular category of usage (*Aktionsart*) as underlying the entire tense usage (aspect). This is the error of *saying too much*. Statements such as "the aorist means once-for-all action" are of this sort. It is true that the aorist may, under certain circumstances, describe an event that is, in reality, momentary. But we run into danger when we say that this is the aorist's unaffected meaning, for then we force it on the text in an artificial way. We then tend to ignore such aorists that disprove our view (and they can be found in every chapter of the NT) and proclaim loudly the "once-for-all" aorists when they suit us.[10]

3) Another error is to assume that nothing more than the unaffected meaning can ever be seen in a given tense usage. This is the error of *saying too little*. To argue, for example, that the aorist is always the "unmarked" tense, or "default" tense, fits this. This view fails to recognize that the tense does not exist in a vacuum. Categories of usage are legitimate because the tenses combine with other linguistic features to form various fields of meaning.[11]

B. *Types of Action Possible*

Greek has essentially three aspects or types of action: internal, external, and perfective-stative. Admittedly, these terms are not very descriptive. The problem in terminology is that the more descriptive we are, the more we exclude in our definition. It is best to learn what is entailed in these terms rather than use labels that are inappropriate or address only part of the data.

Perhaps an illustration might help. More than one grammar has suggested the "parade analogy" to describe the various aspects.[12] To sit in the stands as a spectator and watch a parade as it is passing by is an *internal* perspective: One views the parade in its progression, without focusing on the beginning or end. To view the parade from a blimp as a news commentator several hundred feet in the air is an *external* perspective: One views the whole of the parade without focusing on its internal makeup. To walk down the street after the parade is over as part of the clean-up crew is a *perfective-stative* view: While recognizing that the parade is completed (external), one stands in the midst of the ongoing results (internal)!

---

[10] F. Stagg, "The Abused Aorist," *JBL* 91 (1972) 222-31, did some seminal work to disabuse the aorist of this "once-for-all" approach.

[11] Stagg went a bit too far at times in his "Abused Aorist" in arguing only for the aorist's unaffected meaning in many contexts. Even more extreme is C. R. Smith, "Errant Aorist Interpreters," *GTJ* 2 (1980) 205-26.

[12] See, e.g., Porter, *Idioms*, 24.

1. **Internal (or Progressive)**

    The internal portrayal *"focuses on* [the action's] *development or progress and sees the occurrence in regard to its internal make-up, without beginning or end in view."*[13] This is the detailed or open-ended portrayal of an action. It is sometimes called *progressive*; it "basically represents an activity as in process (or in progress)."[14]

    The tense-forms involved are the *present* and *imperfect*.

2. **External (or Summary)**

    The external portrayal *"presents an occurrence in summary, viewed as a whole from the outside, without regard for the internal make-up of the occurrence."*[15]

    The tense-form involved is the *aorist*. As well, the *future* apparently belongs here.[16]

3. **Perfective-Stative (a.k.a. Stative, Resultative, Completed)**

    The unaffected meaning is a combination of the external and internal aspects: The *action* is portrayed *externally* (summary), while the *resultant state* proceeding from the action is portrayed *internally* (continuous state).[17]

    The tense-forms involved are the *perfect* and *pluperfect*.

---

[13] Fanning, *Verbal Aspect*, 103. Italics in the original. "Linear" (or "durative") is the old description with which most are familiar. Recent research has suggested that this is a particular phenomenological usage rather than an ontological description. That is to say, it describes a few uses of the present tense but not the basic idea of the present.

[14] McKay, "Time and Aspect," 225. Although this gives one a better handle on the idea, it is often too restrictive in its application.

[15] Fanning, *Verbal Aspect*, 97. Cf. also McKay, "Time and Aspect," 225. Again, it is important to remember that this is a definition of the aorist's *aspect*, not its *Aktionsart*, for the latter is a combination of this ontological meaning with other features of the language. Thus, in a given context and with a given verb in the aorist tense, an author may indicate something of the internal make-up of the occurrence.

[16] The future is often listed by grammarians as having an internal portrayal at times. Thus its aspect is listed as occasionally internal, occasionally external. This tense is still something of an enigma. It is the only tense that is always related to time, regardless of mood. And although its forms were no doubt derived from the aorist (note, for example, the sixth principal part), there are occasions in which an internal idea seems to take place (thus it appears to share some similarities with the present). However, it is probably best to see the future as the temporal counterpart to the aorist: Both are summary tenses that can be used to describe an iterative or progressive action, but only in collocation with other linguistic features. The future tense's unaffected meaning does not appear to include an internal portrayal.

[17] There is a basic agreement among grammarians about the force of the perfect (viz., that two elements are involved, completed action and resultant state), although there is some disagreement over the particulars of the definition. McKay, for example, sees the perfect as an aspect, while Fanning sees it as intrinsically involving aspect, time, and

C. *Portrayal Vs. Reality of Aspect*

1. Lack of Precise Correspondence

There is a genuine difference between *portrayal* of action and the real *progress* of the action. An author may *portray* the action as summary, or he may portray the action as progressive, stative, etc. In some respects, it may be helpful to see the various aspects as analogous to photography. The aorist would be a *snapshot*, simply viewing the action as a whole without further ado. It would be the establishment shot, or the portrayal that keeps the narrative moving at a brisk pace. The imperfect would be a *motion picture*, portraying the action as it unfolds. This is more of an "up close and personal" kind of portrayal.

This can be seen in narrative literature easily enough. For example, Mark has more than twice as many verses as Matthew in the *narrative* sections. To him the narrative *is* the story. To Matthew narrative functions more as stage-setting for the great discourses of Jesus. Thus, Matthew usually uses the aorist tense to simply point out that an event took place. Mark may use the imperfect to describe the same event, showing more specifically how it happened.[18] (There are more than twice as many imperfects in Mark as there are in Matthew.[19]) Thus, Matthew might say, "They went out from Jerusalem," while Mark would say, "They were going out from Jerusalem."

Even within one Gospel, the same event might be portrayed with two different tenses. This illustrates the fact that *an author often has a choice in the tense he uses* and that *portrayal is not the same as reality*. For example:

Mark 12:41   πλούσιοι **ἔβαλλον** πολλά
            the rich **were casting in** much
                    The imperfect is used because the scene is in progress. Thus it looks at
                    the incident from the inside.

Aktionsart. Fanning suggests that "the perfect in NT Greek is a complex verbal category denoting, in its basic sense, a state that results from a prior occurrence. Thus, it combines three elements within its invariant meaning: the Aktionsart-feature of stative situation, the tense-feature of anteriority, and the aspect of summary viewpoint concerning the occurrence" (ibid., 120). Although I would quibble over whether the perfect (or any tense) has an *invariant* meaning (i.e., one that is always present), this threefold description offers some helpful insights.

[18] Cf., e.g., Matt 13:57 with Mark 6:4; Matt 9:10 with Mark 2:15; Matt 12:10 with Mark 3:2; Matt 4:16 with Mark 3:12; Matt 16:6 with Mark 8:15; Matt 19:2 with Mark 10:1; Matt 26:39 with Mark 14:33; Matt 26:47 with Mark 14:43. Often, however, Mark's additional imperfects are in phrases or sentences that find no parallel in Matthew (cf., e.g., Mark 1:21, 45; 2:2, 4, 13; 3:8, 11; 4:21, 24; 5:9, 20; 6:6; 10:10; 14:57). Both might introduce a pericope with an aorist; Mark then supplies extra details with an imperfect.

[19] According to *acCordance*, there are 293 imperfects in Mark to 142 imperfects in Matthew. Percentage-wise, the imperfects are over three times as frequent in Mark (22.6 imperfects per 1000 words to 6.75 per 1000 words in Matthew).

Mark 12:44 πάντες γὰρ ἐκ τοῦ περισσεύοντος αὐτοῖς **ἔβαλον**

> For these all, out of their abundance, **cast** (their money) **in**

>> The aorist is now used at the conclusion of Jesus' story as a summary of the event just witnessed.

2. The Issue of Choice

a. Selected by the Speaker

A basic issue in the tense used is *how much* a speaker wants to say about the progress or results of an action, or what he wants to *emphasize*. This is not a question of accurate description vs. inaccurate description, but of fuller description vs. simple statement of action, *or* of one emphasis vs. another of the *same* action. For example:

Rom 3:23 πάντες γὰρ **ἥμαρτον**

> for all **have sinned**

>> The *aorist* is used here, leaving the action in some sense undefined. However, it is an equally true statement that: "all sin" (present–customary) *and* "all have sinned" (perfect–past action with continuing results). Therefore, the choice of the aorist by Paul was used to emphasize one aspect or possibly to say less (or to *stress* the *fact* of humanity's sinfulness) than the present or perfect would have done. However, any of these three tenses could have been used to describe the human condition. An author's portrayal is thus selective at times and simply brings out the aspect that he wants to emphasize at the time rather than giving the full-orbed reality of the event.

b. Restricted by the Lexeme, Context, etc.

Many actions are shut up to a particular tense. For example, if a speaker wishes to indicate an action that is intrinsically *terminal* (such as "find" or "die" or "give birth to"), the choice of tense is dramatically reduced. We would not usually say "he was finding his book." The imperfect, under normal circumstances, would thus be inappropriate.[20]

On the other hand, if an author wished to speak of the unchanging nature of a *state* (such as "I have" or "I live"), the aorist would normally not be appropriate. Indeed, when the aorist of such stative verbs is used, the emphasis is most frequently on the *entrance into the state*.[21] Thus, for example, ζάω ("I live") occurs as a present or imperfect indicative 29 times in the NT, all of which have a stative meaning (e.g., ἐν οἷς καὶ ὑμεῖς περιεπατήσατέ ποτε, ὅτε **ἐζῆτε** ἐν τούτοις [among whom you also formerly lived, when **you were living** among them] in Col 3:7). Conversely, seven of the eight aorist

---

[20] For example, in the NT there are 71 instances of εὑρίσκω as an aorist indicative and only four as an imperfect indicative, all four in the same idiomatic expression.

[21] Fanning, *Verbal Aspect*, 137.

indicatives have an ingressive force (e.g., Χριστὸς ἀπέθανεν καὶ ἔζησεν [Christ died and **came to life**] in Rom 14:9).[22]

The point is that often the choice of a tense is made for a speaker by the action he is describing. At times the tense chosen by the speaker is the *only* one he could have used to portray the idea. Three major factors determine this: lexical meaning of the verb (e.g., whether the verb stem indicates a terminal or punctual act, a state, etc.), contextual factors, and other grammatical features (e.g., mood, voice, transitiveness, etc).[23] This is precisely the difference between aspect and *Aktionsart*: Aspect is the basic meaning of the tense, unaffected by considerations in a given utterance, while *Aktionsart* is the meaning of the tense as used by an author in a particular utterance, affected as it were by other features of the language.

IV. Appendix:
An Assessment of Time In Verb Tenses

This section is *advanced material*. Intermediate students should normally skip over it, at the discretion of the teacher.

Traditionally, NT grammars have viewed time as a part of the Greek tenses, when such tenses combine with the indicative mood.[24] In recent years, however, this view has been challenged, principally by S. E. Porter[25] and K. L. McKay. Since the traditional view is pervasive in the literature–and in fact *assumed* to be true[26]–this section will focus on the arguments for the nontemporal view, followed by an evaluation.[27]

---

[22] Ibid., 138.

[23] The major work in this area is Fanning, *Verbal Aspect*, especially ch. 3: "The Effect of Inherent Meaning and Other Elements on Aspectual Function," 126-96. He views inherent lexical meaning as the major influence (126). His material on this topic is particularly helpful (127-63). One should also note Silva, "A Response to Fanning and Porter," for an emphasis on *grammatical* intrusions on verbal aspect.

[24] However, these same grammars usually point out that time is secondary and that *originally* the Greek tenses did not grammaticalize time (so *BDF*, 166 [§318]).

[25] Porter's *Verbal Aspect* (1989) was done at almost the same time that Fanning's work bearing almost the same title was completed. Both were originally doctoral dissertations done, respectively, at Sheffield and Oxford. Although there are many agreements between Porter and Fanning (especially over the aspectual force of the various tenses), there is a fundamental disagreement as to whether tense involves time.

A. *Arguments for Tense without Time*

There are principally four arguments for the view that the Greek tenses do not grammaticalize time.[28]

1. Phenomenology

Several categories of tenses in the indicative involve no time or an unexpected time: e.g., historical present, futuristic present, proleptic aorist, gnomic tenses. These examples are difficult to explain on the assumption that time is an element of the indicatives tenses.

2. Diachronics

Older Greek (e.g., Homer) has examples of nonaugmented aorist indicatives that are used for past time, as well as augmented aorists that are not.

3. Linguistics

In narrative literature, the imperfect is used for foregrounding, while the aorist is used for backgrounding. That is to say, the imperfect dwells on the event, while the aorist simply summarizes it, moving the narrative along. The augment, then, does not indicate time, but becomes a literary device.

4. Morphology

The pluperfect, in Hellenistic Greek, does not always have the augment. Thus augment is not a time marker.

---

[26] There is irony to the fact that occasionally the nontemporal view is now *assumed* by some, without an attempt to offer proof for it. McKay begins his essay on "Time and Aspect" with this line: "If it is true, as now appears to be certainly the case, that the inflexions of the ancient Greek verb signal aspect (as well as voice and mood) but not time ...." (209). Elsewhere McKay put forth arguments for the nontemporal view, but he usually restricted his case to exceptional instances (i.e., argument from phenomenology) rather than linguistic principle (for references, see McKay, "Time and Aspect," 209, n. 1). There is a major flaw in this approach, as we will demonstrate below.

[27] There have been some critiques of the nontemporal view, but nothing yet that is systematic. See especially the essays by Fanning, Schmidt, and Silva in *Biblical Greek Language and Linguistics*.

[28] Our interaction is primarily with Porter, for his arguments are the most systematic. McKay admits that although he agrees with Porter in principle, "I had formed opinions intuitively rather than logically," while Porter has attempted a systematic, linguistically informed exposition of this view (McKay, "Time and Aspect," 209-10).

B. An Evaluation of the Nontemporal View

Although the above arguments are presented briefly, there are usually many details to back them up. Porter, for example, works through the various tense uses, systematically noting the deficiencies in the temporal view. Nevertheless, there are some serious problems with the nontemporal view. Our evaluation will first address the four arguments presented above, followed by some additional critiques of this view.

1. Phenomenology

There are two major problems with the argument from phenomenology.

a. Analogies with English

Although it would be linguistically absurd to assume a point-for-point correspondence between English and Greek, some analogies are appropriate. In particular, both English and Greek have a historical present and a futuristic present. Yet in English, time is involved in the tenses. Suppose two thousands years from now English has become a dead language. And suppose, further, that a linguist in c. 4000 CE concludes that the English tense system did not grammaticalize time as evidenced by the historical present and futuristic present. We all can see that such an argument would not be valid. Why, then, should we consider it to be valid for ancient Greek?

b. Affected Usages Vs. Unaffected Meaning

All of the examples of nontemporal uses involve *affected* meanings (i.e., phenomenological uses instead of ontological meaning). We might even say that such categories are less than routine.[29] As we have asserted earlier, one should never base an ontological meaning on a selective reading of phenomenological data.[30] Indeed, these are the exceptions that seem to prove the rule—for they are unexpected, even to a Greek ear.[31] (As an illustration, the historical present seems to have become a colloquialism that looked at an event as though it

---

[29] For example, Fanning breaks down the present indicative uses into three broad categories: those that have a narrow time frame, those that have a broad time frame, and *special* uses–i.e., those that appear to be exceptions to the temporal view of the present (*Verbal Aspect*, 199). It should be kept in mind that by categorizing the nontemporal presents as unusual, Fanning is not giving a polemical or dogmatic argument against Porter, for Fanning's work was completed before Porter's was published.

[30] This is precisely what happened in the late 1800's when extrapolations were made about the *essential* differences between the aorist and present in prohibitions. The notion that the aorist meant, *in essence*, "Don't start X" and the present meant, *in essence*, "Stop X," was based on rather limited and selected data. To be sure, in certain situations, these nuances can be pressed. But they are not at the root of the different prohibitions.

[31] Even Porter admits that the historical present is quite emphatic and used especially for the sake of vividness (*Verbal Aspect*, 195-96).

were present from the speaker's viewpoint. The very fact that Luke, the literary writer, virtually refused to use it while it is frequent in Mark [the less educated author] fits in far better with the idea that the Greeks thought of historical presents much the same way we do today.)[32]

2. Diachronics

There are two basic problems with the argument from diachronics. First, both in lexicography and grammar, synchronic evidence is considered to be far more relevant than diachronic. Indeed, those who offer this diachronic argument elsewhere support the supreme value of synchronics.[33] The diachronic argument suffers as well from the great distance between the NT and Homer: What the augment was doing in 900 BCE may not be what it ended up doing in the Hellenistic or even classical era.

Second, parallels with Homer suffer another disadvantage, viz., a difference in genre. Homeric Greek is *poetry* (where meter may be a factor), while the NT is by and large prose. In the least, in Greek as well as in other languages the poetic devices of that language control the form of presentation so much that there is *almost always* some suspension of normal grammatical rules.[34]

3. Linguistics

The fact that the imperfect is derived from the present's principal part and the pluperfect from the perfect's principal parts suggests that there must be some similarity and some difference between such corresponding tenses. The nontemporal view does not easily handle either. Since the imperfect and pluperfect do not occur outside the indicative, what is to explain the differences between them and their corresponding primary tenses if not time? The traditional view is that time occurs only in the indicative and that these secondary tenses have virtually an identical *aspect* with their corresponding primary tenses; hence, the imperfect and pluperfect would be superfluous outside the indicative.

---

[32] More troubling is the gnomic aorist, for this finds no ready analogy with English (but are there not English tense uses that find no ready analogy with Greek?). Nevertheless, there are explanations for this use of the aorist within the temporal view of the tenses (e.g., that such aorists were originally standard, past-referring aorists that became proverbial and timeless through repetition). The paucity of such aorists seems to attest to their exceptional nature.

[33] E.g., Porter, *Idioms*, 13.

[34] Cf., e.g., V. Bers, *Greek Poetic Syntax in the Classical Age* (New Haven, Conn.: Yale University Press, 1984); A. C. Moorhouse, *The Syntax of Sophocles* (Leiden: E. J. Brill, 1982) 1, 10, 13, 135, 143, 177; N. Cosmas, "Syntactic Projectivity in Romanian and Greek Poetry," *Revue roumaine de linguistique* 31 (1986) 89-94.

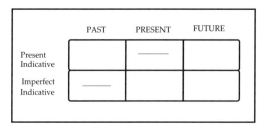

Chart 47
Time-Aspect Similarities in Present & Imperfect Indicative

As can be seen in the chart above,[35] if the "time boxes" were removed, there would be no difference between these two tenses. This makes one of them unnecessary for oblique moods. (A similar chart could be produced for the perfect and pluperfect.)

To sum up: The nontemporal view does not easily handle the issue of redundancy of tenses (e.g., why have a present and imperfect if both share the same aspect?), nor the fact that two tenses disappear outside the indicative. If the "imperfective" tenses (i.e., both present and imperfect) are used for foregrounding, then one of them would seem to be unnecessary. Why then are both often seen in the same contexts? It does not explain why the pluperfect and imperfect only occur in the indicative. The traditional view is that since time is relevant only in the indicative, and since these tenses have a virtually identical aspect with their respective counterparts (imperfect-present, pluperfect-perfect), outside the indicative such secondary tenses are unnecessary.

In addition, there are two other problems with this approach:

- Most grammars regard the *aspectual* value of the historical present to be reduced to zero. The verbs used, such as λέγει and ἔρχεται, normally introduce an action in the midst of aorists without the slightest hint that an internal or progressive aspect is intended. Yet if the nontemporal view of tense were true, we would expect the aspect to be in full flower.[36]

---

[35] The pictorial representation of the first principal part as linear is only meant to show that the present and imperfect parallel each other aspectually, not that this is the fundamental meaning of the aspect. (It is difficult to represent an "internal" portrayal.)

[36] Porter argues that this is indeed the case: "On the basis of the place of the historic Present within the Greek verbal network, the historic Present is to be considered aspectually imperfective" (*Verbal Aspect*, 195). Yet in his description he argues for *vividness* (rather than a progressive portrayal) as the force of the aspect. This seems better suited to the temporal view: The writer uses the present tense in a highly vivid manner, as though the event occurred simultaneously with the time of writing. Thus, in our view, the historical present has suppressed its aspect, but not its time. But the time element is rhetorical rather than real.

- If the aorist indicative is not linked to time, we should expect to see the aorist indicative regularly used for an instantaneous present event. The gnomic aorist occurs, but does the "instantaneous aorist"? Further, we would not expect to see an instantaneous present (in which the aspect is entirely suppressed and the present time element is all that remains).[37] How can the nontemporal view handle, for example, ἁρπάζω ("snatch") in the present tense in Matt 13:19 or John 10:29?

4. Morphology

The argument from morphology is that the pluperfect dropped its augment. Although this did happen with increasing frequency,[38] it was probably due to the fact that (1) the secondary endings of the pluperfect were distinct enough from the perfect that its nature would always have been revealed; and (2) since the pluperfect has a complicated morphology,[39] the tendency for secondary speakers of Greek to drop the augment was most likely due this complicatedness, urged along as it were by the clear secondary features of the tense at the end of the verb.[40]

5. Ancient Greeks' Perception of the Tenses

Several ancient Greek writers (e.g., Protagoras, Aristotle, Dionysius Thrax) distinguished tense forms and described them in terms of time.

---

[37] In Fanning's approach there also seems to be a problem. He argues that the time element is "compressed" but not "suppressed" (*Verbal Aspect*, 202). His rationale is that "the stress [is] on the *exact simultaneity* with the time of speaking. Outside of the indicative, the aorist is used for such instantaneous occurrences, since the temporal value of simultaneity does not interfere" (ibid., 205). Two critiques are in order: (1) The instantaneous present does not seem to have an internal perspective in that it portrays the action as *completed* at the moment of speaking (Fanning even defines it as "'done' at the moment of speaking" [202]); (2) the instantaneous aorist participle does occur as a *simultaneous* action to a main verb (note the redundant participle in the well-worn expression ἀποκριθεὶς εἶπεν [cf. Matt 4:4; 12:39; 25:12; Mark 6:37; 11:14; Luke 4:12; 5:22; 9:20; 19:40, etc.]).

[38] By the time of the NT, it was becoming more and more frequent to drop the augment. Still, even in this corpus there were more augmented pluperfects than nonaugmented (*contra* Porter, *Idioms*, 42, who says that the *augmented* form is used only occasionally).

[39] Even Porter admits that the pluperfect has an "unwieldy morphological bulk" (*Idioms*, 42).

[40] This finds a *partial* analogy in the "helper verbs" such as δύναμαι, θέλω, κτλ. For the classical form had an *epsilon* at the front of the nonaugmented form, while the augment lengthened this to an *eta*. In Koine Greek the *epsilon* dropped out for the primary tenses and the augmented form vacillated between *eta* and *epsilon*. A diachronic examination of the Greek language thus reveals that *some augment changes took place more because of convenience than principle*. Technically, ἐδυνα- would have been read as a present stem in Attic, but in fact was often an imperfect in Koine. This is not much different from a pluperfect verb, whose endings are longer and more cumbersome than other verb forms (not to mention, quite distinct), dropping its augment.

Although we cannot base too much on the ancient Greeks' perception of their own language (they demonstrate their lack of sophistication in many areas), it does not seem too much to expect them to know whether their verb tenses grammaticalized time.

6. Occam's Razor

As McKay correctly notes, "The test of any hypothesis therefore is not that it resolves all doubts but that it offers the most consistent explanation, leaving few anomalies."[41] But there seem to be too many problems and inconsistencies in the nontemporal approach. Further, of two competing theories that both explain the data, the simplest is the best (known as Occam's razor, named after the medieval philosopher, William of Occam). Which view is the most streamlined, yet accounts sufficiently for the data? In our view, the traditional approach (with some modifications) is still to be preferred. Note, for example, McKay's summary of how to determine time in Greek:

> Ultimately we need to weigh up the evidence of the whole context, verb forms, time markers, sentence structure, the nature of the paragraph, the chapter, even the book, and beyond that the personal, social, political and other assumptions which the writer brought to his task.[42]

This view involves too many complexities and subtleties. Not only does it not employ Occam's razor, but it implies two things: (1) One needed massive doses of context and preunderstanding if an ancient Greek utterance was to have been understood in its temporal reference. This puts too much of a burden on the communicants. (2) In daily discourse, conversational speech, and minimally contextualized utterances, we should have expected a great deal of ambiguity as to the time meant, but there seems to be little or no evidence for this.[43]

7. Root Fallacy

Finally, the nontemporal view hurts itself by forcing the verb's aspect onto every example. (We have already noted that the historical present most likely involves zero aspect.) On the other hand, traditionalists also err in *constantly* seeing an "invariant" meaning for the tenses. Surely the time element can be entirely suppressed, on occasion, by other factors,

---

[41] K. L. McKay, "Aspect in Imperatival Constructions in the New Testament Greek," *NovT* 27 (1985) 214. This is approvingly quoted by Porter (*Verbal Aspect*, 75) as he begins his chapter, "A Systemic Analysis of Greek Verbal Aspect."

[42] McKay, "Time and Aspect," 227-28.

[43] McKay notes that for the modern interpreter, "It is obvious that we sometimes lack crucial information, and likely that some of our reconstructions are not accurate . . ." (ibid., 228). But if this is true for the modern interpreter, it would also presumably be true for the ancient interpreter. A desideratum for the nontemporal view, it seems, is to produce examples of temporal misunderstandings in recorded conversations, papyri letters, and the like (in short, any kind of material that involves rapid subject changes).

even as the aspect can be suppressed.[44] Linguists have long noted the etymological fallacy when it comes to word meanings. But grammarians tend to hang on to a controlling nuance for the various syntactical forms.[45]

In our view, *the unaffected meaning of the tenses in the indicative involves both aspect and time. However, either one of these can be suppressed by lexemic, contextual, or grammatical intrusions.*[46] Thus, a proper view of language does not attempt to weave a thread of meaning through all the instances of a given form. Too many other linguistic features are vying for power.

Because root fallacy is still prevalent in grammars (not just regarding the tenses), it might be helpful to note a few English examples that involve either suppression or serious alteration of basic syntactical behavior.[47]

- "Those kids will come up here and throw rocks every day" (the use of the future for a customary event in past time)

- "I could care less" (the negative has dropped out, most likely for euphony's sake)

- "near miss" (Shouldn't we expect a "near miss" to mean that two objects actually struck one another, although just barely?)

- The use of the present infinitive for a perfect infinitive: "Yesterday, when the game started, he would have liked *to see* the roster ahead of time."

- "If I was a pirate" (the past indicative is used for the past subjunctive in unreal conditions)

- "You don't know nothing" (a double negative that functions like an emphatic negative in Greek)

- The use of the future for the future perfect: "If he wins the next race, he will break the school record" (instead of "if he wins the next race, he will have broken the school record")

---

[44] We have already noted our disagreement with Fanning over the instantaneous present (see discussion under "Linguistics").

[45] Silva offers a similar critique of both Porter and Fanning ("A Response to Fanning and Porter," 78-79):

> The desire to come up with a clear cut, comprehensive definition of aspect is certainly understandable, but I have to wonder whether it is misguided. In Porter's case, the problem comes to expression by his unwillingness to admit exceptions: proposal after proposal is rejected on the grounds that it does not explain every instance. Fanning, for his part, often speaks about the need to identify an "invariant" meaning for the various aspects. Given the fluidity of language, however, the goal seems unrealistic.

[46] These will be developed in the chapters on the various tenses.

[47] Thanks are due to my colleague, R. Elliott Greene, for supplying some of the following English analogies.

- "are" is used with a plural subject; but is commonly used with the first person singular in contractions: "I'm doing a good job, aren't I?"[48]

- "Can I have some milk?" in which "can" is used for permission (="may")

- The use of the objective case for the subjective, especially after pronominal subjects: "It is me" (cf. also "who" for "whom")

- In older English "was, is" was correctly used of the second person singular to distinguish it from the second person plural ("you was" instead of "you were")

We all recognize the evolution of the English language, both in its lexical and its grammatical uses. My argument is simply that English is not isolated; all languages change with time. Greek is no exception. We need to look at the verb tenses as part of that change and not insist on a stable core of meaning that cannot be altered.[49] Thus, to see aspect as always present, or to see time as always present in the indicative, is an artificial distinction that smacks of root fallacy.

---

[48] This example and scores of others can be found in Bill Bryson, *The Mother Tongue: English and How It Got That Way* (New York: William Morrow, 1990) 134-46. Cf. also *The Oxford Guide to the English Language* (Oxford: Oxford University Press, 1984) 137-91.

[49] This finds an analogy in Hebrew. Biblical Hebrew, strictly speaking, did not mark time in the tense. However, "Mishnaic and Modern Hebrew are much closer to being strictly tensed languages" (B. K. Waltke and M. O'Connor, *An Introduction to Biblical Hebrew Syntax* [Winona Lake, Ind.: Eisenbrauns, 1990] 347, n. 110).

The Present Tense

Overview of Uses

Select Bibliography

BDF, 167-69, 172, 174 (§319-24, 335-36, 338-39); **Burton**, *Moods and Tenses*, 7-11, 46, 54-55 (§8-20, 96-97, 119-131); **Fanning**, *Verbal Aspect*, 198-240, 325-413; **K. L. McKay**, *A New Syntax of the Verb in New Testament Greek: An Aspectual Approach* (New York: Peter Lang, 1994) 39-42; **idem**, "Time and Aspect in New Testament Greek," *NovT* 34 (1992) 209-28; **Moule**, *Idiom Book*, 7-8; **Porter**, *Verbal Aspect*, 163-244, 321-401; **idem**, *Idioms*, 28-33; **Robertson**, *Grammar*, 879-92; **Turner**, *Syntax*, 60-64, 74-81; **Young**, *Intermediate Greek*, 107-13.

Introduction: The Basic Meaning

Aspect

With reference to *aspect*, the present tense is *internal* (that is, it portrays the action from the inside of the event, without special regard for beginning or end), but it makes no comment as to fulfillment (or completion). The present tense's portrayal of an event *"focuses on its development or progress and sees the occurrence in regard to its internal make-up, without beginning or end in view."*[1] It is sometimes called *progressive*: It "basically represents an activity as in process (or in progress)."[2]

Time

With reference to *time*, the present *indicative* is usually present time, but it may be other than or broader than the present time on occasion (e.g., with historical present and gnomic present respectively).

Aspect + Time (The Unaffected Meaning)

What is fundamental to keep in mind as you examine each of the tenses is the difference between the unaffected meaning and the affected meaning and how they relate to each other. Part of this difference is between aspect and *Aktionsart*. (The other part has to do with the temporal element of tense [restricted to the indicative mood].) Together, aspect and time constitute the "ontological meaning" or unaffected meaning of a given tense in the indicative. In this case, it is the meaning the present tense would have if we could see such a tense in a vacuum—without context, without a lexical intrusion from the verb, and without other grammatical features (either in the verb itself or in some other word in the sentence that is impacting the tense). In other words, the unaffected meaning of the present tense is its *basic idea*. However, this unaffected meaning is only theoretical. No one has ever observed it for any of the tenses, simply because we cannot observe a tense that is not attached to a verb (which has lexical value): -ω is a morpheme, while πιστεύω is a present tense verb. The unaffected meaning, then, is something that has been extrapolated from actual usage.

By analogy, we say that contract verb stems end in either *alpha*, *epsilon*, or *omicron*. Yet you will not find ἀγαπάω, φιλέω, or πληρόω in their uncontracted state

---

[1] Fanning, *Verbal Aspect in New Testament Greek*, 103 (italics in original).
[2] McKay, "Time and Aspect," 225. Although this gives one a better handle on the idea, it is often too restrictive in its application.

in the NT.[3] We extrapolate such uncontracted forms on the basis of observed patterns of behavior. This is similar to our descriptions of the basic idea of the tenses.

What is the value of having such a theoretical knowledge of the tenses? It helps us in at least two ways. (We will illustrate its value by applying this discussion to the historical present.)

1) Since the affected meanings are what we call "Specific Uses," the more we know how the tense is affected, the more certain we can be of its usage in a given passage. *The three intrusions mentioned above (lexical, contextual, grammatical) are the staple things that make up affected meanings.* The more we analyze such intrusions, the better we can predict when a given tense (or case or voice or any other morpho-syntactic element of the language) will fit into a particular category of usage. For example, all undisputed examples of the historical present occur in the indicative mood (a grammatical intrusion), in the third person (a grammatical intrusion), and in narrative literature (contextual intrusion). Further, they only occur with certain kinds of verbs (lexical intrusion).

   Thus if you wanted to identify a particular present tense as a historical present, you would want to check it against the various features of other *known* historical presents. It would not do simply to want a particular present tense to be a historical present. In order to so label it you would have to find sufficient semantic parallels[4] between the present tense in question and known historical presents. Lacking such parallels (especially if they are well defined as with the historical present), you would be hard pressed to call the present tense in question a historical present. Some think that the *first person* present tense verb, εἰμί, in John 8:58 is a historical present. But since all undisputed historical presents are third person, and since none involve the equative verb, this is rather doubtful.[5]

2) It is important to understand that *the unaffected meaning can be overridden–to some degree but not entirely–by the intrusions.* That is to say, it is not correct to say that the unaffected meaning will always be present in full force in any given context. *The unaffected meaning is not, therefore, the lowest common denominator of the tense uses.* But neither will it be completely abandoned. An author

---

[3] The analogy is not perfect of course: In classical Greek some of the dialects did have uncontracted verb forms.

[4] Again, I am referring to the lexical, grammatical, and contextual intrusions.

[5] As much as one might want the theology of a text to be a certain way, just to pull a grammatical category out of the hat–to employ it without regard for its normal semantic situation–is not responsible grammatical exegesis. Yet we all do this–partially because we are accustomed to doing exegesis on the basis of hunches rather than a detailed knowledge of how the language works (a knowledge that was not easily feasible until computer programs made it so), and partially because there are no unbiased exegetes (though some are more biased than others). But an increasingly better grasp of the parameters of Koine Greek is helping all students of the NT to gain a valid interpretation of the NT message. This "valid interpretation" is beyond what is merely possible; it has to do with what is probable.

chooses his particular tense for a reason, just as he chooses his mood, lexical root, etc. All of these contribute to the meaning he wishes to express. They are all, as it were, vying for control. Again, take the historical present as an example. An author uses the present tense in narrative for some reason. The options are really quite simple: either for its aspect or for its time. Most scholars are of the opinion that the aspect of the historical present is no different from an aorist's. If that is so, then an author has chosen the present tense for its *temporal* significance. The author does not use the historical present to indicate real time, of course, but for dramatic effect–for the sake of vividness.[6]

In sum, it is imperative that one pay close attention to the various influences affecting the meaning of the tense. All of these influences, in combination with the present tense, contribute to the specific category of usage under question.[7]

Specific Uses

The specific uses of the present tense can be categorized into three large groups: narrow-band presents, broad-band presents, and special uses. "Narrow band" means that the action is portrayed as occurring over a relatively short interval; "broad band" means that the action is portrayed as occurring over a longer interval; "special uses" include instances that do not fit into the above categories, especially those involving a time frame that is *other than* the present.[8]

I. Narrow-Band Presents

Definition

The action is portrayed as being in progress, or as occurring.[9] In the *indicative* mood, it is portrayed as occurring in the present time ("right now"), that is, at the time of speaking. This involves two particular uses of the present: instantaneous and progressive.

---

[6] Ironically, then, we would say that the historical present is the use of the present in which the aspect is diminished but the time element is still in force, though not literally.

[7] The major work in this area is Fanning, *Verbal Aspect*, especially ch. 3: "The Effect of Inherent Meaning and Other Elements on Aspectual Function," 126-96. He views inherent lexical meaning as the major influence (126). His material on this topic is particularly helpful (127-63). One should also note Silva, "A Response to Fanning and Porter," for an emphasis on *grammatical* intrusions on verbal aspect.

[8] Pragmatically, it is helpful to think in terms of *time* when thinking through these categories. This is not because the present tense always includes a temporal marker, but rather because most present tenses (as other tenses) are found in the indicative. Further, some uses are restricted to the indicative (such as historical present); such can only be thought of in terms of time.

➡ A. Instantaneous Present (a.k.a. Aoristic or Punctiliar Present)[10]

1. Definition

The present tense may be used to indicate that an action is completed at the *moment* of speaking. This occurs *only* in the *indicative*. It is relatively common.

2. Clarification

The element of *time* becomes so prominent that the progressive aspect is entirely suppressed in this usage. The instantaneous present is typically a lexically influenced present tense: It is normally a verb of *saying* or *thinking* (a *performative* present).[11] The act itself is completed at the moment of speaking. (One can readily see why verbs of saying or thinking routinely belong here. When "say," "promise," or "tell" introduces an utterance, the time frame of the introductory verb is concluded once the utterance is over. For example, "I **tell** you the truth, 'This is the last minute of the game.'")

Past	Present	Future
	•	

Chart 48
The Force of the Instantaneous Present

Note: The diagrams used for the tenses that have time indicators relate absolutely only to the indicative mood. The time element is included because of the relatively large percentage of indicative tenses. For those uses that have examples outside the indicative, one should simply ignore the time frame.

3. Illustrations

Mark 2:5   ὁ Ἰησοῦς . . . λέγει τῷ παραλυτικῷ· τέκνον, **ἀφίενταί** σου αἱ ἁμαρτίαι.[12]
Jesus . . . said to the paralytic, "Child, your sins **are forgiven**."

---

[9] The alternative title, "durative" present, to describe both the instantaneous and progressive present is hardly an adequate description for the instantaneous present, since the aspectual force of the present tense is entirely suppressed. We use it only for the sake of continuity with other grammars.

[10] Instantaneous present is a much more satisfactory term since aoristic and punctiliar continue erroneous views about the aorist–viz., that it in reality refers to a momentary act.

[11] Fanning, *Verbal Aspect*, 202. Fanning notes a second type, viz., an act that is simultaneous to the time of speaking but is not identical with it. For our purposes, we can treat them both simply as instantaneous presents.

[12] ἀφέωνται is found in several MSS, including $\mathfrak{P}^{88}$ ℵ A C D L W Γ Π Σ 579 700 892 f^1 *Byz*; ἀφέονται is in G Φ 0130 828 1010 1424 f^{13} *et pauci*; ἀφίονται is read in Δ; ἀφίωνται is the reading of Θ.

John 3:3   ἀμὴν ἀμὴν **λέγω** σοι
              verily, verily, **I say** to you

Acts 9:34   εἶπεν αὐτῷ ὁ Πέτρος· Αἰνέα, **ἰᾶταί** σε Ἰησοῦς Χριστός
              Peter said to him, "Aeneas, Jesus Christ **heals** you."

Acts 25:11   Καίσαρα **ἐπικαλοῦμαι**
              I appeal to Caesar

Cf. also Matt 10:42; Mark 5:7; Acts 19:13; 24:14; Rom 16:1; Rev 1:8.

➡ B. *Progressive Present (a.k.a. Descriptive Present)*

1. Definition

The present tense may be used to describe a scene in progress, especially in narrative literature. It represents a somewhat broader time frame than the instantaneous present, though it is still narrow when compared to a customary or gnomic present. The difference between this and the iterative (and customary) present is that the latter involves a *repeated* action, while the progressive present normally involves *continuous* action.[13] The progressive present is common,[14] both in the indicative and oblique moods.

2. Key to Identification: *at this present time, right now*

Past	Present	Future
	——	

Chart 49
The Force of the Progressive Present

3. Illustrations

Matt 25:8   αἱ λαμπάδες ἡμῶν **σβέννυνται**
              our lamps **are** [right now] **going out**
                  It is also possible to take this as a conative present: "our lamps are about to go out."

Mark 1:37   πάντες **ζητοῦσίν** σε
              all **are** [right now] **searching for** you

---

[13] This is due to two things: (1) Lexically, the verbs that take progressive presents are often stative; (2) contextually, the time frame is often so narrow that the action can be portrayed as uninterrupted.

[14] The descriptive present, in many grammars, is presented as different from the progressive present. The difference is that the descriptive involves a narrower sequential band than does the progressive present. We have put both together for convenience' sake.

Acts 2:8   πῶς ἡμεῖς **ἀκούομεν** ἕκαστος τῇ ἰδίᾳ διαλέκτῳ ἡμῶν;
            How is it that **we are hearing**, each in our own dialect?[15]

Acts 3:12   ἡμῖν τί **ἀτενίζετε**;
            Why **are you staring** at us?

Rom 9:1   ἀλήθειαν **λέγω** . . . οὐ **ψεύδομαι**
            I am telling the truth . . . **I am** not **lying**

> What follows is a discourse about Paul's sorrow over the nation of
> Israel.

Cf. also Matt 5:23; 8:25; 27:12; Mark 2:12; 3:32; 4:38 (unless this is tendential); Luke 11:21;
John 4:27; Acts 4:2; 14:15; 1 Cor 14:14; Gal 1:6; 1 Thess 5:3.

II. Broad-Band Presents

Definition

The following four categories of the present tense include those that are used to
indicate an event or occurrence taking place over a long interval, or an extended
sequence of events.

A. Extending-from-Past Present (Present of Past Action Still in Progress)

1. Definition

The present tense may be used to describe an action which, begun in the
past, continues in the present. The emphasis is on the present time.

Note that this is different from the *perfect* tense in that the perfect speaks
only about the *results* existing in the present time. It is different from the
progressive present in that it reaches back in time and usually has some
sort of temporal indicator, such as an adverbial phrase, to show this
past-referring element.[16] Depending on how tightly one defines this category, it is either relatively rare or fairly common.[17]

---

[15] It seems best to describe this as a descriptive present since the time element is so
collapsed (as opposed to an extension-from-the-past present). Fanning, for example,
would not take it as extending from the past, for in his view this usage "always includes
an *adverbial phrase* or other time-indication with the present verb to signal the past-time
meaning" (Fanning, *Verbal Aspect*, 217). Brooks-Winbery, however, dispute this (*Syntax*,
77).

[16] Fanning, *Verbal Aspect*, 217.

[17] Fanning takes it to be a rare category, limiting it by description: "it always includes
an *adverbial phrase* or other time-indication" (*Verbal Aspect*, 217). McKay is somewhat more
vague in his description, though he includes little that Fanning would not (*New Syntax of
the Verb*, 41-42). Brooks-Winbery are broader still, but their example from 2 Cor 12:9 is
debatable (*Syntax*, 77; see discussion in Fanning, *Verbal Aspect*, 217, n. 30).

2. Key to Identification

The key to this usage is normally to translate the present tense as an
English present perfect. Some examples might not fit such a gloss, however.

Past	Present	Future
•———	———	

Chart 50
The Force of the Extending-from-Past Present

3. Illustrations

Luke 15:29   τοσαῦτα ἔτη **δουλεύω** σοι
              I have served you for these many years

2 Pet 3:4   πάντα οὕτως **διαμένει** ἀπ᾽ ἀρχῆς κτίσεως
              all things thus **continue** [as they have] from the beginning of
              creation

1 John 3:8   ἀπ᾽ ἀρχῆς ὁ διάβολος **ἁμαρτάνει**
              the devil **has been sinning** from the beginning

Cf. also Luke 13:7; John 5:6;[18] Acts 15:21; 27:33;[19] 1 Cor 15:6 (possible).

➡ B. *Iterative Present*

1. Definition

The present tense may be used to describe an event that *repeatedly* happens. (The *distributive* present belongs here, too: the use of the present
tense for individual acts distributed to more than one object.) It is frequently found in the imperative mood, since an action is urged to be
done. The iterative present is common.

This use of the present is different from the customary present in terms
of time frame and regularity. The intervals are shorter with the iterative,
and less regular. However, several passages are difficult to analyze and
could conceivably fit in either category.

2. Key to Identification: *repeatedly, continuously*

---

[18] This instance is also the use of the present tense retained in indirect discourse.

[19] Fanning claims that these two examples from Acts are the only two in the book
(*Verbal Aspect*, 218).

Past	Present	Future
	· · · · ·	

Chart 51
The Force of the Iterative Present

3. Illustrations

Matt 7:7   Αἰτεῖτε . . . ζητεῖτε . . . κρούετε
                Ask . . . seek . . . knock

> The force of the present imperatives is "Ask repeatedly, over and over again . . . seek repeatedly . . . knock continuously, over and over again."

Matt 17:15   πολλάκις **πίπτει** εἰς τὸ πῦρ
             often **he falls** into the fire

Luke 3:16   ἐγὼ ὕδατι **βαπτίζω** ὑμᾶς
            I baptize you in water

> This is an instance of a distributive present: John baptizes each person only once, but the action is repeated.

Acts 7:51   ὑμεῖς ἀεὶ τῷ πνεύματι τῷ ἁγίῳ **ἀντιπίπτετε**
           you **are** always **opposing** the Holy Spirit

1 Thess 5:17 ἀδιαλείπτως **προσεύχεσθε**
            pray [repeatedly] without ceasing

> The idea of the present imperative is not that believers are to pray every minute of every day, but that we should offer prayers to God repeatedly. We should make it our habit to be in the presence of God.

Cf. also Mark 3:14; John 3:2, 26; Acts 8:19; Rom 1:9 (or customary), 24; 1 Cor 1:23; Gal 4:18; Phil 1:15.

➡ C. *Customary (Habitual or General) Present*

1. Definition

The customary present is used to signal either an action that *regularly occurs* or an *ongoing state*.[20] The action is usually *iterative*, or repeated, but not without interruption. This usage is quite common.

The difference between the customary (proper) and the iterative present is mild. Generally, however, it can be said that the *customary* present is *broader* in its idea of the "present" time and describes an event that occurs *regularly*. The customary present is an iterative present with the temporal ends "kicked out."

---

[20] So Fanning, *Verbal Aspect*, 206, n. 12: "The general or customary present need not be iterative. If the lexical character of the verb is stative or denotes a process which can be extended at length, the sense is that of unbroken continuation . . . ." Some grammarians prefer to distinguish the *stative* present from the customary. We have lumped them together for convenience' sake.

There are two types of customary present, repeated action and ongoing state. The stative present is more pronounced in its temporal restrictions than the customary present or the gnomic present.

2. **Key to Identification:** *customarily, habitually, continually*

The two types of customary present are lexically determined: One is repeated action (habitual present [*customarily, habitually*]), while the other is ongoing state (stative present [*continually*]).

Past	Present	Future
. . . .		
	or	
_____	_____	

Chart 52
The Force of the Customary Present

3. **Illustrations**

   a. **Clear Examples**

Luke 18:12 **νηστεύω** δὶς τοῦ σαββάτου
I [customarily] **fast** twice a week

John 3:16 πᾶς ὁ **πιστεύων** εἰς αὐτὸν μὴ ἀπόληται
everyone who [continually] **believes** in him should not perish
> This could also be taken as a gnomic present, but if so it is not a prover-bial statement, nor is it simply a general maxim. In this Gospel, there seems to be a qualitative distinction between the ongoing act of believ-ing and the simple fact of believing.

John 14:17 παρ' ὑμῖν **μένει** καὶ ἐν ὑμῖν ἔσται
he **continually remains** with you and he shall be in you

1 Cor 11:26 ὁσάκις γὰρ ἐὰν **ἐσθίητε** τὸν ἄρτον τοῦτον καὶ τὸ ποτήριον **πίνητε**, τὸν θάνατον τοῦ κυρίου **καταγγέλλετε** ἄχρι οὗ ἔλθῃ.
For as often as **you eat** this bread and **drink** the cup, **you proclaim** the Lord's death until he comes.

Heb 10:25 μὴ **ἐγκαταλείποντες** τὴν ἐπισυναγωγὴν ἑαυτῶν, καθὼς ἔθος τισίν[21]
not [habitually] **forsaking** our assembly, as is the habit of some

Cf. also John 1:38; 4:13, 24; Acts 15:11; 27:23; 1 John 2:8.

   b. **Debatable Examples**

> Cf. 1 John 3:6, 9 for a theologically debatable example (which we are taking as gnomic, but which older commentators considered to be customary). See discussion below under "Gnomic Present."

---

[21] ἐγκαταλίποντες is the reading of ℵ* 90 436; καταλείποντες is found in 𝔓[46] D*.

➡ D. Gnomic Present

1. Definition

The present tense may be used to make a statement of a general, timeless fact. "It does not say that something *is* happening, but that something *does* happen."[22] The action or state continues without time limits. The verb is used "in proverbial statements or general maxims about what occurs at *all* times."[23] This usage is common.

2. Semantics and Semantic Situations

The gnomic present is distinct from the customary present in that the *customary* present refers to a regularly recurring action while the *gnomic* present refers to a general, timeless fact. It is distinct from the stative present (a subcategory of the customary) in that the stative present involves a temporal restriction while the gnomic present is generally *atemporal*.

There are two predominant semantic situations in which the gnomic present occurs.[24] The *first* includes instances that depict *deity or nature as the subject of the action*. Statements such as "the wind blows" or "God loves" fit this category. Such gnomic presents are true *all* the time. There is a *second* kind of gnomic, slightly different in definition: the use of the present in *generic* statements to describe something that is true *any* time (rather than a universal statement that is true *all* the time).[25] This kind of gnomic present is more common. Thus, pragmatically, it is helpful to note a particular grammatical intrusion: *A gnomic verb typically takes a generic subject or object*. Most generics will be subjects (but note the first example below). Further, the present participle, especially in such formulaic expression as πᾶς ὁ + *present participle* and the like, routinely belong here.[26]

3. Key to Identification

One key is to add *as a general, timeless fact*. But this does not cover all situations. Another rule of thumb is to translate the verb as *does* rather than *is doing*. Further, one should especially note whether the subject is generic (a common key is the indefinite pronoun τις, substantival participle [especially with πᾶς], or a substantival adjective).

---

[22] Williams, *Grammar Notes*, 27.

[23] Fanning, *Verbal Aspect*, 208.

[24] See Fanning, *Verbal Aspect*, 208-17, for seminal work in this regard.

[25] Ibid., 209.

[26] Ibid. Cf. Matt 5:32; 7:21; Luke 6:47; 16:18. We have listed John 3:16 as belonging under "Customary Present" because of the stress in John on continual belief. There are other instances of πᾶς ὁ + present participle used for customary or iterative ideas (cf., e.g., Luke 18:14; John 4:13; Rom 2:1).

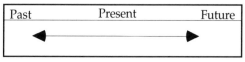

Chart 53
The Force of the Gnomic Present

4. Illustrations

a. Clear Examples

Matt 5:32   πᾶς ὁ **ἀπολύων** τὴν γυναῖκα αὐτοῦ[27]
            everyone who **divorces** his wife

Mark 2:21   οὐδεὶς ἐπίβλημα ῥάκους ἀγνάφου **ἐπιράπτει** ἐπὶ ἱμάτιον παλαιόν
            no one **sews** a piece of unshrunk cloth on an old garment

John 3:8   τὸ πνεῦμα ὅπου θέλει **πνεῖ**
            the wind **blows** where it desires

2 Cor 9:7   ἱλαρὸν γὰρ δότην **ἀγαπᾷ** ὁ θεός
            God **loves** [as a general, timeless fact] a cheerful giver

> That the gnomic present speaks of something that **does** happen, rather than of something that **is** happening, can be seen from this example: God **does love** a cheerful giver (rather than "God **is loving** a cheerful giver").

Heb 3:4   πᾶς οἶκος **κατασκευάζεται** ὑπό τινος
            every house **is built** by someone

> As illustrated here, the gnomic present often focuses on an action proverbial in character.

Cf. also Luke 3:9; John 2:10; Acts 7:48; 1 Cor 9:9; Gal 3:13; 1 John 2:23; 3:3, 20.

b. Debatable Examples

1 John 3:6,9   πᾶς ὁ ἐν αὐτῷ μένων οὐχ **ἁμαρτάνει**· πᾶς ὁ **ἁμαρτάνων** οὐχ ἑώρακεν αὐτὸν οὐδὲ ἔγνωκεν αὐτόν. (9) Πᾶς ὁ γεγεννημένος ἐκ τοῦ θεοῦ ἁμαρτίαν οὐ **ποιεῖ**, ὅτι σπέρμα αὐτοῦ ἐν αὐτῷ μένει, καὶ οὐ **δύναται ἁμαρτάνειν**, ὅτι ἐκ τοῦ θεοῦ γεγέννηται.

Everyone who remains in him **does not sin**. Everyone who **sins** has not seen him nor has he known him. (9) Everyone who has been born of God **does** not sin, because his seed remains in him, and he **is not able to sin**, because he has been born of God.

> Many older commentaries have taken the highlighted presents (as well as others in vv 4-10) as customary (a view especially popularized by British scholars, principally Westcott): *does* not *continually sin . . . does* not *continually sin . . . does* not *practice* sin . . . *is* not *able to habitually sin*. Taking the presents this way seems to harmonize well with 1:8-10, for

---

[27] Instead of the participial construction, D E G S U V (0250) 579 *et plu* have ὅς ἂν ἀπολύσῃ.

to deny one's sin is to disagree with God's assessment. But there are several arguments against this interpretation: (1) The very subtlety of this approach is against it. (2) It seems to contradict 5:16 (ἐάν τις ἴδῃ τὸν ἀδελφὸν αὐτοῦ **ἁμαρτάνοντα** ἁμαρτίαν μὴ πρὸς θάνατον [if anyone sees his brother **sinning** a sin not unto death]). The author juxtaposes "brother" with the *present* tense of ἁμαρτάνω with the proclamation that such might not lead to death. On the customary present view, the author should not be able to make this statement. (3) Gnomic presents most frequently occur with generic subjects (or objects). Further, "the sense of a generic utterance is usually an *absolute* statement of what each one does once, and not a statement of the individual's customary or habitual activity."[28] This certainly fits the pattern.

How should we then take the present tenses here? The immediate context seems to be speaking in terms of a projected eschatological reality.[29] The larger section of this letter addresses the bright side of the eschaton: Since Christians are in the last days, their hope of Christ's imminent return should produce godly living (2:28-3:10). The author first articulates how such an eschatological hope should produce holiness (2:28-3:3). Then, without marking that his discussion is still in the same vein, he gives a proleptic view of sanctification (3:4-10)–that is, he gives a hyperbolic picture of believers vs. unbelievers, implying that even though believers are not yet perfect, they are moving in that direction (3:6, 9 need to be interpreted proleptically), while unbelievers are moving away from truth (3:10; cf. 2:19). Thus, the author states in an absolute manner truths that are not yet true, because he is speaking within the context of eschatological hope (2:28-3:3) and eschatological judgment (2:18-19).

1 Tim 2:12   διδάσκειν γυναικὶ οὐκ **ἐπιτρέπω** οὐδὲ αὐθεντεῖν ἀνδρός

I **do** not **permit** a woman to teach or exercise authority over a man

If this were a *descriptive* present (as it is sometimes popularly taken), the idea *might* be that in the future the author would allow this: *I do not presently permit. . .* However, there are several arguments against this: (1) It is overly subtle. Without some temporal indicator, such as ἄρτι or perhaps νῦν, this view begs the question. (2) Were we to do this with other commands in the present tense, our resultant exegesis would be both capricious and ludicrous. Does μὴ μεθύσκεσθε οἴνῳ . . . , ἀλλὰ πληροῦσθε ἐν πνεύματι in Eph 5:18 mean "Do not *for the moment* be filled with wine, but be filled *at the present time* by the Spirit" with the implication that such a moral code might change in the future? The normal use of the present tense in didactic literature, especially when introducing an exhortation, is not descriptive, but a general precept that has gnomic implications.[30] (3) Grammatically, the present tense is used with a generic object (γυναικὶ), suggesting that it should be taken as a gnomic present. (4) Contextually, the exhortation seems to be rooted in creation (note v 13 and the introductory γάρ), rather than an address to a temporary situation.

---

[28] Fanning, *Verbal Aspect*, 217.

[29] Sakae Kubo comes close to this when he argues for an ideal setting (S. Kubo, "I John 3:9: Absolute or Habitual?", *Andrews University Seminary Studies* 7 [1969] 47-56).

[30] Cf. Rom 6:11, 12, 13; 12:2, 14; 13:1; 1 Cor 3:18, 21; 6:9, 18; 10:14; 15:34; 2 Cor 6:14; Gal 1:8; 5:13, 16; Eph 4:25; 5:1-3; 6:1-2; Phil 2:5, 12, 14; 4:4-9; Col 3:2, 16; 1 Thess 5:15-22; 1 Tim 3:10, 12; 4:7; 5:1, 22; 6:11; 2 Tim 1:13; 2:1, 8, 22; 3:14; 4:5; Titus 2:1; 3:1, 14.

III. Special Uses of the Present Tense

Five uses of the present tense do not easily fit into the above categories. These include the historical present, perfective present, conative present, futuristic present, and present retained in indirect discourse. The first four may be viewed temporally for pragmatic purposes (as most of them occur only in the indicative), moving from *simple past* (historical present), to *past + present result* (perfective present), to *presently incomplete or potential* (conative present), to *futuristic* (futuristic present). The fifth category, the present retained in indirect discourse, is technically not a syntactical category but a structural one.

➡ ## A. Historical Present (Dramatic Present)[31]

1. Definition

The historical present is used fairly frequently in narrative literature to describe a past event.

2. Amplification/Semantics

a. Reason for Use: Vivid Portrayal

The *reason* for the use of the historical present is normally to portray an event *vividly*, as though the reader were in the midst of the scene as it unfolds.[32] Such vividness might be *rhetorical* (to focus on some aspect of the narrative) or *literary* (to indicate a change in topic).[33] The present tense may be used to describe a past event, either for the sake of *vividness* or to *highlight* some aspect of the narrative. It may be *intentional* (conscious) or *unintentional* (subconscious) on the part

---

There do not seem to be *any* exhortational instances of a first person present verb followed by an infinitive (such as *I want you to, I urge him to*) in the *corpus Paulinum* in which the present tense first-person verb should be taken as *right now, but not later*. (1 Cor 7:7 might fit this description, however, but the context also seems to specify a temporal limit [v 26].) These tenses fit some other category, principally gnomic. Cf., e.g., Rom 1:13; 11:25; 16:19; 1 Cor 7:32; 10:1; 11:3; 12:1; Phil 4:2; Col 2:1; 1 Tim 2:1.

[31] We could almost call this the "Walter Cronkite" present or the "You Are There" present. But this description dates me. Generation X students would probably speak of the "Quantum Leap" present, or the "Bronx" present (alluding to the vivid manner of speech in that part of the country).

[32] Although there has been much discussion on the use of the historical present (in Greek as well as other languages) in recent linguistic literature, the most recent works on verbal aspect in the NT are in agreement that *vividness* or *dramatic narration* is the *raison d'être* of this usage. See Fanning, *Verbal Aspect*, 226 (discussion of historical present overall is on 226-39); Porter, *Verbal Aspect*, 196 (discussion of historical present overall is on 189-98).

of the speaker. If intentional, then it is probably used to show the prominence of the events following. If unintentional, then it is probably used for vividness, as if the author were reliving the experience.[34]

However, with λέγει and other verbs introducing (in)direct discourse, the historical present is for the most part a stereotyped idiom that has lost its original rhetorical powers.[35] λέγει/λέγουσιν is by far the most common verb used as a historical present, accounting for well over half of all the instances.[36]

b. Time Vs. Aspect

The *aspectual* value of the historical present is normally, if not always, reduced to zero.[37] The verbs used, such as λέγει and ἔρχεται, normally introduce an action in the midst of aorists without the slightest hint that an internal or progressive aspect is intended.[38] The historical present has suppressed its aspect, but not its time. But the time element is rhetorical rather than real.[39] The diagram below reflects this.

---

[33] Fanning notes that "this portrayal often works its way out by *drawing attention to crucial events* or *highlighting new scenes or actors* in the narrative" and that it often displays "a clear pattern of discourse-structuring functions, such as to highlight the beginning of a paragraph, to introduce new participants into an existing paragraph, to show participants moving to new locations" (*Verbal Aspect*, 231-32).

[34] This does not mean, of course, that the author is truly reliving the experience. Otherwise we would have to say that the evangelist was present when Jesus was tempted by the devil (Matt 4:1-10) and some disciples tagged along with the women who discovered the empty tomb (John 20:1-2)!

[35] So BDF, 167 (§321); Fanning, *Verbal Aspect*, 231-32.

[36] Cf. J. C. Hawkins, *Horae Synopticae: Contributions to the Study of the Synoptic Problem*, 2d ed (Oxford: Clarendon, 1909) 144-49. In addition, note J. J. O'Rourke, "The Historical Present in the Gospel of John," *JBL* 93 (1974) 585-90 (although his list is marred by inclusion of a few present tenses retained in indirect discourse and other nonhistorical presents). Fanning (*Verbal Aspect*, 234, n. 75) has tabulated that 286 of the 430 historical presents in Matthew–Acts are verbs of speaking (thus, almost exactly *two-thirds* of the instances).

[37] So BDF, 167 (§321); Robertson, *Grammar*, 867 (though he says that some instances are equal to an imperfect); Fanning, *Verbal Aspect*, 227-31.

[38] If the nontemporal view of tense were true, we would expect the aspect to be in full flower. Porter argues that this is indeed the case (*Verbal Aspect*, 195). Yet in his description he argues for *vividness* (rather than a progressive portrayal) as the force of the aspect. This seems better suited to the temporal view: The writer uses the present tense in a highly vivid manner, as though the event occurred simultaneously with the time of writing.

[39] Fanning has arrived at similar conclusions (*Verbal Aspect*, 228): "The point of the historical present is not how the occurrence is viewed, but that it occurs (rhetorically) 'now.'" He goes on to say that "the *temporal* meaning predominates and neutralizes the *aspectual* force." Although we fully agree, it does seem that this description goes against the grain of Fanning's "invariant meaning" for the tenses (in this case, that the present tense has an invariant meaning of an internal aspect).

Past	Present	Future
•		

Chart 54
The Force of the Historical Present

c.   **Usage and Genre**

The historical present occurs mostly in less educated writers as a function of colloquial, vivid speech. More literary authors, as well as those who aspire to a distanced historical reporting, tend to avoid it. John has it 162 times, Mark 151 times. Matthew has 93 at most, while Luke has a mere 11, mostly found in the parables of Jesus (with another 13 in Acts). The historical present is preeminently the story-teller's tool and as such occurs exclusively (or almost exclusively) in *narrative* literature.[40]

3.   **Clarification/Semantic Situation**

Although the historical present has already been defined, it needs to be clarified here–in terms of the semantic situation in which it occurs.[41]

a.   **With Reference to Person**

The only person in which the historical present occurs is the *third* person (either singular or plural). Cf., e.g., John 4:11, 15, 19, 21, 25, 26, 28, 34, 49, 50; 20:1 (twice), 2 (thrice), 5, 6, 13 (twice), 14, 15 (twice), 16, 18, 19, 26, 27, 29, etc.[42]

---

[40] Porter (*Verbal Aspect*, 197) finds some examples outside of narrative (principally in Romans and Revelation). His example from Rom 11:7 is disputed by McKay ("Time and Aspect," 210-12). Those from Revelation seem to belong to a different category altogether, for the use of the tenses in *apocalyptic* (in which the *future* is portrayed vividly, sometimes as a present, sometimes as a recent past event) can hardly be compared to other genres.

[41] This is based on John Hawkins' *Horae Synopticae*, where virtually all the historical presents (415) are listed. There is no analysis of the kinds of verbs used in Hawkins (for his purposes were otherwise). But a simple observation of his examples reveals certain facts.

[42] This might also be the case for other Greek literature. See R. L. Shive, "The Use of the Historical Present and Its Theological Significance" (Th.M. thesis, Dallas Theological Seminary, 1982).

On occasion, a first-person verb is listed among historical presents in the NT. But almost invariably, this represents a confusion between historical present and present retained in indirect discourse: Both are translated the same (as far as temporal value is concerned) in English, but the semantics and semantic situation are different. (See discussion below under "Present Retained in Indirect Discourse.")

b. With Reference to Types of Verbs

Because the historical present occurs in *narrative*, it is natural that it be used only in the third person. As well, since it is used for vividness or highlighting, it is equally natural that it use verbs of *action*. λέγω is by far the most predominant verb used as a historical present (in fact, in the references mentioned above [i.e., from John 4 and 20], fifteen of the twenty-three historical presents are the verb λέγω). ἔρχομαι comes in a distant second (in the references mentioned above from John 4 and 20, of the eight non-λέγω historical presents, five are ἔρχομαι).

Significantly, the *one* verb that is *not* used as a historical present is the *equative verb* (εἰμί).[43] Also, when γίνομαι functions as an equative verb, it is not used as a historical present. However, it may function as other than an equative verb at times.[44]

c. With Reference to Mood

Since time is an element of tense only absolutely in the indicative, it stands to reason that the historical present can only legitimately be used in the *indicative* mood. Since the participle takes its cue from the main verb with reference to time, it is not really correct to say that the participle can be a historical present–even when it is related to a historical present main verb.[45]

4. Illustrations

a. Clear Examples

Matt 26:40   **ἔρχεται** πρὸς τοὺς μαθητὰς καὶ **εὑρίσκει** αὐτοὺς καθεύδοντας, καὶ **λέγει**
he came to the disciples and found them sleeping, and he said . . .

Mark 1:41   αὐτοῦ ἥψατο καὶ **λέγει** αὐτῷ
he touched him and said to him . . .

> Other examples of λέγει include Matt 4:6, 10; 8:4, 7, 20; 12:13; 16:15; Mark 6:31, 38; 9:5; 10:23; Luke 11:45; John 1:21; 2:4, 5, 7, 8, 10; 4:7, 9, 11, 15; 18:4, 5, 17; 19:4, 5, 6, 9, 10.

---

[43] Although the copula may be used as a present tense retained in indirect discourse, which is an entirely different idiom. Much confusion has arisen over the similarities in *translation* between these two.

[44] Hawkins lists two or three instances with γίνομαι; in neither instance is it functioning as an equative verb (cf. Mark 2:15).

[45] Early editions of the NASB erred in labeling (via an asterisk) a present participle as a historical present simply because it is related to a historical present main verb (in John 20:1 οὔσης is dependent upon ἔρχεται for its relative time; it should simply be called a temporal participle of contemporaneous time). On two other occasions, they labeled an aorist indicative as a historical present.

Mark 6:1   ἐξῆλθεν ἐκεῖθεν καὶ **ἔρχεται** εἰς τὴν πατρίδα αὐτοῦ, καὶ **ἀκολουθοῦσιν**
            αὐτῷ οἱ μαθηταὶ αὐτοῦ[46]

            he went out from there and **came** into his homeland, and his disci-
            ples **followed** him

> Other examples of ἔρχεται include Matt 26:36; Mark 1:40; 3:20; 5:22;
> 10:1; 14:17; Luke 8:49.

b. Debatable Texts

1) John 8:58

The text reads: πρὶν ᾽Αβραὰμ γενέσθαι ἐγὼ **εἰμί** ("before Abraham
was, **I am**"). On this text, Dennis Light wrote an article in
defense of the *New World Translation* in the *Bible Collector* (July-
December, 1971). In his article he discusses ἐγὼ εἰμί, which the
New World Translation renders, "I have been." Light defends this
translation by saying, "The Greek verb *eimi*, literally present
tense, must be viewed as a historical present, because of being
preceded by the aorist infinitive clause referring to Abraham's
past" (p. 8). This argument has several flaws in it: (1) The fact
that the present tense follows an aorist *infinitive* has nothing to
do with how it should be rendered. In fact, historical presents
are usually wedged in between aorist (or imperfect) *indicatives*,
not infinitives. (2) If this is a historical present, it is apparently
the only historical present in the NT that uses the equative verb
εἰμί. The burden of proof, therefore, lies with one who sees εἰμί
as *ever* being used as a historical present. (3) If this is a historical
present, it is apparently the only historical present in the NT that
is in other than the third person.[47]

The translators of the *New World Translation* understand the
implications of ἐγὼ εἰμί here, for in the footnote to this text in the
NWT, they reveal their motive for seeing this as a historical
present: "It is not the same as ὁ ὤν (*ho ohn´*, meaning 'The Being'

---

[46] For ἔρχεται, A (D) E F G H K M N S U V Y Π Σ Φ Ω 0126 *f*[1, 13] 28 33 565 579 700 *Byz*
have ἦλθεν. The present indicative is supported by ℵ B C L Δ Θ 892 2427 *et pauci*.

[47] To be sure, εἰμί is sometimes considered to be a historical present as is the first person verb, but most reject these identifications in the passages suggested. (Cf. the treatments of this issue in R. L. Shive, "The Historical Present in the New Testament," and
D. B. Wallace," John 5,2 and the Date of the Fourth Gospel," *Bib* 71 [1990] 177-205.) A
proper syntactical approach must be based on legitimate, undisputed examples. Disputed examples must fit into the contours of such clear instances or be judged suspect.
This is not to say that it is *impossible* for εἰμί to be a historical present in, say, John 8:58. But
it is to say that the burden of proof rests with the one who makes such a claim. Unfortunately, a typical approach to grammar in such disputed passages is (a) to locate a category
of usage that fits one's preconceived views, and (b) to ignore the semantic situation of the
category and to argue on the basis of context (which must be construed) and ingenuity.
Context, of course, has its rather large place in exegesis–larger for the most part than
grammar–but our contention is that grammar is often relegated to a mere pool of options.

or 'The I Am') at Exodus 3:14, *LXX*." In effect, this is a negative admission that if ἐγὼ εἰμί is *not* a historical present, then Jesus is here claiming to be the one who spoke to Moses at the burning bush, the I AM, the eternally existing One, Yahweh (cf. Exod 3:14 in the LXX, ἐγὼ εἰμι ὁ ὤν).[48]

2) John 5:2

The text reads: **ἔστιν** δὲ ἐν τοῖς ʿΙεροσολύμοις . . . κολυμβήθρα ("Now there *is* in Jerusalem . . . a pool"). Since εἰμί is nowhere else clearly used as a historical present, the present tense should be taken as indicating present time from the viewpoint of the speaker.[49] The implication of this seems to be that this Gospel was written before the destruction of Jerusalem in 70 CE.[50] Although many object to a pre-70 date for John's Gospel, they must, in support of their view, reckon with this text.

3) Romans 7:14-24

Throughout this section of Romans, Paul speaks in the first person singular in the present tense. For example, in 7:15 he declares, "For that which I am doing I do not understand; for I am not practicing what I would like to do, but I am doing the very thing I hate" (ὃ γὰρ κατεργάζομαι οὐ γινώσκω· οὐ γὰρ ὃ θέλω τοῦτο πράσσω, ἀλλ᾽ ὃ μισῶ τοῦτο ποιῶ). Some would see the presents here as dramatic or historical presents. But since Paul is speaking in the first person, this label is not at all likely. In other words, one cannot appeal to the idiom of the historical present for support of the view that Paul is referring to his past, non-Christian life in this text.[51] If one wants to hold the view that Paul is either not describing himself in this text, or else he is

---

[48] More nuanced is the view that εἰμί is a present tense extending from the past (so McKay, *New Syntax*, 42). However, John 8:58 lacks sufficient parallels to be convincing.

[49] So McKay, *New Syntax*, 40.

[50] By arguing that ἐστίν is a stative present, we are admittedly going against the tide of NT scholarship. Generally, NT scholars have attempted to circumvent the *prima facie* force of ἐστίν by adopting one of five approaches in this text: (1) ἐστίν is a historical present (so Schnackenburg, Knabenbauer, Carson, *et al.*); (2) ἐστίν is an anomalous present (McNeile); (3) the author erred, not knowing that the pool had been destroyed (Bleek?); (4) the pool of Bethesda must have survived the Jewish War (Plummer, Dods, Tholuck, Weiss, *et alii* suggest this, but prefer the historical present view [but Jeremias assumes it]); (5) the redactional view: John 5:2 belonged to an earlier stratum of the Gospel, only to go uncorrected in the final publication (MacGregor, Brown?). Each of these views has severe problems. See Wallace, "John 5,2," 177-205.

[51] Cf. Shive, "Historical Present," 67-70, 74, for a critique of the historical present view in Rom 7:14-25. Cranfield, *Romans* (ICC) 1.344-45, has the right instincts against these verbs being historical presents, but his argument could have been strengthened had he been aware of the semantic situation.

speaking corporately (so as to include himself only in a general way), syntax is not the route to get there.[52]

B. *Perfective Present*

1.   Definition

The present tense may be used to *emphasize* that the results of a past action are still continuing. This usage is not very common.

2.   Clarification

There are *two types*: one lexical, the other contextual. The *lexical* type involves certain words (most notably ἥκω, which almost always has a perfective force to it).[53] The other type is *contextual*: This use of the present is especially frequent with λέγει as an introduction to an OT quotation.[54] Its usual force seems to be that although the statement was spoken in the past, it still speaks today and is binding on the hearers.[55]

Past	Present	Future
• (———————)		

Chart 55
The Force of the Perfective Present

Note: The symbol (———) indicates the *results* of an action.

---

[52] I have struggled with this text for many years (in more ways than one!), and have held to three different views. My *present* view is that the apostle is speaking as universal man and is describing the experience of anyone who attempts to please God by submitting the flesh to the law. By application, this could be true of an unbeliever or a believer. The present tenses, then, would be *gnomic*, not historical, for they refer to *anyone* and describe something that is universally true. This view sees no shift in the person in the "I" of vv 7-13 and 14-25 (which is a basic problem for other views) and is able to handle vv 9, 14 and 25 under one umbrella. The biggest problem for it is that "I" then is figurative, not literal. Further, the interplay between syntax and rhetorical language is a conundrum that deserves greater exploration.

[53] According to Fanning, the following verbs also occasionally function as perfective presents: ἀπέχω, ἀκούω, πάρειμι (*Verbal Aspect*, 239-40, for a discussion). Note also γινώσκω in Luke 1:34.

[54] This usage is so distinct that it could be given a different label, something like the *introductory formula present*.

[55] In some respects it could be treated as a *testimonium* present, which is followed by a content clause: "This is the statement of scripture. . . ." Cf. John 1:19 (αὕτη ἐστὶν ἡ μαρτυρία τοῦ Ἰωάννου).

3. Illustrations

Luke 1:34   εἶπεν δὲ Μαριὰμ πρὸς τὸν ἄγγελον, Πῶς ἔσται τοῦτο, ἐπεὶ ἄνδρα οὐ **γινώσκω**;

But Mary said to the angel, "How shall this be, since **I have** not **known** a man?"

Rom 10:16   Ἡσαΐας γὰρ **λέγει**· κύριε, τίς ἐπίστευσεν τῇ ἀκοῇ ἡμῶν;

For Isaiah **says**, "Lord, who has believed our report?"

> The way in which Paul introduces the quotation from Isa 53 implies that Isaiah's words were still applicable to Paul's situation. Typically quotations of the OT, other than prophecies, are introduced by γέγραπται, "It stands written." It is difficult to assess the difference in force between these two introductory formulas, but it is *possible* that the connotation of the tenses is the following: (1) γέγραπται, being a perfect tense, stresses the abiding *authority* of scripture; (2) λέγει, being a present tense, stresses the *applicability* of scripture to the present situation.

Eph 4:8   **λέγει**

[God] **says** *or* [scripture] **says**

> Occasionally the NT writers do not name the subject of λέγει when introducing a quotation from the OT. A most probable explanation is that to them, what the scripture says is what God says and, consequently, there is no difference between scripture and God's word. A significant text, in light of this discussion, is Eph 5:14. Although λέγει introduces the quotation, it is probably not from the OT. Rather, it may well be a quotation of an early Christian creedal hymn.

1 Tim 5:18   **λέγει** ἡ γραφή· βοῦν ἀλοῶντα οὐ φιμώσεις

the scripture **says**, "You shall not muzzle the ox while it is treading out the grain"

1 John 5:20   ὁ υἱὸς τοῦ θεοῦ **ἥκει**, καὶ δέδωκεν ἡμῖν διάνοιαν

the Son of God **has come** and has given us understanding

> The perfective present is here joined by καί to a perfect tense, illustrating its force.[56]

For *lexical* perfective presents, cf. also Matt 6:2; Luke 15:27; John 8:42; 2 Thess 3:11.

For *contextual* (introductory formula) perfective presents, cf. also Rom 9:15; 10:8, 11, 19; 11:9; 12:19; 2 Cor 6:2; Gal 3:16; 4:30; Jas 4:5, 6.

---

[56] Some instances of ἥκω are linked to an aorist; there is some doubt about whether they are perfective in such places (cf. Luke 15:27; John 8:42), though most likely they are perfective even here.

C. Conative (Tendential, Voluntative) Present

Definition

This use of the present tense portrays the subject as *desiring* to do something (*voluntative*), *attempting* to do something (*conative*), or at the point of *almost doing* something (*tendential*).[57] This usage is relatively rare.[58]

We will break this down into two categories: in progress, but not complete (true conative); not begun, but about/desired to be attempted (voluntative, tendential).

This general category needs to be distinguished from the futuristic present, which typically connotes certainty that an action will be carried out.

1. In Progress, but not Complete (True Conative)

a. Definition

The present tense is used to indicate that an *attempt* is *being made* in the present time (indicative mood). Often it bears the connotation that the action will *not* be completed; it is thus an unsuccessful attempt in progress.[59]

b. Key to Identification: *is attempting (unsuccessfully)*

Past	Present	Future
		———O

Chart 56
The Force of the (True) Conative Present

Note: The symbol O is used for all actions that are either not accomplished or not begun.

c. Illustrations

Acts 26:28 ὁ Ἀγρίππας πρὸς τὸν Παῦλον· ἐν ὀλίγῳ με **πείθεις** Χριστιανὸν ποιῆσαι.[60]

Agrippa [said] to Paul, "In a little while, **you are trying to persuade me to become a Christian!**"

This text has been variously interpreted. Other renderings include: "In a moment you *will persuade* me" and "Are you *trying to persuade* me, in

---

[57] Williams, *Grammar Notes*, 28.

[58] Nevertheless, the conative present fits well the genius of the present tense, for it views the action *internally*, without regard for its culmination.

[59] This is not always the case: note, e.g., Rom 2:4; 2 Cor 5:11.

[60] For πείθεις, codex A reads πείθῃ.

a brief moment, to become a Christian?" Regardless of the rendering, the conative present is involved.

Gal 5:4   οἵτινες ἐν νόμῳ **δικαιοῦσθε**
[you] who **are attempting to be justified** by the Law

> If this were a durative present of some sort, the translation would be, "you who *are being justified* by the Law"! Obviously, such a meaning for this text would contradict the whole point of Galatians. Paul is not declaring that they *are* being justified by the Law, but that they *think* they are (or they are trying to be), though their attempt can only end in failure.

Cf. also Rom 2:4; 2 Cor 5:11; Gal 6:12.

2. Not Begun, but About/Desired to be Attempted (Voluntative/ Tendential)

a. Definition

The present tense is used to indicate that an *attempt* is *about to be made* or one that is *desired to be made* in the present time (or, very near future time). The action may or may not be carried out.

b. Key to Identification: *about to*

Past	Present	Future
		O

Chart 57
The Force of the Tendential Present

c. Illustrations

John 10:32   διὰ ποῖον αὐτῶν ἔργον ἐμὲ **λιθάζετε**;
For which of these works **are you about to stone** me?

John 13:27   ὃ **ποιεῖς** ποίησον τάχιον
what **you are about to do**, do quickly

➡ D. Futuristic Present

Definition

The present tense may be used to describe a future event, though (unlike the conative present) it typically adds the connotations of immediacy and certainty.[61] Most instances involve verbs whose *lexical* meaning

---

[61] To be sure, some examples can be taken as either conative or futuristic present. Fanning, for example, regards νίπτεις in John 13:6 as tendential (thus, *you are* not *about to wash my feet, are you?*), while we take it to be a negated futuristic present (*you will* not *wash my feet, will you?*). There is little difference between the two.

involves anticipation (such as ἔρχομαι, -βαίνω, πορεύομαι, etc.).[62] This usage is relatively common.

1. Completely Futuristic

a. Definition

The present tense may describe an event that is *wholly* subsequent to the time of speaking, although as if it were present.

b. Key to Identification: *is soon going to, is certainly going to, will*

Past	Present	Future
		•

Chart 58
The Force of the Completely Futuristic Present

c. Amplification

Only an examination of the context will help one see whether this use of the present stresses *immediacy* or *certainty*. In this respect, the ambiguity of the semantic nuance of the completely futuristic present is akin to the ambiguity of the lexical nuance of μέλλω (which usually means either "I am about to" [immediacy] or "I will inevitably" [certainty]).

d. Illustrations

John 4:25　Μεσσίας **ἔρχεται**
　　　　　Messiah **is coming**
　　　　　　　The idea at least includes certainty, and possibly immediacy.

Rom 6:9　Χριστὸς . . . οὐκέτι **ἀποθνῄσκει**
　　　　　Christ **is** not **going to die**
　　　　　　　Obviously, the stress here is on certainty, as evidenced by οὐκέτι.

Rev 22:20　ναί, **ἔρχομαι** ταχύ
　　　　　Yes, **I am coming** quickly.
　　　　　　　This is a difficult text to assess. It may be that the stress is on the certainty of the coming or on the immediacy of the coming. But one's view does not hinge on the futuristic present, but on the adverb ταχύ. The force of the sentence may then mean, "Whenever I come, I will come *quickly*," in which case the stress is on the *certainty* of the coming (cf. Matt 28:8). Or, it may mean, "I am on my way and I intend to be there very *soon*." If so, then the stress is on the *immediacy* of the coming.

Cf. also Luke 3:16; John 11:11; 1 Cor 16:5; 2 Cor 13:1.

---

[62] For a detailed and nicely nuanced discussion, see Fanning, *Verbal Aspect*, 221-26.

2. **Mostly Futuristic (Ingressive-Futuristic?)**

a. **Definition**

The present tense may describe an event *begun* in the present time, but completed in the future. Especially is this used with verbs of coming, going, etc., though it is rarer than the wholly futuristic present.

b. **Key to Identification**

Often the verb can be translated as a present tense (e.g., *is coming*).

Past	Present	Future

Chart 59
The Force of the Mostly Futuristic Present

c. **Illustrations**

Mark 10:33 ἀναβαίνομεν εἰς Ἱεροσόλυμα
We are going up to Jerusalem.

John 4:23 ἔρχεται ὥρα καὶ νῦν ἐστιν
An hour **is coming** and is now here.
> The addition of καὶ νῦν ἐστιν defines the coming hour as having already *partially* arrived.

Cf. also Matt 26:45; Acts 20:22.

➡ E. *Present Retained in Indirect Discourse*

1. **Definition**

Generally speaking, *the tense* of the Greek verb in indirect discourse is *retained* from the direct discourse.[63] (Indirect discourse occurs after a verb of perception [e.g., verbs of saying, thinking, believing, knowing, seeing, hearing]. It may be introduced by a declarative ὅτι, λέγων, εἶπεν, etc.[64]) This is unlike English: In indirect discourse we usually push the *tense* back "one slot" from what it would have been in the direct discourse (especially if the introductory verb is past tense)–that is, we render a simple past as a past perfect, a present as a past tense, etc.

---

[63] There are exceptions to this general rule, especially with the imperfect standing in the place of the present. See Burton, *Moods and Tenses*, 130-42 (§334-56).

[64] For a general discussion of the indicative mood in declarative ὅτι clauses, see "Indicative Mood."

In Greek, however, the tenses of the original utterance are retained in the indirect discourse. The *present* tense is one of these. This usage is very common, especially in the Gospels and Acts.

This use of the present tense is not, technically, a syntactical category. That is to say, the present tense also belongs to some other present tense usage. The retained present is a *translational* category, not a syntactical one.

2. Analogy

Suppose a mailman came to my door and said, "I *have* a package for you." I open the package only to discover that it is for a neighbor. The next day I remind the mailman of our conversation: "Remember yesterday when you said that you *had* a package for me? Well, it was really for my neighbor." In English the tense in the direct discourse ("I *have* a package") is replaced by a tense one step removed from the actual time ("that you *had* a package"). It is typically introduced by *that* (just as in Greek indirect discourse is frequently introduced by ὅτι). In Greek, however, both the direct discourse and the indirect use the same tense.

3. Clarification

A retained present is usually progressive, but not in the present time (that is, according to *English*). Do *not* confuse this with the historical present, however. Equative verbs are frequently used in indirect discourse (and thus be translated as a past tense, though present in Greek); they do not occur as historical presents, however.

4. Illustrations

John 5:13   ὁ δὲ ἰαθεὶς οὐκ ᾔδει τίς **ἐστιν**

Now the man who had been healed did not know who he **was**

> Here the equative verb in the present tense is translated as a past tense, though there is no ὅτι. Nevertheless, the clause is in indirect discourse, which simply does not have an introductory conjunction, a common enough occurrence in Greek.[65]

Mark 2:1   ἠκούσθη ὅτι ἐν οἴκῳ **ἐστίν**

It was heard that **he was** at home

> Note that although the equative verb ἐστίν is here translated as a past tense, it is *not* a historical present. The semantics of historical presents are quite different from the present tense retained in indirect discourse. In particular, the verb εἰμί does not occur as a historical present in the NT.

---

[65] Most English translations properly render ἐστιν as "was," recognizing the construction as indirect discourse (cf., e.g., KJV, NKJV, ASV, NASB, RSV, NRSV, NIV, JB).

John 4:1   ὡς ἔγνω ὁ Ἰησοῦς ὅτι **ἤκουσαν** οἱ Φαρισαῖοι ὅτι Ἰησοῦς πλείονας μαθητὰς **ποιεῖ** καὶ **βαπτίζει** ἢ Ἰωάννης

when Jesus knew that the Pharisees **had heard** that Jesus **was making** and **baptizing** more disciples than John

> This text involves indirect discourse embedded within *another* indirect discourse. It affords a good illustration of the differences between English and Greek. The Greek retains the tenses from the direct discourse, while English moves them back one slot. Thus, ἤκουσαν is translated *had heard* even though it is aorist (the original statement also would have been aorist: "the Pharisees have heard . . ."). And both ποιεῖ and βαπτίζει, although present tenses, are translated as though they were imperfects (the original statement would have been "Jesus *is making* and *baptizing* more disciples than John").

> Once again, it is important to distinguish the historical present from the present tense retained in indirect discourse. For one thing, historical presents are aspectually "flat"–that is, they are translated just like an aorist, as a simple past tense. But ποιεῖ and βαπτίζει are naturally translated as though they were imperfects.

John 5:15   ὁ ἄνθρωπος . . . ἀνήγγειλεν τοῖς Ἰουδαίοις ὅτι Ἰησοῦς **ἐστιν** ὁ ποιήσας αὐτὸν ὑγιῆ

the man announced to the Jews that Jesus **was** the one who made him well

Acts 4:13   θεωροῦντες τὴν τοῦ Πέτρου παρρησίαν καὶ Ἰωάννου καὶ καταλαβόμενοι ὅτι ἄνθρωποι ἀγράμματοί **εἰσιν** καὶ ἰδιῶται, ἐθαύμαζον

When they saw the boldness of Peter and John, and when they discerned that **they were** unlearned and ignorant men, they were amazed

Cf. also Matt 2:16; 5:17, 21, 33; 20:30; 21:26; Mark 3:8; 6:49, 52; Luke 8:47; 17:15; 19:3; John 4:47 (with a perfective present, ἥκω); 6:22, 64; 11:27; Acts 8:14; 23:24; Phlm 21; 1 John 2:18; Rev 12:13.

The Imperfect Tense

Overview of Uses

Select Bibliography

BDF, 169-71 (§325-30); **Burton**, *Moods and Tenses*, 12-16 (§21-34); **Fanning**, *Verbal Aspect*, 240-55; **K. L. McKay**, *A New Syntax of the Verb in New Testament Greek: An Aspectual Approach* (New York: Peter Lang, 1994) 42-46; **idem**, "Time and Aspect in New Testament Greek," *NovT* 34 (1992) 209-28; **Moule**, *Idiom Book*, 8-10; **Porter**, *Verbal Aspect*, 198-211; **idem**, *Idioms*, 28, 33-35; **Robertson**, *Grammar*, 882-88; **Turner**, *Syntax*, 64-68; **Young**, *Intermediate Greek*, 113-16; **Zerwick**, *Biblical Greek*, 91-93 (§270-76).

Introduction

As a tense of the first principal part, the imperfect mirrors the present tense both in its general aspect and its specific uses (the only difference being, for the most part, that the imperfect is used for past time). Hence, our treatment does not need to be as detailed as the present tense's discussion.

Like the present tense, the imperfect displays an *internal aspect*.[1] That is, it portrays the action from within the event, without regard for beginning or end. This contrasts with the aorist, which portrays the action in summary fashion. For the most part, the aorist takes a *snapshot* of the action while the imperfect (like the present) takes a *motion picture*, portraying the action as it unfolds. As such, the imperfect is often incomplete and focuses on the *process* of the action.[2]

With reference to *time*, the imperfect is almost always *past*. (Note that since the imperfect only occurs in the indicative mood [1682 times in the NT], this tense always grammaticalizes time.) However, occasionally it portrays other than the past time (e.g., the conative imperfect may have this force to it sometimes; also the imperfect in second class conditions connotes present time—but such is due more to the aspect than the time element of the tense).[3]

In general, the imperfect may be diagrammed as follows:

Past	Present	Future
————		

Chart 60
The Basic Force of the Imperfect[4]

Specific Uses

I. Narrow-Band Imperfects

The action is portrayed as being in progress or as occurring in the *past time* (since all imperfects are in the indicative). This involves three specific types of imperfect: instantaneous, progressive, and ingressive.

---

[1] For a discussion on the difference between unaffected meaning and specific uses, see the introduction to the present tense.

[2] On the different aspectual forces of the aorist and imperfect, see "Portrayal Vs. Reality of Aspect" in the chapter, "The Tenses: An Introduction."

[3] See discussion below (on these respective uses) for reasons on the use of the imperfect to indicate other than past time.

[4] The pictorial representation of the imperfect as linear is itself imperfect. But it is difficult to represent in a generic picture the "internal" aspect.

A. Instantaneous Imperfect
(a.k.a. Aoristic or Punctiliar Imperfect)

1. Definition

The imperfect tense is rarely used just like an aorist indicative, to indicate simple past. This usage is virtually restricted to ἔλεγεν[5] in narrative literature.[6] Even with this verb, however, the imperfect usually bears a different nuance.

Past	Present	Future
.		

Chart 61

The Force of the Instantaneous Imperfect

2. Illustrations

Matt 9:24   **ἔλεγεν**· ἀναχωρεῖτε, οὐ γὰρ ἀπέθανεν τὸ κοράσιον ἀλλὰ καθεύδει.[7]

He said, "Depart, for the little girl is not dead, but is sleeping."

Mark 4:9   καὶ **ἔλεγεν**· ὃς ἔχει ὦτα ἀκούειν ἀκουέτω.

And **he said**, "Let the one who has ears to hear [with] listen!"

> This pronouncement is at the end of a discourse on parables by Jesus. Thus, it is difficult to see the imperfect as ingressive ("he began saying"), progressive ("he was saying"), or iterative/customary ("he would say").

Mark 5:30   **ἔλεγεν**· τίς μου ἥψατο τῶν ἱματίων;[8]

He said, "Who touched my garments?"

> There is evident emotion in this question. The imperfect is often the tense of choice to introduce such *vivid* sayings. In this respect, it parallels the historical (dramatic) present. Further, one is hard-pressed to account for the imperfect on the basis of intrinsic aspectual force (unless it is iterative), for the context argues for a staccato-like effect.

---

[5] It could also occur with the plural ἔλεγον, but there is usually the possibility of a distributive force to the plural, putting it virtually in the *iterative* category.

[6] *Contra BDF*, 170 (§329): "The aorist serves for a simple reference to an utterance previously made (especially for a specific pronouncement of an individual); the imperfect for the delineation of the content of a speech." Many examples of the imperfect fit this description (cf., e.g, Mark 4:21, 26; 6:10; 7:9; 12:38; Luke 5:36; 6:20; 9:23; 10:2; 21:10), but not all (e.g., Matt 9:11; Mark 4:9; 8:21, 24). Further, the imperfects that seem to be used aoristically also frequently have the aorist indicative (εἶπεν) as a textual variant. This use of the imperfect is akin to the instantaneous present in that it usually involves a verb of saying as well.

[7] A number of witnesses, apparently because of the parallel in Mark's account, have a historical present (λέγει) here instead of ἔλεγεν (so C L N W Θ 𝔐 *et alii*).

[8] The aorist εἶπεν is found in D W Θ 565 700.

Mark 8:24   καὶ ἀναβλέψας **ἔλεγεν·** βλέπω τοὺς ἀνθρώπους ὅτι ὡς δένδρα ὁρῶ περιπατοῦντας.[9]

And he looked up and **said**, "I see people walking about like trees."

Luke 23:42   καὶ **ἔλεγεν·** Ἰησοῦ, μνήσθητί μου ὅταν ἔλθῃς εἰς τὴν βασιλείαν σου.[10]

And **he said**, "Jesus, remember me when you come into your kingdom."

> The imperfect is used to introduce a vivid, emotionally-charged statement. As such, it may be termed a *dramatic* imperfect.

John 5:19   ἀπεκρίνατο ὁ Ἰησοῦς καὶ **ἔλεγεν** αὐτοῖς . . .

Jesus answered and **said** to them . . .

> The juxtaposing of the imperfect with an aorist (when both are describing the same thing) confirms the aoristic force of the imperfect here. Most MSS, in fact, have εἶπεν for the imperfect (cf. A D W Θ Ψ *Byz et plu*).

Cf. also Mark 6:16; 8:21; Luke 3:11; 16:5; John 8:23; 9:9.

➡ B. Progressive (Descriptive) Imperfect

1. Definition

The imperfect is often used to describe an action or state that is in progress in past time from the viewpoint (or, more accurately, portrayal) of the speaker. The action (or state) is broader than that of the instantaneous imperfect, but more narrowly focused than that of the customary imperfect. It speaks either of *vividness* or *simultaneity* with another action.[11]

2. Key to Identification: *was (continually) doing, was (right then) happening*

Past	Present	Future
———		

Chart 62
The Force of the Progressive Imperfect

3. Illustrations

Matt 8:24   σεισμὸς μέγας ἐγένετο ἐν τῇ θαλάσσῃ . . . αὐτὸς δὲ **ἐκάθευδεν**

a massive storm came on the sea . . . but **he was sleeping**

Mark 9:31   **ἐδίδασκεν** γὰρ τοὺς μαθητὰς αὐτοῦ καὶ **ἔλεγεν** αὐτοῖς

for **he was teaching** his disciples and **was saying** to them

> Although this could conceivably be a customary imperfect ("he would teach . . . he would say"), this context suggests a specific occasion.

---

[9] Some witnesses have (instead of ἔλεγεν) the aorist εἶπεν (e.g., 𝔓[45] ℵ C Θ 487 1071 1342 *et pauci*), while others have the historical present λέγει (e.g., D N W Σ *f*[13] 565).

[10] Codex D has εἶπεν for ἔλεγεν.

[11] Fanning, *Verbal Aspect*, 241 (this use of the imperfect is found on 241-44).

Acts 3:2   τις ἀνὴρ χωλὸς ἐκ κοιλίας μητρὸς αὐτοῦ ὑπάρχων **ἐβαστάζετο**
             a certain man, who was lame from birth, **was being carried**

Acts 15:37   Βαρναβᾶς δὲ **ἐβούλετο** συμπαραλαβεῖν καὶ τὸν Ἰωάννην τὸν
             καλούμενον Μᾶρκον
             Now Barnabas **was wanting** to take along also John, who was called
             Mark.

> This is not a conative imperfect, for the conative notion of desire is lex-
> emic. Further, Barnabas did not *try* to desire; he actually did want to
> take John Mark on the journey.

Cf. Matt 26:58; Mark 9:28; Luke 1:62; 6:19; Acts 2:6; 4:21; 6:1; 15:38; 16:14.

➡ ## C. Ingressive (Inchoative, Inceptive) Imperfect

1. Definition

The imperfect is often used to stress the beginning of an action, with the
implication that it continued for some time.

2. Clarification and Amplification

The difference between the ingressive *imperfect* and the ingressive *aorist*
is that the imperfect stresses beginning, but implies that the action *continues*, while the aorist stresses beginning, but does not imply that the
action continues. Thus the translation for the inceptive imperfect ought
to be "began *doing*" while the inceptive aorist ought to be translated
"began *to do*."[12]

3. Semantic Situation

The ingressive imperfect is especially used in narrative literature when
a change in activity is noted. It is possibly the most common imperfect
in narrative because it introduces a topic shift. Many of the following
examples may be treated as progressive imperfects, but the context in
each instance indicates a topic shift or new direction for the action.

---

[12] Some grammarians lump this use of the imperfect with the *conative* imperfect,
though still seeing a distinction between the two. Robertson, for example, says, "Here the
accent is on the beginning of the action either in contrast to preceding aorists (just begun)
or because the action was interrupted (begun, but not completed). . . . In English we have
to say 'began' for the one, 'tried' for the other" (*Grammar*, 885). He is in reality describing
the ingressive, then conative imperfect, and it would be better to separate the two.

4.   Key to Identification: *began doing*[13]

Past	Present	Future
•———		

Chart 63
The Force of the Ingressive Imperfect

5.   Illustrations

Matt 3:5   τότε **ἐξεπορεύετο** πρὸς αὐτὸν ˙ Ἱεροσόλυμα
             then Jerusalem **began going out** to him

Matt 5:2   καὶ ἀνοίξας τὸ στόμα αὐτοῦ **ἐδίδασκεν** αὐτούς
             And when he opened his mouth, **he began teaching** them.

Mark 9:20   πεσὼν ἐπὶ τῆς γῆς **ἐκυλίετο** ἀφρίζων
             He fell on the ground and **began rolling about**, foaming at the
             mouth.

Mark 14:72   καὶ ἐπιβαλὼν **ἔκλαιεν**
             And **he began**[14] weeping[15]

John 4:30   ἐξῆλθον ἐκ τῆς πόλεως καὶ **ἤρχοντο** πρὸς αὐτόν
             They came out of the city and **began coming** to him.

> There is a subtle contrast between the aorist and imperfect here. The
> aorist gets the Samaritans out of Sychar, in a summary fashion; the
> imperfect gets them on the road to Jesus. But it looks at the action from
> the inside. The evangelist leaves the reader hanging with this tantaliz-
> ing morsel: They were coming to Jesus but had not arrived yet. Dramat-
> ically, the scene shifts to the dialogue between Jesus and his disciples,
> leaving the readers with some unfinished business about the Samari-
> tans. They appear on the scene again in a few moments when Jesus
> declares, "Lift up your eyes, for they are white for the harvest" (4:35).
> The Samaritans have arrived.

Acts 3:8   ἐξαλλόμενος ἔστη καὶ **περιεπάτει** καὶ εἰσῆλθεν σὺν αὐτοῖς εἰς τὸ ἱερόν
             leaping up he stood and **began walking about** and he entered with
             them into the temple

Cf. also Matt 4:11; Mark 1:35; Luke 5:3;[16] John 5:10; Acts 7:54; 27:33.

---

[13] This gloss is helpful for seeing the aspectual value of the imperfect, but is often too
pedantic for actual translation.

[14] The meaning of ἐπιβαλών here is problematic, but most likely it has the force of
beginning, having begun (cf. BAGD, s.v. ἐπιβάλλω, 2.b.).

[15] Note the textual variant καὶ ἤρξατο κλαίειν (in D Θ *et pauci*), which makes explicit
the ingressive idea. There are several such textual variations in the NT.

[16] Fanning notes that the imperfect of διδάσκω often has an ingressive flavor (*Verbal
Aspect*, 253).

II. Broad-Band Imperfects

Like the present tense, several imperfects involve a time-frame that is fairly broadly conceived. However, unlike the present tense, there is no *gnomic* imperfect because, most likely, such a usage would seem to transgress into the domain of the gnomic present.[17]

→ ## A. Iterative Imperfect

1. Definition

The imperfect is frequently used for *repeated* action in past time. It is similar to the customary imperfect, but it is not something that regularly recurs. Further, the iterative imperfect occurs over a shorter span of time.

There are two types of iterative imperfect: (1) **Iterative** proper, in which the imperfect indicates *repeated action by the same agent*; and (2) **Distributive**, in which the imperfect is used for *individual acts of multiple agents*.[18]

2. Clarification

Many grammarians make no distinction between the iterative and the customary imperfect.[19] However, while the customary is repeated action in past time, it has two elements that the iterative imperfect does not have: (1) regularly recurring action (or, action at regular intervals), and (2) action that tends to take place over a long span of time. Thus, in some sense, it might be said that the customary imperfect is a *subset* of the iterative imperfect. The difference between these two will be seen more clearly via the illustrations.

3. Key to Identification

Often the gloss *kept on doing, going,* etc. helps the student to see the force of this use of the imperfect, but this is not always the case, especially with distributive imperfects. Another gloss is *repeatedly, continuously doing.*

---

[17] In other words, the gnomic imperfect is unnecessary because the only difference between it and a gnomic present (viz., time) would have been overridden by the gnomic idea (since the usage is essentially omnitemporal). Somewhat different is Fanning's view (*Verbal Aspect*, 249); he says that a gnomic imperfect would have spoken of "*unlimited*, universal occurrence in past time."

[18] See McKay, *New Syntax of the Verb*, 44.

[19] E.g., Robertson, *Grammar*, 884; Fanning, *Verbal Aspect*, 244.

Past	Present	Future
. . . . .		

Chart 64
The Force of the Iterative Imperfect

4. Illustrations

Matt 3:6   ἐβαπτίζοντο ἐν τῷ Ἰορδάνῃ ποταμῷ ὑπ᾽ αὐτοῦ
They were being baptized in the Jordan River by him.
> On this text, Robertson writes, "The aorist tells the simple story. The imperfect draws the picture. It helps you to see the course of the act. It passes before the eye the flowing stream of history. . . . The whole vivid scene at the Jordan is thus sketched. Then Matthew reverts to the aorist (3:7)."[20] This is a good example of the *distributive* iterative imperfect.

Matt 9:21   ἔλεγεν ἐν ἑαυτῇ, Ἐὰν μόνον ἅψωμαι τοῦ ἱματίου αὐτοῦ σωθήσομαι
She was saying within herself, "If only I touch his garment, I will be healed."
> This, of course, may fit some other imperfect category, but the iterative imperfect both fits the context and psychology of the narrative. The picture painted seems to be of a desperate woman who repeats over and over again, "If only I touch his garment," attempting to muster up enough courage for the act. (Note also the parallel in Mark 5:28.)

Matt 27:30   ἔλαβον τὸν κάλαμον καὶ **ἔτυπτον** εἰς τὴν κεφαλὴν αὐτοῦ
They took the reed and **were repeatedly beating** [him] on his head.
> This may also be taken as an ingressive imperfect ("they began beating"). In this instance, the one does not cancel out the other. Further, the scene seems to suggest *both* a distributive and iterative sense (i.e., each soldier would strike more than once).

John 3:22   ἐκεῖ διέτριβεν μετ᾽ αὐτῶν καὶ **ἐβάπτιζεν**
there he was continuing with them and **was baptizing**

John 19:3   **ἔλεγον**, Χαῖρε
they kept on saying, "Hail!"

Acts 2:47   ὁ κύριος **προσετίθει** τοὺς σῳζομένους καθ᾽ ἡμέραν
Every day the Lord **was continuously adding** [to the believers] those who were being saved.

Cf. also Matt 12:23; Mark 12:41 (distributive); Luke 19:47; Acts 16:5; Acts 21:19.

---

[20] Robertson, *Grammar*, 883.

➡ **B. *Customary (Habitual or General) Imperfect***

1.   Definition

The imperfect is frequently used to indicate a *regularly* recurring activity in past time (habitual) *or a state* that continued for some time (general).[21]

The difference between the customary (proper) and the iterative imperfect is not great. Generally, however, it can be said that the *customary* imperfect is *broader* in its idea of the past time and it describes an event that occurred *regularly.*

2.   Key to Identification: *customarily, habitually, continually*

The two types of customary imperfect are lexically determined: One is repeated action (habitual imperfect [*customarily, habitually*]), while the other is ongoing state (stative imperfect [*continually*]). The habitual imperfect can be translated with the gloss *customarily, used to, were accustomed to.*

Past	Present	Future
··············· or ———————		

Chart 65
The Force of the Customary Imperfect

3.   Illustrations

Matt 26:55   καθ᾽ ἡμέραν ἐν τῷ ἱερῷ **ἐκαθεζόμην** διδάσκων
 daily **I used to sit** in the temple, teaching

Mark 4:33   τοιαύταις παραβολαῖς πολλαῖς **ἐλάλει** αὐτοῖς
 with many parables like this **he used to speak** to them

Luke 2:41   **ἐπορεύοντο** οἱ γονεῖς αὐτοῦ κατ᾽ ἔτος εἰς Ἰερουσαλήμ
 his parents **used to go** to Jerusalem each year

Acts 3:2   ὃν **ἐτίθουν** καθ᾽ ἡμέραν
 whom **they used to set down** daily
> Note that often a κατά + acc. phrase is used to clarify that the imperfect is customary, but cf., e.g., John 21:18.

Rom 6:17   **ἦτε** δοῦλοι τῆς ἁμαρτίας
 you were [continually] slaves of sin

Gal 1:14   **προέκοπτον** ἐν τῷ Ἰουδαϊσμῷ
 I was [continually] advancing in Judaism

Cf. also Luke 6:23; 17:27; John 11:36; Acts 11:16 (unless iterative); 1 Cor 6:11; Gal 1:13 (ἐδίωκον).

---

[21] Some grammarians distinguish between stative imperfects and habitual imperfects. In terms of type of action portrayed, this is a legitimate distinction. In terms of timeframe, the two are close together. Like the customary present, we have lumped them together for convenience' sake.

III. Special Uses of the Imperfect

Three uses of the imperfect tense do not naturally fit into the above categories. These include the "pluperfective" imperfect, conative imperfect, and imperfect retained in indirect discourse. The first two are true syntactical categories, while the third is technically not a syntactical category but a structural one.

A. "Pluperfective" Imperfect

1. Definition

The imperfect is infrequently used to indicate a time *prior* to the action occurring in the narrative. It thus indicates time *antecedent* to that of the main verb (which also indicates past time).[22] The difference between this and a pluperfect is that the imperfect's *internal* portrayal is still intact.

2. Illustrations

Mark 5:8 **ἔλεγεν** γὰρ αὐτῷ . . .

for **he had said** to him . . .

> The imperfect is referring back to a previous statement that is only implicit in the context. So RSV, NRSV, et al.

Mark 6:18 **ἔλεγεν** γὰρ ὁ Ἰωάννης τῷ Ἡρῴδῃ ὅτι οὐκ ἔξεστίν σοι ἔχειν τὴν γυναῖκα τοῦ ἀδελφοῦ σου

For John **had been telling** Herod, "It is not lawful for you to have your brother's wife."

> John was beheaded two verses earlier; hence, this must be an imperfect used to refer to a prior time!

Luke 8:29 πολλοῖς γὰρ χρόνοις συνηρπάκει αὐτὸν καὶ **ἐδεσμεύετο** ἁλύσεσιν καὶ πέδαις . . . διαρρήσσων τὰ δεσμὰ **ἠλαύνετο** ὑπὸ τοῦ δαιμονίου

For many times [the unclean spirit] had seized him; and **he had been bound** with chains and shackles . . . breaking the bonds, **he would be driven away** by the demon.

> This sentence functions as an editorial aside for the sake of the reader, after Luke's comment that Jesus commanded the demon to come out of the man. What is significant is that the lead-off verb is pluperfect (συνηρπάκει), thus setting the stage for an event prior to the one in view in the narrative. The following imperfects are both iterative and "pluperfective."

Cf. also Matt 14:4.[23]

---

[22] See McKay, *New Syntax of the Verb*, 45.

[23] Matthew 14:4 finds a parallel in Mark 6:18, with the difference being that John was still alive in Matthew's portrayal of events.

B. *Conative (Voluntative, Tendential) Imperfect*

Definition

This use of the imperfect tense occasionally[24] portrays the action as something that was *desired* (*voluntative*), *attempted* (*conative*), or at the point of *almost happening* (*tendential*).[25]

We will break this down into two categories: in progress, but not complete (true conative); not begun, but about/desired to be attempted (voluntative, tendential).

1.   In Progress, but not Complete (True Conative)

a.   Definition

The imperfect tense is used to indicate that an *attempt* was *being made* in the past time. The implications are that it was not brought to a successful conclusion.

b.   Key to Identification: *was attempting (unsuccessfully)*

Past	Present	Future
———O		

Chart 66
The Force of the (True) Conative Imperfect

Note: The symbol O is used for all actions that are either not accomplished or not begun.

c.   Illustrations

Matt 3:14   ὁ δὲ Ἰωάννης **διεκώλυεν** αὐτόν
             but John **was trying to prevent** him

---

[24] Nevertheless, the conative imperfect is much more common than the conative present. Fanning suggests that this is due to its natural contrast with the aorist indicative, while the present has no ready counterpart (*Verbal Aspect*, 249-50, n. 111). McKay sees their frequency as due to genre: "These effects are much more commonly found in the imperfect than in the present . . . , but only because past-oriented narrative tends to offer more scope for them than present-oriented dialogue" (McKay, *New Syntax of the Verb*, 44). Another reason for the increased frequency may be that the outcome is often revealed in narrative contexts, thus permitting the reader to see that the action did not succeed (while with the present indicative often the verdict is still out).

[25] Williams, *Grammar Notes*, 28.

Mark 15:23 **ἐδίδουν** αὐτῷ ἐσμυρνισμένον οἶνον· ὃς δὲ οὐκ ἔλαβεν

They were attempting to give him wine mixed with myrrh, but he did not accept it.

Acts 26:11 αὐτοὺς **ἠνάγκαζον** βλασφημεῖν

I kept trying to make them blaspheme

Cf. also Luke 9:49; Acts 7:26; 27:17 (unless this is ingressive); Gal 1:13 (ἐπόρθουν); Heb 11:17.

2. Not Begun, but About/Desired to be Attempted (Voluntative/Tendential)

a. Definition

The imperfect tense is used to indicate that an *attempt* was *about to be made* or one that was almost *desired to be made*. The action, however, was not carried out. Often the notion conveyed is that the action was contemplated more than once (hence, the imperfect is naturally used).

What is portrayed with this usage frequently is *present* time in which the action is entirely unrealized in the present. The imperfect seems to be used to indicate the unreal present situation.[26]

b. Key to Identification: *was about to, could almost wish*

Past	Present	Future
O O O		

Chart 67
The Force of the Tendential Imperfect

c. Illustrations

Luke 1:59 **ἐκάλουν** αὐτὸ ἐπὶ τῷ ὀνόματι τοῦ πατρὸς αὐτοῦ Ζαχαρίαν

They wanted to call him by the name of his father, Zachariah.

This is possibly an example of a true conative imperfect: "they kept trying to call."

---

[26] This force is also found with the imperfect used in the second class condition. See Burton, *Moods and Tenses*, 15 (§33); Fanning, *Verbal Aspect*, 251.

Rom 9:3   **ηὐχόμην** γὰρ ἀνάθεμα εἶναι αὐτὸς ἐγώ
          For **I could almost wish** myself accursed.
          > Here, the tendential or "desiderative" imperfect is used.[27] Paul is *not*
          > saying, "For I was wishing" (progressive), or "For I was attempting to
          > wish" (true conative).

Cf. also Acts 25:22; Gal 4:20; Phlm 13 (unless this is true conative).

➡ ## C. Imperfect Retained in Indirect Discourse

1. Definition

Like the present, the imperfect can be retained from the direct discourse
in the indirect.[28] In English, however, we translate it as though it were a
past perfect. As with the retained present, this is a *translational* category,
not a *syntactical* one.[29]

Indirect discourse occurs after a verb of perception (e.g., verbs of saying,
thinking, believing, knowing, seeing, hearing). It may be introduced by
a declarative ὅτι, λέγων, εἶπεν, etc.[30] This is unlike English: In indirect
discourse we usually push the *tense* back "one slot" from what it would
have been in the direct discourse (especially if the introductory verb is
past tense)—that is, we render a simple past as a past perfect, a present
as a past tense, etc.

2. Illustrations

Luke 1:58   ἤκουσαν οἱ περίοικοι καὶ οἱ συγγενεῖς αὐτῆς ὅτι **ἐμεγάλυνεν** κύριος τὸ
            ἔλεος αὐτοῦ μετ᾽ αὐτῆς
            Her neighbors and relatives heard that the Lord **had shown** his
            great mercy to her.

John 2:22   ἐμνήσθησαν οἱ μαθηταὶ αὐτοῦ ὅτι τοῦτο **ἔλεγεν**
            His disciples remembered that **he had said** this.

John 9:18   οὐκ ἐπίστευσαν οἱ Ἰουδαῖοι . . . ὅτι **ἦν** τυφλός
            The Jews did not believe . . . that **he had been** blind.

---

[27] The desiderative imperfect is used "to contemplate the desire, but fail to bring oneself actually to the point of wishing" (Fanning, *Verbal Aspect*, 251).

[28] There are exceptions to this general rule. Not infrequently, the imperfect stands in
the place of the present. See Burton, *Moods and Tenses*, 130-42 (§334-56).

[29] For a more detailed explanation, see the discussion of tenses retained in indirect
discourse in the previous chapter.

[30] For a general discussion of the indicative mood in declarative ὅτι clauses, see
"Indicative Mood."

Acts 4:13 καταλαβόμενοι ὅτι ἄνθρωποι ἀγράμματοί εἰσιν καὶ ἰδιῶται, ἐθαύμαζον ἐπεγίνωσκόν τε αὐτοὺς ὅτι σὺν τῷ Ἰησοῦ **ἦσαν**

When they understood that they were uneducated and unlettered men, they began marveling and they came to realize that **they had been** with Jesus.

> This verse has two indirect discourse clauses, the first with a retained present and the second with a retained imperfect. As well, two imperfects introduce the second ὅτι clause (ἐθαύμαζον, ἐπεγίνωσκον), both of which are most likely ingressive.

Cf. also Mark 11:32; John 4:27 (possible);[31] 6:22; 8:27; 9:8; Acts 3:10; 17:3.

---

[31] The imperfect in John 4:27 is probably best taken as progressive after a causal ὅτι, following a common idiom (cf., e.g., Matt 14:5; Mark 6:34; 9:38; Luke 4:32; 6:19; 8:37; 9:53; 19:3, 4; John 3:23; 5:16, 18; 7:1; 9:22; 16:4; 18:18; 19:20, 42; Acts 2:6; 4:21; 6:1; 10:38; 1 John 3:12; Rev 17:8; 18:23). Several modern translations treat ὅτι as declarative, but translate ἐλάλει as a progressive imperfect (see ASV, RSV, NRSV; NIV, JB, NEB seem to follow this too: His disciples "were surprised to find him talking with a woman"). This may be based on the assumption that ἐθαύμαζον is transitive (cf. Mark 15:44; Luke 7:9; 11:38; John 3:7; 5:28; Acts 7:31; Gal 1:6; Jude 16), in which case ὅτι would introduce the direct object. Though frequently so, θαυμάζω is just as frequently intransitive (cf. Matt 8:10, 27; 9:33; 15:31; 21:20; 22:22; 27:14; Luke 1:63; Acts 13:41). Incidentally, the KJV ("And upon this came his disciples, and marvelled that he talked with the woman") commits multiple syntactical errors: ἐθαύμαζον is treated as a simple past; ὅτι is taken as declarative; ἐλάλει is considered retained, but translated as a simple past; and μετὰ γυναικός is considered definite). For more discussion, see the treatment of this text in the chapter on "Moods: Indicative," under "The Indicative with Ὅτι."

The Aorist Tense

Overview of Uses

Select Bibliography

BDF, 169-75 (§329, 331-35, 337-39); **Burton**, *Moods and Tenses*, 16-31, 46-47, 52-53, 59-70 (§35-57, 98, 113-14, 132-51); **Fanning**, *Verbal Aspect*, 255-90, 325-416; **K. L. McKay**, *A New Syntax of the Verb in New Testament Greek: An Aspectual Approach* (New York: Peter Lang, 1994) 46-49; **idem**, "Time and Aspect in New Testament Greek," *NovT* 34 (1992) 209-28; **Moule**, *Idiom Book*, 10-13; **Porter**, *Verbal Aspect*, 163-244, 321-401; **idem**, *Idioms*, 35-39; **Robertson**, *Grammar*, 830-64; **F. Stagg**, "The Abused Aorist," *JBL* 91 (1972) 222-31; **Turner**, *Syntax*, 68-81; **Young**, *Intermediate Greek*, 121-26; **Zerwick**, *Biblical Greek*, 78-90 (§242-69).

Introduction: The Basic Meaning

A. *Aspect and Time*

1. Aspect: "Snapshot"

The aorist tense "presents an occurrence in summary, viewed as a whole from the outside, without regard for the internal make-up of the occurrence."[1]

---

[1] Fanning, *Verbal Aspect*, 97. Cf. also McKay, "Time and Aspect," 225.

This contrasts with the present and imperfect, which portray the action as an ongoing process. It may be helpful to think of the aorist as taking a snapshot of the action while the imperfect (like the present) takes a motion picture, portraying the action as it unfolds.[2] The following analogy might help.

> Suppose I were to take a snapshot of a student studying for a mid-term exam in intermediate Greek. Below the picture I put the caption, "Horatio Glutchstomach *studied* for the mid-term." From the snapshot and the caption all that one would be able to state *positively* is that Horatio Glutchstomach studied for the mid-term. Now in the picture you notice that Horatio has his Greek text opened before him. From this, you cannot say, "Because the picture is a snapshot rather than a movie, I know that Horatio Glutchstomach only had his Greek text opened for a split-second"! This might be true, but the snapshot does not tell you this. All you really know is that the student had his Greek text open. An event happened. From the picture you cannot tell for *how long* he had his text open. You cannot tell whether he studied for four hours straight (durative), or for eight hours, taking a ten minute break every 20 minutes (iterative). You cannot tell whether he studied successfully so as to pass the test, or whether he studied unsuccessfully. The snapshot does not tell you any of this. The snapshot by itself cannot tell if the action was momentary, "once-for-all", repeated, at regularly recurring intervals, or over a long period of time. It is obvious from this crude illustration that it would be silly to say that since I took a snapshot of Horatio studying, rather than a movie, he *must* have studied only for a very short time!

2. Time

In the *indicative*, the aorist usually indicates *past* time with reference to the time of speaking (thus, "absolute time"). Aorist *participles* usually suggest *antecedent* time to that of the main verb (i.e., *past* time in a *relative* sense). There are exceptions to this general principle, of course, but they are due to intrusions from other linguistic features vying for control (see section below).

Outside the indicative and participle, time is not a feature of the aorist.[3]

---

[2] There is a difference between seeing the aorist as undefined and seeing it as a summary tense, though the two are closely related. In our view the aorist summarizes. It is thus not undefined or unmarked. That is to say, it is not *necessarily* the "default" tense that one would use unless he or she had reason to use another. The key issue, it seems, is the tense-mood combination. Outside the indicative, the aorist is hardly unmarked (statistically, the present runs neck-and-neck with it).

However, in the indicative, the aorist does appear to function this way, at least in narrative literature. The imperfect, (historical) present, perfect, and pluperfect are all used in narrative, along with the aorist. But the aorist is by far the most common. Thus, the analogy with a snapshot seems appropriate, enabling the student to get a handle on the basic notion of the aorist's aspect.

[3] Indirect discourse aorist infinitives are an exception to this rule. But this is because such aorists *represent* an indicative of the direct discourse. See chapter on "Moods" for discussion.

Past	Present	Future
•		

Chart 68
The Force of the Aorist Indicative

B. *Thawing Out the Aorist: The Role of the Context and Lexeme*

The aorist is not always used merely to summarize. In combination with other linguistic features (such as lexeme or context) the aorist often does more.

Some actions, for instance, are shut up to a particular tense. If a speaker wishes to indicate an action that is intrinsically *terminal* (such as "find," "die," or "give birth to"), the choice of tense is dramatically reduced. We would not usually say "he was finding his book." The imperfect, under normal circumstances, would thus be inappropriate.[4]

On the other hand, if a speaker wants to speak of the unchanging nature of a *state* (such as "I have" or "I live"), the aorist is not normally appropriate. Indeed, when the aorist of such stative verbs is used, the emphasis is most frequently on the *entrance into the state*.[5]

The point is that often the choice of a tense is made for a speaker by the action he is describing. At times the tense chosen by the speaker is the *only* one he could have used to portray the idea. Three major factors determine this: lexical meaning of the verb (e.g., whether the verb stem indicates a terminal or punctual act, a state, etc.), contextual factors, and other grammatical features (e.g., mood, voice, transitiveness, etc.).[6] This is the difference between aspect and *Aktionsart*: Aspect is the basic meaning of the tense, unaffected by considerations in a given utterance, while *Aktionsart* is the meaning of the tense as used by an author in a particular utterance, affected as it were by other features of the language.

The use of the aorist in any given situation depends, then, on its combination with other linguistic features.

---

[4] For example, in the NT there are 71 instances of εὑρίσκω as an aorist indicative and only four as an imperfect indicative, all four in the same idiomatic expression.

[5] Fanning, *Verbal Aspect*, 137. See also our discussion in "The Tenses: An Introduction."

[6] The major work in this area is Fanning, *Verbal Aspect*, especially ch. 3: "The Effect of Inherent Meaning and Other Elements on Aspectual Function," 126-96. He views inherent lexical meaning as the major influence (126). His material on this topic is particularly helpful (127-63).

C. The Abused Aorist: Swinging the Pendulum Back

There are two errors to avoid in treating the aorist: saying too little and saying too much.

First, some have *said too little* by assuming that nothing more than the unaffected meaning can ever be seen when the aorist is used. This view fails to recognize that the aorist tense (like other tenses) does not exist in a vacuum. Categories of usage are legitimate because the tenses combine with other linguistic features to form various fields of meaning.[7]

Second, many NT students see a particular category of usage (*Aktionsart*) as underlying the entire tense usage (aspect). This is the error of *saying too much*. Statements such as "the aorist means once-for-all action" are of this sort. It is true that the aorist may, under certain circumstances, describe an event that is, in reality, momentary. But we run into danger when we say that this is the aorist's unaffected meaning, for then we force it on the text in an artificial way. We then tend to ignore such aorists that disprove our view (and they can be found in every chapter of the NT) and proclaim loudly the "once-for-all" aorists when they suit us.[8]

Specific Uses

➡ I. Constative (Complexive, Punctiliar, Comprehensive, Global) Aorist

A. Definition

The aorist normally views the action *as a whole*, taking no interest in the internal workings of the action. It describes the action in summary fashion, without focusing on the beginning or end of the action specifically. This is by far the most common use of the aorist, especially with the indicative mood.

The constative aorist covers a multitude of actions. The event might be iterative in nature, or durative, or momentary, but the aorist says none of this. It places the stress on the fact of the occurrence, not its nature.[9]

---

[7] Stagg went a bit too far at times in his "Abused Aorist" in arguing only for the aorist's unaffected meaning in many contexts. Even more extreme is C. R. Smith, "Errant Aorist Interpreters," *GTJ* 2 (1980) 205-26.

[8] Stagg, "Abused Aorist," did some seminal work to disabuse the aorist of this "once-for-all" approach. Unfortunately, commentators and pulpiteers still repeat the error, more than twenty years after Stagg's article appeared, of saying such things as "the aorist *means* momentary action," or "the aorist *indicates* a 'once-for-all' idea."

[9] For a discussion of the different lexemes used with the constative aorist, see Fanning, *Verbal Aspect*, 255-61. He includes in this category the "recent past" aorist. We have distinguished this from constative because of its potential exegetical value in some contexts (see below).

B. Illustrations

Matt 8:3   ἐκτείνας τὴν χεῖρα ἥψατο αὐτοῦ
            He stretched out his hand and **touched** him.

John 1:21   ἠρώτησαν αὐτόν, Τί οὖν; Σύ Ἠλίας εἶ;
            They **asked** him, "What then? Are you Elijah?"

John 4:20   οἱ πατέρες ἡμῶν ἐν τῷ ὄρει τούτῳ **προσεκύνησαν**
            our fathers **worshiped** on this mountain

Acts 9:40   ἤνοιξεν τοὺς ὀφθαλμοὺς αὐτῆς, καὶ ἰδοῦσα τὸν Πέτρον ἀνεκάθισεν
            She opened her eyes, and **when she saw** Peter, **she sat up.**

Rom 5:14   ἐβασίλευσεν ὁ θάνατος ἀπὸ Ἀδὰμ μέχρι Μωϋσέως
            death **reigned** from Adam until Moses

2 Cor 11:24   πεντάκις τεσσεράκοντα παρὰ μίαν **ἔλαβον**
            five times **I received** the "forty-less-one" [lashes]

Rev 20:4   ἐβασίλευσαν μετὰ τοῦ Χριστοῦ χίλια ἔτη
            they **reigned** with Christ for a thousand years

> The "thousand years" makes it clear that the event portrayed by the aorist takes place over a long period of time (thus durative). However, the aorist is used only to summarize the action. The force of the tense here, then, is not *how long* they reigned, but *that* they reigned.

Cf. also Matt 1:19; Luke 4:43; Acts 12:23; Rom 1:13; 2 Cor 11:25; Heb 11:23.

→ II. Ingressive (Inceptive, Inchoative) Aorist

A. Definition

The aorist tense may be used to stress the beginning of an action or the entrance into a state. Unlike the ingressive imperfect, there is no implication that the action continues. This is simply left unstated. The ingressive aorist is quite common.

B. Clarification

This use of the aorist is usually shut up to two kinds of verbs: (1) It occurs with *stative* verbs, in which the stress is on *entrance into the state*. (2) It also occurs with verbs that denote activities, especially in contexts where the action is introduced as a new item in the discourse.[10]

Many aorists could be treated as ingressive or constative, depending on what the interpreter sees as the focus. There is not always a hard-and-fast distinction between them.

---

[10] Similarly, Fanning, *Verbal Aspect*, 261-63.

C. **Key to Identification:** *began to do, became*

The force of this aorist may be brought out by the gloss *began to do* (with activities), *became* (with stative verbs). (Recall that the imperfect idea is *began doing*, an expression that connotes continuation of the action.)

D. **Illustrations**

Matt 9:27   ἠκολούθησαν αὐτῷ δύο τυφλοί
     two blind men **began to follow** him
      The following verse makes it clear that an ingressive idea is meant, for
      the blind men are still following Jesus.

Matt 22:7   ὁ δὲ βασιλεὺς **ὠργίσθη**
     now the king **became angry**

John 4:52   κομψότερον **ἔσχεν**
     he **got** better

2 Cor 8:9   δι᾽ ὑμᾶς **ἐπτώχευσεν** πλούσιος ὤν, ἵνα ὑμεῖς τῇ ἐκείνου πτωχείᾳ
     πλουτήσητε
     Although he was rich, for your sake **he became poor**, in order that
     you, by his poverty, **might become rich.**

Rev 20:4   **ἔζησαν** καὶ ἐβασίλευσαν μετὰ τοῦ Χριστοῦ χίλια ἔτη
     they came to life and ruled with Christ for a thousand years
      The first aorist is ingressive; the second is constative.

Cf. also Matt 9:18; Luke 15:32; John 10:38; 11:31; 13:5; Acts 15:13; Rom 14:9; 1 Cor 4:8; Titus 2:12; 1 Pet 2:24; Rev 2:8; 13:14.

→ *III. Consummative (Culminative, Ecbatic, Effective) Aorist*

A. **Definition**

The aorist is often used to stress the cessation of an act or state. Certain verbs, by their *lexical* nature, virtually require this usage.[11] For example, "he died" is usually not going to be an ingressive idea. The context also assists in this usage at times; it may imply that an act was already in progress and the aorist then brings the action to a conclusion. This is different from a consummative perfect, for the latter places the stress on (a) completion of the action, not merely cessation;[12] and especially (b) continuing results after the completion of the action.

---

[11] Fanning notes that it occurs with verbs that indicate climax, accomplishment, activities, and punctual notions (*Verbal Aspect*, 263-64).

[12] Although the consummative aorist can be said to routinely connote completed action. This is more due to the lexical intrusion than the grammatical force of the tense, although since the aorist basically looks at the action *as a whole*, it is not far removed from its essential nature to see the aorist itself as summarizing and concluding.

B.   Illustrations

Mark 5:39   τὸ παιδίον οὐκ **ἀπέθανεν** ἀλλὰ καθεύδει
             the little girl **has** not **died**, but is sleeping

> Many modern translations render this "the little girl **is** not **dead**, but is sleeping." The whole point of the narrative is to come to this conclusion. The difference between the aorist and the present are clearly seen in this dominical saying: Her life is not at an end (aorist); there is more to come (present).

Luke 19:16   **παρεγένετο** δὲ ὁ πρῶτος λέγων . . .
             Now, **when** the first man **arrived**, he said . . .

> Παραγίνομαι is a lexically-colored verb that almost always has a consummative force to it. It occurs 37 times in the NT, 33 of which are in the aorist. The three present forms are all historical presents (and thus, equivalent to an aorist aspectually [cf. Matt 3:1, 13; Mark 14:43]). The only other form is imperfect, functioning iteratively/distributively (John 3:23–"the people **were coming** and were being baptized" [παρεγίνοντο]).

John 1:42   **ἤγαγεν** αὐτὸν πρὸς τὸν Ἰησοῦν
             he brought him to Jesus

Acts 5:39   **ἐπείσθησαν** αὐτῷ
             they were persuaded by him

Rev 5:5   **ἐνίκησεν** ὁ λέων ὁ ἐκ τῆς φυλῆς Ἰούδα
             the Lion from the tribe of Judah **has overcome**

John 2:20   τεσσεράκοντα καὶ ἓξ ἔτεσιν **οἰκοδομήθη** ὁ ναὸς οὗτος
             this temple **was built** forty-six years ago

> Several grammars list this as a constative aorist, to the effect that it should be translated, "This temple was built in forty-six years."[13]
>
> The usual assumption is that ναός refers to the temple precincts. Josephus indicates that the temple precincts were not completed until Albinus' procuratorship (c. 62-64 CE), in which case the precincts were still in the process of being built when the statement in John 2:20 was made. The idea then would be, "This temple has been in the process of being built for the last forty-six years." There are several problems with this, however, including the meaning of ναός in John, the use of the dative's temporal referent, and the use of the aorist. The force of the aorist here *may* have some impact on the date of the crucifixion.[14]
>
> First, the NT normally makes a distinction between the ἱερόν and the ναός: The ἱερόν refers to the temple precincts (including the courts) while the ναός refers to the holy place or sanctuary proper.[15] If that distinction obtains in John 2:20, then the aorist verb οἰκοδομήθη would refer only to the sanctuary. Notably, the sanctuary was completed in c. 18-17 BCE.[16] Forty-six years later would be 29-30 CE.
>
> Second, the dative (τεσσεράκοντα καὶ ἓξ ἔτεσιν) most naturally refers to

---

[13] E.g., Robertson, *Grammar*, 833; Dana-Mantey, 196 (§180); Moule, *Idiom Book*, 11; Young, *Intermediate Greek*, 123.

[14] See H. W. Hoehner, *Chronological Aspects of the Life of Christ* (Grand Rapids: Zondervan, 1977) 38-43, for a discussion of the implications on the date of the crucifixion.

a point in time, rather than an extent of time.[17] This would fit well with a completion date of the sanctuary ("was built [at a point in time] forty-six years ago").

Third, there is some difficulty with taking the aorist to speak of an action that was still in process ("this temple has been [in the process of being] built for the past forty-six years"). The imperfect would be more natural,[18] but not at all required.[19]

These strands of evidence suggest that the aorist is more naturally taken as consummative. If so, and if this pericope occurred in the first year of Jesus' ministry (as its location in John 2 suggests), then Jesus was probably crucified three years later, in 33 CE.[20]

Cf. also Matt 1:22; 27:20; Acts 17:27; 27:43; Rom 1:13; 1 Cor 4:6; 1 Pet 3:18.

---

[15] See BAGD, s. v. ἱερόν, ναός. Although they cite five references in which ναός is apparently used of the entire edifice, two of these are the Synoptic counterparts to John 2:20, placed during the passion week. John uses ἱερόν ten times, all with reference to the general structure (2:14, 15; 5:14; 7:14; 7:28; 8:20, 59; 10:23; 11:56; 18:20). His use of ναός is restricted to this pericope (2:19, 20, 21). Hoehner, *Chronological Aspects*, 40-41, notes that Josephus also makes this distinction.

[16] See discussion in Hoehner, *Chronological Aspects*, 38-40.

[17] The dat. naturally is used for point (see chapter on the dative case), although with ἔτος extent is a viable option. BAGD cite this text and Acts 13:20 for the dat. of ἔτος to refer to extent of time (the only two references in the NT to ἔτος in the dat. without a prep. [Luke 3:1 has ἐν]). They are correct on the latter passage, but John 2:20 is questionable.

In the LXX, the dat. of ἔτος normally indicates a *point* in time: Gen 14:4; Exod 21:2; 40:17; Lev 19:24; 25:4; Num 13:22 (a strong parallel to John 2:20–"Hebron was built/completed [aor. ᾠκοδομήθη] [at a point in time] seven years before Zoan"); 1 Kings 6:1; 22:41; 2 Kings 18:13; 2 Kings 23:23; 2 Chron 35:19; Esdr 1:20; 5:54; Esther 2:16; 2 Macc 13:1; 14:4; Hag 1:15; Dan 9:2.

On the side of a dat. of extent, a parallel to John 2:20 is found in 1 Kings 7:38 ("Solomon was building [aor.] his own house thirteen years" [RSV]). However, the rest of the verse says, "and he finished his entire house" (RSV). Thus, although this is extent, the aorist is *not* durative or internal. It is complexive. This is the only dat. of extent with ἔτος in the LXX.

[18] L. Morris, *The Gospel According to John* (NICNT) 200, n. 81, feels that "the application of this tense to an edifice that was not to be completed for many years is not easy." He does note the important parallel in 2 Esdras (Ezra) 5:16 (ἀπὸ τότε ἕως τοῦ νῦν ᾠκοδομήθη καὶ οὐκ ἐτελέσθη ["from that time until now it (the temple) has been (in the process of being) built, and it is not yet finished"]).

[19] Fanning, *Verbal Aspect*, 257-58.

[20] This is the argument of Hoehner, *Chronological Aspects*, 38-43. To be sure, he bases his view on more than one verse. His main argument includes many strands of evidence (95-114).

There are two problems with the use of John 2:20 for the date of the crucifixion, however. First, if the aorist is consummative, what is the point being made? To argue that "this temple has stood for forty-six years, yet you will raise it up in three days?" seems to be a *non sequitur*. This is not as weighty as it at first appears, however. All that is required is an understanding of an implicit point: If it has stood for a long time, it is well built. Hence, how could Jesus rebuild it in three days? The idea could easily be "this temple has stood the test of time." The second problem is that the pericope is possibly out of chronological sequence. The temple-cleansing in the synoptic accounts occurs in the passion week. If this is referring to the same event, then a consummative aorist would *confirm* rather than deny a 30 CE crucifixion date!

IV. Gnomic Aorist

A. Definition

The aorist indicative is occasionally used to present a timeless, general fact.[21] When it does so, it does not refer to a particular event that *did* happen, but to a generic event that *does* happen. Normally, it is translated like a simple present tense.[22] This usage is quite rare in the NT.

B. Clarification

Robertson suggests that "the difference between the gnomic aorist and the present is that the present may be durative."[23] But the aorist, under certain circumstances, may be used of an action that in reality is iterative or customary.[24]

C. Illustrations

Matt 23:2   ἐπὶ τῆς Μωϋσέως καθέδρας **ἐκάθισαν** οἱ γραμματεῖς καὶ οἱ Φαρισαῖοι

the scribes and the Pharisees **sit** on Moses' seat

> Some treat this as a dramatic aorist, perhaps due to the Semitic influence.[25]

1 Pet 1:24   **ἐξηράνθη** ὁ χόρτος, καὶ τὸ ἄνθος **ἐξέπεσεν**

the grass **withers** and the flower **falls off**

Cf. also Luke 7:35; Jas 1:11.

V. Epistolary Aorist

A. Definition

This is the use of the aorist indicative in the epistles in which the author self-consciously describes his letter from the time frame of the audience. The aorist indicative of πέμπω is naturally used in this sense. This category is not common, but it does have some exegetical significance.

---

[21] Some grammarians do not see this usage in the NT (so Moule, *Idiom Book*, 12-13).

[22] For a discussion of the gnomic aorist, on the assumption that the aorist indicative grammaticalizes time, see Fanning, *Verbal Aspect*, 265-69. On the assumption that Greek tenses have no temporal value, see Porter, *Verbal Aspect*, 221-25.

[23] Robertson, *Grammar*, 836.

[24] In this respect it is not very different from a customary *present*, but is quite different from a customary *imperfect*. The gnomic aorist is not used to describe an event that "used to take place" (as the imperfect does), but one that "has taken place" over a long period of time or, like the present, *does* take place.

[25] So Fanning, *Verbal Aspect*, 278.

B. Illustrations

Acts 23:30 ἐξαυτῆς **ἔπεμψα** πρὸς σέ

> **I sent** him to you at once

>> This statement about the sending of Paul is in Claudius Lysius' letter to Felix (cf. vv 25-26). Verse 31 indicates that the soldiers then took the letter and Paul to Felix.

Gal 6:11 ἴδετε πηλίκοις ὑμῖν γράμμασιν **ἔγραψα** τῇ ἐμῇ χειρί.

> See with what large letters **I have written** to you, with my own hand.

>> Some dispute that this is an epistolary aorist, taking it back before the immediate context. However, there is ample evidence from amanuensal practices (i.e., the practices of the ancient secretaries who wrote down what an author dictated) to suggest that this note is a brief appendix added by Paul.[26] It is difficult to tell, however, at what point Paul took the pen from his secretary and wrote for himself.[27]

Phil 2:28 **ἔπεμψα** αὐτόν

> **I have sent** him

>> This, of course, is from the standpoint of the readers, for Epaphroditus, the one being sent, was the one who would carry the letter to the Philippians.

Cf. also 1 Cor 9:15;[28] 2 Cor 8:17, 18, 22; 9:3, 5; Eph 6:22; Phlm 12.

There are a number of problem texts in which the aorist may refer to the portion that the author is *presently* composing (thus, truly epistolary), or to the epistle as a whole, or to a previous portion of the epistle just completed (thus, immediate past aorist). Sometimes, in fact, the aorist may refer to a letter written on a previous occasion. For a few of these texts (which have obvious exegetical implications), cf. Rom 15:15; 1 Cor 5:9; Eph 3:3; Phlm 19; 1 John 2:21.

VI. Proleptic (Futuristic) Aorist

A. Definition

> The aorist *indicative* can be used to describe an event that is not yet past as though it were already completed. This usage is not at all common, though several exegetically significant texts involve possible proleptic aorists.

---

[26] See R. N. Longenecker, "Ancient Amanuenses and the Pauline Epistles," in *New Dimensions in the New Testament Study* (Grand Rapids: Zondervan, 1974) 281-97. The discussion of Gal 6:11 is on 289-91.

[27] Ibid., 290. Longenecker suggests that Paul wrote vv 11-18 only.

[28] Referring to a previous portion of the same letter perhaps (thus, immediate past aorist).

B. Clarification

An author sometimes uses the aorist for the future to stress the certainty of the event. It involves a "rhetorical transfer" of a future event as though it were past.[29]

C. Illustrations

Mark 11:24 πάντα ὅσα προσεύχεσθε καὶ αἰτεῖσθε, πιστεύετε ὅτι **ἐλάβετε**, καὶ ἔσται ὑμῖν.[30]

Whatever you pray and ask for, believe that **you have received** [it], and it will be yours.

John 13:31 λέγει Ἰησοῦς· νῦν **ἐδοξάσθη** ὁ υἱὸς τοῦ ἀνθρώπου καὶ ὁ θεὸς **ἐδοξάσθη** ἐν αὐτῷ.

Jesus said, "Now the Son of Man **is glorified** and God **is glorified** in him."

Rom 8:30 οὓς δὲ ἐδικαίωσεν, τούτους καὶ **ἐδόξασεν**

those whom he justified, these **he** also **glorified**

The glorification of those who have been declared righteous is as good as done from Paul's perspective.

Rev 10:7 ὅταν μέλλῃ σαλπίζειν, καὶ **ἐτελέσθη** τὸ μυστήριον τοῦ θεοῦ[31]

whenever he is about to sound [the trumpet], then the mystery of God **is finished**

Cf. also Matt 18:15; John 15:6; 1 Cor 7:28; Heb 4:10; Jude 14.

For some possible but debatable examples, cf. Matt 12:28;[32] Eph 1:22 (ὑπέταξεν); 2:6 (συνεκάθισεν); 1 Thess 2:16.

VII. Immediate Past Aorist/Dramatic Aorist

A. Definition

The aorist indicative can be used of an event that happened rather recently. Its force can usually be brought out with something like *just now*, as in *just now I told you*. This may be lexically colored (occurring with verbs of *emotion* and *understanding*), but more often it is due to

---

[29] Fanning, *Verbal Aspect*, 269. See his discussion on 269-74.

[30] Instead of the aorist ἐλάβετε, most MSS have the present λαμβάνετε (so A F G K U V X Y Γ Σ Ω *f*[13] 28 33 543 *Byz et plu*); others have the future λή(μ)ψεσθε (so D Θ *f*[1] [22] 205 544 565 700 *et pauci*). Such textual data illustrate both the paucity of the proleptic aorist and its semantic force.

[31] The aorist indicative ἐτελέσθη is found in ℵ A C P and another 100 MSS. Another half dozen variants are found among the rest of the MSS, most notably τελεσθῇ and τελέσθει.

[32] If the proleptic aorist is sometimes lexically-colored, it might not be insignificant that the aorist of φθάνω is used in both Matt 12:28 and 1 Thess 2:16.

Semitic coloring, reflecting a Semitic stative perfect.[33] As well, it is sometimes difficult to tell whether the aorist refers to the immediate past or to the present (dramatic).[34]

B. Illustrations

Matt 9:18 ἄρχων εἷς ἐλθὼν προσεκύνει αὐτῷ λέγων ὅτι ἡ θυγάτηρ μου ἄρτι **ἐτελεύτησεν**
A certain ruler came and worshiped him, saying, "My daughter **has just now died.**"

Matt 26:65 ἴδε νῦν **ἠκούσατε** τὴν βλασφημίαν
Behold, just now you **heard** his blasphemy

Eph 3:3 καθὼς **προέγραψα** ἐν ὀλίγῳ
just as **I previously wrote** in part
> The author is here speaking about the revelation that was made known to him by God, that is, the revelation of peace between Jew and Gentile, of one new body. It is probable that the aorist here, then, refers back to 2:11-22 rather than to an unknown epistle.

Cf. also Matt 3:17 (possible); 6:12; Mark 1:8; Luke 1:47; 16:4; John 21:10; Rev 12:10 (possible).

---

[33] Fanning, *Verbal Aspect*, 275-6 (the complete discussion is on 275-81).

[34] Fanning distinguishes these two, calling the first a subset of the constative aorist and the second a dramatic aorist.

The Future Tense

Overview of Uses

Select Bibliography

BDF, 178-79 (§348-51); **Burton**, *Moods and Tenses*, 31-37 (§58-73); **Fanning**, *Verbal Aspect*, 120-24, 317-18; **K. L. McKay**, *A New Syntax of the Verb in New Testament Greek: An Aspectual Approach* (New York: Peter Lang, 1994) 52; **idem**, "Time and Aspect in New Testament Greek," *NovT* 34 (1992) 209-28; **Moule**, *Idiom Book*, 10; **Moulton**, *Prolegomena*, 148-51; **Porter**, *Verbal Aspect*, 403-39; **idem**, *Idioms*, 24, 43-45; **Robertson**, *Grammar*, 870-79; **Turner**, *Syntax*, 86-87; **Young**, *Intermediate Greek*, 117-19; **Zerwick**, *Biblical Greek*, 93-96 (§277-84).

Introduction

With reference to *aspect*, the future seems to offer an *external* portrayal, something of a temporal counterpart to the aorist indicative.[1] The external portrayal "presents an occurrence *in summary, viewed as a whole from the outside, without regard for the internal make-up of the occurrence.*"[2]

---

[1] Not all grammarians agree with this (tentative) assessment. First, some argue that the aspect is sometimes external, sometimes internal. Others regard it as aspectually neutral, the true "unmarked" tense. This tense is still something of an enigma, rendering any statements less than iron-clad. It is the only tense that is always related to time, regardless of mood. In that respect it appears to be a true *tense*. And although its forms were no doubt derived from the aorist (note, for example, the sixth principal part, the characteristic *sigma* in the active and middle forms of both tenses, as well as the similarities between the aorist subjunctive and future indicative), there are occasions in which an internal idea seems to take place, although such are rare (Moule, *Idiom Book*, 10).

With reference to *time*, the future tense is always future from the speaker's presentation (or, when in a participial form, in relation to the time of the main verb).

The future occurs in the indicative, participle, and infinitive forms in the NT. Of the 1623 future forms, there are only twelve participles and five infinitives. The rest are indicatives.[3]

In general, the future tense may be charted as follows (with respect to both time and aspect):

Past	Present	Future
		•

Chart 69
The Force of the Future Tense

Our view that the future is both a true aspect and an exclusively external one is based both on morphology and usage: Its formal link to the aorist suggests that it shares its aspect with the aorist (analogous to the imperfect sharing its aspect with the present, and the pluperfect with the perfect). This would make it a summary tense. Further, just as the aorist can be used in *contexts* that suggest iterative, progressive, or durative action, so too the future can be used in similar contexts. But, just as the aorist has no progressive or iterative nuance in its basic aspect, likewise the future should not be forced into such a mold. It does seem, then, that the future tense's unaffected meaning does *not* include an internal portrayal. (For an excellent discussion on the debate, see Porter, *Verbal Aspect*, 403-16. Our conclusions are not, however, the same [he, like Fanning, argues that the future is aspectually neutral].)

Incidentally, periphrastic futures need to be treated differently. Fanning (*Verbal Aspect*, 317-18) lists eleven legitimate future periphrastics (which use the future indicative of εἰμί and a present participle), one being a *v.l.* found in codex D (Matt 10:22; 24:9; Mark 13:13, 25; Luke 1:20; 5:10; 21:17, 24; 22:69; Acts 6:4 [in D]; 1 Cor 14:9). All of these have an internal aspect, but such is not due to the future per se, but to their combination with the *present* participles.

[2] Fanning, *Verbal Aspect*, 97.

[3] The twelve future participles can be found in Matt 27:49; Luke 22:49; John 6:64; Acts 8:27; 20:22; 22:5; 24:11, 17; 1 Cor 15:37; Heb 3:5; 13:17; 1 Pet 3:13. The five future infinitives are in Acts 11:28; 23:30; 24:15; 27:10; Heb 3:18. All of these are used for subsequent time. Pragmatically, we will restrict our discussion to the indicatives in this chapter, since the nonindicative forms are negligible.

There are a few future subjunctive forms in *v.ll.* in the NT (as in 1 Cor 13:3), but these do not occur in Koine Greek. See our discussion under "Subjunctive Mood"; cf. also *BDF* 15 (§28); Howard, *Accidence*, 219.

Specific Uses

→ *I. Predictive Future*

A. Definition

The future tense may indicate that something will take place or come to pass. The portrayal is external, summarizing the action: "it will happen." The predictive future is far and away the most common use of this tense.

B. Illustrations

Matt 1:21   **τέξεται** υἱόν, καὶ καλέσεις τὸ ὄνομα αὐτοῦ Ἰησοῦν· αὐτὸς γὰρ **σώσει** τὸν λαὸν αὐτοῦ ἀπὸ τῶν ἁμαρτιῶν αὐτῶν.
She will give birth to a son, and you will call his name Jesus, for he **will save** his people from their sins.
> This verse contains three future indicatives: The first and last are predictive; the middle one (καλέσεις) is imperatival ("you are to call . . .").

John 4:14   ὃς δ᾽ ἂν πίῃ ἐκ τοῦ ὕδατος οὗ ἐγὼ **δώσω** αὐτῷ, οὐ μὴ **διψήσει**
Whoever drinks of the water that **I shall give** him **will** never **thirst**.
> The second future tense in this verse could also be considered an emphatic negative future. Usually, the aorist subjunctive is found with οὐ μή; sometimes the future indicative is. In this instance, however, it also has a predictive force.

Acts 1:8   **λήμψεσθε** δύναμιν ἐπελθόντος τοῦ ἁγίου πνεύματος ἐφ᾽ ὑμᾶς καὶ **ἔσεσθέ** μου μάρτυρες
you will receive power when the Holy Spirit comes upon you and **you will be** my witnesses
> The second future may be imperatival.

Acts 1:11   οὗτος ὁ Ἰησοῦς . . . **ἐλεύσεται**
this Jesus . . . **will come**

Phil 1:6   ὁ ἐναρξάμενος ἐν ὑμῖν ἔργον ἀγαθὸν **ἐπιτελέσει** ἄχρι ἡμέρας Χριστοῦ Ἰησοῦ
the one who began a good work in you **will perfect** it until the day of Christ Jesus
> Wedged as it is between the past (ἐναρξάμενος) and an end-point in the future (ἄχρι), the future tense seems to suggest a progressive idea. But the future in itself says none of this.[4]

1 Th 4:16   οἱ νεκροὶ ἐν Χριστῷ **ἀναστήσονται** πρῶτον
the dead in Christ **will rise** first

Cf. also Mark 2:20; 9:31; Luke 2:12; Gal 5:21; 1 Tim 2:15; Heb 6:14; 2 Pet 2:2; Rev 20:7.

---

[4] The aorist, too, is used with ἄχρι at times, even in contexts that would suggest a progressive idea (cf., e.g., Acts 3:21; 22:4; Rom 1:13; Rev 2:25). Yet grammarians are universally agreed that the aorist does not indicate a progressive idea. Why, then, should we treat the future differently?

II. *Imperatival Future*

A. Definition

The future indicative is sometimes used for a command, almost always in OT quotations (due to a literal translation of the Hebrew). However, it was used in this manner even in classical Greek, though sparingly. Outside of Matthew, this usage is not common.[5]

B. Semantics

The force of the imperatival future is not identical with an imperative. Generally speaking, it has a universal, timeless, and/or solemn force to it.[6] One reason for this is that most of the NT examples are quotations from the OT, especially from the legal literature of the Pentateuch. The nature of the commandments in the Pentateuch is often well suited to such a solemn notion, and hence it would be natural to carry this over into the NT. But even when the OT is not behind the command, the force of the imperatival future is emphatic. This is in keeping with the combined nature of the indicative mood and future tense. "It is not a milder or gentler imperative. A prediction may imply resistless power or cold indifference, compulsion or concession."[7]

C. Illustrations

Matt 19:18   οὐ **φονεύσεις**, οὐ **μοιχεύσεις**, οὐ **κλέψεις**, οὐ **ψευδομαρτυρήσεις**
You shall not **murder, you shall** not **commit adultery, you shall** not **steal, you shall** not **bear false witness.**

Matt 6:5   οὐκ **ἔσεσθε** ὡς οἱ ὑποκριταί[8]
You shall not **be** like the hypocrites.
> This is an example of the imperatival future that is other than an OT quotation.

Matt 20:27   ὃς ἂν θέλῃ ἐν ὑμῖν εἶναι πρῶτος **ἔσται** ὑμῶν δοῦλος[9]
Whoever wants to be first among you **shall be** your servant.

Matt 22:37   **ἀγαπήσεις** κύριον τὸν θεόν σου
You shall love the Lord your God

---

[5] For a succinct discussion, see *BDF*, 183 (§362).

[6] This is not to say that the imperative cannot be used this way, just that it would not be as clearly emphatic as the future indicative. Evidence that the imperative is used for such commands can be demonstrated via Synoptic parallels (in which one Gospel has the imperative while the other has the future indicative) and textual variants (in which the imperative is found in some MSS, the future indicative in others).

[7] Gildersleeve, *Classical Greek*, 1.116 (§269).

[8] Most MSS have the singular ἔσῃ, but this does not affect the grammatical point under discussion.

[9] The imperative ἔστω is found in B E G H S V X Γ Λ 28 892 1010 1424 *et alii.*

1 Pet 1:16   ἅγιοι **ἔσεσθε**, ὅτι ἐγὼ ἅγιός εἰμι[10]
You shall be holy, because I am holy.

Cf. also Matt 1:21 (καλέσεις); 4:7, 10; 5:21, 27, 33, 43, 48; 20:26; 21:3; 22:39; 27:4, 24; Mark 9:35; Luke 1:31; 17:4; Acts 18:15; Rom 7:7; 13:9; Gal 5:14; Jas 2:8.

III. Deliberative Future

A. Definition

The deliberative future asks a question that implies some doubt about the response. The question, asked in the *first person* singular or plural, is generally either *cognitive* or *volitional*. Cognitive questions ask, "How will we?" while volitional questions ask, "Should we?" Thus, the force of such questions is one of "oughtness"—that is, possibility, desirability, or necessity. The aorist subjunctive is more common in deliberative questions than the future indicative.[11]

B. Illustrations

Mark 6:37   ἀγοράσωμεν δηναρίων διακοσίων ἄρτους καὶ **δώσομεν** αὐτοῖς φαγεῖν;[12]
Should we buy two hundred denarii worth of food and **give** it to them to eat?

> Frequently, the deliberative future indicative should be translated as a subjunctive. Notice the aorist subjunctive (ἀγοράσωμεν) to which the future indicative is connected by καί.

Rom 6:2   πῶς ἔτι **ζήσομεν** ἐν αὐτῇ;[13]
How **shall we** still **live** in it?

> Paul is not asking here the *means* by which we might live in sin! Rather, he is asking the rightness, the "oughtness," even the possibility of such a lifestyle for one who has died to sin.

Heb 2:3   πῶς ἡμεῖς **ἐκφευξόμεθα** τηλικαύτης ἀμελήσαντες σωτηρίας;
How **shall we escape** if we neglect so great a salvation?

Cf. also Matt 17:17; Rom 3:5; 6:1; 9:14.

---

[10] γένεσθε is found for ἔσεσθε in K P 049 1 1241 1739 *et alii*; γίνεσθε is the verb of choice in L *Byz et alii*.

[11] See "Moods: Subjunctive: Deliberative" for a discussion.

[12] The aorist subjunctive δῶμεν is found instead of δώσομεν in E F G H K S U V W Γ Θ Π Σ Ω *f*¹ 579 700 *Byz*; similarly, the aorist subjunctive δώσωμεν is the reading of ℵ D N *f*¹³ 28 33 565 892 1424.

[13] The aorist subjunctive (ζήσωμεν) replaces the future indicative in 𝔓⁴⁶ C F G L Ψ 33 81 1241 1464 *et alii*.

IV. Gnomic Future

A. Definition

The future is very rarely used to indicate the likelihood that a *generic* event will take place. The idea is not that a particular event is in view, but that such events are true to life. "In the gnomic future the act is true of any time."[14]

B. Illustrations

Matt 6:24   οὐδεὶς δύναται δυσὶ κυρίοις δουλεύειν· ἢ γὰρ τὸν ἕνα **μισήσει** καὶ τὸν ἕτερον **ἀγαπήσει**, ἢ ἑνὸς **ἀνθέξεται** καὶ τοῦ ἑτέρου **καταφρονήσει**.
No one can serve two masters. For either **he will hate** the one and **love** the other, or **he will cling to** the one and **despise** the other.
> The gnomic future idea means here *he would be expected to hate . . . he would be expected to love. . . .*

Rom 5:7   μόλις ὑπὲρ δικαίου τις **ἀποθανεῖται**
scarcely for a righteous man **will** someone **die**
> Paul could have also expressed this in the present: "Scarcely for a righteous man does one die," though the future stresses the likelihood of the event.

Rom 7:3   ζῶντος τοῦ ἀνδρὸς μοιχαλὶς **χρηματίσει** ἐὰν γένηται ἀνδρὶ ἑτέρῳ
she will be called an adulteress if, while her husband is alive, she is joined to another man[15]

V. Miscellaneous Subjunctive Equivalents

The future indicative is sometimes used in situations that are normally reserved for the aorist subjunctive. We have already seen this with the deliberative future. Other categories include emphatic negation (οὐ μή + future indicative [e.g., John 4:14]), ἵνα clauses (e.g., Gal 2:4), and indefinite relative clauses (e.g., Mark 8:35). See "Moods: Subjunctive" for a discussion of the various places where the future appears.

---

[14] Robertson, *Grammar*, 876.

[15] Turner, *Syntax*, says that the future indicative here is almost imperatival: *let her be called* (86).

The Perfect and Pluperfect Tenses

Overview of Tense Uses

Select Bibliography

BDF, 175-78 (§340-47); **Burton**, *Moods and Tenses*, 37-45, 71-72 (§74-92, 154-56); **Fanning**, *Verbal Aspect*, 290-309, 396-97, 416-18; **K. L. McKay**, *A New Syntax of the Verb in New Testament Greek: An Aspectual Approach* (New York: Peter Lang, 1994) 49-51; **idem**, "On the Perfect and Other Aspects in New Testament Greek," *NovT* 23 (1981) 290-329; **Moule**, *Idiom Book*, 13-16; **Moulton**, *Prolegomena*, 140-48; **Porter**, *Verbal Aspect*, 245-90, 321-401; **idem**, *Idioms*, 39-42; **Robertson**, *Grammar*, 892-910; **Turner**, *Syntax*, 81-86; **Young**, *Intermediate Greek*, 126-31; **Zerwick**, *Biblical Greek*, 96-99 (§285-91).

Introduction

As a general introduction, for the most part, the perfect and pluperfect tenses are identical in aspect though different in time. Thus both speak of an event accomplished in the past (in the indicative mood, that is) with results existing afterwards–the perfect speaking of results existing in the present, the pluperfect speaking of results existing in the past.

The **aspect** of the perfect and pluperfect is sometimes called *stative, resultative, completed,* or *perfective-stative.* Whatever it is called, the kind of action portrayed (in its unaffected meaning) is a combination of the external and internal aspects: The *action* is presented *externally* (summary), while the *resultant state* proceeding from the action is presented *internally* (continuous state).[1]

As to **time,** note the treatments below under each tense.

I. The Perfect Tense

Introduction

Although this section on the perfect tense will be brief, one must not assume that the length of discussion corresponds to the significance of the topic. We are brief because the primary uses of the perfect are fairly easy to comprehend, though they are not insignificant. As Moulton points out, the perfect tense is "the most important, exegetically, of all the Greek Tenses."[2] The perfect is used less frequently than the present, aorist, future, or imperfect; when it is used, there is usually a deliberate choice on the part of the writer.[3]

Definition

> The force of the perfect tense is simply that it describes an event that, completed in the past (we are speaking of the perfect indicative here), has results existing in the present time (i.e., in relation to the time of the speaker). Or, as Zerwick puts it, the perfect tense is used for "indicating not the past action as such but the present 'state of affairs' resulting from the past action."[4]

> *BDF* suggest that the perfect tense "combines in itself, so to speak, the present and the aorist in that it denotes the *continuance* of *completed action....*"[5]

---

[1] There is a basic agreement among grammarians about the force of the perfect (viz., that two elements are involved, completed action and resultant state), although there is some disagreement over the particulars of the definition. McKay, for example, sees the perfect as an aspect, while Fanning sees it as intrinsically involving aspect, time, and *Aktionsart.*

[2] Moulton, *Prolegomena,* 140.

[3] It occurs 1571 times: 835 indicatives, 673 participles, 49 infinitives, 10 subjunctives, and 4 imperatives (the perfect optative does not occur in the NT).

[4] Zerwick, *Biblical Greek,* 96.

[5] *BDF,* 175 (§340).

Chamberlain goes too far when he suggests that the perfect sometimes is used to "describe an act that has *abiding* results."[6] The implication that "the perfect *tells* you that the event occurred and *still has* significant results"[7] goes beyond grammar and is therefore misleading. Even more misleading is the notion, frequently found in commentaries, that the perfect tense denotes *permanent* or *eternal* results. Such a statement is akin to saying the aorist tense means "once-for-all." Implications of this sort are to be drawn from considerations that are other than grammatical in nature. One must be careful not to read his or her theology into the syntax whenever it is convenient.

Past	Present	Future
• (―――――)		

Chart 70
The Force of the Perfect

Note: The symbol (――――) indicates the *results* of an action.

The chart shows that the perfect may be viewed as combining the aspects of both the aorist and present tense. It speaks of completed action (aorist) with existing results (present). The basic question to be asked is which of these aspects is emphasized in a given context.

Specific Uses

The uses of the perfect tense may be broken down into three main groups: normative, collapsed, specialized. The *normative* uses involve both the external and internal aspects, but with a slightly different emphasis. The *collapsed* perfects are those that collapse (or suppress) either the internal or external aspect, because of contextual or lexical interference, respectively. The *specialized* perfects are rare uses that detour from the normal usage in a more pronounced way than the collapsed perfects do.

➡ ### A. Intensive Perfect (a.k.a. Resultative Perfect)

1. Definition

The perfect may be used to *emphasize* the results or present state produced by a past action. The English present often is the best translation for such a perfect. This is a common use of the perfect tense.

---

[6] Chamberlain, *Exegetical Grammar*, 72 (italics mine).
[7] Ibid. (italics mine).

2. **Caution**

The average student learning NT Greek typically knows Greek grammar better than English grammar after a couple of years of study. Consequently, the aspect of the Greek perfect is sometimes imported into the English perfect. That is, there is a tendency to see the English perfect as placing an emphasis on existing results–a notion foreign to English grammar. As Moule notes, "the Greek tense is concerned with *result*, while the English tense is concerned solely with the absence . . . of an *interval*."[8] One ought to be careful when translating the perfect into English to resist the temptation to translate it as an English perfect at all times. When so translated, the Greek perfect should be extensive, not intensive.

Along these lines, it should be noted that as many faults as the KJV has, it frequently has a superior rendering of the Greek perfect over many modern translations. (Recall that the KJV was produced during the golden age of English, during Shakespeare's era.) For example, in Eph 2:8 the KJV reads "for by grace are ye saved," while many modern translations (e.g., RSV, NASB) have "for by grace you have been saved." The perfect periphrastic construction is most likely intensive, however. The KJV translators, though not having nearly as good a grasp on Greek as modern translators, seem to have had a better grasp on English. They apparently recognized that to translate Eph 2:8 with an English perfect would say nothing about the state resulting from the act of being saved.[9]

3. **Semantics/Key to Identification**

This use of the perfect does not exclude the notion of a completed act; rather, it *focuses* on the resultant state. Consequently, *stative* verbs are especially used in this way. Often the best translation of the intensive perfect is as a *present* tense. (Nevertheless, many perfects are open to interpretation and could be treated either as intensive or extensive.) The only difference in the chart below and the previous chart (on the unaffected meaning of the perfect) is that the resultant state is here emphasized.[10]

---

[8] Moule, *Idiom Book*, 13.

[9] The KJV seems to translate perfects as resultative more frequently than do some modern translations, such as the RSV. Cf., e.g., Luke 1:1; John 3:21, 28; Rom 13:1; 2 Cor 12:11; Eph 2:5, 8; 1 Thess 2:4; Phlm 7; Heb 10:10; 12:11; 1 Pet 1:23; 2 Pet 3:7; Rev 18:24. To be sure, some of these instances are now antiquated English (e.g., "I am become a fool" in 2 Cor 12:11).

[10] Again, this diagram is restricted to the perfect indicative to show the temporal relations.

Past	Present	Future
. (━━━━━━━)		

Chart 71
The Force of the Intensive Perfect

4. Illustrations

Mark 6:14   Ἰωάννης ὁ βαπτίζων **ἐγήγερται** ἐκ νεκρῶν[11]
            John the baptizer **is risen** from the dead

> This statement by Herod, though a faulty interpretation of Jesus' mira-
> cles, seems to reflect more Herod's concern over the possibility that
> John *was alive* than that John *had been* resurrected. The existing results
> of the resurrection are what troubled him more than the action itself.

Luke 5:20   ἄνθρωπε, **ἀφέωνταί** σοι αἱ ἁμαρτίαι σου
            man, your sins **are forgiven**

John 17:7   νῦν **ἔγνωκαν** ὅτι πάντα ὅσα δέδωκάς μοι παρὰ σοῦ εἰσιν·[12]
            now **they know** that everything that you have given me is from you

> The first perfect (ἔγνωκαν) is intensive, while the second perfect indic-
> ative (δέδωκας) is better seen as extensive.

Rom 3:10   καθὼς **γέγραπται** ὅτι οὐκ ἔστιν δίκαιος οὐδὲ εἷς
            Just as **it is written**, "There is none righteous, no, not one."

> This common introductory formula to OT quotations seems to be used
> to emphasize that the written word still exists. Although just beyond
> the reach of grammar, the exegetical and theological significance of this
> seems to be (in light of how it is used in the NT) that of present and
> binding authority.[13] In other words, γέγραπται could often be para-
> phrased thus: "Although this scripture was written long ago, its
> authority is still binding on us" (a *very* loose paraphrase!).[14]

Heb 4:13   πάντα γυμνὰ καὶ **τετραχηλισμένα** τοῖς ὀφθαλμοῖς αὐτοῦ
            all things are naked and **laid bare** before his eyes

> The emphasis of the perfect participle is clearly on the resultant state,
> accenting as it does the omniscience of God.

Cf. also John 5:45; 11:27; Acts 8:14; Rom 2:19; 5:2; 1 Cor 15:3; 2 Cor 1:10, 24; Phlm 21; Heb
2:18; 3:14; 1 John 4:14; Rev 3:17.

---

[11] Several MSS replace the perfect with the more familiar ἠγέρθη (so C F G K N S U V
W Θ Σ Φ Ω 0269 f[1, 13] 28 *Byz et plu*); others have ἀνέστη (A K Y 110 220 302 465 474).

[12] ℵ has the aorist ἔγνων for ἔγνωκαν; similarly, ἔγνωσαν is found in C U X Ψ f[13] 33
429 700 1241.

[13] As contrasted with λέγει, which seems to emphasize immediate applicability of the
word.

[14] γέγραπται is used ethically and eschatologically. That is, it introduces both commands that are still binding (e.g., Matt 4:4, 7, 10; 21:13; Luke 2:23; 19:46; John 8:17; Acts
23:5; 1 Cor 1:31; 9:9; 1 Pet 1:16) and fulfilled prophecy (e.g., Matt 2:5; 11:10; 26:24; Mark 1:2;
9:12; Luke 3:4; Acts 1:20; 13:33; Rom 9:33; 11:26). γέγραπται occurs 67 times in the NT, 16
of which are in Romans.
  The usage of γέγραπται in John 20:31 is somewhat unusual in that it does not introduce a quotation from the OT, but a concluding remark about the Gospel itself.

➡ B. Extensive Perfect (a.k.a. Consummative Perfect)

1. Definition

The perfect may be used to *emphasize* the completed action of a past action or process from which a present state emerges. It should normally be translated in English as a present perfect. This usage is common.

2. Semantics/Key to Identification

The emphasis is on the completed event in past time rather than the present results. As with the intensive perfect, this does not mean that the other "half" of its aspect has disappeared, just that it does not receive the greater emphasis. For example, ἐγήγερται τῇ ἡμέρᾳ τῇ τρίτῃ ("**he has been raised** on the third day") in 1 Cor 15:4, though extensive, still involves current implications for Paul's audience. (Many perfects are open to interpretation and could be treated either as intensive or extensive.) One key is that *transitive* verbs often belong here.

Past	Present	Future
● (⟶)		

Chart 72
The Force of the Extensive Perfect

3. Illustrations

John 1:34 **ἑώρακα** καὶ **μεμαρτύρηκα** ὅτι οὗτός ἐστιν ὁ ἐκλεκτὸς τοῦ θεοῦ.[15]
I have seen and **I have testified** that this is the elect one of God.
> The portrayal of John's testimony seems to place an emphasis more on the completed event in the past than on the present results. In other words, there is stress on his seeing enough of Jesus [completed action] to make a reliable report.

Acts 5:28 ἰδοὺ **πεπληρώκατε** τὴν Ἰερουσαλὴμ τῆς διδαχῆς ὑμῶν[16]
behold, **you have filled** Jerusalem with your teaching

Rom 5:5 ἡ ἀγάπη τοῦ θεοῦ **ἐκκέχυται** ἐν ταῖς καρδίαις ἡμῶν
the love of God **has been poured out** in our hearts
> This verse is wedged in the middle of the section of Rom 5 that deals with God's work in salvation, setting the groundwork for sanctification. The stress, therefore, seems to be slightly more on what Christ's finished work on the cross accomplished as a solid basis for the believers' present sanctification.

Cf. also Mark 5:33; John 5:33, 36; 19:22; Rom 16:7; 2 Cor 7:3; 2 Tim 4:7; Heb 2:8; 2 Pet 2:21; 1 John 1:10; Jude 6.

---

[15] Though most MSS have υἱός here instead of ἐκλεκτός, internally ἐκλεκτός is a superior reading (though supported only by 𝔓[5vid] ℵ and a few versional witnesses). Neither reading affects how the perfects should be taken.

[16] Instead of the perfect πεπληρώκατε, the aorist ἐπληρώσατε is found in 𝔓[74] ℵ A 36 94 307 1175 *et pauci*.

C. Aoristic Perfect (a.k.a. Dramatic or Historical Perfect)

1. Definition

The perfect indicative is rarely used in a rhetorical manner to describe an event in a highly vivid way. The aoristic/dramatic perfect is "used as a simple past tense without concern for present consequences. . . ."[17]

In this respect, it shares a kinship with the historical present. There are but a handful of examples of this in the NT, occurring only in *narrative* contexts.[18] Thus this use is informed by *contextual* intrusions (narrative). The *key* to detecting a dramatic perfect is the absence of any notion of existing results.[19]

2. Clarification

Robertson suggests that "here an action completed in the past is conceived in terms of the present time for the sake of vividness."[20] Its very paucity in the NT makes it difficult for students to grasp its force. It may be best to think of it as *intensive extensive perfect* used in narrative (i.e., it is an intensive use of the extensive perfect). That is to say, it focuses so much on the act that there is no room left for the results. It occurs in contexts where one would expect the aorist, giving rise to the speculation earlier in this century that the perfect was poorly understood by some writers of the NT.[21]

Past	Present	Future
•		

Chart 73
The Force of the Dramatic Perfect

3. Illustrations

Acts 7:35   τοῦτον ὁ θεὸς. . . **ἀπέσταλκεν**
             this [Moses] God . . . **sent**

---

[17] Fanning, *Verbal Aspect*, 301.

[18] This is not to say that it must occur only in the Gospels and Acts. The examples in 2 Corinthians, for example, are historical narrative embedded within the letter.

[19] Cf. Burton, *Moods and Tenses*, §80, 88. Burton doubts that any genuine examples actually occur in the NT. See now the discussion in Fanning, *Verbal Aspect*, 299-303. Porter apparently does not admit of instances of the aoristic perfect (*Verbal Aspect*, 264-65).

[20] Robertson, *Grammar*, 896.

[21] Cf. discussion in Moulton, *Prolegomena*, 143-47. The Seer of the Apocalypse is especially susceptible of this charge (ibid., 145-47).

2 Cor 11:25 τρὶς ἐρραβδίσθην, ἅπαξ ἐλιθάσθην, τρὶς ἐναυάγησα, νυχθήμερον ἐν τῷ βυθῷ **πεποίηκα**

three times I was beaten with rods, once I was stoned, three times I was shipwrecked, a day and a night **I was adrift** at sea[22]

> Paul indicates no change in temporal referent from the preceding aorists to the perfect. The perfect seems to be used for vividness, almost as if he had said, "I even spent a day and a night adrift at sea!" Support for the conclusion that it is rhetorical is its location in the sentence (placed last for the crescendo).

Cf. also Matt 13:46; 2 Cor 2:13 (narrative within an epistle); Rev 5:7; 7:14; 8:5; 19:3.

➡ D. Perfect with a Present Force

1. Definition

Certain verbs occur frequently (or exclusively) in the perfect tense without the usual aspectual significance. They have come to be used just like present tense verbs.[23] This usage is common.

Past	Present	Future
	——	

Chart 74
The Perfect with Present Force

2. Semantics/Key to Identification

Both in semantics and semantic situation, this use of the perfect is at the opposite end of the spectrum from the aoristic perfect.

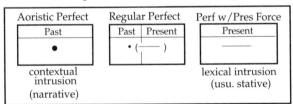

Chart 75
The Aoristic Perfect and Perfect with Present Force Compared

Οἶδα is the most commonly used verb in this category. But other verbs also seem to be used this way: ἕστηκα, πέποιθα, μέμνημαι. The reason why such perfects have the same semantics as presents is frequently that

---

[22] The translation *I was adrift* for πεποίηκα is contextually conditioned. With an acc. of time it can mean *spend, stay* (see BAGD, s.v. ποιέω, I.1.e.δ. [682]).

[23] It should be noted that such perfects are not shut up to the indicative since the issue is not just time but aspect as well. The following chart is restricted to indicatives to show its temporal placement.

there is very little distinction between the act and its results. They are *stative* verbs. The result of knowing is knowing. When one comes to stand he/she still stands. The result of persuading someone is that he/she is still persuaded. Thus this usage occurs especially with verbs where the act slides over into the results. They are resultative perfects to the point that the act itself has virtually died; the results have become the act.

In sum, it is important to remember that (1) this usage of the perfect is always *lexically influenced* (i.e., it occurs only with certain verbs), and (2) a very large number of perfects must be treated as presents without attaching any aspectual significance to them. (Οἶδα alone constitutes over one-fourth of all perfects in the NT!)

3. Illustrations

Mark 10:19 τὰς ἐντολὰς **οἶδας**
            you know the commandments

John 1:26   μέσος ὑμῶν **ἕστηκεν** ὃν ὑμεῖς οὐκ **οἴδατε**[24]
            in your midst **stands** one whom **you do** not **know**

Acts 26:27 πιστεύεις, βασιλεῦ Ἀγρίππα, τοῖς προφήταις; **οἶδα** ὅτι πιστεύεις.
            O king Agrippa, do you believe the prophets? **I know** that you do.

Heb 6:9   **πεπείσμεθα** περὶ ὑμῶν, ἀγαπητοί, τὰ κρείσσονα
            we **are convinced** of better things concerning you

Cf. also Matt 16:28; Mark 5:33; Luke 4:34; 9:27; John 3:2; Rom 8:38; 2 Cor 2:3; Phlm 21; Jas 3:1; 2 Pet 1:12; Rev 19:12.

E. *Gnomic Perfect*

1. Definition

The perfect tense may be used with a gnomic force, to speak of a generic or proverbial occurrence.[25] The aspectual force of the perfect is usually intact, but now it has a distributive value, viz., something that is envisioned on many occasions or for many individuals. Instances in this category are rare.

2. Illustrations

John 3:18   ὁ δὲ μὴ πιστεύων ἤδη **κέκριται**
            but the one who does not believe **has** already **been judged**
            The gnomic perfect here is also extensive. It is gnomic in that a generic subject is in view, extensive in that the focus is on the decisive act of judgment having been carried out.

---

[24] Instead of ἕστηκεν, B L 083 *f*[1] *et pauci* have στήκει; εἰστήκει is the reading of 𝔓[75] (ℵ G [both have ἑστήκει]) 1071 *et pauci*.

[25] For discussion, see Fanning, *Verbal Aspect*, 304.

Rom 7:2   ἡ γὰρ ὕπανδρος γυνὴ τῷ ζῶντι ἀνδρὶ **δέδεται** νόμῳ· ἐὰν δὲ ἀποθάνῃ ὁ ἀνήρ, **κατήργηται** ἀπὸ τοῦ νόμου τοῦ ἀνδρός.
For the married woman **is bound** by law to [her] husband while he is alive. But if the husband dies, she **is released** from the law of the husband.

> The gnomic perfects in this instance are also intensive.

Cf. also John 5:24; 1 Cor 7:39; Jas 1:24.

F. *Proleptic (Futuristic) Perfect*

1. Definition

The perfect can be used to refer to a state resulting from an antecedent action that is future from the time of speaking. (This is similar to one of the strands of the proleptic aorist.) This usage occurs in the apodosis of a conditional clause (either explicit or implicit) and depends on the time of the verb in the protasis. The proleptic perfect is quite rare.[26]

2. Illustrations

Rom 13:8   ὁ ἀγαπῶν τὸν ἕτερον νόμον **πεπλήρωκεν**
the one who loves his neighbor **has fulfilled** the law

Jas 2:10   ὅστις γὰρ ὅλον τὸν νόμον τηρήσῃ πταίσῃ δὲ ἐν ἑνί, **γέγονεν** πάντων ἔνοχος.[27]
For whoever keeps the whole law but stumbles in one point **has become** guilty of all [of it].

> The reason to take this as a proleptic perfect is that the (implied) condition is the equivalent of a future more probable condition. It is also possible to treat this (along with the rest of the examples) as a gnomic perfect since the sinner in view is generic.

1 John 2:5   ὃς δ᾽ ἂν τηρῇ αὐτοῦ τὸν λόγον, ἀληθῶς ἐν τούτῳ ἡ ἀγάπη τοῦ θεοῦ **τετελείωται**
But whoever keeps his word, truly in him the love of God **is perfected**.

Cf. also John 20:23; Rom 14:23.

G. *Perfect of Allegory*

1. Definition

The perfect tense can be used to refer to an OT event in such a way that

---

[26] For discussion, see *BDF*, 177 (§344).

[27] For γέγονεν, Ψ has ἔσται.

the event is viewed in terms of its allegorical or applicational value. This usage is rare, though the author of Hebrews is particularly fond of it.[28]

2. Clarification

To call a perfect an allegorical perfect does not necessarily mean that the biblical author is speaking allegorically; sometimes it focuses on the paradigmatic significance of the OT event. "It was as though this type of Christian interpretation viewed the O.T. narrative as 'contemporary', and could therefore say 'such-and-such an incident *has happened*'. It is, in fact, a logical extension of the Greek Perfect used of a past but still relevant event."[29]

3. Illustrations

John 6:32   εἶπεν οὖν αὐτοῖς ὁ Ἰησοῦς· ἀμὴν ἀμὴν λέγω ὑμῖν, οὐ Μωϋσῆς **δέδωκεν** ὑμῖν τὸν ἄρτον ἐκ τοῦ οὐρανοῦ, ἀλλ᾽ ὁ πατήρ μου δίδωσιν ὑμῖν τὸν ἄρτον ἐκ τοῦ οὐρανοῦ τὸν ἀληθινόν.[30]
Then Jesus said to them, "Verily, verily, I tell you, Moses **has not given** you the bread from heaven, but my Father gives you the true bread from heaven.

> The use of the second person pronoun as indirect object of δέδωκεν indicates that this is a perfect of allegory, as does the parallel with the present tense (δίδωσιν) in the second half of the verse, with the Father as the subject.

Heb 7:6   ὁ δὲ μὴ γενεαλογούμενος. . . **δεδεκάτωκεν** Ἀβραὰμ καὶ τὸν ἔχοντα τὰς ἐπαγγελίας **εὐλόγηκεν**.
But the one who had no genealogy. . . **has received tithes** from Abraham and **has blessed** the one who had the promises.

Heb 11:28   πίστει **πεποίηκεν** τὸ πάσχα
by faith **he has kept** the passover

Cf. also Acts 7:35 (possible);[31] Gal 3:18; 4:23; Heb 7:9; 8:5; 11:17.

---

[28] See discussions in *BDF*, 176 (§342.5); Fanning, *Verbal Aspect*, 305; and especially Moule, *Idiom Book*, 14-15.

[29] Moule, *Idiom Book*, 15.

[30] For δέδωκεν, a few MSS have the aorist ἔδωκεν (so B D L W *et alii*).

[31] So Moule, *Idiom Book*, 14. We have treated this earlier as a dramatic perfect.

II. The Pluperfect Tense

Introduction

As was stated in the general introduction to both the perfect and the pluperfect, for the most part, these two tenses are identical in aspect though different in time. That is, both speak of the state resulting from a previous event–the perfect speaking of existing results in the present (with reference to the speaker), the pluperfect speaking of existing results in the *past* (as this tense occurs only in the indicative mood). Thus, it may be said that *the pluperfect combines the aspects of the aorist (for the event) and the imperfect (for the results).*[32]

To put this another way, the force of the pluperfect tense is that it describes an event that, completed in the past, has results that existed in the past as well (in relation to the time of speaking). *The pluperfect makes no comment about the results existing up to the time of speaking.* Such results may exist at the time of speaking, or they may not; the pluperfect contributes nothing either way. (Often, however, it can be ascertained from the context whether or not the results do indeed exist up to the time of speaking.)

Past	Present
• (———————)	

Chart 76
The Force of the Pluperfect

Note: The symbol (———) indicates the *results* of an action.

There are only 86 simple pluperfects in the NT. In addition, there are a number of pluperfect periphrastic constructions (i.e., εἰμί in the indicative + a perfect participle).[33]

---

[32] So *BDF*, 177 (§347).

[33] Cf., e.g., Matt 9:36; Mark 15:26; Luke 2:26; 4:16; 5:1, 18; 8:2; 15:24; 23:51, 55; John 3:24; 12:16; 18:18; 19:41; Acts 8:16; 13:48; 14:26; 18:25; 22:29; Gal 4:3. The exact number of pluperfect periphrastics is difficult to ascertain because (1) sometimes the finite verb is at some distance from the participle; and (2) a number of perfect participles in such instances could be treated as predicate adjective participles rather than periphrastic. The difference in meaning impacts the temporal sequencing seen in the discourse.

Specific Uses

➡ ## A. *Intensive Pluperfect (Resultative Pluperfect)*

1. Definition

This use of the pluperfect places the emphasis on the results that existed in past time. Its force can usually be brought out by translating it as a simple past tense. This is different from an aorist, however, in that the aorist is not used to indicate a resultant state from the event.[34] It is different from an imperfect in that the imperfect describes the event itself as progressive, while the pluperfect only describes the state resulting from the event as continuing. This usage is relatively common.

Past	Present
• (━━━━━)	

Chart 77
The Force of the Intensive Pluperfect

As with its counterpart, the intensive perfect, some of the examples below might better belong to the extensive usage, since the difference between the two is only one of emphasis.

2. Illustrations

Matt 9:36   ἰδὼν δὲ τοὺς ὄχλους ἐσπλαγχνίσθη περὶ αὐτῶν, ὅτι **ἦσαν ἐσκυλμένοι** καὶ **ἐρριμμένοι** ὡσεὶ πρόβατα μὴ ἔχοντα ποιμένα.
But when he saw the crowds he felt compassion for them, because **they were weary** and **were lying down**, as sheep that do not have a shepherd.
> The periphrastic participles are used to indicate the current status of the crowd when Jesus saw them. There may be a hint in Matthew's use of the pluperfect, esp. in collocation with the shepherd-motif, that this situation would soon disappear.

Luke 4:29   ἤγαγον αὐτὸν ἕως ὀφρύος τοῦ ὄρους ἐφ᾽ οὗ ἡ πόλις **ᾠκοδόμητο** αὐτῶν
they led him to the brow of the hill on which their city **was built**
> This is a good example of what the pluperfect does not tell us: It makes no comment about the present time (from the perspective of the speaker). The pluperfect, being essentially a narrative tense, cannot be employed here to mean that the city no longer stood!

---

[34] *BDF,* 178 (§347).

John 6:17 ἤρχοντο πέραν τῆς θαλάσσης εἰς Καφαρναούμ. καὶ σκοτία ἤδη **ἐγεγόνει** καὶ οὔπω ἐληλύθει πρὸς αὐτοὺς ὁ Ἰησοῦς[35]

They began crossing the sea to Capernaum. Now **it was** already dark, and Jesus had not yet come to them.

> The first pluperfect in this text is intensive (as is evident by the ἤδη); the second one is extensive (ἐληλύθει).

Gal 4:3 ὅτε ἦμεν νήπιοι, ὑπὸ τὰ στοιχεῖα τοῦ κόσμου **ἤμεθα δεδουλωμένοι**

when we were infants, **we were enslaved** to the elementary spirits of the world

> This periphrastic construction is evidently intensive, showing the state that was simultaneous with the main statement (ὅτε ἦμεν νήπιοι). An implication to be drawn from the context (but not from the pluperfect alone) is that the enslavement was now past. The pluperfect is thus well suited for such a notion, but it does not by itself indicate this.

Cf. also Mark 15:7; Luke 4:17; John 11:44; Acts 14:23; 19:32.

➡ B. Extensive Pluperfect (Consummative Pluperfect)

1. Definition

The pluperfect may be used to emphasize the completion of an action in past time, without focusing *as much* on the existing results. It is usually best translated as a past perfect (*had* + perfect passive participle). (Some examples might better belong to the intensive category.) This usage is relatively common, especially in the Fourth Gospel.[36]

Past	Present
• (————)	

Chart 78
The Force of the Extensive Pluperfect

2. Illustrations

Mark 15:46 ἔθηκεν αὐτὸν ἐν μνημείῳ ὃ **ἦν λελατομημένον** ἐκ πέτρας
he placed him in a tomb that **had been hewn** out of a rock

Luke 22:13 εὗρον καθὼς **εἰρήκει** αὐτοῖς
they found it just as **he had told** them

John 4:8 οἱ μαθηταὶ αὐτοῦ **ἀπεληλύθεισαν** εἰς τὴν πόλιν
his disciples **had gone** into the city

---

[35] Instead of καὶ σκοτία ἤδη ἐγεγόνει, ℵ D have κατέλαβεν δὲ αὐτοὺς ἡ σκοτία.

[36] "John does, as a matter of fact, use the past perfect [pluperfect] more frequently than do the Synoptists. He uses it to take the reader 'behind the scenes' and often throws it in by way of parenthesis" (Robertson, *Grammar*, 904-5). More recent grammarians would describe this usage as a *backgrounding* tense usage.

John 9:22   ἤδη γὰρ **συνετέθειντο** οἱ Ἰουδαῖοι
             for the Jews **had** already **agreed**

Acts 8:27   ἰδοὺ ἀνὴρ Αἰθίοψ εὐνοῦχος . . . **ἐληλύθει** προσκυνήσων εἰς Ἰερουσαλήμ
             behold, an Ethiopian man, a eunuch . . . **had come** to worship in
             Jerusalem

> The pluperfect sets up the narrative in which Philip was to meet this
> man: The eunuch had come and was still there in Jerusalem.

Cf. also Mark 14:44; Luke 8:2; John 1:24; 11:13; Acts 4:22 (possible); 9:21; 20:38.

➡ ## C. Pluperfect with a Simple Past Force

1. Definition

Certain verbs occur frequently (or exclusively) in the perfect and pluperfect tenses without the usual aspectual significance. Οἶδα (ᾔδειν) is the
most commonly used verb in this category. But other verbs also are used
this way: ἵστημι, εἴωθα, πείθω, παρίστημι.[37] These are typically stative
verbs; in all cases this pluperfect is due to *lexical intrusion*. Instances are
common in the NT (constituting the largest group of pluperfects). (See
treatment under the perfect tense's counterpart, "Perfect with a Present
Force," for more discussion.)

The periphrastic constructions often resemble an imperfect more than
an aorist in translation.

2. Illustrations

Mark 1:34   οὐκ ἤφιεν λαλεῖν τὰ δαιμόνια, ὅτι **ᾔδεισαν** αὐτόν.
             He would not permit the demons to speak, because **they knew** him.

Mark 10:1   ὡς **εἰώθει** πάλιν ἐδίδασκεν αὐτούς
             as **he was accustomed**, he again taught them

John 1:35   τῇ ἐπαύριον πάλιν **εἱστήκει** ὁ Ἰωάννης καὶ ἐκ τῶν μαθητῶν αὐτοῦ δύο
             on the next day, again John **stood** along with two of his disciples

Acts 1:10   ἄνδρες δύο **παρειστήκεισαν** αὐτοῖς
             two men **stood** by them

Acts 16:9   ἀνὴρ Μακεδών τις **ἦν ἑστώς**[38]
             a certain man of Macedonia **was standing**

Rev 7:11   πάντες οἱ ἄγγελοι **εἱστήκεισαν** κύκλῳ τοῦ θρόνου
             all the angels **stood** around the throne

Cf. Luke 5:1; John 1:33; 5:13; 6:6, 64; 7:37; 18:18; Acts 23:5.

---

[37] See Fanning, *Verbal Aspect*, 308-9. He notes that the pluperfects of οἶδα occur 32
times, ἵστημι (14), εἴωθα (2), πείθω (1), and παρίστημι (1).

[38] The imperfect ἦν is omitted in D* E 3 90 209* 463 *et pauci*.

The Infinitive

Select Bibliography

BDF, 196-212 (§388-410); **J. L. Boyer**, "The Classification of Infinitives: A Statistical Study," *GTJ* 6 (1985) 3-27; **Brooks-Winbery**, 119-29; **Burton**, *Moods and Tenses*, 143-63 (§361-417); **Dana-Mantey**, 208-20 (§187-94); **K. L. McKay**, *A New Syntax of the Verb in New Testament Greek: An Aspectual Approach* (New York: Peter Lang, 1994) 55-60; **Moule**, *Idiom Book*, 126-29; **Moulton**, *Prolegomena*, 202-21; **Porter**, *Idioms*, 194-203; **Robertson**, *Grammar*, 1051-95; **Smyth**, *Greek Grammar*, 411, 437-54 (§1845-49, 1966-2038); **Turner**, *Syntax*, 134-49; **C. W. Votaw**, *The Use of the Infinitive in Biblical Greek* (Chicago: by the Author, 1896); **Young**, *Intermediate Greek*, 165-78; **Zerwick**, *Biblical Greek*, 132-36 (§380-95).

Introduction

Definition and Basic Characteristics

The infinitive is an *indeclinable verbal noun*. As such it participates in some of the features of the verb and some of the noun.

Like a verb, the infinitive has tense and voice, but not person or mood. It can take an object and be modified by adverbs. Its number is always singular. Like the oblique moods (i.e., non-indicative moods) the infinitive is normally negated by μή rather than οὐ.

Like a noun, the infinitive can have many of the case functions that an ordinary noun can have (e.g., subject, object, apposition). It can function as the object of a preposition, be anarthrous and articular, and be modified by an adjective. Although technically infinitives do not have gender, often the neuter singular article is attached to them. So, from a structural perspective, it would be appropriate to speak of infinitives as neuter (though this is never a part of the parsing).

The *neuter* article really has no other significance than a formal attachment (though the *case* of the article at times may be important to observe[1]): One ought not to read into a given infinitive any impersonal idea simply because the neuter article is used!

The infinitive often occurs after *prepositions*. When it does so, the infinitive is *always articular*. However, it would be incorrect to assume that the infinitive is for this reason functioning substantivally. One needs the broader picture here: Prepositional phrases are routinely attached to verbs, and hence adverbial in nature. When the infinitive occurs after a preposition, the preposition combines with the infinitive for an adverbial force.

Structure Vs. Semantics?

Our approach is first to lay out the infinitive by its *semantic* categories (e.g., purpose, result, cause, time, etc.). A discussion of these categories will help the student see the different shades of meaning that each can have. This is important for a general understanding of how infinitives function. However, this approach is not very helpful when one begins with the *text*.

Suppose you were studying 1 Thessalonians and you came across εἰς τὸ ἀναπληρῶσαι in 1 Thess 2:16. How should the infinitive be taken? You may know well your semantic categories, but this does not limit the field. What are the normal possibilities that *this structure* can have? Another approach is needed as well. Hence, at the end of this chapter is an outline of the *structures* in terms of the semantics that each can have. The structural priority scheme is more user-friendly to the person working in the text.[2]

We start with the semantic priority, then, to give definitions of the semantics. Once you have mastered those basic meanings, however, you will most likely turn first to the structural priority system when doing exegesis.

---

[1] Yet even here Boyer argues that (1) since most substantival infinitives are either nom. or acc., the neuter article is of no value in case identification, and (2) the gen. articular inf. "is used for *every* case function" (Boyer, "Infinitives," 24-25 [here quoting 25]). However, his one example of a gen. articular inf. as subject (Acts 10:25 ["Infinitives," 4, n. 9]) is better treated as indicating contemporaneous time.

[2] Most grammars that break down the inf. down by structural categories have two broad groupings, anarthrous and articular. This follows Votaw's scheme. (He noted, for example, that there are 1957 anarthrous infinitives and 319 articular infinitives in the NT [*Infinitive in Biblical Greek*, 50]; *acCordance* revealed another 15 infinitives, either overlooked by Votaw or not in the Westcott-Hort text. Boyer, using *Gramcord/acCordance* [based on UBS³], counted 1977 anarthrous infinitives and 314 articular ones.) This is helpful, but it does not go far enough. We have organized it somewhat differently. See the section on "Structural Categories."

Semantic Categories

The infinitive, as we noted above, partakes of the noun and the verb. True to its nature, we can organize it around these two parts of speech. When the infinitive has a verbal emphasis, it is normally dependent–i.e., it is adverbial in nature. On rare occasions, it can be independent verbally. When its emphasis falls on the nominal side, it likewise can be dependent (adjectival) or independent (substantival). This semantic categorization is visualized in the chart below. (However, because of the relative rarity of the independent verbal and adjectival uses, we will follow a different pattern of organization.)

	Verbal	Nominal
Independent	**(Verbal)** Imperatival Absolute	**(Substantival)** Subject, object, etc.
Dependent	**(Adverbial)** Purpose, Result, Cause, Means, etc.	**(Adjectival)** Epexegetical

Chart 79
The Semantic Range of the Infinitive

I. Adverbial Uses

There are six basic adverbial uses of the infinitive: purpose, result, time, cause, means, and complementary.

→ ## A. Purpose [to, in order to, for the purpose of]

1. Definition

The infinitive is used to indicate the purpose or goal of the action or state of its controlling verb. It answers the question "Why?" in that it looks ahead to the anticipated and intended result. This is one of the most common uses of the infinitive.[3]

Sometimes it is difficult to distinguish this usage from result. Not a few texts are impacted by the decision, however.

---

[3] Votaw counts 294 purpose infinitives in the NT, 261 of which are anarthrous (*Infinitive in Biblical Greek*, 46-47). The simple inf. accounts for 211 of these. He treats infinitives that are objects of prepositions in a different category, but these too can indicate purpose (especially εἰς τό + inf.).

2. **Structural Clues**

The purpose infinitive can be expressed by one of the following structural patterns:

a) Simple or "naked" infinitive (usually following an [intransitive] verb of motion)

b) τοῦ + infinitive[4]

c) εἰς τό + infinitive

d) πρὸς τό + infinitive

The following two constructions only rarely express purpose in the NT:

e) ὥστε + infinitive[5]

f) ὡς + infinitive

3. **Key to Identification**

Although a simple *to* idea will in most instances be the most appropriate translation, you should expand on this for the sake of testing to see if the infinitive in question fits another category. If you suspect a purpose infinitive, insert the gloss *in order to* or *for the purpose of* (and translate the infinitive as a gerund), *in order that*.

4. **Illustrations**

Matt 5:17   μὴ νομίσητε ὅτι ἦλθον **καταλῦσαι** τὸν νόμον
            Do not think that I came **to destroy** the law

> This text illustrates some of the features of the purpose infinitive well. We see a simple infinitive after an intransitive verb of motion. Further, we could expand the translation to "… I came *in order to* destroy" without changing the meaning.

Matt 27:31 ἀπήγαγον αὐτὸν εἰς τὸ **σταυρῶσαι**
            they led him away **to crucify** [him][6]

John 1:33   ὁ πέμψας με **βαπτίζειν**
            the one who sent me **to baptize**

> This text illustrates (1) that the controlling verb of an infinitive is not

---

[4] The 33 instances of the gen. articular inf. used for purpose noted by Votaw occur almost exclusively in Matthew, Luke, and Acts (Votaw, *Infinitive in Biblical Greek*, 21).

[5] Seven of the eight instances of ὥστε/ὡς + inf. to indicate purpose (Matt 10:1 [*bis*]; 15:33; 27:1; Luke 9:52 [ὡς]; 20:20 [ὥστε; *v.l.* is εἰς τό]; Acts 20:24 [ὡς]) are disputed by Boyer, "Infinitives," 11-12. He regards these as probably indicating result. The lone example of ὥστε + inf. for purpose, according to Boyer, is found in Luke 4:29 (with a *v.l.* of εἰς τό). Takamitsu Muraoka, "Purpose or Result? Ὥστε in Biblical Greek," *NovT* 15 (1972) 205-19 (esp. 210-11), is open to the possibility of several others.

[6] The careful reader will notice what appears to be a discrepancy in the use of italics in the Greek for prepositions and conjunctions and words in bold in the English translation (as in this example from Matthew). In reality, the εἰς τό is merely a helper to the inf.; the inf. σταυρῶσαι, by itself, means *to crucify*. Only when the prepositional phrase bears a meaning that is not also implied by the inf. will we italicize anything in the English translation (see examples under inf. of time).

necessarily the main verb of the sentence (in this case, a substantival participle); and (2) that the gloss *in order to* is for testing purposes only, as it would be too clumsy if made the final translation ("the one who sent me in order to baptize").

Eph 6:11   ἐνδύσασθε τὴν πανοπλίαν τοῦ θεοῦ **πρὸς τὸ δύνασθαι** ὑμᾶς στῆναι
            put on the full armor of God **in order that** you **may be able** to stand

1 Pet 3:7   οἱ ἄνδρες ὁμοίως, συνοικοῦντες κατὰ γνῶσιν . . . **εἰς τὸ μὴ ἐγκόπτεσθαι** τὰς προσευχὰς ὑμῶν
            husbands, likewise, dwell [with your wives] according to knowledge . . . **in order that** your prayers **might** not **be hindered**

> Is this text saying that the purpose of the husband's understanding is that his prayers might get past the ceiling, or is such a *result* of his understanding? εἰς τό + inf. can be used for either purpose or result. Other exegetical considerations need to be brought to bear on the question.

Cf. also Matt 6:1; Mark 14:55; Luke 4:16, 29; 22:31; John 4:9; Acts 3:2; 7:19 (or result), 42; Rom 4:11; 1 Thess 2:12; Jas 3:3.

→ ## B. Result [so that, so as to, with the result that]

1. Definition[7]

The infinitive of result indicates the outcome produced by the controlling verb. In this respect it is similar to the infinitive of purpose, but the former puts an emphasis on intention (which may or may not culminate in the desired result) while the latter *places the emphasis on effect* (which may or may not have been intended). This usage is relatively common.

2. Clarification

The result infinitive may be used to indicate either *actual* or *natural* result. *Actual* result is indicated in the context as having occurred; *natural* result is what is assumed to take place at a time subsequent to that indicated in the context. A number of instances (especially where natural result is potentially in view) are difficult to distinguish from purpose infinitives, leaving room for exegetical discussion.[8] As a general guideline, however, if in doubt, label a

---

[7] There are really two kinds of result infinitives: One is the actual, chronologically sequential result of the controlling verb, the other is the implication or significance of what the controlling verb actually accomplishes (almost an epexegetical idea, but not quite like the epexegetical inf. Its gloss would be "this is what the controlling verb means" or "here's what I mean when I say X" [cf. Heb 11:8; Rom 6:12 for examples]).

[8] Boyer lists Mark 7:4; Luke 1:25; 24:16, 45; Acts 7:19; 10:47; 15:10; 20:30; Rom 1:24, 28; 11:8 (*bis*), 10; 2 Cor 10:16 (*bis*); Gal 3:10; 1 Thess 3:3; Rev 16:9, 19 (Boyer, "Infinitives," 12, n. 25). This is just the tip of the iceberg. He suggests, as we have for the corresponding ἵνα-clause, that the inf. might do double duty at times (ibid., 25).

given infinitive as purpose (it occurs about three times as often as result).[9]

3. Structural Clues

a) Simple or "naked" infinitive (usually following an [intransitive] verb of motion)

b) τοῦ + infinitive

c) εἰς τό + infinitive[10]

d) ὥστε + infinitive (most frequent structure for result infinitive)[11]

e) ὡς + infinitive (rare)

f) ἐν τῷ + infinitive (rare)[12]

It should be observed that these first three parallel the first three structures of the purpose infinitive.

4. Key to Identification

Unlike the purpose infinitive, the simple *to* idea will often not be sufficient. In fact, it will frequently be misleading (even to the point of producing a confusing translation). The gloss *so that*, *so as to*, or *with the result that* brings out the force of this infinitive.[13]

5. Illustrations

Luke 5:7   ἔπλησαν ἀμφότερα τὰ πλοῖα ὥστε **βυθίζεσθαι** αὐτά
            they filled both the boats **so that they began to sink**

> This text illustrates the difference between result and purpose. The boats did not *intend* to sink (purpose). But the result was that they were so full of fish they began to sink.[14]

---

[9] Votaw lists 294 purpose infinitives and 96 result infinitives (*Infinitive in Biblical Greek*, 46-47). This does not include the infinitives after prepositions, many of which can go either way.

[10] This is disputed by older works, but it is an established idiom in both the NT and extra-biblical literature. See I. T. Beckwith, "The Articular Infinitive with εἰς," *JBL* 15 (1896) 155-67.

[11] See Boyer, "Infinitives," 11; Votaw, *Infinitive in Biblical Greek*, 14.

[12] Heb 3:12 is apparently the only example of ἐν τῷ + inf. indicating result in the NT.

[13] However, in modern colloquial English, *so that* also indicates purpose.

[14] The example of ὥστε + inf. here also illustrates another feature of the language (which, to some degree, had become lost in the Hellenistic period): ὥστε + inf. in classical Greek indicated *natural* result (a result anticipated, not purposed; but one that may or not have come to fruition), while ὥστε + the indicative indicated *actual* result (a result that definitely occurred, though normally not anticipated). In Koine ὥστε + inf. now does double duty, while ὥστε + the indicative, the rarer construction, is used as it was in the Attic (it occurs but twice in the NT in subordinate clauses, in John 3:16 and Gal 2:13).

Rom 1:20   τὰ γὰρ ἀόρατα αὐτοῦ ἀπὸ κτίσεως κόσμου. . . νοούμενα καθορᾶται. . .
           εἰς τὸ **εἶναι** αὐτοὺς ἀναπολογήτους

           for his invisible nature from the creation of the world. . . has been
           clearly perceived . . . **with the result that** they **are** without excuse

1 Cor 13:2   ἐὰν ἔχω πᾶσαν τὴν πίστιν ὥστε ὄρη **μεθιστάναι**

           if I have all faith **so as to remove** mountains

> This might be called an "implicational infinitive" in that the result is
> not chronologically subsequent to Paul having all faith, but is an impli-
> cation to be derived from it. Several result infinitives fit this subcate-
> gory.

Cf. also Matt 13:32; Mark 1:45; 3:20; Rom 1:24 (unless purpose); 7:3; Eph 6:19; 1 Thess 2:16
(or purpose); Heb 6:10; 11:8; 1 Pet 3:7 (or purpose); Rev 2:20.

→ ## C. Time

This use of the infinitive indicates a temporal relationship between its action
and the action of the controlling verb. It answers the question, "When?"
There are three types, all carefully defined structurally: antecedent, contemporaneous, subsequent. You should distinguish between them rather than
labeling an infinitive merely as "temporal."[15] Overall, the temporal use of
the infinitive is relatively common. Each subcategory should be learned.[16]

1.   Antecedent (μετὰ τό + infinitive) [after . . .]

The action of the infinitive of antecedent time occurs *before* the action of
the controlling verb. Its *structure* is μετὰ τό + the infinitive and should be
translated *after* plus an appropriate *finite* verb.[17]

There is confusion in some grammars about the proper labels of the temporal infinitives. More than one has mislabeled the antecedent infinitive
as the subsequent infinitive, and vice versa.[18] This confusion comes
naturally: If we are calling this use of the infinitive *antecedent*, why then
are we translating it as *after*? The reason is that this infinitive explicitly
tells when the action of the *controlling verb* takes place, as in "*after* he got
in the boat, it sank." In this sentence, "he got in" is the infinitive
and "sank" is the main verb. The sinking comes after the getting in, or

---

[15] For convenience' sake, the structural clues, keys to identification, and illustrations
will all be grouped together, under each type of temporal inf.

[16] The contemporaneous inf. use is by far the most common. The antecedent inf. is
relatively rare, for example, but should be learned in conjunction with the other uses
(hence, all three are marked for memorization).

[17] A cursory search via *acCordance* revealed that the only tenses used in this construction are the aorist (14 times, including the *v.l.* at Mark 16:19) and perfect (once–Heb 10:15).

[18] Cf., e.g., Williams, *Grammar Notes*, 43; Brooks-Winbery, 123-24; Young, *Intermediate
Greek*, 166-67.

conversely, the getting in comes before the sinking. Thus the action of the infinitive occurs before that of the controlling verb.

Students are often confused about this point. Some have even queried, "Then why shouldn't we translate the sentence, 'Before the boat sank, he got in'?" The reason is that there is no word *before*, and the verb is not in the prepositional phrase (where we find the word *after*).[19] It may be helpful to remember it this way: *After the infinitive comes the verb.*

Matt 26:32   μετὰ δὲ τὸ **ἐγερθῆναί** με προάξω ὑμᾶς εἰς τὴν Γαλιλαίαν.
And *after* I **have been raised**, I will go before you into Galilee.

Mark 1:14   μετὰ δὲ τὸ **παραδοθῆναι** τὸν Ἰωάννην ἦλθεν ὁ Ἰησοῦς εἰς τὴν Γαλιλαίαν
Now *after* John **was arrested**, Jesus came into Galilee.

Heb 10:26   ἑκουσίως ἁμαρτανόντων ἡμῶν *μετὰ* τὸ **λαβεῖν** τὴν ἐπίγνωσιν τῆς ἀληθείας
if we sin deliberately *after* **receiving** the knowledge of the truth

Cf. also Mark 14:28; Luke 12:5; 22:20; Acts 1:3; 7:4; 10:41; 15:13; 19:21; 20:1; 1 Cor 11:25.

2.   **Contemporaneous (ἐν τῷ + infinitive)** [*while, as, when . . .*]

The action of the infinitive of contemporaneous time occurs *simultaneously* with the action of the controlling verb. Its *structure* is ἐν τῷ + the infinitive.[20] It should be translated *while* (for present infinitives) or *as, when* (for aorist infinitives) plus an appropriate *finite* verb.[21]

Matt 13:4   ἐν τῷ **σπείρειν** αὐτὸν ἃ μὲν ἔπεσεν παρὰ τὴν ὁδόν
while he **was sowing**, some fell on the road

Luke 3:21   ἐν τῷ **βαπτισθῆναι** ἅπαντα τὸν λαὸν
when all the people **were baptized**

Heb 2:8   ἐν τῷ γὰρ **ὑποτάξαι** αὐτῷ τὰ πάντα οὐδὲν ἀφῆκεν
for *when* he **subjected** all things to him, he left nothing

Cf. also Mark 4:4; Luke 1:8, 21; 11:37; 17:11; 24:51; Acts 2:1; 8:6; 11:15; Rom 3:4; 1 Cor 11:21; Heb 3:15.

---

[19] It is a bit surprising to find some grammars confused on this point, since they recognize that the antecedent *participle* should be translated *after*. The problem arises, however, when they define the time of the controlling verb in relation to the inf., rather than the inf. in relation to the controlling verb ("the action of the main verb takes place before the action expressed by the infinitive" [Young, *Intermediate Greek*, 166]). Such a definition presupposes that the controlling verb is the object of the preposition!

[20] There is at least one instance in the NT of διὰ τό + inf. (Heb 2:15) and one of the gen. articular inf. (Acts 10:25) for contemporaneous time. As well, the dat. articular inf. in 2 Cor 2:13 might fit here (or, perhaps, causal).

[21] A cursory examination of the data via acCordance revealed no other tenses used for contemporaneous time. The present occurs about three times as often as the aorist in this construction. Apart from Luke-Acts and Hebrews, this category is rare in the NT.

3. **Subsequent (πρὸ τοῦ, πρίν, or πρὶν ἤ + infinitive)** *[before . . .]*

The action of the infinitive of subsequent time occurs *after* the action of the controlling verb. Its *structure* is πρὸ τοῦ, πρίν, or πρὶν ἤ + the infinitive. The construction should be *before* plus an appropriate *finite* verb.

There is confusion in some grammars about the proper labels of the temporal infinitives. More than one has mislabeled the subsequent as the antecedent infinitive.[22] This confusion comes naturally: If we are calling this use of the infinitive *subsequent*, why then are we translating it as *before*? The reason is that this infinitive explicitly tells when the action of the *controlling verb* takes place, as in "the rabbit was already dead, *before* he aimed his rifle." In this sentence, "he aimed" is the infinitive and "was (already dead)" is the main verb. The dying comes before the aiming, or conversely, the aiming comes after the dying. Thus the action of the infinitive occurs *after* that of the controlling verb.[23]

Matt 6:8   οἶδεν ὁ πατὴρ ὑμῶν ὧν χρείαν ἔχετε *πρὸ τοῦ* ὑμᾶς **αἰτῆσαι** αὐτόν
            your Father knows what you need *before* you **ask** him

Mark 14:30 *πρὶν ἤ* δὶς ἀλέκτορα **φωνῆσαι** τρίς με ἀπαρνήσῃ
            before the rooster **crows** twice, you will deny me thrice

John 1:48   *πρὸ τοῦ* σε Φίλιππον **φωνῆσαι** ὄντα ὑπὸ τὴν συκῆν εἶδόν σε
            before Philip **called** you, while you were under the fig tree, I saw you

John 4:49   κατάβηθι *πρὶν* **ἀποθανεῖν** τὸ παιδίον μου
            come down *before* my child **dies**

Cf. also Matt 1:18; Luke 2:21; 22:15; John 8:58; 13:19; 14:29; Acts 2:20; 7:2; 23:15; Gal 2:12; 3:23.

➡ D. *Cause*

1. **Definition**

The causal infinitive indicates the reason for the action of the controlling verb. In this respect, it answers the question "Why?" Unlike the infinitive of purpose, however, the causal infinitive gives a *retrospective* answer (i.e., it looks back to the ground or reason), while the purpose infinitive gives *prospective* answer (looking forward to the intended result). In Luke-Acts this category is fairly common, though rare elsewhere.

---

[22] See discussion under infinitive of antecedent time.

[23] For elaboration of this point, see above, under infinitive of antecedent time.

2. Structural Clues

There is one predominantly used structure for this infinitive category, as well as one rarely used structure.[24]

1) διὰ τό + infinitive (most common)
2) τοῦ + infinitive (rare)

3. Key to Identification

Translate this infinitive *because* followed by a finite verb appropriate for the context.

4. Illustrations

Matt 24:12   διὰ τὸ **πληθυνθῆναι** τὴν ἀνομίαν ψυγήσεται ἡ ἀγάπη τῶν πολλῶν
          because lawlessness **will increase**, most people's love will grow cold

Mark 4:6   διὰ τὸ μὴ **ἔχειν** ῥίζαν ἐξηράνθη
        because it **had** no root, it withered

John 2:24   Ἰησοῦς οὐκ ἐπίστευεν αὐτὸν αὐτοῖς διὰ τὸ αὐτὸν **γινώσκειν** πάντας
        Jesus was not entrusting himself to them *because* he **knew** all men[25]

Acts 4:1-2   οἱ Σαδδουκαῖοι (2) διαπονούμενοι διὰ τὸ **διδάσκειν** αὐτοὺς τὸν λαὸν
        the Sadducees (2) [were] disturbed *because* [the apostles] **were teaching** the people

Heb 7:24   ὁ δὲ διὰ τὸ **μένειν** αὐτὸν εἰς τὸν αἰῶνα ἀπαράβατον ἔχει τὴν ἱερωσύνην
        but *because* he **remains** forever, he maintains his priesthood permanently

Cf. also Matt 13:5, 6; Mark 4:5; Luke 2:4; 6:48; 8:6; 9:7; 19:11; Acts 12:20; 18:2; Phil 1:7; Jas 4:2.

E. *Means (ἐν τῷ + infinitive) [by . . . doing, etc.]*

1. Definition

The infinitive of means describes the way in which the action of the controlling verb is accomplished. In some respects this could be called an epexegetical infinitive (but we are reserving that term exclusively for

---

[24] The dat. articular inf. in 2 Cor 2:13 might also display cause (so RSV). But it could equally be considered contemporaneous time.

[25] Though against our normal approach in this grammar, the translation given above is not gender inclusive. This is because in John 2:25 and 3:1 a connection is made between Jesus' knowledge of what was in "man" and his meeting with a certain "man" named Nicodemus. The evangelist is moving from a generic principle in 2:24-25 to a specific illustration of this principle in chapter 3. Gender inclusive translations (such as NRSV) miss this point.

substantival/adjectival infinitives). It answers the question, "How?" Instances are rare.

2. Structural Clues

This usage is almost always expressed by ἐν τῷ + the infinitive. In this respect, its structure is identical to that of the contemporaneous infinitive. However, it is much rarer than the contemporaneous infinitive.

3. Key to Identification

The infinitive should normally be translated with *by* followed by a *gerund* (an "-ing" word).

4. Illustrations

Acts 3:26   ὁ θεὸς. . . ἀπέστειλεν αὐτὸν εὐλογοῦντα ὑμᾶς ἐν τῷ **ἀποστρέφειν** ἕκαστον ἀπὸ τῶν πονηριῶν ὑμῶν.
God. . . sent him to bless you *by* **turning** each [one of you] from your wicked ways.

Ac 4:29-30   δὸς τοῖς δούλοις σου μετὰ παρρησίας πάσης λαλεῖν τὸν λόγον σου, (30) ἐν τῷ τὴν χεῖρά [σου] **ἐκτείνειν**
Grant to your servants [that they might] speak your word with all boldness, (30) *by* **stretching out** your hand.[26]

Cf. also Rom 15:13 (or contemporaneous); Eph 6:17 (*v.l.*);[27] Heb 2:8 (or contemporaneous); 8:13 (or contemporaneous).

➜ F. *Complementary (Supplementary)*

1. Definition

The infinitive is very frequently used with "helper" verbs to complete their thought. Such verbs rarely occur without the infinitive. This finds a parallel in English.[28]

2. Structural Clues

The key to this infinitive use is the helper verb.[29] The most common verbs that take a complementary infinitive are ἄρχομαι,[30] βούλομαι, δύναμαι (the most commonly used helper verb), ἐπιτρέπω, ζητέω, θέλω, μέλλω, and ὀφείλω.[31] The infinitive itself is the *simple* infinitive.

---

[26] Even this example is not always treated as indicating means; NRSV renders it "while you stretch out."

[27] The simple inf. δέξασθαι replaces the imperative δέξασθε in many, especially late MSS (A D^C E K L P *et alii*).

[28] The instances that belong here, in some measure, have implicit counterparts in individual verb-tense uses. For example, ἄρχομαι + inf. is mirrored in the inceptive aorist and imperfect. θέλω + inf. or μέλλω + inf. makes a conative or tendential notion more explicit.

A second clue is that the complementary infinitive is especially used with a *nominative* subject, as would be expected. For example, in Luke 19:47 we read οἱ γραμματεῖς ἐζήτουν αὐτὸν **ἀπολέσαι** ("the scribes *were seeking* **to kill** him").[32] But when the infinitive requires a different agent, it is put in the accusative case (e.g., **γινώσκειν** ὑμᾶς βούλομαι ["I want *you* **to know**"] in Phil 1:12). The infinitive is still to be regarded as complementary.[33]

3. **Key to Identification**: see structural clues

4. **Illustrations**

Matt 6:24   οὐ *δύνασθε* θεῷ **δουλεύειν** καὶ μαμωνᾷ
            you **can**not **serve** God and mammon

Mark 2:19   ὅσον χρόνον ἔχουσιν τὸν νυμφίον μετ᾽ αὐτῶν οὐ *δύνανται* **νηστεύειν**[34]
            as long as they have the bridegroom with them they *can*not **fast**

Gal 3:21   εἰ γὰρ ἐδόθη νόμος ὁ *δυνάμενος* **ζῳοποιῆσαι**
            for if a law had been given that *could* **make alive**

> Here is an instance in which the controlling verb is an adjectival participle. Jude 24 is similar: "Now to him who *is able* **to keep** you from falling" (τῷ δὲ *δυναμένῳ* **φυλάξαι** ὑμᾶς ἀπταίστους).

Phil 1:12   **γινώσκειν** δὲ ὑμᾶς *βούλομαι*, ἀδελφοί, ὅτι τὰ κατ᾽ ἐμὲ . . .
            now I *want* you **to know**, brothers, that my circumstances . . .

1 Tim 2:12 **διδάσκειν** δὲ γυναικὶ οὐκ *ἐπιτρέπω* οὐδὲ **αὐθεντεῖν** ἀνδρός, ἀλλ᾽ **εἶναι** ἐν ἡσυχίᾳ.
            Now I *do* not *permit* a woman **to teach** or **to exercise authority** over a man, but **to remain** in silence.

Cf. also Matt 12:1; Mark 10:28; 15:31; Luke 1:22; 4:42; 13:24; 23:2; John 13:5, 33; Acts 2:4; 15:1; 18:26; 28:22; Rom 8:13; 1 Cor 10:13; 2 Cor 3:1; 2 Tim 3:15; Heb 1:14; 1 Pet 5:1; 1 John 3:9; Rev 1:19; 15:8.

---

[29] It is possible to treat complementary infinitives as direct object infinitives (so Boyer, "Infinitives," 6), thereby substantially increasing their number. We take complementary infinitives as part of the *verbal* idea: Both helper verb and inf. are necessary to communicate the verbal notion. For more discussion, see below under infinitive as direct object.

[30] All instances occur in the Gospels and Acts, except for 2 Cor 3:1.

[31] Boyer, "Infinitives," 6, finds 72 different verbs that take a complementary inf. in the NT. He notes, *inter alia*, that ἔχω frequently takes a complementary inf. (23 times) when it has the force of "have [the ability] to" (ibid., 7).

[32] Cf. also Mark 8:11; 13:5; 15:8; Luke 9:12; John 11:8; Acts 13:44. On a rare occasion, the subject and object involve a reciprocal relationship, with the result that the inf. takes an acc. subject that is the same person as the nom. subject (cf., e.g., Heb 5:5).

[33] For a discussion on the subject of the inf., see the chapter on the accusative case. There it is also noted how to determine, when two accusatives are used with an inf., which is subject and which is complement.

[34] This entire clause is omitted in D U W *f*[1] 33 326 468 700 1525 *et pauci*.

II. Substantival Uses

There are four basic uses of the substantival infinitive: subject, direct object, appositional, and epexegetical.[35] A specialized use of the direct object is indirect discourse. But because it occurs so frequently, it will be treated separately. Thus, pragmatically, there are five basic uses of the substantival infinitive: subject, direct object, indirect discourse, appositional, and epexegetical.

→ ## A. Subject

1. Definition

An infinitive or an infinitive phrase frequently functions as the subject of a finite verb. This category especially includes instances in which the infinitive occurs with *impersonal verbs* such as δεῖ, ἔξεστιν, δοκεῖ, etc.[36]

2. Structural Clues

The infinitive may or may not have the article. However, the usage of this infinitive does not occur in prepositional phrases.

3. Key to Identification

Besides noting the definition and structural clues, one helpful key is to do the following. In place of the infinitive (or infinitive phrase), substitute X. Then say the sentence with this substitution. If X could be replaced by an appropriate noun functioning as subject, then the infinitive is most likely a subject infinitive.

For example, in Phil 1:21 Paul writes, "For to me, to live is Christ and to die is gain." Substituting X for the infinitives we get, "For to me, X is Christ and X is gain." We can readily see that X can be replaced by a noun (such as "life" or "death").

4. Illustrations

Mark 9:5   ὁ Πέτρος λέγει τῷ Ἰησοῦ· ῥαββί, καλόν ἐστιν ἡμᾶς ὧδε **εἶναι**
            Peter said to Jesus, "Rabbi, for us **to be** here *is* good"

---

[35] The epexegetical use might more properly be called adjectival, or dependent substantival.

[36] Technically, there are no impersonal subjects in Greek as there are in English. Instances of the inf. with, say, δεῖ, are actually subject infinitives. Thus, δεῖ με ἔρχεσθαι means "to come is necessary for me" rather than "it is necessary for me to come." One way to see the force of the Greek more clearly is to translate the inf. as a gerund (see our example from Rev 20:3).

John 4:4 ἔδει δὲ αὐτὸν **διέρχεσθαι** διὰ τῆς Σαμαρείας.

Now *it was necessary* for him **to pass through** Samaria

> At first glance the infinitive does not seem to be the subject of ἔδει; rather, it seems to be complementary. But this is looking at the text from the English point of view–from translation rather than from sense. But if we translate the verse, "Now to pass through Samaria was necessary for him," we can see clearly that the infinitive is the subject. In English, however, normal convention requires an indefinite "it" as the subject.

Phil 1:21 ἐμοὶ γὰρ **τὸ ζῆν** Χριστὸς καὶ **τὸ ἀποθανεῖν** κέρδος

For to me, **to live** is Christ and **to die** is gain

> These infinitives could also be translated as gerunds: "living is Christ and dying is gain." This text illustrates two other points of Greek syntax: (1) The subject has the article (in the first clause, since one of the substantives has the article and the other is a proper noun [in Paul], what determines the subject is word order[37]); and (2) the tenses of the infinitives are lexically informed. It is no accident that the first infinitive is present ("to continue living") and the second is aorist ("to die").

Phil 3:1 τὰ αὐτὰ **γράφειν** ὑμῖν ἐμοὶ μὲν οὐκ ὀκνηρόν

To write the same things to you is no hassle to me

> Replacing the infinitive phrase with X shows clearly that this is a subject infinitive: "X is no hassle." Here is an example in which the subject infinitive is anarthrous.

Rev 20:3 μετὰ ταῦτα δεῖ **λυθῆναι** αὐτὸν μικρὸν χρόνον.

After these [events], **releasing** him for a little while *is necessary.*

Cf. also Matt 13:11; 14:4; 15:20; Mark 3:4; 9:11; Luke 20:22; John 4:24; 5:10; Acts 16:21, 30; Rom 7:18; 12:3; 1 Tim 3:2; Heb 2:1; Rev 10:11.

B. Direct Object

1. Definition

An infinitive or an infinitive phrase occasionally functions as the direct object of a finite verb. Apart from instances of indirect discourse,[38] this usage is rare.[39] Nevertheless, this is an important category for exegesis, as the examples below illustrate.

---

[37] See the chapter on the nominative case for a discussion.

[38] It is, of course, possible to treat complementary infinitives as direct object infinitives (so Boyer, "Infinitives," 6), thereby substantially increasing their number. (Boyer counts 892 complementary infinitives in the NT, making this the largest group [ibid., 8].) A better approach is to view the complementary infinitives as part of the *verbal* idea: Both helper verb and inf. are necessary to communicate the verbal notion.

[39] Boyer ("Infinitives," 9) only lists two texts for direct object (2 Cor 8:11; Phil 4:10), apparently overlooking John 5:26; Phil 2:6 and the possibility of Phil 2:13. He adds Rev 13:10 under his category "Object Infintive with Other Verbs," but notes that even this "would not strictly be *object*" (if substantival at all, it would better fit as a predicate nom. use). Note also the *v.l.* in this text.

2. Structural Clues

The infinitive may or may not have the article.[40] However, the usage of this infinitive does not occur in prepositional phrases.

3. Key to Identification

Besides noting the definition and structural clues, one helpful key is to do the following: In place of the infinitive (or infinitive phrase), substitute X. Then say the sentence with this substitution. If X could be replaced by an appropriate noun functioning as direct object, then the infinitive is most likely a direct object infinitive. (This works equally well for indirect discourse infinitives.)

4. Illustrations

John 5:26 ὥσπερ γὰρ ὁ πατὴρ ἔχει ζωὴν ἐν ἑαυτῷ, οὕτως καὶ τῷ υἱῷ ἔδωκεν ζωὴν **ἔχειν** ἐν ἑαυτῷ.

For just as the Father has life in himself, so also he has given to the Son **to have** life in himself.

> This is apparently the only instance in the NT of an anarthrous infinitive functioning as direct object. Another way to look at the infinitive is as an infinitive in indirect discourse (thus, "he has given to the Son, "Have life in yourself." This is awkward, however, and the controlling verb does not fit the normal semantic contours of indirect discourse.

2 Cor 8:11 νυνὶ δὲ καὶ **τὸ ποιῆσαι** ἐπιτελέσατε

but now also complete **the doing** [of it]

Phil 2:6 οὐχ ἁρπαγμὸν ἡγήσατο **τὸ εἶναι** ἴσα θεῷ

he did not consider **equality** with God as something to be grasped

> This is an example of a direct object infinitive in an *object-complement* construction. Here the infinitive is the object and the anarthrous term ἁρπαγμόν is the complement, in keeping with the normal structural pattern of object-complement constructions.[41]

Phil 4:10 ἤδη ποτὲ ἀνεθάλετε **τὸ ὑπὲρ ἐμοῦ φρονεῖν**

now, at least, you have revived your **feeling** for me

Phil 2:13 θεὸς γάρ ἐστιν ὁ ἐνεργῶν ἐν ὑμῖν καὶ **τὸ θέλειν** καὶ **τὸ ἐνεργεῖν** ὑπὲρ τῆς εὐδοκίας

For the one producing in you both **the willing** and **the working** (for [his] good pleasure) is God.

> The syntax of this text is complicated by a number of factors, such as the role of θεός (subject or predicate nom.?–an issue further

---

[40] Though with simple direct object it typically does, while the indirect discourse inf. usually does not.

[41] *Contra* N. T. Wright, "ἁρπαγμός and the Meaning of Philippians 2:5-11," *JTS*, NS 37 (1986) 344, who sees the article as anaphoric to μορφῇ θεοῦ. As attractive as this view may be theologically, it has a weak basis grammatically. See our discussion of this text in "Accusative: Object-Complement."

complicated by the *v.l.* ὁ before θεός in several MSS), whether ἐνεργῶν is here viewed as transitive or intransitive, and the lexical force of ἐνεργέω. Taking ὁ ἐνεργῶν as the subject and θεός as predicate nom. is likely;[42] but the rest of the sentence is in doubt. There are two viable translations: "The one working in you is God, both **to will** and **to work** for his good pleasure," or "the one *producing* in you both **the willing** and **the working** is God." The *transitive* notion of producing is hardly foreign to the Pauline corpus (cf. 1 Cor 12:6, 11; Gal 3:5; Eph 1:11; cf. also Jas 5:16) nor to Paul's view of God's active role in the believer's life. If the infinitives are taken as direct objects of ὁ ἐνεργῶν, the resultant meaning seems explicitly to affirm the divine initiative in the process of sanctification.[43]

➡ C. Indirect Discourse

1. Definition

This is the use of the infinitive (or infinitive phrase) after a verb of *perception* or *communication*. (Technically, indirect discourse is a subcategory of direct object.[44]) The controlling verb introduces the indirect discourse, of which the infinitive is the main verb. "When an infinitive stands as the object of a verb of mental perception or communication and expresses the content or the substance of the thought or of the communication it is classified as being in indirect discourse."[45] This usage is quite common in the NT.[46]

2. Clarification and Semantics

We can see how indirect discourse functions by analogies with English. For example, "I told you to do the dishes" involves a verb of communication ("told") followed by an infinitive in indirect discourse ("to do"). The infinitive in indirect discourse represents a *finite* verb in the direct discourse. The interpreter has to reconstruct the supposed direct discourse. In this example, the direct discourse would be, "Do the dishes." What we can see from this illustration is that the infinitive of indirect discourse may represent an *imperative* on occasion.

But consider the example, "He claimed to know her." In this sentence the infinitive represents an *indicative*: "I know her."

---

[42] See our discussion of this text and the principles involved under "Nominative: Predicate Nominative."

[43] This view in no way contradicts v 12 ("work out your own salvation"), but supplies the basis for how such a command is to be carried out.

[44] Boyer classifies it as a subcategory of the complementary inf. ("Infinitives," 7) and both indirect discourse and complementary under direct object.

[45] Boyer, "Infinitives," 7.

[46] For a general discussion of indirect discourse, see the sections on ὅτι + indicative and ἵνα + subjunctive in the chapter on moods.

From these two illustrations we can see some of the sentence "embedding" in infinitives of indirect discourse. The general principle for these infinitives is that *the infinitive of indirect discourse retains the* **tense** *of the direct discourse*[47] *and usually represents either an* **imperative** *or* **indicative.**[48]

3. Introductory Verbs

The verbs of perception/communication that can introduce an indirect discourse infinitive are numerous.[49] The list includes verbs of knowing, thinking, believing, speaking, asking, urging, and commanding. The most common verbs are δοκέω, ἐρωτάω, κελεύω, κρίνω, λέγω, νομίζω, παραγγέλλω, and παρακαλέω.[50]

4. Illustrations

Mark 8:29 αὐτὸς ἐπηρώτα αὐτούς· ὑμεῖς δὲ τίνα με λέγετε **εἶναι**;
           he said to them, "Who *do you say* that I **am**?"

Mark 12:18 Σαδδουκαῖοι . . . οἵτινες λέγουσιν ἀνάστασιν μὴ **εἶναι**
           Sadducees . . . who **say** **there is** no resurrection

John 4:40 ὡς οὖν ἦλθον πρὸς αὐτὸν οἱ Σαμαρῖται, ἠρώτων αὐτὸν **μεῖναι** παρ᾽ αὐτοῖς
           so when the Samaritans came to him, *they asked* him **to stay** with them

John 16:2 ἵνα πᾶς ὁ ἀποκτείνας ὑμᾶς δόξῃ λατρείαν **προσφέρειν** τῷ θεῷ
           in order that anyone who kills you *will think* that he **is offering** service to God

           The original direct discourse would have been something like, "He will think, 'I am offering service to God.'" The present indicative is thus converted to an infinitive in indirect discourse.

Rom 12:1   *Παρακαλῶ* οὖν ὑμᾶς, ἀδελφοί, . . . **παραστῆσαι** τὰ σώματα ὑμῶν
           I urge you, therefore, brothers, . . . **to present** your bodies

Jas 2:14   τί τὸ ὄφελος, ἀδελφοί μου, ἐὰν πίστιν λέγῃ τις **ἔχειν** ἔργα δὲ μὴ ἔχῃ;
           What is the benefit, my brothers, if someone *claims* **to have** faith but does not have works?

           The direct discourse would have been, "I have faith." If the original discourse had been "I have faith but I do not have works," the subjunctive ἔχῃ would have been an infinitive as well.

---

[47] This is not always the case, however. For example, in Titus 3:12 the aorist inf. παραχειμάσαι represents a *future* indicative of the direct discourse ("I have decided *to spend* the winter there" = "I have decided, 'I *will spend* the winter there'").

[48] It may also represent a subjunctive, but when it does so the subjunctive has an injunctive flavor (e.g., prohibitive subjunctive, hortatory subjunctive).

[49] Boyer has found 82 such verbs, for a total of 362 indirect discourse inf. constructions (ibid., 8).

[50] Ibid., 8-9.

1 Pet 2:11   παρακαλῶ . . . **ἀπέχεσθαι** τῶν σαρκικῶν ἐπιθυμιῶν[51]
               I urge you . . . **to abstain** from fleshly lusts

Eph 4:21-22   ἐν αὐτῷ ἐδιδάχθητε . . . (22) **ἀποθέσθαι** ὑμᾶς . . . τὸν παλαιὸν ἄνθρωπον
               you have been taught in him . . . (22) that you **have put off** . . . the old
               man

> The other translation possibility is, "You have been taught in him that
> you *should* put off the old man." The reason that either translation is
> possible is simply that the infinitive of indirect discourse represents
> either an imperative or an indicative in the direct discourse, while its
> tense remains the same as the direct discourse. Hence, this verse
> embeds either "Put off the old man" (aorist imperative), or "You have
> put off the old man." This is a difficult problem, pregnant with exeget-
> ical implications. As this is an important problem, some discussion of
> it is necessary.
>
> Burton suggests that "there is apparently no instance in the New Testa-
> ment of the Aorist Infinitive in indirect discourse representing the
> Aorist Indicative of the direct form."[52] If so, the text would then mean,
> "Put off the old man."[53] Burton's statement is often quoted as though
> the issue were thereby settled. But Burton does not indicate how fre-
> quently aorist infinitives in indirect discourse occur. Further, he offers
> no analysis of the controlling verb. Recent research,[54] however, has ten-
> tatively concluded that (1) there are at least 150 aorist infinitives in indi-
> rect discourse in the NT, and (2) all of them do indeed seem to support
> Burton's contention. However, further analysis reveals that *all of the
> controlling verbs in such instances imply a command or exhortation.* Hence,
> the statistics may be irrelevant if the semantic situation envisaged here
> is different from all other NT examples. (The fact that διδάσκω, the con-
> trolling verb in Eph 4:22, can refer to the indicatives of the faith as well
> as to exhortations means that the verdict is still out.) There are other
> considerations that help to decide the issue at hand, but suffice it to say
> here that one cannot simply cite Burton as though this exegetical
> conundrum were thereby resolved.[55]

Cf. also Matt 8:18; Mark 5:17; Luke 8:18; 18:40; 22:24; 24:23, 37; John 12:29; Acts 3:3, 13;
10:48; 12:19; 19:31; 27:1; Rom 2:22; 1 Cor 2:2; 3:18; 8:2; 2 Cor 2:8; 11:16; Gal 6:3; Titus 2:6; Jas
1:26; 1 Pet 2:11; Jude 3; Rev 2:9.

---

[51] The *v.l.* has ἀπέχεσθε ($\mathfrak{P}^{72}$ A C L P 33 81 *et al.*), which is a more explicit notion of
command.

[52] Burton, *Moods and Tenses*, 53 (§114).

[53] Not infrequently, exegetes call the infinitives in vv 22-24 "imperatival infinitives."
But this is rather imprecise language. It may be that they *represent* an imperative of the
direct discourse, but this is not the same as an imperatival inf. In the least, it certainly begs
the question to label this as imperatival, for the issue of the meaning of the direct discourse is conveniently bypassed. Surprisingly, Boyer, too, calls these imperatival ("Infinitives," 15, n. 29).

[54] I am indebted to Peter Chiofalo's term paper in the course Advanced Greek Grammar at Dallas Seminary (spring 1991) for this information.

[55] Some other items that may contribute to the understanding include (1) the Pauline
view of the "old man"; (2) the use of διό in 4:25 (usually follows statements, making application of them); (3) the repetition of the ἀποτίθημι in v 25, along with the article before
ψεῦδος (could it be anaphoric, with v 25 being translated, "Therefore, since you have put
off the lie"?); and (4) the shift in tenses used with the infinitives in vv 22-24.

➡ D. Appositional [namely]

1. Definition

Like any other substantive, the substantival infinitive may stand in apposition to a noun, pronoun, or substantival adjective (or some other substantive). The appositional infinitive typically refers to a specific example that falls within the broad category named by the head noun. This usage is relatively common.

This category is easy to confuse with the epexegetical infinitive. The difference is that the epexegetical infinitive *explains* the noun or adjective to which it is related, while apposition *defines* it.[56] That is to say, apposition differs from epexegesis in that an appositional infinitive is more substantival than adjectival. This subtle difference can be seen in another way: An epexegetical infinitive (phrase) cannot typically substitute for its antecedent, while an appositional infinitive (phrase) can. At times, however, even these distinctions get fuzzy. When that is the case, most likely there is little or no exegetical significance to picking one label over the other.

2. Key to Identification

Insert the word *namely* before the infinitive. Another way to test it is to replace the *to* with a colon (though this does not always work quite as well[57]). For example, Jas 1:27 ("Pure religion . . . is this, to visit orphans and widows") could be rendered "Pure religion is this, *namely,* to visit orphans and widows," or "Pure religion is this: visit orphans and widows."

3. Illustrations

1 Thess 4:3 τοῦτο ἐστιν θέλημα τοῦ θεοῦ, ὁ ἁγιασμὸς ὑμῶν, **ἀπέχεσθαι** ὑμᾶς ἀπὸ τῆς πορνείας

this is the will of God, your sanctification, **namely, that** you **abstain** from fornication

> This is an instance of an appositional infinitive in relation to another word in apposition.

Jas 1:27 θρησκεία καθαρὰ . . . αὕτη ἐστίν, **ἐπισκέπτεσθαι** ὀρφανοὺς καὶ χήρας

pure religion . . . is this, **namely, to visit** orphans and widows

---

[56] Also, epexegetical infinitives are not related to pronouns, while appositional infinitives often are.

[57] The reason is that dropping the *to* turns the inf. into an imperative. Only if the context allows for it will this be an adequate translation.

Phil 1:29   ὑμῖν ἐχαρίσθη τὸ ὑπὲρ Χριστοῦ, οὐ μόνον **τὸ** εἰς αὐτὸν **πιστεύειν** ἀλλὰ καὶ **τὸ** ὑπὲρ αὐτοῦ **πάσχειν**

it has been granted to you, for the sake of Christ, not only **to believe** in him, but also **to suffer** for him

> The article with ὑπὲρ Χριστοῦ turns this expression into a substantive functioning as the subject of ἐχαρίσθη. Thus, "the-[following]-on-behalf-of-Christ has been granted to you." This then is picked up by two articular infinitives, πιστεύειν and πάσχειν (the prepositional phrases each time are wedged between the article and inf. for clarity). Thus, the articular infinitives are in apposition to a substantival prepositional phrase functioning as subject.

Cf. also Acts 3:18; 9:15; 15:20, 29; 24:15; 26:16; Rom 14:13; 15:23; 1 Cor 7:25, 37; Titus 2:2 (to an implied pronoun); Rev 2:14.

→ ## E. Epexegetical

1. Definition

The epexegetical infinitive clarifies, explains, or qualifies a noun or adjective.[58] This use of the infinitive is usually bound by certain lexical features of the noun or adjective. That is, they normally are words indicating ability, authority, desire, freedom, hope, need, obligation, or readiness. This usage is fairly common.

This use of the infinitive is easy to confuse with the appositional infinitive. On the distinction between the two, see discussion under "Appositional Infinitive."

2. Illustrations

Luke 10:19   δέδωκα ὑμῖν τὴν ἐξουσίαν τοῦ **πατεῖν** ἐπάνω ὄφεων καὶ σκορπίων

I have given you authority **to tread** on serpents and scorpions

John 4:32   ἐγὼ βρῶσιν ἔχω **φαγεῖν** ἣν ὑμεῖς οὐκ οἴδατε

I have food **to eat** that you are not aware of

1 Cor 7:39   ἐλευθέρα ἐστὶν ᾧ θέλει **γαμηθῆναι**

she is free **to be married** to whom[ever] she desires

Jas 1:19   ἔστω πᾶς ἄνθρωπος ταχὺς εἰς τὸ **ἀκοῦσαι**, βραδὺς εἰς τὸ **λαλῆσαι**

let every person be quick **to hear**, slow **to speak**

Cf. also Luke 22:6; 24:25; Acts 14:9; 1 Cor 9:10; Phil 3:21 (possible); 2 Tim 2:2.

---

[58] Some grammars also say that it can qualify a verb. But when the inf. qualifies a verb, it should be treated as complementary. See our earlier treatment of that category.

III. Independent Uses

There are two independent uses of the infinitive, both quite rare in the NT: imperatival and absolute (as an indicative).

✝ ## A. Imperatival

1. Definition

Very rarely an infinitive may function like an imperative.

2. Key to Identification

Only if an infinitive is obviously not dependent on any other verb can it be treated as an imperatival infinitive. But the following three instances (in two verses) are apparently the *only* examples of this in the NT.[59]

3. Illustrations

Rom 12:15 **χαίρειν** μετὰ χαιρόντων, **κλαίειν** μετὰ κλαιόντων.
Rejoice with those who rejoice; **weep** with those who weep.

Phil 3:16 πλὴν εἰς ὃ ἐφθάσαμεν, τῷ αὐτῷ **στοιχεῖν**.
Only unto that [level of maturity] to which we have attained, **let us walk** by the same standard.
> This example more resembles a hortatory subjunctive than an imperative.

✝ ## B. Absolute

1. Definition

Like a genitive absolute, the infinitive can function independently of the rest of the sentence. It thus bears no syntactical relation to anything else in the sentence. One word, χαίρειν, is especially used as an infinitive absolute. The idea can be expressed as "I greet you" (thus, the equivalent of an indicative), or "Greetings!" (thus, equivalent of an interjection).

---

[59] *BDF* only know of the three examples given here. Boyer, however, finds eleven instances ("Infinitives," 15). But he lumps in the absolute infinitives (Acts 15:23; 23:26; Jas 1:1) and finds dubious examples elsewhere. His examples from Eph 4:23-24 [*sic*: 4:22-24] are better taken as indirect discourse (see discussion of this text earlier); 2 Thess 3:14 is almost surely result; and of Titus 2:9 *BDF* (196 [§389]) argue for an ellipsis of a verb of saying, placing this example in a different category from the classical idiom of imperatival infinitives.

2. Illustrations

Jas 1:1   Ἰάκωβος . . . ταῖς δώδεκα φυλαῖς . . . **χαίρειν**.
          James. . . to the twelve tribes. . . **Greetings**!

Cf. also Acts 15:23; 23:26; Heb 7:9.[60]

Structural Categories

I. Anarthrous Infinitives

The great majority of infinitives in the NT are anarthrous (almost 2000 of the 2291 infinitives).

A. Simple Infinitive

The simple infinitive is the most versatile of all structural categories, displaying eleven of the fifteen semantic uses.

1. Purpose
2. Result
3. Complementary
4. Means (rare)
5. Subject
6. Direct Object (rare)
7. Indirect Discourse
8. Apposition
9. Epexegetical
10. Imperatival (rare)
11. Absolute (rare)

B. Πρίν (ἤ) + Infinitive: Subsequent Time only

C. Ὡς + Infinitive

1. Purpose
2. Result

---

[60] The idiom in Heb 7:9 is classical, following a different semantic situation than that which is found in Jas 1:1.

D. Ὥστε + Infinitive

1. Purpose (rare)
2. Result

II. Articular Infinitives

Of the 314 articular infinitives in the NT, about two-thirds are governed by a preposition. Conversely, all infinitives governed by a preposition are articular.

A. Without Governing Preposition

1. **Nominative Articular Infinitive**

   a. Subject
   b. Apposition (rare)

2. **Accusative Articular Infinitive**

   a. Direct Object
   b. Apposition

3. **Genitive Articular Infinitive**

   a. Purpose
   b. Result
   c. Contemporaneous Time (rare)
   d. Cause (rare)
   e. Direct Object (disputed)
   f. Apposition
   g. Epexegetical

4. **Dative Articular Infinitive**

   There is but one example of this in the NT (2 Cor 2:13). It is either causal or contemporaneous time.

B. With Governing Preposition

1. **Διὰ τό + Infinitive**

   a. Cause
   b. Contemporaneous Time (rare)

2. **Εἰς τό + Infinitive**

    a. Purpose

    b. Result

    c. Epexegetical (rare)

3. **Ἐν τῷ + Infinitive**

    a. Result (rare)

    b. Contemporaneous Time

    c. Means

4. **Μετὰ τό + Infinitive:** Antecedent Time

5. **Πρὸς τό + Infinitive**

    a. Purpose

    b. Result

6. **Miscellaneous Prepositional Uses**

    For a list and discussion of other prepositions used with the infinitive as well as the "normal" prepositions used with infinitives in an "abnormal" way, see Burton's *Moods and Tenses*, 160-63 (§406-17) and Boyer, "Infinitives," 13.

The Participle

Select Bibliography

BDF, 174-75, 212-20 (§339, 411-25); **J. L. Boyer**, "The Classification of Participles: A Statistical Study," *GTJ* 5 (1984) 163-79; **Brooks-Winbery**, 126-38; **Burton**, *Moods and Tenses*, 53-72, 163-77 (§115-56, 418-63); **Dana-Mantey**, 220-33 (§196-203); **K. L. McKay**, *A New Syntax of the Verb in New Testament Greek: An Aspectual Approach* (New York: Peter Lang, 1994) 60-66; **Moule**, *Idiom Book*, 99-105; **Moulton**, *Prolegomena*, 221-32; **Porter**, *Idioms*, 181-93; **Robertson**, *Grammar*, 1095-1141; **Turner**, *Syntax*, 150-62; **Young**, *Intermediate Greek*, 147-63; **Zerwick**, *Biblical Greek*, 125-31 (§360-77).

Introduction

A. *The Difficulty with Participles*

It is often said that mastery of the syntax of participles is mastery of Greek syntax. Why are participles so difficult to grasp? The reason is threefold: (1) *usage*–the participle can be used as a noun, adjective, adverb, or verb (and in any mood!); (2) *word order*–the participle is often thrown to the end of the sentence or elsewhere to an equally inconvenient location; and (3) *locating the main verb*–sometimes it is verses away; sometimes it is only implied; and sometimes it is not even implied! In short the participle is difficult to master because it is so versatile. But this very versatility makes it capable of a rich variety of nuances, as well as a rich variety of abuses.

B. *The Relation of Participles to Exegesis*

The *context* has more influence on participles than on any other area of Greek grammar. In other words, for most participles, one cannot simply look at the structure (the presence or absence of the article is, of course, the most vital structural feature) to determine what kind of participle it is. There will be some clues, however, and the student must master these if he/she is to see the genuine semantic possibilities a participle can have in a given context. One's exegetical skills get tested more with participles than with any other part of speech.

C. *The Participle as a Verbal Adjective*

The participle is a *declinable verbal adjective*. It derives from its verbal nature tense and voice; from its adjectival nature, gender, number and case. Like the infinitive, the participle's verbal nature is normally seen in a *dependent* manner. That is, it is normally adverbial (in a broad sense) rather than functioning independently as a verb. Its adjectival side is seen in both substantival (independent) and adjectival (dependent) uses; both are frequent (though the substantival is far more so).

1.   The Verbal Side of the Participle

a.   Time

The *time* of the participle's verbal nature requires careful consideration. Generally speaking, the tenses behave just as they do in the indicative. The only difference is that now the point of reference is the controlling verb, not the speaker. Thus, time in participles is relative (or dependent), while in the indicative it is absolute (or independent).

	PAST	PRESENT	FUTURE
ABSOLUTE (Indicative)	Aorist Perfect Imperfect Pluperfect	Present	Future
RELATIVE (Participle)	Aorist Perfect	Present (Aorist)	Future
	Antecedent	Contemporaneous	Subsequent

Chart 80
Time in Participles

The *aorist* participle, for example, usually denotes *antecedent* time to that of the controlling verb.[1] But if the main verb is also aorist, this participle *may* indicate contemporaneous time.[2] The *perfect* participle also indicates *antecedent* time. The *present* participle is used for *contemporaneous* time. (This contemporaneity, however, is often quite broadly conceived, depending in particular on the tense of the main verb.) The *future* participle denotes *subsequent* time.[3]

This general analysis should help us in determining whether a participle can even belong to a certain adverbial usage. For example, participles of *purpose* are normally future, sometimes present, (almost) never aorist or perfect.[4] Why? Because the purpose of the

---

[1] We are speaking here principally with reference to adverbial (or circumstantial) participles.

[2] Cf. Robertson, *Grammar*, 1112-13. From my cursory examination of the data, the aorist participle is more frequently contemporaneous in the epistles than in narrative literature. There is also such a thing as an aorist participle of subsequent action, though quite rare.

[3] It would not be correct to say that the future participle represents future time, for often it is used in past-tense contexts. Thus, for example, John 6:64: "Jesus knew from the first . . . **who** it is **that would betray** him" (ᾔδει γὰρ ἐξ ἀρχῆς ὁ Ἰησοῦς . . . τίς ἐστιν ὁ παραδώσων αὐτόν). Cf. also Luke 22:49 (substantival); Acts 8:27; 22:5; 24:11, 17 (adverbial).

controlling verb is carried out *after* the time of the main verb (or sometimes contemporaneously with it). Likewise, *causal* participles will not be in the future tense (though the perfect adverbial participle is routinely causal; the aorist often is and so is the present).[5] *Result* participles are never in the perfect tense. Participles of *means*? These are normally present tense, though the aorist is also amply attested (especially when a progressive aspect is not in view). Many an exegete has gone awry by ignoring these simple guidelines.

b. Aspect

As for the participle's *aspect*, it still functions for the most part like its indicative counterparts. There are two basic influences that shape the participle's verbal side, however, which are almost constant factors in its *Aktionsart*.[6] First, because the participle has embodied two natures, neither one acts completely independently of the other. Hence, the verbal nature of participles has a permanent *grammatical intrusion* from the adjectival nature. This *tends* to dilute the strength of the aspect. Many nouns in Hellenistic Greek, for instance, in a former life were participles (e.g., ἀρχιτέκτων, ἄρχων, γέρων, ἡγεμών, θεράπων, καύσων, τέκτων, χείμων). The constant pressure from the adjectival side finally caved in any remnants of verbal aspect. This is not to say that no participles in the NT are aspectually robust–many of them are! But one must not assume this to be the case in every instance. In particular when a participle is *substantival*, its aspectual force is more susceptible to reduction in force.

Secondly, many substantival participles in the NT are used in generic utterances. The πᾶς ὁ ἀκούων (or ἀγαπῶν, ποιῶν, etc.) formula is always or almost always generic. As such it is expected to involve a *gnomic* idea.[7] Most of these instances involve the present participle.[8] But if they are already gnomic, we would be

---

[4] Some have noted that the aorist participle can, on a rare occasion, have a telic force in Hellenistic Greek, because the future participle was not normally a viable choice in the conversational and vulgar dialect (so A. T. Robertson, "The Aorist Participle for Purpose in the Κοινή" *JTS* 25 [1924] 286-89).

[5] That the present participle could be causal may seem to deny its contemporaneity. But its contemporaneity in such cases is either broadly conceived or the participle functions as the *logical* cause though it may be *chronologically* simultaneous.

[6] For a discussion of the difference between aspect and *Aktionsart*, see our introductory chapter on verb tenses.

[7] See discussion under gnomic present.

[8] The aorist is also sometimes used generically. Cf. Matt 10:39 ("the one who finds [ὁ εὑρών] his life . . . the one who loses [ὁ ἀπολέσας] it"); 23:21, 22; 26:52; Mark 16:16 (a spurious text); Luke 8:12, 14; 20:18; John 5:25; 6:45; 16:2; Rom 10:5; 1 Cor 7:33; Gal 3:12; Jas 5:4, 11, 20. Boyer thus overstates his case when he writes that with the substantival aorist participle, "the identification seems *always* to be specific, not general" ("Participles," 166 [italics added]). Some examples could be taken either way (e.g., 1 Pet 4:1; 1 John 5:1).

hard-pressed to make something more out of them–such as a progressive idea.[9] Thus, for example, in Matt 5:28, "everyone who looks at a woman" (πᾶς ὁ βλέπων γυναῖκα) with lust in his heart does not mean "continually looking" or "habitually looking," any more than four verses later "everyone who divorces his wife" (πᾶς ὁ ἀπολύων τὴν γυναῖκα αὐτοῦ) means "repeatedly divorces"! This is not to deny a habitual *Aktionsart* in such gnomic statements. But it is to say that caution must be exercised. In the least, we should be careful not to make statements such as, "The present participle βλέπων [in Matt 5:28] characterizes the man by his act of *continued* looking."[10] This may well be the meaning of the *evangelist*, but the present participle, by itself, can hardly be forced into this mold.[11]

2. The Adjectival Nature of the Participle

As an adjective, a participle can function dependently or independently. That is, it can function like any ordinary adjective as an attributive or predicate. It also can act substantivally, as is the case with any adjective.

3. Summary

All participles fit one of two categories (in keeping with the fact that they are verbal adjectives): Every participle emphasizes either its verbal or its adjectival aspect. Within each of these emphases, every participle is either dependent or independent. If one can keep this simple grid in mind, he/she will have a broad, organizational understanding of the participle.

	Verbal	Adjectival
Independent	(Verbal) Imperatival Indicative	(Substantival) Subject, object, etc.
Dependent	(Adverbial) Temporal, Causal, Means, Manner, etc.	(Adjectival) Attributive Predicate

Chart 81
The Semantic Range of the Participle

Although every participle fits under either an adjectival emphasis or verbal emphasis and is either dependent or independent, I have not

---

[9] To be sure, the present substantival participle, even when gnomic, can have a progressive force as well. (There is nothing prohibiting an author from speaking about "everyone who continually does.") This seems to be particularly the case with ὁ πιστεύων. See discussion at John 3:16 below.

[10] Lenski, *St. Matthew's Gospel*, 226.

[11] Note the following discussion (620-21, n. 22) on ὁ πιστεύων, in which the progressive notion is argued on the basis of several strands of evidence.

listed one large category of participles (known as participles absolute). These will be treated separately from the above mentioned categories, even though they in fact fit under these categories. The reason for a separate treatment of the participle absolute is that it has particular structural clues (especially a specific case) that require further explanation.

Specific Uses

I. Adjectival Participles

This category involves both the dependent and independent adjectival participles (i.e., both the adjectival proper and substantival). For a structural clue, the student should note the article: If it stands before a participle and functions as a modifying article (normal use) then that participle *must* be adjectival. If the participle does *not* have the article, it *may* be adjectival. Therefore, the first question one needs to ask when attempting to determine the nuance of a particular participle is, *Does it have the article?* If the answer is yes, it is adjectival;[12] if the answer is no, it may be adjectival or any other kind of participle (such as adverbial).

➡ A. Adjectival Proper (Dependent)

1. Definition

The participle may function just like an adjective and either modify a substantive (attributive) or assert something about it (predicate). The attributive participle is common; the predicate participle is rare.[13]

2. Clarification/Key to Identification

The way in which one determines whether a participle is attributive or predicate is exactly the same as when he/she determines whether an *adjective* is attributive or predicate. The adjectival participle may occupy any of the three attributive positions and both predicate positions. You should normally translate the *attributive* participle as though it were a

---

[12] There is one seeming exception to this rule. When the construction is ὁ μέν + participle or ὁ δέ + participle, the article may be functioning like a personal pronoun. In such instances it is not modifying the participle but is the subject of the sentence. The participle will then be adverbial. Cf., e.g., Mark 1:45; 6:37, etc. There are over 100 such constructions in the NT (the vast bulk of which are in the Gospels and Acts). See the discussion of this phenomenon in "The Article, Part I."

[13] Boyer knows of only 20 instances in the second predicate position ("Participles," 166, n. 4) and none in the first predicate position. But several of his examples should be explained otherwise (e.g., the participle in 1 Cor 8:12 is probably temporal; the one in 2 Cor 4:15, means), and he seems to have overlooked a few others.

relative clause (e.g., ὁ πατήρ σου ὁ **βλέπων** ἐν τῷ κρυπτῷ ἀποδώσει σοι ["your Father *who* **sees** in secret will reward you"] in Matt 6:4).

As a refinement, therefore, we should add that a *predicate* participle never has the article (only the attributive and substantival participles do).

3. Illustrations

➡

a. Attributive Participles

Matt 2:7   τοῦ **φαινομένου** ἀστέρος
the **shining** star
> An example in the first attributive position.

John 4:11   τὸ ὕδωρ τὸ **ζῶν**
the **living** water
> An example in the second attributive position. This is the most common construction for attributive participles.

John 4:25   Μεσσίας . . . ὁ **λεγόμενος** χριστός
Messiah . . . **the one called** Christ
> This is in the third attributive position–a frequent construction with participles, but not with adjectives. Cf. also Luke 7:32; John 4:5; 5:2; Acts 1:12; 1 Cor 2:7; 1 Pet 1:7, 21.

John 4:10   ὕδωρ **ζῶν**
living water
> A fourth attributive construction. Cf. also Mark 14:51.

Cf. also Matt 4:16; 6:18; 7:13; 16:16; 17:17; Mark 1:38; 3:22; 6:2; 11:10; Luke 3:7; 15:6; John 1:6; 5:23; Acts 7:55; 13:43; Rom 12:3; 1 Cor 3:7; 2 Cor 8:20; Gal 3:23; 1 Tim 1:10; Heb 6:18; Rev 12:9.

b. Predicate Participles

Acts 7:56   ἰδοὺ θεωρῶ τοὺς οὐρανοὺς **διηνοιγμένους**
Behold, I see heaven **opened**
> This is second predicate position. The perfect (passive) participle, as here, especially seems to function as a predicate participle.[14]

Heb 4:12   **ζῶν** ὁ λόγος τοῦ θεοῦ
the word of God is **living**
> This is an illustration of the first predicate position.

Rom 12:1   παραστῆσαι τὰ σώματα ὑμῶν θυσίαν **ζῶσαν** ἁγίαν εὐάρεστον τῷ θεῷ
present your bodies [as] a sacrifice–**alive**, holy, [and] acceptable to God
> The word θυσίαν is a complement in an object-complement construction and hence a predicate accusative. But the question about ζῶσαν is whether it is attributive or predicate to θυσίαν, not σώματα. If attributive, it should be translated, "Present your bodies as a *living*

---

[14] Cf. also Matt 21:9; 23:39; Mark 11:9, 10; Luke 1:18, 42; 2:36; 18:34; Rom 15:16.

sacrifice ...." The issue is difficult to decide. But since the trailing adjectives are most likely predicate, the participle's close connection with them suggests that it, too, is predicate. This makes the statement more emphatic than an attributive adjective would. Nevertheless, as Robertson points out, "It is not always easy to draw the line between the anarthrous attributive participle and the predicate participle of additional statement."[15]

Jas 2:15   ἐὰν ἀδελφὸς ἢ ἀδελφὴ γυμνοὶ ὑπάρχωσιν καὶ **λειπόμενοι** τῆς ἐφημέρου τροφῆς

if your brother or sister is naked and **lacking** [their] daily food

> The participle is obviously predicate since it is linked by καί to a predicate adjective.

Cf. also Matt 7:14; 21:9; 27:37; Mark 6:2; Luke 12:28; 16:14; Acts 19:37; 2 Cor 6:14; 1 Tim 5:13; Heb 7:3; 2 Pet 1:19.

→ ## B. *Substantival (Independent)*

1. Definition

This is the independent use of the adjectival participle (i.e., not related to a noun). It functions in the place of a substantive. As such, it can function in virtually any capacity that a noun can, such as subject, direct object, indirect object, apposition, etc.[16] This category is found quite frequently in the NT.[17]

2. Key to Identification

First, of course, if the participle has the article it must be either adjectival (proper) or substantival. Second, if it is articular and is not related in a dependent fashion to any substantive in the sentence, then it is substantival. The translation is often *the one who/the thing which* with the participle then translated as a finite verb (e.g., ὁ ποιῶν is translated *the one who does*).

3. Clarification

The substantival participle may or may not be articular, although most are. Its case is determined just like any ordinary noun's case is determined, viz., by its function in the sentence.

---

[15] Robertson, *Grammar*, 1105.

[16] There are, of course, certain substantival categories that are restricted to nouns. The substantival participle does not naturally fit into the adverbial use of nouns, for example, since the adverbial participle is at hand.

[17] Boyer counts 1467 instances of the substantival participle ("Participles," 165, n. 3). It is far more frequent than the adjectival.

4. Semantics

First, in relation to the infinitive, although participles and infinitives are often translated the same (especially when the infinitive is translated as a gerund), there is a distinct difference. "Whereas the infinitive is abstract, speaking of the *act* or *fact* of doing, the participle is concrete, speaking of the *person who* or *thing which* does."[18]

Second, with reference to its verbal nature: Just because a participle is adjectival or substantival, this does *not* mean that its verbal aspect is entirely diminished. Most substantival participles still retain *something* of their aspect. A *general* rule of thumb is that *the more particular (as opposed to generic) the referent, the more of the verbal aspect is still seen.* (See the introduction for detailed discussion.)

Third, the aspect of the *present* participle can be diminished if the particular context requires it.[19] Thus, for example, ὁ βαπτίζων in Mark 1:4 does not mean "the one who continually baptizes" but simply "the baptizer."[20] Indeed, it cannot mean this in Mark 6:14, for otherwise John would be baptizing without a head ("John the baptizer has been raised from the dead")![21] As well, it is probable that Ἰησοῦν τὸν **ῥυόμενον** ἡμᾶς ἐκ τῆς ὀργῆς τῆς ἐρχομένης in 1 Thess 1:10 does *not* mean, "Jesus, the one continually delivering us. . . ," but "Jesus, our deliverer from the wrath that is coming," as is evident by the prepositional phrase that refers to a future time. On the other hand, this passage may be similar to Heb 7:25 in that it could indicate that which (or the one who) continually delivers us from the imminent day of God's wrath.

5. Illustrations

Mark 6:44   ἦσαν οἱ **φαγόντες** τοὺς ἄρτους πεντακισχίλιοι ἄνδρες
those who ate the loaves were five thousand men
> The same rules apply on subject-predicate nominative relations as when both substantives are nouns (viz., if one is articular, it is the subject).

Luke 1:45   μακαρία ἡ **πιστεύσασα**
blessed is **she who believed**

John 3:16   πᾶς ὁ **πιστεύων**
everyone **who believes**
> The idea seems to be both gnomic and continual: "everyone who continually believes." This is not due to the present tense only, but to the

---

[18] Williams, *Grammar Notes*, 50. Cf. also Robertson, *Grammar*, 1101-02.

[19] This is not as common with the participles in other tenses. The reason seems to be that the present participle is well suited to a generic notion, lending itself to a gnomic tense use. The other tenses, however, are usually more specific in their application. For discussion, see Boyer, "Participles," 165-66.

[20] Cf. N. Turner, *Syntax*, 151.

[21] Cf. also Mark 5:15-16.

use of the present participle of πιστεύω, especially in soteriological contexts in the NT.[22]

John 4:13   πᾶς ὁ **πίνων**

everyone **who drinks**

> It may be that the evangelist does have a habitual idea in mind (as well as the gnomic). The present participle is contrasted with the aorist subjunctive of the following verse, as if to say "everyone who continually drinks, but whoever should taste. . . ."

John 6:39   τοῦτο δέ ἐστιν τὸ θέλημα τοῦ **πέμψαντός** με

now this is the will of **the one who sent** me

> This is an instance of a substantival participle functioning as a subjective gen. ("this is what the one who sent me wills").

Acts 1:16   Ἰούδα . . . ὁδηγοῦ τοῖς **συλλαβοῦσιν** Ἰησοῦν

Judas . . . a guide to **those who arrested** Jesus

2 Th 2:6-7   νῦν τὸ **κατέχον** οἴδατε . . . (7) ὁ **κατέχων**

you know that **which is** presently **restraining** [him] . . . (7) the **one who is restraining**

1 Tim 6:15   ὁ βασιλεὺς τῶν **βασιλευόντων** καὶ κύριος τῶν **κυριευόντων**

the King of those **who are reigning** and Lord of those **who are lording it (over)** [others]

> Contrast this with the nouns in Rev 17:14: "Lord of lords and King of kings."

Cf. also Matt 1:22; 5:10; 22:3; Mark 13:13; 14:69; Luke 2:18; 19:32; 20:17; John 1:22; 5:11; 7:33; 18:21; Acts 4:4; 21:20; 1 Cor 12:3; Gal 1:6; 2 Tim 2:4; Jas 5:4; 1 John 3:9; 2 John 1; Rev 22:19.

II. Verbal Participles

This category involves those participles that emphasize the verbal over the adjectival nuance. The category includes both independent and (far more

---

[22] The aspectual force of the present ὁ πιστεύων seems to be in contrast with ὁ πιστεύσας. The aorist is used only eight times (plus two in the longer ending of Mark). The aorist is sometimes used to describe believers as such and thus has a generic force (cf. for the clearest example the *v.l.* at Mark 16:16; cf. also 2 Thess 1:10; Heb 4:3; perhaps John 7:39; also, negatively, of those who did not [μή] believe: 2 Thess 2:12; Jude 5). The present occurs six times as often (43 times), most often in soteriological contexts (cf. John 1:12; 3:15, 16, 18; 3:36; 6:35, 47, 64; 7:38; 11:25; 12:46; Acts 2:44; 10:43; 13:39; Rom 1:16; 3:22; 4:11, 24; 9:33; 10:4, 11; 1 Cor 1:21; 14:22 [*bis*]; Gal 3:22; Eph 1:19; 1 Thess 1:7; 2:10, 13; 1 Pet 2:6, 7; 1 John 5:1, 5, 10, 13). Thus, it seems that since the aorist participle was a live option to describe a "believer," it is unlikely that when the present was used, it was aspectually flat. The present was the tense of choice most likely because the NT writers by and large saw *continual* belief as a necessary condition of salvation. Along these lines, it seems significant that the *promise* of salvation is almost always given to ὁ πιστεύων (cf. several of the above-cited texts), almost never to ὁ πιστεύσας (apart from Mark 16:16, John 7:39 and Heb 4:3 come the closest [the present tense of πιστεύω never occurs in Hebrews]).

commonly) dependent verbal participles. By way of clarification, it should again be stated that the verbal element of *any* participle, whether it be adjectival or verbal in emphasis, is not usually absent (note the partial exceptions above in which the aspect is diminished, even though the voice still retains its force). However, when a participle is labeled as verbal, we simply indicate that its verbal nature is in the forefront.

A. *Dependent Verbal Participles*

This is far and away the larger of the two categories and includes the following subcategories: adverbial (or circumstantial), attendant circumstance, indirect discourse, complementary, periphrastic, and redundant.[23]

1. Adverbial (or Circumstantial)

a. Definition

The adverbial or circumstantial participle is grammatically subordinated to its controlling verb (usually the main verb of the clause). Like an ordinary adverb, the participle modifies the verb, answering the question, *When?* (temporal), *How?* (means, manner), *Why?* (purpose, cause), etc.

b. Terminology

Many grammars prefer to call this participle *circumstantial*. But that title is too vague.[24] To call this participle *adverbial* communicates more clearly and fits the general idea better: Adverbial participles, like adverbs, are dependent on a verb. It has been suggested that this participle "is simply an adjective used to modify a verb, and hence may be appropriately called adverbial."[25] But this is only partially true: The participle is a *verbal* adjective and hence its adverbial nature comes from the verbal side as well as the adjectival.[26]

---

[23] Broadly speaking, of course, all (verbal) dependent participles are adverbial.

[24] The *American Heritage Dictionary* offers for its first two definitions of circumstantial: "1. Of, relating to, or dependent on circumstances; 2. Of no primary significance; incidental." Neither one of these definitions would be an apt description of this use of the participle. As well, labeling this participle circumstantial does not sufficiently distinguish it from attendant circumstance.

[25] Dana-Mantey, 226.

[26] There are, of course, drawbacks to calling this participle adverbial. On the one hand, it is too broad (unlike an adverb, the adverbial participle cannot modify an adjective or other adverb). On the other hand, it is too narrow (several other participles [such as attendant circumstance, indirect discourse, redundant] are also dependent on the verb and may in some sense be called adverbial).

c. Amplification and Key to Identification

First, as we have said earlier, the context plays a major role in determining the force of the Greek participle. This is especially so with the adverbial participle. "The varieties in adverbial use come, not from alterations in the essential function of the participle, but from variations in the relation of its noun to the main verb and the context."[27]

Second, since the subject of the participle is usually the subject of a finite verb, the participle will usually be in the *nominative* case (almost 70% of the time).[28]

Third, there is often a strong translational correspondence between the English participle and the Greek (much more so than for the respective infinitives). In *this* respect, the participle is not too difficult to master.

Fourth, related to this, the English participle is generally more ambiguous than the Greek. Greek participles for the most part follow carefully defined patterns (e.g., word order, tense of participle, tense of controlling verb), allowing us to limit our choices in a given text more than we could if we depended on the English alone. It is for this reason that the student is encouraged to translate the force of the participle with more than an *–ing* gloss.

d. Specific Nuances of the Adverbial Participle

Most adverbial participles belong to one of *eight* categories: temporal, manner, means, cause, condition, concession, purpose, or result.

➡ #### 1) Temporal

a) Definition

In relation to its controlling verb, the temporal participle answers the question, *When?* Three kinds of time are in view: antecedent, contemporaneous, and subsequent. The *antecedent* participle should be translated *after doing, after he did*, etc. The *contemporaneous* participle should normally be translated *while doing*. And the *subsequent* participle should be translated *before doing, before he does*, etc.[29] This usage is common.

---

[27] Dana-Mantey, 226.

[28] According to *acCordance* (with some adjustments made for mistaggings) there are 6674 participles in the NT. Of these, there are 4621 in the nominative case (69%), 957 accusative (14%), 743 genitive (11%), 353 dative (5%), and 1 vocative.

[29] In reality, almost all subsequent participles fit some other category, especially purpose and result. Hence, *before* is not normally a viable translation.

b) Key to Identification

As we have said, the temporal participle answers the question, *When?* As well, if a particular adverbial participle is to be labeled as temporal, this should be the *primary* element the author wishes to stress (because almost all participles, whether adverbial or not, are temporal in at least a secondary sense).[30]

Therefore, once you have identified the temporal force of the participle, you should then go on and ask whether another, more specific semantic value is intended. (Although the temporal participle is commonly found, students tend to appeal to this category too often.) You should probe the participle's usage with questions such as, "Is the author *only* describing when this happened or is he also indicating *why* or *how* it happened?"

For example, Eph 1:19-20 speaks of the power of the resurrection in relation to the believer's sanctification: τὸ ὑπερβάλλον μέγεθος τῆς δυνάμεως αὐτοῦ εἰς ἡμᾶς τοὺς πιστεύοντας κατὰ τὴν ἐνέργειαν τοῦ κράτους τῆς ἰσχύος αὐτοῦ, (20) ἣν ἐνήργησεν ἐν τῷ Χριστῷ **ἐγείρας** αὐτὸν ἐκ νεκρῶν ("the surpassing greatness of his power toward us who believe, according to the working of the strength of his might, which he exercised in Christ **when he raised/by raising** him from the dead"). A temporal participle would focus on the time when God exercised this power (at the resurrection); a participle of means would focus on how God exercised this power. Both are true and the participle conveys both notions. The issue at stake is which one is being emphasized.

c) Amplification

1] Aorist Participle

The *aorist* participle is normally, though by no means always, *antecedent* in time to the action of the main verb. But when the aorist participle is related to an *aorist* main verb, the participle will often be contemporaneous (or simultaneous) to the action of the main verb.

---

[30] Even if a participle is labeled as temporal, this does not necessarily mean that such is its only force. Often a secondary notion is present, such as means or cause. Thus, Heb 1:3, for example, should probably be rendered "**when he made** purification for sin, he sat down at the right hand of the majesty on high" (καθαρισμὸν τῶν ἁμαρτιῶν **ποιησάμενος** ἐκάθισεν ἐν δεξιᾷ τῆς μεγαλωσύνης ἐν ὑψηλοῖς), even though ποιησάμενος is both temporal and causal. To sit down at God's right hand meant that the work was finished, and this could not take place *until* the sin-cleansing was accomplished.

This can be seen in the frequently used redundant participle in the formula ἀποκριθεὶς εἶπεν ("answering, he said"). The answering does not occur before the saying–it *is* the speaking.[31]

We see this in the epistles, too. In Eph 1:8-9 we read ἐπερίσσευσεν [τὴν χάριν] εἰς ἡμᾶς ... γνωρίσας ἡμῖν ("He lavished [his grace] upon us ... making known to us"). It would be difficult to see God's action of making his grace known *to us* (thus, effectual) as other than contemporaneous with his lavishing such grace upon us.[32]

The NT is filled with theologically significant texts related to the temporal participle. Just within Eph 1, note the following: Eph 1:4-5 (ἐξελέξατο. . . προορίσας [are election and predestination simultaneous or sequential?]); 1:13-14 (ἀκούσαντες . . . πιστεύσαντες ἐσφραγίσθητε [does the Spirit seal believers *after* they believe the gospel, or *when* they believe?]);[33] 1:19-20 (although discussed earlier in another context, the issue here would be whether God's power was demonstrated *after* he raised Christ from the dead or *when* he raised him [ἐνήργησεν. . . ἐγείρας]).

With a present tense main verb, the aorist participle is usually antecedent in time.[34]

2] Present Participle

The *present* participle is normally *contemporaneous* in time to the action of the main verb. This is especially so when it is related to a present tense main verb (often, in fact, it follows a present imperative as a participle of *means*). But this participle can be broadly antecedent to the time of the main verb, especially if it is articular (and

---

[31] Cf., e.g., Matt 13:37; 26:23; Mark 11:14; Luke 5:22; 7:22; 13:2; 19:40.

[32] A few MSS, in fact, have the infinitive γνωρίσαι instead of γνωρίσας (so F G 1913).

[33] Although it is certainly possible to translate this last text as "after hearing . . . after believing you were sealed," both the grammatical possibility of contemporaneity and the overall context lead me to believe that the aorist participle is contemporaneous here. Contextually, the threefold praise to the Godhead is in the first two instances due to God's *prior* action (election, redemption). To be consistent, it should be this way for the third leg (in the least, sealing should not follow believing). Further, in the following context (2:1-10), this theme of God's saving grace is given greater articulation. The metaphor of death in that passage as the state from which the elect were delivered gives no confidence that conversion precedes regeneration.

[34] A frequent exception to this is when the controlling verb is a *historical* present and the aorist participle is redundant. Cf. Mark 3:33; 5:7; 8:29; 9:5, 19; 10:24; 11:22, 33; 15:2; Luke 13:8; 17:37; John 21:19.

thus adjectival; cf. Mark 6:14; Eph 2:13). As well, the present participle is occasionally subsequent *in a sense* to the time of the main verb. This is so when the participle has a telic (purpose) or result flavor to it (cf. Eph 2:15). But as Robertson points out, "It is not strictly true that here the present participle means future or subsequent time. It is only that the purpose goes on coincident with the verb and beyond."[35]

3] Future Participle

The *future* participle is always subsequent in time to the action of the main verb (cf. Matt 27:49; Acts 8:27).

4] Perfect Participle

The *perfect* participle is almost always *antecedent* with reference to the main verb. When it is contemporaneous, such is due to either an intensive use of the perfect or to a present force of the perfect in its lexical nuance.[36]

The following chart notes the tenses normally used for the various temporal relations, especially as these relate to the other adverbial uses of the participle.

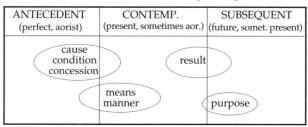

ANTECEDENT (perfect, aorist)	CONTEMP. (present, sometimes aor.)	SUBSEQUENT (future, somet. present)
cause condition concession		
	result	
	means manner	
		purpose

Chart 82
The Tenses of Adverbial Participles

d) Illustrations

Matt 4:2   **νηστεύσας**. . . ὕστερον ἐπείνασεν
           after he fasted. . . he then became hungry

Mark 2:14 **παράγων** εἶδεν Λευὶν τὸν τοῦ Ἀλφαίου
           while going on, he saw Levi, the son of Alphaeus

Mark 9:15 πᾶς ὁ ὄχλος **ἰδόντες** αὐτὸν ἐξεθαμβήθησαν
           when all the crowd **saw** him, they were amazed

---

[35] Robertson, *Grammar*, 1115.

[36] For a more nuanced discussion, see the introduction to this chapter as well as the chapter on the perfect tense.

Eph 1:15-16 **ἀκούσας** τὴν καθ᾽ ὑμᾶς πίστιν. . . (16) οὐ παύομαι εὐχαριστῶν
After I heard of your faith . . . (16) I have not ceased being thankful

Phil 1:3-4 εὐχαριστῶ. . . (4) τὴν δέησιν **ποιούμενος**
I am thankful . . . (4) **when I pray**

Rev 19:20 **ζῶντες** ἐβλήθησαν οἱ δύο εἰς τὴν λίμνην τοῦ πυρὸς
the two were thrown into the lake of fire **while** [still] **alive**

Cf. also Mark 1:19; 3:31; 5:22, 33; Luke 8:8; 10:33; 11:33; John 4:47; 9:1; Acts 1:4; 7:45; 8:40; 11:26; 14:18; Rom 5:10; 1 Cor 11:4; 2 Cor 10:1; Eph 4:8; Heb 1:3; 11:23; Rev 1:12.

2) Manner [*by* + participle of emotion or attitude]

a) Definition

The participle indicates the *manner* in which the action of the finite verb is carried out.

b) Key to Identification

First, there is much confusion between this participle and the participle of means. The reason is that both answer the question, *How?* However, beyond this initial question, there is usually little similarity. The participle of manner is relatively rare in comparison with the participle of means.[37]

Second, pragmatically, the participle of manner refers to the *emotion* (or sometimes *attitude*)[38] that accompanies the main verb. In this sense, it "adds color" to the story. It could appropriately be called *the participle of style*. This contrasts with the participle of means, which *defines* the action of the main verb. The key question that must be asked is, Does this participle *explain or define* the action of the main verb (means), or does it merely add *extra color* to the action of the main verb (manner)?

---

[37] Most grammars and commentaries make either little distinction between these two or define manner in a way that is much closer to our definition of means. (Cf., e.g., Burton, *Moods and Tenses*, 172: "The participle expressing manner or means often denotes the same action as that of the principal verb, describing it from a different point of view.") However, there are usually clear semantic differences. What is at stake is for the most part a terminological issue, not a substantive one. When commentators speak of the "modal participle" (a term that fits both means and manner), it is best to regard most such identifications as participles of *means*.

[38] The attitude, however, may be expressed by a participle of means–if it is an *essential* or defining characteristic of the main verb.

c)   Illustrations

Matt 19:22   ἀπῆλθεν **λυπούμενος**
              he went away **grieving**

> Notice that the participle does answer the question, "How?" but it does not define the mode of transportation. If we were to ask, "How did he go away?" *grieving* would be a participle of manner, while *walking* would be a participle of means.

Luke 8:47   **τρέμουσα** ἦλθεν
              she came **trembling**

Acts 2:13   ἕτεροι δὲ **διαχλευάζοντες** ἔλεγον
              but others **mocking** were saying

Acts 5:41   ἐπορεύοντο **χαίροντες**
              they went on their way **rejoicing**

> This participle gives us quite a bit of the flavor of the narrative; since it adds flavor, it is a "color commentator." This is the function of the participle of manner.

Cf. also Luke 2:48; 7:38; John 20:11; Phil 3:18.

➡️   ### 3)   Means [by means of]

a)   Definition

This participle indicates the means by which the action of a finite verb is accomplished. This means may be physical or mental. This usage is common.

b)   Key to Identification

First, as we pointed out above, both the participle of manner and the participle of means answer the question, *How?* Thus, there is some confusion between the two.

Second, one should supply *by* or *by means of* before the participle in translation. If this does not fit, it is not a participle of means.

Third, there are some further guidelines that the student should employ to distinguish between means and manner:

*   The participle of means answers the question "How?" but here (as opposed to the participle of manner) it seems a more necessary and implicit question.[39]

---

[39] The participle of means gives the *anticipated* answer to the question *How?* while manner normally does not. Thus, to the question, "How did he go to the ballgame?" one could answer "by driving his car" (means) or "hoping for a victory" (manner).

- If the participle of means is absent (or removed), the *point* of the main verb is removed as well (this is not normally true with manner).

- In some sense, the participle of means almost always defines the action of the main verb; i.e., it makes more explicit what the author intended to convey with the main verb.

Fourth, the participle of means could be called an *epexegetical* participle in that it *defines* or *explains* the action of the controlling verb.

c) Amplification and Significance

This participle is frequently used with vague, general, abstract, or metaphorical finite verbs. Further, it usually *follows* its verb.[40] The reason for these two features (one lexical, the other structural) is that the participle explains the verb. If the verb needs explaining, then it is the vaguer term. For example, in Matt 27:4 Judas says, "I have sinned (ἥμαρτον) *by betraying* (παραδούς) innocent blood." The verb comes first and is general in its lexical range. This is followed by the participle of means, which defines more exactly what the verbal action is.

One should note as well that the participle of means is almost always contemporaneous with the time of the main verb. (This, of course, should be obvious, for if the participle of means defines how the action of the main verb is accomplished, then it accompanies it in time.[41])

d) Illustrations

Matt 27:4   ἥμαρτον **παραδοὺς** αἷμα ἀθῷον
I have sinned **by betraying** innocent blood

Acts 9:22   Σαῦλος . . . συνέχυννεν τοὺς Ἰουδαίους . . . **συμβιβάζων** ὅτι οὗτός ἐστιν ὁ χριστός.
Saul . . . confounded the Jews. . . **by proving** that [Jesus] was the Christ.

1 Cor 4:12   κοπιῶμεν **ἐργαζόμενοι** ταῖς ἰδίαις χερσίν
we labor, **by working** with our own hands

---

[40] But cf. Matt 6:27; 2 Pet 3:6.

[41] Sometimes means blends imperceptibly into cause, especially with aorist participles. In such instances, the participle may be used for an action that is both antecedent and contemporaneous to the controlling verb. Cf., e.g., Eph 6:14: "stand, **by having girded** your loins with truth" (στῆτε **περιζωσάμενοι** τὴν ὀσφὺν ὑμῶν ἐν ἀληθείᾳ).

Eph 1:20   ἣν ἐνήργησεν . . . **ἐγείρας** αὐτὸν ἐκ νεκρῶν

             which he exercised . . . **by raising** him from the dead

Eph 2:14-15 ὁ ποιήσας τὰ ἀμφότερα ἕν . . . (15) τὸν νόμον. . . **καταργήσας**

             the one who made both [groups] one . . . (15) **by nullifying** . . . the
             law

Titus 1:11   οἵτινες ὅλους οἴκους ἀνατρέπουσιν **διδάσκοντες** ἃ μὴ δεῖ

             who upset whole houses **by teaching** things that they should not

1 Pet 5:6-7 ταπεινώθητε ὑπὸ τὴν κραταιὰν χεῖρα τοῦ θεοῦ . . . (7) πᾶσαν τὴν
             μέριμναν ὑμῶν **ἐπιρίψαντες** ἐπ᾽ αὐτόν, ὅτι αὐτῷ μέλει περὶ ὑμῶν.[42]

             Humble yourselves[43] under the mighty hand of God . . . (7) **by cast-
             ing** your cares on him, because he cares for you.

> Although treated as an independent command in several modern
> translations (e.g., RSV, NRSV, NIV), the participle should be connected
> with the verb of v 6, ταπεινώθητε. As such, it is not offering a new com-
> mand, but is defining *how* believers are to humble themselves. Taking
> the participle as means enriches our understanding of both verbs:
> Humbling oneself is not a negative act of self-denial per se, but a posi-
> tive one of active dependence on God for help.[44]

Phil 2:7   ἑαυτὸν ἐκένωσεν μορφὴν δούλου **λαβών**

             he emptied himself **by taking on** the form of a servant

> This text satisfies the regular criteria for a participle of means: (1) The
> participle follows the verb; and (2) the verb is vague, almost begging to
> be defined. Taking it as a result participle is problematic, since it is
> aorist; leaving as temporal leaves the meaning of ἐκένωσεν unexplained
> (and such an act is not explained otherwise in the following verses).
> The biggest difficulty with seeing λαβών as means is that emptying is
> normally an act of subtraction, not addition. But the imagery should
> not be made to walk on all fours. As an early hymn, it would be
> expected to have a certain poetic license. Further, Paul seems to have
> hinted at this meaning in his instructions to the saints in v 3: "[Think]
> nothing from selfishness or conceit (κενοδοξίαν)." The Philippians were
> told not to puff themselves up with "empty glory" (κενοδοξίαν),
> because Christ was an example of one who emptied his glory. If this
> connection is intentional, then the *Carmen Christi* has the following
> force:
>
> > Do not elevate yourselves on empty glory, but follow the example
> > of Christ, who, though already elevated (on God's level), emptied
> > his glory by veiling it in humanity.

Cf. also Matt 6:27; 28:19-20; Acts 9:8; 16:16; 27:38; Rom 12:20; Eph 4:28; Phil 1:30; 2:2-4;
1 Tim 1:6; 4:16; 2 Pet 2:15 (unless causal); 3:6.

---

[42] Some MSS, however, have the imperative ἐπιρίψατε for the participle (so 𝔓²⁵ 0206^*vid*
917 1874).

[43] More accurately, "Allow yourselves to be humbled" (as a permissive passive). See
chapter on "Moods: Passive Voice" for discussion.

[44] Michaels, *1 Peter* (WBC) 296.

➡ **4) Cause [because]**

a) Definition

The causal participle indicates the *cause* or *reason* or *ground* of the action of the finite verb. This is a common usage.

b) Key to Identification

This participle answers the question, *Why?* The thought of this participle can be brought out by *since* or *because*. (*Because* is normally preferable, however, in that *since* is often used of a temporal rather than a causal nuance.)

Two further clues (one on the *tenses* used, the other on *word order*) should be noted. (1) Aorist and perfect participles are amply represented, but the present participle is also frequently found here.[45] (2) The causal participle normally *precedes* the verb it modifies. Thus, form follows function (i.e., the cause of an action precedes the action).[46]

c) Illustrations

Matt 1:19   Ἰωσὴφ . . . δίκαιος **ὢν**
            Joseph . . . **because he was** a righteous man

John 4:6   ὁ Ἰησοῦς **κεκοπιακὼς** . . . ἐκαθέζετο
            because Jesus **was wearied** . . . he sat
            Adverbial *perfect* participles almost always belong to this category.[47]

John 11:38 Ἰησοῦς οὖν πάλιν **ἐμβριμώμενος** . . . ἔρχεται εἰς τὸ μνημεῖον[48]
            Then Jesus, **because he was deeply moved** . . . came to the tomb.

---

[45] The aorist also fits several other categories of usage, but the perfect adverbial participle almost always belongs here. The present causal participle may be conceived as broadly contemporaneous with the controlling verb, just as the customary present is broadly contemporaneous with present time. The NT knows of no future causal participles.

[46] We have seen this form-following-function pattern to some degree with the participle of means. It is also true of the participles of result and purpose: These follow the controlling verb.

[47] This is true even of perfects that are used as presents, such as οἶδα. Cf., e.g., Matt 12:25; 22:29; Mark 6:20; 12:24; Luke 8:53; 9:33; 11:17; John 4:45; 7:15; Acts 2:30; 16:34; Rom 5:3; 6:9; 13:11; 1 Cor 15:58; 2 Cor 1:7; 2:3; 4:14; 5:6, 11; Gal 2:16; Eph 3:17 (?); 6:8, 9; Phil 1:16, 25. This lends weight to taking the perfect participle πεφωτισμένους in Eph 1:18 as causal: "since the eyes of your heart have been enlightened."

But the perfect anarthrous participle often belongs to another category (especially periphrastic or predicate adjective), even though it may appear at first glance to be adverbial.

[48] The perfect participle has several competing variants. Chief among them are ἐμβριμησάμενος in C* (K) X 892ˢ 1241 1424 *et pauci* and ἐμβριμούμενος in ℵ A V 296 429 1525 1933.

Acts 7:9   οἱ πατριάρχαι **ζηλώσαντες** τὸν Ἰωσὴφ ἀπέδοντο εἰς Αἴγυπτον
            because the patriarchs **were jealous** of Joseph, they sold him to Egypt

Acts 16:34 ἠγαλλιάσατο πανοικεὶ **πεπιστευκὼς** τῷ θεῷ
            he rejoiced with his whole house **because he had believed** in God

> Although not frequent, causal participles can follow their controlling verbs, as here.

Phil 1:6   **πεποιθὼς** αὐτὸ τοῦτο
            since I am confident of this very thing

Cf. also Luke 9:33; John 4:45; 12:6; 13:3; 18:10; Acts 2:30; Rom 6:6; Phil 1:25; 1 Thess 1:4; 2 Tim 3:14; Titus 3:11; 2 Pet 1:14.

➡️

5) Condition *[if]*

a) Definition

This participle implies a condition on which the fulfillment of the idea indicated by the main verb depends. Its force can be introduced by *if* in translation. This usage is fairly common.[49]

b) Amplification

This participle is almost always equivalent to the third class condition (usually representing some sense of uncertainty) rather than to the first class condition.[50] As well, this usage overlaps with the participle of *means* at times.

c) Illustrations

1] Clear Illustrations

Matt 21:22 πάντα ὅσα ἂν αἰτήσητε ἐν τῇ προσευχῇ **πιστεύοντες** λήμψεσθε.
            Whatever you ask for in prayer, **if you believe**, you will receive it.

Luke 9:25   τί γὰρ ὠφελεῖται ἄνθρωπος **κερδήσας** τὸν κόσμον ὅλον ἑαυτὸν δὲ **ἀπολέσας**;[51]
            For how does it benefit a person **if he should gain** the whole world but **if he loses** himself?

---

[49] Thanks are due to Chai Kim for his work at Dallas Seminary in Advanced Greek Grammar, summer 1991, on the conditional participle.

[50] Cf. Robertson, *Grammar*, 1129. Not only can this be established by sense, but also by Synoptic parallels to some degree. Note, for example, ἐάν. . . κερδήσῃ in Matt 16:26 with κερδήσας in the parallel passage (Luke 9:25). (The problem with this illustration is that one could also show parallels in the Gospels between a first and third class condition, as in Matt 5:46–Luke 6:32.)

[51] Instead of the participles, D* 047 have complementary infinitives (κερδῆσαι, ἀπολέσαι).

Gal 6:9   θερίσομεν μὴ **ἐκλυόμενοι**
            we shall reap **if we do** not **lose heart**

1 Tim 4:4   οὐδὲν ἀπόβλητον μετὰ εὐχαριστίας **λαμβανόμενον**
            nothing is to be rejected **if it is received** with thanks

Cf. also Luke 15:4 (cf. Matt 18:12); Acts 15:29 (or means); 18:21 (gen. absolute); Rom 2:27; 7:3; 1 Cor 6:1; 8:10; 11:29;[52] Col 2:20; 1 Tim 4:6 (or means); 6:8; Heb 2:3; 7:12; 10:26; 11:32; 1 Pet 3:6; 2 Pet 1:10 (or means).

2]   Debatable Texts

1 Tim 3:10   οὗτοι δὲ δοκιμαζέσθωσαν πρῶτον, εἶτα διακονείτωσαν ἀνέγκλητοι **ὄντες**.
            But let them be tested first, then, **if they are** blameless, let them serve as deacons.

> The English translation sounds as if deacons could be selected from a pool of qualified individuals. This reading of the text assumes that ὄντες is a conditional participle and that διακονείτωσαν is a permissive imperative. However, the participle might be substantival and the imperative more likely is a command: "Let them be tested first, then **those who are** blameless **should become deacons**." If so, then *all* those who qualified to become deacons would fill the office.

Heb 6:4-6   ἀδύνατον τοὺς ἅπαξ φωτισθέντας . . . (6) καὶ **παραπεσόντας**, πάλιν ἀνακαινίζειν εἰς μετάνοιαν
            it is impossible to restore again to repentance those who have once been enlightened . . . (6) **if they have fallen away**

> παραπεσόντας is often construed as conditional (a tradition found in the KJV and repeated in most modern translations and by many commentators). But this is unwarranted. The construction of vv 4-6 *approximates* a Granville Sharp plural construction (the only difference being that with the second participle in the construction, γευσαμένους in v 4, the conjunction τε is used instead of καί: τοὺς φωτισθέντας γευσαμένους τε . . . καὶ μετόχους γενηθέντας . . . καὶ . . . γευσαμένους . . . καὶ παραπεσόντας).[53] If this participle should be taken adverbially, then should we not take the preceding two or three participles the same way? The inconsistency has little basis. Instead, παραπεσόντας should be taken as adjectival, thus making a further and essential qualification of the entire group.[54] A better translation, then, is "It is impossible to restore again to repentance those who have once been enlightened . . . **and have fallen away**."

---

[52] It is possible that this is the equivalent of a first class condition (so Robertson, *Grammar*, 1129).

[53] See "The Article, Part II," for discussion of the Sharp construction.

[54] See J. A. Sproule, "Παραπεσόντας in Hebrews 6:6," *GTJ* 2 (1981) 327-32.

➡   6) **Concession**

    a) **Definition**

The concessive participle implies that the state or action of the *main verb* is true *in spite of* the state or action of the participle. Its force is usually best translated with *although*. This category is relatively common.

    b) **Amplification**

First, this is semantically the opposite of the causal participle, but structurally identical (i.e., it typically precedes the verb and fits the contours of a causal participle–i.e., antecedent time and thus aorist, perfect or sometimes present). Second, there are often particles that help to make the concessive idea more obvious (such as καίπερ, καίτοιγε, κτλ.).

    c) **Illustrations**

Mark 8:18 ὀφθαλμοὺς **ἔχοντες** οὐ βλέπετε καὶ ὦτα **ἔχοντες** οὐκ ἀκούετε;
Although you have eyes, do you not see? And **although you have** ears, do you not hear?

Rom 1:21 **γνόντες** τὸν θεὸν οὐχ ὡς θεὸν ἐδόξασαν
although they knew God, they did not honor him as God

Eph 2:1 ὑμᾶς **ὄντας** νεκρούς
although you were dead

1 Pet 1:8 ὃν οὐκ **ἰδόντες** ἀγαπᾶτε[55]
although you have not **seen** him, you love him

Phil 2:6 ὅς ἐν μορφῇ θεοῦ **ὑπάρχων**
who, **although he existed** in the form of God

The translation of this participle as concessive is not entirely clear upon a casual reading of the text. The two options are either causal or concessive.

There are two interpretive problems in Phil 2:6-7 relevant to the treatment of this participle. First, of course, is the grammatical problem of whether this is concessive or causal. Second is the lexical problem of whether ἁρπαγμόν in v 6 means *robbery* or *a thing to be grasped*. The grammatical and the lexical inform one another and cannot be treated separately. Thus, if ὑπάρχων is causal, ἁρπαγμόν means *robbery* ("who, *because* he existed in God's form, did not consider equality with God as robbery"); if ὑπάρχων is concessive, then ἁρπαγμόν means *a thing to be grasped* ("who, *although* he existed in God's form, did not consider equality with God as a thing to be grasped"). As attractive as the first alternative might be theologically, it is not satisfactory. Ultimately, this

---

[55] Instead of ἰδόντες, 𝔓⁷² ℵ B C K L P 81 142 323 630 945 1241 1505 1739 2138 2464 *Byz* read εἰδότες.

verse cannot be interpreted in isolation, but must be seen in light of the positive statement in v 7–"but he emptied himself" (the participle ὑπάρχων equally depends on both ἡγήσατο and ἐκένωσεν). Only the concessive idea for the participle and *a thing to be grasped* translation for ἁρπαγμόν fit well with v 7.[56]

Cf. also John 10:33; Acts 5:7; 2 Cor 11:23; Phil 3:4; Heb 5:8.

➡ ### 7) Purpose (Telic)

a) Definition

The participle of purpose indicates the purpose of the action of the finite verb. Unlike other participles, a simple "-ing" flavor will miss the point. Almost always this can (and usually should) be translated like an English *infinitive*. This usage is somewhat common.

b) Key to Identification/Semantics

First, to *clarify* that a particular participle is telic (purpose), one can either translate it as though it were an infinitive, or simply add the phrase *with the purpose of* before the participle in translation.

Second, since purpose is accomplished *as a result* of the action of the main verb, perfect participles are excluded

---

[56] Perhaps the largest issue of this text is the meaning of ἁρπαγμόν. Is it *something to be grasped for* or *something to be retained*? If the former, the idea would be that although Christ existed in God's form, he did not attempt to become equal to God. If the latter, the meaning would be that although Christ existed in God's form, he did not feel compelled to maintain his equality with God. Both views naturally fit with a concessive participle, though the relation of τὸ εἶναι ἴσα θεῷ to the μορφῇ θεοῦ hangs in the balance.

Appeal has been made to the article with the infinitive, as though it were anaphoric (so N. T. Wright, "ἁρπαγμός and the Meaning of Philippians 2:5-11," *JTS*, NS 37 [1986] 344). If so, then "form of God" means the same thing as "equality with God" and ἁρπαγμόν is *something to be retained*. But, as we have argued elsewhere (see chapters on the accusative and infinitive), the article more probably is used to indicate the object in an object-complement construction. The connection with "form of God" is thus left open. In light of the predominant usage of ἁρπαγμόν as *something to be grasped for*, I am inclined to see a difference between μορφῇ θεοῦ and τὸ εἶναι ἴσα θεῷ. This does not deny an affirmation of the deity of Christ in this text, just that such a notion is found in τὸ εἶναι ἴσα θεῷ. μορφῇ θεοῦ carries that weight by itself (*inter alia*, there is the contextual argument: If one denies that Christ was truly God, one must also deny that he was truly a servant [note μορφὴν δούλου in v 7]). What, then, is the meaning of the infinitive phrase? It seems to suggest hierarchy, not ontology.

Putting the interpretation of all the elements together yields the following. Although Christ was truly God (μορφῇ θεοῦ), two things resulted: (1) he did not attempt to "outrank" the Father, as it were (cf. John 14:28 for a similar thought: "The Father is greater than I am"); (2) instead, he submitted himself to the Father's will, even to the point of death on a cross. It was thus not Christ's deity that compelled his incarnation and passion, but his obedience.

from this category (since they are typically antecedent in time). The future adverbial participle *always* belongs here;[57] the present participle frequently does. The aorist participle also has a representative or two, but this is unusual.[58]

Third, many present participles that fit this usage are lexically influenced. Verbs such as *seek* (ζητέω) or *signify* (σημαίνω), for example, involve the idea of purpose lexically.

Fourth, the telic participle almost always *follows* the controlling verb.[59] Thus, the word order emulates what it depicts. Some participles, when following their controlling verbs, virtually demand to be taken as telic (e.g., πειράζω).[60]

c) **Significance**

This participle, like the participle of cause, answers the question, *Why?* But the participle of purpose looks forward, while the participle of cause looks back. As well, the difference between the participle of purpose and the infinitive of purpose is that the participle emphasizes the *actor* while the infinitive emphasizes the *action*.

d) **Illustrations**

Matt 27:49 εἰ ἔρχεται Ἡλίας **σώσων** αὐτόν
            if Elijah is going to come **[with the purpose of]** saving him

---

[57] There are only twelve future participles in the NT. Five are adverbial, all of which are telic in force. Cf. Matt 27:49; Acts 8:27; 22:5; 24:11, 17. The other seven are substantival (cf. Luke 22:49; John 6:64; Acts 20:22; 1 Cor 15:37; Heb 3:5; 13:17; 1 Pet 3:13).

[58] The aorist participle can, on a rare occasion, have a telic force in Hellenistic Greek, because the future participle was not normally a viable choice in the conversational and vulgar dialect (so A. T. Robertson, "The Aorist Participle for Purpose in the Κοινή," *JTS* 25 [1924] 286-89). Cf. Acts 25:13 (*v.l.* is a future participle, as would be expected).

[59] 1 Cor 4:14 is an unusual exception.

[60] Almost every instance of an adverbial πειράζων in the present tense in the NT that follows the controlling verb suggests purpose (cf. Matt 16:1; 19:3; 22:35; Mark 1:13; 8:11; 10:2; Luke 4:2; 11:16; John 6:6 [8:6, though this text is spurious]). Hebrews 11:17 is the lone exception (temporal); Jas 1:13 has the participle before the verb. Mark 1:13 and Luke 4:2 might also be exceptions (he was in "the wilderness for forty days, *being tested* by the devil"), but the relation of the testing in the wilderness to the leading of the Spirit seems to suggest that these, too, should be taken as telic. (Luke 4:1 makes sense if taken this way: "he was led by the Spirit (2) for forty days *for the purpose of being tested*." Note also Matt 4:1, where the simple infinitive of πειράζω is used to describe the Spirit's activity: ἀνήχθη εἰς τὴν ἔρημον ὑπὸ τοῦ πνεύματος **πειρασθῆναι** ὑπὸ τοῦ διαβόλου).

Luke 10:25   νομικός τις ἀνέστη **ἐκπειράζων** αὐτὸν λέγων· διδάσκαλε, τί ποιήσας ζωὴν αἰώνιον κληρονομήσω;
a certain lawyer stood up **to test** him, saying, "Teacher, what must I do to gain eternal life?"[61]

Luke 13:7   ἰδοὺ τρία ἔτη ἀφ' οὗ ἔρχομαι **ζητῶν** καρπόν
behold, for the last three years I have come **[for the purpose of] seeking** fruit

John 12:33   τοῦτο δὲ ἔλεγεν **σημαίνων** ποίῳ θανάτῳ ἤμελλεν ἀποθνήσκειν.
Now he said this **to signify** by what sort of death he would die.

Acts 3:26   ἀπέστειλεν αὐτὸν **εὐλογοῦντα** ὑμᾶς
he sent him **[for the purpose of] blessing** you

Cf. also Matt 16:1; 19:3; 22:35; 27:55; Mark 1:13; 8:11; 10:2; Luke 2:45; 4:2; 10:25; 11:16; John 6:6, 24; 18:32; 21:19; Acts 8:27; 22:5; 24:11, 17; 25:13; Rom 15:25; 1 Cor 4:14; 16:2.

➡   ### 8)   Result

a)   Definition

The participle of result is used to indicate the actual outcome or result of the action of the main verb.[62] It is similar to the participle of purpose in that it views the *end* of the action of the main verb, but it is dissimilar in that the participle of purpose also indicates or emphasizes intention or design, while result emphasizes what the action of the main verb actually accomplishes. This usage is somewhat common.[63]

b)   Amplification and Semantics

First, the participle of result is not necessarily opposed to the participle of purpose. Indeed, many result participles describe the result of an action *that was also intended*. The difference between the two, therefore, is primarily one of emphasis. The relation between purpose and result might be visually represented thus.

---

[61] The participle ποιήσας is conditional ("I shall inherit eternal life **if I do** what?"), but we have translated it like a hortatory/deliberative subjunctive for smoothness.

[62] Thanks are due to Brian Ortner for his work in Advanced Greek Grammar (Dallas Seminary, spring 1994) on this topic.

[63] Although most grammars do not include this as a separate category (*contra* Young, *Intermediate Greek*, who calls it "rather rare" and a "debated category" [157]), such is not due to linguistic principle. The result participle is usually mixed in with the attendant circumstance participle, following Burton's lead (*Moods and Tenses*, 173-74 [§449-51]). But that is looking at the matter purely from an English viewpoint. The two should be distinguished because of structural and semantic differences. See discussion under "Attendant Circumstance."

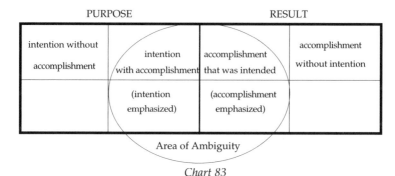

Chart 83
The Semantic Overlap of Purpose and Result Participles

Second, there are *two types* of result participle:

- *Internal* or *Logical Result:* This indicates an *implication* of the action of the controlling verb. It is thus actually *simultaneous*, giving the *logical* outcome of the verb. Thus, John 5:18: "He was calling God his own Father, [**with the result of**] **making** (ποιῶν) himself equal to God."

- *External* or *Temporal Result:* This indicates the true result of the action of the controlling verb. It is *subsequent*, stating the *chronological* outcome of the verb. Thus, Mark 9:7: "a cloud came [**with the result that it**] **covered** (ἐπισκιάζουσα) them."

c) Key to Identification

The result participle will be a *present* tense participle and will *follow* (in word order) the main verb. The student should insert the phrase *with the result of* before the participle in translation in order to see if the participle under examination is indeed a result participle.

d) Illustrations

Mark 9:7   ἐγένετο νεφέλη **ἐπισκιάζουσα** αὐτοῖς
a cloud came [**with the result that it**] **covered** them

Luke 4:15   αὐτὸς ἐδίδασκεν ἐν ταῖς συναγωγαῖς αὐτῶν **δοξαζόμενος** ὑπὸ πάντων.
He taught in their synagogues, [**with the result that he was**] **being glorified** by all.

John 5:18   πατέρα ἴδιον ἔλεγεν τὸν θεὸν ἴσον ἑαυτὸν **ποιῶν** τῷ θεῷ.
He was calling God his own Father, [**with the result of**] **making** himself equal to God.

Eph 2:15   ἵνα τοὺς δύο κτίσῃ ἐν αὐτῷ εἰς ἕνα καινὸν ἄνθρωπον **ποιῶν** εἰρήνην

   in order that he might create in himself the two into one new man,
   [with the result of] making peace

Eph 5:19-21   πληροῦσθε ἐν πνεύματι . . . (19) **λαλοῦντες** . . . **ᾄδοντες** καὶ **ψάλλοντες**
   . . . (20) **εὐχαριστοῦντες** . . . (21) **ὑποτασσόμενοι**

   Be filled with the Spirit . . . (19) **[with the result of] speaking** . . .
   singing and **making melody** . . . (20) **being thankful** . . . (21) **being
   submissive**.

> In this text the five participles are debatable. Some have suggested
> means, manner, attendant circumstance, and even imperatival! As we
> have already seen, manner is not too likely *if* we follow the axiom that
> the idea of the main verb (in this case, πληροῦσθε in 5:18) would not be
> removed if these participles were absent. As we shall see later, atten-
> dant circumstance and imperatival participles are rarely, if ever, found
> in a construction such as the one in this text. Means fits well with the
> grammar of the passage (viz., the participle of means is often used in
> the present tense *after* a present imperative). But it may not fit well with
> the theology of the Pauline epistles[64]–i.e., it would be almost inconceiv-
> able to see this text suggesting that the way in which one is to be Spirit-
> filled is by a five-step, partially mechanical formula![65] Result may fit
> well both syntactically and exegetically: Result participles are invari-
> ably present participles that follow the main verb; as well, the idea of
> result here would suggest that the way in which one measures his/her
> success in fulfilling the command of 5:18 is by the participles that fol-
> low (notice the progressive difficulty: from speaking God's word to
> being thankful for all, to being submissive to one another; such pro-
> gression would, of course, immediately suggest that this filling is not
> instantaneous and absolute but progressive and relative). There are
> other arguments for the idea of result in these participles that we will
> have to forego. Suffice it to say here that the issue is an important one
> in light of the popularity and abuse of the command in Eph 5:18 (espe-
> cially in evangelical circles).

Cf. also Mark 7:13; Heb 12:3; Jas 1:4 (possible); 2:9; 1 Pet 3:5 (unless means); 2 Pet 2:1, 6.

e. Summary of the Adverbial Participle

As we have seen, there are eight kinds of adverbial participles: temporal, manner, means, cause, condition, concession, purpose, and
result. Yet it should be stressed that the participle in itself means
none of these ideas. The participle in Greek follows certain contours.

---

[64] Regardless of what one thinks about the authorship of Ephesians–whether by Paul
or a disciple of his–its theology may justifiably be labeled as "Pauline."

[65] One of the remarkable currents of NT theology is a studied reserve on the *method*
of sanctification. That is, the biblical authors speak positively about the ministry of the
Spirit but typically refrain from telling how that ministry is to be implemented into the
believer's life. Most likely, their theology is rooted in Jer 31:31, 34 (NRSV): "I will make a
new covenant. . . . No longer shall they teach one another, or say to each other, 'Know the
LORD,' for they shall all know me, from the least of them to the greatest, says the LORD."
This new covenant mentality of what might be labeled a "soft mysticism" is prevalent in
the NT.

By observing the tense, word order, context, and lexemes of the verb and participle, you can usually narrow down its possibilities. Paying careful attention to the semantic situation of each adverbial participle is vital to sound exegesis.

➡ **2. Attendant Circumstance**

a. Definition

The attendant circumstance participle is used to communicate an action that, in some sense, is coordinate with the finite verb. In this respect it is not dependent, for it is translated like a verb. Yet it is still dependent *semantically,* because it cannot exist without the main verb. It is translated as a finite verb connected to the main verb by *and.* The participle then, in effect, "piggy-backs" on the mood of the main verb. This usage is relatively common, but widely misunderstood.[66]

b. Clarification

First, we are treating this participle as a *dependent* verbal participle because it never stands alone. That is, an attendant circumstance will always be related to a finite verb. Although it is translated as a finite verb, it derives its "mood" (semantically, not syntactically) from that of the main verb.

Second, it is important to argue from *sense* rather than from translation. In order to see more clearly what the sense of a participle will be, we need to apply the following criterion: If a participle makes good sense when treated as an adverbial participle, we should not seek to treat it as attendant circumstance. This will reduce the instances to those that are undisputed. From that we can extrapolate a "profile" as it were of what this participle should look like.

Third, the confusion has arisen over a couple of things: loose translation[67] and mixing the participle of result in with the attendant circumstance participle (see earlier discussion).

c. Validation

Is the attendant circumstance participle valid? Some grammarians deny its validity; others see it very frequently. In our view, it is both clearly valid and *relatively* frequent. It should be noted that what is

---

[66] Thanks are due to Clay Porr and Jeff Baldwin for their work in Advanced Greek Grammar at Dallas Seminary (spring 1990 and spring 1991, respectively) on the topic of the attendant circumstance participle.

[67] The NIV is notorious for translating many participles as though they were attendant circumstance. This is undoubtedly due more to modern conversational English (on which level the NIV belongs) than to the translators' understanding of the Greek text.

at stake is the interpretation of scores of passages. Hence, the discussion in this section is unusually long.

Consider, for example, Matt 2:13. The angel is speaking to Joseph and says: ἐγερθεὶς παράλαβε τὸ παιδίον καὶ τὴν μητέρα αὐτοῦ καὶ φεῦγε ("Rise and take the child and his mother and flee!"). There is really only one good possibility for ἐγερθείς as an adverbial participle–temporal. (The others, as you can think through them for yourself, make little sense.) If temporal, then it is more than likely antecedent to the action of the main verbs (though in close proximity). But such an idea would not convey the urgency of the command (*"After you have arisen, take . . . and go . . ."*). Such a translation would suggest that the time when Joseph was to rise was an option; it was only that once he did rise, he was to obey the angelic command. The attendant circumstance participle fits far better here–the *mood* of the two main verbs is picked up by the participle (*"Rise and take . . . and go . . ."*). It is apparent that Joseph was commanded not only to take his family and flee, but also to rise immediately.

Matthew 2:13 illustrates several important criteria for the attendant circumstance participle: (1) The context made it clear that no adverbial participial category would do justice to the use of this participle; (2) the context made it equally clear that the true force of this participle (semantically) was that of an imperative–it was *part* of the command; and (3) the participle was related to an imperative. Finally, one should note that in Matt 2:14, we see Joseph's response: ἐγερθεὶς παρέλαβεν . . . νυκτός (he rose and took . . . during the night"). The evangelist uses νυκτός to emphasize immediate obedience to the angelic vision. In other words, the participle in both v 13 and v 14 is attendant circumstance. The difference between the verses is that the mood of the main verb has changed and therefore the "mood" of the participle changes, too.

In conclusion, we can say that Matt 2:13-14 is a clear passage in which the attendant circumstance participle is valid and is valid with both imperatives and indicatives as main verbs.[68]

d. Structure and Semantics

1) Structure

In the NT (as well as other ancient Greek literature) certain structural patterns emerge regarding the attendant circumstance participle. These are not absolute. We might, however, say that they follow a "90% rule." That is to say, *all five of the following features occur in at least 90% of the instances of attendant*

---

[68] Occasionally a particle is used to show the urgency of the whole construction (as in Luke 17:7: εὐθέως παρελθὼν ἀνάπεσε ["**Come in** right now **and** sit down (to eat)"]).

circumstance. The conclusion from this is that if these five features are not present (or if one or two of them are not present), to label a participle as attendant circumstance needs strong corroborative evidence. It is not impossible, of course, but one should double-check the other possibilities before he/she so tags the participle. The five features are:

- The tense of the participle is usually *aorist.*

- The tense of the main verb is usually *aorist.*[69]

- The mood of the main verb is usually *imperative* or *indicative.*[70]

- The participle will *precede the main verb*–both in word order and time of event (though usually there is a very close proximity).

- Attendant circumstance participles occur frequently in narrative literature, infrequently elsewhere.[71]

These criteria can be illustrated with our example from Matt 2:13-14. Verse 13 has an aorist participle (ἐγερθείς) *followed* by an aorist imperative (παράλαβε). Verse 14 has an aorist participle (ἐγερθείς) *followed* by an aorist indicative (παρέλαβεν).

2) Semantics

Two things should be noted about the semantics of this participle. First, the attendant circumstance participle has something of an *ingressive* force to it. That is, it is often used to introduce a new action or a shift in the narrative. This contrasts with the adverbial participles and becomes a key for identifying this usage.

Second, the relative semantic weight in such constructions is that *a greater emphasis is placed on the action of the main verb than*

---

[69] The historical present, however, does occur from time to time. See discussion and texts in note at Matt 9:18 below.

[70] Although the subjunctive does sometimes occur, especially the hortatory subjunctive. (See discussion and examples at Heb 12:1.)

[71] Some of the features are more central than others. Specifically, (1) all or almost all attendant circumstance participles are aorist; (2) almost all attendant circumstance participles come before the verb; (3) most aorist participle + aorist indicative constructions are adverbial, though many are attendant circumstance; (4) in narrative literature, in almost all of the aorist participle + aorist *imperative* constructions, the participle is attendant circumstance (but see Luke 22:32).

These first two features, of course, do not *necessitate* that a participle be attendant circumstance. But the fourth feature is stated to mean just this. In the least, since virtually all aorist participle + aorist *imperative* constructions involve attendant circumstance participles, this casts the most serious doubt on translations of πορευθέντες in Matt 28:19 as "having gone," or worse, "as you are going."

on the particle. That is, the participle is something of a prerequisite before the action of the main verb can occur. Joseph had to get up before he could take Mary and Jesus to Egypt. But the getting up was not the main event–it was leaving town that counted![72]

e. **Illustrations**

1) **Clear Examples**

Matt 9:13   **πορευθέντες** δὲ μαθέτε τί ἐστιν. . .
Now **go and** learn what this means. . .

Matt 9:18a   ἰδοὺ ἄρχων εἷς **προσελθὼν** προσεκύνει αὐτῷ
Behold, a ruler **came and** bowed down before him
> This is an example of an aorist participle followed by an imperfect indicative. Such does occur rarely. Much more common is a *historical present* as the main verb.[73]

Matt 9:18b   ἡ θυγάτηρ μου ἄρτι ἐτελεύτησεν· ἀλλὰ **ἐλθὼν** ἐπίθες τὴν χεῖρά σου ἐπ᾽ αὐτήν, καὶ ζήσεται.
My daughter has just now died, but **come and** place your hand on her and she will live.
> As is almost always the case, the main idea is found in the main verb ("place [your hand on her]"); the coming is a necessary prerequisite, however.

Matt 28:7   ταχὺ **πορευθεῖσαι** εἴπατε τοῖς μαθηταῖς αὐτοῦ ὅτι ἠγέρθη ἀπὸ τῶν νεκρῶν
Go quickly **and** tell his disciples that [Jesus] has been raised from the dead.

Luke 5:11   **ἀφέντες** πάντα ἠκολούθησαν αὐτῷ
they left everything **and** followed him
> Had Luke used two indicatives there would have been more equal weight to them. With the attendant circumstance participle, however, the focus of the text is not on what the disciples left (such was necessary to follow an itinerant preacher), but on their following Jesus.

Luke 5:14   **ἀπελθὼν** δεῖξον σεαυτὸν τῷ ἱερεῖ
Go and show yourself to the priest

Luke 16:6   **καθίσας** ταχέως γράψον πεντήκοντα[74]
Sit down quickly **and** write fifty

---

[72] If an author wished to make both commands truly coordinate, he would normally join two imperatives with καί. This occurs 179 times in the NT.

[73] Cf., e.g., Matt 15:12; Mark 5:40; 8:1; 10:1; 14:67; Luke 11:26; 14:32. This fact tends to support the view that the aspect collapses in historical presents.

[74] καθίσας ταχέως is omitted in D.

Luke 17:19 ἀναστὰς πορεύου
            Rise and go

> Here we have the infrequent structure of aorist participle with *present* imperative.

Acts 5:5   ἀκούων δὲ ὁ Ἀνανίας τοὺς λόγους τούτους **πεσὼν** ἐξέψυξεν
            but when Ananias heard these words, **he fell down and** died

> The participle at the front of the clause is present and temporal; the following aorist participle is attendant circumstance. Again, the semantics here follow the normal contours of this participial usage: The main point was not that Ananias fell down but that he died.

Acts 10:13 **ἀναστάς,** Πέτρε, θῦσον καὶ φάγε.
            Rise, Peter, **and** kill and eat.

Acts 16:9   **διαβὰς** εἰς Μακεδονίαν βοήθησον ἡμῖν
            Come over to Macedonia **and** help us

Heb 12:1   ὄγκον **ἀποθέμενοι** πάντα. . . τρέχωμεν
            let us lay aside every burden . . . **and** run

> Notice that we see two of the five structural guidelines in this text (aorist participle preceding main verb). The three differences here are: (1) the tense of the main verb is present, (2) the mood of the main verb is subjunctive;[75] and (3) this is not narrative. Nevertheless, the primary criterion for determining whether a particular participle is attendant circumstance is sense, not structure. And the sense fits well here: The participle derives its "mood" from that of the main verb (a hortatory subjunctive–which is nevertheless *semantically* equivalent to an imperative). No adverbial participial category does justice to this text.[76]

Cf. also Matt 2:8, 20; 9:6; 11:4; 17:7, 27; 21:2; 22:13; 28:7; Luke 4:40; 7:22; 13:32; 14:10; 17:7, 14; 19:5; 30; 22:8; Acts 1:24; 2:23; 5:6; 9:11; 10:20; 11:7.

2) Disputed Examples

Eph 5:19-21 πληροῦσθε ἐν πνεύματι. . . (19) **λαλοῦντες**. . . **ᾄδοντες** καὶ **ψάλλοντες**. . .
             (20) **εὐχαριστοῦντες**. . . (21) **ὑποτασσόμενοι**
             be filled by the Spirit. . . (19) **and speak**. . . **and sing and make melody** . . . (20) **and be thankful** . . . (21) **and be submissive**

> Some exegetes take these participles to indicate attendant circumstance. But attendant circumstance participles are rarely, if ever, found in a construction such as the one in this text (not only are the participles following the verb, but both main verb and participles are present tense). A distinction needs to be made between result and attendant circumstance. Seeing no distinction between the two would make the participles coordinate commands, while taking them as result would

---

[75] For other examples of an attendant circumstance participle attached to a subjunctive, cf. Matt 2:8; 4:9; 13:28; 27:64; Mark 5:23; 6:37; 16:1; Luke 7:3. My colleague, Elliott Greene, is to be thanked for supplying these examples.

[76] Although temporal might do this justice ("after laying aside every burden . . . let us run"), since the participle introduces a new action into the discourse it is best taken as attendant circumstance.

regard them more as the overflow of one who is Spirit-filled (cf. Gal 5:22-23 for a similar idea).

Mt 28:19-20 **πορευθέντες** οὖν μαθητεύσατε πάντα τὰ ἔθνη, βαπτίζοντες αὐτοὺς εἰς τὸ ὄνομα τοῦ πατρὸς καὶ τοῦ υἱοῦ καὶ τοῦ ἁγίου πνεύματος, (20) διδάσκοντες

Go, therefore, **and** make disciples of all the nations, baptizing them in the name of the Father and of the Son and of the Holy Spirit, (20) teaching. . .

> Several observations are in order. First, notice that the first participle, πορευθέντες, fits the structural pattern for the attendant circumstance participle: aorist participle preceding an aorist main verb (in this case, imperative).
>
> Second, there is no good grammatical ground for giving the participle a mere temporal idea. To turn πορευθέντες into an adverbial participle is to turn the Great Commission into the Great Suggestion! Virtually all instances in narrative literature of aorist participle + aorist *imperative* involve an attendant circumstance participle. In Matthew, in particular, every other instance of the aorist participle of πορεύομαι followed by an aorist main verb (either indicative or imperative) is clearly attendant circumstance.[77]
>
> Third, we must first read this commission in its historical context, not from the perspective of a late twentieth-century reader. These apostles of the soon-to-be inaugurated church did not move from Jerusalem until after the martyrdom of Stephen. The reason for this reticence was due, in part at least, to their Jewish background. As Jews, they were ethnocentric in their evangelism (bringing prospective proselytes to Jerusalem); now as Christians, they were to be *ektocentric*, bringing the gospel to those who were non-Jews. In many ways, the book of Acts is a detailed account of how these apostles accomplished the command of Matt 28:19-20.[78]
>
> Finally, the other two participles (βαπτίζοντες, διδάσκοντες) should not be taken at attendant circumstance. First, they do not fit the normal pattern for attendant circumstance participles (they are present tense and follow the main verb). And second, they obviously make good sense as participles of *means*; i.e., the means by which the disciples were to make disciples was to baptize and then to teach.

3. Indirect Discourse

a. Definition

An anarthrous participle in the *accusative* case, in conjunction with an accusative noun or pronoun, sometimes indicates indirect discourse after a verb of perception or communication.[79] This usage is fairly common (especially in Luke and Paul), but less so in Hellenistic than in classical Greek overall.

---

[77]Cf. Matt 2:8; 9:13; 11:4; 17:27; 21:6; 22:15; 25:16; 26:14; 27:66; 28:7.

[78] For further information on the use of πορευθέντες here, cf. Cleon Rogers, "The Great Commission," *BSac* 130 (1973) 258-62.

[79] Robertson, *Grammar*, 1123. Cf. also Williams, *Grammar Notes*, 57.

b. **Amplification**

As with the infinitive of indirect discourse, the participle of indirect discourse retains the tense of the direct discourse.[80]

c. **Illustrations**

Acts 7:12   ἀκούσας δὲ Ἰακὼβ **ὄντα** σιτία εἰς Αἴγυπτον
             when Jacob heard that **there was** grain in Egypt

Phil 2:3   ἀλλήλους ἡγούμενοι **ὑπερέχοντας** ἑαυτῶν
             by regarding one another **as more important** than yourselves

2 John 7   ὁμολογοῦντες Ἰησοῦν Χριστὸν **ἐρχόμενον** ἐν σαρκί
             confessing Jesus Christ **coming** in the flesh (*or* confessing Jesus
             Christ **to have come** in the flesh; *or* confessing **that** Jesus Christ **has
             come** in the flesh)

Cf. also Luke 14:18; John 4:39 (perhaps); Acts 7:12; 9:21; 17:16; 2 Cor 8:22; Rev 9:1.

4. **Complementary**

a. **Definition**

The complementary participle *completes* the thought of another verb. It is especially used in combination with a verb suggesting a consummative (e.g., "stop" [παύω]) or sometimes a progressive (e.g., "continue" [ἐπιμένω]) idea.[81] The idiom is rare in the NT.

b. **Illustrations**

Matt 11:1   ὅτε ἐτέλεσεν ὁ Ἰησοῦς **διατάσσων**
             when Jesus *finished* **teaching**

Acts 5:42   οὐκ ἐπαύοντο **διδάσκοντες** καὶ **εὐαγγελιζόμενοι** τὸν χριστόν Ἰησοῦν
             they did not *cease* **teaching** and **proclaiming** that the Messiah was
             Jesus

Acts 12:16   ὁ Πέτρος ἐπέμενεν **κρούων**
             Peter *kept on* **knocking**

Eph 1:16   οὐ παύομαι **εὐχαριστῶν**
             I *do* not *cease* **being thankful**

Cf. also Matt 6:16; Luke 5:4; John 8:7 (*v.l.*); Acts 6:13; 13:10; 20:31; 21:32; Gal 6:9; Col 1:9; 2 Thess 3:13; Heb 10:2.

---

[80] Robertson, *Grammar*, 1122.

[81] In classical Greek an ingressive notion with ἄρχομαι + participle occurs. This idiom is not found in the NT.

➡ 5. **Periphrastic**

a. **Definition**

An anarthrous participle can be used with a verb of being (such as εἰμί or ὑπάρχω) to form a finite verbal idea. This participle is called periphrastic because it is a *round-about* way of saying what could be expressed by a single verb. As such, it more naturally corresponds to English: ἦν ἐσθίων means *he was eating*, just as ἤσθιεν does. This usage is common with the present participle and perfect participle, but not with other tenses.[82]

b. **Structure and Semantics**

First, regarding semantics, in classical Greek this construction was used to highlight aspectual force. By the Hellenistic era, and particularly in the NT, such emphasis is often, if not usually, lost.[83]

Second, as to structure, the following should be noted. The participle is almost always nominative case and usually follows the verb.[84] And, as Dana-Mantey succinctly stated long ago,

> This mode of expression, common to all languages, is extensively employed in Greek. It occurs in all the voices and tenses, though rare in the aorist. . . . Certain tense forms in Greek were expressed exclusively by the periphrastic construction; namely, the perfect middle-passive subjunctive and optative. As the finite verb, εἰμί is generally used, though also γίνομαι and ὑπάρχω, and possibly ἔχω in the perfect (cf. Lk. 14:18; 19:20) and pluperfect (Lk. 13:6). The periphrastic imperfect is the form most common in the New Testament.[85]

Finally, various verb-participle combinations are used to constitute a single finite verb tense, as noted in the following table.

---

[82] Boyer ("Participles," 172) counts 153 present participles, 115 perfect participles, and possibly two aorist participles ("very doubtful") in the construction (in Luke 23:19 and 2 Cor 5:19).

[83] Another issue related to the semantics has to do with distinguishing this participial use with the predicate adjective participle. This is particularly problematic with perfect passive participles (in which the simple adjectival idea seems more pronounced than with other participles). See Boyer, "Participles," 167-68, 172-73, for discussion of principles. Essentially he argues that context helps, in particular when the participle is thrown in with adjectives.

[84] There are two examples in the accusative case and 28 instances in which it precedes the verb, according to Boyer, "Participles," 172.

[85] Dana-Mantey, 231.

Finite Verb (of εἰμί)	+	Participle	=	Finite Tense Equivalent
Present	+	Present	=	Present
Imperfect	+	Present	=	Imperfect
Future	+	Present	=	Future
Present	+	Perfect	=	Perfect
Imperfect	+	Perfect	=	Pluperfect

Table 11

The Forms of the Periphrastic Participle

c. Illustrations

1) Present Periphrastic

2 Cor 9:12   ἡ διακονία . . . ἐστιν **προσαναπληροῦσα** τὰ ὑστερήματα τῶν ἁγίων
[this] ministry . . . is **supplying** the needs of the saints

Col 1:6   καθὼς καὶ ἐν παντὶ τῷ κόσμῳ ἐστὶν **καρποφορούμενον**
just as in all the world it is **bearing fruit**

Cf. also Matt 5:25; Mark 5:41; Luke 19:17; John 1:41; Acts 4:36; 2 Cor 2:17; 6:14; 9:12; Col 2:23; Jas 1:17 (possible).[86]

2) Imperfect Periphrastic

Matt 7:29   ἦν **διδάσκων** αὐτούς
he was **teaching** them

Mark 10:32   ἦσαν . . . **ἀναβαίνοντες** . . . καὶ ἦν **προάγων** αὐτοὺς ὁ Ἰησοῦς
they were **going up** . . . and Jesus was **going before** them

Cf. also Matt 19:22; Mark 1:22; 5:5; 9:4; Luke 4:20; 19:47; John 1:28; 13:23; Acts 1:10; 2:2; 8:1; 22:19; Gal 1:22.

3) Future Periphrastic

Because of the combination of the future finite verb and the present participle, the aspect of this use of the future is progressive (unlike its simple tense-form counterpart). This category is rare.[87]

---

[86] Jas 1:17 means either "every perfect gift is from above, coming down . . ." or "every perfect gift from above is **coming** down" (πᾶν δώρημα τέλειον ἄνωθέν ἐστιν **καταβαῖνον**), the latter treating the participle as periphrastic.

[87] Fanning (Verbal Aspect, 317-18) lists eleven legitimate future periphrastics (which use the future indicative of εἰμί and a present participle), one being a v.l. found in codex D (see references above). All of these have an internal aspect, but such is not due to the future per se, but to their combination with the present participles.

Mark 13:25 καὶ οἱ ἀστέρες ἔσονται. . . **πίπτοντες**[88]
and the stars *will be* **falling**

1 Cor 14:9 πῶς γνωσθήσεται τὸ λαλούμενον; ἔσεσθε γὰρ εἰς ἀέρα **λαλοῦντες**.
How will he know what is said? For *you will be* **speaking** into the air.

Cf. also Matt 10:22; 24:9; Mark 13:13; Luke 1:20; 5:10; 21:17, 24; 22:69; Acts 6:4 (in D).

4) Perfect Periphrastic

Luke 12:6 ἓν ἐξ αὐτῶν οὐκ *ἔστιν* **ἐπιλελησμένον** ἐνώπιον τοῦ θεοῦ.
Not one of [the sparrows] *is* **forgotten** before God.

2 Cor 4:3 εἰ δὲ καὶ *ἔστιν* **κεκαλυμμένον** τὸ εὐαγγέλιον ἡμῶν
But even if our gospel *is* **veiled** [or *has become* **veiled**]

Eph 2:8 τῇ γὰρ χάριτί *ἐστε* **σεσῳσμένοι**
For by grace *you have been* **saved** [or *you are* **saved**][89]

Cf. also Luke 14:8; 20:6; 23:15; John 3:27; 6:31, 45; 12:14; 16:24; 17:23; Acts 21:33; Rom 7:14; Eph 2:5; Heb 4:2; Jas 5:15; 1 John 1:4.

5) Pluperfect Periphrastic

Matt 9:36 *ἦσαν* **ἐσκυλμένοι** καὶ **ἐρριμμένοι** ὡσεὶ πρόβατα μὴ ἔχοντα ποιμένα
they were (or *had become*) **weary** and **scattered**, as sheep who do not have a shepherd

Acts 21:29 *ἦσαν* γὰρ **προεωρακότες** Τρόφιμον
for they *had* **previously seen** Trophimus

Cf. also Matt 26:43; Mark 15:46; Luke 2:26; 4:16; 5:17; 8:2; 9:45; 15:24; 23:53; John 3:24; 19:11, 19, 41; Acts 8:16; 13:48; Gal 4:3.[90]

6. Redundant (a.k.a. Pleonastic)

a. Definition

A verb of saying (or sometimes thinking) can be used with a participle with basically the same meaning (as in ἀποκριθεὶς εἶπεν). Because such an idiom is foreign to English, many modern translations simply render the controlling verb.

b. Clarification

Some call this a pleonastic (=redundant) or appositional participle. In a sense, it is a subset of the participle of *means*, for it defines the

---

[88] For πίπτοντες a few MSS read πεσοῦνται (so W Λ^C 213 565 700).

[89] See discussion of this text in the chapter on the perfect.

[90] Especially (passive) pluperfect periphrastics can be confused with predicate adjective participles (e.g., Rev 17:4). Some of these examples might better fit the adjectival category.

action of the main verb. For the most part, it is probably due to a Semitic idiom. It occurs almost exclusively in the Synoptic Gospels.

c. Illustrations

Luke 12:17　διελογίζετο ἐν ἑαυτῷ **λέγων**
he was thinking within himself, **saying**

Matt 11:25　**ἀποκριθεὶς** ὁ Ἰησοῦς εἶπεν
Jesus, **answering**, said

> The construction ἀποκριθεὶς εἶπεν "became to such an extent an empty formula that it is even sometimes used when there is nothing preceding to which an 'answer' can be referred. . . ."[91]

Cf. also Matt 11:25; 12:38; 13:3, 11, 37; 15:22; 17:4; 26:23; 28:5; Mark 9:5; 11:14; Luke 5:22; 7:22; 13:2; 19:40.

B. Independent Verbal Participles

Included in this category are those participles that function as though they were finite verbs and are not dependent on any verb in the context for their mood (thus, distinct from attendant circumstance). The independent verbal participles may function as either indicatives or imperatives, though both of these are extremely rare.

✝ ### 1. As an Imperative (Imperatival)

a. Definition

The participle may function just like an imperative. This use of the participle is not to be attached to any verb in the context, but is grammatically independent. The imperatival participle is quite rare.

b. Clarification and Exegetical Significance

"In general it may be said that no participle should be explained in this way that can properly be connected with a finite verb."[92] This is an important point and one that more than one commentator has forgotten.

c. Illustrations

1) Clear Examples

Rom 12:9　**ἀποστυγοῦντες** τὸ πονηρόν, **κολλώμενοι** τῷ ἀγαθῷ
hate the evil, **cleave** to the good

---

[91] Zerwick, *Biblical Greek*, 127.
[92] Robertson, *Grammar*, 1134.

1 Pet 2:18   οἱ οἰκέται, **ὑποτασσόμενοι**. . . τοῖς δεσπόταις

Servants, **submit yourselves**. . . to your masters

Cf. also Rom 12:10, 11, 12, 13, 14, 16, 17, 18, 19; 2 Cor 8:24; 1 Pet 3:7. It is to be noted that *most* of the NT instances of this phenomenon will be found in Rom 12 or 1 Peter.

2) Doubtful Examples

Eph 5:19-21 **λαλοῦντες**. . . **ᾄδοντες**. . . **ψάλλοντες**. . . **(20) εὐχαριστοῦντες**. . . **(21) ὑποτασσόμενοι**

speaking. . . singing. . . making melody. . . (20) being thankful. . . (21) be submissive

> Although most would consider the first four of these participles as adverbial (see previous discussions of this verse), many, including recent editions of the Greek NT, would consider the last participle as imperatival. Such is doubtful, especially since it too is a present anarthrous participle, as are the first four. The basic rule here is simply this: If a participle can be identified as dependent (i.e., if it can at all be attached to a verb), it should be so considered. Furthermore, it seems that there are two primary reasons why some have considered ὑπο- τασσόμενοι as imperatival here: (1) The original wording of 5:22 apparently lacked the imperative ὑποτάσσεσθε,[93] leaving the verb to be supplied from the preceding line and thus intrinsically connecting v 21 with the following section of material; and (2) it is separated by several words from the preceding participle, which fact seemingly connects it with the following paragraph rather than with the preceding.
>
> In response to this, note the following: (1) Although there is an obvious connection between vv 21 and 22, v 21 can just as easily function as a hinge between the two sections. The thought of vv 15-21 flows right into 5:22-6:9. This section on the (extended) family, whether it starts at v 21 or v 22, is the only major section in the body of Ephesians to begin *without* a conjunction. It is as if the instruction in the former section is meant to be "ringing in the ears" of the hearers as they turn to the issue of the family.[94] Consequently, any dramatic break between the two is overdrawn. The participle belongs equally to both. (2) On a syntactical and stylistic level, this view does not take into account the semantic situation in which an imperatival participle is found (which, among other things, indicates that this is a very rare usage), nor the usage of dependent participles in this letter in particular (cf. Eph 1:13-14, for example, where several dependent participles are strung along). To view any of these participles as imperatival is to view the passage from the English point of view only, ignoring the Greek.

[93] Although the only Greek witnesses to lack any verb are 𝔓[46] and B, the internal reasons are compelling for the omission.

[94] Apparently the reason for no conjunction is that 5:22-6:9 does not advance the argument of the book, but is in fact a parenthesis to it. Without elaborating here, the argument of Ephesians appears to be framed by a chiasmus, focusing on chapter 2 and developing out from there. One implicit question deriving from 2:11-22 (the doctrinal heart of the book) remains to be answered: If there is now spiritual equality between Jew and Gentile in the body of Christ, are all social hierarchies eradicated? 5:22-6:9 answers that question with a resounding "No."

Eph 4:1-3　Παρακαλῶ ὑμᾶς . . . περιπατῆσαι . . . (2) **ἀνεχόμενοι** ἀλλήλων . . . (3) **σπουδάζοντες** τηρεῖν τὴν ἑνότητα

I urge you . . . to walk . . . (2) **forbear** one another . . . (3) **strive** to maintain the unity

> Barth states categorically that "the imperative mood of the added verb 'be' and of the word 'bear' is suggested by the dominating term 'I beseech you' and by the special character of the Greek participle 'bearing'."[95] He assumes "the imperative mood of the participle" in v 3.[96] *BDF* and Robertson also consider these participles to be imperatival,[97] in spite of their warning that such will not occur in contexts in which the participle *can* be linked dependently to a finite verbal form (such as παρακαλῶ . . . περιπατῆσαι in v 1). Moule apparently takes these participles as imperatival because they are in the nom. case[98]–a reason probably assumed by the others who hold this view. Indeed, to see them as other than imperatival requires an explanation about their case: How can we say that these *nominative* participles are adverbial and dependent if they lack concord with ὑμᾶς?

> These participles are, most likely, dependent. The reason for their being nom. is as follows. παρακαλῶ ὑμᾶς περιπατῆσαι is a complete verbal idea expressed by an indicative and infinitive. The infinitive is complementary, completing the thought of the main verb. It would be possible to express this same idea (though more forcefully, less politely) by a simple imperative: περιπατήσατε. Diagrammed, the two clauses would look like this:

(ἐγώ)	παρακαλῶ περιπατῆσαι	ὑμᾶς	=	(ὑμεῖς)	περιπατήσατε

> Thus we have an instance of *constructio ad sensum* (construction according to sense rather than according to strict grammar "rules"). The participles in 4:2-3 are nominative because they agree with the *sense* of the "command," even though it is not syntactically expressed as an imperative. Consequently, these two participles are dependent and adverbial. More than likely they are participles of *means* (remember that present tense participles of means usually follow present or aorist imperatives; here, they follow the *sense* of an imperative): They define how the readers are to walk.

> The resultant idea in this passage, then, is as follows: The author sums up in οὖν (4:1) the indicatives of the faith and commands that some action be taken based on them. The action is "walk worthily of the calling. . . ." The means by which this command is to be carried is twofold: (1) negatively, by "forbearing one another in love"; and (2) positively, "by striving to maintain [not originate] the unity of the Spirit." Ephesians 4:1-3, then, gives us the author's sum of what this little epistle is all about.

Other passages often cited as having imperatival participles that should be seriously questioned include: Eph 3:17; 6:18; Col 2:2; 3:13, 16; 1 Pet 5:7; et al.[99]

---

[95] Barth, *Ephesians* (AB) 2.427.

[96] Ibid., 428.

[97] *BDF*, 245; Robertson, *Grammar*, 946.

[98] Moule, *Idiom Book*, 105.

[99] Cf. Smyth, *Greek Grammar*, 478, for more help on the imperatival participle.

2. As an Indicative (Independent Proper or Absolute)

a. Definition

The participle can stand alone in a declarative sense as the only verb in a clause or sentence. In such instances, the participle may be treated as an indicative verb. This use of the participle is quite rare.

b. Clarification and Amplification

This usage is apparently due to a Semitic influence, for such occurs in Hebrew[100] and Aramaic.[101] (Its occurrence in the Apocalypse is testimony to this view.) It is doubtful that it occurs in classical Greek.[102]

c. Illustrations

Rev 1:16   καὶ **ἔχων** ἐν τῇ δεξιᾷ χειρὶ αὐτοῦ[103]
           and **he had** in his right hand

Rev 19:12 **ἔχων** ὄνομα
           he had a name

Cf. also Rom 5:11; 12:6; 2 Cor 4:8; 5:6; 9:11; Rev 4:7; 10:2; 11:1; 12:2; 17:5; 21:12, 14, 19 for some other *possible* examples.

By way of conclusion on the independent participle (both imperative and indicative), we wholeheartedly affirm the sober assessment by Brooks and Winbery: "*Certainly no participle should be explained as an independent participle if there is any other way to explain it.*"[104]

III. The Participle Absolute

In this final section on participles, we will be dealing with participles that occur in particular case constructions (known as nominative absolute and genitive absolute). These participles do, however, fit under the above two broad categories (adjectival and verbal). They are treated here separately because they involve structural clues related to their cases and, to some degree, they express an *additional* nuance beyond what has been described in the above two major categories.

---

[100] GKC, 357-60.

[101] Rosenthal, *A Grammar of Biblical Aramaic*, 55.

[102] Smyth, *Greek Grammar*, 477.

[103] Instead of the participle, a few MSS have the imperfect indicative εἶχεν (so ℵ* 172 424 2018 2019 2344 *et plu*).

[104] Brooks and Winbery, 138 (italics in original).

A. Nominative Absolute

1. Definition

The nominative absolute participle is in reality simply a substantival participle that fits the case description of *nominativus pendens*. Although it is called "nominative absolute," it is not to be confused with the *case* category of nominative absolute. (This label, which has been the cause of much confusion, probably is derived from the fact this participle has some affinity with the genitive absolute participle.) To refresh your memory, the *nominativus pendens* (pendent nominative) "consists in the enunciation of the logical (not grammatical) subject at the beginning of the sentence, followed by a sentence in which that subject is taken up by a pronoun in the case required by the syntax."[105]

2. Clarification

Although this participle has *some* affinity with the genitive absolute participle, the *nominative* absolute participle is always *substantival* while the genitive absolute participle is always *adverbial* or, at least, dependent-verbal.[106]

3. Illustrations

John 7:38   ὁ **πιστεύων** εἰς ἐμέ . . . ποταμοὶ ἐκ τῆς κοιλίας αὐτοῦ ῥεύσουσιν
              the **one who believes** in me . . . rivers will flow out of his belly

Rev 3:21   ὁ **νικῶν** δώσω αὐτῷ καθίσαι
              the **one who conquers**, to him I will give to sit

Cf. also Mark 7:19; 12:40; Rev 2:26; 3:12.

➡ B. Genitive Absolute

1. Definition

In defining the genitive absolute participial construction, we have two options: We can define it *structurally* or we can definite it *semantically*. We shall in fact define it both ways in order that you might be able to identify the construction and, once identified, understand its semantic force.

a. Structure

Structurally, the genitive absolute consists of the following:

---

[105] Zerwick, *Biblical Greek*, 9.

[106] In light of this, it is somewhat puzzling to see grammarians such as Robertson (*Grammar*, 1130) and Funk (*Beginning-Intermediate Grammar*, 2:675) subsume this participle under the circumstantial participle, even though they recognize that it is never circumstantial!

1) a noun or pronoun in the genitive case (though this is sometimes absent);

2) a genitive *anarthrous* participle (always);

3) the entire construction at the front of a sentence (usually).

b. Semantics

Semantically, there are again three items to notice, once the structure has been identified (note that the above stated structure is not limited to the genitive absolute construction):

1) This construction is unconnected with the rest of the sentence (i.e., its subject–the genitive noun or pronoun–is different from the subject of the main clause);

2) the participle is *always* adverbial (circumstantial) or, at least, dependent-verbal (i.e., it cannot be an adjectival or substantival participle);

3) the participle is normally (about 90% of the time) *temporal*,[107] though it can on occasion express any of the adverbial ideas.[108]

2. Illustrations

Matt 9:18   ταῦτα αὐτοῦ **λαλοῦντος** . . . ἄρχων εἷς ἐλθὼν προσεκύνει αὐτῷ
while he was saying these things, . . . a certain ruler came and bowed down before him

Rom 7:3   **ζῶντος** τοῦ ἀνδρὸς . . . γένηται ἀνδρὶ ἑτέρῳ
while her husband **is still alive** . . . she becomes another man's [wife]

> This is a *somewhat* rare example in that it is found in the epistles (cf. also Eph 2:20). Most gen. absolutes are in the Gospels and Acts.

John 5:13   Ἰησοῦς ἐξένευσεν ὄχλου **ὄντος** ἐν τῷ τόπῳ
Jesus departed **while** a crowd **was** in that place

> This text is a little unusual in that the gen. absolute construction comes at the *end* of the sentence. ὄχλου, however, could be taken as a gen. of separation and ὄντος as adjectival: "from the crowd which was in that place."

Cf. also Matt 8:1, 5, 16, 28; 9:32, 33; 17:14, 22, 24, 26; 18:24, 25 (causal here); 20:29; 21:10, 23; 22:41; 24:3; Mark 5:2, 18, 21, 35; 15:33; Luke 11:14; 18:36, 40; John 4:51; Acts 13:2; 1 Pet 3:20.

---

[107] Cf. Henry Anselm Scomp, "The Case Absolute in the New Testament," *BSac* (January 1902) 76-84; (April 1902) 325-40.

[108] "All the varieties of the circumstantial participle can appear in the absolute participle" (Robertson, *Grammar*, 1130).

Introduction to Greek Clauses

Overview of Chapter

I. Introduction

A. Approach of this Chapter

This chapter is intended to offer little more than an outline of basic clause structure in the NT. Because the specific categories are treated elsewhere in the grammar, a minimal treatment is required here.[1]

B. Definition

Clauses are units of thought forming part of a compound or complex sentence. Each clause normally contains a subject and predicate or a nonfinite verbal form (i.e., either an infinitive or participle).

---

[1] Credit is due to my colleague John Grassmick for supplying the essential framework of this chapter, as well as for many of the examples and definitions.

A *compound* sentence is one in which two or more clauses are connected in a coordinate relation, known as *paratactic* structure.

A *complex* sentence is one in which one or more clauses are subordinate to another clause, known as *hypotactic* structure.

II. Two Types of Clauses

A. Independent Clause

An independent clause is a clause that is *not* subordinate to another clause.

An independent clause normally has for its nucleus: subject–verb–(object).[2] A coordinating conjunction makes two independent clauses coordinate (paratactic) to each other (thus forming a compound sentence).

- "She ate a hot dog *but* he drank milk."
- "He went to the library *and* (he) worked on his assignment."

B. Dependent Clause

A dependent clause is a clause that stands in a substantival or subordinate (hypotactic) relationship to another clause, either an independent clause or another dependent clause.

- "He went to the library *in order to* work on his assignment." (subordinate relation)
- "The student *who* went to the library completed his assignment on time." (substantival relation)

III. Classification of Independent Clauses

A. Introduced by a Coordinating Conjunction

The function of an independent clause is usually determined by the "logical" function of the *coordinating conjunction* introducing the clause.[3] This function may be:

1. *connective*, most often involving καί or δέ
2. *contrastive*, most often involving ἀλλά, δέ, or πλήν

---

[2] The subject may, of course, be embedded in the verb.

[3] See chapter on conjunctions for a more detailed discussion.

3. *correlative,* usually involving μέν . . . δέ or καί . . . καί

4. *disjunctive,* involving ἤ

5. *explanatory,* usually involving γάρ

6. *inferential,* most often involving ἄρα, διό, οὖν, or ὥστε

7. *transitional,* usually involving δέ or οὖν

B. Introduced by a Prepositional Phrase

Sometimes an independent clause will be introduced by a *prepositional phrase* whose function determines the function of the independent clause. For example:

1. διὰ τί–"why?" (cf. Matt 9:11)

2. διὰ τοῦτο–"for this reason" (cf. Matt 13:13)

3. εἰς τί–"why?" (cf. Mark 14:4)

4. ἐκ τούτου–"as a result of this" (cf. John 6:66)

5. ἐπὶ τοῦτο–"for this reason" (cf. Luke 4:43)

6. κατὰ τί–"how?" (cf. Luke 1:18)

7. μετὰ τοῦτο–"after this" (cf. Rev 7:1)

C. Asyndeton (no Formal Introduction)

Occasionally, an independent clause is *not* introduced by a conjunctive word or phrase. This phenomenon is known as *asyndeton* (a construction "not bound together").[4] In such cases the function of the independent clause is implied from the literary context. Asyndeton is a vivid stylistic feature that occurs often for emphasis, solemnity, or rhetorical value (staccato effect), or when there is an abrupt change in topic.[5] Thus, it is found, for example, with:

1. commands and exhortations, put forth in rapid succession (cf. John 5:8; Eph 4:26-29; Phil 4:4-6; 1 Thess 5:15-22)

2. sentences in a series (cf. Matt 5:3-11 [the beatitudes]; 2 Tim 3:15-16)

3. sentences unrelated to each other/topic shift (cf. 1 Cor 5:9)[6]

---

[4] For a general discussion of asyndeton, see *BDF*, 240-42 (§459-63).

[5] *BDF*, 241 (§462): "Although asyndeton lends solemnity and weight to the words, it is not a conscious rhetorical device. . . . There are, however, many and, in part, brilliant examples of rhetorical asyndeton in the Epistles, particularly Paul's. . . ."

IV. Classification of Dependent Clauses

Dependent clauses can be analyzed in terms of structural form or syntactical function. There are four basic structures (infinitival, participial, conjunctive, and relative clauses) and three syntactical functions (substantival, adjectival, and adverbial clauses).

A. *Structure*

Four kinds of constructions are involved in dependent clauses.

1. *Infinitival* clauses: contain an infinitive.

2. *Participial* clauses: contain a participle.

3. *Conjunctive* clauses: introduced by a subordinate conjunction.

4. *Relative* clauses: introduced by

   - a relative *pronoun* (ὅς [*who, which*])
   - a relative *adjective* (οἷος [*such as, as*], ὅσος [*as much/many as*])
   - a relative *adverb* (e.g., ὅπου [*where*], ὅτε [*when*]).

   Relative clauses can also be analyzed according to *syntactical function:*[7]

---

[6] There is also occasional asyndeton between paragraphs, though more polished writers usually avoided this. The very casualness of epistolary style sometimes created instances (*BDF*, 242 [§463]).

In Ephesians, a more polished, less emotional letter, we are surprised to find it at the beginning of the "house tables" (5:22): αἱ γυναῖκες τοῖς ἰδίοις ἀνδράσιν ὡς τῷ κυρίῳ (no other paragraph after 1:3 in the body of this letter begins without a conjunction). This verbless command borrows the participle from v 21 (ὑποτασσόμενοι), though the imperative is to be understood. The verbless command, coupled with the lack of a conjunction at v 22, has led many scholars to begin the paragraph at v 21, taking ὑποτασσόμενοι as imperatival (among texts/translations of the NT, note, e.g., NA[27], RSV, NRSV, NIV). This, however, creates more problems: The participle follows a string of present adverbial participles, all dependent on πληροῦσθε in v 18. ὑποτασσόμενοι is most naturally taken with them (in spite of its distance), especially in light of the scarcity of imperatival participles in the NT. Further, v 21 is a programmatic statement ("being submissive to one another in the fear of Christ"), applicable to all in the church in a general sense. Only by exegetical gymnastics can it be made directly applicable to both halves of the three groups in 5:22-6:9 (should parents be submissive to children?).

A better approach sees v 21 as a hinge statement that both summarizes the evidence of Spirit-filling (participle of result) and introduces a *parenthesis* to the argument of the epistle in 5:22-6:9. The house tables thus do not advance the argument per se , but answer an implicit question growing out of 2:11-22, viz., If Jew and Gentile are on equal footing in the body of Christ, does this mean that all social hierarchies are abolished? The answer seems to be a resounding "No."

[7] See chapter on "Pronouns" for a more detailed discussion of relative pronouns.

a. *Definite* relative clause

A definite relative clause contains a verb in the *indicative* mood and refers to a specific individual or group, or to a specific fact, event, or action (e.g., οὐδείς ἐστιν **ὃς** ἀφῆκεν οἰκίαν [*there is no one **who** has left home*] in Mark 10:29). The relative pronoun refers back to its *antecedent* in the sentence (a noun, pronoun, or noun phrase). It has concord with its antecedent in *number* and *gender*, but its *case* is determined by its function in the relative clause.

b. *Indefinite* relative clause

An indefinite relative clause contains a verb in the *subjunctive* mood plus the particle ἄν (or ἐάν) and refers to an unspecified individual or group, or to an event or action (e.g., ὃ ἐὰν ᾖ δίκαιον [*whatever is right*] in Matt 20:4; ὃς ἂν θέλῃ ἐν ὑμῖν εἶναι πρῶτος [*whoever wants to be first among you*] in Matt 20:27). Indefinite relative clauses have *no antecedent*.

B. *Syntactical Function*

There are three broad syntactical functions to dependent clauses: substantival, adjectival, and adverbial.

1. Substantival Clause

In this usage the dependent clause functions like a noun.

a. Structure

This function of the dependent clause can be expressed by the following structural forms:[8]

1) Substantival *infinitive* clause
2) Substantival *participial* clause
3) Substantival *conjunctive* clause
4) Substantival *relative pronoun* clause

b. Basic Uses

1) Subject

a) Substantival *infinitive* (e.g., Heb 10:31)
b) Substantival *participle* (e.g., John 3:18)
c) ὅτι + *indicative mood* (e.g., Gal 3:11)

---

[8] Each of the following structures follows a specific pattern as well. See the respective chapters for details.

      d) ἵνα + *subjunctive mood* (e.g., 1 Cor 4:2)

      e) *Relative pronoun* ὅ (e.g., Matt 13:12)

2) Predicate Nominative

      a) Substantival *infinitive* (e.g., Rom 1:12)

      b) Substantival *participle* (e.g., John 4:26)

      c) ἵνα + *subjunctive* (e.g., John 4:34)

3) Direct Object

      a) Substantival *infinitive* (e.g., 1 Tim 2:8)

      b) Substantival *participle* (e.g., Phil 3:17)

      c) ὅτι + *indicative* (e.g., John 3:33)

      d) ἵνα + *subjunctive* (e.g., Matt 12:16)

      e) *Relative pronoun* ὅ (e.g., Luke 11:6)

4) Indirect Discourse

      a) Substantival *infinitive* (e.g., Luke 24:23; 1 Cor 11:18)

      b) Substantival *participle* (e.g., Acts 7:12; 2 Thess 3:11)

      c) ὅτι + *indicative* (e.g., Matt 5:17; John 4:1)

5) Apposition

      a) Substantival *infinitive* (e.g., Jas 1:27)

      b) ὅτι + *indicative* (e.g., Luke 10:20)

      c) ἵνα + *subjunctive* (e.g. John 17:3)

2. Adjectival Clauses

The dependent clause may function like an adjective and modify a noun, noun phrase, or other substantive.

a. Structure

This function of the dependent clause can be expressed by the following structural forms:[9]

1) Epexegetical *infinitive* clause

2) (Attributive) adjectival *participial* clause

3) *Conjunctive* clause

4) *Relative pronoun* and *relative adjective* clauses

---

[9] See the respective chapters for particular structures that each of these takes (e.g., an adjectival participle is normally articular).

b. Basic Uses

Every adjectival clause *describes, explains,* or *restricts* a noun, pronoun, or other substantive. It has no functional subcategories. The following structural forms express this basic function:

1) Epexegetical *infinitive* (e.g., Rom 1:15)
2) Adjectival *participle* (e.g., 2 Cor 3:3)
3) ὅτι + *indicative mood* (e.g., Luke 8:25)
4) ἵνα + *subjunctive mood* (e.g., John 2:25)
5) *Relative pronoun* clause (e.g., Eph 6:17; 1 John 2:7)

3. Adverbial Clause

In this usage the dependent clause functions like an adverb in that it modifies a verb.

a. Structure

This function of the dependent clause can be expressed by the following structures:

1) *Infinitival* clause
2) *Adverbial Participial* clause
3) *Conjunctive* clause
4) *Relative pronoun* and *relative adverb* clause

b. Basic Uses

1) Cause (all four constructions)

a) *infinitive* (e.g., Jas 4:2)[10]
b) adverbial *participle* (e.g., Rom 5:1)[11]
c) ὅτι + *indicative* (e.g., Eph 4:25)[12]
d) *relative pronoun* οἵτινες (e.g., Rom 6:2)

2) Comparison (conjunctive and relative clauses)

a) καθώς + *indicative* (e.g., Eph 4:32)[13]
b) *relative* adjective ὅσος (e.g., Rom 6:3)[14]

---

[10] Virtually all causal infinitives follow διὰ τό. See chapter on infinitives for discussion.

[11] Most causal participles precede the verb they modify. See chapter on participles for discussion of word order and tenses used.

[12] Ὅτι introduces subordinate clauses 1291 times and subordinate *causal* clauses 433 times, according to *acCordance.* γάρ also is used to introduce subordinate causal clauses 241 times. Another five conjunctions are used a total of 61 times.

3) Concession (all four constructions *except infinitive* clauses)

   a) adverbial *participle* (e.g., Phil 2:6)[15]

   b) εἰ καί + *indicative* (e.g., Luke 11:8)[16]

   c) *relative pronoun* οἵτινες (e.g., Jas 4:13-14)

4) Condition (all four constructions *except infinitive* clauses)[17]

   a) adverbial *participle* (e.g., Heb 2:3)

   b) conjunctive clause:

   1] In the *first class condition* the speaker assumes that the condition stated in the protasis (the "if" clause) is true for the sake of argument, and thus the content of the apodosis (the "then" clause) follows, naturally and logically (e.g., εἰ + *indicative* in Gal 5:18, 25; Luke 4:3). Frequently the protasis is in fact *not* true, but is still presented by the speaker as true for the sake of argument (e.g., Matt 12:27-28; 1 Cor 15:14).

   2] In the *second class condition* the condition is assumed to be *not* true (contrary to fact). The speaker then states in the apodosis what would have been true had the protasis been true (e.g., εἰ + *past tense* in the *indicative* mood in John 5:46; 11:32). The protasis can, of course, be true, but this is either not known to be the case by the speaker (as in Luke 7:39) or is presented with some irony (no examples in the NT).

   3] In the *third class condition* there is a wide variety of nuances found in the protasis, from hypothetical to probable. Some examples also involve a "present general" reality. (Cf. ἐάν + *subjunctive* in Matt 9:21; 1 Cor 13:1-3; 1 John 1:7, 9).

---

[13] καθώς introduces a subordinate comparative clause 174 times (according to *acCordance*). This is followed in frequency by ὡς (107), ὥσπερ (29), καθάπερ (11), et al.

[14] The use of the relative to introduce a comparison is rare in the NT. The correlative adverb is more common (e.g., οὕτως).

[15] See chapter on participles for a discussion of this text.

[16] εἰ καί is used more frequently in concessive clauses than any other structure (except for adverbial participles, though they often involve no structural clues). Boyer regards 18 of 22 instances of εἰ καί as concessive, noting that the four exceptions involve an intermediary conjunction (δέ or γε) (J. L. Boyer, "Adverbial Clauses: Statistical Studies," *GTJ* 11 [1991] 71-96 [here, 81]). Concessive conjunctions also occur, but these are rare (eight times total in the NT [καίπερ (all five times with a concessive participle), καίτοιγε, καίτοι]).

[17] For a more detailed discussion, see chapters on "Moods" and (especially) "Conditional Sentences."

    c)   *relative adjective* ὅσοι (e.g., Rom 2:12)

5) Complementary (infinitive and conjunctive clauses)

    a)   *infinitive* (e.g., 1 John 3:16)[18]

    b)   ἵνα + *subjunctive* (e.g., Luke 6:31; John 8:56)

6) Location (conjunctive and relative adverb clauses)

    a)   οὗ + *indicative* (e.g., Rom 4:15)

    b)   *relative adverb* ὅπου (e.g., Mark 4:5)[19]

7) Manner/Means (*all* four constructions *except conjunctive* clauses)

    a)   articular *infinitive* (e.g., ἐν τῷ + *infinitive* in Acts 3:26)[20]

    b)   adverbial *participle* (e.g., Acts 16:16)[21]

    c)   *relative pronoun* ὅν (e.g., Acts 1:11)

8) Purpose (*all* four constructions)

    a)   *infinitive* (e.g., 1 Tim 1:15)[22]

    b)   adverbial *participle* (e.g., 1 Cor 4:14)[23]

    c)   ἵνα + *subjunctive* (e.g., 1 Pet 3:18)

    d)   *relative pronoun* οἵτινες (e.g., Matt 21:41)

9) Result (*all* four constructions)

    a)   *infinitive* (e.g., Gal 5:7)

    b)   adverbial *participle* (e.g., John 5:18)[24]

---

[18] Complementary infinitives are used hundreds of times in the NT. They follow certain kinds of "helper" verbs, such as δύναμαι, ὀφείλω, etc. See chapter on infinitives for discussion. These can also be treated as an essential part of the verbal idea, rather than as adverbial modifiers, subordinate to the verb.

[19] The use of ὅπου (ἄν) to introduce a local subordinate clause is more frequent than any other means for this semantic category, occurring 82 times. This is followed by οὗ/οὗ ἐάν (23 times) and ὅθεν (7 times).

[20] The infinitive of means is normally expressed by ἐν τῷ + infinitive. However, this construction is more often used of contemporaneous time.

[21] Means and manner need to be distinguished for participles, in light of resultant exegetical differences. See chapter on participles for discussion.

[22] The infinitive of purpose occurs hundreds of times in the NT, but is being replaced in Koine Greek by ἵνα + subjunctive. See chapter on infinitive for discussion of the kinds of infinitives (e.g., whether articular or anarthrous) used to express purpose.

[23] The most frequently used participle to express purpose is the present adverbial participle. All five future adverbial participles also express purpose; the aorist is used only once or twice for purpose. See chapter on participles for discussion.

    c) ἵνα + *subjunctive* (e.g., Rom 11:11)

    d) *relative adverb* ὅθεν (e.g., Heb 8:3)

  10) Time (*all* four constructions)

    a) articular *infinitive* (e.g., πρὸ τοῦ + *infinitive* in Matt 6:8)[25]

    b) adverbial *participle* (e.g., Matt 21:18, 23)[26]

    c) ὅτε + *indicative* (e.g., Matt 19:1)[27]

    d) *relative pronoun* clause (e.g., ἀφ᾽ ἧς . . . in Col 1:9; ἐν ᾧ . . . in Mark 2:19)

C. *How To Classify a Dependent Clause*

1. Identify the structural *form* of the clause:

    Infinitival? Participial? Conjunctive? Relative?

2. Identify the syntactical *function* of the clause by classifying the key structural marker in the clause (viz., the infinitive, participle, conjunction, or relative pronoun). This involves two steps:

    a) Identify the main functional category: substantival, adjectival, or adverbial.

    b) Identify the appropriate functional subcategory under the main category (e.g., under *Adverbial*, is it cause, condition, purpose, result, time, etc.?)

3. Note the word or words in the context to which the dependent clause is related. For example, in Phil 1:6 ὅτι introduces a conjunctive clause that is substantival in apposition to τοῦτο (v 6a).

---

[24] The participle of result is sometimes confused with the attendant circumstance participle. But the structure and semantics of each type of participle are different. See chapter on participles for a discussion.

[25] The infinitive of time involves antecedent, contemporaneous, and subsequent time. The temporal infinitive is far less common than the temporal participle. See chapter on infinitive for discussion of structures and meaning.

[26] Virtually all adverbial participles are temporal, although some are *only* temporal. Like the infinitive, these can indicate antecedent, contemporaneous, or subsequent time. See chapter on participles for a discussion.

[27] According to *acCordance*, there are 364 instances of subordinate temporal conjunctions in the NT. The most common are: ὅταν + subjunctive (123), ὅτε + indicative (103), ὡς + indicative (69), ἕως + indicative or subjunctive (40).

The Role of Conjunctions

Overview of Chapter

Select Bibliography

BAGD, *passim* (see under specific conjunctions); *BDF*, 225-39 (§438-57); **Burton**, *Moods and Tenses*, 83-116, 119-25, 126-42 (§188-288, 296-316, 321-56); **Dana-Mantey**, 239-67 (§209-42); **Robertson**, *Grammar*, 1177-93; **Turner**, *Syntax*, 329-41.

Introduction

A. Definition

The term *conjunction* comes from the Latin verb *conjungo*, which means "join together." A conjunction is a word that connects words, clauses, sentences, or paragraphs, and as a result links the component parts and/or the thought-units of a language together. It is a linking word.[1]

B. Characteristics of Conjunctions

The primary characteristic of conjunctions is that of making connections in a language. They can make two types of structural connections: coordinate (paratactic) or subordinate (hypotactic). The *coordinate* conjunction links equal elements together, e.g., a subject (or other part of speech) to a subject (or other part of speech), sentence to sentence, or paragraph to paragraph.[2] The *subordinate* conjunction links a dependent clause to an independent clause or another dependent clause, either of which supplies the controlling idea that the subordinate conjunction and its clause modifies. Some English examples are supplied below followed by Greek examples.

---

[1] Thanks are due to my colleague, John Grassmick, for supplying the essential framework of this chapter, as well as many of the examples and definitions.

[2] Although the two elements might be equal *syntactically*, there is often a *semantic* notion of subordination. For example, on the surface "I went to the store *and* I bought bread" involves two coordinate clauses joined by *and*. But on a "deep structure" level, it is evident that coordinate ideas are not involved: "I went to the store *in order that* I might buy bread."

Semitic languages are especially paratactic, as are the lower echelons of Hellenistic Greek. Narrative literature often reflects this, even among the more literary writers. Among NT books, Revelation (103 instances of καί per 1000 words) and Mark (84/1000) have the greatest frequencies of καί. Luke comes in a distant third with 66 per 1000.

Among other things, the abundance of parataxis illustrates the limited value of diagramming sentences, especially in narrative literature. Paratactic structure (i.e., when whole clauses are joined) may or may not reflect the true semantic relationship. Hypotactic structure, on the other hand, does reflect the deeper structure: One does not use hypotactic structure when parataxis is meant, because the more nuanced category reflects the true intention of the author more accurately.

John **and** Jim are Greek scholars.

> *And* is a coordinate conjunction linking two nouns, both of which are subjects.

I study Greek **in order to** improve my Bible study skills.

> *In order to* is a subordinate conjunction introducing a clause that modifies the controlling idea, "I study Greek." The dependent clause gives the **purpose** for my study of Greek.

John 1:1   Ἐν ἀρχῇ ἦν ὁ λόγος, **καὶ** ὁ λόγος ἦν πρὸς τὸν θεόν

In the beginning was the Word, **and** the Word was with God.

> **καί** is a coordinate conjunction linking two independent clauses.

John 3:16 Οὕτως **γὰρ** ἠγάπησεν ὁ θεὸς τὸν κόσμον, **ὥστε** . . . , **ἵνα** πᾶς ὁ πιστεύων. . . .

For God so loved the world, **with the result that** . . . , **in order that** everyone who believes. . . .

> **γάρ** is a coordinate conjunction linking this sentence to the previous idea in John 3:14, explaining why God makes eternal life available. **ὥστε** is a subordinate conjunction, introducing the result of God's love for the world, namely, he gave his Son. **ἵνα** is a subordinate conjunction, introducing the purpose God had in giving his Son, viz., that everyone who believes in him might have eternal life.

C. *The Use of Conjunctions in Exegesis*

Conjunctions are important in exegesis because they relate the thoughts of a passage to one another. A key to determining their use is identifying the two sets of ideas that the conjunction links together. One must determine the controlling idea the conjunction modifies, that is, the element in the sentence or larger literary unit to which the conjunction is to be connected. Often more than one possible connection exists. When this situation occurs, context and authorial expression are two key ways to determine the most likely connection.

> I walked home and studied Greek **in order to** be able to watch the baseball game tonight.
>
> > In this sentence it is unclear whether the subordinate clause introduced by "in order to" gives the purpose for walking home, the purpose for studying Greek, or the purpose of both.

Contrast this example with the earlier example from John 3:16. In that passage it is clear that the ἵνα clause gives the purpose for which God gave his Son and not the purpose for which God loved the world, because the latter idea does not make contextual sense. Sometimes, however, the elements that a conjunction (particularly a subordinate conjunction like ἵνα or ὅτι) connects together can be disputed. That is why it is necessary to state clearly what ideas a conjunction links together and the nature of the connection. When there are several possible connections, try to be aware of the options. Test each option with an interpretive translation in determining the best one.

D. *Common Greek Conjunctions*

The most common *coordinating* conjunctions are (in order):

καί, δέ, γάρ, ἀλλά, οὖν, ἤ, τε, οὐδέ, οὔτε, and εἴτε.[3]

The most common *subordinating* conjunctions that usually govern the *indicative* mood are (in order):

ὅτι, εἰ, καθώς, ὡς, γάρ, and ὅτε.[4]

The most common *subordinating* conjunctions that usually govern the *subjunctive* mood are:

ἵνα, ὅταν, ἐάν, ὅπως, ἕως, μή, and μήποτε.[5]

Specific Semantic Categories

The following survey gives some of the major categories of usage for Greek conjunctions.

Preface

Conjunctions can be organized three ways: semantically, structurally, and lexically.

1. Semantic (Functional) Categories

Conjunctions can be divided into three semantic/functional categories: *substantival*, *adverbial*, and *logical*. The *substantival* category refers to *content* uses, such as direct and indirect discourse, or to epexegetical uses. The *adverbial* category includes uses indicating time, place, purpose, result, or other ideas that are commonly regarded as adverbial.

---

[3] According to *acCordance*, there are 33 different coordinating conjunctions used in the NT, with a total of 14,183 instances. The ten listed above account for 13,777 of these (or 97%). καί is used as a coordinating conjunction in over half of the instances.

Some of the conjunctions so-called by *acCordance* are other parts of speech *functioning* like conjunctions. The data need to be adjusted accordingly. Nevertheless, the general pattern is still the same: There are almost two conjunctions per verse, on average, in the NT.

[4] There are 4107 instances of subordinating conjunctions in the NT (*acCordance*), involving 44 different conjunctions. About three-fourths govern an indicative verb. Again, not all that *acCordance* labels as a conjunction is such, but the general patterns are not affected by this.

[5] The above listings presents only the basic category in which a conjunction belongs. Some conjunctions can function in more than one category.

The *logical* category includes uses indicating a movement of thought in the passage in terms of addition, contrast, conclusion, transition, or other such relationships.

2. **Structural Categories**

    It is also possible to divide conjunctions into two broad structural categories: *coordinate* and *subordinate*. But these are not as helpful to the student exegetically as the more semantically sensitive divisions given here.

3. **Lexical Categories**

    Finally, conjunctions can be organized lexically, i.e., alphabetically according to their form. A lexicon takes this approach. It is important that students use a lexicon such as BAGD when working with conjunctions. The outline of conjunctions given in this chapter is intended to supplement, not supplant, the description of conjunctions in the standard lexica.[6]

Our approach is to organize the data by the broad semantic/functional categories of logical, adverbial, and substantival.[7]

I. Logical Conjunctions

These conjunctions relate the movement of thought from one passage to another by expressing logical relationships between the connected ideas. For the most part, coordinate conjunctions are used here.

A. Ascensive Conjunctions [even]

1. **Definition**

    This use expresses a *final addition* or *point of focus*. It is often translated *even*. This classification is usually determined by the context. Conjunctions that function this way are καί, δέ, and μηδέ.

---

[6] Besides supplying a rich bibliography and a few exegetical insights, BAGD attempt, in most cases, to "cover all the bases" of usage. Such an approach contrasts with this chapter, which only addresses the basic categories of usage.

[7] For an outline of the broad structural categories, see the chapter, "Introduction to Greek Clauses."

2. Illustrations

1 Cor 2:10 τὸ πνεῦμα πάντα ἐραυνᾷ, **καὶ** τὰ βάθη τοῦ θεοῦ
the Spirit searches all things, **even** the deep things of God

Eph 5:3 πορνεία δὲ καὶ ἀκαθαρσία πᾶσα . . . **μηδὲ** ὀνομαζέσθω ἐν ὑμῖν
but do **not** let immorality and all uncleanliness . . . **even** be named
among you

B. *Connective Conjunctions (continuative, coordinate) [and, also]*

1. Definition

This use simply *connects an additional element* to a discussion or adds an
additional idea to the train of thought. It is translated *and*, though if it is
emphatic, it can be translated *also*, indicating a key addition. This latter
use (*also*) is sometimes called **adjunctive**. The major connective conjunctions are καί and δέ. δέ as a connective conjunction may often be left
untranslated.

2. Illustrations

Eph 1:3 εὐλογητὸς ὁ θεὸς **καὶ** πατὴρ τοῦ κυρίου ἡμῶν Ἰησοῦ Χριστοῦ
blessed be the God **and** Father of our Lord Jesus Christ

Luke 6:9 εἶπεν **δὲ** ὁ Ἰησοῦς πρὸς αὐτούς
and Jesus said to them

C. *Contrastive Conjunctions (adversative) [but, rather, however]*

1. Definition

This use suggests a *contrast* or opposing thought to the idea to which it
is connected. It is often translated *but, rather, yet, though,* or *however*.
Major contrastive conjunctions include: ἀλλά, πλήν, καί (if indicated by
context), δέ (if indicated by context).

2. Illustrations

Matt 5:17 οὐκ ἦλθον καταλῦσαι, **ἀλλὰ** πληρῶσαι
I did not come to destroy, **but** to fulfill [the Law]

Matt 12:43 διέρχεται δι᾽ ἀνύδρων τόπων ζητοῦν ἀνάπαυσιν **καὶ** οὐχ εὑρίσκει
[An unclean spirit . . .] goes through waterless places seeking rest
but it does not find [it]

John 15:16 οὐχ ὑμεῖς με ἐξελέξασθε, **ἀλλ᾽** ἐγὼ ἐξελεξάμην ὑμᾶς
you did not choose me, **but** I chose you
The contrast between Jesus and the disciples is categorical: Election

was accomplished by him, a point strengthened by the ἀλλά. A comparative contrast would mean, "You did not choose me as much as I chose you," but that is foreign to the context.

D. Correlative Conjunctions (paired conjunctions)

1. Definition

These are *paired conjunctions* that express various relationships. Such pairs include: μέν . . . δέ (*on the one hand . . . on the other hand*); καί . . . καί (*both . . . and*); μήτε . . . μήτε (*neither . . . nor*); οὔτε . . . οὔτε (*neither . . . nor*); οὐκ . . . ἀλλά or δέ (*not . . . but*); οὐ . . . ποτέ (*not . . . ever*); ποτέ . . . νῦν (*once . . . now*); τε . . . τε (*as . . . so*) or (*not only . . . but also*); ἤ . . . ἤ (*either . . . or*).

2. Illustrations

Matt 9:37   ὁ **μὲν** θερισμὸς πολύς, οἱ **δὲ** ἐργάται ὀλίγοι

On the one hand, the harvest is plentiful, **but on the other hand**, the laborers are few.

> A smoother translation should normally be used: "The harvest is plentiful, but the laborers are few." The above was given to show the contrast in balance that the μέν . . . δέ construction suggests.

Mark 14:68   **οὔτε** οἶδα **οὔτε** ἐπίσταμαι σὺ τί λέγεις

I **neither** know **nor** understand what you are saying

Luke 24:20   ὅπως **τε** παρέδωκαν αὐτὸν οἱ ἀρχιερεῖς καὶ οἱ ἄρχοντες ἡμῶν εἰς κρίμα θανάτου **καὶ** ἐσταύρωσαν αὐτόν

how our chief priests and rulers **both** betrayed him to a sentence of death **and** crucified him

E. Disjunctive (Alternative) Conjunctions [or]

1. Definition

This use gives an *alternative* possibility to the idea to which it is connected. It is translated *or*. The major disjunctive conjunction is ἤ. It can suggest opposite or related alternatives.

2. Illustrations

Matt 5:17   μὴ νομίσητε ὅτι ἦλθον καταλῦσαι τὸν νόμον **ἢ** τοὺς προφήτας

Do not think that I came to destroy the Law **or** the prophets

Matt 5:36   οὐ δύνασαι μίαν τρίχα λευκὴν ποιῆσαι **ἢ** μέλαιναν

you are not able to make one hair white **or** black

F. Emphatic Conjunctions [*certainly, indeed*]

1. Definition

This use appears in various forms and is determined by the context. It usually involves *intensifying* the normal sense of a conjunction. Examples are as follows: ἀλλά intensified is translated *certainly*; οὐ with μή becomes *certainly not* or *by no means*; οὖν becomes *certainly*. True emphatic conjunctions include: γε, δή, μενοῦνγε, μέντοι, ναί, and νή.

2. Illustrations

Rom 8:32   ὅς **γε** τοῦ ἰδίου υἱοῦ οὐκ ἐφείσατο
who **indeed** did not spare his own Son

Phil 3:8   ἀλλὰ **μενοῦνγε** καὶ ἡγοῦμαι πάντα ζημίαν εἶναι
but **indeed** also I count all things to be loss

G. Explanatory Conjunctions

1. Definition

This use indicates that additional information is being given about what is being described. It can often be translated *for, you see,* or *that is, namely*. Key conjunctions here are: γάρ, δέ, εἰ (after verbs of emotion), and καί.

2. Illustrations

John 3:16   οὕτως **γὰρ** ἠγάπησεν ὁ θεὸς τὸν κόσμον
for God so loved the world

John 4:8   οἱ **γὰρ** μαθηταὶ αὐτοῦ ἀπεληλύθεισαν εἰς τὴν πόλιν
for his disciples had gone into the city

H. Inferential Conjunctions [*therefore*]

1. Definition

This use gives a *deduction, conclusion,* or *summary* to the preceding discussion. Common inferential conjunctions include: ἄρα, γάρ, διό, διότι, οὖν, πλήν, τοιγαροῦν, τοινῦν, and ὥστε.

2. Illustrations

Rom 12:1   παρακαλῶ **οὖν** ὑμᾶς . . . παραστῆσαι τὰ σώματα ὑμῶν
I urge you **therefore** . . . to present your bodies

Rom 15:7   **διὸ** προσλαμβάνεσθε ἀλλήλους, καθὼς καί . . .
therefore receive one another, even as also [Christ received you]

I. Transitional Conjunctions [now, then]

1. Definition

This use involves the change to a new topic of discussion. It can often be translated *now* (though οὖν is frequently translated *then*). Major conjunctions with this force are: οὖν and δέ. δέ is by far the most common. The use of οὖν is reserved for narrative material, especially John.

2. Illustrations

Matt 1:18   τοῦ **δὲ** Ἰησοῦ Χριστοῦ ἡ γένεσις οὕτως ἦν

Now the birth of Jesus Christ was as follows

John 5:10   ἔλεγον **οὖν** οἱ Ἰουδαῖοι τῷ τεθεραπευμένῳ

Then the Jews were saying to the one who had been healed

> The transitional force of οὖν sometimes comes close to the inferential force, as here. But to label a conjunction as transitional is to regard the connection to be more chronological than logical. Cf. also John 1:22; 2:18, 20; 3:25; 4:33, 46; 5:19; 6:60, 67; 7:25, 28, 33, 35, 40; 8:13, 21, 22, 25, 31, 57; 9:10, 16.

II. Adverbial Conjunctions

These conjunctions amplify the verbal idea in a specific way. These uses usually involve *subordinate* conjunctions.

A. Causal Conjunctions [because, since]

1. Definition

This use expresses the basis or ground of an action. Major conjunctions used this way are: γάρ, διότι, ἐπεί, ἐπειδή, ἐπειδήπερ, καθώς, ὅτι, and ὡς. They are often translated *because* or *since*.

2. Illustrations

Luke 1:34   Πῶς ἔσται τοῦτο, **ἐπεὶ** ἄνδρα οὐ γινώσκω;

How can this be, **since** I do not know a man?

John 5:27   ἐξουσίαν ἔδωκεν αὐτῷ κρίσιν ποιεῖν, **ὅτι** υἱὸς ἀνθρώπου ἐστίν

he gave authority to him to render judgment, **because** he is the Son of Man

B. *Comparative Conjunctions (manner)*

1. Definition

This use suggests an *analogy* or *comparison* between the connected ideas or tells how something is to be done. Major conjunctions used this way are: καθάπερ, καθώς, οὕτως, ὡς, ὡσαύτως, ὡσεί, and ὥσπερ. They are often translated *as, just as, in the same way, thus,* or *in this manner.*

2. Illustrations

1 Cor 2:11   **οὕτως** καὶ τὰ τοῦ θεοῦ οὐδεὶς ἔγνωκεν εἰ μὴ τὸ πνεῦμα τοῦ θεοῦ
In the same way also no one has known the things of God except the Spirit of God.

> The comparison here is to the spirit of a human being knowing a human being's thought (v 10).

Eph 4:32   γίνεσθε εἰς ἀλλήλους χρηστοί . . . χαριζόμενοι ἑαυτοῖς **καθὼς** καὶ ὁ θεὸς ἐν Χριστῷ ἐχαρίσατο ὑμῖν
Be kind to one another, forgiving each other, **just as** God in Christ has forgiven you.

C. *Conditional Conjunctions [if]*

1. Definition

This use introduces a condition in the presentation of the speaker that must occur before a certain action or conclusion can occur. This conditional clause may not reflect reality, but rather simply the writer's presentation or perception of reality. As part of a conditional clause this conjunction introduces the **protasis** (or *if* part of the *if . . . then* statement). εἰ and ἐάν are the major conditional conjunctions. They are translated *if.*[8]

2. Illustrations

1 Cor 2:8   **εἰ** γὰρ ἔγνωσαν, οὐκ ἂν τὸν κύριον τῆς δόξης ἐσταύρωσαν
For **if** they had known [the wisdom of God], [then] they would not have crucified the Lord of glory.

John 5:31   **ἐὰν** ἐγὼ μαρτυρῶ περὶ ἐμαυτοῦ, ἡ μαρτυρία μου οὐκ ἔστιν ἀληθής
If I testify concerning myself, [then] my testimony is not true.

---

[8] See chapter on conditional sentences for a detailed discussion.

D. Local Conjunctions (sphere)

1. Definition

This use gives the location or sphere (metaphorically), that is, the context in which an action takes place. Major conjunctions used this way are: ὅθεν, ὅπου, and οὗ. Translations include *where*, *from where*, or *the place which*.

2. Illustrations

Matt 6:19   μὴ θησαυρίζετε ὑμῖν θησαυροὺς ἐπὶ τῆς γῆς, **ὅπου** σὴς καὶ βρῶσις ἀφανίζει

     Do not store for yourselves treasures on the earth, **where** moth and rust destroy.

Rom 4:15   **οὗ** δὲ οὐκ ἔστιν νόμος, οὐδὲ παράβασις

     but **where** there is no law, there is no transgression

      Note the difference between the conjunction (οὗ) and the negative adverb (οὐ).

E. Purpose Conjunctions [in order that]

1. Definition

This use indicates the goal or aim of an action. Major conjunctions for this category are: ἵνα, ὅπως, μήπως (the negative purpose), μήπου (negative purpose), and μήποτε (negative purpose). By far the most common is ἵνα. Translations for this use are: *in order that, with the goal that, with a view to, that*.

2. Illustrations

John 3:16   τὸν υἱὸν τὸν μονογενῆ ἔδωκεν, **ἵνα** πᾶς ὁ πιστεύων εἰς αὐτόν . . .

     he gave his only Son, **in order that** everyone who believes in him [should not perish but should have eternal life]

John 5:34   ἀλλὰ ταῦτα λέγω **ἵνα** ὑμεῖς σωθῆτε

     but I say these things **in order that** you might be saved

Acts 9:24   παρετηροῦντο δὲ καὶ τὰς πύλας ἡμέρας τε καὶ νυκτὸς **ὅπως** αὐτὸν ἀνέλωσιν

     And they were also watching the gates, both day and night, **in order that** they might kill him

F. Result Conjunctions [so that, with the result that]

1. Definition

This use gives the outcome or consequence of an action. The focus is on the outcome of the action rather than on its intention. Major conjunctions used this way are: ὥστε, ὡς, ὅτι, and less frequently, ἵνα. This use can be translated *that*, *so that*, or *with the result that*. By far the most common is ὥστε.

2. Illustrations

John 3:16 οὕτως γὰρ ἠγάπησεν ὁ θεὸς τὸν κόσμον, **ὥστε** τὸν υἱὸν τὸν μονογενῆ ἔδωκεν

for God so loved the world, **that** he gave his only Son

John 9:2 τίς ἥμαρτεν . . . **ἵνα** τυφλὸς γεννηθῇ;

Who sinned . . . **with the result that** [this man] was born blind?

G. Temporal Conjunctions

1. Definition

This use gives the time of the action. Major conjunctions used this way are: ἄχρι, ἕως, ὅταν, ὅτε, οὐδέποτε (negative temporal), οὐκέτι (negative temporal), οὔπω (negative temporal), ποτέ, and ὡς. Translation varies depending on the conjunction used.

2. Illustrations

Luke 21:24 Ἰερουσαλὴμ ἔσται πατουμένη ὑπὸ ἐθνῶν, **ἄχρι οὗ** πληρωθῶσιν καιροὶ ἐθνῶν

Jerusalem will be trampled under foot by the Gentiles **until the time when** the times of the Gentiles be fulfilled

John 6:24 **ὅτε** οὖν εἶδεν ὁ ὄχλος ὅτι Ἰησοῦς οὐκ ἔστιν ἐκεῖ

now **when** the crowd saw that Jesus was not there

III. Substantival Conjunctions

These uses are limited to instances where the conjunction introduces a noun content clause and to epexegesis.

A. Content Conjunctions [that]

1. Definition

This use involves a conjunction that introduces a subject, predicate nominative, direct object, or an appositional noun clause. Direct and indirect discourse are specialized object clauses following verbs of expression or perception.

Major conjunctions here include: ἵνα, ὅπως, ὅτι, and ὡς. ἵνα and ὅτι are the most common.[9] This use of the conjunction is translated *that* or, if introducing direct discourse (e.g., a *recitative* ὅτι), it is left untranslated.

2. Illustrations

1 Cor 4:2   ζητεῖται ἐν τοῖς οἰκονόμοις, **ἵνα** πιστός τις εὑρεθῇ
            That a person be found faithful is sought in stewards.
            This is a *subject* clause.

1 Cor 15:3 παρέδωκα γὰρ ὑμῖν . . . **ὅτι** Χριστὸς ἀπέθανεν ὑπὲρ τῶν ἁμαρτιῶν ἡμῶν
            For I passed on to you . . . **that** Christ died for our sins.
            This is a *direct object* clause.

John 4:17   Καλῶς εἶπας **ὅτι** Ἄνδρα οὐκ ἔχω
            [Jesus said to her], "Correctly you have said, 'I do not have a husband.'"
            This is a direct discourse object clause.

John 4:19   κύριε, θεωρῶ **ὅτι** προφήτης εἶ σύ
            Sir, I perceive **that** you are a prophet.
            This is an indirect discourse object clause.

B. Epexegetical Conjunctions [that]

1. Definition

This use involves a conjunction introducing a clause that completes the idea of a noun or adjective. It often functions like an epexegetical infinitive. Major conjunctions used this way are ἵνα and ὅτι. The normal translation for this use is *that*.

2. Illustrations

Luke 7:6   οὐ ἱκανός εἰμι **ἵνα** ὑπὸ τὴν στέγην μου εἰσέλθῃς
            I am not worthy **that** you should enter under my roof.

Matt 8:27   ποταπός ἐστιν οὗτος **ὅτι** καὶ οἱ ἄνεμοι καὶ ἡ θάλασσα αὐτῷ ὑπακούουσιν;
            What sort of man is this **that** both the winds and the sea obey him?

---

[9] See chapter on moods, under indicative (for ὅτι) and subjunctive (for ἵνα) for a more detailed discussion.

Conditional Sentences

Overview of Chapter

I. Introduction

A. *Importance of Conditional Sentences in the New Testament*

1.   Quantity

There are over 600 *formal* conditional sentences in the NT (i.e., with an explicit *if*). This works out to an average of about one per page in Nestle[27]. Besides these formal conditions, there are hundreds of implicit conditions. Thus, a proper understanding of conditions impacts one's exegesis at every turn of the page.[1]

2.   Quality

It is no overstatement to say that some of the great themes of biblical theology cannot be properly understood apart from a correct understanding of conditions.

---

[1] Against our usual custom, the *Select Bibliography* is placed in the appendix to this chapter rather than at the beginning. The bibliographical materials on conditional sentences are quite daunting, as is the topic itself. So as to make the topic of conditions more inviting to intermediate students, it was felt that the entire bibliography should go in the appendix.

Widespread misunderstanding persists about the Greek conditions. On any Sunday misinformation about conditional clauses is communicated from pulpit to pew. Whole theological systems and lifestyles are sometimes built on such misunderstandings.

By way of a crude illustration, several years ago a student at a Christian college in a major midwestern city was reading the Sermon on the Mount. This pious young man came across Matt 5:29 ("if your right eye offends you, pluck it out"). His understanding of Greek was that since this was a first class condition, it meant *since*. And, obedient to scripture, he proceeded to gouge his eye with a screwdriver! The young man survived the self-mutilation, but lost his eye.[2] A particular understanding of conditions certainly impacted his lifestyle!

B. *How to Approach Conditional Sentences*

There are essentially three approaches we can take in analyzing conditional sentences: structural, semantic, and pragmatic. The *structural* (or formal) approach looks at the conditional particle (whether εἰ or ἐάν) and the moods and tenses used in the protasis (*if* clause) and apodosis (*then* clause). From these structural groups emerge the basic meanings that conditions display.

The *semantic* (or universal grammar) approach asks essentially what the two halves of conditions mean. That is, how do they relate to each other? This approach begins with the basic structure (*if . . . then*), but addresses more general issues that are true of all conditions, such as whether the relationship of protasis to apodosis is cause to effect or something else.[3]

The *pragmatic*[4] (or speech act theory) approach examines what people are trying to communicate when they use conditional sentences in a very broad way. This approach is not concerned with how the two halves relate to each other, but whether a conditional sentence is uttered as a veiled threat, request, command, and the like.

All of these are valid approaches to conditional sentences. We will focus on the first two since the pragmatic approach is too far removed from form for us to get an easy handle on it; that is, it more properly belongs to discourse analysis than to syntax.[5]

---

[2] This is a true story I learned from one of the young man's classmates.

[3] What we are calling the *semantic* approach could also be labeled the *logical* approach in that it especially focuses on the logic of conditional clauses.

[4] We are here using "pragmatic" in its linguistic sense–i.e., that field of linguistics that is concerned with the entire context in which an utterance is spoken, comprising not only the textual context, but other things, such as the historical, political, and social context.

[5] A brief treatment of this approach is found in the appendix, along with suggested reading.

II. Conditional Sentences in General

Certain features of conditional sentences are true of all languages. In a given instance, such features are intuitively recognized. But these need to be brought out in the open initially to overcome several misconceptions about how conditions behave in cherished texts.

A. *Definition*

Conditional sentences can be defined structurally or semantically.

1. Structurally

A conditional sentence has two parts: an "if" part and a "then" part. "IF" = protasis; "THEN" = apodosis.

2. Semantically

Conditions can be defined semantically in terms of the overall construction as well as the individual components.

a. The Meaning of the Construction (i.e., the Relation of the Protasis to the Apodosis)

There is often a tacit assumption that the protasis of a condition indicates the *cause* and the apodosis tells the *effect*. But this is not the only relation the two can have. In essence, there are three basic relations that a protasis can have to an apodosis: cause-effect, evidence-inference, and equivalence. It is a profitable exercise to examine the biblical text in light of these basic nuances.

1) Cause-Effect

The first relation the two parts can have is that of cause and effect. "IF" = cause; "THEN" = effect. For example:

- "If you put your hand in the fire, you will get burned."
- "If you eat three pounds of chocolate every day for a month, you will look like a blimp!"

The NT has its share of illustrations as well:[6]

Rom 8:13   εἰ κατὰ σάρκα ζῆτε, μέλλετε ἀποθνήσκειν.
            If you live according to the flesh, you are about to die.

---

[6] This cause-effect relationship is not shut up to a particular class of conditions. It occurs across the board, in the first, second, and third class conditions (as the illustrations show).

Matt 4:9 ταῦτά σοι πάντα δώσω, ἐὰν πεσὼν προσκυνήσῃς μοι.
I will give you all these things, if you fall down and worship me.

1 Cor 2:8 εἰ ἔγνωσαν, οὐκ ἂν τὸν κύριον τῆς δόξης ἐσταύρωσαν.
If they had known, they would not have crucified the Lord of glory.
> This is an "unreal" condition, in which a statement is presented as not true. But the cause-effect relationship can still be seen: Knowledge (of the wisdom of God) would have caused the rulers of this world not to crucify the Lord of glory.

2) Evidence-Inference

The second relation the protasis can have to the apodosis is that of ground, or evidence, to inference. Here the speaker infers something (the apodosis) from some evidence. That is, he makes an induction about the *implications* that a piece of evidence suggests to him. For example,

- "If it's Tuesday, this must be Belgium" (title of an old movie).
- "If she has a ring on her left hand, then she's married."

Notice that the protasis is not the *cause* of the apodosis. In fact, it is often just the opposite: "If she gets married, she will wear a ring on her left hand." Thus, often, though not always, the ground-inference condition will semantically be the *converse* of the cause-effect condition.

Rom 8:17 εἰ δὲ τέκνα, καὶ κληρονόμοι
Now if [we are] children, then [we are] heirs.

1 Cor 15:44 εἰ ἔστιν σῶμα ψυχικόν, ἔστιν καὶ πνευματικόν.
If there is a physical body, there is also a spiritual [body].
> Obviously, the physical body does not *cause* the spiritual one; rather, Paul simply infers that there must be a spiritual body from the evidence of a physical one.

3) Equivalence

The third relation the two parts can have to one another is one of equivalence. That is, we could put this formula this way: "If A, then B" means the same thing as "A = B." (This often looks very similar to evidence-inference.) For example,

- "If you are Henry's son, then Henry is your father."
- "If you are obedient to God, you are living righteously." (more loosely equivalent)

Gal 2:18 εἰ γὰρ ἃ κατέλυσα ταῦτα πάλιν οἰκοδομῶ, παραβάτην ἐμαυτὸν συνιστάνω.
For if I build up again those things that I have destroyed, I demonstrate that I am a transgressor.

Jas 2:11   εἰ . . . φονεύεις δέ, γέγονας παραβάτης νόμου.
             But if you commit murder, you have become a law-breaker.

4) Principles

A few principles emerge from this brief analysis.

- The three types of conditions are not entirely distinct. There is much overlap between them.[7]

- Nevertheless, it is important exegetically for the student to *try* to distinguish, if possible, these three nuances. We will see this more clearly when we examine the "General Guidelines" section.

- *A compound protasis does not necessarily mean that both conditions have the same relation to the apodosis.* Note, for example, the following illustration:

  Suppose a quarterback tells his tailback, "If you veer right and go ten yards, you'll make a first down." But both protases do not have the same relation to the apodosis. The tailback could also veer left or plow straight ahead. The essential thing, though, is that he make ten yards!

b. The Meaning of the Components

Basically, the meaning of the components is that of supposition-consequence. Specifically:

1) *Apodosis*

The apodosis is *grammatically independent, but semantically dependent.* That is, it can stand on its own as a full-blown sentence (e.g., "If I die, *I die*"), but it depends for its "factuality" on the fulfillment of the protasis ("If he wins this race, he'll be the new champion").

2) *Protasis*

The protasis, on the other hand, is *grammatically dependent, but semantically independent.* That is, it does not form a complete thought (*"If I go swimming tomorrow,* I'll catch a cold"), but its fulfillment is independent of whether the apodosis is true.

---

[7] The equivalence type especially can often be treated as a specific kind of evidence-inference construction. Not all evidence-inference constructions, however, involve equivalence (e.g., 1 Cor 15:44).

B. General Guidelines for Interpreting Conditional Sentences

1. The Conditional Element

Only the *protasis* is the conditional element. That is, the contingency lies with the *if*, not the *then*. If the protasis is fulfilled, the apodosis is also fulfilled.

2. Relation to Reality

What is the relation of the conditional statement to reality? This fits into the larger issue of the relation of language to reality. As we have argued throughout this work, *language is essentially a **portrayal** of reality*. The portrayal is never a *complete* picture of reality. This does not necessarily mean that it is incorrect, but neither is the portrayal necessarily correct either.

The implications of this for grammar in general and conditional clauses specifically are significant. By way of illustration, in Matt 18:8 the evangelist portrays the Lord as saying, "If your hand causes you to stumble, cut it off!" He uses the *first* class condition. But Mark, in the parallel passage (9:43), portrays the Lord as saying this in the *third* class condition. Now it is possible that one of the two writers got his information wrong. But it is equally likely that the semantic domains of first and third class conditions are not entirely distinct. Perhaps they are elastic enough that both of them can be used, at times, to speak of the same event.

3. Converse of the Condition (Semantically)

The converse of "If A, then B" is "If B, then A." The significance? Just that *the converse of a condition is not **necessarily** true*. For example, the converse of "If it is raining, there must be clouds in the sky" is "If there are clouds in the sky, it must be raining." The converse in this instance is patently false.

Applied to the biblical text, notice the following:

Rom 8:13 εἰ κατὰ σάρκα ζῆτε, μέλλετε ἀποθνῄσκειν.
  If you live according to the flesh, you are about to die.
    The converse of this is not necessarily true: "If you are about to die, you must have lived according to the flesh." There may be other reasons one is about to die besides living according to the flesh.

Gal 3:29 εἰ ὑμεῖς Χριστοῦ, ἄρα τοῦ Ἀβραὰμ σπέρμα ἐστέ
  If you belong to Christ, then you are Abraham's seed.
    The converse is not necessarily true: "If you are Abraham's seed, then you belong to Christ." There might be others who are Abraham's seed who do not belong to Christ.

Rom 8:14 ὅσοι γὰρ πνεύματι θεοῦ ἄγονται, οὗτοι υἱοὶ θεοῦ εἰσιν.
  For as many as are led by the Spirit, these are the sons of God.
    This is an implied condition (with no formal "if"), but a condition

nonetheless. The converse may or may not be true, but the grammar does not tell us: "If you are the sons of God, you are led by the Spirit." Whether the converse is true needs to be established on grounds *other than* the syntax of the condition.

Clear thinking in this area will enable you to avoid faulty interpretations of scripture in several passages.

4. Reverse of the Condition (Semantically)

By the reverse of the condition, I mean the opposite of the condition. The reverse of the condition, "If A happens, B happens" is "If A does *not* happen, B (still) happens."

The significant point to remember is that *the reverse of the condition is not necessarily false*. The *reason* for this is twofold: (1) Not all conditions are of the cause-effect type, and (2) even among the cause-effect type of condition, the stated cause does not have to be a necessary or exclusive condition. That is, if the condition is not fulfilled, this does not necessarily mean that the apodosis *cannot* come true.

- In the statement, "If you put your hand in the fire, you will get burned," the negation of this is not necessarily true. That is, "If you *don't* put your hand in the fire, you will not get burned"–for you could put your *foot* in the fire (or your hand in the oven, etc.).

- Or: "If I die, my wife will get $10,000." Negative: "If I don't die, my wife will *not* get $10,000." (This is not necessarily true: She could rob a bank. . . .)

Biblically, consider the following examples.

1 Tim 3:1   εἴ τις ἐπισκοπῆς ὀρέγεται, καλοῦ ἔργου ἐπιθυμεῖ.
If anyone aspires to the episcopate, he desires a noble work.
> Obviously, this does not mean that if someone does *not* aspire to the office, he does not desire a noble work.

Jas 2:9   εἰ προσωπολημπτεῖτε, ἁμαρτίαν ἐργάζεσθε
If you show partiality, you commit sin.
> It is, of course, possible to sin in other ways than by showing partiality.

Rom 10:9   ἐὰν ὁμολογήσῃς ἐν τῷ στόματί σου κύριον Ἰησοῦν καὶ πιστεύσῃς ἐν τῇ καρδίᾳ σου ὅτι ὁ θεὸς αὐτὸν ἤγειρεν ἐκ νεκρῶν, σωθήσῃ
If you confess with your mouth that Jesus is [the] Lord and believe in your heart that God has raised him from the dead, you shall be saved.
> One way to look at this text is to consider the confession *with the mouth* as the ground or *evidence* upon which the inference "you shall be saved" is based. But it is not the *cause*. The cause is in the second part of the condition, "If you believe in your heart. . . ." It is not necessary to treat each protasis as bearing the same relationship to the apodosis.

5. Summary

If the reverse of a condition is not necessarily false and the converse is not necessarily true, then what do conditions mean? To put this another way, if the apodosis of the condition does not *necessarily* in every case depend upon the fulfillment of the protasis in order to be fulfilled, then what is the purpose of a conditional statement anyway?

The answer to this is related to *presentation. As far as it is **presented**,* although sometimes the apodosis *may* be true without the protasis being true, the apodosis *must* be true when the protasis is true. That is to say, as far as portrayal is concerned, if the protasis is fulfilled, the apodosis is true. Thus, "If you put your hand in the fire, you will get burned" is saying that if you fulfill the condition, the consequence is true. All of this can be summarized as follows:

a) Conditional statements refer to the portrayal of reality rather than to reality itself. However, within those parameters the following may be said:

b) If A, then B ≠ if B, then A (converse not necessarily true).

c) If A, then B ≠ if non-A, then non-B (reverse not necessarily false).

d) If A, then B *does not deny* if C then B (condition not necessarily exclusive or condition not necessarily causal).

III. Conditional Sentences in Greek (especially the NT)

Now that we have looked at the logical function of conditions, we are in a better position to interpret the various structures of Greek conditions.

A. *Ways to Convey the Conditional Idea in Greek*

Conditions may be conveyed *implicitly* (i.e., without the formal structural markers) or *explicitly* (i.e., with the formal structural markers).

1. Implicitly

a. Circumstantial Participle

The circumstantial participle can be used to indicate condition.

Heb 2:3   πῶς ἡμεῖς ἐκφευξόμεθα τηλικαύτης **ἀμελήσαντες** σωτηρίας;
How shall we escape **if we neglect** so great a salvation?

b. Substantival Participle

There is no *syntactical* category of "conditional substantival participle," but the notion of condition can still be implied with substantival participles. This often follows the formula ὁ + participle (+ participle) + future indicative (see examples below).

Matt 5:6   μακάριοι οἱ πεινῶντες καὶ διψῶντες τὴν δικαιοσύνην, ὅτι αὐτοὶ χορτασθήσονται.

Blessed are those who hunger and thirst for righteousness, for they shall be filled.

> Stated as an explicit condition: "Blessed are you if you hunger and thirst for righteousness, for you will be filled."

Mark 16:16 ὁ πιστεύσας καὶ βαπτισθεὶς σωθήσεται

The one who believes and is baptized shall be saved.

> This is a part of the longer ending of Mark, a text most likely not original (but still valuable for illustrative purposes). Stated conditionally: "If you believe and are baptized, you will be saved."

> This text may illustrate another point about conditions. As you recall, the two conditions in the protasis do not necessarily bear the same relation to the apodosis. One might be cause, the other might be ground or evidence. If that is the case here, "If you believe" is the cause and the fulfillment of the apodosis depends on it; "and are baptized" is the evidence of belief and the apodosis does *not* depend on it for fulfillment. This would explain the following sentence: "The one who does not believe shall be condemned."

c. Imperative

The imperative can indicate a condition.

John 2:19   **λύσατε** τὸν ναὸν τοῦτον καὶ ἐν τρισὶν ἡμέραις ἐγερῶ αὐτόν.

If you destroy this temple, in three days I will raise it up.

d. A Relative Clause

This usually involves an indefinite relative, but not always.

Matt 5:39   **ὅστις** σε ῥαπίζει εἰς τὴν δεξιὰν σιαγόνα σου, στρέψον αὐτῷ καὶ τὴν ἄλλην·

If anyone strikes you on your right cheek, turn to him the other also.

1 Cor 7:37   **ὃς** δὲ ἕστηκεν ἐν τῇ καρδίᾳ αὐτοῦ ἑδραῖος . . . καλῶς ποιήσει.

But **whoever** (= "if anyone") stands firmly in his heart . . . will do well.

e. A Question

On a rare occasion, a direct question can be used with a conditional force.

Matt 26:15   τί θέλετέ μοι δοῦναι, κἀγὼ ὑμῖν παραδώσω αὐτόν;
What will you give me **if** I deliver him over to you?

f.   The Semantics Involved

The implied conditions are normally equivalent to the third class condition. This has a bearing on the exegesis of several passages.[8]

2.   Explicitly

Explicitly, conditions are expressed with the *if* stated in the protasis. The Greek has two words for *if* that are used most often–εἰ and ἐάν. The rest of this chapter will focus on the explicit conditions.

B.   *Structural Categories of Conditional Sentences*

Explicit conditional sentences follow four general structural patterns in the Greek NT.[9] Each pattern is known as a *class*; hence, first class, second class, third class, and fourth class. See the section on semantics for the meaning that each conveys.

Type	*Protasis ("if")*	*Apodosis ("then")*
First Class	εἰ + indicative mood any tense (negative: οὐ)	any mood any tense
Second Class	εἰ + indicative mood past tense aorist . . . imperfect . . . (negative: μή)	(ἄν) + indicative past tense . . . aorist (past time) . . . imperfect (present time)
Third Class	ἐάν + subjunctive mood any tense (negative: μή)	any mood any tense
Fourth Class	εἰ + optative mood present or aorist	ἄν + optative mood present or aorist

Table 12
The Structure of Conditions

---

[8] See discussion under conditional participle in the chapter on participles.

[9] We are here combining the third and fifth class condition because the fifth class is a subset of the third class structurally. If we were to distinguish them structurally, we should also distinguish the two types of second class condition structurally.

C. *Semantic Categories of Conditional Sentences*

➡   **1.   First Class Condition (Assumed True for Argument's Sake)**

    a.   Definition

> The first class condition indicates *the assumption of truth for the sake of argument*. The normal idea, then, is *if–and let us assume that this is true for the sake of argument–then.* . . . This class uses the particle εἰ with the indicative (in any tense) in the protasis. In the apodosis, any mood and any tense can occur. This is a frequent conditional clause, occurring about 300 times in the NT.[10]

    b.   Amplification

        1)   Not "Since"

> There are two views of the first class condition that need to be avoided. First is the error of saying too much about its meaning. The first class condition is popularly taken to mean the condition of reality or the condition of truth. Many have heard this from the pulpit: "In the Greek this condition means *since*."[11]
>
> This is saying too much about the first class condition. For one thing, this view assumes a direct correspondence between language and reality, to the effect that the indicative mood is the mood of fact. For another, this view is demonstrably false for conditional statements: (a) In apparently only 37% of the instances is there a correspondence to reality (to the effect that the condition could be translated *since*[12]). (b) Further, there are 36 instances of the first class condition in the NT that cannot possibly be translated *since*. This can be seen especially with two opposed conditional statements.[13] Note the following illustrations.

---

[10] Boyer ("First Class Conditions," 76-77, n. 5) tentatively counts 306 first class conditions, though cautiously noting that a precise count is difficult because "some are mixed (part first class and part second class); some are incomplete (where the protasis or apodosis is left unexpressed); and some are uncertain (where the verb is left unexpressed)."

[11] Grammarians such as Gildersleeve, Roberts, Robertson, *BDF*, etc., have looked at conditions in light of the mood used and have argued that the indicative mood in first class conditions is significant. But their language has often been misunderstood: "assumption of truth" has been interpreted to mean "truth."

[12] We will argue that the first class condition should *never* be translated *since* (see the third section, "Assumed True for the Sake of Argument").

[13] For a detailed discussion of these points, see Boyer, "First Class Conditions," especially 76-80.

Mt 12:27-28 εἰ ἐγὼ ἐν Βεελζεβοὺλ ἐκβάλλω τὰ δαιμόνια, οἱ υἱοὶ ὑμῶν ἐν τίνι ἐκβάλλουσιν; . . . (28) εἰ δὲ ἐν πνεύματι θεοῦ ἐγὼ ἐκβάλλω τὰ δαιμόνια, ἄρα ἔφθασεν ἐφ᾽ ὑμᾶς ἡ βασιλεία τοῦ θεοῦ.

If I cast out demons by Beelzebul, by whom do your sons cast them out? . . . (28) But **if** I cast out demons by the Spirit of God, then the kingdom of God has come upon you.

> Obviously it is illogical to translate both sentences as *since I cast out*, because the arguments are opposed to each other. And it would be inconsistent to translate the first participle *if* and the second *since*.

1 Cor 15:13 εἰ δὲ ἀνάστασις νεκρῶν οὐκ ἔστιν, οὐδὲ Χριστὸς ἐγήγερται

> But **if** there is no resurrection, then Christ has not been raised.

> It is self-evident that the apostle Paul could not mean by the first class condition *"since* there is no resurrection"!

Cf. also Matt 5:29-30; 17:4; 26:39 with 26:42; John 10:37; 18:23; 1 Cor 9:17; 15:14.

2) Not Simple

Because of the compelling evidence that the first class condition does not always correspond to reality, some scholars have assumed that it is just a simple condition.[14] This view goes back to a classical scholar, W. W. Goodwin: "When the protasis *simply states* a particular supposition, implying nothing as to the fulfilment of the condition, it has the indicative with εἰ."[15] The first class condition, in this view, is sometimes called the "simple condition," "condition of logical connection," or "neutral condition." One might call this the "undefined condition" in that nothing can be said about the reality of the supposition.

But this view says too little. At bottom, it assumes a *point* of meaning for a syntactical structure, ignores the mood used (the indicative means *something*),[16] and makes no distinction between the various conditions.[17] Virtually all conditions can be said to make a logical connection between the two halves (e.g., the third class condition in Mark 8:3–ἐὰν ἀπολύσω αὐτοὺς νήστεις εἰς οἶκον αὐτῶν, ἐκλυθήσονται ἐν τῇ ὁδῷ ["If I send them to their homes starving, they will faint on the way"]). This is the nature of conditions in general, not just the first class condition.

---

[14] For a critique of this view, see the appendix.

[15] Goodwin-Gulick, *Greek Grammar*, 294 (§1400).

[16] This approach agrees that the indicative assumes the untruth of a proposition in the second class condition (Boyer, "Second Class Conditions," 82: "they enjoy more agreement on the part of the grammarians than the other types and are less problem [*sic*] for the exegete"). To argue that the indicative mood is a key indicator of meaning in one condition but not in the other argues against the validity of the overall scheme.

[17] Boyer argues that the logical connection view fits "every one of the 300 NT examples and are equally true of every one of them" ("First Class Conditions," 82). But this is a minimalist statement that could be said of *all* conditions–first, second, third, or fourth class.

The question is not how little the first class condition says, but how much. What are its distinctives?[18]

3) Assumed True for the Sake of Argument

The force of the indicative mood, when properly understood, lends itself to the notion of *presentation* of reality. In the first class condition the conditional particle turns such a presentation into a supposition. This does *not* mean that the condition is true or means *since*! But it does mean that as far as the portrayal is concerned, the point of the argument is based on the assumption of reality.

Several examples will be provided to demonstrate this point. But three points need to be added.

- First, even in places where the argument is apparently believed by the speaker, *the particle εἰ should not be translated since*. Greek had several words for *since*, and the NT writers were not opposed to using them (e.g., ἐπεί, ἐπειδή). There is great rhetorical power in *if*. To translate εἰ as *since* is to turn an invitation to dialogue into a lecture.[19] Often the idea seems to be an encouragement to respond, in which the author attempts to get his audience to come to the conclusion of the apodosis (since they already agree with him on the protasis). It thus functions as a tool of persuasion. Note some of the illustrations below that demonstrate this point.[20]

- Second, how can we tell whether a speaker would actually affirm the truth of the protasis? Context, of course, is the key, but a good rule of thumb is to note the apodosis: Does the logic cohere if both protasis and apodosis are true? Often when a question is asked in the apodosis, the author does not embrace the truth of the protasis. These are only simple guidelines. Where in doubt, check the broader context.

---

[18] In Boyer's treatment of conditions, he appeals to classical scholarship: "The classical grammarians along with the older NT scholars had the right idea" ("First Class Conditions," 83). But this is a misleading statement, for Boyer is appealing to a particular view *within* classical scholarship, viz., Goodwin's, that was itself a reaction to the standard view that went back to Gottfried Hermann. Gildersleeve took Goodwin to task for his avant garde position and rightly criticized him for ignoring the mood. Many if not most classical scholars sided with Gildersleeve against Goodwin.

[19] Although many translations do this in various places, such translations miss the literary force of the conditional statement.

[20] This usage could be considered one of the pragmatic functions of conditions. Because of the high frequency in the NT of this *responsive* or *persuasive* protasis with first class conditions, however, we are equally justified in placing this usage here.

- Third, not infrequently conditional sentences are used rhetorically in a way that goes beyond the surface structure. Hence, on one level the structure might indicate one thing, but on another level, an entirely different meaning is in view. For example, suppose a mother says to her child, "If you put your hand in the fire, you'll get burned." We could analyze the condition on a structural or logical level. These ought not to be ignored. But the pragmatic meaning of the statement is, "Don't put your hand in the fire!" It is, in effect, a polite command, couched in indirect language. (This approach is addressed briefly in the appendix.)

Mt 12:27-28 **εἰ** ἐγὼ ἐν Βεελζεβοὺλ ἐκβάλλω τὰ δαιμόνια, οἱ υἱοὶ ὑμῶν ἐν τίνι ἐκβάλλουσιν; . . . (28) **εἰ** δὲ ἐν πνεύματι θεοῦ ἐγὼ ἐκβάλλω τὰ δαιμόνια, ἄρα ἔφθασεν ἐφ᾽ ὑμᾶς ἡ βασιλεία τοῦ θεοῦ.

If I cast out demons by Beelzebul, by whom do your sons cast them out? . . . (28) But **if** I cast out demons by the Spirit of God, then the kingdom of God has come upon you.

> We have already seen with this couplet that the particle cannot consistently be translated *since*. But leaving it as a mere simple condition is not saying enough. The force is "**If**–*and let's assume that it's true for the sake of argument*–I cast out demons by Beelzebul, then by whom do your sons cast them out? . . . But **if**–*assuming on the other hand that this is true*–I cast out demons by the Spirit of God, then the kingdom of God has come upon you." This yields satisfactory results for both halves.

Matt 5:30 **εἰ** ἡ δεξιά σου χεὶρ σκανδαλίζει σε, ἔκκοψον αὐτὴν καὶ βάλε ἀπὸ σοῦ

If your right hand offends you, cut it off and throw it from you!

> Jesus often put forth a number of challenges to current Jewish orthodoxy, such as that appendages and external things are what defile a person. Reading the text in light of that motif yields the following force: "**If**–*and let us assume that this is true for argument's sake*–your right hand offends you, then cut it off and throw it from you!" The following line only enforces this interpretation ("For it is better for you that one of your members should perish than that your whole body should be cast into hell"). Jesus thus brings the Pharisees' view to its logical conclusion. It is as if he said, "If you really believe that your anatomy is the root of sin, then start hacking off some body parts! After all, wouldn't it be better to be called 'Lefty' in heaven than to fry in hell as a whole person?"
>
> The condition thus has a provocative power seen in this light. Just the opposite of Jesus' affirming that appendages cause sin (as many have assumed, since a first class condition is used here), he is getting the audience to sift through the inconsistency of their own position. It is not the hands and eyes that cause one to sin, but the heart.

Luke 4:3 εἶπεν αὐτῷ ὁ διάβολος· **εἰ** υἱὸς εἶ τοῦ θεοῦ, εἰπὲ τῷ λίθῳ τούτῳ ἵνα γένηται ἄρτος.

The devil said to him, "**If** you are God's Son, tell this stone to become bread."

> The force of this is "**If**–*and let us assume that it's true for the sake of argument*–you are God's Son, tell this stone to become bread." Apparently, the devil was from Missouri (the "Show Me" state)!

1 Th 4:14   εἰ γὰρ πιστεύομεν ὅτι Ἰησοῦς ἀπέθανεν καὶ ἀνέστη, οὕτως καὶ ὁ θεὸς
τοὺς κοιμηθέντας διὰ τοῦ Ἰησοῦ ἄξει σὺν αὐτῷ.

For **if** we believe that Jesus died and rose again, even so God will
bring with him those who are asleep through Jesus.

> Many modern translations render the particle *since*. Although it is cer-
> tainly true that Paul embraced this as true, to translate it as *since* keeps
> the audience at an arm's length. The sentence becomes a lecture rather
> than a dialogue. By translating it *if*, the audience is drawn into the argu-
> ment of the apodosis. Their response would be something like, "If we
> believe that Jesus died and rose again? Of course we believe that! You
> mean that this indicates that the dead in Christ will not miss out on the
> rapture?" In such instances it is not the protasis that is in doubt, but the
> apodosis. (Further, to say that the connection is merely logical hardly
> does such texts justice.) Not infrequently in the NT, the speaker draws
> his audience to just such a connection, basing his argument on what
> both speaker and audience already embrace as true. These instances are
> not without exegetical significance. Cf., e.g., Rom 3:29, 30; 5:17; 2 Cor
> 5:17; Gal 3:29; 4:7; 2 Tim 2:11; Phlm 17; Heb 2:2-3; 1 Pet 1:17; 2:2-3; 2 Pet
> 2:4-9; 1 John 4:11; Rev 13:9; 20:15.

Rom 8:9   ὑμεῖς δὲ οὐκ ἐστὲ ἐν σαρκὶ ἀλλὰ ἐν πνεύματι, **εἴπερ** πνεῦμα θεοῦ οἰκεῖ
ἐν ὑμῖν.

But you are not in the flesh but in the Spirit, **if indeed** the Spirit of
God dwells in you.

> Here the conditional particle is a spin-off of εἰ, strengthening the ascen-
> sive force. This looks very much like 1 Thess 4:14—i.e., it too seems to be
> a "responsive" condition. The audience would most likely respond
> along these lines: "If the Spirit of God dwells in us? Of course he does!
> And this means that we are not in the flesh but in the Spirit? Remark-
> able!"

Cf. also Mark 14:29; Luke 4:9; 6:32; 19:8; John 10:24; 18:23; Acts 5:39; 16:15; 25:5; Rom 2:17;
4:2; 6:5; 7:16, 20; 2 Cor 3:7, 8; 11:15; Gal 2:18; 5:18; Phil 2:17; Col 3:1; 1 Tim 5:8; Heb 12:8; Jas
4:11; 2 John 10; Rev 14:9.[21]

➡   **2.   Second Class Condition (Contrary to Fact)**

    a.   Definition

The second class condition indicates *the assumption of an untruth (for
the sake of argument).*[22] For this reason it is appropriately called the
"contrary to fact" condition (or the *unreal* condition). It might be better to call it *presumed* contrary to fact, however, since sometimes it
presents a condition that is true, even though the speaker assumes it
to be untrue (e.g., Luke 7:39). In the protasis the structure is εἰ +
indicative mood with a secondary tense (aorist or imperfect usually). The apodosis usually has ἄν (but some examples lack this particle),[23] and a secondary tense in the indicative mood. There are
about 50 examples of the second class condition in the NT.[24]

---

[21] For a complete list, with Greek and English texts laid out, see Boyer, "First Class
Conditions," 83-114.

b. Amplification: Past and Present Contrary-to-Fact

There are two types of second class conditions: *present* contrary-to-fact and *past* contrary-to-fact.[25]

The *present* contrary-to-fact condition uses the *imperfect* in both the protasis and apodosis.[26] It refers to something that is not true in the present time (from the speaker's portrayal). A typical translation would be *If X were . . . then Y would be* (as in "If you were a good man, then you would not be here right now").

The *past* contrary-to-fact uses the *aorist* in both the protasis and apodosis. It refers to something that was not true in the past time (from the speaker's portrayal). A typical translation would be *If X had been . . . then Y would have been* (as in "If you had been here yesterday, you would have seen a great game").

c. Illustrations

Luke 7:39   οὗτος εἰ ἦν προφήτης, ἐγίνωσκεν ἂν τίς καὶ ποταπὴ ἡ γυνὴ ἥτις ἅπτεται αὐτοῦ, ὅτι ἁμαρτωλός ἐστιν.

If this man *were* a prophet, *he would know* who and what sort of woman this is who is touching him, that she is a sinner.

John 5:46   **εἰ** *ἐπιστεύετε* Μωϋσεῖ, *ἐπιστεύετε* ἂν ἐμοί

If *you believed* Moses, *you would believe* me.

The idea is "If you believed Moses—but you do not. . . ." This involves the imperfect tense, a present contrary-to-fact condition.

---

[22] For the NT, it is unnecessary to add "for the sake of argument" since the speaker/author of every second class condition in the NT apparently embraces the untruth of the protasis. But this is partially due to the paucity of examples. On a larger scale it would be helpful to make this distinction because an author can embrace the truth of the protasis, even though he presents it as untrue (especially in sarcastic contexts: "If the Dallas Cowboys had done better in 1995, they would have gone to the Super Bowl in 1996").

Boyer argues that the second class is not semantically the opposite of the first class because with the second class condition the speaker always believes the untruth of the proposition, while with the first class he does not always believe the truth of the proposition ("Second Class Conditions," 83-84). By arguing that they are not semantic opposites, he is able to treat the indicative as significant in the second class condition but as irrelevant in the first. But such an approach is to confuse a phenomenological usage with an ontological meaning: In *neither* condition does the indicative imply *fact*. This is to confuse language with reality or, in the least, with the perception of reality.

[23] Thirty-six of the instances have ἄν while 11 lack it (Boyer, "Second Class Conditions," 82, n. 6).

[24] Boyer, "Second Class Conditions," 81, counts 47 in the NT.

[25] On five occasions the pluperfect is used in the protasis of the second class condition (cf. Matt 24:43; Luke 12:39; John 4:10; 8:19; Acts 26:32). In four of these the pluperfect of οἶδα (ᾔδειν) is used (all except Acts 26:32), functioning apparently like a simple past tense.

[26] Apparently, not all imperfect + imperfect second class conditions indicate *present* contrary-to-fact; most of the exceptions involve the imperfect of εἰμί in the protasis (cf., e.g., Matt 23:30; John 11:21; Gal 4:15). See discussion in Boyer, "Second Class Conditions," 85-86.

1 Cor 2:8   εἰ ἔγνωσαν, οὐκ **ἂν** τὸν κύριον τῆς δόξης ἐσταύρωσαν
              If *they had known, they would* not *have crucified* the Lord of glory.

Cf. also Matt 11:21; 23:30; 24:22; Mark 13:20; Luke 10:13; 19:42; John 5:46; 9:33; 15:19; Acts 18:14; Rom 9:29; 1 Cor 11:31; Gal 1:10; 3:21; Heb 4:8; 8:4, 7; 1 John 2:19.

➡ ### 3. Third Class Condition

   #### a. Definition

   The third class condition often presents the condition as *uncertain of fulfillment, but still likely.* There are, however, many exceptions to this. It is difficult to give one semantic label to this structure, especially in Hellenistic Greek (note the discussion below). The structure of the protasis involves the particle ἐάν followed by a *subjunctive* mood in any tense. Both the particle (a combination of εἰ and the particle ἄν) and the subjunctive give the condition a sense of contingency. The apodosis can have any tense and any mood.[27] This is a common category of conditional clauses, occurring nearly 300 times in the NT.[28]

   #### b. Clarification and Semantics

   The third class condition encompasses a broad semantic range: (a) a *logical connection* (if A, then B) in the present time (sometimes called *present general condition*), indicating nothing as to the fulfillment of the protasis; (b) a mere *hypothetical* situation or one that probably will not be fulfilled; and (c) a *more probable future* occurrence.[29]

   Technically, the subjunctive is used in the **third class condition** as well as the **fifth class condition.** Structurally, these two are virtually identical: The *fifth* class condition requires a present indicative in the apodosis, while the *third* class can take virtually any mood-tense combination, including the present indicative.

   Semantically, their meaning is a bit different. The *third* class condition encompasses a broad range of potentialities in Koine Greek. It depicts what is *likely to occur* in the *future,* what could *possibly occur,* or even what is only *hypothetical* and will not occur. In classical Greek the third class condition was usually restricted to the first usage (known as *more probable future*), but with the subjunctive's

---

[27] For data, see Boyer, "Third (And Fourth) Class Conditions," 164.

[28] Boyer "Third (And Fourth) Class Conditions," counts 277 third class conditions (163, n. 1).

[29] Boyer gives the third class condition eight semantic categories, from "fulfillment certain" and "fulfillment probable" to "fulfillment improbable" and "no indication of probability" (ibid., 168-69). His largest category is "no indication of fulfillment" (with 120), followed by "fulfillment probable" (63; in combination with "fulfillment certain" this comes to 82).

encroaching on the domain of the optative in the Hellenistic era, this structural category has expanded accordingly.[30] The context will always be of the greatest help in determining an author's use of the third class condition.

The *fifth* class offers a condition the fulfillment of which is realized in the *present time*. This condition is known as the *present general condition*.[31] For the most part this condition is a *simple* condition; that is, the speaker gives no indication about the likelihood of its fulfillment. His presentation is neutral: "If A, then B."

Because of the broad range of the third class condition and the undefined nature of the fifth class, many conditional clauses are open to interpretation. But for the most part, the present general condition addresses a *generic* situation in the present time (broadly speaking), while the *more probable future* addresses a *specific* situation in the *future* time.[32]

c. Illustrations

Matt 4:9   ταῦτά σοι πάντα δώσω, **ἐὰν** πεσὼν *προσκυνήσῃς* μοι
I will give you all these things, **if** *you will* fall down and *worship* me.
This is a true third class since the apodosis involves a future indicative.

Mark 5:28   ἔλεγεν ὅτι **ἐὰν** *ἅψωμαι* κἂν τῶν ἱματίων αὐτοῦ *σωθήσομαι*
She was saying [to herself], "**If** only *I touch* his garments, *I will be healed*."
This woman, who had been hemorrhaging for a dozen years, was desperate. She had gotten worse by doctors' hands. The imperfect ἔλεγεν is perhaps iterative: "She was saying over and over again," as if to muster up enough courage and enough faith. Thus, in Mark's portrayal, there seems to be a great deal of doubt in this woman's mind that such an act would even heal her.

---

[30] See discussion of this in the chapter on moods.

[31] Although many grammarians, especially those of the Goodwin school, treat the first class condition as the "simple" condition, this label more appropriately belongs to the fifth class. See discussion above, under first class condition, as to why "simple condition" is inappropriate for the first class.

[32] Boyer argues against the present general condition, stating that all conditions with ἐάν + subjunctive in the protasis involve the element of futurity. His basis for this is the mood used: "[An author's] choice to use the subjunctive points to the common element. They are both undetermined, contingent suppositions, future in time reference" (Boyer, "Third (and Fourth) Class Conditions," 173). But the subjunctive idea does not necessarily involve uncertainty about *time*; frequently, it is used for uncertainty as to the *subject* (e.g., in indefinite relative clauses). Thus, the subjunctive is well suited to any condition where uncertainty is in view, either a specific situation in the future or a general situation in the present (see, e.g., John 11:9 below).

John 3:12   εἰ τὰ ἐπίγεια εἶπον ὑμῖν καὶ οὐ πιστεύετε, πῶς **ἐὰν** εἴπω ὑμῖν τὰ ἐπουράνια *πιστεύσετε*;

If I have told you earthly things and yet you do not believe, how *will you believe* if *I should tell* you heavenly things?[33]

> This is a third class condition, embedded within a deliberative question. It follows a first class condition in which the apodosis is a denial of belief. In light of this parallel, as well as the context, we should read the third class condition as follows: "If I should tell you heavenly things–and it is likely that I will–how is it possible for you to believe?"

John 11:9   **ἐάν** τις *περιπατῇ* ἐν τῇ ἡμέρᾳ, οὐ *προσκόπτει*

If anyone *walks* in the day, *he does* not *stumble*.

> This is an example of the present general condition. There is no hint of uncertainty about this event occurring, nor is it something presented as an eventuality. This is a principle, a proverb. The subjunctive is used because the subject is undefined, not because the time is future.

1 Cor 14:8   **ἐὰν** ἄδηλον σάλπιγξ φωνὴν *δῷ*, τίς *παρασκευάσεται* εἰς πόλεμον;

If the trumpet *should give* an indistinct sound, who *will prepare* for battle?

> Although Paul puts his condition in the third class, he does not expect a bugler to play an inarticulate sound on the verge of battle! Due to the subjunctive's encroaching on the optative in Koine, it has come to cover a multitude of conditional situations.

1 Cor 13:2   **ἐὰν** *ἔχω* προφητείαν καὶ *εἰδῶ* τὰ μυστήρια πάντα καὶ πᾶσαν τὴν γνῶσιν καὶ **ἐὰν** *ἔχω* πᾶσαν τὴν πίστιν ὥστε ὄρη μεθιστάναι, ἀγάπην δὲ μὴ *ἔχω*, οὐθέν εἰμι.

If *I have* a prophetic gift and *I understand* all mysteries and all knowledge, and if *I have* all faith so as to remove mountains, but *do* not *have* love, I am nothing.

> The fourfold condition is used in a very broad way. Paul builds his argument from the actual (he does have prophetic powers) to the hypothetical (he does not understand all mysteries nor have all knowledge [otherwise, he would be omniscient!]). This is his pattern in the first three verses of 1 Cor 13–an argument from the actual to the hypothetical. It is therefore probable that Paul could speak in the tongues of human beings, but *not* in the tongues of *angels* (v 1). 1 Cor 13:1, then, offers no comfort for those who view tongues as a heavenly language.

1 John 1:9   **ἐὰν** *ὁμολογῶμεν* τὰς ἁμαρτίας ἡμῶν, πιστός *ἐστιν* καὶ δίκαιος, ἵνα ἀφῇ ἡμῖν τὰς ἁμαρτίας καὶ καθαρίσῃ ἡμᾶς ἀπὸ πάσης ἀδικίας.

If *we confess* our sins, *he is* faithful and just to forgive us our sins and to cleanse us from all unrighteousness.

> This verse is frequently seen to be a more probable future condition. As such, it is sometimes viewed as referring to unbelievers who have not yet confessed their sins (though the *we* is problematic[34]). More likely, it is a present general condition in which the subject is distributive ("if any of us").[35] The subjunctive is thus used because of the implicit uncertainty as to who is included in the *we*.

---

[33] Instead of πιστεύσετε in the second protasis, πιστεύετε is found in 𝔓[75] *et pauci.*

Cf. also Matt 6:22, 23; Mark 4:22; 10:30; Luke 5:12; John 6:44; 8:31; Acts 9:2; 15:1; 26:5; Rom 2:25; 7:2-3; 10:9; 1 Cor 6:4; 11:15; 14:28; Col 4:10; 1 Thess 3:8; 1 Tim 3:15; 2 Tim 2:5; Heb 10:38; Jas 2:17; 5:15; 1 John 1:8, 10; 4:12; Rev 2:5; 3:20.[36]

4. Fourth Class Condition (Less Probable Future)

a. Definition

The fourth class condition indicates a *possible* condition in the future, usually a remote possibility (such as *if he could do something, if perhaps this should occur*). The protasis involves εἰ + the *optative* mood. The *optative* is also used in the apodosis along with ἄν (to indicate contingency). Because of the increasing use of the subjunctive and decreasing use of the optative in Hellenistic Greek, it should come as no surprise that there are no complete fourth class conditions in the NT.

Sometimes the conditional clause is mixed, with a non-optative in the apodosis (e.g., Acts 24:19). On two other occasions, there is an apodosis, but a verbless one (1 Pet 3:14, 17). On other occasions, no apodosis is to be supplied, the protasis functioning as a sort of stereotyped parenthesis (e.g., 1 Cor 14:10; 15:37).[37]

b. Semantics

The semantic significance of the fourth class condition, even though it is never complete in the NT, must not be overlooked. As we have pointed out, the subjunctive has increasingly encroached on the domain of the optative in Koine Greek.[38] Thus, the subjunctive's

---

[34] *We* typically falls into one of three categories of usage: editorial (referring just to the author), exclusive (referring just to the author and his associates), or inclusive (referring to the author, his associates, and the readers). To see the *we* in 1 John 1:9 as referring to unbelievers would be to take the pronominal referent to mean "you, but not me." Such is not impossible, of course, but it is highly unlikely and apparently otherwise unexampled in the NT. See chapter on "Person and Number" for discussion of the use of the first person plural.

[35] A more probable future condition, however, is perhaps supported by the *v.l.* to καθαρίσῃ; the future indicative καθαρίσει is found in A 33 2464 *et alii*. The future indicative could be connected to ἐστίν (thus, "he is faithful and righteous . . . and he will cleanse us"), but it can just as easily be joined to ἀφῇ ("he is faithful and righteous to forgive us and cleanse us"). Along these lines, it is interesting that in Johannine literature the future indicative does occur after ἵνα more frequently than in any other writer (cf. John 7:3; Rev 3:9; 6:4, 11; 8:3; 9:4, 5, 20; 13:12; 14:13; 22:14). Nevertheless, the reading is most likely a later addition.

[36] For a complete list, see Boyer, "Third (and Fourth) Class Conditions," *passim.*

[37] See Boyer, "Third (and Fourth) Class Conditions," 171-72, for discussion.

[38] One measure of this is the shift in frequency between LXX and the NT. There are 516 optatives in the LXX and only 68 in the NT. Proportionately, if the optative's frequency had remained stable, we might have expected about twice as many optatives (c. 125) in the NT.

semantic domain has broadened. But this does not mean that there is overlap in *both* directions; the optative still functions within its more narrow confines. This is due to the principle that when an author chooses the rarer form (in this case, the optative), he does so consciously.[39] The illustrations below will note the significance of this point.[40]

c. Illustrations

The first illustration includes just the protasis of the fourth class condition; the last two include just the apodosis.

1 Pet 3:14   εἰ καὶ *πάσχοιτε* διὰ δικαιοσύνην, μακάριοι[41]

Even **if** *you should suffer* for righteousness, [you would be] blessed.

> This text comes as close as any to a complete fourth class condition in the NT. *Prima facie*, the readership of this letter has not yet suffered for righteousness, and the possibility of such happening soon seems remote. The author reinforces this point in v 17, again with the protasis of a fourth class condition: "It is better to suffer for doing good than for doing evil, **if** the will of God *should* so *will* it (**εἰ** θέλοι τὸ θέλημα τοῦ θεοῦ). Although the occasion of 1 Peter is frequently assumed to involve suffering on the part of the readership, this text seems to argue against that. It is probably better to see the author in the midst of suffering, out of which experience he offers his counsel to believers who may have been insulated from it thus far.

Luke 1:62   ἐνένευον τῷ πατρὶ αὐτοῦ τὸ τί ἂν **θέλοι** καλεῖσθαι αὐτό

they were making signs to his father as to what **he would want** to call him

---

[39] This can be seen via analogy with lexical choice. A child might speak of a "book," while an adult, whose vocabulary is presumably richer, might say "booklet," "tome," "volume," etc. In grammar, the difference between colloquial speech and literary speech is also pronounced (e.g., "who" for "whom" in colloquial speech, but not vice versa).

[40] Boyer has correct instincts when he observes that the issue of the comparative meanings of third and fourth class conditions among NT grammarians tacitly assumes that the subjunctive and optative were used with the same frequency in the Hellenistic period ("Third(and Fourth) Class Conditions," 171-72). That is to say, most NT grammarians simply transfer the classical meanings of the third class and fourth class to the Koine period, assuming that nothing has changed. But Boyer goes too far when he argues that "such [meanings for these conditions] can have no application to NT Greek, for the obvious reason that the NT has no fourth-class conditions" (ibid., 171). This is an inaccurate assessment on three levels: (1) Although there are no *complete* fourth class conditions, the incomplete conditions (either protasis or apodosis) do occur in the NT; (2) to argue that the third class condition has broadened out does not imply that the fourth class condition has likewise broadened out, simply because the overlap is moving in one direction; (3) as we have argued, since the optative is dying out in the Koine period, when an author uses it, he is presumed to be doing so for a reason. For these reasons, we have suggested that the fourth class condition still retains its force of "less probable future," while the subjunctive has broadened in scope to include this meaning as well as others.

[41] A few MSS supply the indicative verb ἐστε after μακάριοι (so ℵ C), in which case we should read the text, "Even if you should suffer for righteousness, you *are* blessed."

The implicit protasis is, "If he had his voice back so that he could call him some name." There is little expectation this will happen, however (note their reaction in v 65 when this occurs).

Acts 17:18   τινες ἔλεγον· τί ἄν **θέλοι** ὁ σπερμολόγος οὗτος λέγειν;
Some [of the philosophers] were saying, "What **would** this babbler **say**?"

The implicit protasis is, "If he could say anything that made sense!" It is evident that the philosophers do not think such is likely.

Cf. also Acts 5:24; 8:31; 17:27; 20:16; 24:19; 27:12, 39; 1 Cor 14:10; 15:37; 1 Pet 3:17.

Appendix on Conditional Sentences: Advanced Information

Select Bibliography

J. K. Baima, "Making Valid Conclusions from Greek Conditional Sentences" (Th.M. thesis, Grace Theological Seminary, 1986); *BDF*, 182, 188-91, 194-95, 237 (§360, 371-76, 385, 454); **J. L. Boyer**, "First Class Conditions: What Do They Mean?" *GTJ* 2 (1981) 76-114; **idem**, "Second Class Conditions in New Testament Greek," *GTJ* 3 (1982) 81-88; **idem**, "Third (and Fourth) Class Conditions," *GTJ* 3 (1982) 163-75; **idem**, "Other Conditional Elements in New Testament Greek," *GTJ* 4 (1983) 173-88; **A. F. Braunlich**, "Goodwin or Gildersleeve?" *AJP* 77 (1956) 181-84; **Burton**, *Moods and Tenses*, 100-116 (§238-88); **C. J. Fillmore**, "Varieties of Conditional Sentences," *Proceedings of the Third Eastern States Conference on Linguistics*, ed. F. Marshall (Columbus: Ohio State University, 1987) 163-82; **M. L. Geis**, "Conditional Sentences in Speech Act Theory," *Proceedings of the Third Eastern States Conference on Linguistics*, 233-45; **D. G. Gibbs**, "The Third Class Condition in New Testament Usage" (Th.M. thesis, Dallas Theological Seminary, 1979); **B. L. Gildersleeve**, "On εἰ with the Future Indicative and ἐάν with the Subjunctive in the Tragic Poets," *TAPA* 7 (1876) 5-23; **W. W. Goodwin**, *Greek Grammar*, rev. C. B. Gulick (Boston: Ginn & Co., 1930) 292-302 (§1392-1436); **idem**, "On the Classification of Conditional Sentences in Greek Syntax," *TAPA* 4 (1873) 60-79; **idem**, "'Shall' and 'Should' in Protasis, and Their Greek Equivalents," *TAPA* 7 (1876) 87-107; **J. H. Greenlee**, "'If' in the New Testament," *BT* 13 (January 1962) 39-43; **W. R. Hintze**, "The Significance of the Greek First Class Conditional Sentence in the Structure and Interpretation of the Gospels" (Ph.D. dissertation, Southwestern Baptist Theological Seminary, 1968); **R. C. Horn**, "The Use of the Subjunctive and Optative Moods in the Non-Literary Papyri" (Ph.D. dissertation, University of Pennsylvania, 1926); **J. J. Kijne**, "Greek Conditional Sentences," *BT* 13 (October 1962) 223-24; **C. D. Morris**, "On Some Forms of Greek Conditional Sentences," *TAPA* 6 (1875) 44-53; **Moule**, *Idiom Book*, 148-52; **H. C. Nutting**, "The Order of Conditional Thought," *AJP* 24 (1903) 25-39, 149-62; **idem**, "The Modes of Conditional Thought," *AJP* 24 (1903) 278-303; **Porter**, *Idioms*, 254-67;

W. K. Pritchett, "The Conditional Sentence in Attic Greek," *AJP* 76 (1955) 1-17; **J. W. Roberts**, "The Use of Conditional Sentences in the Greek New Testament as Compared with Homeric, Classical and Hellenistic Uses" (Ph.D. dissertation, University of Texas, 1955); **Robertson**, *Grammar*, 1004-27; **J. B. Sewall**, "On the Distinction Between the Subjunctive and Optative Modes in Greek Conditional Sentences," *TAPA* 5 (1874) 77-82; **J. R. Searle**, *Speech Acts: An Essay in the Philosophy of Language* (Cambridge: Cambridge University Press, 1969) especially 60-71; **Smyth**, *Greek Grammar*, 512-39 (§2280-2382); **E. A. Sonnenschein**, "Horton-Smith's Conditional Sentences," *Classical Review* 9 (1895) 220-23; **E. C. Traugott, A. ter Meulen, J. S. Reilly, C. A. Ferguson**, editors, *On Conditionals* (Cambridge: Cambridge University Press, 1986); **C. L. Tune**, "The Use of Conditional Sentences in Hebrews" (Th.M. thesis, Dallas Theological Seminary, 1973); **D. R. Waters**, "Conditional Sentences in Romans" (Th.M. thesis, Dallas Theological Seminary, 1976); **M. Winger**, "If Anyone Preach: An Examination of Conditional and Related Forms in the Epistles of St. Paul" (M.Div. thesis, Union Theological Seminary, 1983); **idem**, "Unreal Conditions in the Letters of Paul," *JBL* 105 (1986) 110-12; **R. A. Young**, "A Classification of Conditional Sentences Based on Speech Act Theory," *GTJ* 10 (1989) 29-49; **idem**, *Intermediate Greek*, 227-30; **Zerwick**, *Biblical Greek*, 101-13 (§299-334).

I. Introduction

William Shakespeare put into the mouth of one of his characters: "'If' is [a] peacemaker . . . [there is] much virtue in 'If.'" By this he meant, of course, that contingencies and compromise are the essence of peace-making. However, if Shakespeare were alive today, he would say that "If" is anything *but* a peace-maker among Greek grammarians. One might say that the issues involved have brought on a *first class* war among grammarians!

A. The Battle of Conditions

In general, the battle has been over which has priority in determining the semantics of conditional sentences, the *mood* or the *tense*. Two schools of thought have emerged. Both schools are oriented to classical Greek. However, NT students have often taken up sides without always thinking through the differences between the classical and Koine eras. Our treatment will be a brief assessment of these schools, especially as they relate to the Greek of the NT. But perhaps we should begin with a look at a third alternative.

B. Parenthesis: Conditions and Speech Act Theory

As we pointed out in the main section of this chapter, there are three approaches that scholars have taken with regard to conditions: structural, semantic (logical), and pragmatic (speech act theory). The first of these is restricted to *Greek* conditions; the latter two are complementary approaches, addressing conditions in terms of universal grammar. Not all see the issues this way, however.

In NT circles, R. A. Young has criticized the debate over Greek conditions as focusing too heavily on the structure of conditions without due regard for more broadly defined semantic issues. His approach is to analyze conditions on the basis of "speech act theory."[42] The speech act theory (or pragmatic) approach examines the communicative intention when conditional sentences are employed. This view is concerned with whether a conditional sentence is uttered as a veiled threat, request, command, and the like. This approach to language in general, and to conditions in particular, is not new.[43] But Young has both applied it to the NT and has argued that this view renders the debate over structure virtually obsolete.[44]

How shall we assess the pragmatic (or speech act theory) approach to conditional sentences? Briefly, two points can be made, one positive and one negative.

First, much exegetical value can be gleaned from this approach. The simple recognition that conditional sentences are often employed to communicate *indirectly* what would be harsh if communicated directly is a helpful insight.[45] In John 11:21, Martha's statement to Jesus, "Lord, if you had been here, my brother would not have died," although *formally* a second class condition, is intended as a *rebuke*. It is as if she had said, "Lord, you should have been here!" Sometimes the protasis "is a mitigator or politeness marker."[46] As such, it is often used to make an implicit request, sometimes even an

---

[42] See especially his article, "A Classification of Conditional Sentences Based on Speech Act Theory."

[43] Note in the bibliography especially works by Searle, Geis, and Traugott, Meulen, Reilly, and Ferguson.

[44] The article frequently has "either–or" type statements, such as "Speech act theory yields more meaningful results than traditional approaches" (29), and "Speech act theory categorizes utterances according to function rather than form. There is greater exegetical and homiletical value in classifying conditionals in this way" (39). To be sure, Young also states that "the analysis of conditionals in light of mood, tense, and particles is not wrong, but it only examines part of what contributes to meaning" (47). But for the most part he gives the impression that such structural approaches are wrong-headed. For example, in his opening volley under the section "Inadequacy of the Traditional Understanding," he argues that the meaning derived from a structuralist approach for Gal 4:15 "is nothing more than a truism that does not say anything at all" (32-33).

[45] The illustrations and categories are taken from Young, "Speech Act Theory," 36-46. There is much excellent and stimulating material in this essay for NT students.

[46] Ibid., 42.

impossible one. Thus, Jesus' plea in the Garden, "If it is possible, let this cup pass from me" (Matt 26:39), though formally a first class condition, is, on a deeper level, an expression of agony.[47] It is an implicit request that already knows it cannot be filled. Conditions are also used to exhort (1 John 4:11), manipulate (Matt 4:3), lament (Matt 11:21), persuade or argue (Matt 12:27-28), assert (Mark 8:12), and mock (Matt 27:40).

Such insights are both helpful and necessary for students to grasp the full sense of scripture. Beneath the surface of the text are deeper meanings that modern linguistic approaches are helping to dig out.

Second, this approach also has certain weaknesses. As we have noted, sometimes the practitioner of speech act theory gets so enthused over its value that the structure becomes meaningless.[48] Although we would agree that in the traditional approach it is wrong-headed to see a one-to-one correspondence between form and meaning, it is equally wrong to abandon the structural conventions of the language and seek meaning elsewhere. In analyzing Jesus' prayer in the Garden ("If it is possible, let this cup pass from me"), the choice of first class condition means *something*. The second class would not convey the same meaning, for example. The structures still need to be analyzed if we are to better understand language.

In our view, the pragmatic approach to conditions does not supplant the structural approach, but *complements* it. Indeed, it must *assume* a certain structuralist approach before it can make any further assessments. To the extent that those initial assumptions are incorrect, the inferences drawn from pragmatics are liable to be invalidated.[49] Speech act theory is, for the most part, extra-syntactical. This is not wrong, but neither is it syntax. Grammarians do not argue that syntax is the sum of all meaning, just that it provides a necessary foundation for assessing meaning. Speech act theory is one of the buildings erected on that foundation. This school, as well as several other

---

[47] We can see this in the quotation of Psalm 22:1 from the cross. "My God, my God, why have you forsaken me?" though formally a question, is really an expression of profound pain.

[48] Recall that Young defined speech act theory as categorizing "utterances according to function *rather than* form" ("Speech Act Theory," 39 [italics added]) and that he saw this approach as the way out of the quagmire of the structuralist debate.

[49] Ironically, Young has to assume certain traditional schools of thought on conditions as he makes his case for the irrelevance of these schools. He seems to argue, for example, that the indicative is the mood of reality, that the first class condition can and should be translated *since* on occasion, that aorists in the second class condition indicate past contrary-to-fact (judging by his translation of Gal 4:15), and that there is overlap in the semantic range of the four structural conditions. All of these opinions, whether accurate or not, depend largely on a prior assessment of the structures involved. At some points we might take issue with him over the structural interpretation. For example, to say that the first class condition should ever be translated *since*, in our view, is incorrect, robbing the linguistic form of some of its rhetorical power (see discussion earlier in this chapter under "First Class Conditions"). But the point we are making here is that his pragmatic approach *depends* on a certain structuralist view rather than denies its validity.

linguistic schools, is making an increasingly profound impact on biblical studies. But the greatest progress is made only when the head does not say to the foot, "I have no need of you."

II. The Controversy Between
Systems of Classification

The controversy over structural classification has been a hundred years' war. This debate focuses on the best system for classifying the structures and the meanings of the Greek conditional sentences.[50]

By way of background, there are several possible ways to classify conditions:

1) According to **form**

2) According to **time**

3) Whether the condition is **particular** (i.e., individual) or **general** (i.e. generic)

4) According to the meaning of the **moods** involved.

Out of these schemes emerged two predominant views in classical studies.

A. *Statement of the Two Views*

1. W. W. Goodwin

William Watson Goodwin, a classical Greek grammarian, wrote some provocative articles in *Transactions of the American Philological Association,* appearing in the 1870s. His view of conditions took the following approach:

a) General (third class, fourth class) vs. Particular (first class, second class)

b) Time (future in third and fourth class, present in first class)

c) Vividness of portrayal (third class is future more vivid; fourth class is future less vivid)

d) Simple condition or logical connection (first class) vs. meaningful choice of mood in third and fourth class.

In other words, the first class is used for particular and present situations. The third class condition is used for general and future notions; in relation to the fourth class, it expresses a future more vivid idea. The fourth class is used for future less vivid statements. The first class makes

---

[50] Credit is due to Buist M. Fanning for his input into this section.

no comment about the likelihood of fulfillment, while the moods in the other classes are at least significant, though not along the lines of fulfillment.

2. **B. L. Gildersleeve**

Basil Lanneau Gildersleeve was also a classical Greek grammarian with a tremendous wit. He was very much a scientific grammarian. Gildersleeve wrote in reaction to Goodwin's system in subsequent issues of the *Transactions of the American Philological Association* as well as the *American Journal of Philology* (the journal of which he was editor and founder).

The primary facet of Gildersleeve's system was in reference to fulfillment vs. unfulfillment. Another way to put this is that Gildersleeve made a strong link between the conditional sentence and the *mood* in which it was expressed.

B. *Critique of the Two Views (especially in relation to NT)*

1. **Of Goodwin's System**

There are four major objections to Goodwin's system, at least as it relates to the NT.[51]

a. **The reference to general (third class) vs. particular (first class) is not an ontological distinction.**

- εἰ + the indicative does not *always* refer to something particular, i.e., to a particular person or situation. In the NT, there are more than sixty general *first* class conditions (out of the 300+). In other words, about 20% of the first class conditions are general rather than particular. These especially are seen when the indefinite pronoun τις is used in the protasis. For example, in 1 Cor 8:2 we read, "If anyone thinks that he knows anything, he has not yet come to know exactly as he ought to know." Cf. also Matt 16:24; Mark 4:23; 9:35; Luke 14:26; Rom 8:9; 1 Cor 3:12, 15, 17; 7:13; 14:37; 16:22; 2 Cor 5:17; 11:20; Gal 1:9; 6:3; Phil 2:1; 3:4; 2 Thess 3:10, 14; 1 Tim 3:1; 6:3; Jas 1:5, 26; 3:2; 1 Pet 4:11; 2 John 10; Rev 11:5; 13:10; 14:9; 20:15 (N.B. *all* the first class conditions in Revelation are general).

- ἐάν + and the subjunctive does not *always* equal something general. For the most part, this usage is restricted to instances in which a present indicative is in the apodosis (as Goodwin argued). But specific, concrete situations are sometimes in view

---

[51] It should be kept in mind that not all of these critiques are of the school per se, but of its relevance to Hellenistic Greek in general and the Greek NT in particular.

even when the present indicative is in the apodosis. For example, in John 19:12 we read, "If you release *this man*, you are no friend of Caesar's" (ἐὰν τοῦτον ἀπολύσῃς, οὐκ εἶ φίλος τοῦ Καίσαρος). Cf. also Matt 21:26; John 13:8; 14:3; 15:14; 1 Cor 9:16.

b.   **The time criterion is not an ontological criterion.**

It is not true that the first class condition always refers to present or past time. There are over twenty instances of the *future* indicative in the protasis of a first class condition in the NT. See, for example, Matt 26:33; Mark 14:29; Luke 11:8; Rom 11:14.

c.   **The concept of "vividness" is vague and not clearly based on morpho-syntactic categories.**

On what basis is the subjunctive more *vivid* while the optative is less vivid? Is vividness an element of the mood? Further, in the NT, the notion of distinction between these two classes evaporates largely because of the paucity of optatives. There are no complete fourth class conditions. Thus, one would be hard-pressed to suggest that, in the NT at least, the biblical writers always made a clear distinction between the third class and fourth class conditions with reference to vividness.

d.   **Goodwin's system does not adequately take into account the moods involved in the conditions.**

To argue, as Goodwin did, that the first class condition is entirely neutral, implying nothing as to the affirmation of the protasis, is to misunderstand both the opposing school's view of things and to ignore the moods used in conditions. The Gildersleeve school did not argue that the first class condition meant *since*, but that the mood used had to do with presentation, not reality. And to see the first class condition as a mere logical connection does not seem sufficiently to take into account its counterpart in the second class condition (which also uses the indicative mood), nor does it say anything that is distinctive of the first class condition.[52]

Further, as to the subjunctive and optative, the ontological force of each of these moods is related to potentiality, not vividness. It may be that vividness is sometimes attached to a *tense* usage (as in the historical present), but to see such in the moods is to treat moods in conditional clauses in a way that is at odds with their normal function.

---

[52] See our treatment of this issue in the sections on the first and second class conditions.

2.   **Of Gildersleeve's System**

Gildersleeve's system has also been scrutinized. The following are major critiques of the school that are often put forth.

a.   **The protasis of the first class condition does not always, or even usually, *state* its hypothesis as a fact.**

The common misconception that it does so, even that it *usually* does so, has led to serious exegetical errors. Others have said it before, though none so convincingly as Boyer in his 1981 article. He pointed out that only 37% of first class conditions could be accurately presented as meaning "since." It needs to be emphatically stated here that *the first class condition does not mean "since."* One of the best demonstrations of this is seen in Matthew 12:27-28, discussed earlier.

There are a number of such couplets of opposites in the NT in which the first class condition is used in *both* arguments. It is impossible, in such passages, to claim that the first class condition means *since* both times. Cf. John 10:37-38; 15:20 (twice); 18:23 (twice); Acts 25:11 (twice); Rom 8:13 (twice); 1 Cor 9:17 (twice); 2 Cor 7:8-9; 2 Tim 2:12 (thrice); 1 Pet 2:20 (twice).

Nevertheless, in defense of Gildersleeve, he argued that the indicative mood was related to the portrayal not the reality of the event.[53] Hence, he would agree with the above criticism.

More convincing is the charge that the first class condition does not always put forth an argument. Jesus' prayer in the Garden is an illustration of this point. "If it is possible, let this cup pass from me" hardly means "If–*and let us assume that it is true for the sake of argument*–it is possible, let this cup pass from me." There is no argument in these words, just agony.

b.   **The distinction between third and fourth class conditions is not entirely valid.**

There are two problems here: (1) To say that the third class condition presents something as "more probable" or likely to happen misses the mark in many passages. For example, in 1 Cor 13:2 the third class condition is used to describe something impossible: "If I should know all mysteries and have all knowledge. . . ." (2) Although Gildersleeve may be right for classical Greek, he surely is not for Koine. This is not meant to be a criticism of Gildersleeve, but of NT grammarians who have uncritically adopted Gildersleeve's approach

---

[53] Boyer, "First Class Conditions," 78-81, in his critique of the Gildersleeve school (he does not call it by this name, but deals with it under three different labels) assesses its view correctly, then says that since NT students have not properly understood the view, it must be abandoned!

even though the language has gone through some dramatic shifts with regard to moods and conditions.[54]

Descriptions of the subjunctive and optative moods in standard grammars sometimes tacitly assume that the optative is still in full flower in the Koine period. But it is in fact dying out. The reason is that it was too subtle for people acquiring Greek as a second language to grasp fully.[55] In the Hellenistic era *the subjunctive is encroaching on the uses of the optative*. The third class condition thus, at times, is used for mere *possibility* or even *hypothetical* possibility (as well as, at other times, probability). As Gibbs has noted, the third class condition in Hellenistic Greek "is simply a large basket made to hold any future condition, likely or unlikely, possible or absurd."[56]

c. **Time does seem to play a part in the conditions.**

This can be seen with the second class condition, for example. It does not refer to the future. Also, the fourth class condition does not refer to past time. There are also tendencies in the first class condition (usually present time) and third class condition (present general and specific future, but not past). Conditions are thus linked to time, to some degree.

3. **Summary**

In summary, Gildersleeve's system is more accurate in that it is based, for the most part, on the normal uses of the *moods*. That is, his view is truer to the genius of the Greek language. But it has some flaws in it, especially in terms of relevance for Koine Greek.

---

[54] As we noted in the main body of this chapter, it is not valid to argue that the lack of complete fourth class conditions in the NT is grounds for obliterating all distinctions between third and fourth class. This is due to the fact that (1) although the third class condition has broadened in its usage, the fourth class has not–the overlap is moving in one direction; (2) since the optative is dying out in the Koine period, when an author uses it, he presumably does so for a reason. For these reasons, the fourth class condition still retains its force of "less probable future," while the subjunctive has broadened in scope to include this meaning as well as others. For other arguments on the distinction between third and fourth class conditions, see earlier sections.

[55] Moulton, *Prolegomena*, 165, notes: "No language but Greek has preserved both Subjunctive and Optative as separate and living elements in speech, and Hellenistic Greek took care to abolish this singularity in a fairly drastic way."

[56] Gibbs, "Third Class Condition," 51.

C. A Proposed Solution

1. The Alternatives (Logically)

From a logical standpoint we have at least four options:

1) Reject Goodwin's system, and accept Gildersleeve's.
2) Reject Gildersleeve's system, and accept Goodwin's.
3) Reject both systems and come up with another system.
4) Accept *parts* of each system, but not the entirety of either.

This last approach is advocated here.

2. Structure and Semantics

How is it *possible* to accept elements of each system?

First, both schools have *assumed* that if they could find exceptions to the other's system, no matter how small, they could throw out the entire system. If such an approach were taken in other areas of grammatical study, we would have to be agnostic about virtually everything in grammar. Just because a system is not infallible does not mean that it is thoroughly corrupt.

Second, to argue on the basis of a supposed *inherent idea* for each class condition that is *always* present in every instance is a faulty approach. This is analogous to word usage. Words change in their meaning; so do grammatical structures.

Third, grammatical structures, like words, can have fields of meaning, rather than simply points of meaning. For example, ἀφίημι does *not* mean only *forgive*. It also means *permit, let go, allow, divorce, leave, abandon,* etc. A grammatical example is the infinitive. The infinitive does not indicate only purpose; it may also indicate result, means, time, command, cause, etc. To recognize that the different classes of conditions *may* have fields of meaning, rather than points, will go a long way in helping us solve the problem of the meaning of the conditions.

At the same time, we should recognize both that occasionally the field of meaning that one class condition has can overlap with another (e.g., cf. Matt 18:8 and Mark 9:43: "If your [right] hand causes you to stumble"–first class in one, third class in the other),[57] and that the choice of a particular class condition by an author is never arbitrary. That is, although there may be overlap in meaning, the two are never entirely synonymous.

---

[57] Winger also demonstrated this point with first and second class conditions. See his "Unreal Conditions," 110-12.

3.   Summary

Our view embraces the notion that conditional clauses have some over-lap in usage rather than entirely distinct, compartmentalized, singular meanings. The basic points to be summarized are as follows:

- The *moods* in the conditions need to be taken seriously and consis-tently with how they are used elsewhere. The indicative, though often misunderstood to be the mood of reality, is the mood of asser-tion. The other moods are all potential. Specifically, in Koine Greek the subjunctive is broadly conceived, ranging from probability to hypothetical impossibility. The optative, because of its paucity, is chosen consciously by speakers and hence is used for the most part as it was in classical Greek: It indicates a remoter possibility in the future.

- Both the *first class* and *second class* condition basically suggest "assumption of truth/untruth for the sake of argument." This is in keeping with the force of the indicative. This condition is primarily used as a tool of persuasion. Often the speaker agrees with the argu-ment of the protasis. But even in such cases the first class condition should not be translated *since*. This is due to the persuasive nature of this condition: It draws the reader into the discussion. "Since" puts the reader at arm's length; "if" invites the reader to dialogue.[58]

To be sure, such a nuance can be overridden by other factors such as context, genre, etc. But even here, the first class condition has *some* meaning. The example given earlier of Jesus' prayer in the Garden now needs to be evaluated in this light.[59] "If it is possible, let this cup pass from me" is a conditional clause that, on one level, may be say-ing, "If it is possible–and I suspect it is–let this cup pass from me." The inner turmoil of Jesus is thus seen in the very structure of the condition, not in spite of it: He struggles because the temptation to circumvent the cross was very real. The fourth class condition, for example, would hardly have communicated the same point.[60]

---

[58] For discussion, see earlier section on "First Class Conditions."

[59] Those who disagree with the Gildersleeve school often use this example as a trump card. Both Boyer and Young, for example, use it to point out the absurdity of the "assump-tion of truth for argument's sake" view.

[60]This is not saying all that there is to Jesus' statement here, of course. Young is correct to point out that Jesus' expression is more of an unrealizable request than a logical argu-ment. But the agony is more vivid because it is in the first class condition.

We are not arguing that the cross was unnecessary as a means of salvation. But even granting the Gethsemane prayer its full-blown soteriological significance–and that the cross is essential to save sinners–a prior question needs to be asked: Is it necessary that God saves anyone? Perhaps this is the struggle seen in the Garden. In the least, to deny any turmoil, any internal struggle, is to deny the full humanity of Christ. We will surely never grasp the depths of the nature of the theanthropic Person, but the saints long ago rejected Docetism as an explanation.

- The *third class* condition uses the subjunctive to indicate either a potential *action* or a potential *actor*. Not all third class conditions are thus future; a large percentage are present general. The *present general* condition (sometimes called *fifth class* condition) thus usually has in view a generic subject or a distributive subject. This comes as close as any of the conditions to an "aoristic" condition or logical-connection condition. Its force is simply "If A, then B" with no hint about the prospects of the fulfillment of the protasis (because, with a distributive subject in view, some fulfill it and some do not).

  When a *future* situation is envisioned, it ranges (as does the subjunctive in Koine) from more probable future to mere hypothetical situation. The context is determinative. One cannot therefore argue, for example, that Paul most likely spoke in a heavenly language because 1 Cor 13:3 uses the third class condition. The parallels in vv 1-2 argue decisively against this view.

- Finally, the *fourth class* condition indicates a remote possibility in the future time. It is the *less probable future* condition.

For specific details and examples of our approach, see the main body of this chapter.

Volitional Clauses (Commands And Prohibitions)

Overview of Chapter

Select Bibliography

BDF, 172-74, 183-84, 195-96 (§335-37, 362-64, 387); **J. L. Boyer**, "The Classification of Imperatives: A Statistical Study," *GTJ* 8 (1987) 35-54; **Fanning**, *Verbal Aspect*, 325-88; **K. L. McKay**, "Aspect in Imperatival Constructions in New Testament Greek," *NovT* 27 (1985) 201-26; **Moule**, *Idiom Book*, 135-37; **Porter**, *Idioms*, 220-29; **idem**, *Verbal Aspect*, 335-61; **Young**, *Intermediate Greek*, 141-45.

Introduction: The Semantics of Commands and Prohibitions ("Do Not Start" vs. "Stop Doing"?)

Commands and prohibitions are vital to understand. They shape the attitudes and behavior of the believing community. It is imperative (pardon the pun!) to grapple with their meaning as best we can.

Beyond their obvious pragmatic value, volitional clauses comprise a fascinating area of study in Greek grammar that has been retooled in recent years. Some breakthroughs on the use of the tenses in general, and the use of the present and aorist in imperatives in particular, have changed the way grammarians and exegetes have looked at commands and prohibitions in the NT.[1]

A. *The Origin of the View*

For over eighty years, students of the NT assumed a certain view about the semantics of commands and prohibitions. This view is often traced to a brief essay written in 1904 by Henry Jackson.[2] He tells of a friend, Thomas David-son, who had been struggling with commands and prohibitions in modern Greek:

> Davidson told me that, when he was learning modern Greek, he had been puz-zled about the distinction, until he heard a Greek friend use the present impera-tive to a dog which was barking. This gave him the clue. He turned to Plato's *Apology*, and immediately stumbled upon the excellent instances 20 E μὴ θορυβήσητε, before clamour begins, and 21 A μὴ θορυβεῖτε, when it has begun.[3]

In other words, an Englishman learning modern Greek noted that the aorist in prohibitions meant *do not start*, while the present in prohibitions meant

---

[1] This chapter focuses on the tense-mood combination used in commands and prohi-bitions. It does not address modality in any detail. For a discussion, see the chapter on moods.

stop doing. He quickly looked at his copy of Plato and found that the same distinction was true in classical Greek.

This view was promoted two years later in Moulton's *Prolegomena*,[4] in which he speaks of the aorist as prohibiting an action not yet begun and the present as prohibiting an action that is in progress. From there this "already/not yet" view of the present and aorist prohibitions made its way into many of the textbook grammars of the NT for the next several decades, spreading by analogy to positive commands.[5]

Up until recently, this view was the accepted hypothesis on the essential meaning of prohibitions in NT Greek.

B. The Corrective by McKay and Others

In 1985 K. L. McKay challenged this view in his important essay, "Aspect in Imperatival Constructions in New Testament Greek."[6] He argued that "it seems axiomatic that the aspectual system found in the imperative and in the jussive uses of the subjunctive may be expected to be essentially the same as that found in the indicative. . . ."[7] What is that aspectual system found in the indicative? "The difference between the aorist and imperfective

---

[2] "Prohibitions in Greek," *Classical Review* 18 (1904) 262-63. The suggestion found here had already been communicated by Jackson to Walter Headlam, who noted it in passing in an earlier essay ("Some Passages of Aeschylus and Others," in *Classical Review* 17 [1903] 295, n. 1). Jackson's source was misunderstood, prompting the explanation by Jackson in *Classical Review* 18. The following year, Headlam expanded on the topic more completely ("Greek Prohibitions," *Classical Review* 19 [1905] 30-36). But Headlam and Jackson were not the first to suggest such differences between the aorist and present in prohibitions. As Headlam notes in his first essay, Gottfried Hermann had made, nearly a century earlier, the observation that was to become so popular (in his *Opuscula* [Lipsiae: G. Fleischer, 1827] 1.269), though it took Headlam and Jackson to resurrect the notion and put it in English dress. (For the sake of historical accuracy, it should be noted that Jackson did not get the idea from Hermann, though Hermann had suggested it prior to Jackson.) Ironically, the protests of H. D. Naylor ("Prohibitions in Greek," *Classical Review* 19 [1905] 26-30)–whose views were far more sober–went unheeded.

[3] Jackson, "Prohibitions in Greek," 263.

[4] Moulton, *Prolegomena* (first edition of 1906) 122. Unless otherwise specified, all other references to Moulton's *Prolegomena* in this book are to the third edition (1908).

[5] Dana-Mantey are representative. They give as their basic definition of each tense usage the following: "(1) Thus a prohibition expressed with the *present tense* demands the cessation of some act that is already in progress" (301-2); "(2) A prohibition expressed in the *aorist tense* is a warning or exhortation against doing a thing not yet begun" (302). Similar are the remarks of Brooks and Winbery, 116; Chamberlain, *Exegetical Grammar*, 86. Robertson, too, commends Moulton's canon on one page, but backpeddles for three more on the exceptions (*Grammar*, 851-854). For similar treatments, cf. also Turner, *Syntax*, 76-77; H. P. V. Nunn, *A Short Syntax of New Testament Greek*, 5th ed. (Cambridge: University Press, 1938) 84-86.

[6] *NovT* 27 (1985) 201-26.

[7] Ibid., 203.

[including present and imperfect] aspects is that the former represents an activity as a total action, in its entirety without dwelling on its internal details; while the latter represents an activity as a process going on, with the focus on its progress or development."[8] McKay then produced numerous examples from which he extrapolated that "in the imperative the *essential* difference between the aorist and the imperfective is that the former urges an activity *as whole action* and the latter urges it as *ongoing process*."[9] Whether or not the action had already begun is not a part of the ontology of either tense of the imperative.

This more basic understanding of the imperative paved the way for others.[10] In rapid succession, work by James L. Boyer, Stanley E. Porter, and Buist M. Fanning argued essentially the same point that McKay had made. The traditional view has thus been shown to be faulty. Nevertheless, older grammatical works (before 1985), which have so much good material in them on other fronts, need to be used judiciously when it comes to commands and prohibitions.[11]

C. *A Critique of the Traditional View*

The problems with the traditional view are as follows. First, it was not based on Hellenistic Greek. A clue from modern Greek was quickly found to be valid in one text (!) in classical Greek, then foisted upon several texts in the NT. This is a *diachronic* approach to the language of the worst kind, for it has an anachronistic starting point.

Second, as McKay pointed out, the traditional view did not approach the imperative from the larger framework of the unaffected meaning of tense. It isolated imperatives from indicatives, infinitives, participles, and so on—as though basic ideas about tense needed to be suspended in this case. It assumed that imperatives, by their nature, were exceptions to the rule.[12]

Third, the fundamental problem with the traditional approach was that it took a legitimate phenomenological usage (i.e., a meaning affected by lexical, contextual, or other grammatical features)[13] and assumed that such affected meanings expressed the unaffected or basic idea. But the sampling

---

[8] Ibid., 203-4.

[9] Ibid., 206-7.

[10] McKay was not the first to break from the Jackson-Moulton pack, however. J. P. Louw, "On Greek Prohibitions," *Acta Classica* 2 (1959) 43-57, had argued a similar view. Credit is given to McKay for bringing this more sure-footed linguistic approach to the attention of NT students.

[11] For this reason, our bibliography includes only two items before 1985.

[12] As we have seen, a similar inconsistency has plagued the Goodwin school with respect to conditional clauses.

[13] See our discussion of affected vs. unaffected meanings in the introduction to tenses and in the introduction to the present tense.

was not large enough to make meaningful conclusions about the *essential* differences between aorist and present. A hunch was promoted. When certain passages did not fit the view, they were ignored, abused, or conveniently called exceptions.

Fourth, as the colloquial aphorism goes, "The proof of the pudding is in the eating." The results of the traditional approach are almost comical. Exegetical and expository literature in the past several decades is filled with statements that are less than credible. Applying the traditional canon to Eph 5:18 results in: "*Stop being drunk* with wine, but *continue to be filled* with the Spirit" (μὴ μεθύσκεσθε, πληροῦσθε). On this view, one could ask, "Why stop getting drunk if it does not prevent one from getting Spirit-filled?" Further, if Ephesians is a circular letter, why are specific judgments made in it? Note, for example: "*Stop provoking* your children to wrath" (μὴ παροργίζετε in 6:4); "*Stop grieving* the Holy Spirit" (μὴ λυπεῖτε in 4:30); "*Stop being foolish*" (μὴ γίνεσθε in 5:17).[14] Or consider John 5:8: "Take up [aorist: ἆρον] your mattress and *continue walking* [present: περιπάτει]." But how could the lame man *continue* walking if he had not done so for thirty-eight years?[15]

In sum, the *basic* force of the aorist in commands/prohibitions is that it views the action *as a whole*, while the *basic* force of the present in commands/prohibitions is that it views the action *as ongoing process*. This basic meaning may, of course, be shaped in a given context to fit, say, an ingressive idea for the aorist. Thus if the conditions are right, the aorist prohibition may well have the force of "Do not start." This is an affected meaning or specific usage. But to call this the *essential* idea is not correct.

---

[14] See in particular Kenneth Wuest's *Word Studies in the Greek New Testament*, for examples of a slavish adherence to this canon.

[15] Other texts are equally absurd, if the traditional canon is followed. The following examples include translations that are patently ridiculous. For the present tense, note, e.g., Matt 4:10 ("Continue to go away, Satan"); 5:44 ("Continue to love your enemies" [when the audience had not yet begun]); Matt 7:23 ("Continue to depart from me"); Mark 5:41 ("Continue to rise"); 7:10 ("Let the one who speaks evil of his father or mother continue to die"); Luke 8:39 ("Continue to return to your home"); John 10:37 ("If I do not do the works of the Father, stop believing in me"); 19:21 ("Stop writing" the title on the sign above Jesus' name–v 19 states that this was already a completed act). For the aorist, note, e.g., Mark 9:43 ("If your hand offends you, begin to cut it off"); Luke 11:4 ("Begin to forgive us our sins"); John 3:7 ("Do not start to marvel" [Nicodemus already was marveling]); Heb 3:8 ("Do not start to harden your hearts" [their hearts were already getting calcified]). Frequently the aorist is used of an action that has not yet occurred, but the whole is exhorted (e.g., Jesus' rebuke of the demon, "Come out of him" in Mark 9:25; cf. Mark 9:22, 47; 10:37, 47; 14:6; Luke 3:11; 4:9, 35; 7:7; 11:5; John 4:7, 16; 10:24; 11:44).

Specific Uses

I. Commands

Commands are normally expressed in one of three tenses in Greek (each having a different nuance): future, aorist, present.[16]

A. *Future Indicative (a.k.a. Cohortative Indicative, Imperatival Future)*

The future indicative is sometimes used for a command, almost always in OT quotations (due to a literal translation of the Hebrew).[17] However, it was even used in classical Greek, though infrequently. Outside of Matthew, this usage is not common.[18] Its force is quite emphatic, in keeping with the combined nature of the indicative mood and future tense. It tends to have a universal, timeless, or solemn force to it. (But again, this is largely due to quotations of OT legal literature.) "It is not a milder or gentler imperative. A prediction may imply resistless power or cold indifference, compulsion or concession."[19]

Matt 4:10   κύριον τὸν θεόν σου **προσκυνήσεις** καὶ αὐτῷ μόνῳ **λατρεύσεις**.
             You shall worship the Lord your God and **serve** him only.

---

[16] The perfect imperative occurs only rarely in the NT. Cf. Mark 4:39 (πεφίμωσο); Acts 15:29 (ἔρρωσθε); 23:30 (ἔρρωσθε [*v.l.*, found in P 1241], ἔρρωσο [*v.l.*, found in ℵ *Byz et plu*]; the lack of a final "farewell," though the reading of only a few MSS [A B 33 *et pauci*], is obviously superior since the *v.ll.* are predictable in this context]); Eph 5:5; Heb 12:17; Jas 1:19. In these last three texts, ἴστε could be either perfect active imperative or indicative. Even with these examples, not all are imperatives of command (note the instances in Acts). The perfect imperative is also rare in the LXX, occurring only twenty times (cf. 2 Macc 9:20; 11:21, 28, 33; 3 Macc 7:9 [all have ἔρρωσθε]; and 15 other perfect imperatives, such as κέκραξον in Jer 22:20; 31:20; 40:3 [33:3]. In the last text it functions as a conditional imperative: "Cry out to me and I will answer you"). In addition, there are other ways to express a command in Greek: imperatival ἵνα, imperatival infinitive, and imperatival participle. All of these are rare in the NT. As well, indirect commands are found in other constructions, such as complementary infinitives with verbs of desiring or exhorting (as in "I want you to know"), attendant circumstance participles with imperatives, optative of obtainable wish, and various indirect discourse constructions after verbs of exhorting. For discussion of all these phenomena, see the respective morpho-syntactic sections throughout this grammar.

[17] See also the chapter on the future tense for a discussion. This section simply duplicates the main points of the relevant material in that chapter, for convenience' sake.

[18] For a succinct discussion, see *BDF*, 183 (§362).

[19] Gildersleeve, *Classical Greek*, 1.116 (§269).

Matt 22:37   ἀγαπήσεις κύριον τὸν θεόν σου ἐν ὅλῃ τῇ καρδίᾳ σου καὶ ἐν ὅλῃ τῇ ψυχῇ σου καὶ ἐν ὅλῃ τῇ διανοίᾳ σου

You shall love the Lord your God with all your heart and with all your soul and with all your mind.

1 Pet 1:16   ἅγιοι **ἔσεσθε**, ὅτι ἐγὼ ἅγιός εἰμι[20]

You shall be holy, because I am holy.

Cf. also Matt 5:33, 48; 22:39; Mark 9:35; Gal 5:14.

B. Aorist Imperative

The basic idea of the aorist imperative is a command in which the action is viewed as a whole, without regard for the internal make-up of the action. However, it occurs in various contexts in which its meaning has been affected especially by lexical or contextual features. Consequently, most aorist imperatives can be placed into one of two broad categories, ingressive or constative.

Further, the aorist is most frequently used for a *specific* command rather than a general precept (usually the domain of the present). Thus, "in general precepts . . . concerning attitudes and conduct there is a preference for the present, in commands related to conduct in specific cases (much less frequent in the NT) for the aorist."[21] Why is the aorist singled out for specific commands? "A specific command normally calls for action viewed as a single whole, for action to be done in its entirety on that occasion, and the aorist is natural for this."[22]

1. Ingressive

This is a command to *begin an action*. It is a common usage. The stress is on the *urgency* of the action. This may be broken down into two subcategories.

a. Momentary or Single Act

Here a specific situation is usually in view rather than a general precept.

---

[20] γένεσθε is found for ἔσεσθε in K P 049 1 1241 1739 *et alii*; γίνεσθε is the verb of choice in L *Byz et alii*.

[21] *BDF*, 172 (§335). Cf. also Fanning, *Verbal Aspect*, 327-35.

[22] Fanning, *Verbal Aspect*, 329. Fanning displays a table showing the usage of the tenses in fifteen NT books (Luke, Acts through Titus, James, and 1 Peter). Overall, the statistics are as follows. For general precepts: 449 presents and 145 aorists (3 to 1 ratio); for specific commands: 280 aorists and 86 presents (3.3 to 1). Thus, this rule is merely a guideline, although the exceptions do fall into definable patterns (ibid., 332).

Mark 9:25 ἐγὼ ἐπιτάσσω σοι, **ἔξελθε** ἐξ αὐτοῦ
I order you, **come out** of him!

John 19:6 **σταύρωσον σταύρωσον**[23]
Crucify [him], **Crucify** [him]!
> The stress is on the urgency of the action and it is viewed as a single event–that is, the part that *others* play in crucifying a man is a single event, while his hanging on the cross is durative.

Matt 6:11 Τὸν ἄρτον ἡμῶν τὸν ἐπιούσιον **δὸς** ἡμῖν σήμερον.
Give us this day our daily bread.
> This is also both urgent and momentary. The aorist is the common tense used in prayers and petitions.[24]

b. Pure Ingressive

The stress is on the beginning of an action that the context usually makes clear is *not* a momentary action.

Rom 6:13 μηδὲ παριστάνετε τὰ μέλη ὑμῶν ὅπλα ἀδικίας τῇ ἁμαρτίᾳ, ἀλλὰ **παραστήσατε** ἑαυτοὺς τῷ θεῷ
Do not present [present tense] your members as instruments of unrighteousness to sin, but **present** [aorist tense] yourselves to God.

Phil 4:5 τὸ ἐπιεικὲς ὑμῶν **γνωσθήτω** πᾶσιν ἀνθρώποις.
Let all men [come to] **know** your forbearance.

Jas 1:2 Πᾶσαν χαρὰν **ἡγήσασθε,** ἀδελφοί μου, ὅταν πειρασμοῖς περιπέσητε ποικίλοις
Consider it all joy, my brothers, when you encounter various trials. . . .
> The idea here seems to be, "Begin to consider. . . ."

2. Constative

This is a solemn or categorical command. The stress is *not* "begin an action," nor "continue to act." Rather, the stress is on the *solemnity* and *urgency* of the action; thus "I solemnly charge you to act–and do it now!" This is the use of the aorist in general precepts. Although the aorist is here transgressing onto the present tense's turf, it adds a certain flavor. It is as if the author says, "Make this your top priority." As such, the aorist is often used to command an action that has been going on. In this case, both solemnity and a heightened urgency are its force.[25]

John 15:4 **μείνατε** ἐν ἐμοί, κἀγὼ ἐν ὑμῖν.
Remain in me, and I in you.

---

[23] The second imperative is omitted in 𝔓[66*] 1010 *et pauci.*

[24] The parallel in Luke, however, has the present δίδου.

[25] The difference between the aorist and the future indicative in such general precepts seems to be that urgency is used with the aorist while the future indicative does not stress this element.

> Obviously the command is not ingressive: "Begin to remain in me."
> Nor is it momentary and specific. This is a general precept, but the force
> of the aorist is on urgency and priority.

1 Cor 6:20   ἠγοράσθητε τιμῆς· **δοξάσατε** δὴ τὸν θεὸν ἐν τῷ σώματι ὑμῶν.

You were bought for a price. Therefore, **glorify** God with your body.

2 Tim 4:2   **κήρυξον** τὸν λόγον

Preach the word!

> The idea here is hardly "**Begin** to preach the word," but, "I solemnly
> charge you to preach the word. Make this your priority!" (as the follow-
> ing context clearly indicates).

In summary on the constative aorist imperative, it can be said as a general rule that this command says nothing about beginning or continuing
an action. It basically has the force of, "Make this your top priority." Our
knowledge of the author and the context will help us see if the audience
has made it *any* priority at all, or if they have neglected it entirely.

C. Present Imperative

The present imperative looks at the action from an internal viewpoint. It is
used for the most part for general precepts–i.e., for habits that should char-
acterize one's attitudes and behavior–rather than in specific situations.[26] The
action may or may not have already begun. It may be progressive, iterative,
or customary.

The present tense is also used for specific commands at times, however. In
such contexts it is usually ingressive-progressive.

1. Ingressive-Progressive

The force here is *begin and continue.* It is different from the pure ingressive aorist in that it stresses both the inception and progress of an action
commanded while the pure ingressive aorist imperative stresses only
the inception, making no comment about the progress of the action.

Matt 8:22   **ἀκολούθει** μοι καὶ ἄφες τοὺς νεκροὺς θάψαι τοὺς ἑαυτῶν νεκρούς.

Follow me and leave the dead to bury their own dead.

> Here Jesus urges a would-be disciple to begin and continue following
> him.

John 5:8   ἆρον τὸν κράβατόν σου καὶ **περιπάτει**

Take up your bed and **walk**

> The momentary aorist is used, followed by an ingressive-progressive
> present. The force of this clause is, "Take up [right now] your bed and
> [begin and continue to] walk."

---

[26] For discussion and differences with the aorist, see under "Aorist Imperative."

Eph 4:28   ὁ κλέπτων μηκέτι κλεπτέτω, μᾶλλον δὲ **κοπιάτω**
            Let him who steals no longer steal, but rather let him **work**.

> Here the present prohibition is first used ("no longer steal") with the obvious force of "stop stealing" (aided by μηκέτι), followed by the ingressive-progressive present, "Let him begin and continue to work."

2. Customary

The force of the customary present imperative is simply *continue*. It is a command for action to be continued, action that may or may not have already been going on. It is often a character-building command to the effect of "make this your habit," "train yourself in this," etc. This is the use of the present imperative in general precepts.

Matt 6:9   οὕτως οὖν **προσεύχεσθε** ὑμεῖς
            you should therefore **pray** as follows . . .

> The focus is not on urgency, nor on a momentary act. This initial command at the beginning of the Lord's Prayer means, "Make it your habit to pray in the following manner."

Luke 6:35   **ἀγαπᾶτε** τοὺς ἐχθροὺς ὑμῶν καὶ **ἀγαθοποιεῖτε**
            Love your enemies and **do good** [to them].

Eph 5:2   **περιπατεῖτε** ἐν ἀγάπῃ
            Continue to walk in love.

> It is only the context of the whole book of Ephesians that indicates that this is a customary present rather than an ingressive-progressive present. In 1:15 the author notes that the Ephesians already "have love for all the saints." Thus he is here simply exhorting them to *continue* in that love.

3. Iterative

The force of an iterative present imperative is *repeated action*. That is, "do it again and again." It is not continuous action that is commanded, but a repeated act. Normally, a good rule of thumb is that when an *attitude* is commanded, the force of the present imperative will either be *ingressive-progressive* or *customary*; when an *action* is commanded, the force of the present imperative will usually be *iterative*. It is, however, difficult to distinguish this usage from the customary present.

Matt 7:7   **Αἰτεῖτε** . . . **ζητεῖτε** . . . **κρούετε**
            Ask . . . **seek** . . . **knock** . . .

> The force of these commands is, "Keep on asking . . . keep on seeking . . . keep on knocking . . ."

1 Cor 11:28 **δοκιμαζέτω** δὲ ἄνθρωπος ἑαυτὸν καὶ οὕτως ἐκ τοῦ ἄρτου **ἐσθιέτω** καὶ ἐκ τοῦ ποτηρίου **πινέτω**·

> But **let** a person **examine** himself and thus **let him eat** from the bread and **drink** from the cup

>> The idea is that whenever the Lord's Supper is observed, this examination (and eating, drinking) needs to take place.

II. Prohibitions

Prohibitions, like commands, are normally expressed by one of three tenses in Greek: future, aorist, present.

A. Future Indicative (+ οὐ or sometimes μή)

This is simply the force of the future indicative for commands in the negative. It is typically solemn, universal, or timeless. See, for example, the Ten Commandments (LXX) in Exod 20 and repeated often in the NT. (Note discussion above under "Commands.")

Matt 19:18   οὐ **φονεύσεις**, οὐ **μοιχεύσεις**, οὐ **κλέψεις**, οὐ **ψευδομαρτυρήσεις**
          you shall not **murder, you shall** not **commit adultery, you shall** not **steal, you shall** not **bear false witness**

Matt 6:5   οὐκ **ἔσεσθε** ὡς οἱ ὑποκριταί
          you shall not **be** like the hypocrites
            This is an example that is other than an OT quotation.

Cf. also Matt 4:4, 7; 5:21, 27, 33; Rom 7:7; 13:9.

B. Aorist Subjunctive (+ μή)

The aorist in prohibitions is almost always in the subjunctive mood. With the second person, this is always the case.[27]

The prohibitive aorist is normally used, like its positive counterpart, in specific situations. The force of the aorist is used to prohibit the action as a whole. Hence, because of this, it sometimes has an *ingressive* flavor: *Do not start.*

But not all aorist prohibitions are used this way. Especially when used in general precepts, it seems to have the force of prohibiting an action *as a whole.* Yet, even here, the ingressive notion may be part of the meaning. This is due to the fact that the prohibited action is normally not yet engaged in, as the context shows.

The difficulty of deciding between these two notions is seen in the illustrations below. At bottom, the ingressive and summary perspectives of the aorist blend into one another at almost every turn.

Matt 1:20   μὴ **φοβηθῇς** παραλαβεῖν Μαρίαν τὴν γυναῖκά σου·
          Do not **fear** to take Mary as your wife.

---

[27] There are, by my count, only eight instances of the aorist imperative in prohibitions, all in the third person (Matt 6:3; 24:17, 18; Mark 13:15 [*bis*], 16; Luke 17:31 [*bis*]).

Matt 6:13   μὴ **εἰσενέγκῃς** ἡμᾶς εἰς πειρασμόν
             Do not **lead** us into temptation.

Luke 6:29   ἀπὸ τοῦ αἴροντός σου τὸ ἱμάτιον καὶ τὸν χιτῶνα μὴ **κωλύσῃς**.
             From the one who takes away your coat, **do** not **withhold** even your
             shirt.

2 Th 3:13   μὴ **ἐγκακήσητε** καλοποιοῦντες
             Do not **become weary** in doing good.

C. Present Imperative (+ μή)

1. Cessation of Activity in Progress (Progressive)

Here the idea is frequently progressive and the prohibition is of the "cessation of some act that is already in progress."[28] It has the idea, *Stop continuing.* μὴ φοβοῦ is thus naturally used as the formula to quell someone's
apprehensions.[29]

Matt 19:14   **μὴ κωλύετε** αὐτὰ ἐλθεῖν πρός με
             Stop preventing them from coming to me.
             What indicates that cessation of an activity is in view is the previous
             verse, where we are told that the disciples were disturbed that some
             wanted to bring children to Jesus.

Luke 1:30   εἶπεν ὁ ἄγγελος αὐτῇ· μὴ **φοβοῦ**, Μαριάμ
             The angel said to her, "**Do** not **be afraid**, Mary. . . ."
             The typical opening line of an angelic visitor is, "Do not fear." The sight
             is evidently sufficiently startling that the individual would already be
             moving in the direction of apprehensiveness. For other instances
             (including nonangelic announcements), cf. Luke 2:10; 8:50; John 6:20;
             Acts 18:9; 27:24; Rev 1:17.

John 2:16   μὴ **ποιεῖτε** τὸν οἶκον τοῦ πατρός μου οἶκον ἐμπορίου.
             Stop **turning** my Father's house into a marketplace.

Rev 5:5   εἷς ἐκ τῶν πρεσβυτέρων λέγει μοι· μὴ **κλαῖε**
             One of the elders said to me, "Stop **weeping**."

2. General Precept (Customary)

The present prohibition can also have the force of a *general precept.*
This kind of prohibition really makes no comment about whether
the action is going on or not.

John 10:37   εἰ οὐ ποιῶ τὰ ἔργα τοῦ πατρός μου, μὴ **πιστεύετέ** μοι
             If I do not do the works of my Father, then **do** not **believe** me.

---

[28] Dana-Mantey, 302.

[29] Of the 50 instances in the NT of μή + imperative or subjunctive, 40 use the present
imperative, while only ten use the aorist subjunctive.

1 Cor 14:39   τὸ λαλεῖν μὴ **κωλύετε** γλώσσαις
               Do not **forbid** the speaking in tongues.

Eph 6:4   οἱ πατέρες, **μὴ παροργίζετε** τὰ τέκνα ὑμῶν
               Fathers, **do not provoke** your children to wrath.

2 John 10   εἴ τις ἔρχεται πρὸς ὑμᾶς καὶ ταύτην τὴν διδαχὴν οὐ φέρει, μὴ **λαμβάνετε**
               αὐτὸν εἰς οἰκίαν
               If any comes to you and does not bring this teaching, **do** not **receive**
               him into [your] home.

In many of the NT letters the force of a particular present prohibition will not always be focused on the cessation of an activity in progress. It is *not*, then, safe to say that when an author uses the present prohibition the audience is being indicted for not heeding this command. Other factors–especially the overall context and *Sitz im Leben* of the book–must be taken into account.

Syntax Summaries

The following material summarizes the basic categories found in the body of this work. Every category is mentioned by title; for some, the key to identification is also listed (in italics); for others, other helpful information is supplied. Every category that has at least relatively frequent occurrences in the NT is listed in **bold** print. As well, the rarest categories and disputed categories are listed in smaller type. The pages where the section can be found are listed in parentheses. At the end of this summary is a "Cheat Sheet" with titles in small type.

Nouns and Nominals

The Cases

Nominative
(specific designation)

Primary Uses (38-49)

1. **Subject**: subject of finite verb (38-40)

2. **Predicate Nominative**: approximately same as subject; can be in convertible or subset propositions (40-48)

3. **Nominative in Simple Apposition**: two adjacent substantives that refer to the same thing/person (48-49)

Grammatically Independent Uses of the Nominative (49-60)

1. **Nominative Absolute**: in introductory material (not sentences) (49-51)

2. *Nominativus Pendens* **(Pendent Nominative)**: logical rather than syntactical subject at beginning of a sentence (51-53)

3. **Parenthetic Nominative**: subject of an explanatory clause within another clause (53-54)

4. Nominative in Proverbial Expressions: in proverbial expressions that have no finite verb (54-55)

5. **Nominative for Vocative** (Nominative of Address) (56-59)

6. Nominative of Exclamation: exclamation without grammatical connection to rest of sentence (59-60)

Nominatives in Place of Oblique Cases (61-64)

1. Nominative of Appellation: a title that functions like a proper name, as if in quotes (61)
2. Nominative in Apposition to Oblique Cases (62)
3. Nominative After a Preposition: ἀπὸ ὁ ὤν in Rev 1:4 only (62-64)
4. Nominative for Time (64)

Vocative

(direct address & exclamation)

Direct Address (67-70)

1. **Simple Address**: without ὦ (except in Acts) (67-68)
2. Emphatic (or, Emotional) Address: with ὦ (except in Acts) (68-69)

Exclamation (70)

Exclamation with no grammatical connection

Apposition (70-71)

Two adjacent substantives that refer to the same thing/person

Genitive

(qualification & [occasionally] separation)

Adjectival (78-107)

1. **Descriptive Genitive**: *characterized by, described by* (79-81)
2. **Possessive Genitive**: *belonging to, possessed by* (81-83)
3. Genitive of Relationship: family relationship (subset of possessive) (83-84)
4. **Partitive Genitive ("Wholative")**: denotes the whole of which the head noun is a part–*which is a part of* (84-86)
5. **Attributive Genitive**: specifies an *attribute* or innate quality of the head substantive; convert genitive into an attributive adjective (86-88)
6. **Attributed Genitive**: semantically opposite of attributive genitive; convert head noun into adjective modifying the genitive noun (89-91)
7. Genitive of Material: *made out of, consisting of* (91-92)
8. **Genitive of Content**: *full of, containing* (related to noun or verb) (92-94)

9. **Genitive in Simple Apposition**: genitive substantive adjacent to another genitive substantive, referring to the same thing/person–*namely, which is* (94)

10. **Genitive of Apposition (Epexegetical)**: genitive states a specific *example* of which the head noun names a category–*namely, which is* (95-100)

11. Genitive of Destination (a.k.a. Direction or Purpose): *for the purpose of, destined for, toward,* or *into* (100-101)

12. Predicate Genitive: simple apposition in genitive case made *emphatic* by *participial* form of the *equative* verb (102)

13. Genitive of Subordination: specifies that which is *subordinated* to or under the dominion of the head noun–*over* (103-104)

14. Genitive of Production/Producer: genitive *produces* the noun to which it stands related–*produced by* (104-106)

15. Genitive of Product: genitive is the *product* of the noun to which it stands related–*which produces* (106-107)

Ablatival Genitive (107-12)

1. Genitive of Separation: genitive indicates that from which the *verb* or sometimes head noun is *separated*–*out of, away from,* or *from* (107-109)

2. Genitive of Source (or Origin): the *source* from which the head noun derives or depends–*out of, derived from, dependent on,* or "*sourced in*" (109-10)

3. **Genitive of Comparison**: genitive after a *comparative adjective*, translated *than* (110-12)

Verbal Genitive (i.e., Genitive Related to a Verbal Noun) (112-21)

1. **Subjective Genitive:** functions as *subject* of verbal idea implicit in head noun (113-16)

2. **Objective Genitive:** functions as *direct object* of verbal idea implicit in head noun (116-19)

3. Plenary Genitive: both subjective and objective (e.g., "Revelation of Jesus Christ" = "revelation *about* and *from* Jesus Christ") (119-21)

Adverbial Genitive (121-30)

1. Genitive of Price or Value or Quantity: the price paid for the word to which it is related–*for* (122)

2. **Genitive of Time (kind of time)**: *within which* or *during which* (122-24)

3. Genitive of Place (where or within which): the place *within which* the *verb* to which it is related occurs (124-25)

4. Genitive of Means: the means by which the verbal action is accomplished–*by* (125)

5. Genitive of Agency: the *personal* agent by whom the action in view is accomplished; related to –τος adjective; *by* (126-27)

6. **Genitive Absolute**: see participles (127)

7. Genitive of Reference: *with reference to* (127-28)

8. **Genitive of Association**: *in association with* (128-30)

After Certain Words (131-36)

1. **Genitive After Certain Verbs (as a Direct Object)**: especially after verbs of *sensation, emotion/volition, sharing, ruling* (131-34)

2. Genitive After Certain Adjectives (and Adverbs): certain adjectives (such as ἄξιος, "worthy [of]") and adverbs normally take a genitive "object" (134-35)

3. Genitive After Certain Nouns: occurs after certain nouns whose lexical nature requires a genitive (135)

4. **Genitive After Certain Prepositions**: certain prepositions take the genitive after them (see chapter on prepositions) (136)

Dative

(personal interest, reference, position, & means)

Pure Dative Uses (140-53)

1. **Dative Indirect Object**: dative noun is that to or for which the action of a *transitive* verb is performed–*to, for* (140-42)

2. **Dative of Interest (including Advantage [*commodi*] and Disadvantage [*incommodi*])** (142-44)

   a. **Advantage**: *for the benefit of* or *in the interest of* (142-44)

   b. **Disadvantage**: *for/unto the detriment of* or *to the disadvantage of* or *against* (142-44)

3. **Dative of Reference/Respect**: *with reference to* (144-46)

4. Ethical Dative: the person whose feelings or viewpoint are intimately tied to the action–*as far as I am concerned, in my opinion* (146-47)

5. Dative of Destination: the "to" idea when a nontransitive verb is used (147-48)

6. Dative of Recipient: would be an indirect object, but it appears in *verbless constructions* (such as in titles and salutations) (148-49)

7. Dative of Possession: that to which the subject of an equative verb belongs–*belonging to* (149-51)

8. Dative of Thing Possessed (disputed): *who possesses* (151)

9. Predicate Dative: simple apposition in dative case made *emphatic* by *participial* form of the *equative* verb (152)

10. **Dative in Simple Apposition**: dative substantive adjacent to another dative substantive, referring to the same thing/person (152-53)

Local Dative Uses (153-58)

1. Dative of Place: see dative of sphere (with which it is combined) (153)

2. **Dative of Sphere**: the sphere or realm in which the word to which the dative is related takes place or exists–*in the sphere of* (153-55)

3. **Dative of Time (when)**: the *time when* the action of the main verb is accomplished–usually a *point in time* (155-57)

4. Dative of Rule: the standard of conduct to which a person conforms–*according to*, or *in conformity with* (157-58)

Instrumental Dative Uses (158-71)

1. **Dative of Association/Accompaniment**: the person or thing one associates with or accompanies–*in association with* (159-61)

2. Dative of Manner (or Adverbial Dative): the manner in which the action of the verb is accomplished (answering "How?")–*with, in* (161-62)

3. **Dative of Means/Instrument**: the means or instrument by which the verbal action is accomplished–*by means of, with* (162-63)

4. Dative of Agency: the *personal* agent by whom the action of the (passive) verb is accomplished–*by* (163-66)

5. Dative of Measure/Degree of Difference: *by* before a quantitative word in the dative (typically, πολλῷ [dative] + μᾶλλον) (166-67)

6. **Dative of Cause**: the cause or basis of the action of the verb–*because of, on the basis of* (167-68)

7. Cognate Dative: cognate to the verb either formally or conceptually; translate like an *adverb* (168-69)

8. Dative of Material: the material that is used to accomplish the action of the verb; a *quantitative* word–"I write with pen (means) and *ink* (material)" (169-70)

9. Dative of Content: the content that is used by a verb of *filling*–*with* (170-71)

Dative After Certain Words (171-75)

1. **Dative Direct Object**: dative direct object, often involving personal relationship (171-73)

2. Dative After Certain Nouns: after a *verbal* noun; personal interest usually present; dative often corresponds to direct object–"service to the saints" = "serve the saints" (173-74)

3. Dative After Certain Adjectives: several adjectives take a dative; personal relation usually involved; no set pattern of translation (174-75)

4. **Dative After Certain Prepositions**: certain prepositions take a dative (see chapter on prepositions) (175)

Accusative

(extent or limitation)

Substantival Uses of the Accusative (179-99)

1. **Accusative Direct Object**: the immediate object of the action of a transitive verb (179-81)

2. **Double Accusatives** (181-89)

    a. **Person-Thing**: certain verbs take two direct objects, one a person and the other a thing (e.g., teaching, anointing, asking ["I teach you Greek"]) (181-82)

    b. **Object-Complement**: one accusative is the object, the other is its complement; equivalent to subject-predicate nominative ("I call him lord") (182-89)

3. Cognate Accusative (Accusative of Inner Object): direct object that shares lexically or conceptually the idea of the verb ("do not treasure treasures") (189-90)

4. Predicate Accusative: simple apposition made emphatic by a *copula* in *participial* form *or infinitival form* (an accusative related to subject of infinitive) (190-92)

5. **Accusative Subject of Infinitive**: accusative of reference that functions like subject of infinitive ("I want *you* to know") (192-97)

6. Accusative of Retained Object: the *accusative of thing* in a double accusative person-thing construction with an active verb *retains its case* when the verb is put in the *passive* ("I taught you *the lesson*" becomes "You were taught *the lesson* by me") (197)

7. Pendent Accusative (*Accusativum Pendens*): accusative thrown forward to the beginning of the clause, followed by a sentence in which it is replaced by a pronoun in the case required by the syntax–*with reference to* (subset of acc. of reference) (198)

8. **Accusative in Simple Apposition**: accusative substantive adjacent to another accusative substantive, referring to the same thing/person (198-99)

Adverbial Uses of the Accusative (199-205)

1. Adverbial Accusative (Accusative of Manner): *qualifies* the action of the verb rather than indicating *quantity* or extent of the verbal action (δωρεάν is most frequent–*freely*) (200-201)

2. **Accusative of Measure** (or Extent of Space or **Time**): *for the extent of, for the duration of* (rare with space, common with time) (201-203)

3. Accusative of Respect or (General) Reference: restricts the reference of the verbal action–*with reference to* (203-204)

4. Accusative in Oaths: the person or thing by whom or by which one swears an oath (204-205)

Accusative After Certain Prepositions (205)

Certain prepositions take the accusative after them

The Article

(basically a conceptualizer & identifier, not a definitizer)

Regular Uses of the Article

1. *As a Pronoun ([partially] Independent Use)* (211-16)

   a. **Personal Pronoun**: functions as *third* person pronoun in *nominative* in μὲν. . . δέ construction or with δέ alone (211-12)

   b. Alternative Personal Pronoun: *the one . . . the other* (almost always in μὲν. . . δέ construction) (212-13)

   c. **Relative Pronoun**: *who is, which is* (the article with second and third attributive positions in which the modifier is *not* an adjective) (213-15)

   d. Possessive Pronoun: *his, her* (used in contexts in which possession is implied) (215-16)

2. *With Substantives (Dependent or Modifying Use)* (216-31)

   a. **Individualizing Article** (216-27)

      1) **Simple Identification**: distinguishes one individual from another ("drip-pan" category) (216-17)

      2) **Anaphoric (Previous Reference)**: points out something mentioned earlier in the text, by way of reminder (217-20)

      3) Kataphoric (Following Reference): points to something in the text that immediately follows (220-21)

      4) **Deictic ("Pointing" Article)**: points out an object or person which/who is *present* at the moment of speaking; demonstrative force–*this* (221)

      5) *Par Excellence:* object is "in a class by itself" (222-23)

      6) **Monadic ("One of a Kind" or "Unique" Article)**: identifies "one-of-a-kind" noun (223-24)

7) **Well-Known ("Celebrity" or "Familiar" Article)**: well known, but for reasons *other* than the above categories; that which is familiar to the readers (225)

8) **Abstract (i.e., the Article with Abstract Nouns)**: identifies a quality or abstract concept (e.g., love, salvation, peace, faith); article is rarely used in translation (226-27)

b. **Generic Article (Categorical Article)**: distinguishes one class from another (227-31)

3. *As a Substantiver (With Certain Parts of Speech)* (231-38)

Turns another part of speech into a substantive; conceptualizes the idea of that part of speech

a. Adverbs (232-33)

b. Adjectives (233)

c. Participles (233-34)

d. Infinitives (234-35)

e. Genitive Word or Phrase (235-36)

f. Prepositional Phrase (236)

g. Particles (237)

h. Finite Verbs (237)

i. Clauses, Statements, and Quotations (237-38)

4. *As a Function Marker* (*often has semantic force as well; see categories above*) (238-43)

a. To Denote Adjectival Positions: especially to denote the second attributive position (without separate semantic weight) (239)

b. With Possessive Pronouns: when αὐτοῦ and the like are attached to a noun, the article is almost invariably found as well (239)

c. In Genitive Phrases: both the head noun and the genitive noun normally have or lack the article (Apollonius' Canon) (239-40)

d. With Indeclinable Nouns: article indicates the case of the noun (240-41)

e. With Participles: to denote substantival (or adjectival) function of the participle (241)

f. With Demonstratives: a demonstrative in *predicate* position to an *articular* noun has an attributive relation; demonstratives do not modify anarthrous nouns (241-42)

g. With Nominative Nouns: to denote subject (242)

h. To Distinguish Subject from Predicate Nominative and Object from Complement: subject/object have the article so as to distinguish them from PN/complement (242-43)

i. With the Infinitive to Denote Various Functions: see section on infinitive (243)

Absence of the Article

(may be indefinite, qualitative, or definite)

1. ***Indefinite*** (244)

    Refers to one member of a class, without specifying which member; lacks referential identity

2. ***Qualitative*** (244-45)

    Stresses quality, nature, or essence; focuses on class traits

3. ***Definite*** (245-54)

    Stresses individual identity; has unique referential identity

    a. **Proper Names**: definite with or without the article (245-47)

    b. **Object of a Preposition**: object can be definite, qualitative, or indefinite (247)

    c. **With Ordinal Numbers**: number specifies *amount* of substantive, making it definite (248)

    d. **Predicate Nominative**: if PN *precedes* copula, it *may* be definite (248)

    e. **Complement in Object-Complement Construction**: if the complement *precedes* the object, it *may* be definite (248)

    f. **Monadic Nouns**: one-of-a-kind nouns do not need the article to be definite; this applies to nouns that are referentially unique due to modifiers (e.g., adjective [as in πνεῦμα ἅγιον] or genitive [υἱὸς θεοῦ]) (248-49)

    g. **Abstract Nouns**: love, joy, peace, etc. are often anarthrous, but not indefinite (249-50)

    h. **A Genitive Construction (Apollonius' Corollary)**: anarthrous head noun with anarthrous genitive noun: both usually have the same semantic force (usually definite or qualitative) (250-52)

    i   **With a Pronominal Adjective**: nouns with πᾶς, ὅλος, etc. do not need the article to be definite, for either the class as a whole ("all") or distributively ("every") is being specified (253)

    j. **Generic Nouns**: the whole class is in view; little semantic difference between this and articular generic nouns (253-54)

Special Uses and Non-Uses of the Article

A. **Anarthrous Pre-Verbal Predicate Nominatives (Involving Colwell's Rule)** (256-70)

1. **Statement of the Rule**: a definite predicate nominative that precedes the verb is usually anarthrous (257)

2. **Clarification of the Rule**: the converse is *not* true; anarthrous pre-verbal PNs are usually *qualitative*. θεός in John 1:1c is probably qualitative (thus, not identifying the λόγος with the person of ὁ θεός, but stressing that their natures are the same: "What God was, the Word was" [NEB]). (259-62)

B. **The Article with Multiple Substantives Connected by Καί (Granville Sharp Rule and Related Constructions)** (270-90)

1. **Statement of the Granville Sharp Rule**: both substantives (nouns, participles, adjectives) refer to the same person in the article-substantive-καί-substantive (TSKS) construction when:

   - both are personal
   - both are singular
   - both are non-proper (i.e., common terms, not proper names)

   Example: ὁ θεὸς καὶ πατήρ (Eph 1:3) (271-72)

2. **Validity of the Rule Within the New Testament**: always valid; Titus 2:13 & 2 Pet 1:1 impacted. Exceptions outside the NT are capable of linguistic explanation and do not affect the christologically significant texts (273-77)

3. **TSKS Constructions Involving Impersonal, Plural, and Proper Nouns** (277-90)

   a. Proper Names: always distinct individuals (e.g., "the Peter and James") (277-78)

   b. **Plural Personal Constructions**: three different semantic groups possible: (1) distinct, (2) identical, (3) overlap (three subgroups). This breaks down:

      - participle + participle = identical
      - noun + noun = distinct or overlap (affects Eph 2:20; 4:11)
      - adjective + adjective = identical or overlap
      - mixed constructions: mixed semantic values (278-86)

   c. **Impersonal Constructions**: three different semantic groups possible: (1) distinct, (2) identical, (3) overlap (three subgroups). All are represented, though #2 (identical) is rare. Affects Acts 2:23; 20:21; 2 Thess 2:1; etc. (286-90)

Adjectives

"Non-Adjectival" Uses of the Adjective

The Adverbial Use of the Adjective (293)

Usually reserved for special terms

The Independent or Substantival Use of the Adjective (294-95)

Usually articular

The Use of the Positive, Comparative, and Superlative Forms of the Adjective

A. **The Use of the Positive Adjective** (297-98)

1. **Normal Usage**: only one object in view (297)

2. Positive for Comparative: implicit comparison between two substantives (297)

3. Positive for Superlative: implicit comparison between three or more substantives (298)

B. **The Use of the Comparative Adjective** (298-301)

1. **Normal Usage**: explicit comparison between two; adjective usually followed by genitive or ἤ (299)

2. Comparative for Superlative: comparison of three or more (299-300)

3. Comparative for Elative: *very* + positive form of adjective; no comparison is made (thus, ἰσχυρότερος would be *very strong* rather than *stronger*) (300-301)

C. **The Use of the Superlative Adjective** (301-305)

1. **"Normal" Usage**: the extreme in a comparison of three or more (301-302)

2. **Superlative for Elative**: *very* + positive form of the adjective (303)

3. **Superlative for Comparative**: only two are compared; frequent with πρῶτος, rare with other terms (303-305)

The Relation of Adjective to Noun

A. **When the Article Is Present** (306-309)

    1. **The Attributive Positions**: adjective modifies the noun (306-307)

        a. **First Attributive**: article-adjective-noun (ὁ ἀγαθὸς βασιλεύς = the good king) (306)

        b. **Second Attributive**: article-noun-article-adjective (ὁ βασιλεὺς ὁ ἀγαθός = the good king) (306-307)

        c. Third Attributive: noun-article-adjective (βασιλεὺς ὁ ἀγαθός = the good king) (rare with adjectives, more common with other modifiers) (307)

    2. **The Predicate Positions**: adjective makes assertion about the noun (307-309)

        a. **First Predicate**: adjective-article-noun (ἀγαθὸς ὁ βασιλεύς = the king is good) (307-308)

        b. **Second Predicate**: article-noun-adjective (ὁ βασιλεὺς ἀγαθός = the king is good) (308)

B. **When the Article Is Absent** (309-14)

    1. **The Anarthrous Adjective-Noun Construction**: usually attributive, sometimes predicate (309-10)

    2. **The Anarthrous Noun-Adjective Construction**: usually attributive, sometimes predicate (310-11)

Pronouns

Semantic Categories: Major Classes

A. **Personal Pronouns**: ἐγώ, σύ, αὐτός (320-25)

    1. **Nominative Uses** (321-23)

        a. **Emphasis** (321-23)

            1) Contrast: kind (antithetical) or degree (comparison) (321-22)

            2) Subject Focus: to identify, give prominence to, clarify, etc.; contrast not prominent, though sometimes present (322-23)

        b. Redundancy: sometimes as a "switch-reference" device, to show alternating subjects; other times, merely stylistic (323)

    2. **Oblique Cases** (324-25)

        a. **Normal Use: Anaphoric**: to stand in the place of a noun or other nominal (324)

        b. **Possessive**: *genitive* of the personal pronoun (324)

        c. Reflexive: *himself, herself, itself* (324-25)

B. *Demonstrative Pronouns*: pointers–οὗτος, ἐκεῖνος, ὅδε (325-35)

    1. **Regular Uses (as Demonstratives)** (325-28)

        a. **οὗτος (Proximity)**: *this* (326-27)

        b. **ἐκεῖνος (Remoteness)**: *that* (327-28)

        c. ὅδε (anticipatory/proleptic): *the following* (328)

    2. For Personal Pronouns: οὗτος and ἐκεῖνος sometimes have diminished demonstrative force; equivalent to third person personal pronouns (328-29)

    3. Unusual Uses (from an English perspective) (329-35)

        a. Pleonastic (Redundant, Resumptive): unnecessary use, sometimes for rhetorical effect (329-30)

        b. *Constructio ad Sensum (construction according to sense)*: natural gender or number is used instead of grammatical gender or number (as in τὰ ἔθνη . . . οὗτοι ["the Gentiles . . . these"]) (330-35)

           1) Gender: lack of concord in gender between pronoun and antecedent (331-32)

           2) Number: lack of concord in number between pronoun and antecedent (332-33)

        c. **Conceptual Antecedent or Postcedent**: neuter of οὗτος routinely used to refer to a phrase or clause (333-35)

C. *Relative Pronouns*: ὅς and ὅστις labeled relative pronouns because they relate to more than one clause (335-45)

    1. **ὅς** (336-43)

        a. **Regular Use**: link a substantive to the relative clause, which either describes, clarifies, or restricts the meaning of the substantive (336-37)

        b. **"Unusual" Uses**: "glitch" in concord, identification of antecedent, etc. (337-43)

           1) **Natural Gender vs. Grammatical Gender (*constructio ad sensum*)** (337-38)

2) **Case** (338-39)

    a) **Attraction (a.k.a. Direct Attraction)**: attracted to the case of the antecedent (338-39)

    b) **Inverse Attraction (a.k.a. Indirect Attraction)**: antecedent attracted to the case of the RP (339)

3) **Antecedent Complexities** (339-43)

    a) Omission of Antecedent: due to embedded demonstrative or poetry (339-42)

    b) **Adverbial/Conjunctive Uses**: after a *preposition*; adverbial/conjunctive force; no antecedent, or antecedent is conceptual (342-43)

2. **ὅστις (called Indefinite; better: Generic or Qualitative)** (343-45)

    a. **Generic**: focuses on the whole class (thus, *whoever = everyone who*) (343-44)

    b. **Qualitative**: focuses on the nature or essence of the person or thing in view (*the very one who, who certainly, who indeed*) (344)

    c. Confusion with ὅς: functions like a definite RP (344-45)

D. *Interrogative Pronouns* ask a question: τίς & τί , ποῖος, πόσος (345-46)

    1. **τίς & τί**: asks *identifying* question (*Who? What?*) in direct and indirect questions. Sometimes τίς asks *What sort?* (qualitative), and τί asks *Why?* (adverbial). (345-46)

    2. ποῖος & πόσος: asks *qualitative* (*What sort?*) and *quantitative* question (*How much?*), respectively. (346)

E. *Indefinite Pronouns*: introduces a member of a class without further identification (τις, τι) (347)

    1. **Substantival**: *anyone, someone, a certain* (347)

    2. **Adjectival**: *a(n)* (347)

F. *Possessive Pronouns (Adjectives)*: no distinct form in Greek, but (348):

    1. **Possessive Adjective** (ἐμός, σός, ἡμέτερος, ὑμέτερος) *lexicalizes* possession (348)

    2. **Personal Pronoun in Genitive** (αὐτοῦ) *grammaticalizes* possession (348)

G. *Intensive Pronoun*: αὐτός (348-50)

    1. **As an Intensive Pronoun**: *himself, herself, itself* (in *predicate* position to an articular noun) (349)

   2. **As an Identifying Adjective**: *same* (modifying an articular substantive in the *attributive* position) (349-50)

   3. **As a Third Person Personal Pronoun**: *he, she, it* (348)

H. **Reflexive Pronouns**: ἐμαυτοῦ (*of myself*), σεαυτοῦ (*of yourself*), ἑαυτοῦ (*of himself*), ἑαυτῶν (*of themselves*); used to *highlight the participation of the subject* in the verbal action, as direct object, indirect object, intensifier, etc. (350-51)

I. **Reciprocal Pronouns**: ἀλλήλων (*of one another*) used to indicate an interchange between two or more groups; thus, always *plural* (351)

Lexico-Syntactic Categories: Major Terms

A. *ἀλλήλων:* reciprocal (352)

B. *αὐτός:* personal, possessive (gen.), intensive (352)

C. *ἑαυτοῦ:* reflexive (352)

D. *ἐγώ:* personal, possessive (gen.) (352)

E. *ἐκεῖνος:* demonstrative, personal (352)

F. *ἐμαυτοῦ:* reflexive (352)

G. *ἡμεῖς:* personal, possessive (gen.) (353)

H. *ὅδε:* demonstrative (353)

I. *ὅς:* relative pronoun (definite) (353)

J. *ὅστις:* relative pronoun (indefinite) (353)

K. *οὗτος:* demonstrative, personal (353)

L. *ποῖος:* interrogative (qualitative) (353)

M. *πόσος:* interrogative (quantitative) (353)

N. *σεαυτοῦ:* reflexive (353)

O. *σύ:* personal, possessive (gen.) (353)

P. *τίς:* interrogative (353)

Q. *τις:* indefinite (354)

R. *ὑμεῖς:* personal, possessive (gen.) (354)

Prepositions

A. Ἀνά (Accusative) (364)

    1. Distributive: *in the midst of* (ἀνὰ μέσον + G); *each, apiece* (with numbers)

    2. Spatial (in composition with verbs): *up, motion upwards*

B. Ἀντί (Genitive) (364-68)

    1. Substitution: *instead of, in place of*

    2. Exchange/Equivalence: *for, as, in the place of*

        The notions of exchange and substitution are quite similar, often blending into each other.

    3. Cause (debatable): *because of*

C. Ἀπό (Genitive): *separation from, from, of* (368)

    1. Separation (from place or person): *away from*

    2. Source: *from, out of*

    3. Cause: *because of*

    4. Partitive (i.e., substituting for a partitive gen.): *of*

    5. Agency (rare): *by, from*

D. Διά (Genitive, Accusative) (368-69)

    1. With Genitive (368)

        a. Agency: *by, through*

        b. Means: *through*

        c. Spatial: *through*

        d. Temporal: *through(out), during*

    2. With Accusative (369)

        a. Cause: *because of, on account of, for the sake of*

        b. Spatial (rare): *through*

E. Εἰς (Accusative) (369-71)

    1. Spatial: *into, toward, in*

    2. Temporal: *for, throughout*

    3. Purpose: *for, in order to, to*

    4. Result: *so that, with the result that*

    5. Reference/Respect: *with respect to, with reference to*

    6. Advantage: *for*

7. Disadvantage: *against*

8. In the place of ἐν (with its various nuances)

F. **'Ek** (Genitive): *from, out of, away from, of* (371-72)

1. Source: *out of, from*

2. Separation: *away from, from*

3. Temporal: *from, from* [this point] . . . *on*

4. Cause: *because of*

5. Partitive (i.e., substituting for a partitive gen.): *of*

6. Means: *by, from*

G. **'Ev** (Dative) (372-75)

1. Spatial/Sphere: *in* (and various other translations)

2. Temporal: *in, within, when, while, during*

3. Association (often close personal relationship): *with*

4. Cause: *because of*

5. Instrumental: *by, with*

6. Reference/Respect: *with respect to/with reference to*

7. Manner: *with*

8. Thing Possessed: *with* (in the sense of *which possesses*)

9. Standard (=Dative of Rule): *according to the standard of*

10. As an equivalent for εἰς (with verbs of motion)

H. **'Eπí** (Genitive, Dative, Accusative) (376)

1. **With Genitive**

    a. Spatial: *on, upon, at, near*

    b. Temporal: *in the time of, during*

    c. Cause: *on the basis of*

2. **With Dative**

    a. Spatial: *on, upon, against, at, near*

    b. Temporal: *at, at the time of, during*

    c. Cause: *on the basis of*

3. **With Accusative**

    a. Spatial: *on, upon, to, up to, against*

    b. Temporal: *for, over a period of*

I. Κατά (Genitive, Accusative) (376-77)

    1. With Genitive (376)

        a. Spatial: *down from, throughout*

        b. Opposition: *against*

        c. Source: *from*

    2. With Accusative (377)

        a. Standard: *in accordance with, corresponding to*

        b. Spatial: *along, through* (extension); *toward, up to* (direction)

        c. Temporal: *at, during*

        d. Distributive: "indicating the division of a greater whole into individual parts"[1]

        e. Purpose: *for the purpose of*

        f. Reference/Respect: *with respect to, with reference to*

J. Μετά (Genitive, Accusative) (377-78)

    1. With Genitive (377)

        a. Association/Accompaniment: *with, in company with*

        b. Spatial: *with, among*

        c. Manner (Attendant Circumstance): *with*

    2. With Accusative (377)

        a. Temporal: *after, behind*

        b. Spatial (rare): *after, behind*

K. Παρά (Genitive, Dative, Accusative) (378)

    1. With Genitive: in general, *from (the side of)* (with a personal object)

        a. Source/Spatial: *from*

        b. Agency: *from, by*

    2. With Dative: in general, *proximity* or nearness

        a. Spatial: *near, beside*

        b. Sphere: *in the sight of, before* (someone)

        c. Association: *with* (someone/something)

        d. Virtually equivalent to simple dative

    3. With Accusative

        a. Spatial: *by, alongside of, near, on*

        b. Comparison: *in comparison to, more than*

        c. Opposition: *against, contrary to*

---

[1] BAGD, s.v. κατά II.3 (406).

L. **Περί** (Genitive, Accusative) (379)

    1. **With Genitive**

        a. Reference: *concerning*

        b. Advantage/Representation: *on behalf of, for* (= ὑπέρ)

    2. **With Accusative**

        a. Spatial: *around, near*

        b. Temporal: *about, near*

        c. Reference/Respect: *with regard/reference to*

M. **Πρό** (Genitive) (379)

    1. Spatial: *before, in front of, at*

    2. Temporal: *before*

    3. Rank/Priority: *before*

N. **Πρός** (Accusative almost exclusively) (380-82)

    1. Purpose: *for, for the purpose of*

    2. Spatial: *toward*

    3. Temporal: *toward, for* (duration)

    4. Result: *so that, with the result that*

    5. Opposition: *against*

    6. Association: *with, in company with* (with stative verbs)

O. **Σύν** (Dative) (382)

    Expresses accompaniment/association: *with, in association (company) with*

P. **Ὑπέρ** (Genitive, Accusative) (383-89)

    1. **With Genitive** (383)

        a. Representation/Advantage: *on behalf of, for the sake of*

        b. Reference/Respect: *concerning, with reference to* (= περί)

        c. Substitution: *in place of, instead of* (= ἀντί)
           (such instances also involve representation)

    2. **With Accusative** (383)

        a. Spatial: *over, above*

        b. Comparison: *more than, beyond*

Q. ʽΥπό (Genitive, Accusative) (389)

   1. With Genitive

      a. (Ultimate) Agency: *by*

      b. Intermediate Agency (with active verbs): *through*

      c. Means: *by* (rare)

   2. With Accusative

      a. Spatial: *under, below*

      b. Subordination: *under* (the rule of)

Verbs and Verbals

Person and Number

Usual examples of concord are not covered in this chapter; the following are, for the most part, unusual & exegetically significant uses.

Person (391-99)

   A. First Person for Third Person ("I" = "Someone"): for the sake of vividness when a more universal application is in view (391-92)

   B. Second Person for Third Person ("You" = "Someone")?: no clear examples in NT (392-93)

   C. First Person Plural Constructions: The Scope of "We" (393-99)

      1. Editorial "We" (Epistolary Plural): first person plural by an author when he is only speaking about himself (394-96)

      2. Inclusive "We" (Literary Plural): first person plural includes both author(s) and audience (397-99)

      3. Exclusive "We": first person plural restricts the group to the author and his associates (397-99)

Number (399-406)

   A. Neuter Plural Subject with Singular Verb: neuter plural subjects *normally* take singular verbs since impersonal things are usually in view; treated as a collective whole; when they take a *plural* verb, individual identity is stressed (399-400)

   B. Collective Singular Subject with Plural Verb: when words such as ὄχλος take plural verb, individual identity is stressed (400-401)

   C. Compound Subject with Singular Verb: *first-named* subject is stressed (e.g., "Jesus and the disciples *comes*") (401-402)

D. The Indefinite Plural: "They" = "Someone" (convert plural into a *passive* in which the object becomes the subject; "Have they discovered a cure for cancer?" = "Has a cure for cancer been discovered?") (402-403)

E. The Categorical Plural (a.k.a. Generalizing Plural): "They" = "He, She" (like indefinite plural, but can be used with plural *nouns*); focuses more on action than actor (403-406)

Voice

(indicates how subject is related to the action [or state] expressed by the verb)

Active (410-14)

Subject *performs, produces,* or *experiences* the *action* or exists in the *state* expressed by the verb

A. **Simple Active**: subject performs or experiences the action (411)

B. **Causative Active (a.k.a. Ergative)**: subject is not directly involved in the action, but is the ultimate source of it (411-12)

C. **Stative Active**: subject exists in the state indicated by the verb (412-13)

D. **Reflexive Active**: active verb + *reflexive pronoun* (subject acts upon himself or herself) (413-14)

Middle (414-30)

Subject *performs* or *experiences the action* expressed by the verb in such a way that *emphasizes the subject's participation;* subject acts with a *vested interest*

A. Direct Middle (a.k.a. Reflexive or Direct Reflexive): verb + *self* (as direct object); subject acts *on* himself or herself (416-18)

B. Redundant Middle: the use of the middle voice in a reflexive manner with a *reflexive pronoun* (418-19)

C. **Indirect Middle (a.k.a. Indirect Reflexive, Benefactive, Intensive, Dynamic)**: subject acts *for* (or sometimes *by*) himself or herself, or in his or her *own interest*; key: like active verb + *reflexive pronoun* in *dative* (419-23)

D. Causative Middle: subject *has* something done *for* or *to* himself or herself (423-25)

E. Permissive Middle: subject *allows* something to be done *for* or *to* himself or herself (425-27)

F. Reciprocal Middle: verb with *plural subject* to represent interaction among themselves (427)

G. **Deponent Middle**: generally, no active *form* but active *meaning;* specifically, no active form for a particular *principal part* in *Hellenistic* Greek, and one whose force in that principal part is evidently active (428-30)

Passive (431-41)

The subject is *acted upon* or *receives the action* expressed by the verb

A. **Passive Constructions** (431-39)

    1. **The Passive With and Without Expressed Agency** (431-38)

        a. **With Agency Expressed** (431-35)

            1) **Ultimate Agent:** usually ὑπό (+ gen.), sometimes ἀπό (+ gen.) or παρά (+ gen.), indicating the person who is ultimately responsible for the action (433)

            2) **Intermediate Agent:** διά (+ gen.), indicating the person who carries out the act for the ultimate agent (433-34)

            3) **Impersonal Means:** ἐν (+ dat.), simple dative, or sometimes ἐκ (+ gen.), indicating the means an agent uses to perform an act (434-35)

        b. **With No Agency Expressed**: various reasons why agency is unexpressed (such as: obvious from context, focus on subject, nature of some verbs requires none, equative verbs, implicit generic agent, obtrusiveness of an explicit agent, rhetorical effect; *divine passive* is not a separate category, but may belong to several of the previous ones) (435-38)

    2. Passive With an Accusative Object: especially with accusative of thing (in person-thing double accusative construction) as a retained object; thing stays as accusative when verb becomes passive; person becomes subject (e.g., "She taught you *the lesson*" becomes "You were taught *the lesson*" by her") (438-39)

B. **Passive Uses** (439-41)

    1. **Simple Passive**: subject receives the action (439-40)

    2. Causative/Permissive Passive: implies consent, permission, or cause of the action of the verb on the part of the subject receiving the action (440-41)

    3. **Deponent Passive**: generally, no active *form* but active *meaning*; specifically, no active form for a particular *principal part* in *Hellenistic* Greek, and one whose force in that principal part is evidently active (441)

Moods

*(present [the speaker's portrayal of his affirmation of certainty of] the
verbal action or state with reference to its actuality or potentiality)*

Indicative (448-61)

The mood of assertion, or *presentation of certainty*

1. **Declarative Indicative**: presents assertion as a noncontingent (or unqualified) statement (449)

2. **Interrogative Indicative**: question of fact; expects a *declarative* indicative in response (449-50)

3. **Conditional Indicative**: indicative with εἰ in protasis–first class: *assumed true for sake of argument*; second class: *assumed false (for sake of argument)* (450-51)

4. **Potential Indicative**: semantically equivalent to a *potential* mood, due to verbal root; found in verbs of obligation, wish, or desire (such as ὀφείλω, δεῖ, θέλω), followed by infinitive (451-52)

5. Cohortative (Command, Volitive) Indicative: *future* indicative is sometimes used for a command (452-53)

6. **The Indicative with** Ὅτι (453-61)

   a. **Substantival** Ὅτι **Clauses** (453-59)

      1) Subject Clause: functions as subject of verb (453-54)

      2) **Direct Object Clause**: functions as direct object of verb (454-58)

         a) Direct Object Proper: direct object of a transitive verb that is *not* a verb of perception (454)

         b) **Direct Discourse (a.k.a. Recitative** Ὅτι **Clause,** Ὅτι *Recitativum***)**: after verb of *perception*; in place of ὅτι, put in *quotation marks* (454-55)

         c) **Indirect Discourse (a.k.a. Declarative** Ὅτι **Clause)**: after verb of *perception*; ὅτι clause contains *reported speech* or *thought*; translation: *that* (456-58)

      3) **Apposition** (to noun, pronoun, or other substantive): *namely, that* (can be substituted for its antecedent) (458-59)

   b. Epexegetical: *explains* or *clarifies* or *completes* a previous word or phrase (similar to apposition, but cannot be substituted for its antecedent) (459-60)

   c. **Causal (Adverbial)**: *because* (introduces a dependent causal clause) (460-61)

Subjunctive (461-80)

Generally represents the verbal action (or state) as uncertain but probable; however, since it encroaches on the optative's domain in Koine, it has broadened out to include possible, hypothetical, and impossible

1. **In Independent Clauses** (463-69)

   a. **Hortatory Subjunctive (a.k.a. Volitive; but this also means imperatival)**: *let us* (*first person plural* used to exhort oneself and one's associates); rarely, first person *singular* is used (*let me*) (464-65)

   b. **Deliberative Subjunctive (a.k.a. Dubitative)**: asks either a *real* or *rhetorical* question; a hortatory subjunctive turned into a question; asks about *possibility, necessity,* or *moral obligation* (465-68)

   c. **Emphatic Negation Subjunctive**: οὐ μή plus the *aorist subjunctive* (strong negation, *not even possible*) (468-69)

   d. **Prohibitive Subjunctive**: usually μή + *aorist subjunctive*, typically in the *second* person; equivalent to μή + imperative: *Do not* (rather than *You should not*) (469)

2. **In Dependent (Subordinate) Clauses** (469-80)

   a. **Subjunctive in Conditional Sentences**: subjunctive with ἐάν in protasis–*third class condition* (may indicate more probable future, mere possibility, or hypothetical situation); *fifth class condition* (a.k.a. *present general condition*) (indicates a generic situation in the present time) (469-71)

   b. **῞Ινα + the Subjunctive** (471-77)

      1) **Purpose ῞Ινα Clause (a.k.a. Final or Telic ῞Ινα)**: *in order that, so that* (indicates the purpose or intention of the controlling verb) (472)

      2) Result ῞Ινα Clause (a.k.a. Consecutive or Ecbatic ῞Ινα): *so that, with the result that* (indicates a consequence of the verbal action that is *not intended*) (473)

      3) **Purpose-Result ῞Ινα Clause**: indicates *both the intention and its sure accomplishment* (473-74)

      4) **Substantival ῞Ινα Clause (a.k.a. Sub-Final Clause)**: ἵνα clause indicates some substantival function (474-76)

         a) Subject Clause (475)

         b) Predicate Nominative Clause (475)

         c) Direct Object Clause (a.k.a. Content ῞Ινα Clause): answers *What*? not *Why*? (475)

         d) Apposition Clause: *namely, that* (475-76)

      5) Epexegetical ῞Ινα Clause: after a *noun* or *adjective* to explain or clarify that noun or adjective (476)

6) Complementary Ἵνα: *completes* the meaning of a helping verb such as θέλω, δύναμαι (total verbal meaning is usually *purpose*) (476)

7) Imperatival Ἵνα: equal to a *command* (could be treated as an independent use of subjunctive since the ἵνα clause is not subordinate to a main verb) (476-77)

c. Subjunctive with Verbs of Fearing: μή plus the subjunctive can be used after verbs of *fearing, warning, watching out for* to serve as a warning (477)

d. Subjunctive in Indirect Questions: follows the main verb, but appears awkward in the sentence structure (reflects a deliberative subjunctive from the direct question) (478)

e. **Subjunctive in Indefinite Relative Clause**: after ὅστις (ἄν/ἐάν) or ὅς (δ᾽) ἄν; construction indicates a *generic* or *indefinite* subject; translate like an *indicative* (since the contingency is of the person, not the action) (478-79)

f. **Subjunctive in Indefinite Temporal Clause**: after a *temporal adverb* (or *improper preposition*) meaning *until* (e.g., ἕως, ἄχρι, μέχρι) or *whenever* (ὅταν), indicating a future contingency (479-80)

Optative (480-84)

Generally portrays an action as *possible*

1. **Voluntative Optative (a.k.a. Optative of Obtainable Wish, Volitive Optative)**: expresses an *obtainable wish* or a *prayer* (e.g., μὴ γένοιτο–*may it never be!*) (481-83)

2. **Oblique Optative**: used in *indirect questions after a secondary tense* (substitutes for an *indicative* or *subjunctive* of the direct question) (483)

3. Potential Optative: with the particle ἄν in the *apodosis* of an *incomplete* fourth class condition; protasis needs to be supplied (e.g., [*If he could do something,] he would do this*) (483-84)

4. Conditional Optative: in the *protasis* of a *fourth class* condition (with εἰ) to indicate *remote possibility* (e.g., *if he could do something, if perhaps this should occur*) (484)

Imperative (485-93)

The mood of *intention* (in the realm of *volition* rather than cognition)

1. **Command**: commands an action to be done, usually from a superior to an inferior in rank (485-86)

2. **Prohibition**: μή + imperative; forbids an action, usually from a superior to an inferior in rank (487)

3. **Request (a.k.a. Entreaty, Polite Command)**: used to make a request rather than a demand, especially from an inferior in rank to a superior (487-88)

4. Permissive Imperative (Imperative of Toleration): used in response to an act being done or already done; *permission, allowance,* or *toleration* (488-89)

5. Conditional Imperative: state a condition (protasis) on which the fulfillment (apodosis) of another verb depends; almost always *imperative + καί + future indicative*; imperative is is still "commanding" (489-92)

6. Potential Imperative (debatable category): imperative in apodosis of implied condition with a conditional imperative in protasis (492)

7. Pronouncement Imperative: imperative in the *passive voice* equivalent of a statement that is fulfilled at the moment of speaking (492-93)

8. As a Stereotyped Greeting: injunctive force suppressed; used for *exclamation* (e.g., χαῖρε [*Greetings!*]) (493)

Tense

(indicates the speaker's presentation of the verbal action [or state] with reference to its aspect and, under certain conditions, its time)

Present (513-39)

Portrays the action as an internal or progressive event, without regard for beginning or end; in indicative, present time (generally)

I. **Narrow-Band Presents** (516-19)

    A. **Instantaneous Present (a.k.a. Aoristic or Punctiliar Present)**: action occurs at the moment of *speaking*; usually a *performative* statement (e.g., "I *tell* you the truth, the Rams won the game"); *indicative* only (517-18)

    B. **Progressive Present (a.k.a. Descriptive Present)**: *at this present time, right now* (describes a scene in progress, esp. in narrative literature) (518-19)

II. **Broad-Band Presents** (519-25)

    A. Extending-From-Past Present: describes an action which, begun in the past, continues in the present; translate like an *English present perfect* (519-20)

    B. **Iterative Present**: *repeatedly, continuously* (describes an event that *repeatedly* happens [*indicative* if in present time]); includes *distributive* present (individual acts distributed to more than one object) (520-21)

    C. **Customary (Habitual or General) Present**: signals either an action that *regularly occurs* or an *ongoing state* (broader, more regular than iterative) (521-22)

    D. **Gnomic Present**: *does happen* (rather than *is happening*); states a general, timeless fact, often proverbial in character (523-25)

III. **Special Uses of the Present** (526-39)

   A. **Historical Present (Dramatic Present)**: describes a *past event* in narrative literature (only *indicative, third person*; used for vividness; λέγει most common; εἰμί does not occur; aspectually equivalent of aorist) (526-32)

   B. **Perfective Present**: used to *emphasize* that the results of a past action are still continuing (*lexical* type [e.g., ἥκω] and *contextual* type [to introduce OT quotations]) (532-33)

   C. **Conative (Tendential, Voluntative) Present**: portrays subject as *desiring* to do something (*voluntative*), *attempting* to do something (*conative*), or at the point of *almost doing* something (*tendential*) (534-35)

      1. In Progress, but Not Complete (True Conative): *is attempting (unsuccessfully)* (attempt is being made in the present time [indicative mood]) (534-35)

      2. Not Begun, but About/Desired to be Attempted (Voluntative/Tendential): *about to* (an *attempt* is about to be made or is desired to be made in the present time [or, very near future time]) (535)

   D. **Futuristic Present**: describes a future event, typically adding the connotations of *immediacy* and *certainty* (usually with verbs whose lexical nuance includes anticipation) (535-37)

      1. **Completely Futuristic**: *is soon going to, is certainly going to, will* (536)

      2. **Mostly Futuristic (Ingressive-Futuristic?)**: describes an event *begun* in the present time, but completed in the future (such as *is coming, is going*) (537)

   E. **Present Retained in Indirect Discourse**: after verb of *perception*; tense retained from the direct discourse when the saying is put in indirect discourse; translate as though *imperfect* when main verb is past tense ("they heard that he *was* at home") (537-39)

Imperfect (540-53)

Portrays the action as an *internal* or *progressive* event ("motion picture"), without regard for beginning or end; occurs only in *indicative, past time* (generally)

I. **Narrow-Band Imperfects** (541-45)

   A. **Instantaneous Imperfect (a.k.a. Aoristic or Punctiliar Imperfect)**: in narrative, ἔλεγεν is sometimes equivalent to an aorist (= "he said") (542-43)

   B. **Progressive (Descriptive) Imperfect**: *was (continually) doing, was (right then) happening* (in progress in past time) (543-44)

C. **Ingressive (Inchoative, Inceptive) Imperfect**: *began doing* (stresses the beginning of an action, with the implications that it continued for some time; frequent in narrative to note a topic shift) (544-45)

II. **Broad-Band Imperfects** (546-48)

A. **Iterative Imperfect**: *kept on, repeatedly* (*repeated* action in past time) (546-47)

B. **Customary (Habitual or General) Imperfect**: *customarily* or *habitually* (habitual), *continually* (general); indicates a *regularly* recurring activity in past time (habitual) *or a state* that continued for some time (general) (548)

III. **Special Uses of the Imperfect** (549-53)

A. **"Pluperfective" Imperfect**: indicates time *antecedent* to that of the main verb (which also indicates past time) (549)

B. **Conative (Voluntative, Tendential) Imperfect**: portrays the action as something that was *desired* (*voluntative*), *attempted* (*conative*), or at the point of *almost doing* something (*tendential*) (550-52)

1. In Progress, but Not Complete (True Conative): *was attempting (unsuccessfully)* (attempt made in past time) (550-51)

2. Not Begun, but About/Desired to be Attempted (Voluntative/Tendential): *was about to, could almost wish* (an *attempt* was *about to be made* or one that was almost *desired to be made*) (551-52)

C. **Imperfect Retained in Indirect Discourse**: after a verb of *perception*; tense retained from the direct discourse when the saying is put in indirect discourse; translate as though *pluperfect* ("the Jews did not believe that **he had been** blind [ὅτι ἦν τυφλός]") (552-53)

Aorist (554-65)

Presents action *as a whole; summary* tense; takes a *snapshot* of the action; past time in the indicative

A. **Constative (Complexive, Punctiliar, Comprehensive, Global) Aorist**: views the action *as a whole*, taking no interest in its internal workings; describes the action in *summary* fashion (557-58)

B. **Ingressive (Inceptive, Inchoative) Aorist**: *began to do, became* (stresses the *beginning* of an action, or the *entrance* into a state) (558-59)

C. **Consummative (Culminative, Ecbatic, Effective) Aorist**: stresses the cessation of an act or state (559-61)

D. Gnomic Aorist: presents a timeless, general (generic) fact; translate like simple present tense (562)

E. Epistolary Aorist: aorist *indicative* in the *epistles* in which the author self-consciously describes his letter from the time frame of the audience (562-63)

F. Proleptic (Futuristic) Aorist: describes an event that is not yet past as though it were already completed (563-64)

G. Immediate Past Aorist/Dramatic Aorist: *just now* (describes an event that happened rather recently or at the present moment) (564-65)

Future (566-71)

External portrayal (like aorist) in *future* (subsequent) time

A. **Predictive Future**: indicates that something will take place or come to pass (568)

B. Imperatival Future: used for a command, almost always in OT quotations (569-70)

C. Deliberative Future: asks a question that implies some doubt about the response—one of possibility, desirability, or necessity (570)

D. Gnomic Future: indicates the likelihood that a (true to life) *generic* event will take place (571)

E. Miscellaneous Subjunctive Equivalents: sometimes used in situations normally reserved for the aorist subjunctive (571)

Perfect (572-82)

Describes an event which, *completed* in the past (we are speaking of the perfect indicative), has *results* existing in the present time; *combines aorist and present*

A. **Intensive Perfect (a.k.a. Resultative Perfect)**: *emphasizes* the *results* or present state produced by a past action (often best translated like English present); frequent with *stative* verbs (574-76)

B. **Extensive Perfect (a.k.a. Consummative Perfect)**: *emphasizes* the *completed action* of a past action from which a present state emerges (best translated like English present perfect); frequent with *transitive* verbs (577)

C. Aoristic Perfect (a.k.a. Dramatic or Historical Perfect): rhetorical use of the perfect as a *simple past* without concern for results; in *narrative* literature, *contextually* conditioned (578-79)

D. **Perfect with a Present Force**: focus on *present state* in which the completed action is not in view; *lexically conditioned* (e.g., οἶδα, ἕστηκα) (579-80)

E. Gnomic Perfect: speaks of a *generic* or proverbial occurrence; normal aspect, but *distributive* subjects/actions (580-81)

F. Proleptic (Futuristic) Perfect: refers to a state resulting from an antecedent action that is future from the time of speaking (581)

G. Perfect of Allegory: OT event is viewed in terms of its allegorical or applicational value (Melchizedek *"has received tithes* [δεδεκάτωκεν] from Abraham") (581-82)

Pluperfect (583-86)

Existing results in the past (it occurs only in the indicative); *combines aorist and imperfect*

A. **Intensive Pluperfect (Resultative Pluperfect)**: emphasizes *resultant state* that existed in past time (translate as simple past) (584-85)

B. **Extensive Pluperfect (Consummative Pluperfect)**: emphasize the completion of an action in past time (*had* + perfect passive participle) (585-86)

C. **Pluperfect with a Simple Past Force**: focus on *past state* in which the completed action is not in view; *lexically conditioned* (e.g., ἤδειν, εἰστή-κειν) (586)

Infinitive

(indeclinable verbal noun)

Semantic Categories

Adverbial (590-99)

A. **Purpose**: *to, in order to, for the purpose of* (indicates the purpose or goal of the action or state of its controlling verb) (590-92)

B. **Result**: *so that, so as to, with the result that* (indicates the outcome produced by the controlling verb; emphasis on *effect*, whether intended or not) (592-94)

C. **Time** (594-96)

   1. Antecedent: μετὰ τό + infinitive; translate *after* + appropriate finite verb (594-95)

   2. Contemporaneous: ἐν τῷ + infinitive; translate *while, as, when* + appropriate finite verb (595)

   3. Subsequent: πρὸ τοῦ, πρίν, or πρὶν ἤ + infinitive; translate *before* + appropriate finite verb (596)

D. **Cause**: διὰ τό + infinitive; indicates the *reason* for the action of the controlling verb; translate *because* + appropriate finite verb (596-97)

E. **Means**: ἐν τῷ + infinitive; describes the *way* in which the action of the controlling verb is accomplished; translate *by . . . doing, etc.* (597-98)

F. **Complementary (Supplementary)**: used with a "helper" verb (the most common are ἄρχομαι, βούλομαι, δύναμαι, ἐπιτρέπω, ζητέω, θέλω, μέλλω, ὀφείλω) to complete its thought (598-99)

Substantival (600-609)

A. **Subject**: functions as subject of verb, especially with *impersonal verbs* such as δεῖ, ἔξεστιν (600-601)

B. **Direct Object**: occurring after *other than* a verb of perception or communication (601-603)

C. **Indirect Discourse**: specialized direct object after a verb of *perception* or *communication*; represents a finite verb of direct discourse ("I told you *to do* the dishes" in the direct discourse would have been, "*Do* the dishes"); retains the *tense* of the direct discourse and usually represents either an *imperative* or *indicative* (603-605)

D. **Appositional**: *namely*; stands in apposition to a noun, pronoun, or substantival adjective (or some other substantive); *defines* the substantive (606-607)

E. **Epexegetical**: *clarifies, explains,* or *qualifies* a noun or adjective (words that indicate ability, authority, desire, freedom, hope, need, obligation, or readiness) (607)

Independent (608-609)

A. Imperatival: functions just like an imperative; not dependent on any other verb (do not confuse with indirect discourse infinitive) (608)

B. Absolute: bears no syntactical relation to anything else in the sentence; (e.g., χαίρειν = Greetings!) (608-609)

Structural Categories

I. *Anarthrous Infinitives* (609-10)

    A. **Simple Infinitive** (609)

        1. Purpose

        2. Result

        3. Complementary

        4. Means (rare)

        5. Subject

        6. Direct Object (rare)

        7. Indirect Discourse

        8. Apposition

        9. Epexegetical

        10. Imperatival (rare)

        11. Absolute (rare)

    B. Πρίν (ἤ) + Infinitive: Subsequent Time (609)

C. ʾΩς + Infinitive (609)

   1. Purpose

   2. Result

D. ῞Ωστε + Infinitive (610)

   1. Purpose (rare)

   2. Result

II. Articular Infinitives (610-11)

  A. Without Governing Preposition (610)

    1. Nominative Articular Infinitive (610)

      a. Subject

      b. Apposition (rare)

    2. Accusative Articular Infinitive (610)

      a. Direct Object

      b. Apposition

    3. Genitive Articular Infinitive (610)

      a. Purpose

      b. Result

      c. Contemporaneous Time (rare)

      d. Cause (rare)

      e. Direct Object (disputed)

      f. Apposition

      g. Epexegetical

    4. Dative Articular Infinitive (610)

      Only 2 Cor 2:13: either causal or contemporaneous time

  B. With Governing Preposition (610-11)

    1. Διὰ τό + Infinitive (610)

      a. Cause

      b. Contemporaneous Time (rare)

    2. Εἰς τό + Infinitive (611)

      a. Purpose

      b. Result

      c. Epexegetical (rare)

    3. ᾽Εν τῷ + Infinitive (611)

      a. Result (rare)

      b. Contemporaneous Time

      c. Means

    4. Μετὰ τό + Infinitive: Antecedent Time (611)

5. **Πρὸς τό + Infinitive** (611)

    a. Purpose

    b. Result

6. **Miscellaneous Prepositional Uses** (611)

Participle

(declinable verbal adjective)

I. *Adjectival Participles*: *adjectival nature is emphasized over verbal*; if the participle is articular, it *must* be adjectival; if anarthrous, it *may* be adjectival (617-21)

    A. **Adjectival Proper (Dependent)** (617-19)

        1. **Attributive Participles**: *who, which*; functions like an attributive adjective, in any standard attributive position (618)

        2. Predicate Participles: functions like a predicate adjective in predicate position (though usually in predicate position, the participle is adverbial) (618-19)

    B. **Substantival (Independent)**: *the one who, the thing which*; functions in the place of a substantive; can perform virtually any function a noun can; *verbal aspect* usually retained (619-21)

II. *Verbal Participles*: *verbal nature is emphasized over adjectival*; only with anarthrous participles, usually nominative and dependent on main verb (621-53)

    A. **Dependent Verbal Participles** (622-50)

        1. **Adverbial (or Circumstantial)**: modifies the verb, answering the question *When?* (temporal), *How?* (means, manner), *Why?* (purpose, cause), etc. (622-40)

            a. **Temporal**: answers the question *When?* May be antecedent (*after doing, after he did*), contemporaneous (*while doing*), or subsequent (*before doing, before he does*) (623-27)

            b. Manner: answers the question, *How?* by + participle of *emotion* or *attitude* (easily confused with *means*) (627-28)

            c. **Means**: *by means of* (answering the question, *How?*); indicates the means by which the action of a finite verb is accomplished; *defines* or *explains* the controlling verb; usually *follows* the verb (628-30)

      d. **Cause**: *because* (answers the question, *Why?*); indicates the *cause* or *reason* or *ground* of the action of the finite verb; usually *precedes* its verb (631-32)

      e. **Condition**: *if* (implies a condition on which the fulfillment of the idea indicated by the main verb depends) (632-33)

      f. **Concession**: *although* (implies that the state or action of the *main verb* is true *in spite of* the state or action of the participle) (634-35)

      g. **Purpose (Telic)**: translate like an *infinitive* or *with the purpose of* (indicates the purpose/intent of the action of the finite verb); usually *follows* main verb (635-37)

      h. **Result**: *with the result of* (indicates the actual outcome or result of the action of the main verb); can be *internal* (logical) or *external* (temporal); *follows* main verb (637-39)

2. **Attendant Circumstance**: translate as finite verb + *and* (it describes an action that, in some sense, is coordinate with the finite verb; "piggy-backs" on mood of main verb); *five structural clues* usually found:
- tense of participle: *aorist*
- tense of main verb: *aorist*
- mood of main verb: *imperative* or *indicative*
- participle *precedes the main verb* (both in word order and time of event)
- frequent in *narrative*, infrequent elsewhere (640-45)

3. Indirect Discourse: anarthrous participle in the *accusative* case, in conjunction with an accusative noun or pronoun, sometimes indicates indirect discourse after a verb of perception or communication; retains tense of direct discourse

4. Complementary: *completes* the thought of another verb; e.g., "I do not cease *praying* for you" (646)

5. **Periphrastic**: anarthrous participle used with a verb of being to form a finite verbal idea; see table below for various combinations (647-49):

Finite Verb (of εἰμί)	+	*Participle*	=	*Finite Tense Equivalent*
Present	+	Present	=	Present
Imperfect	+	Present	=	Imperfect
Future	+	Present	=	Future
Present	+	Perfect	=	Perfect
Imperfect	+	Perfect	=	Pluperfect

6. Redundant (Pleonastic): verb of saying (or thinking) used with a participle with basically the same meaning (as in ἀποκριθεὶς εἶπεν) (649-50)

B. Independent Verbal Participles (650-53)

1. As an Imperative (Imperatival): functions just like an imperative; participle not to be attached to any verb in the context, grammatically independent (650-52)

2. As an Indicative (Independent Proper or Absolute): functions like declarative indicative; participle stands alone in a declarative sense as the only verb in a clause or sentence (653)

III. *The Participle Absolute* (653-55)

A. Nominative Absolute: substantival participle that fits the case description of *nominativus pendens*–logical rather than syntactical subject at beginning of a sentence (654)

B. **Genitive Absolute**: anarthrous genitive participle with genitive substantive, functioning adverbially (usually temporal), but grammatically independent of verb in main clause (654-55)

Clauses

Clauses (in General)

I. *Independent Clauses: a clause that is not subordinate to another clause* (657-58)

A. **Introduced by a Coordinating Conjunction**
B. **Introduced by a Prepositional Phrase**
C. **Asyndeton (no Formal Introduction)**

II. *Dependent Clauses*: a clause that is subordinate to another clause (659-65)

A. **Structure** (not all occur with every syntactical function) (659-60):

1. *Infinitival* clauses
2. *Participial* clauses
3. *Conjunctive* clauses
4. *Relative* clauses (both definite and indefinite)

B. **Syntactical Function** (660-65)

1. **Substantival Clause**: can function as a subject, predicate nominative, direct object, indirect discourse, apposition

2. **Adjectival Clause**: attributive function only; *describes, explains*, or *restricts* a substantive

3. **Adverbial Clause**: modifies a verb as follows: cause, comparison, concession, condition, complementary, location, manner/means, purpose, result, time

Conjunctions

I. *Logical Functions*: relate the movement of thought from one passage to another by expressing logical relationships (670-74)

    A. **Ascensive**: *even* (final addition or point of focus); καί, δέ, and μηδέ (670-71)

    B. **Connective (continuative, coordinate)**: *and, also* (if emphatic [adjunctive]); (*connects an additional element* to a discussion); καί and δέ (671)

    C. **Contrastive (adversative)**: *but, rather, however* (*contrast* or opposing thought to the idea to which it is connected); ἀλλά, πλήν, sometimes καί and δέ (671-72)

    D. **Correlative**: paired conjunctions expressing various relationships; e.g., μέν . . . δέ (*on the one hand . . . on the other hand*); καί . . . καί (*both . . . and*) (672)

    E. **Disjunctive (Alternative)**: *or* (suggests an *alternative* possibility to the idea to which it is connected); ἤ (672)

    F. **Emphatic**: *certainly, indeed* (involves *intensifying* the normal sense of a conjunction); ἀλλά (*certainly*), οὐ μή (*certainly not* or *by no means*), οὖν (*certainly*); true emphatic conjunctions include γε, δή, μενοῦνγε, μέντοι, ναί, and νή (673)

    G. **Explanatory**: *for, you see*, or *that is, namely* (conjunction indicates additional information being given to what has been described); γάρ, δέ, εἰ (after verbs of emotion), and καί (673)

    H. **Inferential**: *therefore* (gives a deduction, conclusion, or summary to the preceding discussion); ἄρα, γάρ, διό, διότι, οὖν, πλήν, τοιγαροῦν, τοινῦν, and ὥστε (673)

    I. **Transitional**: *now, then* (involves the change to a new topic of discussion, especially in narrative); οὖν and especially δέ (674)

II. *Adverbial Functions*: amplify the verbal idea in a specific way (usually subordinate conjunctions) (674-77)

    A. **Causal**: *because, since* (expresses the basis or ground of an action); γάρ, διότι, ἐπεί, ἐπειδή, ἐπειδήπερ, καθώς, ὅτι, and ὡς (674)

    B. **Comparative (manner)**: *as, just as, in the same way, thus*, or *in this manner* (suggests an *analogy* or *comparison* between the connected ideas or tells how something is to be done); καθάπερ, καθώς, οὕτως, ὡς, ὡσαύτως, ὡσεί, and ὥσπερ (675)

C. **Conditional**: *if* (introduces a protasis of a conditional clause); εἰ and ἐάν (675)

D. **Local (sphere)**: *where, from where*, or *the place which* (gives the location or sphere [metaphorically], that is, the context in which an action takes place); ὅθεν, ὅπου, and οὗ (676)

E. **Purpose**: *in order that* (indicates the goal or aim of an action); ἵνα, ὅπως, μήπως (the negative purpose), μήπου (negative purpose), and μήποτε (negative purpose) (676)

F. **Result**: *so that, with the result that* (gives the outcome or consequence of an action); ὥστε, ὡς, ὅτι, and less frequently, ἵνα (677)

G. **Temporal**: translations vary (indicates the time of the action); ἄχρι, ἕως, ὅταν, ὅτε, οὐδέποτε (negative temporal), οὐκέτι (negative temporal), οὔπω (negative temporal), ποτέ, and ὡς (677)

III. *Substantival Functions*: the conjunction introduces a noun content clause and epexegesis (677-78)

A. **Content**: *that* (conjunction introduces a subject, predicate nominative, direct object, or an appositional noun clause; direct and indirect discourse are specialized object clauses following verbs of expression or perception); ἵνα, ὅπως, ὅτι, and ὡς (678)

B. **Epexegetical**: *that* (conjunction introducing a clause that completes the idea of a verb, noun, or adjective); ἵνα and ὅτι (678)

Conditional Sentences

I. *Conditional Sentences in General*: there are three common relationships that the protasis can have to the apodosis (regardless of whether the condition is first class, second class, etc.) (682-84):

A. **Cause-Effect**: protasis indicates the cause of which the apodosis is the result (682-83)

B. **Evidence-Inference**: protasis indicates the evidence from which the apodosis supplies the inference (683)

C. **Equivalence**: both halves are saying the saying the same thing ("If A, then B" means "A = B") (683-84)

II. *Conditional Sentences in Greek (especially the NT)* (687-701)

A. **First Class Condition**: *the assumption of truth for the sake of argument* (does not mean *since*, nor is it a simple, logical condition); protasis: εἰ + indicative (in any tense)/apodosis: any mood, any tense (689, 690-94)

B. **Second Class Condition**: *the assumption of an untruth (for the sake of argument)*; protasis: εἰ + indicative of secondary tense (aorist or imperfect usually)/apodosis: ἄν (usually) + secondary tense in indicative (689, 694-96)

C. **Third Class Condition**: range of nuances: (a) a *logical connection* (if A, then B) in the present time (*present general condition* or *fifth class condition*), (b) *hypothetical* situation, and (c) *more probable future* occurrence; ἐάν + subjunctive, any tense; apodosis: any tense, any mood (present indicative for present general condition) (689, 696-99)

D. Fourth Class Condition (Less Probable Future): *possible* condition in the future, usually remote possibility (such as *if he could do something, if perhaps this should occur*); protasis: εἰ + *optative*; apodosis: *optative* + ἄν (689, 699-701)

Volitional Clauses

(commands & prohibitions)

I. *Commands* (718-22)

A. Future Indicative (a.k.a. Cohortative Indicative, Imperatival Future): usually a quotation from OT (718-19)

B. **Aorist Imperative**: views action *as a whole* (719-21)

1. **Ingressive**: focus on beginning of action, used for *urgency* especially (719-20)

    a. **Momentary or Single Act**: specific occurrence in view (719-20)

    b. **Pure Ingressive**: focus on beginning of action that will not be completed immediately (720)

2. **Constative**: stress on a *solemn, categorical* command; "Make this your top priority and do it now!" (720-21)

C. **Present Imperative**: views action *as ongoing process* (721-22)

1. **Ingressive-Progressive**: *begin and continue* (721-22)

2. **Customary**: *continue*; command for action to be continued, action that may or may not have already been going on; general precept, character-building command (722)

3. **Iterative**: *repeated action*; difficult to distinguish from Customary (shorter intervals, less regular) (722)

II. *Prohibitions* (723-25)

A. Future Indicative (+ οὐ or sometimes μή): negative command, typically solemn, universal, or timeless (and usually OT quotation) (723)

    B. **Aorist Subjunctive (+ μή)** (723-24)

        1. **Ingressive:** *Do not start* (723-24)

        2. **Constative:** *Don't do* (723-24)

    C. **Present Imperative (+ μή)** (724-25)

        1. **Cessation of Activity in Progress (Progressive):** *Stop continuing* (724)

        2. **General Precept (Customary):** makes no comment about whether prohibited action is already in progress (724-25)

Cheat Sheet

Cases

Nominative

Subject
Predicate Nominative
Nominative in Simple Apposition
Nominative Absolute
Nominativus Pendens (Pendent Nominative)
Parenthetic Nominative
Nominative in Proverbial Expressions
Nominative for Vocative
Nominative of Exclamation
Nominative of Appellation
Nominative in Apposition to Oblique Cases
Nominative After Preposition
Nominative for Time

Vocative

Simple Address
Emphatic (or Emotional) Address
Exclamation
Apposition

Genitive

Descriptive Genitive
Possessive Genitive
Genitive of Relationship
Partitive Genitive ("Wholative")
Attributive Genitive
Attributed Genitive
Genitive of Material
Genitive of Content
Genitive in Simple Apposition
Genitive of Apposition (Epexegetical)
Genitive of Destination
Predicate Genitive
Genitive of Subordination
Genitive of Production/Producer
Genitive of Product
Genitive of Separation
Genitive of Source (or Origin)
Genitive of Comparison
Subjective Genitive
Objective Genitive
Plenary Genitive
Genitive of Price or Value or Quantity
Genitive of Time
Genitive of Place
Genitive of Means

Genitive of Agency
Genitive Absolute
Genitive of Reference
Genitive of Association
Genitive After Certain Verbs (as Direct Object)
Genitive After Certain Adjectives
Genitive After Certain Nouns
Genitive After Certain Prepositions

Dative

Dative Indirect Object
Dative of Interest
   Advantage (*commodi*)
   Disadvantage (*incommodi*)
Dative of Reference/Respect
Ethical Dative
Dative of Destination
Dative of Recipient
Dative of Possession
Dative of Thing Possessed
Predicate Dative
Dative in Simple Apposition
Dative of Place: see sphere
Dative of Sphere
Dative of Time
Dative of Rule
Dative of Association/Accompaniment
Dative of Manner
Dative of Means/Instrument
Dative of Agency
Dative of Measure/Degree of Difference
Dative of Cause
Cognate Dative
Dative of Material
Dative of Content
Dative Direct Object
Dative After Certain Nouns
Dative After Certain Adjectives
Dative After Certain Prepositions

Accusative

Accusative Direct Object
Double Accusative
  Person-Thing
  Object-Complement
Cognate Accusative
Predicate Accusative
Accusative Subject of Infinitive
Accusative of Retained Object

Pendent Accusative (*Accusativum Pendens*)
Accusative in Simple Apposition
Adverbial Accusative (Manner)
Accusative of Measure (Space, Time)
Accusative of Respect or (General) Reference
Accusative in Oaths
Accusative After Certain Prepositions

Article

Regular Uses
As a Pronoun
  Personal Pronoun
  Alternative Pronoun
  Relative Pronoun
  Possessive Pronoun
With Substantives
  Individualizing Article
  Simple Idenitification
  Anaphoric (Previous Reference)
  Kataphoric (Following Reference)
  Deictic ("Pointing")
  Par Excellence
  Monadic ("One of a Kind")
  Well-Known ("Familiar")
  Abstract
  Generic (Categorical)
As a Substantiver of:
  Adverbs
  Adjectives
  Participles
  Infinitives
  Genitive Word or Phrase
  Prepositional Phrase
  Particles
  Finite Verbs
  Clauses, Statements, & Quotations
As a Function Marker
  Denote Adjectival Positions
  With Possessive Pronouns
  In Genitive Phrases
  With Indeclinable Nouns
  With Participles
  With Demonstratives
  With Nominative Nouns
  To Distinguish S from PN & Object from Complement
  With Infinitive (various functions)

Absence of the Article
Indefinite
Qualitative
Definite
  Proper Names
  Object of Preposition
  With Ordinal Numbers

Predicate Nominative
Complement in Object-Complement Construction
Monadic Nouns
Abstract Nouns
Genitive Construction (Apollonius' Corollary)
With Pronominal Adjective
Generic Nouns

Special Uses/Non-Uses of the Article
Anarthrous Pre-Verbal PNs (involving Colwell's Rule)
Article with Multiple Substantives Connected by καί (Sharp's Rule & related constructions)

Adjectives

"Non-Adjectival" Uses of Adjective
Adverbial
Substantival

Positive, Comparative, Superlative
Positive
  Normal Use
  Positive for Comparative
  Positive for Superlative
Comparative
  Normal Use
  Comparative for Superlative
  Comparative for Elative
Superlative
  "Normal" Use
  Superlative for Elative
  Superlative for Comparative

Relation of Adjective to Noun
When Article is Present
  Attributive Positions
    First Attributive
    Second Attributive
    Third Attributive
  Predicate Positions
    First Predicate
    Second Predicate
When Article is Absent
  Anarthrous Adjective-Noun Construction
  Anarthrous Noun-Adjective Construction

Pronouns

Personal Pronouns
Nominative Uses
  Emphasis: contrast, subject focus
  Redundancy

Oblique Cases
  Normal Use: Anaphoric
  Possessive
  Reflexive

Demonstrative Pronouns
Regular Uses (as Demonstratives):
οὗτος, ἐκεῖνος, ὅδε
For Personal Pronouns
Unusual Uses
  Pleonastic (Redundant, Resumptive)
  Constructio ad Sensum: Gender, Number
  Conceptual Antecedent/Postcedent

Relative Pronouns
ὅς
  Regular Uses (as RP)
  "Unusual" Uses
    Natural vs. Grammatical Gender
    Case
      Attraction
      Inverse Attraction
    Antecedent Complexities
      Omission of Antecedent
      Adverbial/Conjunctive
ὅστις
  Generic
  Qualitative
  Confusion with ὅς

Interrogative Pronouns
τίς/τί: identifying
ποῖος, πόσος: qualitative, quantative (respectively)

Indefinite Pronoun
Substantival
Adjectival

Possessive "Pronoun"
Possessive Adjective
Personal Pronoun in Genitive

Intensive Pronoun: αὐτός
Intensive Pronoun
As Identifying Adjective
As Third Person Personal Pronoun

Reflexive Pronoun

Reciprocal Pronoun

Prepositions
(see main section of Syntax Summaries)

Person & Number
Person
First for Third Person
Second for Third Person

First Plural Constructions
  Editorial "We" (Epistolary Plural)
  Inclusive "We"
  Exclusive "We"
Number
  Neuter Plural Subject, Singular Verb
  Collective Singular Subject, Plural Verb
  Compound Subject, Singular Verb
  Indefinite Plural
  Categorical Plural

Voice
Active
Simple Active
Causative Active (Ergative)
Stative Active
Reflexive Active

Middle
Direct Middle
Redundant Middle
Indirect Middle
Causative Middle
Permissive Middle
Reciprocal Middle
Deponent Middle

Passive
Passive Constructions
  With & Without Agency Expressed:
    Ultimate Agent
    Intermediate Agent
    Impersonal Means
    No Expressed Agency
  With Accusative Object
Passive Uses
  Simple Passive
  Causative/Permissive Passive
  Deponent Passive

Moods
Indicative
Declarative Indicative
Interrogative Indicative
Conditional Indicative
Potential Indicative
Cohortative(Command,Volitive) Indicative
Indicative with Ὅτι
  Subject
  Direct Object
    Direct Object Proper
    Direct Discourse
    Indirect Discourse
  Apposition
  Epexegetical
  Causal

Subjunctive

Independent Clauses
  Hortatory Subjunctive
  Deliberative Subjunctive
  Emphatic Negation Subjunctive
  Prohibitive Subjunctive
Dependent Clauses
  Subjunctive in Conditional Sentences
  Ἵνα + Subjunctive
    Purpose
    Result
    Purpose-Result
    Subject
    Predicate Nominative
    Direct Object
    Apposition
    Epexegetical
    Complementary
    Imperatival
  Subjunctive with Verbs of Fearing
  Subjunctive in Indirect Questions
  Subjunctive in Indefinite Relative Clause
  Subjunctive in Indefinite Temporal
    Clause

Optative

Voluntative Optative (Obtainable Wish)
Oblique Optative
Potential Optative
Conditional Optative

Imperative

Command
Prohibition
Request (Entreaty)
Permissive Imperative (Toleration)
Conditional Imperative
Potential Imperative
Pronouncement Imperative
Stereotyped Greeting

Tense

Present

Instantaneous Present
Progressive Present
Extending-From-Past Present
Iterative Present
Customary Present
Gnomic Present
Historical Present
Perfective Present
Conative Present
  In Progress, but not Complete
  Not Begun, but About/Desired to be At-
    tempted

Futuristic Present
  Completely Futuristic
  Mostly Futuristic
Present Retained in Indirect Discourse

Imperfect

Instantaneous Imperfect
Progressive (Descriptive) Imperfect
Ingressive Imperfect
Iterative Imperfect
Customary Imperfect
"Pluperfective" Imperfect
Conative Imperfect
  In Progress, but not Complete
  Not Begun, but About/Desired to be At-
    tempted
Imperfect Retained in Indirect Discourse

Aorist

Constative Aorist
Ingressive Aorist
Consummative Aorist
Gnomic Aorist
Epistolary Aorist
Proleptic Aorist
Immediate Past/Dramatic Aorist

Future

Predictive Future
Imperatival Future
Deliberative Future
Gnomic Future
Miscellaneous Subjunctive Equivalents

Perfect

Intensive Perfect (Resultative)
Extensive Perfect (Consummative)
Aoristic (Dramatic, Historical) Perfect
Perfect with Present Force
Gnomic Perfect
Proleptic Perfect
Perfect of Allegory

Pluperfect

Intensive Pluperfect (Resultative)
Extensive Pluperfect (Consummative)
Simple Past Pluperfect

Infinitive

Adverbial Uses

Purpose
Result
Time
  Antecedent
  Contemporaneous
  Subsequent
Cause

Means
Complementary (Supplementary)

Substantival
Subject
Direct Object
Indirect Discourse
Appositional
Epexegetical

Independent
Imperatival
Absolute

Participle
Adjectival Participles
Adjectival Proper
   Attributive
   Predicate
Substantival

Verbal Participles
Dependent Verbal
   Temporal
   Manner
   Means
   Cause
   Condition
   Concession
   Purpose
   Result
   Attendant Circumstance
   Indirect Discourse
   Complementary
   Periphrastic
   Redundant (Pleonastic)
Independent Verbal
   Imperatival
   Indicative

Participle Absolute
Nominative Absolute
Genitive Absolute

Clauses
Clauses (in General)
Independent Clauses
Dependent Clauses
   Substantival
   Adjectival
   Adverbial

Conjunctions
Logical Functions
Ascensive
Connective
Contrastive (Adversative)

Correlative
Disjunctive (Alternative)
Emphatic
Explanatory
Inferential
Transitional

Adverbial Functions
Causal
Comparative (Manner)
Conditional
Local (Sphere)
Purpose
Result
Temporal

Substantival Functions
Content
Epexegetical

Conditional Sentences
In General
Cause-Effect
Evidence-Inference
Equivalence

In Greek
First Class
Second Class
Third Class
Fourth Class

Volitional Clauses
Commands
Future Indicative
Aorist Imperative
   Ingressive
      Momentary or Single Act
      Pure Ingressive
   Constative
Present Imperative
   Ingressive-Progressive
   Customary
   Iterative

Prohibitions
Future Indicative
Aorist Subjunctive
   Ingressive
   Constative
Present Imperative
   Cessation of Activity in Progress
   General Precept

Subject Index

Q

V

Greek Word Index

This index includes all the words and several phrases found in this grammar that are in themselves important for the grammatical discussion being made. Sometimes a nonlexical form of the word is listed because of that form's particular connection to the syntax under discussion. Occasionally the particular term listed here is not actually found on the page listed, but is obvious from the context or English description (e.g., ὁ will be listed in this index for pages that only speak of the article). In most instances of this sort, the page number will be put in parentheses.

Scripture Index

This scripture index is designed to enable the student to gain quick access to the discussions of the exegetically significant texts. If a page number is both bold and in italics, there is an extended treatment of the passage on that page (or, in some instances, a brief analysis of an exegetically significant text in which the syntactical point stressed makes an obvious impact on the meaning of the text). The second level discussion is found on pages that are put in italics (but not bold type). Such treatments involve either minimal exegetical implications or are fairly lengthy but oriented primarily toward syntax (i.e., the text in question is gleaned mostly for its illustrative value of the syntactical point). Finally, all the rest of the pages are in normal roman type; such type represents everything from mere reference to quotation of the verse. This system can be summarized as follows:

123 important/extended discussion of exegetically significant text
123 some impact on exegesis noted or text is exploited for its syntactical value
123 mere citation, quotation, etc.

For additional textbooks on New Testament Greek look for these outstanding titles.

Basics of Biblical Greek

Second Edition Grammar
and Workbook

William D. Mounce

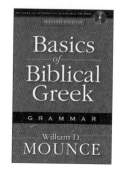
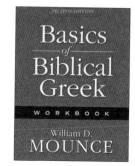

Grammar

Basics of Biblical Greek is an entirely new, integrated approach to teaching and learning New Testament Greek. It makes learning Greek a natural process and shows from the very beginning how an understanding of Greek helps in understanding the New Testament. Written from the student's perspective, this approach combines the best of the deductive and inductive methods.

A prominent feature is the strong tie-in between the lessons and the biblical text. From the beginning, the students work with verses from the New Testament.

Workbook

The workbook contains a parsing section. Translation exercises are taken directly from the New Testament. Unusual constructions and exegetical insights are explained in footnotes. The workbook is perforated and punched for loose-leaf binders.

Computerized Teacher Packet and Flash-Card Program

A computerized **Teacher Packet** with quizzes, tests, answers for all exercises, and overhead materials is available at no charge to instructors who use Basics of Biblical Greek as their textbook, as well as **Flashworks™**, a computerized flash-card program.

Hardcover: 978-0-310-25087-6
Workbook: 978-0-310-25086-9

Pick up a copy today at your favorite bookstore!

A Graded Reader of Biblical Greek

A Companion to *Basics of Biblical Greek* and *Greek Grammar Beyond the Basics*

William D. Mounce

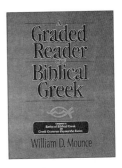

This companion volume to the *Basics of Biblical Greek Grammar* and *Workbook* contains annotated readings from the New Testament designed for second-year Greek students. By working with verses from the New Testament instead of made-up exercises, students are able to deepen their understanding of the New Testament while learning the fundamentals of Greek. Sections from the Greek New Testament are presented in order of increasing difficulty. Unfamiliar forms and constructions are annotated.

This book can also be used in conjunction with Wallace's *Greek Grammar Beyond the Basics*.

Softcover: 978-0-310-20582-1

Pick up a copy today at your favorite bookstore!